Charles Hornsby is an international manager with a multinational corporation. He completed his D.Phil. on Kenyan politics at St Antony's College, Oxford in 1986, and has since combined a professional career in information technology with a deep engagement with Kenya. He has published several articles on Kenyan politics and co-authored with David Throup the influential *Multi-Party Politics in Kenya* (1998). He has been a journalist or election observer during most of Kenya's recent elections and lived and worked in Ghana in 1995–8 and Kenya in 1999–2001. He currently lives in Malaysia.

'This is the first full history of Kenya's half-century of independence. And it is more than that. Hornsby roots independent Kenya's problems in its many colonial crises, particularly the brutally divisive Mau Mau war. Since then Kenya has experienced rapid change, not least its explosive population growth, and crises, often resolved, at least temporarily, by illegal government action. But the underlying continuities are extraordinary. What were patched-up, ad hoc, responses at independence had become settled political conventions a few years later. Hornsby shows how Kenya's most recent tragedy, the killings and evictions that followed the 2007 general election, can be traced back to these political deals of decolonisation, inscribed in disputed African access to the departing white settlers' land. His case is made all the stronger by his close attention not only to political but also to economic and social history, agrarian and international affairs. But, unusually, Hornsby also shows that political philosophy has mattered – as much as the intrigue, ethnic patronage, and corruption that are the conventional stuff of less well informed commentaries on recent African history. A fundamental choice was available to Kenya's leaders 50 years ago. They were divided over which path to follow, "socialist" or "capitalist". Choosing the capitalist road but calling it African socialism, Kenya's later history has always been dogged by an undertow of ideological dissent, difficult to define precisely, impossible for leaders to banish from their nightmares. In Hornsby's hands there is here a deep politics at work in a long process, under the high politics of the every day. One of many continuities has been the apparent absence of the army from direct political involvement – an a-political tradition that has emerged from a series of abortive interventions in earlier years. This is not the same as saying that the state has retained a legitimate monopoly on the exercise of force. It has not: political assassination has from time to time served regime interests; the police have often acted as a vigilante gang; vigilante gangs act as local police forces and political enforcers. To explain such ambiguities in the Kenyan nation and state is not easy. But with great thoroughness, edged with sometimes startling insight, Hornsby has done just that.'

John Lonsdale, Emeritus Professor of Modern African History,
University of Cambridge

'Charles Hornsby has followed Kenya intensely for decades and watched the twists and upsets of its dramatic politics. Now he has written a heavyweight and lucid history of this fascinating and important country. His account is a grand narrative full of sharp insights.'

Richard Dowden, Chairman Royal African Society

'The definitive study of independent Kenya. Hornsby has an encyclopaedic knowledge of Kenyan politics and politicians.'

David Throup, Senior Associate, Africa Program,
The Center for Strategic and International Studies, Washington, DC

KENYA

A History Since Independence

CHARLES HORNSBY

I.B. TAURIS

LONDON · NEW YORK

Published and reprinted in 2012 by I.B.Tauris & Co Ltd
6 Salem Road, London W2 4BU
175 Fifth Avenue, New York NY 10010
www.ibtauris.com

Distributed in the United States and Canada Exclusively by Palgrave Macmillan
175 Fifth Avenue, New York NY 10010

ISBN: 978 1 84885 886 2

A full CIP record for this book is available from the British Library
A full CIP record is available from the Library of Congress

Library of Congress Catalog Card Number: available

Typeset by JCS Publishing Services Ltd, www.jcs-publishing.co.uk
Printed and bound by CPI Group (UK) Ltd, Croydon, CR0 4YY

Contents

Tables, Figures and Illustrations

Tables

Figures

Acknowledgements

This book is like most such endeavours, a labour of love; the result of 27 years of research and immersion in Kenya's politics, economy and society. To all those who gave their time to talk – endlessly, at times – of Kenya and its history, I hope it is worth the wait.

Special thanks are due to Susanne Mueller for reading and critiquing the entire first draft and to John Lonsdale for his ideas and support throughout. Chapters were also reviewed by and ideas debated with (among others) Patrick Smith, Steve Orvis, Lauren Ploch, Peter Kagwanja and Sebastian Elischer. A broad debt of gratitude is owed to David Throup, whose inputs on the colonial era and the 1960s and 1970s were invaluable. Many of my ideas have evolved with him over a decade, and some of his thoughts have probably become my own. Thanks are also due to Mike Kirkwood and Kenneth Ombongi for their editorial work, to my anonymous reviewers, to the editorial team at I.B.Tauris and to my editor Jessica Cuthbert-Smith.

Other acknowledgements should go to those politicians, academics, journalists and economists who took the time to discuss ideas with me, including Robert Shaw, Marren Akatsa, Tony Killick, the late Judy Geist, Marcel Rutten, Sally Healy, François Grignon, Mutegi Njau, Tom Wolf, Lazarus Muema, John Nellis, Richard Dowden, James Long and Ben Kipkorir. Thanks are due also to David Anderson, for organising the seminar in honour of John Lonsdale in 2004, where some of the ideas in this book received their first outing.

Over the years, the book also owes much to the opportunity to work with the National Election Monitoring Unit and later the Institute for Education in Democracy. Particular debts are due to Grace Githu (who sadly passed away in 2002) and to Koki Muli for their support, enthusiasm and challenge. There are older debts too: to the universities who provided space and materials (particularly Oxford, Cambridge, Nairobi and SOAS), to Tony Kirk-Greene for originally inspiring me about Africa (though I chose the 'wrong side') and to those who helped me during my thesis, all those years ago. Thanks are also due to Wouter de Vries and Hetty ter Haar, who provided me with a house and home in Kenya during 1992–3. More recently, I have learnt from and borrowed the houses of Isaac and Jane Omolo-Okero, Edward and Lilian Torgbor, Wanjohi and Wamuyu Kangangi, and Michael and Jennifer Murungi. My thanks go to them and their families for their practical assistance and critical challenge on the realities of Africa.

Particular thanks should go to the Nation Group and particularly Charles Mallei for many years of access to their archives, and to my employer for basing me in Nairobi during 1999–2001. More recently, I would like to acknowledge the Public Records Office at Kew, which never ceases to please with its efficiency, the Institute for Commonwealth Studies in London, and the IED, which – with the support of the Westminster Foundation for Democracy – gave me a base and a role in 2002 and on many other occasions.

This book is dedicated to Gifty, Edith and Peter, for their patience through those long lost evenings; to my mother, brother and sister, without whom much would be very different, and to my deeply missed father, whose experience and enthusiasm gave me support and focus over the years. It is also dedicated to the people of Kenya, who, despite many challenges, continue to struggle with undimmed optimism to improve their country.

The views expressed in this book are entirely the author's and should not be considered in any way the views of his employer. No information gained in the course of the author's duties has been used in this work.

Abbreviations and Acronyms

4Cs	Citizens Coalition for Constitutional Change
ACK	Anglican Church of Kenya
ADB	African Development Bank
ADC	Agricultural Development Corporation
AEMO	African Elected Members Organisation
AFC	Agricultural Finance Corporation
AFL-CIO	American Federation of Labor-Congress of Industrial Organizations
AGOA	African Growth and Opportunity Act
AIC	African Inland Church
AIDS	acquired immune deficiency syndrome
ALCS	African Liaison and Consulting Services
APP	African People's Party
BAT	British-American Tobacco
BHC	British High Commission
CBK	Central Bank of Kenya
CCK	Communications Commission of Kenya
CDC	Commonwealth Development Corporation
CDF	Constituency Development Fund
CIA	Central Intelligence Agency (US)
CID	Criminal Investigation Department
CITES	Convention on International Trade in Endangered Species
CJPC	Catholic Justice and Peace Commission
CKRC	Constitution of Kenya Review Commission
CLARION	Centre for Legal Aid and Research International
CMC	Cooper Motor Corporation
CNU	Coalition of National Unity
CO	Colonial Office
COGS	Chief of General Staff
COMESA	Common Market for East and Central Africa
COTU	Central Organisation of Trade Unions
CPK	Church of the Province of Kenya
DANIDA	Danish International Development Agency
DC	district commissioner
DDDG	Donors for Development and Democracy Group
DFCK	Development Finance Company of Kenya
DFRD	District Focus for Rural Development
DP	Democratic Party
DPF	Deposit Protection Fund

EAA	East African Airways
EAC	East African Community
EACSO	East Africa Common Services Organisation
EAD	East Africa Department, UK Foreign and Commonwealth Office
EAI	East African Industries
EALA	East African Legislative Assembly
EAP&L	East African Power and Lighting Company
EAP&T	East Africa Posts and Telecommunications
EAR	East African Railways
EAR&H	East African Railways and Harbours
EATEC	East Africa Tanning and Extract Company
ECK	Electoral Commission of Kenya
EEC	European Economic Community
EPZ	export processing zone
ESAF	enhanced structural adjustment facility
EU	European Union
FAO	United Nations Food and Agriculture Organisation
FCO	Foreign and Commonwealth Office, London
FERA	February 18th Revolutionary Army
FGM	female genital mutilation (also female circumcision or clitoridectomy)
FKE	Federation of Kenya Employers
FORD	Forum for the Restoration of Democracy
FORD-Asili	Forum for the Restoration of Democracy-Asili
FORD-Kenya	Forum for the Restoration of Democracy-Kenya
FORD-People	Forum for the Restoration of Democracy-People
Forex-C	Foreign exchange bearer certificate
GB£	British pounds
GDP	gross domestic product
GEMA	Gikuyu Embu and Meru Association
Gema	Gikuyu, Embu and Meru ethnic groups
GNU	Government of National Unity
GPT	graduated personal tax
GSU	General Service Unit
HELB	Higher Education Loans Board
HFCK	Housing Finance Company of Kenya
HIV	human immunodeficiency virus
HoROR	*House of Representatives Official Report*
IBRD	International Bank for Reconstruction and Development (World Bank)
ICC	International Criminal Court
ICDC	Industrial and Commercial Development Corporation
ICFTU	International Confederation of Free Trade Unions
ICI	Imperial Chemical Industries

IDB	Industrial Development Bank
IED	Institute for Education in Democracy
IFES	International Foundation for Electoral Systems
IFI	international financial institutions (World Bank, IMF)
IIEC	Interim Independent Electoral Commission
ILO	International Labour Organization
IMF	International Monetary Fund
IPK	Islamic Party of Kenya
IPP	independent power producer
IPPG	Inter-Parties Parliamentary Group
IREC	Independent Review Commission
IRI	International Republican Institute
ISP	Internet service provider
K£	Kenyan pounds (20 shillings)
KACA	Kenya Anti-Corruption Authority
KACC	Kenya Anti-Corruption Commission
KADU	Kenya African Democratic Union
KAF	Kenya Air Force
Kamatusa	*Ka*lenjin, *Ma*asai, *Tu*rkana and *Sa*mburu ethnic groups
KANU	Kenya African National Union
KAR	King's African Rifles
KASA	Kenya African Socialist Alliance
KAU	Kenya African Union
KAWC	Kenya African Workers Congress
KBC	Kenya Broadcasting Corporation
KBL	Kenya Breweries Limited
KCA	Kikuyu Central Association
KCB	Kenya Commercial Bank
KCC	Kenya Cooperative Creameries
KCPE	Kenya Certificate of Primary Education
KCSOP	Kenya Civil Society Observation Programme
K-DOP	Kenya Domestic Observation Programme
KEDOF	Kenya Elections Domestic Observation Forum
KENDA	Kenya National Democratic Alliance
KFA	Kenya Farmers Association
KFL	Kenya Federation of Labour
KFRTU	Kenya Federation of Registered Trades Unions
KGB	Komityet Gosudarstvyennoi Biezopasnosti (USSR)
KGGCU	Kenya Grain Growers Cooperative Union
KHRC	Kenya Human Rights Commission
KIE	Kenya Industrial Estates
KLFA	Kenya Land and Freedom Army (also LFA)
KLGWU	Kenya Local Government Workers Union
KMC	Kenya Meat Commission

KNA	Kenya News Agency
KNAC	Kenya National Assurance Company
KNC	Kenya National Congress
KNFU	Kenya National Farmers Union
KNP	Kenya National Party
KNTC	Kenya National Trading Corporation
KNUT	Kenya National Union of Teachers
KPA	Kenya Ports Authority
KPC	Kenya People's Coalition
KPCU	Kenya Planters Co-Operative Union
KPF	Kenya Patriotic Front
KPLC	Kenya Power and Lighting Company
KPTC	Kenya Posts and Telecommunications Corporation
KPU	Kenya People's Union
KR	Kenya Railways
KRA	Kenya Revenue Authority
KSC	Kenya Social Congress
Ksh.	Kenya shilling
KTDA	Kenya Tea Development Authority
KTDC	Kenya Tourist Development Corporation
KTN	Kenya Television Network
KVDA	Kerio Valley Development Authority
KWAL	Kenya Wine Agencies Limited
KWS	Kenya Wildlife Service
LDP	Liberal Democratic Party
LNC	Local Native Council
LSK	Law Society of Kenya
MI5/6	Military Intelligence Section 5/6 (UK)
MoU	memorandum of understanding
MP	Member of Parliament
NAC	National Alliance for Change
NAK	National Alliance (Party) of Kenya
NAOR	*National Assembly Official Report*
NARC	National Alliance Rainbow Coalition
NARC-Kenya	National Alliance Rainbow Coalition-Kenya
NAU	New Akamba Union
NBK	National Bank of Kenya
NCA	National Convention Assembly
NCC	National Construction Corporation
NCCK	National Council of Churches of Kenya
NCEC	National Convention Executive Council
NCPB	National Cereals and Produce Board
NCWK	National Council for Women of Kenya
NDC	National Disciplinary Committee

NDI	National Democratic Institute
NDP	National Democratic Party
NEC	National Executive Committee
NEMU	National Election Monitoring Unit
NGO	non-governmental organisation
NHC	National Housing Corporation
NHIF	National Hospital Insurance Fund
NIB	National Irrigation Board
NKP	New Kenya Party
NOCK	National Oil Corporation of Kenya
NORAD	Norwegian Agency for Development Cooperation
NPCP	Nairobi People's Convention Party
NPK	National Party of Kenya
NSE	Nairobi Stock Exchange
NSIS	National Security Intelligence Service
NSSF	National Social Security Fund
NYS	National Youth Service
OAU	Organisation for African Unity
ODM	Orange Democratic Movement
ODM-Kenya	Orange Democratic Movement-Kenya
OECD	Organisation for Economic Cooperation and Development
OP	Office of the President
PAC	Public Accounts Committee of the National Assembly
PC	provincial commissioner
PCEA	Presbyterian Church of East Africa
PICK	Party of Independent Candidates of Kenya
PFLP	Popular Front for the Liberation of Palestine
PNU	Party of National Unity
PRGF	Poverty Reduction and Growth Facility
PSC	Parliamentary Select Committee
PTA	Preferential Trade Agreement
RAF	Royal Air Force (UK)
SAOR	The Senate Official Report
SAP	structural adjustment programme
SAS	Special Air Service (UK)
SDP	Social Democratic Party
SDR	Special Drawing Right
SPLA	Sudan People's Liberation Army
Supkem	Supreme Council of Kenya Moslems
TI	Transparency International
TLB	Transport Licensing Board
TRDC	Tana River Development Company
TSC	Teachers' Service Commission
TV	television

UDI	unilateral declaration of independence
UDM	United Democratic Movement
UK	United Kingdom (also Great Britain)
UN	United Nations
UNDP	United Nations Development Programme
UNEP	United Nations Environment Programme
UNESCO	United Nations Educational, Scientific and Cultural Organisation
UNHCR	United Nations High Commissioner for Refugees
UNICEF	United Nations Children's Fund
US(A)	United States of America
USAID	US Agency for International Development
USSR	Union of Soviet Socialist Republics
VAT	value-added tax
VoK	Voice of Kenya
WTO	World Trade Organization
YK'92	Youth for KANU '92

Chapter 1

Introduction

Introduction

This book is a history of the state of Kenya since its independence in December 1963. 'Kenya' was a colonial invention, and its history has been dominated by the disruptive changes that followed the British conquest at the turn of the twentieth century. However, while many histories of colonial rule and particularly of the Mau Mau conflict of the 1950s have been written, there are few histories of independent Kenya. There have been many edited collections of papers and many scholarly works on Kenya's economy, but most have focused on the colonial era or on specific post-independence topics. British rule lasted 60 years; Kenya has been a sovereign state for 47. Kenya should be assessed not only as a colonial invention, but also for the successes and failures of its own making. This book tries to do this. It is a history of one country, not a comparative history of Africa. It seeks to explain what has happened in Kenya since independence and to align academic understandings of post-colonial development with the experiences and perceptions of Kenyans about their country. Others will compare this story with that of other states, and I hope, use it to understand Africa better.

Kenya's history has not been one of war, military rule, mass murder or state collapse; neither has it been one of improving living standards, industrialisation, growing national pride and the establishment of a key role in the world economy. It has been rather a story of endurance: of political and economic structures inherited from colonial days, of unfulfilled promise and weighty historical baggage. It is a story that blends both politics and economics, a struggle to create and consume resources that involved Western powers and Kenyans in a complex web of relationships; a tale of growth stunted by political considerations, of corruption and of money.

It is also a story about people, about a few powerful individuals whose choices have so influenced Kenya's future. Few of them come out of the story entirely unblemished, though many made great sacrifices in the struggle for what they believed right. Hindsight is a wonderful thing and retrospective assessments of people's choices seldom take account of the circumstances and perceptions of their world at that time. To lead requires difficult choices and compromises, and the role of a politician in a less-developed society (in which nothing is easy and nothing is safe) is a challenging one. However, the rewards of success are great.

This is also a tale of people as communities and their collective behaviour, in which ethnicity plays a strong role – a topic that often evokes strong responses. Kenyan politics cannot be understood without understanding Kenyan ethnicity. It is not, however (and never was) a primordial constant, but an arena for conflict, based around genuine differences of language, culture and economic interest between the peoples living within the boundaries of the nation state, but always changing. Ethnicity is about shared communities, gradations of us-ness from the nuclear family to the language family, but also about conflict and difference. In Kenya, a certain form of ethnic conflict has been enduring, despite many efforts to build a national identity. It has shaped the political system, and has in turn been shaped by Kenya's politicians and the institutions they inhabit. Sometimes, it has been associated with violence. The problem of ethnically focused political violence in Kenya has come to world attention in 1969, 1991–3 and 2007–8; each time worse than the last. Its origins lie elsewhere – in land rights, poverty, elite survival strategies and state abuses – but the recourse to violence takes on its own logic, and the risk of further trouble remains real.

Inevitability and Contingency in Kenya's History

The history of any country is the consequence of a number of elements. Some – population, geography, economic structure and technological level – are the products of the past and are relatively inflexible. Such structural forces place a country in a particular global position, limiting the options available to its leaders. Broad economic, cultural and social forces will drive a gradual evolution across whole continents, changeable by the acts of a few great individuals, but with huge inertia.[1] Other parts of a history are more contingent and may mask, modify or redirect these broader forces. Although the outlines of a country's history may be predictable, unplanned events and the actions of influential individuals, particularly during periods in which change has already begun, remain critical to the actual outcome. As Bruce Berman and John Lonsdale wrote in 1992, it is essential not to 'write history backwards' from outcomes to inevitable antecedents, but to accept contingencies and accidents alongside deeper social and economic forces.[2]

Kenya's independence history is no different. As in much of Africa, the new, weak political institutions and externally oriented economic system inherited from colonial rule permitted a greater contingency and unpredictability than in more mature states, as the impact of individual actors and accidents was proportionately greater. Nonetheless, the probable trajectory of its future was clear. It was likely at independence that the new states of East Africa would have difficulty in standing alone on the world stage and that they would fall into a dependent economic, political and military relationship with the world powers (at that time the USA and USSR). It was likely that Kenya, with its stronger economy and greater Western investment, would perform better than its neighbours. 'Tribalism' and ethnicity (reflecting the existence of at least 42 ethnic groups in Kenya, with different languages, traditions and economic interests, and the country's fractured history during and after the Mau Mau war) were always going to be challenges. A powerful and coercive bureaucracy, built to maintain order, defend British rule and repress a violent revolt, would inevitably play a major and self-interested role in the country's future. As Chris Allen has argued, there were only a few 'basic histories' in independent

Africa, 'frequently repeated and causally entwined sequential patterns of political development'.[3] Most states followed a pattern of one-party rule and clientelism, matched and mitigated by centralised, bureaucratic politics, unless disrupted by war or military coups and a catastrophic descent into 'spoils politics'. This phase was followed in the 1990s by an externally driven restoration of democratic forms and liberalisation of the state and the economy, if the state had not imploded entirely. Kenya followed this pattern closely, with one difference: it never experienced a period of state failure or overthrow. From the British withdrawal until today, the Kenyan state has endured, its grip looser or tighter, but always present, with great continuity in structure, accountabilities and personnel. Events reached a crisis at least a dozen times, but were always settled conservatively. Despite constitutional and economic change, party splits, murder, repression, a coup attempt, politically motivated ethnic clashes and mass civil disobedience, the country's political and economic system has endured.

Nonetheless, the precise shape of Kenya after 47 years of independence could not have been predicted with confidence. Kenya could easily have ended up under military rule, or could have disintegrated for a decade, as Uganda did. With good luck and better governance, it might have leapfrogged onto a path of sustainable growth as an 'African tiger'. Prime Minister and then President Jomo Kenyatta's strategy for rule, with its state capitalist, pro-Western orientation, could have been very different if he had emerged from nine years of false imprisonment with greater bitterness towards the British. The murder of Tom Mboya in 1969 and Daniel arap Moi's accession to the presidency in 1978 both demonstrated the power of contingency, and the impact of decisions by a few influential men. The first speeded Kenya's move towards rule by a Kikuyu oligarchy, political and economic decay; the second shifted the country onto a trajectory of ethnic tension and resource redistribution. The failure of the 1982 coup probably diverted a descent into military rule and instead set Kenya on a path of Kalenjin-led authoritarianism. The reintroduction of multi-party democracy under Western pressure a decade later was probably inevitable, but the consequences, including the ethnic clashes and the Goldenberg scheme to loot the Treasury, were not. Ten years later, Moi's decision to back Jomo's son Uhuru Kenyatta for the presidency was a catastrophic mistake that destroyed the Kenya African National Union (KANU) and gave victory to an uneasy alliance of its opponents. Little had changed either economically or institutionally since the opposition's defeat in 1997, but as individual alliances shifted, their supporters followed and the result was entirely different.

More predictably, during 2003–5, an opportunity for national renewal was squandered by bad luck and a legacy of ethnic and personal tensions. Kenya's primary political cleavage reverted to the same two divisions that had dogged it in the 1960s: epitomised by the relationship between the Luo and Kikuyu communities and – independently – between the Kikuyu and Kalenjin, each representing a different path for Kenya. Raila Odinga's ability to retain a cross-ethnic alliance even after his party split, and the narrowness of Mwai Kibaki's disputed electoral victory in 2007, inspired a violent backlash that split the country in two and forced a division of powers that had been demanded and rejected many times before. Kibaki and Odinga were forced into a power-sharing deal that avoided the horror of civil war, but it was an unhappy arrangement, a sticking plaster to allow the wounds of 2007–8 to heal.

Politics and Economics

This book, unusually, is not presented as a sequence of separate essays on economics, political institutions, security, agriculture and foreign policy, but as a historical narrative that draws together these subjects and shows how the relationships between them have evolved over the five decades of independence. It is probably the first attempt at an inclusive political and economic history of independent Kenya. There are two reasons for this approach: first, in Kenya, politics and economics are so deeply entwined that you cannot discuss one without discussing the other; second, policy and practice are not ahistorical, but vary over time. Events must be understood in their historical context. It is no more logical to treat the Kenyatta, Moi and Kibaki governments' policies as constant than it would be to describe British history since 1963 without distinguishing between the policies of Harold Wilson, Margaret Thatcher and Tony Blair and the circumstances in which they operated.

Although sometimes appealing, a sharp distinction between the economic and the political sphere has limited value, particularly in Africa. Both are the collective products of individual choices and much (though not all) political conflict is about economic issues. The dependency between the two spheres is deep. A country such as Kenya does not improve its infrastructure and social services, produce more, or become richer independent of its political system, but as a direct consequence of it. To give one example: agricultural productivity is a function not only of farmers' individual decisions and world prices, but also of land policy, ownership patterns, the degree of state marketing and price support for particular crops, the degree of predation on profits from regulatory and marketing organisations and the disruptive effects of land-related violence. All are political issues. In the same vein, Kenya's various redistributive and growth-oriented economic policies can only be understood in the context of who was benefiting from them at a particular time. The importance of wealth as a route to power, and of political power as a route to acquire both wealth and access to state resources has also meant that the same elites dominate both politics and economics and fight their battles in both spheres. Through control of the state, political power becomes economic power; through patronage politics, economic power becomes political power. Corruption is simultaneously an economic, political, administrative and social process.

At the macro level, Kenya's economic performance has also been driven by Western political pressure. Good relations and alignment on international issues encourage investment and tourism. The granting and withholding of foreign aid and budgetary support is a political process, driven by the degree of alignment between the ruling elite and Western interests, and by the behaviour of the elite. As the history of structural adjustment shows, the granting and withholding of aid is only loosely related to the actual reforms introduced by governments. Foreign investment, a key driver of growth, is a fickle, fearful thing that can be frightened away by corruption, violence and nationalism alike. Mass tourism, although it helped Kenya become more prosperous, also tightened the links between politics and economic performance, as political problems hurt tourist bookings and therefore national prosperity. Global communications have similarly amplified the knock-on effects of domestic problems on foreign audiences, and therefore on tourism, aid and investment alike.

A Stable State?

Kenya in 2011 remained recognisable as a natural evolution of the nation created at independence. Unlike most African states, it had avoided military rule, social instability, warlord-ism, mass murder or social collapse. Religious divisions have not led to violence, and attempts at secession have been defeated or deterred. Kenya has never gone to war. In almost every crisis over the years, the outcome was a more gradual shift away from the existing course of events than in neighbours such as Uganda, Ethiopia, Somalia and Sudan. Why did Kenya show such continuity that the same governing party could run the country for nearly 40 years? The army remained loyal, constitutional process was followed and losers did not (generally) resort to violence. The 2008 coalition government was headed by a president who had been part of the government at independence and a prime minister who was the son of the first vice-president. The economy remained based on the colonial pattern, with an externally oriented cash-crop sector, a large smallholder agricultural sector and modest industrial development. Despite mass urbanisation, education, social change and global communications, the political system was built around the same institutions and with the same focus on ethnicity as in 1963. The command and control system and authoritarian political culture, the 'guided' democracy and the huge gulf between rich and poor remained (though the rich elite itself had changed). The same families appear to run the country, and the same arguments over land, ethnicity, presidential authority, corruption and foreign intervention seem to continue decade after decade.

The answer to the question of why this is the case is a difficult one. Clearly, one reason is simply luck: that the crises of the nation-state were settled with moderation rather than coups and murder was sheer accident. More interesting is the possibility that inherited social and economic structures and direct external influence held Kenya on a more stable course. The command and control system that the British created to maintain order was propagated into the independent state almost unchanged.[4] Kenyatta and his advisers were concerned from the first about Kenya's security and the desire for political order was one of their core motivating forces. There was an effective bureaucracy at least for the first two decades of independence, which helped temper political excess. The defeat of Mau Mau left a population fearful of the state and accustomed to obedience. The substantial wealth in the country, originally European and Asian, but later also African, the tight links which emerged between the economic, political and administrative elites and the patron–client structures of political power meant that many had investments in the existing social and economic order, and that truly radical change was supported by few in positions of power. There was something substantial to fight over, and most actors in the drama agreed that any action that would destroy the commercial farming sector, tourism or the foreign support on which the country depended was not worth the price.

The absence of strategic minerals was a blessing in disguise, unlike for example Angola, the Congo, Nigeria and Sudan. The physical and population geography of the country also discouraged ethnic separatism. Kenya had too many ethnic groups, and the misalignment of communities and boundaries left by the Europeans meant no partition of the country was viable, while only the Maasai and Somali could plausibly have seceded to join a neighbour.

Western involvement also played a role. The large foreign investments and number of foreign citizens living in Kenya at independence acted as stabilising forces, both for good and ill. British finance, military support and advice actively contributed to the survival of the Kenyatta government. Foreign advisers have continued to serve in little-noted but influential positions ever since. In the 1970s, the decade of self-reliance, Western intervention was less overt, but thousands of aid workers, teachers and other foreign professionals continued to work in Kenya. Foreign aid sustained the country's economy from the moment of independence, providing a buffer for the errors of its leadership and a safety net that was guaranteed by Kenya's pro-Western orientation. In the 1990s, with the fall of communism, attitudes changed. Western governments and international finance institutions placed tighter constraints on what the state could 'get away with', and donors drove a reform agenda that unwound most of the economic structures created in the 1960s and 1970s, but aid continued.

Continuity also owed something to the *dramatis personae* of the early days: Kenyatta himself, Charles Njonjo, Moi and Kibaki. All were conservative figures, patriarchal and authoritarian, but always pragmatists, willing to turn back from the brink at moments of crisis. Although all have been accused of corruption, authoritarianism and self-interest, all subscribed to a paternal vision of the rights and duties of power, which included the preservation of the country they had inherited. They each felt a degree of accountability to the 'will of the nation', if not to its electoral expression.

After a brief period of instability in 1963–5, the nation-state was set on its course, driven by both active commitment and growing inertia down a single path. Kenyatta's age and autocratic inclination created a political system that began to see its perpetuation as its primary reason for existence. The conservative and authoritarian political culture he nurtured was sustained into the twenty-first century under Moi, who truly followed in the footsteps of his patron, though with very different consequences. This state ideology was overlaid, often forcibly, on a more egalitarian, democratic, racist, populist and nationalist public opinion. Many of Kenya's challenges have been grounded in deep differences between the way the governing elites have seen the interests of the country and the opinions of the electorate.

While Kenya has been one of the most stable states in Africa, this is not necessarily a term of approbation. Although today's Kenya would be easily recognisable to Kenyatta or Mboya, they would be disappointed by what they saw. Kenya's competitive advantage within Africa has been frittered away, while the continent as a whole has been left behind. Economically the equal of Singapore and Tunisia in 1963, in 2005 the country's gross domestic product (GDP) per head was lower than that of Chad or Mauritania.[5] Kenya has failed to make a transition to a new model of economic development or a higher level of material benefit for its people. In the absence of bloody, discontinuous change, politicians have continued to fight the same battles, decade over decade, and have failed to deliver the basic services that even a liberal state provides in other societies.

The country has also been stable because it has found institutional change to be hard. The state's growing incapacity and a zero-sum mental model of political competition amongst Kenya's citizens left the country struggling to implement new policies. The mould hardened before the work was finished, trapping the country with a set of institutions that no longer matched the challenges it faced, but every attempt at reinvention failed because of the vested interests it might harm and the neo-patrimonial and ethnic lenses through which actions were seen. The shambles of 13 years of pressure for constitutional reform showed this most clearly, as institutional incapacity combined with a legacy of class, ethnic and personal tensions to create a veto on change, until it was forced through violent confrontation. Kenya is therefore less a *stable* state than a *brittle* state: resistant to change, but liable to fragment if social pressure exceeds the tolerance of its inflexible shell. For a while, in January 2008, it seemed that this shell might fracture completely.

It is clear that the real Kenya has changed, however. Despite popular rhetoric suggesting the continuity of presidential authoritarianism, Kenya in 2011 is a very different country from that of its first decade. The economy's prosperity no longer relies on the state; multi-party democracy is here to stay and presidential demands provoke as much resistance as obedience. Even the constitution is changing, as this book goes to press, creating new opportunities and risks. A fourth generation of political leadership is coming onto the scene, with fewer ties to the past. It is unclear, though, what will replace presidential authoritarianism in the long term. Devolution has dangers, and ethnicity, money politics and populism have created a cocktail of expectations and constraints that will be hard for any leader or structure to satisfy.

Themes of Conflict

Since the foundation of the state, five themes of conflict have continued to influence the country's direction, threading through and shaping historical events.

Centralism versus Majimbo (Regionalism) and the Politics of Land Ownership

The choice between a centralised constitution (with its focus in the executive presidency) and a decentralised constitution with competing or layered sources of authority dominated Kenya's politics in 1961–4 and has re-emerged since 1991 as the key fault line in Kenya's polity. It encapsulates and is powered by a deeper debate between what became known as 'minority' and 'majority' groups over the right of 'willing buyers' to purchase land in the 'ancestral lands' of others. Land was not the only issue at stake, but it was certainly the most important. Within this lay a third debate, over the bodies in which rights resided: individuals in the liberal democratic citizenship model, as the state formally espoused, or ethnic communities or collectives, as supporters of federalism often argued.

After a decade of neglect, the shift of leadership and state preference to the Kalenjin ethnic community in 1978 reawoke the challenge to the centralised model of presidential authoritarianism and to the willing buyer, willing seller land model, resulting in a gradual rollback of the black settler land rights that had been established in the 1960s. The reintroduction of multi-party democracy in 1991 re-established land as a key cleavage between settled communities (particularly the Kikuyu, but also the Luo, Gusii and Luhya) and Kalenjin and Maasai pastoralists, and powered the subsequent violence. This dispute was fought during the 1990s both on the ground in the Rift Valley and through party politics and the constitutional review process. The killing fields of 2007–8 in the Rift were the same farms over which Kikuyu, Kalenjin and Luhya had competed in the 1960s and 1990s. The underlying tension remained: was land something to be bought and sold, and could Kenyans live anywhere in the country, or was land a collective asset, held in trust for future generations, and were strangers who bought land simply '*ahoi*' (tenants), who could be evicted at will?

Socialism versus Capitalism and Individualism versus Egalitarianism

Kenya has also experienced enduring tension between supporters of a more communal, egalitarian or socialist path, and proponents of a more individualised, capitalist and unequal view of what was right for the country. The tension was most visible during 1963–5, but proponents of a more egalitarian or socialist view continued to seek expression through the Kenya People's Union (KPU) in 1966–9, the unofficial opposition of the 1970s, Oginga Odinga's socialist party of 1982, Mwakenya, the struggle for multi-party democracy and even the Orange Democratic Movement of 2007. Kenya's 'left' has seldom had the opportunity to set policy or even articulate its views without harassment, but there have always been individuals ready to make a case for change, whether harking back to pre-colonial communal societies or to Marxist models of development.

Kenya's African socialism was never truly socialist, and its capitalism was never of an American free-enterprise liberal type. Kenya's was an interventionist, 'state capitalist' regime, in which the state owned, managed or indirectly controlled the majority of productive activity and private capitalists were either foreign multinationals or the politicians themselves and their allies, forms of 'crony capitalism'. During the 1980s, the government's unpopularity and rent-seeking undermined Western-led attempts at reform. In the early 1990s, after the collapse of communism, the international finance institutions forced a more externalised, openly capitalist model on Kenya, against strong popular and state resistance. Even now, most Kenyans remain more pro-regulatory, egalitarian and communal than either their elites or Western governments might prefer. The fault line between economic liberals and those of a more social democratic perspective remains deep, and sometimes aligns with the sensitive 'marker' of ethnicity (pro-state intervention and anti-capitalist political elites are often Luo, and the most open espousers of free market liberal ideologies are often Kikuyu).

Neo-Patrimonialism, Ethnicity and the 'Fruits of Uhuru'

The third theme of cleavage (which has overshadowed others in public perceptions) has been over which individuals and which ethnic groups get to 'eat the fruits of *Uhuru*' (a Kenyan metaphor for the benefits of independence). At every level of state and society and in every institution, the process of neo-patrimonialism continues to shape political and economic activity, as loosely structured factions based around powerful patrons compete for power and resources. These informal structures of authority and competition lie within and often conflict with formal bureaucratic-legal institutions and explain much of Kenya's politics since 1963. Institutions and the formal 'rules of the game' provide a structure within which this competition takes place, and have been strong in Kenya (by African standards), but neither rational-choice nor institutional frameworks can fully explain events, because the real beneficiaries may not even be visible. Ethnicity provides a frame for some of this competition, but not all.

At the national level, this struggle for power and resources coalesced into a three-way cleavage, epitomised by three ethnic groups: the Kikuyu, Luo and Kalenjin. The first two decades of independence saw the incorporation (on junior terms) of the Kalenjin into Kenyatta's Kikuyu-centred alliance, and the gradual marginalisation of the Luo, alongside the embedding of a series of advantages for the Kikuyu community. There was no inevitability about the cleavage created in 1963–9 between Kikuyu and Luo: it was a by-product of a competition over other issues, which gradually assumed an ethnic flavour. Similarly, the densely populated, agricultural Luhya ended up inclined towards the Kalenjin or 'minority' side for reasons that were as much accidental and personal as anything else. However, a view of politics as an ethnically driven competition for resources, a survival of the fittest where the prize was control of the resources of the state, was built into the country from independence. It was reinforced by almost every act of Kenyatta, Moi and Kibaki, each seeking to rule a fractious community of sub-nationalities by a combination of patronage, incorporation and reliance on their own ethnic community for their security. The rewards of power were sweet and the consequences of defeat severe, and winning became a goal in itself for both the individual and the community. Increasingly, an individual's success or failure was interpreted as victory or defeat for an entire ethnic community.

Once the struggle for power of 1980–3 was resolved, the presidency of Daniel arap Moi saw a shift in the balance of state benefit away from the Kikuyu and towards a new and more fragile Kalenjin-dominated pastoralist alliance. Unlike Kenyatta, Moi had to take away before he could give, since many of the 'fruits of Uhuru' had already been eaten, and the resulting fracture between the Kikuyu community and the Kalenjin continues to echo through the country's politics today. The failed coup attempt of 1982 set him on a path of absolutist control and increasing Kalenjinisation. During the 1980s and 1990s, the government 'forced' the emergence of a new Kalenjin economic and political elite. In the multi-party era, ethnic tensions were reinforced by the consolidation of political party support along ethnic lines. Moi's Kalenjin were always the core of the 'government', the Kikuyu of the 'opposition', leaving the Luo community united but uncertain whether to back 'the Kikuyu' or 'the Kalenjin'. Raila Odinga's deal with KANU in 1999 represented a realignment of forces, a western alliance of Kalenjin, Luhya and Luo, but it fell apart when faced with Moi's preference for an older, more incorporative strategy. His choice of Uhuru Kenyatta, the old president's son, as KANU's presidential candidate in 2002 and Odinga's return to the opposition destroyed KANU.

The victory of Kibaki and of the National Alliance Rainbow Coalition (NARC) ended Moi's 'pastoralist era', but the conflicts over which individuals and communities would benefit most from access to state resources continued, and the perception re-emerged that the state, through covert bureaucratic means, was favouring the 'Mount Kenya peoples' (Kikuyu, Embu, Meru) over all others. By 2005, Odinga had rebuilt the western alliance under a new banner, with support in the east and on the coast as well, strong enough to take on and arguably defeat Kibaki's Mount Kenya-centred government. The 2007 elections ended in chaos, with three very Kenyan problems: electoral abuses, political violence and land powering a crisis that focused world attention on the country once more.

This struggle for resources at the centre has defined and structured ethnic identities as much as vice versa. Where in the pre-independence and early post-independence era ethnic identities aggregated themselves on a national scale to challenge for the state, the post-independence struggle for control has seen further aggregation. Thus, the Gicugu became part of the greater Kikuyu community, then in turn the 'Gema tribes' (the Gikuyu, Embu and Meru communities) and the 'Mount Kenya peoples' (sometimes expanded further to include the Kamba). Likewise, the Cherang'any of the Rift Valley became the Marakwet, then the Kalenjin and briefly the 'Kamatusa' (*Ka*lenjin, *Ma*asai, *Tu*rkana and *Sa*mburu) supra-ethnic aggregate. The levelling effects of development are taking their toll, laying the foundation in one to two generations for new ethnic identities to emerge. Although county-based devolution could delay this, in the long term the political identities of Kenyan peoples will probably continue to aggregate, creating 'identities' such as Western-Nilotic, Kamatusa, Mount Kenya, Coastal and Northern, as economic and political divisions absorb and subsume older differences of language, culture and history.

Internationalism versus Nationalism and Self-Reliance

The choice of whether to seek autonomy from or incorporation into the world economy and culture has also threaded its way through Kenya's history. The first decade of independence was dominated by the desire to Africanise skilled jobs and assert Kenya's African identity and demonstrate the country's ability to control its destiny against strong influence from the old colonial power, the Americans and Eastern bloc. A similar tension existed over whether to create protected local industries, providing jobs and saving foreign exchange, or to gamble on the roulette wheel of free trade. The cultural debates of the first two decades contained the same fault line: whether Africans should remain close to their own cultural heritage and consensus-based, elder-led political structures, or immerse themselves fully in the emerging Western/world culture and the atomised individualism it represented.

To some extent, this fault line has been overtaken by events. Since 1963, Kenya has been buffeted by the vagaries of oil prices, Cold War politics, technological change and globalisation. The perception of national autonomy that most governments try to portray – that they can decide the nation's policies independently of outside forces – was always an illusion. There was always a strong relationship between Kenya and foreign governments, and the British played the role of patron and guardian uncle to Kenya for the first decade of its independence. As the influence of the UK diminished in the 1970s, it was replaced by the United States as a more powerful but less reliable patron. External as much as internal pressure forced the reintroduction of multi-party democracy in 1991. By the mid-1990s, the debate over Kenya's dependence on foreign interests had shifted to the 'tyranny' of the international financial institutions (the World Bank and the International Monetary Fund). The balancing act and the conflict continued however: should Kenya follow its own course or open its borders and adopt ideas from elsewhere? How far should local farmers, industries and elites be protected against foreign factories, capitalists and farmers? In many cases, those in power have discovered that their choices are far more limited that those on the outside believe.

Moi as a man embodied a 'heartland' culture of African identity and resistance to externally imposed ideas. He and many other Kenyans have felt themselves to be victims of and powerless towards the Western powers, subject to their whims of policy and fashion. While Kenyatta emphasised the form of self-reliance, though perfectly willing to compromise on the substance, other Kenyans have sought a more thorough accommodation with the West. Tom Mboya represented an early example of a politician deeply attuned to international opinion who saw no particular virtue in economic or social autarky. Others who sought stronger links with Western interests included Njonjo and, since the 1980s, many in the NGO sector who have made use of both Western ideas and money to drive domestic change.

Inside Kenya, although Africans have dominated the political sphere for four decades, the economy remains dominated by non-Africans. While the settlers and administrators of the 1950s have gone, today's aid workers, diplomats and executives constitute a large, privileged and influential social tier. Multinational businesses come and go, but Kenya's high degree of externalisation means it must accommodate to the outside. The Chinese are the latest opportunity and challenge. Even the role of the Kenyan Asian community has not been fully resolved. Although there are now only about half as many people of Indo-Pakistani origin in Kenya as at independence, they continue to wield a disproportionate economic influence and face systemic discrimination. The fears and frustrations over Asian economic power were reawoken by the scandals of the Moi era, in which Asian executives' names featured with disturbing frequency.

Democracy and Autocracy

The African men (they were all male) who replaced their British (male) rulers in 1963 inherited a highly stratified society and then perpetuated it. Although they had used electoral democracy to rise to power, they soon jettisoned it in the interests of a more hierarchical model, in which they, despite their youth, became Kenya's 'elders', elevated by their education and experience to speak on behalf of their less-educated, less-fortunate brethren. Indeed, the idea of electoral democracy as an open individual choice between competing parties was far from universally accepted as a social 'good': many believed it produced waste, caused conflict and heightened ethnic tensions. With a brief and shallow tradition of democratic accountability, there was a natural tendency amongst Kenya's new rulers to see their interests as identical to those of the country. They soon demonstrated they had little interest in the opinions of the poor, less educated, more ethnically parochial peasants, urban workers or the growing underclass of poor and landless. They were supported in this paternally autocratic approach by Western governments, which often encouraged policies that were unpopular inside Kenya, believing these to be in Kenya's best interests in the long term.

As president, Kenyatta was the aged king whose word was law, and Moi inherited and adapted the model of authoritarianism and the administrative structures that supported it. Although Kenya is one of the few states in Africa to have conducted regular elections, it was a constrained pseudo-democracy until 1992, and even thereafter, elections remained far from fair, even where they were free. A tension still remains in public and elite opinion over the merits of a strong leader and a powerful authoritarian state that can direct popular energies into developmental channels (*'Maendeleo'*) versus a fully democratic state, better representing the diversity of popular opinion, but with greater conflict, resource wastage on competitive politics (*'Siasa'*) and a weaker leader. The 2007 elections were a watershed in this evolution, inaugurating an era in which popular and populist politicians and policies played a greater role than in any previous contest. However, the rapid emergence of political families, the inheritance of parliamentary constituencies and a general resignation to the fact that political power will always be exercised by a wealthy, closed, connected elite, all conflict with contemporary rhetoric of popular choice.

Since the early 1990s, representative democracy has also been associated with a greater political role for women, as voters, then as parliamentarians and even presidential candidates. But the rhetoric of empowerment often conflicts with the reality; despite the active leadership of a cadre of women in NGO and political roles, most women remain in supporting roles economically and politically.

Within the state, there has been a three-way struggle between predatory policies that would benefit the elite alone; utilitarian policies that should benefit the majority, even if they increased inequality; and those that were popular, even if they might be economically ineffectual. Because Kenya remained nominally a democracy, and its presidents were alert to the risks of popular dissatisfaction, the tendency of the elite to rule in its own interest was tempered by the need to seek legitimacy, and therefore by recourse to popular policies, even when these were difficult to defend on economic grounds. This was one of the key functions and benefits of the electoral system and the single-party parliament, as they ensured that the voice of the majority could sometimes be heard. Western governments steered Kenya towards rational-technocratic options and away from both populism and predation.

During the 1980s, however, Moi's elite rigged elections and drove redistributive policies that did not always prove to be in the interests of the masses either. The result was a shift in the grounds of debate, so that the interests of the majority aligned better with the interests of the Kikuyu elite than with the new Kalenjin, Luhya, Kamba and Asian 'state class'. The tension in the 1990s on structural adjustment concealed a tension over whether policies should benefit the majority of Kenyans or ensure that resources continued to flow primarily to the elite, even at the expense of the majority. The 2003 Kibaki regime was to offer growth once more, at the expense of growing inequality, but was near eviscerated in 2008 by accusations of election-rigging to sustain itself in office against the popular will.

Security, Impartiality and Growth

Alongside these five themes of conflict, independent Kenya's history has been dominated by the need to deliver three key 'public goods' that cross the boundary between politics and economics. These were *security and stability* (as contrasted with foreign invasion, internal violence and civil disorder), *bureaucratic impartiality and efficiency* (as contrasted with corruption, 'tribalism', non-economic resource allocation and neo-patrimonialism) and *economic growth and development* (as contrasted with economic decline, service failure, poverty and starvation). These were the core values of the Kenyatta state and the foundation of its success. Despite the battles over 'who got what', as long as Kenyatta and his allies could retain a secure state, ensure there was more to go around and maintain a civil service in which corruption and tribalism did not dominate, they would survive. More centralised, capitalist, Kikuyu-focused, internationalised and elitist policies and practices were all justified on the basis that such choices would deliver these key public goods. Neo-patrimonialism – although it resulted in non-economic decision-making, centralised and personalised authority and bloated bureaucracy and ethnic conflicts – was constrained by a recognition that it must not be allowed to rot the state from within.

In the long term, however, Kenya's governments could consistently deliver none of these. By the mid-1970s, economic growth was slowing, and corruption and tribalism were worsening, though the state retained its ability to maintain order into the 1990s. The growth that Kenyatta delivered was founded on rising indebtedness and was never truly secure. In turn, the real failures of the Moi government lay in its inability to deliver any of these three public goods. The need to build up new ethno-regional factions as alternative sources of power to the existing Kikuyu elite led to massive state-sanctioned corruption, non-economic decision-making and a collapse of bureaucratic efficiency. Poverty worsened and food security was a constant concern for half of the country. The desire to defend Rift Valley pastoralist land rights and to neutralise the political impact of immigrant communities led to the clashes of the 1990s, which destroyed much of Moi's residual legitimacy. A combination of external events and a decline in bureaucratic efficiency led to a spiral of economic inefficiencies, resource misallocation and Western hostility, which destabilised an already-shaky economy and eventually undermined the KANU government's will to live.

Kibaki's presidential victory appeared to be a platform for radical change, but the problems of the Kenyatta and Moi states lingered on. During 2003–7, NARC delivered greater growth, resource efficiency and security (though security proved the most intractable). However, its achievements were overshadowed by its insensitive and arrogant behaviour, resulting in a growing clamour over devolution and power-sharing and a resurgence of ethnicised conflicts over 'who gets what'. Corruption remained endemic, the economy struggled to support popular expectations, the poor remained poor, the executive presidency was still a point of division and politics remained ethnic, personalised, violent and accumulative.

The Colour of Money

Kenya's history has been dominated by the struggle for and the exercise of political power. This has been the most visible view of Kenya, and its narration – of presidential authoritarianism and centralism, ethnic conflict and struggles for office – has been the main strand of history and journalism both inside the country and outside. Kenya's second history was the story of the state's struggle to maintain the public goods that sustained its legitimacy. Behind this was a third storyline that underpinned and fuelled the successes and failures of four decades: of money.

At independence, Kenya was a poor country with great expectations, determined to be independent, but without the financial means. Its leadership needed both foreign expertise and money to meet the (exaggerated) expectations that the settler class had shown them were possible. Its patron, Great Britain, wished to 'wash its hands' of its client as quickly as it could, and though willing to provide money, advice and support, did not intend to contribute more than was essential. However, Kenya never achieved financial independence; its budgets always depended on foreign gifts and loans, and its strategy of encouraging inwards investment was of limited effectiveness. When in the late 1980s its behaviour led the donors to close their wallets, the government could do little but obey. The multi-party Moi era of 1993–2002 was dominated by an endless dance over money with Western governments, as investments were tied to both political and economic reforms. Kibaki's first government tried to break this dependence, but with limited success. Although better economic performance weakened the donors' influence, new debts to new allies created new dependencies.

Money also permeates Kenya's internal history. The perception of politics as a zero-sum competition grew, in which one man and one community's gain was another's loss. Inherent constraints and politicised resource allocation drained resources from more productive to less productive sectors and a succession of figures saw their positions as a licence to accumulate. Much of what happens in Kenya can only be understood as a struggle within the elite for personal reward and to direct resources towards specific communities for their political benefit. Money and elite corruption to acquire it sit at the nexus of politics and economics.

Competing Narratives of History

The history of independent Kenya is encrusted with myth and there is little consensus on even basic subjects. The limited scholarship on contemporary events until the 1990s, and the focus on issues of relevance to foreigners amongst international journalists, plus the state's reluctance to permit historical research, has led to the creation of 'imagined histories' in Kenyan discourse. History has been rewritten by successive winners, leaving both events and their meaning confused. The histories of Mau Mau, of Kenyatta and of the Kikuyu community's rights to land were rapidly rewritten and other stories erased in the 1960s. Leaders such as Mboya and Ronald Ngala became forgotten men after their deaths. After Daniel arap Moi's accession to the presidency, the role of the kingmaker Njonjo was downgraded and the land rights of the 'indigenous inhabitants' of the Rift Valley and Coast reasserted. Older histories were lost in the late 1980s, when being a professor of government was a career that led only to the prison cell. More recently, Raila Odinga's history has been one of continual reinvention, from coup plotter and dissident to statesman via seven different political parties.

Two enduring and conflicting narratives have dominated perceptions of Kenya's history. Caricatured for effect, the first is that of political conservatives and of foreign governments. Kenya was a shining star in Africa; Kenyatta was a wise and benevolent ruler. However, corruption and tribalism became a growing problem as his grip loosened, and the second president's tribalism, corruption and redistributive policies pushed Kenya off the path to growth. Only economic liberalisation – which needed liberal democracy in order to be sustainable – could change it. Western governments did their best to push Kenya into reform, but it failed to respond. Support and pressure from the donors and the IFIs saved Kenya from itself in the 1990s, but tribalism, corruption and incompetence continually drag it backwards. Kibaki's new broom brought liberalisation, growth and greater inequality, but its leadership remained corrupt and the divisive pressures of ethnicity a looming danger.

Kenya's alternative history is of popular resistance to an alliance of comprador elites and foreign rulers. This history was sustained by academics, socialists and nationalists, who believed that the leadership had made fundamental errors from the first. This narrative begins with resistance to the colonial conquest, then the struggle for land and identity leading to the Mau Mau war. It challenges the concept of 'development' as growth and argues that Kenya has been exploited and abused by Western powers. After independence, the victory of the conservative 'home guards' was a betrayal of independence, and attempts to reverse this civilian coup led to repression and murder. In the 1980s, the closure of all critical thought created martyrs and a deep-seated anger that exploded when foreign support for the regime was withdrawn. Intellectuals kept alive a flame of dissent throughout, though they struggled to reconcile the dual roles of the West as both the source of Kenya's problems and its liberator. In the 1990s, reflecting the changes in the world, this school of thought moderated its socialism and redirected its anger towards elite rule and presidential authoritarianism, placing its faith in the ability of ordinary people to do the right thing if they were not exploited and misdirected by their political masters. This narrative remains egalitarian, hostile to liberalisation and sceptical of integration into the world economy. From this perspective, Kibaki proved that presidents were incapable of ruling without corruption, self-serving ethnic mobilisation and electoral abuse, and only radical, discontinuous change would bring renewal. This conflict has led to economies with history on both sides, although, as Lonsdale suggests, 'much of Africa's written history has certainly taken the part of its rulers rather than that of its people'.[6]

Sources

This book is based on 25 years of research on Kenya and, as a result, its sources are many and eclectic. The first source has been the rich and varied secondary material: the many books and articles on Kenya's politics, economics and international relations, including a growing number of biographical memoirs. Its second source has been Kenya's press, particularly its English-language newspapers from 1961 onwards, mostly in paper form in the *Daily Nation* archives, consulted between 1992 and 2005. Since 1997, they have been partially and since 2005 fully available in electronic form. Weekly magazines (the *Weekly Review* from 1975, many others after 1990) provide an essential counterpoint to the daily press. While living in Kenya during 1999–2002, it was possible to acquire 'grey' or flimsy publications, although they are seldom available outside the country.

The third source has been the British government records on Kenya from 1961 to 1975 in the National Archives in Kew. The Foreign and Commonwealth Office (FCO) records are the most significant, but Cabinet records (CAB), papers from the Prime Minister's Office (PREM), the Colonial Office (CO) and the Ministry of Defence (DEFE) all contain valuable material. More are released every year, but as I moved to live in the Netherlands in 2005, 1975 was a natural end-point, matching the gradual diminution of British influence. Kenyan government documents have also been invaluable, including National Assembly Official Reports, Kenya Gazettes, Select Committee reports and Statistical Abstracts. An essential source of primary data on constituency and electoral politics was the Institute for Education in Democracy's archives between 1993 and 2005. All this has been filtered and structured from personal experience of Kenya since 1985, and from interviews and engagements with Kenyan politicians, academics, journalists and businesspeople. In the 1992, 1997 and 2002 elections, the author was respectively a journalist, external monitor and internal monitor, and at times an actor as well as observer.

Telling Kenya's story is not always easy. There are few truly authoritative sources of information, perceptions differ wildly and some stories (such as Njonjo's) have never been written at all. For most of the 1960s and 1970s, there were few sources to challenge the official view, apart from the works of a few academics. In the 1980s, this paucity of evidence worsened, with even the simplest matters politicised and virtually all information secret. In the 1990s, the situation reversed, as liberalisation, democracy and press freedom resulted in an explosion of media comment, much of it violently polemical. Meanwhile, official sources of information became suspect, even on such fundamental issues as population, GDP, forest cover or exports, and were supplemented or supplanted by international institutions' and donors' reports, creating multiple, often competing 'truths'. Given that little of this information makes its way into the public sphere, and that many politicians have a limited understanding of the country's economic circumstances, some decisions were made with limited knowledge of the 'facts'. There is also a tendency towards conspiracy theories in the popular imagination. As a result, it is sometimes necessary to introduce generally accepted beliefs (though these may be false), rumour and gossip if such beliefs drive behaviour. In politics, perception is often reality.

The remainder of the book is divided into 13 chapters, structured by distinct periods of policy and practice. Chapter 2 introduces Kenya's history up to independence, focusing on the late colonial period and showing how decolonisation established the themes of conflict seen since. Chapter 3 describes the first giddy years of independence, the rush for growth, the impact of the land settlement schemes, the establishment of single-party rule and the growing tension over the country's course. Chapter 4 describes the second period of multi-party competition, which ended with Mboya's death and the re-establishment of one-party rule. Chapter 5 takes us into the 1970s, the 'golden years' of the Kenyatta era, in which his conservative, bureaucratic but authoritarian writ was still law, although the country's problems were deepening. The declining years of the monarch are covered in Chapter 6, which shows how power slipped into other, equally authoritarian hands. It describe the struggle for the presidential succession and – partly as a consequence – how tribalism, corruption and economic performance worsened.

Chapter 7 describes the instabilities of the early Moi years, in which a younger, non-Kikuyu president sought to change Kenya's course, but was driven by his need for survival to concentrate power in his own hands, close political space and create a new ethnically centred power structure. Chapter 8 recounts the dark days of the late 1980s, the missed opportunities for economic reform and growing corruption and political repression. Chapter 9 presents the seismic changes of 1990–2, during which Kenya was forced onto a new economic and political trajectory, which also saw the emergence of state sponsored ethnic and political violence. Chapter 10 describes the period 1993–7, during which a reinvigorated KANU presided over a gradual political and economic liberalisation, but this took place alongside corruption, tribalism and state decay. Chapter 11 recounts the dying days of the Moi administration, with the president a 'lame duck', and KANU weakened by years of misrule, but still able to dominate, entice or divide its opponents, until Moi's cataclysmic mistake of 2002 in selecting his successor, which handed victory to his opponents.

Chapter 12 describes the first Kibaki presidency, and how NARC's victory in 2003 resulted in the return of economic rationality and of growth, but how its achievements were frittered away in apparently ideological but ethnically underpinned conflict. This ended with the 2007 elections, the shattering violence of January–February 2008 and its aftermath in the creation of Kenya's first true coalition. An epilogue, Chapter 13, covers events since April 2008. The 'grand coalition' endured, but struggled to solve Kenya's problems, with the notable exception of a new constitution, which was inaugurated in 2010 with great hope but with huge risks as well. Chapter 14, the conclusion, reprises the themes of the book. It weaves together a picture of how Kenya's politics have been dominated by a struggle to deliver security, efficiency and growth, but how a few divisive political themes and the legacies of the past have undermined their achievements, making the long-term future of Kenya's institutions and the security of the country's people far from certain.

Chapter 2

Independence!

Introduction

Independent Kenya did not emerge suddenly in 1963, as a blank slate on which its new leaders could write, but as the organic evolution of decades of development, conflict and change, both under British rule and before the colonial incursion. Independence was a critical symbolic step, but the process of decolonisation had begun six years before and continued for a decade thereafter. In order to understand independent Kenya, we must understand how the colony emerged with its unique form and challenges, and how many of the problems of the independent state had their origins in choices made in the colonial period. Following the defeat of the Mau Mau revolt, the shape of the country's accelerated decolonisation in 1960–3 reflected a complex combination of African pressure and divisions, the legacies of war, settler land fears, changing metropolitan strategy (blown by an anti-colonial 'wind of change') and Cold War security concerns. The colonial government was far from happy about such a rapid transfer of sovereignty, but it ensured that the institutions that Kenya inherited at independence were based on British and colonial (rather than revolutionary) stock, and that most of its successors had been educated in the British view of the world. These institutions reflected a history of centralised, arbitrary political authority, on which had been recently overlaid a shallow set of democratic and then federal institutions. The country's political divisions similarly had their roots in a combination of the opinions of a few talented individuals, Cold War politics and deeper-rooted differences in the interests of the various ethnic groups in the country. The decisions made at this time, and the issues on which political competition centred, have dominated Kenya's history ever since.

Independence!

On 12 December 1963, Kenya attained independence from the United Kingdom (UK). At a ceremony on 11 December, in front of the Duke of Edinburgh, Colonial Secretary Duncan Sandys and 200,000 Kenyans, Jomo Kenyatta received Kenya's articles of independence (see Figure 2.1).

At midnight that night, in front of 250,000 revellers, the duke and ex-Mau Mau generals, the Union Jack was lowered and the black, green and red flag of Kenya rose. Kenya was one of the last British colonies in Africa to achieve independence, and the last in East Africa. The delay was a legacy of European settlement, powerful European interests and the Mau Mau war of 1952–6. When change came, however, its pace had proved overwhelming. Nonetheless, the British, who had often viewed

2.1: Kenyatta signs the Articles of Independence, December 1963

Courtesy: Nation Group Newspapers

Kenya's prospects with pessimism, negotiated a transition that proved comfortable both for them and for their successors.

The People and Geography of Kenya

Geography and Boundaries

Kenya is one of the most varied countries in Africa, with coastlines, forests, mountains, deserts, the huge Lake Victoria in the west and the Rift Valley. It has an Indian Ocean coastline and five countries as neighbours – Tanzania to the south, Uganda to the west, Sudan and Ethiopia to the north and Somalia to the north-west. The country contains five agricultural and climatic zones.[1] The coast is low-lying, fertile and hot. It blends into the eastern plateau, mostly semi-arid, stretching inland for several hundred miles. That is succeeded by the Rift Valley and neighbouring highlands (1,000–3,000 metres high), which run across the country north to south, creating a region of cool, fertile agricultural land around the valley itself. To the north and north-west lie semi-desert and desert. In the west, the land slopes down from the Rift Valley to a second small, fertile, humid zone bordering Lake Victoria. Less than 20 per cent of Kenya's land is suitable for agriculture or intensive livestock production, 10 per cent is agriculturally marginal and the remaining 70 per cent desert or semi-desert.

The rough boundaries of Kenya were set more than a century ago, once the division of East Africa into German and British spheres was complete. Most of what is now Kenya came under British administration with the establishment of the East Africa Protectorate in 1895, and control transferred to the Colonial Office in 1905. However, Kenya's boundaries have changed six times since then. The most significant was the transfer of Kisumu and Naivasha Provinces from Uganda to Kenya in 1902. The protectorate was renamed Kenya Colony in 1920, save for the 10-mile-deep coastal strip that Britain administered under the sovereignty of the Sultan of Zanzibar until they were merged at independence. In 1924–5, the British gave 'Jubaland', a northern buffer between British and Italian zones, populated by migratory Somali, to Italian Somaliland. In 1926, Kenya expanded to include northern Turkana.[2] More boundary changes took place after independence. None of the country's borders matched local languages, communities or physical geography; Kenya was an artificial creation, delineated by the British for their purposes, lumping together neighbours, enemies and some communities that had previously had no contact whatsoever.

The People of Kenya in 1963

Kenya's population at independence was 8.6 million people, less than one-quarter of its population today. Most people's involvement in the formal sector economy was limited and they were (on paper) poorer as a result, living a primarily agricultural or pastoral life. Despite Kenya being the most urbanised country in East Africa, 92 per cent of the population lived in the rural areas. Although life had changed dramatically under British rule, most Kenyans remained smallholders or pastoralists. Most land ownership was still familial, communal or collective. Average life expectancy was only 35, mostly due to very high childhood mortality rates, and half the population was under 16, reflecting the rapid population growth of the mid-twentieth century.

The African peoples of Kenya were then (and remain) classified linguistically into three main groups. The Bantu-speaking peoples constituted roughly two-thirds of Kenyans, including the Kikuyu, Embu, Meru, Kamba, Luhya, Gusii, Mijikenda, Taita and Pokomo communities. The second group consisted of the Lake, Plains and Highland Nilotes ('people of the Nile'): the Luo, Kalenjin, Maasai, Turkana and Teso peoples. Finally, there was a smaller Eastern Cushitic-speaking community in the north: the Boran, Orma, Rendille and Somali. The new nation's boundaries included five large ethnic groups (or 'tribes', as they are universally known in Kenya): communities of shared language, ancestral origin and culture with a common name, together comprising two-thirds of Kenya's people, but at least 40 smaller communities.[3] Most were relatively recent arrivals in their area, displacing or absorbing older communities and languages between the fifth and seventeenth centuries.[4] Mobility was continuous until the arrival of the British, and the region was a mosaic of different communities, moving and assimilating under the pressures of food shortages, war, population growth and disease. Community boundaries were blurred and changing significantly as late as 1850.

The largest ethnic community in 1963 was the Kikuyu (or Gikuyu) of the central highlands. Having moved from the north and east over a period of 400 years, the related Kikuyu, Embu, Mbeere, Meru and Tharaka peoples had settled around Mount Kenya. They had then expanded south along the ridges of the highlands, on land cleared or purchased from hunter-gatherers, until they met the Maasai and the ancestors of the Kamba people. They were relatively recent arrivals, and only settled southern Kiambu district in the mid-nineteenth century.[5] Colonial rule stopped their further growth, as the white newcomers took Kikuyu and Maasai land for themselves. The Kikuyu constituted 19 per cent of Kenya's population in 1962. Their close linguistic cousins the Meru accounted for another 5 per cent (see Figure 2.2). Some placed the Gicugu and Ndia communities of Kirinyaga as separate sub-groups or with the Embu, but most considered them part of the broader Kikuyu.

The second largest community at independence was the Luo of Lake Victoria. They had migrated into central and south Nyanza from the north-west between 1490 and 1790, forcing out or assimilating the previous occupants.[6] Although there were at least 34 Luo clans, their tight geographical position and recent arrival meant there was less regional differentiation among the Luo than in some other communities. Their low-lying, humid territories and distance from the highlands also meant the Luo were unaffected by colonial land alienation. To the east of the Luo, in the small, fertile highlands south of the Rift in Nyanza Region, lived the Gusii people (commonly known as the Kisii). A Bantu community linguistically close to the Meru and Kuria but surrounded by Nilotic (Luo and Maasai) neighbours, they arrived in what was now Kisii District around 1820.

The Luhya (also known as the Abaluhya or Abaluyia – *aba* meaning people in the Bantu languages) to the north of the Luo, in contrast, were a looser federation

2.2: 1962 census results

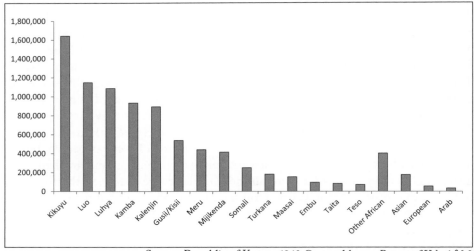

Source: Republic of Kenya, *1962 Census Advance Report of Vols. 1 & 2*

of communities who also constituted 13 per cent of the population, mostly living in Western Region. There were 17 or 18 distinct Luhya 'sub-tribes' or sub-groups, ranging from the largest – the Bukusu of Bungoma and the Maragoli of Kakamega – through the monarchical Wanga to the tiny Kisa and Marama. The complex substructure of the Luhya was attributable in part to their recent history of migration, conflict and absorption of other groups.[7]

Fourth largest were the Kamba (or Akamba), Bantu speakers whose 'reserves' (in the language of their conquerors) were east of Nairobi in Machakos and Kitui Districts, collectively known as Ukambani.[8] Kamba families had also settled on the trade routes to the coast before the British arrival, and acted as ivory hunters and intermediaries between upcountry communities and Arab and Swahili traders. The Kamba too suffered from European land alienation around Machakos.

The fifth largest community was the Kalenjin family of peoples in the Rift Valley. These semi-nomads probably migrated into the area in the seventeenth century, assimilating and influencing existing inhabitants, including the forest-dwelling Ogiek.[9] The Kalenjin consisted of seven major sub-groups: the Kipsigis, Nandi, Tugen, Keiyo (or Elgeyo), Marakwet, Pokot and Sabaot. Some, such as the Kipsigis and Nandi, had become farmers, while most Tugen and Pokot remained pastoralists. These 'sub-tribes' themselves consisted of distinct communities or extended families, and in the early years of colonial rule they were subdivided further in ethnography and sometimes administration.[10] The Kalenjin were the least unified of the big communities, and censuses did not identify them as a 'tribe' (the term used in government documents) until 1979.

Other communities living in what had become Kenya included the once-powerful Maasai, though they constituted less than 2 per cent of the population.[11] In the nineteenth century, these warlike cattle-herders had controlled most of the Rift Valley grasslands from Tanganyika to Samburu, Laikipia and Uas Nkishu (anglicised to Uasin Gishu) in the north-west, an area equivalent to that of the European settlers who followed them. The Maasai had traded and intermarried with their agricultural neighbours, particularly the Kikuyu, but retained a distinctive military orientation, cattle economy and identity. Their control of the Rift Valley ended with the arrival of the British. Most of the Maasai were now in the south, following colonial relocations, with only a few Maasai and the Samburu (who spoke a dialect of Maa) in the north. North and west of the Samburu were the Turkana, very recent arrivals.

Much of the Kenya coast was populated by nine Bantu communities, each centred on a hilltop fort and clearing known as a *kaya*. These were the Mijikenda peoples. They shared inland areas with the Bantu Pokomo and Cushitic Orma in the north and with the Taita in the south. The coast itself was unique, however, in the influence of Omani and Zanzibari Arab culture and the development of a distinctive Swahili identity, which merged Bantu cultures and peoples with Arab and Islamic influences. Trading caravans had also brought the Swahili language into the interior, and it became widely spoken in the colonial era.

The British had ruled the Somali-speaking peoples of Kenya's north-west for 60 years, but most Somali still viewed themselves as part of a greater Somalia.

Kenya's Somali-speakers shared a common language and Islamic religion, but were divided into (often hostile) clans. Most were camel-pastoralists, unfettered by national boundaries, and most only arrived in Kenya in the twentieth century. The British made few attempts at either administration or development, seeking only to maintain order and to restrict their movement south and west. As for the Kalenjin, censuses recorded the Somali under their families or clans (for example, Ajuran, Degodia, Garre or Murille) until the 1980s.

The new colonial power tried to maintain order (and secure their own people's land rights) by fixing administrative boundaries based on the ethnic differences they saw between communities. To do this, they defined communal 'native' land rights in 24 reserves, each dedicated for occupation by specific ethnic groups. They also discouraged or banned outright cross-border settlement and land-buying by Africans. These Reserves hardened boundaries between communities and ended long-term migrations such as the southern march of the Turkana and the movement of the Tugen from the Baringo hills into Maasai-controlled grazing, which had been under way when the British arrived.

Other Recent Migrants

A unique feature of Kenya within East Africa was the high number of European immigrants in the country, encouraged over five decades by an open land frontier, government support and the promise of a colonial lifestyle. Mostly British or South African, Europeans had soon acquired much of the most fertile lands, inspired by glowing reports of the opportunities in the region. Although their numbers had grown rapidly, there were still only 56,000 Europeans in 1962, less than 1 per cent of the population.[12]

Immigrants from India arrived alongside Europeans at the turn of the century, adding their numbers to the Indian merchants trading along the coast.[13] Having built the railway, a few thousand stayed on and other tradesmen, clerks and workers followed. With immigration unrestricted, the community grew rapidly, taking advantage of the opportunities that colonial rule brought in trade and small-scale production, creating clusters of Indians of Gujerati, Punjabi or Goan origin throughout East Africa. The relative ease of travel from India meant that 'Asians' (as they became known in Kenya) maintained their caste and social structures more easily than elsewhere in Africa. By 1962, there were 177,000 Asians in Kenya, of whom half were Hindu, one-quarter Muslim and the remainder Sikh or Christian.[14] Most of Kenya's Asians and Arabs lived in urban areas.

The Fluidity of Ethnicity

The ethnic labels ascribed to peoples in the early twentieth century were not always identical to those used today. Although the collective identity of the Kikuyu was well established, as was that of the Luo, some communities were only just beginning to adopt a 'tribal' rather than a 'sub-tribal' label. This was particularly clear amongst the

Kalenjin, Luhya and Coastal peoples, who each identified themselves at a sub-group level (Nandi, Samia or Giriama, for example), rather than as a 'national' ethnic bloc. The name 'Luhya', for example, was coined in the 1930s, meaning 'those of the same fires', as a way of asserting a common identity large enough to entitle them to a share of the national 'cake'. The name 'Kalenjin' (a term for people whose languages include the phrase 'I tell you') dated from the 1940s or early 1950s, and its use was similarly driven by the desire to obtain bargaining power at the national level.[15] The Mijikenda retained separate identities as Rabai, Giriama, Kauma and Digo throughout the colonial period, and only in the build-up to independence did their political elite assert a 'Mijikenda' identity, reflecting a broadening conception of kinship driven by the creation of the nation-state.

The 'tribes' of pre-colonial Kenya were not hard, immutable collectives, but reflected gradations of shared origin, language and culture. Many if not most ethnic groups had clans whose rituals, language or history indicated recent absorption from another community. The Kikuyu, Embu and Meru of central Kenya, for example, spoke (mostly) intelligible languages, and people living on the borders between such communities might be unaware of their own 'tribe'. At an individual level, ethnic identities were not genetic, but fluid and incorporating.

There were also processes of cultural assimilation and aggregation under way, which were gradually reducing the number of recognised and self-ascribed ethnic groups. These processes were accelerated by the creation of district boundaries and by British expectations of 'ethnographic purity' within each tribal unit.[16] In South Nyanza district, for example, the Abasuba (or Basuba) peoples of Mfangano and Rusinga islands and the mainland Wagasi, all Bantu speakers, were still separately identified in the 1962 census, but were being absorbed linguistically and administratively into the Luo, leaving many 'Basuba' both Luo and Basuba.[17] The simplifying force of colonial rule was seen everywhere. The scattered forest-dwelling hunter-gatherer Ogiek (or Okiek, also known by the British as Ndorobo), were gradually driven to adopt a recognised identity.[18] As their ethnic and geographical status on the boundaries of Kikuyu, Maasai and Kalenjin was unclear, members of the community increasingly defined themselves as Kalenjin after independence, though many probably had common ancestors with those calling themselves Kikuyu. The Terik (or Nyangori) sub-group of the Kalenjin effectively ceased to exist after independence, fully assimilated into other Kalenjin communities. Similarly, the northern Sakkuye are today being absorbed into the Borana, and will probably cease to exist as an independent ethnic identity in the next few decades.

Early Years, 1888–1930

Over six decades, Kenya Colony was transformed from a lightly populated pastoral and agricultural area with no fixed borders or broad political authority into a functioning twentieth-century state. It was an artificial creation, following no natural boundaries, built through the imposition of will and technology by a small number of Europeans on a reluctant African population, directing African and Asian labour.

Conquest and Colonisation, 1888–1910

The British colonial invasion was a gradual event, lasting more than a decade. It began with private enterprise and the formation of the Imperial British East African Company in 1888. Then, in 1895, with the 'scramble for Africa' at its height, the British declared a protectorate over the land from the coast to the Rift Valley. The main impetus for settlement and commerce was the construction of the railway from the coast to Uganda, which began in the deep-water port of Mombasa in 1895 and reached Kisumu on Lake Victoria in 1901.

The railway was designed to protect the headwaters of the Nile in Uganda, but once completed, it needed both justification and defence, and from 1903 white settlers provided both, changing Kenya's future irrevocably. Britain believed it had a potential colony in Kenya, and many Europeans emigrated there to farm and live the life of adventure in the highlands, which were cool and generally free from disease. Many of the first settlers came from the British aristocracy and the military. Accustomed to command and with deeply engrained prejudices against foreigners, these imperial settlers were convinced that they were the natural rulers of Kenya (as of everywhere else) and that Africans were their feudal subjects.[19]

The existing inhabitants of the region resisted colonial rule, and the British employed large-scale violence to subdue them. There was conflict between East African Company forces and the Kikuyu during the first contacts of 1888–92. There was more sustained violence between colonial forces and the Nandi, Gusii, Luhya, Luo and Teso in the west between 1895 and 1908. It was a one-sided contest of spears against guns, mass slaughter and a population cowed into sullen obedience. The Gusii were not defeated until 1908, while the Giriama revolted as late as 1914.[20] Even where lands were unsuitable for white settlement (there were few mineral reserves to stir avarice), the imposition of colonial order had its own logic. The British were few in number, and relied on non-European armies to fight their battles. Some were mercenaries from overseas; more were local allies, persuaded by the promise of spoils or the defeat of their enemies. The Kamba were preferred for their loyalty and obedience, as were the Maasai and the Luhya Wanga in the west. The more paternal element of British culture was seen in their abolition of slavery in the sultan's dominions in 1907.[21]

The 30 years before the British arrival had seen drought, brutal wars amongst the Maasai and outbreaks of rinderpest and smallpox, which had depopulated much of the central Rift Valley and Kiambu and killed most Maasai cattle. Finding the highlands lightly populated and suitable for European agriculture, the British 'alienated' (took for themselves) most of the centre of the country, from Machakos to the Uganda border. Between 1902 and 1915, 7.5 million acres (3.1 million hectares) or 20 per cent of the best land in the country was declared Crown property and reserved for white immigrants only. The government then leased, sold or gave it to white settlers under a British-style individual land title system, creating what became known as the 'white highlands' or the 'scheduled areas' (see Figure 2.3). In 1915, to secure the position of the settlers, who demanded further support from the state, their land lease terms were extended from 99 to 999 years.

Compensation to the previous users or occupants was minimal, and some Kiambu Kikuyu and Kamba found themselves transformed overnight from landowners to 'squatters' (semi-feudal tenants with land-use rights in return for work). There were particular problems in southern Kikuyu areas, stemming from grants of land to Europeans around Limuru and Thika, though there were disputes about how much of the alienated land had been cultivated before the European invasion, and who had really 'owned' it, as such issues affected their land rights.[22] There was clear evidence of uncompensated land losses by some Kikuyu families, while others had 'sold' land to the British, believing they were only giving them 'use rights'. Although only about 4 per cent of Kikuyu and 2 per cent of Kamba lost land, their growing population was trapped in their small 'reserves'.[23]

Others experienced more substantial losses. The Nandi and Kipsigis Kalenjin to the west also lost land, while the Maasai lost the entire central Rift Valley. Three-quarters of the alienated lands had been Maasai-controlled until 1890.[24] The British signed controversial treaties with the Maasai and Sabaot Kalenjin in 1904, alienating their land for European settlement. Some of these treaties were for 99 years, considered a polite fiction at the time, but which proved an issue on their expiry a century later.[25] After the first treaty, the British moved the Maasai of Nakuru and Naivasha north to Laikipia 'in perpetuity'. In 1911–13, however, to extend white farms and ranching north, the governor drove all 10,000 Maasai from Uasin Gishu, Trans-Nzoia, Laikipia and Nakuru into the southern Maasai reserve, which later became Kajiado and Narok Districts. Both deportations were justified by agreements with (illiterate) Maasai elders, but were repudiated later as having been signed under duress.[26]

The Introduction of European Administration

Before the imposition of colonial rule, Kenya had no trans-ethnic and few ethnic political structures. Authority was personal and local, a function of age, lineage, supernatural abilities, wealth and leadership skills, supported by the communal wisdom of elders and the physical power of young men.[27] Age sets or grades (communities of similarly aged men) collectively moved into new roles as children became warriors, then elders and senior elders. Some communities created semi-elective chiefs, but most did not choose a formal head. All societies were gerontocratic and relatively egalitarian, and all relations were personalised.

The region's new rulers overlaid on this a different model: the provincial administration, a structure that they used to govern their colonies throughout Africa. They divided the country administratively into provinces, the provinces into districts, and the districts into divisions, locations and sub-locations. The new state drew these boundaries based on the needs of the white settlers and their understanding of African ethnic groups. The formalisation of the African 'reserves' in 1915 hardened boundaries that had been fluid, reinforcing separate development policies for black and white and for different ethnic groups.

Lacking the numbers to administer the colony directly, the British ruled through local representatives, and appointed 'chiefs' and 'senior chiefs' to administer African communities – often inventing such leadership positions in the process.[28] They also created local courts to apply customary law and a local tribal police to enforce it. British civil servants administered these fiefdoms as provincial commissioners and district commissioners (PCs and DCs) and district officers down to the divisional level, below which African chiefs were appointed and salaried. Although they provided a buffer and communication channel between white rule and the population, these new chiefs (often traders, interpreters or early Christians) were widely disliked, and their establishment caused structural changes in patterns of wealth and influence. Many took advantage of their new gatekeeper positions to acquire land and money; early examples of the use of central authority to acquire local resources corruptly.

2.3: The 'white highlands'

Source: Government of Kenya

Alongside the provincial administration came technical services such as agricultural extension officers, labour officers and vets, working for the central ministries. All reported to the governor, a London appointee, and his small central government. The result was a structure of command and control that tried to maintain order and encourage development while delegating most authority to the district level. The Colonial Office in London decided overall policy, but relied on local officials for virtually everything else.

Racial segregation was embedded into the colony from the first, with Africans seen as a resource to be exploited, not as having rights equal to those of the European settlers. There was also tension within the colonial state between wholehearted support for white settler power and privilege, and support for African rights and economic development.[29] These tensions grew as changes in Kenya's society and economy caused economic differentiation, education spread, wage labour grew and the mythical monolithic 'tribal identity' that underlaid the indirect rule model disintegrated.[30]

The colonial government administered its new African subjects in differing ways. In the pastoral north and south there was little interest in development, and the key issues were livestock control and the maintenance of security. In the densely populated agricultural areas the settlers and therefore the government wanted labour for the new white farms. Taxation began early, with the government collecting a tax on every hut in the colony before the First World War, as a means to raise funds, but also as a way to force Africans into wage labour. Seeking ways to make the colony and railway pay, the government helped the settlers draw African labourers onto their under-utilised land, to work as squatters. There had been few significant Kikuyu settlements inside the Rift Valley before the arrival of the British, but under colonial rule the Kikuyu spread widely through the valley, working on European farms in return for the right to live, cultivate crops and graze sheep and goats inside the 'white highlands'. The majority of squatters in the southern Rift and Laikipia were Kikuyu, the largest number from Kiambu, but there were many Bukusu squatters in Trans-Nzoia, and Nandi, Keiyo and Kipsigis in the west. Many Luo, Luhya and Gusii, in contrast, moved to live as short-term contract workers on the tea estates around Kericho or on the sisal estates of the coast, a choice that had long-term implications for Kenya's future.

Gradually, the country developed from a scattering of foreigners with guns into a functioning state and economy, built on settler agricultural exports, mostly to the UK. Policy and practice encouraged the build-up of large ranches, plantations and farms.[31] Towns grew up, based on the railway network and European forts. An internally focused subsistence economy was overlain with an export-driven cash-crop agricultural economy, structured around a British-derived capitalist system.

During the 1920s, both maize and wheat became successful exports for white farmers. The search for profitable crops also saw the introduction of tea, coffee and sisal. While Europeans were the main initiators and beneficiaries, there were significant trickle-down benefits to their African subjects, with new tools such as hoes and ox-ploughs, and new crops permitting greater food production. Maize cultivation grew rapidly, and maize soon became the staple food. Roads, standardised weights and measures, higher-yielding crop varieties and powered grain-mills improved the lot of many Africans. The area of land under African cultivation increased, as farmers could now cultivate land previously left empty for reasons of defence.[32] However, the state reserved the (particularly profitable) growing of coffee for Europeans, ostensibly to reduce the risk of disease and maintain quality, but also to maintain racial segregation and to encourage Africans into wage labour.

In 1906, the government set up an appointed Legislative Council to make laws and represent white settler opinion. In 1919, 6,000 European men and women 'of pure descent' chose their first elected representatives. Indian and Arab constituencies were added in 1924, but representation was not extended to Africans. In 1925, recognising the need for Africans to have some responsibility for their own affairs, the Legislative Council established local native councils (LNCs) to help administer the reserves. While they had taxation powers and could mobilise significant resources, most members were government appointees and the councils were primarily discussion fora for the communication of grievances to the DCs who chaired them. A key focus for the councils' efforts was access to European-style education, and they invested heavily in establishing local primary schools. The government also used the LNCs to channel dissent into more constructive activity.

The New Religions

Before the arrival of Europeans, most Kenyans had practised either Islam or animist 'traditional religions', a collective name for various forms of worship of gods, spirits or ancestors. Islam had recently spread inland from the coast with the Arabs and from the north with the Somali. Indian immigrants also brought new forms of Islam and the Hindu religion into urban areas.

Although Christianity first arrived in Kenya during the sixteenth and seventeenth centuries, it had little impact until the twentieth century. The British conquest saw the Bible arrive alongside the gun, as missionaries moved into Kenya in the 1890s and 1900s. The result was the rapid growth of competing evangelical missions from European Christian communities. These included the Anglican Church Missionary Society, the Presbyterian Church of Scotland Mission, the African Inland Mission/Church, Methodists, Pentecostal churches, Quakers and the Catholic Church. There was a rapid Christianising of the population, a 'race for Christ', with the lure of access to medical services and a basic education in the mission stations.[33] The Kikuyu, whose religion was monotheist, were particularly well served by competing churches. Some churches absorbed elements of local religions into their beliefs and practices, and African independent churches emerged as offshoots of Protestantism.

Development and Dissent in the 1920s

After the carnage of the First World War, in which many Kenyan Africans died, there was a stronger assertion of settler influence over the fledgling Kenyan government. African wages were cut by a third in 1921, and labour conditions were harsh. From 1919 until 1947, for purposes of identification and labour control, Africans had to wear a much-hated pass (*kipande*) around their necks when travelling outside the reserves.

After the war, the trickle of white immigrants became a stream. In December 1919, 1,500 soldier-settlers arrived on one ship alone, granted land by a grateful Britain. Many came with the aim of establishing a white state and society, on the pattern of Canada, Australia, New Zealand and South Africa. Many Britons believed that their civilising influence could only be of benefit to East Africans, whom they saw as amongst the most backward communities in the world, 'without a history, culture or religion of their own'.[34] New land alienations continued until 1919–20, when parts of the Nandi Reserve and Kericho were excised and allocated, contrary to previous commitments to the inviolability of the reserves.

It was amongst the Kikuyu and particularly those from southern Kiambu that the effects of land alienation and economic development were most pronounced. Rapid urbanisation in nearby Nairobi created both markets for agricultural produce and work in the factories.[35] The end of the First World War brought the first stirrings of Kikuyu resistance to colonial rule. Elders from Kiambu founded the first such body, to help protect *githaka* (extended family) land rights from European alienation. However, the best known was the East African Association, a Kikuyu-led young men's protest movement founded in 1921, helped by Indian businessmen unhappy with the increasingly white-supremacist direction of the colony. The consequence was stronger African protest – against land alienation, the hut tax, the *kipande*, wage cuts, restrictions on coffee growing and the lack of political representation. The protests ended in 1922 with the detention without trial of Kiambu agitator Harry Thuku and the killing by troops of dozens of Kikuyu protesters in Nairobi.[36] This took place only 27 years after the protectorate was established. Taxes were reduced soon after. However, an archetype had been established of Kikuyu-led popular protest, violent repression and subsequent compromise.

The tensions were not solely between 'white' and 'black'. With a large Indian population, the British briefly considered making the colony 'the America of the Hindu', but this idea fell out of favour as white numbers grew, and the scheduled areas remained 'whites only'. Still, there were twice as many Asians as Europeans in the 1920s. The period 1918–23 saw more disputes between Asians and Europeans than over the position of the African majority.[37] In 1923, facing evidence of conditions of near-slavery for African workers and serious tensions between white and Indian immigrants, the Colonial Office made a key decision, known as the Devonshire Declaration. This asserted that in Kenya the interests of the African majority would always be paramount, and that there would be no settler dominion of government as in southern Africa. The 'white highlands' would remain white, though, and there would be no Indian land settlement or common electoral roll. The three-layer racial hierarchy would endure.

There was little indication in practice of African paramountcy. The government remained dominated by settler opinion, racial segregation remained universal and the treatment of African labour appalling. Discrimination against Africans and to a lesser extent Asians was institutionalised in practice, though rarely enshrined in law.[38] Kenya was becoming a dual state and society: a settler economy, with its crops, land, society, politics and form of government, coexisting alongside its African equivalents.

Meanwhile, the country developed rapidly as towns grew, roads were built, the railway extended (to serve European settlers) and new crops spread. The 1920s were a boom era for settler agriculture, and the land under European cultivation tripled. While the settlers were the most visible face of Europe, British capital also invested in primary production for export (tea, tobacco, wattle and soda ash). Africans were encouraged or forced to sell their labour by taxation, low wages, direct coercion, bans on cash-crop growing and the opportunity to purchase new goods. One-fifth of the adult male population was part of the labour force by the early 1920s – one of the highest rates in Africa.[39] Nonetheless, many communities resisted wage labour or integration into the money economy, and there was a labour shortage throughout the 1920s. Enforced communal labour was widely used to terrace land and build roads. Administration was closer and coercion more common than elsewhere in British Africa. The economy therefore evolved under the competing influence of both settler and metropolitan capital interests, periodically constrained by British humanitarian concerns and administrative commitments to fair play.[40] Relations between the colony and London were often as poor as with the 'natives'.

By 1928, there were more than 100,000 squatters on white farms, cultivating far more land than were the Europeans. Initially, the government had supported African squatting, as they knew the Europeans could not farm alone, and conditions were better for the migrants than in the crowded reserves. During the 1920s, attitudes changed and regulations tightened. Squatters' rights to land and livestock were restricted and settler demands for compulsory labour grew.[41] The state and more efficient European farmers were working towards an end to squatting and its replacement by wage labour, fearing that long-term cultivation by Africans would inevitably create de facto land rights in the highlands.

Before the twentieth century there were no settlements in Kenya larger than for-tified villages outside Mombasa and the coast. Urban life in upcountry Kenya was a colonial phenomenon. Nairobi and Mombasa were the main trans-ethnic 'melting pots'. Nairobi was built near the meeting point of Kikuyu, Kamba and Maasai lands. It soon developed from a railway yard into a major urban, industrial and commercial centre. The country's capital moved there in 1907, a critical decision in the evolution of the state, as it centred politics and the economy on the whites and the upcountry Kikuyu (and Kamba), and away from the coast and the Swahili. Nairobi grew spec-tacularly quickly, with the population reaching over 110,000 by the first census in 1948. More than one-third of its inhabitants were Asian, fewer than 10 per cent were European. Mombasa, four centuries older, was Kenya's second town, populated by a mixture of Muslim Arabs, Swahili, Mijikenda and growing numbers of upcountry workers, particularly Luo and Kamba, working around the port. Smaller settlements included Kisumu and Nakuru. Originally, the urban areas were designed for permanent European and Asian occupation only, with Africans regarded as temporary visitors. This policy soon broke down, but strict racial segregation was still observed, and most urban land was European or Asian owned until the 1960s. Urbanisation resulted in growing formal and informal incomes, but alongside this came crime, prostitution and disease.

Kikuyu dissatisfaction deepened once educated Kikuyu discovered that their reserve had been declared the property of the state and that the Colony would give no legal recognition to *githaka* land rights. Protracted debates in the administration over the merits of allowing individual land title for Africans produced no result. Thuku's efforts were followed in 1924–5 by the formation of the Kikuyu Central Association (KCA) by educated farmers and traders from Central Province (the home of most Kikuyu, Embu and Meru). Its aims were both political and economic: the return of Kikuyu land, an end to the ban on Africans growing cash-crops and the repeal of the hut tax. The KCA also adopted the Kikuyu practice of oaths of loyalty to an association, which was to evolve into one of the tools used in the Mau Mau revolt. The Luo also established protest groups in the 1920s and political associations emerged amongst other agricultural communities in the 1930s.[42] The British never accepted the legitimacy of such associations, however, believing that the provincial administration and their local government structures made them unnecessary.[43] They were also careful to ensure that these groups remained regional or ethnic, a policy that had long-term consequences for the independent state.

In 1929, a Kikuyu from Gatundu in Kiambu was financed by local contributions to sail to Europe to press their land claims on the British. He was named Kamau wa Ngengi, who had taken the Christian name Johnstone and was later to be known as Jomo Kenyatta. His history dominated that of Kenya for the next 50 years. At this time, the flamboyant Kenyatta was in his mid-30s, mission-educated and with a job in Nairobi.[44] He had become the full-time secretary of the KCA in 1928 and editor of its Kikuyu-language newsletter *Muigwithania* (the reconciler or unifier). After 20 months in Europe, having had little success in influencing the government, Kenyatta returned to Kenya. In 1931, however, he returned to the UK and was to remain abroad until 1946.

Social and Cultural Change

Pre-colonial labour in all Kenyan communities was divided by gender, with men generally responsible for cattle-keeping, hunting, land clearance and war, and women for agriculture, cooking and child rearing. Polygyny amongst wealthier men was common, as was the payment of bridewealth to the family of the bride in recompense for her agricultural labour. Marriage was an economic and social arrangement between families as well as individuals. Women could not inherit property, and mostly took a subservient social and political role. Most African communities followed an age-set model of authority, which saw leadership as moving from generation to generation. The transition to adulthood was for most male and female youth an experience of genital excision, which symbolised their readiness for adult responsibilities. The largest community that did not practise male circumcision was the Luo, a distinction that took on political significance later, because of the association of circumcision with adulthood in other communities.

The growing numbers of adherents to the Christian missions in central and western Kenya were now challenging this model, and church mission schools – teaching Christianity, reading, writing, arithmetic and basic technical skills – allowed them access to jobs that the majority did not have. Even amongst non-English or Swahili speakers, the Christian message spread, as the churches translated the Bible into African vernacular languages. Areas where European administration came late, where pastoralism made permanent schools impossible or where initial responses were hostile were later at a significant educational disadvantage. The introduction of the money economy (replacing livestock as the main measure of wealth and medium of exchange) also changed social relations, weakening bonds between elders and youth, and the first 'urbanised' Africans emerged, who had lost their links with their local lineages (and often their land rights with it). In Central Province, fertile and close to Nairobi, commercial agriculture was threatening the *mbari* system of patron–client tenancies. Population growth, land purchases by chiefs and other wealthy men and pressure from commercial farming led to the first landlessness by the 1930s. Elsewhere, land-holding remained communal and land sales rare.

A major controversy emerged in 1929–30 concerning the practice of female circumcision (also known as clitoridectomy or female genital mutilation) as a rite of passage into adulthood for young Kikuyu women. The tensions within the Kikuyu over this custom catalysed the emerging conflict within the community. The European-led Protestant missions had campaigned increasingly assertively against female circumcision, and in 1929 they demanded that Christians abandon the practice entirely. The KCA opposed the missions and most Kikuyu supported their stand. The issue became a symbol of Kikuyu dissent against colonial rules and the European churches.[45] Concerned about native (especially Kikuyu) political activity, the government used legislation to restrict public meetings and limit fund collections, but it was unwilling to ban female circumcision entirely.

The crisis resulted in the breaking away of Kikuyu, Embu and Meru churches to form independent African Christian churches. It also strengthened the independent schools, which were an increasingly radical influence in Central Province and amongst Kikuyu squatters in the Rift. Despite state hostility, the independent schools movement (unfunded and with only African teachers) grew rapidly. By 1936, there were 44 independent schools in Central Province. In 1939, Chief Koinange wa Mbiyu of Kiambu also established an independent African Teachers' Training College at Githunguri.

Another key establishment for the future of Kenya was also sited in Kiambu – Alliance High School at Kikuyu, established by Protestant missions in 1926. The school took the best African Protestant secondary students from around the country, and educated most of the leadership that took Kenya to independence and beyond. These included Chief Koinange's son Mbiyu, Eliud Mathu, James Gichuru, Oginga Odinga, Jackson Angaine, Charles Njonjo, Ronald Ngala, Jeremiah Nyagah, Charles Rubia, Ngala Mwendwa, Paul Ngei, Dawson Mwanyumba, Munyua Waiyaki and Julius Kiano.[46]

New Forms of Trade and Industry

There had been barter trade between communities before the British arrival – in food, livestock, pots and baskets, skins, weapons, tools, salt, ivory, poisons and slaves. The introduction of industrial mass production, high-speed rail transport and new markets overlaid on this a larger-scale pattern of production and trade. The design of Kenya's new road and rail networks was oriented towards the transport of raw materials from settler farms to the urban areas and the coast. Kenya's main exports were crops such as coffee, sisal and tea, while it imported most industrial goods from the UK. Asian merchants soon dominated retail and small-scale trade in imported goods, again overlaid on longer-established trading patterns amongst African communities in locally produced goods.

There had been small-scale industries in the pre-colonial period such as iron smelting, basketry and pottery, but these too were supplanted by the mass production of goods using factories, labour specialisation and electric power. Industrialisation began with the processing of local raw materials, producing beer, soap, dairy products, tea, coffee, sisal, meat and cement. Industrial development remained modest, however. Until the 1940s, British policy was against the local production of industrial goods; instead, the country was seen as a market for British exports.

Colonial Maturity but Rising Tensions, 1930–52

Kenya Colony was free to make policy under only the broadest guidelines from the Colonial Office, as long as it remained financially self-sufficient and did not cause concern at home. The state as a political and economic actor was not a monolithic entity, but responded to the pressures of several communities – British investors, white settlers, British domestic opinion, its own interests and what it believed were the interests of the African peasantry. It remained decentralised and responsive to local issues, though it rarely articulated Asian or African opinion explicitly.[47] However, the government and particularly the provincial administration continued to treat most opposition as akin to subversion. They did whatever they could to discourage, discredit or suppress it. For most Africans, the state remained alien and of little legitimacy, its laws arbitrary and its decisions made without their consent or involvement.

Agricultural Development in the 1930s

The 1930s and the global depression saw a fall in both agricultural exports and prices. Indebted white farmers needed government loans, rebates and cuts in African wages to keep afloat and to protect them against African competition. Their over-dependence on maize and wheat inspired a diversification into new crops such as pyrethrum flowers, used for insecticide.

Agricultural cooperatives now processed and marketed most European crops. White farmers had formed the first cooperative in 1908 for marketing, sharing farm inputs and lobbying. Cooperatives offered farmers collective buying power and distribution and marketing economies. The three main cooperatives – the Kenya Planters Co-Operative Union (KPCU), the Kenya Cooperative Creameries (KCC) and the umbrella Kenya Farmers Association (KFA) – were registered in 1931. The KFA campaigned for high standards of products and growing (and against African competition in agriculture); the KCC processed and marketed milk, while the KPCU marketed settler coffee. Africans increasingly participated in this movement and built their own local agricultural cooperatives.

African agriculture began to receive serious administrative attention in the 1930s. There were efforts to improve yields and force communities to introduce terracing and soil conservation measures, and the government posted the first agricultural extension officers to the reserves. There was wider use of new ploughs, hoes and plant breeds. Some workers began to invest their wages in agricultural improvements, including 'grade' (high milk-yielding, imported) cattle. A few wealthier Africans, mainly in Central Province, began to engage in true cash-crop commercial agriculture, producing for sale rather than selling surpluses. Maize-growing was now near universal, while wattle (the bark from wattle trees) to tan hides became an important crop in Central Province.[48] Other crops began to be cultivated in larger quantities, including tobacco and cotton. The state permitted coffee growing by progressive farmers in the Kisii, Embu and Meru highlands by the mid-1930s, though they limited the scale of plantings, in part to minimise the social disruption caused by cash incomes.[49] Coffee-planting remained banned in Kikuyu Central Province, the area closest to European coffee farms, however, until 1951. The state wished to minimise competition between European and African farmers and discouraged the emergence of large African commercial farmers until the 1950s.[50] In their worldview, they had to maintain the bifurcation between African peasants in the reserves and large commercial white farms. By the late 1930s, though, there was already significant economic differentiation – at least in Central Province – with teachers and government officials enlarging their holdings. Colonial chiefs in Kiambu were particularly assertive in using their status to acquire land.[51]

Pastoralism had been a feature of East African life for centuries. Most communities practised agro-pastoralism (the keeping of animals as an adjunct to agriculture). The true pastoralists of Kenya, however, were the nomadic cattle-herding Maasai, Samburu, Turkana and Pokot and the camel-herding Somali, Oromo and Rendille. These communities had no permanent home, but moved from place to place and lived primarily from the consumption and barter of livestock products. Pastoral practices also changed during the colonial era. With less warfare, better disease control, and broader access to markets there were rapid increases in stock numbers. This was counteracted, however, by the limitations on land availability and animal ownership imposed by the government. There was a growing problem of soil erosion, caused by what experts believed was 'overstocking', although the true causes included the restriction on stock movement for disease control and the closure of grazing in the highlands. Concern over the carrying capacity of the rangelands led to land rehabilitation programmes and forced destocking amongst the Kamba and Tugen during the 1930s, and resulting political ferment.[52] Settlers also engaged in their own form of agro-pastoralism, with the development of beef ranching, mostly in Laikipia.

Land Tensions, the Second World War and Kenyatta, 1933–45

In 1932, the British appointed a Land Commission to adjudicate African claims against the government and white settlers and to define the boundaries of the white highlands. Its 1933 report accepted KCA and other submissions that some Kikuyu had lost land through European alienation, and slightly enlarged the Kikuyu and Kamba Reserves. However, it refused restitution for most land alienations, rejected *githaka* land title and ruled that squatter settlement on white farms in the European reserve would never offer them legal title. Kikuyu squatters were bitterly disappointed, as many had believed until then that they had customary land tenure rights. The real struggle over land had begun. From 1937 onwards, regulations defined squatters as labourers, not tenants and gave powers to settler district councils to regulate native stock and labour. Nonetheless, squatter numbers continued to grow. By the end of the 1930s, there were more than 150,000 Kikuyu living and working on European farms, many of who had lost land rights in the crowded Kikuyu Reserve. There were also communities of Kikuyu scattered across other reserves, living, trading and cultivating lands without formal title.

Meanwhile, Johnstone Kenyatta, now calling himself Jomo, lived and worked from hand to mouth in the UK. He studied in London and in 1938 wrote a well-received and well-publicised book on the Kikuyu people, *Facing Mount Kenya*, one of the first anthropological treatises on an African people written by someone from that community.[53] He represented Kenyan African grievances in London, though as the years passed he became isolated from events at home. While in Europe, his political views matured; he campaigned for African interests with European Christians and liberals and with intellectuals from other African countries, but remained something of a loner. He visited Moscow twice and spent 1932–3 in Russia, studying under a pseudonym and supported by Soviet funds.[54] Despite his apparent flirtation with communism, however, he was disillusioned by his time in the east, and was more influenced by the conservative, pragmatic and consensus-driven British approach to politics.[55] He even married a second, British wife. Kenyatta's lengthy absence from his home country, although it isolated him, also allowed him to escape the divisions in the KCA and pressures on it to compromise with the state. With the outbreak of the Second World War, the government banned the KCA and linked associations in Ukambani and Taita in 1940 as potentially subversive and detained 22 KCA officials without trial.

The war was the trigger for fundamental change in Kenya's economy and society, beginning a 20-year boom for the colony. The conflict with the Italians in East

Africa was swift and victorious, and King's African Rifles (KAR) units were freed for service elsewhere in the empire. The government supported agricultural exports in every way, including subsidies for settlers and forced African labour. Both settler and African agriculture blossomed, with the need to feed Allied armies abroad. Between 1942 and 1952, the output of large farms doubled, driven by mechanisation, high and fixed world prices and bulk export deals. Kenyan agriculture already had a large number of statutory boards, to develop and market crops, and the demands of war strengthened them further. With the dangers and costs of maritime trade high, the country was also forced to create several new import substitution industries.

Post-War Development and Change

After the Second World War, British involvement became more active, and grants, loans and investments poured into the colony. The period saw the fastest formal sector growth in Kenya's history, estimated at 13 per cent a year between 1947 and 1954.[56] The welfare state and the managed economy were the dominant political themes in Great Britain, and London encouraged the colonies to invest in development and social welfare for all their peoples (not just Europeans). In Kenya, however, a wealthy and assertive settler community increasingly dominated the governor and his Council of Ministers.[57] There were calls for settler self-government, and growing tensions between their demands, a sceptical Labour government and the interests of African farmers.

In the same period, state regulation of (mostly settler) agricultural crops was further institutionalised, with the creation of more regulatory and marketing boards, including the Coffee Marketing Board, the Maize and Produce Board, the Kenya Meat Commission, the Tea Development Authority, the Wheat Board, the Sisal Board and the Pyrethrum Board. The aim was the same: standardisation of product quality, support for distribution and marketing and price stabilisation, though the profitability of export crops depended on world prices, which the boards could not control. The settlers and government were convinced that this structure minimised price instability, cut out middlemen and increased the predictability of agro-industrial investment.[58] These agricultural parastatals (a form of state-owned enterprise) were also quiet vehicles for settler influence and state control of the sector. Kenya's agricultural sector did not evolve as a private sector capitalist system, but as an administered public–private partnership in which the private sector mostly produced, but the state priced, planned and marketed.[59]

The formal sector of the economy (recorded, taxed and administered) remained almost entirely immigrant owned and operated, with the Asian community dominating small-scale manufacturing and trade and Europeans owning most commercial farms and large businesses. However, a few African entrepreneurs were beginning to establish small businesses in the reserves. The labour force was changing too. By the 1940s, 30 per cent of men were in paid employment. Central Province – particularly Kiambu and Fort Hall (later renamed Murang'a) – and the Luo and Luhya were the main labour sources. Those with education, contacts or special skills could earn salaries vastly greater than those of labourers. As a result, by 1952, there was a clear differentiation between the mass of peasants and pastoralists, and a small class of better-educated teachers, traders, clerks and workers with greater incomes and access to capital, and therefore to land. This emerging middle class was not a distant elite, but well embedded in their rural milieu.

The state still hankered after the simplicity of indirect rule. British administrators individually controlled their districts, trying to treat their peoples as if they were homogeneous and segregated tribes, but migration, landlessness and economic and social change were all undermining this image.[60] The Second World War introduced further seeds of change, with many thousands of East Africans serving outside Africa. Returning soldiers, their horizons widened, used to fighting alongside Europeans and with money to invest, started small businesses, challenging the status quo in the reserves. Differentiation was particularly rapid in the Kikuyu Reserve. The Kikuyu chiefs were the most obvious beneficiaries of economic change, and were lauded by the British as 'progressive' cash-crop farmers. Many of the new rural elite were also involved in the campaign for greater political representation.

From 1947–8, accepting the impossibility of retaining the African majority in a communal state, and desperate to rebuild the shattered British economy, the improvement of African agriculture became a priority. The population was growing and land in the reserves deteriorating.[61] Since there could be no African land ownership in the highlands, the state instead focused on improving the 'carrying capacity' of the reserves and again enforced terracing in Fort Hall and amongst the Tugen, Bukusu and Kamba. It also enforced African cattle dipping and compulsory destocking. This led to protests by a tiny but influential group of African proto-politicians, who opposed such improvements as racially motivated and diverting attention from the real problem of the highlands. The state ended most bans on African cultivation of cash-crops, which had kept incomes below those in neighbouring states. Tea, sisal and pineapple production were all encouraged, but coffee growing picked up most quickly. Racial discrimination remained institutionalised in jobs, housing and schooling, however, and the emerging African elite's resentment at their lower status was a source of enduring discontent.[62]

De facto individual land tenure was now widespread in Central Province, and landlord–tenant relations in Kikuyu areas deteriorated further, resulting in the expulsion of tenants, and frequent litigation. Increasing land sales combined with the forced return of squatters from the Rift to cause landlessness and tension. The growing number of landless was to be the main source of Mau Mau support in the reserves. This change was not unique to Central Province, however. By 1950, Gusii and Kipsigis farmers were also fencing 'their' lands even without formal tenure, agreeing with the settlers that this was the key to agricultural productivity.[63] There was still no legal basis for this, as Europeans had little confidence in the productivity of African agriculture, and a deep fear of both detribalisation and landlessness. Plans for formal individual land tenure trials began, but were slow to mature.[64]

Another source of tension was the changing attitude towards squatters. By 1948, there were 220,000 Kikuyu squatters, nearly one-quarter of the Kikuyu population, on farms in the white highlands and nearby forests.[65] However, agricultural prosperity, closer European settlement and a shift to dairy farming were reducing settler dependence on their labour, and European farmers were forcing squatters off their lands and back to Nairobi and the reserve, limiting their cattle or turning them into wage labourers.[66] By 1948, facing the imminent destruction of their way of life, the squatter movement had become more militant. The failure of the 1940s settlement scheme in Olenguruone in Nakuru, where the government had settled 12,000 Kikuyu ex-squatters on land taken from the Maasai, was a key driver for anti-European oathing and subversion.[67] The same processes took place, in a more muted form, amongst the Kalenjin and Luhya of Trans-Nzoia and Uasin Gishu. Here, however, the commitment to squatter life was less permanent, there was more land in the reserves, settler influence was weaker and European dependence on squatter labour was greater.[68]

African pressure for political representation was growing. The governor appointed the first African, a British-educated teacher from Kiambu named Eliud Mathu, to the Legislative Council in 1944. In the same year, the Kenya African Study Union was formed – the first explicitly national African political organisation. It took a constitutionalist line in representing African grievances and supported Mathu. In 1946, with the war over, it was renamed the Kenya African Union (KAU), and became more assertive. Its leaders included another Kiambu teacher James Gichuru as president, journalist Francis Khamisi from Mombasa and J. D. Otiende, a Luhya teacher from Kakamega.[69]

Although KAU's leadership was moderate and well educated, the government had little time for such 'rabble-rousers'. Kenya was expected to remain a colony indefinitely. The administration believed that economic and social development must precede political development, and that premature African political activity would imperil their gradual advance towards civilisation.[70] Influenced by the new Labour government in the UK, the government granted greater African representation in the Legislative Council, with four nominated members by 1948, but there were no African elections. In April 1952, for the first time, the government decided that the LNCs might elect African candidates for six Legislative Council constituencies, from whom the governor would select representatives. The Emergency was to intervene, however.

Kenyatta, KAU and 'Mau Mau', 1946–52

The Kikuyu community was under increasing pressure from population growth, land shortages, squatter evictions, internal inequalities and settler proximity. Although banned, the KCA continued to operate amongst squatters and in the reserve. By 1946, Kikuyu were swearing new versions of traditional oaths to resist anti-squatter rules.[71]

In 1946, Kenyatta finally returned to seek a leadership role in the nationalist movement. With the Second World War over, as the exhausted British Empire gave up its crown jewel of India, Kenya too appeared ripe for change. On his return, Kenyatta received an overwhelming response from the Kikuyu. Local people had maintained his memory, and believed that he had returned to break European control over the highlands and cash-cropping. He immediately resumed campaigning for change. He took the *mbari* oath (the main Kikuyu oath of unity) and a more aggressive KCA oath. He maintained close relations with the influential and increasingly anti-British Koinange family in Kiambu, both Chief Koinange and his American-educated son Peter Mbiyu.[72] To cement their alliance, Kenyatta took one of the chief's daughters as a third wife.

In 1947, Kenyatta was chosen to replace Gichuru as KAU's president, while also serving as head of the Githunguri Teachers' Training College. He used both positions to build African nationalist sentiment. Kenyatta was a natural leader, but some saw him as arrogant and dictatorial, an opportunist who had been parachuted into the leadership of organisations built by others.[73] Others noted his desire for money and his difficulties in separating his personal financial affairs from those of Githunguri College.[74] His strengths and weaknesses were to help set the direction taken by the independent state.

Gradually, the KCA and KAU began to merge in Kikuyu areas. The overwhelming majority of KAU supporters were Kikuyu, and KAU never established a mass presence outside the Kikuyu, Embu and Meru. Kenyatta certainly tried, and he built links into Luo, Luhya, Kamba, Ugandan and Tanganyikan elites. In practice, though, a mass following amongst the Luo and pastoral communities eluded KAU. Its key demand was the return of 'stolen lands', but this had less appeal in other communities, less affected by land alienation or economic differentiation. Growing Kikuyu violence did not elicit a positive response amongst other communities, while the colonial state did what it could to limit KAU's influence. The state restricted KAU's public meetings and prevented it from visiting the northern 'Outlying Districts'. These factors, plus the moderate nature of KAU's campaign, its shortage of money and the local nature of most African politics in the period meant that their mass support was limited.[75] By 1948, KAU was in decline, unable to show tangible gains for its campaigns and collections.

While change was occurring elsewhere, nationalist forces in Kenya were stunted by the settlers' influence over the state, and there were few avenues for legitimate protest. Administrators persisted in believing that political agitation was the cause of popular unrest, rather than a symptom of it.[76] By 1947–8, the result was organised underground resistance, inspired by long-running land and status grievances, given impetus by growing social and economic differentiation and the influence of younger, more militant Kikuyu. The fledgling African press (much of it in Gikuyu) challenged many of the precepts of white rule. Religious attitudes were also changing, with growing resistance to the European-dominated mainstream churches. New Christian sects and radical preachers preached 'liberation theology'.

Despite growing violence and pressure for change from London, the settler-dominated state was adamant. There would be no elections for Africans and no review of the land situation. Kenya would stay a 'white man's country'. There were moves for reform amongst some Europeans in the late 1940s, but they were too little, too late. Although decolonisation was beginning elsewhere, most Kenya settlers looked south for their inspiration. Partition was not feasible because of the dispersed geography of the highlands. Instead, there was talk of a new East African Dominion, linked to Rhodesia and South Africa. To the settlers, Kenyatta represented a dangerous force, and as early as 1948 they were calling for his arrest. Rejecting the opportunity to incorporate him into the political system, and fearing his communist connections, the colonial government chose instead to believe that he was leading underground resistance to white rule.

In 1950, responding to the growing pressure for political representation, the government introduced true local government for Africans. The LNCs were reconstituted as 33 African district councils with significant revenues (from taxation, property leases and forest royalties). They were responsible for most government services, including roads, health services, water, education and agricultural extension. They also provided a legitimate outlet for political activity. However, there were no elections for the new councils until 1958 because of the Emergency. In the white highlands, the situation was very different, as the seven white districts had their own county councils on the British model. There, the voice of African squatters remained weak and their rights non-existent.

Meanwhile, Nairobi was growing, as both the landless and educated came to find work. The British king declared Nairobi a city in 1950, and by 1962 the population had reached 250,000. The city was a unique environment within which European, Asian and African ethnic groups (mainly Kikuyu, Kamba, Luo and Luhya) interacted, but its planners had given little thought to their accommodation or needs. Rising prices, poor living conditions, overcrowding and unemployment bred crime. By 1947, the administration had virtually lost control of the African areas of Nairobi to Kikuyu gangs and militant trade unionists.[77]

The late 1940s were years of rising tension amongst the Kikuyu, although most other Kenyans remained politically passive. Kenyatta and the ex-KCA leaders had oathed older, wealthier Kikuyu into KAU in 1947–8, and oathing amongst both squatter and reserve Kikuyu spread rapidly. By 1950, mass oathing was under way in Nairobi, Kiambu, Fort Hall and Nyeri. A convergence of interest between squatters, the Central Province poor and Nairobi activists was emerging that was to lead to open revolt.[78] The consent amongst the people of central Kenya to be ruled was breaking down. In 1948, the Europeans first came to hear of a new movement, 'Mau Mau', a name of uncertain origin, which became shorthand for the growing anarchy, and which they believed was a revolutionary secret society. Although the administration was increasingly worried, it was out of touch with African opinion and unable to recognise the relationship between their policies and the growing dissent.

With colonial policy changing, trade unions were fully legalised in Kenya in 1942–3. Supported by the first minimum wage ordinances, Kikuyu- and Asian-led trade unions exerted their authority in mass general strikes in 1947 and 1950, with both political and economic objectives.[79] However, the nationalist movement was far from united. Kenyatta and the national party opposed the 1950 general strike and denounced violence, but behind Kenyatta were more confrontational figures. Demobilised Kikuyu ex-soldiers, including Bildad Kaggia, Fred Kubai, Waruhiu Itote and Stanley Mathenge, and Kamba such as J. D. Kali and Paul Ngei had been liberated and radicalised by their experiences in the British army, and were ready to fight for land and freedom.[80] The Nairobi branch of KAU was the most militant. There was a tight relationship between trade union leaders and Nairobi KAU, with communists such as Makhan Singh working alongside 'hardliners' such as Kubai and Kaggia to rouse dissent. After the 1950 general strike and the banning of the East African Trades Union Congress, they infiltrated and took over the moribund KAU in Nairobi and initiated a campaign of mass oathing of Nairobi's poor and disaffected.[81] During 1951, the militants developed an underground network linked to Nairobi's criminal underclass and established a Kikuyu-only Central Committee (the *muhimu*) inside KAU to direct oathing, violence and anti-European activities.[82]

European concern at Kikuyu subversion was rising. By 1950, the British had already developed an Emergency Scheme for the colony in the event of mass unrest.[83] During 1950–1, oathing multiplied and killings increased in the Rift Valley, the Kikuyu Reserve and Nairobi as the radicals consolidated their hold. By 1952, between 75 and 90 per cent of Kikuyu men had taken some form of oath (many against their will) to support the movement and never to sell land to Europeans and Asians, on pain of death. Whatever their reasons for taking the oath, most Kikuyu believed it was binding, with death the inevitable consequence of betrayal (either supernaturally or at the hands of their recruiters). The most militant were taking *batuni* (platoon) oaths committing them to fight their enemies and recover stolen lands, although there was little true military preparation. European-owned cattle were mutilated and fires started, several Europeans killed or wounded and chiefs, police informers, non-Kikuyu headmen and oath-resisters were murdered.

By 1952, the frightened settlers were demanding sterner action and the repression of all African nationalism, though Governor Sir Philip Mitchell still believed there was no serious risk of insurrection. The state made little effort to win 'hearts and minds' or to build alternative non-Mau Mau Kikuyu alliances, but instead expanded its intelligence and security forces in order to disrupt the militants' oathing, underestimating their determination and support.[84] The European-led and mostly Kamba, Luo and Kalenjin police tried to restore order through curfews and mass arrests, and built a network of informers within the movement. By September 1952, the courts had jailed more than 400 for membership of Mau Mau. However, preparations for rebellion were advancing, and in August–September 1952 several groups of Kikuyu (including ex-soldiers) left for the Aberdare Mountains to prepare for war.[85]

Kenyatta, campaigning for non-violent change, found himself trapped, discredited amongst his supporters by the lack of progress in changing settler attitudes, but feared by the British. Under pressure from the authorities, he denounced Mau Mau at public meetings during 1951–2, but found his situation increasingly difficult, as a moderate leader who was losing control of a revolt that was using KAU as a cover. The radicals conceded that Mau Mau needed Kenyatta's experience and authority, and continued to support him in public, but privately they were contemptuous. His own involvement in oathing and meetings with young Kikuyu about to enter the forests showed that Kenyatta drew a fine line between violent and non-violent protest.[86] His speeches, monitored by the police, similarly trod a narrow path between radicalism and moderation, demonstrating an ambivalence that led European observers to disbelieve his anti-Mau Mau protestations. In their view, Kenyatta and Chief Koinange were the masterminds behind Mau Mau, despite the fact that many Kikuyu saw Kenyatta as a force for moderation. As his denunciations of Mau Mau became more open during July and August 1952, however, the radicals insisted that he cease. In late 1952, Kenyatta was called before the Central Committee for the first time and warned he must fall silent or die. He cancelled his remaining meetings.[87]

The Mau Mau Rising

The Mau Mau guerrilla war of 1952–5 was a key event in Kenya's history, and shaped its future political, economic and social structure. It was an unstructured, violent revolt amongst Africans – mostly Kikuyu – against foreign rule, land alienation and political and economic inequality. It escalated rapidly with the detention of the nationalist leadership in 1952, but had been brewing for at least five years and its antecedents went back to the first European land seizures. It was an unconventional war, fought to win by any means by both sides. It was also a war of clashing moralities, as both the Europeans and the Mau Mau believed completely in the rightness of their cause. In the end, the British triumphed, but their victory had a high price.

The 1952 Insurrection and the Trial of the 'Kapenguria Six'

Once Governor Mitchell had retired and left Kenya in June 1952, the last impediment to a decisive strike against KAU was gone. Under intense settler pressure, led by European Legislative Council leader Michael Blundell, the government agreed to impose a State of Emergency and to arrest Kenyatta and other KAU leaders.

On 7 October 1952, activists shot dead Kiambu Senior Chief Waruhiu wa Kungu, a prominent Christian anti-Mau Mau leader. This was the final trigger for action. Believing they were facing a revolutionary movement and possible civil war, on 20 October Governor Sir Evelyn Baring, new to Kenya and with the unanimous support of the British Cabinet, declared a State of Emergency.[88] The state initiated operation 'Jock Scott' and arrested more than 180 political leaders across the country, and deployed a battalion of British troops on active service for the first time. Most African newspapers were banned. The Mau Mau Central Committee and the radicals were taken by surprise, and 'the secret organisation within KAU was decapitated'.[89] Amongst the detainees were six KAU Executive Committee members, arrested as organisers of the violence. The six – Kenyatta, Kaggia, Kubai and Kungu Karumba (all Kikuyu), KAU Secretary 'Ramogi' Achieng-Oneko (Luo) and Ngei (Kamba) – were soon to become a national symbol of resistance to colonial rule.

The British thought that the emergency would be short-lived, but they were wrong. After the initial chaos, during which the rebels engaged in brutal violence against Kikuyu unwilling to support them, the 'police action' became a guerrilla and civil war. The mass arrests, troop deployments, punitive sweeps of Central Province and eviction of Kikuyu squatters from white farms resulted in open conflict in Central Province and the Rift Valley as thousands joined the rebel camps in the forests.

The war was fought mainly in the northern Kikuyu districts of Nyeri and Fort Hall and the mountains, particularly the dense bush of the Aberdares.[90] However, the Mau Mau maintained close supply and communication links with Kikuyu in the reserve and Nairobi. Up to 30,000 joined the struggle in various capacities. Some were landless or had been driven away from the white highlands; others were educated workers in Nairobi. Their reasons for involvement in the war varied and there was no single vision of the future for which they were fighting. Many of the most prominent Mau Mau leaders, including Kimathi, Mathenge and 'General China' Waruhiu Itote came from Nyeri, the most northern of the Kikuyu districts, which had experienced little land loss. The acephalous nature of the resistance caused confusion in the government and the enraged settlers. The rebels had few guns, bullets or reliable food sources and little national organisation, with their mostly illiterate leadership relying on personal or clan alliances for support.[91] 'Jock Scott' had seized most of their political leadership before they developed national communication and control structures. Although otherwise isolated rebel groups did cooperate in some raids, efforts to form a unified military command failed. The Mau Mau also failed to destroy key transport and communication services such as the railway.[92]

The rebels' main targets were those they could not trust within their own communities: those Kikuyu, Embu and Meru who worked for and with the government, who refused to take the oath, or who were on the other 'side' of fault lines that had emerged over the previous decade. In response, the government encouraged, then armed and financed a loyalist self-defence force, the Kikuyu 'Home Guard', recruited from amongst those who had the most to lose from a Mau Mau victory (or gain from its defeat), whose Christianity set them against Mau Mau rituals, or who opposed the corrosive effect of violence on Kikuyu social order. The initially inchoate, often personalised violence coalesced into a civil war, as individuals were forced to choose a side.[93] The conflict created and reinforced a division within the Kikuyu community that endured for decades, and propelled loyalists into positions of power after independence.

The government did not try to compromise, and despite doubts in Whitehall, they accepted the settler view that Mau Mau was a disease, and that honour and security could only be secured by its complete defeat. Following early Mau Mau successes, military professionals took over control of operations in mid-1953 and the experience gained in defeating insurgencies elsewhere in the empire was put to use.[94] In all, 55,000 British troops served in Kenya, along with RAF bombers and KAR units from other parts of East Africa. The British also made use of press censorship and relentless propaganda to convince both foreigners and Africans of the justness of their cause. Officially, however, there was no war, only a civil disturbance involving individual criminal acts, and the normal rules for prosecutions held.

The brutal violence of early attacks convinced the Europeans that they were dealing with people who were mentally ill, their minds warped by the rituals of oathing. Every Kikuyu became a potential enemy, and Mau Mau fighters were systematically dehumanised as 'vermin' or 'animals', for whose condition death was the only cure. In the view of most Europeans, the revolt was not a nationalist movement but an 'African terrorist movement rooted in black magic', perverted and primordial, its origins unrelated to economic or political repression.[95] The beleaguered position of rebel groups after 1954 led to more extreme oaths involving sexual acts and cannibalism. These in turn provided ammunition for British propaganda and discouraged sympathisers.[96] If Mau Mau did have real roots, most white settlers believed they lay in the Kikuyu's inability to adapt to the demands of modernisation. The debate over why the rebellion occurred, and the roles of ethnicity, class and social differentiation in its origins, has continued for decades.[97]

The different experiences of different ethnic groups, robust government action and the violence and ethno-centricity of the revolt meant it did not become a generalised war of liberation, but remained centred on the Kikuyu community. They did not fight entirely alone. There were Mau Mau supporters from other communities in Nairobi, some Maasai and Ndorobo fighters, and the movement gained support amongst the Kamba in 1954, but most Kenyans watched passively or took advantage of the opportunities the conflict offered. Extensive use was made of Kamba and Kalenjin as soldiers, of Samburu as trackers, and of Luo, Nandi and Kipsigis as prison warders. The government watched the Kamba (Bantu neighbours of the Kikuyu, with a strong presence in the military) particularly carefully and invested heavily in ensuring the community remained loyal.

In January 1954, the military wounded and captured guerrilla leader Itote, head of the Mount Kenya forces. Itote led an attempt at a negotiated ceasefire in March–April, which proved abortive, but could have changed the face of Kenya if successful. He ended up in the same cells as Kenyatta in Turkana. By early 1954, the rebels had been driven out of most white farms, and the tide was turning in the government's favour. In April 1954, the War Council executed Operation Anvil, in which troops, police and the Home Guard seized and screened the entire African population of Nairobi.[98] Twenty-four thousand Kikuyu, Embu and Meru without proper papers or who were deemed potential Mau Mau supporters were detained without trial in special camps, set up to hold suspects who had not been convicted in court. It was a decisive blow. Soon after, the government began to cut the rebels' supply lines by enforced villagisation of the entire Kikuyu population. In 1955, on the offensive inside the forests, the government made use of pseudo-gangs, teams of ex-Mau Mau on death row who had been 'turned' by the Special Branch intelligence unit to hunt down their old comrades.

The war aroused concern in the emerging developing world and within the communist countries, which portrayed the revolt as a nationalist struggle. The United States (US) was ambivalent, sympathetic to anti-colonial revolts but fearful of both communism and barbarism. There was growing opposition to the state's repressive behaviour in the British Labour Party, resulting in angry House of Commons debates in 1955 over alleged atrocities, though most Britons believed the government line. Unlike many other guerrilla wars, Mau Mau received little or no external support.

Although they had agents abroad (including Mbiyu Koinange) and some funds may have made their way from India, they had no foreign offices or propaganda machine. Remote from supply lines, anti-European and with unclear aims, the movement found no foreign military ally. Forced to manufacture homemade guns in the forests, starving and hunted by counter-terrorist bands, the rebels could do little but survive. By late 1955, the war was over. It officially ended with the capture and execution of Kimathi, the most senior Mau Mau leader in October 1956, but bands of rebels continued to live in the forests, occasionally attacking others, until after independence.[99]

The war led to the death of at least 14,000 Africans, 29 Asians and 95 Europeans. Most were Mau Mau supporters. Although official figures in the Corfield Report of 1960 recorded 11,503 Mau Mau dead, the numbers were underestimated to disguise the ferocity of the state response.[100] A thousand were judicially hanged and many more were killed by troops in the forests, without any records.[101] There were extrajudicial executions by police and Home Guard units, and settler fury at the crimes of their enemies and the slowness of the law's response led to a collapse of legal standards. The beating and torture of Kikuyu suspects was commonplace, and the security forces murdered hundreds.[102] Particularly notorious were the white settler Kenya Regiment and Police Reserve, the police General Service Unit (GSU) and the Home Guard. The Home Guard in Central Province grew to 25,000 men by 1954, a formidable counter-insurgency force under the control of local chiefs, the provincial administration and local settlers, which used its power both to repress Mau Mau and to benefit itself.[103] Although it was never official policy, senior officials were aware of the police and Home Guard's excesses, but concealed their violence and acquisitiveness in order to maintain morale.

The repression of Mau Mau was brutally effective, but the treatment of suspects and detainees was a stain on the British presence in Kenya. Between 150,000 and 320,000 Africans were detained for varying lengths of time in more than 50 detention and work camps.[104] A quarter of the adult male Kikuyu population probably passed through the system at some point between 1952 and 1958.[105] Treatment in the camps, staffed by little-trained non-Kikuyu, loyalist Kikuyu and European settlers, was often brutal. Information on what was happening there was carefully controlled, and the Colonial Office and the governor systematically denied reports of mistreatment.[106] The British relied on the Home Guard to run a 'rehabilitation pipeline' through which detainees passed until their release back into society as 'reformed'. The detainees were forced to undergo what was called 're-education', combining psychological warfare, violence, forced confessions, manual labour and inculcation in the virtues of Christianity.[107] Most of the camps – apart from those maintained for 5,000 or so 'hard core' detainees who refused to confess their sins and who were never expected to be freed – were closed down by 1958.

Views of the Mau Mau revolt have varied; while some have condemned its atavistic savagery, others hailed it as a war of liberation. Some have viewed it as a fundamentally Kikuyu affair, others as a prototypical nationalist movement. Similarly divergent have been the arguments as to its causes (though clearly land lay at the heart) and its consequences. Some argued that Mau Mau was the cause of Kenya's independence, others that it delayed it. The British were technically victorious since the revolt was completely defeated, but the international attention it inspired, and the need to summon so many British troops, showed that the settler monopoly of power was unsustainable in the long term. The Corfield Report estimated it had cost GB£55 million to contain the Emergency, making the economic case for change unanswerable.[108] The state's response also damaged the moral legitimacy of Kenya's government in the eyes of Western liberals. Though Mau Mau did not lead directly to independence, it forced a reassessment of policy that set Kenya on that course and eliminated any remaining chance that Kenya might go the way of Rhodesia and South Africa to become an independent, white-ruled state.

While the British repressed the insurgency, Kenyatta and the other five senior Mau Mau suspects (the 'Kapenguria six') had been jailed in April 1953 after a show trial held at Kapenguria in Pokot, far from the nearest Kikuyu settlement (to avoid the intimidation of witnesses). Despite an internationally publicised trial, a strong defence case and expert legal assistance, the court found Kenyatta and the others guilty of oathing and leadership of an illegal organisation. Even though there had been years of surveillance, there was almost no evidence that Kenyatta had been the leader of Mau Mau, but colonial officials genuinely believed he was dangerous. The government therefore bribed witnesses to provide false evidence, and the ex-settler British judge was paid GB£20,000 (10 years' salary) to facilitate a conviction.[109] The government believed they needed such tactics to demonstrate their resolve and to counter the fear that Mau Mau created. Kenyatta, Kaggia, Kubai and the others were sentenced to seven years' hard labour, with indefinite detention thereafter.[110]

The Economic Impact of the War and the Swynnerton Plan

The war not only weakened settler rule, it also led to a restructuring of Kikuyu society, its fracture into hostile interests and the creation of a popular ideal of Kikuyu ethnonationalism. The state's aggressive response wholly changed the shape of Central Province. The region was closed to visitors, and counter-terrorism techniques applied based on those developed in Malaya. These including the creation of stockaded villages from June 1954, within which the population could be better defended and controlled. By October 1955, the government had forced more than a million Kikuyu and Embu into 854 new villages, built by forced labour.[111] The land of at least 2,000 guerrillas and detainees was confiscated and their houses and shops demolished, and those who admitted taking an oath were fined.[112] The government closed all the Kikuyu independent schools or transferred them to the control of Christian missions. In the white highlands, most Kikuyu squatters were driven out or detained, and were replaced with seasonal labour from the Luhya, Luo, Kipsigis and Kamba. Funds flowed into Central Province, to offer inducements for loyalty. Coffee-growing licences and educational bursaries were available only to Home Guards, and medical supplies, sugar and other services were only offered to villages declared free of Mau Mau. Jobs in the administration and Tribal Police were for loyalists only.

The need to consolidate military success through 'hearts and minds' also inspired radical policy changes. Winston Churchill's Conservative government, more willing to use force, was also more favourable to individual land tenure than its Labour predecessor had been. The result was a land consolidation and agricultural improvement programme begun in 1954, known as the Swynnerton Plan. This would convert communal land ownership to individual land title, beginning in Central Province, where individual land tenure already informally existed, and where villagisation and unlimited state power had created an ideal opportunity.[113] This programme had explicitly political as well as agricultural objectives. The process of adjudicating 750,000 land fragments, consolidating multiple small plots into farms, demarcating the farms and registering individual freehold land titles involved a fundamental change to land law and to land tenure rights for Africans. The process was slow and marked by malpractice, especially in Fort Hall, where loyalists used their positions of authority to extend their holdings, but during 1956–60 it restructured Kikuyu society, creating a community of landholders who had a long-term interest in the development of their land, and who could use it as collateral for loans. The goal was a rapid increase in agricultural productivity that would divert attention from the highlands and provide a safe outlet for Kikuyu labour. This innovative but controversial programme gave Kikuyu loyalists a head start in the 'dash for growth' of the 1960s. It also implied that many would become landless labourers on the cash-crop farms of others. Land consolidation proceeded rapidly in Nandi as well, the most agriculturally advanced Kalenjin district.

The Swynnerton Plan also committed the state to support 'progressive' African farmers. Alongside land consolidation and registration, the state would provide agricultural assistance, marketing and inputs, and encourage African cash-cropping of coffee, pyrethrum, maize and tea. Government expenditure on agricultural administration nearly tripled from 1952 to 1960. From the early 1950s, Arabica coffee production jumped, despite resistance from settlers still concerned about price undercutting and quality. The value of the cash-crops produced by African smallholders doubled between 1954 and 1963. While Nyanza and Central Provinces had been roughly equal in African cash-crop production until 1957, from that time on, Central Province took a growing lead.[114]

Perhaps strangely, despite the troubles, the 1950s saw heavy British investment and rapid industrial growth within a centrally planned framework. Many Kenyan household names date from that time, including Unilever's East African Industries, East African Tobacco, East African Breweries, Unga, Coca-Cola, Sadolin Paints, Schweppes, Bamburi and East African Portland Cement, Kabazi Canners and Metal Box.[115] Most were import substitution investments (which received tariff protection or duty refunds on imported materials) to produce consumer goods or to process agricultural products for export to the UK. Government policy was to make East Africa self-sufficient as far as possible. By the mid-1950s, manufacturing industry produced nearly 10 per cent of Kenya's gross domestic product (GDP), making it by far the most industrialised country in the region, though it produced few capital goods. There was a tendency for industries in East Africa to be dominated by one or two suppliers, competition limited by the small size of the market. The influx of British capital also placed labour relations on a more normal footing.

Between 1945 and 1963, the African business community also grew, diversifying into commodity production, shops and trading. This was now encouraged by the state, which provided training and modest loans to African businesses, and by metropolitan capital, keen to build markets for their consumer goods.[116] However, such changes were still small-scale. More than two-thirds of the share capital of the businesses registered between 1945 and 1963 was European, less than a quarter Asian, and less than 1 per cent African.[117] Although there were a few well-known African businesses, most remained small or of extremely uncertain profitability. Kenya's various Asian communities still dominated local trade, acting as middlemen in the 'pecking order' between black and white and between the big European-owned industries and the farmer. They had not invested heavily in manufacturing industry until the 1950s, but there was now rapid investment from this community also. By independence, family-owned Asian manufacturers dominated textiles and clothing, furniture making, soap, metalworking and engineering sectors.[118]

Religion, Education and Social Change in the 1940s and 1950s

Meanwhile social change continued, with more women drawn into the money economy, and practices such as female circumcision and arranged marriages began to decline. Villagisation particularly accelerated change amongst the Kikuyu.

Most Africans were now Christian, and church attendance was high, although witchcraft and traditional religions remained widely practised, often in parallel. The churches provided health and education services where the government did not offer them directly. Politically, the churches took an uncertain course during the 1950s. They supported multiracialism and interracial cooperation, but also opposed Mau Mau, and Kikuyu Christians played key roles in the detention camps and the rehabilitation programme.[119] The main denominations were close to the settler establishment, although the umbrella National Council of Churches of Kenya (NCCK) was more liberal.[120] The vast majority of Christian ministers were European, but in the late 1950s several young African ministers were appointed who – like the independence elites in other areas – were to dominate their respective churches after independence.[121]

Initially, Western mission education had been unpopular, amongst pastoralists, communities less integrated into the colonial economy and those who wished to avoid contact with the European invaders. However, attitudes changed as the financial benefits became obvious. Government and mission elementary, primary and secondary education spread, with 2,600 secondary students in 1956.[122] Four secondary schools for Africans in 1950 had become 82 by 1963. Chiefly families in every community were the first and most active in educating their sons. Girls were not seen as suitable educational material, as children and 'homemaking' were still their primary roles, and jobs were virtually non-existent. Education remained racially and religiously segregated, since most private schools were built and managed by

Christian, Islamic or Hindu groups. There was no post-secondary education in the colony, but from 1950 onwards Makerere College in Uganda (East Africa's centre of higher learning) began to offer a few degree places to Kenyans. In 1956, the Royal Technical College in Nairobi (which became a college of the University of London in 1961) began to meet more of the demand. For the richest, cleverest and luckiest Kenyans, however, a foreign university education was the real goal. By 1955, there were 902 Kenyans studying abroad, including 132 Africans.[123]

Africans also benefited from a dramatic improvement in access to medical services. Until the 1920s there were virtually no 'Western' medical services for anyone except Westerners, and the country had suffered from new diseases (including plague, sleeping sickness, smallpox and influenza). From the late 1920s on, rudimentary medical services reached Africans for the first time.[124] Conditions were still poor, but infant mortality rates fell dramatically. The result of this and of greater food production and economic opportunity was a rapid rise in population. Between 1948 (the first proper census) and 1962, the population grew by 3.4 per cent a year. At the arrival of the British, there were less than four million inhabitants within Kenya's borders. By 1963, there were nearly 9 million. This was an extraordinarily rapid increase, and was to have a profound impact on the independent state.

The Fight for Majority Rule, 1953–60

Until the late 1950s, political institutions had evolved as tools for the white settler community to influence colonial policy. They had been adapted to give a voice to the various Asian communities, but the African majority still had no direct representation, and in 1953 all African political organisations had been banned. From 1954, however, despite settler hostility, the British began trying to encourage 'responsible' and moderate African leaders. Their goal was to find a long-term solution to the crisis, through a three-pronged approach: military victory, agricultural reform and the encouragement of 'legitimate' African leadership and only then, substantive political change. By late 1956, there were eight nominated Africans in the Legislative Council, though few Africans saw them as their legitimate representatives.

Trade Unions and Mass Action, 1953–6

With political parties banned and a guerrilla war under way, trade unionism was one of the few legitimate avenues of mass protest. However, most of the existing union leadership was in detention. The resulting vacuum was the catalyst for the emergence of a new non-Kikuyu union movement, less militant but equally committed to change. They were determined to improve pay and conditions for African workers, but were equally determined to use the trade unions – which had hard-fought Western credentials as a legitimate expression of protest and economic power – to push for political change under the protection of Western liberalism.

Tom Mboya, a young Luo-Abasuba health inspector from South Nyanza, was at the centre of this process. In 1951–2, this gregarious student organiser had created, from scattered staff associations, a new trade union – the Kenya Local Government Workers Union (KLGWU), and in 1953, he became its full-time General Secretary.[125] The KLGWU then affiliated with the Kenya Federation of Registered Trades Unions (KFRTU), formed in 1950. In a period of great difficulty, the British tried to foster what they termed 'responsible' non-political trade union activity. Mboya was always a politician, however. Incensed by the 'Jock Scott' arrests, he had joined KAU in October 1952, and had risen rapidly to become National Treasurer of the party, as arrests decimated the movement.[126] In October 1953, aged only 23, this outstanding organiser and speaker became the general secretary of the KFRTU, a position he retained until he joined Kenyatta's Cabinet nine years later.

Over the next two years, Mboya won a series of victories for trade unionism. As one of the few remaining voices for Africans, he propelled himself into the national spotlight, resolving a series of industrial protests in a way that promoted both union recognition and wage increases. Although he took pride in being a Luo, Mboya spoke Gikuyu and Kikamba, denounced tribalism and appealed to Kenyans of every ethnic group.[127] His colleagues and allies in the union movement included several figures who were later to achieve national prominence, including Clement Lubembe, Arthur Ochwada and Martin Shikuku amongst the Luhya, and in the Luo, Denis Akumu of the Dock Workers Union and Ochola Mak'Anyengo of the Petroleum Oil Workers Union. As a result of this activism, the need of international capital for a stable workforce and the government's desire to stabilise the country during and after Mau Mau, African real wages doubled between 1955 and 1964.[128] Increasingly, Mboya also led the KFRTU into politics, although national political organisations remained illegal. In 1955, with his dominance over the movement complete, the KFRTU was renamed the Kenya Federation of Labour (KFL).

The Americans, looking for allies in a post-colonial world, identified Mboya as someone to watch, and he built close ties with influential African Americans and the American labour unions. The American Federation of Labor-Congress of Industrial Organizations (AFL-CIO) was a major contributor to the International Confederation of Free Trade Unions (ICFTU), of which the KFL was a member, and which assisted the penniless Kenyan unions and Mboya both financially and morally. Mboya also built links with the British trade union movement, which supported African labour leaders to speak and study overseas. These links, which Mboya cherished, ensured that Africans retained a voice during the dark days of the Emergency, and that Western audiences heard a different side of the story from the savagery of Mau Mau. Mboya ensured that the labour movement retained enough support overseas to ward off an outright ban, despite settler hostility.

While the British did not find Mboya's ability comfortable, they recognised his importance. He was given a scholarship to Ruskin College in Oxford, which he took up in 1955–6.[129] By 1956, his vision for socialist, but not revolutionary, change in Kenya and the removal of European privilege was firmly established. He continued to run the union movement throughout the 1950s, though with increasing difficulty, and it remained his primary constituency. His close links with the AFL-CIO and his use of their cash in his conflicts with labour opponents gave him power, but also left him vulnerable to accusations of being a tool of the American Central Intelligence Agency (CIA), which was believed to be financing the moderate labour unions. However, much as Kenya's government was to do after independence, Mboya treated this relationship pragmatically; willing to say whatever was needed to persuade those with funds to provide them.[130] With money in short supply, access to resources for organisation, transport and publicity was key to political success.

New African Political Parties and the 1957 Elections

Following the British strategy of reform to win 'hearts and minds', Colonial Secretary Oliver Lyttleton forced through a new multiracial constitution in 1954, to take effect once the Emergency was over. All Kenya's races and religions would be represented, but with separate elections, privileges and roles. As well as restructuring the government into a formal ministerial structure, it introduced a (restricted) African franchise for the first time. In 1956, the details were published of this scheme to elect eight African members directly.[131] Although white members would still constitute an overall majority, many Europeans robustly opposed these reforms, and a struggle began within the white community, between 'moderates', led by Blundell, and a larger number of 'die-hard' opponents that was to last until 1963. Neither one thing nor the other, the Lyttleton Constitution was equally opposed by Africans as racially separatist and failing to reflect their overwhelming numerical dominance. A couple of nominated African Legislative Council members accepted positions in the government, but most African opinion was hostile.

By 1955–6, reform was under way in many areas of Kenya's society and economy, though the government and the settler-dominated Legislative Council seldom conceded it graciously. While some settlers still called for partition, a 1955 British Royal Commission declared the goal of eliminating all racial barriers to the free movement of land, labour and capital and called for an end to the 'white highlands' for the first time. There was a gradual diminution of the informal colour bar: moves to integrate the military and judiciary and the first professional and business appointments for Africans returning from European universities. Colonial policy was pushing Kenya towards a multiracial future whereby the 'races' would formally share power, maintaining the disproportionate influence of the smaller European and Asian immigrants.

With Mau Mau defeated and the first African elections in the pipeline, in June 1955 the government permitted the re-establishment of African district-based political parties, although national organisations remained banned. The colonial power wished to ensure that politics functioned on a sub-national and ethnic basis, while encouraging the development of new, moderate, local leaders. Dozens of ethnic and regional African political associations emerged (outside Central Province, where all political activity was still banned). The decision to direct African political activity through regional structures was to reverberate throughout independent Kenya, the foundation of the alignment of political orientation and ethnicity. Multi-ethnic Nairobi was the main place where a cross-ethnic organisation could exist. There, a

Luo lawyer named 'Clement' Argwings-Kodhek, the first Kenyan African to qualify as a barrister, founded the Nairobi African District Congress in 1956 (it had to be renamed from 'Kenya' to 'Nairobi' on colonial orders). It was challenged in 1957–8 by the Nairobi People's Convention Party (NPCP), the political wing of Mboya's labour movement.

Political activity remained regulated, however. Under the 1950 Public Order Ordinance and the 1952 Societies Ordinance, the state decided which entities it would register as political parties, and the registrar of societies could ban any organisation if in his opinion it constituted a risk to 'peace, welfare or good order'. Membership of unregistered organisations was an offence and unlicensed meetings of ten or more persons were illegal.

The first elections for African members of the Legislative Council took place in March 1957, less than seven years before independence.[132] There were 37 candidates for eight seats, elected by Africans on a complex and limited franchise, which gave multiple votes for wealth, age and military and government service. Amongst the Kikuyu, Embu and Meru, only those who could demonstrate their loyalty could vote, and constituency boundaries were designed to minimise the influence of Mau Mau.[133] There were no national parties and the key campaign platforms for candidates were their personal achievements, the encouragement of education as a route to modernity, access to land and racial equality. Most candidates supported a gradualist approach, with few calling for independence from Britain.

Two key figures entered electoral politics for the first time. Elected for the Central Nyanza seat was a 46-year-old Luo, Oginga Odinga. Already known for his anti-colonial zeal and anti-authoritarian attitudes, he was an Alliance and Makerere-educated teacher. He had come to prominence through his Luo Thrift and Trading Corporation business, the first significant African-owned commercial enterprise in Luoland.[134] Odinga also played a key role in the Luo Union, the Luo social welfare and cultural organisation, of which he had become leader in 1953. He began to be referred to as Jaramogi (following the ideals of Ramogi, the fabled leader of the Luo people). In Nairobi, the new councillor was Mboya, who defeated rival Argwings-Kodhek with the support of the KFL to become the sole African representative of the capital in the run-up to independence.[135]

No one was elected from the Kikuyu, one-quarter of Kenya's population. The veteran Kikuyu Mathu lost in Central Province to Meru teacher Bernard Mate, as the loyalty conditions were applied more strictly to the Kikuyu than the more accommodating Meru, leaving 20 per cent of the province's population with half its votes.[136] The Coast was now represented by Mijikenda headmaster Ronald Ngala, the Luhya by Bukusu intellectual Masinde Muliro, and the southern Luo, Gusii and Kipsigis by a Luo, Lawrence Oguda. Ukambani elected the little-known nominated member James Muimi. The only other survivor amongst the nominated African members was Daniel Toroitich arap Moi. A primary school teacher from Baringo, Moi won the Rift Valley seat on the votes of his Kalenjin community. The cast of Kenya's independence drama was assembling, though key figures – including Kenyatta – remained in jail.

The eight victorious Africans had little truck with multiracialism, agreeing before the polls that they would refuse office under the Lyttleton Constitution and would use their new platform to campaign for further reform. Although they had no common political party, they formed an African Elected Members Organisation (AEMO), with Mboya as secretary and Odinga as chairman, and used their elected status to challenge European dominance openly and as equals for the first time. Their defiance in refusing to join the government during 1957–8 and their eloquent speeches exposed the hollow nature of multiracialism.[137] The Kenya government under Baring now viewed Mboya with fear and dislike, referring to him as 'the Kenyan Nkrumah', and seeing the evil hand of the British Labour Party in his actions, reflecting the divide that existed between conservative settlerdom and more socialist Britain.[138] However, the AEMO's determination, the need to avoid another revolt, and pressure from home forced the government to reconsider. Following consultations, the Lyttleton Constitution was abandoned and Alan Lennox-Boyd, British colonial secretary since 1954, proposed a second round of constitutional changes.

The Lennox-Boyd Constitution and the AEMO, 1958–60

The resulting 'Lennox-Boyd Constitution' of April 1958 expanded the number of African elected representatives to 14, giving them numerical equality with European elected members. Multiracialism continued, however, with separate electoral rolls and racial representation. The new constitution also added 12 'Specially Elected' members to be chosen by the Legislative Council directly: four from each of the 'three races'. Both Britain and the white Kenyans still rejected absolutely a single common voting roll. Mboya, Odinga and the others, in contrast, continued to oppose piecemeal reform. They trod a narrow line between incitement of the African crowd (which might lead to their arrest and the loss of credibility with their international supporters) and acquiescence to European pressure (which would destroy their credibility with their constituents).

They took every opportunity to increase their numbers. Elections were held for the six new African seats in March 1958, which brought into national politics other figures of the independence era. These included loyalist and chief's son Jeremiah Nyagah in Nyeri-Embu, Justus ole Tipis for the Maasai, Kipsigis Council clerk Taita arap Towett and Julius Kiano for south Central Province, the first Kikuyu elected to the Assembly, a young academic and ally of Mboya. All backed the AEMO's rejection of the constitution. For the first time, their campaigns made widespread use of the slogan of *Uhuru* (independence) for Kenya.

Ghana was already independent, and in 1958, Tanganyika too started on the road to independence, but Kenya remained trapped in no-man's land by its history of violence and by the white settler establishment. Rather than leaving, Europeans were still arriving, taking the white population up from 42,000 in 1953 to 54,000 by 1956.[139] Racial segregation and European dominance remained entrenched. Both the settlers and the British expected that Kenya would remain a 'white man's country' for years.

In January 1959, the East African governors were expecting Kenya's independence to take place sometime after 1975.[140]

By late 1958, the AEMO was boycotting the Legislative Council to strengthen pressure for reform. The Kenyan government was frustrated by the ability of their opponents (particularly Mboya) to leverage British and American support to their cause. The AEMO and its Asian and European allies even travelled to London to put their case directly to the colonial secretary. Buoyed by his successes abroad, Mboya's NPCP was active outside Nairobi, building a national political party 'under the covers'. As a result, the government initiated a sweep against the NPCP in March 1959, and arrested 39 of its members, searching for evidence of sedition. Times had changed, however, and although several lesser leaders were charged, Mboya was untouched and unbowed.

However, divisions inside the AEMO were becoming apparent. The African members were each extremely influential, but had no common party or obvious common interests apart from hostility to the colonial state. There was personal resentment of Mboya by other leaders, particularly the older Odinga and Muliro. His brilliance and arrogance made Mboya the effective leader of the African members, assisted by a press campaign that left him internationally famous, but little liked by colleagues.[141] There were also tensions over the stance they should take on the future of the white highlands, particularly between Kalenjin and Kikuyu, and over the return of the Kikuyu to Nairobi, the highlands and active politics.

Between 1957 and 1960, two factions emerged from the network of district parties, trade unions and other African organisations, which were to prove the foundation of Kenya's political system. The leadership of the two largest ethnic groups – the Kikuyu and Luo – took a more confrontational stance against colonial rule than the less-developed, more fragmented Kalenjin, Mijikenda, Luhya and northern pastoralists. The split in the AEMO was formalised in 1959, and was encouraged by the Colonial Office, which was looking to create a new multiracial centre party to take Kenya to self-government. The largest faction, led by Muliro, Moi, Nyagah, Towett and Ngala, worked through the multiracial Kenya National Party (KNP), which included sympathetic non-African members and was allowed to establish itself as a national party. The other faction, known as the Kenya Independence Movement, consisted only of Mboya, Odinga, Oguda and Kiano, but – more significantly – all the Kikuyu and Luo members. They took a more anti-European line, denouncing multiracialism and demanding independence faster than the KNP. They called for the opening of the highlands to African settlement, but opposed any deal to sell white settler land to Africans. This split within the new elite was driven in part by differences of strategy and personality differences (particularly between Mboya and Muliro), but was underlaid by diverging long-term regional and ethnic goals. This confluence of ethnic, organisational and personal interests amongst a dozen individuals created divisions that were to dominate the next four decades.

Meanwhile, the 'Kapenguria six' remained in prison or in detention camps – as did 1,600 hard-core ex-Mau Mau. The Emergency remained in force. Even the admission by the state's key witness in 1958 that he had been bribed to lie at the trial was unable to free Kenyatta. There was growing disquiet in liberal circles in the UK about Kenyatta's conviction, but in Kenya the settlers remained obdurate.

In 1958, this view was challenged for the first time. Odinga, who had met Kenyatta in the early 1950s, was the first member to call in the Legislative Council for Kenyatta's return to political life.[142] The Europeans and the government were horrified by Odinga's reassertion of Kenyatta's significance and the suggestion that he might return to lead the country. Odinga's call for Kenyatta's rehabilitation was not much more popular in the AEMO: either its members came from non-Mau Mau communities or, if they were Kikuyu, Embu or Meru (like Kiano and Nyagah), they had been elected by the loyalists, the only ones able to vote. There was no natural constituency for Kenyatta until Odinga created it. Between 1958 and 1959, Odinga led a reassessment of Kenyatta amongst the fledgling political elite that transformed him into a leader-in-waiting. For the ambitious Mboya to assert the primacy of Kenyatta and the old guard was a bitter pill, but one he eventually swallowed.[143] After 1959, most African leaders and pan-African conferences supported the cause of Kenyatta's freedom. Odinga later suggested that others had warned him that the real Kenyatta was not all that he hoped for, but Odinga chose to seek his freedom and leadership nevertheless.[144] Odinga's commitment was to change the direction of Kenya's history.

The Emergence of the Independence Elite

A few hundred young African men were now in a position of great importance. Having achieved a European-style secondary education, some had managed to obtain further education abroad, and the first students were emerging with degrees from Makerere, India or South Africa, and a very few from the colonial home itself. Many were the children of chiefs, such as the Mwendwa family of Kitui and the Njonjo, Koinange and Waiyaki families of Kiambu, or came from important Christian families, but others had achieved their goal purely through ability, family sacrifice, tenacity and good luck.[145] After completing their education, they had gone into the few professions open to them, as teachers, clerks, council officials, health workers or lawyers. They were far from conservative figures – their radicalism kept aflame by the racial segregation they faced – but most focused on the need for Africans to decide their own fate, rather than on a specific ideology such as communism. This community was to merge with a few dozen ex-Mau Mau detainees, a few elders and traditional chiefs, an even smaller number of self-made businessmen and the trade union leadership to create the cadre that led Kenya to independence and beyond.

With self-government moving closer, the British began to Africanise the senior civil service for the first time. In 1960, there were no African PCs, DCs, permanent secretaries, deputy secretaries or even under-secretaries, and very few district officers. From 1960 on, however, bright, disciplined young Africans were identified and sent for training in the UK, then appointed as understudies or assistants to white officials.

By independence three years later, Africans held roughly 19 per cent of senior posts.[146] As the pace of change speeded up, so did the careers of this alternate elite. Key individuals groomed by the British to run the country included Kenneth Matiba, Simeon Nyachae, John Michuki, Charles Koinange, Jeremiah Kiereini, Geoffrey Kariithi, Robert Ouko, Paul Boit and John Matere Keriri. Again, many came from the educated loyalists of Central Province or from chiefly families elsewhere. The exposure of this young cadre to colonial administration was brief, with most holding a bewildering array of short-term posts over three to four years before being elevated to leadership roles at independence. Nonetheless, they emerged with a belief in law and order as a precondition for development and an ethos of discipline, hard work and public service.[147]

In the same period, a major expansion was taking place in the future size of the African elite, driven by the Cold War between communism and capitalism. External interest in Africa was growing, particularly in the US. With four successful lecture tours and meetings with American dignitaries including Senator John F. Kennedy and Vice-President Nixon between 1956 and 1960, Mboya built tight relations between the US and Kenyan nationalism.[148] Between 1958 and 1961, Mboya, helped by Kiano and others, organised mass airlifts of 'O'-level African students to US universities on scholarship programmes. Despite some harassment from the colonial government, they sent more than 1,000 students on programmes funded by American donations. The Kenyans were given free or subsidised tuition, and lived in local communities. The spirit of pan-Africanism contributed immensely to this intellectual enfranchisement of the future leaders of Kenya, and cemented Mboya's political credibility. These American 'airlifts' produced many of the second-generation elites of the 1970s and 1980s, including politicians, academics and journalists such as George Saitoti, Elijah Mwangale, Josephat Karanja, Zachary Onyonka, Joseph Kamotho, Wangari Maathai, Jonathan Ng'eno and Hilary Ng'weno.[149]

In response, building on the pro-African liberation stance of the Eastern Bloc countries, Odinga sought similar assistance. During 1960, he travelled extensively in the East, visiting China, the USSR, East Germany, Yugoslavia and Nasser's Egypt, much to the disquiet of the British. During these visits, he arranged for a similar, more controversial, study programme, in which between 500 and 1,000 students were sent to study in the Eastern Bloc.[150] By July 1963, there were 400 students in Russia, Poland, Bulgaria and Czechoslovakia who had travelled there secretly (as the British denied Africans any direct contact with the communist states). Amongst those who went overseas on Russian scholarships – most to Moscow – were Kipng'eno arap Ng'eny, Moses arap Keino and Oburu and Raila Odinga, Jaramogi's sons.[151] Odinga also arranged scholarships to Indian universities. As a result of all these programmes, by 1963, there were 3,900 Kenyan students studying overseas, including 1,900 Africans.

The Return of the Detainees and the End of the Emergency

Kenya was gradually returning to a peacetime model. During 1956–8, 55,000 detainees were freed, to return to Central Province and the highlands.[152] Many came back to find their assets gone and their lives transformed, fertile ground for legal and illegal protest. By 1958, rural Kikuyu and Embu were organising once more, with a new secret society known as Kiama Kiu Muingi (Society or Council of the People) opposing land consolidation and representing a continued thread of support for the ideals of Mau Mau. Kikuyu oathing again became widespread. As they returned, ex-detainees became increasingly influential in local politics. Concern at the risk of insurrection lay behind many of the reforms in the Legislative Council in 1958–9. At the same time, repression in Kikuyu areas reintensified, with detentions, loyalist screening committees and curfews re-established.[153]

To assuage discontent and help build the moderate middle class they believed would provide Kenya with stability, in October 1959 the government finally lifted the ban on African land ownership in the white highlands. The 'colour bar' was replaced by a 'good husbandry' rule, which permitted only a tiny number of wealthy allies to acquire land. However, the pace of change was growing. The Conservative government of Prime Minister Harold Macmillan recognised the changes sweeping through the world and the decline of British imperial power, and pushed a hostile Kenyan settler community and administration into a rapid programme of reform. A key event in this reappraisal was the beating to death of 11 hard-core detainees by warders at Hola detention camp in Tana River in March 1959 and the subsequent cover-up. When exposed in the House of Commons, it forced a fundamental reassessment of Kenya policy, a change also driven by imminent independence in Tanganyika.

In January 1960, the governor finally lifted the State of Emergency and released most remaining detainees. Restrictions on Kikuyu movement ended, leading many to travel to the highlands seeking work. However, the squatter system was gone, providing only 4 per cent of agricultural employment in 1963.[154] Rural wages fell and social conditions were difficult, leading to labour unrest and illegal squatting. Many Kikuyu ex-squatters were returning to the highlands not only to work, but to establish their land rights in the expectation that these would be confirmed after independence by the subdivision of European farms. By this time, African elites too knew that a redistribution of the white highlands was inevitable, and were positioning themselves for the competition. While the Maasai and Kalenjin based their claims on pre-colonial usage, the Kikuyu based theirs upon their colonial tenure. Kikuyu squatters now moved north-west as far as Uasin Gishu and Trans-Nzoia, which had previously hosted few Kikuyu. The experience of Mau Mau appeared to have changed Kikuyu perceptions of the Rift Valley, creating a more expansionary view that treated much of the white highlands as theirs, by virtue of their struggle and sacrifice, despite the historical record.[155] Recognising that any subdivision based on pre-colonial occupation or spheres of influence was unlikely to give them the lion's share, senior Kikuyu began to consider 'willing buyer, willing seller' options. Well before Kenyatta's release, Gichuru and others were clear that, after independence, there would be no free land.[156]

Lancaster House, the 1961 Elections and the KADU Government

The First Lancaster House Conference, 1960

African pressure and changing British attitudes now led to a moment of sudden, shocking change: the first Lancaster House Conference in London of January–March 1960. Macmillan, a reluctant Conservative Party and the new British Colonial Secretary Ian Macleod agreed that Britain could no longer withhold independence in Kenya simply because of the white settlers. Although the Conservative Party was the 'party of empire', Macmillan had no personal loyalty to Kenya's Europeans. Since multiracialism could not offer a long-term solution, the legitimacy of African nationalism must be accepted.[157] Liberated by his October 1959 re-election, in February 1960 Macmillan declared Britain's intent to withdraw from all its remaining colonies and recognised a 'wind of change' blowing across the continent that the colonial powers could no longer hold back. Although they feared their African colonies were not ready for independence, the British judged the dangers of delay – violence, radicalisation and a turn to communism – to be a higher risk. As part of the package of changes under way, a newcomer, Sir Patrick Renison, replaced Governor Baring.

The Lancaster House Conference saw the Legislative Council meet with Macleod to chart a new course. Ngala, Muliro, Odinga and Mboya led the African delegation. To some surprise, even amongst African members, the conference laid down the goal of Kenyan independence under majority rule for the first time.[158] It restructured the Legislative Council, establishing an overall African majority of one, with 33 open seats, 20 seats reserved for Asian, European and Arab candidates, and 12 national members elected by Parliament. Macleod also widened the African franchise significantly. Although the African councillors were not happy, they accepted the plan. European opinion was not so forgiving, and die-hards bitterly criticised Blundell on his return. Many settlers felt abandoned by the British, with no guarantees of what would happen to their land. Unless they were willing to resort to violence, however, the colony would move towards majority rule.

Although independence was almost guaranteed, the British and Kenyan governments were still concerned to halt the spread of Soviet and Chinese influence, which would weaken Western leverage as well as (in their view) threaten Kenya's prosperity. To do this, the British steered African nationalist opinion towards moderation and sought opportunities to bring more moderate Africans into positions of influence. Four elected AEMO members (Ngala, Muimi, Kiano and Towett) now joined the government. The harder-line members led by Odinga, in contrast, rejected this arrangement until Kenyatta was free.[159]

The Formation of KANU and KADU

The state also relaxed the ban on colony-wide African political parties. At Lancaster House, the African elected members had agreed to unite under the banner of a new party, but such ideals swiftly evaporated. Instead, two new parties emerged, centred on the existing groups within the African members.

On 14 May 1960, the Kenya African National Union (KANU) was founded, in its symbolic home in Kiambu. Its name, black, red and green flag and symbols were chosen as a direct successor to those of KAU. KANU's leadership was dominated by representatives from the larger, land-constrained, more rapidly differentiating Kikuyu, Luo, Embu, Meru and Kamba. It favoured rapid decolonisation, social reform, a prominent state role in the economy and open competition for land and resources, unfettered by ethnic boundaries, in which their communities would perform relatively well. Gichuru was chosen as its acting president, while Odinga was the prime mover in the party's formation, and was elected vice-president. Mboya, with some reluctance on all sides, brought in his NPCP and was elected secretary-general (by only one vote). However, there was little love lost between Mboya and the other founders, and had circumstances differed only slightly, Mboya might have struck out alone, creating a three-way (rather than two-way) split, which would have changed the shape of the independence settlement. As it was, the meeting not only founded the alliance that was to seize power; by choosing Gichuru as president, it also raised expectations that, once free, Kenyatta would become its leader.

Fears of Kikuyu and Luo domination, desire for personal status, and European encouragement had already deepened the division within the African leadership to the point of no return. Ngala and Moi were elected *in absentia* as KANU officials, but the decision to split had already been made. Immediately after the formation of KANU, negotiations began to establish an alternative party. On 25 June 1960, the leaders of four regional alliances – the Kalenjin Political Alliance of Moi and Towett; the Coast African People's Union of Ngala; John Keen and John Konchellah's Maasai United Front; and Muliro's Kenya Africa People's Party – plus Somali leaders agreed a merger to create a competing national coalition: the Kenya African Democratic Union (KADU). The new party chose the 37-year-old Ngala as its leader, Muliro as deputy leader, Moi as chairman and Keen as secretary. As with KANU's leaders, each politician's district parties followed their leaders *en masse*.

Both parties were unstable, temporary structures, built in the expectation of power, centred around a few national-level 'champions' and supported by their various local ethno-regional bases. Because of the significance of ethnicity as a point of political cleavage, the personalisation of politics around a few leaders, and the low level of awareness amongst most voters, KANU always had the support of most Africans. KADU was also hampered by its lack of a clear ideological position, relying on 'protection for minorities' and by its more ambiguous commitment to the release of Kenyatta. Its key assets were its position on land, and the desire of the (more socially conservative) coastal and pastoral communities to avoid dominance by the Kikuyu and Luo – themes that continued to dominate post-independence politics. KADU also had European backing. It appeared supportive of liberal economic policies and willing to grant more protection to the settlers than KANU. Ex-Governor Baring and Blundell were amongst those Europeans who quietly assisted KADU, seeing it as a bulwark against Kikuyu radicalism and as more likely to 'do a deal' on the settlers' land.[160]

The situation on the Coast was particularly complex because of the size and influence of the Muslim Arab-Swahili community, many of whom saw little future in an African-dominated Kenya, and who campaigned from 1957 for coastal autonomy or *Mwambao*.[161] Roughly half the coast was Christian, half Muslim; a complex mosaic that made any coordinated political position difficult. Ngala represented the Christian Mijikenda community and, increasingly, a middle ground of regional autonomy. However, his remit amongst Muslim Arab, Swahili, Shirazi and Bajuni peoples was weaker, since he supported the integration of the coastal strip into Kenya proper. These communities represented the dominant economic, political and cultural force in the region, but were divided and uncertain as to whether to back union with Zanzibar or Ngala's regionalism.

Meanwhile, Kenyatta and his compatriots remained in Turkana. He had completed his prison sentence, but remained subject to indefinite detention. The government remained determined to erase Kenyatta from Kenya's memory. They had destroyed his house and dispersed his family. Most officials remained convinced that he had masterminded Mau Mau and believed that moderate leaders such as Ngala and Mboya should be encouraged instead. In May 1960, Governor Renison, new to Kenya and under pressure from settler leaders, reasserted that Kenyatta would remain under restriction and would never be permitted to re-enter politics. To Renison, Kenyatta was a 'leader to darkness and death'.[162] Such obduracy only reaffirmed Kenyatta's legitimacy in African eyes. The pressure grew on the British (at the United Nations and elsewhere) to release him.

For Kenyatta personally, these were difficult times. Relations had deteriorated between the Kapenguria prisoners as the years passed, and the elderly Kenyatta had become isolated from the younger, more radical, detainees.[163] He had narrowly survived an attempt on his life in 1957 by a young Mau Mau prisoner, Kariuki Chotara (probably organised by his prison colleagues), during which Itote and Ngei saved his life, which cemented Kenyatta's loyalties to these two individuals thereafter.[164]

Immigrant Fears, Economic Crisis and the First Settlement Schemes

Kenya's Asians and Europeans were now facing the prospect of radical change. African calls for imminent independence roused fears amongst the security forces and the 61,000-strong white community. The violence of the Congo in 1960 after Belgium's withdrawal deepened these fears. In 1961, more than 6,000 Europeans left, and in 1962 and 1963 the annual outflow was more than 8,000 (although 3,000 immigrants also arrived each year).[165] Political uncertainty hit the economy hard. New capital investment and building virtually ceased in 1960, British money began to shift back home and unemployment increased.[166] Share and land prices fell, and agricultural production declined with reduced investment and a severe drought in 1961. The idea of eventual independence also exposed the fragile nature of Kenya's economy, dependent on a few cash-crops and on external financing to cover even current expenditure.[167]

Politically, the white community remained divided between those who believed change was inevitable and hoped to manage it, and those who remained committed to a white dominion for East Africa. Many Asians were equally concerned about the future. Some had supported African nationalists financially and morally, but the community included many wealthy and privileged individuals and had a poor reputation for business ethics and the treatment of Africans. They too began to cut their investments. The avoidance of mass emigration, in order to preserve the technical and material basis of the colony, became a key objective for both British and African leaders. Mboya, Gichuru and others saw how dependent they were on European support to avoid collapse during the transition. The British too were extremely concerned to avoid 'another Congo', and to ensure that a future African-led government would respect the rights and interests of British citizens who chose to remain.

From February 1960, the key issue for the European settlers was land, and the need to agree a programme of land purchase and African settlement that would either buy them out entirely or permit them to continue farming safely after independence. The creation of such a programme was one of Blundell's conditions for his support for the transition to majority rule. There were approximately 3,600 European-owned agricultural holdings, of which 2,680 were 'mixed' farms, the remainder being ranches or plantations. However, progress was slow. African leaders were unwilling to agree to settler demands for financial guarantees for their land, though their own policies were not yet fully developed. The government struggled to develop proposals that could satisfy everyone, as both they and the settlers were opposed to mass land subdivision and settlement, believing it would destroy the economy and the value of the land for those Europeans who stayed on. South African-born Minister of Agriculture Bruce McKenzie's first settlement proposals in 1960–1 were small, concerned the highest-quality land, and were based on a large-farm model, which would never meet the political demand for land. However, they contained the key ingredients of the final deal. The funds to buy out the white farmers would come from British and international loans, and the loans would have to be repaid by African farmers.[168]

After months of negotiation, two further schemes were established. A total of 180,000 acres (73,000 hectares) would be settled at a cost of GB£6–8 million. Britain would provide the money for land purchase, two-thirds by loan, one-third by grant. Loans to fence and improve the properties would come from the World Bank (the International Bank for Reconstruction and Development), West Germany and the British-funded Commonwealth Development Corporation.[169] A new Land and Settlement Board would choose settlers (who would later have to be 'confirmed' by the presidents of the regional assemblies). Candidates had to have capital and farming experience, and the schemes were not designed to settle the landless but to Africanise the highlands, mixing African and European farmers and stabilising the land market.[170] The designers planned two main types of scheme. The 'yeoman' scheme would create large farms for experienced farmers, to which the recipient had to contribute GB£500. The 'peasant' scheme was designed to create smaller farms, to which the settler contributed GB£100. While the yeoman farms would be interspersed with European farms, the peasant schemes were planned for the borderlands between the reserves and the highlands. In practice, by 1962 the two schemes had merged. The schemes were small scale and the land quite expensive, partly because they had to meet World Bank economic (rather than Kenyan political) criteria, and probably favoured European sellers over African buyers. The land was priced on its 1959 value, before the economic crisis had cut prices in half.

The state had also resettled several thousand families in small land settlements in non-European lands. The government used detainee forced labour during 1956–62 to build three high-density settlement schemes based on irrigation. The largest, the Mwea rice irrigation scheme, eventually supported 20,000 Kikuyu families, mostly ex-detainees. There were other less-sensitive settlement schemes, settling vacant Crown land with people from elsewhere in the country, such as the Shimba Hills and Baringo settlements, but most attention was on the well-developed white farms.

The 1961 Elections

The February 1961 elections were Kenya's first true national elections and produced the first African majority on the Legislative Council. They reflected and reinforced the growing polarisation in the country. Although both parties were committed to independence, the numbers were in KANU's favour. Nonetheless, Kenya's first African government was not formed by the winners, but by the losers. The polls began four years of confrontation between centralism and federalism and saw the entrenchment of ethnicity as the key driver of political preference. They led inexorably to the release of Kenyatta, but also deepened the divide in KANU between Mboya and Odinga, which increasingly aligned with a division over future economic policy and Cold War alliances.

The polls were the first fought on a common voters' roll, though Africans did not yet have universal suffrage.[171] The boundaries of the 33 open seats (effectively for Africans) were based on the existing districts. The effect was to over-represent the larger, lightly populated pastoral regions in the number of voters per seat, a disparity that was to continue for decades. To counterbalance this, the most densely populated districts were allocated two seats.[172] In the 20 seats reserved for non-Africans, only candidates from one 'racial' group were permitted. Europeans would represent the highlands from Uganda to Ukambani, while most of the coastal strip was reserved for Arabs and Asians. Here, there would be a racially or religiously 'pure' primary, after which everyone, including Africans, would choose from amongst the candidates who had received at least 25 per cent support in the primaries.

KANU's rallies focused on the release of Kenyatta and immediate independence, while KADU called for much the same, but in more moderate, pro-Western terms.

Blundell's New Kenya Party (NKP) quietly supported KADU. During the campaign, there was no real national contest, and neither KADU nor KANU made significant inroads into each other's core ethnic areas. In KADU-dominated areas, KANU could muster virtually no candidates, and KADU was in a similar position in Central Province and Nyanza. The power of ethnicity and regional alliances was so strong that in only 10 of the 33 open seats did both parties even field a candidate, and in only six was there a true contest.

2.4: 1961 election results

Source: Adapted from Republic of Kenya, 1961 Constituency Boundary Map

KANU was widely expected to win, but the party was divided internally. There were already policy disagreements over the importance of Western capital investment, the means to acquire land from the Europeans, and how to distribute this land thereafter. While Gichuru and Mboya were willing to compromise with the British in the interests of economic efficiency and a secure transfer of power, Odinga and others demanded rapid nationalisation, land expropriation and a commitment to socialism. Odinga and some members of the Kenyatta family also believed that Gichuru and Mboya were equivocal over Kenyatta's release, as they would have to surrender their hard-fought dominance to the ageing detainee. The conflict within KANU grew to the point where Gichuru suspended Odinga from the party, and he and Mboya demanded Odinga's expulsion just before the election.[173] The crisis was papered over and Odinga's vice-presidency of KANU reaffirmed, but Odinga's 'ginger group' of activists were increasingly influential. The battle was as much within the party as between KANU and KADU. In 'KANU zones' pro-Odinga KANU supporters stood as independents against pro-Mboya party nominees, and vice versa. Munyua Waiyaki, a young radical doctor from a well-known Kiambu family, opposed Mboya in the Nairobi open seat. Odinga backed him quite openly.

The poll itself saw mass voter illiteracy, and presiding officers ended up marking the ballots for most voters. There was a huge turnout of 885,000 voters, nearly 84 per cent of the electorate. In the African open seats, KANU won a decisive victory, with 19 seats and 67 per cent of the vote, while KADU took 11 seats with only 16 per cent of the vote. Minor parties and independents took the remaining three seats (see Figure 2.4). Patterns of ethno-regional political alignment were crystallising and would endure for decades. KADU secured the support of the Kalenjin and Maasai, the coastal Mijikenda and sections of the Abaluhya. KANU took the votes of the Luo and the Kikuyu, and most of the Taita, Gusii and Kamba. In the urban seats, Mboya routed his opponents in Nairobi, supported by what was now a mostly Kikuyu electorate. KANU won the open Mombasa seat, while KADU's Wafula Wabuge, a Luhya, won multi-ethnic Nakuru Town.

In the European seats, honours were shared between the NKP and the anti-independence Kenya Coalition. As a result, the small parties, the independents and the white, Arab and Asian councillors held the balance of power between KANU and KADU.

KADU Leads Kenya's First African Government, April 1961

Victorious in the elections, KANU expected that a deal for the release of Kenyatta would follow. However, Renison (with the support of the British Cabinet) refused to release Kenyatta until an African government had been established and 'found workable'. KANU therefore declined to form a government. The result was deadlock. Officials privately approached both Mboya and Gichuru to become prime minister, but they refused.[174] Renison did, though, move Kenyatta closer to Nairobi and allowed visits from politicians, churchmen and journalists, in an attempt to reduce the political significance of his detention.

After some manoeuvring, KADU broke the deadlock. In return for a promise to build a house for Kenyatta, his release 'in due course' and effective control of the government, on 18 April 1961 KADU joined an alliance with the NKP and the Kenya Indian Congress to establish Kenya's first African-led government. Ngala became leader of government business (the title that Nkrumah had held in Ghana). Moi, Muliro and Towett joined him as ministers, alongside white and Asian leaders. In order to provide this curious alliance with a working majority in the council, Renison nominated 11 more appointees.

Kenyatta, meanwhile, had been allowed to give his first press conference in April 1961, which was covered by the world's press. He emerged as a very different figure from the bogeyman constructed by the settlers, smart, eloquent and reasonable. He denied association with Mau Mau and committed himself to non-violence and constitutional independence. He also rejected any Russian associations, stressing there was no place for communism in Africa, denied he had ever demanded the eviction of Europeans from the highlands and stated that the land titles of productive European settlers would be secure under an independent Kenyan government.

Meanwhile, Ngala's government could not re-establish confidence. Its survival rested on the support of the governor and the settlers, and KADU found itself voting against KANU motions to release Kenyatta.[175] In parallel, Blundell, the NKP and white farmers were negotiating directly with the British for money for large-scale land purchase and African settlement. Neither KANU nor KADU's land position was yet clear. In August 1961, a series of meetings between the parties concluded with a resolution supporting the sanctity of both ethnic and private property rights and the need for fair compensation for any land acquisitions.[176]

Kenyatta's Release, August 1961

Mounting African discontent forced the British to accept the inevitability of KANU's taking office. Kenyatta's detention, however, remained an insuperable obstacle. As the government prevaricated, Kenyatta entertained a series of visitors, playing the role of leader in exile. By July 1961, Renison and the Macmillan government were convinced that his release was essential to an orderly transfer of power and that his continued detention was more risky than his release.[177]

Finally, Renison announced Kenyatta's release on 1 August 1961. Soon after, Kenyatta returned home, to a hero's welcome. The British also freed the last remaining hard-core detainees. Many thought Kenyatta would reunify KANU and KADU and create a united nationalist party once more.[178] He even considered creating a third political party. However, he was eventually persuaded to accept the leadership of KANU. On 28 October 1961, Kenyatta duly replaced Gichuru as president of KANU, a post he held for the rest of his life. He felt little loyalty to the leaders who had campaigned for his release, though, and tried to maintain a balance between the Odinga and the Mboya factions. He soon proved to be more politically conservative than either Mboya or Odinga.[179]

British opinion was becoming used to the idea that Kenya would not remain a colony for long, and negotiations began for a faster transfer of power. In November 1961, Macmillan commented, 'it is quite impracticable to contemplate ruling Kenya for an extended period'.[180] Hostility to Kenyatta was still strong, but colonial officials could see little chance of bringing forward alternative leaders in time. Although the British Cabinet remained deeply unhappy with the idea of this 'evil man' leading an independent Kenya, they recognised his presence was essential to any settlement.[181] As a result, they followed a twin-track policy. Within weeks, they were speeding Kenyatta's move to the Legislative Council, changing the rules to allow the ex-detainees to register when the voters' rolls were closed, and changing the law barring prisoners convicted of sentences of over two years from standing for the Council. In January 1962, Kenyatta duly took a seat in the Legislative Council unopposed.[182] In parallel, they tried to limit the risk that KANU and Kenyatta posed by encouraging federalism, both within Kenya and across East Africa.

The Majimbo *Debate and the Struggle for the White Highlands, 1961–3*

The campaign for federalism had already begun. In September–October 1961, advised by the NKP, KADU's Peter Okondo put forward proposals for an entirely new constitutional structure. Recognising that they were unlikely to win power at the centre, KADU proposed that independent Kenya should adopt a federal system under a *majimbo* (regional) constitution, which would create elected regional assemblies with taxation powers and responsibility for housing, local government, social services, education and the police. This would leave the National Assembly with control only over defence, foreign affairs, macro-economic policy and the national budget. This Swiss- or American-style arrangement promised to leave KADU in command of the Rift and the Coast even if KANU came to power in Nairobi.[183] This was critically important, as a Rift Valley region would probably include most of the ex-white highlands. Many white settlers supported such an arrangement, partly for their own protection, partly in order to avoid a violent confrontation over control of the unitary state.[184] Colonial officials in contrast were sceptical, as they believed regionalism made little economic sense. KANU, too, was entirely opposed to any form of regional autonomy. The same debate – between region and centre – was to take centre-stage again in the late 1990s and 2000s, with many of the same forces arrayed against each other. Notions of efficiency, individualism and the free movement of peoples warred with the concepts of communal land rights, local government as more accountable and the need to share resources equitably.

While the political sphere took most attention, serious economic, social and security problems continued in the highlands. Land was the real issue underlying the *majimbo* debate, and the white farms and unoccupied Crown lands were becoming a battleground between settlers, the landless and the new African leaders. This competition for land increasingly took on an ethnic flavour, just as politics was doing. KADU's position was that the sanctity of land titles should apply to ethnic communities as well as to individuals.[185] Tensions mounted between the Kikuyu and the Kalenjin and in 1962, Kipsigis leaders ordered all Luo workers in Kericho to leave the Rift. The first sales of white farms under the settlement programme in November 1961 led to unemployment for existing workers. There was deep concern amongst Kikuyu farm workers that regionalism might mean their expulsion from the Rift, and they were determined to seize what they believed was theirs while they could.

The result in 1961–2 was the growth of informal radical Kikuyu groups, a continuation of the activities of the Kiama Kia Muingi, sometimes known by the old Mau Mau name, the Kenya Land and Freedom Army (KLFA).[186] Again, landless Kikuyu in the Rift oathed, protested, and stockpiled arms, and there were isolated killings. Their goals were now *Uhuru* and the expropriation of land from the whites without payment. Evictions proved futile and white farmers were told in 1962 to abandon attempts to remove these squatters. With the prize of independence moving closer, the landless in the forests and villages of Nakuru and Thomson's Falls were increasingly unwilling to obey European authority. More and more KLFA supporters in the Rift were also KANU officials, much as the KCA and KAU had interrelated a decade before. Radical Kikuyu activists such as Mark Mwithaga and Kaggia (freed from detention) took up leadership roles in KANU branches in Nakuru, Naivasha and Laikipia. These branches supported mass squatting on white lands that were due for sale, threatening the government's gradualist plans.

On land, KANU remained divided. Only gradually did the majority come to accept settler proposals for a large-scale, foreign-funded buy-out. In contrast, Odinga, Kaggia, Ngei and others opposed any pre-independence deal, since they believed it would entrench European interests, and they campaigned against the sale of any European land to Africans.[187] The economic importance of the European farming sector was demonstrated by the rapid decline in land prices and productivity during 1961–2, as white farmers cut plantings and investments. By January 1962, Kenyatta was clear that a deal must be done. The British must fund a large-scale resettlement programme that would settle the landless, using long-term loans with easy repayment conditions.[188] He, Gichuru and other KANU leaders needed a deal urgently to begin resettlement and had reluctantly concluded that land would have to be bought. They were therefore unhappy with the promises by some KANU branches of 'free land' at independence. In their view, this threatened the deal with the British, the resettlement programme, their own personal authority and the economic stability of the country. Kenyatta's explicit opposition to 'free things' reflected his view of Kenyans as hard-working, self-made people. From his release onwards, Kenyatta also made clear that law and order was a priority, and that his would not be a 'gangster government'. As he warned people, 'If you cannot obey the present laws how will you be able to obey our own laws when we have them?'[189]

Concerns over the risk to the transition eventually led the government – by now a coalition – to intervene. In September 1962, police raids arrested dozens of Kikuyu and found homemade guns and ammunition. Hundreds of Kikuyu were expelled from KANU for supporting the KLFA. KADU demanded even sterner action in the

Rift Valley, but a full-scale security crackdown was politically impossible, as it would have broken the shallow consensus between KANU and the British. Instead, the state used the land settlement programme to divert the political pressure.

A New Constitution and Coalition Government, 1962–3

Meanwhile, the 'wind of change' blew through Africa. Most of British-ruled West Africa was independent and Somalia, Tanganyika and Uganda had all followed suit by 1962.

The Second Lancaster House Conference, 1962

In November 1961, the British agreed to a second constitutional conference on Kenya. They were increasingly concerned that the political impasse and weak KADU-led government would drive KANU left into the arms of Odinga, the Eastern Bloc and communism. From 14 February to 6 April 1962, the second Lancaster House Conference took place, under another new colonial secretary, Reginald Maudling. The conference saw lengthy disputes between the two main African parties, now led by Kenyatta and Ngala. Despite British doubts and KANU's hostility, the conference hammered out a deal for self-government based on KADU's regionalism. The British government favoured KADU's views, mostly because of concerns at the future of the white settlers and the economy under KANU, but also because KADU represented the ethnic groups that had remained loyal during the Emergency, and had taken office when KANU refused. It also represented many of the most warlike of Kenya's peoples, and Maasai and Kalenjin leaders including Tipis, William Murgor and Marie John Seroney threatened civil war if their demands were not met.

The new structure devolved substantial powers to six regions (excluding Nairobi), with most civil servants and the police employed by the regions and much of the state's revenue directly accruing to them. The 1962 agreement also transferred much of the 'Westminster model' of parliamentary government to the soon-to-be independent state, including the role of a prime minister and single-member 'first past the post' constituencies. It converted the Legislative Council into a bicameral National Assembly, with a Senate alongside the House of Representatives, and the Council of Ministers became the Cabinet. The 41 districts would continue to serve as the basis of representation, each with a senator and one or more MPs, with constituency boundaries drawn to reflect ethnic boundaries as far as practicable. As a result, the semi-arid districts had a representation far outweighing their population (Kakamega had more than 10 times the population of Samburu, for example).

The idea of the second chamber was KADU's, and was supported by both European and Asian communities, to protect minorities and safeguard the Regional Constitution. According to Maudling, its goal was 'partly to ensure proper representation of geographical views and interests, partly to act as a revising and reforming house, and also, possibly most important, to act as a fundamental protector of individual rights and liberties'.[190] Based on the British House of Lords, the Senate had limited ability to initiate legislation, a limited veto and no power to choose the government. However, it required 75 per cent of senators to support any change to the Constitution and 90 per cent to change the specially entrenched provisions defining the regions, districts and 'tribal authorities', individual rights and citizenship. There was a detailed Bill of Rights, including protections against discrimination and nationalisation. The Constitution was to be overseen by an independent judiciary little different from that of the colonial era. The Constitution was said to be the longest and most complex created by the British for a newly independent country.[191] Many British civil servants were sceptical, but political necessities dominated the debate.

The conference also agreed the outline of Kenya's independence land deal. KANU and the settlers agreed there was a desperate need for the rapid expansion of the land purchase and settlement programme. While Rift Valley KADU leaders, including Moi and Tipis, defended the historical right to land of the Rift Valley peoples and the centrality of community land rights, which would give the Maasai and Kalenjin most of the white highlands, KANU and especially its Kikuyu supporters (both loyalists and ex-detainees) were implacably opposed. They argued that historical claims to land ownership were of little interest; that Kikuyu labour had helped develop most of the farms; and that only central control of land would ensure that it would be freely available to all.

The deal (which was based on a proposal from European farmers) was that regionalism would be accompanied by a dramatic extension of settlement. While most ranches and plantations would remain intact in European hands, a million acres of mixed farms (half the total) would be taken over and used to settle Africans. This would be funded by British and international loans, and executed through private land purchase. Both KADU and the settlers had favoured a more limited settlement approach. KADU also feared that the Central Land Board that was proposed to manage the transfer of white-owned lands would favour the Kikuyu, and it therefore ensured that the regions would play a role in this board.[192] Crown lands became the responsibility of the regions, and the un-demarcated ex-reserves were handed over to the new county councils to allay fears about their future. The Maasai, who attended the conference in a unique status because of the 1904 and 1911 treaties, were left with little apart from promises of the ethnic purity of their districts. Their delegation refused to sign, claiming a second British betrayal, although this had no practical effect.[193]

This compromise suited the British well, as failure to resolve the issue before independence would have left them with serious liabilities in the event of future expropriation.[194] Kenyatta and KANU reluctantly agreed. Not only was there a risk that some of their allies might defect to join KADU in government if they did not take office soon; they had successfully retained key elements of a central land distribution system. They also believed that they would be able to change the Constitution once they took power, and that power would soon come.

In April 1962, the KADU-NKP government resigned, to be replaced by a KANU-KADU coalition, which would supervise the transition to self-rule, headed by the governor. British hopes of splitting off 'moderate' KANU leaders such as Mboya from 'the extreme group – men of violence and of Communist contacts – led by

Kenyatta, Odinga and Ngei' came to nothing.[195] Kenyatta became minister of state for constitutional affairs and economic planning. He brought with him Gichuru as finance minister, Mboya as labour minister and Lawrence Sagini from Kisii, Timothy Chokwe from the Coast, Fred Mati from the Kamba and white settler McKenzie as minister of lands and settlement. As minister of state for constitutional affairs, Ngala's ministers were Moi, Towett, Muliro and Mate. Despite his importance, Odinga was excluded from the government on Maudling's insistence, partly because of his opposition to African land purchase, but mostly because he was in contact with and receiving money from communist governments.[196] Odinga had been open since 1960 that he received financial support from the Russians.[197] The British believed he represented both Russian and Chinese interests, and the consequence was a campaign against Odinga in the settler and international press, which accused him of seeking revolution. Odinga's failure to receive a ministry in the coalition was a defining moment, with Kenyatta accepting his exclusion as a price for power. In Odinga's words: 'Kenyatta succumbed. He did so without even a single fight to uphold our position.'[198]

Over the next year, the coalition government did its best to administer Kenya during a difficult transition, and to prepare for another round of elections. Each new minister now had to lead and Africanise bureaucracies that were almost entirely European and Asian in the middle and upper ranks, and contained many who were hostile to their objectives, while at the same time maintaining their party and nationalist credentials. The economy remained shaky, dependent on Asian and European capital and expertise, and its agricultural performance dependent on the settler farms. The country faced an uncertain political future, with an under-defined system of regional government, little money, few experienced African administrators or professionals; no clear political settlement and facing a loss of investor confidence.

Kenyatta's Deal with the British

Kenyatta was now the dominant figure in the emerging independence settlement, and the British saw him as a man with whom they could do business. It was now clear that Kenyatta was a relatively conservative nationalist, without strong ideological views. He had been propelled by force of personality, his demonisation by the British and the efforts of others into a position of critical importance, but was perfectly suited once there to secure his position and to work without prejudice with those willing to support him.

The colonial government's change in attitude between 1961 and 1963 was extraordinary, and preceded the conversion of the settlers to Kenyatta's cause by at least a year. The secret of much of Kenya's future lies in this change of relationship between colonial state and African political prisoner. Neither Kenyatta's biographers nor historians have given a full explanation of this volte-face. The key probably lies in Kenyatta's 'forgive and forget' attitude and his genuine respect for the British. From the moment of his release, he showed himself committed to a moderate course. It also lies in Realpolitik. Kenyatta was willing to compromise over the economy and land in return for power and for British support for Kenya. Odinga, less happy to make such an arrangement, suggested that the British had promised Kenyatta their support in return for their remaining his chief advisers and their continued military presence.[199] Whether such a conversation ever took place is doubtful, but the evidence suggests Odinga was correct in his summary of the arrangement that was reached.

New Regional Boundaries, 1962

It was now necessary to resolve some of the thorny issues that might hinder Kenya's advance towards independence. Key among these was the determination of the regional boundaries that would accompany the introduction of *majimbo*. In July 1962, Colonial Secretary Maudling appointed a commission to redesign the old provinces to create six new regions. This was a critical moment in the evolution of the independent state.

The Regional Boundaries Commission, which took testimony from many delegations and all parties, rejected KANU's appeals to leave the existing provinces intact and gave greater weight to KADU's claims and to the importance of ethnicity in defining administrative boundaries.[200] They abolished the Southern Province, and created a new Eastern Region with the Kamba joining the Embu, Meru and the Oromo-speaking peoples of the north. They shrunk Central Province to move the Embu and Meru out, at the request of these communities, who were claimed to fear the radicalism and numbers of the Kikuyu. This left the Kikuyu alone in Central Region, but the Commission added to it European areas in Thika, Nyeri and the Aberdares (and ruled that the people of Kirinyaga should henceforth be treated as Kikuyu). However, they moved settler Nanyuki District out to join an enlarged Laikipia in the Rift Valley. Maasai claims to Laikipia were disregarded.

Western Region was carved off from Nyanza, separating the Luo and Gusii from the Abaluhya. Fragments of settler lands were transferred into Nyanza to alleviate land shortages, but they were small. Small areas of Maasailand were also transferred into Luo Nyanza to reflect their long-standing occupation. The Kamba of Machakos acquired European lands to the south and east of Nairobi. The Luhya obtained their own Western Region, extended to include some European farms in Kakamega and Bungoma, but most of Luhya-dominated Trans-Nzoia remained in the Rift Valley. The Rift Valley was extended by the addition of the Maasai, the Samburu, and the Kipsigis from Nyanza, which brought all Kalenjin-speakers together, bar the Sabaot. Most of the former white highlands remained in the Rift, leaving it dominated by KADU and the Europeans, to KANU's discomfort. The Coast remained intact. The Somali, who had declared that they did not wish to be part of Kenya at all, were designated part of Coast Region in the interim (see Figure 2.5).[201]

The boundaries created by the Commission were to prove extraordinarily long lasting and drove regional politics. The creation of a seventh North-Eastern Region in March 1963 was the sole major change in the next 45 years. The 1962 redistribution also had huge implications for land rights, as the restructuring gave de facto control to the ethnic groups who dominated a particular region over ex-settler land placed

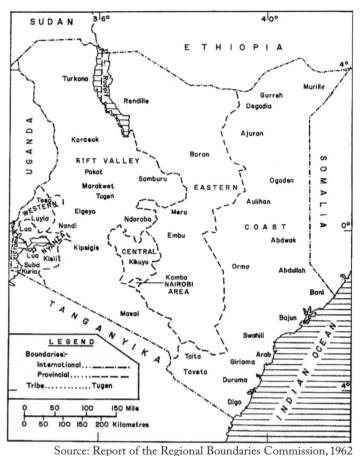

2.5: New regional boundaries and ethnicity, 1962

Source: Report of the Regional Boundaries Commission, 1962

within it. While the newly titled Nyandarua District (the Aberdares) was given to the Kikuyu, the Commission left Nakuru and Laikipia as Kikuyu-dominated outposts in the Rift Valley, a curious decision. This was probably part of a broader exercise to provide security for the white farmers, as observers expected the Rift Valley to remain KADU-dominated. It also asserted clearly that the Kikuyu did not have pre-eminence in land claims on these areas.

The 'Million-Acre' Scheme, October 1962

With independence coming close, the British government came under intense pressure from Africans, white farmers and British politicians alike to speed up the land transfer plans. After lengthy negotiations, they agreed the details of their new larger scheme. Its objectives were explicitly political: to secure an orderly transition to independence without destroying the large farm sector and foreign aid opportunities, and to avoid a land grab or a new emergency.

The October 1962 agreement established a 'million-acre' scheme for land purchase and settlement, to take place between 1962 and 1967. This was to be financed mostly by the British and staffed mainly by British officials. The goal was now to buy and subdivide nearly 1.5 million acres (0.5 million hectares) of European-owned mixed farmland, roughly one-sixth of the total, into 'high-density' subsistence farms. Another sixth would be sold intact to wealthy Africans. There would be no 'free land' and the 35,000 or so families to be settled would have to repay the loans they received. Settlers were supposed to be landless and unemployed, but long-term workers on the farms purchased had priority, provided they were 'acceptable to the regions' (i.e. of the right ethnic group). The provincial administration selected the remaining settlers by lot.

The cost of the various programmes was now estimated at GB£25.5 million, of which the British would give or loan GB£21 million for the land, to be repaid over 30 years. West Germany, the Land and Agriculture Bank, the Agricultural Finance Corporation (AFC) and the UK contributed development loans, but the World Bank declined, uncomfortable with the proposals. One-third of the cost ended up as a grant, while the settler had to repay the remaining two-thirds. The situation was confused by the continuation of the older schemes, which merged in practice with the high-density scheme.

The administration of this settlement process was central to the new government's survival. In the new KANU-led government of June 1963, the Agricultural Settlement Fund trustees (Minister of Finance Gichuru, Minister of Lands and Settlement Jackson Angaine and Minister of Agriculture McKenzie) would liaise with the British and control the fund into which all settlement money was paid. The purchase of land was the responsibility of a nominally autonomous Central Land Board, chaired by a Briton and with regional representation. The settlement of the landless was the role of the Ministry of Lands and Settlement, though in practice the ministry took over most of the functions of the Land Board. As well as appointing McKenzie, Kenyatta ensured that a European farmers' leader became parliamentary secretary for lands and settlement, to reassure the UK and white settlers.

Reflecting the increasing tension around land allocations, the million-acre scheme took an ethnic approach to the high-density schemes, allocating European land within their 'sphere of influence' to each of the major ethnic groups. Few if any schemes were multi-ethnic. The farms chosen for purchase and subdivision were selected less by which Europeans wished to sell, than by which ethnic group's land hunger needed assuaging first. At least 40 per cent of the land was reserved for Kikuyu settlement in the Aberdares and Nyeri in the new Central Region, and 20 per cent for the Abaluhya within Western Region.[202] There was a strong theme of ethnic partitioning; with Kikuyu squatters and workers evicted from the Lugari settlement scheme in Western to make way for Luhya, and non-Kikuyu in the Aberdares were similarly removed.[203] Reflecting their numerous, landless and angry status, the scheme was put into effect first in 1963 to settle the marginal lands of the Aberdares. This 'accelerated Kikuyu settlement scheme' aimed to compress all the land purchases for Central Region within three years.[204]

Most of the central Rift Valley around Nakuru, Kitale and Eldoret remained as large farms. The new government and its colonial masters agreed that, for these, a 'willing buyer, willing seller' arrangement was the only practicable one. Despite the ethnic orientation of the high-density schemes, this land would not be reserved for specific communities, but would be sold on the open market. The UK made extra funds available through the Land and Agriculture Bank to provide loans for Africans to buy these farms.

The land deal remained an uneasy compromise. The fact that land loans needed to be repaid remained infuriating to many Africans, who believed that it had been their land before colonial rule, and that African labour had developed the farms to their current productivity. Many Kalenjin and Maasai, meanwhile, saw the farms as stolen goods, and were unhappy about the possibility of their purchase by people from other ethnic groups. As most of the land purchase payments left the country, the result was a net drain on the economy, which had to be matched with productivity increases. Many experts doubted that these smallholdings could be more productive than the large farms they replaced. These early loans, massive by contemporary standards (roughly equivalent to GB£350 million) began a cycle of reliance on external financing for development that was to dog Kenya for decades. The four-year delay in beginning repayments, though it dulled this pain, stored up problems for the future, as some senior Kenyans did not actually expect to repay the foreign loans. Many African settlers did not intend to pay the government back, either.

The reasons for the African leadership's willingness to make this deal, which was to drive post-independence politics, remain controversial. In part, the land deal was the price Kenya had to pay for the support of the West and the peaceful and rapid departure of the British. The land transfer programme was proof that the new government was a trustworthy client to the international financial and political network to which it sought membership.[205] It remains uncertain, however, whether Kenyatta, Kiano, Mboya, Gichuru and Koinange would have sought any other course even if it had been possible. They genuinely believed this was the only stable and prosperous future for Kenya. The new government also believed that the economic interests of the country lay in a gradual transition to black land ownership. The country was in crisis. After a decade of growth, Kenya had lost over 80,000 formal sector jobs between 1960 and 1963. The European-owned farms, ranches and plantations produced 80 per cent of exports and employed nearly half the workers in the country. Kenyatta and his allies had to demonstrate a commitment to a managed land-acquisition programme to avoid a panic, mass abandonment of farms and a collapse in land prices.[206] There may also have been an inverse political effect amongst more conservative KANU leaders, as to support expropriation without compensation would have raised the standing of their more radical opponents. The agreement ensured that Kenyatta and those around him would eventually have to take on the radicals.

On the ground, the situation was still difficult. The police continued to hunt the Land and Freedom Army, but the betrayal of their hopes of free land put further power behind the movement. There was harassment of those who took the government's terms for settlement plots, and defiance of eviction orders, forcing a heavy police presence in some areas. The security forces specifically targeted KLFA activists to exclude them from land settlement programmes.[207] In December 1962, African and European members of the government discussed the KLFA and its links with Kaggia, who – like Odinga – had been left out of the coalition. They were concerned that the KLFA was planning to put up candidates in the 1963 elections to compete against KANU's candidates, especially in Central Region.[208]

Meanwhile, new Colonial Secretary Duncan Sandys, unhappy with the lack of progress, had replaced Renison with Malcolm MacDonald as governor. MacDonald, who took up his post in January 1963, had little experience of Africa, but played a key role during the transition and in maintaining relations between Britain and Kenya after independence. He drove an immediate escalation of negotiations and preparations for a rapid transfer of power.

Labour and Employment

Another risk to the fledgling government came from the trade unions. The industrial sector in Kenya was still tiny and the number in formal employment small – 50,000 in urban-based industrial manufacturing, 150,000 in the public sector, plus plantation and other agricultural workers. Politically, however, it was a key constituency. In 1962–3, with African rule coming closer, there was a new outbreak of militancy. Mass strikes with both political and economic objectives were the result, putting the economy and Mboya as labour minister under severe pressure. The 'poacher turned gamekeeper' Mboya was adept at balancing the interests of workers against that of the wider economy, but he risked being outflanked by the radicals, who were associated with Odinga through trade unionists such as ex-detainee Kubai.[209]

One of Mboya's key achievements was the creation in 1962 of an Industrial Relations Charter. This formalised a three-way negotiation process between government, Kenya's 68 trade unions and employers, and provided a structure for wage negotiations, of which the independence government would make full use. The right to strike remained, but only as a last resort. In 1963, after joining the government, Mboya finally handed over his decade-long leadership of the KFL to a supporter, Nairobi Senator Clement Lubembe.

Although there were no proper records of the unemployed or underemployed, it was clear that the economy was expanding too slowly to accommodate the number of school leavers entering the labour market. The population had grown very rapidly in the 1950s, creating an inflationary boom in people, concealed by the dislocations of Mau Mau, which bubbled through the education system in the 1960s and the labour market in the 1970s. This demographic time bomb was a long-term risk to Kenya's stability and in the short term, tens of thousands of educated unemployed were a threat to any government. Little could be done, however, but to hope for rapid growth after independence.

Borders and Boundaries

As if the struggles over policy, land and power were not enough, Kenya also faced a potential secessionist threat. In 1962, the British Northern Frontier Commission had surveyed whether the peoples of the north wished to join Somalia or Kenya. It found that while other northerners wished to remain Kenyan, over 85 per cent of Somali wanted union with Somalia.[210] However, with independence imminent, the British decided to leave the issue in Kenyan hands. On 8 March 1963, under pressure from African politicians who were determined to take over Kenya intact, Sandys decided to support a Kenyan future for the Somali.

The result was mass protest in the Somali-populated districts of Wajir, Garissa and Mandera and in the town of Isiolo. The government of Somalia, committed to creating a 'Greater Somalia', including all ethnic Somali in Ethiopia, Kenya and Djibouti, broke off diplomatic relations with the UK in March 1963.[211] The GSU was deployed in North-Eastern, but the situation worsened. All the Somali chiefs resigned their posts in March, and no one stood in the elections for the National Assembly or the North-Eastern Regional Assembly.

Calls for armed secession began in April, and attacks on police camps began at the same time. Somali murdered a DC in July, all firearms licences in the area were withdrawn in August, and by October 1963 there were regular attacks on police, officials and other communities. In response, the KANU government moved more troops to the Somali border and detained without trial several Somali separatist leaders. Somalia was reported to be increasing its army to 20,000 men, with Russian support, while Mogadishu accused the Kenyans of genocide. Although Kenyan and British ministers discounted the possibility of war, the stage was set for a confrontation at independence.

Two other boundary issues also created problems in this interregnum. The first was whether Luhya-dominated Trans-Nzoia and Kitale should remain in the Rift Valley, as the Regional Boundaries Commission had decided, or join the rest of the Luhya in Western Region. Muliro and the Bukusu Luhya campaigned to have Trans-Nzoia transferred, but Kalenjin KADU leaders were opposed, as there were many Kalenjin in the east of the district. On 8 March 1963, Sandys announced that Kitale would stay in the Rift, as the two parties could not agree. A revision of boundaries was agreed later in the year, but Odinga as home affairs minister vetoed the change at the last minute, following attacks by Sabaot on Bukusu around Mount Elgon. This decision was to remain a vexatious anomaly for Luhya 'nationalists' for the next 45 years. On the same day, Sandys also announced that the 10-mile coastal strip, still legally the property of the sultan of Zanzibar, would become a full part of the independent state in December. Kenya needed the coast, and particularly Mombasa, too much to risk a federal model. The Arab community was abandoned to the mercies of the new government, in return for guarantees of freedom of religion to Muslims and the entrenchment of Arab land ownership in the coastal strip, at the expense of local Mijikenda. Issued at the same time as the announcement of self-government, both decisions passed without crisis.

Party Reorganisations, Splits and Manoeuvres, 1962–3

With the lure of imminent power, KANU and KADU skirmished while they worked together in the coalition government, preparing for the showdown. Talks about the *majimbo* constitution proved divisive and unproductive, and faction fighting in the parties also intensified, particularly within KANU, as both West and East identified KANU as most likely to lead Kenya to independence. Mboya as secretary-general was the key figure in preparing KANU for the polls. He was assisted and shadowed by Joe Murumbi, KANU's national treasurer and executive officer, but no friend to Mboya. Odinga remained party vice-president to Kenyatta's president, his socialism tinged with Luo nationalism, just as Kenyatta's nationalism was Kikuyu-oriented.

There was no simple East–West divide, however. Kenyatta was increasingly concerned about Mboya's pre-eminence, and worked with the radicals to control him. Odinga was still receiving funds from Communist countries, some of which ended up in Kenyatta's hands. Odinga and Kenyatta ran a secret joint bank account, used by the radicals, including Odinga's Luo allies, Murumbi, Asian ex-detainee Pio da Gama Pinto and Kaggia. Between August and October 1962, Kenyatta also denounced those who accepted foreign money as 'insects' at a rally in Mboya's constituency, then helped Kubai in an abortive coup against Mboya in the KFL. In response, Mboya threatened to take the Luo and the labour movement out of KANU, a gamble that he won since his position was reaffirmed.[212] Nonetheless, there was little love lost between KANU leaders.

Even in 1962–3, it was clear that Kenyatta was looking to the state as his primary source of authority. From the moment that he assumed KANU's presidency, he saw the party as a political not an administrative entity. By early 1963, despite the funds that were making their way to the future leaders of Kenya, the party's credit had been exhausted and its organisation consisted of virtually nothing apart from the personal machinery of the three key leaders – Odinga, Kenyatta and Mboya. Weak, ethnically based and personalised political parties were part of Kenya's history from the first.

In November 1962, intrigue burst into the open, with the establishment of a new political party. But it was an ethnic, not a policy-based, fracture. Ex-detainee Ngei abandoned KANU to form the African People's Party (APP). The primary drivers for Ngei's actions were personal. KANU had been reluctant to accord Ngei the position to which he felt entitled after his release. He had been refused permission to attend the Lancaster House Conference, and the Kamba leadership declined to vacate a seat for him as had been done for Kenyatta. Ngei also saw the opportunity to hold the balance of power between KANU and KADU.[213] KANU lost the support of most of the Kamba community, a serious blow. However, the APP had little impact outside Ukambani, and Ngei's decision was probably a mistake. It was not the last time, however, that a trans-ethnic coalition would be split by the defection of a single leader.

Inside KADU, there were also tensions, with the Luhya's commitment to the party uncertain, given their potential land conflicts with the Kalenjin. However,

Muliro's influence and his antipathy towards Mboya kept most of the Luhya in KADU during this key period.

Elections and Self-Government, May–December 1963

The eight months between May and December 1963 saw the consummation of the changes begun in 1960–2 and the formation of the government that took Kenya to independence.

The Independence Elections, May 1963

The elections for the national and regional assemblies under the *majimbo* constitution took place in May 1963. This was a key moment in the life of the independent state, which decided whether it would become a unitary or federal nation. The prize was self-government, an idea proposed by MacDonald. The polls saw a replay of the 1961 elections, minus the fancy franchises and racial constituencies. The electoral system was that used in the UK, the first past the post system in single-member constituencies. The 117 House of Representatives constituencies were delineated based on a combination of ethnic boundaries, natural features and district boundaries.[214] The Senate seats were the 41 districts (varying in size from 8,000 voters in Marsabit to 260,000 in Central Nyanza). Although the National Assembly soon became unicameral, this system remained almost unchanged into the twenty-first century. The use of ethnicity as a criterion for constituency design and of the district as a unit of representation (whatever its population) were institutionalised from the country's birth.

There were 266 candidates for the House, of which 88 were formal KANU nominees and 57 KADU. Well before the polls, it was clear that KANU would be the largest party. As in 1961, KADU was unable to field candidates in most of Central or Eastern Region or Luo Nyanza. Although KADU made an election pact with the APP, and several APP candidates stood down for KADU at the last minute, it did not change the result.

While ethnicity was politically crucial, it was not the sole criterion for candidate selection. Far more than was possible thereafter, KANU put up candidates who were not members of the dominant community in that region. Thus, half-Maasai John Keen stood in Luhya-dominated Trans-Nzoia, and KANU's candidates in three of the four Nakuru District seats, dominated by Kalenjin and Kikuyu, were Luo or Luhya. In Nairobi, there were only three Kikuyu candidates standing, compared to 22 from other communities. Asians played a significant role in all parties, with five Asian candidates in Nairobi, a level of direct political involvement that soon became impossible.

On 18 April, KANU launched its election manifesto, 'What a KANU Government Offers You', which committed Kenya to early independence as a republic within the Commonwealth. It also supported non-alignment, pan-Africanism and federation in East Africa. What it did not commit to was more significant: there were no

2.6: KADU's manifesto, 1963

Courtesy: Charles Hornsby

promises of mass nationalisation or land expropriation, but rather a commitment that land settlement would not take place at the expense of high agricultural standards. KANU was also emphatically opposed to the new Regional Constitution. KADU's election manifesto was both more liberal and more socially conservative, favouring fewer, better-managed resettlement schemes, opposing any 'grandiose scheme of nationalisation of land' and stressing the importance of traditional 'spheres of influence' in land matters.[215] KADU's key campaign issue was the *majimbo* constitution, which they feared KANU would abandon if they won (see Figure 2.6). In Ngala's words, 'If you vote Kanu you are voting for a party that will destroy the constitution.'[216]

As in 1961, the election also saw factional contests within KANU, between supporters of Mboya and Odinga in Nyanza, Nakuru and Nairobi, and between Home Guards and 'freedom fighters' in Central Region. There were (unsuccessful) attempts to prevent radicals such as Kaggia from being nominated as KANU candidates.[217] Murumbi, who ran KANU headquarters, suggested, 'the real election struggle took place within K.A.N.U. itself and in K.A.N.U. controlled areas . . .'[218] The parties' sources of funding for the election were not disclosed, but KANU believed that Europeans were still backing KADU. Kenyatta's nephew and Nairobi KANU candidate Njoroge Mungai, for example, suggested that 'Kadu is led by a European called Michael Blundell who wears a black face called Ngala.'[219] KANU raised funds locally from the Asian community. It also sent Murumbi on a fundraising mission overseas, which supplemented the money that Mboya and Odinga had raised from their sponsors. British intelligence records suggest that while Mboya had GB£30,000–40,000 from the Americans and Odinga GB£70,000 from the Russians, Pinto had somehow brought GB£160,000 into the country through the Indian High Commission.[220]

The campaign saw extensive intimidation and several deaths, but the polls themselves passed off peacefully. The main problem was in Isiolo, where four people died as Somali tried to enforce their boycott over local Meru and Turkana.[221] Campaigning was sometimes crudely ethnic – a Mombasa KADU candidate repeatedly declared, for example, that all Kikuyu and Luo civil servants and hawkers would be repatriated upcountry unless they supported KADU.[222] The possibility of election-rigging by the provincial administration was not even considered. Although the government had no particular desire for a KANU victory, it knew it was likely. At the local level, KANU transported voters from Central Region to register and vote in the Rift Valley, because 'KANU had relatively few voters in Nakuru, Kitale, Eldoret and Kericho and . . . the party's success in the area would depend to a large extent on the availability of voters from outside the area.'[223] While there were complaints of press bias against KANU and some hints of bias amongst British officials, the fact that it was likely to win maintained balance. The *Nation* newspaper even declared for KANU in an eve of poll message.

The result was a decisive victory for KANU. In the House, KANU won 64 seats, KADU 32, the APP 8 and other small parties and independents 8, giving KANU an overall majority. Since in practice the independents backed the winner, KANU was close to a two-thirds majority. In the Senate, KADU did better, losing 16–18 seats to KANU, with two seats held by independents and two by the APP, leaving KANU short of an overall majority.[224] In the regional elections, KADU took control of three regions (Coast, Rift Valley and Western) and KANU three (Central, Eastern and Nyanza). Moi was elected president of the Rift Valley and Ngala president of the Coast.

As in 1961, KANU won the votes of almost all the Kikuyu, Embu, Meru, Luo, Taita and Gusii. Kenyatta, Gichuru, Kiano, Koinange and most other KANU candidates in Central Region were unopposed. KADU won the votes of almost all the Kalenjin and Mijikenda and half of the Luhya (see Figure 2.7). However, not all communities were indissolubly wedded to one party. Key figures in the Maasai and Luhya changed sides in the last few months, resulting in split votes in these swing areas. Turnout amongst the 2.7 million registered voters was very high in contested seats, averaging over 80 per cent. Turnout was near zero in Isiolo and Marsabit, however, where few risked breaking the Somali boycott.

Once the elections were over, KANU used the 12 Specially Elected seats to bring several Europeans into Parliament and the government. These included McKenzie, the ex-air force officer and farmer who was to play a critical role in the first decade of independence.

The political elite that was to lead the country to independence was young and entirely male, well educated by African standards, but without strong financial resources and inexperienced in both government and parliamentary politics. Jomo Kenyatta (in his late 60s), and Angaine and Koinange (in their 50s) were the oldest MPs. More than one-third had been teachers, with many others coming from clerical roles or trade unions, and only a small group of professionals – lawyers, doctors and academics. It was also a relatively radical group. Half of KANU's Central Region MPs were ex-detainees or forest fighters, as were three of four Nakuru members and several Meru and Kamba MPs.

2.7: 1963 election results

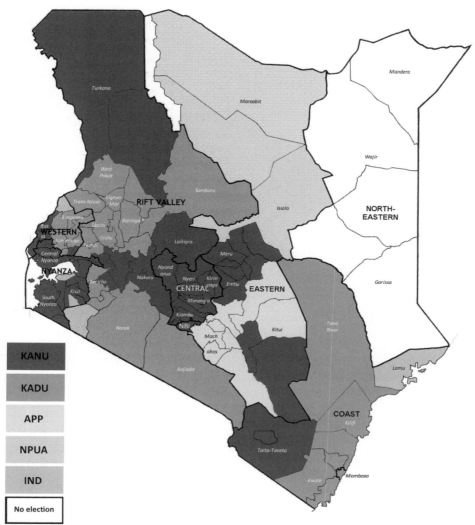

Source: Adapted from 1963 Constituency Boundaries Commission Map

The New Cabinet and the Timetable for Independence

The Cabinet that Kenyatta as Kenya's first prime minister announced on 30 May 1963 contained 15 ministers and 15 parliamentary secretaries, selected from amongst MPs. Determined on a rapid transition to independence, MacDonald immediately delegated full responsibility for defence, external affairs and internal security to the prime minister.

The two biggest KANU-voting ethnic groups dominated the new administration. There were six Kikuyu (including Kenyatta), four Luo and six ministers from other communities, each with one representative. The introduction of this informal ethno-regional quota for appointments established a precedent that was to continue thereafter. The government was also balanced between KANU factions. The old-time KAU-era Kiambu Kikuyu included Kenyatta, Koinange and Gichuru. Home Affairs Minister Odinga and Minister for Information and Broadcasting Achieng-Oneko represented the Luo 'radicals'. The third group were the 'Mboya men' of the 1950s, including Mboya himself, Kiano and Samuel Ayodo from South Nyanza. Mboya took the Justice and Constitutional Affairs Ministry, responsible for the changes to the Constitution that KANU was demanding. McKenzie took the post of agriculture minister a week later, once elected by the House. At the same time, Kenyatta promoted his old KAU ally Angaine from Meru to become minister for lands and settlement. Three of the five men who had sat with Kenyatta in the Kapenguria dock joined the government: Achieng-Oneko (who had been Kenyatta's private secretary since his release) became a minister, while Kubai and Kaggia became parliamentary secretaries. While the government was almost entirely African, however, 15 of the 20 permanent secretaries were still European.[225]

A little-noted appointment at the time was Kenyatta's choice of Charles Njonjo as attorney-general, Kenya's chief legal officer. Njonjo, another Kikuyu from Kiambu, was already deputy public prosecutor. Educated in Uganda, South Africa and the UK, he had been a barrister in London until his return to Kenya in 1955. Marked out by the British, he was the son of Josiah Njonjo, a prominent Kiambu chief. Njonjo was to play a defining role in ensuring a stable, conservative and pro-Western Kenya over the next 20 years. He also sat in the Cabinet (see Figure 2.8) and the National Assembly as a non-voting member.

The new administration contained many able individuals. Ten ministers had been students at the Alliance High School (as had nine permanent secretaries).[226] The Cabinet also reflected the Kiambu core of Kenyatta's support. It included five Kikuyu from Kiambu families, one from Murang'a (Kiano) and none at all from Nyeri. There was only one senator in the 34-man government, indicating KANU's distrust of the two-chamber system.

The new National Assembly was designed to mimic the Legislative Council and the British House of Commons, with opposed benches for government and opposition. All its powers, privileges and processes were modelled on Westminster, from debating etiquette, the speaker's wig and the parliamentary mace to the three readings of bills and the names and functions of parliamentary committees. A speaker presided over each House, elected by Parliament. MPs had immunity from legal proceedings for words spoken in the Assembly, although they were subject to its collective discipline if they behaved inappropriately.

On 1 June, known henceforth as Madaraka Day, Kenya became a self-governing colony. In his acceptance speech, Kenyatta launched a new slogan for the country – *Harambee* – a Swahili word meaning 'Let's pull together' or 'Let's put our shoulders together', reflecting his belief in the virtues of hard work and the need to make

2.8: The independence Cabinet

Courtesy: Nation Group Newspapers

people responsible for the improvement of their own lives. For six months more, Kenya continued as a colony under self-government, with the role of the British rapidly reducing in importance. On 2 July, Sandys announced that Kenya would become independent on 12 December 1963. Zanzibar's independence was fixed for two days before. The choice of dates was driven by expectations that a federation of East Africa would come into effect at the end of the year. However, how could Kenya enter a federation when it already had its own federal constitution – one, moreover, that its government repudiated?

Towards a Single Centralised Party and Nation-State, June–December 1963

In the short period between June and December 1963, much of the future of Kenya was decided. Committed to the abolition of the Regional Constitution, KANU did everything it could to maintain central control. With parts of the new Constitution in place, on 7 June the district commissioners were renamed regional government agents, answerable to the regional assemblies, and the (British) provincial commissioners became civil secretaries, chief executives of the regions. However, most regional powers were only to be transferred after independence. The central government resisted all attempts by the regional assemblies to assert their own identities. Home Affairs Minister Odinga was crucial in counteracting moves to devolve finances and administration. He visited the regions after the election and announced there would be no transfer of staff or funds to regional control until the regional administrations could administer them responsibly. This of course never happened. Instead, officials were only 'seconded' to the regions.[227] Fiery speeches by Moi and Ngala demanding autonomy for the Rift and Coast were met with warnings that the full rigour of the law would be used against them if they overstepped the borders of legality. Meanwhile, Odinga was Africanising officials in the former provincial administration and his ministry, targeting Europeans unwilling to accept African authority. In his words, 'some deportations were necessary to bring home to the expatriates the reality of the transfer of power.'[228]

KANU also demanded changes to the Constitution, particularly the provisions relating to central control of the police and civil service, and to its amendment procedure, as the party believed the requirement for a 75 per cent vote in the House and 90 per cent in the Senate to modify the entrenched provisions were too high. KADU remained obdurate, and the talks that had begun in June continued inconclusively for months. The British increasingly supported Kenyatta, concerned about the security situation, and doing little to interfere with the new government's constitutional manipulation. KADU walked out of the talks on 23 August, refusing to discuss fundamental changes to the Constitution, but discussions between the other parties and MacDonald continued.

The country was also showing signs of a move towards a one-party state. With so much up for grabs in this period of change, to be outside the government was to be disadvantaged for decades. On 12 September 1963, the APP disbanded and Ngei led his team across the floor to join KANU en masse.[229] The APP's defection gave the government the 75 per cent majority it needed in the House to change the Constitution, even under the current rules. Immediately after the elections, several MPs had defected to KANU, and Kalenjin KADU leaders Murgor and Seroney also crossed the floor in November 1963.

The New Army and Military Relations

Radical change was needed in the military as well as the political sphere. Kenya's military forces were far from ready to assume their duties, and compromises had to be made here also. Kenyan units of the KAR, the main African military force, were being hurriedly shaped into the nucleus of the new Kenyan army, inheriting its command structure and ethos. The British had mainly recruited the KAR's Kenyan battalions from the ethnic communities they had seen as 'martial races', the Kamba, Nandi and Samburu, commanded by a few British officers.[230] It had remained isolated from recent political ferment. Since the Mau Mau war and British regional strategy had positioned large British military forces in Kenya, little had been done to prepare the KAR to metamorphose into the armies of three independent states.[231] The development of an African officer corps did not begin until 1956–8, and the first African officers were not admitted to Britain's Sandhurst for training until 1959. In early 1963, the Kenyan KAR consisted of only 2,700 men, starved of materiel since independence in Tanganyika and Uganda.

With the failure of efforts to retain an East African-wide army after Tanganyika's independence, the British were forced into a hasty Africanisation programme. They instituted rapid promotion and special training for promising Kenyans during 1962–3, but at independence only 80 of 165 commissioned officers in the KAR were African.[232] As in Uganda and Tanganyika, the Kenyan military would have to remain partly British-led. The new governments had little choice: they would have had to disband part of their armies if the Europeans left, and, since the British continued to pay the salaries of expatriate officers, their services were effectively free.[233] The British also wished to ensure that the KAR remained as divorced as possible from local political pressure. During 1962–3, Odinga had won political capital by pressing for changes to army recruiting quotas and by representing rank-and-file grievances over pay and conditions and the need to Africanise the military. The British were increasingly concerned that he and Ngei were inciting dissatisfaction.[234] Kenyatta and the Kikuyu insiders around him also needed to secure their position from an ethnic perspective. By September 1963, Kenyatta had quietly changed the army's recruitment policy to require that one-third of all new recruits were Kikuyu.[235]

The British military command had been surprised by the speed of recent change. Their hopes of retaining a permanent military base in Kenya, a strategic location for imperial defence since 1957, foundered with KANU's victory in 1963. While Kenyatta might have considered a deal, Mboya was publicly determined that 'there is no question of negotiating a military pact with Britain.'[236] By June 1963, therefore, Britain was committed to closing all its bases within a year of independence. KANU's demands for the withdrawal of British troops did not mean the end of British assistance, however. In October 1963, there were still 7,500 British troops in the country, including a RAF base at Eastleigh in Nairobi. As independence grew closer, it became clear that Kenya's fledgling army could not defend the country's Somali or Ethiopian borders without British help.[237]

As early as May 1963, Kenyatta was dropping hints that Kenya might still be willing to negotiate a post-independence defence pact. This was driven by two factors: the necessity of retaining British military aid, equipment and personnel to keep the army running, and the additional stability that their presence would offer in a situation of social upheaval. While other countries were willing to provide military assistance, only Britain appeared willing to donate both the staff and money needed to train and equip the new army. The British were also willing to help Kenya build a navy and an air force, 'as an inducement to their granting us [the RAF] staging, maintenance and communications facilities at Eastleigh'.[238]

The British were not the only source of military assistance, however. An inner circle in KANU including Kenyatta and Odinga was using the student airlifts as a cover for secret military training in Israel and the Eastern Bloc. This began in 1962, and took place without the knowledge of most of the other members of the coalition government. Between June and November 1962, 11 Kikuyu students, led by ex-detainee J. M. Kariuki, received training in security and intelligence in Tel Aviv.[239] In November, the recently released 'General China' Itote led a larger military team to Israel, concealed by fake agricultural training courses.[240] The wholly Kikuyu nature of the 30-man team indicates their loyalties were to KANU, Kenyatta and the Kikuyu leadership, and it was rumoured that Itote would become the armed forces head at independence. Whether their original purpose was to fight a KADU-led independence, create a private defence unit or serve as the nucleus of the new army is uncertain but, in practice, Kenyatta's agreements with the British took Kenya down a different course. By the time the students returned, Kenyatta had decided that he did not wish to rely on ex-Mau Mau forces. He required those trained in Israel to be retrained by the British during 1964 to ensure their discipline and loyalty. Most eventually left the military.[241]

KANU leaders also covertly sent Kenyans for military training to China, Bulgaria, Czechoslovakia and other Eastern Bloc countries. Odinga played a key role in arranging this, and many nominees were Luo.[242] Bizarre political machinations on this issue continued even within the KANU government. On 6 November 1963, Odinga, Mboya, Mungai and other ministers secretly replaced the students chosen by Otiende's Ministry of Education for training in Bulgaria with 55 KANU youth wingers. The switch was made on the airport tarmac, leaving the real students behind. Otiende was furious and demanded to know 'how many governments exist in this country'.[243] It is near certain that these youth wingers were clandestinely receiving military training. As they returned, these Eastern Bloc-trained cadres were to become a major source of tension.

Land Grabs and Kikuyu Settlement, 1963

After self-government, the scramble for land in the highlands became acute, as the landless squatted, in the hope that their occupation would be regularised after *Uhuru*. The economic position declined, farming became increasingly dangerous for the white settlers and farms fell idle during their purchase, demarcation and distribution. The arrival of the first wealthy Africans (generally ex-loyalists) from the reserves on the newly demarcated large farms also caused resentment amongst the landless. Many of the new gentry were prevented from taking over their land, and it was only after independence that this process was fully implemented.

Meanwhile, there was a crisis brewing in Central Region. State calculations in February 1963 suggested that there were enough workers already on the white farms to fill the entirety of the settlement schemes in Nyandarua and northern Nyeri, without settling a single landless Kikuyu from the reserve. In the last few months of 1963, there was a mass 'land grab' in Nyandarua. Many landless Kikuyu had moved into the area to squat on European farms, while the first settlement schemes had displaced many of the original squatters with new Kikuyu from the reserve. The displaced and the passed-over were trying to take over farms in the Ol Kalou area. With independence imminent and fears of anti-European violence growing, the British government was forced into further concessions in November.[244] In addition to the Ol Kalou scheme, developed as cooperative farms, the British agreed to finance a special accelerated scheme for Central Region. As a first step, 4,000 landless Kikuyu families were settled in six weeks in southern Nyandarua on land deemed economically marginal. It was a nakedly political gesture.

Foreign Policy and Federation

In the run-up to independence, Kenya's past and future leaders worked to ensure a smooth transfer of power. Foreign policy was the responsibility of Governor MacDonald, and he occasionally exercised this right, particularly over the Somalia issue. In general, however, the new ministers set the policy framework, and it was strongly pan-African. One key plank was opposition to the continuation of white rule in Africa. Mboya demanded that Portugal give up its African territories. Trade and Industry Minister Kiano tried to enforce a boycott of South African goods, and ministers banned over-flights by South African planes, refused to admit their athletes and threatened to close their consulate. Although relations with the UK were good, this did not preclude robust criticisms of British South African policies. Mboya threatened that if the UK granted independence to settler-dominated Rhodesia, Kenya would leave the Commonwealth.

Relations with East and West were already becoming a source of tension. The Cold War was at its height and, with so many new countries emerging, there was a second 'scramble for Africa' as East and West competed for political and economic influence. The division in KANU was becoming clearer between 'radical' African politicians, committed to a more socialist or egalitarian society, and the numerically larger 'moderates', economically more liberal, who were committed to independence but willing to compromise in order to achieve it. Odinga was the most senior figure (though not always the leader) of one wing, Mboya most visibly represented the other, and each had a clear sponsor. The US Kennedy administration followed a policy of denial towards all left-leaning African political movements, to limit Soviet and Chinese influence, while the communist states worked to build their footprint in the region. The Americans saw Kenya as part of Great Britain's sphere of influence, however, and apart from their support for Mboya, their investments were moderate and their initiatives cautious.[245] It was Britain, not the US, which was on the front line of the Cold War in Kenya.

In most African states, the colonial powers handed over power on a timetable and under a political system partly of their choosing. As a result, most African governments' policies at independence were guardedly pro-Western, though critical of colonial support for white settler regimes. The East was forced to become the aggressor, aiming to upset the status quo by building a case for radical change, and supporting military assistance to rebel movements where democratic processes appeared unlikely to deliver it. Kenya was in the front line of this conflict, and the period saw lobbying, propaganda and gift giving by the Americans, Chinese and Russians. The British, meanwhile, still controlled much of the civil service, and worked quietly to ensure that Kenya started on a path of stability, bureaucratic efficiency and economic growth. Since they believed this could only be achieved under a non-communist system, they 'educated' the new government in the need for moderation.

At the same time, the leaders of Kenya, Uganda and Tanganyika were committed to an East African federation. While most attention was focused at the nation-state level, the links between countries in the region were strong. For decades, they had shared common administrative systems, markets and tariffs as well as cultures, languages and history. In 1919, the British had introduced a common currency, the East African shilling, followed by common law courts. Since 1927, Kenya, Uganda and Tanganyika had been part of a customs union. From 1948–9, the East African High Commission had provided common railways, harbours, aviation, customs, income tax, post and telephone services. In 1961, with Tanganyika's independence looming, the High Commission had been restructured to become the East Africa Common Service Organisation (EACSO), funded from tax revenues. It had its own Central Legislative Assembly, able to approve legislation and expenditure on common issues. As independence came to each country, the key question was, would they become independent states or build on these regional arrangements? Most East Africans expected federation after independence, and some hoped it would extend to Rwanda and beyond. On 5 June 1963, the three mainland leaders announced that they intended to establish a political federation before the end of 1963.[246] The British warmly supported this, and promised their 'fullest support and cooperation'.[247]

In practice, events quickly moved in the opposite direction, a choice that was to have long-lasting consequences. Federation meant the creation of a single political structure with a single president. Having only recently established their power bases, all three leaders were reluctant to abandon them for an uncertain position within a federation. Since Uganda and Tanganyika were already independent, federalism implied a loss of authority for their presidents and autonomy for their countries, especially since Kenyatta was the most likely federal president. Tanganyika and Uganda were also concerned about union with a powerful, European-dominated Kenya. Nairobi was the administrative and commercial centre of East Africa, and Kenya had gained most from the common market. Many felt that the differences in economic development between the states would continue to work to Kenya's advantage.

Differences of opinion opened up over federation after a meeting in August 1963, and Ugandan Prime Minister Milton Obote's refusal to attend the heads of state meeting in September 1963 killed the issue until after Kenya's independence. There was little real will to unite, and disputes over the site of the federal capital, citizenship and language were simply pretexts. Little progress had been made by the time Kenya's independence came.

Final Preparations for Independence, September–November 1963

A third and final constitutional conference from 25 September to 19 October 1963 in London saw a successful effort by KANU to weaken the *majimbo* constitution. As Ngala had predicted, the party wished to increase central control of the police and public service, and to reduce the majority needed to change the Constitution. Justice and Constitutional Affairs Minister Mboya's case was simple: whatever they had agreed to under duress, Britain should not let Kenya go into independence with a constitution that most voters opposed.

KADU's team in London, led by Ngala, desperately resisted such changes, but it was clear once negotiations began that the British, led by Sandys, were inclined to compromise with KANU. During October 1963, Kenya came close to insurrection. After a near-walkout from the conference by KADU, Seroney sent a telegram to Rift Valley President Moi: 'Dishonourable betrayal of majimbo agreement by Britishers. Alert Kalenjin and region and Kadu to expect and prepare for worst. Partition and operation Somalia only hope.'[248]

The security forces went onto high alert, as KADU leaders announced plans to set up a Sovereign Federal Republic of Kenya with Ngala as president, Moi as vice-president and Nakuru as their new capital. There were reports that the Kalenjin under Moi were arming for a war of secession, and there was talk of alliances with Kenya's Somali.[249] However, the British were desperate to avoid civil war or a delay to independence and could see little alternative but to do a deal with KANU. They therefore provided BBC facilities for Kenyatta to broadcast on Kenyan radio a reassurance that the government was in control and a warning to troublemakers that aired throughout 10 October 1963.[250] The colonial secretary also warned KADU that British troops would be used against them if they acted unconstitutionally.[251] When neither the British nor Kenyatta blinked, KADU backed down. Ngala was concerned that Moi, by releasing a partition map and threatening a unilateral declaration of independence (UDI), was pushing events out of control, and dispatched Luhya MP Shikuku back from London (again with British assistance) to pacify Moi and the hotheads. On 14 October, Ngala 'postponed' KADU's partition plan.

KANU now in turn threatened a walkout and a UDI if its demands were not met. By 19 October, with chaos in the British government following the resignation of Macmillan, Sandys had given Kenyatta what he required. The police and civil service would remain centrally managed, and the special protection rules for the Constitution would remain only for the rights of individuals, citizenship, regional boundaries, the Senate and control of Trust Land.[252] All other issues (including the powers of the regional assemblies) would be subject to a 75 per cent majority in both houses. On 19 October, the conference ended and Kenya's leaders returned to Nairobi to prepare for independence. Regionalism was crippled before it was born.

KADU was furious, and Ngala accused Sandys of dishonesty by breaking pledges that he and Maudling had made. He suggested that since KANU and Britain had violated the Constitution, KADU would not be bound by it either. Returning to Kenya, Ngala announced, 'The time for action has arrived.'[253] Nonetheless, KADU's bluff was again called; it did not have the mass support or the secure territory that partition would require. Three days later, Ngala announced that KADU had shelved its secession plan. Instead, he called for Kenyatta to show good faith and implement the remainder of the Constitution as he had promised the British, whereby most regional powers would be handed over on 1 December 1963, with the remainder coming into effect on 1 January 1964.[254] It was a vain hope, but Kenyatta needed to console the losers. Trying to assuage the fears of the minority communities, on 20 October, he gave 'a categorical assurance that, under the Constitution, all tribal land is entrenched in the tribal authority, and no-one can take away land belonging to another tribe'.[255] This – in effect a promise not to introduce a 'willing buyer, willing seller' arrangement in the ex-reserves – was soon abandoned.

Another last-minute issue for the new nation was its relationship with its residents of foreign origin. At Lancaster House, KANU demanded and the British agreed that the Constitution would not permit dual citizenship. Within two years of independence, all Kenyans with foreign passports would have to choose one nationality, with the expectation that life would become tougher for those who did not become Kenyan. On the side of inclusiveness, ministers rejected backbench demands that only Africans should be permitted to be Kenyan citizens. In November 1963, the Citizenship Act was passed, entitling residents of any colour at independence and all those born in Kenya to citizenship.

Conclusions

The key decisions that would drive the new state for the next four decades had been made. Kenya would come to independence led by Jomo Kenyatta, the man the British had hated and jailed, heading a broad-based alliance of leaders from the Kikuyu, Luo and more densely populated regions. The transition would be gradual and the demands of the more radical elements in KANU would be controlled. The UK would remain Kenya's patron and protector. Economic decisions about the need for development, aid and security would push Kenya's foreign relations towards an accommodation with the West, and this in turn drove domestic policy. A Western-funded settlement programme would assuage African desires for land in the short term while building a stable landowning society, mainly at the expense of the pastoralists and the poor.

Despite this supportive structure, the new leadership faced daunting challenges. It needed to build upon Kenya's industrial and agricultural base, keeping overseas capital flowing in, while simultaneously Africanising much of the economy. It would inevitably struggle to meet the expectations of the mass of Kenyans, who expected independence to bring jobs, land and prosperity. There was a legacy of violence, repression and social divisions, and growing ethnic tension. It was saddled with a devolved Constitution that it was committed to abolish, and had to work within a political system that was personalised, factionalised and already built around ethnicity. KANU itself was divided, held together only by its common opponents and the lure of power. The country had a small army of doubtful efficacy, which relied on foreign officers and equipment, and faced insurrection in the north-east. Over the next five years, Kenyatta and his allies were to address all these issues, building a stable, secure, centralised, increasingly prosperous, increasingly African-led and mostly united Kenya. These achievements would come at a high price.

Chapter 3

Struggle for the State, 1964–1965

Power at Last

Kenya's new government faced many challenges, under the watchful eye of its ex-colonial master. There were great hopes and great expectations, which it would inevitably struggle to meet. The next two years were a period of rapid growth, alongside deepening tensions within the political system and a rapid recentralisation of power.

The country's new ruling coalition was an uneasy combination of competing interests. The political kingdom had been captured, with British consent, by a small and well-educated group of politicians, newly promoted administrative cadres and a fledgling business community. This group of a few hundred young, able but poor men remained at the centre of events for three decades. Many came from chiefly families or the first generation of educated youth, picked by their community or the British as suitable for leadership. However, KANU's leadership also contained many more radical individuals who wished to nationalise foreign-owned corporations, seize white settler farms without compensation and follow a more pro-Eastern foreign policy. Many Kenyans had similar sympathies, determined to see Kenya set its own direction, or looking for equity in the distribution of the fruits of *Uhuru*. The 'radicals' were most clearly represented by Oginga Odinga and Bildad Kaggia, while Jomo Kenyatta and Tom Mboya led the 'moderate' or 'conservative' camp.[1] In retrospect, the resulting Odinga–Kenyatta clash appears near inevitable, the product of a deep division that was papered over in order to secure the transfer of power.

The period from independence until late 1965 was therefore one of conflict and change. As the struggle raged for control of the state, decisions based on short-term expediency were interspersed with fundamental directional choices. Kenya soon returned to a command and control leadership model strikingly similar to that of the colonial era. Decisions about development, money and military protection drove foreign relations, domestic policy and land policy, which in turn drove greater centralisation and a conservative social and political model that combined individual accumulation with a partisan, interventionist state. As Henry Bienen noted elsewhere in Africa, there was 'a speeded up, highly telescoped process of deradicalization'.[2] The political and administrative structure Kenya inherited was based on the British model of parliamentary democracy. A non-partisan civil service would serve the elected politicians, who would periodically be replaced by their opponents through multi-party elections. However, it had only recently been grafted onto more authoritarian stock. Kenya's new leaders, like those throughout the continent, soon and conveniently concluded that this model was unworkable (as the British had felt until 1960), and that the country's interest would better be served under the unity offered by a benevolent dictatorship.

Moves towards political unity were counterbalanced by a deepening divergence of opinion amongst this elite on economic policy, relations with Britain and the US, the land settlement programme and the responsibilities of the government towards the poor and landless, particularly those who had suffered during Mau Mau. The *majimbo* debate was over by the end of 1964, and battle instead joined around control of a centralised state. Differing interests and views aligned around a single confrontation, forcing individuals to choose a side. The result was a conflation of issues that positioned Chinese and Russian connections, support for compensation for the Mau Mau, nationalisation, land seizure without compensation from Europeans, egalitarianism, populism, trade unionism and Luo identity on one side. On the other stood those supporting capitalism, growth, centralism, gradualism, pro-British and American policies, elite dominance, Kikuyu identity and the maintenance of law and order. It culminated in the exclusion of the radicals at the rigged KANU Limuru conference of 1966. This represented the end, not the beginning, of the real struggle for power.

Political Unity and the End of *Majimbo*, 1964

Kenya had achieved independence with a more decentralised set of political institutions and administrative system than it had known under British rule. The Regional Constitution had little legitimacy, though, and KANU was determined to dismantle it before it could become effective. Kenya's history of centralised bureaucracy, the fragility of the new state and the realities of power all drove the government to abolish regionalism.

As minister for justice and constitutional affairs, Mboya played a central role in restoring the unitary state, assisted by Attorney-General Charles Njonjo.[3] The regional authorities (particularly the KADU-dominated Coast and Rift Valley) tried to establish their identities, responsibilities and powers, but the central government undermined them at every opportunity. The central government continued to budget for the entire civil service, despite the constitutional paperwork stating otherwise. The transfer of powers to the regions had been scheduled for 1 December 1963, with full implementation on 1 January 1964. Some services were transferred to regional control, but the delegation of financial authorities was administratively delayed until 1 July 1964. In May 1964, with talk of a new republican constitution brewing, the transfer of fiscal responsibilities was postponed again, to 1 December 1964. These delays were probably illegal, but no one challenged them in court, which reflects the low level of institutionalisation of the rule of law and the broad support for the restoration of unitary government. The questionable commitment of the government to the Constitution was also evident in December 1963, when the North-Eastern Region Emergency proclamation was before the Senate. On 31 December, Mboya declared that that government would impose emergency regulations whatever the Senate decided, even if it violated the Constitution. All 14 remaining KADU senators voted against legitimising the emergency, and the motion failed to achieve the 65 per cent vote required, but after frantic negotiations, it was re-presented and passed.[4]

By December 1964, Kenyatta's promises to the British regarding the Constitution in October 1963 forgotten, the first and second constitutional amendments had abolished most of the *majimbo* constitution. The provisions for entrenched voting rights were watered down, the police, public service and local government fully returned to central responsibility and the regions made fiscally dependent on the centre. All land vested in the regions was transferred back to central control and the government acquired the right to take over Trust Land (ex-reserves, held in trust for ethnic groups as collective bodies) without compensation. The regional assemblies were left to rot, with no power or money. Few questioned this at the time.

Multi-party democracy, too, lasted less than a year. Opposition parties throughout Africa were collapsing, with both scholars and politicians arguing that they were shallow, ethnically based, unnecessary or economically inefficient.[5] Only a single mass party could overcome the threat of tribalism. Contemporary assessments of the challenges to nationhood viewed national identity and stability as key, and these were seen as threatened by the divisiveness that an electoral contest would create. Prime Minister Kenyatta's attitude to parliamentary opposition was never that of a democrat. As soon as Parliament had assembled in July 1963, he was threatening that 'Negative and destructive opposition can only do harm to democracy, and – what is more – it can quickly lead to the destruction of the privileges and rights of the opposition itself.'[6] By August 1964, he was arguing that a one-party state was 'inevitable'. KADU was a 'splinter club' of 'conceited grasshopper politicians' with nothing to contribute.[7] The mood of the time focused on the need for the new states of Africa to penetrate the rural periphery and reinforce their control.[8] Six short years of elections and parliamentary politics had not created deep-rooted values of liberty and popular participation, the legitimacy of opposition or of accountability to the popular will.

From the first, the state did not accept the legitimacy of open debate on political matters. In January 1964, after the army mutiny, the government banned public meetings in several districts and this became nationwide in April, though Kenyatta could authorise exemptions to it. When the ban was lifted in June 1964, Mboya warned that meetings must not be used to 'undermine established authority' or for 'destructive criticism'.[9] KADU protested that the ban was directed at it and that ministerial *barazas* (public meetings) were unaffected.

KADU's collapse was therefore unsurprising. The party had been defeated electorally twice, and faced a state determined to consolidate its authority and abolish the Regional Constitution. This left it with little to offer its supporters, while the government made it clear that resources would flow according to its priorities, and that those in opposition would have little role in shaping them. Under pressure from its constituents and the state, KADU's members of parliament one by one defected to KANU. By October 1964, KADU had only 23 members left in the Assembly, but it still had 35 per cent of the Senate – enough to block any constitutional change.

In early November, three more KADU senators defected, finally giving KANU the numbers it needed. On 10 November 1964, facing the inevitable, KADU's remaining leaders Ronald Ngala and Masinde Muliro led the party across the floor (Chairman Daniel arap Moi had recently defected as well). KADU dissolved itself, leaving Kenya a de facto one-party state.[10] The dissolution of KADU was a critical moment, setting the stage for three decades of single-party rule. Kenyatta rewarded Ngala with the chair of the Maize Marketing Board and he entered the Cabinet in 1966, but his authority never recovered. It is uncertain whether KANU truly wanted a single-party state at this time or not. Martin Shikuku later claimed that KANU was only after a two-thirds majority and had not intended to destroy the opposition.[11] However, both pronouncements of the time and subsequent events suggest KANU was never happy with public challenge, especially given its internal divisions, and, like the colonial government, wished to direct Kenya's energies from *siasa* (confrontational politics) into *maendeleo* (disciplined and loyal development). Thus, within the space of two years, both the Regional Constitution and the multi-party democracy that the British had stitched together during 1961–3 were dead.

The Shifta War, 1964–7

One of the new state's first challenges was to control its borders. With an alienated and violent Somali population, militarily supported by Somalia, the government faced a real threat of war in its first days in office. Kenya's army was a small, volunteer force of only 2,700 men, led by 200 British and African officers.[12] There seemed a serious risk that Somalia might use independence as an opportunity for military intervention to enforce secession.

During November and December 1963, Somali attacks on police posts and army camps had become more frequent. Although each attack was small, within four days of independence there had been five more incursions. On 25 December, two weeks after independence, the Cabinet declared a State of Emergency in North-Eastern Region, and Governor-General Malcolm MacDonald took powers under the Preservation of Public Security Ordinance to detain people without trial.[13] A week later, the National Assembly reluctantly endorsed the Emergency. A five-mile 'Prohibited' zone was established along the 400-mile border with Somalia, in which no settlements or movements were permitted. The violence continued, however, and it became clear that Somalia was training and providing bases for up to 2,000 *shifta* (from the Amharic word for bandit) guerrillas.

The resulting unofficial border war with Somalia continued for several years, and spread into Coast Region, with Lamu and Tana River joining the North-East as 'Prescribed' (closed) areas in April 1964, as the pastoralist Orma community increasingly backed the *shifta*. Emergency powers were extended to Marsabit, Isiolo, Lamu and Tana River Districts in 1966. The *shifta* used guerrilla tactics, including hit-and-run attacks and mining of roads. In response, the Kenyans adopted British counter-insurgency techniques that had been used during Mau Mau, including the establishment of collective villages surrounded by barbed wire and guarded by troops. There were widespread beatings and killings of civilians and mass confiscations of livestock. The Prohibited zone was deepened to 15 miles along the border, and anyone found within it was deemed hostile. As with the Kikuyu in 1953–5, every Somali was seen as a potential *shifta* and treated accordingly, although there was no equivalent of the detention camp pipeline, and the loyalists were not so well rewarded. The government used its ability to detain without trial anyone it believed (without evidence to satisfy a court of law) to be helping the *shifta*. Permanent Secretary for Information and Broadcasting Peter Gachathi and the Voice of Kenya (VoK) also ran a 'psychological operations' propaganda campaign to weaken resistance, developed by a British colonel and based on the Mau Mau experience.[14]

No official death figures were published for the conflict, which received little international attention, but at least 3,000 Kenyans and *shifta* died. By 1966, the Kenyans had gained the upper hand, supported by a 'shoot to kill' policy, but there were no clear military victories and the country was spending K£3–5 million a year on the war. British forces continued to support the Kenyans, and Somalia in turn received military support from the Russians, who helped train the *shifta*, but the two Cold War armies never engaged directly.

The conflict established patterns of suspicion and hostility between ethnic Somali and other Kenyans that were to endure for decades. Development in the colonial era in North-Eastern had been non-existent and this changed little after independence. The state treated Kenyan Somali as subjects rather than citizens, and the region as a military-ruled colony. Travel to and from the North-East was restricted, Kenyan Somali had to have special passes, human rights simply did not apply, and nomads in general and Somali in particular were forcibly repatriated if they strayed outside provincial boundaries. Conditions were harsh for those suspected of supporting the *shifta*, with most ethnic Somali, Muslim Boran and Sakkuye kept in emergency camps and subject to mass herd confiscations.[15] In 1962, Isiolo District had 55,000 occupants, but by 1969 the population had fallen to 30,000, the rest having fled or been killed.[16] The troubles also began the sedentarisation of the Boran and Gabbra, restricted by the war from their grazing lands.

Securing the Security Forces

Facing internal tensions and external threat, Kenyatta's government depended on the loyalty and effectiveness of Kenya's security forces. However, these had been designed for very different duties. Initially, there was suspicion between the security forces and their political masters, partly because the army was mostly still British-led and Kamba and Nandi-manned. This soon proved a blessing in the light of the growing tensions in KANU.

The January 1964 Mutiny

Almost as soon as independence dawned, all four East African countries suffered army mutinies. In Kenya, on 24 January 1964, there was a strike by several hundred soldiers of the Kenya Rifles 11th Battalion, based in Lanet near Nakuru. It followed those in Uganda and Tanganyika between 20 and 23 January, and the coup in

Zanzibar two weeks before. The mutineers were driven by disgruntlement over pay and conditions, fear of their future under a KANU government, the continued command of expatriate British officers and the mutineers' recent successes in Tanganyika.[17] On the day of the Kenyan mutiny, Kenyatta had ordered a commission of inquiry into army pay and conditions, and announced plans to speed up the Africanisation of the officer corps. He knew something was about to happen, but offered too little, too late.

The Kenyans were not the only military force inside Kenya. There were still 5,000 British troops in the country, concentrated near Nairobi and at Gilgil in the Rift Valley. Without reference to the Cabinet, Kenyatta appealed for and received the support of the British army units in the area, and this and other threatening gestures were enough to restore order without significant bloodshed.[18] The mutineers surrendered the next day. There were rumours that there had been Russian influences behind the mutiny that did not emerge in public. Kenyatta personally ordered Odinga not to leave Nairobi on that day.[19] Most believe, though, that the revolt was a spontaneous protest by a few individuals at their personal circumstances.[20] Kenyatta was nonetheless determined to make an example of the mutineers: 43 soldiers were court-martialled, and the court jailed 16 'ringleaders' for a total of 197 years.[21] The battalion was disbanded. This severe response reflected the government's fragility and fears that the mutiny could have grown into a coup or a revolutionary example, even though the mutineers had not planned this.[22]

After the mutiny and the Zanzibar revolution, Kenyatta was increasingly aware of the possibility of a military coup. He improved conditions, announced pay rises to the military, speeded Africanisation and instructed the intelligence services to infiltrate and watch the army for signs of disaffection. Kenyatta also increased his commitment to his British 'patrons' for military training, equipment and personal and regime protection. This abortive protest therefore helped secure the government, as it instilled a healthy paranoia about military intentions, without weakening its legitimacy. The maintenance of public order was to be one of Kenyatta's priorities for the rest of his life.

The Defence Agreement of 1964 and Military Relationships with Great Britain

Discussions began in March 1964 between Kenyan ministers and British Secretary of State for Commonwealth Relations Duncan Sandys on defence matters. They concluded with a formal defence agreement on 3 June 1964. According to the agreement, all British troops stationed in Kenya would withdraw by 12 December 1964. In the meantime, the British would help build the Kenya Rifles into a proper national army. They would resource and train a new Kenya Air Force (KAF), and create a small Kenyan navy. Overall, the British would commit nearly US$40 million to Kenya's defence. In the meantime, the RAF and British land units would continue to shore up internal security in the north-east. British troops would help the Kenyans free of charge, as long as the army continued to be led by a British officer. The UK would relinquish rights to most of their military properties and cancel more than

GB£6 million in military loans. The British also agreed to continue training Kenya's officer corps. In return, the Kenyans would allow British aircraft to overfly and stage in Kenya and the fleet to visit Mombasa. The British could continue to use communications facilities until 1966, and their forces would be able to train in Kenya twice a year.

The British also agreed to 'continue, subject to any prior commitment and to prior authorisation, to make available British troops stationed in Kenya to assist the Kenyan Government in dealing with internal disturbances'.[23] Even in 1964, the British and Kenyans feared trouble from within, and Britain was prepared to commit troops to support Kenyatta. Soon after this, and independently of the main defence agreement, the British secretly provided a SAS team to train Kenyatta's personal bodyguard, the all-Kikuyu Ichaweri (the name refers to the location of Kenyatta's home in Gatundu), in counter-subversion techniques. The British wished to protect their man against any communist trouble to come.

This agreement was to prove mutually satisfactory throughout the 1960s, and the Kenyans were keen to continue with the arrangements as long as possible. British assistance helped keep defence costs below 7 per cent of the budget during the decade. The KAF was duly equipped with British-donated aircraft and inaugurated in June 1964. The navy became operational in 1967 with the arrival of three patrol craft, another gift from the British. As well as helping to build a professional and politically neutral military, Britain had shown it would support Kenyatta against internal or external threat. As *Pathé News* in 1964 trumpeted, 'Without British help, Kenya might easily be a prey to communist forces.'[24] The benefit to the British was less clear. It can best be seen in the context of the Cold War, and the fear that if Britain were to cease support for the Kenyan military, it would be replaced by communist forces or lay Kenya open to a coup. The sums owed to Britain in loans and the many British citizens in Kenya loomed large in this assessment.[25] It also allowed the UK to retain substantial influence inside the country. British officers ran the army until 1966 and the navy and air force until 1972, and Britain provided many seconded officers and remained Kenya's main supplier of equipment and training until the mid-1970s.

As soon as independence dawned, the British experienced problems with their non-offensive military support to Kenya in North-Eastern Region. A British officer was injured by *shifta* in January 1964 and several incidents saw British troops involved in defensive operations. In April, in a significant escalation, the British government agreed to allow infantry and aircraft to be used on active service against the *shifta*, under tight controls.[26] The British Foreign Office was extremely concerned about the risk of being drawn into open war with Somalia, if British and Somali regular troops engaged in open combat. Within a few weeks, however, British aircraft had made several unauthorised incursions over the Somali border that could have led to a rapid escalation of violence. The UK government also believed that the more assistance they provided, the less likely Kenya was to seek a negotiated settlement.[27] The British were particularly concerned in May 1964 about reports that Kenya was planning 'highly objectionable' forced removal of villagers and livestock and the poisoning of water supplies. They made it clear that they were unlikely to allow their forces to be associated with such operations. They also rejected Kenyatta's request that RAF aircraft be employed offensively in the prohibited zone. However, they agreed to provide additional scout cars (under the aid programme), approved the use of British aircraft for reconnaissance and leaflet dropping (as long as the Kenyans paid for them) and provided helicopters for casualty evacuation.[28] The British believed that this support was important if they were to obtain long-term military facilities in Kenya; the Kenyan government deeply appreciated their contribution.

A Kikuyu-led Police Force

Independent Kenya's police force was modelled on British lines, but with many unusual characteristics. It was a relatively large force, numbering more than 12,000. The Mau Mau insurgency had resulted in a doubling of numbers, closer policing and the introduction of an aggressive paramilitary orientation, which reflected its frontline role in the fight.[29] Education and training levels were low, and few were of Kikuyu origin, as they had not been trusted during the Emergency. At independence, the police were still seen as an instrument of social control, violent and arbitrary, a negative image reinforced by the poor alignment between formal law and local practice. Little changed during the transition to independence. Although the police fell under regional control during 1963–4, they were restored as an integrated force in 1964. As in the military, Africanisation of the officer corps had been slow and many senior British and Asian officers stayed on. Sir Richard Catling, the British head of the police throughout Mau Mau, remained police commissioner until 1965.

Kenya also retained the Tribal Police (renamed the Administration Police in 1958), which reported to the local chief and the DC. It was used for less-serious and less-structured conflict resolution, and in Central Province had been a key institution in the fight against Mau Mau. Plans to abolish it at independence were reversed by Kenya's new rulers, keen to retain institutions of central authority. Kenya also retained its Police Reserve, a volunteer force of several thousand to bolster the police during emergencies.

During 1964, the situation in the police force became increasingly tense as Minister for Home Affairs Odinga used his patronage to promote supporters and less 'establishment' figures inside the police. In July and August 1964, without Kenyatta's approval, he ordered the sacking and deportation of several British police officers who had helped repress Mau Mau. Although some expected a crisis, Kenyatta did nothing openly, but Odinga's change of portfolio with the introduction of the Republican Constitution soon removed him from control of this sensitive service.[30]

From December 1964, as Africanisation intensified, conservative Kikuyu dominated the security establishment. Bernard Hinga was a key figure, a Kikuyu colonial police officer directly loyal to Kenyatta, also from Kiambu and an Alliance High School alumnus. He was appointed as chief commissioner of police on 31 December 1964, aged only 33, and he remained in his post throughout the Kenyatta era. The paramilitary police GSU was upgraded to become a significant military force, trained by the Israelis, and recruited many Kikuyu. Kenyatta wished to balance the police and GSU against the armed forces, to avoid concentrating military power in army hands. The GSU remained British-led until May 1967, when Kenyatta appointed the 35-year-old Ben Gethi, a Kikuyu from Laikipia, another colonial police officer (who had trained in Israel) as GSU head.[31]

The Special Branch, which dealt with matters of intelligence and state security, was soon Kikuyu-led as well. Its director from January 1965 until 1991 was James Kanyotu, a Kikuyu from Kirinyaga. Aged only 28 when appointed, he was another Alliance graduate, and he too had been a colonial police officer. At Kenyatta's request, Special Branch continued to work closely with the British security services even after independence. Meanwhile, another Kikuyu from Kenyatta's Gatundu division of Kiambu, Bernard Njiinu, led Kenyatta's personal bodyguard the Ichaweri (technically part of the police Presidential Escort Unit) from 1964 until after Kenyatta's death. The Criminal Investigations Department (CID), the plain-clothes police unit that investigated serious non-political crimes, became the sole non-Kikuyu-led security force when a Luo, Peter Ochieng, replaced its European head in 1965.

The Failure of East African Federation

One of the early decisions facing the government was how far and how fast to proceed with East African federation. At the opening of Parliament on 13 December 1963, Kenyatta once more committed Kenya to political union.[32] How this was to be accomplished was unclear, however, as the Kenyans seemed to take federation less seriously now they had achieved *Uhuru*. Rather than weakening the nation-state, the government appeared to be strengthening it in relation to both its regions and its neighbours. Uganda, meanwhile, was absorbed in its internal struggles between Prime Minister Milton Obote and the Kabaka of Buganda.

Almost immediately, the government had to face the consequences of the 12 January 1964 coup and bloodbath in Zanzibar, which had been delayed until Kenya was independent to reduce the likelihood of British intervention. The situation in Zanzibar was profoundly unstable, with a deep-rooted African antagonism towards the entrenched Arab minority – a more severe version of the problem Kenya faced in the coastal strip. While the primary goal of the coup was to bring the country under African leadership, the British and Americans were certain that communist forces had backed the coup.[33]

During 1964, the pressure grew on the government to commit to federation, reflecting the pan-Africanism of the time. This was linked to the struggles inside KANU, as the radicals believed that tighter links with more socialist Uganda and Tanganyika would strengthen their cause. This current was strengthened when Tanganyika and Zanzibar stunned the world by announcing their political union. On 27 April 1964, the new federation of Tanzania came into existence, with Julius Nyerere as president. By mid-1964, the Kenyan government was clearly reluctant to proceed further, with Kenyatta insisting that any announcement be delayed until 'all the facts have been fully exposed and considered', a classic delaying tactic. Mboya later noted the threat to a fragile national identity that regional integration represented. However, on this issue, the government struggled to control the Assembly. In June 1964, it was defeated in the House by an alliance of KANU and KADU backbenchers when it tried to avoid a commitment to immediate federation.

There was little sign of change, though. In August 1964, Kenyatta suggested (in Swahili) that the June 1963 federation meeting had been intended to trick Britain into speeding up Kenya's independence by using Federation as bait.[34] He and senior civil servants appeared reluctant to subordinate their capitalist, pro-Western, successful economy to the economic drags and socialist orientations of Nyerere and Obote. In any case, Uganda too was now hostile to union and the political climate in East Africa was worsening. In May 1965, the Kenyans seized a convoy of 75 tonnes of Chinese arms that was secretly being transported through Kenya by Ugandan troops. Although Obote apologised, this inflamed tensions inside Kenya, as some suggested that the arms had been intended for Odinga's supporters. Kenya's differences with Nyerere were also growing, as Tanzania took an increasingly anti-Western stance and turned to communist China for assistance. Although Nyerere was still talking of federation in 1965, by the end of 1964, the idea was dead.

If federation was no longer an option, an economic alliance or common market still seemed plausible. The new nations had a common currency; there was free movement of peoples and a vibrant set of regional institutions. The EACSO ran the post, telecommunications, aviation, railways and ports, the East African Court of Appeal and medical, agricultural, livestock and fisheries research. It collected income tax (more than half of which came from Kenya) and distributed funds to the national governments. It also collected excise duties, more evenly split between the three countries.

The key obstacle to regional integration was the better-developed economy of Kenya, and the fact that free trade and regional-scale manufacturing was most likely to benefit Kenya's businesses and their British and Asian owners. The Kampala Agreement of 1964 tried to rebalance trade and promote the siting of industries outside Kenya, but when the Kenyans failed to ratify the proposal, Uganda and Tanzania imposed quotas on Kenyan imports.[35] In September 1965, still keen to show progress towards economic integration, the three East African presidents established the Philip Commission, a special committee of their cabinets. Mboya, James Gichuru and Bruce McKenzie were Kenya's representatives. Between September 1965 and May 1966, the Commission defined the structure of what would later become the East African Community.

Regional and International Relations

Despite its close links with its neighbours, Kenya quickly assumed all the attributes of a sovereign nation-state, keen to distance itself symbolically from its ex-colonial master. Foreign relations were the prerogative of the prime minister and later the president, with the power to negotiate treaties with foreign nations, declare war and recognise states without requiring approval by the Assembly. Internationally, Kenya publicly supported a non-aligned, pan-African foreign policy, combined with Commonwealth membership. However, from the first it was friendlier to West than East, reflecting the views of Kenyatta and Mboya and the realities of development aid and finance.

At independence, Kenyatta set about creating a diplomatic corps, and appointed Kenya's first ambassadors and high commissioners. His choices reflected the balance of ethnic groups and factions in his government. Representatives of Kikuyu interests included Josephat Karanja, a 32-year-old from Kiambu and Alliance High School graduate, who became high commissioner to London. He was to become Kenya's vice-president 25 years later. Representatives of a different perspective included Burudi Nabwera, a pro-Odinga KANU official from Western Region, who became Kenya's UN and US ambassador. Kenya became the 111th member of the UN, and joined the Organisation for African Unity (OAU). However, Kenyatta was not a globetrotter; after a visit to the UK for a Commonwealth conference in 1964, he never left Africa again.[36] He preferred to focus on domestic issues, while his high blood pressure made long-distance flights hazardous.

Relations with the British

Relations with the UK were extremely close, the cornerstone of Kenya's foreign policy. Kenyatta's friend MacDonald served as Kenya's governor-general for another year, since the country initially retained the queen as head of state. As well as military support and the aid and settlement programmes, the UK was Kenya's largest trading partner. There were tens of thousands of British citizens living in Kenya, and Britons still staffed hundreds of key administrative and technical posts. Most Europeans now saw Kenyatta as their defender rather than their enemy, epitomised in MacDonald's foreword to Kenyatta's book *Harambee!*, eulogising his 'strong, wise, unifying' leadership.[37]

Unable to travel, Kenyatta managed relations with the UK through two key intermediaries: the European minister of agriculture, McKenzie, who held a covert security brief from Kenyatta that left him in charge of military relations with the UK, and the anglophile Njonjo. Both were well-regarded in Britain. Daniel arap Moi also on occasion reflected and transmitted the British view of events.[38]

Kenyatta's personal relations with the British deepened, and their commonality of interest became clearer. The elderly leader was surrounded by ambitious lieutenants who owed him little, and who had close ties with the leading actors in the Cold War drama. Kenyatta needed a patron and the British were seeking to retain Kenya within their sphere of influence. Kenyatta had lived for many years in Britain, as had Njonjo, creating an unstated commonality of understanding. Kenyatta and the British seem to have delivered on their deals to each other. The British promised help to Kenyatta in 1964–5 in the event of a left-wing coup and provided military assistance against Somalia. They donated arms, aid, personnel and technical support. In return, Kenyatta delivered a stable, Western-oriented government that would protect British land and employment interests, and support a moderate line in the OAU and UN, at a time when Western governments were beset by both the communist threat and anti-colonial pressure. The close economic, political and military relations between the countries were the source of deep frustration elsewhere in the government and party; many saw them as evidence of a dependent and neo-colonial relationship that would forever threaten Kenya's self-reliance.

In most international fora, Kenya therefore took a quiet, non-aligned position. The one issue where it did take a leading role was white rule in South Africa and Rhodesia. There were frequent public and private clashes over Britain's 'softly, softly' policy towards both states. Kenyatta spoke often and openly about the threat of apartheid and in 1964 criticised the life imprisonment of Nelson Mandela. On 17 June 1964 he pledged, 'Kenya will do all that is within its power to bring about the liberation of South Africa.'[39] In practice, however, the Kenyans did little. The most visible signs of change were the closure of the South African consulate and the eviction of the Portuguese. Trade with South Africa was banned, but South African goods still entered Kenya via other countries.

When white-led Rhodesia unilaterally declared its independence in November 1965, it enraged both conservative and radical Kenyans. All East Africa imposed trade sanctions on Rhodesia, ended air connections, seized Rhodesian goods in transit and refused to recognise the new regime. They also demanded that Britain intervene militarily to crush the rebellion. Britain refused, crippled by both domestic public opinion and the realities of remote military operations with South Africa so close. While Tanzania followed the OAU in breaking off relations with the UK, Kenya did not. Instead, in 1965–6, Kenya hosted British fighters and supply planes that airlifted fuel and supplies to landlocked Zambia. Kenyatta also provided a moderate 'sounding board' for British policies over Rhodesia.[40] He regularly castigated the British, but eventually decided to keep Kenya in the Commonwealth.

Relations with the US

Relations with the US were warm, although the superpower had few economic interests in Kenya. Kenya received little direct American investment after independence, as the region had few major extractive industries and exported nothing essential to the US.[41] Aid also remained low, as the US was reluctant to accept the mantle of developing Africa. The US took the view that Kenya had a defence agreement with the UK and needed no additional military assistance, despite Kenyan requests for help. The main aid that Kenya received from the US was educational: the student programme continued and there were more than 1,000 Kenya students in the US in 1964, but numbers declined after 1966.

The 1963–8 Johnson administration continued Kennedy's support for self-determination for those African countries not yet free. However, the Americans too struggled with the Rhodesia problem and were unwilling to intervene in South Africa. The primary US objective in sub-Saharan Africa remained to prevent the region from falling under communist domination. Thus, US policy focused on strengthening African ties to the West and on providing sufficient aid to make turning to the Soviet bloc less attractive. The fact that five Kenyan ministers (Mbiyu Koinange, Julius Kiano, Njoroge Mungai, Lawrence Sagini and Samuel Ayodo) were US-educated helped maintain cordial relations.

Relations were far from smooth, however. A particularly dangerous moment in US–Kenyan relations occurred during the 1964 Congo crisis. After the murder of radical leader Patrice Lumumba in 1961, the country had begun to fall apart. In 1964, a pro-Lumumba communist-backed rebellion captured large areas of the country and took hundreds of foreign hostages. The US-supported prime minister, Moise Tshombe, responded with white mercenary-led troops and both East and West armed their proxies. The OAU asked Kenyatta to mediate. The Americans attended talks in Nairobi over the summer of 1964 but they remained determined to rescue the hostages. In November, they assisted an attack by Belgian paratroops, which freed most hostages, but left many Congolese dead.[42] Kenyatta was furious at the US deception; there were anti-US demonstrations in Nairobi in late 1964 and even threats that Kenya might sever relations.[43]

Looking to the East, 1964

Relations with the communist world were also contested, a sign of a growing rift in the government. The Russians, Chinese and Czechs had all set up embassies in Kenya at independence, and worked assiduously to cultivate their African hosts. Without colonies in Africa themselves, they had a natural anti-colonial constituency, and could align themselves against white rule in southern Africa with ease. However, they were internally divided, with the Russians trying to prevent China gaining an upper hand in the region. Odinga was the most closely aligned with the Eastern Bloc, and was known to be receiving money from the East, though he always denied being a communist, claiming that these allegations were smear tactics by his enemies. Kenya had declared its non-aligned strategy, but Kenyatta, Mboya, Njonjo and others viewed the communists with suspicion. Nonetheless, Kenya's development strategy in early 1964 was genuinely 'non-aligned', as Kenyan leaders, both conservative and radical, sought assistance from both East and West.

Between 18 April and 11 May 1964, Odinga and Joe Murumbi led a six-person delegation on a key trip to Moscow and Peking, to seek assistance from the East. During the trip, they met Nikita Khrushchev personally and negotiated an economic agreement with the Soviet Union, which offered funding for nine projects, including a hospital in Kisumu, agricultural improvements, a technical college and (most worrying for the West) a radio station.[44] Kenyatta, who still wished to keep his options open, personally approved the Russian offer before Odinga accepted it.[45] Moving on to Peking, Odinga then met Mao Tse-Tung and made a pro-Chinese speech supporting the cause of revolution in Africa. The Chinese also made offers to Odinga, including a US$15 million loan for an irrigation project in Tana River. There are also reports that radical ex-detainee Pio da Gama Pinto organised a secret meeting between Odinga, Murumbi and Chinese Premier Zhou Enlai. The meeting discussed the possibility of a socialist or communist revolution in Kenya, and the Chinese may have offered some form of military assistance.[46] The Americans were worried by the size and sophistication of the Russian and Chinese offers, though the British were more sanguine. Kenya also signed trade pacts with other Eastern Bloc countries. A serious effort was under way to diversify Kenya's sources of assistance, and ministerial-level contacts with the East continued throughout 1964.

How far Kenya might have moved to the left if Kenyatta had died in this period, if the communists had provided better aid offers, or if he had been convinced by the radicals' arguments, is hard to tell. Under Odinga as president, Kenya would certainly have taken a different course, on land, nationalisation and private accumulation, though whether this might have resulted in a 'better' society or economic collapse is unknowable. The chances of a decisive turn to the left were never strong, however. Kenyatta was deeply influenced by the British, while Mboya saw Odinga's ideas as threatening not only Kenya's economy but also his own survival. The British were delivering economically and militarily, and firmly supported Kenyatta. The military and civil service were loyal, and the moderate or conservative faction in KANU controlled roughly two-thirds of the party and of Parliament.

President, Parliament, Provincial Administration and Party

The period 1964–5 saw fundamental changes to the structures created by the independence settlement, concentrating power in the unitary state and in the hands of one man. From the moment of self-government until the reintroduction of multi-party democracy in the 1990s, one of the main features of the Kenyan political system was the aggregation of powers to central government and especially to the presidency.

The Move to a Republic, December 1964

In August 1964, Prime Minister Kenyatta announced that the government would be submitting a set of constitutional amendments designed to transform Kenya into a republic and remove the last vestiges of *majimbo*. These were drafted to avoid hitting the specially entrenched constitutional provisions while undermining their fundamental intent. KADU had opposed the legislation until its implementation was inevitable, at which point Ngala had led the remaining KADU leaders across the floor.

On 12 December 1964, like many other countries at the time, Kenya became a republic, with the position of prime minister abolished and Kenyatta elevated to president, head of the armed forces and symbol of national identity as well as political leader. As president, Kenyatta retained all the functions of the prime minister, including the appointment of the Cabinet. He was to be elected, however, in a curious parliamentary–presidential hybrid, not by voters but by the National Assembly, from amongst its members. Although he was on paper an elected MP, he no longer attended the National Assembly except on ceremonial days, to reinforce the perception that he was above party or petty conflict. At the same time, most of the remaining fragments of the *majimbo* constitution were removed, and control of land returned to the centre. Governor-General MacDonald departed, to return as high commissioner a few weeks later (as Kenya remained in the Commonwealth). Henceforth, 12 December was known as Jamhuri (Republic) Day.

Kenyatta used the declaration of the republic to make a major reshuffle of portfolios, signalling a decisive shift to the right. He moved Odinga from home affairs to the new post of national vice-president (matching his vice-presidency of KANU). In theory, Odinga was now only the proverbial heartbeat away from the top. However, it was an appointed, not an elected position, according to Njonjo's and Mboya's amendments, with few formal duties. Odinga was bitter about this stripping of his responsibilities, later describing his position as that of 'a naked cock' with nothing to do.[47] It appeared that Kenyatta's suspicions of Odinga were now greater than of Mboya. To some surprise, ex-KADU Chairman Moi entered the Cabinet, replacing Odinga as home affairs minister. He was the sole KADU leader to be made a minister, indicating that Kenyatta had already marked him out for preferment. He was less confrontational than Muliro or Ngala, a populist, but conservative and pro-Western. He was to play a major role in the war against Odinga's radicals. Paul Ngei also joined the Cabinet at last. With the major constitutional changes completed, Mboya moved from the Ministry of Justice closer to his natural home, in charge of economic planning and development.

'King' Kenyatta

The monarchical nature of Kenyatta's rule was now becoming apparent. His photo was in every shop and on the currency, the state broadcast media followed his every move, and the roads were cleared of moving vehicles as the Presidential Escort passed. Kenyatta's style was evident in November 1965, when, clad in leopard-skins, he opened Kenya's new House of Representatives in Nairobi with its vast statue of himself in front of it. His attire for the Jamhuri Day celebrations mixed the regalia of an African chief and a European monarch (see Figure 3.1). Kenyatta had always been a showman and mythmaker, and he used these skills in 1963–5 to elevate himself further and further above his colleagues. In the process, he built a structure of power, organised around himself, his ethnic community and their interests, and a broad coalition of others whose interests he assisted. Because this coalition delivered development, others acquiesced.

Kenyatta as a man, a political prisoner and an independence leader has been extensively studied, though biographers glided over events after his accession to power.[48] Kenyatta had written a sociological thesis in 1938, but he was not a political philosopher. In response to the intellectualism of the time, he published two collections of speeches, but he was a pragmatist rather than an intellectual. He concentrated his energies on the exercise of authority. As both charismatic leader and founding father, Kenyatta needed no philosophy of rule. He was the king, or the elder of the nation who had suffered for his people, and his right was near divine. In

3.1: Kenyatta and Colonel Ndolo, December 1965

Source: Nation Group Newspapers

1965, there were even references during the 20 October celebrations of Kenyatta Day to his 'last supper' with colleagues before his arrest. His style was no longer that of a man of the people – he was a man apart, to whom access was carefully controlled by bodyguards and supporters.

Kenyatta was also developing his personal fortune. As prime minister and president, he was the recipient of many gifts and the subject of many requests for favours, and the enormous wealth of the Kenyatta family – which remained 30 years after his death – began in this period. He was a man who enjoyed the good life, with a cavalier attitude to debts.[49] By December 1963, he had already ordered a luxury customised Mercedes for his use without state budgetary provision or personal intent to pay, leaving the local agents pleading helplessly for recompense.[50] Both he and Ngei became notorious for requisitioning goods and asking for the bills to be sent to the state, or ignoring them completely. After so many years in the wilderness, Kenyatta enjoyed the exercise of power, and acquired a collection of cars, land and property, much of it by unclear means. He also made full use of the powers vested in the President to make grants of unalienated government land.[51] By 1965, the Kenyatta family was buying numerous settler farms as they came on the market and using Kenyatta's position to excise and allocate government forest in Kiambu to themselves. His fourth and final wife, 'Mama' Ngina, the daughter of Kikuyu chief Muhoho, was a particular beneficiary of this largesse. Kenyatta therefore found it difficult to control similar proclivities amongst his allies, who also began to amass wealth via legitimate and not-so-legitimate activities, using their connections to acquire businesses, extract commissions and win contracts. Although this became a matter of public protest in the 1970s, the foundations were laid in the 1960s.

The Provincial Administration and the President

Rather than ruling through the party, as was the fashion in many African states, Kenyatta chose instead to restore and work through the provincial administration. African political parties in Kenya had always been regional, personalised and factionalised, and both this and the greater radicalism amongst KANU officials led Kenyatta down this path. The calculating and practical Mboya concurred. He knew that the political position they had taken was not particularly popular amongst the masses, and so they needed to ensure that their views dominated the political agenda. The administration could deliver this more securely than could the party. There was also a degree of arrogance and a need for personal security amongst many in the new government. The ladders that the African elites had used to climb to power – popular protest, mass parties, politicised trade unions, free elections and political bargaining – were kicked away before others in turn could climb them.

The provincial administration was unusually powerful in Kenya, a legacy of settler rule, the Mau Mau period and the rush for development of the 1950s. After a brief interregnum in 1964, provincial and district administrators exerted nearly as much power after independence as they had before. The 'little kings', who had ruled their fiefdoms with paternal authoritarianism, were refocused on maintaining a new elite's rule. Through the local security and intelligence committees, their development functions, their control of meetings and the police, they dominated the countryside.[52] The British had trained most provincial officials, and they inherited a mindset that saw their role as the patriarchal heads of their communities and their priority as the maintenance of law and order. Some genuinely believed, as their predecessors had, that political conflict was unproductive, and tried to divert effort into cooperative development.

The independent state soon echoed its colonial parent's repressive attitudes to dissent. Susanne Mueller has traced this back to years of bureaucratic centralisation under colonial rule, weak party structures and a lack of respect for the Constitution engendered by its rapid change in the late 1950s.[53] The government retained the colonial legal framework, which allowed it to control political activity in the countryside through legislation such as the Public Order Act and the Chiefs Act. The police force was under the control of the (pith-helmeted) provincial commissioners, and the provincial and district commissioners were responsible to the Office of the President (OP), rather than to MPs or local authorities. In the words of Muliro in 1967, 'Today we have a black man's Government, and the black man's Government administers exactly the same regulations, rigorously, as the colonial administration used to do.'[54]

While the civil service ran the country, it was controlled by its presidential master, and from the first, Kenyatta hired and fired permanent secretaries and ministers alike on the radio. Officials generally arrived to find empty offices, with no effective handover.[55] Although ministers were gradually gaining experience of office, the power of the Cabinet was already in decline by December 1964, with decisions made by caucuses of ministers close to Kenyatta, and communicated to the Cabinet for ratification.

The Decline of KANU and the Rise of Clientelism

Although it retained a local organisational and patronage role, the central party was soon little more than an irritant. National leaders abandoned or ignored their party jobs and accountabilities and focused rather on their state roles. KANU was part of the emerging patron–client structure of rule, but an unstable and dangerous part.

KANU's substantial legitimacy gave it the ability to mobilise popular feeling, but Kenyatta and Mboya made no effort to mobilise the population through the local party apparatus, which was (not coincidentally) dominated by a more activist, populist and socialist 'cadre'. Instead, KANU's national officials disregarded the party constitution and avoided all efforts to hold elections. In 1964, radical National Organising Secretary John Keen and Assistant Executive Officer John O'Washika wrote to Kenyatta, cataloguing the decline of the party and calling for its Governing Council to meet. Nothing was done. The incorporation of KADU into KANU forced reorganisations and new elections over much of the country, and these were used as pretexts for delaying the summoning of the Delegates' Conference or the National Executive Committee. In the meantime, several centrally inspired branch coups took place, ensuring that delegates would be more pliable if these bodies ever met.[56] In March 1966, with the conflict between conservatives and radicals becoming open, Keen described the state of the ruling party as 'appalling' in an open letter to Kenyatta. He complained that there had been no Annual Delegates' Conference since 1962, the Secretariat had not met since February 1964, the party was K£20,000 in debt, telephones had been cut off at party headquarters and staff had not been paid.[57] Most branches and head office were illegally in office, having failed to file annual returns, but the state did not deregister them. It did not want an active party, but still needed the party to exist on paper.

The reasons for this approach included the strength of the provincial administration, Kenyatta's personal dominance of politics and his lack of deep linkages to his own party. Kenyatta encouraged the growth of a neo-patrimonial system rather than a party-state, partly because he could not reliably control KANU.[58] Mboya was more equivocal: disappointed at the decline of the party, but unwilling to reactivate it. The overlap in positions between top party and state leaders meant they had little time for party activities and blurred the lines between state and party functions.[59] More fundamentally, the party was more radical than the government was becoming, and the pro-Odinga faction was the keenest on keeping the party alive and holding party elections. Mboya, particularly, could not risk elections until Odinga had been weakened.

Factionalism, meanwhile, was endemic in party branches and sub-branches. Well before independence, local disagreements had been fought out in party and local elections. Factions had split into different parties (the APP, KADU and KANU) and then reunited, but the basis for conflicts – personalities, ethnicity, access to resources and alignment with national-level coalitions – remained. This was encouraged by the tensions at the top. While the party had little practical power, it retained significant legitimacy, chose the delegates to central meetings and placed its stamp of approval on candidates for parliamentary and civil elections. These were valuable assets. Factionalism was not a simple pro- and anti-radical divide, but a multi-layered process, personalised and based on local and economic interests and loyalties.[60] The pro- and anti-Odinga divide did 'align the poles' briefly, but there was never a monolithic set of loyalties to institutions or organisations beyond the personal.

The outlines of Kenya's patron–client political system were becoming clear. Political leaders would seek support locally and reward it though the channelling of resources to their clients, while the leadership in the centre (Nairobi), as personalised in central party officials, ministers and civil servants, would maintain the support of key communities by allowing their representatives access to the opportunities that the centre controlled. Such coalitions were built from the bottom up and the top down simultaneously. This process also reflected a personalisation of politics, which had its origins in Kenya's history, African leadership traditions, and the lack (in some arenas) of other bases for factional competition. It was reinforced by the first past the post electoral system and a deliberate destruction of ideology and class as the basis for political competition. This method of rule was to become characteristic of 1970s Kenya, but, again, its outline was clear by 1965.

A Guided Democracy

A democratic Assembly based on the popular vote, able to choose the government and decide policy had been one of the key deliverables of independence. The National Assembly was imbued with legitimacy in part because of the struggle Africans had experienced to achieve membership, then control. However, after independence, its significance declined. Although it remained the centre of debate and of public attention, the Assembly never exerted its power to hold the government to account, nor did it force significant changes to the government's legislative programme or policies.

While the state wanted an active parliament in order to demonstrate its legitimacy, it did not want it to force the agenda on policy issues. Like the party, the Assembly was more radical on most issues than the country's circumstances would permit. Therefore, efforts were exerted to prevent it from passing private members' bills (though the president still had to give his assent, a final control) and private members' motions, even when passed by the House, were deemed non-binding on the government. Debate was often animated and even vitriolic, but there was no risk that the government would fall or lose its legislation. In June 1965, for example, angry at backbenchers' pro-federation activism and their effrontery in interfering with government policy, Kenyatta declared the KANU backbenchers group disbanded and replaced it with a broader Parliamentary Group. His wish was law.

Another thing the government did not want was unfettered access by politicians to the people. Apart from a few months from mid-1964 to mid-1965, there was no relaxation of the colonial regulations requiring those wishing to hold rallies, including MPs, to obtain a licence from the police. Such licences could be refused for 'security reasons' or withdrawn at the last minute. This ensured that, through the provincial administration, the state could control how politicians addressed the voters, and ensured that, while some would have unfettered access, more radical messages could be muffled. Partly as a result, there was immediate hostility between MPs and the provincial administration, both claiming a mandate to rule, which was to deepen as the decades passed.

The third constitutional amendment of May 1965 completed the destruction of the *majimbo* constitution. It removed the specially entrenched provisions entirely, and cut the 75 per cent support requirement for other changes to 65 per cent. The 65 per cent majority required to declare a State of Emergency was reduced to a simple majority, and the period within which this assent had to be granted was lengthened to three weeks. At the same time, the regions became provinces again and the provincial administration was officially reborn. Civil secretaries became provincial commissioners once more, and regional government agents reverted to being district commissioners. The regional assemblies were retitled provincial councils and the salaries to their members ended, making them little more than paper entities.[61] The remaining provisions relating to local control of agricultural land were also removed. The Assembly had no problems in passing what Mboya described as 'technical' changes.[62]

The first single-party elections took place in August 1965, with the rotation of one-third of the senators. Turnout was atrocious, influenced by the decline of KANU and the absence of party competition. The Senate had been given little authority by the Constitution and less by the government, and it became increasingly redundant. Although Njonjo promised in 1965 that 'the Government has no intention of securing the abolition of the Upper House,' it survived only one more year.[63]

Problems in Local Government

With the *majimbo* constitution, Kenya had also acquired a new structure for local government. A hierarchy of elected county councils, area and location or urban councils had been established, with an elected chairman or mayor replacing the colonial DC. Education, health, social services and roads were all handled at county council level, funded by the graduated personal tax (GPT), a form of income tax, by rates, taxes on local produce and licence fees, topped up by central government grants.

However, around independence, with uncertainty in the air, many people had refused to pay tax, forcing councils to borrow to finance their activities. By 1965–6, most were in serious difficulties, as the demands on their services massively exceeded their income. Kakamega County Council was dissolved as insolvent as early as 1965, and the responsibility for collection of GPT moved to the provincial administration. The finances and administration of local government were to remain a problem for the next four decades.

Nairobi City Council remained an exception, unique in wealth and importance. Its mayor from 1962 to 1967 was Murang'a Kikuyu businessman Charles Rubia, who used his role to springboard himself into national politics. By 1965, however, even

Nairobi Council was experiencing difficulties, which deepened as the years passed. There were concerns over corruption in tendering procedures and tensions between elected councillors and council officers over accountabilities and duties, tensions that would continue for decades.[64] On the positive side, the city, flush with cash, was paving roads and building new sanitation, electricity and lighting services.

State Control and the Media

The mass media were key tools for the new government, but also a potential threat. As a result, censorship, particularly self-censorship, was endemic and investigative journalism almost unknown. The media were expected to contribute to development, not to challenge their political masters.

The nation inherited a single radio and TV broadcaster, the Kenya Broadcasting Corporation (KBC), which operated on a public broadcasting and licence fee basis. However, the KBC was soon in financial difficulties. In mid-1964, the government 'nationalised' the KBC and renamed it the Voice of Kenya (VoK), bringing all radio and TV services under its editorial control in Achieng-Oneko's Ministry of Information, Broadcasting and Tourism. This decision was explicitly political. A British ex-official suggested that the Chinese government, believing it was supporting nationalisation, contributed US$1 million to the acquisition, one of the outcomes of Odinga's visit to Peking in 1964.[65] Reflecting the new state's instability, its control mentality and pseudo-socialist orientation, all private ownership of broadcast media was banned. The radio (broadcasting in English, Swahili and local languages) was a key tool in influencing the rural areas. Television in contrast was virtually irrelevant. At independence, almost all televisions were white-owned and in Nairobi.

Print journalism was a more open field, but the Emergency had seen significant censorship and the closure of all African vernacular magazines and newspapers. The sector was now dominated by two private-sector groups: the long-standing settler-focused *East African Standard*, and the new more nationalist Nation Group, publishing the English-language *Daily* and *Sunday Nation* and their Swahili sister papers, founded in 1959–60. The Aga Khan, the Ismaeli spiritual head, was the paper's financier and sponsor. These two media groups were to continue their rivalry for the next five decades. Smaller, less professional competitors did not last long, and the only local weekly news magazine, the *Kenya Weekly News*, ceased publication in 1969. In the ferment of independence, many other African- and Indian-owned newspapers were also established, including papers in Gikuyu and Dholuo, but these soon faded out.

The freedom of the press was far from guaranteed at independence. Legislation from 1960 gave the government significant powers over the media. The new elite warned the press that it must respect the government and cease to expose its internal divisions. In June 1963, Mboya orchestrated the burning of copies of newspapers that KANU deemed hostile, and in July, Achieng-Oneko announced that any attempt by the press 'to promote disunity, to slight our Prime Minister or other members of the Government in any way will not be tolerated . . .'[66] There was a deep insecurity and fear of public challenge in the new leadership, reflected in its search for status, financial security and media obeisance alike. Few of the new ministers or civil service heads had worked their way up through the system. However able, they knew little of government, and were dependent on a fragile popular consensus and on European and foreign expertise. There was also a streak of authoritarianism in Kenyatta, Mboya and others, which power accentuated.

As a consequence, the government sought to strengthen its control over the press and the news it reported. With Achieng-Oneko driving policy, in December 1963 the government established its own news agency with Czech and Russian assistance, and discontinued BBC news feeds.[67] The government placed its Kenya News Agency (KNA) between the newspapers and the Reuters East Africa service. This gave them the ability, by law, to control most of the foreign news reaching the local press, and KNA made good use of it to kill critical stories. Over the next two years, Achieng-Oneko regularly attacked the dailies for being too critical of an independent Kenya and supporting 'settlers and imperialists'. He even attempted to close down the *East African Standard*, which came under strong pressure to toe the line. Instead, in May 1967, the British Lonrho group bought the *Standard*. Lonrho followed a policy of aligning its business directions with government and elite interests, and ensured that the *Standard* took a pro-government line throughout the 1960s and 1970s. The *Nation*, too, was increasingly subject to overt and covert state influence, its British journalists fearful of deportation. In 1965, at the height of the East–West struggle, the newspaper appointed a new editor-in-chief. He was George Githii, a 29-year-old Kiambu Kikuyu, combative freethinker and – not coincidentally – previously Kenyatta's press secretary.

'Mau Mau' No More

The legacy of Mau Mau amongst the Kikuyu was one of the most difficult and divisive challenges for the new government. Central Region was at this time still a post-conflict society, in which ex-guerrillas and ex-Home Guards were trying to reach new accommodations in a state whose leaders included representatives of both movements.[68] Kenyatta's response was to bury all discussion of the war as far as practically possible. Those ex-freedom fighters and detainees who wished to join the new Kenya would be welcome – bygones would be bygones – but they received no compensation or special privileges. Before independence, Kenyatta had pardoned the remaining detainees in prison, and issued an amnesty for fighters to leave the forests and surrender their weapons. More than 2,000 did so in the first weeks after *Uhuru*, far more than the British had expected.[69] Tensions soon arose as some ex-Mau Mau began to act as if they now led the country. Many loyalists initially lived in fear, in the belief that the British departure would inevitably lead to reprisals. Beatings took place in Kikuyu areas, and Mau Mau leaders publicly flogged an MP and a senator for such crimes as 'failing to give them a lift in their car'.[70] Kenyatta had to demand the cessation of the wearing of 'quasi-military uniforms'.

Most of the remaining guerrillas had left the forests at independence, but some soon returned. The amnesty for Mau Mau expired in January 1964, after which they were treated as common criminals. There was open fighting between Mau Mau units and security forces in Meru, where guerrillas rejected the new land settlement arrangements. The government alternated between exhortations, promises and direct action, with a final month-long amnesty when the republic was declared in December 1964. By early 1965, most of the remaining hard-core fighters had been captured or killed.

Although on paper Kenya acknowledged the role Mau Mau had played in the struggle for independence, his government persistently downgraded its importance and did nothing to reward the pro-Mau Mau Kikuyu who had suffered. Despite Kenyatta's promise in 1964 that the land confiscated during the Emergency would be returned, nothing happened. The British removed and hid most records of the war on the eve of independence, to protect loyalists from reprisals and themselves from demands for compensation for atrocities. Ex-Mau Mau were given no preference in access to land or jobs, and their lack of education and resources made it difficult to acquire them by normal means. Some of the more compromised colonial chiefs were compulsorily retired, and some Mau Mau (such as those in Meru, Jackson Angaine's home district) were settled on land schemes, but they received the same terms as other settlers. Ex-Mau Mau received no senior military roles, and the government tried to keep all mention of Mau Mau or of favours for the Kikuyu quiet.[71] There were no monuments raised, Mau Mau leaders were not buried in state and their families and descendants received nothing. Motions in Parliament to recognise and recompense those who suffered were defeated or ignored. There was no reunion of former guerrillas until the political imperatives of the Moi government demanded it in 1986. John Lonsdale and Atieno Odhiambo describe this as a 'political culture of orderly amnesia'.[72]

There were good reasons for this approach. Kenyatta's involvement in the struggle had been ambiguous, and some of his closest allies had been Home Guards. National unity was his goal, and Mau Mau was divisive on several levels: between Africans and Europeans; between Kikuyu and non-Kikuyu; and between ex-Mau Mau and ex-loyalists. In September 1962, Kenyatta had made his views clear when he said, 'Mau Mau was a disease which had been eradicated, and must never be remembered again.'[73] By 1964, the anniversary of the 1952 crackdown on 20 October had become a national holiday, but rather than 'Mau Mau Day', it had become 'Kenyatta Day'.

To reward the Kikuyu fighters would have raised tensions with the ex-KADU leadership. It would have antagonised the white settlers more than any other action he could have performed. By late 1964, once Kenyatta was on a course of confrontation with the radicals, recognition of Mau Mau was also a problem for reasons of narrow political calculation. The radical politicians of Central Province and the Rift were ideologically closer to the fighters of 1952–6 than to Kenyatta's KANU, which had become a 'stepchild' of the colonial government. To have rewarded the ex-fighters would be to help some of those most opposed to his gradualist approach. As a result, Mau Mau had to be sacrificed. The children of the loyalists were the main inheritors of the colonial state. As Odinga put it in 1966, 'I am deeply perturbed that in Kenya today those who sacrificed most in the struggle have lost out to people who played safe in our most difficult days.'[74] Nonetheless, the legacy of struggle was also part of the justification for the Kikuyu's claims to a greater share of the national cake. This allowed Kikuyu elites in the 1960s and 1970s to claim and disclaim Mau Mau allegiances (couched as the 'struggle for independence') whenever they wished.

To counterbalance this, an alternative narrative of history grew up in the 1960s and 1970s that emphasised Kenya's history of oppression and resistance to colonialism.[75] This view rejected Christian education and British contributions to development, stressing instead traditional religions, social organisation and political structures. Marxist class-struggle interpretations of Mau Mau were common and it became a betrayed national war of liberation.

Land, Settlement and the Highlands, 1963–7

The successful completion of the land settlement programme was the primary objective of both British and Kenyan governments in the first years of independence. The British goal was to ensure that its citizens were not driven off the land, that its investments remained safe and that its ex-colony remained stable and anti-communist. The Kenya government needed land and cash to buy out the settlers, to meet the pent-up demand for land and to buy political support. Pressure for compulsory land acquisition was resisted and land nationalisation (as in Tanzania) was never seriously considered. Both recognised that, in the long term, this could not solve the problems of landlessness and unemployment, and that only industrial development could absorb the growing workforce. Nonetheless, it provided a critical breathing space. The combination of the settlement programme and land registration and consolidation in the reserves was one of the most rapid and significant changes to land tenure systems in the continent.

The Settlement Schemes

The arrangements put in place to finance, buy, subdivide, allocate and sell white-owned land continued with only minor changes after independence. Between 1962 and 1965, the UK provided GB£18 million to fund the acquisition of European mixed farms, on which no interest was due until 1969. McKenzie, Gichuru and Angaine were the key figures in obtaining and spending this money. Kenyatta had appointed McKenzie as minister of agriculture in 1963, and he remained in office throughout the 1960s. The sole European in the Cabinet and the voice of European interests, he was a larger-than-life figure – hunter, pilot, farmer and politician – of legendary energy, with close British security contacts. Gichuru was his trusted Kiambu lieutenant, while Angaine was a conservative Meru politician, an ex-detainee, and like Njonjo and Koinange, the son of a senior chief. Kenyatta trusted him to manage settler selection and settlement.

Although the schemes were politically essential, they were also a source of many difficulties. There were ethnic sensitivities from the first, as almost all the schemes were intended to be ethnically homogeneous and to respect ethnic 'spheres of influence'.[76] The Kikuyu settlement of Nyandarua District was the largest, forcing the government to reallocate resources from other areas. Elsewhere, Kakamega and Bungoma Districts acquired 150,000 acres of farms, which were settled almost exclusively by Luhya. The Kamba reacquired European-farmed land in Machakos. The Luo, who had not suffered significantly from European land alienation, received only 10 small settlement schemes covering 77,000 acres, although Luo farmers also privately bought into farms on the Rift–Nyanza border. The Maasai got nothing, while the Kalenjin received small areas around Sotik in Kericho and Nandi, but were otherwise encouraged to direct their ambitions towards private land purchase in Uasin Gishu and Trans-Nzoia. With the collapse of regionalism, the DCs selected those settled, on advice from Angaine's ministry. However, the government refused to disclose the ethnicity of those allocated land. This left to the imagination how the ethnicity of land distribution was changing in practice.

Economically, the schemes were a risky proposition, and most assessments concluded that they were designed more for political than agricultural purposes.[77] Some of the land used for high-density settlement, particularly in Nyandarua, was of poor quality. With the limited inputs and support for the high-density plots, it was hard to create a profitable farm, and some were unsuitable for cash-crops. Maize yields were low and internal politics delayed the supply of inputs to new farmers. Many of the larger 'willing buyer, willing seller' farms and low-density plots were bought by influential absentee farmers, who soon became recognised as some of the least productive. There was also a long-running dispute over the valuation process for land, as Africans protested that the valuations put on land by settlement officers, generally European, were too high.

The settlement schemes continued to represent a key line of cleavage between 'radicals' and 'moderates'. While most radicals rejected the idea of buying land back from the Europeans, the moderates accepted its necessity and aimed to obtain the most benefit for the country as possible. Those who supported socialism and nationalisation of industry generally supported the seizure of white-owned land. The creation of cooperatives to farm ex-white farms was also controversial, enmeshed in the power struggles of 1964–5. At this time, the government was committed to cooperative farming, and it allocated 200,000 acres (80,000 hectares) of the land it purchased to cooperative farms. Most prominent of these was the Ol Kalou scheme in Nyandarua, where 2,000 families were allocated land in 1964–5, each with 2.5-acre private plots, with the rest of the farm worked in cooperative farms.

The government also had to deal with the squatter problem. Across the highlands, there were families demanding that the land they were cultivating become theirs, if possible for free. Some squatters who had settled less-productive empty Crown lands received title deeds years later, but most of those who squatted in the ex-white highlands were eventually evicted. During 1964–5, the Land and Freedom Army continued to dominate KANU in Nakuru and elsewhere in the Rift, and supported

Kikuyu squatters in their ambitions. Demonstrations in Nakuru demanded free land, oathing continued, and violence was never far away. The KLFA had to be politically neutralised, and the squatters had to be bought off or turned off the land. In the majority of settlement schemes in Nakuru and Nyandarua, the existing squatters were simply removed by force, with new claimants chosen to occupy the plots.

The initial success of these land schemes, coupled with the social revolution of land titles and consolidation that had begun during the Emergency, helped to mask and weaken the deep Mau Mau-era divisions amongst the Kikuyu. It also served to provide a graceful exit for many white settlers. By the end of 1965, when the first tranche of funds ran out, there were only 1,100 European mixed farmers left.

The Sale of Larger Farms and the 'Willing Buyer, Willing Seller' Model

While the subdivision of white-owned farms and their sale to the landless had been a political necessity, few in government believed it was economically wise. Once the immediate pressure began to lift, the government tried to enlarge plot sizes with lower-density schemes, and support the transfer of whole farms into the hands of wealthier Africans. Not only would this ensure the continuation of a commercial farming sector, but it would create a land-owning 'middle class' as a conservative and stabilising force. Over a decade, one-sixth of the settler lands were sold intact to the emerging African elite. Kenyatta, his wife and children, Moi, Koinange, Ngala Mwendwa, Odinga (through Luo Thrift and Trading), Kiano, J. M. Kariuki, Muliro and Ngei were amongst MPs who bought farms, many very cheaply, during 1964–6.[78] Many of these farms remain intact to this day, though their owners have changed with the balance of power within the state.

Land was a key source of political patronage, and the government's primary tool in controlling dissent. The choice of farms to buy was political, as was the choice of plot size, the price and the selection criteria for who would get it. At every stage, officials could and did intervene. Influential Africans did not even need much money to buy settler farms, as they were also able to raise loans from government bodies such as the Agricultural Finance Corporation (AFC) and the Land and Agriculture Bank. Nor was there a limit on how much land an individual could own. Although a ceiling was a popular idea amongst peasants, it would have required the subdivision of all large farms, which the government did not support for both economic and personal reasons. All attempts in the National Assembly to push such a policy were rejected. Yet the large farm policy was criticised from all sides as the years passed and the evidence grew that large farms owned by absentee owners were less, not more, productive than subdivided settlement schemes.

In the new settlements, several hundred white farmers' houses and 100-acre plots around them were kept intact and reserved, by Angaine's (i.e. Kenyatta's) instruction in May 1964, for sale to senior community figures.[79] These 'Z plots' were a way to preserve the farmhouses, but also to provide assets for acquisition by the political elite. There was no competitive pricing for their sale, and many were sold to ministers, MPs, ambassadors, permanent secretaries and PCs, men with little farming experience, using British settlement funds. British officials refused to pay, but the process continued. For those closest to the centre of power, there were other opportunities. In February 1965, for example, Kenyatta issued a directive to the Agricultural Settlement Fund trustees that a Z plot house and land worth GB£2,800 be given to his ex-personal secretary and leader of the National Youth Service J. M. Kariuki, as a reward for his efforts in the 'fight for independence'. This was done, and as the directive demanded, it was immediately written off as a bad debt. Officials in charge of administering the fund ignored this blatant theft.[80] It is unsurprising that the Z plots had a very poor loan repayment record.[81]

The Stamp Report and the Second Scheme

By 1964, the Kenyans were already pushing the British for a second 'million-acre scheme', which would focus on large farm transfers.[82] However, the British were reluctant and insisted on a review, known as the Stamp Mission. This reported in October 1965, and damned the schemes: not only did they result in a drain on the economy, as most of the money paid to the white farmers left Kenya; they also diverted resources from developing the 80 per cent of high-productivity land in the ex-reserves. Although it was political dynamite and was kept secret, the report concluded that land transfers should be slowed and agricultural consolidation and production in the reserves encouraged instead.

The British now wished to reduce their financial commitments to the settlement programme, which they considered to have been a failure. This led to lengthy arguments with the Kenyans, led by McKenzie, during which they made clear the political implications of a failure to fund new schemes. Eventually, an arrangement was agreed for a new programme of GB£18 million in loans from 1966 to 1970. Of these, only GB£6 million was to be used for farm buy-outs. Only 100,000 acres a year could be taken over, far less than before, of which 20,000 acres would be reserved for subdivision and settlement schemes. The Agricultural Development Corporation (ADC) would buy the remainder as single farms, and would gradually transfer them into private African hands. From now on, the majority of farms would be sold intact.

Land Registration and Consolidation in the Former Reserves

Whilst most attention was focused on the former white highlands, individual land registration, consolidation and the issue of land titles continued in the former reserves, with equally dramatic effects. The new government believed, as had the old, that individual title and the consolidation of fragmented holdings were essential for long-term agricultural improvement, and reduced the cost of land litigation and the fear of land expropriation. The colonial government had virtually completed consolidation in Kiambu, Kirinyaga and Nyeri, but it had proceeded more slowly in Murang'a (previously known as Fort Hall), where opposition to individual title was stronger and corruption in the first round forced a complete re-demarcation and re-registration.[83] In general, studies suggested the process slightly favoured 'the rich, the powerful and the loyal'.[84] Not only had some pro-Mau Mau Kikuyu lost their land rights, if they had them at all (many had been *ahoi* tenants), but the complex bureaucratic processes used favoured those with money, education and contacts. In Murang'a particularly, inequalities in land access were significant, with 39 per cent of all land in holdings of 10 acres and above.[85] Many of the consolidated plots were smaller than administrators believed were viable (7.5 acres).

By 1965, registration and consolidation was also under way in Embu and Meru, Kakamega and Bungoma, and parts of the Rift Valley, but most of the ex-reserves remained communally owned, the occupants technically tenants of the state. British loans and expertise continued to support the programme. Some districts were registered without consolidation. Wherever officials tried to adjudicate areas where other communities had acquired land inside ex-reserves, there was trouble as the 'indigenous' inhabitants tried to extinguish the use rights of the interlopers.[86] In Central Nyanza, clan and community organisations mounted sustained opposition to land consolidation, which Odinga supported, and the process proceeded slowly. In the large pastoral ex-reserves such as Maasailand, where land had never been an individual asset, consolidation and registration were even more difficult. There was also a political obstacle to overcome. It was now clear, with the defeat of regionalism, that land would not be reserved for specific ethnic groups, but could be bought by anyone, once it was demarcated and registered. Kenyatta had promised in 1963–4 that 'there is no-one at all – including the Government – who will take the Masai land.'[87] However, with regionalism dead, a new order flourished.

Another issue was that the registration system created alongside the land consolidation programme was proving inadequate. In practice, the majority of land sales and inheritances were not registered, but executed informally on the ground, to avoid paying fees, to bypass restrictions on plot subdivision, or simply because of ignorance.[88] A growing divergence between the formal position and the actual transactions emerged, which led to growing fragmentation, land litigation and corruption as the years passed.

Border Troubles and Ethnic Clashes

Trouble between ethnic communities where their lands bordered or grazing overlapped had been a continual problem for the colonial government, and such clashes (often caused by cattle raiding) continued throughout the 1960s. Fighting was endemic in the north – in the Somali North-East and also amongst the Turkana, Merille, Samburu, Borana, and Ethiopian and Sudanese pastoralists. In the south, there were several clashes and raids between Gusii and Kipsigis, and between these communities and the Kuria and Maasai. There was fighting between Maasai and the growing number of Kipsigis immigrants in Narok and between Kamba and Maasai on the border of Machakos district in 1967. The exact nature of such violence was to become a matter of debate after the 'ethnic clashes' of the 1990s. All the northern and southern pastoral districts were still administered under the Special Districts

(Administration) Act, another colonial instrument, which prohibited outsiders entering them without permission, to control stock theft and raiding.

While the political division that had fired conflicts in 1961–3 had become less visible, ethnic trouble continued, driven mainly by border disputes. The GSU had to patrol the border between Rift Valley and Western regions in July 1964, after violence between Kalenjin and Luhya left at least one dead and many huts burnt. The clarification of boundaries between Western and Nyanza regions also caused controversy, as the Luo and Luhya communities were deeply intermixed in Western Butere and Nyanza Gem, and ethnicity did not always match geography. Communities on the border took it upon themselves to decide within which region they would be administered, and the Luhya left in Nyanza quickly found their lands and security under threat. From the start, political boundaries were associated with ethnicity and ethnicity with violence.

Africanisation and Kenyanisation

Another key plank of the government's policy was Africanisation. This was a nationalist programme to reduce Kenya's economic, political and military dependence on foreigners, and to restrict the roles that foreigners could hold in the economy. It was a political necessity, to maintain legitimacy and show that Kenya was run by and for indigenous Kenyans. However, it was economically risky, and required a careful balancing of competing pressures. Without the Europeans and Asians, Kenya in 1964 would have had virtually no professionals, no functioning government, virtually no large private business and little commercial agriculture. Too rapid a process of change would scare off white and Asian capital and expertise, but slower change would raise pressure for violent or precipitate action. Kenyatta always saw his first priority as 'an efficient and effective machine of government'.[89] He spoke the language of rapid change, but acted with care.

The Future of the Immigrants

Although 'Africanisation' was the term most often used, the pressure was formally on non-citizens, and was less-emotively described as 'Kenyanisation' (favouring citizen employment). The government was constitutionally required to guarantee equal treatment for all citizens, irrespective of their race. The Constitution did not prohibit discrimination against non-citizens, however. There was a deep-rooted anger at the systematic disadvantaging of Africans in the colony, and a desire to redress the balance. The new government was not averse to showing its power against openly racist Europeans and Asians, and deported several who had shown insufficient respect towards Kenya's flag, president or African majority. The government, though, had to balance its interests and those of its supporters against the risk of alienating their European patrons.[90] The Asian community was not so well defended.

Kenya's Constitution gave non-African residents at independence until December 1965 to decide whether to register as Kenyan citizens.[91] The responses to this offer varied by community and by their perceptions of prospects in the new Kenya. Most Europeans preferred to remain British; 50,000 Asians took up the offer, and another 13,000 were naturalised as Kenyans, but the majority declined or were ineligible, and instead obtained or retained a British passport. It took four more years for thousands of late applications to be scrutinised, creating more uncertainty.

In 1963–5, one of the key questions regarding Kenya's future concerned the future of the European community, whose response to the new government was critical to its success. For many of them, independence was a vast risk, in which they had little confidence. There was a widespread fear of dictatorship and of the divisive impact of African ethnicity. Books such as Carey-Jones's *The Anatomy of Uhuru* – written a year after independence – expressed the fear that inefficiency and low competence levels due to over-rapid African promotions would lead to chaos.[92] Carey-Jones also showed concern about the unfolding East–West struggle in Africa, and its effect on ordinary people. Many Europeans' fears of independence were as much fears of communism. The language of these works appears archaic, but some of the issues raised – administrative competences, politicisation of the civil service, the role of the state and of minority communities – are debated to this day.

There is no doubt that the white settler community was extremely conservative, even by British standards (British officials felt that many would be more at home in South Africa or Rhodesia). Even in the late 1960s, old-fashioned racism remained common. Nonetheless, to keep European skills, capital and international credibility, compromises were made. Although European numbers declined from 56,000 in 1962 to 41,000 in 1969, the transition was gradual and well managed. As the land acquisition process proceeded, so Europeans also departed one by one from the administration, handing over to successors they had helped nurture. The European community remained well represented economically and had a voice in the Cabinet through McKenzie, while European politician Humphrey Slade served as speaker of the National Assembly until 1970. Active equalisation and positive discrimination policies were adopted in the public sector, but inequalities in the private sector and the professions, less amenable to legislation, continued for decades.

The future of the Asian population was more difficult to resolve. There were 180,000 Asian residents in Kenya at independence, three times the number of 'whites'. The various Asian communities had retained their separate traditions and religious beliefs (Christian, Muslim, Sikh or Hindu), and rarely married into different Asian communities and virtually never with Europeans or Africans.[93] Amongst Muslims there were further divisions between Sunni and Shi'ite, and sub-groups such as the Ismaelis retained a distinct identity.[94] Nairobi was the centre of Asian activity, and in 1969, 13 per cent of the city's population was Asian, but Asian traders were scattered throughout Kenya.

The community had been pro-government and anti-Mau Mau, and faced accusations of exploitation and racism. Many found the equality of Africans difficult to accept. Their thriftiness, family orientation and willingness to work long hours for low margins had allowed them to generate significant capital, but they had been ill served by the independence political settlement. Thousands lost their jobs with Africanisation in the EACSO (more than 90 per cent of all clerks had been Asian until 1962). There was considerable resistance to integration on both sides. The government criticised the Asian community for racism, separatism, restrictive commercial practices and unwillingness to commit themselves to Kenya. Asians in turn saw the state as institutionally racist, and felt that, whatever the Constitution said, discrimination would not end if they became citizens. It was now virtually impossible for Asians to find jobs in government service or parastatals. In a vicious circle, the Asian community tried to broaden its options, ensuring sufficient funds flowed overseas to allow them to survive expropriation, but this capital flight was in turn used as evidence of their lack of commitment to Kenya. There were a few open defenders of the Asian community, particularly Njonjo, who rigorously upheld the non-discrimination clauses of the Constitution, but most Africans were hostile.

On the Coast, there were also more than 30,000 Kenyans of Arab origin, although centuries of trade and settlement had left the boundaries of Arab and Swahili communities blurred. Some Arabs were large landowners in the coastal strip. Again, their status was uncertain and their prospects bleak. Most Arabs, however, chose to take Kenyan citizenship.

Africanisation of the Civil Service, Commerce and the Professions

Africanisation of the civil service had begun in 1960, but it was far from complete by 1963. As in many other African countries, there was a desperate shortage of African professionals. In 1962, there had been only 18 Africans amongst the top 89 central government posts and only 180 among the 3,000 senior professional and technical staff.[95] In other parts of the economy, the situation was equally dangerous. In 1965, *Sessional Paper No. 10* noted, for example, that only 50 of 811 doctors in Kenya were African, and two of 25 surveyors.[96]

Despite claims that it proceeded too slowly, in practice Kenya citizenised its administration rapidly and without losing continuity. Odinga led the charge as home affairs minister, replacing all the key DC and PC positions by the end of 1964 with Africans (and retiring most colonial-era chiefs as well). Many expatriates chose to leave as soon as they could. From 1964, all central government workers' terms and conditions of employment were managed by the Public Service Commission, a committee of presidential appointees who appointed and promoted civil servants on the advice of ministries. This allowed an active and centrally led programme of Africanisation, limited mostly by the lack of educated and technically qualified Africans capable of appointing to these posts. By November 1966, citizens staffed 89 per cent of the civil service, but the proportion was still lower in the senior grades.[97] Similar processes were seen in the parastatals. In some cases, such as the Kenya Meat Commission (KMC), performance suffered as a result, with inexperienced managers and politicised decisions leading to falling profits and rising costs. In other cases, the transition was smooth.[98] As Kenyatta claimed in 1967, 'Despite this rapid Africanisation, there has been no fall in the standards of efficiency.'[99]

The rapid promotion of personnel as a result of the Africanisation of government positions was the foundation of the careers of a generation of Kenya's leaders. The administrative elites selected by the British and later by Kenyatta for preferment during 1961–6 were given enormous opportunities at a young age, and many converted this into enduring political, economic and financial power. Men like Kenneth Matiba, Njonjo and Simeon Nyachae made the leap forward that was to leave them at the apex of government in their thirties, and was to secure their dominance for three decades. Many were the sons of chiefs and had been students at Alliance High School. At least half were Kikuyu (see Table 3.1), and by 1964 there was already disquiet amongst other communities that Africanisation was 'Kikuyuisation' in disguise.

Table 3.1: Civil servants who converted rapid promotion into enduring power

Name	Age in 1961	Role in 1961	Role in 1966	Later Achievements	Ethnicity
Gethenji, Joseph	26	Student	Assistant director of personnel	Director of personnel, 1968–78; permanent secretary, 1978–87; MP, 1992–7.	Kikuyu
Karanja, Josephat	29	Student	High commissioner to London	Vice-chancellor of University of Nairobi, 1970–9; vice-president, 1988–9; MP, 1992–4	Kikuyu
Kariithi, Geoffrey	36	District officer	Permanent secretary	Head of the civil service, 1967–79; assistant minister, 1988–91	Kikuyu
Keriri, John Matere	25	Student	Deputy-secretary	Permanent secretary; managing director DFCK, 1972–82; assistant minister, 1988–92, 1997–2002; state house controller, 2003–4	Kikuyu
Komora, Yuda	28	Teacher	Deputy chief education officer	Director of Education, 1970–4; permanent secretary, 1974–9; Kenatco general manager, assistant minister, 1992–7	Pokomo
Kyalo, John	29	District officer	Permanent secretary	Permanent secretary, 1966–78; minister, 1990–5	Kamba
Mahihu, Eliud	36	District officer	Provincial commissioner	Provincial commissioner, 1964–80; parastatal head; nominated MP, 1988–92	Kikuyu
Mathenge, Isaiah	31	District officer	Provincial commissioner	Provincial commissioner, 1965–79; MP, 1992–7	Kikuyu
Matiba, Kenneth	29	Education officer	Permanent secretary	Breweries managing director; minister, 1983–8; presidential candidate, 1992; MP, 1992–7	Kikuyu

Name	Age in 1961	Role in 1961	Role in 1966	Later Achievements	Ethnicity
Mbathi, Titus	33	Lecturer	Permanent secretary	Permanent secretary, 1964–70; minister, 1980–3	Kamba
Michuki, John	30	District officer	Permanent secretary	Permanent secretary to 1970; KCB chairman, 1970–9; MP, 1983–8 and 1992 on; minister, 2003 on	Kikuyu
Murgor, Charles	36	District officer	Provincial commissioner	Provincial commissioner, 1966–9; MP, 1969–83	Kalenjin
Mwendwa, Kitili	32	Assistant secretary	Solicitor-general	Chief Justice, 1968–71; MP, 1984–5	Kamba
Mwendwa, Kyale	35	Education officer	Chief education officer	Director of education, 1968–77; minister, 1986–8	Kamba
Njenga, Jonathan	33	Community development officer	Commissioner of community development & social services	Principal immigration officer, 1972–9; MP 1982–8	Kikuyu
Njonjo, Charles	41	Senior Crown counsel	Attorney-general	Attorney-General, 1963–80; minister, 1980–3	Kikuyu
Nyachae, Simeon	29	District assistant	Provincial commissioner	Provincial commissioner, 1965–79; permanent secretary, 1979–84; chief secretary, 1984–6; minister, 1993–9, 2004–7; presidential candidate, 2002	Gusii
Omanga, Andrew	29	Assistant secretary	Permanent secretary	Permanent secretary, 1964–74; minister, 1979–88	Gusii
Omolo-Okero, Isaac	32	Barrister	EA commissioner of customs and excise	Minister, 1969–79; Kenya Airways chairman, 1996–2005	Luo
Ouko, Robert	29	Student	Permanent secretary	Permanent secretary, 1964–9; minister, 1969–90	Luo
Shako, Juxon	43	District officer	Permanent secretary	Permanent secretary, 1966–8; minister, 1969–74	Taita
Wamae, Eliud Matu	23	Student	Deputy general manager, Central Bank of Kenya	Executive director ICDC, 1969–79; MP, 1983–8, 1992–2002	Kikuyu
Wanjigi, Maina	30	Student	Director of settlement	Executive director ICDC, 1968–9; assistant minister, 1969–79; Kenya Airways chairman, 1980–3; minister, 1983–90	Kikuyu

Source: Various

From the start, Kenyatta stressed his commitment to multi-racialism (not African supremacy) and the equality of all citizens, whatever their colour. While civil service and parastatal roles were quickly Kenyanised, technical positions, the private sector and the professions remained disproportionately white and Asian for many years. In the private sector, citizens held less than 25 per cent of senior managerial and technical posts in 1967. This reflected a combination of longer professional qualification periods, access to technical skills only available overseas, the slow equalisation of educational achievement, the importance of family businesses and family capital, and genuine 'closed shop' ethnic biases. The government was cautious, recognising this was probably unavoidable. The 1965 *Sessional Paper* explicitly accepted that Kenya must supplement its 'meagre supply of domestic, trained manpower with large numbers of skilled people borrowed from abroad. It is a choice between rapid growth and little or none . . .'[100]

Education was one of the key tools available to make the situation more equitable. One immediate action taken was the desegregation of schools, so that schools previously reserved for non-Africans were required to be at least 50 per cent African by 1967. Nonetheless, it took many years for imbalances to be rectified. In 1967, 32 per cent of University of Nairobi students were Asian and 5 per cent European, when together they constituted less than 2 per cent of the population.[101]

Most people of every colour accepted the need for change and for positive discrimination such as loans for Africans who wished to buy out Asian businesses.[102] The trade unions, backbenchers and many others called for the government to move faster (by lowering educational standards and qualifications to take up professional posts, and reducing or eliminating prior experience as a condition for employment), and called for access to jobs to be based on ethnicity rather than citizenship. The government balanced these populist but risky demands against those of business, investment and equity, supporting rapid change only where qualifications and prior experience were more selection barriers than true necessities.

In the manufacturing industry, there was no forced action to favour African entrepreneurs. This reflected the capital-intensiveness and economic importance of such businesses. Most government departments followed strict tendering processes and did not openly favour African-owned businesses, though the Ministry of Works did prefer Africans for smaller contracts from 1967. In trade, however, Africanisation was actively encouraged, and in April 1965 the Kenya National Trading Corporation (KNTC) was launched as a subsidiary of the state-owned Industrial and Commercial Development Corporation (ICDC). Its task was to Kenyanise wholesale and retail trade, providing goods directly from overseas to retailers and bypassing Asian middlemen. It was given a monopoly on imports of sugar, rice, soap, detergent and second-hand clothes (and exported surplus crops). Inevitably, it was led by a Kiambu businessman, Peter Kinyanjui. From 1964, there was a jump in the percentage of new African-owned businesses, though it was not until the mid-1970s that Africans owned the majority of new ventures.[103]

The Legal System

The legal system Kenya inherited was conservative and European dominated, and Kenyatta did nothing to change this. As attorney-general, Njonjo was the government's chief law officer. He drafted all legislation and served as chief prosecutor, with the power to initiate and halt cases without (on paper) being subject to any higher authority. He was also a Cabinet minister and the government's legal adviser. The head of the judiciary was the chief justice, charged with the direction of all judges. Independent Kenya's first chief justice was a European, John Ainley. While the president appointed the chief justice, all other ranks were appointed on the advice of a Judicial Service Commission. Judges were appointed for life.

The independence legal system remained modelled on the British model, with the Constitution as a supreme underlying law. The confused colonial-era system of racially separate courts was restructured in 1967, so that a single structure now governed criminal law and other major subjects. However, for personal and civil matters, three different legal systems remained in effect: the formal and common law; customary law, which continued to govern local community problems; and *sharia* (Muslim religious) law, which governed Muslims' relations with other Muslims, as agreed in the deal over the coastal strip. *Sharia* courts were retained as subordinate courts to the High Court, and the authority of the Muslim chief kadhi continued to be recognised. The 1967 legislation reconfirmed that customary law (varying according to ethnic tradition) and Islamic law were binding in the absence of a statute to the contrary.[104] Trial by jury, which had existed for Europeans but not Africans in the colonial era, was scrapped and all decisions rendered by judges.

In general, during the 1960s and 1970s, Kenya maintained high levels of formal adherence to law, and as long as political considerations did not intervene, the legal system remained effective and relatively fair. However, the Public Order Act restricting assemblies, the detention legislation, the Societies Act, sedition laws and restrictions on the media significantly weakened constitutional guarantees of individual freedom. Virtually no effort was made to challenge the constitutionality of any legislation affecting individual rights and, from the first, security and public order took precedence over civil liberties. The Law Society of Kenya (LSK) and individual lawyers said little. In Yash Ghai and J. P. W. McAuslan's words, 'the Bar has not in the past represented, and does not now represent, any sort of effective pressure-group for constitutionalism and the Rule of Law . . .'[105] The reasons for this related primarily to the racial origins of Kenya's lawyers. At independence, the legal fraternity and its trade union the LSK was almost exclusively white and Asian. Settler domination of the legal system and its high academic standards had made it hard for African lawyers to qualify or operate, and in 1959 there were only eight Africans in private practice. As with the military, the British forced a crash programme on a reluctant colony, but its implementation was incomplete by 1964.[106] For such a privileged community, 96 per cent of whom were Asian or white, to criticise the state would have been treated as a sign of open disloyalty. It was only in the 1980s that the legal profession, by then mostly African, was willing to challenge the state.

The Economy

In the economic sphere, the government faced a near-impossible task: to satisfy African demands for growth and for equality with whites and Asians, while retaining non-African skilled manpower and capital and encouraging inward investment. Expectations were at fever pitch; with the belief that a welfare state, free education, free medical services and other public goods would spontaneously come into existence at independence. On 10 June 1964, Kenyatta launched Kenya's first Development Plan for 1964–70, based on optimistic assumptions of rapid growth.

In practice, for a short period, the government succeeded in delivering growth, improved services and Africanisation alike. During 1964–9, Kenya managed 6 per cent annual growth in GDP. Despite the rapid rate of population growth, real GDP per person grew at more than 3 per cent a year. Fiscal policy remained conservative and inflation rates low, which helped support a sharp increase in production, driven in part by new investment and in part by the restoration to productive use of assets that had suffered from under-utilisation and under-investment during the transition.

Foreign Investment and African Socialism

It was already clear that the indigenous resources available through taxation were insufficient to sustain the level of development that Kenyans desired. The state was constrained in what it could build by access to capital. Kenya had productive projects, but was unable to generate the cash indigenously, either from private African millionaires (of whom there were none) or from the state itself, whose resources were constrained by the low level of taxation and difficulties in its collection outside the tiny formal sector. In fact, the colony was in financial difficulties at independence, as it had for some time been supported by British development loans, military forces, flood and famine relief, overseas civil servants' salaries and grants to cover budget deficits, as well as development aid from the World Bank and others. Spending was expected to increase rapidly, but there were few sources of untaxed revenue to mine. All sides in the debate over economic policy therefore viewed access to foreign money as critical to the future. Only foreign aid or private investment could offer the capital needed. In 1964–5, foreign aid accounted for 95 per cent of the government's development expenditure. Scarce revenues, their allocation (or misallocation) and the need to supplement them with foreign aid were central political issues for the next four decades.

During 1964–5, the government developed a policy that, in line with the terminology of the time, it referred to as 'African socialism', but which might better be described as 'state capitalism'. Led by Mboya, the government created a mixed model of development that attempted to satisfy domestic aspirations for African ownership, growth and social services without discouraging foreign investors. Mboya was convinced that social justice could only be delivered through growth, and that the only way to obtain the funds needed for development was through foreign investment. His policy had strong continuities with colonial strategy since the 1950s.

Private sector forces would drive growth, but the state would plan what would be built, regulate the market and provide starter capital for investments that the private sector might hesitate to make alone. Most of the government explicitly rejected the compulsory nationalisation of foreign assets as discouraging investment (there was no expectation that public ownership might be intrinsically less efficient or more prone to misallocation and corrupt practices than the private sector). Instead, between 1964 and 1966, there was an explosion of new state boards and authorities – where they did not already exist – covering virtually every aspect of agriculture and industry, to tax, regulate and encourage their development. Foreign aid would be encouraged, but only if it was without strings (although the state recognised there were still 'subtle obligations'). Private inward investment would be encouraged by liberal taxation policies, tariff protection and licensing rules to limit competition. However, the state would have the final say. This was most clearly articulated in 1965's *Sessional Paper No. 10*, but by mid-1964 this direction was already clear. The 1964 Foreign Investment Protection Act reaffirmed the deal with the West and helped end the capital outflow. This provided for dividend remittances and full compensation in the rare event of nationalisation.

This was the view of the majority of the government, but it was not the view of Odinga, Kaggia, Fred Kubai, Achieng-Oneko and a large chunk of KANU. They had campaigned on a radical platform in 1963, and remained determined that Kenya would not become a Western satellite. They campaigned publicly and privately for more aggressive nationalisation, repudiation of the 1962 land deal, faster Africanisation and a non-aligned foreign policy. Their economic policies were less cogently expressed than Mboya's, but they were clearly more socialist than official government policy, although neither Odinga nor his supporters ever proposed Soviet or Chinese-style communism, with nationalisation of land and collective ownership of all the means of production.

The case for a pro-Western economic policy was hard to challenge in practice, however. Private investment in Kenya continued to be disproportionately European in origin – nearly 50 per cent of the nominal capital invested in new firms in 1963–6 was European, mostly British. Foreign aid, solicited from both East and West, was also coming in more rapidly from the West. The Soviet Union and the People's Republic of China, although keen to initiate large projects, did not have private businesses that could invest alongside the state. Worse, most of their projects were to be funded not by the transfer of hard currency but by the gift of goods, which would have to be sold on the Kenyan market (possibly damaging local businesses) to raise funds for the projects' construction. This disparity in responses helped shift many waverers against the Eastern Bloc during 1964. The pro-British and American elements in the Cabinet and their Western advisers stressed this disparity as demonstrating Kenya's need to take a 'moderate' international course. As the balance of power shifted against Odinga during 1964–5, most of the Eastern Bloc projects stalled.

In this period, most policy-makers and economists believed development and GDP growth should be the primary goal of state investments. Projects should be judged by their ability to promote growth, as trickle-down effects in jobs and incomes would follow. Concerns about the side-effects and the concept of underdevelopment were a decade away.[107] However, doubts remained even amongst pro-Westerners. There was certainly no consensus that a fully open economy was desirable. Even after the defeat of the radicals in 1965, foreign assistance was not universally accepted, and rich and poor Kenyans alike treated basic features of international capitalism such as the repatriation of dividends with suspicion. In every aspect of the economy and society, although encouraging external investment, the government wished to retain controls that would allow it to manage the process.

Industrial Development in the early 1960s

The independent state inherited both the benefits and the costs of greater industrialisation than its neighbours had achieved. Without coal, oil or valuable minerals, Kenya's agro-industrialisation under British rule had been powered by the white settlers' agricultural production and their market, and protected by tariffs and licensing rules. In 1964, manufacturing contributed 10 per cent of the nation's GDP, a far higher level than in most of Africa. Nairobi was the regional centre, with Mombasa a distant second. Keen to deliver growth in both GDP and jobs, the new government supported continued industrial development, to move further away from the export of primary products into agricultural processing for export and import-substitution.

The basis of this post-independence development plan was a partnership between government and business. The Kenyan government welcomed foreign multinational investment and was willing to provide incentives for it through joint venture arrangements, and also encouraged investments by foreign governments and the British Commonwealth Development Corporation (CDC). It protected such investments by banning or limiting imports that competed with local products, as well as providing duty remissions and support for exports. The aim was to become more self-sufficient in manufactured goods, create employment, develop skills and conserve foreign exchange. This process, a continuation of the 1950s expansion, was relatively successful, though there was scepticism even at the time that local markets would be too small to produce some products efficiently.[108] Industries established in the early 1960s included the Mombasa oil refinery, the General Motors car plant and agro-industrial enterprises such as the tea factories built by the Kenya Tea Development Authority, Kisumu Cotton Mills, two sugar factories and Kenya Canners (canning pineapples for export).[109]

Finance for Development

Kenya needed money to build its economy, as well as to acquire stakes in foreign-owned businesses and to buy settler land. The solution chosen was the creation of a series of financial parastatals. These strategic investors loaned money from abroad or from state funds to Kenyans and invested directly in new projects. It was an audacious programme, but yielded mixed results, hampered by low levels of repayment and some poor investment choices.

For industrial development, the key finance institutions were the Development Finance Company of Kenya (DFCK) and the colonial Industrial Development Corporation, rebranded and rechartered as the Industrial and Commercial Development Corporation (ICDC) in 1964. Together, they provided the core long-term finance for industrial development in the absence of a large or liquid capital market (the Nairobi Stock Exchange was far too small). The ICDC provided loans for industrial and commercial projects and helped Kenyans acquire foreign-owned businesses. It also acted as the holder of the government's share in equity partnerships with foreign companies. It soon became the most significant industrial development organisation in the country. The DFCK, meanwhile, had been formed in 1963 to help develop agro-processing, industry and commerce, as a joint venture between the ICDC, the CDC and other Western development agencies. The ICDC also established Kenya Industrial Estates (KIE) in 1967, providing loans for manufacturing in designated industrial estates. There was some overlap between the projects these entities supported, but they were all apparently profitable.

To finance agricultural development, the government had established the AFC in 1963, to also offer Africans buying European farms loans to buy cattle and farm machinery. The AFC absorbed the Land and Agriculture Bank in 1966, which had been the main lender to settlers before independence. It was funded through grants and loans from international institutions and bilateral donors such as USAID (the US Agency for International Development), and by government revenue. The process of approval for loans from the AFC and local agricultural committees and loans boards was widely believed to favour the wealthy and influential.[110] Its performance proved disappointing, and its assets were worn away by massive defaults. The AFC was joined in 1965 by the ADC, responsible for investing in agro-industrial enterprises such as the sugar factories, as well as buying and managing farms. It too was funded by loans from foreign governments, mainly Britain, and British officials helped administer the fund. The ADC too generated poor financial returns, partly a consequence of its hidden role of granting credit to assist Africanisation, which was not reflected in its financial returns.

Four more finance parastatals were established in these early years. The CDC and the government jointly established the Housing Finance Company of Kenya (HFCK) in 1965. This non-bank financial institution had a simple purpose – to take deposits from the public and re-loan them as mortgages. Also established in 1965 was the Kenya Tourist Development Corporation (KTDC), to invest in new tourism projects and promote tourism. In 1968, the government created a new retail bank, the National Bank of Kenya (NBK), as a competitor to foreign private banks. The government also established the Cooperative Bank in 1968, to give the movement easier access to credit than was forthcoming from the commercial banks.

Kenya tried to grow quickly, mostly using Western investments, loans and gifts, with much of the work done through these finance parastatals. As a result, there was a huge jump in the level of state credit available to those Africans able to take advantage of the opportunity. However, the country never achieved the take-off point where such investments yielded returns many times their seed capital. Many of these investments were not repaid by the recipients or were misallocated or misused. The result was that Kenya's long-term foreign liabilities rose year by year.

Agricultural Expansion in the 1960s

Although industry was the main recipient of foreign capital, agriculture remained the mainstay of Kenya's economy. Virtually all agriculture was rain-fed, and Kenya's prosperity and its people's security were driven by the vagaries of rainfall, with poor rains almost inevitably leading to famine. While most European production was marketed centrally, most African produce was still grown for domestic consumption and did not pass through any formal exchange. Roughly one-third of GDP was non-monetary; mostly agricultural produce.

As in many independent African states, the minds of Kenyan leaders and their European advisers were focused more on industrialisation and large development projects – dams, roads and infrastructure – than on smallholder pricing or rural credit. Nonetheless, Kenya's prospects remained bound to its agricultural performance, particularly of its export crops. Kenyatta soon proved a strong advocate of wealth creation through small-scale agriculture, and the state successfully supported both peasant and commercial agriculture during the 1960s. It did this in myriad ways, including price stabilisation policies, investments in agricultural processing, fertiliser subsidies, seasonal credit, advice for farmers, veterinary assistance, training, support for cooperatives, loans for development, feeder roads and crop research. Fertiliser use doubled between 1964 and 1970. The result was a jump in cash-crop production, led by smallholders, to some extent in the new farms in the highlands but mostly in the ex-reserves, where the potential for growth was even greater. It was one of the greatest achievements of the Kenyatta government, though it did not occur without tensions between the requirement for quality controls on cash-crops and popular pressure for unrestricted expansion. Peasant producers in consolidated areas where land was suitable for coffee, tea or pyrethrum gained a substantial economic advantage over other communities.[111]

Coffee and Tea

Coffee was Kenya's most profitable crop at independence and remained its top foreign exchange earner until 1989. The Coffee Board of Kenya regulated the industry, with a second parastatal, the Coffee Marketing Board, acting as the wholesaler, financier for farmers and manager of the crop's sale for export. Most smallholder coffee was produced with the help of and marketed through the cooperative movement. The beans were milled by the KPCU, which also acted as wholesale buyer. The coffee was sold at auction and exported, mainly to Western Europe.

At independence, Kenya's Arabica production was growing rapidly. However, its exports were managed according to the 1962 International Coffee Agreement, a producers' cartel and quota system. Under this agreement, Kenya would grow and

Western countries buy a fixed amount of coffee, 45,000 tonnes in 1963–4, which matched Kenya's current production, but was far lower than the 70,000 tonnes expected when newly planted trees matured (after six to eight years). There were markets elsewhere, but they were small and prices were lower. As a result, even before independence the government had banned all new coffee planting, fearing over-dependence on a crop with few growth opportunities. Nonetheless, overproduction was inevitable, as controls on plantings broke down during the rush to independence.

Smallholder coffee acreage expanded between 1961 and 1967 to 130,000 acres – nearly double the 75,000 acres of European estates. By the late 1960s, smallholders produced nearly 60 per cent of Kenya's coffee. Most smallholder growers were in Central Province, Embu and Meru, where land consolidation was more advanced and growers had the incentive to invest in slow maturing, high-yielding crops. The government tried to limit smallholder plantings, but enforcement was weak. There was a growing conflict of interest between small producers and European estates (who were generally higher-quality producers), as more coffee meant unsold stocks or lower prices. There was widespread resistance to planting controls, especially in Murang'a, where land consolidation problems had delayed coffee planting. Particularly tricky was the fact that many of the largest growers were ex-Home Guard and chiefly families. The government had to broker between the long-term interests of the sector and the interests of its supporters. In 1967, Kenyatta compromised, abandoning the uprooting of illegal plantings.[112] An outbreak of disease in 1967–8 gave the government breathing space (see Figure 3.2), as production fell, retrospectively rationalising Kenyatta's political decision.

Tea was Kenya's third export at independence after coffee and sisal, mainly produced on large higher-altitude plantations by British multinationals and exported to London. The Brooke Bond group, Liptons and other European concerns dominated the industry and controlled blending, packing, marketing and export. The Tea Board of Kenya set policy.

As with coffee, Kenya embarked on a significant expansion of tea production in 1964, to be grown by smallholders and managed by the new Kenya Tea

3.2: Coffee and tea production, 1961–70

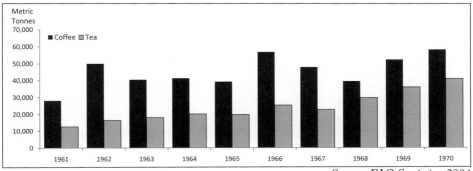

Source: FAO Statistics, 2004

Development Authority (KTDA). Funded by the CDC, West Germany and the Kenyan government, the KTDA was more administratively self-contained than most parastatals. It also incorporated elected growers' representatives in its management.[113] Over the next few years, it established a network of tea factories around the country for African smallholders. Between 1963 and 1970, production doubled and smallholder tea grew from 6 per cent of production in 1964–5 to 20 per cent in 1969–70. The result was a dramatic expansion in exports, earning Kenya 18 per cent of its foreign exchange by 1969.[114]

The Sugar Industry

Sugar cane had been grown in Kenya in small quantities since 1902, and two small Asian-owned sugar mills had been built at Miwani near Kisumu and at Ramisi on the coast, but Kenya imported most of its refined sugar requirements. Now, the government led a dramatic expansion in the industry. Cane production tripled between 1963 and 1969, as new sugar factories and sugar-growing schemes provided opportunities for import substitution, cash-crop farming and local employment alike. The government's target was sugar self-sufficiency by 1970. The country was expected to be a relatively low-cost producer once the factories were completed and the estates matured.

The process began with the construction of two large projects at Chemelil and Muhoroni, both in Central Nyanza. The Chemelil factory was built between 1965 and 1968 with British and West German aid. Managed by Booker Tate but owned by the government, it could process 2,000 tonnes of cane a day, and provided a market for private 'outgrowers' (local farmers under contract) in Nyanza and Nandi. Its smaller neighbour Muhoroni (part-owned by the Mehta group) began operating in 1966. Work also began on a large factory at Mumias, originally to be built by the Russians, an idea abandoned in 1964. The government considered the Mumias scheme marginal financially, but was keen to develop western Kenya for political reasons.[115] There was no cosy British 'stitch-up' of such investment opportunities, but rather open competition between British, West German, Italian and Chinese companies and governments to fund and build the scheme.

Other Cash-Crops

Other cash-crops of significance to Kenya did not follow the same pattern of investment and steady growth, but rather cycles of growth and decline, reflecting unstable world trading conditions and local production constraints. Sisal was grown mostly for export, on large estates in marginal lands, with the largest production in Taita-Taveta district. As with tea, most estates were British-owned and most exports went to London. Demand was in decline at independence, however, and the product was unsuitable for smallholder agriculture. Production fell from 70,000 tonnes in 1963 to fewer than 50,000 tonnes in 1970. Another traditional export was wattle bark, which had been planted both on large estates and by Central Province smallholders, but here too demand was in long-term decline.

In the colonial era, some Nyanza and Coast farmers had grown cotton for export. It was also becoming a favourite of state irrigation schemes, run by the new National Irrigation Board. Production was expected to grow rapidly under the direction of its parastatal, the Cotton Lint and Seed Marketing Board, but in practice returns remained low, and, after a jump in 1964–5, production remained flat at 15,000 tonnes until the 1970s.

Other important cash-crops included horticultural products, particularly pineapples grown for the Thika cannery, and cashewnuts, mostly grown on the Coast. Finally, there was pyrethrum, grown by smallholders at the highest altitudes in Central Province, the Rift Valley and Mount Elgon. Inevitably, a Pyrethrum Board controlled production, and a Pyrethrum Marketing Board controlled marketing and processing. In 1963, Kenya was the world's largest producer of pyrethrum.

Food and Famine

As with export cash-crops, the 1960s saw growth in food production, both in informal 'off book' home consumption and local trade (which could only be estimated), and formal sector production, mainly from the large farms, which passed through the marketing boards. The sale of agricultural products across district borders had been discouraged or banned by the colonial government, which emphasised local food security over integration into the market economy and the protection of settler markets. Although it rarely appeared on the export list, one food crop was critical to the survival of most Kenyans: maize. The Maize Marketing Board controlled the storage, distribution and marketing of maize, with prices set by the Agriculture Ministry to protect growers, with a goal of national self-sufficiency. From 1964 on, the government encouraged the use of higher-yielding maize varieties in the ex-white highlands. Other important food crops included rice, wheat, sorghum, millet, beans, potatoes, bananas, peas, sweet potatoes and cassava, while on the lake and at the coast, fishing was a key economic activity.

In 1965, the country suffered from food shortages and near-famine, following a year of low rains, which was exacerbated by the command and control economic structure and abuses in the marketing boards that ran maize distribution. More than a quarter of the country was affected and hundreds died. There was deep frustration at this, as a lack of storage facilities meant that surplus maize had been exported in 1964. On the positive side, Kenya imported maize from the US and Tanzania, created a national famine relief committee and solicited food aid from relief agencies. Aid, combined with a strong government response, with convoys of famine relief sent to affected areas, avoided many deaths. It was the first of many cycles of boom and bust in the maize industry.

Meat and milk products were also important sources of nutrition. Most meat was consumed locally, but a small proportion was marketed and exported, mainly from large British-owned beef ranches and the pastoral areas. Most beef and pork passed through parastatals for slaughter and processing. Milk and dairy production was another growth sector. The industry remained dominated by the KCC, which handled more than 90 per cent of formal-sector dairy sales (most produced in the ex-scheduled areas), although most milk was still consumed locally. 'Africanisation' of the dairy industry was actively supported by the state, with improved milk-producing stock, veterinary services, cattle dips and husbandry advice for smallholders, particularly in Central Province.

Cooperatives in Trouble

The country inherited a strong agricultural cooperative movement, closely linked with the marketing boards. It promoted cooperatives to help fulfil its development promises, and between 1963 and 1966 nearly 200 were registered every year. By 1967, there were 1,800 cooperatives, though probably only half were operating.[116] Almost all small-farm coffee, pyrethrum and dairy production went through the cooperatives, which were most active in Central and Nyanza provinces.

While the large super-unions such as the KPCU and KCC flourished, however, many local cooperatives were soon in trouble. Many failed because they were too small, under-capitalised or operated in hostile environments, while others were politicised or mismanaged. State regulation was weak, and some suffered from repeated embezzlement by officials.[117] The 1966 Cooperatives Act sought to clean up the situation. What had been free market entities were now subject to the organising hand of the state, from primary producers through district-wide unions to the national societies. The district unions became a key part of the government's agricultural policy machinery.[118]

Labour and the Trade Unions

The new government faced a significant trade union 'problem'. The unions were well organised and influential. They had resources, foreign contacts, an independent agenda and the power to affect the economy directly. Moreover, most workers' organisations had a more natural affinity with the socialist inclinations of the 'Odinga wing' than the Kenyatta or Mboya line. Now, facing a government determined to stamp its authority on society, which was also the largest employer in the country, the unions were unable to prevent the destruction of their freedoms and of the collective bargaining system built under British rule.

Controlling wages and avoiding industrial action was an immediate government priority. Ex-labour leader Mboya now took the view that trade unionists were a 'relatively small, privileged minority'.[119] In February 1964, the government initiated the first of three tripartite agreements with the Federation of Kenya Employers (FKE) and the trade unions. It promised extra jobs for the rising number of unemployed, to be provided by employers increasing their staffing by 10 per cent and the government by 15 per cent. In return, the unions agreed to a wage freeze and a no-strike deal for a year. According to official figures, 40,000 of the 205,000 registered unemployed obtained some sort of job in the next year, though how many were later discharged is unknown. The real benefit of such schemes was extremely questionable.

Meanwhile, the conflict between the pro-Mboya and pro-Odinga factions in the KFL became more acute. Clement Lubembe had taken over from Mboya as secretary-general, and continued to support the KFL's link with the ICFTU, which in turn continued to support the moderate unions financially. Other unions, led by Luo firebrand Denis Akumu of the Dock Workers' Union in Mombasa, opposed this 'neo-colonialist' linkage. Factionalism was at its peak during 1964–5, when the national struggle was at its height, as Mboya's enemies tried to weaken his control over the movement.[120] Ethnicity played a part in the structure of these factions, but they were rarely mono-ethnic.[121]

Despite the government's refusal to recognise the legitimacy of splinter unions, in April 1964 Akumu led the creation of a competing union federation to the KFL, the Kenya Federation of Progressive Trades Unions, later renamed the Kenya African Workers Congress (KAWC). The new federation's leadership, which openly targeted Mboya, was a roll call of Odinga supporters.[122] It affiliated to the World Federation of Trades Unions, the socialist/communist union body, and received funding from there and from Odinga. The KAWC also received some support from Kenyatta, as he was still concerned about Mboya's power in 1963–4.[123] The KAWC achieved some success, rallying more unions to its cause, and the conflict with the KFL continued until June 1965, when the government banned meetings by either organisation and appointed a cross-factional ministerial committee to recommend a long-term solution. By this time, however, Kenyatta was unwilling to see Odinga's team victorious.

In September 1965, the government imposed a unification of the warring factions and simultaneously took over the trade union movement. It deregistered both the KFL and KAWC and established a new organisation, the Central Organisation of Trade Unions (COTU). This was a 'union of unions' of the Eastern European variety, where the president ratified the election of its leaders. Kenyatta announced that COTU would affiliate with neither East nor West, and appointed leaders from both factions to the new organisation, trying to limit dissent. The election-winner Lubembe became COTU secretary-general, while Akumu became his deputy. State influence over the unions grew and union leaders began to be incorporated into the patron–client system. While a superficial unity was imposed, however, the roots of the dispute remained, in national politics and in perceptions of the role of trade unionism in an African state.

The same year, the Trades Disputes Act extended the colonial ban on strikes in essential services and barred sympathetic strikes. It provided for forced arbitration, and allowed the minister for labour to ban strikes that did not follow the proper procedure.[124] The Industrial Court, established in 1964, was the venue for this arbitration. In compensation, the check-off system was mandated, whereby union dues were deducted from wages at source. The split in the union movement meant they could not unite to oppose these changes. The limits of union power compared to the late colonial days were already clear.

Harambee!

Despite the disputes about political and economic direction, all agreed that Kenya was developing and that independence was delivering some of the expectations it had nurtured. However, it could never deliver them all. KANU had promised a heady cocktail of 'medical and hospital services, old age and disability benefits, free and universal primary education, benefits for the unemployed, and financial aid to all who need and merit it for university work'.[125] In practice, many of the promised services were jam tomorrow, not today. There was some free medical care and free university education, but only for the very few who could obtain it. Primary and secondary education remained mostly fee-paying, and available only to a minority. As the government admitted, 'to provide them fully and freely now would bankrupt the nation and mortgage economic growth for generations'.[126]

Facing impossible demands for access to services and particularly to education, the government encouraged a system of self-help known as *harambee* in Swahili. *Harambee* was Kenyatta's rallying cry and approach: the use of collective fundraising and voluntary work to build schools, cattle dips, clinics and dispensaries where the state was unable to provide them. *Harambee* offered three advantages as a state philosophy. First, it provided a real avenue for local development, responsive to local priorities, in a situation where the state was unable to deliver. Second, it diverted expectations away from the government, and therefore earthed tensions that might have sparked protest. Third, it established a culture whereby the wealthy and influential would contribute to their rural communities rather than spending funds in the cities or abroad, reinforcing the emerging patron–client structures.[127] Since virtually all funds were spent in the location where they were collected, *harambee* was effectively a redistributive savings scheme, reinvesting its collections into local services.

Rural women's groups were the core of the *harambee* movement. Self-help groups had long provided local communal functions (such as land clearing and rotational *shamba* work). These were now deemed to be *harambee* activities, regulated by the local community development officer. From the start, although most efforts and most contributions were local, projects were also sources of political credit, both for local politicians through their initiation and fundraising (as evidence of their wealth and connections), and for national-level leaders (if they were subsequently taken over and funded by central government). *Harambee* also posed real problems, because its unplanned nature meant that some projects were unsustainable, or competed for scarce resources with other operations. As the years passed, many projects failed or were taken over by the state, and few large projects remained genuine self-help operations in the long term.

The projects created through *harambee* varied with the needs of the community. At independence, rural health services were often far away, and only for those who could afford to pay. Dispensaries and health centres were therefore a common demand. Given the choice, though, education was how Kenyans chose to spend their money, and *harambee* was the foundation of a huge increase in the number of schools in the 1960s. Kenya's pre-independence history had demonstrated the 'first mover advantage' of education.

The Dash for Education in the 1960s

At independence, the country was in desperate need of a better-educated African workforce. Kenyatta had committed to fight against 'poverty, ignorance and disease', and improving African access to education was a critical tool in achieving all of these. Over the next seven years, the numbers passing through primary education increased by 45 per cent, while secondary education increased four-fold (see Figure 3.3). This was a political necessity, but it was expensive. The percentage of the budget devoted to education rose from less than 10 to 20 per cent by 1972. KANU had promised seven years of free primary education, and that secondary education would be available for half the eligible students. However, in practice, it could barely keep up with the growth in the population.

In 1964, a special Education Commission was established, to review how the education system could be used to build national identity, encourage racial and ethnic intermixing and support development. The resulting Ominde Report recommended a unified education system for all races and a common curriculum, with all church high schools under government control. It also proposed the use of English as the primary language for teaching, with Swahili supported as a national language. The integration of religious and racially specific schools happened quickly on paper, but it took a decade to create true integration.[128]

Under colonial rule, primary education had begun anywhere between the ages of six and 15, depending on exposure to Christianity, the proximity of a school, the availability of cash for fees, children's cattle-herding obligations and *moran*-ship. It was mostly the

3.3: Primary and secondary school enrolment, 1960–70

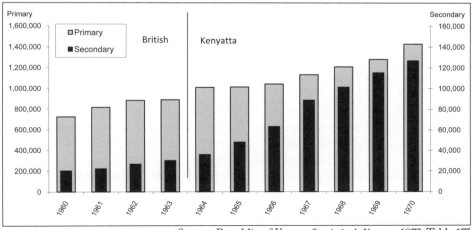

Source: Republic of Kenya, *Statistical Abstract*, 1972, Table 175

responsibility of the churches, councils and local communities. By 1965, the state could report that enrolments had reached one million pupils. In 1967, the Education Ministry introduced a new Certificate of Primary Education and a standardised syllabus. State control increased with the 1968 Education Act, which converted most church schools into state institutions. By 1970, nearly 1.5 million children were in primary school (see Figure 3.3). These were significant changes, but the goal of universal primary education was still far away, and school fees remained in effect. Access to primary education also remained uneven by both region and gender. Most school-age Kikuyu in Central were in primary school, but the proportion was far lower in the Rift Valley, Coast and North-East.[129] Only a third of primary pupils were girls.

The change was even more dramatic at the secondary level. Until independence, only a tiny proportion of children could aspire to secondary schooling, which began anywhere from the ages of 14 to 20. Now, the number of government-funded secondary schools tripled between 1963 and 1968, reflecting the growing numbers flowing through the primary system and the intense demand for further education, as secondary leavers were generally successful in getting jobs. However, no more than a quarter of primary leavers could go to secondary school.

Harambee was particularly important in the establishment of secondary schools. Parents, churches and local communities funded much of Kenya's education boom. Of the 783 secondary schools in 1970, more than half were unaided, almost all built since independence.[130] The Kikuyu areas were the most committed, reflecting their long history of private schools. Private businesses also competed with state and *harambee* schools by building fee-paying schools. Kenyans invested much of their newfound wealth in the 1960s and 1970s in education, although this decision, curiously, may not have been to their collective advantage in the absence of a booming job market. The individual advantages of education declined once many had access to it.

While building a *harambee* school was easy, funding its teachers and services was harder, and a high proportion of peasant incomes went into school-building and school operation. Quality was extremely variable, and some districts saw competing building projects pushed by political factions, consuming resources to uncertain benefit.[131] By 1966, Mboya was demanding that *harambee* school-building cease entirely and by 1968 the regulations surrounding unaided schools had tightened. In the same year, the state reluctantly agreed to offer limited aid and inspection services for *harambee* schools. It was also possible for the government to take over schools entirely and incorporate them into the state system, but this was not common.

In 1967, the government introduced a new East African Certificate of Education as the secondary leaver's qualification. The school curriculum was modified from colonial times, emphasising African rather than European history and placing more emphasis on technical and science subjects. The last two years of secondary education (Forms V and VI) were declared free in 1965. These ended in 'A'-levels and, for around 80 per cent of those who qualified, university.

Access to secondary education remained even more unequally distributed. Two-thirds of students were male, as girls were less likely to have gone to primary school, or to be funded for secondary education. Indeed, the percentage of female secondary pupils fell during the 1960s, from 35 per cent in 1960 to only 25 per cent in 1967, as families who could now afford to send one child to secondary school sent a boy first. Amongst government-assisted secondary schools, regional inequalities in access to education also grew. The advantage that Central and Nyanza Provinces had in 1960 was perpetuated, and Central's lead grew further.[132] The nomadic pastoralists had virtually no schools at all. This limited the opportunities for formal sector employment and the trickle-down development of these regions.[133]

The rapid increase in schools and pupils also required more teachers, of which there was a huge shortage. In 1967, the government established a Teachers' Service Commission, responsible for the recruitment, promotion and pay of public teaching staff. At this time, foreign teachers provided the backbone of higher education, with US Peace Corps and the Commonwealth schemes supplementing local staff. Between 1963 and 1966, the percentage of secondary school teachers with a degree or equivalent qualification fell from 67 to 52 per cent. Most *harambee* schools could not afford good enough teachers or facilities and the pass level in secondary examinations fell between 1965 and 1970, after *harambee* schools began entering children.

As a partial replacement for secondary education, the government launched the National Youth Service (NYS) in 1964. It was billed as an opportunity for unemployed young men to learn self-reliance by engaging in military training and development projects. Its real aim was probably to offer a constructive outlet for radical Kikuyu youth.[134] It was led by a prominent school head, but Kenyatta's private intelligence chief Waruhiu Itote was assistant-director and Kikuyu MP J. M. Kariuki was its chairman. The churches too sought to help jobless primary leavers, establishing village polytechnics to teach useful trades. The state also provided technical training at the Kenya Polytechnic and trade schools.

Access to university education expanded rapidly as well. With the establishment of the University of East Africa in 1963, the Royal Technical College became University College Nairobi. For those that could get there, university education was free, a luxury Kenya was later unable to afford. Enrolments to Nairobi quadrupled to over 2,000 between 1963–4 and 1969–70, and many Kenyans also attended Dar-es-Salaam and Makerere colleges. Although racially unbalanced, the university did not suffer from obvious tribalism or ethnic quotas. A university education abroad remained the main prize, however. The state issued bursaries to deserving students, while others were helped by the continuation of the Mboya and Odinga airlifts. There were 2,900 Kenyans studying abroad in 1967, far more than before independence, though possession of a university degree still placed its owner in a tiny, privileged elite.

The 'Reds' and the 'Blacks'[135]

Most political and economic choices during 1964 and 1965 were dominated by the growing conflict between 'radicals' and 'conservatives' inside KANU. Odinga, Kaggia and Achieng-Oneko represented the radicals, with Odinga the centre of attention as

Kenyatta's potential successor. Kenyatta and Mboya (supported by Njonjo, Mungai, Koinange, McKenzie, Gichuru, Kiano and Moi) came to represent the conservatives, with Kenyatta swinging gradually towards the West during 1964. It was a complex alignment of personal interests, external alliances and underlying disputes over political direction.

Odinga was the centre of this storm. He was the leader of most of the Luo community, a gifted orator though not a great organiser. Kenyatta owed his freedom and his presidency to Odinga's courage in 1958, and Odinga had given him unstinting support since. Odinga's links with the Eastern Bloc, which were to prove his downfall, were an asset as long as Kenyatta believed they would be used to help Kenya and to counteract Mboya's pro-American influence. Much depended on the Eastern Bloc's ability to deliver material assistance and on Odinga's personal loyalty. The government had decided on its pro-British, gradualist course during 1962–3, however, and a change of direction was increasingly difficult. Kenyatta had long been suspicious of Odinga's communist links, in part from his own experience of the Comintern in the 1930s. In late 1964 or early 1965, advised by the British, Kenyatta decided that Odinga and the radicals must go.

Kenya briefly became a battleground in the Cold War, and the US CIA, the Israelis, the British, the Russians, the Chinese and the East Europeans all installed intelligence agents in their Nairobi embassies. Kenya was the safest and easiest centre for East African operations, given the high number of Europeans in the country and its comparative development. More importantly, it was far from clear what course the country was going to take. The British had outflanked the 'reds' in 1962–3 by allying with Kenyatta, but there were still many opportunities. The result was a competition of increasing aggressiveness, involving phone tapping, propaganda, diplomatic lobbying and even violence, which peaked in 1964–5. The British favoured Kenyatta and Njonjo. The Russians and Chinese backed Odinga and Kaggia. The Americans backed Mboya. These alignments reinforced and deepened internal differences on policy and came in time to dominate them.

The conflict had been building since 1960, but the crisis of 1964–5 was to skew Kenyan politics for decades, split KANU in two and create a gulf between Luo and Kikuyu communities that continues to this day. Rightly or wrongly, Kenyatta came to believe that Odinga and the radicals were not just campaigning for a more left-wing policy, but plotting to oust him. When this personal threat was combined with Kenya's military dependence on Britain, its need for financial support from the West and the criticality of sustaining his land settlement policy, Kenyatta was forced to take a side.

Mboya, Odinga, Kenyatta and Kaggia

The emerging conflict between Odinga and Kenyatta and between communism and capitalism overlapped with different disputes over leadership within the Luo and Kikuyu. There had been little love lost between the most senior Luo leaders Odinga and Mboya, and they had intrigued against each other since 1958. While Odinga represented a rural, nationalist Luo identity, Mboya reflected a more detribalised, cosmopolitan, worker-oriented future. Odinga never accepted that Mboya, 15 years his junior, could lead him, underestimating his determination. As he admitted later, 'I never took Mboya seriously.'[136] But Mboya proved an implacable foe. In the same way, Kaggia was one of the few remaining challenges to Kenyatta's pre-eminence amongst the Kikuyu. He and Kenyatta had been detained together, but Kaggia had genuinely been a Mau Mau organiser. Their relationship in detention had deteriorated and there was no love lost after their release.

There was, however, an imbalance between the two forces in both their levels of elite support and their personal qualities. Odinga and Kaggia were noted for their speaking abilities, their openness and concern for the common man, but neither was noted for his organisational skills or political tactics. The pro-Western leaders had captivating speakers too, Kenyatta and Mboya particularly, while Mboya and Njonjo gave them a crucial organisational edge. They too believed right was on their side, but that theirs was a more difficult truth to present. Therefore, they needed to ensure that the 'right' answer prevailed, even though it was less palatable to the African majority, for whom the simpler messages of redistributive socialism had great appeal. This would not, therefore, be a fair fight.

Struggles in Murang'a and the Sacking of Kaggia in 1964

In Murang'a, there was a particularly bitter conflict during 1964 with local and national ramifications. Factional political conflict had surfaced in 1962 between Julius Kiano and others who backed Kenyatta's 'forgive and forget' strategy, and the returning ex-detainees. In 1963, Kaggia had been elected as the KANU MP for Kandara in Murang'a, and Kenyatta had appointed him as a parliamentary secretary (while Kiano became a minister). However, Kaggia was openly dissatisfied with the government's land and settlement policies and the prominence of former Home Guards within the administration. Local issues and factional struggles added to the growing national divide.

Kaggia's time in government was brief, as he soon transgressed on several fronts. First, he was a strong campaigner for East African federation. In May 1964, Kaggia chaired the meeting of Kenyan and Tanzanian delegates that resolved on immediate federation. More fundamentally, he was dismissive of the independence land deal, and critical of the use of 'willing buyer, willing seller' arrangements to transfer large farms into African hands. He wanted white settler land confiscated and used to resettle landless Africans on cooperative farms. His protests extended as far the organisation of active resistance to land registration and consolidation in Murang'a. This infuriated Kenyatta. In May 1964, Kenyatta warned Kaggia that he was 'seriously concerned at your repeated attacks on the policies of the Ministry of Lands and Settlement, and with your interference with land consolidation at Fort Hall'.[137] Kaggia refused to give assurances of future obedience, and on 15 June 1964 Kenyatta sacked him. It was a portent of the greater crisis to come.

The pro- and anti-Kaggia struggle in Murang'a continued. The radicals won KANU branch elections in August 1964, but the result was two competing sets of party officials. The conflict spilled over into the cooperatives and community development organisations, an example of the fluid, multilayered competition that was to become characteristic of Kenyan politics, in which short-term alliances and personal interests could counterbalance or overcome longer-term differences.

The Lure of the East

Both the Soviet Union and China saw East Africa as fertile ground for revolutionary change, and had built good relations and financial links with many African leaders before independence. Odinga is believed to have accepted large sums of money – up to US$1 million – from the Russians and Chinese, though such claims are hard to verify. Conservatives such as Moi regularly claimed that the radicals had access to communist funds, a view that was shared by Kenyan, British and American intelligence. In March 1966, for example, Moi claimed that Odinga had used GB£400,000 in an attempt to subvert the government during 1964.[138] In return, the Russians and Chinese – in competition more than cooperation – saw a potential future president of Kenya. They encouraged him to seize power democratically or, if necessary, by more direct means.

Although he was the frontman for the radicals, Odinga was far from alone. Many others in KANU such as Keen were open communists. Keen had visited Russia in 1962, and had helped obtain military training for students in Eastern Europe and Russia.[139] Ngei too was an ally at this time; Odinga and Ngei jointly addressed a rally in Machakos in September 1964 where a Russian also spoke, publicly cementing their socialist alliance.

A key figure in Odinga's camp was Pio da Gama Pinto. A young Goan journalist, trade unionist and activist with ties to China and the Soviet Union, he was unique amongst Kenyan Asians in his personal commitment to the nationalist cause. Pinto was alleged by the British security services to have been involved in several murders in 1952–3 and to have helped obtain arms for Mau Mau.[140] He was detained until 1959, one of the few Asians to be held by the British for involvement in Mau Mau. Even before independence, the British were monitoring the activities of KANU radicals with Eastern Bloc links, and they watched Pinto particularly closely. He had helped organise the Russian student airlifts, and had helped finance KANU's 1963 election campaign. An avowed communist, he ran the pro-radical Pan-African Press, and was a close ally of Odinga's.[141] Elected as a Specially Elected MP in 1964, he was also popular amongst backbenchers.

The British-led and trained security forces were also watching Odinga before independence, and surveillance intensified during 1964–5. Odinga's work to secure military training for Kenyan youth was of particular concern. In the build-up to independence, more than 400 Kenyans, the majority of them Luo, had received military training in communist countries, and this process continued thereafter. It is unlikely however, that this was a Luo pro-Odinga strike force, as has sometimes been implied. On 24 April 1964, another group of Kenyan 'students' left for Eastern Europe for military training. Just as with the Bulgarian airlift of November 1963, these were not predominately Luo: 79 of the 105 were Kikuyu; only nine were

Luo.[142] Again, the airlift was organised without the knowledge of the ministries of Education or Defence. Despite the deal with the British, it seems that some KANU leaders were still trying to build alternative security forces loyal to them, using the Eastern Bloc rather than the West.

Western Anti-Communist Activity in Kenya

The struggle in Kenya merged with the broader anti-communist crusade of the US during Lyndon Johnson's presidency (1963–8). US CIA activities in East Africa remain classified, but were extensive during 1964–6. Worried that communists had made significant progress in the region, American concern grew after the Zanzibar coup and Nyerere's turn to the East.

American aid was now explicitly a tool of US foreign policy, a 'political weapon' to assist their friends.[143] The Americans were therefore keen to fund projects such as the National Youth Service, to avoid them becoming communist 'indoctrination' groups.[144] The US also provided humanitarian support via USAID and the Peace Corps, and used the Voice of America to build support for its worldview, along with cultural exchanges and scholarship programmes. The scale of this should not be over-emphasised, though; this was a political, not an economic or military conflict. Kenya was not an American military ally or even of particular strategic interest, and USAID's aid to Kenya was less than US$4 million in 1966. There was no direct military assistance, though visits by US warships to Mombasa helped remind Kenyans of their 'powerful friends'.[145]

However, the US did provide covert assistance – financial, intelligence and organisational – to help defeat Odinga and the leftists, whom they saw as irredeemably associated with communism and therefore a legitimate target.[146] How much assistance they provided and in what form is uncertain. The Americans are known to have passed on intelligence – when it suited them – to the Kenyan security services on communist activity. Mboya was their major conduit for financial support. Mboya's biographer David Goldsworthy revealed that Mboya continued to receive US donations from covert sources throughout 1965, despite Kenyatta's requests that US labour funding for him cease. He was alleged to have distributed GB£15,000 at political functions in South Nyanza in the crucial month of February 1965.[147] Radicals sometimes referred to him as the 'American Ambassador'.[148] The US also organised and funded the Peace with Freedom cultural organisation. This built up an academic and cultural infrastructure in 1963–4, including the Jomo Kenyatta Educational Institute and the East African Publishing House, to establish an anti-communist but African set of institutions that would ensure that 'there is no other gap which some other country or ideology could fill.'[149] It was probably a CIA front.

The British also took an anti-communist view, though in a more guarded form. They concentrated their advice and support on Kenyatta, Njonjo and McKenzie. Kenyatta had given them effective command of the army, and relied on them for military and intelligence support, which left them in an unrivalled position to influence the establishment. They were far more influential than the higher-profile Americans, whose heavy-handed and (to their eyes) uninformed initiatives they often resented.

The Israelis were also involved in a covert contest with the Chinese security services inside Kenya. Israel had built military links with the Kenyans in the early 1960s, and assisted Kenya's government by disclosing information on China's intelligence operations.[150] In 1965, based on Israeli or American intelligence, Kenya closed the Nairobi offices of the New China News Agency, and expelled several Chinese diplomats for spying in 1967.

The Lumumba Institute

In December 1964, KANU established a new training centre for party officials in Nairobi, known as the Lumumba Institute. It was designed ostensibly to strengthen the party, and Kenyatta and Odinga were its joint trustees. However, it was also another move in the 'grand game' that was unfolding inside KANU. Its chairman was Kaggia, and its board membership was a roll call of radicals, including Pinto and Murumbi. KANU Secretary-General Mboya was explicitly excluded from its leadership.[151]

Although the institute was genuinely a training school, it also had hidden objectives: to inculcate African socialist and communist principles. The Soviet Union and East Germany funded and equipped the institute directly, and its lecturers included Russians and Kenyans trained in Russia. The institute's first and only course ran from March to June 1965. To attend it, Odinga and Kaggia selected more than 100 KANU district officials. Not only was the institute a platform for the radicals in their fight with Mboya, it may also have been preparing a cadre of students for mass action. Although Odinga himself denied such a hidden agenda, there were allegations that Chinese and South African communists were using the institute as a training ground for radicals to take over KANU.[152] Almost immediately after its foundation, the US warned Kenyatta of the risks he was taking. It was to be the last time Kenyatta associated himself with any radical initiative.

Military Preparations?

By the end of 1964, a crisis was brewing. Despite his loyalty to Odinga, Kenyatta was increasingly aligned with the pro-Western group. His security forces – fed by Western intelligence – were convinced that the radicals were considering direct action. Some believed that Odinga and his allies were preparing the Eastern Bloc-trained KANU youth for trouble and importing weapons to arm them.

In October 1964, Police Chief Hinga reported to Kenyatta that Special Branch officers had discovered a secret flight bringing 21 Kenyans back from military training in Czechoslovakia. They were taken to Odinga's Home Affairs Ministry, to disperse and wait until they were called for. Airport officials were refused access to the cargo. The aircraft offloaded cases and boxes, at least one of which the British reported as containing Russian heavy machine guns, which were delivered to the Home Affairs Ministry.[153] These rumours were made public in the British *Sunday Telegraph* in

November, though their access to such sensitive intelligence increases the possibility that the stories were 'plants' prepared by British intelligence to convince Kenyatta of Odinga's intentions. Odinga claimed later that he, Kenyatta and Murumbi had jointly ordered the weapons before independence, to allow the government to equip the police independently of Britain.[154] It is still not clear where the truth lies. In December 1964, Odinga was also using his Eastern Bloc-trained forces to lead 'forest clearance' exercises in Nyanza, which the British believed disguised paramilitary force training.[155] There is evidence that Odinga was planning some form of action, but, equally, there is also evidence that the British and Americans were trying to convince Kenyatta that this was occurring, as a way of turning Kenyatta to the right.

The Crisis of February–April 1965

With the growing polarisation in the country, the hostile camps prepared for a showdown. Over a few weeks in February–April 1965, a possible military threat to Kenyatta's government was deterred, and Kenya's commitment to a pro-Western development and security strategy was decisively reaffirmed.

In early 1965, Kenyatta instructed Economic Planning and Development Minister Mboya and his assistant minister, Nyeri-born Nairobi MP Mwai Kibaki, to prepare a policy paper on African socialism. Its goal was to make explicit that Kenya would chart the mixed capitalist route, rather than the more radical brand Odinga supported.[156] This was to become *Sessional Paper No. 10*. First drafted by an American expatriate adviser to the Kenyan government, it described a mixed socialist and capitalist model, rejecting both Marxism and *laissez-faire* capitalism, and stressing African traditions, equality and social justice. Kenyatta made it clear in his introduction to the paper that the intent was not to stimulate discussion on Kenya's economic policy, but to end it.[157]

In response, Odinga called a secret meeting at the Lumumba Institute that included MPs and trade unionists Achieng-Oneko, Kaggia, J. D. Kali, Akumu, Oprong Oduya, Ochola Mak'Anyengo, Henry Wariithi, and Tom Okelo-Odongo. All bar Wariithi were later to join the opposition. The group agreed that Pinto would prepare a competing paper, to be tabled at the same time, and resolved to organise backbench MPs to reject the government paper. The plan was then to move a motion of 'no confidence' in the government, and Wariithi and Pinto were asked to approach backbenchers to seek their support.[158] Kenyatta became aware of their plans soon after (the security services were bugging at least one of Odinga's houses). Before the launch of the sessional paper in April 1965, however, much had changed.

On 24 February 1965, Pinto was murdered outside his home in Nairobi. Special Branch officers or auxiliaries loyal to Kenyatta almost certainly carried out the killing, though nothing was ever proven.[159] There were echoes of recent high-profile assassinations in the US. Two youths were arrested and charged, and one, 21-year-old Kamba Kisilu Mutua, was convicted and sentenced to death in June 1965. His sentence was commuted to life imprisonment, and he remained in jail for the next 37 years.

That politics was behind the killing was clear. Wanyoike Thungu, Kenyatta's bodyguard, had recently warned Pinto that he would be killed if he did not flee the country. A few hours before his murder, Pinto told his house servant 'a man had been offered money to kill him, Kaggia and Kali.'[160] Thirty years later, more details emerged as to how and why Pinto had died, as part of an attempt by the Moi government to remind Kenyans of the darker side of the Kenyatta regime. Mutua always claimed that police officers had murdered Pinto and had used him (a vegetable seller who had been arrested before for minor offences) as their fall guy. Special Branch had recruited him as an informer and had placed him at the scene of the crime. This was known to other policemen, including Chief Inspector Patrick Shaw, the feared white police officer who was involved in many controversial events, and who took Mutua's first statement.[161] This statement (allegedly seen by a *Nation* reporter in the police archives) indicates police officers were involved in the killing and that he was framed.

Elements in the leadership or intelligence forces ensured the investigation did not proceed too far. Ten fingerprints on Pinto's car were not identified, and a getaway vehicle for the two or three Africans seen running from the scene was never traced. Individuals alleged to be police officers were arrested at the scene of the crime, yet released without charge and without police even recording their names.[162] Even when sentencing Mutua, trial judge Chief Justice Ainley accepted that he did not pull the trigger, but placed him at the murder scene as a companion of the killer, and convicted him on that alone.

Pinto's death removed a key figure in Odinga's camp. The murder also shocked many Kenyans, including Pinto's close friend Murumbi. It was an end of innocence for independent Kenya, and demonstrated the determination of Kenyatta's government to cling to power by any means, and of the commitment of Western countries to ensure that Kenya did not fall under communist influence. The British and US governments – in later years so outspoken on political issues – said nothing.

In early April 1965, the split between radicals and conservatives became open, as ministers battled each other in public and in the press over Kenya's commitments to socialism and non-alignment. On 2 April, the internal Assembly election to replace Pinto saw the shock defeat of KANU candidate Ndolo Ayah by an independent. The radicals were incensed, as the moderates had backed an independent, since Ayah was a Luo from Central Nyanza and close to Odinga. Radical Teso MP Oduya suggested this was evidence that KANU was finished, called on Kenyatta to resign and suggested it was time to start a new party.[163] At the same time, a conservative Kamba MP tabled a motion in the House that suggested that the trouble went even deeper. Thomas Malinda's motion alleged a plot to overthrow the state:

In view of the evidence that arms and ammunition are continuously being smuggled from communist and other foreign countries into or through Kenya for the purpose of staging an armed revolution to overthrow our beloved Government, or involving us in external conflict, this House urges the Government to use all means at its disposal to ensure that this secret plan is revealed and made public . . .[164]

The stakes were rising. Ngala claimed that foreign embassies were smuggling weapons into Kenya, and reports emerged that students studying in communist countries were receiving military training in order to overthrow the government.

Assistant minister Okelo-Odongo and minister Mboya were the main protagonists in the resulting media battle. In a speech at the Lumumba Institute on 6 April 1965, Okelo-Odongo proposed that Kenya 'must bend a little more to the Eastern Bloc at this moment' and suggested that some interpretations of African socialism seemed little different from capitalism.[165] Mboya countered in the press. Kenya was trading with both East and West, but policy must be based pragmatically on economic development, not on emotional and political considerations. The West was Kenya's main market, and Kenya had received far more aid from the UK, West Germany and the US than from elsewhere. Others preferred the public platform, with Kiano leading a rally in Murang'a that attacked 'troublemakers' wanting to destroy the government, while Achieng-Oneko claimed the British were inciting an ideological conflict and warned of civil war between Kikuyu and Luo. Everywhere, the two sides held rallies attacking communism or the free allocation of land, or demanding nationalisation of hotels, schools and industries. At the same time, Odinga and others were still trying to paper over the cracks, desperate to avoid a direct conflict with Kenyatta. Odinga denied on several occasions that there was a crisis in government, and scotched rumours that police had searched his offices.

On 11 April, Mboya admitted in public that factionalism was rife in the party and in Parliament. The same day, Kenyatta travelled to Murang'a to denounce Kaggia in Kandara. It was a decisive commitment to the conservative cause. He had heard talk of revolution in Kenya, Kenyatta suggested, but 'if any African wants to fight me, let him try.'[166] Then, in a widely quoted denunciation, he turned on Kaggia:

> We were together with Paul Ngei in jail. If you go to Ngei's home, he has planted a lot of coffee and other crops. What have you done for yourself? If you go to Kubai's home, he has a big house and has a nice shamba. Kaggia, what have you done for yourself? We were together with Kungu Karumba in jail, now he is running his own buses. What have you done for yourself?[167]

Although intended to reaffirm the virtues of investment and hard work, it was also a clear statement of the acquisitiveness of the elite, and of Kenyatta's rejection of the radicals. Facing calls to resign from KANU, Kaggia's response was firm: 'I was not elected to Parliament to obtain a big farm, a big house or a transport business. I was elected to represent my people.'[168] The police banned his next rally on 18 April, on government orders.

By early April 1965, Kenyatta, Njonjo and McKenzie had evidence that Odinga and his allies were planning some form of military action. Kenyatta had at least one agent in the Odinga group, who kept him informed of his opponents' plans. The government began to prepare for a coup attempt, which they expected in mid-April.[169] British Cabinet papers from the period confirm what was suspected: the British were willing to commit troops to defend Kenyatta's government.

Njonjo was the conduit for a request, made through MacDonald on 4 April, for the British to make troops and warships available to assist the government. The British Defence and Overseas Policy Cabinet Committee agreed to the request on 12 April.[170] The British were particularly concerned that Ngei – with his links to Kamba in the military – was in league with Odinga. Although they doubted that Odinga would actually strike, on 14 April 1965, the British confirmed, 'Ministers have agreed that Kenyatta may now be informed that in principle we would be ready to respond to a request for troops.'[171] They offered two infantry battalions, plus aircraft as a show of strength. This was subject to typically British conditions – the troops would not be used in active operations against the radicals, only to free up Kenyan forces to fight. The British also agreed to redeploy the SAS team training the police to defend Kenyatta in the event of an attempt on his life. They told Njonjo this on 14 April.[172]

As the crisis grew, the government sent the GSU into Central Nyanza between 8 and 10 April. There was a press blackout on their activities, which included house searches, beatings and rapes, which were only made public at the end of the month, when angry Luo MPs raised the issue in Parliament.[173] It was clear that the GSU were doing two things: searching for weapons and intimidating the Luo to forestall a rebellion. It was reported that arms were found in the house of a Gusii leader in Nyanza and at least one person was arrested, though what happened remains shrouded in secrecy. On 14 April, Njoroge Mungai, as defence minister, denied that any arms caches were found. However, the nature of his denials was made clear by his aside that the security forces could handle 'anything that comes along from any individuals'.[174] The British believed that 'three or four of Odinga's important supporters in Nyanza (such as the Russian-trained President of the Youth Wingers there) have been detained and that in raids on houses and other places some incriminating documents and arms have been found.'[175]

Meanwhile, on the night of 8 April, army units also searched the Home Office, and found crates of arms, including grenades and machine guns.[176] More searches uncovered weapons elsewhere in Nairobi, while the security forces sought urgent intelligence from the West about the youth who had received military training in the Eastern Bloc.[177]

The crisis was also associated with the arrival of a shipload of Russian weapons. Although the truth remains unclear, it is possible that the tanks, artillery, mortars, machine guns and ammunition aboard the freighter *Fizik Lebedev* may not originally have been intended for the army, but for the planned revolution. Radical politicians of the time confirm off the record that some form of action was planned. Mombasa was a centre of radicalism, and the Luo-led trade unions were extremely influential there. Odinga, who had organised the shipment with the Russians, only informed other ministers of their dispatch after the consignment was already at sea. In early April, Mungai denied rumours that the weapons were to be diverted away from the army and, by this time, it was probably true. Although a veneer of public relations was attached to the issue, it was a subject of extreme sensitivity and it is hard to explain events without a Cold War interpretation. It was arranged, for example, that

British and American warships would dock in Mombasa just before the Russian ship's arrival. HMS *Albion* arrived in harbour on 14 April, and the USS *Greenwich Bay* docked as the Russian ship was due to enter harbour.[178] Meanwhile, a 17-man Russian military delegation had also arrived in Nairobi on 15–16 April, headed by a KGB general.[179]

But the freighter was missing. It was due to arrive on 17 April, but for unexplained reasons the ship sailed on to Dar-es-Salaam instead.[180] When it finally appeared in Mombasa a week later, security forces sealed off the port. The *Nation* commented tellingly that the ship was riding very high in the water.[181] A complete news blackout was imposed until 28 April, when it was reported that the ship had finally berthed to discharge its consignment. Again, there was a revealing denial – that no cargo had been unloaded onto floating lighters while she was waiting to berth.[182]

Kenyatta met the Russian team on 28 April, briefed to expect trouble. Advised by the British as well as the Kenyan military, he insisted that the Russians hand over their arms to British, not African, officers (as they wished to do). The Russians then asked to be permitted to train the Kenyan army in the use of their weapons, but Kenyatta again refused – he (perhaps cynically) suggested he had been told it was a gift with no strings attached. Increasingly unhappy, Kenyatta then used reports that much of the equipment was of Second World War vintage to demand that the Kenyans inspect it before it was unloaded.[183] Under tight security, Mungai, Murumbi, McKenzie and British officers including army commander Brigadier Hardy inspected the weapons on board, and confirmed that much of the material was of little use without training, or duplicated equipment the army already had. When this was reported back, there was an intense argument between Odinga and Kenyatta, which nearly ended in blows.[184] On 29 April, Kenyatta called a press conference and officially rejected the weapons as they were 'old, secondhand, and would be of no use to the modern army of Kenya'.[185] The Russian ship sailed away, shadowed by the British security services. The Soviet military mission was ordered to leave, and British troops in Kenya kept on stand-by until they had departed.

The rejection of the weapons – combined with the internal crisis – was a crucial event. If the arms were for the revolution, they had been intercepted (though there were reports in May that more arms had come across Lake Victoria from Tanzania into Nyanza). The British army noted in military communiqués that the tanks on the ship had been fuelled, watered and 'ready to go', and that the small arms were ready for use.[186] Timothy Parsons in *The 1964 Army Mutinies* notes that 14 of the Czech-trained Kenyans had been trained on the same model of T-34 tanks as had arrived in Mombasa.[187] If the Russians had genuinely intended the weapons to go to the government, their hopes of breaking the British monopoly had failed. Their behaviour had angered Kenyatta, who believed the Russian ambassador had lied to him. It also led to serious doubts about Odinga amongst the Russians and Chinese. With this crisis over, and the government firmly in control, buttressed by military guarantees from the West, and with Odinga's credibility with Kenyatta irreparably damaged, the radicals' days inside KANU were numbered, a year before the formal break.

The government launched *Sessional Paper No. 10* on 27 April 1965. Kenyatta, Mboya, Kibaki and (curiously) Achieng-Oneko presented it to the House as government policy. It was overwhelmingly adopted, but privately many MPs were unhappy. The paper described a planned economy similar to that sought after in Europe at the time, with strong rent, price and wage controls, and duties and taxes used to direct the use of private property and limit profits. The government would determine which industries would be established. It accepted the right to nationalise unproductive assets or those that threatened the national interest, but rejected nationalisation of land or property indiscriminately or without compensation. While more industry was needed, it should not involve the replacement of labour by capital. The paper explicitly addressed the choice of development versus equality, and accepted that investment would be concentrated in the areas likely to lead to the greatest benefit for the country as a whole, even if this involved unequal treatment between regions. It flatly denied the existence of social classes: 'No class problem arose in the traditional African society and none exists today amongst Africans. The class problem in Africa, therefore is largely one of prevention.' [188]

Overall, the paper was a cogent statement of Kenya's problems and prospects, and offered an explicit state capitalist vision of development. It was far more left wing than the government was to become in practice, with headlines such as 'The marketing boards will be used to promote a socialist organisation of the country's economy.' [189] Like the KANU manifesto, *Sessional Paper No. 10* undertook that the government would 'consider the need and practicability of establishing ceilings on individual ownership of property'. [190] It emphasised cooperative farming, taxation policies to promote equality, development partnerships and a planned economy. Whether this approach represented the genuine beliefs of Kenyatta and others or a deliberate outflanking of the radicals is open to opinion. Its rosy view of the future was to suffer disappointment after disappointment over the decades, with most of its promises still not delivered 45 years later. In its emphasis on an open economy, however, and its encouragement of foreign investment, Kenya's strategy was to remain unaltered for decades.

Two days after, the radicals counterattacked. On 29 April, 50 students of the Lumumba Institute issued a press statement attacking the paper. It was to be a brief victory. Despite determined opposition from radical MPs, the next day Parliament passed a motion authorising the government to take over the institute from the party. With the security forces increasingly suspicious of its intentions, the institute represented too much of a threat. After the passing out of the first and only set of graduates (shouting, 'Kenya and Communism') the government closed it down. [191]

No Way through from Within, May–December 1965

The incorporation of KADU into KANU during 1964–5 had accelerated the process of division within the governing party and strengthened the conservatives. Ngala and the KADU leaders were more economically liberal and less socialist than Odinga or even Kibaki and Mboya, and their influx into the party – though not on generous terms – swung the balance against the radicals. Moi was chosen to lead the integration of KADU into KANU in the Rift Valley, and Ngala on the Coast, setting a conservative agenda in these regions. There was open conflict in areas such as Nakuru as the reorganisation proceeded during 1965, with the national party trying to force changes on officials in pro-Odinga KANU branches.

Odinga still controlled a dozen of Kenya's 41 party districts, mostly in the old KANU heartlands, but Secretary-General Mboya worked tirelessly to ensure that both radicals and personal opponents were removed from party posts by any means, gradually purging much of the leadership. Odinga was invulnerable in Central Nyanza, and Mboya could not dislodge Ngei or Muliro. Elsewhere, however, there was coup after coup. Between August 1964 and December 1965, KANU branch elections chose new officials in Murang'a, Kitui, South Nyanza, Mombasa, Machakos, Nakuru and Kisii districts, all radical areas. These coups were assisted by the use of police support to arrest troublesome opponents if needed. In Murang'a, Kaggia was removed in a coup in May 1965, and Achieng-Oneko was ousted from the Nakuru branch in August, while in Kisii, radical MP Zephaniah Anyiene's supporters were ousted by a coup organised by Gusii ministers. Invariably, the losers cried foul, claiming that Mboya and Njonjo (as the boss of the registrar of societies) were rigging the polls, resulting in two competing party branches in many districts.[192] Kenya was witnessing the emergence of its own bizarre combination of bureaucratic legalism and blatant illegality, executed in tandem by the same individuals.

Despite their numbers in the Assembly and their popular support, the pro-Odinga faction were unable to parry the government's tactics. Their patronage resources were limited, and they struggled to counter the combination of Kenyatta's personal and institutional authority and Mboya's brilliance and control of the party machinery. Many non-aligned backbenchers were fearful for their future and unwilling to challenge their patrons openly.

On 4 July 1965, the radicals tried a party coup of their own, when 27 radicals (including ex-Lumumba Institute students) took over KANU headquarters and called for the replacement of KANU's national officials. Officials from 22 district branches argued that, since no national elections had been held for years, nor any delegates' conference summoned, KANU's national officers were in office illegally. They therefore called their own KANU elections at the institute, which Muliro and Anyiene amongst others contested. The polls replaced all KANU officials except Kenyatta and Odinga. The radicals then moved to KANU headquarters to announce their coup at a press conference.[193] There, however, the police arrested them and charged them with illegally taking over the party's offices. Njonjo's response was harsh, with 24 of the accused jailed for up to 18 months. There was little doubt that the KANU officials were indeed illegally in office, but the government did not intend to allow it to become a public issue. Soon after, the government expelled a Chinese diplomat who had aided the operation.

Kenyatta's rejection of Odinga and his allies was now open. In early 1965, Kenyatta ceased wearing his Luo beaded cap, a symbolic rejection. Despite this, the Odinga faction continued to blame Mboya for their problems. With what seems a curious innocence in retrospect, they hoped that Kenyatta would eventually intervene to protect them.[194] For a long time, the Odinga faction did not realise the extent to which the president's own hand lay behind their troubles. Pro-Westerners did everything to equate Odinga's stance with communism and enslavement to the Eastern Bloc, and British and American diplomats continually warned Kenyatta of dangers from the left. On Madaraka Day, 1 June 1965, Kenyatta made a major speech that explicitly warned of 'imperialism from the east' and made it clear that 'To us Communism is as bad as imperialism.'[195] Soon after, Kenyatta replaced Odinga as the head of the Kenyan delegation to the Commonwealth Prime Ministers' Conference in London.

Although the government had not tried to legislate a one-party state, they certainly did not wish to face any formal opposition. By December 1964, Njonjo and the (European) registrar of societies had embarked on a quiet campaign to deregister all existing political organisations, to remove opportunities for the radicals to adopt them or for political activity to occur outside controlled channels. In March 1965, the Baluhya Political Union, KADU, the Taita-Taveta Union and several North-Eastern parties were all deregistered. Most of the remaining entities were closed down between May and December 1965.[196] Although they were completely legal, the registrar similarly refused all attempts to form new political parties, turning down applications from the Tana and Lamu African Political Party in December 1964, the Suba United Party in February 1965, the Kenya Socialist Party in August and the Continental African People's Party in September.

As the year continued, the Odinga faction became more isolated within both government and Parliament. Where they did manage to go to the country – as in the 1965 Senate by-elections – they were quite successful, as their criticism of the government's performance remained popular.[197] However, they were undermined within the state apparatus and their access to channels of communication and mobilisation restricted. Government rhetoric was increasingly strident, with its critics presented as trying to undermine it, and this in turn was portrayed as seditious and therefore criminal. Nonetheless, Odinga continued to speak out, condemning British and American imperialism and accusing the West of subversion. In June, there were calls for his resignation, and verbal battles continued for the rest of the year. In July 1965, the KANU Parliamentary Group elected new officers. In a familiar pattern, the radicals were edged out and Ngala (described bitterly by Odinga as 'one of the most obedient protégés of the colonialists') replaced him as its vice-chairman, while Kali was removed as chief whip.[198] The Assembly also reconstituted the Sessional Committee (which decided the order of business in the House), removing Achieng-Oneko and other Odinga allies. By late 1965, KANU officials critical of the government were being denied licences to speak in Central Province for security reasons.[199]

On 27 December 1965, a final Cabinet reshuffle stripped Odinga and his allies of key responsibilities. Achieng-Oneko lost tourism to Mboya's ally Ayodo, while Attorney-General Njonjo took over the supervision of elections, Odinga's last material function as vice-president. Home Affairs Minister Moi acquired the police, internal security and immigration. Amid rumours of corruption, Ngei's Ministry of

Cooperatives and Marketing was abolished and he was moved elsewhere. Although Odinga remained vice-president, his supporters had been cut down and his power whittled away. It was now only a question of time before they were driven out of KANU.

Conclusions

The first and most important competition over the direction of the independent state was over. By the end of 1965, Kenya had restored the 'command and control' system that the British had tried to replace as independence dawned. A system of state regulation would dominate an otherwise capitalist society, with the president at the apex of power. Although regionalism was dead, ethnicity would still be a crucial element in the political system. The tension between socialism and capitalism and to a lesser extent between Kikuyu and Luo that had begun before independence had deepened, and the foundations of Kikuyu dominance had been established. Political structures and economic institutions would continue to mirror the pre-independence model, with a new elite at the apex rapidly arrogating to itself the wealth and privileges that the Europeans had enjoyed. State security and economic development would be the primary targets, with equality only an aspiration. Beneath the ideological and ethnic struggles for the state, the distribution of land in the Rift Valley remained a potent political issue, only temporarily masked by the creation of a shallow political unity, the safety valve of the settlement schemes and the shift of the allocation of land from political to bureaucratic processes.

The Americans and British had won the Cold War skirmish for control of the government, driving KANU to the right. The West would support Kenyatta, and would 'turn a blind eye' to the actions needed to ensure that Kenya did not fall to communism. Kenya would remain closely tied to its British patron and, in return, would protect foreign interests when needed. Its security forces would remain loyal to Kenyatta. The radicals and Odinga supporters who had challenged the gradualist strategy since the early 1960s were isolated. Kenyatta was convinced that his old friends had planned to strike against him. Unable or unwilling to act, Odinga and his allies were exposed for the *coup de grâce*.

Chapter 4

Multi-Party, but not Democracy, 1966–1969

The Consolidation of the Kenyatta State

Jomo Kenyatta, Tom Mboya and their allies were now ready to strike against the Odinga faction and the radicals. They did so decisively, leaving them no choice but to leave KANU. The resulting period of multi-party competition never took a democratic form. The constitutional amendment that led to the Little General Election, the extension of detention without trial, the refusal to register the opposition Kenya People's Union (KPU)'s branches, the banning of its meetings, the arrests and jailing of activists, and threats against KPU members all reflected a partisan state, both able and willing to eliminate opposition.[1] As a result, KANU drove the KPU back into its sole secure area, the party's ethnic heartland in Nyanza. This conflict alienated the Luo community from the Kenyatta state and created an antipathy between Kikuyu and Luo that was to endure for decades.

An increasingly-authoritarian and nepotistic governing elite appeared entrenched in power, buttressed by its ability to deliver growth and security. Western governments and businesses remained supportive of Kenyatta and the Kenya model. The economy was booming, backed by strong foreign investment, the *shifta* insurrection was defeated and, though there were warning signs of elite corruption and bureaucratic decline, these had not yet undermined the functioning of the state.

With the Luo and the radicals driven out of power, the late 1960s began to entrench the advantages that the Kikuyu had recently reasserted in the exploitation of state resources. Bureaucratic centralism based around a powerful presidency was enshrined in both law and practice. The contest for the presidential succession continued, but was now between the 'Gatundu group' of Kiambu insiders and Mboya and his allies. This second, lower-key power struggle ended with Mboya's murder in 1969. This took Kenya into a dangerous period – mass ethnic violence or civil insurrection was a real possibility – that ended in mass detentions, the banning of Odinga's opposition party and a return to single-party rule. But the government weathered these storms and closed out the 1960s in full control: Kenyatta's rivals fully incorporated into the political system, dead or in detention.

Encircled and Isolated

January 1966 opened quietly. Behind the scenes, however, Oginga Odinga and the radicals were under attack. In January 1966, Kenyatta set up a secret Cabinet Security Committee, consisting of the conservative inner circle of Njoroge Mungai, James Gichuru, Daniel arap Moi and Bruce McKenzie. Its remit was to identify and respond to the main threats to Kenya's security. Kenyatta explicitly directed the committee that the threat was internal and came from Odinga. He also instructed them to use the UK to source any training or equipment required. The committee reported just before the crisis broke, and duly accused Odinga and his allies of subversion.[2]

The Split Becomes Public, February–March 1966

On 15 February 1966, without warning, Mboya introduced a motion of confidence in the president and his government in Parliament that also condemned 'dissident and confused' socialist groups. There was confusion as to whether it was a government or a private member's motion, as Leader of Government Business Odinga denied he had ever heard of it. During the resulting debate, Mboya denounced dissidents in the party and challenged them to quit KANU. There was an open confrontation between Mboya and Odinga, during which Mboya made it clear that Kenyatta had authorised the move.[3] Odinga stormed out of the House. Radical and moderate MPs clashed repeatedly and Mboya suggested that failure to pass the motion would lead to a general election.[4] Although the House passed the motion, it was irrevocably divided; it was also clear that the Odinga group was in the minority. The next day, the position of leader of government business was declared non-existent.

On 23 February 1966, with an open split looming, Kenyatta suspended Paul Ngei from office over allegations of corruption. Ngei had headed the Maize Marketing Board until December 1964 and had then overseen it as minister for cooperatives and marketing. A commission of inquiry had been set up in January to investigate events at the three maize boards, which were merged into a single Maize and Produce Board. There was evidence of mismanagement, politicised distribution and exploitation by officials.[5] The inquiry found that Ngei had used his powers to divert maize to a milling company owned by his wife, and appointed a firm owned by his brother as the ministry's sole agent.[6] Officials later suggested that Ngei and at least one other minister were also taking kickbacks from the sale of maize. It was not a coincidence that Ngei, who had demanded the expropriation of European land without compensation, was a supporter of the radicals in Cabinet. However, he was restored to office after a second investigation exonerated him. Some suspect this investigation was directed to acquit Ngei, in return for his loyalty.

The Cold War implications of the Cabinet split were equally clear. The British fleet was soon back in Mombasa, and the government broke off talks with the Russians on the projects they had proposed to fund (apart from Kisumu hospital, which was already under construction), and announced it would seek help elsewhere.

The conservatives now decided the time was right for the *coup de grâce*. On 27 February 1966, Mboya announced in the press that KANU would hold a National Delegates' Conference in Limuru on 12–13 March, where Kenyatta would outline new plans for the party and introduce a new party constitution.[7] After four years of inactivity, the party would now meet, without warning, and hold elections. It was a stunning blow. One-third of the parliamentary party (51 MPs) backed Odinga in an immediate protest, arguing that the conference was unconstitutional, undemocratic (as it would legitimise Mboya's recent branch coups), and a transparent attack on Odinga and the radicals.[8] However, 99 MPs wrote another letter to Kenyatta, pledging full support for the conference. Kenyatta then summoned a meeting of the parliamentary party, and on 11 March MPs voted 85:30 for the new constitution – which, it now emerged, would abolish Odinga's post of party vice-president – and the conference continued. It was a transparent political trick, but in their weakened circumstances, the Odinga faction could do little but prepare for the worst.

The March 1966 Limuru KANU conference saw 400 delegates vote on the new party constitution and elect eight new provincial vice-presidents. Notwithstanding the recent KANU branch elections, which had replaced radicals with more amenable delegates, several pro-Odinga delegates were refused admission and substituted with more pliable individuals. The selection of the vice-presidents saw a clean sweep for the 'conservatives'. Mwai Kibaki was elected for Nairobi, Jeremiah Nyagah for Eastern, Moi for the Rift Valley, Ronald Ngala for the Coast and ex-KADU Luhya MP Eric Khasakhala for Western. In the key battlegrounds, Mboya's ally Lawrence Sagini from Kisii was elected for Nyanza (unopposed, because Odinga did not bother to run), while Gichuru 'defeated' Bildad Kaggia to become Central vice-president. When Kaggia inconveniently beat Gichuru in the first poll, delegates were substituted and a rerun held to produce the desired result.[9] Kenyatta was re-elected as president and Mboya beat Masinde Muliro to remain secretary-general. Kenyatta followed a policy of ethno-regional balance in the allocation of the remaining leadership posts, an approach emulated in all subsequent KANU elections.

US Ambassador William Attwood was actively involved in these events. He later claimed that the conference was summoned so suddenly because Odinga could have bought votes with US$150,000 he had received from the Chinese.[10] The British High Commission also believed Odinga was still receiving Chinese money.[11] This truth is unknown, but their belief reinforced the determination of British and American intelligence to help Kenyatta. What Attwood did not say was that American money had probably funded the conference, and the Americans had helped organise it.[12] Odinga alleged that delegates had been accommodated and lavishly entertained by someone at a time when KANU had no money at all.[13]

The Formation of the Opposition and the State's Response

Unable to continue the fight from within, Odinga and his allies decided that constitutional opposition was their only recourse. They were too proud to beg Kenyatta for forgiveness, and too popular to abandon a position they felt was just. A few days after the Limuru conference, a group of individuals, including pro-Odinga activist Oyangi Mbaja, applied to register a new political party: the Kenya People's Union (KPU).[14] However, the government was not ready to accept Odinga's departure with equanimity. In March 1966, the government banned a series of his meetings, claiming he did not have meeting licences. Soon after, Moi alleged that 'foreign powers' had poured money into Kenya to overthrow the government. Several

4.1: Oginga Odinga (*left*) and Tom Mboya (*right*)

Courtesy: Nation Group Newspapers (*left*) and Flamingo (*right*)

communist diplomats and journalists were expelled during March, a clearing-out of suspected spies or conduits of funds to Odinga.

On 14 April 1966, Odinga (Figure 4.1) finally resigned as vice-president, and one by one, he and his allies resigned from KANU. His resignation statement explained that he refused to be part of a government ruled by 'underground masters' serving foreign interests, and accused the Limuru conference of being rigged.[15] On 25 April, Luo Information and Broadcasting Minister Ramogi Achieng-Oneko also resigned, the only minister to join Odinga. He too attacked Kenyatta's government as no longer non-aligned, but capitalist and linked militarily with Britain, and rejected Kenyatta's policies on land, foreign affairs, federation and agriculture. On 26 April, Odinga announced that his group had joined the KPU.

The goal of the KPU leadership was to create a more left-wing party, to oppose the growing conservatism and Western orientation of the KANU leadership and to restructure politics along class and socio-economic grounds.[16] Odinga was forced into this position by the ideological differences, leadership struggles and repression of dissent inside KANU. These in turn stemmed from the key policy decisions made on land, defence and Western investment during 1962–5. It was a decision he did not make easily. He could have chosen to suffer Kenyatta's humiliations, and perhaps worked his way back into favour, but Kenyatta's hostility appeared implacable, and Odinga's intemperance and sense of betrayal ensured that the conservatives would fight the remainder of the confrontation on a battlefield of their choosing. The split also symbolised a final break between socialism and nationalism, and showed how fully Mboya, Kenyatta and the insiders around them had aligned themselves with the West. With the formation of the KPU, Odinga took a massive gamble – that

Kenyatta and KANU would play by the rules, and that the West would ensure that they did so. Both bets proved ill-judged. The three short years of multi-partyism that followed were marred by more serious abuses than were conducted against a political party at any time before or since in Kenya's history. His Western patrons said and did nothing, tacitly endorsing Kenyatta's tactics.

One-fifth of the parliamentary party – 31 MPs – declared their loyalties to the KPU. Ten of them, including Kaggia, Achieng-Oneko, Oprong Oduya, J. D. Kali, Zephaniah Anyiene and Assistant Minister Tom Okelo-Odongo, were true 'radicals'. Six more were allies and clients of Odinga from Central Nyanza, supporters since the days of Luo Thrift and Trading. More surprising, half the defectors were senators and MPs from pastoralist areas such as Baringo, who appeared to be backing Odinga more as a protest against government neglect than ideological sympathy.[17] Okelo-Odongo suggested he had the names of 62 MPs (more than a third of Parliament) who had agreed to cross the floor, but the government's harsh reaction soon whittled this number down. The initial plan was to force a general election by bringing down the government, but several allies such as Kamba assistant minister Gideon Mutiso changed their minds.[18] Muliro and Martin Shikuku, too, were closet supporters, but decided not to join Odinga. Ngei was a more overt ally. He refused to attend KANU parliamentary group meetings in this period, and several of his allies defected, but he did not take the jump himself, probably because he had been promised his ministerial post back. Assistant Minister Munyua Waiyaki (from Kiambu, but representing Mathare in Nairobi) resigned from the government, but renounced his defection to the KPU at the last minute.

The new party was even stronger in the trade union movement, although COTU itself remained under Mboya's control. Odinga's resignation from KANU was followed by that of 13 senior trade unionists, including COTU Deputy Secretary-General Denis Akumu and Ochola Mak'Anyengo of the Petroleum and Oil Workers' Union. COTU suspended then sacked them all. The Dock Workers' Union and others duly walked out of COTU.

Kenyatta did not intend to permit fair and open competition between KANU and the KPU. Believing the threat they faced from Odinga was real, KANU's leaders were playing to win. In a radio broadcast on 26 April, Kenyatta branded the KPU leaders as arrogant dissidents, whose goal was to 'destroy national stability'.[19] KANU also played the tribal card, accusing Odinga of being a Luo-only leader. Officials seized the passports of many who had resigned, with Moi commenting (in a phrase he would never tire of repeating) 'Passports are not a right but a privilege . . .'[20] The government sacked all KPU members from parastatal posts.[21] Allegations were made that the KPU had promised K£150,000 to ex-Mau Mau forest fighters to take up arms against the government, while Kenyatta thundered, 'Those who tried to play with the government will be trampled on like mud.'[22] Moi and Ngala claimed that Odinga was holding secret meetings with the Tanzanian government, which both parties denied.[23]

At the same time as the state was wielding the 'stick', the 'carrot' was also in use. Politicians from Baringo District, for example, were told that if they remained loyal, 'some of the projects we have been promised will now be set up in Baringo.'[24] By the night of 27 April, with news circulating of an amendment to the Constitution, 13 of the defectors had already changed their minds. The line-up that occupied the opposition benches when Parliament resumed on 28 April lasted only a day. The same day, the government introduced the fifth constitutional amendment, which forced MPs who resigned from a political party to seek a new mandate from the electorate at the end of a parliamentary session. This was a very different view from that which Kenyatta had taken two years earlier, when KADU's MPs were defecting to his camp. But it was a political masterstroke.

The opposition in the House melted away, as MPs scurried for cover in KANU rather than face an election. Mboya and the government forced the amendment through the Assembly on 28–9 April. In the House it passed by 97 votes to 11 on the second reading and 95 to 8 on the third, exposing how shallow Odinga's support now was.[25] This amendment remained in effect for the next 44 years. Within moments of its passage, Kenyatta ended the parliamentary session months early and the speaker declared 29 seats vacant.[26] The stage was set for the first post-independence multi-party election, known as the Little General Election.

The loss of two ministers and two assistant ministers forced a government reshuffle, and on 3 May 1966 Kenyatta announced his new administration (see Figure 4.2). A surprise decision was the appointment of the intellectual and relative radical Joe Murumbi as vice-president. Chosen, unlike Odinga, because he was not

4.2: The May 1966 Cabinet

Courtesy: Nation Group Newspapers

a threat, Murumbi knew nothing of his preferment until it was announced.[27] His appointment was an appeal to those in KANU who had sympathies for Odinga's views, showing that they still had a home in the party.

The reshuffle increased the number of ministers to 22, with five newcomers, all representing more conservative opinions. Ngala finally joined the Cabinet, alongside Clement Argwings-Kodhek (now a Mboya ally), Luhya James Osogo and Nyagah. The 35-year-old Kibaki, who had received a first-class degree from the London School of Economics and had lectured at Makerere, also joined the Cabinet, at Commerce and Industry. Kenyatta took the foreign affairs portfolio himself in the OP.

The Little General Election, June 1966

The Little General Election took place between 11 and 26 June 1966. Polls were held in 10 Senate and 19 House seats. Voting was based on the 1962 register of voters, updated in 1965, using the unusual 'one ballot box per candidate' system that had been used in 1961. The KPU nominated all the MPs who had defected to contest their seats. Their KANU opponents were generally local notables with good party connections.

The KPU, though weakened by the impact of recent government actions, still had the support of a wide sector of the country. There were KPU MPs in almost every district, although the party was strongest amongst the Luo of Central Nyanza. As well as its bedrock in the Luo, the views of Odinga, Kaggia and Achieng-Oneko had many supporters, while others were simply unhappy with Kenya's Western tilt. The government was particularly concerned by the KPU's potential support amongst former Mau Mau supporters in the Kikuyu peasantry.

In line with the views of the radicals since 1960–1, the KPU's manifesto promised to nationalise foreign-owned industries and to 'break the foreigners' grip on the economy'. In the KPU's view, KANU's African socialism was 'neither African nor socialism. It is a cloak of the practice of total capitalism.'[28] The KPU criticised Kenyatta's land policy, neo-colonial influences and the way in which KADU leaders had taken places in the KANU hierarchy. They called for the reallocation of resources to assist the poor and landless, and more cooperative settlement schemes, with land seized without compensation or at the cost of the British. They accepted the irreversibility of land consolidation, but demanded a ceiling on land holdings. Their manifesto had to be published abroad and smuggled into Kenya, as no local printer would touch it for fear of the consequences.

In response, KANU defended its policies and achievements since independence. Its spokesmen pointed out that nationalisation would only drain the country's coffers, defended individual property rights, and criticised the KPU's proposals as economically disastrous. The association, which it had worked hard to establish, of radicalism with communism was well-mined. Indeed, both parties accused each other of being in the pay of foreign powers. With only 29 seats contested, there was no chance, even if the KPU won every seat, for it to form the next government.

This left it vulnerable to claims that a vote for the party was only a protest vote.[29] To fund its campaign, KANU turned to the business community (much of it Asian or British). The KPU's sources of funding are unknown.

The election campaign was far from fair, with the Voice of Kenya imposing a near-blackout on KPU statements and meetings, while reporting KANU affairs in full. The KPU did receive press coverage, however. The registrar of societies did not recognise the KPU formally until 21 May, nomination day, limiting its ability to campaign. Throughout April and early May, the KPU was barred from holding any meetings at all, on the direct orders of the president to provincial commissioners.[30] This made it extremely difficult to organise, recruit or advertise its programme. There was violence during the early stages of the elections, especially in the Rift Valley and in Kaggia's Kandara, where seven people were killed amid intimidation by KANU youth wingers, since Kenyatta had committed himself to Kaggia's defeat.[31]

In general, KPU leaders did not criticise Kenyatta personally but the advisers surrounding him. KANU in turn stressed its loyalty to Kenyatta, and in Kikuyu areas focused on how Kaggia had backed the Luo against his own people. Kenyatta led an eve-of-poll rally in Kandara, where he attacked Kaggia, stressed the government's omnipotence and threatened the 'jigger' (burrowing flea) of the KPU that it would be 'trampled on like flour'.[32]

The results were declared on 27 June. Ethnicity and state power proved stronger than either ideology or dissatisfaction at the government's performance. The KPU polled slightly more votes than KANU in both the House and Senate, but their regional focus meant they won only nine seats to KANU's 20. In the pastoral and semi-arid areas of Baringo, West Pokot, Marsabit and Tana River districts, the vote for the KPU candidates collapsed (see Figure 4.3). In these marginal areas, political consciousness remained low and the wishes of the state were paramount. Despite Kalenjin fears about their lands, Moi ensured that Kalenjin voters supported the Kikuyu incumbents over the Luo challengers.

Only in Odinga's Central Nyanza did the KPU vote hold up. There, the KANU machinery had defected en masse and KANU had trouble finding candidates to stand.[33] Despite threats by ministers that voting for the KPU would mean their isolation from development projects, communal solidarity triumphed. Odinga's victory was cemented by his personal popularity and the support of local elders; a vote for the KPU was a vote for Odinga. There was a strong sense of solidarity in adversity against Odinga's perceived mistreatment by Kenyatta, and the Luo's apparent loss of government largesse. There was also a powerful egalitarian streak to the KPU's Nyanza campaign, which was in stark contrast to KANU's rampant individualism. Elsewhere, only in Machakos District did the KPU perform well. Ngei's position remained ambiguous and both his Kamba KPU allies retained their seats.[34]

The vote and count saw abuses by government officials, particularly in Kandara, which recorded the highest turnout of the election, and where Kaggia polled only 10 per cent of the vote. Kaggia claimed later that the result was fixed, ballot boxes stuffed and KPU votes counted for KANU.[35] Others suggested that Kaggia's defeat represented a rejection of his policies by smallholders with new economic

4.3: Performance of KPU candidates in 1963 and 1966 Little General Election

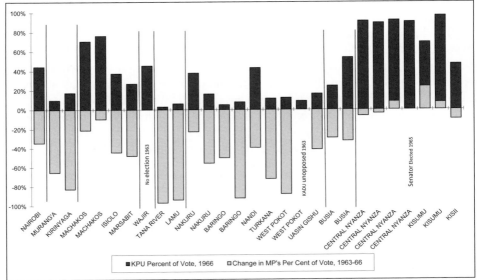

opportunities, state influence, or a Kikuyu rejection of a Luo-led alliance.[36] On 28 June, Odinga claimed rigging had affected 21 seats, alleging that KANU had used the government machinery and public money to campaign, but when the KPU losers petitioned against 16 of the results, all were dismissed on technicalities.

The Kenyatta Succession

Kenyatta was now impregnable and his word was law. Around him, younger politicians intrigued, currying favour and hoping to succeed Mzee ('the old man', as he was known) when the inevitable happened. Kenyatta was around 70, and illness and the pressures of government were taking their toll.[37] He suffered his first stroke or thrombosis in mid-1966, later confirmed by his biographer Jeremy Murray-Brown. Nothing was made public in Kenya until Kenyatta appeared at the end of August announcing that rumours of his illness were false, and, 'I'm not in a *sunduku* [coffin] yet.'[38] However, from this time on, his health was a continual concern and the succession a source of intrigue.

Kenyatta also needed a new vice-president. Chosen as a compromise candidate in 1966, Murumbi soon found his position untenable. Out of sympathy with the strident propaganda of the day and still shocked by Pinto's murder, Murumbi soon asked to be relieved of his position and to retire from politics. On 21 September 1966, his departure was made public, and the race was on to succeed him. In January 1967, Kenyatta announced that his successor would be 43-year-old ex-KADU Chairman Daniel arap Moi.[39] The rationale for his choice, which was to change the direction of Kenya's history, were never made public, but Moi had several advantages. He was not a threat to the Kikuyu insiders; his Tugen people were a small sub-tribe of the Kalenjin, with little influence in Nairobi – there were fewer than 400 Tugen in the city at the time. As a Kalenjin, his appointment meant that he must support the government's land settlement plans. He also represented the conservative ex-KADU wing of the party and was more reliable and pliable than either Ngala or Muliro. According to Moi's biographer Andrew Morton, Njonjo first proposed him to Kenyatta, and he was backed by a group of influential executives and politicians centred on McKenzie.[40] The decision was a great disappointment to Mboya and Mungai, who both had designs on the role. Indeed, this was probably Kenyatta's reason for bypassing them. At the same time as Moi took over the vice-presidency (while remaining minister for home affairs), Mbiyu Koinange moved to take control of the provincial administration inside the OP, which he ran for the next 12 years.

Although Moi was now Kenyatta's deputy, few actually expected him to replace Mzee. At this time, McKenzie and the British thought Gichuru the most likely successor, being well respected, a Kiambu Kikuyu and relatively elderly. However, drink and diabetes were affecting him physically. Mboya and Mungai were also candidates, with Moi running fourth.

Securing the Political System, 1966–8

With a loyal Moi by his side, Kenyatta's grip on the nation was unchallenged, and 1967–8 was a period of relative calm. Once it had been used to destroy Odinga and secure Kenyatta's authority, KANU was again relegated to a venue to fight private quarrels and a robe of legitimacy for the monarch.

The Bureaucratic-Executive State

Kenyatta appeared convinced of his own right to rule, and gave no indications of plans to retire or to share executive authority. He was now above both law and challenge. Power was increasingly centralised in Nairobi and in the OP: formally through the constitutional changes, the detention legislation and emergency powers in North-Eastern and the subordination of elements of the legal system to political imperatives; informally through networks of state patronage and personal loyalty. By 1968, PCs controlled all government officers in their provinces as representatives of the president. For Kenyatta and his allies, the provincial administration was the 'machine' by which policy would be implemented; the National Assembly and the party were communication tools, vents for protest and emergency alarms. This was partly a reflection of Kenyatta's unique 'founding father' position, but, as Anyang' Nyong'o pointed out,

> Strong presidents have not imposed themselves on society simply by individual cunning and expertise; social forces in society, and the conflicts among such forces, provide the context in which such presidents acquire and retain power, and, in certain cases, even end up using this power against the very social forces that propelled them into the power.[41]

Tensions between KANU MPs and the provincial administration grew, both sides believing they had the right to lead their area. Kenyatta, however, continued to focus his attention on the administration, giving it control of local land boards, district agricultural committees, loan committees, settler selection, tax collection, *harambee* organisation and appointment of chiefs.[42] By 1967–8, a 'bureaucratic–executive alliance' was already in place.[43]

The emergence of the executive presidency in Kenya reflected a long history of powerful (British) bureaucracy, a cultural respect for elders, the economic dominance of the state and the lack of a wealthy baronial class, able to challenge the monarchical presidency. It also reflected Kenyatta's unique combination of age, ability and authority, his ability to rely on a shield of able, educated Kikuyu allies, and the decisions taken at independence, which required a strong executive to sustain unpopular policies. This bureaucratic-executive state speeded up the development of a neo-patrimonial system (in which personalised, patrimonial and clientelist forces coexisted with a formal bureaucracy and state institutions) when the state was used to impose Kenyatta's will, but also limited its predatory tendencies, since bureaucratic norms of efficiency remained relatively strong.

4.4: Kenyatta and Moi, Jamhuri Day, 1967

Courtesy: Nation Group Newspapers

The Role of Parliament in the 1960s

Although Kenyatta had rebuilt the colonial tradition of centralised executive power, he and his ministers still paid close attention to Parliament. It served a legitimising function, demonstrating popular consent – in principle – to be governed by KANU. As a debating chamber, it publicised the concerns of society. It retained the paper authority to unseat him and, as long as the government could be criticised in the House, it appeared that the country was still a democracy.[44] Kenyatta did not need to retain the National Assembly as it was – on occasion, it was positively inconvenient – but he understood the importance of such a lightning rod for dissent. He could have increased the number of nominated members, or strengthened party approvals of candidates at any time after 1965, but chose not to do so.

The Kenyan Assembly was more active than most African assemblies, and retained a critical and sometimes hostile approach to poorly prepared government policies. It struggled to hold the government to account, however. While debate had been open and sometimes acrimonious before the KADU defections, and even more so during the struggle between left and right in 1965, once the KPU was isolated, the party whip controlled most dissent. All the processes of a Parliament continued – the Sessional Committee, which decided the business of the house; the Select Committee on Standing Orders, which managed parliamentary processes; the Public Accounts Committee, which reviewed government spending; the Powers and Privileges Committee, which controlled members' behaviour – but as an institution, the Assembly never asserted its independence. It did reject or force the withdrawal of a few bills in 1966–8, but, overall, its legislative contribution was marginal.[45] It also failed to limit executive encroachment into the powers of other bodies and into the commitments made at independence. The fourth constitutional amendment of 1966, for example, included the extension of emergency powers against the *shifta*. It also made explicit that all civil servants (except those protected by the Constitution) sat at the 'pleasure of the President' and that he could appoint and dismiss them at will. The amendment removed the automatic right to citizenship for Commonwealth citizens after five years residency that had been offered at independence. Finally, it further vested control of county council land in central government and the commissioner of lands. The House approved it under protest by 86:11 on the second reading, with only backbencher Shikuku and Odinga's supporters opposed. Nandi lawyer and intellectual Marie Seroney, already concerned at the tendency of the House to parrot the government line, openly referred to Parliament as a 'Reichstag' and suggested MPs were 'rubber stamps' for the government.[46]

Most parliamentary debates consisted of appeals for government resources: roads, schools, factories, loans and water for MPs' constituencies. MPs were supplicants to the state, begging for development projects and pleading for exemptions to government rules to assist their communities. This did not mean the Assembly was entirely supine. Verbal pyrotechnics continued; backbenchers criticised the pace of Africanisation, challenged the government's closeness to the British, criticised their land and settlement policy and called for immediate East African federation. The reaction of the administration to such pleas, however, was to ignore them. Even when the Assembly passed private members' motions, the government did not treat them as binding unless they related to the Assembly. A rare exception was the 1968 Hire Purchase Act, the sole legislation for decades to be enacted via a private member's bill (introduced by J. M. Kariuki). After 1968, even if Parliament passed private members' legislation, the President vetoed it.

Inside Parliament, the KPU was grudgingly given the privileges of an official opposition. Odinga became chairman of the Public Accounts Committee, and opposition motions received priority over backbench ones. The KPU used this platform as best it could to challenge the executive, but facing a 161:9 majority, it had no chance of changing policy. The doctrine of collective responsibility was still imposed, though it made less sense outside a true Westminster system. Though frequently they played no part in decisions (the president was not bound by Cabinet decisions or even required to consult it), all government members were bound to support their government in their speeches and during divisions. The speaker did not permit motions of 'no confidence' against individuals, only against the whole government. While ministers, particularly the Kikuyu core, had significant powers, Kenyatta gave little authority to the role of parliamentary secretary (renamed assistant minister in December 1964). Although bound by collective responsibility, assistant ministers had no access to state secrets, nor did they act as ministers in the absence of their bosses. They had a public profile and a higher salary, but were otherwise 'window dressing and white washing'.[47]

The state's expanding powers of patronage were also used to reward its parliamentary loyalists, giving them money, public platforms and patronage opportunities of their own.[48] By 1969, 15 of the 18 main agricultural boards had at least one MP sitting on them and MPs chaired more than a dozen non-agricultural boards. Board members were required to support government policy for their industry. Again, there was an element of ethnic balancing, with the state responding to requests for regional or ethnic representation and MPs usually representing the main producer regions for particular commodities.

While the KANU–KPU split dominated politics, the division between the government and its backbench was equally strong, albeit based on different grounds. Although MPs such as Shikuku and Muliro were far from allies of Odinga, they had little time for Kenyatta's pro-Kikuyu policies either, but were forced to choose the lesser of two evils. The political class showed characteristics of what Richard Sandbrook called 'amoral pragmatism'.[49] They were working in (and building) a political culture that did not have a strong set of values. In a system that rejected checks and balances and constraints on elite action (from accounting rules to press freedom) as 'Western' or 'colonial', most politicians and civil servants accepted their situation and set out to make the best of it.

The Abolition of the Senate, December 1966

In December 1966, the final vestige of federalism was scrapped when the seventh constitutional amendment abolished the Senate, and the senators became MPs in a new unicameral legislature.[50] Almost as soon as it had come into being, the bicameral legislature had been under threat. The Senate had been designed as a forum for minority and community rights and a brake on government excesses, but in practice its impact was minimal. The government ignored most of its motions, while the House of Representatives defined virtually every bill as a 'money bill' and refused to accept Senate amendments.

In the resulting constituency boundary redistribution, the semi-functioning Electoral Commission of Kenya (ECK) allocated each senator a seat in the new House, carved from within his district. The House of Representatives was expanded by 41 seats and retitled the National Assembly, but without any other substantive changes. The House had already approved a boundary redistribution, but this was cancelled, leaving the Assembly at 158 seats, as it was to remain for the next 20 years.[51] It was not coincidence that the ECK had recommended the expansion of several densely populated pro-KPU districts.

The other key change in this amendment was the extension of the life of Parliament. Using the justification that some newly elected senators had terms that would give them tenure until 1971, while the House was due to go to the polls in 1968, the Act extended the lifetime of the National Assembly until 1970 (unless dissolved earlier by the president).[52] It had the convenient side-effect of delaying the time when the KPU could challenge the government in a national election.

KANU and the KPU, 1966–8

Once it had expelled the KPU, KANU reverted to local factionalism and central lethargy. Despite the competitive pressures of multi-party democracy, there was no period of party revitalisation, as in practice the state was running the anti-KPU campaign. The National Governing Council did not meet until 1968 and there were no further party elections. Factional struggles continued as groups inside KANU built influence locally and used this to oust their opponents from positions of authority or resource control, then sought legitimisation from central officials, who would grant or refuse this according to their own interests.[53]

The KPU tried to take on KANU as a nationalist and socialist opposition, but few believed that Odinga would be Kenya's next president. Although the KPU offered a challenge to KANU's monopoly of power and a critique of its strategy, there was little chance after May 1966 that the KPU would win electoral victory. The government's clean-up campaign in 1964–5 had squeezed the middle ground of doubters, while the allocation of state resources in their favour and the 1966 elections had driven most Kikuyu into Kenyatta's arms. If KANU represented any political philosophy at this time, it was a middle-class ethos of personal advancement and opportunity, under a paternalist, interventionist government, but in general, it simply represented 'the establishment'.

Further Repression, 1966–8

Over the next three years, the use and misuse of legal powers, coercion and state patronage weakened the KPU nationally, although the party retained its Luo bedrock of support. Many of the state's actions and attitudes were reminiscent of the colonial response to African nationalist opinion, but to secure itself, the state expanded even further its ability to control and coerce, further limiting the space in which independent forces could operate.

Detention without Trial

On 24 May 1966, in the middle of the election campaign, KANU proposed a change to the law: the introduction of preventive detention without the need to declare an emergency. On 5 June 1966, Kenyatta gave his assent to the resulting Preservation of Public Security Act. It provided the state with wide powers of detention without trial, and allowed control of free movement, the imposition of curfews, and press censorship. The only restriction on these powers was that regulations made under the Act had to be renewed by Parliament every eight months. The Act, an updating of the colonial legislation, was a crucial weapon in the elite's armoury. Emergency powers had been used in North-Eastern since 1963, but now they could be used against the KPU. An associated constitutional amendment provided that if the president detained people, their constitutional rights would not be violated. Only one MP opposed the legislation (since the KPU's seats were already vacant), but George Githii's *Daily Nation* savaged the bill (and was castigated publicly by politicians and privately warned not to go too far).[54]

The government did not hesitate to use this power to strike at the organisational and intellectual foundations of the KPU, though it left the opposition's MPs untouched. With the election over, on 5 August 1966, the state arrested and then detained (without reason given) six KPU supporters, including Mbaja, head of the KPU Youth Movement, and several trade unionists. Akumu (administrative secretary of the KPU) and the party's Nairobi branch secretary protested, but found themselves amongst a second group of 12 detainees on 10 August. Odinga's personal secretary and the KPU Secretary-General Chris Makokha followed. After a lull during 1967, four more KPU officials followed them into jail in 1968, including youth winger Ochola Achola and Odinga's bodyguard, while Odinga's assistant Israel Agina was jailed for sedition in 1969.[55] The British had not attempted such open repression since 1954. The state-dominated media made no comment, and there was no public word from Europe. The churches too said little, although some Kikuyu and Luo priests preached sermons supporting the ideals of the KPU. Most KANU MPs supported the detention of their opponents since it improved their own electoral chances.

Registration of Branches and Restrictions on Public Meetings

The government also made use of its power to constrain the space in which the KPU could operate, to ensure that it was beaten back from a national party to a ethno-regional one. There was no pretence of administrative neutrality. The police and the attorney-general's office were openly declared to be tools of the incumbent government.

One way that the KPU was administratively constrained was by restricting its ability to organise locally by delaying or refusing certificates of registration to its branches. The 1952 Societies Ordinance had empowered the registrar of societies to register all societies, including political parties. An unregistered society was unlawful, and its meetings a criminal offence. These rules had been retained at independence. Although the KPU branches in Nairobi, Nyanza and Central Province were well established and registration could not be refused without a crisis, the periphery was more vulnerable. The registrar rejected more than 40 per cent of KPU branch registration applications between 1967 and 1969, compared to less than 2 per cent of KANU's.[56] The increasingly influential Attorney-General Njonjo was the architect of this policy. When called to account for the registrar's decisions, he claimed that the applications contained bogus addresses for their offices. In 1968, the Societies Act extended the 1952 Ordinance, removing the remaining restrictions on the registrar's actions, and increased the penalties for being a member of or attending a meeting of an unlawful society.[57] By October 1969, only half the country's districts had legal KPU branches. The 1968 law requiring that a political party endorse all candidates for office prevented the KPU from putting up candidates in areas where it had no registered branch.

The state also did what it could to prevent the KPU from campaigning, and again it used colonial legislation to achieve this. Until a branch was registered, all meetings were illegal. Any meeting of 50 or more people anywhere required a licence, while the police could cancel or break up any meeting of between 10 and 50 people at will. This power derived from legislation passed in 1948. Again, the Cabinet had considered repealing it during the pre-independence interregnum in July 1963, but decided on advice from the British to retain it.[58] Soon after the Little General Election, the KPU held a large rally at Mombasa, but it was permitted no other meetings until 1969.[59] The state denied a blanket ban existed, but cancelled every event on security grounds such as the 'interests of public order'. The government even banned the legally required annual party conferences of the KPU until 1969. In contrast, government ministers did not require licences to speak, and most KANU meetings were unaffected (though some troublesome KANU backbenchers were given the KPU treatment). KPU national officials were also barred from entering North-Eastern Province, much of the Rift Valley and even Meru under the Outlying Districts Ordinance.[60]

Instead, the KPU leaders were forced to use funerals, *Harambee* meetings, Parliament and press conferences to publicise their platform. Even then, they were followed by police looking for opportunities to arrest them. In a celebrated case, Deputy Leader Kaggia was sentenced to a year in prison in April 1968, simply for holding an unlicensed meeting. Some had doubts about this. On 2 July (European) Acting Chief Justice Denis Farrell halved the magistrate's sentence to six months, saying the original term was too severe. Farrell had replaced Chief Justice Sir John Ainley on his retirement in 1968, and his confirmation as chief justice had been imminent. Within hours, however, Farrell was forcibly retired (though the state could not do this legally). The next day, Kenyatta appointed Kitili Mwendwa, solicitor-general and brother of minister Eliud Ngala Mwendwa, as the new chief justice.[61] The message had come from the top: in the legal system, as elsewhere, no quarter would be given to the KPU.

Administrative Harassment

There were other tools in the state's armoury. Local council employees and teachers were told that 'participation in politics' (i.e. support for the KPU) would be grounds for immediate dismissal. Since the government was a KANU government, they were told, its employees had a duty to support KANU's policies. More than 35 civil servants were sacked for supporting the KPU, and others demoted.[62] KPU members, including Odinga himself, were unable to travel abroad because their passports had been withdrawn. In the private sector, too, companies that employed KPU supporters were warned to dismiss them or face the state's wrath.[63]

Local officials were equally partisan. In 1966, some councils expelled all their KPU members without any legal right to do so.[64] In 1967, the government legitimised this by forcing through legislation that applied the 'crossing the floor' rules they had used in Parliament to local councils. KPU supporters were threatened with losing land in settlement schemes, loans and trade licences, and were removed from land consolidation committees. One KPU ex-MP reported that chiefs in Baringo had been instructed not to issue famine relief to KPU supporters.[65] The government also tried to intimidate the opposition. Kenyatta consistently incited violence against his opponents, demanding they be trampled like 'snakes in the grass', 'crushed like powder' or 'ground up'. During 1967, as the police looked on, ministers Julius Kiano and Ngala led groups of KANU youth wingers to destroy local KPU offices, just as KANU was to do in 1992. Only in Luo Nyanza was communal solidarity strong enough to counterweigh the fear and discrimination.

The Voice of Kenya had meanwhile become the voice of KANU. The state used its media monopoly to ensure that no competing views were heard. Information and Broadcasting Minister Osogo made it clear that the VoK would speak only with the voice of the government.[66] KANU consistently portrayed the KPU as the tool of foreign powers, building a perception of any relationship with the Russians or Chinese as illegitimate, while refusing to accept any challenge to their own links with the UK. The private print media challenged nothing, reporting government broadcasts as fact and handling KPU-related materials with care. Foreign journalists working in Kenya knew their work permits depended on not antagonising the government, while media owners feared nationalisation; though even this does not explain how supine the press was in 1966–9 in comparison to 1991–5. There was a real fear that the government would physically harm any journalist, editor or publisher who did not conform. There was also a quiet commonality of interest, in that the private media had little interest in an Odinga victory. Expatriate British journalists, who still dominated Kenya's press, were unlikely to challenge the status quo. The government also declared several communist publications seditious and banned them completely, making possession of them a criminal offence.

Even the university, beginning to experience the unrest and political activism that was so dominant in the West, saw the same processes at work. Students rebelled in January 1969 when the government twice banned Odinga from speaking to them, on Kenyatta's personal instruction. The government's response was to close the

University of Nairobi for two weeks and demand that students sign undertakings not to participate in unauthorised demonstrations before they were allowed to return. It was the first of many such confrontations.

As well as the 'sticks' he had borrowed from the British, Kenyatta also had 'carrots' to offer defectors.[67] The legacy of the colonial forced development of the economy and the lack of a large African private sector meant that the political and administrative insiders around the president controlled more than half of the senior jobs available to Africans. They also controlled land, properties, contracts, licences, educational bursaries and loans. The selective disbursement of such resources was another tool to entice back defectors and reward loyalists.

The most blatant abuse of all came in the local government elections of July–August 1968. Fearing or simply refusing to accept an open nationwide contest, on Kenyatta's instruction Mboya and Njonjo ensured that the civil service disqualified almost all the 1,800 KPU candidates for improper completion of their nomination papers.[68] Nearly every KANU candidate was elected unopposed. Deposits were raised from K£5 to K£10 just before the nominations, dates were changed and, in areas where there were no registered KPU branches, all candidates were disallowed. Where papers were successfully submitted, the initials (rather than signature) of party leader Odinga on the nomination forms were rejected. In unreliable Kisumu and Nairobi, the more independent town clerks were replaced as returning officers by the DCs, and all the KPU candidates then duly disqualified. There were rumours that all DCs had been ordered to disqualify the KPU or lose their jobs.[69] The KPU was furious. Odinga accused Kenyatta of wanting to become 'King of Kenya', and withdrew the few candidates who had managed to be nominated. Without the backing of Western governments, though, there was little more he could do. British newspapers called it a 'hollow victory' but the UK appears to have lodged no formal protests with the Kenyans. However, British officials internally described the government's actions as a 'farce' that 'can only tarnish the image of both Kenyatta and his government'.[70] It was an example of the bizarre constitutionalism that Njonjo now epitomised: the discriminatory application of the law and the use of legal technicalities to control political activity.

In this way, the KPU was weakened and driven back into its heartland in Luo Nyanza. After 1967, there was a steady stream of defections back to KANU, including two of its (non-Luo) MPs and its deputy secretary-general. In its heartlands, however, it held firm.

Corruption, Tribalism and Elite Dominance

The Challenge of Corruption

There were other aspects in which the governing elite was finding it harder to distinguish its own interest from that of the nation. In the late 1960s, concern began to be voiced over the way in which the political and civil service elite was enriching itself. In a process that paralleled experiences elsewhere in Africa, the inner circle had begun to take advantage of their gatekeeper and resource allocation positions for personal gain, lured by the differential between their modest financial status and the expectations they and their supporters had. As Odinga and others had warned, Kenya was splitting into a 'have' and 'have not' culture. The new African political and bureaucratic elites were merging with the commercial and landowning elites to form not a propertied middle class – as the British had planned – but a new ruling class that saw the state as its primary fount of resources.

The origins and extent of corruption in independent Kenya is a sensitive subject. It is clear that the misuse of public office for private gain was built into the indirect model of colonial rule, for example in the opportunities a chiefly role offered. During Mau Mau, Kikuyu Home Guards systematically extorted funds from others. Late colonial history also suggests that theft or embezzlement of funds was common amongst self-help groups and cooperatives. The British did not consider it a national problem, mainly because Africans' access to resources was so limited. However, they frequently investigated or dismissed chiefs, clerks and other gatekeepers for financial abuses.[71] Europeans too were involved in corrupt activities, with backhanders paid for construction contracts and city officials issuing contracts to companies they owned.[72] Accounting standards were lax and leaders often found it difficult to account for funds. Kenyatta had been accused of failing to distinguish between collective and personal income, and there were rumours that Odinga had misappropriated funds from the Luo Union or Luo Thrift and Trading.[73]

Popular attitudes to such resource diversions were inconsistent. Attitudes to theft of government or collective funds seemed more relaxed than to theft from individuals (which was heavily sanctioned). Although corruption was generally viewed negatively, many local communities assumed that their politicians were not serving them disinterestedly, but would play the system to their benefit. Writing of the Bukusu in the 1960s for example, De Wolf was clear that 'Relations concerned with larger units are not conceived in moral terms, unlike those in the family and community.'[74] In other words, to steal from the government was not a real crime, and no one was surprised when councillors allocated themselves sites for shops and loans to buy tractors. Some were sacked or jailed, but this was considered bad luck, more than just desserts. The situation in the civil service seems to have been better than in politics. Nonetheless, misappropriation was common. Njonjo admitted that 130 civil servants had been sacked for theft or financial irregularities in 1965 alone.[75]

Part of the problem seems to have been simple opportunity. There was more to steal than in most other African states, a structure of capital that had commanding heights by African standards. The state also controlled most of these heights, creating the ability to intervene. There also appears to have been an arrogance amongst some African elites and a need to differentiate themselves from the masses. Kenya had had a ruling class (the Europeans) for many years, creating an aspiration to emulate that class. There was also a limited internalisation of respect for or obedience to law for its own sake. Hence, in a situation where there was an opportunity to get something from the apparently inexhaustible pit of state funds, and it was not coming from one's own 'affective community', it was fair game. Corruption was also easy to hide.

The state was short of accountants, and those accused of misbehaviour could always claim tribalism in their defence.

Some forms of acquisition were protected from the top. It was in this period for example that Kiano acquired the nickname 'Mr Ten Per Cent'. One expatriate civil servant prepared a dossier on Kiano's involvement in Japanese textile imports, on which he was paid a 10 per cent commission. Njonjo, on instructions from Kenyatta, declined to take action.[76] Although Kenyatta was infuriated by public exposure of corruption, he was less concerned about abuses that remained private. The Kenyatta family too was rapidly enriching itself, and it was not alone.[77] Although ministerial salaries were modest, by the late 1960s, the British noted that even 'their' man McKenzie had gone from rags to riches in a few years.

Finally, those who asked why the press was not more active in exposing corruption received a firm riposte from the *Sunday Nation* in 1968: 'Such an objection overlooks the stringent libel laws as well as the Preventative Detention Act which are sufficient to ensure that the Press does not become over-enthusiastic in the execution of its duties.'[78]

Ethnic Preference and Tribalism

'Tribalism', the pattern of behaviour in which individuals in positions of authority give or are alleged to give systematic preference to a specific ethnic group in appointments or access to resources such as jobs, land or loans, was already a concern by 1964. More specifically, the Kikuyu and above all the Kiambu Kikuyu were seen to be disproportionately reaping the 'fruits of *Uhuru*'.

The state refused to disclose the ethnic origins of civil servants, but by 1965 a pattern of preference had already emerged for jobs requiring the personal confidence of the president. The perception grew during 1964 that KANU's victory meant that the Kikuyu and Luo dominated top appointments, while the KADU regions received few posts. As the struggle within KANU then played out, the Luo too were marginalised, leaving the Kikuyu dominant in politics, the administration and the security forces, leavened by a few Kamba soldiers and Kalenjin loyal to Moi. The nominally independent Public Service Commission was not immune from accusations of partisanship. In 1966, for example, Shikuku named civil service head Duncan Ndegwa (from Nyeri) as the 'architect of tribalism'.[79] This belief was itself a form of tribalism, when individuals identified other communities as the collective source of their individual frustrations.

The key question remains, however, whether such allegations were true. The evidence for systemic bias in the late 1960s is inconclusive, in part because Kenyatta (unlike Moi later) did not need to demonstrate open bias to achieve his goal. In the civil service, the Kikuyu were the largest group. Making up 20 per cent of the general population, they held at least 35 per cent of top civil service positions by 1969. They were also over-represented in the educated elites from whom the civil service was drawn.[80] The government consistently denied favouritism, claiming that appointments were made on merit alone. Calls for civil service jobs to be allocated on an ethnic quota basis were vehemently rejected.[81] The evidence suggests that bias was not systemic throughout the administration, but that some positions were allocated with explicit regard for ethnicity – and it became more obvious higher up the pyramid of power.

The Emerging Elite

The immediate pre- and post-independence period had seen a giddy rise to prominence for a lucky few. The Africanisation of the civil service, easy access to land, the success of coffee farming, rapid economic growth and access to cheap loans all combined to force the emergence of a political, administrative, economic and social elite, acquiring houses, cars, land and businesses. Many of their farms and businesses were modest in size or of uncertain profitability, but they were laying foundations that would blossom in the 1970s. This proto-elite was young, educated and predominantly Kikuyu, Embu and Meru.

Amongst it were a few whose fortunes were more deeply entrenched. The top rank of the political and administrative system included several children of colonial chiefs, including Simeon Nyachae (son of Chief Musa Nyandusi), Njonjo, Mbiyu Koinange, Nyagah, John Michuki, Eliud Mwendwa, Paul Ngei and Jackson Angaine.

Regional and International Relations

The mid- and late 1960s were a period of growing cynicism and loss of innocence worldwide. The Kennedy assassination in the US was followed by the enlargement of the Vietnam War. In Africa, South Africa continued to pursue apartheid, Mozambique and Angola remained white-ruled, and Rhodesia declared unilateral independence and survived. The year 1967 saw war in Nigeria and coups elsewhere. To Western countries, Kenya appeared a rare gem: a stable, growing, pro-Western black-ruled country; and they responded accordingly.

International Relations

Britain's relationship with Kenya remained extremely close. Britain continued to provide technical assistance and CDC investment, as well as aid for development and land redistribution, and was by far Kenya's largest donor and military partner. The main issue between the two countries was Rhodesia, as Kenya believed that Britain's weak reactions to the white-led government's 1965 UDI made it complicit in the repression of its African majority. Although Kenya initially supported the use of force to defeat the white Smith regime, it eventually accepted that this was impractical. As an ally, the UK expected Kenya to listen to its views carefully, even where the countries did not agree, and Kenya's foreign policy consequently reflected a tension between domestic pressure to support independence for white-ruled African states and non-alignment, and pressure to support Western interests. As a result,

Kenya played a quiet, reactive role in most international events. The problems that Kenyatta had experienced at home and the support Egypt, Russia and China gave the *shifta* buttressed Kenya's pro-Western diplomatic stance.

The British were satisfied with their close relations. Economically, Kenya was a useful supplier of cash-crops and a customer for British manufactured exports (a third of Kenya's imports came from the UK). For the UK, the future of the Asians, the security of the remaining British citizens and the completion of the land transfer programme were the key issues. Geopolitically, the UK was satisfied that it had helped deny Kenya to the communists. Although they believed that Kenya was stable, the British were still concerned about the long-term risks to their citizens. In 1968, the military established a secret contingency plan for the evacuation of foreigners from Kenya in the event of a collapse of law and order. It covered 43,000 Europeans and 188,000 Asians, and involved parachute landings and the seizing of Kenyan airports.[82] The plan was updated in 1969 after the murder of Mboya, but it was clear that it was a last resort, since it would inevitably provoke a violent response.

With relations so close, the British High Commission and the Foreign and Commonwealth Office (FCO) were extremely concerned about the risks of even casual contacts between their officials and KPU leaders, whose policies they deplored. The FCO therefore strongly discouraged officials from meeting opposition leaders. There were virtually no meetings with the opposition until late 1969.[83] The KPU was seen as unlikely to form a government, and therefore the potential benefits of a better relationship were outweighed by the risk of Kenya ministers 'jumping to the conclusion that we were hedging our bets – or, still worse, actively encouraging their opponents'.[84]

Relations with the US were good, and the US was Kenya's third largest donor after the UK and the World Bank. After the defeat of the radicals, US policy towards Kenya was to encourage peaceful conflict resolution, fight communism and encourage regional cooperation. CIA covert operations petered out with the shift of US attention to Vietnam and the declining communist threat. Most US bilateral aid was replaced by multilateral aid through the UN and the World Bank. The US remained popular in Kenya because of its anti-colonial stance, but there were strong lobbies that relations should not become too close. The publication of Ambassador Attwood's book *The Reds and the Blacks* in 1967 – revealing America's involvement in the fight against Odinga – caused great embarrassment. The book was banned in Kenya. There was also a significant gap between American verbal commitments to the end of white rule, and its economic and geopolitical interests, which linked it closely with the UK and South Africa, while its discrimination against black Americans continued to anger Kenyans.

In contrast, after the split with Odinga, Kenya entered into a period of open confrontation with the communist states, which lasted for the rest of Kenyatta's life. This became public in 1966 when Kenyatta, Gichuru and Moi made a series of vitriolic attacks on the Soviets and Chinese. Continued Chinese support to Odinga reinforced Kenyatta's hostility, and economic links were minimal after 1966. Although diplomatic relations continued, in 1967 the government banned the works of Mao Tse-Tung and expelled three Chinese diplomats. During 1966–9, Kenya also expelled a dozen Russian diplomats and journalists suspected of spying or aiding Odinga.

Uganda, Tanzania and the EAC

Within East Africa, relations with Uganda and Tanzania remained close but troubled. The leaders of the three states had personal differences, but divergent economic and development policies were more significant challenges. Tanzania now viewed Kenya as a puppet of the West, while Kenya was concerned about Chinese involvement in Tanzania escaping Julius Nyerere's control and the impact of Tanzania's nationalisations.

Another problem was the growing violence in Uganda. Once President Milton Obote had abrogated the constitution, Baganda MPs refused to take the oath, and the independent Baganda Parliament refused to recognise Obote's new constitution. On 24 May 1966, at the height of the KPU crisis in Kenya, Obote sent in the army, killing more than 1,000 and driving the Kabaka into exile. Uganda was on the verge of civil war, and Kenya responded by closing its borders. Relations were also affected by the Kenyan government's belief that Uganda provided tacit support for the KPU. However, Kenya continued to treat Uganda as a friend, and in 1967 Kenyatta promised Obote troops, if necessary, to perform internal security duties. McKenzie presciently noted at the time that Obote appeared to be frightened, 'largely on account of his failure to dominate Brigadier Amin, the Army Commander.'[85]

Although federation had proved impossible, economic integration was an easier task. In June 1967, the three East African presidents finally signed a Treaty for East African Cooperation. The East African Community (EAC) replaced the EACSO on 1 December 1967. It provided for an economic union analogous to the Common Market of Europe, but without real efforts towards political union or harmonisation of policies. The EAC was the most developed regional integration scheme of its day in Africa, but the treaty was a stage on the road to disintegration, not unity, because of the high degree of existing integration between the colonial territories. By 1965, the common currency was dead and national trade quotas had already undermined the customs union.[86]

With the creation of the EAC, the three countries agreed to continue to manage jointly the railways, harbours, postal service and telecommunications, while the East African Industrial Court would deal with trade disputes, and parastatals such as East African Airways (EAA) would remain common services. A common customs tariff system would be maintained, though there was little done to harmonise national tax systems. The treaty had some redistributive features. The first was the introduction of a transfer tax to help protect Ugandan and Tanzanian industries against Kenya, which resulted in several cases where competing businesses were established in each country. Second, an East African Development Bank was set up to allocate investments disproportionately in favour of Uganda and Tanzania. Finally, the headquarters of two of the common service organisations were moved from Kenya

(Harbours to Tanzania and East African Posts and Telecommunications (EAP&T) to Uganda). The political headquarters of the EAC moved to Arusha in Tanzania, the geographical centre of East Africa.[87]

The treaty created new institutions to administer the community, with a secretariat and a minister and assistant minister from each country. An East African Legislative Assembly (EALA) replaced the Central Legislative Assembly. The Ugandan and Kenyan Presidents chose to appoint their countries' representatives, however, limiting the EALA's significance. Ultimate authority rested with the three presidents, each with veto power over central legislation. The EAC soon attracted applications from Zambia, Ethiopia, Somalia, Burundi and Rwanda, but never accepted a new member (in this incarnation).

Widespread public goodwill existed for the community. However, Kenya soon began to regret some of these decisions. Although central services were administered reasonably efficiently, Kenya felt constrained by its slower-growing neighbours. There were political issues between the Kenyans and the socialist governments of the other two countries that inhibited new common infrastructure projects.[88] Other regional institutions were already in decline. The University of East Africa splintered, for example, as nationalist aspirations led to increasing duplication of facilities between the colleges. This ended with a formal split into three national universities in 1970.

Regional Relations and the End of the Shifta Struggle

Relations with Somalia remained hostile. In 1966–7, the British estimated there were still 2,000 *shifta* operating in North-Eastern and the risk of full-scale war was ever-present. The Somali however, were tiring of a struggle that was producing little. In 1967, following a change of government in Somalia, Zambian President Kenneth Kaunda mediated a peace deal that culminated in a 'Memorandum of Understanding' between Kenyatta and the Somali prime minister at Arusha in October 1967. Kenya established a diplomatic mission in Mogadishu and the fighting gradually wound down as Somalia withdrew support for the *shifta*. Kenya gave little to Somalia in return. Some of the emergency regulations were suspended in 1968; in 1969, the Kenyans granted amnesty to political offenders, released their remaining Somali detainees and partially reopened the border. To avoid claims from its own citizens for compensation, the Kenya government maintained the fiction that the troubles were an internal problem and that the *shifta* were 'Kenyan citizens who were misbehaving within Kenya'.[89] Despite the normalisation of relations, Kenya remained concerned about the prospect of a Somali invasion and minor skirmishes continued for years.

While relations with Somalia were poor, they were correspondingly good with Ethiopia, which faced the same 'Greater Somalia' threat. In December 1963, Kenya and Ethiopia had ratified a mutual defence pact and Emperor Haile Selassie was the first leader to pay a state visit to Kenya in 1964. Kenya's relations with its other northern neighbour, the Sudan, were quiet.

Military Relations

Security remained one of Kenyatta's primary concerns, and as well as defeating the Somali secession, his government successfully deterred potential military coups. Kenyatta's personal authority made a coup against him difficult. Other stabilising factors included the dominance of non-aligned ethnic communities in the army, and the continued control of key posts by British officers, with the implied threat of a British military response to protect Kenyatta.

On 1 December 1966, three years after independence, direct British control of the Kenyan army ended. Brigadier Hardy was replaced as army commander by Joseph Ndolo, a Kamba colonial soldier; the British considered him a friend. Jackson Mulinge, another Kamba KAR soldier, replaced Ndolo as deputy army commander (see Table 4.1).

Although both the army and the Ministry of Defence (through Kenyatta's cousin and personal physician Mungai) were now under African command, the British retained a key role. Having learnt his lesson, Kenyatta was determined to rely on the British on security issues. A defence review in 1966, conducted by a British officer, had recommended significant changes to the Kenyan military. As a result, within a month of Ndolo's elevation, Kenyatta appointed Major-General Penfold, a British officer and ex-KAR commander, to the new role of Chief of General Staff (head of the armed forces). This roused protest in the National Assembly, with a KPU

Table 4.1: Military heads, 1964–71

Chief of General Staff	Major-Gen. R. B. Penfold	1966–9	British
	Brigadier Joseph Ndolo	1969–71	Kamba
Commander of Kenya Army	Major-Gen. Ian Freeland	1963–4	British
	Brigadier A. J. Hardy	1964–6	British
	Brigadier Joseph Ndolo	1966–9	Kamba
	Brigadier then Major-Gen. Jackson Mulinge	1969–78	Kamba
Deputy Commander of the Army	Col. Joseph Ndolo	To 1966	Kamba
	Lt. Col. Jackson Mulinge	1966–9	Kamba
	Col. Peter Kakenyi	1969–n/a	Kamba
Commander of Kenya Air Force	Group Capt. Ian Stockwell	1964–7	British
	Group Capt. Fred Rockwell	1967–71	British
	Group Capt. John Edwards	1971–3	British
Commander of Kenya Navy	Commander E.M.C. Walker	1964–7	British
	Commander Pearce	1967–9	British
	Commander Hall	1969–72	British

Source: Various

motion criticising British influence: 'This man is a foreigner; he has no allegiance to the President of this Republic. He has no allegiance to Kenya . . .'[90] But Penfold remained as Chief of Staff until 1969. He also assumed duties on the new permanent Cabinet Security Committee on defence and internal security in 1967.[91] The high level of trust between the British and Kenyan governments is revealed by the fact that the secretary to this committee was a British MI5 officer, with full access to Kenyan Special Branch files.[92] In 1966, Penfold was supported by 100 British officers and 240 other ranks, while the SAS continued to train Kenyatta's bodyguard and the GSU. This reliance on the British, though not exactly hidden, was certainly not made public.

In May 1969, a second wave of replacements of European officers occurred when Penfold handed over command of the General Staff to Ndolo (see Figure 4.5). The holders of all three top posts – Ndolo, Army Commander Mulinge and Deputy Army Commander Kakenyi – were now Kamba. However, British officers continued to head the navy and air force.

Kenyatta maintained a close interest in the military, gradually promoting Kikuyu officers without destabilising the professional command structure, which might have precipitated the coup he wished to avoid. Despite recruitment quotas, the Kamba and Kalenjin still dominated the lower ranks, with the Kamba making up 11 per cent of the population and 21.4 per cent of the army and the Kalenjin with 10 per cent of the population providing 22.5 per cent of the army.[93] It was only in 1969 that Kenyatta ordered a shift from ethnic to district-based recruiting quotas.[94] Kenyatta also used the Kamba dominance of the officer corps to counterweigh

4.5: The military chain of command, 1969. *Front row, left to right:* Mungai, Mulinge, Kenyatta, Ndolo; *back row, left to right:* Matu, Kakenyi and Nzioka

Courtesy: Nation Group Newspapers

Kikuyu political hegemony, providing an opportunity for patronage to the Kamba and helping to control the chauvinists in his own community. The community most under-represented in the army and completely absent from its leadership was the Luo, historically not seen as 'warlike' by the British, and now massively disadvantaged by state suspicion over their support for Odinga.[95]

The continued threat of attack from Somalia, discounted by the British, but of deep concern to Kenya, was to become the subject of the third defence arrangement between the two countries. During the 1964 defence discussions, Duncan Sandys had informally indicated that Kenya did not need to build up its armaments to compete with Somalia, as the British would find it difficult to stand by if Kenya was invaded. In January 1967, with Somalia receiving arms and jet aircraft from the Soviet Union, Kenyatta raised this issue formally and secured from a reluctant Harold Wilson a written commitment that Britain would look favourably on a request for military assistance in the face of a Somali attack. The British high commissioner handed the note to Kenyatta in his Bamburi beach hut, leading this secret deal to be known as the 'Bamburi Understanding'. It said:

> Kenya Government may be sure that if Kenya were the victim of outright aggression by Somalia the British Government would give the situation the most urgent consideration. While, therefore, the British Government cannot in advance give the Kenya Government any assurance of automatic assistance, the possibility of Britain's going to Kenya's assistance in the event of any organised and unprovoked attack by Somalia is not precluded.[96]

Although Kenyatta chose to treat this as a near-unconditional guarantee, the British were characteristically careful to leave their options open.[97]

A Growing Economy

The Triumph of 'African Socialism'

The late 1960s were a good time for Kenya's economy. The crises of independence had been overcome; the land question resolved (after a fashion) and rapid growth delivered (see Figure 4.6). There was an expectation that Kenya, short of capital but not of investments, would soon take off and would no longer need to rely on foreign aid. This was the age of development planning, in which a disinterested elite was expected to use the levers available to them to build a modern economy in the interests of all. Mboya's Ministry of Economic Planning and Development planned state investments in roads, schools, housing, irrigation and utilities, all coordinated through a national Development Plan (a second version of which was produced in 1966).

The victory of the self-styled 'moderates' had signalled that Kenya was open for Western investment, both private and government-to-government. Their economic policy had been articulated in the 1965 Sessional Paper, which had appropriated the popular term 'socialism' to the pro-Western cause. Nationalisation such as that taking place in Tanzania after the Arusha Declaration – of commercial banks, millers, breweries and other major industries – was not on the agenda. It was a policy of encouraging development over equality, accepting differentiation as a side-effect of growth: in Njonjo's possibly apocryphal words, a 'man eat man' rather than a 'man eat nothing' culture.

Nonetheless, there remained a strong nationalist and socialist element in Kenya's state and society, reflecting a consensus – echoed in Europe – that state ownership was good, and private enterprise (especially foreign) a necessary evil. Even amongst Kenyatta's closest allies there was some suspicion of foreign ownership. Although there was no compulsory nationalisation, the government's investment vehicles built a portfolio of part or complete ownership in power, transport and communications, manufacturing and finance. This protected foreign investors, but also ensured they depended on state support and allowed the government to share in their success. By the late 1960s, most aspects of the economy were under the direct or indirect control of the central ministries. As well as import licences and access to foreign exchange, the government controlled tax and duty rates and tariffs. It set prices for many goods. The agricultural statutory boards were in practice subject to the government's instructions. It could influence overall credit levels and could grant or withhold it directly through the AFC, the DFCK and some banks. It owned firms in many industries and could decide who could own a business through its Africanisation policies.

4.6: Real GDP growth, 1964–70

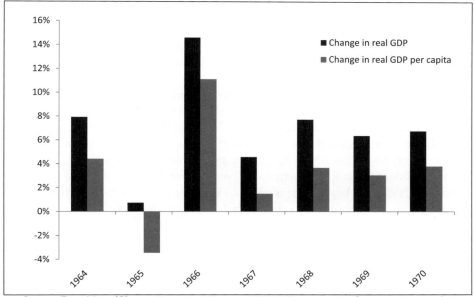

Source: Republic of Kenya, *Statistical Abstracts*, 1968–1974, per capita figures are interpolations from census data

In retrospect, though, the achievements of the period were more modest than originally believed. Foreign companies did invest more in Kenya than elsewhere in Africa, but did not generate the flow of capital needed to build the economy fast enough to satisfy expectations, while Western gift aid was modest. Regional integration was limited by the export-orientation of colonial infrastructure, which meant it was virtually impossible to ship goods by land between most countries (with the rare exception of the EAC, which itself was no longer a common market). Aid could mask but could not override the changing terms of trade. The global balance of power between primary producers and manufacturers was changing. Between 1954 and 1964, Kenya had to pay 10 per cent more per unit for imports and received 14 per cent less for its exports.

Debate had also begun on the impact of globalisation. Already an issue during the 1930s, the inexorable march of manufacturing technology was creating increasingly complex products. These required more specialisation to produce and a broader market to make economic sense. In Europe, products such as civil aircraft were already global businesses, and industries such as cars were heading the same way. The challenge for Kenya was whether it could sustain and develop regional markets for its own less-complex manufactures, or protect them from the growing scale of world competition.

Fiscal Fragmentation and a New Central Bank

Despite the formation of the EAC in 1967, the economic cracks were widening rather than narrowing between the states. Rather than establishing a Central Bank for East Africa, as the British had hoped, during 1965–6 the three countries abandoned their common currency (the East African shilling) and introduced exchange controls. Tanzania was the first to issue its own notes in 1965 and Uganda followed. In September 1966, Kenya too began to issue its own currency, the Kenya shilling and the Kenya pound (£1 = Sh20), alongside the establishment of the Central Bank of Kenya (CBK).

The CBK's main functions were to issue and manage the currency, to act as the government's banker and to manage exchange rates, foreign reserves (with a target of enough foreign exchange to cover four months of imports) and exchange controls. It also regulated the commercial banks, ensuring their stability and proper operation. The CBK managed the government's bank account, known as the Consolidated Fund, into which all government income was paid and from which the National Assembly's permission was needed to make withdrawals (via the budget and supplementary estimates when the budget was exhausted). For the first time, the state now had the power to manage domestic credit and the money supply directly. An expatriate from the International Monetary Fund (IMF) initially became governor of the bank, as skills in fiscal policy were rare in Kenya. He was replaced in 1967 by Duncan Ndegwa, civil service head since 1963, who remained in the role for the next 20 years.

Aid Partners and Sources of Government Money

Money lay at the heart of Kenya's problems, particularly the lack of sufficient tax and revenue surplus from the country's operations to finance its development. Income taxes from the country's few formal sector employees provided the largest domestic source of revenue, between K£15 and K£30 million a year. Other direct taxes were tiny in comparison. Indirect taxes provided more money – import duties drew in K£17–22 million a year, excise duties and tariffs another K£6–12 million.[98] Total state revenue nearly doubled, from K£40 million in 1964–5 to K£76 million in 1969–70, but these sums were still minuscule. The state now financed all its recurrent spending and some development spending directly, but still relied on foreign loans and gifts for the rest.

Kenya needed aid. The country was a favoured site for Western assistance in Africa, and an influx of funds in the 1960s helped deliver significant improvements in living standards and services. Almost all this aid was bilateral and government-to-government. By far Kenya's largest aid partner until the 1980s was the United Kingdom. In 1964, the British reported that they had invested more in Kenya since 1945 than in any other colony.[99] The independence settlement offered still more help. Under technical and teaching schemes, 1,500 Britons continued to work in Kenya. When added to the settlement schemes (GB£12 million), expatriate pensions and compensation (£13 million) and technical assistance (£10 million), the British contributed another £45 million to Kenya over the next three years. However, there were capital outflows matching this. The pension expenditure and much of the settlement fund money left the country, and debt repayments had already begun. The balance of trade was in Britain's favour, leading to a net outflow of funds by 1966.

The CDC was Kenya's second major bilateral investor, again mainly with British funds. It invested in potentially profitable projects such as the KTDA tea factories, the Tana River Development Company, and house building. As a pseudo-commercial entity, it needed to charge interest on its loans, something many Kenyans disliked. The US provided some direct private investment, but their main contribution was in aid form. In the first four years of independence, the US Embassy reported that the US had given US$64 million of aid to Kenya, including $15 million in long-term loans. US technical personnel continued in various roles, while 1,500 Kenyans were still studying in the US.[100] The next largest bilateral aid partner was West Germany, offering long-term loans to the ICDC, the DFCK and other parastatals.

Multilateral aid mainly came through the World Bank. From 1960–1 on, the bank had loaned Kenya K£5 million for roads and land settlement, and in 1965–6 it invested K£27 million in East African Roads and Harbours (EAR&H) and communications upgrades in EAP&T. The UN agencies (UNESCO, the UN Food and Agriculture Organisation – FAO – and UNICEF) also had programmes in Kenya. Finally, there were the African banks, the East African Development Bank and the African Development Bank (ADB). It was a complex but generous support structure.

By 1967, there were already signs that the optimistic assumptions of aid in the early years of freedom were not going to be met. Although foreign investors and donors were willing to contribute to Kenya's development, it was never for entirely altruistic reasons, and much aid was in loan form. Where foreign governments did invest, there was an inevitable requirement for supervision of those investments, and this was already seen as bordering on interference in domestic affairs. The result was also a steady increase in public debt. Government borrowings doubled between 1964 and 1970. Bond issues and loans from Britain dominated its portfolio, but there was growing use of short-term borrowing (mainly by selling Treasury bills). In the same period, the debt servicing costs – how much the Kenyans had to pay back for their loans and interest – also doubled, though the increase was delayed by the deferred repayment terms for many of the early settlement loans.

Commerce and Industry Minister Kibaki warned that the country was showing signs of a dependence mentality. Kenyans appeared to believe they could never develop through their own resources and efforts, but only by foreign aid. This debate – over the criticality of external pump-priming investments and the degree to which Kenya should adjust its policies to ensure they continued – was to continue for decades.

Foreign Private Investment: The Rise of the Multinationals

The mid- to late 1960s saw substantial foreign investments in the country. K£25 million a year (net) flowed into the country during 1966–8.[101] Most investments were tariff-jumping import substitution projects, reducing Kenya's dependence on imports, creating jobs and saving foreign exchange, though at the cost of production inefficiency and higher consumer prices. Most foreign investment was matched by the government. Manufacturing output increased by 50 per cent between 1964 and 1970. Despite this investment, however, the sector barely changed its share of GDP, rising from 10.4 per cent in 1964 to 10.8 per cent in 1970.[102] There was no mass shift to export-oriented manufacturing and processing of Kenyan agricultural products dominated the sector.[103]

One of the biggest foreign investments was the acquisition of Kenya Canners by the American Del Monte Corporation in 1968. This followed its 1965 takeover of the Thika pineapple plant, the first substantial US investment after independence (though the Treasury later used it as an example of a deal that was not in Kenya's interest).[104] British and British-linked groups were more assertive. A major new entrant was Anglo-African giant Lonrho, which invested heavily in Kenya, buying up several British-owned firms during 1967–9. These included the *Standard* newspaper's parent, farms, distributors, the East Africa Tanning and Extract Company (EATEC) wattle estates and a large vehicle importer.[105] In 1967, ICI and the DFCK set up Triangle Fertilisers, building a plant in Mombasa. However, the risks were high where competing multinational investments clashed. The Rothmans investment of 1966–7, during which the British-South African Group invested heavily in the Kenyan market, led to a marketing war with British American Tobacco (BAT), and ended with Rothmans admitting defeat (as Castle Breweries would do 35 years later) and selling out to its rival. Another mid-1960s investment was the Kenya National Assurance Company (KNAC), an insurance company established by the DFCK, British and other overseas investors. In 1967, the government took a controlling share in the business, converting it into a parastatal. This provided both stronger control and more patronage opportunities: soon after, it insisted that all government bodies, parastatals and cooperatives insure through KNAC.

Asian capital, in contrast, though local and ready to invest, was discouraged for political reasons. Kenyan Asians did not qualify as foreign investors, but neither did they receive the credit preference that Africans received. The result was an underinvestment in mid-size manufacturing during the 1960s.[106] In this area, at least, equity was preferred over growth.

The ICDC and Finance for Investment

In the late 1960s and 1970s, the ICDC was a key instrument of government policy, using state funds to encourage both Africanisation and economic growth. Its primary role was to hold equity in large investments on behalf of the government. It owned and managed shareholdings in hundreds of firms, including complete ownership of Kenatco and KNTC, majority holdings in General Motors and Kenya Wine Agencies and minority shareholdings in Kenya Cashewnuts and East African Industries (EAI). It also spun off its own subsidiaries, including the DFCK, the ICDC Investment Company and Kenya Industrial Estates, all supported by foreign loans. In this way, the state acquired stakes in virtually every major new business, encouraging the growth of protected public–private partnerships, often with local production or import monopolies.

The other role of the ICDC was to provide loans for Africans to establish or expand their businesses, including financing the buy-out of Asian businesses. The ICDC's small commercial and industrial investors' programme was initially seen as a success. However, it was less well regarded in the long term. At this time, many African businessmen were inexperienced in business, had difficulties distinguishing credit from income, tried to do too much themselves and faced pressures from family members. Some sold their businesses back to Asians, and became sleeping partners and frontmen. As with other small-scale credit systems, the loans programme was hamstrung by the popular view that debts to the government could be ignored if funds were not available, as repayment was not an obligation, and they would eventually be written off. The ICDC was extremely reluctant to foreclose on investments. The larger loans generally went to the country's few existing capitalists and to civil servants – those with the best security, connections and experience. The non-commercial nature of such loans was explicit, and by its nature this was a high-risk process. Although profitable on paper, the ICDC paid no dividends between 1964 and 1977. At the time, however, it was under pressure for being too restrictive, rather than too lax, in its lending. Its first three executive directors were all Kikuyu. Joe Wanjui (Kiambu) led it until 1968, when he joined

EAI. Civil servant Maina Wanjigi (from Murang'a) replaced him for a year, and he in turn was succeeded by Matu Wamae (from Nyeri) in 1969. All became wealthy and influential.

Commercial bank lending was also a problem. Banks made loans to many businesses, but there were tensions between commercial good practice and the political pressure to loan funds on limited security. Many African wholesale, retail and manufacturing businesses were highly geared, running with loans twice the size of their assets. Foreign-owned banks dominated commercial banking. Barclays, National and Grindlays Bank and Standard Bank were all British owned, and together held 85 per cent of bank assets. Smaller foreign banks included the Bank of Baroda and Bank of India, the Ottoman Bank and the Commercial Bank of Africa.[107] The only significant locally owned finance institutions were the East Africa Building Society and the state-owned Cooperative Bank and National Bank of Kenya.

The capital market was still in its infancy. A few private companies went public through share offerings on the Nairobi Stock Exchange in 1969–70.[108] However, there still were too few wealthy Africans to buy these shares, and Asian families bought most with cash they could not remit abroad. In 1967, stockbrokers estimated that 95 per cent of their transactions were with Europeans or Asians.

The Energy Sector

In the capital-intensive energy sector, public–private partnerships dominated. Kenya's electricity supply and demand were both modest. Half its power came from Uganda's Owen Falls dam, bought by the Kenya Power Company, a public–private joint venture, and then distributed and sold to consumers by East African Power and Lighting (EAP&L). EAP&L was a private business, but the government was its largest shareholder and set electricity prices. Kenya's big growth opportunity was in hydroelectric power. In 1964, the Tana River Development Company (TRDC) was established as a joint venture between the government, the CDC, other foreign investors, and EAP&L. In 1968, it completed the first stage of the huge Seven Forks hydroelectric project on the Tana River. This state-controlled three-partner structure for electricity generation and distribution continued until the 1990s.

The centre of the oil industry was the Mombasa oil refinery, a 50–50 government and oil company joint venture that opened in 1964.[109] At the time, it was the biggest industrial investment in East Africa, and (extended and modernised) it remained functional 45 years later. The refinery proved to be one of Kenya's strongest export earners, exporting refined petroleum products to Uganda, Rwanda and beyond. Oil distribution and marketing were dominated by multinationals, including Shell/ BP, Esso, Mobil, Caltex and Agip. Fortunately or unfortunately, Kenya had no oil reserves, although Shell continued drilling in the north without success.

Developments in Transport

Kenya's transport network was growing and services improving. Much of it was built, owned and operated by the three East African governments. EAR&H ran both Mombasa harbour and the railway (from Mombasa through Nairobi and Nakuru to Kisumu and Uganda). This extensive network was seen as a huge competitive advantage for the country (to move bulk produce to the coast for export) and 'the physical life-line without which Kenya's economy would quickly perish'.[110] However, no new lines were laid after independence. The railways were showing signs of financial distress, hurt by the growing quality of road transport, but new passenger services were still being introduced – in 1963, the first passenger service was run between Nairobi and Dar-es-Salaam – and both railways and harbours were still profitable in 1969.[111] EAA was the main regional airline. It had been established in 1946 as a joint investment between the three East African governments, and was profitable and stable. Nairobi airport, able to handle jet aircraft, was the hub for both Kenya and East Africa.

The colonial government had also built an extensive network of murram (untarred) roads. Few new roads were built during the 1960s, but bituminisation accelerated rapidly. The Mombasa–Nairobi highway was fully tarred for the first time in 1968. Road construction and maintenance was the responsibility of the Ministry of Works. Most commercial road transport was privately owned, although the state also had its own transport business, Kenatco.

Small Businesses and the Informal Sector

While there were virtually no large African-owned enterprises yet, the ICDC, KNTC, banks and district loan boards were pumping resources into the smaller-scale African private sector and Kikuyu employers were their main beneficiaries. A survey in 1966–7 showed that 64 per cent of the ICDC's small industrial loans and 44 per cent of commercial loans since independence had gone to Kikuyu businessmen. Many had used political connections to get them, but this bias was also linked to a higher level of mobility and greater commercial focus in the Kikuyu community.[112] As well as moving into the white highlands, Kikuyu entrepreneurs were setting up shops and businesses in Luo, Luhya, Gusii and Kamba areas. It was the same route that Asians had travelled half a century before, and – like the Asians before them – these new immigrants were not always welcome.

Loosely linked with such pump-priming investments was the rise of the small-scale African manufacturing and service sector. Emerging on the margins of the urban areas, it was populated by moderately educated people who had left formal sector employment, many having learnt their trade in Asian-owned businesses.[113] By the late 1960s, the sector was growing rapidly, absorbing many migrants into lower-income, less skilled jobs. Some of these businesses were official, registered and taxed; others existed in the grey area of undocumented employment. They were part of the informal sector, which began to be recognised in the 1970s as a key element in Kenya's economy, providing opportunities for those unable to obtain formal sector jobs or to cultivate the land.

The Changing Business Elite

The best analysis of Kenya's industries in the 1960s was conducted by the NCCK, which published the book *Who Controls Industry in Kenya?* in 1968. It concluded that the economy remained – unsurprisingly – dominated by firms established in the colonial era. Most were British owned and led mainly by white Kenyans.[114] Less common were businesses owned and led by other foreign interests (such as Bamburi Cement, Coca-Cola, Esso, Sadolin paints and the Bata shoe group). Asian businesses dominated textiles, small manufacturing, property companies, bakeries and smaller import–export businesses.

Among large companies, the top 50 directors in 1968 were almost entirely white or Asian.[115] Nairobi Mayor Charles Rubia was one of the few exceptions, a director of the ICDC, DFCK, Block Hotels, the Cooperative Bank and East African Breweries. Most other African directors were seconded from the government, to oversee its investments. Permanent secretaries Michuki at the Treasury and Joseph Kibe and Kenneth Matiba at Commerce and Industry (all Kikuyu from Murang'a) sat on the board of virtually every company that had government equity. In contrast, the agricultural parastatals were mostly chaired by ex-opposition politicians such as Ngei (Maize Marketing Board 1963–4), Ngala (Maize Marketing Board 1964–6), Muliro (Cotton Lint and Seed Marketing Board 1965–6 and Maize and Produce Board 1966–9) and Towett (Dairy Board 1965–8) or by foreign professionals. Kikuyu elites led the big cooperatives (most notably the KCC) and large private companies such as BAT. There was no dominance by a single ethnic group; there were many non-Kikuyu 'political' directors, such as Walter Odede, Mboya's Luo father-in-law. However, there were almost no Kamba, Kalenjin, Mijikenda, Maasai or northern pastoralist business or parastatal executives.

Employment and the Labour Movement

One curious fact about the 'rush to growth' of the 1960s was that it created no growth in private sector wage employment at all. The number of private sector jobs stood at 412,800 in 1962, and did not return to this level until 1971 (see Figure 4.7). All the new jobs of the 1960s were in the public sector, particularly central government, which doubled its establishment between 1963 and 1971. The central administration expanded so fast in part because of the creation of new departments and parastatals and growing demand for services, in part as a response to patronage pressures.[116] With 40 per cent of the recurrent budget devoted to salaries, the funds available for development from internal resources were already under strain. By 1970, there were 250,000 public sector workers. The country's four largest commercial employers were all state owned: EAR&H, Cargo Handling Services, Nairobi City Council and EAP&T, with the private sector's EAP&L and Lonrho next.[117]

4.7: Wage employment, 1960–73

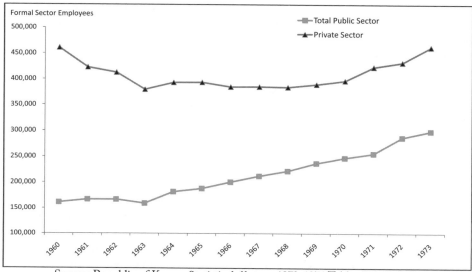

Source: Republic of Kenya, *Statistical Abstract*, 1972, 1976 Tables 221–2, Collier and Lal:
Labour and Poverty in Kenya, p. 69

Wages rose faster than inflation for those in formal sector jobs. In the early 1960s, public sector salaries had grown fastest, but with the Kenyanisation of the late 1960s shortages of skilled Africans pushed private sector salaries up as well. By 1970, average African salaries in real terms were double those of 1961.[118] This was not the result of private bargaining, but a state-controlled process. Wage controls had been in place since 1951, and by 1969 there were 15 wage regulation orders for specific industries.[119] In 1967, under union pressure, the state raised the minimum wage, and extended it to all workers over 18.

The creation of COTU, the Industrial Court and the rise in wages all quietened labour protest. The man-days lost to strikes fell rapidly from the 1965 peak. Despite this, there was no natural congruence of interests between unionised workers and the state, and they remained in a difficult relationship, shaped by the state's role as the country's largest employer. Formal sector workers were still a privileged minority, since only a quarter of the labour force were in paid employment (most were subsistence farmers or pastoralists), and half of that quarter were in informal or short-term jobs.

The KPU split had blown apart the fiction of trade union unity, and the government's response to union dissent had been harsh. Once control was restored, those willing to conform could be well rewarded. Released from detention in May 1967, for example, by February 1969 Akumu was COTU secretary-general once more, now part of the Gatundu group's campaign against Mboya.[120] Although centralised on paper in COTU, the trade union movement was far from monolithic. As well as representing varying political views, it was divided by ethnicity and patron–client relations, and by the differing interests of workers in different sectors.[121] Mass activism at a national level was carefully restricted, although individual unionists were free to launch political careers based on workers' votes. In 1969, in another recourse to administrative fiat, the government ordered the Kenya Civil Servants Union and the Kenya National Union of Teachers (KNUT) to disaffiliate from COTU.[122] At the same time, it announced legislation to make it compulsory for other unions to affiliate to COTU, and an offence for any strike to take place without COTU's approval. Defiantly, 30,000 teachers struck in November 1969, but Kiano declared their strike illegal. The leaders were arrested and charged with incitement, and the strike soon collapsed.

Tourism and Wildlife

Kenya had been developing a small, elite tourist business since the 1920s, based on its settler connection and development. Wealthy and powerful individuals visited Kenya for its wildlife viewing and big-game hunting, but numbers were small: only 65,000 tourists visited Kenya in 1963. The development of international tourism was not initially the most visible priority for the government, but in the long term it proved a great success. With internal political tensions resolved and state credit easily available, 1967 was the year when mass tourism took off, with visitors almost tripling between 1966 and 1968 (see Figure 4.8). Gross foreign exchange earnings from tourism tripled between 1963 and 1972 and tourism was soon second only to coffee as a foreign exchange earner.

Wildlife hunting continued, with visitors able to buy licences to shoot elephant, rhino, lion, leopard and buffalo. Elephant numbers were so high that the government considered a cull of Tsavo's 15,000 elephants. However, there was already concern that Kenya's wild animals might need greater protection from the growing human population. The 1945 National Parks Ordinance had set aside areas exclusively for the use of wildlife. At independence, there were five national parks (the largest,

4.8: International arrivals and game park visits, 1962–72

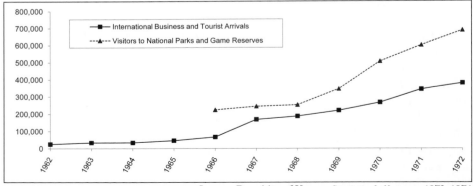

Source: Republic of Kenya, *Statistical Abstracts*, 1972, 1976

Tsavo, covering most of Taita-Taveta District) and several more reserves under local management in Maasailand and Meru. With the settlement of previously under-used European farms and ranches, however, the pressure on Kenya's wildlife grew rapidly. In response, between 1964 and 1969, the government gazetted six new national parks, a policy that was supported by local councils in the hope of greater revenue from tourism, but with limited benefit to local communities in practice.[123]

In the colonial era, foreign capital had dominated the industry, and nearly all the hotels had been in private hands. Now, the government took stakes in most big developments. The largest hotel chain was Block Hotels, part owned by the ICDC. The Hilton hotel opened in 1969 and the Intercontinental hotel was under construction, as were several safari lodges. The KTDC acted as the main government investor, taking equity stakes in the Intercontinental, Hilton, Pan-Afric and Kenya Hotels and Safari Lodges.

More Changes in Land and Agriculture

Food and Cash-Crops

The 1960s saw massive extensions of government support for smallholder and commercial agriculture, particularly export cash-crops. Better roads helped farmers bring their produce to market, credit was easily available and cooperatives helped market their produce. The result was a rapid growth in marketed output, especially of coffee, tea and pyrethrum, which raised living standards for those producers able to participate. Marketed output from small farms increased by a phenomenal 12.6 per cent per annum between 1964 and 1970, an unprecedented jump in production caused by the introduction of cash-crops into areas where political conditions had limited their growth, by government support, and European farm purchase and subdivision. By 1967, the value of marketed output from small farms (smallholdings in the reserves or the settlement schemes) exceeded that from large farms (the former white highlands).

Coffee remained the dominant cash-crop, its earnings more than double those of its next competitor, tea. Kenya's relatively open economy depended heavily on these two products, exposing the country to 'boom and bust', as world prices and demand varied. African cash-cropping was focused on a few agriculturally rich, densely populated districts: particularly Kiambu, Murang'a and Nyeri in Central Province and Kisii in Nyanza. By 1969, more than one-third of smallholders in these districts were growing coffee and 10 per cent were growing tea. Central Province also dominated smallholder dairy and pyrethrum production. In other districts, far from urban and export markets, subsistence agriculture and pastoralism remained the norm.[124]

Maize remained Kenya's food staple. Most maize was consumed or bartered locally; the rest was sold via the Maize and Produce Board, which had the monopoly over its purchase, storage, distribution and sale of maize, and its agent the KFA.

4.9: Maize imports and exports, 1963–2003

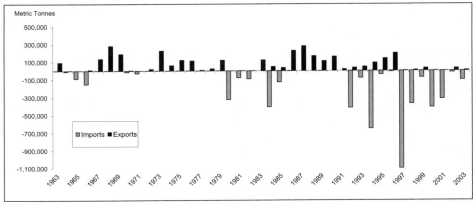

Source: FAOStat data, 2004

Kenya was not a particularly efficient producer and the government kept maize prices above world prices. Until 1966, Kenya was a net maize importer, but from 1967 until the 1980s the country was self-sufficient and often exported maize (see Figure 4.9). Maize movements between districts were still controlled and maize pricing and policy remained politicised and sensitive.

A similar system applied to wheat, mostly grown on large farms in Uasin Gishu and Nakuru and sold through the KFA and the Wheat Board. Facing growing demand for bread, the government supported the expansion of wheat farming into Narok, and production doubled between independence and 1969.

Settlement in the Rift Valley

The former white highlands continued to be the destination for tens of thousands of immigrants from other parts of Kenya, through settlement schemes and 'willing buyer, willing seller' land purchases. Between 1960 and 1968, more than 2 million acres (800,000 hectares) of former European farms were taken over;[125] 45,000 to 50,000 families (at least 250,000 people) were settled on 1.1 million acres of settlement schemes. By 1970, when most schemes ended, more than two-thirds of the original European mixed farming area was African owned. The remaining third was still in European hands, as were 4 million acres of ranches and plantations, for which there were no foreign funds for a buyout.

'Willing buyer, willing seller' was now the main acquisition method. By 1969, Africans had bought out 1,200 farms directly.[126] The ADC also took over some white-owned farms itself. However, the settlement schemes never entirely ended. After the end of the million-acre scheme, the UK continued to finance some lower density settlement throughout the decade. In 1966, the Kenyans set up their own scheme for squatters ineligible for the main schemes. This, the *haraka* scheme, settled another

13,000 families on small subsistence plots on abandoned or mismanaged farms, though the results were a disappointment economically.[127] The state continued to drip feed the occasional subdivision of a farm or forest area, to keep land hopes alive. As Gary Wassermann drily noted, 'In Kenya, land is the opium of the masses.'[128]

Nyandarua, Nakuru and Laikipia were the main settlement areas for the Kikuyu. Their moves north of Nakuru were more disputed. Tensions swirled around Moi, who, as the most senior Kalenjin in the government, was seen as selling out to the Kikuyu by allowing them to purchase white-occupied land outside their 'traditional' areas. By 1969, 27 per cent of Kikuyu lived outside Central Province: in the Rift Valley, the urban areas and elsewhere. In Nakuru District, more than half the large farms were now Kikuyu owned.[129] It is a misconception, however, that there was a mass migration of Kikuyu to the mixed farming belt of Nakuru, Uasin Gishu and Trans-Nzoia after independence. In fact, this did not occur: 59 per cent of Nakuru District was Kikuyu in 1962, 61 per cent in 1979. In these 17 years, the percentage of Kikuyu in Uasin Gishu fell from 33 to 19 per cent and in Trans-Nzoia from 12 to 10 per cent.[130] The Kikuyu were already established in these districts by 1962, and much of their land acquisition was by larger farmers, not smallholders, barely changing the ethnic composition of the districts. The Kalenjin, meanwhile, moved into Trans-Nzoia, Uasin Gishu and northern Nakuru. Between 1962 and 1969, the Kalenjin population of Uasin Gishu tripled.

Although observers have disagreed with the economics or decried the class implications of the settlement programme, most accept that it achieved its short-term goals. Kenyatta repeatedly used the acquisition of European farms when defending the government's performance, and one analysis describes it as 'one of the most successful and socially profitable examples of land reform in the world.'[131] Economically, it was controversial: while it demonstrated the viability of peasant production, most of the farms did not achieve the targeted returns. Assumptions made about productivity were optimistic, and far from being landless, some plot owners had actually obtained second farms through the schemes, and divided their efforts between the ex-reserves and the highlands. As the most lucrative cash-crops took years to mature, there was little coffee or tea in the settlement schemes in the 1960s. Half the loans made for land purchase consistently remained unpaid.[132] In fact, non-farm incomes were the main way Kenyans paid back settlement scheme loans.[133] Although larger farms were more profitable, land could not generate a sufficient surplus to fund the improvements needed to become sustainably profitable. The settlement schemes satisfied those who obtained land and diverted protest with the promise of more, but the numbers settled were modest. Only a complete end to the large farm sector could have made a real inroad on landlessness.

In practice, Kenya was driving in the opposition direction. By the late 1960s, government policy and administrative processes quietly favoured larger farms, despite the political pressure in favour of subdivision. Partnerships and cooperative ownership was fine, but purchase for subdivision was discouraged, driven by the desire to maintain large-scale commercial agriculture. The number of farms larger than 100 hectares in the ex-scheduled areas, having fallen from 3,000 to fewer than

2,000 between 1962 and 1966, rose slightly between 1966 and 1970.[134] There was a growing tension in agricultural policy between vote-winning, redistributive choices, and elite-oriented activities that favoured inequality for greater production. Policy oscillated between differing views of development and equity, but was guided by Western advice and bureaucratic norms towards a less-populist model that aimed to maximise production whatever the effects on equality.

Kenya had at this time no overt class of robber barons, and the rural populace and its profitability were the cornerstone of Kenya's political and economic system. Inequalities in land ownership and in farm returns were growing, but there was a strong egalitarian element in popular culture, which meant that such unequal relationships needed to be disguised or rationalised. This was achieved in part through patron–client linkages that provided trickle-down benefits to smaller farmers from patron accumulation. It was also executed through bureaucratic processes (land control, credit policy, trade licences and agricultural extension rules) that were opaque to most people. In this way, inequalities could grow without disrupting popular support.

Although land registration continued, its implications remained controversial. In 1967, Parliament passed the Land Control Act, which provided for strict control on all land purchases to mitigate the side-effects of individual land title. The new land control boards could veto land acquisitions – a paternalist response to the concern about landlessness – and tried to minimise subdivision. The boards also further entrenched ethnicity in land ownership, as they ensured that within most ex-reserves (unlike the white highlands), land would normally change hands only within the local ethnic community. While non-citizens were banned from buying agricultural land, the government forced through an exemption process allowing – with their permission – foreign businesses to own land. European farmers and companies were not only selling land; they were buying it as well.

Continuity and Change in the Pastoral Regions

While shrinking farm sizes tended to push farmers in central and western Kenya away from pastoralism, or towards 'zero grazing' (feeding cattle in stalls), the northern pastoralists such as the Turkana and Samburu, who derived almost all their income and sustenance from naturally foraging livestock, were less affected by the changes of the 1960s. The semi-arid areas were not so well suited to milk production because of their distance from markets and poor infrastructure.

Northern pastoralists were also poorly represented politically, and there was little investment in these regions. Pastoralism amongst the Somali had been disrupted by the *shifta* war, and the provision of famine relief around permanent water sources further encouraged the creation of permanent settlements. For the Maasai, closer to Nairobi, the closure of the national parks, population growth and land registration created a long-term challenge to their communal land-owning, nomadic, cattle-based economy.[135] The late 1960s saw a new form of tenure in pastoral areas, backed by the World Bank, to encourage the more productive use of lightly populated pastoral lands. The 1968 Land (Group Representatives) Act allowed land to be registered by ethnic communities as corporate entities, with communal land ownership and grazing reserved for section members only, and the possibility of land improvements and of using land as security for loans. Land was wealth now, even more than cattle. These ranches expanded to cover most of the Maasai lands by the early 1980s. In parallel, however, western Narok was being privately registered by Maasai elites and sold to Kipsigis immigrants, and many Kikuyu and Luhya were buying into Kajiado and north Narok. This was to cause much trouble later, as the Maasai found it difficult to accept the long-term implications of such settlement.

Growing Pressure on the Asians, 1967–9

While white settlers were leaving as their farms were acquired, there was no equivalent foreign-funded programme for the economic centre of Asian life: small and medium-sized businesses.

Africanisation was rapidly reducing job opportunities for non-citizens. By 1970, 95 per cent of those in public and private sector jobs were citizens, up from 89 per cent in 1963. The future of the Asians who did not become Kenyan, and more worryingly for the region, of all Asians whatever their citizenship, was the 'Asian question' that was so influential in Anglo-Kenyan relations and internal politics in the 1960s and 1970s. By 1967, although in law the goal was Kenyanisation, the real goal was Africanisation – the practice of positive discrimination and the replacement of as many non-Africans by Africans as possible. It was unconstitutional, but politically popular (at least until the economic consequences became clear).[136] Kenyatta, like many other Kenyan Africans, was not well disposed towards the Asian community, though he tried to balance equity and economics. Many Asians believed that it was only their commercial and financial muscle and the likely effect on foreign investment that stopped them being driven out entirely. There had been successes, but ownership in the commercial sector was changing only slowly and there was a gradual shift from 'levelling the playing field' to direct legislative intervention.

The 1967 Immigration Act and the 1968 Trade Licensing Act were the most radical legislative initiatives yet. The Immigration Act tightened the rules covering work permits, to force non-citizen Asians to become Kenyan or leave. The focus was on semi-skilled clerical and manual jobs. The Act also established a Kenyanisation Bureau, to stop foreigners being employed to do a job that a Kenyan could do, and to scrutinise land sales to foreigners. The Trade Licensing Act was intended to Africanise the distribution trade, previously dominated by Asian families. It progressively excluded non-citizens from trading in rural areas and specified a list of goods to be sold by citizens only. It forced Asian non-citizens to close down their businesses or sell them to Africans. The policy also provided an opportunity for discretion or corruption, since licences could still be granted in special circumstances. Odinga was an opponent of this populist legislation, warning that unemployment would result and questioning the logic of replacing an Asian elite with an African one. Most African leaders, however, found Asians an easy target: for Kenyatta in a speech on 8 February 1968, Asians were 'swarms of locusts'.[137] In July 1968, notice was given that non-citizens outside urban areas had six months to wind up their wholesale and retail businesses and on 1 January 1969, 3,000 traders were ordered to close down.

The state also adopted other pro-African policies. Procurement practices began formally to favour Africans in tendering; the Maize and Produce Board started to drive Asian traders out of the maize flour market; and the KNTC drove Asian traders out of their import intermediary role in favour of African distributors. The KNTC even refused to supply some Asian-owned shops with commodities.[138] However, like the ICDC, the KNTC later paid the price of granting too many loans to politically connected Africans inexperienced in business, and bad debts mounted.[139] The Transport Licensing Board (TLB), the regulator, increasingly restricted commercial vehicle licences to citizens, and in 1967 it declared that 90 per cent of passenger road transport was now 'African'. The National Construction Corporation (NCC), founded in 1968 to provide capital and support to African building contractors, played a similar role. It was a well-understood and consistent programme of gradually increasing discrimination that often failed to distinguish between skin colour and citizenship. Several state bodies were taken to court for discriminating against non-African citizens.

The result was panic and a gradual exodus. At least 50,000 Asians left in the first five years of independence. By the 1969 census, there were only 139,000 left. The effects were seen in several sectors, where costs rose and production fell. Small urban centres where Asians had provided most retail and distribution services were severely affected. During 1967–8, GB£25 million of Asian capital left the country, weakening the balance of payments.[140]

Britain, meanwhile, was becoming extremely concerned about the prospect of mass East African Asian immigration to the UK. In February 1968, fearing a British clampdown on Asian UK passport holders' immigration rights, nearly 10,000 Kenyan Asians left the country, and Nairobi airport was jammed with families trying to flee. On 1 March 1968, the Labour government passed the British Commonwealth Immigrants Act, which imposed controls on the rate of entry of East African Asians holding British passports. Ironically, the bill was based on a private member's bill from the architect of Kenyan independence, Duncan Sandys. The British government justified the decision – which was extremely unpopular worldwide and resulted in mass demonstrations – by the domestic social consequences of failing to do so, and blamed the East African states for their restrictive citizenship policy. The result was a slow-motion crisis; 80,000 Kenyan Asians were now effectively stateless, without Kenyan citizenship but unable to enter the UK either. To manage the flow, the British operated a quota system, admitting only 1,000 families a year from Kenya.

A key plank of British policy in East Africa over the next few years was therefore to ensure that Kenya did not force Asians out too quickly. As the British stated in 1970, 'Owing to the difficulty of honouring our commitment it is necessary to try to prevent action by the Kenyans which would force British Asians out of Kenya at a faster rate than they can be assimilated into Britain.'[141] The British recognised that domestic politics would prevent them from accepting large numbers of Kenyan Asians, and legally they now had no obligation to do so, but most officials accepted a moral responsibility. The Kenyans' negotiating position was simply that the non-citizens were British and not their problem.

Social Changes

Kenya in the 1960s was a nation undergoing dramatic and unplanned social changes. Rapid urbanisation, social differentiation and economic growth combined with the freedoms created after independence to create great opportunities: for the clever and the well connected, it was a period of unparalleled social mobility.

Population and Urbanisation

By 1965, planners were already concerned that Kenya's rapidly rising population would place intolerable burdens on the cost of education and on the labour market. The growth range estimated in their plans was 1.7–3 per cent per annum, but the real rate proved even higher. Since compulsory registration of births and deaths was only introduced gradually during the 1960s, there was no way to estimate Kenya's population until the country conducted its first census, which took place in August 1969. The results showed that the population had reached 10.9 million: a 3.3 per cent compound annual growth rate since 1962. The limited family planning education available made little difference: Kenya was experiencing the classical model of falling child mortality, but unchanged perceptions of the right number of children. Average lifetime fertility per woman rose from 6.8 children in 1962 to 7.6 in 1969. The knock-on effects were to hit Kenya in the 1970s and 1980s, creating one of the highest ratios of unproductive to productive individuals in the world.[142] This placed a burden on the country that was always going to be difficult to escape.

Ethnically, amongst the African communities there were few major changes since 1962 (see Figure 4.10). The most notable was the slow growth of the Somali and fall in Boran numbers, a consequence of the *shifta* war. The Asian, European and Arab populations had all fallen since 1962 as non-citizens left the country.

The census confirmed Kenya's migration trends. As well as the growing urban areas, Nyandarua District showed an 8.4 per cent annual increase since 1962. The Rift Valley had also experienced rapid in-migration, taking 110,000 migrants born in Central Province, 90,000 from Western and 75,000 from Nyanza.[143]

Rapid urban growth was placing tensions on local services. Nairobi's population more than doubled from 250,000 to 509,000, a growth of over 10 per cent a year. This was partly due to the removal of emergency movement restrictions, the pressure of land consolidation and the resulting displacement of tenant farmers, and low rural wages, reflecting the widespread availability of unskilled labour. By 1969, 10 per cent of Kenyans lived in urban areas.

4.10: Population growth by ethnic and racial group, 1962–9

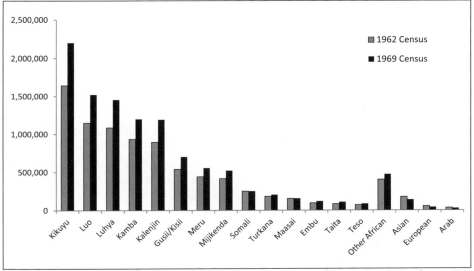

Source: Republic of Kenya, *Kenya Population Census 1962* and *Kenya Population Census 1969*

Unemployment worsened. In response, the 1968 Vagrancy Act was enacted to remove 'loafers' in towns. Already by 1967, there were reports in the press of 'street children' robbing women. Urban life for the poor became increasingly congested and difficult. While the private sector built new development for middle-income urban Kenyans, the (often single, migratory) urban poor had little help. This changed in 1966, when Nairobi City Council and Mombasa Municipal Council built numerous housing estates. Rent tribunals were introduced in 1967, to keep house rents affordable. In 1965, the government had also established the National Housing Corporation, to build low-cost houses and provide loans for private housing projects. Pre-independence patterns of racial land zoning were gradually replaced by income-based segregation in housing.

These processes had not yet broken the relationship between the city and rural areas whereby male wage earners were a key source of income for rural families. There were 50 per cent more men than women in Nairobi according to the census, reflecting the greater opportunities available to men in the city, reinforced by their broader access to education. Nearly 90 per cent of male urban migrants sent money home regularly in 1974.[144] Most Africans were not city-born, but migrated there as adults. When they retired, they returned to the rural areas, and virtually every city dweller wanted to own a *shamba* in their home district. In the words of Colin Leys, these were 'partly urban-based peasants' not a 'proletariat'.[145] However, the risks and opportunities of urban life were encouraging a 'get rich quick' sentiment, with an accompanying greater willingness to risk social exclusion in return for material gain. There was an increasing recognition of wealth for its own sake. Amongst Kikuyu adults, business was now the most admired occupation, with previous community leaders such as teachers far down the popularity scale.[146]

Health

Just as with education, the government faced almost unlimited demand for medical facilities. Tuberculosis, bilharzia, malaria, tetanus and leprosy remained common, though sleeping sickness, cholera and plague had been controlled. Poor hygiene and overcrowding in urban settlements helped spread disease. Nutrition remained poor for many Kenyans. Again, the country had to compromise between what it wanted and what it could afford (even though there was substantial foreign aid to the sector). In 1965, some fees for state medical services were removed, but other services (and most private services) were still fee-based, and provision remained limited. The number of hospital beds (private and public) increased, but only from 11,344 in 1963 to 14,537 in 1970 (a 28 per cent rise).[147] Most doctors were European or Asian and practised in the urban areas. While hospitals might not be affordable, smaller rural health centres were, and 250 were built (many on a *harambee* basis) between 1966 and 1979.[148] The Ministry of Health also took over many church-run facilities after independence.

As a result of better primary and preventive services and improved economic conditions, child mortality reduced and life expectancy jumped sharply, from 35 years in 1962 to 49 in 1969.

The Role of Women and Gender Issues

At independence, most Kenyans were polygynous, with wealthier men taking additional wives to reflect their status. Most communities were patrilineal, inheriting from the father's side; widows could not inherit land or cattle unless a Christian marriage had been formalised (and not always then). After independence, women remained second-class citizens, both legally and in practice. They held less than 12 per cent of formal sector urban jobs in 1971.[149] Most remained tied to the land in rural areas, and low levels of education meant they had fewer opportunities for work, though this was changing as school enrolments for women rose.[150] Female circumcision was still common, and despite campaigns against the practice by social organisations, 40 years later the practice continued.

In 1964, the National Council for Women of Kenya (NCWK) was founded, merging several racially specific women's groups. It was dominated by the African Maendeleo ya Wanawake (Development for Women), which had been established as a Kikuyu loyalist organisation during Mau Mau. A small group of elite women, mostly Kikuyu and Luo, played a militant role in asserting female equality in Kenya in the late 1960s, but they were extremely isolated.[151] Most rural women accepted their lot, and most men were contemptuous of the movement. No woman had been elected to Parliament since independence. The attitude of most MPs towards women was made clear during a debate in 1966 that called for them to be given special means to enter the Assembly. Most MPs were opposed, believing that unmarried women were unsuited for leadership and that married women should be at home taking care of the children. In minister Mwendwa's pithy phrase:

> The first duty of a woman, any woman, is to get a husband. This is the first qualification of a woman. If she fails to get a husband, she has failed her first examination and she is not worthy to represent anybody . . .[152]

The payment of bridewealth remained common, though its continuance seemed to be driven more by the desire of parents of girls to receive financial advantage from a marriage, than by the desire to create enduring ties between families.[153] Another social change that only took place very slowly was cross-ethnic marriage. Although foreign brides were common in the elite who had lived abroad, it was rare among ordinary Kenyans to marry someone from a different ethnic group. Cross-racial liaisons were even rarer and more unpopular.

Religion

Most Kenyans considered themselves religious, and the majority were Christians of various denominations. Roughly 20 per cent were Catholic, 25 per cent Protestant and 15–20 per cent worshipped at independent churches. People's faith often depended on their ethnic origins, as church followings had grown around the sites of the original church missions.[154] The Anglican community had been favoured by the British and was the largest and most influential church, with over a million members. Most of the rest of the country was either Muslim or professed animist beliefs. Most Christians were tolerant of the views of others, and there was little religious tension or violence.

Unusually for a Kenyan, Jomo Kenyatta was not a religious man. He had been raised as a Protestant, but as president he showed no religious interests. He praised the contribution of the churches to unity and development, but did not attend church services and was buried non-denominationally.

As they had done under colonial rule, the churches retained their own identities, finance and legitimacy. They remained active in helping the community, particularly in health and education, and continued to fill gaps in state provision, for example in the troubled North-Eastern Province. Like most non-governmental organisations in this period, they tried to remain outside politics, and by focusing on personal salvation, national unity and development they implicitly aligned themselves with the government's political agenda.[155]

The Muslim community in Kenya remained systematically disadvantaged. Making up less than 10 per cent of Kenya's population, ethnically and religiously divided and less influenced by commercial agriculture or European settlement, they had played little role in the fight for independence. The *shifta* war, the *mwambao* movement and the association of Islam with Arab and foreign influences placed all Muslims under suspicion.[156] Although Kenyatta was not a Christian, his government was a Christian government, just as its predecessor had been.[157] Not a single Muslim minister, permanent secretary or provincial commissioner was appointed during Kenyatta's 15-year rule.

More Succession Struggles, 1968–9

On the political front, 1968 appeared quiet, but there was a gradual increase in internal tensions, as Kenyatta's age and infirmity fuelled the succession struggle, while the KPU challenge weakened.

A Second Stroke

On 4 May 1968, Kenyatta suffered a cerebral thrombosis during a visit to the coast.[158] As in 1966, his illness was kept secret. The government was in crisis, with the new (Kikuyu) civil service head Geoffrey Kariithi summoning a meeting of provincial commissioners (itself an extraordinary thing, reflecting the huge power of the PCs) to discuss what to do in the event that Kenyatta did not recover.[159] However, he made a rapid recovery. Githii published a story about Kenyatta's 'slight indisposition' in the *Nation* on 8 May, but this led to public concern about the president's illness, which was now described as 'a fever'. Soon after, Githii resigned and left to study overseas. The omnipotent, ever-present figure of Mzee could not suffer life-threatening illness.

From this time on, visitors noted that Kenyatta, whose date of birth was never established, was ageing (he was now around 75). His concentration was intermittent and he increasingly focused his energies on internal affairs. He continued to make key appointments and major decisions, but power began to move gradually into the hands of those close to him. These included Moi, Njonjo and McKenzie amongst the pro-British group, and Koinange and Gichuru amongst those more inclined to a Kikuyu-centric view. Njonjo was Kenyatta's right-hand man, but had little grassroots support and was not a presidential contender in his own right. Mungai and Kibaki were influential but not consistently aligned with any faction. Mboya was extremely important in the party, the House and amongst non-Kikuyu, but clearly did not have Kenyatta's support for the succession. Two Cabinet committees increasingly made decisions: the Economic Committee comprising Moi, Mboya, Gichuru, McKenzie and Kibaki; and the Security Committee, made up of Moi, Mungai, Njonjo and McKenzie.

Changing the Electoral System, June 1968

June 1968 saw another change to the Constitution to increase central control over political activity. The tenth amendment was a radical step, with political overtones to every clause. First, it permanently embedded the provisions for preventive detention, no longer requiring parliamentary approval every eight months. Second, it required all candidates for Parliament to be members of a registered political party, and placed the presidential and parliamentary candidates' names on the same ballot paper, so the two votes were cast together (making it impossible for voters to vote KPU for Parliament and Kenyatta for president). The elimination of independent candidates increased the power of the party over its MPs and kicked off a new cycle of local factionalism. Either the Mboya faction or the 'Gatundu group' controlled most KANU branches, so backbenchers now had no chance of re-nomination unless they had the support of the faction controlling the party branch. The amendment also replaced the 12 Specially Elected Members with 12 presidential nominees.

Most important, the 1968 amendment changed the rules governing elections for the presidency, creating a bizarre hybrid that lasted unchanged until 1992. The electoral position of the president was already anomalous. He had to be an elected MP and, if the presidency became vacant, MPs would choose his successor, acting as an electoral college. However, if Parliament were dissolved at the same time, voters would directly elect the president. From now on, the president would always be chosen by a direct nationwide election. Each party would nominate one candidate. Although the president still had to be an elected MP, he became otherwise independent from Parliament.[160] In the event of his death, resignation or incapacity, a presidential election must be held within 90 days. In the meantime, the vice-president would succeed to his office, but with limited powers.

The target of this change was not Odinga, but Mboya. This was the first, successful 'Change the Constitution' movement, led by Njonjo and Moi, which moved control of the succession from the National Assembly, where Mboya had the support of half the MPs, to the party and the general population.[161] In the event of Kenyatta's death, the interim presidency would now go to Moi, to be followed by a general election. The party would still choose KANU's candidate at a National Delegates' Conference, consisting of the National Executive Committee (NEC) of party officials, KANU MPs and district delegates. This too increased the stakes surrounding control of party branches. There were also two attempts between March and May to raise the minimum age for a presidential candidate from 35 to 40, designed to exclude Mboya, who was only 37. The Assembly blocked both moves.[162]

Tom Mboya

Tom Mboya remained the most significant non-Kikuyu in the government. Always unsure of his constituency in Nyanza, but popular amongst urban voters, he offered a fresh-faced alternative to the acquisitive behaviour and ethnic agenda of the Kikuyu elites. Kenyatta relied on Mboya as KANU secretary-general, minister and intellectual powerhouse of the administration, and he was still the most popular candidate to succeed Mzee. The change to the succession law had reduced but not eliminated his chances, as he was rumoured to control half the party branches.[163] However, his popularity amongst workers had been hurt by his policy of wage restraint and his efforts to control the trade union movement. His personal arrogance had alienated many, and his pragmatic economic policy struck few popular chords.

With Odinga on the defensive, there was a concerted attempt by the Gatundu group to weaken Mboya in turn during 1968–9. Mboya and Moi became the frontmen in a near-open conflict. According to the British, KANU 'A' or the Gatundu group now comprised Njonjo, Mungai, Moi, Koinange, Gichuru, McKenzie and possibly Kibaki. They backed Daniel arap Moi for the succession: in the caustic view of British High Commissioner Edward Norris 'as his capacity for independent action is limited by his modest intellectual ability and his comparatively uninfluential tribal following.'[164] Mboya's KANU 'B' was backed by ministers Samuel Ayodo, Ngala, Nyagah, Sagini, Mwendwa and J. D. Otiende. The situation was rarely clear-cut though. Although most analysts placed Mungai in the Gatundu group, Mungai, who had his own ambitions, was keeping his options open.

There had already been manoeuvring and faction fighting between pro- and anti-Mboya teams. In January 1968, there had been a battle for the KANU Nairobi branch leadership between ex-Mayor Rubia and Waiyaki, who was backed by Mboya. Rubia had won the elections, which saw delegate substitution and vote buying, but Kenyatta had nonetheless endorsed Rubia's victory. Mboya appeared to be losing control of Nairobi for the first time. It was clear that the Kikuyu establishment wanted Mboya out as secretary-general, and a KANU Delegates' Conference was originally planned for 1968, where Rubia was expected to be their candidate. In February 1968, Moi deported four American and German allies of Mboya, who had run 'Peace with Freedom'. They had served as a conduit of funds from the West to the labour movement, and probably to Mboya as well.[165] From mid-1968 onwards, efforts were made to oust Mboya's supporters including Khasakhala (vice-president, Western), Ngala (vice-president, Coast), Mwendwa (Kitui chairman) and Angaine (Meru chairman) from their party posts by providing financial support and backing to their opponents. Most were unsuccessful, but Mboya's control over the party weakened. Election rigging became more common. In March 1969, Ngala's opponents won control of KANU's Mombasa branch. Mboya had now lost control of Kenya's largest urban areas.

In early 1969, the Americans still rated Mboya's chances of succeeding Kenyatta highly. Although on the defensive, he remained an inveterate schemer and according to *The Times* he had 'at least an interest' in 120 of 158 constituencies in the coming elections.[166] However, he remained crippled by his limited Luo support as long as Odinga was around. Since Mboya was an urban man and a Basuba, rural Luo gravitated to Odinga, and only Mboya's organisational skills and funds kept him in control of South Nyanza. The British were more likely to place their bets on Moi. Moi was the only candidate acceptable both to other ethnic groups and to the Gatundu group. He was believed to have the common touch, to be one of the few leaders to build a constituency in the pastoral areas, and to be 'relatively uncorrupt'.[167] As a leader, though, the High Commission did not rate Moi highly. As analyst Richard Edis commented in 1968: 'His typical reaction seems to be clumsily veiled and heavy-handed threats. On present form this would seem to be how he would treat criticism, but probably more ruthlessly, if he were in power.'[168]

Odinga's Defection?

By late 1968, government pressure was wearing down the KPU. Although it was secure in Nyanza, the local government elections had shown that it would never be permitted to win a national election. As a result, Odinga began to hint of his willingness to return to KANU if the conditions were right. He had already written letters to Kenyatta asking for a meeting, which had been ignored. While there was no reference to it in the press, McKenzie briefed the British that Odinga, 'had showed signs of wanting to make his peace with KANU. He had been trying to approach President Kenyatta, but Mboya had insisted that Odinga should approach him rather than the President. The result was at present deadlock.'[169]

Moi made the official position clear in a speech in November 1968 where he refused any negotiations, and said Odinga must return unconditionally and 'swallow the KANU policy as it is today'.[170] Another opportunity was lost, and the battle lines hardened once more. If either side had compromised and the Luo had been reintegrated into KANU without the repression that followed, Kenya's history might have been very different.

Backbench Dissatisfaction and Open Primary Elections

With the KPU in trouble, only the KANU backbench could offer a parliamentary challenge to Kenyatta's wishes, and during 1968–9 they increasingly did so. In late 1968, the government lost several parliamentary votes. Concern also mounted that 'smoke-filled-room' KANU candidate selection meetings were likely to lead to the selection of unpopular candidates and popular disaffection in the upcoming general elections. In December 1968, therefore, Kenyatta announced that KANU would hold open primary elections in each constituency to select its candidate. This idea was believed to have originated with Mboya and was intended to compensate for the removal of independent candidates and meet criticism of the 'increasingly arbitrary manipulation of the party machine by the ruling establishment'.[171]

However, the mechanism for conducting such primary elections was undefined. It was also unclear whether the government's plans applied only to KANU, or would be put through the National Assembly as requirements for all parties, in which case the administration of KPU primary elections by government officials could be another means to cripple the opposition. By March 1969, the process was still shrouded in confusion. On 19 March, Kenyatta proposed an about-turn, in which the party primary rules would apply only to KANU, they would be conducted by a few 'known and trusted' KANU members and he would personally vet their choices.[172] The result was a rebellion by KANU backbenchers and assistant ministers. On 20 April 1969, 19 MPs issued a statement in Nyandarua known as the 'Ol Kalou Declaration' that condemned attempts to sabotage the primary elections. Its supporters included many who later became members of the unofficial opposition, including J. M. Kariuki, Jesse Gachago, four more assistant ministers and KANU's new Chief Whip, Shikuku.

On 29 January 1969, Minister Clement Argwings-Kodhek died, after what was reported to be a car crash in Nairobi. He was the most senior Luo minister after Mboya, and the seventh MP to die on Kenya's roads in six years. Many Luo believed that he had been murdered by government insiders, reflecting the growing alienation and paranoia amongst the community. While his death was a family tragedy, the Gem by-election in Odinga's Siaya District that followed had broader repercussions.[173] In May 1969, the KPU won the seat by a massive majority, KANU's first loss since the formation of the opposition. KANU had tried to turn the by-election into a test of the government's ability to win back Nyanza. They did not attempt to rig the election or to disqualify the KPU candidate. KANU's leadership, meanwhile, was divided. Mboya and other Luo leaders did little to support their candidate, who appeared closer to the Gatundu group. Although the KPU was barred from campaigning (and even funerals were banned), its organisation was intact and the influence of elders and of the Luo Union remained strong. Odinga was presented as the general of the Luo army, defending their land against Kikuyu attack.[174] This defeat was a shock to the Gatundu group, but Kenyatta read the message correctly: victory for KANU would require party members to choose their candidates. It may also have contributed to the growing estrangement between Kenyatta and Mboya.

Some in the government were still hostile to the idea of open primaries and the challenge to central authority that they represented. On 16 May, Rift Valley PC Nyachae banned a public meeting to which 100 MPs had been invited, intended as a demonstration of parliamentary support for the Ol Kalou Declaration. A KANU Parliamentary Group meeting on 19 May saw open rebellion against delegate-selected primaries. As a result, in a second about-turn, Kenyatta agreed that all card-carrying members of the party would participate, and that the candidate's name would not have to be approved by the president. This decision was of huge importance, because once the KPU was banned, this primary was to become the true election, and would serve for 15 years as a key legitimising feature of the one-party state.

The 1969 primaries battle also marked the emergence to prominence of wealthy Kikuyu ex-detainee Josiah Mwangi (J.M.) Kariuki (Figure 4.11), who was becoming the leader of a third KANU faction. Kariuki had been appointed chairman of the Betting Control and Licensing Board in 1966, and an assistant minister in July 1968; his star was in the ascendant. He was backed by media interests and many politicians, especially in Nyandarua and Nyeri, whom his financial standing allowed him to assist.

In July 1969, when the government introduced the primary legislation into the Assembly, it faced fierce opposition. The government initially proposed that only card-carrying party members of registered parties could vote. MPs, led by the influential and controversial Seroney, objected to this and to rules that would allow primaries to be conducted by public queue voting, as an alternative to the secret ballot. The dissenters won a significant victory when Njonjo accepted modifications that provided for a secret ballot of all voters in the primaries. These changes were passed

4.11: J. M. Kariuki

Courtesy: Nation Group Newspapers

into law as the National Assembly and Presidential Elections Act in September 1969. Thus, almost by accident, a primary system was created that could later serve for national elections as well.

The Murder of Mboya, 1969

On 5 July 1969, Tom Mboya was murdered, shot dead in a Nairobi street by a lone gunman. He was 38. The nation entered a period of shock and anger. There was near-insurrection amongst the Luo, already angered by the long-running harassment of the KPU. As soon as Mboya's death became known, violence erupted in Nairobi and Nyanza. There were rumours of Kikuyu involvement in the death almost immediately, and Luo mourners stoned Vice-President Moi when he tried to pay his respects. Within days, the Luo began to coalesce behind their sole surviving national-level leader, Odinga.

Three days after the murder, when Kenyatta arrived at All Saints Cathedral for the Requiem Mass, angry crowds stoned his car and shouted '*Dume*' ('Bull', the KPU slogan). In the resulting melee between predominantly-Luo mourners and police, two people died and 60 were injured (see Figure 4.12), and tear-gas left mourners in the cathedral weeping.[175] Ethnic tensions rose rapidly. As Mboya's two-mile-long funeral cortège passed by road through Kikuyu townships on the outskirts of Nairobi, it was stoned by Kikuyu, angry at the attack on Kenyatta. Two days later, when the cortège reached Nyanza, anti-Kikuyu feeling was intense, and there was a risk of mass violence. The police rounded up all Kikuyu in South Nyanza and took them to Kisii for their own safety.

The government remained calm. Kenyatta said and did little in public, waiting for passions to subside. Foreign observers feared 'tribal war' (as usual), but Kenyans had learnt from the British the power of resolute authority, and the government showed no signs of doubt. Mboya was buried in an emotional ceremony at his family home on Rusinga Island. The world's leaders sent condolences, and Odinga joined Mboya's ministerial allies from western Kenya and J. M. Kariuki at the funeral, but neither Kenyatta nor any Kikuyu minister attended.

The murder was a disaster for the government. British High Commissioner Norris noted,

> For the moment, the Luo have been collectively and decisively alienated. If an election were held tomorrow, K.P.U. would probably win every seat in Nyanza and more elsewhere, particularly in Western Kenya . . . the atmosphere is one of bitterness, uncertainty and suspicion.[176]

Who was responsible for Mboya's murder has never been determined. On 12 July, Moi tried to link the killing to communists, but everyone dismissed this as implausible.[177] As with Pinto's death, the apparent culprit was a petty crook with connections to the intelligence services who was charged with the murder on 21 July. The police arrested him after a tip-off, and conveniently found the murder weapon in his possession. A Kikuyu from Kiambu, Isaac Nahashon Njenga Njoroge had received military training in Bulgaria (he was probably one of the squad sent by Kenyatta before independence). He had become a hired thug and KANU youth winger who had been recruited by the intelligence services in return for an amnesty for his previous crimes.[178]

4.12: Fighting outside the cathedral, 8 July 1969

Courtesy: Nation Group Newspapers

As with the Pinto case, Njoroge's trial was characterised by confusion and a lack of information, but there was strong pressure for a conviction in order to quell Luo protest. The trial was conducted before a respected Scottish judge, Justice Simpson, but left many stones unturned. Njoroge commented after his arrest, 'Why pick me? Why not the big man?' but this was never explained.[179] No motive was suggested, nor was there any evidence that he had fired the murder weapon, although he admitted possessing it. Simpson found him guilty on 10 September and sentenced him to death, but Njoroge left the court 'laughing and smiling'. He appealed to the East African Court of Appeal, claiming that all the evidence was circumstantial. The court dismissed his appeal and he was hanged in prison on 8 November. There were rumours that those for whom he was working helped him escape, but British High Commission records are unambiguous, since the public hangman was an expatriate who described the event to British officials.[180] Njoroge's comments about the 'big man' were never investigated, despite his astonishing claim during the trial that he was with Kenyatta's bodyguards in Gatundu on the morning of the murder.[181]

It has never been discovered who gave the orders to have Mboya killed. In a letter written a few days before his death, Mboya wrote, 'An attempt is obviously to be made to precipitate a crisis – maybe an army coup! Security will become more urgent now . . . things have started . . .'[182] The British High Commission initially received evidence from several sources, including expatriate police officers, suggesting Charles Rubia was involved. He was Mboya's competitor both for the post of KANU secretary-general and for Mboya's Nairobi constituency.[183] However, British confidence in the 'Rubia line' weakened as the weeks passed and evidence grew that the Gatundu group might be more directly involved.[184] Other sources suggested Mungai or Njonjo might have some knowledge of the circumstances behind the killing (although Njonjo had been best man at Mboya's wedding).[185] There were rumours that Mboya had been seeking a rapprochement with Odinga, that Kenyatta had discovered these discussions and that a member of his kitchen cabinet had said, 'You shall not see that little man again.'[186] There had been a Cabinet meeting only days before Mboya's death, where he had been accused of disrespect to Kenyatta and of soliciting funds to topple the government. The timing of Njoroge's execution was also interesting. He was hanged on Njonjo's instructions, and the execution was so sudden that even priests were not present. Njenga was taken by surprise, but kept his secrets. According to Norris,

> The swiftness and secrecy with which the execution was carried out, together with Njenga's alleged surprise and indignation, would seem to be consistent with the possibility that he had been given assurances that his life would be saved, and that he was then summarily dispatched to prevent him opening his mouth.[187]

The death of Mboya was a crucial moment in the life of the independent state. Its consequences included the reinforcement of Kikuyu dominance during the 1970s and the transformation of the succession struggle. The removal of Kenya's most prominent political thinker and political operator also weakened the intellectual foundations of the regime and helped freeze the mould of its economic and social policies. Alive, he was a controversial but towering figure who would never have accepted the decay of the late 1970s. Finally, his death reinforced the disassociation between the Luo and the Kenyan state that was to result in economic stagnation and the community's exclusion from sensitive positions for the next 15 years. As David Goldsworthy noted, Mboya represented an alternative future for Kenya that was written out of history with alacrity by the survivors.[188]

Oathing in the House of Mumbi

Facing revolt amongst the Luo, and growing support for change amongst many horrified by Mboya's murder, Kenyatta's closest allies reverted to their ethnic bailiwicks. There had been reports of oathing as early as December 1968, to force Kikuyu voters to return sitting MPs in the election.[189] From July 1969, however, pressure was applied on a new scale. Delegations of Kikuyu and later of some Embu, Meru and Kamba were taken in their thousands to Kenyatta's house in Gatundu to take 'tea with Mzee' and to swear oaths to keep the presidency in the 'house of Mumbi' (the Kikuyu ethnic community). The centre of the oathing was the Presidential Escort's quarters. This mass oathing continued – with government officials organising events but publicly denying their existence – for two to three months, as tension mounted. The analogy with the events of 1948–50, when Kenyatta and his allies had organised oathing in Kiambu, was clear.[190]

Kenyatta permitted, if he did not initiate, this ritual. A biographer of Kenyatta reported that the president himself persuaded the churches to acquiesce in the way in which lorries of Kikuyu chose to 'express their love for the President'.[191] There were claims that blood and meat were used in the oaths, and that some were told they must be prepared to fight the Luo or to prevent a Luo becoming leader of Kenya.[192] Either Kenyatta was no longer in control of the state, or he had returned to his Kikuyu nationalist and animist roots in order to consolidate power. Little scholarly attention has been paid to this mass oathing or its links with Mau Mau. It remains an unexplained lacuna, but appears to reaffirm the ethnically driven nature of Kenyatta's 'Greater Kikuyu' project.

Church leaders and those from other communities who heard the stories became increasingly concerned. In August, Taita Towett in the *Kenya Weekly News* took up the debate openly, describing how vehicles of Kikuyu were coming from as far away as Kitale to 'greet Mzee', when it was well known that Kenyatta was in Mombasa.[193] The NCCK magazine *Target*, under its combative Luo editor Henry Okullu, also publicised what was happening. In a stunning piece of self-censorship, which demonstrated the media's timidity, all other newspapers and periodicals had said nothing. Finally, questions were asked in the House. KPU MP Okelo-Odongo claimed that those being oathed were stripped naked, tied with a rope around their neck and forced to swear to fight the Luo and not to allow any other tribe to lead Kenya.[194] Labour Minister Mwendwa reported attempts to oath the Kamba to support the Kikuyu, and there were reports of clashes between Kikuyu and Kipsigis in which several died. This led to public denials by Koinange, whom many believe was the organiser, along with Kenyatta's bodyguard Wanyoike Thungu. There was growing resistance from church groups: several Christians who refused to swear lost their jobs, and one Kikuyu Presbyterian Church of East Africa (PCEA) elder was beaten to death.

In early September 1969, the churches reluctantly came out into the open. Mass rallies in Central Province on 11 and 21 September excoriated the oathing, but ambiguously declared the Church's loyalty to Jesus Christ, Jomo Kenyatta and the government.[195] The stakes were mounting, however. There were public protests by Kamba and Luhya MPs. At a press conference on 18 September, assistant minister Mutiso denounced recent attempts to oath his Kamba community around Machakos. Rumours suggested that Ngei had personally oathed Kamba on the Murang'a–Machakos border.[196] With the process now impossible to hide, Moi was forced to launch an investigation and to issue a statement condemning oathing, although he continued to deny it was occurring. It ceased almost immediately, and Kenyatta returned from his six-week stay at the Coast the same day.[197] By that time, almost every Kikuyu adult male had been oathed. Nonetheless, Kikuyu in the government, always sensitive to Western opinions, were furious that the news had broken internationally. Three British newspapermen, including the news editor of the *Nation* and the acting-editor of the *Standard*, were deported on 26 September, a direct consequence of their coverage of Mutiso's press conference.[198] At the same time, Dr Kiano 'warned foreign newspapers and the local Christian publication *Target* to be very careful over what they wrote about Kenya'.[199]

The effect of Mboya's murder and the oathing was a closing of Kikuyu ranks behind Kenyatta. Kaggia and the remaining Kikuyu KPU leaders were forced to rejoin KANU, which they did on 1 August. The party was wiped out in Central Province. Odinga's views on the reasons for Kaggia's choice were clear: 'He was under threat from certain quarters. Chances are that this threat could have been carried out in a fatal manner.'[200] The government meanwhile tried to calm the growing crisis. On 31 July, Kenyatta moved Luo Mboya-ally Joseph Odero-Jowi to fill his mentor's seat at Economic Planning and Development. Luo Permanent Secretary Robert Ouko took the EAC ministerial role, while Luo John Okwanyo became an assistant minister. Kenyatta and Moi both publicly appealed for unity. At the same time, the other vacancy left by Mboya's death was filled by the reliable but unambitious Ngala-ally Robert Matano from Kwale, who became KANU's acting secretary-general, a position he held for the next 16 years.

New Parties and an Approaching Election

Kenya was still nominally a multi-party state, but the government was determined to limit the number of opponents it faced. The last 'independent' political parties had been shut down in 1967 and all new parties were still having their registration refused. In July 1969, amidst increasing tensions, Muliro and Towett were amongst ex-KADU leaders and Mboya supporters who considered the creation of a third force, and overtures were made to Ngala, but this did not succeed either. In the run up to the elections, at least five political parties applied for registration, but the registrar refused every one. Unless there was another mass defection, Kenyatta (through Njonjo) was not going to permit further challenge.[201]

Meanwhile, the election approached. From late 1968 onwards, KANU's coffers had been open, and British High Commission records show how British and Asian firms in Kenya were asked to contribute by the acceptable face of KANU: Njonjo, McKenzie and (to their surprise) retired ex-Governor Malcolm MacDonald. The 'sales pitch' used was that it was in their interest for a pro-Western, pro-business government to win. According to British High Commission reports, most paid up, including ICI, Shell and Metal Box, contributing up to GB£5,000 each.[202] Similar approaches were made to businesses in the UK, led by the chairman of the CDC Evelyn Baring, now Lord Howick. While it did not appear to be official British policy to support KANU, an influential lobby amongst the British 'great and good' clearly did so. The KPU too looked for funds, but received little assistance, since there were widespread fears that support for the KPU would cost supporters dearly.

In January 1969, the KPU issued its most well-known manifesto, the 'Wananchi Declaration' (*wananchi* meaning 'ordinary people'). Amongst other policies, it called for non-citizens to be barred from buying farmland, and for ceilings on landholdings in former settler areas, to allow land to be given freely to the landless and squatters. It also accused the Kenyan government of being controlled by the West. Ironically, the manifesto had to be prepared with external assistance and printed in the UK, as the government had warned Kenyan printers not to touch it.

In June 1969, Kenyatta announced that elections would be held within the year. Voter registration was finished by 30 September, with 3.7 million voters having completed the (voluntary) process. The KANU Governing Council nominated Kenyatta as its presidential candidate in August, while the KPU Delegates' Conference nominated Odinga in September. The Assembly approved the election regulations in early October, and the stage was set for the showdown. Observers believed that the KPU would win only 20–30 seats, mainly in Nyanza, the Coast and Western, notwithstanding recent disasters for the government. There was little chance of a fair election even in Nyanza, however, with all meetings of 10 or more people in Kisumu banned in September and the ban extended to the whole province in the run-up to the polls. Despite this, the government decided that it did not wish to take this chance.

The Hammer Falls, October 1969

The end of the official opposition came on 25 October 1969. Despite the risk of trouble, Kenyatta had decided to visit Kisumu to open the Russian-built Nyanza hospital. The hospital had been operating since 1967, and Kenyatta had twice refused to open it previously, but now, he decided to do so.[203] Odinga was not invited, but he and his supporters came in force anyway. As Kenyatta arrived, the crowds chanted

'*Dume!*' At the dais, as Kenyatta began to speak, fighting broke out. Tear-gas was used, and the Presidential Escort fired on the crowd.

Calm was restored, but a furious Kenyatta returned to the microphone and continued to speak. He violently abused Odinga and the KPU, threatening that he would have them 'crushed like a powder', while Odinga traded taunts with the president. Journalists reported that Odinga then attempted to grab the microphone from Kenyatta and a full-scale riot began (see Figure 4.13). The Presidential Escort and the GSU surrounded the president, shot their way through the 'threatening' crowd, and continued shooting for some miles outside the town.[204] Many dozens were killed, including two police officers shot by the president's security. Virtually all film of the incident was seized and destroyed. Although the official death toll was reported as 11, the new hospital was overflowing with corpses.[205] Kenyatta never set foot in Kisumu again. President Escort Commander Bernard Njiinu later claimed that he narrowly prevented one of his men from killing Odinga.[206]

Within 24 hours, Odinga, the KPU MPs and all the remaining national party officials, 22 men in total, had been arrested and detained without trial. The Voice of Kenya announced: 'The cabinet is satisfied beyond any doubt that these men were the people behind the unruly demonstrations at Kisumu.'[207] The state's position was that the trouble was the result of the 'wanton hot-headedness' of people who 'played with hot fire'. On 28 October, Moi called for the banning of the KPU as a subversive organisation and alleged there were plans to assassinate Kenyatta.[208] On 30 October, only five weeks before the election, the registrar duly banned the party as 'dangerous to the good government of the Republic of Kenya'.[209] A curfew was imposed in Central Nyanza and Siaya and hundreds arrested. There was no significant violence, however and no recorded deaths. Facing an uncompromising opponent, the Luo proved unwilling to take on the state directly.

4.13: The Kisumu incident, 25 October 1969. Kenyatta is circled, surrounded by bodyguards.

Courtesy: CameraPix

It has sometimes been claimed that the Kisumu incident (as it became known) was deliberately incited by the government as a pretext to ban the KPU.[210] The timing was certainly convenient and the government was sensitive to the ethnic tensions and weakening of its authority that a contested election would cause. However, the anxious faces in photographs and the personal risk to Kenyatta during the incident make this unlikely. The government probably took the chance offered by an unexpected crisis. The KPU's banning reflected Kenyatta's fury at his inability to crush his enemy politically. It also reflected his refusal to expose his rule to democratic contest. Although the KPU had little chance of defeating KANU, the illusion of total control that the elites saw as essential to the maintenance of public order (and their place at the top) would have been shattered.

Western reactions were muted. As long as Odinga remained on the stage, the existing regime had to be supported, warts and all. In contrast, the foreign radical press denounced the banning as an 'obvious admission by the President of how utterly discredited he is in his own country and of how impossible it is for him to retain power by democratic means'.[211]

The events of 1966–9 were a radicalising experience for many young Luo. It was not a coincidence that the leadership of the 1982 coup attempt were mainly Luo in their 20s and 30s, who had been teenagers during this period and had seen both injustice and the powerlessness of their leaders to respond constitutionally. The ethnicisation of the power struggle of the 1960s also created an association between Luo identity and anti-government protest that was to endure through the 1980s, and reinforced a communal political solidarity that proved more enduring than that of any other ethnic group. It was to continue through the lives of Oginga Odinga, his second son Raila, James Orengo and many other Luo leaders.

The General Election of 1969

Held in the aftermath of Mboya's murder and the banning of the KPU, the 1969 general election was a referendum on post-independence politics and on recent events. With the opposition out of the way, but a commitment already made to free party primaries, the government decided to allow voters a free choice. There was little or no centrally directed rigging and campaigning was open and lively. The widespread discontent and growing ethnic antagonism of the preceding period was channelled into the selection of a new Assembly and government. The result was both a triumph for the state, in its successful reincorporation and re-establishment of a weakening legitimacy, and at the same time a challenge to it, because of the number of regime critics who were elected.[212]

Initially, it seemed that only KANU members would be able to vote in the KANU primaries, which were all that was left of the 1969 elections. However, by a massive sleight of hand, the government converted the scheduled polls from a closed primary in a multi-party state to an open general election in a single-party state without changing anything apart from administrative procedures. Every registered Kenyan voter could vote, though all candidates had to have been paid-up KANU members for the last six months.[213] As in 1966, the election was not organised by the Electoral Commission of Kenya (as would have been expected), but by the supervisor of elections, an official in the attorney-general's office.[214] The state chose the polling stations, and district commissioners served as returning officers.

In October, civil servants wishing to stand were ordered to resign, to limit their misuse of state resources for campaigning. Although the government asked civil servants not to venture into politics, there was a flood of resignations. Indeed, so many senior figures resigned and lost that the government had to find ways to re-employ them in 1970.[215] Those who tried their hands included ICDC head Maina Wanjigi, ex-Comptroller of State House Eliud Mathu and Nyanza PC Charles Murgor. At least five university lecturers and dozens of trade unionists stood, including Akumu and Juma Boy, assistant secretary-general of COTU. Businessmen and teachers formed the largest groups of candidates.

Candidates without educational qualifications or previous Assembly experience had to pass language boards to establish their proficiency in English, limiting candidates to the better educated. Some of the MPs elected in 1963, when party was the dominant determinant of political performance, did not come from the majority community in the area, and several therefore moved constituency back to their home areas, reflecting an increasing ethnicisation of politics.

On 21 November, KANU national officials reviewed applications and issued 'clearance' certificates to candidates. Only six of the 622 who applied and paid their Ksh10,000 deposit were vetoed. Kenyatta personally exempted Kaggia from the six-month rule, part of the deal that had seen him rejoin the party. As expected, Kenyatta was unopposed as KANU's presidential candidate on 22 November. His sole possible opponent, Odinga, was in detention, so Kenyatta was elected unopposed. Parliamentary nomination day was 26 November, with only four hours for candidates to submit their papers. A few candidates were refused in Nyanza, but there were no mass disqualifications. In all, 600 candidates were nominated, an average of 3.8 per seat. They included only four women. Nine MPs were unopposed, including Kenyatta, Moi and Angaine. To ensure his success, the security forces briefly detained Koinange's main opponent, just before the nominations.

With no choice of president or party, the elections were not now about policy but individuals, with only an indirect impact on policy. Candidates campaigned on their potential or actual contributions to development, and on how their educational and professional qualifications would suit them for high office. Fought without Mboya, Odinga and the KPU, the situation in Luo Nyanza was confused, with personal alliances and interest group and clan issues rising to the fore. There was no obvious attempt to back ex-KPU supporters, and there was – surprisingly in retrospect – no overt poll boycott.

In September 1969, just before the election, Nandi ex-KADU backbencher Seroney issued the manifesto known as the 'Nandi Hills Declaration'. This election pamphlet argued that this settlement area, originally Nandi land, was being opened to all buyers and therefore was being settled by people from outside the district. His argument restated KADU's original case that land should be demarcated as communal spheres of influence, not sold freely to anyone who wanted to buy it. Police arrested Seroney two weeks later and charged him with sedition. He was found guilty in October, just before the polls, but was fined and set free, probably in order to keep the issue of Kalenjin land out of the campaign.

There was some violence in the elections, as there was to be in every poll thereafter, though almost all was locally organised, caused by over-enthusiastic supporters. There was evidence of partiality by local chiefs and officials during the campaign, but little sign of systematic favouritism from the OP. However, there were restrictions imposed on the campaigns of some out-of-favour politicians. The dissident Mutiso was amongst those whom officials prevented from campaigning.

Election day was 6 December. Despite the ban on the KPU, the voters still administered a shock to the government. There was carnage amongst the incumbents elected six years before. The electorate rejected 5 out of 20 Cabinet ministers and 14 out of the 30 assistant ministers standing. The changeover on the backbenches was even more dramatic – only 27 of 109 backbenchers were returned.[216] Many had spent little time in the rural areas, and had failed to fund development projects or *harambee* schools. Old-guard politicians of limited education, selected as candidates in 1963 because of their prominence in the nationalist movement, proved especially vulnerable. If it was a mass rejection of the incumbent elite, it did not affect the most senior: Kenyatta's closest allies were untouched. One reason ministers were more electorally successful was their ability to direct development to their constituencies. This was to evolve into the patron–client system of the 1970s.

Voting was mainly on an ethnic basis in the ethnically mixed constituencies, and on a clan/location basis in mono-ethnic seats. Kalenjin vs. Kikuyu competition was evident in Kericho and Nakuru, as was Luhya vs. Kalenjin voting in Uasin Gishu and Trans-Nzoia. As Goran Hyden and Colin Leys noted, 'Ascriptive group membership was still seen by nearly all voters as the *sine qua non* of acceptability and trustworthiness.'[217]

In Nairobi, with Mboya gone, Rubia won Starehe in a hard-fought battle. Kibaki was narrowly re-elected in Bahati, though he faced allegations that he only won because the GSU prevented some of his opponent's supporters from voting. In Central Province, only eight of the 21 incumbents were returned, but they included old-guard ministers Koinange, Gichuru and Kiano; there were rumours of rigging in favour of Gichuru. Elsewhere, the Kikuyu electorate voted for educated moderates rather than hard-line 'tribalists'. Despite his deal with Kenyatta, Kaggia was defeated, with rumours of state rigging against him. J. M. Kariuki won an enormous victory in Nyandarua North. In Nyanza, Western and Rift Valley provinces, however, the election produced a vote of no confidence in the government. Every incumbent Luo MP who was not in detention was defeated, including ministers Odero-Jowi and Ayodo. The Nyanza electorate voted for a new batch of educated, less-politicised leaders, including Siaya lawyer Isaac Omolo-Okero and lecturer William Omamo. In the Rift Valley, voters reaffirmed support for some outspoken MPs and Muliro and Seroney were victorious. In Western, Shikuku was re-elected in Butere, as were other critics of the government. Elsewhere, Ukambani saw Ngei's dominance reconfirmed, while on the Coast, Ngala did well in the rural areas, but lost Mombasa. The other three ministerial losers were out-of-favour Dawson Mwanyumba in Taita-Taveta, Sagini in Kisii and Otiende in Kakamega.

Each candidate had a ballot box, labelled with his or her name and photo, into which voters placed an unmarked ballot paper. There were no proper records maintained during the count, which took place centrally at a single location for the district, and anecdotal evidence suggests electoral abuses were common. MPs later called them 'a trial by ordeal'.[218] J. M. Kariuki claimed, 'anyone could take in as many ballot papers as he could in his pocket and put them inside the ballot box.'[219] Several officials were found to be in collusion with candidates and there were many allegations of administrative bias. There were reports of boxes being dumped or forcibly emptied en route to the count.

The turnout of 1.7 million voters was low, only 47 per cent of the 3.7 million registered voters – a huge decline compared to 72 per cent at the 1963 independence elections. Two hundred thousand fewer people voted than in the polls for the House of Representatives in 1963. Turnouts were highest in Central Province and lowest in Nyanza and semi-arid areas. Although the government blamed bad weather and the low number of polling stations, in the first poll since independence, the majority of Kenyans had declined to vote. Two weeks after the polls, all KANU's 'primary' victors were nominated as candidates for the non-existent multi-party election, and then deemed elected unopposed.

Western reactions were muted. There were no formal observers present. The British High Commission viewed the poll as generally fair, peaceful and helping to reduce tensions. Officials also noted that, 'the results amount to a vote of no confidence in a Kikuyu-dominated government.'[220] Although the British were still pro-Kenyatta, they were critical of the old guard and more positive about the emerging progressive Kikuyu leadership centred on J. M. Kariuki and Gachago.

The new MPs were an assorted group. At least nine were former KPU members and owed as much loyalty to Odinga as to Kenyatta. Others came from the emerging administrative elites, the first of many to swap business and civil service positions for political careers. For the first time, a woman was elected: Luo Grace Onyango, former mayor of Kisumu. Despite the recent struggle, the new elected Luo leadership immediately stressed their loyalty and commitment to working with the administration.

Some losers did not accept that their defeat had been fair. As a result, the country saw 15 petitions against the election results, which played out in court during 1970. Following British tradition, special petition courts, each manned by three judges, heard the cases. Extraordinarily, Njonjo required that the judges were chosen from the European and Asian members of the judiciary only, allegedly to remove the risk of African partiality. These courts reviewed the evidence and pronounced on whether the result was valid, and whether anyone had committed an election offence. Of the 15 petitions, three were successful.

Conclusions

From July to December 1969, Kenya had lurched from one crisis to the next. The period began with the assassination of Mboya, and ended with the 1969 general election. In the interim, the state had trembled and the country had once again become a one-party state. This time, KANU was to remain the sole party for 22 years.

The successful navigation of the period between October and December 1969 was a masterful recovery from near-chaos. It ensured that a form of democracy was played out in the 1969 KANU primary election, which refreshed the elite, restored some legitimacy, but did not challenge the nature of elite rule, state policy or the president's power. However, victory had come at a high price. Mboya's death in July 1969 removed the man who many believed should have been Kenya's next president. If his opponents had not decided that murder was the answer, Kenya might have taken a less ethnically focused and more economically successful course. These events also demonstrated the refusal of the government to accept challenges to its right to rule, and the reversion of political actors under pressure to their ethnic bastions. The government's monopoly of coercion and administrative power had gradually squeezed and marginalised its opponents to the point where it could crush them without mass unrest or external protest.

Henceforth, Kenya would follow a pro-Western and capitalist foreign and economic policy, with one party but open general elections, and a presidential system in which the unquestioned power of the presidency watched over an unceasing factional battle amongst the elites. This battle would mask, but not conceal, the growing divisions within society and the increasing dominance of a privileged elite. All attempts to introduce class-based politics, or to appeal explicitly to the landless and underprivileged, would be ruthlessly repressed.

By 1969, the team of individuals that had won power in 1961–3 had changed beyond recognition. The 1964 merger and 1966 fission had restructured their ranks, leaving Kikuyu leaders more dominant, the Kamba and Kalenjin well represented, and the Luo marginalised. Egalitarian and socialist elements had been purged. Although the process of elite formation and state control was incomplete, the outlines of the structures that would govern Kenya for the next decade were in place. The Kikuyu would rule, Kenya would develop but with growing social differentiation and inequality. The elites who had captured the resources that the British abandoned – in politics, the civil service, parastatals and business – would become rich. There would be no genuine democracy. There would be a growing discontinuity between the institutions that represented the people of Kenya – however imperfectly – and the institutions that actually governed Kenya.

Chapter 5

'Golden Years', 1970–1974

Entering the 1970s

The crushing of political opposition and the renewal brought about by the 1969 elections initiated a third phase in independent Kenya's existence. The growth and instability of the 1960s gave way to stability, slower development and the entrenchment of Kikuyu power. This was the apex of the Kenyatta state, when the ageing president was still able to control his subordinates and ruled with some legitimacy. Although any direct challenge was crushed, as long as politicians remained in KANU and did not criticise Kenyatta himself, the single-party state was willing to incorporate dissent and capable of co-opting new leaders. A rotation of elites, bartering ethnic and regional support for the government for personal and community rewards, institutionalised a system in which Kenyatta and the central government machinery became the arbiters of every politician's success. The argument that open political contests were wasteful and ethnically divisive centralised competition within a framework controlled by the victors. The country's development strategy, balancing central planning and regulation with support for private enterprise, remained modelled on that of the colonial era. The state's success in delivering growth, Kenyatta's legitimacy as 'father of the nation' and the elite's control of the instruments of coercion all helped sustain stability.

By the mid-1970s, however, the limitations of the Kenyatta model were becoming apparent. The reforms of the 1950s and 1960s had run their course. The economy had stabilised around a balance of smallholder and large farm production, a dominant state and a medium-sized industrial sector, with fewer opportunities for growth. The economy never fully recovered from the 1973 oil shock, while the political mould hardened. With Kenyatta increasingly uninterested in the affairs of government, Tom Mboya dead and the ruling elite divided, the state began to stagnate. Ministers were reappointed, policy changes were minimal and the party left to rot. The state was now run by a predominantly Kikuyu technocratic and political elite, one which itself was deeply divided over the succession. Real policy change was impossible because the risks of failure were too great. Meanwhile, the independence generation from the Luo community had been excluded from the patronage system, its loyalty suspect, and Kenyatta never visited Nyanza or met Oginga Odinga again.

The New Government

The Cabinet that Kenyatta appointed on 22 December 1969 was virtually unchanged. Daniel arap Moi remained vice-president and minister for home affairs and Charles Njonjo attorney-general. Mbiyu Koinange stayed on as Kenyatta's minister of state;

Jackson Angaine at lands and settlement and Paul Ngei at housing. Mwai Kibaki became finance minister, replacing James Gichuru (who moved to defence). Kenyatta appointed the ambitious Njoroge Mungai as foreign minister, restored as a ministry in its own right.

There were six new faces in the Cabinet. Luo MPs Isaac Omolo-Okero and William Omamo from Odinga's Siaya District both received ministerial office. Ex-civil servant Juxon Shako became the Taita minister, and lecturer Zachary Onyonka replaced Lawrence Sagini as joint Gusii 'boss'. Ex-KADU leaders Masinde Muliro and Taita Towett also entered Kenyatta's Cabinet for the first time, making Towett, a Kalenjin from Kipsigis, a regional rival for Moi. These appointments reaffirmed Kenyatta's 'tribal barons' method of rule. All large communities would have at least one representative. Apart from Kiambu, Nairobi and Odinga's dangerous Siaya, each ethno-regional group or sub-group would have one minister (in Ukambani for example, there was a minister for Machakos and a minister for Kitui), responsible for ensuring loyalty and patronage. If rejected by the voters, he would be replaced by the man who beat him, or if the newcomer was insufficiently 'clubbable', by another MP from the same district.

Table 5.1: Ethnic composition of the government, 1969

Ethnic group	Ministers*	Permanent secretaries	Assistant ministers	Population, 1969 census
Kikuyu	7 (30%)	8 (38%)	8 (21%)	20%
Luo	3	3	2	14%
Luhya	2	2	8	13%
Kalenjin	2	2	4	11%
Kamba	2	2	2	11%
Gusii	2	2	2	6%
Mijikenda	1	1	2	5%
Taita and Taveta	1	1	0	1%
Meru and Tharaka	1	0	2	5%
Embu and Mbeere	1	0	1	1%
European	1	0	0	0%
Somali	0	0	2	2%
Maasai	0	0	2	1%
Asian	0	0	1	1%
Other	0	0	2	9%
TOTAL	23	21	38	100%

Source: Various

*Ministers include the president and the attorney-general

Amongst ministers and the senior civil service, there was a similar ethnic allocation system and a similar pattern of Kikuyu dominance (see Table 5.1). Of the six
most sensitive or powerful posts (president, finance, home affairs, defence, attorney-general and the office of the president), five were held by Kikuyu and there
were seven Kikuyu ministers in total. Amongst the 21 permanent secretaries heading
ministries or of equivalent rank, eight were Kikuyu. In contrast, assistant ministerial posts, far less influential, could be spread more widely. This year, new assistant
ministers included several dissenting voices, such as John Keen, Martin Shikuku
and Burudi Nabwera. The only re-elected government member to be dropped was
Gideon Mutiso, the MP who had publicised the forced oathing. Two years later,
Mutiso's frustration was to become apparent.

The appointments of Muliro and Towett seemed designed to incorporate those who
had been on the brink of revolt after Mboya's assassination. Nonetheless, the new government reaffirmed the dominance of the kitchen cabinet surrounding the president.
Most of Kenyatta's closest advisers (including Koinange, Mungai, Njonjo, Gichuru,
Eliud Mathu and Kenyatta's brother James Muigai) came from Kiambu. Of those from
elsewhere, only Kibaki from Nyeri and Moi from the Kalenjin were close to this inner
circle. Although Western reactions to the new government were positive, the British
were concerned at the strengthening of Kikuyu dominance in the government.[1]

J. M. Kariuki was widely expected to become minister for agriculture. However, at
the last minute he was 'spiked' and replaced once more by Bruce McKenzie, reappointed
as a Nominated MP. The refusal to bring Kariuki into the Cabinet was connected
with his emphatic restatement of populist anti-British sentiments between his election
and the formation of the new government. On 10 December 1969, he had asked the
government to freeze all loan repayments for lands bought under the million-acre
scheme, and to write off or reduce the interest charged to farmers.[2] He and allies
Nabwera and Charles Rubia were dissatisfied at receiving only assistant ministerial
posts, and soon moved into a position of opposition from inside the government.

Legitimacy and Opposition

Although the KPU had been destroyed, the debate over Kenya's direction and the
challenge to Kenyatta's rule from a more left-wing perspective continued. There
was strong popular (and some elite) support for more socialism, egalitarianism and
a Kenya-first populism fed by and focused on the continued dominance of non-
Africans. These legacies were often blurred, and were particularly associated with the
Luo, Marxist intellectuals and ex-Mau Mau supporters.

Questions of Legitimacy

After 1969, the legitimacy of Kenyatta and his government was in truth open to
doubt. No one ever voted for Kenyatta directly and he had no intention of submitting
to, let alone losing, a competitive election. He was unopposed in Parliament in 1962,
1963, 1969 and 1974, and he had been handed his leadership of KANU during 1960–1

by Gichuru, Mboya and Odinga. Although KANU had won the 1963 elections under his leadership, it was then a party of protest, far more radical than it had since become. There was an enduring difference in political views between the elites and the masses, which continued through Kenya's independent history. The *wananchi* (ordinary people) were more egalitarian, communal or tribal and pro-self reliance than the elites. Many *wananchi* also believed they should be benefiting more, and their representatives less, from the changes of independence.

The government therefore needed to ensure that politics was never restructured along left–right or class-based lines. Instead, it tried to maintain legitimacy through other routes. These included the maintenance of parliamentary traditions and legal processes; the fig leaf of KANU; the preservation of security and stability; economic progress; the deification of Kenyatta; and the deliberate nuancing of the Mau Mau war (which many members of the ruling elite had opposed or sat out unscathed). Kenyatta brooked no challenge to his rule and was ruthless to those he believed would disrupt Kenya's progress under his tutelage. His Kenya was an authoritarian single-party state, but the illusion of choice and the apparatus of democracy had to be maintained. With policy no longer on the agenda, political activity shifted into the local arena, where a 'who gets what' contest generated elites with local legitimacy who could bring their ethnic communities into the patronage system. Some commentators called it a 'guided democracy' (if that was not a contradiction), while scholars argued for the incorporative effects of 'semi-competitive' elections.[3] Political life remained relatively open and its press apparently free, but self-censorship was universal. The political influence of non-governmental organisations was minimal, with no foreign funds from the West to sustain them and a state determined to control most aspects of associational life.

Legitimacy also had a regional dimension. The government focused development and attention on Nairobi, Central Province, the coast around Mombasa and Nakuru. Ministers and senior civil servants seldom travelled to semi-arid Samburu, Turkana, Marsabit or North-Eastern Province, which were virtually ignored. This was the subject of protest in the Assembly, which, from its origins in the colonial reserves, was far more regionally and ethnically balanced than the administration. The government did not try to alter this, recognising the need for an outlet for dissent and an image of regional balance.

The Backbench Opposition

The early 1970s were the period of greatest parliamentary independence for 20 years. The elections had brought into the Assembly several educated, outspoken young newcomers who sympathised with the message of the banned KPU. The new Parliament contained at least 40 radical MPs, whose critique of the government's policies of growth at the expense of greater inequality and its reliance on Western assistance appealed to intellectuals and the landless alike. In fact, the front bench encountered more focused criticism from the 'informal opposition' than it had ever faced from the KPU. Backbenchers regularly savaged government policy and forced the government to withdraw several items of legislation. Despite Kenyatta's assertion that the National Assembly 'does not exist to oppose or to harass the Government', in February 1970 Parliament rejected its first motion from the government side and tried to force a majority of radical backbenchers onto the Sessional Committee (which set the programme of parliamentary business). Kamba MP Fred Mati was chosen as Kenya's first African speaker without incident, but the Parliamentary Group rejected the government's choice of Kikuyu G. G. Kariuki as chief whip. The government lost two more motions in March 1970 and in May the backbench defeated a bill to introduce the death penalty for armed robbers, to which Kenyatta had given his personal support. Of the 41 bills introduced in 1970, four were defeated and others withdrawn – an unprecedented record. Luo, Luhya and Gusii backbenchers were the core of dissent.[4]

Although they operated within limits, the unofficial opposition consistently spoke out against corruption, tribalism and the growing wealth of the elites. They also represented the more xenophobic side of some Kenyan Africans, reflecting a legacy of resentment at white rule and the government's relations with Britain. The backbench generally represented populist, anti-foreigner, anti-Western, anti-corruption and anti-free enterprise opinions. They demanded more government jobs, ceilings on land holdings and the nationalisation of large companies. While they never risked bringing the government down, they were a vocal safety valve. Throughout the 1970s, the state was in danger of being outflanked by such views, which had widespread support. The government regularly found itself defending unpopular policies in order to attract Western tourism and investment. As leader of government business, Vice-President Moi had the difficult task of controlling Parliament on Kenyatta's behalf. His strongest supporter was Njonjo, the government's most eloquent defender, who generally acted as minder for legislation in the House.

Much of the Assembly's ire was directed at the civil service, whom they saw as having 'gone astray' and become 'big headed'. In Shikuku's words, 'The provincial administration is now a Government within a Government. I do not believe this Provincial Administration can coexist with Parliament . . .'[5] The backbench tried (unsuccessfully) to remove repressive legislation such as the Preservation of Public Security Act and the Public Order Act. They continued to defeat or force the withdrawal of government bills: four in 1971 and at least three in 1972. For some MPs, the frustration was as much personal as political. Behind the scenes, influential dissenters such as Marie Seroney were seeking opportunities for reconciliation, frustrated at their personal exclusion from access to state patronage, but the Kikuyu elite kept them at arm's length.[6]

J. M. Kariuki

J. M. Kariuki was the government's most influential critic, a wealthy Kikuyu insider who nonetheless catalysed the wishes of the poor, landless and those unhappy with the direction Kenya was taking. It was Kariuki who coined the phrase 'we do not want . . . a Kenya of ten millionaires and ten million beggars,' although his oratorical power was undermined by the fact that he was probably one of the 'ten'.[7] A detainee who had spent years in the Mau Mau camps, he had become Kenyatta's private secretary after his release. His popularity was fuelled by his wealth, the origins of which were never clear. Wealthy Europeans, including Jack Block and Lord Delamere, assisted him financially, but he had acquired a very substantial portfolio of business investments. He had shares or interests in Kenya Breweries, Block Hotels, the Nairobi International Casino, Caltex, CMC Motors, Lonrho, BAT and Standard Chartered Bank.[8] He was believed to be the frontman for a syndicate of unnamed investors. He 'owned' racehorses, a tour company, mines and several farms. He was extremely well connected, and knew much more than his position entitled him to know. He also, inevitably, had large state loans.

Kariuki's public persona, however, was that of a radical nationalist and opponent of the government's pro-Western, growth-focused strategy. He was one of the few politicians willing to risk Kenyatta's anger. He called for expropriation of the remaining white-owned land, the abrogation of the British loans, ceilings on land holdings, and the nationalisation of industry – the same issues that Bildad Kaggia had championed. He soon built a following amongst backbenchers, becoming one of the few leaders after Mboya to have cross-ethnic support. Around him gathered a coalition of representatives of the poor and landless, critics of Kiambu dominance and those opposed to Kikuyu settlement in the Rift and Coast. His allies in the Cabinet included James Nyamweya, Onyonka and Shako.[9] As Kenyatta's secretary, he had built a close relationship with Mzee, and often visited Gatundu privately. He clearly had presidential ambitions and was cultivated by both the Americans and some communist states.

By mid-1970, Kariuki was courting dismissal from the government, and in return, his enemies were closing in. In June 1970, he was almost jailed for non-payment of a debt. In October, a reshuffle stripped him of responsibility for hotels.[10] By November, Njonjo was encouraging Caltex to take action to recover the costs of two petrol stations Kariuki had acquired.[11] By 1971, he was informally barred from speaking at any public meetings. In March 1971, police turned 130 guests, including MPs and army officers, away from a birthday party at Kariuki's house, an incident that aroused international attention. Kariuki made no secret that he saw Njonjo as his main enemy, excoriating him in 1971 as 'a third rate lawyer'.[12] By 1973, however, he and his allies were targeting Koinange in the OP as the architect of their misfortunes, including a blanket ban on Kariuki, Seroney and Shikuku speaking anywhere in the country.[13] During 1971–3, Njonjo and the government used the legal system to crack down on their critics. Five MPs were jailed for minor offences, and Kariuki and others had loans called in and faced tax and bankruptcy cases. While there was no doubt that most of the offences had been committed, the double standards involved were clear.

The Retirement of McKenzie, 1970

In October 1970, the British lost their strongest supporter inside the government when Bruce McKenzie resigned from the Cabinet. He had been under pressure for some months from backbenchers, who accused him of absenteeism and of diverting resources in his agriculture ministry to favour the Kikuyu. The real reasons for McKenzie's departure have never been explained. He claimed ill health, but he remained active for years afterwards. It was reported that he wished to concentrate on his businesses, and was expected to take up the regional vice-chairmanship of Lonrho. However, Mungai used his brother's position as high commissioner to London to pursue his growing feud with Njonjo, McKenzie and Moi, and persuaded Tiny Rowland, the owner of Lonrho, not to give McKenzie the job.[14]

There has long been speculation that McKenzie's loyalties were not solely to Kenya. It was well known that he represented settler and British opinion in the Cabinet and he frequently provided information to the British High Commission. He was later alleged to have been a MI6 spy, and to have supplied intelligence detrimental to Kenya's interests to the British.[15] There is evidence that such intelligence links existed. He was a friend of Chapman Pincher, the defence journalist who had close contacts in the security services. Pincher's obituary of McKenzie described him as a 'high level politician, ambassador extraordinary, Intelligence agent . . ., military adviser with close links to Britain's SAS, arms dealer . . .' who had rendered important intelligence services to Britain.[16] However, McKenzie's dual loyalties were well known at Cabinet level and there is no evidence in the High Commission correspondence of actions that were to the detriment of Kenya. Indeed, McKenzie was extremely adept at squeezing resources out of the UK for the benefit of the Kenyans. He has also been accused of being a spy for the Israelis.[17] This stems from his role in organising the Entebbe hostage rescue (see Chapter 7).

From the perspective of the British, the government had now lost two of its strongest ministers – Mboya and McKenzie – and the quality of its decision-making was deteriorating. The frequency of Cabinet meetings was declining; its decisions were uncoordinated and not always implemented. Individual ministers made policy in alliance with influential civil servants and sought direct approval from Mzee. Decisions were made by the inner circle of Moi, Mungai, Njonjo and Koinange, with Kenyatta as final arbiter.

The KPU Leaders Emerge

The ex-KPU detainees began to trickle out of prison in 1970, assisted by pressure from Luo MPs and backbenchers. By December 1970, only seven (including Odinga) were still in prison. The government used one of the first freed detainees to rationalise their repression. In return for his release, a staged press conference was held in April 1970, in which Odinga's ex-ally claimed that Odinga had received over Ksh1 million (US$140,000) between 1967 and 1969 from China, Russia and North Korea; China was the main donor after the Russians became dissatisfied with Odinga's achievements in 1965. He also suggested that Odinga – through bodyguard Ochola Achola – had smuggled arms into Nyanza.[18] Moi then produced documents obtained (possibly illegally) from Odinga's mail, suggesting that Odinga had requested US$200,000 from the Russians to fund the 1966 Little General Election.[19] Their goal was to weaken Odinga's influence and quieten those calling for his release.

A year later, on 2 April 1971, Kenyatta finally released Odinga, to celebrations throughout Luoland, but deep concern amongst the new leaders of the community. Since 1969, Kenyatta had done little to develop Luo Nyanza or to build up anti-Odinga Luo leaders, and appeared to have washed his hands of the community entirely. Although he had released his enemy, Kenyatta ordered the press to give him no publicity. Five months later, on 8 September 1971, Odinga rejoined KANU and declared himself ready to stand for party elections. Despite two years in prison, Odinga appeared fit. He had recently bought a farm, which suggests that he retained substantial resources.

The last four KPU leaders remained in jail, without trial or right of appeal. The Detainees Review Tribunal had recommended their release, but the government resisted.[20] Ochola Mak'Anyengo and Achola were not freed until 1974. Ex-minister Ramogi Achieng-Oneko remained incarcerated until 1975, when he finally agreed to plead for clemency. Wasonga Sijeyo, winner of the Gem by-election, remained in prison until Kenyatta's death.

The 1971 Coup Plot

In early 1971, an Africa-wide wave of military coups finally reached East Africa. The trouble began in Uganda. On 25 January 1971, while Ugandan President Milton Obote was flying home from a Commonwealth summit, army commander Idi Amin seized control of the country. Although the genesis of events was domestic, international politics played a role. Britain was one of the first countries to recognise Amin's government, delighted at Obote's exit, and the Kenyans were also satisfied that he was gone. Obote landed in Kenya and claimed political asylum, but Kenyatta refused, on the advice of Njonjo and McKenzie.[21] In contrast, Tanzanian President Julius Nyerere did give Obote asylum and refused to recognise Amin, making the coup a critical event in the disintegration of the East African Community.

Within months, Kenya too was in difficulties. The likelihood of a military coup in Kenya had been growing since 1969, with senior army officers, including army commander Brigadier Joseph Ndolo, musing on the country's future. The likelihood of military action increased after Amin's intervention. By March 1971, Ndolo's opinions had come to the attention of the British, who discussed the mechanics of a possible attempt in detail: 'In February and March, Ndolo discussed the situation in Kenya with a number of people in terms which clearly indicated that he thought that he would have to mount an Army coup on Kenyatta's death if not before.'[22] The British took Ndolo seriously, believing that there was 'a real possibility of an attempt at an Army coup within the next eighteen months or so'.[23] They concluded that it would not significantly harm British interests, but that Britain would be better served by the survival of the existing regime. They therefore continued to provide discreet advice to make a coup less likely, while further tightening links with the army.[24]

The coup plot exposed in March–May 1971 was only loosely related to the musings of Ndolo, and the true story has never been told. What emerged from the plotters' confessions was a poorly structured Luo–Kamba plot, inspired in part by the events of 1969. It appeared naive and the plotters' testimony is confusing and sometimes incredible. The formal plot – led by Joseph Owino, a Luo soldier who had also been implicated in the 1964 mutiny – probably began in September 1970. In February 1971, the plotters recruited a more senior Luo, university professor Ouma Muga. In early 1971, Muga led a delegation to Nyerere to ask for money and weapons for a coup, and for a Tanzanian mobilisation on the border. Nyerere refused and arrested some of the conspirators.[25] Soon after, Kenyan military intelligence learnt of the plot, possibly through Nyerere himself.[26] On 24 March 1971, Kenyatta ordered the army to return the extra ammunition issued during the Uganda coup.[27] By May, several soldiers were under arrest.

Twelve men, including air force and other officers, were charged with sedition (rather than the capital crime of treason), and were jailed for between six and nine years. All pleaded guilty, having been denied access to legal representation. There were later reports that some were tortured.[28] During the trials, the names of more senior figures emerged, linking the plotters first to MP Gideon Mutiso and then to Chief Justice Kitili Mwendwa and Ndolo, all Kamba. Mutiso later admitted that he had been involved, and was to become 'Chairman of the Revolutionary Council'. He too was jailed for nine years on 23 June after a mock trial presaging those of the 1980s, in which he pleaded guilty and implicated Ndolo.[29] The Kamba head of the new Strikemaster air force unit was detained without trial, as was a Kamba businessman said to have been the intermediary between Ndolo and Mutiso. The plotters' motives appeared to include anger at the 'Kikuyuisation' of Kenya and the oathing of 1969. Some also wished to create a more socialist Kenya. There was talk of making Odinga the head of the government, with Ndolo incongruously designated as his deputy.[30] At least four of those arrested (Muga, Owino, Bernard Mukaya and Oyangi Mbaja) were ex-KPU members and linked to Odinga, but the press and government tried to keep this connection quiet, for unclear reasons.

How much the senior Kamba officers actually knew of the Owino plot remains unknown, but by early June it seemed that Kenyatta, his Kikuyu security advisers (Njonjo, Geoffrey Kariithi, Police Chief Bernard Hinga, intelligence chief James Kanyotu, Koinange, Jeremiah Kiereini and Ben Gethi) and Moi had decided that both Ndolo and Mwendwa must go, and used the trials to implicate them.[31] Kenyatta considered ordering Ndolo's arrest, but was persuaded that to do so might precipitate the crisis he was trying to avoid. Instead, Ndolo was called to State House, informed by Kenyatta that his disloyalty had been discovered, and asked to retire, with a promise of no reprisals against him if he acquiesced.[32]

On 27 June, a loyalty demonstration was organised in Nairobi, attended by between 60,000 and 200,000 people, mostly Kikuyu. At the rally, some carried placards denouncing Mwendwa, which the *East African Standard* publicised. Moi briefed the British that Mwendwa was behind the coup, as the High Commission's records show (see Figure 5.1). As a result, he too was forced to resign on 7 July 1971. Some suspected that the opportunity was taken by those hostile to Mwendwa to tar him with the same brush as other senior Kamba. Njonjo was known to be

5.1: Transcript of British High Commission report on the coup plot, 1971

> TO IMMEDIATE F C O TEL NO 1803 OF 24 JUNE, INFO DAR ES SALAAM AND KAMPALA.
>
> MY TELNO 1787 OF 23 JUNE: THE CONSPIRACY CASE.
>
> VICE PRESIDENT TOLD ME THIS MORNING THAT THE PRESIDENT HAS SAID THAT HE WILL NOT ALLOW GENERAL NDOLO TO BE PROSECUTED. HE CONSIDERS THAT HE HAS BEEN MISGUIDED AND STUPID BUT NOT VICIOUS AND HIS 37 YEARS OF LOYAL SERVICE SHOULD BE TAKEN INTO ACCOUNT. IF HE IS ALLOWED TO RETIRE HE WILL HENCE-FORTH BE LOYAL AND THIS IS IMPORTANT SINCE HE IS AN IMPORTANT FIGURE IN THE KAMBA TRIBE. IN ANY CASE, MOI SAID, NDOLO WAS NOT CLEVER ENOUGH TO HAVE WORKED OUT A PLOT. THE MINISTERS WERE CONVINCED THAT THE CHIEF JUSTICE, MWENDWA, HAD BEEN ADVISING HIM. INDEED THERE WAS A SIGNIFICANT PATTERN OF VISITS BETWEEN NDOLO AND MWENDWA WITHIN 12 HOURS OF NDOLO'S CONTACTS WITH THE CONSPIRATORS. UNFORTUNATELY HOWEVER THERE WAS NOT SUFFICIENT EVIDENCE TO BRING ANY CHARGE AGAINST MWENDWA.

Source: Telex from Norris to FCO, No. 1803, 24 June 1971,
in FCO 31/856, Political Detentions in Kenya, 1971

campaigning to remove Mwendwa, and his family believed Njonjo instigated both the placards and Mwendwa's resignation.

Ndolo retired on 24 June. Soon afterwards the pro-British army head Jackson Mulinge was promoted to major-general. However, the post of Chief of General Staff was left vacant, leaving the service heads reporting directly to Defence Minister Gichuru. With Mwendwa disgraced, James Wicks, a British citizen, took over as chief justice.

Heeding the warning, Kenyatta thereafter spent more time with the army and paid tribute to them more actively. The threat of trouble gradually receded, checked by Kenyatta's careful treatment of Ndolo, his active management of the officer corps, continued close British military links, his use of the GSU as a counterweight to the army, and the damaging consequences of Amin's actions on Uganda.

The Security Forces in the early 1970s

The Military

The Kenyan military remained relatively efficient and with combat experience in the north-east. The army could muster 430 officers and 5,900 men, it was mostly British-equipped and organised on British lines, and morale remained good. However, it had no tanks, whereas Somalia and Tanzania had Russian or Chinese armoured units.[33]

Kenya was also the only country in the region without jet fighters, since Tanzania and Somalia had acquired Soviet MiGs. In 1969, the government agreed, after lengthy negotiation, to buy six BAC 167 Strikemaster jet fighters from Britain. The Russians offered to supply MiG-19 fighters free of charge, which the Kenyans used as a negotiating tactic with the UK, but in reality they were unwilling to accept

Soviet assistance. Pressure from the High Commission and the FCO to provide lower prices and better credit was resisted by the UK Treasury, which argued that there were no longer security reasons to offer special terms to Kenya.[34] By this time, British military interests lay elsewhere, and Kenya was a normal commercial customer.

The Strikemasters were not enough. Somalia's admission to the Arab League led Kenyatta to fear that Arab countries would support a Somali attack. The Kenyans were also worried by Uganda's growing instability and feared a joint northern and western assault. In 1973, under pressure from the Kenyans, who – through the still-present McKenzie – threatened to buy Mirages from France if a deal was not forthcoming, the British agreed a second GB£12 million deal, which for the first time gave Kenya jet interceptor capability. This agreement supplied Kenya with six Hawker Hunter fighters, plus patrol craft, radar, vehicles, arms and ammunition. Kenyatta negotiated the deal personally, which included a GB£2 million gift from the British.

The British dominance of the Kenyan military gradually weakened in the 1970s. The navy and air force remained under the command of British officers until 1972–3, but British army staff had fallen from 70 in 1968 to only six by 1971. With the risk of attack or subversion low, the British also allowed the internal security guarantee made in 1965 to lapse in 1971.[35] However, they continued to provide the looser guarantee against Somali attack, with the Bamburi understanding reaffirmed by both Edward Heath in 1970 and Harold Wilson in 1974.[36] The British also continued to train most Kenyan officers and to use Kenya as an intelligence base, with MI6 officers stationed there throughout the 1970s. Defence purchases still came primarily from Britain, but gradually became more diverse.[37] Kenyatta wanted the British defence relationship to continue, having his eye on the Soviet military presence in the Middle East and internal security at home. As a result, in the early 1970s, a small permanent British defence liaison team was set up to coordinate training missions. This would help the Kenyan armed forces, but would also 'promote the continued purchase by Kenya of British equipment and would favourably influence the maintenance of our defence rights'.[38]

Defence policy was set by a special Defence Committee, an extremely stable Kikuyu, Meru and Kamba group consisting of Gichuru (Kikuyu, minister of defence, 1970–9), James Njeru (Meru, assistant minister for defence, 1966–79), Jeremiah Kiereini (Kikuyu, permanent secretary, 1970–9), Mulinge (Kamba, army commander, 1969–80), the air force and navy commanders, and the Chief of Staff (Kamba). The British military adviser often attended their meetings.

There was now a strong trend to promote young Kikuyu officers.[39] As the British commanders left, the Kamba–European line-up was replaced by a Kamba–Kikuyu one (see Table 5.2). Lucas Matu was Kenyatta's man, and was expected to succeed Mulinge. There were no Luo above the rank of major. The British remained tightly linked with Kenya's security establishment; most senior military (and police) officers had trained in and were friendly to the UK.

Table 5.2: Military heads, 1969–78

Role	Name	Dates	Ethnicity
Chief of General Staff	Brigadier Joseph Ndolo	1969–71	Kamba
Commander of Kenyan army	Major-General Jackson Mulinge	1969–80	Kamba
Deputy army commander	Colonel Peter Kakenyi	1969–72	Kamba
	Brigadier Lucas Matu	1972–4	Kikuyu
Chief of Staff at MoD	Colonel Lucas Matu	1969–72	Kikuyu
	Brigadier Peter Kakenyi	1972–4	Kamba
Commander of Kenya air force	Group Captain Edwards	1971–3	British
	Colonel Dedan Gichuru	1973–80	Kikuyu
Commander of the navy	Commander William Hall	1969–72	British
	Lieutenant-Colonel Jimmy Kimaro	1972–8	Taveta

Source: Various

The Police and GSU

The police force was far larger than the army, with 13,500 ranks, roughly the same number as at independence. They were lightly armed, and though their professionalism was somewhat dubious, they enjoyed good training facilities and retained expatriate Britons in key appointments (there were nearly 50 in 1974).[40]

The paramilitary GSU, although part of the police, was increasingly autonomous. Its members wore military uniforms and were barely distinguishable from a military unit. The GSU could muster 1,500–1,600 men, alongside 150–200 in the Presidential Escort Unit and 60 Ichaweri.[41] According to the British, by 1971, the GSU was predominantly Kikuyu. The Ichaweri, Kenyatta's private bodyguard and also formally part of the police, were all handpicked Kikuyu, led by ex-Mau Mau activist Wanyoike Thungu (also chairman of KANU's Kiambu branch). They were notorious for their violent behaviour, and had been involved in the 1969 oathing.[42] The British SAS continued training the Presidential Escort Unit and the Ichaweri in counter-subversion and internal security until 1971, and as late as 1974 a British expatriate still nominally led the unit.

The civilian security heads showed the state's ethnic bias more clearly than in the military (see Table 5.3). The Kikuyu insiders who had been appointed between 1964 and 1967 continued to lead the security services until Kenyatta's death. The most senior Luo, CID head Peter Okola, was replaced in 1973 by yet another Kikuyu, Ignatius Nderi from Nyeri, another colonial police officer and son of a senior chief. Nderi, Kanyotu and Gethi all built close working relationships with the increasingly powerful Njonjo, who straddled the police, the legal fraternity, the civil service and politics. It was a conservative, pro-British and ethnically chauvinist group. Most were ex-colonial police officers who had seen action against Mau Mau.

5.2: Bernard Hinga and James Kanyotu

Courtesy: Nation Group Newspapers

Table 5.3: Police heads, 1969–78

Role	Name	Dates	Ethnicity
Commissioner of police	Bernard Hinga	1965–79	Kikuyu
Head of Special Branch	James Kanyotu	1965–91	Kikuyu
Deputy-director of intelligence	Stephen Muriithi	1965–82	Kikuyu
Head of the GSU	Ben Gethi	1967–78	Kikuyu
Head of the CID	Peter Okola	1965–73	Luo
	Ignatius Nderi	1973–84	Kikuyu
Head of the Presidential Escort Unit	Bernard Njiinu	1964–80	Kikuyu

Source: Various

The Second Asian Crisis

The 'European problem' of the early 1960s – the struggle for African self-determination and racial equality with the British – was effectively solved by the mid-1970s. Most of the white settlers had sold up. While the government was still buying land from Europeans in Uasin Gishu and Trans-Nzoia, the settlers retained only a shadow of their old influence. Although Europeans still controlled huge chunks of the economy, it was mainly through multinational firms rather than local white-owned businesses. While African entrepreneurs might not yet be able to compete with or control these organisations, the government certainly could.

Further Restrictions on Non-Citizens

However, the 'Asian problem' had not disappeared. Kenya was gradually driving out non-citizens and even some unemployed citizens. Nonetheless, Asians were not leaving as fast as most Africans wished. Many had become citizens, but popular concern was racial, not national. Asians, whether Kenyan or not, were excoriated as 'paper citizens' with few ties to the country, keen only for short-term profits, which they would take offshore. Their values, colour, customs and religions all set them apart.

The lines of dispute on this subject were confused. While Kenyatta often appeared anti-Asian from his speeches, his government had no desire to evict the Asian community too quickly. They recognised the risk to the economy, given the Asians' wealth and dominance of manufacturing, at least until Africans were ready to take over. They were also concerned about the British response. Populists took the opposite view, demanding expropriation and expulsions. Backbench radicals such as Wafula Wabuge accused Asians of 'breeding too quickly' and Shikuku and Eric Bomett were amongst those who demanded that all non-citizen Asians leave Kenya entirely. Some MPs even demanded the expulsion of all Asians.

During 1971–3, non-citizen Asian wholesale and retail traders were steadily forced out of rural areas, handing over their businesses to Africans. In March 1972, Africanisation extended to the printing and building industries, and in May, 300 urban businesses were given notice that they would be taken over. This drove a second crisis in 1972, as non-citizens prepared for flight. The British quietly increased the quota of families they would admit to 1,250 a year.

Amin's Expulsions

In late 1972, however, the situation changed unexpectedly; the decision of a single disturbed man. On 26 August 1972, Idi Amin did what some Kenyans had talked of: he drove out, without compensation, the entire Ugandan Asian community of 80,000 people. Amin announced that God had told him in a dream to drive out all Asians from Uganda within 90 days, and this he proceeded to do without mercy. Asians' bank accounts were frozen and their property seized. Shuttle diplomacy between the British, Amin and other African leaders was an abject failure. Eventually, the UK was forced to accept those Ugandans who had British passports, and the Amin regime and ordinary Ugandans helped themselves to the assets of these businessmen, lawyers, doctors, accountants and technicians. With Western aid frozen and diplomatic relations with Britain and the US broken off, Uganda began to collapse.

The Kenyan Government's Response

Events in Uganda made clear the scale of the risk in Kenya, where even larger numbers of Asians lived. Of the Asians who held foreign passports, 35,000–40,000 (plus dependants) had British passports and 5,000 had Indian passports, and there were more than 40,000 Kenyan citizens. The Kenyan elite therefore tried to mute tensions, refusing to debate the issue or become enmeshed in Uganda's actions. Fearful of the domestic consequences, Kenyatta refused to accommodate any fleeing Asians and resisted British requests to persuade Amin to change his plans.

Kenya could not insulate itself entirely from the chaos over its border, however. There was pressure in 1971–2 to seize Asian-owned land in Nyanza and to allocate it to local people. Both Moi and Kenyatta had to reassure Kenyan Asians that the government did not wish to drive them away. Generally, the government took a more moderate approach on the Asian question than its own supporters or the backbench wished. It commissioned a report in 1972 on Africanisation, which reported that Asians had been taking citizenship without any real commitment to the country, 'to facilitate their continued exploitation of the country from the privileged positions they now monopolise . . .' [43] But the government then concealed the report.

Africanisation continued. Between 1972 and 1974, the programme eliminated non-citizens from most commercial sectors, especially in the countryside. In late 1972, Tourism Minister Shako announced that no travel agents or curio sellers would be licensed if they were not majority Kenyan-owned (he also declared that state ownership of the entire tourist industry was the government's goal). Another 1,200–1,400 quit notices were given to Asian businesses in 1973, forcing them to hand over to Africans. The ICDC financed these takeovers, with the inevitable allegations of corruption and favouritism in the choice of those who would inherit the businesses.[44] After changes to the Trade Licensing Act in 1974, even some citizen Asians (including the owners of a supermarket chain) and non-citizen owners of large manufacturing firms were issued with quit notices. This was a tactic by (Kikuyu) businessmen to gain control of these investments, though most such grabs were successfully resisted by appeals to their impact on investment and the fact that they were probably illegal.[45] Asian and Arab-owned businesses without influential Kikuyu partners were under growing pressure, but the state resisted calls for wholesale expropriation. One reason for this was Uganda; that country's collapse after the expulsion of the Asians was a warning that change must be gradual. Domestically, the experience of Africanisation had been disappointing, since many African owners had struggled to maintain the businesses they had inherited, though this was a political 'hot potato' and not admitted in public.

Equally important, Kenya used the Asians as a bargaining tool. Relations with the UK between 1968 and 1974 were dominated by the British need to ensure a controlled flow of Asian immigrants to the UK. The British came under intense pressure to admit more of the British passport holders finding life in Kenya difficult. The Kenyans in turn used the British to make capital at home, blaming them for their failure to honour their responsibilities. Despite British pressure for what they called 'compromise' (delays to Africanisation and the enforcement of existing laws), Mungai, Kibaki and others remained obdurate. As Kibaki said in 1970 when British nationalists tried to link Kenya's aid from the UK to their stance on the Asians, 'The Asians are British – they are your problem.'[46] Less well known was that Kenyatta had made a secret agreement in 1973 with the British that, despite this posturing, no further increase in entry quotas would actually be required, in return for the gift of GB£2 million worth of arms.[47] During 1974–5, with another relaxation of British entry policies, the crisis gradually abated. By 1974, more than 98 per cent of all government posts and 92 per cent of private sector jobs were held by Africans (although these proportions were all lower at senior levels). By 1979, the

Asian population was down to 78,000, of which 50,000 or so were Kenyan and the remainder UK passport holders, a sharp fall from the 139,000 of 1969.

Regional and International Relations, 1970–4

Kenya retained its reputation as a safe place to experience Africa, buttressed by its close links with the UK. Although Kenyatta was hardly a democrat and there were growing concerns about the sustainability of its model and the emergence of a two-tier society, Western countries said nothing as long as Kenya remained stable and pro-Western. Under Mungai, Kenya's foreign policy was more assertive than in the 1960s. Regionally, however, Kenya was becoming isolated.

Regional Troubles

The East African Community (EAC) was already experiencing economic problems. Both Uganda and Tanzania saw Kenya as the community's main beneficiary, as the regional base for industries serving the three markets. They both continued to apply tariff or quota restrictions to Kenyan imports. In 1973, the EAC also decided to decentralise the collection of income tax, which would now be collected nationally, and the tiny EAC component paid to Arusha, rather than the other way round. By 1974, the level of economic integration between the three countries was lower than it had been before the EAC was formed.

However, the most obvious problems were political. Tanzania's dislike of Kenya's expatriates and capitalists (and particularly of Njonjo) was open. Kenya viewed Tanzania's socialism as a drag on progress and was concerned about the presence of Chinese technicians and advisers, while growing Chinese imports into Tanzania replaced Kenya's exports. Tensions with Uganda had already been inflamed by Obote's Ugandanisation in 1970 of unskilled jobs, forcing 10,000 Kenyans out of Uganda. The 1971 Amin coup worsened the situation dramatically. The three presidents never met again as a corporate entity, as Nyerere never recognised Amin as the head of state, which led to an open estrangement between Uganda and Tanzania. The Tanzania–Uganda border was closed and skirmishes took place in late 1971. In September 1972, Ugandan exiles launched an unsuccessful invasion from Tanzanian soil. Fighting a small-scale war was not conducive to economic union.

Meanwhile, the trouble in Uganda spilled over into Kenya. Kenya had initially welcomed Amin's coup, helped reorganise the Uganda police and assisted Amin in the OAU. Thereafter, Kenyatta tried to avoid any direct criticism of his mercurial neighbour, despite the problems Kenyans were having in Uganda and the difficulty of getting Kenyan money out of that country. Nonetheless, Amin's growing ties with Russia, China, Libya and Egypt caused Kenya concern, as did his erratic interventions in international affairs. The Asian expulsions started a spiral of decline in Uganda that cut Kenya's throughput and export trade. Amin (a Muslim) also expelled all Israeli nationals in 1972, causing more tensions as they passed through Kenya. There were killings of Kenyans by Ugandan soldiers on the border in 1973, and senior Ugandans, seeing the violent and arbitrary nature of Amin's rule, began to slip across the border. In June 1974, ex-freedom fighter Kungu Karumba's unexplained disappearance in Uganda was a further flash point.[48] Kenyatta and Amin met in June 1974, but the chill between the states continued.

Relations with the West

Relations with the UK remained close, but by the mid-1970s the British influence was weakening and the UK's economic decline limited their ability to give preferential treatment to the Kenyans. With the British military commitments near an end and the land acquisition process nearly complete, dealings between the two countries began to approximate a normal state–state relationship. McKenzie's departure and the reduction in the number of expatriates in the government also meant that Britain's access to inside information declined. However, the British retained a close interest in Kenya's politics and the military, trying to ensure that whatever government emerged after Kenyatta's departure would remain friendly. The British also retained an intelligence interest in Kenya, with their 'counter-subversion fund' and the Ariel Foundation (which was believed to have assisted both Kenyatta and Mboya covertly in the early 1960s) still looking for 'projects' to fund in 1971.[49]

Britain remained Kenya's largest aid donor throughout the 1970s, though some of its assistance – such as the funds to build a dam on the Tana River – was tied aid, to be spent with British contractors. The UK also continued to pay pensions to colonial civil servants, finance the CDC, and provide GB£10–15 million a year in other aid. The biggest change in relations came in 1973, when the UK joined the European Economic Community (EEC). This required a renegotiation of all preferential trade arrangements with the UK. In the end, the Kenyans followed the 'Yaoundé option' for aid and trade, and structured their relationship with the UK and the rest of the EEC along the lines developed for the French colonies. They later became beneficiaries of the 1975 Lomé Convention, which standardised preferential supply relationships for African, Caribbean and Pacific countries with Europe, without preferential concessions for European exports in return.

The major source of strain with the UK was still its relations with southern Africa. Kenyan policy on this issue was somewhat schizophrenic. Most of the government remained committed to combating apartheid, and Kenya campaigned against British and French arms sales to South Africa. Despite British wooing, Mungai criticised Western links to South Africa in a way that embarrassed the UK on several occasions. Although the Kenyan government had no wish to take action on the South African issue, it was so prominent that they had to do something to stave off local criticism.[50] Nonetheless, the UK government privately viewed Kenya as one of the more reasonable African countries on this issue.[51] Mungai and Kenyatta secretly agreed, for example, to participate in dialogue with South Africa as long as the South Africans publicly accepted the eventual equality of races, even without a timetable. Kenyatta was also a personal friend of Hastings

Banda in Malawi, whose willingness to do business with South Africa aroused international protest. Rhodesia also caused friction, particularly after the British-led 'independence deal' of 1971, which failed to achieve the minimum conditions laid down by the OAU. Mungai severely criticised the British over this, and Kenya committed itself to support Zimbabwean freedom fighters, albeit without doing much in practice.[52]

While relations with the UK remained strong, Kenya and the US maintained friendly but low-level relations. The 1970s were a period of US disillusionment with Africa. With the aid and trade still low, US regional attention focused on South Africa, Nigeria and the Congo. Apart from Cold War issues, its commitments were sparse. 'Put simply, Washington sought politically viable and economically friendly states with which to conduct normal relations.'[53] This required active anti-communist agendas, but little else.

Other International Relations

Kenya continued to play a moderate, non-aligned role in the Organisation of African Unity and the United Nations (UN), and it was compensated accordingly. In 1972, it was elected to the UN Security Council, backed by both African states and the West, and consequently played a high-profile role internationally over the next two years. This was a personal triumph for foreign minister Mungai. In 1973, the UN also established its Environment Programme (UNEP) in Nairobi. It was the first major UN body sited outside the developed world, and Mungai described it as a sign of the world's endorsement of the president's policies. The UN Centre for Human Settlements (Habitat) followed UNEP to Nairobi in 1978.

Although Kenya supported a negotiated settlement of the Middle East crisis, and had long-standing military links with Israel, it broke off diplomatic relations in November 1973, as the OAU demanded. The oil crisis of 1973–4 had a serious effect on the economy, and Mungai was probably trying to obtain economic concessions from Arab states in return for Kenya's support. Cooperation with Israel became covert, but continued.

Kenya's relations with communist states (particularly China) remained very tense and trade was minimal. However, Russia still maintained 40 diplomatic staff and a significant intelligence presence in Kenya. They hoped that relations might improve after Kenyatta's death.

A Maturing Economy

The 1970s saw a continuation of Kenya's development strategy. In the posthumous words of Tom Mboya in the *Development Plan 1970–74*, 'The primary objective of the KANU government is the development of our economic resources to achieve the goal of economic independence, together with social justice and a steadily improving standard of living for all.'[54] However, while they hoped both to accelerate growth and to redress inequalities, the reality proved less satisfactory. With a 3.4 per cent annual growth in population, the country had to run economically merely in order to stand still. Growth in real GDP began a downwards trend (see Figure 5.3). The limited data available also suggested that income inequality was growing fast in both rural and urban areas.[55]

There was now a stronger focus on central planning and state investment in industrial development, with the ICDC leading the drive towards a dominant position for the state in industry and tourism as well as infrastructure and agriculture. Not only did this reflect the growing support for socialist central planning models worldwide, it also reflected the decline of foreign private investment into Kenya and the near-infinite demand for state patronage.

Kibaki as finance and economic planning minister from 1970 until 1978 was the architect of this strategy, criticised by socialists for being capitalist (in the 1970s) and by capitalists for being socialist (in the 1990s). Feted by *Time* magazine as one of 150 future world leaders in 1974, he was noted for 'playing a long game' and rarely responded directly to criticism. Occasionally, he was accused of pro-Kikuyu tribalism (under his ministry, for example, the head of every state-owned bank was Kikuyu), but in general he was well respected. He was also unusual amongst Kenyan politicians, as few had much interest in macroeconomic policy, which they left to the technocrats. Indeed, Kenyatta's Kenya was unusual in Africa in the degree to which the 'technocrats' (macroeconomic policy-makers) were insulated from both populist and sectional political pressures. Kenyatta felt no strong need to buy popularity after 1966, and there was apparent alignment between the national interest (as seen by most policy-makers) and the interests of the ruling elite.

Kenya's Trade Balance and the Oil Price Shock of 1973–4

Kenya's trade balance and balance of payments deficit remained manageable, but the gap between imports and exports was growing. Until 1971, the negative balance of trade was matched by a strong inflow of capital, mainly private investment. From

5.3: Real GDP growth, 1964–80

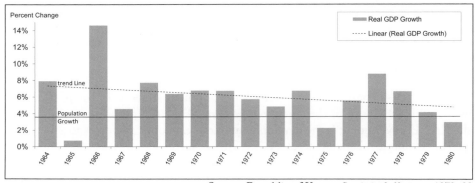

Source: Republic of Kenya, *Statistical Abstracts*, 1972–82

5.4: Imports and exports, 1964–78 (in US$ per annum)

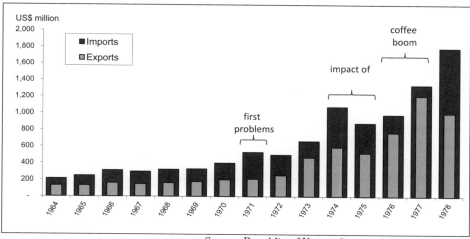

Source: Republic of Kenya, *Statistical Abstracts*, 1972–82

this time on, however, foreign capital inflows declined. There was a mini balance of payments crisis in 1971 and more serious problems began in 1973. The oil price shock associated with the Arab–Israeli war of October 1973 caused structural change to Kenya's balance of payments and substantial damage to its economy, as oil prices quadrupled between 1973 and 1974. Import costs rose and the budget deficit (after investments and loans to parastatals) more than doubled from US$90 million in 1970–1 to US$210 million in 1974–5. Despite calling on the IMF for short-term support, foreign exchange reserves fell to dangerously low levels.[56]

The government's response was to limit domestic demand in order to sustain the balance of payments at a fixed exchange rate. During 1971–3, it introduced a comprehensive licensing system in which some types of import were banned entirely (unless special licences were issued), import duties on cars rose to 100 per cent and duties increased on luxuries such as watches, cameras, clocks, radios and televisions in order to sustain the shilling.

Inflation and Exchange Rate Policy in the 1970s

Inflation also began to rise. Having failed to persuade the Middle East to give Kenyans cheap oil, Kibaki had the onerous duty of raising most prices in the 1974 budget, and the knock-on effects continued into 1975. Consumer prices were increasingly controlled by the Finance Ministry. Basic commodities such as maize, bread and sugar were made subject to price controls in 1971 and these were extended in 1974 to cover 150 more commodities. Nonetheless, this could not prevent a rapid rise in inflation, driven by rising import costs: from 7.7 per cent in 1972 to 18 per

5.5: Inflation rates, 1963–78

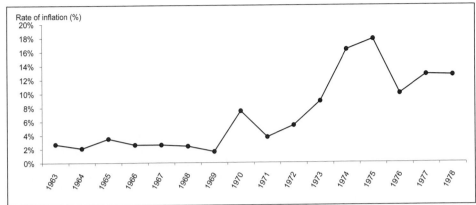

Source: CBS Statistics http://www.cbs.go.ke/, 2006

cent in 1975 (see Figure 5.5). This inflationary bubble, fuelled by problems in Western economies, the oil crisis and worsening terms of trade, also did sustained damage to the economy.

During the 1970s, the state regulated interest rates and kept them low by world standards (4 per cent until 1974). They were increased to 5.6 per cent in 1974, but this was still well below inflation. The result was negative real rates, a strong demand for loans and a disincentive to Kenya's traditionally high level of saving.[57]

The Central Bank fixed foreign exchange rates at the direction of the Treasury and they remained stable. In 1971, Kenya and the other EAC countries decided to peg their currencies against the dollar, moving away from sterling. In 1975, abandoning the dollar after only four years due to world currency instability, Kenya instead tied the shilling to the IMF Special Drawing Right (SDR), a weighted average of world currencies. In 1978, the shilling was worth almost exactly the same against the dollar (7–7.5 shillings per US$) as it had been in 1967. Access to foreign exchange was state controlled and allocated by committee. During shortages, the government ordered the CBK to refuse all requests for foreign currency to buy goods that were made locally, offering complete protection for local industries.

Too Little Money, Too Many Demands

Government spending grew, with the growth funded through higher taxation and larger borrowing. Although government revenue also rose as a percentage of GDP and Kenya was funding more of its development budget than in the 1960s, the state was still systematically short of funds. Opportunities to raise more revenue remained constrained by the small size of the private sector, the high level of off-book production and consumption and Kenya's dependence on export crops whose prices were set by the world market. While indirect taxes (sales, import and export taxes) had provided 43 per cent of current revenue in 1970, by 1974 this had risen to 54 per cent.[58] The state's options were limited. Kenya just did not produce or consume enough and what it did produce was hard to estimate and hard to tax. Despite its nominal capitalism, the government was concerned about being too dependent on foreign investment and suspicious of indigenous Asian capital. It was only the Kikuyu insiders and a few multinationals that could offer a safe source of private capital, but Westerners were often reluctant to invest without cast-iron guarantees.

With few politically acceptable opportunities to increase taxation, the government resorted increasingly to deficit financing and borrowing (see Figure 5.6). It also diversified its sources of loans away from the UK. In 1972, for the first time, Kenya borrowed from an international commercial bank, taking US$15 million from the First National Bank of Chicago for budgetary support. The government's strategy was now to use its own income to fund recurrent expenditure – mostly civil service salaries – and to fund most development out of aid and loans. The risk – as Kenya was to discover – was that loans required repayment, and unless the investment generated self-sustaining returns, the result would be greater impoverishment in the future. Poor planning and execution of externally funded investments was a key reason for Kenya's troubles in the 1980s.

Foreign aid continued to drive much of Kenya's growth. Donors funded between 30 and 60 per cent of the development budget during 1969–74, mostly in loan form.[59] In 1970, another aid agreement was reached with the UK for GB£11.5 million for the period 1970–4. As well as direct financial support, 1,500–2,000 British technical and advisory personnel continued to work for the government, and European advisers continued to fill specialist posts in key ministries. However, there was growing domestic resistance to the presence of expatriate advisers and the number fell rapidly during the 1970s. There was real anger, for example, at the degree to which donors influenced development policy.[60] The government's relationship with overseas investors also came under attack from the backbench. J. M. Kariuki and other MPs regularly attacked the recruitment of expatriates to run organisations such as Kenya Canners, Chemelil Sugar factory and Mumias Sugar (particularly if they were Asian). Many nationalist Kenyans believed that foreign managers had no special skills, and that their jobs could easily be Africanised, suggesting they were impeding Africans from standing on their own feet.[61] Some even demanded that all expatriates be expelled.

State Control of the Economy

While officials encouraged investment and free enterprise, the presumption was that foreign private enterprise was dangerous and required careful control. Kenya's African socialism in the 1960s had been dominated by the need to keep the West sweet, and founded on infusions of private capital. However, during the 1970s, with more emphasis on self-reliance and the worldwide trend towards socialism, civil servants and politicians alike demanded majority state ownership of most new investments, in order to kick-start a more industrialised economy and absorb the growing numbers of unemployed.

5.6: Government deficit, 1964–75 (after investments and parastatal loans, in US$ million)

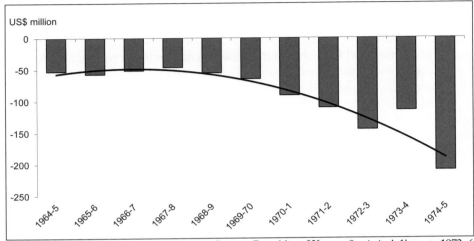

Source: Republic of Kenya, *Statistical Abstracts*, 1972–6

The state gradually built a web of permits and structures to allow it to control major projects and to ensure that Kenyan interests would dominate those of foreign investors. In 1971 the Treasury established a Capital Issue Committee to vet all issues of stock, unhappy that some foreign-owned businesses were selling shares to Kenyans and then repatriating funds to their home countries. Africanisation rules now required the vast majority of jobs to be local, while industrial importers had to obtain 'No Objection' certificates showing that no similar product was manufactured locally before they were allowed to import. Although Kenyan industry was more capital intensive than in many other African states (a legacy of European investment), there was sustained pressure from business, universities and government to create more labour-intensive solutions, which were believed to be more appropriate to a low-wage, high-unemployment country. Donors, many of them following the same policies at home, did not challenge Kenya's import substitution or protectionist policies.

Another example of Kenya's evolving development strategy came with demands to nationalise the banks. The National Bank of Kenya (NBK) already belonged to 'the people', while the Cooperative Bank was owned by the cooperatives. The others – Standard Bank, Barclays Bank, National and Grindlays Bank, the Bank of Baroda, Bank of Netherlands, and the Bank of India – were now castigated as foreigners whose only interest was to make a profit, who were reluctant to make loans to Africans, something the government intended to change. In 1970, the government acquired a 60 per cent stake in the British-owned National and Grindlays Bank, which it renamed the Kenya Commercial Bank (KCB). Under its (Kikuyu) chairman, John Michuki, the KCB expanded its lending to Africans by 225 per cent between January and September 1971, an extraordinary change in operating practice.[62] In

1972, the government also tried to force a merger of the other large private banks, Standard Bank and Barclays, and to take a controlling interest in the resulting bank. However, the Union Bank Bill was thrown out by MPs, fearing that the government would use its control of the banking sector to discriminate against its critics.

The ICDC remained the core vehicle for state control of the economy, holding an equity stake in businesses including East African Breweries, EAI, Firestone, Block Hotels, NAS Airport Services, Uchumi Supermarkets and Union Carbide. The commercial success rate of these ventures was uneven: while some large ventures prospered, several majority-owned subsidiaries faced severe financial problems by the late 1970s, and many small investments collapsed completely. The government seemed determined on a 50–50 share in most large businesses. In sectors they considered strategic, however, such as power, they demanded not just equity but control. In 1971, the state acquired ownership of the Kenya Power Company and a controlling interest in the Tana River Development Company. In 1972, they bought a controlling interest in East African Power and Lighting and increased their stake in the Mombasa oil refinery to 51 per cent.

On 1 January 1970, the central government also took over the responsibilities of the county councils for roads, primary education, health care, agricultural extension and water. For some time, councils had been struggling to meet the demand for services on a limited income base and with weak collection mechanisms. The responsibilities of rural councils were reduced, but they remained financially dependent on central government.

Import Substitution and the Growth of Manufacturing Industry

Although relatively industrialised by African standards, manufacturing in Kenya still accounted for only 10–11 per cent of GDP. Food processing was dominant, alongside drinks, tobacco, wood, paper, rubber and petrochemicals. To increase this contribution, the government provided significant support for foreign investment to meet the growing needs of the domestic (and EAC) market, reduce imports, create jobs and save foreign exchange.

The period 1967–72 was one of strong multinational investment, with K£77 million of new foreign private long-term capital moving into the country.[63] Most were joint ventures, designed to support both economic development and self-reliance. As a result, between 1970 and 1978, manufactured goods fell from 26 to 17 per cent of total imports. By 1975, imports of food, drink and tobacco had fallen to virtually zero.[64] These investments included Firestone East Africa, which began operating in 1971, manufacturing tyres locally and importing specialist tyres. Firestone was granted duty exemptions and a monopoly on local production, a deal that was later criticised as favouring the company, in part because of corrupt benefits to individuals. A second major project was Pan-African Paper Mills (paper and pulp producers) in Bungoma District in Western Province, a joint venture between the ICDC, American and Indian investors. Construction began in 1972 and production started in 1974.[65] In 1974 the government announced another public–private partnership, a joint venture with British

Leyland and Cooper Motor Corporation to build a plant at Thika to assemble Land Rovers, trucks and Volkswagens, again with protection from competing imports. Two more assembly plants were approved in the same year – an ICDC–General Motors joint venture in Nairobi and a Lonrho-led consortium. In 1973, the ICDC established another subsidiary, the Industrial Development Bank (IDB). The IDB's goal was to finance large industrial projects – competing with both the DFCK and the ICDC – but its speciality was the acquisition and disbursement of World Bank loans.

There was increasing concern, however, that Kenya's manufacturing industries were inefficient, working below capacity and producing goods that were more expensive than equivalent international products. This was partly a result of the small size of the Kenyan market and the growing difficulties in exporting to its neighbours.[66] In many cases, manufacturing businesses were effectively local monopolies, with one large company either a joint venture or closely linked to the government in either legal or de facto control of the market. Foreign investors preferred such arrangements, as they would be protected from competition through import bans, tariff protection or duty waivers. The result was a high level of effective protection, which encouraged inefficient production for domestic use over production for export.[67] Given the degree of risk involved in African investments, multinationals expected to recover their investments in 5–6 years, which increased the cost for Kenya of such projects. Worse, some ventures were rigged against Kenya through management contracts or component import agreements that permitted transfer pricing or other remittances on top of dividends.[68] The generous terms of some deals may have been linked to gifts to ministers and officials.[69] As in other less-developed countries, such investments also tended to be poorly integrated with the rest of the economy, using capital-intensive production methods and dependent on imported spares and inputs. The government knew this was undesirable, but accepted it as unavoidable, though they pressed firms to Africanise their sourcing.

Transport and Communications

There were also growing pains in the transport and communications sector. After the Ministry of Works took over responsibility for all roads outside urban areas, there was a 28 per cent increase in road mileage during 1970–4 and 37 per cent more roads were tarred. Like many other issues, road building soon became tribalised, with allegations that Central Province roads were favoured at the expense of areas such as North-Eastern, which still had no tarred roads at all.[70] By 1974, road quality was already becoming a problem and attention was shifting towards the problem of maintaining roads rather than building them. Better roads did not mean safer driving. Lack of upkeep and poor driving skills contributed to a tripling of deaths and serious road injuries between independence and the mid-1970s. A major innovation took place in June 1973, when Kenyatta legalised the *matatu* industry, allowing private minibuses to transport passengers along defined routes. The intent was to Africanise the transport sector, but the state thereby created a monster that it could barely control.

In the aviation sector, there was a similar mix of improving services but warning signs of problems to come. The first jumbo jet landed in Kenya in 1971, the first in Africa and a precursor to the mass tourism boom of the 1970s. EAA, however, was now in serious trouble. In May 1973, the East African Legislative Assembly published a damning report suggesting the organisation was near collapse due to poor investments and over-expansion, over-rapid promotion of Africans into senior technical positions, high costs, mismanagement and corruption. A rescue deal had to be put together in 1973. A profitable entity at independence now required substantial cash just to keep it operating.

In 1974, a similar deal was needed for East African Railways (EAR). Although the British had run the railways as a viable undertaking, the EAC could not. Traffic volumes and profitability were hurt by competition from bituminised roads, which poached the high-value traffic and left the railways carrying uneconomic bulk products.[71] Lack of capital led to deteriorating rolling stock, and the administration of the organisation was less efficient under its new structure. Political problems delayed remittances from Tanzania to the railways' Nairobi headquarters, and Tanzania claimed that Kenya was neglecting the railways in favour of its private road haulage industry. It seemed that the railways might break up completely, but eventually the partners agreed to inject new capital, restructure the lines around national boundaries and bring in a foreign management team.

Employment and Unemployment

Kenya was now suffering from its earlier success in education, with increasing numbers of school leavers entering a job market that offered few opportunities. There were 200,000 new jobs created between 1969 and 1974, a 27 per cent increase in the private sector and 39 per cent in public sector; but more than 600,000 left school in the same period. Manufacturing output was growing, but through higher productivity and better utilisation of machinery, rather than through hiring more workers. The relatively high salaries of formal sector workers, and industry's preference for a skilled, stable workforce over an unskilled, unstable one combined to discourage new hires. Independently, there was a fall in formal agricultural employment, mostly due to productivity improvements and the decline of the sisal industry.

Under-employment had long been widespread, but because most adults remained in the rural areas, labouring on family lands, it could be managed. Now, with a better-educated generation coming onto the labour market, little growth in jobs and growing landlessness, the situation had changed. While 85 per cent of the 1965 school leavers were in employment or further education in 1966, for the 1969 crop this number had fallen to 67 per cent. There was little prospect that the situation could be reversed, creating a massive long-term unemployment problem that no subsequent government has been able to solve. Many school leavers would have to work the land, take 'informal sector' roles, live on family charity or turn to crime. Attempts were made to stem the drift to the cities and provide jobs in the rural areas, but they had little effect. Both Africanisation and the government's reluctance to subdivide the remaining large farms worsened the problem.

The state's solution – like that of most other countries at the time – was Keynesian and interventionist, legislating for more employment and investing in labour-intensive rather than capital-intensive industries. The plan was that jobs, any jobs, would earn incomes, which would then be spent on local products, which would provide more jobs. Kenyatta's second tripartite agreement of 1 June 1970 required that all businesses, including the government, employ 10 per cent more people. In return, there would be another year of no strikes and wage restrictions. Job seekers swarmed to registration centres, but businesses ignored the order or converted casual labour into permanent employees until the government's attention was elsewhere.[72] The National Assembly's approach was little different. It wanted more Africanisation, income control, labour-intensive investments and agricultural subsidies.[73]

At the government's request, the International Labour Organisation (ILO) conducted a major study during 1971–2 into unemployment and poverty in Kenya. Its report in November 1972 challenged the state's employment and development policies, and called for the redirection of resources away from the cities, formal sector employees and the most developed areas. It also called for large-scale income redistribution, including salary freezes for the better-off, progressive taxation, and a more critical attitude to foreign investment and suggested that tribalism and nepotism were undermining development. It also placed the 'informal sector' of small, unregistered, untaxed manufacturing and service businesses squarely on the agenda, arguing that the government's focus on the formal sector (which employed only a fifth of working-age men) was causing it to miss opportunities elsewhere. The problem was not unemployment (because many of those unemployed were on the streets hawking, working in small businesses or cultivating land owned by others) but low incomes and lack of productivity.[74] The report also argued for the break-up of the large farms, since the smallholder sector was at least equally productive and politically and socially more beneficial.

The state responded with its *Sessional Paper on Employment* in 1973, promising greater equality and broader access to services, but without addressing most of the structural issues, since many of the ILO's proposals struck at the fundamentals of its strategy for development and its leaders' personal interests.[75] The paper committed the government to labour-intensive rather than capital-intensive investments, and increased tariffs on capital goods to encourage employment. There was to be more emphasis on increasing rural incomes, but no land reform. In retrospect, it is far from clear that this was the best advice to give, or the best response.

Labour Relations and Trade Unionism

In the 1970s, the world labour movement was at the zenith of its power and industrial strife was near-universal. Kenya was no exception, and the country's 50 unions mounted numerous strikes and protests. However, in comparison with the UK, where industrial action brought down the government, the Kenyan unions never seized the national agenda or made public policy.

Part of the reason for the relative quiescence of organised labour was that COTU remained partially government controlled. MPs Denis Akumu as secretary-general and Fred Omido as chairman dampened the ardour of the radicals and used their authority to grant or deny support to industrial action. There was a tight structure of wages advisory boards and councils that ensured that wages could be reviewed without striking. The Industrial Court continued to arbitrate the 10 per cent of disputes that could not be settled amicably. Its charter was amended in 1971 to give it more power to reinstate or compensate workers wrongfully dismissed. The Ministry of Labour retained the right to declare strikes illegal and to use force if necessary to break them up.

Facing mass unemployment, urban workers were easily cowed by the threat of dismissal. The government kept wage increases well below the rate of inflation, quietly eroding the position of formal sector workers to reverse the effects of the 1950s and 1960s. They hoped thereby to reduce rural–urban wage differentials, improve industrial competitiveness and create jobs.[76] Reflecting their fragile position, the trade unions placed more emphasis on keeping the jobs of their members than in aggressive wage pressure.

The unions – a surrogate in political battles as well as an institution in their own right – still suffered from endemic factionalism. The government found it difficult to develop a coherent policy on the union movement, concerned about losing control but unwilling to risk a revolt by imposing Kikuyu leadership on one of the few sectors that was not Kikuyu-dominated. In 1972, these divisions led to a second split in COTU. A long-running dispute between the All Workers Group (led by Akumu) and the Kenya United Group (led by Kikuyu James Karebe) involved overlapping divisions over relations with the government, factional interests, personal positions and ethnicity. In October 1972, Karebe, Clement Lubembe and others created a competing Federation of United Trades Unions (FUTU). However, the rebellion ended in a return to the fold in 1974, and Akumu was triumphantly re-elected as COTU head.

Despite these restraints, 1974 saw mass industrial action, including disputes at East African Railways, Harbours and EAA. There were strikes by bank staff in July and August. At the same time, university students went on strike for the second time that year. When there were wildcat strikes at Embakasi airport, and teachers announced a national strike, the government had had enough. On 16 August 1974, Kenyatta banned all strikes in a presidential decree, threatening severe action against anyone who organised or participated in one. Extraordinarily, COTU supported the ban.[77] The legality of a presidential decree was never questioned.

Land and Agriculture

Agriculture remained the mainstay of the economy, contributing more than a third of GDP. From 1972 onwards, however, the growth in output was slower than the growth in population, as the agricultural boom slowed, hurt by rising oil prices. Bad weather in 1974 caused the first fall in agricultural GDP since independence.

The spread of cash-crop farming and the planting of improved crop varieties continued. Small farm production continued to grow, supported by farm subdivision, better roads, better seeds and greater use of fertilisers. Most farmers, though, still produced both for their own use and to sell surpluses. Relatively few farms were purely commercial. Rather than being driven out, small-scale family-based agriculture was expanding, through the settlement schemes and informal large-farm subdivision. This 'peasantisation' was sustained by high-input, high-return cash-crops.[78]

Boom and Bust in the Maize Industry, 1971–4

The early 1970s were a period of food shortages, particularly of maize, most of which was grown and consumed by smallholders. In 1971, after the rains failed, 180,000 northern Kenyans were receiving famine relief. In part, their plight could be traced to government policies. Food prices and distribution were both state regulated (maize could not be transported across district boundaries by anyone except the government, unless specially licensed). When the state set purchase prices below the level that Kenya's higher-cost (and indebted) farmers could produce profitably, farmers diversified, sold products at higher prices 'off book', or exported illegally. Kenya had to import grain from the US and sell it at a loss, and to raise maize purchase prices twice during 1971 to above export parity.[79] When the ban on maize movement was partially lifted, production increased rapidly, and 1972 was a boom year.

A Parliamentary Select Committee on the maize industry was set up in 1972, to investigate these recurrent problems. When it reported in November 1973, by which time maize and wheat were in short supply once more, it became embroiled in a classic conflict between workers' and farmers' lobbies in Parliament. Its recommendations of price rises and liberalisation faced strong opposition because they would disadvantage the urban poor. Its investigation had also revealed significant administrative incompetence. Both Shikuku and the committee argued that the government should remove all restrictions and create a free market in maize, but the government defeated the report. In January 1974, the Maize and Produce Board was declared the sole buyer of maize from farmers and distributors. Food pricing and distribution and politics would continue to be uncomfortable bedfellows for three decades.

Milk and Meat

Growth in the livestock industry flattened out, limited by controls on consumer prices for meat and milk, which were kept below world market prices. While herd numbers on large farms were stable, smallholder and pastoralist herds continued to expand (although most meat and milk production and consumption was unrecorded).[80]

The 1973 maize shortage coincided with drought in the north, which caused a glut of meat, as pastoralists tried to sell undernourished animals. The drought, which continued for several years, was at its worst in 1975. Many northern pastoralists were forced to seek help around the market towns of the region. Amongst the poorest, the process of sedentarisation (losing their cattle, ceasing to be nomadic and taking up permanent homes and occupations) had begun.[81]

Some state agricultural processing organisations were also experiencing problems. The Kenya Meat Commission (KMC), the parastatal abattoir, faced competition from the mid-1970s with the licensing of several competitors, and its throughput and profitability declined. The 1973 drought also damaged the KCC, its effects worsened by inflexible pricing and poor management, and it made losses for several years. Farmers, however, were protected by increases in milk producer prices.

The Land Frontier in the 1970s

The flood of land-hungry Kikuyu, Luhya, Kalenjin, Kamba, Meru and Gusii out of their ex-reserves continued. The primary areas for settlement were under-utilised lands in the Rift Valley, parts of Eastern Province and the Coast.

The process of land acquisition now took four forms. The main form was the 'willing buyer, willing seller' process, whereby anyone with money could buy land from those willing to sell. Kenyatta also allowed politicians and civil servants to buy farms in Uasin Gishu and Trans-Nzoia from the ADC, which continued to acquire a few European-owned farms. Less-wealthy individuals bought farms in partnerships and subdivided them later. More land was sold by private sale intact than was bought and subdivided, with clear implications for land ownership patterns. It also had ethnic implications. The inequality in access to finance – not only was the Kikuyu community richer, but it had better access to loans and better protection from default – meant that the first generation of land purchase from whites in the Rift Valley was mostly by wealthy Kikuyu and Meru. Nakuru and Uasin Gishu were the primary areas for this settlement, but by 1973 Kikuyu (or Gikuyu), Embu and Meru (known in shorthand as 'Gema') settlers were also moving into what had once been Kipsigis lands. The preferential access to land enjoyed by the wealthy led to public protests. Seroney tried to introduce legislation to ban speculative land dealings in 1971, which the House narrowly voted down. For Kipsigis MP Moses arap Keino, by 1973 the ministry of lands and settlement had become the 'Ministry of "Settling the Rich"'.[82]

The second method was the formal settlement schemes. The government developed a few new schemes in the 1970s, mainly by excising forestland in less densely populated districts. The Lands and Settlement Ministry still operated the successors of the million-acre and *haraka* schemes, but neither was a great success. Most settlements were small, the number of people settled was unknown, and the process of choosing settlers was corrupt and chaotic. By the late 1960s, the government had quietly changed policy, no longer supporting large-scale subdivision. Agricultural policy now emphasised the importance of large farms as the only economic means of producing wheat and sisal, and a reasonably efficient way to grow sugar, tea and coffee. However, opinions on their efficiency were divided, and the debate was given impetus by the political implications of mass landlessness. In practice, many argued, smallholder returns per hectare were little different or even greater, with the main advantage of large farms being the easier provision of processing facilities for the crops.[83]

The decision to deprioritise subdivision and settlement was never clearly articulated or debated inside Kenya. It was driven in part by the lack of foreign funds for further schemes, but other factors included the elite's desire to acquire large farms and the poor performance of the settlement schemes, which were often overpriced, rarely achieved the target incomes and experienced large-scale defaults.[84] Many who had bought plots were unable to service their loans. Some beneficiaries did not even distinguish between cash and income and immediately spent their loans.[85] In the Lugari settlement scheme in Western Province for example, by 1977, 80 per cent of the original smallholders had forfeited their land because of loan defaults. Most were bought by absentee urban owners.[86] No freehold was given until the loans were cleared, and even 20 years later many settlers were still without title deeds. The British rescheduled and eventually wrote off some loans.[87] This problem was not confined to the settlement schemes. Many 'willing buyers' were also unable to service their AFC loans, and some absentee farmers with political connections made no attempt to repay. Arrears to the AFC were immense, with reports that repayment of half its loan capital was in arrears, let alone interest. There were persistent rumours that most AFC loans went to Kikuyu and Kalenjin, and that many were later written off under a rigged 'guaranteed minimum returns' scheme that compensated farmers when results were poor.

In the early 1970s, rather than creating new settlement schemes, the government focused on cooperative or collective farms. The new *shirika* scheme was designed to settle 30,000 unemployed and landless families on 200,000 hectares of formerly British-owned lands between 1971 and 1976. *Shirika* was based on cooperative ownership, with individual plots and a central pool of land for cooperative crop production. In contrast to their attitude in the early 1960s, the British backed it with a GB£2.5 million gift rather than a loan. Even so, it was not a success. Members did not fulfil their collective obligations, preferring to take their labour elsewhere or work their own plots, and the cooperatives lacked modern farming tools and the capital to invest. By 1983, both the *shirika* schemes and the original Ol Kalou cooperative farms had been fully subdivided. According to Christopher Leo's calculation, the various settlement schemes now totalled 2 million acres (800,000 hectares), on which 80,000 families had been settled.[88] With an influx of landless relatives and informal subdivision, up to 500,000 people were now living on the schemes, mixing cash-crop and subsistence farming.

The final (and increasingly important) means for land buying was collective land purchase through land-buying companies. Groups of peasants pooled resources and bought 'shares' in a company, which then promised to buy white-owned farms, subdivide them and convert them into peasant plots. Hundreds of such companies were established in the 1970s, mainly in Central Province and the Rift Valley, to buy land in Nakuru and Laikipia. Laikipia's population doubled between 1969 and 1979, as at least 40,000 Kikuyu moved into the area.[89] One of the most famous land-buying companies was the Ngwataniro group, led by Kikuyu politician Kihika Kimani. There was rampant fraud, however, as directors stole peasant contributions, while the government discouraged the subdivision of farms even after their purchase.

There was ethnic competition between groups of peasants and between peasants and wealthy individuals over who would acquire specific farms. The competition for land between the Kalenjin and the Kikuyu (and to a lesser extent the Luhya) simmered under the surface throughout the Kenyatta era. The Kikuyu had acquired Nyandarua, Laikipia and most of southern Nakuru, the Luhya western Trans-Nzoia and Lugari and the Kalenjin eastern Trans-Nzoia and northern Nakuru. All three communities shared Uasin Gishu, with the Kalenjin dominant in the east and west, the Kikuyu in the south and the Luhya in the north-west.

'Foreign' settlement in the ex-reserves of other communities remained deeply unpopular. Despite official policy, commentators noted: 'for most of our people – even those who move to individual land tenure systems, the view of land as being owned by the tribe will still remain.'[90] Although the centre promulgated the spirit of 'one nation', the reality was quite different. Virtually every large community believed that ethnic purity in their ex-reserves was desirable. In 1970, for example, Kamba MPs demanded that the state withdraw all non-Kamba primary teachers from Ukambani.[91] Every community feared Kikuyu immigration, and land boards were hostile to Kikuyu land purchase over most of the country.

Nonetheless, the Kikuyu and Meru expansion continued. This process was administered by Jackson Angaine, who headed the Ministry of Lands and Settlement continuously from 1963 until 1979. The proactive role that Angaine was playing in facilitating Gema settlement was clear – one MP in 1973 criticised him, saying 'Is he only interested in the lands they are grabbing from the Kalenjin people in the Rift Valley? The Kalenjin land is already finished in the Rift Valley'.[92] In 1974, a Kalenjin MP demanded his sacking and referred to him as 'a leader to hell and darkness'.[93] It was widely believed that Moi had abandoned any attempt to restrict Gema settlement. While he could not challenge the process publicly though, Moi worked behind the scenes to help Kalenjin farmers compete with the Kikuyu to buy settler farms when they came on the market.[94] Towett similarly pressurised Europeans to sell their land to Kalenjin within the Kalenjin sphere of influence.[95]

After independence, the Maasai lands south of Nairobi, which had been closed to outsiders during the colonial era, also became targets for 'willing buyer, willing seller' land purchases by Kikuyu and Kipsigis.[96] Although there were few white settlers to buy out here, the Maasai were encouraged to establish title to land. In 1969–71, group ranches were adjudicated in Kajiado and Narok, covering nearly a million acres.[97] Better-watered areas around Ngong town and Kilimanjaro in Kajiado were also demarcated, then sold and converted to settled agriculture (reducing the pasturelands available for the remaining pastoralists). Kikuyu, Luo and Kamba moved in large numbers into Kajiado District, and by 1989 the Maasai were a bare 57 per cent of the district's population (see Figure 5.7).

Tensions grew in both Kajiado and Narok as high-potential land was settled both legally and illegally by non-Maasai. Pitched battles were fought in 1975–6 between

Luo and Luhya immigrants and Maasai in Narok, presaging further troubles to come.[98] Smaller, localised but bloody conflicts continued between the Maasai, Kipsigis, Kisii, Luo and Kuria over land and cattle. These predated colonial rule and continued into the 1990s.[99]

Land on the coastal strip remained an even more intractable problem. Arab, Swahili and Asian families had acquired much of the 10-mile wide strip during the sultan's days, and had land titles to prove it. After independence, they retained ownership, as guaranteed in the Lancaster House settlement. However, much of the land had been settled by local Mijikenda and ex-slaves who believed it to be government land or unoccupied. There was no buyout of land as had happened with the Europeans, as no one was willing to pay for it. The problem pitted the sanctity of private property against the political imperative to find land for local people, and was worsened by the financial muscle of the Arab community, which was well represented in the corridors of power. Once land registration and consolidation began in Kwale and Kilifi in 1971–3, squatters were living on borrowed time before the surveyors declared their occupation illegal and confirmed the title of their landlords.

The problem was worsened by the growing commercial value of the land. The formal owners sold land for tourist development and the government made grants of coastal land suitable for tourism, often in areas already occupied by Mijikenda, resulting in mass evictions. In the early 1970s, to help move ownership of these plots into African hands, Kenyatta issued a presidential edict that barred the sale of all beach plots without his permission. The result was to move control of these assets entirely into presidential favour, a process administered by Coast PC Eliud Mahihu, who could now decide who could and could not buy coastal plots. Political insiders, ministers, PCs and the administrative elite acquired beachfront land, properties and businesses from European, Asian and Arab sellers, laying the foundation for further disputes.[100]

5.7: The ethnic composition of Kajiado District, 1962–89

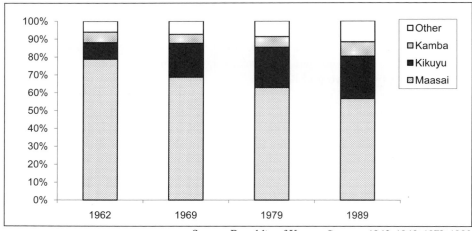

Source: Republic of Kenya, *Censuses*, 1962, 1969, 1979, 1989

There were also tensions between settlers and indigenous peoples in Shimba Hills in Kwale District, where 3,000 upcountry people had been settled in one of the first colonial settlement schemes. At independence, Kwale County Council took over the scheme as Trust Land, which it leased to the settlers for 33 years, leaving them with no title deeds and therefore no security for loans. The local Digo and the county council were hostile to accepting the permanent rights of these settlers, who included many Kamba. This ensured that there was little further immigration to Kwale after 1969. Many Kenyans also settled in Taveta constituency around independence, believing they were squatting on government land. Much of the constituency (three large sisal farms) was, however, acquired in 1972 by the Greek Criticos family, in a joint venture with Jomo Kenyatta himself. This meant that no one could erect a permanent building or enclose land, another source of long-running tension.

During the 1960s, several *haraka* schemes had been established on the coast, providing land for around 5,000 squatters, and more small settlements took place in Kilifi in the 1970s. In Lamu District, a larger programme began in 1973, the Lake Kenyatta Settlement Scheme, supported by West German aid. Between 1969 and 1979, the district's population rose by more than 80 per cent, with nearly 10,000 Kikuyu (including ex-Mau Mau veterans) now making up 20 per cent of the district. The indigenous Bajuni became a minority (see Figure 5.8). As a consequence, the immigrants also began to exercise political influence, with Kikuyu parliamentary candidates contesting the seat from 1979 onwards.

A similar situation was seen in the Garsen, Bura and Hola irrigation schemes in Tana River District. Again, the state chose an under-utilised ex-KADU coastal district for upcountry settlement. By 1981, there were 1,000 Kikuyu families settled in Bura. While such schemes were significant both politically and economically, however, it is important not to overemphasise their impact. The mass immigration of 10,000 Somali nomads in the 1970s changed the character of the district more than any settlement scheme.

5.8: The ethnic composition of Lamu District, 1962–89

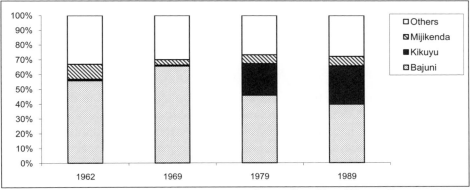

Source: Republic of Kenya, *Censuses*, 1962–89

A comparable process was under way in part of Isiolo District in Eastern Province. The Ministry of Lands and Settlement had allocated land to Meru settlers in 1971 in the hills near Isiolo, driving Boran pastoralists away. But once again, while the settlement schemes received more attention, Samburu and Somali immigration from the north was changing the population of previously Boran Isiolo far more than the Gema settlers would do.

Elite Rule

By the mid-1970s, Kenya was ruled by an elite: aloof, complacent, capable and Western-oriented, which dominated politics, the civil service, business, large-scale farming, parastatals and most formal and informal power structures. A gradual bifurcation in the African elite was taking place, between a multi-ethnic middle class of managers, clerks, small businessmen and junior civil servants, and this small ruling class. There were no hard boundaries, and social mobility was still common, but there was a gradual separation between the lives and prospects of a few thousand families and the rest of the formal, non-manual sector.

Many of this 'super-elite' occupied positions that had been reserved for Europeans in the colonial era, replicating their greater salaries and prospects.[101] They had leveraged the one-off opportunity of Africanisation in the 1960s and early 1970s. Many had studied together or knew each other. Most were Kikuyu, particularly from Kiambu, lived in Nairobi and were active supporters of Kenyatta and his allies. Most straddled several roles: they were civil servants, politicians, farm owners, landlords and businessmen, all at the same time. Although this concentrated resources in their hands, this 'straddling' also ensured that – through their interest in cash-cropping – farmers received a reasonable return. As David Leonard noted,

> The class structure of Kenya gives its rulers a set of interests in export agriculture as well as commerce and industry. They therefore balance the interests of the sectors better than Tanzania does and are unlikely to 'kill the goose that laid the golden egg'.[102]

Large and small farmers were also bound together by the patron–client system and competitive electoral politics.

The Kikuyuisation of Kenya

Although the state continued to talk of Kenya as one nation, and to de-emphasise ethnicity in its public statements and policies on land, service delivery and jobs, the unifying rhetoric of nationhood concealed a less palatable truth. The 1970s saw the entrenchment of Kikuyu power via a web of both formal and informal networks. As with the security forces, the senior civil service was increasingly Kikuyu dominated. The crucial posts of provincial commissioners, for example, were held by a small group of conservative insiders, more than half of whom were Kikuyu from 1967 until Kenyatta's death, and three of whom were sons of chiefs (see Table 5.4). Appointments to statutory boards and parastatals showed the same trend

These men were powerful, educated, intelligent and able, and they effectively ran Kenya in the interest of Kenyatta, themselves (they all had substantial business investments) and the country. Just as their colonial predecessors had done, they disliked local politicians, whom they treated as competitors, and made no pretence of democracy. Mahihu was particularly well known for his dictatorial attitude and concern with development. As he said in 1998: 'About calling us governors, I had no problem . . . we were employed to govern our provinces and we did.'[103] Simeon Nyachae was in a class of his own as the most able, politically astute non-Kikuyu PC with direct personal loyalty to Kenyatta (though he had married a wife from Nyeri). His governorship of Central Province was a critical ethnic balancing act. Moi's influence was seen in the appointment of two Kalenjin PCs, and Kenyatta took care to ensure that the Luo were governed not by a Kikuyu but by a Kipsigis.

The same pattern was seen elsewhere. In the central government, Geoffrey Kariithi (a Kikuyu from Kirinyaga and educated at Alliance High School) headed the civil service from 1967 to 1979. Other senior figures included Kiereini (ex-Alliance,

Table 5.4: Kenyatta's key provincial commissioners

Name	Position	Background
Paul Boit	PC Central, Western and Nairobi 1964–80	Kalenjin – Nandi, son of chief
Isaiah Cheluget	PC Nyanza Province 1969–80	Kalenjin – Kipsigis.
Charles Koinange	PC Central and Eastern 1967–80	Kikuyu from Kiambu, son of senior chief, Mbiyu Koinange's brother and Kenyatta's brother-in-law
Eliud Mahihu	PC Eastern and Coast 1964–80	Kikuyu from Nyeri, colonial administrator and ex-Home Guard
Isaiah Mathenge	PC Coast, Rift Valley and Eastern 1965–82	Kikuyu from Nyeri, ex-Home Guard and detention camp warder
John Godhard Mburu	PC Coast, North-Eastern, Nairobi, and Western 1964–79	Kikuyu from Murang'a
Simeon Nyachae	PC Rift Valley and Central 1965–79	Gusii, son of senior chief

Source: Various

also from Kirinyaga and an ex-detention camp warden) who ran the Ministry of Defence. Peter Gachathi (Alliance, Kiambu) was education secretary from 1969 to 1979. Duncan Ndegwa (Alliance, Nyeri) was governor of the Central Bank. Joseph Gethenji (Nyeri) was director of personnel from 1968 to 1978, while Joseph Kibe (Murang'a) was permanent secretary for commerce and industry. Of course, there were powerful civil servants who were not Kikuyu, but they generally played a secondary role.[104] A study of top civil service posts in 1972 showed that Kikuyu now held 50 per cent of the top jobs, a rapid increase since the 1960s.[105] There were reports that a Posting Committee in the OP made civil service appointments in advance of interviews by the Public Service Commission, and that this committee was dominated by ex-Home Guard Kikuyu.

The situation was little different amongst the parastatals. Many heads of parastatals, appointed by Kenyatta or his ministers, were also Kikuyu (see Table 5.5).

Table 5.5: Senior Kikuyu parastatal heads in the 1970s

Name	Role	Background
Ephantus Gakuo	Director-general of East African Railways (later Kenya Railways), 1967–1970s	Murang'a
Bethwell Gecaga	Chairman, Industrial Development Bank, 1976–9	Murang'a
Julius Gecau	Managing director, East Africa (later Kenya) Power and Lighting Company, 1970–84	Kiambu
James Karani Gitau	General manager, Kenya National Trading Corporation, 1969–79	Kiambu
Stanley Githunguri	Executive chairman, National Bank of Kenya, 1976–9	Kiambu
Charles Karanja	General manager, Kenya Tea Development Authority, 1970–81	Kiambu
John Matere Keriri	General manager then managing director, Development Finance Company of Kenya, 1972–82	Kirinyaga
Peter Kinyanjui	Chairman of East African Harbours Corporation (later Kenya Ports Authority), 1970–80	Kiambu
John Michuki	Executive chairman, Kenya Commercial Bank, 1970–9	Murang'a
Philip Ndegwa	Chairman, Agricultural Finance Corporation to 1974	Kirinyaga
Matu Wamae	Executive director, Industrial and Commercial Development Corporation, 1969–79	Nyeri

Source: Various

There is no doubt that these were intelligent, competent individuals. Many had gone through the elite forcing-ground at Alliance High School and knew each other well. Whether they were the best men for the job is another question, as personal loyalty to Kenyatta was critical. Kenyatta was lucky that he had an educated, able cadre of loyalists to choose from, a luxury that Moi did not have a decade later.

Amongst private sector organisations not led by Europeans or Asians, Kikuyu dominance was equally strong. Francis Thuo (Murang'a) was chairman of the Nairobi Stock Exchange during 1970–83. Joseph Wanyoike (Murang'a) was managing director of Kenya Cooperative Creameries from 1968 until 1978. Bethwell Gecaga (Murang'a) chaired BAT from 1967 until 1995. His son and Kenyatta's nephew Udi Gecaga was now Lonrho chairman. Ex-permanent secretary Kenneth Matiba (Alliance, Murang'a) ran Kenya Breweries until 1984, while Joe Wanjui (Kiambu) ran East African Industries until 1993.

This Kikuyu dominance at the top filtered down to other levels. Each appointment generated power and income for its holder and a trickle-down to their home area through contracts, jobs for clients and preferential allocation of development funds. A self-reinforcing structure of privilege was built which 22 years of Moi's rule never fully dismantled. In October 1973, Shikuku presciently warned that if the Kikuyu did not share the fruits of *Uhuru* with others, they would eventually be 'eaten' by the other 41 tribes 'like a satisfied hyena was eaten up by hungry hyenas'.[106] Not every job was set aside for the Kikuyu, however. The ethnic sifting process worked much the same way when a non-Kikuyu ran an organisation. There were protests in 1970, for example, that EAA, the National Housing Corporation (NHC) and the KNTC were all the 'monopoly of Abaluyias'.[107]

The Luo received little preference from the state. The 1965–6 split and the KPU era had alienated Kenyatta permanently from the community and as, *Kenya Times* suggested:

> Henceforth, the Luos became second class citizens of Kenya. They were viewed with suspicion in all quarters and they were given the lowest rating whenever it came to jobs. Apart from the Kisumu-Busia, Kisumu Kericho and Kisumu Kisii roads, Luo Nyanza roads were not tarmacked.[108]

While the Kamba had the military, the Luo – with some of the best-educated and most active elites at independence – had few avenues for their energies. They had no large settlement schemes and most of Luo Nyanza was unsuitable for coffee and tea. They could go into business, but the commercial sector was tilted in favour of the Kikuyu and they had little capital. Distrusted in the military, parastatals and politics, they focused instead on the civil service, the professions, trade unionism and religion. Luo increasingly blamed their marginalisation, both real and apparent, on the Kikuyu, and built a mythology of resistance and social cohesion around opposition to the Kikuyu elite's political and economic goals.

It was now clear that the Kikuyu and to a lesser extent their Mount Kenya neighbours in Embu and Meru were embedding a sense of pre-eminence in their collective culture. There was a growing assumption of their right to rule. Many Kikuyu believed they were smarter, more entrepreneurial and had suffered more under colonialism. They compared themselves with Europeans, and viewed other Kenyans as backward and likely to destroy the economy if given power. Their widespread antipathy to the Luo was not based on their failure to practise male circumcision (though it was a genuine point of cultural tension), but on the threat they posed because of their numbers and history of recent conflict. By the 1980s, under Moi, the Kikuyu had become firmly associated in the popular imagination with competitive differentiation and 'money grabbing', while their Luo counterparts had come to epitomise indolence, poverty, socialism and rebellion.[109] Odinga and Kenyatta symbolised this cleavage: Odinga was the dispossessed; Kenyatta the benevolent dictator but simultaneously 'the chief architect and patron of the Greater Kikuyu Community'.[110]

The Cult of 'Mzee'

The cult of presidentialism deepened. As he aged, Kenyatta became more intolerant of dissent, and the centralisation of power around him encouraged sycophancy and exploitation. By 1971, Kenyatta's was the only portrait permitted in shops and business premises. In 1973, businesses, sports, political and ethnic associations were required by law to stop using the title 'president' for their heads. The word could now only refer to the head of state. Increasingly, Kenyatta operated with little concern for the niceties of law, travelling with his inner circle from residence to residence like a medieval monarch and issuing orders and proclamations that his functionaries had to find means to put into legal effect. The circle around him closed tighter, and it became impossible for most politicians, even some ministers, to see him privately. A KANU Governing Council conference on 4 July 1974 declared Kenyatta KANU's 'life president', a non-existent role, but one that reflected the reality at the time.[111]

An early example of this monarchical trend occurred in 1969, when Kenyatta had by presidential proclamation (with no constitutional basis) extended Kenya's sea boundaries from three to 12 miles. Legislation had to be introduced in 1972 to ratify this. In a similar case, in July 1971, Kenyatta met a delegation of councillors and 'postponed' local government elections from 1972 (when they were due) to 1974. Njonjo suggested the decision might be illegal, to which Kenyatta is said to have responded 'to the devil with the law'.[112] Local Government Minister Julius Kiano had to introduce a bill legalising what had already happened.

Another 'Kenya first' presidential diktat came in July 1971, when Kenyatta demanded that the Voice of Kenya broadcast only locally produced material. This led to a rare dispute in Cabinet, which eventually settled on a ratio of 75 per cent local content. Since the edict took effect immediately, there were weeks of chaos as VoK tried to commission or find local material. In 1973, Kenyatta went further, dictating that television programmes must concentrate on national events depicting African culture and Kenya's achievements, and demanding further reductions in imported programming.

In another step to limit foreign influences, the 1974 Governing Council meeting also resolved to make Swahili Kenya's national language. This was not as popular as might be expected, as many Kenyans at this time (including some MPs) did not speak Swahili, which had not been universally taught under British rule. Kenyatta demanded that the National Assembly debate only in Swahili, but faced stiff opposition, since the Constitution specified that English would be the language of the Assembly, and it remained the language of government documents. Despite Kenyatta's instructions, MPs refused to speak Swahili on 9 July 1974, and the government was humiliatingly defeated in a motion of adjournment.[113] The next day, the thirteenth constitutional amendment was introduced, making Swahili the Assembly's sole language, and was forced through a reluctant Parliament.[114] It was to last only five years.

Personal Relations are Political Issues

The Kenyan elite, like others before them, used relationships as a tool to cement alliances. As in medieval families, bonds were sometimes sealed with marriage. Bethwell Gecaga was married to Kenyatta's cousin, and their son Udi Gecaga married Kenyatta's daughter. PC Isaiah Mathenge's daughter married Kenyatta's nephew Ngengi Muigai in 1976, and Njoroge Mungai's daughter (briefly) married Senator Wamalwa's son Michael.

The acquisition of wives (under Muslim or customary law) remained a traditional way of demonstrating success, and just as Kenyatta had had four wives (though Mama Ngina was dominant), Paul Ngei had five, Mbiyu Koinange and Nyachae four and J. M. Kariuki three. The Moi faction was less liberal with its affections – Charles Njonjo had married an English woman, Kibaki had one official wife, while Vice-President Moi separated from his only wife in the mid-1970s. He had been married since 1950 to Helena (Lena), who came from a wealthy and politically active Baringo family. Lena had borne him seven children, but their relationship was now under severe strain. At a New Year's Eve dance on 31 December 1973, there was a public crisis. It has been variously described: either Lena refused to dance with Kenyatta, citing her increasingly vocal Christianity, or Moi chose to take another woman onto the dance floor.[115] Either way, a furious row ensued in front of Kenyatta. Although unreported in the press, Moi banished Lena to a farm in the Rift Valley, where she was kept securely for 25 years. He spent the next three decades as a bachelor.

Factionalism, the Patron–Client system and Parliamentary Politics

Factionalism Becomes Self-Sustaining

As the 1970s continued, the endemic factionalism in KANU, which had briefly aligned with an ideological debate in the mid-1960s, became an end in itself; machine politics was the norm.[116] In the terminology of the time, Kenya was now an 'oligarchical praetorian' state, where political competition was now no longer about what should happen, but about who should benefit from the unchallengeable policies of the state. In the absence of genuine political differences, the competition for control of constituencies, districts and ethnic power blocs, which had always been personalised, now became almost entirely so.

If both critics and supporters agreed that Kenya was an unequal, elitist, colonially influenced polity, it was also one in which people could and did participate in the political process. The high level of rural participation in politics was driven by the agricultural basis of Kenya's prosperity and the patron–client structure of Kenyatta's rule.[117] Voters cared deeply about who led them, and the effect of the electoral system, skewed towards the rural areas, helped moderate policies that might seriously harm local agriculture. The government was not hated, though it was hardly loved. The limited evidence available suggests that most Kenyans believed that, since independence, the government had acted in their interests and that most had benefited.[118] Few argued, though, that the people could influence policy. The state was fixed on its course and calls for change were ignored, unless to head off rebellion on a minor item.

The centre (around Kenyatta) allowed the factional conflicts that spread across KANU, Parliament, local councils, cooperatives, self-help groups and virtually every other institution to play themselves out, except where openly socialist politicians appeared to be gaining ascendancy or Odinga's influence could be felt. Ministers generally had the upper hand at home, secure in the knowledge that they had Kenyatta's confidence and the tacit support of the provincial administration. However, most incumbents faced an 'out' team of opponents who could sometimes mobilise grassroots protest to defeat them. Personal interests blended with ethno-regional competitions for pre-eminence, reinforcing and sometimes creating new lines of cleavage, which then in turn became the basis of electoral competition.

One area of Kenya was unique: Luo Nyanza. Throughout the 1970s, there was a struggle in Luoland between supporters of Odinga – driven out of active politics but still extremely influential – and their opponents, led by ministers Omamo, Omolo-Okero and (after 1974) Mathew Ogutu, who represented a younger, more capitalist and accommodating strain of Luo identity. The region was divided into two camps, one backed by the state, the other by the majority of Luo. Most Luo factional competition in the period can be traced back to this divide, which was fought through KANU, parliamentary elections and the Luo Union alike. Although the anti-Odinga team dominated, they were too closely associated with the Kikuyu and never achieved mass popularity. The result was that neither side was victorious, leaving the Luo with neither the unquestioned ethno-regional leadership that could bring them back to the centre of politics nor a decisive victory for the radicals with the support to mount a real challenge to the throne.

The Patron–Client System

With the early 1970s came the maturing of the neo-patrimonial and patron–client system, over which Kenyatta presided as patron-in-chief. In this personalised system, an informal asymmetrical exchange of goods and services formed the basis of most political activity. Patrons (politicians, senior civil servants, business elites) offered security (or the threat of its withdrawal) and resources such as jobs and money to their clients by manipulating both their formal authority and informal connections. In turn, their clients would vote for them, support them in their competition with others, allow them preferential access to local resources and offer them physical protection and support. This system emerged in the absence of other forms of competition as the dominant feature of politics in the 1970s.[119]

Patron–client relations were visible in every aspect of society, but were most obvious in the political sphere, where the confluence of poverty, multiple ethnicities, traditions of clientelism, *harambee* and an authoritarian political system created an unusually clear form. They politicised every institution that controlled resources, including local government, trade unions, cooperatives and the civil service. They had underlain the political disputes of the 1960s, deepening as the resources available to the leaders improved. This was the importance of Odinga's communist funds and Mboya's US links. Until the state was theirs to command, the resources to build such patronage networks were limited. Once independence came, Kenyatta, who now had the deepest pockets, undermined each challenger until his dominance was complete. Kenyatta's Central Province, and Kiambu district particularly, was the beneficiary of a disproportionate amount of government investment and *harambee* contributions alike.

While kinship relations were often seen in patron–client networks, they were not necessary: enduring links could be built and serviced across many forms of commercial and professional relationships. Mboya's early networks were based on the labour movement and, later, on his access to central resources, and they were sustained in the absence of a single guiding ethnicity. Kenyatta's own network was the most extensive of all, crossing most ethnicities, and some of his senior lieutenants (particularly Moi) also built cross-community networks. However, for most Kenyan politicians, ethnicity was a building block for their communities, usually at the sub-tribe or clan level. Such patron–client links weakened the emergence of overt class-based politics in Kenya, because they created competing vertically integrated communities of interest. They provided a stable, relatively reliable means of transacting business, in a situation where state and political institutions were weak and the rule of law far from guaranteed. They also offered a competing, informal structure for the exercise of power, acquisition of status and allocation of benefits beneath the nominally bureaucratic-rational state, which Goran Hyden called the 'economy of affection'.[120] They were expensive, because they undermined economic decision-making and encouraged corruption, but as long as the level of abuse remained modest, it was a 'tax' which was accepted as a necessary evil.

In this 'Kenya model' of clientelism, politicians rewarded their constituents and supporters through contributions from themselves and their 'friends' towards *harambees*, and by channelling state and private funds to their constituencies. Elections were a key 'delivery' moment in the system.[121] This combination of a no-party state, a competitive single-member electoral system and limited rigging helped keep politicians tightly linked to peasant aspirations. At the national level, this also converted (loosely) into a hierarchy within the legislature. The president was sacrosanct; his ministers performed well, assistant ministers better than average, and the backbench MP, with few resources at his disposal, was the least likely to return to the house.[122] Rather than a rapid turn-over of personnel, Kenyatta's patrimonialism produced an extremely stable system in which ministers could hold the same job for a decade and had real authority, even though it still depended on the trust of Mzee.

Since 1964, it had been clear that the Kenyan civil service served the government rather more directly than was envisaged in the Westminster model. Senior civil servants were appointed by politicians; did business with politicians; married the relatives of politicians; and in many cases became politicians after they retired. Of 21 permanent secretaries in December 1969, for example, 12 later stood for Parliament. Positions at the head of parastatal organisations were also part of the patron–client system. The president and ministers appointed the chairmen, directors and members of several hundred authorities, enterprises and regulatory boards, ambassadors and councils. Politicians were often the beneficiaries of appointments, with chairmanships reserved for defeated ministers (including Otiende and Sagini in 1969 and Omamo, Mungai and Shako in 1974) and others who had done the elite special favours.[123]

The patron–client model was also key to the changing role of the single-party Parliament. The National Assembly was not truly a legislative organ, but remained a representative one, linking Nairobi with the rural areas. As well as acting as rural representatives in the centre, MPs acted as a transmission belt for government policy and a way to whip up support for the state. Few members now saw debating legislation as their primary role, and much of their time consisted of competitive lobbying, publicly and privately, for resources.

A factional patron–client system is inefficient and requires fuel. Access to that fuel – money, jobs and influence – was limited and unequally distributed. Although it became more extreme later, the hand-out culture, whereby voters expected to be paid in one form or other to support a candidate, was already well embedded. The result, when these costs were piled on top of the costs of financing an election campaign and transportation of voters, left a number of politicians in serious debt.[124] This increased their dependence on wealthy backers and those civil servants, lawyers and politicians who could protect them from debt collectors and bankruptcy proceedings. The most notorious example was Kenyatta's old cellmate Paul Ngei, who was renowned for using his position to obtain money and goods without paying.[125] In 1974–5, his political career in trouble, he only narrowly escaped bankruptcy.[126]

Corruption and Acquisitiveness

Growing Corruption

By the early 1970s, corruption was a serious problem, in both the civil service and in private business. The relaxation of financial controls since independence, official myopia and the patron–client system all encouraged the use of public positions for private gain. By 1973, it was public knowledge, for example, that to do business in the Ministry of Commerce and Industry you had to give *chai* ('tea', or a bribe), and that officials would not approve import licences until they were paid. State land was also a valuable asset, although the commissioner for lands (a European until 1975 and henceforth a Kikuyu) ensured there was no mass theft. Rubia and J. M. Kariuki both alleged in 1974 that ministers, permanent secretaries and PCs had been allocated government farms in Maasailand. There were also allegations that 'big people' were getting loans from the NHC to buy multiple properties. Others organised the allocation to their families and proxies of houses owned by Nairobi City Council. One area of corruption specific to East Africa was 'fronting' for Asian businesses. Non-citizens, unable to obtain licences, were willing to pay African frontmen to put their names on the applications. Inevitably, many such deals ended in chaos.

The growing lack of restraint was driven from the top, where the Kenyatta family continued to enrich itself. In 1974, the High Commission reported that meetings with the president required a donation of GB£2,000–£5,000 for a 10-minute audience, to be paid to a charity of his choice (cheques left blank).[127] Attempts to require Kenyatta to pay for the fuel he was using at his farms led to the deportation of the American managing director of Esso in 1974. With the first family's noses in the trough, there was little to stop his allies from doing the same. Although he retained a good public image, insiders also viewed Moi as 'extremely corrupt'.[128] In 1974, a tanker overturned in Nyanza, and was found to contain rice en route to Uganda, where prices were higher. It was suspected that the 'big man' behind this was Moi, and that the tanker was being escorted by police working for Nyanza PC Cheluget, Moi's ally.[129] Moi's name was also mentioned in connection with charcoal smuggling to Saudi Arabia through his personal assistant Nicholas Biwott, and there were reports that Kenyatta publicly denounced his corruption at a Cabinet meeting in 1972.[130] In 1972, Paul Ngei, Coast MPs and PCs Mahihu and Mathenge were named in Parliament as involved in a cloves and maize smuggling racket between Zanzibar and Kenya. Lamu MP Abu Somo was the source of the information. Somo soon retracted the allegations, claiming the people who had given him the information now denied doing so, but he was found guilty of 'giving false information to public officers' and jailed.[131] Several ministers alleged the smuggling and hoarding of commodities during 1974. The fact that this was only necessary because of price imbalances was not fully recognised at the time.

The acquisitiveness of the elite was not confined to Kenyan-owned resources, though it was easier to keep the assets if foreign interests were not involved. The ruby mines scandal was a classic case, in which American prospector John Saul and a partner had discovered rubies in Tsavo National Park in 1973. In January 1974, they registered their find and were given permission to mine and export the rubies. It was reported that they brought in Moi, Tourism and Wildlife Minister Shako and Natural Resources Minister Omamo as partners for political protection, and allocated them 51 per cent of the profits.[132] It was not enough. With the value of the two mines now recognised, the Kenyatta family moved in. Acting for Mama Ngina and Kenyatta's niece Beth Mugo, George Criticos, Kenyatta's Greek-Kenyan partner, approached the Americans to demand their share. A day later, on 18 June 1974, Saul was deported. The same day, the mining claims register was mysteriously lost. The first entry in the new register was the discovery of ruby mines by George Criticos. The

American Embassy protested vigorously, and after hostile press coverage in the US and UK, the Kenyans backed down. The Criticos licence was revoked in December, and Mama Ngina returned one of the mines, though the other remained in family hands.[133] Compensation was only paid to the Americans when Kenya needed US military assistance in 1976.

Acquisitiveness and Waste in the Civil Service

In 1970, a commission of inquiry was appointed to investigate the organisation, conditions, remuneration and recruitment of the public service, chaired by CBK head Duncan Ndegwa. The report, published in 1971, recommended organisational changes, pay increases for senior staff, the trimming of some parastatals and the appointment of an ombudsman. Most controversially, it permitted civil servants to engage in private business alongside their official duties, as long as it did not lead to a conflict of interest.[134] This legitimised an emerging reality. It also reflected the need to avoid their wholesale defection to the private sector.

The government immediately implemented most of the report's recommendations (except the ombudsman), but it was kept from Parliament for three years because of the sensitivity of its proposals. When it finally reached the Assembly, it faced serious opposition, and was damned by MPs as encouraging corruption.[135] Nabwera for example called it 'a cancer which will systematically destroy this country'.[136] Parliament adopted the report on 5 June 1974 by only four votes, showing the strength of the unofficial opposition.[137] Whatever its original intent, the Ndegwa Report soon became a licence to exploit public sector roles for private gain.

The controller and auditor-general (who monitored state spending for its proper use) and the National Assembly's Public Accounts Committee (PAC) were now castigating the government for unapproved spending and misallocation of resources. In its 1970–1 report, the PAC criticised the lack of basic financial controls in some ministries.[138] Expenditure above the approved budget was rising, to K£4.5 million in 1971–2. The PAC criticised procedural weaknesses and the government's tendency to invest without clear purpose or financial rigour. At every level, there were cases of unauthorised expenditure, diversion of resources, personal arrangements and abuse of procedures, with officials looking for ways to bypass the system. Complex accounting problems and compromises on process would somehow leave the taxpayers disadvantaged but individuals in government or their patrons better off. Although the amounts concerned were small, it was apparent that the state did not feel it was subject to parliamentary approval. The PAC had no capability to force the government to take action. The auditor-general did not even have the right to examine the accounts of the parastatals, where much of the waste was occurring.

In March 1971, a rare event occurred. A senior civil servant was charged with corruption and was jailed, for seven years. He was the permanent secretary for tourism and wildlife under J. M. Kariuki, and was – perhaps inevitably – Luo.[139] Under Kenyatta, no senior Kikuyu official was ever charged with, let alone convicted of, corruption.

Press, Parliamentary and Church Resistance

The backbench did not go down without a fight. Shikuku, the 'people's watchman', as he was now known, led the charge, but was frustrated at every turn by state hostility. In 1971, for example, Parliament set up a Select Committee on corruption, tribalism and nepotism. However, Kenyatta then summoned the KANU Parliamentary Group and 'explained' that the committee would be prevented from making investigations, and that the police had been ordered not to cooperate. The Parliamentary Group allowed the committee to lapse.[140] In 1974, the Assembly passed a second such motion, and demanded that civil servants declare their assets, but this died with the dissolution of Parliament.

The churches too criticised the elite's acquisitiveness, including a confidential report to Kenyatta by the Church of the Province of Kenya (CPK) in 1970, which criticised his land policy, failure to deliver social services, corruption and elitism.[141] However, church censure remained behind closed doors.

The Assembly did have an ally: the international press. In late 1974, there were a series of uncomplimentary reports in the *Daily Telegraph*, *Newsweek* and elsewhere, driven by the ruby mines scandal, that infuriated the elites and led to the interception of several editions as they arrived in Kenya. Foreign concerns were far more important than domestic pressures.

Urbanisation, Social Change and Crime

In December 1973, Kenya celebrated a decade of independence. Most observers judged the independence era a success, but noted that Kenya's national identity was only slowly emerging and continued to be challenged by socio-economic and ethnic tensions. Kenyan society was also becoming more aggressive and acquisitive. The 'dog eat dog' model of development reinforced the desire to get to the top by any means. At the same time, growing numbers of foreign tourists brought with them the aspirational lifestyle of luxury hotels and safaris, while urbanisation was breaking older bonds to the land and community. These changes were breeding a distinct 'Nairobi' political culture, which – in classic capitalist form – was more acquisitive, atomised, and inegalitatarian than the heartlands of rural Kenya.

By the early 1970s, the challenges of urbanisation were really beginning to affect Kenya. More than 10 per cent of Kenyans were now urban residents. To meet growing demand, local councils, private developers and the central government built houses for the emerging middle class. At the same time, the urban poor were building shanties and slums in Kibera, Mathare Valley and elsewhere. In January 1970 Nairobi City Council responded. City council *askaris* burnt to the ground several slums, leaving 50,000 inhabitants homeless. Nonetheless, the flood to the cities continued. By the mid-1970s, more than 25 per cent of Nairobi's population was living in overcrowded 'temporary' settlements, where the prevalence of unemployment led to theft, illegal brewing and other social problems. Hawking (mobile or temporary selling of goods), which had been a problem since the colonial era in the city, was a growing challenge.

As unemployment rose and the elites prospered, so crime increased. Even Kenyatta's own farm was robbed.[142] Although the scale was modest in comparison to the chaos of the 1990s, personal security began to become a concern. The National Assembly had rejected the death penalty for armed robbery in 1970. Nonetheless, infuriated by his inability to control the streets and the possible effect on investment, Kenyatta demanded at rallies in 1971 that armed robbers be hanged in public, and tried to force the change through Parliament. The Assembly was unimpressed, and though it eventually passed the Criminal Law (Amendment) Act to execute violent robbers, it specified that they must have committed grievous bodily harm. It also mandated that executions take place in private, influenced by Njonjo's opposition to public killings, which he termed 'barbaric, sadistic and inhuman'. It was a rare case of parliamentary resistance to presidential authority.

Kenyatta was back on the stump with his own draconian solutions to the problem of crime in 1972, demanding that theft also become a capital offence: 'My brothers, let us say it loudly, thieves shall be hanged; hanged until they die.'[143] It was crucial that no quarter be given to the poor if they turned to crime. Kenyatta's wish was eventually implemented in a second amendment in 1973, which mandated the death penalty for robbery with violence. The death penalty for armed robbery (even without violence) was introduced in 1975, and remains on the statute book to this day. For the first time, the police were armed and ordered to 'shoot to kill'.

However, there was already concern about the loss of discipline and corruption in the force. Njonjo admitted that, by 1972, 60 per cent of crimes went undetected or were not investigated.[144] The state of Kenya's prisons was also a cause for concern, highlighted by an incident in 1972 in which warders killed up to 30 prisoners. There was little public outcry. The lives of criminals had little value to Kenyans. Indeed, prisoners were routinely used as forced labour on the farms of ministers and civil servants.

The senior judiciary, meanwhile, remained mostly European and Asian. All Kenya's magistrates were African, but there were only three African High Court judges, with Attorney-General Njonjo explicit that appointments would be made on merit, not ethnic criteria. Many African lawyers disagreed, believing his maintenance of high standards of conduct and qualifications deliberately discriminated against them (and thereby also built a constituency for Njonjo amongst Europeans and Asians). Nonetheless, in every aspect of the criminal and judicial system, problems were growing. By 1972 there was a substantial backlog in cases (2,000 awaiting High Court hearing), with the number of cases consistently exceeding the number of judges available. The problems of the 1990s were already present.

The Insatiable Demand for Education

The Long Road to Free Primary Education

Education was essential for participation in the formal sector, and the competition for limited places remained intense. The 1969 KANU manifesto and the *Development Plan, 1970–74* had promised seven years of free primary education for all, the same promise Kibaki was to make more than 30 years later. However, to fund the growing demand, fees were soon increased, to mass protest. The political system struggled to reconcile the imperative to increase educational provision (which the backbench supported) with the cost (which was the government's primary concern).

In 1974, primary enrolment jumped dramatically from 1.8 million to 2.8 million (see Figure 5.9). This followed a presidential decree in December 1973 that primary education would now be free for Standards I to IV. It was a popular but risky move. There was severe pressure on classrooms and teachers, and a growing concern that Kenya's investment in education, one of the highest in the world as a proportion of GDP, might be unsustainable.[145] The abolition of primary school fees left huge holes in school budgets, and led to the creation of new activity, building and equipment levies.

The differences in primary educational provision by region and therefore by ethnicity continued. The 1969 *Economic Survey* had shown that while 134 per cent of 6–12-year-old Nairobi children were in primary school and 102 per cent in Central Province, Nyanza's figure was 56 per cent, the Rift Valley 43 per cent and North-Eastern an appalling 5 per cent.[146] During the 1970s, however, the situation equalised somewhat, as other provinces caught up. North-Eastern's primary numbers quadrupled between 1970 and 1980 and the Rift Valley's tripled.[147]

Secondary Education

While most could aspire to primary education, secondary education remained the preserve of the few. The numbers in secondary school quadrupled again between 1970 and 1980 to over 400,000, but there were even more children coming through the primary system. For 70 per cent of primary school leavers, education was over. Even when secondary places were available, it did not mean that the state was providing them. State policy was to limit the expansion of secondary education,

5.9: Primary and secondary school enrolments, 1963–78

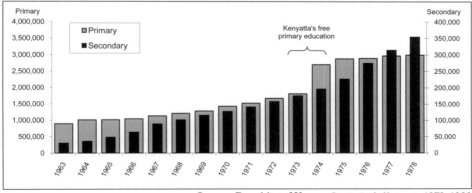

Source: Republic of Kenya, *Statistical Abstracts*, 1972, 1982

as there were too few formal sector jobs. However, *harambee* schools continued to undermine their efforts. By 1977, there were more than a thousand *harambee* and private schools providing places for 200,000 secondary pupils, compared to 120,000 in 450 government-aided schools. *Harambee* schools were a mixed blessing. Most supported the poorer parts of the community, but were small, inefficient and charged higher fees than state schools. To some extent, the *harambee* system increased regional inequality, as wealthier regions could afford to fund more schools. There were doubts, however, about the standard of education they offered, and the quality gap between aided and unaided schools widened. A two-tier system was emerging and it was far from clear that Kenya was getting the best value for money.

Inequalities in the provision of secondary education also continued. While 77 per cent of 1977's Standard VII students in Nairobi had places in 1978's secondary classes, and 46 per cent in Central, the numbers fell to 35 per cent in the Rift Valley and 25 per cent in North-Eastern.[148] Each district set its academic target for admission based on available services. As teacher training places had not risen as fast as the number of children, the percentage of untrained teachers also increased. Again, Central Province and particularly Kiambu did best.[149] Quietly, the Education Ministry also ensured that racial integration continued and that Africans would not be discriminated against in access to secondary education, issuing instructions in 1975 that all schools must admit at least 95 per cent Kenyans, of which 90 per cent should be African.[150] Secondary education was also a predominantly male affair: 42 per cent of primary students were girls by 1972, but only 30 per cent of secondary pupils. Older prejudices continued, sustained by the cost of education and the 'high risk, high reward' economic system.

The cost to families of secondary education was rising. While the government provided bursaries to some poor pupils, most students in Form I to Form IV had to pay school fees, tuition, uniform and examination fees. In 1969, Kenya offered free education for those few who could find a place and get the grades at Form V and VI. This too was short-lived: by 1973, the Education Ministry had imposed tuition and examination charges here, and admitted it could not finance the last two years of secondary school without contributions from parents.[151]

In its campaign to keep costs down, the government had virtually abandoned secondary school building by 1974, taking over *harambee* schools instead. However, there were inequalities here too. In 1980, the government disclosed that it had taken over more *harambee* schools in Central Province than in any other province – another benefit to the Kikuyu.[152]

The Harambee Institutes of Technology

As overall education levels improved, this raised the ante for access to white-collar jobs. By 1970, a secondary qualification no longer guaranteed employment. Partly in response, the early 1970s saw a new educational phenomenon, the *harambee* institutes of technology. Communities across the country decided that – given the increasing need for technical skills and the shortage of places for such study – they should establish vocational institutes of science and technology.[153] In the end, 15 such *harambee* institutes were established, each funded through house-to-house collections, *harambees* and donations from cooperative societies, trade unions and abroad. Most achieved little, being primarily prestige projects, and only 11 survived into the 1980s.

As well as doubts over whether local communities could fund such complex projects, the institutes had implications for national identity. They were political tools and were structured on an ethno-regional basis, in an open competition between communities for resources. Kenyatta, for example, presided over the first fundraising for the Murang'a Institute in 1971 and laid the foundation stone for the Kiambu Institute in 1974, while Kibaki led the fundraising drive for the Kimathi Institute in Nyeri, and Moi did the same for the Rift Valley Institute of Science and Technology. The most notorious, however, was the Ramogi Institute of Advanced Technology in Kisumu.[154] This project was launched in 1971 with huge fundraising events amongst urban Luo and was linked to the Luo Union and chaired by Luo politicians. However, like so many other Luo development projects, it became enmeshed in machinations over the Odinga issue, leading to disputes over ownership and misappropriated funds. It opened in 1976–7, sadly diminished from the original plans.

The government also ran other technical and vocational institutions, including polytechnics and teacher training colleges. Again, there was evidence of inequalities in access, with 42 per cent of admissions to Githunguri teacher training college during 1971–3 coming from Central Province.[155]

University Education

In 1970, the University of East Africa had broken up and University College became the University of Nairobi, issuing its own degrees. Jomo Kenyatta appointed himself university chancellor and in turn, appointed Kiambu diplomat and Princeton Ph.D. Josephat Karanja as vice-chancellor, over the heads of several Luo professors. The same pattern of preference was emerging as elsewhere. As early as 1970, Luhya MPs Elijah Mwangale and Muliro alleged that 75 per cent of the African university intake was from Central Province.

Nairobi University expanded dramatically; doubling student numbers from 2,800 to 5,400 between 1970 and 1977 (though fewer Kenyan students attended Makerere or Dar-es-Salaam than before). The decision to expand the university so fast reflected the huge demand (more than 4,000 Kenyans were studying overseas at the time) and broader access to secondary education, but also a reassertion of national identity and efforts to assert Africa's independence from Western history, culture and dominion. The late 1960s and early 1970s saw a flowering of research into the pre-colonial history and traditions of Kenyan communities. The department of history became one of the leading departments in the university, as African scholars published a series of works based on their sociological and anthropological theses. However, Mau Mau remained off limits and critical analysis of contemporary events was even less popular.

Here too, money and its equitable and productive use was now a problem. In 1974 the government ceased paying grants for living costs and introduced student loans, though it continued to pay tuition costs, accommodation and food fees.[156] This was the first step towards an end to free university education, long before structural adjustment, and was bitterly resented at the time. In a typical reaction, however, few Kenyans actually repaid these loans once they had left university, leaving the government to foot the bill.

Kenya's students were not isolated from the changes taking place in the West and were increasingly dissatisfied with Kenya's political direction. Kikuyu–Luo, socialist–capitalist and radical–conservative tensions were played out on the university campus throughout the decade. In 1971, the university experienced its first student riots, which led to students being expelled and jailed. There were more protests in 1972 and the socialist (and predominantly Luo-led) student union was banned. In 1974, students struck again, demanded the sacking of an expatriate lecturer, nullification of exam results and the readmission of sacked students.[157] The university was closed for five months. Karanja remained in the post until 1979, but his handling of relations with students led to accusations that he was arrogant and out of touch, charges which returned to haunt him when he achieved high office in the late 1980s.

KANU and GEMA

KANU lapsed further into disarray. The party remained technically an illegal organisation throughout the decade, having failed to hold national elections as required by its constitution. It had not held an annual Delegates' Conference since 1966; it had no elected secretary-general and the Governing Council and NEC had not met since 1969. The government maintained a conspiracy of silence about this inconvenient fact. Attempts by the unofficial opposition to publicise it were dodged by Njonjo, who placed the burden of submitting annual returns to the registrar at branch level, and refused to answer any questions on the party's national position. KANU's purpose was to serve as a (weak) basis for legitimacy, a venue for factional competition, a platform for publicity and a means of rewarding and punishing local dignitaries. It decided nothing, organised nothing, and did nothing. It was a convenient fiction (more convenient than not having a political party). Its sole operational role came in regulating electoral competition, where it could filter out a few undesirables.

June 1970 saw the first attempt to declare a formal one-party state, with a parliamentary motion proposed by Kirinyaga backbencher James Njiru (which had been agreed with Ngei, Moi and Kibaki beforehand). It was rejected by the majority of backbenchers. Politicians saw that there was little prospect of advancement outside KANU for now, but wished to keep their options open for the post-Mzee era.[158] Kenyatta appeared to favour a formal one-party state, but was unwilling to legislate it against the will of the majority.

Meanwhile, to quiet protests, in April 1970 Kenyatta had announced the establishment of a special KANU Reorganisation Committee led by Vice-President Moi, to revitalise the party. When it reported in August 1971, it recommended that the eight provincial vice-presidents created just five years before to undermine Odinga be abolished and a single vice-president restored. The party organisation was realigned to match districts and parliamentary constituencies (to stabilise the political hierarchy) and the composition of party committees changed. No changes were made to the way KANU's presidential candidate would be elected, however, leaving it in the hands of the National Delegates' Conference. The party announced that grassroots elections would begin in March 1972, but there was nothing to suggest that the party would adhere to its new organisation any more than it had to the old.

Campaigning soon began for the new posts. True to form though, Kenyatta did not actually intend to hold such elections; March 1972 came and went, and the polls were deferred, with the pathetic excuse that the All-African Trade Fair was on at the time. The real reasons related to the ability of each faction to defer the polls if it felt it might lose, and to the low number of KANU members. The paid-up membership of the party was believed to be no more than 340,000. Such low figures reflected not only the irrelevance of the party, but also the factional nature of membership, as officials were frequently accused of denying membership to those unlikely to vote for them.

As KANU declined, so a new organisation emerged, the Gikuyu, Embu and Meru Association (GEMA), whose name was to become a shorthand for the commercial and political aspirations of the ethnic groups living around Mount Kenya. First formed in 1971 under the leadership of Kiano and incumbent MPs, GEMA was reconstituted as a more broad-based welfare union for the Kikuyu, Embu and Meru peoples in 1973.[159] Kenyatta himself was patron, self-made timber merchant and beer and cigarettes distributor Njenga Karume (Kiambu) became its chairman, governor of the Central Bank Ndegwa (Nyeri) was vice-chairman, and land-buying company chairman Kihika Kimani (Nakuru) was organising secretary. Less-prominent Embu and Meru leaders became treasurer and secretary-general (part of a consistent pattern, in which Kikuyu leaders would mobilise the Embu and Meru around their collective identity, but allocate the lion's share of the spoils to themselves). The 1973 GEMA elections were heavily contested, as it was clear the organisation would play a key role in ethno-regional politics. GEMA also established a commercial subsidiary with a public shareholding, to invest in land-buying and businesses. It was clear that GEMA was intended to be another means by which the Kikuyu elites would advance their interests. In 1973, for example, backbencher Mwangale warned that GEMA must not turn into 'KANU A'.[160]

GEMA itself may have contributed to the deferral of the KANU elections. The British were told confidentially that in August 1972 GEMA leaders met Kenyatta and asked that the elections be postponed, as they did not feel confident that enough sympathetic candidates would win.[161]

The Succession Crisis Grows

The main internal problem the regime faced was the question of the succession. By 1971, the British government had already prepared telegrams from their queen and prime minister for Kenyatta's death. Although he was still alert, he was nearly 80, suffering from vomiting and sores, and likely to have another stroke at any time.

With Mboya dead and Odinga neutralised, speculation and intrigue centred on Vice-President Moi and his chances to succeed Mzee. Although Kenyatta had chosen Moi as his nominal successor, he did not appear to accept his own mortality, and he did nothing to anoint or to delegate authority to Moi. His ambivalence left the succession open, keeping the pressure off him and on the struggle to succeed him. Moi was the most likely candidate as interim president, but analysts felt that the longer Kenyatta lasted, the less likely Moi was to be able to stave off the 'family' candidate Njoroge Mungai. At this time, most foreign observers and many Kenyans felt that only a Kikuyu could rule Kenya, because of the numerical strength, economic and political power and vice-like grip that they had had on the state since independence.

Views of Moi were inconsistent – some saw him as 'weak and ineffectual', others as 'strong, but not particularly smart'. His sincerity and capacity for hard work were assets, but his intellectual limitations were evident; there were rumours of corruption; and he had shown an autocratic streak as home affairs minister. He had the support of most Kalenjin MPs and the guarded endorsement of ex-KADU leaders such as Muliro, Ngala and Maasai MP Stanley Oloitipitip. He also had good personal relations with Western governments and intelligence services. Nonetheless, he was not one of the real insiders. Many expected that even if Moi did emerge as titular president, the Kikuyu would wield real power behind the scenes. Some saw Njonjo – who was backing Moi for the succession but had little popular base himself – as a potential prime minister to Moi's president.

In fact, Mungai was the British High Commission's preferred successor. It commented in 1970 that he had 'outstandingly the best presidential credentials'.[162] Mungai was one of the Kiambu elite, related to Kenyatta, clever, ambitious and well funded. However, he was not particularly popular and lacked a national base outside the Kikuyu. The bitterness between the Moi–Njonjo and Mungai camps was open by 1971, and in 1972, the Lonrho representative was deported amid rumours that he was supplying funds to Mungai.

Amongst the Kikuyu, both Charles Rubia and J. M. Kariuki were seen as future contenders. However, both were long shots. Kariuki's ego and aggression marked him out – in the prescient words of a pastoralist MP in 1971 – as a 'better assassination prospect than a presidential one'.[163] Neither Koinange nor Njonjo, although key 'behind the scenes' operators, was a plausible president. Njonjo was unpopular and not a politician. Koinange was elderly and unlikely to step out from Kenyatta's shadow. James Gichuru too was old, and increasingly unwell. Another name occasionally mentioned was Nyeri Finance Minister Kibaki, seen as ambitious, likeable and intelligent, but also as lazy and lacking a firm political base. Amongst the non-Kikuyu, Ngala was highly rated by the Americans, but by few others outside the coast. Although he had been Kenyatta's equal in the early days, and retained leadership of the Giriama, he was not a confidante of Kenyatta, a national player or known for his administrative effectiveness.

The growing tension over the succession was exposed in a debate about whether Kenya should create a position of prime minister as leader of the government in Parliament. Although it was in the 1990s that this issue came to dominate the national stage, discussions were under way on such a division of powers 20 years before. Supporters of such a post included the unofficial opposition, who were unhappy that the president was never in the House to be challenged. Others campaigning for a prime minister included the group opposed to Moi. If they could not replace him as vice-president, perhaps they could establish a third position, as master of the House, and leave the vice-president's role as ceremonial? If so, Mungai was the obvious candidate. Just as was to happen decades later, the role became inextricably associated with its expected occupant. In February–March 1971, the issue became public after a British journalist wrote a story suggesting that Kenyatta had agreed to a prime minister being established and that Mungai would get the job, and called Moi a 'mediocrity'.[164] This led to explosions of anger from Moi and Njonjo. The latter put the issue down firmly in Parliament, claiming the suggestion was near treasonable – 'There is no inheritance from a living man' – the same argument he was to use in 1976.

On 25 December 1972, Kenya lost another senior politician when Ronald Ngala was fatally injured in another road accident. He died two weeks later in hospital, aged 49. The inquest revealed that the driver had been trying to avoid wildebeest on the road, and had lost control of the vehicle.[165] There were rumours for decades that his death was not accidental, coming so soon after Mboya's murder, and reflecting the confusion surrounding the car-crash.[166] Ngala did not receive a state burial, although 100,000 mourners attended his funeral. His death removed Kenya's only national-level Mijikenda leader, but his eldest son Noah Katana Ngala followed in his footsteps and was elected to Parliament in the 1974 election.

The 1974 General Election

In 1974, Kenya held its second post-independence national elections, in an atmosphere of confrontation between the government and the informal opposition. Again, the elections provided a mechanism by which the regime could incorporate new blood, remain connected with local issues and legitimise its power. With the elections held for the first time on the regular five-year cycle, the build-up to the polls was a long phoney war. This ended in August when Kenyatta dissolved Parliament and the polls were announced for 14 October.

No Competing Parties

Despite the paper commitment to a multi-party system, it was still administratively impossible to register a competing political party. Between 1970 and 1972, the registrar refused applications to register at least three more parties.[167] Nevertheless, plans were under way to break these bonds. As early as May 1973, Moi told a rally that disgruntled MPs opposed to Kenyatta wished to form another party, almost certainly a reference to J. M. Kariuki and his allies.[168]

Kenyatta's efforts to deter such a move again revealed his intolerance and propensity to violence. At the end of March 1974, at a rally in Nakuru, he declared,

'We will not allow the formation of another party.'[169] Using religious and traditional catechisms of obedience, he demanded subservience:

> Kanu is the father and mother of the Government. The Government I lead is a Kanu offspring, All the Holy Scriptures enjoin children to respect their parents. And I insist on unswerving respect for the party for without it there would be no Government.[170]

The stadium was asked to display weapons and to chant '*Choma, moto!*' (Burn quickly) to the party's enemies. At the Madaraka Day celebrations on 1 June 1974, with military chiefs alongside him, Kenyatta announced that some MPs 'were dreaming of starting another party' and threatened to 'grind them like flour'.[171] In Thika on 11 June, he threatened to 'crush like sand' anyone trying to form another party. A few days later, he was in Nakuru declaring that foreign powers were funding disgruntled elements to undermine the government, but 'the day of reckoning is coming when we shall crush them.'[172] In the end, in the face of Njonjo's roadblocks and Kenyatta's threats, there was no rebellion.

Changes to the Electoral System

A symptom of the growing sclerosis in the political system was the reluctance of the government to change constituency boundaries. As required every 10 years, the Electoral Commission (now known as the Boundaries Review Commission) produced a report in 1973 with a new set of boundaries, also increasing the number of seats. For the second time, however, Kenyatta shelved the commission's work, so the election was fought on the 1966 boundaries.

A new feature of the 1974 elections was the use of a single ballot box to hold all votes, rather than one box for each candidate, a system that had proved open to abuse. The change was a response to a rare private member's bill to modify the electoral system, introduced by Seroney. It was finally passed in early 1974, steered through the house by Shikuku, Seroney and J. M. Kariuki against government resistance. However, Kenyatta refused to give his assent to the bill – partly because of clauses that provided for freedom of assembly during the campaign, and which removed the requirement that all candidates be members of a party. Equally important, Kenyatta and his allies did not wish MPs to take on the power to create legislation.[173] Instead, Njonjo introduced a similar government bill. The July 1974 National Assembly and Presidential Elections Act changed the ballot box system and introduced new procedures to help illiterate voters, but excluded the other more radical reforms. The age of voting was also reduced from 21 to 18 in a Constitutional Amendment in 1974.

A complete re-registration of voters was conducted in April–May 1974, extended twice because of low response. There were now 4.5 million registered voters (76 per cent of Kenya's estimated 5.9 million adults). The estimate of the number of adults was reduced to 4.4 million in May, when it looked as if registration figures would be lower, then raised again, which demonstrates the malleability of government statistics.

There were numerous anomalies and reports of multiple registrations (undetectable, as the register was manual). Some candidates bought or stole voters' cards to use them to vote on polling day. The election materials were produced locally, with the prisons constructing wooden boxes and the government printer producing the ballot papers. Rather than the Electoral Commission running the polls, Njonjo's 'supervisor of elections' again administered the process.

Nominations

As in 1969, civil servants had to resign to stand, independent candidates were not permitted, and candidates had to abide by the rules of the party to obtain nomination. There was disappointment for Odinga and his team, who had quietly reintegrated themselves within KANU. Months before the election, the 4 July KANU Governing Council had warned the ex-KPU detainees that KANU would bar each of them from standing unless he had been a KANU member for three years since his release and had 'fully identified himself with the Government and party policies and programmes of development'.[174] This was criticised by some Luo politicians and by the unofficial opposition, including Kariuki, who called it 'a cowardly move aimed at barring certain people'.[175] Although it was clear that Kenyatta would not accept their applications, the ex-KPU leaders demanded the right to contest anyway. Unsurprisingly, the Governing Council barred 14 ex-detainees on 21 August, including Odinga, Luke Obok and Tom Okelo-Odongo. The decision was Kenyatta's personal instruction;[176] it was widely reported in the Western press, without comment or government censure. KANU also refused permission to stand to a dozen other candidates, including Koinange's sole opponent.

Kenyatta was again nominated unopposed as KANU's presidential candidate. For parliament, 733 candidates were nominated, 15 of whom were women, the highest percentage yet (2 per cent). Five MPs were unopposed, including Koinange, Moi, Ngei and Kenyatta himself, who did not even bother to turn up in Gatundu, submitting his papers by proxy from Mombasa. Excluding incumbents, 60 per cent of the candidates were businessmen, teachers or civil servants. As in 1969, in the rural areas almost all candidates were members of the ethnic group and sub-group that dominated the constituency. Only local men were considered qualified to represent an area. One of the rare constituency movers was Kibaki, who chose discretion over valour and decamped from Nairobi to his home seat of Othaya in Nyeri, which he continued to represent for most of the next 40 years.

The Campaign

The election proved a trial of strength between the unofficial opposition and the government. J. M. Kariuki was still the main state target. In June 1974, he was before the bankruptcy courts again over debts to the state-owned NBK, which would have barred him from being an MP.[177] All but one of his election rallies were cancelled by a government of which he was technically still a member.[178] At his sole rally he made a speech attacking greed, corruption, injustice and KANU's failure to meet independence-era promises such as free education. He called for a land commission and a ceiling on land ownership. Kenyatta clearly had Kariuki in his sights when he warned *wananchi* in September to be on the lookout for a few 'disgruntled elements' and threatened that Kenyans were ready to shed blood to protect their independence.[179]

Other backbenchers under attack included Nakuru MP Mark Mwithaga, Shikuku, Seroney, Nyeri MP Waruru Kanja and Assistant Minister Rubia, who experienced an attempt on his life during the campaign. The freedom of the radicals to campaign was restricted. PCs, for example, were instructed to ensure that candidates did not make 'baseless and scandalous allegations' against the government. According to Mahihu, 'We are determined to see that candidates do not interfere with the remarkable achievements that the Kenya Government has achieved during the last ten years.'[180] Parliamentary newcomer Koigi wa Wamwere in Nakuru was arrested and refused bail in September for breach of the peace after he attacked the influential Kimani. Kenyatta campaigned personally for Kimani, attending the opening of the Ngwataniro Harambee School at the height of Kimani's campaign.[181] GEMA and its money played a key role in elections in Central Province, the Kikuyu Rift and Nairobi. It campaigned openly for a 'clean sweep' of Nairobi seats for the Kikuyu.

It was clear that this would be Mzee's last election, and the election was also being fought over the succession. A particularly intense contest was fought between Mungai, minister for foreign affairs, and Dr Johnstone Muthiora, a novice political science lecturer, in Dagoretti in peri-urban Nairobi. It was particularly unusual because the *Daily Nation* actively campaigned against Mungai, under the control of returned editor George Githii and of Njonjo, who financed Muthiora's campaign.[182] In response, the police (led by the pro-Mungai Hinga) arrested Muthiora for holding a private party in his own home, while Mungai denounced 'a campaign to distort the truth, to vilify my person and discredit my achievements . . .'[183]

As in 1969, KANU issued a campaign manifesto. Amongst many platitudes, it proclaimed 'the duty of *wananchi* to support the party in every aspect.' There were virtually no policy issues raised in the campaign. Candidates campaigned on their personalities, their likelihood of ministerial office, their financial resources and their connections. Alliances with councillors, cooperatives, women's organisations, youth clubs and local businesses were critical in maintaining links with electors. Cross-constituency ethnic alliances were common.[184] There was some violence and vote buying and widespread use of *harambee* meetings for campaigning. In Nyeri and some other areas, however, there was still a countervailing anti-wealth lobby, represented by ex-Mau Mau such as Kanja, who attacked corruption, land grabbing and 'money sickness'.

Election Day and the Results

Election day, 14 October, was a public holiday. Polling proceeded smoothly in the 4,000 polling stations, although there were many problems with the register. The police arrested over 300 people for voting offences, but there was no obvious evidence of organised presidential intervention. There were also no external observers.

5.10: Njoroge Mungai and Charles Njonjo

Courtesy: Nation Group Newspapers

When the results were finally published, the electorate had rejected four ministers. The most important was the defeat of Mungai. His campaign had been poorly run, and he had demonstrated little affinity with his impoverished constituents. This was a critical event, since it meant that as Kenyatta moved into the last years of his life, Mungai was no longer a candidate for the presidency (unless he could find a seat elsewhere). Ministers Omamo, Ngala Mwendwa and Shako were also unseated. Omamo's defeat was a response to the barring of Odinga, which some Luo believed he had engineered. Most other Luo MPs also lost, reflecting disenchantment with the exclusion of the Odinga team and the limited impact of their replacements.[185] Kibaki received a massive endorsement in Othaya, and Gichuru and Kiano were also re-elected. J. M. Kariuki won easily, receiving 75 per cent of the vote in the settlement zone of Nyandarua North. Many of his allies were also victorious, including Rubia and Shikuku.

Moi did not have a good election. He was unopposed in Baringo Central, but Seroney won Tinderet in Nandi District easily, even though Moi had openly attacked him and despite the fact that Seroney was not allowed to address any meetings.[186] Seroney's allies won most Nandi-populated seats. Moi's Kalenjin competitor Taita Towett also won, while Moi's assistant Nicholas Biwott, a 33-year-old Keiyo, was defeated on his first attempt in Kerio South.

The national turnout was 2.65 million voters, or 63 per cent in the contested seats, still below expectations, but better than 1969. Partly because of the barring of the ex-KPU leaders, the turnout in Luo Nyanza was below 50 per cent. Central Province turnouts in contrast were high, averaging 74 per cent. Though only four ministers were defeated, the losses were again greater amongst lower-ranking posts: 18 of 35 assistant ministers and 61 of 102 backbenchers lost their seats.[187] The 1974 election completed the transition to a full patron–client model, in which Kenyans judged the performance of their parliamentarians primarily on their capacity to bring 'pork' back to their constituencies. Although this resulted in peacock-like inflationary competitive displays of wealth and influence, it also ensured that MPs were deeply aware of local issues and that problems in the periphery would be raised in the centre.[188]

There was evidence of localised malpractice, with bizarrely inconsistent turnouts from adjacent seats. There were 39 election petitions, disputing the legitimacy of a quarter of the Assembly. These exposed a catalogue of abuses, including the mass oathing of voters to support candidates in Ukambani. As a consequence, nine MPs lost their seats in 1975. Four of them were also barred from standing for five years for election offences.

The new House did not differ fundamentally from its predecessor. Four women were elected to Parliament, a significant increase but still a tiny number. Four trade unionists were also elected, reflecting the importance of the labour movement in the period. The average age of MPs rose to 41, as voters preferred their MPs older, wealthier and more experienced. Reflecting the strength of Kikuyu influence at this time, all eight Nairobi MPs and all four Nakuru MPs were now Kikuyu (something Kenyatta was said to be very unhappy with, as it was far too public a demonstration of the underlying reality).

Despite their concerns, Western governments remained committed to their ally. The Western press remained mostly supportive of Kenya's single-party but open electoral system, though in London *The Times* suggested that the results were a 'last warning' to Kenyatta that he must address corruption, tribalism and land distribution policies.[189]

Conclusions

The stage was now set for the last period of Kenyatta's rule. The election had not resolved any of the structural issues facing Kenya: the succession, economic performance, unemployment, inequality, land rights, tribalism or corruption. An elderly president and his Kikuyu advisers would continue to rule the country, protecting the interests of the elite and of Western investors against populist and xenophobic sentiments, and would continue to exploit their position for their own benefit. Electoral democracy was a tool for legitimacy, but would not be allowed to challenge their control. Opposition had been kept inside the no-party state, but was increasingly assertive and ready to challenge Kenyatta directly.

The implications of Kenya's economic, social and political strategy were becoming clearer. The mostly benign despotism of Kenyatta's rule had brought growth, security, stability and a greater degree of bureaucratic efficiency than elsewhere in Africa, relying on Western investment, expertise and endorsement. However, the currents were shifting. Kenya was trying to become less dependent on foreigners (though it was borrowing more at the same time). Western private investment was no longer driving development and the state was becoming increasingly protectionist and interventionist. The protective mantle of British military and financial support was being withdrawn, while the regional environment was becoming more difficult. Kenya now had to stand on its own feet in an increasingly hostile world.

Chapter 6
Rigor Mortis, 1975–1978

Storm Clouds on the Horizon

At the end of 1974, Kenya still appeared stable and prosperous, a beacon of calm in a continent of coups, wars, famine and economic weakness. However, the country's political system was increasingly sclerotic, a consequence of Kenyatta's declining energy, the success of his strategy for the first decade of independence, the conservative influence of Western governments, the power of the Kikuyu elite, and the state-led nature of Kenyatta's economic and social policy. Over the next four years, with their uncrowned monarch ageing, ministers and civil servants were open in their exploitation of the state and protected their dominance through threats, arrests and detention without trial. There were few economic innovations, signs of decay in some institutions and a further entrenching of Kikuyu dominance in both public and private sectors. Kenya's state-led development model showed signs of an impending crisis and its tourism and aid dependency were an increasing concern, distorting both state and society. Western support continued, but the UK was no longer able to play the role of patron fully and Kenya's focus began to shift towards the US and its relations with the international financial institutions.

Kenyatta's death in 1978 was the crucial, long-expected opportunity for change and a vast challenge for a divided political class to overcome. Despite plots and even murder, the succession struggle (which had begun in 1967) ended with the incumbent Vice-President Daniel arap Moi, a Kalenjin, winning the presidency, and the victory of the pro-British, technocratic faction over the claims of the Kiambu 'family'.

No Change at the Top

The new Cabinet of October 1974 changed little. Kenyatta kept Moi, Mbiyu Koinange, Julius Kiano, Mwai Kibaki, Jeremiah Nyagah, James Gichuru, Jackson Angaine, Isaac Omolo-Okero and Charles Njonjo in their jobs, the most stable ministerial team Kenya has ever seen. Kenyatta appointed only five new ministers. He brought in Munyua Waiyaki, who had resigned in 1966 in sympathy with Odinga, to replace Njoroge Mungai as foreign minister. Daniel Mutinda replaced Eliud Mwendwa as the minister for Ukambani. Maasai Stanley Oloitipitip, Luo Mathew Ogutu (replacing William Omamo) and Taita Eliud Mwamunga were the other new arrivals. Kenyatta also appointed Kenya's first female assistant minister, Dr Julia Ojiambo, predictably to Housing and Social Services. Geoffrey Kariithi remained permanent secretary in the Office of the President and secretary to the

Cabinet, and more than half the permanent secretaries were Kikuyu. Kenyatta and the government were sworn in on 5 November (see Figure 6.1).

Amongst Kenyatta's 12 nominations to Parliament were two representatives of Kenya's increasingly influential ethnic or tribal unions: Njenga Karume, chairman of GEMA, and Mulu Mutisya, leader of the New Akamba Union (NAU). Mutisya, an illiterate businessman and ex-detainee, had formed NAU in 1961, and used it to entrench his influence amongst the Kamba. He was to remain a nominated MP for the next 18 years. Njenga Karume too was a self-made businessman who wielded great influence in government and amongst the Kikuyu. Another ex-detainee, he had become one of the largest beer distributors in Kiambu.[1] Amongst those excluded was Mungai, since Kenyatta had promised that he would not nominate any defeated MPs back to Parliament. Although Mungai persuaded his sister to resign her nomination to create a vacancy for him in 1975, he was unable to find a parliamentary seat that he was confident he could win. He was therefore not eligible for the presidency or vice-presidency.

The unofficial opposition was finally excluded from the government, as Kenyatta dropped re-elected assistant ministers J. M. Kariuki, Charles Rubia, Burudi Nabwera and Martin Shikuku. The pro-Odinga Luo also received little consideration. Omolo-Okero retained his ministerial position, and even Omamo, defeated in Bondo, was nominated to Parliament in 1975. Another opportunity to change direction had been lost. Although Kenyatta projected authority in public,

6.1: Kenyatta's swearing-in, November 1974

Courtesy: Nation Group Newspapers

he found it increasingly hard to lead the government, yet there seemed little chance that anyone would take the reins of power gently from the old man's hands. Despite recurrent blood clots and bouts of unconsciousness, Kenyatta declined to prepare for the inevitable.

Opposition Becomes Open

It was soon clear that the government was going to have trouble controlling the National Assembly. When it reassembled on 6 November 1974, the uncontroversial Speaker Fred Mati was re-elected easily, but, to the government's horror, dissident Marie John Seroney was the sole candidate for the post of deputy speaker. Kenyatta summoned a secret session of Parliament to try to delay the election; he failed, and immediately prorogued Parliament.

There were rumours that Kenyatta had threatened Seroney with detention (and had also allocated him a farm), but the opposition was galvanised by recent corruption allegations, the election results and increased Western attention (including protests by the US ambassador at the mistreatment of US citizens). When Parliament reassembled in February 1975, Seroney was duly elected deputy speaker, as the government had feared, and the Assembly's mood remained hostile for the rest of the year. Several government bills were so heavily criticised, generally on nationalist or populist grounds, that they had to be withdrawn. The state's demands that backbench opposition be 'constructive' no longer had much effect.

Although Seroney was the focus of conflict, J. M. Kariuki remained the unofficial opposition's leader, spearheading the fight against capitalism, corruption, the land deals with the UK, and the increasing wealth of the business, political and administrative elites. Although many saw him as inheriting Bildad Kaggia's role as a defender of socialism, collectivism and the Kikuyu underclass, Odinga was unequivocal: 'Like Kenyatta, he loved wealth and possessions.' Odinga suggested he had been quickly corrupted, and had used his connections and talents for personal enrichment.[2] Kariuki was an unlikely popular martyr.

Bombs and Murders, March 1975

In early 1975, the first bombs to strike independent Kenya exploded. In February, there were two blasts in central Nairobi, inside the Starlight nightclub and in a travel bureau near the Hilton hotel.[3] The day after the second explosion, J. M. Kariuki revealed in Parliament that his car had been hit 'by what seemed to be bullets'.[4] There were rumours of a botched attempt on his life. They were followed by a more serious blast in a Nairobi bus on 1 March, which killed 30 people (see Figure 6.2). Despite a massive public outcry and a police manhunt, no arrests were made. For several days thereafter, the city lived in fear, destabilised by numerous telephone bomb hoaxes. Someone was creating a climate of fear.

6.2: Bus explosion,
1 March 1975

Courtesy: Nation Group Newspapers

The Murder of Kariuki

On 2 March 1975, the day after the bus blast, security officials including GSU commander Ben Gethi publicly accosted J. M. Kariuki outside the Hilton hotel. He had been followed by the police throughout the day, including European police reservist Patrick Shaw. Gethi asked Kariuki to accompany the security officials into a convoy of cars and took him to an unknown destination. The next day, Maasai herdsmen discovered his tortured and mutilated corpse in the Ngong hills near Nairobi. His fingers had been cut off and his eyes gouged out before he was shot dead. The killers had burnt his face with acid to prevent identification of the body, as his fingerprints were gone. However, the acid had deterred scavengers, and his body was still identifiable. Nonetheless, police sent the corpse to the mortuary as an unknown victim.

After Kariuki's disappearance, there was a lull of five days while friends and family tried to discover his whereabouts. There were rumours that he had been detained. Finally, on 7 March, Assistant Minister Justus ole Tipis admitted to the Assembly that Kariuki was missing and appealed for anyone knowing his whereabouts to cooperate with police. The same day, Kenyatta, returning to Nairobi from a month-long stay in Nakuru, made a veiled speech that appealed for order, and warned 'the government would have no mercy on any individual or group that attempted to disrupt peace and harmony in Kenya.'[5] Kenyatta knew what was to come.

On Saturday 8 March, the *Daily Nation* reported that Kariuki was in Zambia, although the news desk already had sworn statements that the corpse in the mortuary was his; editor-in-chief George Githii ordered a reluctant news desk to print this misinformation.[6] On 11 March, nine days after his abduction, Kariuki's wife identified his body in the mortuary, after which armed GSU sealed off the building. At the same time, Moi was making a statement, reporting that Kariuki's whereabouts were still unknown. On 12 March, Police Commissioner Bernard Hinga finally confirmed that Kariuki was dead, killed by two bullet wounds. He claimed that the 'partial decomposition' of the body had made identification impossible.[7]

The result was a mass outbreak of popular anger. As soon as Kariuki's death became public, angry students demonstrated, but were dispersed by the GSU (see Figure 6.3). Large crowds gathered and police cordoned off roads into Nairobi. Most shops and schools closed. Several ministers removed the flags of office from their cars and fled in fear.

Kariuki's death also roused the National Assembly into open hostility. MPs immediately demanded an investigation into the murder. Moi publicly abased himself before Parliament, swearing that he had had no idea that Kariuki was dead, and was only repeating what officials had told him: 'I did it in good faith. I am sorry, I am sorry.'[8] On 14 March, Parliament appointed a Select Committee to investigate the killing. Its chair was backbencher Elijah Mwangale from Bungoma, and it included Shikuku, Seroney and other friends of Kariuki. The government appeared to have lost control of Parliament completely; there was talk of the murder as being Kenya's Watergate. In the meantime, Kenyatta, furious at his ministers' weakness, had summoned an emergency Cabinet meeting, where, one by one, he forced each minister to declare continued loyalty.[9]

Kibaki was the only minister to attend Kariuki's funeral, stressing he was there as a friend. Central PC Simeon Nyachae bravely represented the government, but faced deep hostility and was unable to read Kenyatta's condolences. Even the churches were roused into opposition, with a young Kikuyu Anglican cleric, David Gitari, particularly outspoken in his criticism in a series of live radio broadcasts. Kenyatta and senior ministers lay low, avoiding public events.

6.3: Students demonstrate after murder of J. M. Kariuki, 17 March 1975

Courtesy: Nation Group Newspapers

The Kariuki Select Committee

For two months, the Select Committee investigated the killing, but the police and civil service, orchestrated by Koinange at the OP, obstructed them at every turn. Police officers including Hinga and CID Director Ignatius Nderi refused to cooperate, and Koinange declined to respond to the committee's summons. Waruhiu Itote, Kenyatta's intelligence adviser, who also headed the National Youth Service, threatened to shoot anyone who summoned him to testify. They discovered in passing that Kariuki's last resting place was a well-known execution spot and that three more bodies had been dumped there since July 1974.[10] One of those present during Kariuki's arrest was detained by the government (to prevent him testifying), and other witnesses were beaten, tortured and prepared by police before testifying to the committee, a pattern that would be repeated in the Ouko case 15 years later. Still, the committee discovered much it was not supposed to know. As part of an internal power struggle, Special Branch officers apparently leaked much of the information that formed the committee's findings.[11]

The committee's report, tabled in Parliament on 3 June 1975, was an indictment of the government. It accused Koinange, Kenyatta's bodyguard Wanyoike Thungu and Gethi of involvement in the murder itself or the cover-up. Also accused of collusion were Hinga and Assistant Commissioner of Police Sokhi Singh. When Kariuki's watch was found in a police barracks, it was claimed that Singh warned those who found it to keep quiet and collected the watch himself. No attempt was made to determine how it might have got there. Also accused was the assistant commissioner of police in charge of the Rift Valley, James Mungai, while Githii was accused of publishing false statements about Kariuki's whereabouts. Just before distribution, the report was presented to Kenyatta, who personally tore off the back page, which contained the name of Koinange and a senior Kikuyu security official from the master copy of the report, commenting that to name Koinange was to name Kenyatta and 'and I won't allow that'.[12] The report was published without its last page.

Attorney-General Njonjo led the government's defence, moving that Parliament should 'note' rather than adopt the report, which he called 'biased and prejudicial'. However, the government was defeated. On 11 June, backbenchers, supported by Minister Masinde Muliro and Assistant Ministers John Keen and Peter Kibisu (who defied a government whip), voted to accept the report by 62 to 59. Kenyatta immediately sacked all three dissenters.[13] Muliro spent the rest of his life in the political wilderness. Although the Kariuki file remained open, no arrests were made and the police were unwilling to discuss the case. Hinga, Gethi and the others stayed in their posts, apparently unaffected. The murder was an open sore for the next 30 years.

Who Murdered Kariuki, and Why?

It was never clear whether Kenyatta had sanctioned Kariuki's murder. It is unlikely that it was planned, given the public nature of his arrest. The true story may never emerge, but a series of exposés 25 years later presented for the first time a plausible account of what might have happened. A *Nation* article in 2000 alleged that Gethi was the man who first shot Kariuki in the arm, at Special Branch Headquarters in central Nairobi. During the interrogation of Kariuki after his 'arrest', Thungu had assaulted Kariuki and smashed out his front teeth. Kariuki drew a hidden weapon and attempted to shoot Thungu, but Gethi, although a friend of Kariuki, fired first.[14] Nderi was alleged to have been present, as were Shaw and Itote. A group of police informers were nearby, ready to testify against Kariuki, and it was this group that allegedly committed the murder. Kariuki, bleeding, was packed into a meat van and taken to his death. A man named Pius Kibathi was one of those reported to have been involved.[15] Almost all those implicated were police, police informers or senior Kikuyu intimates of Kenyatta.

There is also strong circumstantial linkage between the bombings and Kariuki's murder. Githii claimed that the bombs were the work of communists.[16] The most likely explanation, however, is that Kenya's security services themselves built and detonated the bombs, in order to 'set up' Kariuki to be blamed. After the bus explosion, senior police officers were on hand within minutes. Nderi admitted to the Select Committee that he had been investigating links between Kariuki and the bombings, on the evidence of a 'police informer'. Kariuki was a director of the Starlight club, the site of the first bomb. There is one more association between the bombings and the Kariuki murder: Kibathi. A police informer and ex-police trainee from Gatundu, he had been released from a prison term for bank robbery just before Kariuki's death, and was known to have political protection.[17] He was the informer who had linked Kariuki with the bombings. On 6 March, police arrested an unnamed man for making hoax bomb calls, after which they came to a halt – a photograph on the front page of the *Nation* of the arrested man is clearly of Kibathi.[18] Kibathi was bailed and vanished. The *Nation* reported in 2002 that Special Branch head James Kanyotu believed Kibathi was part of a plan orchestrated by Koinange and others to discredit Kariuki.[19]

The Kariuki murder demonstrated once more that there was a parallel security network beneath the formal one, often involving men with police or military training and originating from Kiambu. This shadowy network of informers and reservists was linked to Kikuyu CID and Special Branch figures, and acted for them outside formal channels. Its primary purpose may have been to eradicate armed robbery, but it could be turned to darker purposes. The murder also showed that Kenyatta (unlike Moi and Kibaki after him) was unwilling to turn against his closest allies, even when they had committed such crimes. Ironically, Kariuki's brutal murder may have brought down those responsible. The widespread popular revulsion at the involvement of the Kiambu elite in his death helped tip the balance amongst 'non-aligned' politicians sufficiently to ensure that Moi succeeded Kenyatta in 1978.

A 'Hawk amongst the Chickens', 1975–6

The period immediately after the Kariuki murder was the first time that it seemed Kenyatta's government might fall to popular discontent or military action. The regime's reputation was severely damaged amongst the Kikuyu, especially in Nyandarua and

Nyeri, Kariuki's family home. Dissent had to be controlled and order re-established. Although he had been in Nakuru at the start of the crisis, Kenyatta held his ground robustly on his return. On Sunday 23 March 1975, two weeks after the murder became public, Kenyatta organised a massive show of force in downtown Nairobi. As KAF jets overflew the city centre and passers-by scattered, fearing a coup, Kenyatta stood on a temporary dais and took the salute. The army, navy and air force marched past en masse, with Moi, Army Commander Jackson Mulinge, KAF Commander Dedan Gichuru, Navy Commander Jimmy Kimaro and Chief of Police Hinga at Kenyatta's side.[20] The message was clear: the government was still in control of the means of coercion.

Political control also needed to be re-established. Kenyatta and his allies used GEMA to lead their counterattack. Just as in 1969, they played on the fear that, divided, the Kikuyu would be defeated. A series of loyalty demonstrations were organised in Central Province, Embu, Meru and Nakuru during May–June 1975, in parallel with the hearings of the Select Committee. They were led by Kikuyu MP Kihika Kimani, Kenyatta's 'eyes and ears' in Nakuru. These rallies denied the government's association with the murder, called for unity and attacked 'rumour mongers'. In a rare public speech, Koinange reassured those with doubts that 'The Kenya Government is the best in the whole world under the leadership of President Kenyatta who is being led by God.'[21] Kenyatta too mobilised his fading energies. Usually speaking in Swahili, he once more threatened death and destruction to anyone wanting to 'ruin our independence'. *Africa Confidential* quoted him in Nakuru: 'We shall have to trample the wreckers underfoot, to finish them off completely . . . we shall mow them down like grass . . .'[22] In Mombasa, he hit the same note: 'Those who speak ill of the government and propagate rumours . . . should realise that pangas are still in stock and could be put to use if the need arises.'[23]

While Kiambu and Nakuru were soon calm, Nyeri and Nairobi remained recalcitrant. In May 1975, for example, three Nairobi MPs – including Rubia and Waiyaki – refused to join a delegation to Kenyatta, in the pointed words of the *Standard*, 'without apology'.[24] Many students and intellectuals were also hostile. In April 1975, following the curious death by septicaemia of Mungai's 1974 nemesis Johnstone Muthiora, students rioted in protest; 90 were arrested and the university closed. Trouble broke out again in May, and Vice-Chancellor Karanja again used the police to crush student protests, leading to another national outcry. Student riots were to continue on the anniversary of Kariuki's death for the rest of the Kenyatta era. A generation of elites were being radicalised.

The Fall and Rise of Paul Ngei

November 1975 brought Kenyatta further difficulty. His old cellmate Paul Ngei, who had saved his life in Turkana, was again in trouble, brought down as a result of his supporters' conduct during the 1974 elections. During the campaign in his Kangundo constituency, his sole opponent had been intimidated into leaving Ngei unopposed. A coffin for his opponent had been paraded around the constituency on nomination day and the returning officer was threatened with violence if he permitted any

6.4: Paul Ngei

Courtesy: Nation Group Newspapers

opposition to Ngei. It was purely a matter of prestige, as Ngei was in no danger of defeat. In a revealing speech, Ngei summarised what was at stake: 'If I am opposed we as a tribe will have a very bad position in the government and if I am returned unopposed we will have a better say.'[25] Local police advised Ngei's opponent to stand down, as they could not protect his life.

With the election over, his opponent petitioned against the result, backed by Ngei's local factional opponents. To great surprise, Ngei's election was nullified by the High Court, led by Chief Justice James Wicks, and he was barred from standing for Parliament for five years. He was the first full minister to lose his seat because of an election petition.

Ngei was unbowed. Aware of what was to come, his response to journalists was 'Slipping is not falling. I have only slipped.'[26] Kenyatta immediately summoned Njonjo and demanded that he find some way to pardon Ngei. In just two days, a reluctant attorney-general pushed the fifteenth constitutional amendment through the House. This permitted the president retrospectively to pardon convicted election offenders. There were only two dissenting voices (backbenchers George Anyona and Chelegat Mutai). With a monarchist's faith, Moi supported the amendment because 'If we say that the President is above the law, why should we say that he be denied these (new) powers which rightfully belong to him?'[27] Within days of the bill sailing through, Kenyatta had pardoned Ngei. He won the by-election his own barring had caused, and was reappointed to the Cabinet. Once again, Kenyatta had demonstrated that where his wishes and the law were in conflict, the president would triumph. The episode also cast a light on the hidden succession battle. Ngei was aligned with the anti-Moi team, while the judiciary took their advice on sensitive cases from Njonjo.

Restoring Order

Over the next year, Kenyatta gradually rebuilt his authority and the country settled back into a mood of sullen resignation. However, Kariuki's murder had ended the regime's tolerance for dissent in the media, academia and the backbenches. Now, all signs of Marxism, radicalism or appeals to Kikuyu peasant aspirations were classed as support for communism and therefore sedition. Despite their successes in mobilising opposition to the government in 1975, the unofficial opposition were eliminated one by one. Over the next two years, six troublesome MPs – Seroney, Shikuku, Mutai, Kibisu, Mark Mwithaga and Anyona – were detained or jailed on dubious grounds, while others decided that it was time to fall silent.

Kenyatta's right to rule still rested, at least in theory, on his party position. As a result, it was unwise to point out the appalling state to which KANU had declined, since this would also challenge Kenyatta's legitimacy. On 9 October 1975, however, during a parliamentary debate Shikuku commented in passing that 'anyone who tries to lower the dignity of Parliament is trying to kill Parliament the way KANU has been killed.' This was little different from what many MPs had said in the past, but when Shikuku was challenged to substantiate that KANU was dead, Seroney's ruling as deputy speaker was that 'there is no need to substantiate what is obvious.'[28] This aroused the government's fury. The result was a parliamentary walkout by the front bench, led by Moi, singing the party song 'KANU Builds the Nation'.

The *Standard*'s first response was an editorial, 'King versus Parliament'; the *Nation* too favoured the backbench, suggesting that Moi had abdicated his responsibility. But the government had had enough. On 15 October 1975, police entered Parliament, seized and then detained Seroney and Shikuku, in a blatant violation of members' immunity from prosecution for their speeches in the Assembly.[29] The two MPs lost their parliamentary seats and remained in solitary confinement until Kenyatta's death, without adequate food, medical attention or family visits. Seroney never recovered. The British reaction was typically muted, with the UK press referring to Kenyatta's detentions as a crafty move that had 'skilfully broken the back of his opponents', a very different reaction to political detentions in the Moi era.[30]

In August 1975, Kikuyu Nakuru North parliamentary aspirant Koigi wa Wamwere was also detained. The causes included his public criticism of Kenyatta, his socialist sympathies and his opposition to the Ngwataniro land-buying companies and the Kiambu clique in Nakuru.[31] In the same month, Nyeri backbencher Mwithaga, vice-chairman of the Kariuki Select Committee, was jailed for having struck his ex-wife two years before. He had already lost his seat after an election petition. Kibisu, who had voted against the government on the Kariuki report, was jailed for assault in October, having been charged on the same day he was sacked. He too lost his seat.

On 16 October 1975, Kenyatta summoned MPs to a private KANU Parliamentary Group meeting. He warned dissidents, of whom he had a list of 20 to 30, that henceforth they must obey or he would crush them. In his words, 'People appear to have forgotten that the hawk is in the sky and ready to swoop on the chickens . . .'[32]

6.5: Marie John Seroney and Martin Shikuku

Courtesy: Nation Group Newspapers

To the horror of the regime, his threat was published in the international press, and a second crisis ensued as they tried to discover which MP had committed the sin of talking to foreign journalists. The chief suspect, Mutai, departed from Parliament four months later. She was jailed for incitement to violence after she had called publicly for the uprooting of sisal plantations, and was sentenced by the same magistrate who had jailed Mwithaga. As with the others, she was denied visits while in jail (the right to prison visits was controlled by Moi), and served her sentence without remission.

The dissidents had nowhere to turn, as it remained impossible to register an opposition party. In March 1976, a minor politician was detained after submitting to Njonjo the papers required to register a new party, and a Democratic Party was refused registration in July 1976. Njonjo admitted in the House that no party would be registered that might 'disrupt social and political stability'.[33]

April 1977 saw further evidence of the collapse of tolerance. Anyona, a young, radical Gusii MP, had been an irritant to the government since his election in 1974. He was an eloquent speaker in the House and had already had all his meetings banned. In 1977, he went too far. Just before the East African Community collapsed, a Ksh200 million (US$25 million) tender for railway locomotive spare parts had been issued. A British Railways subsidiary failed to pre-qualify and the tender committee selected a Canadian company instead. In April, Anyona tabled documents in Parliament suggesting that Omolo-Okero, Njonjo and Bruce McKenzie had colluded with the British high commissioner to have the tender suspended.[34] On 4 May, the police once more invaded Parliament and Anyona joined Shikuku and Seroney in detention. Njonjo warned the House that if MPs protested too much, the powers and privileges legislation that protected them (in theory) from such attacks would be repealed entirely. Western NGO Amnesty International declared Anyona a prisoner of conscience.

On 31 December 1977, the novelist Ngugi wa Thiong'o was also arrested and detained. This followed preparations to stage an anti-capitalist and pro-Mau Mau play in Gikuyu and the publication of his novel *Petals of Blood*, which angrily criticised the emerging shape of Kenya's society (although it had been launched by Kibaki). His anti-capitalist stance had angered Njonjo, but his detention still appears ham-fisted, revealing the depth of the leadership's insecurity. It inspired much more anti-government writing over the years. Indeed, this was a feature of virtually every detention: the survivors were left with a deep anger that fuelled far stronger opposition to the state than before their jailing.

By mid-1976, Kenyatta and his government had re-established control. However, it had been Mzee's final exertion. His popularity was permanently damaged, and the 85-year-old was no longer in full control of the government. In the words of Kariithi, 'There was no hiding that Kenyatta was not the same man . . . He was no longer in total command.'[35] The Kikuyu elites in politics and the civil service used Kenyatta, aged and out of touch, to ratify decisions already made. Although he continued to meet visiting delegations, there was little dialogue. Kenyatta now spent almost all his time in Nakuru or Mombasa, and his main interests were tribal dancers and choirs, and debates on Kikuyu tradition with Koinange. The Cabinet was of little relevance. In practice, the government was run by Njonjo, Kariithi and Koinange, a few key ministers, permanent secretaries including Jeremiah Kiereini, the provincial commissioners (particularly Isaiah Mathenge and Eliud Mahihu) and police bosses (almost all of them Kikuyu). Civil servants were increasingly resistant to ministerial orders. No meaningful policy innovation was possible since there was no leadership from the top and the elite was irreparably divided.[36]

Development and Underdevelopment

Kenya's GDP continued to rise, but apart from the coffee boom of 1976–7, the rate of growth declined. The economy remained generally well managed, with no hyperinflation or vastly overvalued currency, but structural problems were emerging that the government could not resolve. The effects of the oil crisis continued to stress the economy. With high levels of imports and exports, and a fixed exchange rate, 1975 was a difficult year. World inflation drove domestic inflation, and worsened Kenya's terms of trade significantly. Kibaki was forced to raise prices and even to devalue the shilling (which had been almost static since independence). However, this was followed by an unexpected boom in 1976–7, caused by jumps in world prices for coffee and tea. This helped sustain the state, and solved the balance of payments problem in the short term, but the after-effects, which included higher consumption, easier credit and more government borrowing, were to haunt Kenyatta's successor in 1979–81.

Imports and Exports

Since 1964, Kenya's three main export earners – coffee, tea and petroleum products (from the Mombasa refinery to Uganda and beyond) – had accounted for 50–60 per cent of exports. This changed from 1975 with the oil price rise and the coffee and tea boom, so that at its peak in 1977 these three products collectively delivered 75 per cent of export earnings (see Figure 6.6). Rather than diversifying its exports, Kenya was entirely dependent on their performance. The government had tried rather ineffectually to boost exports; it had introduced an export compensation scheme, refunding some duties and taxes paid on intermediate imports to help industrial exporters, but it was to take decades to mature. In practice, export volumes stagnated, facing weak demand and protectionist barriers in industrialised countries. Although Kenya was making more money, it was not exporting more; it was just getting better prices for what it sold.

Historically, imports had come predominantly from Western Europe, especially the UK, but this too changed after the oil shock. The value of imports from the Middle East (almost all oil) rose from 9 per cent in 1973 to 35 per cent in 1981. To help the balance of payments, in the interventionist fashion of the time, Commerce and Industry Minister Kiano further restricted imports of goods that competed with those manufactured locally. Duties were raised to restrict imports of capital goods and encourage more labour-intensive production techniques.

With the coffee boom, Kenya's current account moved into surplus, with such large foreign reserves that the government struggled to justify further foreign aid. However, this too was transitory. The government did not tax export earnings from coffee or tea directly, so the temporary gains went straight into farmers' pockets. Kenyatta personally made the decision not to introduce a windfall tax or stabilisation

6.6: Export earnings by value from coffee, tea and petroleum products, 1964–84

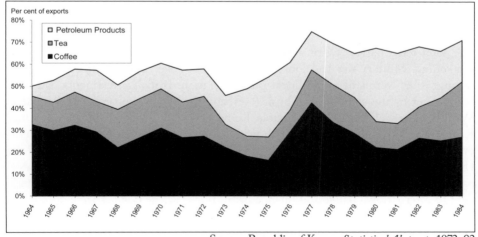

Source: Republic of Kenya, *Statistical Abstracts*, 1972–82

fund. Instead, the government tried to use regulatory methods to control the resulting demand.[37] This K£250 million jolt of natural resource income led to an unsustainable surge in domestic credit in 1977–8, while the government and councils embarked on huge spending plans.[38] These in turn fuelled the demand for imports and relaxation of quotas.[39] The result was a second, worse, balance of payments crisis in 1978–80 when exports returned to normal and oil prices rose for a second time.

Taxing More and Spending More

By 1978–9, the government taxed and spent 10 times (in shillings) what it had taken in 1964–5. It had kept spending and taxation roughly synchronised, but was finding the balance hard to maintain. Import duties had provided 40 per cent of recurrent revenue in the early 1960s, but this had declined to 20 per cent by 1980–1, a side-effect of the success of the import substitution programme.[40]

Growing state revenues were matched by higher spending on oil imports, services to the growing population, the costs incurred with the breakup of the EAC, over-optimistic spending during the coffee boom, and rising defence costs. Still, capital investment remained high as a percentage of total resources (25 per cent in 1977, up from 16 per cent in 1964), indicating that Kenya was investing in its economy.[41] Most analysts commended Kenya for avoiding the prestige projects and unproductive investments of other African countries. Development expenditure as a percentage of total government spending peaked at this time at 35 per cent, up from 20 per cent in the mid-1960s. Not all development spending was productive, however, as the category included loans to and equity in parastatals, the long-term value of which was beginning to be questioned. Long- and short-term capital movements in some years dampened and in others magnified the impact of the current account on foreign exchange reserves.[42] The government also consistently underestimated spending and overestimated foreign aid, making fiscal management harder.

Aid, Donors and Debt

The long-term patron–client relationship between Kenya and the UK was now weakening. Military ties had loosened, there were fewer British citizens in Kenya (though they were still a significant presence), more British investments had been bought out by the state or local businesses, and the 'Asian problem' had dissipated. With Britain itself in economic trouble, Kenya no longer had a reliable patron. Once Kenyatta finally departed, the British were happy to wash their hands of the debts of history and treat Kenya like any other ex-colony. While Kenya's debts to the UK (both financial and emotional) were declining, its debts to other countries – particularly the US, West Germany and Japan – were growing, as was its multilateral debt to international banks and finance institutions (whose policies were dominated by Washington). There is a sense in which, to oversimplify, Kenya began to change patrons in the late 1970s – from Britain to the US.

In 1974, under pressure from rising oil prices, Kenya began its love–hate relationship with the IMF. The IMF offered short-term loans to deal with balance of payment crises, in return for which it required authorities to review their exchange rate policies to ensure fiscal stability. Kenya drew down on its IMF reserves in 1974–5 and took on large borrowings from the fund in 1976. These loans included conditions requiring that Kenya rectify structural imbalances caused by the government's policies. Kenya was the first country to use this new scheme. The World Bank, which provided long-term low-interest loans for development projects, also chipped in US$30 million. Nonetheless, at this time the demands of the IMF and World Bank (the international finance institutions or IFIs) were modest. Although they encouraged lower tariffs, higher interest rates and lower government spending, their loan conditionalities were short-term and focused on domestic credit and government borrowing. Neither fundamental economic change nor 'governance' intruded. In the event, the coffee and tea boom meant Kenya did not need to use all its loans.[43]

Annual overseas aid (grants and loans) grew significantly in the late 1970s (see Figure 6.7). Between 1973 and 1976, Kenya received at least US$738 million in aid of various types, with the World Bank the largest donor and the UK second, making it one of the most favoured nations in Africa for aid.[44] Agriculture, water and transportation were the main sectors supported, through more than 400 individual projects, each with its own disbursements, audits and controls. From 1976–7, with the UK's accession, the European Economic Community (EEC) also began to support projects in rural Kenya, including a new arid and semi-arid lands programme and contributions to Tana River hydroelectric schemes. Other country development agencies, particularly the Scandinavians, funded projects elsewhere.

Gradually and systematically, this emerging aid 'system' helped Kenya's people. As a by-product, however, it weakened Kenya's state: offering better salaries and opportunities than the civil service; making state development planning or investment prioritisation almost impossible; and most importantly, divorcing service delivery from taxation or from government decision-making. Such projects also reinforced a dependency culture, which made local nationalists despair. As one 1982 critique suggested:

> ... Turkana is ceded to the USAID (USA), NORAD (Norway), the FAO (UN), and the EEC. Machakos is in the hands of the EEC which experiments in 'integrated rural development'. CIDA (Canada) meanwhile surveys and develops the rangelands, Belgium supplies water to Marsabit district, the World Bank plans and finances urban housing and waste disposal. Isiolo district is in a British sphere, whilst West Pokot is a Dutch one and Baringo a dual mandate of the World Bank and USAID's marginal lands project.[45]

There was also growing dissatisfaction at the outcome of many rural development projects. While some (such as the sugar outgrowers' schemes) seemed sustainably productive, others left few benefits after the foreign workers had left. A combination

6.7: Total overseas development aid, 1970–8

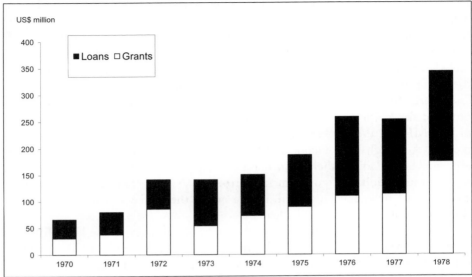

Source: O'Brien and Ryan, 'Kenya', in Devarajan, Dollar and Torgny:
Aid and Reform in Africa, pp. 520–1

of bureaucracy, Kenyan rent-seeking and poorly judged projects (the Norwegian-funded Lake Turkana fish factory was a notorious case) meant the returns on many investments were low. Kenyans were also the victims of changing fashions in aid and – just as NGOs were to do in the 1990s – the government played along for the money.[46] But while half of the cash was an outright gift, more than half was in loans that developments were supposed to repay.

The government also made use of short-term domestic borrowing – impractical in the 1960s because of the lack of local capital – and issued bonds to fund its debt, mostly bought by institutional investors.[47] It also continued borrowing commercially abroad, including large borrowings from Lloyds Bank. The result was a debt burden in shillings that tripled between 1970 and 1978 (see Figure 6.8). Dollar debt repayments increased eightfold between 1963–4 and 1977–8, though debt remained within 8–10 per cent of government spending.

Banking and Debt

Kenya's large and relatively sophisticated financial sector performed well in the 1970s. The key retail banks were now the KCB, Barclays, Standard Bank and the NBK, together holding 70 per cent of deposits. Non-bank financial institutions included the HFCK (the state-owned mortgage company) and a few Asian-owned private institutions. There was a rapid rise in deposits in 1971–9, reflecting growing private wealth, but also greater access to and trust in banks.

6.8: Government debt, 1964–78

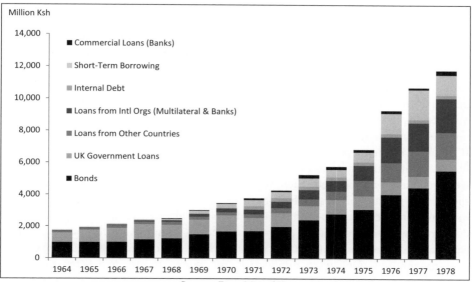

Source: Republic of Kenya, *Statistical Abstracts*, Various years

The financial parastatals had greater independence from government control than in other sectors, and were successful in retaining market share, with the NBK growing the fastest.[59] Despite this, signs were emerging of a long-term debt problem. In 1979, for example, the NBK wrote off Ksh153 million in bad debts. Part of the reason was that state financial institutions could be pressured to give large loans to influential individuals, including their own chairmen and officials. These banks also acted as bankers to the parastatal sector, taking on risks that a commercial entity would never have accepted. This problem was to come to the forefront of public attention in the 1980s, but the seeds of trouble had already been sown.

State Capitalism and the Role of Multinational Companies

Manufacturing output had now tripled since independence, although equally rapid agricultural growth meant its share of GDP rose only slightly. Many foreign companies found it easier to reinvest their capital in industrial expansion than remit it overseas, but there were few major new investments after 1973–4. World recession and more restrictive rules on foreign investments, inspired by pressure to keep local control, discouraged new investors. There was some local private capital available, but much of it went into buying out foreign concerns. Quantitative restrictions on imports continued, although technocrats knew the risks of over-protecting local markets. Increasingly complex administrative regulations stifled local private investment.

The state continued to serve as a surrogate capitalist, investing both foreign loans and its own revenue in commercial businesses.[48] By the late 1970s, there were nearly 200 parastatals, and they employed as many people as the central government.

There has been disagreement on the extent to which the government's industrial development arms contributed to development or actually diverted resources into unprofitable protected cul-de-sacs. The ICDC was accused in the 1970s of favouring large, capital-intensive firms selling to a protected internal market, and of being beholden to its partners. It made some of its more doubtful investments on explicit instructions from the government. The ICDC and the DFCK apparently prospered, but their loan portfolios included many slow-to-mature or failed enterprises. Half the ICDC's investments paid no dividends at all during the 1970s.[49] As the government was an equity partner, it has been argued that its partners' case for greater protection were generally well received. There were textbook cases of protected local industries, such as the production of sisal bags at three times the landed costs of the equivalent imported product.[50] On the other hand, it was not always the case that parastatals – even when protected by tariffs – were less efficient than private companies.[51] But it was clear that management in many parastatals was even more lax than in the central government, functions were duplicated and worse, as emerged after Kenyatta's death, there was 'clear evidence of prolonged inefficiency, financial mismanagement, waste and malpractices in many parastatals.'[52] A problem was emerging that only a government with a clear mandate, strong resolve and a willingness to challenge historical orthodoxy could address.

One rare new foreign investment was the Rivatex textile mill in Eldoret, which began operating in 1977. This was a classic joint venture, in which a multinational textile company provided capital, management and expertise, while the government took an 80 per cent stake and offered a protected market and tax and duty exemptions. Its products were widely criticised as being of low quality, but to protect it, the government had to crack down on textile smuggling and then ban imports of second-hand clothes entirely.[53] An even worse example was the Ken-Ren Fertiliser Company in Mombasa, a joint venture with an American company in 1975. This ended in complete failure and the loss of Ksh420 million (US$50 million), blamed by some on an unrealistic proposal, by others on the desire of Kiambu 'family' members to continue to profit from fertiliser imports.[54] Unpaid foreign loans relating to Ken-Ren were still on Kenya's books 30 years later.

In the 1970s, scholars were increasingly critical of the long-term implications of investments by multinational corporations. Most Marxist analyses saw multinational investments as harming, not developing, countries such as Kenya. With international attention focusing more on basic needs, employment and the reduction of inequality than on growth per se, multinationals were becoming villains rather than saviours. The case for the 'prosecution' was strong: the products that multinational subsidiaries produced were more expensive and required more foreign inputs and less labour than lower-quality domestic equivalents. Multinationals retained the attitudes and business practices of the West, rather than responding to domestic imperatives, and perpetuated inequality.[55] They had created a profitable, capital-intensive Nairobi-focused set of businesses, paying high wages, which created and satisfied Western consumer tastes, protected and sustained by a close association with government.[56] The Kenyan state was characterised as an agent of foreign capital and a willing partner in Kenya's exploitation. Less attention was paid to the alternative: whether private African entrepreneurs or the state would have done a better job, and whether the real alternative to multinational investment was no investment at all. Consumer choice was accorded little attention.

Over the years, views have changed, but the underlying dispute – over the degree to which foreign investment and the resulting compromises on economic policy were to the benefit of Kenya – continues. The remedies offered at the time were more nationalisation and a more critical approach to foreign investment. Government policy itself began to shift in the late 1970s. Many of the elite were embedded in commercial relations with multinationals, but some 'technocrats' too were becoming sceptical of the virtues of foreign multinational investment.[57]

There were two major new infrastructure developments in the period. The building of a new international airport began in 1974 and finished in 1978, funded by the World Bank and the government, to replace the overstretched facilities at Wilson and Embakasi. It was renamed Jomo Kenyatta International Airport (JKIA) after Kenyatta's death. In 1973, the Kenya Pipeline Company was formed to build an oil pipeline from the Mombasa refinery to Nairobi, moving tankers off the Nairobi–Mombasa road. Inevitably, such a large contract inspired elite competition. While the nominally retired McKenzie supported a proposal from Shell to manage the line and fund the construction from Grindlays Bank, Mungai and others backed a Lonrho proposal using Kuwaiti money.[58] In the end, financed in part by the World Bank, the pipeline began operating in 1978, one of the largest infrastructure projects since independence.

Underdevelopment, Dependency and the Role of the Elite

In the late 1970s, a vigorous debate raged over whether Kenya's capitalist, import-substituting, growth-oriented strategy was in fact a route to long-term disaster and impoverishment. Few disputed that the colonial economy had been designed around cash-crop exports and import-substitution industries, or that the independence government had further encouraged this. It was also agreed that Kenya was more open to foreign investment than most other African countries. The discussion concerned whether these were unusually good policies for Africa or unusually bad. In line with the mood of the times, Marxism and dependency theory dominated the debate. Critics argued that the Kenyan model was fundamentally flawed and that Kenya must seek some form of revolutionary break with the past.[60] They also argued that the tight relationship between the new African elite and foreign interests was dangerous. In *Underdevelopment in Kenya*, Colin Leys suggested the bond was 'parasitic', and the elite was serving as an 'auxiliary of foreign capital', creating a political and economic structure hostile to the needs of most people.[61] There were also debates on whether an indigenous African capitalist class existed, or whether the few that had achieved these heights were just middlemen for foreign capitalists. Similarly disputed was the issue of whether this emerging class (growing as a consequence of Africanisation) would act in its collective interest, and whether it could survive in the absence of state protection.

However, in the late 1970s and early 1980s, the evidence grew to suggest that this argument, while capturing the inequitable relationship between African states and the capitalist world, was incomplete. There was little evidence that capitalist development automatically resulted in poverty and dependency for developing countries, though it certainly implied that inequality would increase. Where domestic and foreign capital conflicted, the state often favoured domestic interests, and international business did not control economic policy. Kenya's public-private partnership model seemed to function as much for the benefit of the state and the individuals who controlled it as for foreign investors.

Less attention was paid to the Asian commercial class. Despite state neglect and sometimes hostility, the community strengthened its control of larger manufacturing concerns in the 1970s as its dominance of trade weakened, moving up the value chain into businesses requiring more capital and expertise. This gave them more time before African businessmen (many of whom preferred to invest in land) could compete on equal terms.[62]

The state was now actively seeking to promote domestic ownership and limit foreign influences. By 1972, just under half the equity in a sample of firms sending funds abroad was already owned by citizens or by the state.[63] There were further restrictions on firms not owned by citizens after 1974, including tougher dividend remittance rules and limitations on domestic borrowing by multinationals.[64] Taxes on company profits rose to 45 per cent in 1974 and a capital gains tax was introduced in 1975. The state restricted acquisitions by foreign firms and ensured that divesting companies such as Brooke Bond Liebig sold shares to the Treasury or to local investors, not to foreigners.[65] In the mid-1970s (against the advice of the CDC and World Bank), the Kenya Tea Development Authority set up a new parastatal – Kenya Tea Packers – to take over tea-packing and local marketing in Kenya, driving multinationals including Brooke Bond out of the market.[66] In 1975, the law was changed to require that citizens appointed by the KNTC distribute all goods manufactured by foreign firms. In 1976, the Foreign Investment Protection Act was amended to specify that foreign investors would be refunded profits and investments at current exchange rates, not original dollar rates, further disincentivising investment.

A study by Nicola Swainson in the mid-1970s showed that the change in the composition of company directorships since 1967 had also been dramatic: 18 of the top 49 directors were now Africans, most prominent among them GEMA head Karume. There had also been a dramatic Africanisation of senior management positions, leaving European managers and directors in a minority. Shares were increasingly owned by Africans, including senior civil servants whose interests straddled directorships in international companies, administrative positions and private investments. The 1970s and early 1980s saw further private capital accumulation by these elites, based in part on their roles as foreign proxies but leveraging their positions in the state bureaucracy. Leys took the view later that they were not purely proxies, but key actors in building and sustaining indigenous capital. He also stressed – as the state had done for decades – the importance of productive foreign investment as the route to growth. The role of multinational enterprises continued to be controversial, however, with others still arguing that multinationals extracted too much surplus to support development, and that local elites were too closely identified with international interests.

Lonrho, one of the largest international firms in Kenya, was a classic example of the challenge. In the mid-late 1970s, Lonrho (owner of the *Standard* and many other businesses) was among the few big investors in new ventures, including a textile mill and the vehicle assembly plant. Its alliance with the Kenyatta family was open: Lonrho offered financial and media support in return for preference and protection for its businesses. This was not a one-sided deal. Individual elites also leveraged their positions to extract resources. Their East Africa chairman Udi Gecaga, for example, profited significantly from the Lonrho relationship, an example of how African elites could use multinationals to support their own investments, taking part-shares in companies their employer owned, or using the assets, name or influence of their employer to obtain loans and other benefits for themselves.[67]

During the 1980s, the debate over the role of multinationals died down, and there was a wave of buy-outs of foreign firms, as domestic capital replaced foreign investors. By the 1990s, the nature of the debate had changed. State control was no longer seen as an inherent social good; the evidence of domestic private capital formation and independent state action to sustain it was overwhelming; and multinational businesses were playing such a vigorous role on the world stage that there was little prospect of major new developments without them.

Tourism and Wildlife

Kenya continued to develop its tourism business, with the wildlife safaris of the 1960s supplemented by large investments in beach tourism, which soon made up 60 per cent of the industry. Kenya catered for everyone, from wealthy Americans to backpackers. Increased affluence in the West, mass air travel and the development of package holidays coincided with Kenya's positive investment climate, and visitor numbers increased by 75 per cent between 1969 and 1976 (see Figure 6.9). However, tourism figures flattened out during the world recession and did not return to 1976's height until the 1980s, affected in part by the collapse of the EAC. Game park visits, a key indicator of tourist spending, declined in 1975–6.

The increase in tourist spending was a cash cow for those with capital and connections. The KTDC funded most hotel construction: its 'soft' loans to consortia with African participation were another means to transfer resources from government into elite hands. Between 1970 and 1980, Kenya added 10,000 hotel beds in 500 hotels. The KTDC also bought a controlling share in African Tours and

Hotels, which as a parastatal then took control of several smaller hotels and built several more. Several foreign companies established big coastal hotels in alliance with Kenyan elites. EAB chairman Kenneth Matiba was one of the few with the experience, ability and contacts to raise the capital needed. In 1970, a year after he had been appointed a director of the KTDC, Matiba and two Europeans established Alliance Hotels.[68] Mixing private and government roles inextricably, he was at the same time chairman of Kenya Safari Lodges and Hotels, a KTDC-owned hotel operator. Matiba's chain prospered and in 1978, Alliance built its own hotel on the south coast. In some sectors at least, domestic and international capital were now competing equally.

While beach tourism was growing, it was less high profile than the country's wildlife market. Kenya needed to protect its wildlife from both poaching and people. Rather than shrinking under the pressure of the growing population, Kenya's national parks expanded in size in the 1970s. In 1974, Lake Nakuru National Park doubled in area and Nairobi National Park was extended in 1976. Although they were essential in protecting wildlife, the parks remained controversial. While they provided jobs and income opportunities, most of the revenue from park fees went to the state, many of the employees came from elsewhere and most of the profits from the lodges went to foreign companies and elite investors. In several parks, including Amboseli and Bogoria, local people were moved off their land, losing access to grazing and water for their cattle, causing long-running disputes.

Other challenges to the long-term benefits of mass tourism included the foreign ownership of many hotels and the limited trickle-down of incomes; the disruptive social effects of wealthy foreigners; the opportunity cost of funds and labour invested in this sector rather than elsewhere; and the risk of dependence on fickle customer perceptions of country risk. Nonetheless, tourism was to remain a core component of Kenya's economic strategy, and was now Kenya's second largest foreign exchange earner after coffee.

6.9: Tourism indicators, 1969–79

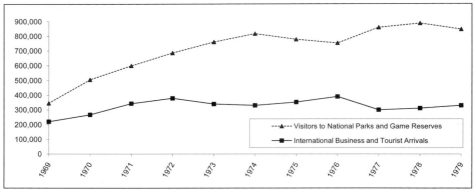

Source: Republic of Kenya, *Statistical Abstract*, 1972, 1976, 1982

Agriculture, Land and Class

Fuelled by a price boom in export crops, the late 1970s were good years for Kenya's farmers. Maize, tea, coffee, pineapples, cotton, sugar cane and cashewnuts all performed well. Small farms (of 12 hectares or less) now produced more than half of all marketed production by value. Pricing, however, was an increasing concern to experts, concerned that throughout Africa, governments were keeping agricultural producer prices artificially low.[69] In Kenya, while export crop prices were set by international markets (and producers received most of their earnings), the state controlled both producer and consumer prices for maize, milk, beef, wheat and sugar. Policy in the 1960s had been gradually to reduce prices, but food pricing in the 1970s was politicised and inconsistent.[70] Most prices were set below import parity (the cost of importing the same products), but there was no consistent strategy favouring rural producers or urban consumers. Peasants, larger farmers, bureaucrats, consumers, political elites and business interests all influenced policy in different directions. The Kenya National Farmers Union (KNFU) continued to represent farmers' interests, particularly those of large farmers, and was the main lobby group on the government for higher prices and more state services. The marketing boards were sometimes left 'holding the baby' of producer price increases with frozen consumer prices. Marketing costs as a proportion of prices paid to farmers were also rising. The cooperatives and marketing boards had little incentive to manage costs, with the increases serving the interests of employees, of those politicians who influenced appointments and of local businesses who held contracts with them, rather than working to the benefit of farmers.[71]

Instead of dampening price instability, marketing boards sometimes caused market instabilities. As an example, following unexpectedly large maize price increases in 1976, production boomed in 1976–7, but the Maize Board ran out of space to store the surplus, leading them to refuse to buy grain. When restrictions on the private transfer and storage of grain were briefly lifted, private traders bought surpluses cheaply, undercutting the board. Other farmers were left with unsaleable surpluses and cut back on production in response. The surplus grain was eventually exported at a loss, and prices cut once more.[72]

The Coffee Boom, 1975–7

In July 1975, unseasonable frosts in Brazil killed many young coffee plants, and the result was worldwide shortages in 1976. Coffee prices increased four- to five-fold in a few months, and Kenyan growers and brokers made millions. International Coffee Agreement quotas had already lapsed, and Kenya's production, which had been stable at 60,000–70,000 tonnes a year, increased to 100,000 tonnes in 1977. Export earnings jumped sharply during 1976–7 as a result (see Figure 6.10). This was not to last. Prices halved in late 1978 and by 1979, with heavy rains, production was back down to 75,000 tonnes. Tea production also grew, as the smallholder plantings of the early 1970s matured. At the same time, world tea prices doubled during 1976–8.

6.10: Coffee and tea exports, 1964–79 (by value)

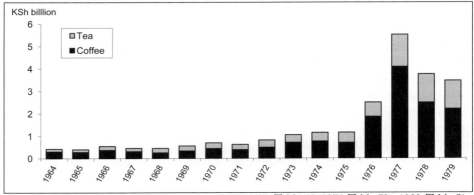

Source: Republic of Kenya, *Statistical Abstracts*, 1972, Table 60; 1976. Table 58a; 1982, Table 51a.

The boom resulted in an influx of easy money, which conveniently flowed mainly into Central Province, the centre of smallholder coffee growing. Farmers' incomes jumped, as did savings and investment, then construction and consumer prices. The mini-boom that resulted helped sustain Kenyatta's regime at what would otherwise have been a difficult time, and allowed it to delay some difficult decisions.

The more easily money was acquired, the more it corrupted, and the new 'black gold' inspired new forms of crime – robbers routinely looted coffee lorries. The collapsing Ugandan state was unable to reward its own growers, and so Kenyans stepped in to organise illegal imports. Probably 15,000 tonnes of 1977's exports had actually been smuggled into Kenya. Both police and Coffee Board officials were implicated in smuggling. According to Njonjo, 'There was a total breakdown of the law. Those who were responsible for administering the law were themselves involved.'[73] Huge sums were made by those able to buy police immunity.

The Sugar Industry

Although the government had built the Muhoroni and Chemelil factories, there was still a large gap between sugar supply and demand. To meet this, the government established three more sugar factories in the 1970s, all in Western and Nyanza, part of a strategy of import substitution, employment and wealth creation in western Kenya. Construction of Mumias Sugar Factory in Kakamega began in 1973, Nzoia Sugar Factory was built in Bungoma between 1975 and 1978, and the last of the big factories, South Nyanza (Sony) Sugar Company in Migori was constructed in 1978–9. State-set sugar producer prices nearly tripled between 1970 and 1977, to support the industry. As a result, Kenya moved from being a net sugar importer in 1966 to self-sufficiency by 1979.

These predominantly state-owned but internationally managed factories made little use of mechanisation, deliberately adopting high-labour input methods to ensure local employment. The factories soon became the largest employers in much of Nyanza and Western Province, and local politics became deeply intertwined with their performance.[74] Tens of thousands of small outgrowers grew cane as a cash-crop to feed the factories, alongside the nucleus estates of factory-owned land. As a side-effect, local food production declined.

The Thinning Land Frontier

The African elites and land-buying companies continued to struggle to acquire the few remaining white-owned farms coming onto the market. By 1978, the pressure to buy soon was peaking, as there was 'a general feeling that, when Mzee dies, policy over land distribution and ownership could change drastically'.[75] Kimani's Ngwataniro land company was particularly important as both a political and a commercial entity, settling more than 50,000 families in Nakuru and Laikipia between 1974 and 1980.[76] Many other peasant families had bought share certificates entitling them to land that had not yet been bought (and might never be).

By 1978, 95 per cent of all European-owned mixed farms had been acquired, roughly half for formal settlement schemes; a quarter as large individually owned farms and the rest as group farms or for informal subdivision. By the time British funding for land purchase schemes ended in 1979, 1,400 farms covering 3.5 million acres (1.4 million hectares) had been bought at a cost to the UK of GB£31 million.[77] In 1979, the Department of Settlement estimated that there had been at least 225 settlement schemes, settling 90,000 families on 2 million acres (800,000 hectares) of land.[78] While in the 1960s, Central Province had been the largest beneficiary, by 1979, the Rift Valley and Central Province each held a third of the land demarcated and sold.

The *Development Plan, 1974–78* had followed the ILO's recommendations of a return to support for small farmers (at least in principle). After 1976, most of the farms that had begun as cooperatives or land-buying company farms were subdivided, but the process was painful, with long arguments over costs and contributions. The marketed output of large farms fell only gradually, from 59 per cent in 1964 to 44 per cent in 1978.[79] Pressure to help the small farm sector more, or to acquire and subdivide African-owned large farms was resisted and promises of a land tax similarly came to nothing. By 1978, the number of large farms (more than 100 hectares) in the ex-scheduled areas was higher than in 1964.[80]

Land Registration

Land consolidation and registration in the Trust Lands (ex-reserves) continued: 500,000 hectares a year were demarcated and allocated between 1971 and 1977, after which the process slowed. It was increasingly affected by disputes over ownership and difficulties in defining individual rights in clan-owned lands. While the adjudication of Central Province was finished in the 1960s, and Western Province was largely complete by 1974, adjudication of Kalenjin and Maasai areas was only mid-way through. The Coast and Eastern Province, meanwhile, had seen little progress, nor had work begun in the North-East.[81]

By 1974, probably half Kenya's smallholders had individual freehold title to their land, though this excluded many who had acquired land in the settlement schemes, where the issue of individual title was delayed by subdivision and group occupation. Most land was registered under male names, giving the eldest male in most households the legal right to sell family land. The land control boards still had to approve sales, and could intervene if they believed the result would not be equitable for all family members.[82] The state required all land sales to be formally registered, but many failed to comply.

Rural Credit

Land title was a key asset in acquiring rural credit. Angelique Haugerud showed that in 1979–80, 15 per cent of the farms in her Embu study were acting as security for loans.[83]

The AFC was one of the biggest lenders, helping farmers to buy farms, as well as lending to smallholders and ranchers and funding the seasonal credit system. As it had no depositors, the AFC had less incentive to retain its capital base. Its poor performance required large investments of capital, and it was sustained only by interest-free loans and grants. It made relatively few loans, two-thirds by value of which were to buy large farms, which resulted in high default rates.[84] Some believe that its real purpose was to serve 'as a mechanism to transfer resources from the exchequer to the AFC's clientele'.[85] The AFC's performance improved after 1977. However, its poor administrative procedures and appalling record in loan collection continued to endanger its viability and it consistently under-provided for bad debts. Its officers were heavily pressured to make loans to clients of politicians, with little prospect of collection if the borrowers remained influential.

Other state lenders to the agriculture sector included the Cooperative Bank, the Cereals and Sugar Finance Corporation and the ADC. Their funds too were used for non-commercial as well as commercial investments. In 1979–80, for example, the ADC made 77 per cent of its total investments at the specific direction of the Ministry of Agriculture, though it still showed a paper profit.[86] Commercial banks were chary of lending to farmers; the risks were so high that in 1975–6, the Central Bank was forced to mandate that private banks lend at least 17 per cent of their deposits to the agricultural sector. Few met this target even then.[87]

Class Formation and Agricultural Development

During the 1960s, the cash-cropping of coffee, tea, pyrethrum, maize and milk had made Central Province and parts of Embu, Meru and Kisii one of Africa's most successful examples of smallholder agriculture. This success was based on labour-intensive cultivation, with little mechanisation. There was extensive debate about why Kenya had been so successful, and about the implications for social differentiation.

Everyone agreed, though, that Kenya paid a far higher proportion of the export value of cash-crops to its producers than Uganda or Tanzania, and that this had encouraged growth.

Although most believed that land registration and consolidation had energised agricultural innovation and productivity, others argued that it had diverted resources that could have been used for real agricultural improvement. Most farmers did not actually obtain credit even after registration, and although the programme had encouraged the consolidation of land into fewer larger farms, extensive off-book land subdivision had taken place, undermining the principle of clear land title anyway.[88] Plots were divided between children or leased to others without registration, reducing average farm sizes below what was considered commercially viable in the 1960s.

There was much debate on whether greater inequality, cash-crop farming and individual land title was leading to 'class formation'. The key focus was the Kikuyu peasantry, seen as the driving force for growth, but also the victim of rapid differentiation, an experimental sandpit in which violent social forces had been at play since the 1940s. Analyses of the colonial and early post-colonial era by Gavin Kitching, Apollo Njonjo, Sharon Stichter, Nicola Swainson and others suggested that class formation and capitalist accumulation, at least in Kikuyu areas, appeared thus far to resemble the processes seen in other countries. Nationwide, two rural surveys in 1974–5 and 1978–9 suggested a pattern of growing economic differentiation. Although data were patchy, the number of small farms continued to grow, to approximately 1.5 million in 1975, of which 500,000 (30 per cent) were very small (less than 0.5 hectares). Analyses of the results showed greater differentiation between the wealthy (combining agricultural and urban incomes, investing in cash-cropping and diversifying) and a proletarianised poor (unable to survive on the land and forced to sell their land and labour, if they were lucky). Kenya was clearly an extremely unequal society. However, all figures were made hard to interpret by informal inheritance and subdivision, shared cultivation of farms and the large farms in the ex-reserves, which appeared in neither the small farm nor the ex-scheduled areas statistics.[89] Other studies suggested that at least in Central Province cash-crop production had actually reduced inequality, as the 'middle peasantry' had been able to use their moderate land holdings to good effect in export crop production.[90] The proportion of landless people in Central Province seemed to be falling, helped by migration into the Rift, a safety valve that was now closing.

The 1978–9 rural survey also confirmed the importance of Central Province. It produced 30 per cent of all smallholder production, including half of all smallholder tea, while 92 per cent of smallholder coffee came from Central Province, Embu, Meru and Kisii. The success of these cash-crops drove the development of these districts, which had seen higher than average agricultural incomes over the last 20 years.[91] However, while the government and most aid agencies supported the growth of cash-cropping to raise incomes and speed development, others argued that the move from food production to cash-crops was a dangerous mistake.

Evidence mounted that for peasant farmers, diversification was the key to long-term success, whether between crops (to allow switching to respond to price or marketing problems) or between farm and off-farm incomes. For decades, remittances from urban workers had provided capital for agricultural improvements. This had been the engine of growth in Central Province and the area around Nairobi.[92] Those families able to straddle formal sector roles and cash-cropping had been able to enlarge their farms and invest in higher-value crops, which in turn increased incomes and created a beneficial cycle of differentiation. In practice, however, much of the accumulated capital was not reinvested in agriculture, but spent on education, consumption and housing, or invested into trade and urban businesses.[93] Worse, as real wages in the formal sector declined in the 1970s, the flow of remittances fell. Accumulative straddling, using urban wages to invest at home, was replaced by subsistence straddling, using farm incomes and small-scale trade to supplement formal sector wages.[94]

The proportion of Kenyans in absolute poverty had declined as a consequence of cash-cropping, and most development indicators suggested health, services and incomes had improved. Living standards had improved little, though, for those unable to grow cash-crops, and had worsened for some small farmers in Coast, Western and Nyanza, pastoralists, the landless and the unemployed.[95] Districts such as Siaya and Kisumu in Nyanza, once relatively prosperous, had been outpaced because of their unsuitability for smallholder production and the poor performance of cotton as a cash-crop.[96] There was now a 15-year difference in life expectancy at birth between Central Province and Nyanza.

Although the elite tried to conceal it, there were class issues in Kenya that now crosscut ethnic and regional interests. There is little doubt that the interests of the administrative, political and economic elite, a small community of a few thousand, perhaps half of them Kikuyu, dominated Kenya. Agricultural interests were well represented in the political system, though there were still tensions between the interests of commercial farmers, cash-cropping smallholders, subsistence peasants and pastoralists. However, all these interests were mediated through this elite, whose social and economic status and orientation were closer to those of the West than of their own farmers. The bureaucrats, who used their gatekeeper role to extract rents and represent their own interests, and who merged with the socio-political elite at the top, were at the zenith of their power.

Health and Social Change

The late 1970s saw some of the highest per capita incomes and the best services for the middle classes and better-off peasants in Kenya's history. The rapid growth of the 1960s had slowed, and population growth was gradually overwhelming the capacity of services, but for the wealthier, the electricity, water and telephone services usually worked, and there was optimism about the future. Few foresaw the scale of the problems to come.

Water, Health and Nutrition

In health services, considerable improvements had been achieved since independence, with death rates dropping from 20 per thousand in 1963 to 14 in 1982, and infant mortality rates halved. As a result, life expectancy improved to 53 by 1979. Funds per person for health provision remained stable and the number of hospital beds nearly doubled between 1970 and 1978. Statistics for doctors per 1,000 people were good, though 90 per cent of these doctors practised in the urban areas. Malaria remained endemic in the west and at the coast, but sleeping sickness, smallpox and cholera were virtually eradicated.

The health infrastructure formed a pyramid: local community health centres; district hospitals (with limited facilities); bigger hospitals in each province; and Nairobi's Kenyatta National Hospital as the final reference hospital. The Ministry of Health ran all state medical facilities, set policy, acquired drugs and equipment, recruited staff, administered the National Hospital Insurance Fund (NHIF) and controlled the budget. Health care in state hospitals was mostly free, though outside specialist units it would be considered poor by contemporary standards. The Health Ministry was already renowned as corrupt and incompetent. There were sometimes no drugs or only out-of-date stock, while in the rural areas there were stories of wild dogs eating dead bodies in hospital mortuaries, and of hospitals infested with bedbugs. In parallel, there was a network of private and church medical services, which in the urban areas provided some of the best fee-paying medical care in Africa, and half the country's hospital beds.

Nutritional surveys in 1974–5 and 1977 showed that, on average, both urban and rural Kenyans received adequate nutrition. But there were pockets of deep regional poverty, and one-third of Kenyans were still nutritionally deficient. This was the background to Moi's free school milk programme of 1979.

There had been a significant improvement since independence in both rural and urban access to potable water. Reflecting the importance of water for health, the government established a new Ministry of Water Development in 1974, responsible for water supplies, sewage and pollution control. In 1970, the government had promised potable drinking water to all Kenyans by the year 2000. It was an ambitious target: in 1975, only 10 per cent of rural households had access to piped water. Central Province was easily the best served: it was small, well-watered, able to fund *harambee* schemes, close to Nairobi and favoured for investment.

Kenya's birth rates were still rising, while death rates continued to fall, giving the country the second-fastest population growth (3.4 per cent compound a year) in the world during the 1970s. However, there was no consensus on the need to reduce this rate. Although Sweden was providing Kenya with US$6 million a year for birth control, contraceptive use was deeply unpopular, and many MPs rejected Western-led population control policies. Shikuku, for example, made a typically xenophobic prophecy: 'The world war is approaching. Who will fight in the war? We must produce more children . . .'[97] Another MP claimed that the aim of family planning was to 'destroy the African population. We want to encourage our people to have as many children as they can so we can have a big population in this country.'[98] Only the arch-elitist Njonjo was willing to support population control in Parliament, and was much derided as a result. Kenyans were to pay the price for their independent thinking in the next two decades.

Changing Social Custom and the Role of Women

During the 1970s, more of the country began to experience the social changes and dislocations that Central Province had experienced in the 1950s and 1960s; a result of urbanisation, higher incomes and socio-economic differentiation. New attitudes led to the decline of age-grade initiation ceremonies and of respect for elders and the loosening of clan ties. The traditional controls on and outlets for youth energies began to break down and the community social security system for the less fortunate eroded.

The debate about the degree to which Kenyans should retain their distinctive traditions continued. Some leaders (often Kikuyu) represented and espoused an urban, detribalised, Western-oriented Kenya; others wished to emphasise the positive aspects of traditional culture and to preserve Kenyan music, dance and art from the Western influences that were causing their decline. Kenya had no formal cultural policy. Nonetheless, foreign influences were a real concern. Those determined to keep Kenya 'African' mounted public opposition to Western innovations such as mini-skirts. Parliamentary debates were full of attacks on beauty contests, wigs and eye shadow as 'un-African'. The hippy era was in full swing, and Kenya's puritanical self-reliance clashed with its need to encourage tourism. Vice-President Moi decreed in March 1972, for example, that immigration officials would no longer admit 'hippies' to the country, asking them to be on the lookout for longhaired men who 'need a wash'. He also blamed hippies for introducing a drug culture into the country. Marijuana use was certainly widespread, but predated Western hippies (more than 3,000 Kenyans were jailed in 1965 for possession). Kenya was already a significant marijuana producer and exporter.

Another Western value that was challenged in Kenya was the concept of female equality. In law as well as in practice, women still did not have equal rights. The vast majority of women were working (mostly cultivating their small farms), and Nairobi even had a female mayor, Margaret Kenyatta, during 1970–6. However, female formal sector employment was extremely low: women held only 18 per cent of such jobs in 1981. Women were not allowed to join the National Social Security Fund (NSSF) until 1977 and did not have identity cards until then. The state refused to legalise abortion or to provide contraception for women.

The fate of a key piece of legislation, the Marriage Bill, which aimed to provide stronger protection for women, symbolised their lower status. Introduced in 1976, it was rejected by the (mostly male) MPs then and again on its reintroduction in 1979. It aimed to unify the legal codes governing marriage and to rectify institutional biases that disadvantaged women. The bill criminalised adultery, clarified the status of traditional marriages, established joint ownership of property and the ability of women to inherit property in traditional marriages and tried to outlaw the 'traditional' right of men to beat their wives. However, there was little support in the Assembly for such 'un-African' changes. In the words of MP Wafula Wabuge in 1979, 'if you do not slap a woman, you will note that her behaviours will not appeal to you. Just slap her and she will know you love her.'[99] Its defeat meant that multiple socio-legal systems remained, and under both customary and Muslim law, women remained legally inferior.

State and Society

Although dominated by the state, Kenya contained many interests groups, opinion formers and non-governmental organisations (NGOs), including the churches, the media and ethnic unions. Their tacit and sometimes active support helped sustain Kenyatta's hierarchical structure of politics and social affairs.

Church and State

The relationship between the Christian churches and the government was one of agreed spheres of influence. The churches focused their material efforts on small-scale development activities, organising thousands of smaller projects. The state did not interfere in Church matters, in the main, while the churches said little publicly about politics. A rare critic of this relationship was (Luo) Bishop Henry Okullu, whose book, *Church and Politics in East Africa*, suggested that the independent church had a 'too comfortable relationship with the State', which meant its role 'to be the "nation's conscience" has gone unheard'.[100] For Okullu, the demand that churches should stay out of politics was a call for it to support the status quo.[101] He also criticised the concentration of power in Kenya and the absolutism of Africa's rulers, and denounced the often-repeated idea that the state 'granted' the church freedom of worship.

In the 1960s, churches had been mainly European-led. As this changed, ethnicity played a role in appointments, but in this domain, selection processes favoured less confrontational (and fewer Kikuyu) figures. The first African archbishop of the (Anglican) Church of the Province of Kenya was Festus (Festo) Olang', chosen in 1970. Olang', a non-confrontational Luhya, was preferred for the post over Bishop Obadiah Kariuki (Kenyatta's brother-in-law), in part because he was not Kikuyu and the Church wished to keep some distance from the government.[102] The Presbyterian Church of East Africa (PCEA), in contrast, with its 'home' in Central Province, remained Kikuyu led and Kikuyu dominated. In the Catholic Church, the pope appointed Archbishop Maurice Otunga as Kenya's first cardinal in 1973. Otunga, also Luhya, also had a humble approach. By 1976, however, frustration at the direction of social change and at Kenya's leadership was growing. Gradually, the churches assumed a more critical role. Outspoken clerics Okullu and Gitari both became bishops in 1974–5. In 1977, long before the schism of 1986, the NCCK declared itself a 'forum for alternative political viewpoints' in the absence of other parties, challenged Anyona's detention and called for a ceiling on land holdings.[103]

Although Christianity dominated political and social discourse, between 6 and 8 per cent of Kenya's population was Muslim.[104] In the mid-1970s, in line with the growing wealth and influence of Islam after the oil crisis, this community became more politically active. More coastal students were studying at Islamic universities in the Middle East, returning to disseminate fundamentalist perspectives on Islam. In 1973, a new umbrella body to represent Muslim interests was founded, the Supreme Council of Kenya Muslims (Supkem). Supkem was led by MPs and by the Central Bank's deputy governor, and was strongly pro-government. It was a new part of Kenyatta's top-down patron–client structure and was designed to play a similar role to the tribal unions of the upcountry communities. It too supported the separation of 'Church' and State.[105]

The Media

The media in the 1970s remained relatively open but self-censoring, and the government allowed little criticism into the country. Foreign newspapers containing critical articles were intercepted on arrival, and foreign correspondents who strayed too far were deported. Moi continued to make it plain that the government would not tolerate 'destructive criticism' from the media, local or foreign. Domestic television and radio remained government-controlled. All content was sanitised, and the Voice of Kenya was known ironically in the National Assembly as the 'Voice of Provincial Commissioners'.

The *Nation* papers now slightly outsold the *Standard* stable, though the *Nation*'s reputation was hurt by its misstep after the Kariuki murder. There was also the *Sunday Post*, East Africa's oldest Sunday newspaper, until its closure in 1974. The *Weekly Review*, launched by Hilary Ng'weno in February 1975, only days before Kariuki's murder, was the sole source of analytical – though rarely investigative – political journalism. The NCCK also published its monthly magazines *Target* and *Lengo*, which were occasionally critical on social issues. In 1977, the press presence was enhanced with the arrival of the *Nairobi Times*, a new daily launched by Ng'weno, though it did not last long.

Western views of Kenya's press were surprisingly positive – the *Guardian*, for example, called Kenya's press 'black Africa's only truly free press' in 1977.[106] Western journalists preferred to base themselves in Nairobi, since it had the best transport and information links in the region and the most congenial lifestyle. The space for dissent was limited, though. No criticism was tolerated, however slight, of the president. Permanent Secretary for Information and Broadcasting Darius Mbela actively instructed editors how to run their newspapers, and many times, ministers and civil servants ordered stories to be buried or changed. On one occasion, police arrested a *Nation* editor simply for reporting what had been said in Parliament. None of this was reported in the local press.[107]

In reality, the only factor keeping press freedom alive was the hostility between the *Nation* (once more edited by George Githii from 1972 until 1977) and the pro-'family' *Standard*. Both were linked to the business and political elites, but reflected different wings of the coalition. In early 1976, in an attempt to take control of the *Nation*, the 'family' sought to install Kenyatta's favourite nephew, 31-year-old Ngengi Muigai, at the top of the Nation Group in Kenya, which would have given them control of both national newspapers. However, concerned about the impact on press freedom and the commercial future of the company, the *Nation*'s owner, the Aga Khan, backed by his managers and the Moi–Njonjo–Kibaki axis, successfully resisted Kenyatta's request.[108]

'Tribal' Unions

Ethnic or 'tribal' unions, self-help civil society organisations to develop their home districts, sustain community identities and represent the interests of their ethnic groups in national affairs, had been a collective response to urbanisation in the mid-colonial period. The Luo Union had been one of the first and most influential, and the New Akamba Union had also proved successful as a local development agency in Ukambani. There was also a less well-known Abaluhya Association, a Kalenjin Association and a Mijikenda Union. These national-level 'ethnic voices' also helped small businesses, sponsored football teams and organised *harambees*. In urban areas, they sat alongside the numerous small clan and locational committees, which each offered communal solidarity and *harambee* support to group members in distress.[109]

In the late 1970s, partly in reaction to the decline of KANU, the ethnic unions began to represent their communities more actively in the conflict over Kenya's future direction. In 1973, the Kikuyu, Embu and Meru had established their own union, GEMA (see Chapter 5). The activities of all unions had a political context, since any group mobilising resources, offering leadership positions and able to direct its supporters became politicised. But GEMA was the most powerful. It openly declared itself for a Kikuyu succession to Kenyatta, and suggested that in the KANU elections, all seats bar that of the president should be contested (i.e. that Moi should be opposed). Moi replied combatively, suggesting 'Welfare organisations should serve *wananchi* in their areas, but should not be involved in political matters,' or they would be banned.[110] Moi and Njonjo saw GEMA as a clear threat to their plans.

The Luo Union was also a political tool, for different reasons. Luo politics remained dominated by the Odinga issue, with supporters and opponents skirmishing at every opportunity. Although Odinga was elected KANU chairman in Siaya District in 1975 and again in 1976, party headquarters and the registrar refused to ratify his election. The Luo Union experienced regular pro- and anti-Odinga intrigues. In April 1977, the majority of Luo politicians issued the 'Oyugis declaration', calling on the Luo to accept Odinga as their spokesman once more. Omolo-Okero was active in February–June 1978 in countering this on behalf of the existing Luo leadership. In April 1978, nearly half a million Luo joined a loyalty delegation to Kenyatta in Nakuru. It was organised by the Luo Union as part of a strategy of reconciliation between Odinga and Kenyatta, but was taken over and its purpose reversed by Nyanza PC Isaiah Cheluget and loyalist Luo and Gusii leaders. These skirmishes ended rather with the ousting of the elected

Union leadership by a pro-government team. There would be no reconciliation with Odinga while Kenyatta lived.

At every level, ethnicity remained a key frame of reference and attribute for Kenyans, visible in names, appearance, skin colour and accents. Even football was organised on ethnic lines, as many club names directly reflected ethnicity (such as Abaluhya Football Club or AFC Leopards) or were associated with one part of the country (Gor Mahia and the Luo). During the 1970s, the government tried to detribalise sport, but the association endured.

Surveys and analysts noted a high degree of ethnic hostility between Kikuyu and Luo, which appeared to reflect events since independence.[111] The divisions of the 1960s were becoming institutionalised. A feeling of marginalisation amongst the Luo deepened, reinforcing an alienation from other settled agricultural communities and particularly from the Kikuyu, which left them in a unique position of both real and perceived disadvantage.[112]

Cankers within the State

Kenya was now a place of increasing corruption and inequality. Civil servants enthusiastically exploited the opportunity that the Ndegwa Report had given them to engage in business. The Kikuyu-dominated *wabenzi* (Mercedes-Benz people) prospered, protected by the state and unrestrained by Parliament. The 'action' was now in resource extraction: poaching, charcoal and mining.

Poaching

The 1970s were the worst period of poaching in Kenya's history. With the support of senior government figures, Kenya's abundant wildlife was slaughtered for the export of ivory and skins to the Middle and Far East. In mid-1973, at least 500 elephants were killed legally each month. However, receipts in destinations such as Hong Kong suggested that at least 345 tonnes of ivory had been exported from Kenya in 1973, indicated the death of at least 15,000 elephants in a year, three times the official number.[113] There were wide discrepancies between estimates of the number of elephants left, from 150,000 to only 40,000. Ten thousand rhinos were killed during 1973–9, 80 per cent of the remaining population. Sport hunting was still legal, but in 1973, Chief Game Warden John Mutinda finally withdrew all elephant-hunting licences. Western concern over poaching was rising, with television reports and articles devoted to Kenya's problem and its causes in state corruption. There were high-profile arrests, including a Somali picked up with the tusks of 525 elephants in his baggage en route to Hong Kong.

Eventually, Tourism Minister Juxon Shako had banned ivory export by anyone except the government in August 1974. However, exports continued. One problem was that the Kenyatta family itself was implicated in both poaching and ivory exports. Margaret Kenyatta, Kenyatta's daughter, was chairman of the United African Company, one of at least 10 companies exporting ivory despite the ban.[114] Ivory could earn Ksh300 (US$36) per kilogram, making one elephant worth thousands of dollars. Other valuable items included zebra pelts (5,000 of these animals were shot illegally within 320 miles of Nairobi in six months during 1975) and colobus monkey skins. In 1975, two men were found in possession of 26,000 colobus monkey skins (more than the total remaining population today).[115] However, dealers could buy both police inaction and the needed documentation, of which there was an inexhaustible supply. The monkey skin owners were acquitted after they produced 'valid' permits.

It was widely believed that much of the poaching that decimated the elephant and rhino populations was organised and carried out by the Ministry of Tourism and Wildlife. An expatriate official identified both assistant ministers – one being J. M. Kariuki – as buying ivory direct from game department headquarters for export.[116] There were later suggestions that officials, police sharpshooters and the Kenyatta family were involved in a vertically integrated poaching cartel. A Samburu MP alleged in Parliament that there were in fact very few poachers *outside* the ministry. In 1976, Parliament established a Select Committee to probe malpractices at the ministry, but nothing came of it in the face of state obstruction.

In May 1977, all sport hunting was banned. However, the loss of hunting revenue further damaged the ability of the ministry to combat poaching. Bizarrely, Mau Mau veterans, denied most forms of recompense for their losses, had been allowed to poach since the 1960s, through the issue of 'collectors' permits', which allowed them to carry as much ivory as they wished, under the polite fiction that it was of Mau Mau vintage. These permits were finally cancelled in 1977 under pressure from environmentalists.[117] In the same year the African elephant was listed under Appendix II of the Convention on International Trade in Endangered Species (CITES).

Destruction of Kenya's tree cover, soil erosion and changing rainfall patterns also became public issues. The felling of trees for land settlement and the production of charcoal were particular problems. Charcoal was now worth K£1,000 per tonne in the Middle East, and 80,000 tonnes a year was exported by 1975. Eventually, after dockworkers refused to load more ships, the government was forced to introduce a total ban on charcoal exports, to replace the partial ban in force (which meant that only senior figures such as PCs could carry out the trade).

Growing Corruption

Kenyatta's fading grip made corruption both easier and safer. Civil servants' freedom to conduct business allowed officials to reward themselves and to misuse state resources for private gain. Bribery was now required to obtain most licences, permits or quotas, particularly for foreigners. By 1975, the government itself was inveighing against the collapse in civil service mores. The Ndegwa Report was widely blamed:

> Overnight, Government offices became 'official' quarters for commercial transactions and heavy private deals. Government vehicles became means of private interests. Government 'stamps' and licenses became commercialised…Massive corruption had finally crept with devastating impact into one of the most prestigious of Civil Services in Africa.[118]

Parastatals were particularly prone to abuse, especially the EAC's organisations, as the victim was remote.[119] For different reasons, the big urban councils were even more corrupt and incompetent than central government, since they were less internationally visible and accounting standards were lower; Mombasa Municipal Council was dissolved in 1977, while in the same year the first probes began into Nairobi City Council's procurement practices.

Land grabbing – the process of selling or giving state land to private individuals, to develop or sell – was becoming more common, though it was less politically charged than it was to become under Moi, when the supply of undeveloped land had run out. When Kenyatta's nephew Muigai married Isaiah Mathenge's daughter in 1976, for example, Kenyatta's wedding present was a large tract of government land. Such technically legal processes were supplemented illegally in most local lands offices, as cartels stole land, destroyed and forged documents, and sold the resulting plots on to others.

In August 1975, the British *Sunday Times* ran a series of exposés of the avarice of the Kenyatta family. It detailed how the family had forced the sale of the Inchcape trading group (which included the Ford vehicle franchise) to a consortium including Udi Gecaga, Muigai and Kenyatta's son Peter Muigai Kenyatta, the price to be paid in instalments out of profits. The article included an excellent display of the Kenyatta family, which has been updated and extended in Figure 6.11. It further exposed the family's involvement in ivory exports, and the impossibility of collecting debts owed by the 'royal family', as they were now known. It also detailed how Kenyatta personally approved the purchase of large farms by his family, exempting them from review by land control boards. It listed the vast farms the family had acquired in the Rift Valley, including six farms owned by Kenyatta himself, a 26,000-acre farm owned by Mama Ngina in Kiambu, and her farm in Rongai next to Kenyatta's own.[120]

The *Sunday Times* described how Mama Ngina had been buying land on the coast that was used to build two hotels, while Kenyatta himself built Leopard Beach Hotel, which was registered in a Swiss company's name. It revealed that in 1972, Mombasa Municipal Council had waived all rates on properties owned by the president and his family, and had listed 11 more properties in the area. The paper also described how the family operated through overseas frontmen such as George Criticos and Asian lawyers and accountants. The international casinos were also of interest. In 1967, a company for Italian investors linked to the Mafia had established the Nairobi International Casino, with Fred Kubai and later Peter Muigai Kenyatta and James Gichuru as shareholders.[121] In 1973, it faced competition from another casino on the outskirts of Nairobi. The *Sunday Times* revealed that while Kenyatta's name did not appear on the registration papers, he owned the site and the building, and received a third of its profits.[122] Kenyatta's niece Beth Mugo, meanwhile, had become involved in the gemstone business, and had obtained the right to sell gems to foreigners at Nairobi airport.

Just as the Kenyatta family was becoming rich, so those close to Mzee also demonstrated their power. The *Sunday Times* named Coast PC Mahihu as owning

6.11: The Kenyatta family

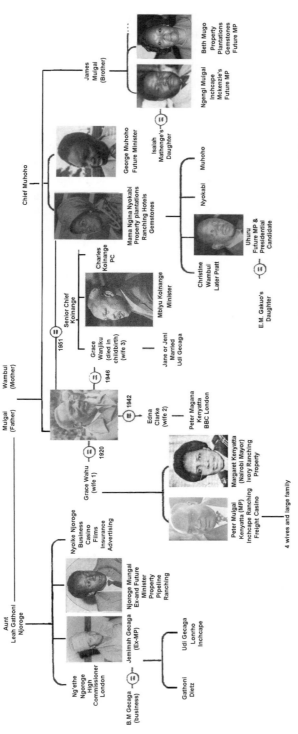

Source: *Sunday Times*, 17 August 1975 and subsequent information

the Bahari Beach Hotel and Rift Valley PC Mathenge as owning the Coral Beach Hotel. Eliud Wamae part-owned the Kenya Beach and the Ngong Hills hotels. John Michuki and Mugo, meanwhile, were involved with a German hotel group.

The backbench put up a determined but futile fight against this trend. In May 1975, in its post-Kariuki murder peak of independence, the Assembly defeated government opposition to establish a third anti-corruption Select Committee; Martin Shikuku became its chairman, and for the first time in Kenya's history, all its members – including minister Omolo-Okero – declared their wealth. However, the government soon undermined it, and on 24 June, Parliament killed the committee it had established only weeks before.[123] Parliament could no more control the elite's depredations than could the government itself. The Public Accounts Committee continued to castigate ministries for overspending against budgets, with the figure rising to US$13 million in 1974–5.[124] Ministries were criticised for failing to recover loans, bypassing tender procedures, misusing grants, uneconomic investments and poor accounting. Although lip service was paid to efficiency, the political will for root and branch reform was missing. The churches too complained at the growing 'get rich quick' culture and the damaging effects of corruption and nepotism, but the elite were beyond moral censure.

Patronage and nepotism were increasingly the way business was done. If you did not know someone, then business would be very difficult. It was common for politicians to ensure that allies, friends, relatives and people from the same ethnic group and sub-group as themselves received jobs or contracts, which would provide them with income and in turn buttress the politician's career. Indeed, it was almost essential that this happened: if everyone else was doing the same thing, failing to do so would disadvantage your community and weaken your finances and electoral viability. Ministers also prioritised government projects to assist their own constituencies or districts. It was common for water projects to be sited in the constituency of the water minister, roads in the district of the public works minister and so on. Kenyatta permitted this, as it stabilised and channelled conflict and patronage, and left him and the central bureaucracy as arbiters of who would gain and lose.

Elite Rule

Intertwined with the losing battle of those outside the government against corruption and poaching was the demand for greater equality in the distribution of the 'fruits of Uhuru'. All agreed that inequality was growing as fast as the economy, if not faster. The inner circles were becoming rich. There was a tight network of directorships and hidden interests that ran through virtually every major company with local ownership, linking it with one senior politician or another through nominee accounts, Asian supporters or overt directorships. This elite, particularly the Kikuyu, were notorious for their closed business practices, their love of golf and their emulation of colonial British behaviour. There was a growing alignment of political, administrative and economic power, creating something close to a ruling class for the first time. Although some saw all Kikuyu as exploiters, there were differences between northern

(Nyeri) and southern (Kiambu) Kikuyu, which widened after the Kariuki murder. Meanwhile, Kenyan society remained characterised at the top by the conspicuous consumption of the Europeans. Although most of the 50,000 Europeans in Kenya were now expatriate businessmen or diplomats and their families, fragments of the old settler culture endured.[125]

The close links between the business, political and security elites were shown in the ownership of a company called African Liaison & Consulting Services Limited, formed in 1977, whose directors were Gethi, Kanyotu, McKenzie and Julius Gecau, the managing director of Kenya Power and Lighting. Shareholders included Moi and Kibaki.[126] It was the pinnacle of Kenya's small security–political–executive complex, and it took a leading role in acquisitions and investments during the late 1970s and early 1980s. McKenzie's business interests were wide-ranging since his retirement: he sat on the boards of Kenya Airways, CMC Holdings and a dozen other companies. Kanyotu too was also involved in private business, possibly as a nominee for others, including Firestone, Sheraton Holdings and Sameer Investments, the business of Asian executive Naushad Merali. Njonjo, Gecau, Philip Ndegwa, Kariithi, Kiereini, Mungai and others also invested in a competing company named Heri Limited, which invested in vehicle franchises, property and the Stock Exchange.

Such wealth met with little public support, as Kenyans retained a strong egalitarian streak. Although wealth and exploitation were considered normal in the urban environment, rural elites who prospered too quickly and too openly sometimes found their cattle dead or their chickens stolen.[127] There was widespread dissatisfaction at the growing gap between rich and poor, and had such issues ever been put to the public in an election, it is likely that they would have supported radical change. Egalitarianism was still popular in Parliament. In 1974, for example, Mwangale led a call for a 10,000-acre maximum land holding. Rubia attacked 'land grabbing' and the ownership of more than three farms or businesses (though he himself would have exceeded this level). Parliament was fatally weakened, however. The state was set on its course, and both Western development orthodoxy and personal advantage cautioned against such redistributive measures. While politicians often referred to the *wananchi* as the justification for their conservative attitudes and decisions, few politicians were willing to allow the peasants actually to make such decisions, and they much preferred to buy their support with gifts and promises.

In January 1978, a first sign emerged that this might change. Ministers, MPs and civil servants were summoned to a meeting at the Kenya Institute of Administration, at which Moi represented Kenyatta. The meeting signalled the beginning of a reappraisal within the state, and an acceptance of the growing time bombs of unemployment, inequality and land hunger. The conference's speeches and resolutions defended what it called the government's 'participative centralism' strategy, but accepted that public accountability was in decline.[128] It also reasserted the 'Africa first' model, calling for more Kenyanisation and more stringent controls on foreigners entering the country. In the event, little changed before Kenyatta's death, but Moi took some of these themes forward.

Regional and International Relations

Kenya's strong security forces, non-interventionism and policy of armed neutrality had left it the only country in the region not fighting a war, either internally or with a neighbour. Even so, the late 1970s were one of the most difficult times in Kenya's history, as most of its neighbours collapsed, forcing the country into formidable expenditure on the military. Military and foreign policy issues also grew in significance.

Relations with the UK remained warm, but there was no longer the special relationship of the 1960s. Britons continued to vote with their feet, with 6,000 to 10,000 leaving every year. In contrast, relations with the US warmed. Henry Kissinger visited Kenya for talks with Kenyatta, culminating in the countries' first military agreement in August 1976, although trade remained modest and few American chose Kenya as their permanent home.

Relations with South Africa remained contentious. In 1976, Kenya boycotted the Montreal Olympic Games when the International Olympic Committee refused to ban New Zealand, whose rugby team was touring South Africa. However, pragmatic considerations and personal relations led Kenyatta and Njonjo to follow a parallel policy of quiet *détente* with South Africa, which infuriated Foreign Minister Waiyaki.[129] Kenya welcomed Portugal's belated decolonisation, and Kenyatta assisted in the peace deal that paved the way for independence in Angola in 1974–5.

The Entebbe Incident

There were more problems closer to home, in Uganda. On 27 June 1976, a plane flying from Tel Aviv was hijacked by Popular Front for the Liberation of Palestine (PFLP) terrorists. Idi Amin (a Muslim) allowed the PFLP to land and set up a base in the old Entebbe airport in Uganda. By 2 July, the hijackers had freed the non-Jewish and elderly prisoners, leaving 105 Jewish hostages. It then became known that Amin was not just providing a place for the drama to play out, but was actively assisting it as a means to gain prestige. He had provided extra weapons to the terrorists, allowed more colleagues to join them, helped draft their demands, and was jointly guarding the victims with his own troops.

The Israelis decided to act. On the night of 3–4 July 1976, Israeli commandos, paratroopers and planes attacked Entebbe and freed the hostages. They killed several dozen Ugandan soldiers and destroyed 13 Ugandan fighter planes on the ground. However, a direct return flight to Israel was logistically impossible, and, despite their lack of diplomatic relations, the Israelis were allowed to land in Nairobi to refuel and drop off their wounded. Israeli intelligence figures helped organise the attack from Nairobi. According to some, this included Israeli commandos operating from Kenya and the refuelling of the attack planes before as well as after the raid.[130] McKenzie was a key figure in organising the raid. It is almost certain that Njonjo and GSU commander Gethi, who had been trained in Israel, also helped McKenzie. UK intelligence author Chapman Pincher later suggested that Kenyatta did not even know of the planned raid, but once it was executed could do nothing – to reveal his ignorance would have exposed his weakness.[131] At an OAU heads of state summit, Moi called the Israelis aggressors, and complained of 'blatant violation of our airspace'. He may have been unaware of the truth.[132] In contrast, grateful US Secretary of State Kissinger offered Kenya his support in handling any repercussions with Uganda and positioned an aircraft carrier group off Mombasa to deter Amin.[133]

What is less well known is that this was the second incident involving Kenya and the PFLP that year. In January 1976, three Palestinians had entered Kenya and set up Russian hand-launched anti-aircraft missiles at the perimeter of the airport, before the expected arrival of a jet belonging to Israeli airline El Al. However, Israeli intelligence had alerted the GSU, and they captured the men before they could fire. Their vehicle contained machine guns, grenades and pistols that appeared to have come from Uganda. Two more suspects were arrested later that week. These people were amongst those the Entebbe hostage-takers wanted freed.[134] One reason why the Kenyans were happy to help Israel in the Entebbe raid was this evidence of Ugandan complicity in terrorism inside Kenya.

Two years after the Entebbe raid, on 24 May 1978, Bruce McKenzie was murdered, in circumstances that suggested revenge. He had visited Uganda in a private plane for business reasons and had met Amin at State House, Entebbe. On the way back, the plane exploded in the air, destroyed by a time bomb. There are several theories behind the murder. Most likely, it was Amin's revenge; according to his assistant, Amin had given McKenzie a stuffed lion's head to take back to Nairobi. This may have been the bomb.[135] It is also possible that it was a Palestinian revenge attack for Entebbe (although the Palestinians denied it).[136] Amin too denied involvement, claiming that McKenzie had been a friend. Others pointed fingers at a business deal gone sour with one of Amin's lieutenants.

The Collapse of the EAC

By this time, the East African Community had collapsed. During 1975–7, all the central services broke apart. In 1976, Uganda established its own airline to compete with the insolvent East African Airways, and in February 1977 Kenya set up its own state-owned Kenya Airways, with two leased planes. East African Railways had been carved up in 1975, leading to the creation of Kenya Railways (KR) and the Kenya Ports Authority (KPA) – running Mombasa port – and Kenya Posts and Telecommunications Corporation (KPTC) followed. The same process occurred in the private sector, as East African Breweries became Kenya Breweries, for example. It was a bitter divide. Tanzania closed its border with Kenya in February 1977, and all three countries seized EAC assets on their soil. Following the failure to agree a new Community budget, in July 1977, Kenya withdrew its workers from the EAC's Arusha headquarters, and on 1 August Nyerere closed it down. The Community was dead before its tenth birthday.[137]

There were many reasons for its failure. In terms of the Community's economics and institutions, the transfer tax (as intended) fostered national-level duplication in industrial development. In some sectors, such as tourism and road transport, Kenya benefitted disproportionately. Another problem was the increasing role of state trading corporations, which as state bodies 'could be directed and might be expected even without direction to discriminate in favour of domestic suppliers'.[138] This undermined a key objective of the treaty. The states failed either to allow *laissez-faire* private enterprise or to plan cooperatively. The Community also required settlement of intra-country trade balances in foreign currency. With the balance of payments problems caused by the oil price shocks, import restrictions were applied to EAC countries as well. This led to restrictions on the transfer of funds to the headquarters of the common services, which disrupted these central bodies.

The key problem was political, however, since the institution relied on good relations between the three presidents, which had ceased to exist after the 1971 Amin coup. The EAC secretariat's powers were limited, and the Community worked on unanimity, not majority rule. With relations frozen between Uganda and Tanzania, the three leaders – collectively the executive authority of the EAC – never met again. Relations between Kenya and Tanzania were hostile by 1975, while Uganda was in open confrontation with both Kenya and Tanzania. Njonjo told Parliament in 1975 that the EAC had already failed, and advised that it should be dissolved.

Neither could the treaty do anything about the divide between Kenya's capitalism and Tanzania's socialism. A third of Kenya's exports were going to its EAC neighbours, one of the best examples of intra-African trade on the continent, but the imbalances this created were not appreciated. The tendency to base regional investments in Kenya led to the perception that multinationals were exploiting Tanzania. Overall, the three partners behaved as if the Community was a zero sum game whereby one country's gain was at the expense of the rest. Given that Kenya's growth was partially driven by its embrace of foreign investment, in contrast to Tanzania's, 'the equalising mechanisms of the Treaty were attempting to swim against a strongly flowing stream.'[139] Together these issues were too much for the Community to bear.

With the end of the EAC, Kenya returned to the splendid isolation policy that its collective psyche seemed to prefer. Njonjo and McKenzie celebrated with champagne on 29 June 1977.[140] Kenya, cushioned by the coffee boom, was sanguine about the collapse, underestimating the impact of the loss of the Tanzania and Zambia export markets. The failure of the Community did more damage to Kenya's economy than expected. Kenya's trade with Tanzania fell from US$55 million in 1976 to US$5 million in 1978.[141] It has been alleged that Njonjo and McKenzie had acted as 'agents of British capital' whose economic interests lay in the collapse of the EAC.[142] It is certainly possible that McKenzie and Njonjo encouraged the break-up so as not (in their view) to delay Kenya's progress. However, Britain had always encouraged regional institutions in East Africa, and British interests in Kenya by the late 1970s were minimal, a fact that Kenyans often failed to recognise.

Encircled and Isolated

Uganda, meanwhile, became more brutal and chaotic, with extrajudicial killings common. Unable to sustain the economy after the Asian exodus and Western ostracism, Amin protected himself through loyal troops, 'black magic', torture and mass murder. Amnesty International estimated that he was responsible for the murder of half a million people in his eight-year reign.

In February 1976, Amin laid claim to much of western Kenya (trying to reverse the 1902 boundary changes). Kenya reacted aggressively, and Kenyatta led rallies nationwide promising to defend Kenyan soil. After the disappearance of Kenyan students and the nationalisation without compensation of many Kenyan assets, Kenya recalled all its nationals studying in Uganda. The sole supplier of fuel and other essentials to its landlocked neighbour, Kenya cut off fuel supplies for non-payment, and in response Uganda launched minor incursions into Kenyan territory. There was a troop build-up on the border following the Entebbe crisis as Amin considered a strike against Kenya, and reports of massacres of Kenyans inside Uganda. However, quiet US support deterred Amin and the OAU brokered a settlement in August 1976, which averted war.

Kenya also faced problems in the north. Relations with Ethiopia were good until 1974. In 1974, however, Ethiopia experienced a military coup, which left the aged Emperor Haile Selassie powerless. A military council took power and developed close relations with the USSR. In 1977, the Ethiopian revolution became more radical, nationalising businesses and land. The military government (the Derg) engaged in mass murder to secure its position and introduced a radical Marxist-Leninist ideology. In April 1977, the Ethiopians closed all American military facilities and military relations ended.

Somalia was even more of a concern. In 1969, Siad Barre had seized power in a coup, but the new regime had maintained its predecessor's policy of avoiding further confrontation with Kenya. The independence of Djibouti in 1977 upset the delicate balance in the region, as Djibouti was part of greater Somalia for the Somali, but was also Ethiopia's key port and railway terminus. Once the USSR began to provide military assistance to Ethiopia, relations deteriorated sharply. On 2 July 1977, Somalia invaded Ethiopia, and the Ogaden war began. Over the next few months, Somalia conquered much of eastern Ethiopia. Kenya protested vigorously, fearful of Somali expansionism and Kenyan forces engaged with the Somali military several times in 1977. The Kenyans also gave military assistance to rebels fighting the Barre regime. In April 1978, a Somali colonel and his allies, implicated in an unsuccessful coup, fled to Kenya, where Kenyatta gave them sanctuary. The colonel claimed that he met Kenyatta and Moi several times, and that Moi 'facilitated the airlift of Somalia fighters through Kenya to Ethiopian bases'.[143] With Ethiopia also a Soviet client, Somalia's relationship with the USSR soon soured, and in November 1977 Somalia expelled its Soviet advisers and sought assistance from Muslim states instead. An Ethiopian and Cuban army counterattacked in February 1978 and by April had recovered all the lost territory. At the same time though, Ethiopia faced open revolt in Eritrea, which limited its capacity to continue the war. Eventually, the fighting ended, with little gain for either side.

Security Developments

Facing a hostile environment, Kenya's military spending increased sharply in the 1970s. Once Selassie had fallen, Kenya was encircled by collapsing regimes (Uganda), old enemies (Somalia) and socialist states (Ethiopia and Tanzania). All had larger armies or better equipment, or both.[144] Although Uganda was unlikely to strike alone, because of Kenya's supply stranglehold, the Kenyans still feared a Somali tank assault, which could seize North-Eastern Province in days.

In September 1974, Kenyatta commissioned the British to conduct a defence review. It concluded that Kenya needed to increase the size of its army and to re-equip. The military was well trained, but was too small and lacked essential equipment. The review recommended a major increase in air force size and capability, and that the army be expanded to two brigades and acquire its first tanks and field artillery.[145] The consequence was a huge growth in military capability (and cost) between 1975 and 1982. The army doubled in size from 6,500 to 13,000, and defence spending rose from 5–6 per cent in the 1960s to 15 per cent of the budget by 1978.

The US now became Kenya's main military partner. Following two years of negotiations, in August 1976 Kenya entered a US$75 million agreement with the US, its first major defence agreement with a country other than the UK. Kenya agreed to host a US military presence in the region, and to provide access to Mombasa harbour for the US navy, in return for which the US would supply advanced military equipment, training and assistance. This included US$65 million of credit to buy 12 new Northrop F-5 fighters, giving the air force better interceptor capability. The F-5s arrived in 1978 and remained in service until the turn of the century. Kenya also bought 32 Hughes helicopters, which arrived in 1980–1.

Kenya continued to retain military links with the British, though these were limited by the lack of British generosity on terms. Kenya purchased more than 60 Vickers battle tanks, 12 Hawk trainers and six Buffalo transport planes in the late 1970s. The British army continued to train Kenyan officers and Kenya hosted annual British training exercises and a small permanent liaison team at the Nanyuki base. These faced nationalist hostility, however. COTU, for example, called in 1975 for the withdrawal of all foreign troops.

The Kenyan army was still observing quotas on military recruitment, but the rules had changed. By the late 1970s, 19 per cent of the army was Kikuyu and 12 per cent Kamba, with all other communities below 10 per cent.

While the army remained relatively apolitical and balanced between Kikuyu and Kamba, the police were both politicised and divided over the succession. Many senior officers were associated with the anti-Moi forces. At the top, Police Commissioner Bernard Hinga was an ally of Mungai, while Rift Valley Assistant Commissioner James Mungai was also a Kikuyu anti-Moi man. In contrast, the 2,000-strong GSU, though predominantly Kikuyu, was led by Gethi, an ally of

Njonjo and Moi. The head of Special Branch, Kanyotu, also supported the Moi–Njonjo team, as did CID head Nderi. In contrast, the recently established 250-man anti-stock-theft unit included an Israeli-trained team with military equipment and parachute experience; 80 per cent of the team came from Kiambu, and it appeared to be designed as a 'family' counterweight to the GSU.[146] These were dangerous times, but no one would strike as long as Kenyatta was alive. Once he was dead, all bets were off.

The Succession Crisis, 1976–7

As Kenyatta's death became imminent, the inner councils and many other Kikuyu showed increasing concern over the possible succession of Vice-President Moi. Since 1968, the Constitution had specified that, on the president's death, the vice-president had 90 days as acting president before an election had to be held. The position of Moi – the loyal compromise candidate – had become increasingly secure. He had the support of key figures in the state apparatus and of influential businessmen. Most Western diplomats believed he represented Kenya's best chance of stability. His alliance with Njonjo made it unlikely that he could be bypassed, defeated or intimidated into standing down. To replace him, the Constitution had to be amended, which required at least the neutrality of Kenyatta and a two-thirds majority in the Assembly. Nonetheless, tales of impending crisis were common.[147] Moi represented important interests, but had little executive power and was kept outside the inner counsels. Few could imagine that the succession could be anything but a Kikuyu affair, with Moi a stopgap, and there were concerns that a contested transition would inspire violence. This was worsened by Kenyatta's reluctance to anoint anyone – including Moi – as his successor.

Moi and the Kiambu 'Family'

Moi's greatest assets were the support of Njonjo and the Kikuyu technocracy, and the absence of a single clear opponent. Most of the competitors of the 1960s were dead or out of contention. Ngei had the will but his questionable financial position made him an unlikely choice. Kibaki was a potential contender but appeared to be backing Moi. Amongst the 'family' itself, Mungai was the leading light. He clearly wished to challenge for the presidency, backed by the family and business interests including Lonrho (led by Udi Gecaga), and Inchcape (led by Muigai), but as a nominated MP was formally ineligible. Ex-Nairobi Mayor Margaret Kenyatta appeared unwilling to take on the challenge. Kenyatta's son Peter Muigai was also a MP but not a national figure. There was only one family member with both the power and position to seize the throne: Mbiyu Koinange.

An enigmatic figure throughout the 1970s, the role of Koinange has been the subject of much dispute. Some believed he was the power behind the throne and a possible successor to Kenyatta. Others saw him as Kenyatta's court jester and friend, whose role was to support him and to 'tell traditional stories by the fire'.[148] Kenyatta and Koinange had much in common. Both were elderly and from Kiambu. Like Kenyatta, Koinange had been one of the first overseas-educated Kenyans. They had become friends in 1936, when Koinange was on a scholarship to Cambridge.[149] Koinange was also Kenyatta's brother-in-law. He had been a minister since 1963, but it was as minister of state in the Office of the President from 1970 to 1978 that Koinange's role became the subject of controversy. Despite his soft-spoken style, the unofficial opposition hated him for his tight control of the provincial administration. Although Koinange was never elected to any KANU post, he attended all KANU Governing Council and NEC meetings, without anyone risking a comment on his presence. He was with the president at all times, whether Kenyatta was receiving foreign ambassadors or traditional dancers.

Koinange was not averse to using his power. He was unopposed in the 1974 election, as his opponent had been arrested the night before the parliamentary nominations (and was released as soon as they were completed). His style was one of silence, conspiracy and personal authority. However, there are two sides to every story. The Koinange family benefited little financially from his position. Geoffrey Kariithi reports that Kenyatta diligently kept their personal relationship apart from matters of state and that Kenyatta would not delegate the most sensitive files to him. 'People who say Koinange ruled for Kenyatta don't know what they were talking about.'[150]

The pressure on Moi grew, trying to force him to protest, resign from his post or otherwise disgrace himself. He was regularly harassed when travelling through Nakuru by Rift Valley police boss James Mungai. Mungai mounted roadblocks and even sent police to the vice-president's Kabarak home to search it for arms. Mungai was reported to have physically assaulted Moi at least twice.[151] PC Mathenge also harassed Moi, searching his motorcade when it traversed the province. In October 1975, at the height of the repression of dissidents, responsibility for the police and the GSU was transferred from Moi's Home Affairs Ministry to Koinange's Office of the President.[152] Odinga had been stripped of his powers in the same way in 1964. Nevertheless, Moi bided his time, accepting the humiliation. As heir-apparent, he had only to endure.

The Change the Constitution Movement

At the end of September 1976, the challenge to Moi became open. In two huge rallies in Nakuru on 26 September and Limuru on 3 October 1976, ministers in the Gema inner circle demanded a change to the Constitution to remove the provision for the vice-president's automatic succession. Their focus was openly on Moi, whom they believed (for reasons including his abilities and ethnic origins) to be unfit to be Kenya's president. More than 20 MPs attended the Nakuru meeting, including ministers Angaine (Meru), Gichuru (Kikuyu), Ngei (Kamba) and Towett (Kalenjin), plus Njoroge Mungai, Karume and several Gusii MPs.[153] It was fronted by Nakuru strongman and GEMA Organising Secretary Kihika Kimani. Odinga's ally Achieng-Oneko also attended, suggesting an emerging alliance between the

Luo ex-KPU team and the Kikuyu elite based on their shared dislike of Njonjo and Moi, whom they blamed above all for their detentions and harassment.[154] The aim of the movement was to use a series of meetings as a springboard to raise the issue in Parliament, after which they would propose a constitutional amendment to share power amongst ministers. Ngei put their case for change bluntly when he said, 'If you give me that period [90 days as acting president] . . . I can really teach you a lesson and I would assure you it would not be a pleasant lesson.'[155]

But Moi had many defenders. Kibaki and Njonjo were his allies, as were key bureaucrats Kariithi and Kiereini (all Kikuyu). The 'ex-KADU' communities were with him, as were many Luhya. Close allies included coastal leaders Robert Matano (Mijikenda) and Shariff Nassir (Arab) and Maasai leaders Oloitipitip and Tipis. Another key supporter was Nyachae, who as PC for Central Province, 'used his position to frustrate the change-the-constitution group by denying them licences to hold rallies in that province' after their first meeting.[156] In many ways, the Moi faction, although they later presented themselves as the 'underdogs', were the incumbents while the 'family' were the challengers. The views of the population were, of course, irrelevant. Kenyatta's all-important views on the matter were also unknown; he characteristically played his cards close to his chest.

Kenyatta said nothing in public about the open rift in his government. Moi too remained silent, but on 6 October, Njonjo issued a statement from Nakuru (where Kenyatta was) warning, 'it is a criminal offence for any person to compass, imagine, devise or intend the death or deposition of the President.' This would be punishable by a mandatory death sentence, and 'Anyone who raises such matters at public meetings . . . does so at his peril.'[157] Though the legality of his statement was very questionable, the movement's leaders were forced onto the defensive. They issued a pledge of loyalty on 7 October, refuting Njonjo's arguments and claiming their proposals enjoyed public support. On 9 October, with Lonrho backing the movement, the pro-family *Standard* called the attorney-general's statement 'The Big Bluff'. The *Nation*, aligned with Njonjo, pronounced the Change the Constitution group's actions to be 'on the borderline of treason'.[158]

On 8 October, after feverish organisation, Oloitipitip called a press conference where he claimed that he had the signatures of 98 MPs to a document opposing the amendment. His list included, he claimed, 10 Cabinet ministers, amongst whom he named Onyonka (Gusii), Kiano (Kikuyu) and Daniel Mutinda (Kamba).[159] The movement's leaders now tried to get those who had put their names to the 'Group of 98' document to withdraw them, and the *Standard*'s headline on 9 October was '40 MPs Quit the 'Other Faction''.[160] Amid frantic manoeuvring, the movement held its climactic rally in Meru on 10 October, led by Kimani and Gichuru. Angaine, Ngei, Karume and Mungai again all spoke in favour of change and a dozen other MPs attended.[161] Kimani criticised a 'shadow government' within the state, and linked their demands to the suffering of the Kikuyu during Mau Mau, castigating their opponents as collaborators.[162] Mungai and Ngei also linked the succession with the struggle for independence, suggesting they would never allow Kenya to be ruled by someone who had not 'fought for freedom'.

Everything now turned on Kenyatta's wishes. Following their third rally, on 8 October, the Change the Constitution leaders had presented their case to Kenyatta in Nakuru. However, reports suggest that Kenyatta scolded them and refused to allow them to use his name in their campaign. Another rally in Mombasa (apparently to be addressed also by Odinga), was banned by PC Mahihu.[163] On 11 October 1976, the Cabinet met in Nakuru and endorsed Njonjo's ruling, which it now described as 'its earlier statement'. The movement had misjudged Kenyatta's reluctance to enshrine Kiambu dominance. Kenyatta's ambivalence, Njonjo's support and popular discontent at instituting a monarchical system left Moi still holding the vice-presidency when the inevitable happened.

Party Elections, 1976–7

Nonetheless, the struggle continued. KANU had last held national elections in 1966 to drive out Odinga. In December 1976–January 1977, as a continuation of the struggle over the succession, the party finally held national elections. Starting at local, then sub-branch (constituency), then branch (district) level, party members selected new officers as a prelude to the first National Delegates' Conference (NDC) in 10 years. The elections divided the ruling party into two rival camps, known as 'KANU A' and 'KANU B', associated respectively with the Kiambu elite and the Moi team. As in 1964–6, both factions sought to establish nationwide followings, despite there being no obvious ideological differences between the tickets. Although ethnicity remained the most important single factor, with most Kikuyu, Embu, Meru and Kamba politicians supporting the Change the Constitution forces, KANU A and KANU B both constructed national coalitions. Odinga was again barred from contesting. Mungai beat Rubia to become Nairobi branch chairman, but the pro-Moi forces overcame their challengers in districts such as Mombasa and Laikipia. Moi's allies Matano (acting secretary-general), Tipis (treasurer) and Nathan Munoko (national organising secretary) assisted significantly in this. There were numerous complaints of rigging and electoral abuses.

With the branch elections completed, attention moved to the showdown at the national level. Towett took on Moi for KANU's vice-presidency, while Gichuru or Mungai was slated to contest the post of national chairman against Kibaki. Matano was expected to lose his post to Ngei or Muliro from the Change the Constitution team. Both sides prepared and spent feverishly. The elections were due to begin on 3 April 1977, but were again cancelled without explanation, this time over the radio the night before their commencement, although the delegates were already in Nairobi. Three possible reasons have been advanced for the decision. The most likely was a sudden deterioration in Kenyatta's health. Another was that chaos was about to ensue, as there was no agreed list of party delegates. The final suggestion was that the cancellation came because the Change the Constitution group realised that they were going to lose.[164]

As a result, the two factions never openly contended for control of the party or the succession, and paralysis continued to cripple the state's operations. The bitterness between the factions was open, however. Relations between Njonjo and Mungai were so poor that Kenyatta's bodyguard Wanyoike Thungu had to intervene to prevent a fist-fight between the two in August 1977.[165] The struggles between the factions continued in the press, Parliament, local government and the Cabinet for another 18 months, but Moi remained vice-president.

Kenyatta's Death and the Succession, August–October 1978

Time had run out. On 21 August 1978, Kenyatta retired to rest at State House, Mombasa, after watching traditional dancers in Kwale District. His physical and mental state had been deteriorating since 1977, and he had collapsed earlier that day. After supper, Koinange flew to Nairobi, and was due to rejoin him the next day. Although he was attended to by a doctor, Kenyatta's condition worsened, and he died at 3.30 a.m. on 22 August.

The timing of Kenyatta's death in Mombasa, with most of his retinue absent, allowed Moi to secure power without open opposition. The man to whom Moi probably owed his presidency was Coast PC Mahihu. Mahihu immediately informed civil service head Kariithi, Moi and Kanyotu of what had occurred – with the cryptic 'the country has lost its eyes'– and Moi left his Kabarak home for Nairobi in an armed convoy, fearful of an immediate attack.[166] Mahihu also informed Kibaki, who was staying locally. Only then did he call Koinange and Kenyatta's relatives, at around 4 a.m., to instruct them to come to Mombasa. Koinange is said to have met Kenyatta's family on the runway and only then to have realised that Kenyatta was dead. It may never be known how close Moi came to a physical attack. There were reports that forces loyal to the Kiambu elite threw up roadblocks on Nakuru roads less than an hour after Moi passed on the way to Nairobi.[167] If Kenyatta had died in Nakuru, events might have proceeded very differently. A Kikuyu successor might have led Kenya past the instability and restructuring over which Moi presided, but they would have struggled as much as Moi with the precepts of structural adjustment, while the institutionalisation of Kikuyu rule would have made widespread ethnic violence more likely in the long term. The Kenyan state had also shown its robustness, the risk of a coup or unrest averted by quick, constitutional action by a few senior individuals.

Once in Nairobi, Moi had to be sworn-in as acting president. Ministers gathered during the morning for an emergency Cabinet meeting. There were reports that Ngei, Mungai and Muigai considered methods by which Moi's accession could be prevented, including a motion of no confidence, and canvassed ministers about their willingness to block Moi. But the pro-Moi forces were too strong, and the Cabinet endorsed Moi's selection in the afternoon of 22 August. The decision was not a formality, and involved extensive debate. This followed frantic organisation by Kariithi and Kanyotu to delay the meeting until Moi and enough of his supporters had arrived in Nairobi.[168] Later that day, Chief Justice Wicks swore in Moi as acting president, in kingmaker Attorney-General Njonjo's office. Moi now had 90 days to secure his position, after which a presidential election would be held. In the interim, he could not dissolve Parliament, detain anyone, or sack any minister without the explicit support of the Cabinet.[169]

The period of official mourning for Kenyatta lasted 30 days, during which all public meetings were banned and all bars and places of entertainment closed. This was the period during which factions jostled for power and the succession was finally determined. Although an image of calm and unity was maintained, it was only a firm hand on the state apparatus, and the absence of a convincing alternative that secured Moi's uncontested election. Those who had opposed Moi's succession were fearful of their future and that of their community and the country. In the first few days, Karume, Koinange and Ngei all called in interviews and press conferences for the presidential election to be contested, but these were cut from press and TV broadcasts on Kariithi's instructions.[170] Those around Moi saw Koinange as the greatest threat to the new government, but it was not to be. Whether deterred by the growing authority of Moi and Njonjo or personally unwilling to front the anti-Moi group, a few days after Kenyatta's death Koinange issued a statement: 'There is no truth whatsoever in the rumours spreading abroad that I or any respectable politician I know of in this stable land of ours will be opposing the President.'[171]

There were other attempts to prevent Moi from being sworn in automatically. Lawyers Paul Muite, Amos Wako and others tried to demand an open presidential election. Again, the media were ordered not to print or air the calls. The lawyers later claimed they were only saved from detention on Njonjo's instruction because the detention legislation had expired with the old president.[172] Publicly, however, the nation was unanimous: the succession would take its course, with a Kalenjin leader steered by respected conservative Kikuyu insiders.

Kenyatta received a state burial on 31 August 1978. Half a million Kenyans and dignitaries from 85 countries attended. Tributes poured in from around the world. He was buried in a mausoleum constructed next to Parliament, according to plans prepared a decade before. The respect that the British accorded him was shown by the fact that Kenyatta's body was drawn by the same gun carriage that had carried Winston Churchill 13 years earlier (see Figure 6.12). Not everyone mourned; there were reports of spontaneous celebration in Luo Nyanza after the announcement of his death.

The day after Kenyatta's funeral, Moi announced a special National Delegates' Conference would be held in October, to elect a new party president and nominate KANU's candidate for the presidency. He appealed for unity and for an end to tribalism, and promised to follow in Kenyatta's footsteps (using the Swahili word '*nyayo*' for 'footsteps'). The next day, Nassir called for Moi's unopposed election as KANU president and for Kibaki's election as party vice-president. The first stage in the building of a 'bandwagon' had begun. On 1 September, the Cabinet passed a motion of loyalty to Moi. During September, delegation after delegation from around the country pledged their loyalty and prominent Kenyans one by one expressed their support, including Moi's long-time opponents such as Odinga and Kimani. On 23 September, the NEC selected Moi as the party's sole nominee, and on 3 October 1978, 2,000 NDC delegates unanimously endorsed him as KANU's presidential

6.12: Kenyatta's funeral, 31 August 1978

Courtesy: Nation Group Newspapers

candidate. With the nomination in the bag, Moi announced that his choice of vice-president was the man who was to replace him 25 years later, Kibaki.

On 10 October, no other nominations from political parties having been received (as there were none), Moi was elected unopposed. On 14 October 1978, Chief Justice Wicks swore him in as Kenya's second president. A new era in Kenya's history had dawned.

Conclusions

Kenya's father figure was dead, but the dutiful son Daniel arap Moi had smoothly taken his place, buttressed by the critical support of Njonjo and other key Kikuyu allies. This had not been a foregone conclusion. The murder of J. M. Kariuki in 1975 not only removed another potential contender, but also damaged the credibility of Moi's Kiambu opponents. Similarly, if the enigmatic Kenyatta had chosen to keep the presidency in the family, or Njonjo had wavered in his commitment, the 1976 Change the Constitution movement might have succeeded. Even then, when Kenyatta died in 1978, the fact that he did so in Mombasa rather than Nakuru may have saved Moi's presidency.

For years, watched over by an increasingly corrupt and authoritarian state, but calmed by rising incomes and improved services, the population had acquiesced in a system of unequal exchange between patrons and clients that nevertheless promised something for all (except the Luo). They had survived without war or serious civil disorder, even though the external environment had become more difficult. They were now embarking on a dangerous transition, during which the social contract of the 1970s would be challenged by a change at the top, at the same moment that Kenya's economy would face its most severe test.

Chapter 7

Too Many Cooks, 1978–1983

A New Broom or a 'Passing Cloud'?

Daniel arap Moi came to power as the titular head of a coalition opposed to the continued dominance of the Kenyatta family and the Kiambu elite, although he had been sustained by Kenyatta's ambivalent support. Once in power, he broadened Kenyatta's Kikuyu–Kalenjin–Kamba alliance to create Kenya's first true coalition of ethnic interests. In his first fragile year in office, he was sustained by the support of key Kikuyu allies Charles Njonjo and Mwai Kibaki. This team drew national and international praise for their smooth assumption of power. Moi was relatively young (only 55), and promised Kenyans what Kibaki was to offer 25 years later: a new openness, an end to the corrupt rule of a tribal elite, a more inclusive, active and caring government and free primary education. The new deal of 1978–80 was that in return for their support, Moi would broaden the Kenyatta-era social contract to include less-advantaged groups, without challenging Kikuyu pre-eminence. Kenyatta's Kikuyu-conservative-bureaucratic state would continue, under a new master.

Under pressure from many sides, Moi soon found events moving out of his control. The economy was soon in crisis and the political system in flux. Many saw his presidency as an interregnum before the real rulers of Kenya, the Kikuyu, reasserted themselves. However, they underestimated both the power that the presidency gave Moi and his advisers, and their determination to hold on to it at any cost. Moi weathered the storms of this period by dividing his opponents, and used to his advantage popular dissatisfaction with Kikuyu rule. When the challenge came, it was from amongst his closest allies. Njonjo's bid for political power in 1980–1 divided the Kikuyu elite and led directly to the 1982 coup attempt and the presidential authoritarianism and de-Kikuyuisation of the mature Moi state.

A New Cabinet and KANU Leadership, 1978

On 11 October 1978, the day after he became president, Moi reshuffled the Cabinet. He made few changes, knowing that national elections were due next year. His main act was to remove control of the police and provincial administration from Mbiyu Koinange, sidelining his nemesis to a minor ministry.[1] At the same time, Moi appointed Kibaki as vice-president, maintaining Kikuyu representation in two of the three top positions (Njonjo remained attorney-general). Moi's Maasai ally Stanley Oloitipitip took over his Home Affairs Ministry. The reasons why Moi chose Kibaki remain confidential, but it was an obvious choice. He was a key ally:

clever, respected, at the centre of government, Kikuyu and unlikely to scheme against his new leader. Moi is thought to have also considered Jeremiah Nyagah and Julius Kiano for the role, and Njonjo may have been the one who persuaded Moi to pick Kibaki. It appears, though, that Moi was never entirely happy with his right-hand man. Kibaki's popularity in Nyeri meant he was independent of the still-insecure president. Kibaki was also a reserved man, ill at ease with the *wananchi* or populist policies, an intellectual, more interested in official business than the speeches and walkabouts that Moi loved.

The key concern for Moi, Njonjo and their team at this time was the reaction of the Kikuyu, who dominated the civil service, the security forces, parastatals, business and cash-crop production. Although the press refused to publish direct criticism of the new government, there were oblique references during 1978–9 to the Moi government as a 'passing cloud', soon to be followed by a sunnier (Kikuyu-led) period, and rumours of coup plots. To quiet concerns, Moi promised that he would follow in Kenyatta's footsteps (*Nyayo*), eschewing radical changes in policy. Indeed, although known for his openness and generosity, the new president was just as conservative and hostile to socialism as his predecessor had been.

With a new president, KANU also needed new leadership. The first KANU National Delegates' Conference for 12 years had already elected Moi as party president. When the remaining elections took place three weeks later, they were organised in a way that would soon become familiar. A small group of power brokers, based around Njonjo and Moi's Kikuyu 'fixer', G. G. Kariuki, prepared a regional slate of candidates, ensuring that every province had at least one rep-

7.1: Moi's first Cabinet, 1978

Courtesy: Nation Group Newspapers

resentative and building a 'ticket' that was printed on cards distributed to all attendees.[2] Nonetheless, every seat was contested.

On 28 October, Kibaki defeated Nyagah by 3:1 in a secret ballot, to become KANU vice-president. Nyagah's ability to contest the polls despite Moi's clear preference for Kibaki indicates the degree of openness at this time (although Nyagah was unpopular for a while as a result). There were no more contested KANU vice-presidential elections during Moi's years in office. Isaac Omolo-Okero (Luo) was elected chairman, while Moi allies took the other senior posts, with Robert Matano (Mijikenda) confirmed as secretary-general, Justus ole Tipis (Maasai) as treasurer, and Nathan Munoko (Luhya) as organising secretary. The remaining jobs were also allocated on provincial and ethnic lines. Oginga Odinga was barred from standing again, on the bizarre ground that his life membership certificate was fake.[3] There was widespread protest (including a claim by Masinde Muliro that the NEC had cleared Odinga's candidature, only to have it reversed from above) and prescient warnings that barring Odinga would only make him stronger.

Moi's Honeymoon

The first months of Moi's presidency were a political honeymoon. Kenyans congratulated themselves on being the first black African state to transfer power peacefully and constitutionally from one president to another. Government Road in central Nairobi was renamed Moi Avenue in celebration. Outside the Kikuyu elites, the nation welcomed a younger, more vibrant and less Kikuyu-dominated government. Moi's openness and populism were a radical departure from the somnolent and regal days of Kenyatta's decline. Moi loved public appearances at schools and *harambee* projects, and in the early months of his rule he toured the country tirelessly, explaining the government's policies at open meetings. The *Weekly Review* described him as 'a brother to Kenyans', part of a deliberate effort to build his legitimacy.[4] He fostered the image of a humble, honest, Christian man who would stamp out corruption and the misuse of power. An austere near-workaholic, he was at his desk by 5 a.m., often continuing until late in the evening. His physical energy and constant activity were in stark contrast to most of his colleagues.

The 12 December 1978 Jamhuri Day national address was Moi's first opportunity to declare his priorities. He followed Kenyatta's example by unilaterally introducing a third popular but outdated tripartite agreement between employers, government and trade unions, requiring a further 10 per cent increase in the number of employees. He also announced the introduction of free milk for all primary school children and abolished school fees for Standard VI, the next stage towards free primary education.

Moi also released all Kenyatta's 26 political detainees, including George Anyona, Martin Shikuku, Marie Seroney, Koigi wa Wamwere and Ngugi wa Thiong'o, to universal acclaim. A discordant note was struck, however, by his response to Amnesty International, which had been calling for just such a step. Reflexively resisting external pressure, Moi emphasised that he had kept the provision for detention without trial on the statute book.[5] He declared that he would only use it as a last resort, but it was only four years before he turned to it himself. In fact, Moi and Njonjo had already quietly renewed the Preservation of Public Security Act for the new president, laying new regulations before Parliament on 3 November 1978.[6]

Moi's Underlying Problems

Moi's transition from brother to monarch took four years, but the change was almost inevitable if he was to survive, and it was less of a conversion than a change of focus, as his authoritarianism had long been apparent. From a minority community, with little education or international exposure, a poor public speaker, lacking the legitimacy that leading the country to independence had brought Kenyatta and without the economic opportunities that had permitted Kenyatta to rule over a period of prosperity, he faced daunting obstacles.

First, Moi was unlucky in his timing economically. He came to power just as the tea and coffee boom of 1976–7 ended. The one-off benefits of cash-crop planting, land registration and white farm purchase were over and state patronage was harder to find. Kenya's state-led development model was struggling. Unemployment was mounting, the bureaucracy creaking and the economy suffering from the EAC's collapse and, soon after, a world recession.

Second, Moi was not Kikuyu, and many Kikuyu resented the elevation of an ex-KADU teacher to replace 'their' president. Key Kikuyu elites had backed Moi, but he was unpopular in Central Province, which was also suffering from falling coffee prices. Moi's efforts to broaden Kenya's development base and to reward his allies in the Rift Valley, Western and Coast soon alienated many Kikuyu, accustomed to both leadership and preference.

Third, Moi was personally isolated. Unlike Kenyatta, he did not have a coterie of educated, able, experienced and trusted tribesmen around him. There were still virtually no Kalenjin parastatal executives, businessmen or even senior politicians at this time. Indeed, there were few Kalenjin in Nairobi (apart from his assistant Nicholas Biwott) on whom he could rely. As a result, Moi was dependent on the support of five key Kikuyu: Njonjo, Kibaki, civil service head Geoffrey Kariithi, Permanent Secretary Jeremiah Kiereini and G. G. Kariuki. While Moi was the frontman, the influence of this group was obvious. Njonjo, Kariuki and Biwott regularly travelled with Moi in the presidential limousine, and some openly referred to Njonjo as the 'other president'. There were stories of those early days that suggested that Moi personally feared Njonjo, who referred in conversation to 'my government'. Unless Moi was to be a puppet, there was bound to be a crisis.

Finally, Moi was not a charismatic father figure like Kenyatta. He had held onto the vice-presidency for 11 years because he was a compromise candidate. He had survived through loyalty, good networks amongst the non-Kikuyu, alliances with individuals better connected than he, and a patient, unassuming and non-confrontational posture. Few of these characteristics would serve him well as president.

Securing Moi's Position

Security and the Ngoroko Plot, 1978–9

Moi's first priority was to secure his position and to weaken his most vociferous Kikuyu opponents. Under Njonjo's direction, the security forces began trailing some Kikuyu leaders and monitoring their meetings, while Njonjo relentlessly castigated the police for corruption. On 26 October 1978, Njonjo sensationally announced (inside Parliament, protected by privilege from libel suits) that (Kikuyu) Rift Valley Police Chief James Mungai had formed an assassination squad – based around the Nakuru Anti-Stock Theft Unit (bandits or *ngorokos*, as Njonjo called them) – to murder Moi and himself and seize power. Soon afterwards, the unit was disbanded and fearing arrest, Mungai fled overseas.

These events were given more publicity in 1980 by *The Kenyatta Succession*, a book by two Nairobi journalists. This described the tensions between Moi and the Kiambu elites, the Change the Constitution movement, and the history of the Anti-Stock Theft Unit.[7] It supported suggestions that the unit might have been planning a *coup d'état* and the murder of Moi, Kibaki and Njonjo. Since then, doubt has been cast on some of its claims (the book was probably part of the grand game Moi and Njonjo were playing, using the print media for their own purposes), although it is very likely that the people Mungai represented would have prevented Moi's presidency if they could. After the 1979 elections, the new civil service head Kiereini declared the *ngoroko* affair closed (having achieved its purpose of weakening the Kiambu elites).[8] Mungai returned to Kenya but was never charged.

Years later, Deputy Public Prosecutor James Karugu reported that he had written to Special Branch head James Kanyotu, asking for their dossier on the *ngorokos*. Kanyotu wrote back expressing his views clearly: 'My department (the Directorate of Security Intelligence) has absolutely nothing on Mungai and his alleged assassination squad. If at all something like that exists, the person best placed to discuss the matter with you is the Attorney-General (Njonjo).'[9]

By December, Moi and Njonjo had removed other senior police officers whose loyalty was doubtful. One of the first to go was Police Commissioner Bernard Hinga, who had held the role for 13 years. Moi replaced Hinga with Ben Gethi on 1 November 1978, while a protégé of Gethi's replaced him as GSU commandant.

Moi and the military

In the military too there were changes at the top. In November 1978, Moi promoted Jackson Mulinge from army commander to lieutenant-general and Chief of General Staff, the role of armed forces head that Kenyatta had abolished in 1971. Another Kamba, Brigadier Kathuka Nzioka replaced Mulinge. Lieutenant-Colonel John Sawe, a Kalenjin and head of the transport services, was promoted to deputy army commander, creating a curious situation whereby a colonel commanded brigadiers, his superior officers. Three brigadiers, including Lucas Matu, were then retired to head parastatals, clearing the way for Sawe, who was made brigadier in 1979. Matu died in suspicious circumstances soon afterwards. There were mutterings of tribalism when Nzioka also died in 1979 and Sawe was promoted to head the army, having jumped from lieutenant-colonel to major-general in a year (see Table 7.1).

The Kenyan military was now at an all-time high in influence and expenditure. The army numbered 13,000 and spent nearly US$300 million a year, and was still investing heavily in new equipment, including Vickers tanks, French armoured

Table 7.1: Military positions during the transition

Chief of General Staff	Lt.-Gen. then Gen. Jackson Mulinge	1978–86	Kamba
Army Commander and Deputy COGS	Lt.-Gen. John Sawe	1981–6	Kalenjin
Armed Forces Chief of Staff	Brig. Lucas Matu	to 1979 (retired)	Kikuyu
	Brig. Wilson Shigoli	1979–n/a	Luhya
	Brig. Cromwell Mkungusi	*circa* 1983	Coastal
	Major-Gen. Joseph Musomba	*circa* 1983–4	Kamba
Army Commander	Lt.-Gen. Jackson Mulinge	1971–8 (promoted)	Kamba
	Major-Gen. Joseph Kathuka Nzioka	1978–9 (died)	Kamba
	Brig. then Major-Gen. John Sawe	1979–81 (promoted)	Kalenjin
	Major-Gen. Mahamoud Mohamed*	1981	Kalenjin
Deputy Army Commander	Brig. Peter Kakenyi	To 1978 (retired)	Kamba
	Col. then Brig. John Sawe	1978–9 (promoted)	Kalenjin
	Brig. then Major-Gen. Mahamoud Mohamed*	1979–82	Somali
	Major-Gen. James Lengees	1983–6	Samburu
Kenya Air Force then '82 Air Force	Brig. Dedan Gichuru	1973-80	Kikuyu
	Brig. then Major-Gen. Peter Kariuki	1980–2 (jailed)	Kikuyu
	Major-Gen. Mahamoud Mohamed	1982–6	Somali
Kenya Navy	Brig. Jimmy Kimaro	1972–8 (died)	Taveta
	Col. then Major-Gen. Simon Mbilu	1978–88	Kamba

Source: Various

*indicates that there were inconsistencies in reports of leadership positions at this time.

7.2: Defence spending as percentage of total budget, 1969–2002

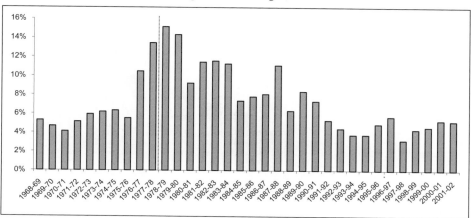

Source: Republic of Kenya, *Statistical Abstracts*, 1972–2007

cars, artillery and armoured personnel carriers. The air services too were growing in capability, with new Hawk and F5 fighters and French and American helicopters.[10]

Kenyatta's last years had seen military spending rise to absorb 15 per cent of the budget. The government now began to cut back defence provisions and managed to reduce their percentage of the budget for most of the next decade (see Figure 7.2).

Moi believed that close ties with the US were critical for Kenya's security, and following the Iranian revolution of 1979, Kenya's strategic importance to the US rose, because of the country's proximity to the Middle East oil routes. Between 1976 and 1982, Kenya purchased US$150 million worth of American military equipment and training, financed by US loans. US statistics show a sharp rise in military and economic assistance after 1975 (see Figure 7.3).

In February 1980, during the first visit by a Kenyan president to the US, Moi granted the US naval facilities and use of Kenya's airfields. In return, the Americans promised US$27 million in military assistance and economic aid worth US$50 million. The deal included the construction of a dock and dredging so that US aircraft carriers could use Mombasa harbour, and modifications to the landing strip in Mombasa airport so that C-5s could land (also enabling commercial 747s to use the airport). During the 1980s, the Americans continued to give grants and loans for the purchase of US equipment and training in its use, creating a dependency similar to Kenyans' dependency on the UK in the 1960s. The US spent more than US$250 million on military aid to Kenya from 1975 to the 1990s.[11]

Kenya was now an American client and loyalty was demanded in return. In solidarity with the US, Kenya boycotted the 1980 Moscow Olympics over the Soviet invasion of Afghanistan. However, the government still feared a backlash, as links with the US were far from popular, and refused a US request to carry out military exercises in Kenya in July 1980. For the same reason, the 1980 agreement was never made public in Kenya.

7.3: US grants and loans to Kenya, 1969–84

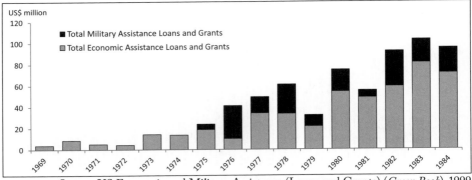

Source: US Economic and Military Assistance (Loans and Grants) (*Green Book*), 1999

The Changing of the Guard

The period 1979–81 was one of gradual de-Kikuyuisation of the administration. On taking office, Moi retired several of Kenya's ambassadors, including Kiambu relatives of Kenyatta, and promoted coastal and Kalenjin figures in their places.[12] Many senior Kikuyu decided to retire from the civil service and parastatals. In September 1979, for example, Kariithi retired as head of the civil service (he was replaced by Njonjo's friend Kiereini). Although Moi was deeply loyal to his Tugen tribesmen, he proved willing to sacrifice his Kikuyu allies to political expediency. In 1980, Kikuyu Coast PC Eliud Mahihu, who had secured Moi's succession in 1978, was fired (he learnt of it over the radio). By 1982, all eight of Kenyatta's provincial commissioners were gone, quietly replaced by new, lesser-known and mostly non-Kikuyu figures. In January 1981, the Kikuyu exodus was symbolised by the departure of Udi Gecaga (Kenyatta's son-in-law) as Lonrho East Africa chairman.

To fill these vacancies, Moi brought a few loyal Kalenjin into parastatal posts, including Kipng'eno arap Ng'eny (a Kipsigis) as chairman of KPTC in 1979, but there was no sudden mass influx of Kalenjin. Instead, there was a broadening of leadership. Moi appeared to be seeking alliances with influential Kikuyu elites from Murang'a, including Kiano, Joseph Kamotho, Charles Rubia and Maina Wanjigi, as a counterbalance to historical Kiambu and Nyeri dominance, while Njonjo's hand was seen in Kikuyu and non-Kikuyu appointments alike.

During 1979, the new team made life difficult for their most vocal opponents. They dissolved Kiambu's local council for maladministration and the 'Kiambu mafia' came under attack in Kiambu's KANU branch. They purged Kihika Kimani's Nakuru KANU branch, Kimani's Ngwataniro farms came under police scrutiny and he was evicted as the company's managing director. The treatment of land also changed with Moi's accession. The sale of beach plots, previously the preserve of Kenyatta and the Kikuyu elites, was frozen and existing allotments reviewed.

Politics and Business

Just as they were cleaning up opposition in the military and politics, so Moi, Njonjo and their nominees were making their mark in the corporate world. Chains of nominees and private companies were used to obfuscate ownerships, but it is clear that their business interests were closely aligned and blossomed in this period. For example, P. K. Jani, an Asian with close links to Njonjo, joined the board of African Liaison and Consulting Services (ALCS) in 1979, and Kiereini joined him soon after.[13] Njonjo already had interests in banking (including Standard Bank), travel agencies, Cooper Motor Corporation (CMC) and air services. At some point, Moi also took part-ownership in these businesses. In the late 1970s and early 1980s, through ALCS and linked companies, Njonjo, Moi, Gethi, Kiereini and others acquired major interests in leading public companies including the Credit Finance Corporation, Barclays Bank, Heritage Insurance Company and CMC.[14]

Nicholas Biwott, too, was ramping up his investments. Having formed Lima Limited with Moi in 1975 to import farm machinery, in 1978 he teamed up with Israeli businessman Gad Zeevi, who owned a construction company. Together, they built a business empire (the HZ group) over the next decade, including construction, petroleum distribution, aircraft, banking, retail businesses, hotels and manufacturing.

The 1979 Elections

Although KANU remained the sole political party, the November 1979 elections were the most open since 1963.[15] Kenyatta's former associates had to face their constituents without the backing of the provincial administration, while Moi was still basking in his popularity. There was a feeling that these elections, known as the *Nyayo* elections (echoing Moi's promise to follow in Kenyatta's footsteps or *nyayo*), would provide an opportunity for Kenya to take a new path.[16]

Campaigning had been under way in all but name since Moi's accession, but the elections formally began with the dissolution of Parliament on 25 September. This time, civic elections were held at the same time as the parliamentary polls. To control the spread of 'money politics', new regulations set a limit on campaign expenditure of Ksh40,000 (US$5,500). Following a 1979 constitutional amendment to allow English to be spoken alongside Swahili once more in the Assembly, candidates now had to be conversant with both languages. Constituency boundaries remained unchanged, as the Electoral Commission abandoned its work to update them for the third time.[17] This year, candidates were required to be life members of KANU, having paid Ksh1,000 (US$140) and received a life membership certificate (which could prove difficult to obtain if your opponent ran the branch or was a national official). Moi justified this rule, which restricted politics to those with money, as candidates should not be 'easily bribed'.[18]

When the re-registration of voters took place in June–July 1979, 5.5 million voters registered, roughly 85 per cent of those eligible, which was better than in

1974 but below expectations. There was extensive transport of voters from rural to urban constituencies and many other complaints of abuses.

Primaries and Nominations

Despite the end to detention without trial, KANU once more barred several senior ex-KPU leaders from standing in the elections. The Governing Council meeting of 4 October 1979 (the first since 1974) decided to bar seven ex-detainees – including Odinga, Ramogi Achieng-Oneko, Luke Obok and Anyona. The reasons given were obviously spurious. The origin of the decision remains obscure – some suggested that it originated in senior Luo politicians who would be disadvantaged by the return of the KPU to political prominence. Other fingers pointed at Njonjo. This decision was the first souring of the romance between Moi and the Kenyan people. It led to student protests and the closure of Nairobi University.

On 16 October 1979, Moi was declared the sole candidate for Kenya's presidency. Two days later, 744 candidates were nominated to contest the 158 parliamentary seats, leaving seven MPs unopposed, including Moi, Kibaki and Tipis. Only 2.5 per cent were women, barely more than in 1974. The growing importance of money in politics was evident in the proportion of businessmen standing for Parliament, rising from 21 per cent of candidates in 1974 to 30 per cent, and dominating Central Province and Nairobi. Many Kikuyu civil servants and parastatal heads decided to resign and enter politics, buttressed by the wealth they had acquired over a decade. These included University Vice-Chancellor Josephat Karanja, Permanent Secretary Peter Gachathi and several of Kibaki's appointees including John Michuki, head of the KCB and Matu Wamae, head of the ICDC.

The Campaign

The campaign saw the repetition of the tactics developed in 1969 and 1974 – a combination of promises of development and trumpeting of achievements, leveraging ethnicity, personal abilities and connections.[19] Clanism or localism (seeking support from specific clans or geographical parts of a seat) was a key electoral weapon in most ex-reserves, while ethnic-based campaigning dominated the settlement zones and the cities. There were now a few candidates from immigrant communities outside the former white highlands as well, with a Kikuyu candidate in Lamu West, a Kamba in Taveta, a Luhya in South Nyanza and a Meru in Isiolo. However, the ex-reserves of the larger ethnic groups remained ethnically pure.

The campaign was peaceful and no deaths were reported. However, it was far from free. No criticism of the government was tolerated. As one district officer publicly warned, for a candidate to attack the government would be 'digging his own grave'.[20] There were also no opinion polls. The *Weekly Review*, which started a write-in poll to help predict who might win the elections, was blacklisted from government and parastatal advertising in October 1979, until it toed the line.[21] The government had little interest in the opinion of Kenya's citizens, and certainly did not want independent assessments of candidates' electoral prospects.

There was more money 'poured' by wealthier candidates, in gifts of sugar, beer and cash, despite the rules barring treating and the limit on campaign expenditure, which were generally ignored. *Harambee* meetings had been increasing in number and cost since 1977, as candidates demonstrated their political virility by their delivery of resources to the constituency. Moi had forced the suspension of such meetings in October, but voters were open about judging a candidate's ability by his delivery, without much concern for how this largesse had been obtained. Apart from a few exceptional personalities, poor candidates could not finance a campaign or treat voters, and most voters saw them as unsuitable for office.

The new president campaigned for a slate of allies nationwide, in a way that Kenyatta had never done. While warning MPs against sponsoring candidates, Moi publicly intervened in at least 20 contests. He called for G. G. Kariuki and Kibaki to be elected unopposed, ran a slate through Baringo, and helped Tipis secure the decision by opponent William ole Ntimama to stand down in Narok North. In Buret in Kericho, Moi attacked Taita Towett, the only other Kalenjin in the Cabinet. He backed Robert Ouko and Okiki Amayo in Nyanza, Julia Ojiambo in Busia and Isaac Salat in Kericho.[22] At the same time, concerned about the growth of socialist influences in Kenya, both Moi and Kibaki campaigned against what they called 'foreign ideologies', including Marxism, across the country.

Moi did not explicitly refer to the events of the past few years, but for his Kikuyu supporters such as Rubia, G. G. Kariuki, Kamotho and George Githii, the Change the Constitution movement was a godsend, as it allowed them to portray their opponents as anti-*Nyayo*. Influential ex-editor Githii even took on Njoroge Mungai directly in Dagoretti. The government made determined efforts to ensure that both Koinange and Kimani were defeated. In Kiambaa, Koinange faced GEMA stalwart Njenga Karume, who was backed by Moi in a curious alliance of self-interest. In a similarly odd alliance, Kimani was opposed in Nakuru North by ex-detainee Wamwere. Wamwere, released from detention on 12 December 1978, was summoned three days later to meet G. G. Kariuki, who told him he had the government's support in taking on Kimani. The new Nakuru KANU Chairman Kariuki Chotara organised for all the other five candidates to stand down in favour of Wamwere just before polling day.[23]

Within the 'in-team', however, there were already tensions between Kibaki allies and other Moi loyalists in some seats, including Mbiri in Murang'a, where Breweries Chairman Kenneth Matiba faced Minister Kiano, a Moi supporter. Although Moi appeared neutral between the two heavyweights, he already had his eyes upon Matiba as a potential challenger for the presidency.[24] It was clear that relations between Kibaki and Njonjo had cooled, and there were rumours that some Kibaki allies were on Njonjo's list of anti-*Nyayo* leaders. To help win a clear mandate, Moi and Njonjo set up a secret joint bank account to fund *Nyayo* supporters.[25]

Moi's personal assistant since 1971, Biwott, was unopposed in Kerio South (see Figure 7.4). Biwott, a Keiyo, was a key Moi confidant, hard working, intelligent and

7.4: Nicholas Biwott

Courtesy: Nation Group Newspapers

unscrupulous. He had learnt his trade as personal assistant to Bruce McKenzie in the 1960s, and had been intimately involved in Moi's rise. The incumbent MP was persuaded that to fight the president's choice was unwise and duly stood down. As compensation, he was appointed to three senior parastatal posts in succession.

Polling Day and the Results

Polling day was 8 November and was a national holiday. As before, each count took place at district headquarters. In Parliament, the Moi slate performed reasonably well. Seven ministers lost, of which only two – Kiano (defeated by Matiba) in Murang'a and Munoko in Bungoma – were close to Moi. Kenyatta-era insiders Jackson Angaine and Koinange both lost.[26]

Nairobi's winners included the first elected white MP since independence: Philip Leakey, son of Louis and brother of wildlife expert Richard, who took the affluent Langata suburb. An MP of Asian origin was also elected for the first time since 1963. Both were signalled as symbols of a new era of racial openness. Mungai beat Githii in Dagoretti. In contrast to 1974's clean sweep, only four of Nairobi's eight seats returned Kikuyu representatives. In Central Province, surprisingly little changed, with the incumbents re-elected in 17 of the 21 seats, including Kibaki, Gichuru, Kamotho and Arthur Magugu in Githunguri. Few of the big names retiring from the civil service were successful. Karanja lost in Githunguri, Wamae in Nyeri, Gachathi in Kiambaa, and Michuki in Murang'a. The sole radical arrival in the province was the former secretary-general of the Union of Kenya Civil Servants, Kimani wa Nyoike, in Nyandarua. Little changed on the Coast either, where 12 out of 18 incumbents were re-elected, including Moi's allies Shariff Nassir and Matano.

Although 1979 saw high turnouts and free votes in most seats, and the election of several independent non-conformists, the elections also revealed Moi's authoritarian tendencies. Only 15 Rift Valley incumbents were re-elected, while there were 23 newcomers. All four Nakuru MPs were evicted, damned by their Change the Constitution associations, to be replaced by a more radical team, including Kikuyu prison graduates Mark Mwithaga and Wamwere. The results were rigged in several seats where senior Kenyatta-era figures did not owe direct loyalty to Moi. In Trans-Nzoia, Moi's old colleague Muliro was 'defeated' by fellow-Luhya Fred Gumo, ex-mayor of Kitale, in an election that involved administrative favouritism during the campaign and a rigged count in which the returning officer issued a different result from that delivered by the ballot boxes.[27] Muliro appealed to the supervisor of elections, who agreed to a recount, but then changed his mind on 'instructions from above'.[28] In Nandi, the DC and KANU Chairman Ezekiel Barngetuny ensured that newcomer Henry Kosgey 'defeated' Seroney in Tinderet. Seroney, who had been expected to win easily, conceded without petitioning, commenting, 'despite grave irregularities . . . no useful purpose will be served in filing an election petition.'[29] Towett was also 'defeated' in Kericho by Dr Jonathan Ng'eno, the man he had beaten 4:1 in 1974, on a turnout that almost doubled the number of voters. There was a similarly high level of change in Western Province, where only four incumbents survived. Unlike Seroney, however, ex-detainee Shikuku returned to the House, recovered and reinvigorated.

Nyanza voters again elected several pro-Odinga candidates in Siaya and Kisumu. Minister Omolo-Okero was defeated in Gem by one of Odinga's sons-in-law, Peter Oloo-Aringo was re-elected in Alego and Odinga's proxy again humiliated William Omamo in Odinga's home seat of Bondo. Amongst the Gusii, minister James Nyamweya lost, while Abuya Abuya – an ally of the barred Anyona – was elected in Anyona's stead.

Turnout was up from 1974: 3.7 million Kenyans voted, a respectable 67 per cent turnout. This was the only election between 1963 and 2007 in which more than half of all adults voted. Turnout was strangely inconsistent, however, and registration figures were not published alongside the election results. Baringo North, for example, showed a turnout of more than 100 per cent. On 22 November, all 158 MPs were formally nominated as KANU's parliamentary candidates, and then declared elected unopposed.

For the third time since independence, the elections had provided a means by which voters could judge the performance of their representatives. Individual victories or defeats had little effect on policy, but the electoral process tightened the elite's dependence on popular support. It also maintained the pattern of regional, and therefore ethnic, competition for resources. It increasingly favoured the wealthy and powerful, since their financial strength, organisational acumen and personal authority helped persuade voters that they would be effective local patrons.[30] Single-party elections also placed checks on the excesses of the elite, forcing them to conceal more extreme corrupt practices and to share their wealth with their constituents. Though 'big men' (financially and usually physically), now dominated the more developed areas, they were *local* big men and there was no automatic election for anyone except the president's closest allies. In 1979, for example, losing candidates included four ex-permanent secretaries, two ex-PCs, the principal immigration officer and several ex-DCs and ambassadors. Voters wanted leaders who would both reward them and – if necessary – take a stand on behalf of local interests, whether on the wearing of traditional dress, cattle rustling, brewing of local liquor or land sales to outsiders.[31] There was still a tension between the desire to be led by a 'big man' – who could directly finance the constituency and might bring development, but would be more beholden to central interests – or a 'small man', a beggar at the national table but more committed to defending his community.

There were no foreign or domestic election observers, but Western countries heralded the elections as free and fair. However, there was the usual crop of losers claiming electoral abuses: there were 31 petitions against the 1979 polls, covering 20 per cent of the contests. Again, only non-African judges heard the petitions, as Njonjo's ruling that only Asian or European judges could be trusted with such cases still held. Nine MPs eventually lost their seats, including three ministers: Daniel Mutinda, James Osogo and Mathew Ogutu. As usual, the petitions revealed a catalogue of abuses, including bribery, oathing, campaigning by civil servants, threats, stolen ballot papers and rigged polls and counts.[32] Election malpractice was becoming a standard tool in the armouries of politicians.

The New Government

In Moi's new government of November 1979, Kibaki remained vice-president and minister of finance, but much else changed. Twelve new ministers entered the Cabinet, as Agriculture and Education were split in two and new ministries of Energy, Industry, Transport and Communications and Environment and Natural Resources were created. The government ballooned, as Moi sought unity through the incorporation of every community and interest (see Figure 7.5).

Although there were more ministers, more functions moved into the Office of the President. Biwott and G. G. Kariuki both became ministers of state in the OP. Moi abolished the ministries of Defence and Lands and Settlement, moving these departments to report to him directly. Two new regional authorities, the Lake Basin Development Authority covering Nyanza and part of Western and the Kerio Valley Development Authority (KVDA) covering Turkana, West Pokot, Baringo and Elgeyo-Marakwet, were set up within the OP. These had briefs to develop these river basins, part of a broader plan to diversify development. By 1983, the KVDA was planning a huge dam, hydroelectric plant and irrigation project at Turkwell Gorge, between Turkana and West Pokot, which was to prove one of the most controversial projects in Kenya's history.

Moi increased the number of assistant ministers from 30 to 47, including at least one from every district and incorporating pastoralists such as the Boran and Turkana, never before considered government material. Indeed, MPs explicitly referred to it as a national government, in contrast to the Kenyatta era. His new assistant ministers included influential dissenters who had lost their place at Kenyatta's table such as Shikuku, John Keen, Waruru Kanja and Mwithaga, who had all had on-off relationships

7.5: The Cabinet, January 1980

Courtesy: Nation Group Newspapers

7.6: The ethnic composition of the Cabinet, 1963–83

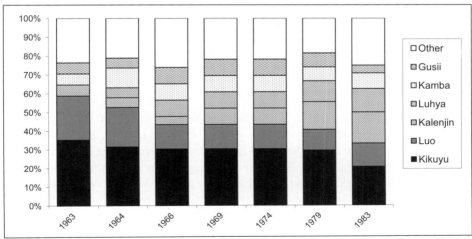

Source: Various

with Moi when he was vice-president. The ethnic composition of the Cabinet changed little, however (see Figure 7.6). The percentage of Kikuyu ministers was unchanged, as newcomers included Rubia, Magugu, G. G. Kariuki and Kamotho. The number of Kalenjin doubled from two to four (Moi, Biwott, Kosgey and Ng'eno).

Local and international responses were positive, though the 1979 government later became controversial because of Njonjo's influence on the appointments list. On 28 November, for example, the increasingly pro-Njonjo *Standard* commented that in making appointments, Moi 'has also been conferring with his top legal and constitutional advisers headed by the Attorney-general, Mr Charles Njonjo'.[33] There is no doubt that many of the so-called Moi loyalists were Njonjo loyalists as well.

Amongst senior civil servants, Moi's most important appointment was the move of Simeon Nyachae, his ally and business partner, from Central Province PC to permanent secretary in the OP. Kiereini remained as secretary to the Cabinet. Moi also made extensive use of parastatal appointments as consolation prizes to election losers, particularly to placate his Kikuyu supporters. Kiano was appointed chairman of the IDB, for example, while Wanjigi became chairman of Kenya Airways.

An Uncertain Path, 1979–80

With the political and economic fabric of the country adjusting to its new leader, 1979–80 saw confused and cross-cutting trends. Increasingly, the image of the government was one of policy inconsistency and internal tensions, as populist and redistributive interests warred with conservative and technocratic views, much as had occurred in 1963–5 and was to happen once more in 2003–5. Several initiatives seemed to presage real change in the state. Shikuku led demands for all politicians and civil servants to declare their wealth (although no legislation was introduced to require it). As local government minister, Rubia took action against local government corruption in plot and house allocations. Leaders stressed the end of *chai* (tea, or bribery) and the beginning of a new era. In November 1980, in a symbolic move, the withdrawal of the Kenyatta-era currency began and the CBK issued a new set of notes and coins, with Moi's head printed on them.

Famine, 1979–80

Not all was well agriculturally. The state still seemed unable to halt a cycle of instability in food production. After a year of drought in 1979, by March 1980, food queues were appearing, there was famine in northern Kenya and widespread violation of the controlled prices for maize. Many Boran and Turkana abandoned their dying animals and entered relief camps set up by Western aid agencies. This was worsened by the interventions of the Maize and Produce Board, which had exported surplus stock and cut prices in 1978 after the bumper harvest of 1977, and commercial growers had cut their plantings as a result.

In response, during 1979–80 the government raised purchase prices for maize twice, while restraining consumer price increases, with the Treasury bearing the resulting shortfall.[34] During his trip to the US, Moi also arranged emergency imports of maize. The government took direct control of the Maize Board and the KFA's storage depots and transportation, running maize deliveries to shortage areas as a military operation. Local buying centres were set up throughout the maize-growing regions of Western Province and Nandi, a significant redirection of state resources into these areas.[35] The government also secretly leavened stocks of maize flour with wheat, which was not in such short supply.[36] The drought lowered water levels in the hydroelectric schemes, causing power shortages. Although few people starved, it was a disastrous start for the government. There were allegations that the Kikuyu were deliberately instigating these crises in order to drive Moi from power, and Kikuyu farmers were accused of hoarding their crops. In June 1980, the new *Standard* chairman, Githii, blamed the maize shortage on Kibaki and Agriculture Minister Nyagah, to which Kibaki retorted, 'We know who some of these newspapers are working for . . .'[37]

Legitimacy and Ideology

With his rule validated by the electoral process, Moi had less need for the legitimacy that KANU brought his government, and KANU held no further elections until 1985. Although the Delegates' Conference met more often, KANU technically remained an illegal organisation. Instead, Moi tried to fit himself into the 'skin' of presidentialism that Kenyatta had evolved, as the country's new omnipotent 'big man' and super-patron, though this proved a slow and difficult task. He used and abused presidential power as his master had done, rewarding allies and punishing opponents through formal and informal institutions. A cult of personality gradually built up around him, but it was weaker than Kenyatta's monolithic edifice had been.

Moi's speeches were stronger than Kenyatta's in expressing his distrust of 'foreign ideologies', particularly Marxism, but he included Western capitalism in this as well. Moi represented a strand of political thought that was instinctively hostile to both foreign ideas and foreign influence, and in common with his socialist critics, disliked Kenya's cultural and economic dependence on the West. His particular ire was reserved for Marxism in the universities, however, and the feeling was mutual as support for the government weakened in the face of evidence that little had changed. There were more student riots in February and May 1980.

Moi also sought legitimacy through the churches. As a vocal and active Christian, and a member of the conservative African Inland Church (AIC), Moi had long enjoyed good relations with church leaders. Now, he presented himself (in contrast to his predecessor) as an active defender of Christianity. Indeed, his *Nyayo* philosophy of 'peace, love and unity' – Moi's attempt to build a legitimating ideology – was based directly on Christian principles.[38] He also called on the churches to play a more active role in the life of the state. The churches' public posture was still implicitly supportive of the state, as they generally focused on personal salvation and national development, and they said little publicly during the troubles of 1981–2.

Ethnicity and Culture

Moi was also more concerned than Kenyatta had been by the loss of Kenyan cultures, and took several steps to protect indigenous cultural artefacts. He created a Department of Culture in May 1980 and a Ministry of Culture and Social Services; he reactivated the Kenyan National Cultural Council in 1980 and appointed a National Music Commission in 1982. Moi also made use of music to 'sell' his government, commissioning several songs praising him that were broadcast during 1978–82.[39] Muungano, a new national choir that was formed in 1979, composed many songs in his honour. In March 1980, following in Kenyatta's footsteps of a decade before, the Ministry of Information decreed that 75 per cent of all music on the Voice of Kenya had to be of Kenyan origin. However, there was still too little material available, and listeners preferred Western pop. Two weeks later, the decree had to be withdrawn.

More generally, state policy began to emphasise the distinct cultural practices of Kenya's ethnic groups, reflecting Moi's more parochial background (unlike Kenyatta, he had not spent a decade abroad) and the Kalenjin's strong sense of tradition. In 1981, the Ministry of Higher Education introduced oral literature in the secondary school syllabus, despite concerns that this would reinforce tribalism.[40] Moi also encouraged the speaking of mother tongues in primary education. The debate over local traditions and foreign influences in this period was complex and multi-layered. Many African writers were now writing in their vernacular languages, blending traditional stories with critiques of Western culture and state corruption, which they generally blamed on foreign influences. As Bethwell Ogot suggested, 'The conflicts between indigenous and foreign cultures, between past and present, run through almost all of the literature of Kenya.'[41]

With the change of regime, previously unmentionable differences in service provision between regions and ethnic groups could be brought into the open. For the first time, MPs could criticise Kikuyu domination openly. The government began publishing statistics showing that Central Province had previously received the lion's share of resources, and suggesting it would no longer do so. During an Assembly debate on parastatals, for example, it emerged that more than 60 per cent of the ICDC's employees were Kikuyu. A redistributive agenda was becoming part of the legitimising ideology of the government.

The Role of Parliament

The period 1980–2 was a more open period for parliamentary activity, reflecting the factional instability inside the government and the lack of firm presidential control. Four bills were withdrawn under backbench pressure during 1981–2. Formal divisions were rare, however, and no legislation was actually defeated during the fourth Parliament. Kenya's Assembly was relatively strong and had built more popular legitimacy than in most African states, but the executive still saw its authority stemming not from Parliament but from other, deeper, sources. In the main, the

House acted as an advisory council of influential notables whose authority stemmed from who they were as much as from the elected post they held.

Styles amongst incumbent politicians differed, reflecting the nature of their support and the way in which they viewed their responsibilities. A few, particularly Shikuku, saw it as their duty to serve the nation inside Parliament. For the majority, however, pork barrel politics was the foundation of their success. In the words of one wealthy MP, Matiba,

> I was not greatly interested in routine parliamentary duties . . . I was aware that not many crucial decisions were made in the chamber itself. I saw my role as an elected member who had authority to oversee development and practical issues on behalf of the people of Kiharu.[42]

MPs were now expected to perform as development coordinators and employment exchanges, pressurising government departments and private industry to find jobs for their constituents.[43] The Assembly's business was dominated by requests for help from ministries, competing for limited funds, and a systematic lack of quorum.

Where they did pick up national issues in their parliamentary contributions, it was generally from a nationalist and protectionist perspective. MPs criticised Asian 'profiteering' and the continued presence of expatriates in the law, private business and parastatals and challenged tariff reductions and demanding protection for local industries suffering from foreign competition. Kikuyu tribalism, corruption and inequality were also a focus of protest, with many attacks on ostentatious displays of wealth.

Members of Parliament did not represent just their constituencies, but also particular agro-industrial interests which were important to their seat and region. Sugar-belt MPs in Western and Nyanza, for example, always debated issues affecting the sugar industry, and represented outgrowers, while the government usually took the side of the state-owned sugar factories. Pastoralist MPs represented stockholders on disease control, boreholes and abattoirs. MPs from coffee-growing areas supported the interests of small coffee farmers and criticised coffee institutions and policies. Business interests, both large and small, were well represented throughout. There were several trade unionists in Parliament, including Juma Boy (COTU secretary-general and head of the Dock Workers Union), Fred Omido (COTU chairman) and wa Nyoike. This should have resulted in a strong workers' lobby in the House, but in practice they achieved little more than in the Kenyatta era, reflecting the weakness of organised labour in general and their personal enmeshment in the patronage system. They could not prevent Moi's banning of the Civil Servants Union for 'over-indulgence in politics' or of the University Academic Staff Union in 1980, after it organised demonstrations against the US military deal.

Throughout the 1970s and 1980s, MPs salaries ran at eight times average public sector wages, before fringe benefits.[44] Although wealthy by local standards, MPs believed they were grossly underpaid, given their obligations to *harambee*, school fees and other assistance to their constituents, and the rising costs of elections. In 1979, candidates needed Ksh65,000–100,000 (US$8,000–15,000) to have a reasonable chance of success in a rural constituency.[45] Being a politician was now a financial drain and MPs struggled for years to repay the debts they incurred while campaigning. After 1979, indebted parliamentarians included figures close to Moi such as Nassir, whose car was taken in 1981, and who only narrowly avoided bankruptcy. In 1983, Phoebe Asiyo was nearly jailed for non-payment of lawyers' fees, while Ojiambo had her property seized for a debt to a car dealer.[46]

Even ministers were not immune. Paul Ngei, whose finances remained legendary, nearly lost his ministerial seat and his job several times between 1980 and 1982. He had faced bankruptcy in 1975–6, but the process had been suspended once Kenyatta pardoned him. Now, a new demand was presented in 1980, with 44 creditors together claiming he owed them Ksh5.1 million (US$600,000). Bailiffs could find no property that Ngei owned. A year later, in July 1981, Justice Alan Hancox declared him bankrupt, but Ngei appealed. He survived because an unknown source provided him with the money to pay off all his debts (Ksh6.4 million by this time).[47]

Njonjo's Bid for Power, 1980–2

After a reasonably successful start, the government soon found itself in trouble. Moi faced a reinvigorated left, economic difficulties, a sceptical Kikuyu community and a set of senior Kikuyu officials who believed his presidency was their doing. He found it difficult to gain the respect he felt he deserved as president, and there was growing dissension at the top.

Njonjo Enters the Political Kingdom

The early 1980s were dominated by factional conflict amongst the new ruling team, as Njonjo challenged Kibaki for the vice-presidency and for control of policy. Conflict had broken out almost as soon as Moi took office. Njonjo's supporters quietly warned that Kibaki had too much power as both vice-president and minister of finance, and blamed him for the deteriorating economic situation. Kibaki, who appeared happier in economic debates than in cut-throat politics, looked increasingly at risk. By March 1980, the existence of political groupings and the competition between Kibaki and Njonjo was public knowledge, although the battle lines were confused by the continued importance of 'old guard' Kikuyu such as Mungai and Karume who were aligned with neither side. Kibaki admitted to the growing crisis when he denied to a KANU National Delegates' Conference in 1980 that he was opposing Moi, and accused those who wanted to seize the vice-presidency for themselves of sponsoring such rumours.[48]

In April 1980, having reached the age of 60, Charles Njonjo duly retired as attorney-general, and entered electoral politics. For more than a decade, he had been interested in an active political role, but had been held back by his loyalty to

Kenyatta and lack of a popular base.[49] Married to an English woman, dressed in a three-piece suit with a rose and watch chain, and a stickler for correct English usage, 'Sir Charles' or the 'duke of Kabeteshire' (as he was sometimes nicknamed) was the antithesis of the 'rough and ready' Kenyan politician. His contempt for the less able of his fellows was well known, and he was said to have a particular dislike of the Luo. Nonetheless, he had been one of the most powerful people in the government since the mid-1960s. His influence was unrivalled, built on close alliances with senior Kikuyu, Europeans and Asians in the police, military and the law. He had helped put Moi on the throne, perhaps in the expectation that he would one day replace him. Now, the time had come to enter the political snake pit. He lasted only three years.

The day before Njonjo resigned from the civil service, the MP for Kikuyu constituency, his home seat, resigned to create a vacancy for him. He was compensated with a Ksh160,000 (US$20,000) cash payment and a parastatal chairmanship. A massive development programme began in the constituency, and a few weeks later, Njonjo was elected unopposed as MP, all the other candidates having decided to support him or suddenly obtained jobs elsewhere. His campaign manager was another Kiambu lawyer who was to become a household name later in the decade, Paul Muite. On 25 April, James Karugu, yet another Kiambu lawyer and deputy public prosecutor, replaced his mentor as attorney-general. Those congratulating Njonjo on his victory did not include Kibaki or ex-Change the Constitution leaders such as Gichuru. Njonjo was still far from popular amongst the Kikuyu, although his ministerial allies included Magugu (the son of another prominent colonial chief from Kiambu) and Kamotho.

On 20 June 1980, as expected, Moi reshuffled the Cabinet. Speculation that Njonjo had his eye on a constitutional amendment and the position of prime minister or even the vice-presidency proved premature, and instead he became minister for home and constitutional affairs, a new post (see Figure 7.7). This allowed Njonjo continued control of the law and judiciary, plus the CID, prisons, elections and constitutional change.

As the implications of the change rippled throughout the country, the pressure on Kibaki grew. Njonjo seemed to be trying to position himself as the pre-eminent Kikuyu leader. There were suggestions in *Africa Confidential* that Kibaki was going to resign and was struggling to counter Njonjo's influence over Moi.[50] Kibaki twice had to call press conferences and make a public statement in the National Assembly to rebut such stories. Kibaki and his allies in return accused unnamed opponents of distancing the president from the people and of deciding who was more loyal. By July 1980, Moi was warning that there was no collegiate presidency, and that no leaders were indispensable. It seemed that his relations with those who had placed him on the throne were becoming more difficult.[51]

In November 1980, Moi sacked Nyeri assistant minister Kanja, after Kanja alleged in Parliament that Njonjo and G. G. Kariuki had armed bodyguards to protect them because of their crimes.[52] Kanja, an ex-Mau Mau veteran, was not a Kibaki ally, but he blamed many of Kenya's problems on Njonjo, and indirectly alleged that Njonjo was implicated in the murders of Pio da Gama Pinto, Tom Mboya and J. M. Kariuki.

7.7: Njonjo's swearing-in, June 1980. *From left to right:* Kiereini, Moi, G. G. Kariuki, Njonjo

Courtesy: Nation Group Newspapers

In June 1981, a pro-Kibaki MP was jailed for breach of the peace after declaring in a hotel bar that he expected Kibaki to become president of Kenya at some point. Such a suggestion was now a criminal offence. Everywhere, the hand of Njonjo was seen or imagined, moving pieces into place for his takeover. He appeared to be the real power in the state. In 1980, Bishop Manasses Kuria was elected by the Anglican CPK synod to replace Festo Olang' as Kenya's second archbishop. The shadow of politics was visible in this too, with Kuria (a Kikuyu) said to have been backed by Njonjo, a senior CPK lay member.[53] Njonjo and other Kikuyu Anglicans were unhappy with the outspoken government critic Luo Bishop Henry Okullu, the most prominent alternative candidate.

It is unclear how much the instability of 1980–2 was a consequence of Njonjo's moves to undermine Kibaki and Moi (as the press have presented it), or whether Moi was actually encouraging Njonjo to undermine Kibaki. Years later, some insiders suggested that Moi deliberately incited the conflict, telling both they were his preferred successor, giving him time to develop non-Kikuyu alliances to sustain him when the break with the Kikuyu came.[54] In retrospect, it may have been part of his strategy for survival to divide the Kikuyu: first weakening the Kiambu elites through Njonjo, then dividing Kiambu and Nyeri, before finally – with Kiambu weakened and Njonjo gone – striking at Nyeri.[55]

For now, though, Moi and Njonjo were still allied and working to defeat their old guard opponents. A leaders' conference at the Kenya Institute of Administration in July 1980 decided to abolish all Kenya's tribal unions, in the interests of 'peace, love and unity'. Other cultural and ethnic associations such as the New Akamba Union and the Luo Union had to go, but the real target was GEMA. Over the next three months, all the tribal associations were dissolved. Despite Karume's protests, GEMA could do little.[56] Obedience to the decision became a litmus test of loyalty, and Njonjo's influence strengthened as a result. However, the concept of ethnic solidarity did not vanish with its institutional expression. The 'Gema tribes' and their common political and economic interests were at the core of the government's problems over the next decade, and the concept of Gema as a community remained a potent political symbol.

Political tensions were also spilling over into violence. On New Year's Eve, 31 December 1980, the Norfolk Hotel in central Nairobi was partially destroyed by a bomb. Fifteen people were killed and more than 80 wounded. The bomb is usually seen as the work of Palestinian terrorists in revenge for the Entebbe incident, since a pro-Palestinian group claimed responsibility; the hotel, part of the Block Hotels group, was owned by a Kenyan of Jewish origin. However, conspiracy theorists also had ammunition. Rumours suggested that Kibaki was due to speak at the hotel that night or even that Njonjo was in the building at the time.[57]

In April 1981, moves to discredit Njonjo surfaced with the treason trial of Kikuyu businessman Andrew Muthemba, Njonjo's cousin, for trying to overthrow the government.[58] Muthemba had attempted to smuggle arms out of Nanyuki air force base in January 1981, and was accused of founding a group with the aim of removing the 'big man'. Njonjo was mentioned several times as Muthemba's contact, but denied everything. Muthemba was acquitted in May 1981 after offering the surprising defence that he had been selflessly testing the quality of Kenya's security defences. Judge Alfred Simpson criticised the prosecution as politically motivated to smear Njonjo, but there were suggestions that senior legal and police figures ensured that key evidence was withheld, so that the case collapsed.[59] It remains unclear whether these were genuine coup preparations by the Njonjo team or a botched attempt by opponents in the security services to smear Njonjo. The case fostered further insecurity and anti-Kikuyu feeling. Within eight weeks, Attorney-General Karugu (who had consented to the prosecution) had resigned; the consequence of Njonjo's displeasure. He was replaced in July 1981 by James Kamere, again from Kiambu. In 1982, long-serving British Chief Justice Wicks also retired and was replaced by Simpson, who was also close to Njonjo.

Odinga's Failed Reintegration and the Repression of Socialism, 1979–81

Despite a decade of disenfranchisement, Odinga remained a key figure amongst the Luo, a symbol of Luo identity and socialist integrity in its conflict with Kikuyu hegemony. Although Odinga had supported the Change the Constitution movement, blaming Moi and Njonjo more than the 'Kikuyu nationalists' for his troubles, there was still a chance for reconciliation. In 1979, Moi had appointed Odinga as chairman of the Cotton Lint and Seed Marketing Board, his first government post since 1966. He also appointed a number of Odinga's allies, including Obok and Achieng-Oneko, to parastatal jobs, while Odinga's protégé Oloo-Aringo became a minister in 1980. In July 1980, Odinga was finally readmitted to KANU as a life member. Moi seemed to be leading a new accommodation, in return for which Odinga would help sustain him in power.

An unwise comment and latent tensions undermined this reconciliation at the last minute, changing Kenya's future. In March 1981, Odinga was ready after 12 years to re-enter Parliament. His proxy, the Bondo MP, resigned his seat to allow Odinga to stand. However, Odinga's plan was derailed at the last moment. He made unguarded comments at a rally on 4 April 1981 that Kenyatta had been a 'land grabber'. Seizing the opportunity, Njonjo led a campaign against Odinga's return, using the *Standard* as his mouthpiece. The campaign was supported by senior Luo including Omamo and Ouko, determined that the ex-KPU team would not return to power. After public condemnations by Moi, KANU again barred Odinga from standing for election. Omamo was elected as Bondo MP, the emergency pro-Odinga candidate's nomination also having been conveniently annulled. When the *Nation* suggested Odinga's banning was unconstitutional, the government warned, 'The persistent rebellious attitude of those concerned with the selection of editorial matters within the *Nation* newspapers cannot be viewed as being in the interests of the state.'[60] Its sensitivity was now so acute that after the *Nation* suggested that a KANU statement was 'anonymous', its top six journalists were arrested and its editor-in-chief fired.[61] Unless journalists were willing to risk their lives, the media were becoming pawns of the state.

This failed reintegration and the continued demonisation of Odinga were open incitements to direct action by radical forces. There were already stirrings in the military, which was experiencing a rapid decline in its facilities. In late 1980 and early 1981, a group of mostly Luo junior officers in the KAF, hearing rumours of Kikuyu military preparations, began to prepare a coup of their own. Despite the arrest of a leading figure, military intelligence was unable to penetrate their plans, allowing the plot to proceed.[62]

The state was concerned by its weakening hold on political discourse, while the growing influence of the radicals seemed to revive the spectre of socialist revolution. With the rapprochement with Odinga over, a crackdown followed in late 1981. Inside Parliament, seven left-wing MPs – the 'seven bearded sisters': Wamwere, Orengo, Abuya, Onyango Midika, Chibule wa Tsuma, Lawrence Sifuna and Mashengu wa Mwachofi – were the government's main target. These backbenchers had consistently attacked Njonjo and the government's policies, especially Kenya's relationship with Western powers. In September 1981, in a replay of the events of 1972, police questioned 10 radical MPs over their parliamentary mileage claims, and raised a warrant for the arrest of MP Chelegat Mutai for mileage fraud. She fled to Tanzania. A few days later, Kanja was jailed, having been found in possession of foreign currency more than 24 hours after an overseas trip. For this crime, he served a year in jail, without remission. Again, the law was being used to punish dissenters.

Relations with the university had also worsened. The greater openness of 1978–81 had encouraged long-repressed dissent, which the government now wished to quash. The university was dominated by a group of able, critical and socialist academics, including David Mukaru Ng'ang'a, Apollo Njonjo, George Katama Mkangi, Willy Mutunga, Gibson Kamau Kuria, Atieno Odhiambo, Michael Chege and Peter Anyang' Nyong'o. They led a sustained critique of Kenya's capitalist development path in the 1970s and early 1980s, and many had links with pro-Odinga politicians. Now, there were searches of lecturers' offices and homes for seditious publications, and in October 1981 police picked up Ng'ang'a over the distribution of clandestine leaflets. Academic repression grew, as publication of anything with political content became unwise. This confrontational relationship drove many intellectuals into open anti-government politics in the 1980s and 1990s.

As political tensions increased, so electoral processes began to suffer. In 1981, ministers-to-be Omamo in Bondo and Peter Okondo in Busia were both elected unopposed in by-elections, as all competition was dissuaded or their opponents were denied KANU clearance. After Kanja was jailed, KANU also barred controversial lecturer and NCWK chairperson Wangari Maathai from standing in the resulting by-election.[63] The 1982 by-election in Nakuru North following Wamwere's detention (see below) was rigged to ensure that his Kikuyu ally was defeated, leading to a Kalenjin MP representing one of the most radical Kikuyu-dominated areas of Nakuru (but, critically, one that also contained Moi's home).

Njonjo's Strength Grows, 1981

By late 1981, Njonjo's strength was reaching its peak. He represented a direct line of both policy and style from colonial days. He was everything African nationalists hated: pro-South African, a disciplinarian and supporter of state control and bureaucratic efficiency. Much of the anti-government protest in Luo, academic and radical circles targeted Njonjo rather than Moi. As the years of co-rule passed, their paths diverged; Moi was a populist, while Njonjo gloried in his elitism. Although equally anti-communist, Moi was more supportive of a pan-African policy than Njonjo. Most clearly, as long as Njonjo was around, Moi was never going to be an 'effective head of state both at home and abroad'.[64]

By October 1981, Njonjo probably had 60 MPs in his camp. All, to varying degrees, understood that the objective was to replace Kibaki, and possibly Moi. There were Njonjo and Moi camps in diplomatic and business circles. He was consistently supported by the *Standard*, edited by Githii, which printed his photo on its front page so often that one minister nicknamed it the *Kibichiku Times*, in a reference to Njonjo's birthplace.[65] The *Nation*, too, now followed the Njonjo line, after public disputes with the minister during 1980–1.[66] Every day, donations poured in from European and Asian firms to the Kikuyu constituency, Njonjo was conducting *harambees* throughout Central Province and the Coast, and his supporters were active everywhere.

Kibaki and his allies were increasingly frustrated. In November 1981, both Kibaki and his ally Munyua Waiyaki indirectly attacked Njonjo. They were not aware of any other vice-president, they announced, and while anyone was welcome to be a candidate for the post, rivals should campaign openly. They emphasised that no one was 'Minister for screening loyalty to the President'.[67] Githii took on Kibaki in response in a *Standard* editorial, accusing him openly of tribalism and disloyalty.[68] Moi knew there was trouble coming. In late October, he had called for 'an end to political groupings' and said, 'Loyalty to me should be direct and not through groupings . . .'[69] Unable to stamp his authority on the Cabinet, however, Moi found events drifting beyond his control. He complained in early 1982 that the civil service was distorting his intentions, that people were misinterpreting his attitude as weakness, and that no one should claim that they 'help me to rule'.[70] The administration increasingly ignored his directives, and it seemed his time in power might be near an end.

The Economy in the Transition

Not only was the political system in crisis, but the economy too was in trouble. Moi had inherited a slow-motion economic crisis not of his making, but which his initial expansionary and inclusive policies had worsened. With the coffee boom over, public spending rising, the land frontier closed, the oil crisis and the EAC gone, the early 1980s saw food shortages, price rises, foreign exchange crises, budget shortfalls and growing debt. Growth slowed, interest rates rose and capital formation declined. GDP growth fell from 8 per cent in 1977 to 3 per cent in 1980. The years 1980–1 saw unsustainably high taxation, borrowing and deficits; growth in the industrial and commercial sectors in 1982 was the lowest since independence. The development model of the 1970s was stalling, fuelling the authoritarianism of the time.

External Shocks and Pressures

There were several external causes of this crisis, which was particularly severe for Kenya because its economy was relatively open, with a high level of imports and exports compared to GDP. The most obvious was the jump in oil prices. The Iranian revolution caused petrol shortages in 1979, and spot prices hit nearly US$40 per barrel, up from US$14 in 1978. By late 1980, oil was absorbing half of Kenya's foreign exchange. Petrol prices rose rapidly, with a knock-on effect on inflation, which jumped from 13 per cent in 1981 to 22 per cent in 1982. Other challenges included a global recession in 1979–81, dampening demand for Kenya's exports. Kenya's terms of trade had changed fundamentally. The purchasing power of coffee overseas had fallen by 50 per cent and that of tea by 68 per cent between 1964 and 1981, with the resulting need to slash imports or increase exports to avoid a crisis. The drought of 1979–81 also cut cash-crop production, reducing foreign exchange inflows at the exact moment when the government needed stable finances to consolidate its position. The vulnerability of Kenya's economy to world price instability was evident.

Further problems were caused by the closure of the Tanzania border and the restrictions on trade with Uganda, Rwanda and the Congo caused by the collapse of Uganda. Kenyan manufactured exports, which had enjoyed a protected market in the EAC, suffered. Searching for new regional outlets for its manufactures, in 1981 Kenya signed up to the new Preferential Trade Agreement (PTA) for Eastern and Southern African states. However, it took years to build alternative markets and in the meantime the loss of a regional market discouraged new foreign investment.

Structural Problems in Public Spending

There were also structural problems within the economy. The state-led model of planned development was reaching a crisis. The government spent more and more, either diverting money from productive use or allocating it on non-economic criteria. Government spending peaked at 44 per cent of GDP in 1980–1, compared to 21 per cent in 1964–5.[71] The government was growing larger and larger, trying to deliver more and more services to a growing population, mostly without user charges. It could not sustain this growth without new sources of revenue, and its opportunities to raise taxes were severely restricted.

Part of the problem was the size of the public sector, which had tripled since independence, and rose sharply after Moi's accession (see Figure 7.8). Although in comparison with some African states, Kenya's private sector was larger and freer, it was being overwhelmed by the heavy hand of the state and its taxes and non-economic policy-making. The state was also suffering from a hangover from the 1977 coffee boom, which had rippled through in 1978–81 into greater demand for consumer imports, large-scale construction and capital investment and unsustainable public spending, soon wiping out most of the gains from the boom.[72] The new government's political fragility made it slow to respond.

Not only was the government spending more, it was not spending it effectively or wisely. The Civil Service Review Commission that Moi had appointed in October 1979, led by S. N. Waruhiu, had severely criticised Kenya's 'seriously overmanned' and politicised civil service for corruption and the erosion of discipline since the Ndegwa report, and recommended changes to terms and conditions, including a declaration of interests and a ban on all directorships in private companies.[73] Despite these brave words, no such policies were implemented. The government was still buying short-term support by expanding the civil service, and ethnicity and patronage still drove this recruitment. For example, Moi's old friend and Luhya ally Moses Mudavadi massively expanded Western Province admissions into teacher training colleges as minister for basic education in 1979–80, and as minister of water development he recruited so many new employees that some had to be laid off after he was transferred.[74]

The government initially appeared to have the will to address these problems. In February 1979, Moi had appointed a working party chaired by respected civil service economist Philip Ndegwa to investigate the performance of statutory boards and cooperatives.[75] It reported in May 1979 with a set of administrative improvements familiar to any business, including better financial controls, budgeting, planning and procurement.[76] More fundamentally, the report challenged the foundations of the 'parastatal state'. It identified many government investments that were producing minimal returns and would have to be written off. The report proposed tighter rules

7.8: Public sector workforce, 1955–84

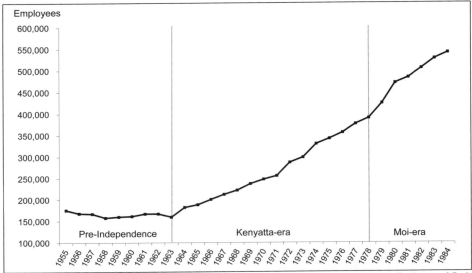

Source: Republic of Kenya, *Statistical Abstracts*, 1972–88, Collier and Lal:
Labour and Poverty in Kenya, p. 69

for future public investments, and a clearer separation of duties between regulatory and productive functions. Finally, the report proposed that no new parastatals be established 'unless the need for it is indisputable', suggested some organisations be abolished, and proposed an inquiry into malpractices in specific boards.[77] For the first time, Kenya's government was talking of a rollback of the state. While talk was cheap, though, action was to prove more difficult.

The Foreign Exchange Crisis and Structural Adjustment, 1979–82

With the shilling stronger than it would have been under free market conditions, the result of the economy's difficulties was uncompetitive exports, a growing deficit and a foreign exchange shortage. The deficit (after investments in and loans to parastatals) widened from 5 per cent of GDP in 1976–7 to 12 per cent in 1981–2.[78] Under pressure from the IMF and World Bank, Kenya devalued the shilling in September 1981 and again in 1982. The value of the currency halved in four years from 8 to 16 to the dollar. This helped Kenya's exports and depressed import demand, but it also fed inflation, hurt urban consumers and doubled the domestic value of Kenya's foreign debt.

In 1979, Kenya had made use of its credit from the IMF. Facing a balance of payment crisis, in 1980 Kenya turned to the World Bank for help. The result was Africa's first structural adjustment loan, worth US$70 million, and large IMF stand-by loans.[79] The World Bank focused on long-term lending for development; the IMF on short-term (one- to two-year) loans for fiscal stabilisation, but their loan conditions were increasingly aligned around a belief in free markets rather than state planning. At their prompting, Kenya adopted a policy of higher and more flexible interest rates, to create incentives for saving and to support the shilling. A 1980 Sessional Paper and related agreements proposed to cut the deficit and manage public debt better, with a ceiling on government borrowing, and to replace quantitative import restrictions (bans and quotas) by tariffs. Thus began the era of structural adjustment or structural adjustment programmes (SAPs), shorthand for World Bank- and IMF-driven programmes of economic liberalisation, privatisation and market reforms, with low-interest loans as the carrot. However, the conditions imposed by the IFIs remained mild. Indeed, the World Bank took a protective policy towards Kenya at this time, seeing it as one of the best governments in the region from an economic perspective.[80] Nonetheless, Kenya had grave difficulties in meeting the IFIs' conditions, mainly because of excessive state spending, and the credits were lower and slower to arrive than expected. In 1981 the IMF agreement was abandoned.[81]

The limited changes the government had conceded had little effect. Real interest rates remained negative, rewarding borrowers. Foreign currency rationing and pre-import cash deposit rules caused damage throughout the country. The balance of payments gap reached a new high, foreign exchange for imports of fertilisers, spares and equipment was virtually unavailable, and there was open corruption in its acquisition. In 1981, foreign exchange reserves could cover only 1.6 months of imports, an all-time low. With a nine-month wait in 1982 between a request for foreign currency to import and its granting, and no clear policy to decide who got it and who did not, industry began to seize up.

There were ineffective cuts in public expenditure and rises in taxes. However, tax increases further repressed demand, while high domestic borrowing restricted credit for the private sector. The government seemed caught in a vicious circle. The revenue shortage became so severe that the government had to beg large companies to pay their taxes in advance, to enable it to pay civil servants their February 1982 salaries. Parastatals fell months behind in their payments to farmers. In March 1982, Moi again stressed strict control of government spending. Supplementary budgets to regularise overspends were no longer acceptable, and cash constraints began to shut down services while unpaid bills piled up on the desks of senior managers.

To help face the crisis, Kenya requested emergency funds from the IMF, the US, UK, France, West Germany and the Netherlands. Kenya was still a favoured nation in Africa and the donors were willing to help, but relations were still far from easy. A new IMF agreement was agreed in January 1982 for US$175 million, in return for cuts in government spending and liberalisation of import controls, but payments lasted only a few months before the government exceeded ceilings on bank borrowing and payments were halted.[82] A US$131 million World Bank structural adjustment loan followed in July 1982. This was based on commitments to trade liberalisation and agricultural reforms, but it too was suspended in 1983 in the face of government intransigence on maize marketing reform. Aid, it seemed, was sometimes used as an alternative to structural reform in Kenya, rather than a driver for it. It was also already apparent that the IFIs would struggle to convert their theoretical prescriptions into consistent, viable, well-sequenced sets of policy changes. The stop-start aid game had begun and was to prove a destabilising factor in Kenya, both politically and economically, for the next two decades.

The Growing Debt Burden

One of the government's most severe growing problems was its debt burden. This had been rising steadily since independence, and it rocketed up from 1977–8 (just before Moi took over). Kenyatta had borrowed to fund land purchase, development and defence, but the investments had generated insufficient growth in GDP or exports to repay the loans. Now, Moi did the same thing. He needed new sources of funds to ensure fiscal stability during the transition, and, like a compulsive shopper, Kenya hurried from bank to bank. Where in 1978 Kenya had owed US$35 million in commercial debt to eight finance institutions, by 1983 it owed $340 million to 14 different sources (mostly banks) keen to lend out their petrodollars. Kenyatta and Moi had also signed huge defence loans with the US, constituting 15 per cent of 1979's debt.

As a result, the debt repayment burden tripled in dollar terms between 1977–8 and 1982–3 (see Figure 7.9), despite the fact that three-quarters of Kenya's external debt was low-cost lending from bilateral and multilateral sources.

7.9: Dollar debt servicing costs, 1963–84

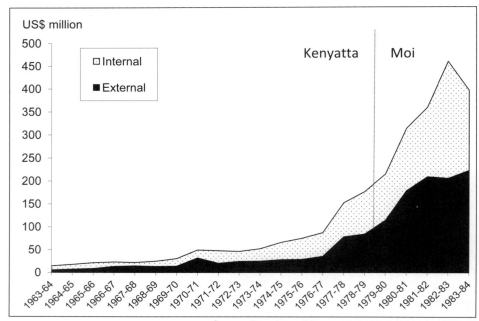

Source: Republic of Kenya, *Statistical Abstracts*, 1972–88

By 1983, control of this debt and the need to fund further development from domestic capital rather than foreign loans was a key part of government plans. However, the state could do little but borrow even more from abroad to finance the deficit. In the words of the *1984–8 Development Plan*: 'Radical curtailment of external borrowing is simply not feasible economically.'[83] Moi was to spend the rest of his time in office grappling with the implications for Kenya's economic policy and for the influence that this gave foreign governments and the IFIs over the country's direction.

Infrastructure and Energy

Despite these problems, new infrastructure investments were still coming on stream, mostly funded by donors. The Nyali Bridge connecting Mombasa to the north coast, for example, was built in the late 1970s with Japanese aid, and the World Bank funded several new highway projects. Mombasa was the most modern and efficient port between the Middle East and South Africa.

Things were not going so well in the rail or aviation sectors. The British-built narrow-gauge rail network had changed little since the 1960s, apart from the conversion from steam to diesel locomotives. Rail freight and passenger traffic increased until 1981, but then fell off. By the mid-1980s, unit costs were rising and the network was entering a decline from which it never recovered.[84] Forced to compete with road traffic, Kenya Railways was hampered by special tariffs dictated by the government to subsidise exports of fluorspar, sugar, sisal, soda ash, maize and wheat, and by having to pay for infrastructure maintenance where road users did not. In 1983, the government waived repayment of Ksh533 million in loans and interest just to keep it operating. Kenya Airways, meanwhile, had been in trouble since its formation. Undercapitalised, with old planes, it struggled to compete with international airlines. By 1983, it was insolvent, with accumulated losses exceeding capital by 40 per cent. Without foreign exchange to buy new planes, it could do little.[85]

For electricity, Kenya still relied on the majority state-owned East African Power and Light, renamed the Kenya Power and Lighting Company (KPLC) in 1983 as sole distributor, and the Kenya Power Company and Tana River Development Company as generators. On the supply side, responding to recent oil shocks, major hydroelectric and geothermal investments were under way. A large hydroelectric plant was being constructed at Kiambere, funded by World Bank loans, and a European bank loaned US$9 million to extend the Ol Kaaria geothermal scheme in 1981–2.[86] Meanwhile, the UK- and West German-funded Masinga Dam and hydro scheme on the Tana River was finished in 1981, and in 1982 the Tana and Athi River Development Authority joined the other government bodies as a supplier of power. In 1983, hydroelectricity produced 72 per cent of Kenya's electricity – a major achievement. On the demand side, in 1974, Kenya had introduced a rural electrification programme that connected most district headquarters to the national grid. However, progress was painfully slow; only 6 per cent of Kenya's population had access to electricity.

In the oil and gas sector, the Mombasa refinery remained the core of Kenya's strategy. The Kenya Power Company pipeline now delivered most fuel to Nairobi, and was run both efficiently and profitably. Despite its commitments, in 1981 the government created another parastatal, the National Oil Corporation of Kenya (NOCK) to increase state control of the oil industry. By 1988, NOCK was importing 30 per cent of Kenya's crude and selling to the marketing companies, weakening the influence of the multinationals. The Kisumu Molasses Project (see below) was also under construction, designed to produce ethanol for use in cars. In the informal sector, wood, charcoal and kerosene remained the main energy sources, and Kenya's tree cover was declining under pressure from a growing population's demand for wood.

Manufacturing Industry

Kenya had continued to develop its manufacturing capacity, but in the 16 years since independence, its contribution to GDP had only risen from 10 to 13 per cent, and it had created few new jobs. Although dozens of import-substitution and material-processing factories had been established, and Kenya was one of the most sophisticated economies in Africa, there was no take-off into capital goods production apart from car kit assembly. What Kenya did manufacture was for domestic consumption or for its African neighbours. Its products were not of sufficiently high quality or low price to compete globally (owing to shortages of skilled technical labour, the labour-intensive nature of industry and limited technology transfer by multinationals). The limitations of the import substitution model were becoming apparent, especially since the collapse of the EAC had shrunk its protected market. Structural adjustment was bringing with it a new industrial strategy, with more stress on exports and reduced protection. In practice, though, these policies were pursued half-heartedly to avoid damaging local industries, and little had changed by the mid-1980s. The main side-effect was a reduction in state finance for industrial loans. Since the domestic credit market was small and the cost of foreign loans was climbing, the result was a shortage of funds for industrial development.[87]

The cash crunch and shortage of spare parts and materials of 1980–2 hit industry hard. Several businesses were forced to close down, including Kisumu Cotton Mills and the controversial Kisumu Molasses Project, which collapsed in 1981 after consuming US$130 million in construction costs. The plant, the only one of its kind in sub-Saharan Africa, was designed to produce power alcohol from sugar residues, using an old Brazilian ethanol refinery. It was formed in 1977 as a joint venture between the government (which held 51 per cent), the Madhvani Group and investors from Luxembourg, Switzerland and Panama, some of whom appeared to be 'briefcase companies'. It seems to be an early example of a project designed to extract funds from the Treasury through management fees and transfer pricing; it relied on government subsidies and would never have been profitable at 1980s fuel prices.[88] The government ended up with the entire debt when the project was put into receivership in 1983.

Employment and Trade Unionism

The employment situation continued to worsen. Manufacturing employment had barely doubled since independence and only constituted 2 per cent of a labour force of nearly 6 million. Probably 10 per cent of the labour force was formally unemployed, most in the urban areas; many others were in informal or temporary low-income jobs, and there was massive under-employment amongst farm workers.[89] The civil service, in contrast, had seen dramatic increases, particularly after the 1978 tripartite agreement, which had led to a 14 per cent jump in numbers and was a valuable source of short-term patronage. By 1983, this was recognised as a structural mistake.

Despite the nominal power of the 33 registered trade unions and of COTU, the laws requiring compulsory mediation and cool-down periods made striking legally very difficult. One exception came in 1981, when new rules demanding that state doctors give up private practice caused a nationwide doctors' strike in May 1981. Other strikes brought bank employees and industrial workers onto the streets. Unions were banned and strikes were broken up, but 1980–2 was the most serious period of industrial disruption since 1974.

Land and Agriculture

Agriculture's share of GDP was now stabilising at just under a third. The key planks of government agricultural policy were food self-sufficiency, increased cash-crop exports and – as time passed – a commitment to increase producer prices to achieve this (at the cost of consumers). Despite calls from the IFIs for structural changes to the role of the agricultural boards, they retained their monopoly positions as suppliers of inputs, marketers of produce and tax collectors.[90]

The processing services for smallholder cash-crops – including coffee, cotton, sugar, milk and tea – experienced significant predation from central and local interests in the early 1980s, bringing some close to collapse.[91] While on paper their influence should have allowed such bodies to lobby for better pricing or protection, they proved unable to do so. Short-term political pressures kept processing charges and prices low, while the new elites extracted surpluses to secure their positions, or used the factories as sources of patronage, increasing costs.

Food Production

The performance of Kenya's food-crops was uneven, with production and prices fluctuating, a function of drought, international supply and demand and state policy. In the key maize sector, producer prices were raised after the famine in 1980, but poor weather meant that production did not recover until 1982 (see Figure 7.10). Wheat was less affected by the drought, but production remained below demand (which was increasing with urbanisation and new tastes for bread), forcing large imports.

7.10: Maize and wheat production, 1964–84

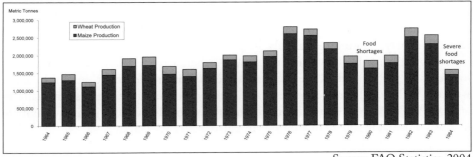

Source: FAO Statistics, 2004

In 1979, as recommended by the Ndegwa report, the poorly performing Wheat Board and the Maize and Produce Board were merged to form the National Cereals and Produce Board (NCPB), responsible for the purchase, distribution, storage and sale of both maize and wheat. Its aim was to manage price fluctuations and to provide buffer storage to deal with surpluses and shortages. Although it claimed a monopoly on maize marketing, in practice it handled 30 per cent of Kenya's maize production (most from the old European large farms), while 60 per cent was consumed directly and 10 per cent was sold privately quasi-legally.[92] Long-distance movement of maize remained illegal without a permit.

The government resisted IMF pressure to end the state monopoly of grain marketing, for reasons including fear of famine and the desire to protect both consumers and producers. The government strongly supported a policy of national food self-sufficiency throughout the 1980s, a view that was reinforced by the severe drought of 1984. However, this conflicted with economists' calls to maximise cash-crop production instead; to earn foreign currency that could be used to buy foreign food and other products. In practice, rather than focusing on one high-value crop, as economics would suggest (since profits per acre were generally larger), most small farmers diversified. To reduce the risk of weather, cooperative and board malpractice, payment delays, and unstable international crop prices, many combined cash-crops such as coffee and cotton with food crops. This remained a rational choice, even though inefficient, because of the uncertain prices and availability of food.

Encouraged by the World Bank, producer prices were increased to close to import parity. Maize, wheat, rice and sugar prices all increased by 50 per cent or more (in shilling terms) between 1981 and 1983, and farmers responded to these incentives. All price controls were removed on some products, including beef, increasing prices, production and incomes for producers. The World Bank invested heavily in agricultural development programmes, and to support farmers, the government offered large (unsecured) loans to farmers through the AFC.

Cash-Crops

Coffee and tea remained Kenya's most important export crops. International Coffee Agreement quotas were reimposed in 1980, limiting Kenya's exports to 83,000 tonnes, below its actual production. There was a mounting stock of unsold produce and little encouragement for further plantings. Tea production remained flat after the expansion of the late 1970s (at under 100,000 tonnes per annum) until the bumper year of 1983. The crop was more important as a smallholder activity than ever before, however, with 150,000 KTDA-managed smallholders by 1982.

Amongst Kenya's other crops, pyrethrum went through a brief period of boom and bust. After two decades of stability, production peaked in 1983 at nearly 30,000 tonnes. In that year, however, both world prices and demand collapsed, and the Pyrethrum Board was unable to pay growers. Output fell to only 6,000 tonnes in 1986. On the positive side, horticultural exports (flowers, fruit and vegetables), though small, were growing rapidly, with smallholders replacing the old plantations as the main suppliers.

In the sugar industry, the early 1980s saw the investments of the previous decade come to maturity. With South Nyanza (SoNy) and Nzoia sugar factories coming on stream in 1979–80, the cane crushed doubled between 1977 and 1980.[93] In 1980, refined sugar output exceeded 400,000 tonnes and Kenya exported almost 95,000 tonnes. Kenya was finally self-sufficient in sugar. Nearly half the cane was grown by Luo and Luhya smallholders, providing a valuable source of income.[94] However, problems were already emerging, especially with the newest factories, which were seriously under-capitalised and with a pricing structure that made Kenya's relatively expensive and labour-intensive processing economically marginal. Cooperative outgrower service organisations suffered from predation and poor management. Fixed prices in a period of rapid inflation left the factories with losses in 1980 and 1981. By 1981, cane was rotting in the fields because prices were too low for it to be worth farmers supplying, and payment delays in Nzoia and SoNy were so severe that farmers could not rely on the income. Although prices increased thereafter, an opportunity to create a sustainable import substitution market was receding, due to under-capitalisation, poor management, high distribution and processing costs, pricing, low capacity utilisation and lack of foreign exchange. The government was both the perpetrator and the victim. Although management contracts were in the hands of foreign agents, the state owned more than 90 per cent of the five main factories.[95]

Cotton too experienced problems. Cotton growing was increasingly a smallholder activity, with 100,000 producers in South Nyanza and Western Province producing half Kenya's crop. Production had finally taken off in the late 1970s, with a new scheme to achieve self-sufficiency in textile production, in which the government provided free seed and free credit, combined with higher producer prices. The state also invested in cotton via the National Irrigation Board (NIB), which managed the large irrigation schemes, including the Bura project in Tana River District, which began production in 1982–3. Cotton production in 1980 reached a record of 38,000 tonnes, but the performance of the Cotton Lint and Seed Marketing Board, which had a monopoly on purchases and sales, was extremely poor. By 1981, it was struggling to pay farmers. The market for cotton was also weakening, due to the importation of second-hand clothes and the gradual move towards synthetic materials. Finally, inefficiency and low investment left production costs well above world levels and quality levels low. By the late 1980s, many growers had abandoned the crop and the board was moving towards complete collapse. It was the first of many such crises to come.

The Closed Land Frontier

The land frontier was now closed, and there were few new settlement schemes, although occasionally the state would drip-feed a farm for settlement as a political reward, or subdivide and allocate ex-Crown lands in marginal areas to squatters. However, the peasantisation of agriculture continued. Subdivision of the *shirika* and group-owned farms accelerated in 1978–83, and the Ol Kalou salient was broken up into individual plots. During 1982–5, the number of farms in the ex-white highlands classified as 'large farms' fell by 20 per cent, the first substantial decline since 1966.[96] At the same time, the large European-owned ranches and coffee plantations began to be bought out by Africans in earnest.

In 1983–4, there were numerous legal cases against Kikuyu land-buying companies, since at least 70,000 contributors had still received no plots. Anti-corruption populism and anti-Kikuyu elite activities conveniently coincided. In 1986, Moi demanded the shutdown of all the 1,000 remaining land-buying companies and the subdivision of the farms they had bought, claiming they had cheated the public. There were more grants of government lands to well-connected individuals and speculators, although now the beneficiaries were connected with Moi rather than Kenyatta. Indeed, land was a key tool by which Moi bought loyalty throughout his presidency. By 1979, he was already using G. G. Kariuki to ensure that when state-owned farms in Nakuru were subdivided and allocated, chunks were reserved for senior settlement and security officials.[97] Settlement schemes were often used to settle parachuted outsiders, while local officials, ministers and civil servants allocated some plots to themselves or their families.[98] The result was often violent disputes, legal cases and land left idle as a result. Local politicians faced a difficult choice, trying to placate their constituents while not upsetting a patronage system of which they themselves were often the beneficiaries.

In the meantime, the land adjudication and registration process slowed, as roughly two-thirds of agricultural land had been demarcated by 1980 (see Figure 7.11). The remainder was mostly pastoral land, grazed in common and far harder to demarcate. There were few individual or group title registrations after 1983, leaving North-Eastern Province, Marsabit, Isiolo, Turkana, Samburu and much of the Coast un-adjudicated.

The problem of Coast Province and its Arab landlords was a particular concern. The *Development Plan, 1979–83* had promised a review of land rights, which had

7.11: Annual land registration and adjudication, 1966–89

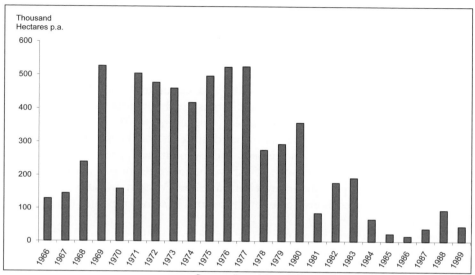

Source: Republic of Kenya, *Statistical Abstracts*, 1972–2001

not taken place because of the inevitable problems. Only by sticking rigorously to the 'willing buyer, willing seller' model and insisting on the sanctity of individual title, however obtained, could the government keep the lid on popular protest. The ethnicity of land ownership remained a potent issue, though any resort to violence in its name was repressed. Trouble flared up in December 1981, when Nandi and Luhya farmers fought over land on the borders of Nandi and Kakamega districts.[99] There was also violence between Maasai and immigrants in Narok, during which several thousand Kipsigis immigrants were driven out of the district – another warning of troubles to come in the 1990s.[100]

Socio-Economic Differentiation and Agricultural Development

As the processes of social differentiation continued, so did the debate as to whether Kenya was becoming a society of rich landowners and a landless proletariat, or whether the smaller and medium-sized farms would endure. The data on farm sizes and incomes were unreliable, but suggested that proletarianisation was occurring, albeit at a different pace in different regions. Subdivision was cutting the number of large farms, but this was counteracted by land sales from the poor to the wealthy.

The number of sales remained relatively low, however. Kenyans' emotional attachment to land (even if economically irrational on paper) encouraged the continuation of a smallholder model, even though it left many farms too small to produce economically. Cash-cropping had also delayed differentiation, because small plots could be profitable with coffee and other high-input cash-crops. Rather than selling up, many smaller farmers 'straddled' instead, combining on- and off-farm income. Indeed, the main means for most families to accumulate capital since the 1950s had been to combine salaried employment, businesses and crop production. Studies of Kisii and Embu in the 1980s suggested that straddlers were the only families extending their land holdings. However, the movement from peasant to straddler was becoming harder, institutionalising the decisions and accidents of the independence period.[101]

In Central Province, the process of land consolidation into fewer hands was most advanced. There was increasing rural landlessness, with a quarter of the population probably landless by 1978. Concerns about population growth, inequality and the questionable productivity of large farms all drove calls for further subdivision and ceilings on land holdings by academics and by politicians such as Orengo and Wamwere. The state resisted such a policy change, reflecting a combination of factors, including the personal interests of the elites, Western pressure to retain the free land market, the economic case for large farms in some crops and the high cost of land reform.

Despite two decades of innovation, most farmers still relied on family labour, and no large-scale agricultural labour market had emerged outside the plantation sector. Even in Central Province, less than 10 per cent of the labour invested in agriculture was hired. Not only was family labour cheap, but there was too little cash to support labourers between harvests, and little incentive to produce efficiently for absentee landowners.[102] Despite the British- and World Bank-led reforms of the 1950s and 1960s, Kenya had never fully transitioned to a market economy for land. Those wishing to buy land often could not do so because of the lack of credit and informal embargos on land sales to those from other ethnic groups. Land purchases were also risky because of uncertainty about the rights of tenants, family members and squatters and because of unofficial subdivision. The rental market had also failed to take off, as land titles remained in limbo between pre-colonial use-based and full capitalist property rights.[103] With a growing population, informal land sales and increasing corruption in the land registration and legal systems, land litigation was widespread.

Pastoralists – Still Second-Class Citizens

Although Moi had far better connections with the pastoral areas than had Kenyatta, the camel- and cattle-herding pastoralists of the north remained second-class citizens in many ways. Development in northern Somali, Gabbra, Boran, Rendille, Samburu and Turkana lands was almost non-existent in the 1970s. There were still few schools and no industry. Pastoralists were barely mentioned in analyses of Kenya's economy and scarcely seen as playing a role in deciding the country's future.

Over much of the country, pastoralism entered the 1980s in decline as development (including education) reached semi-arid lands and at the same time drought devastated herds, forcing nomads to seek other means of survival. The practice of stock theft or cattle rustling was growing rather than dying out, and there was increasing use of modern weapons acquired from neighbouring countries. Donors and aid agencies had tried repeatedly to improve the lot of pastoralists through irrigation projects that encouraged the Turkana and Boran to become farmers, or which carved out private land holdings from the rangelands, in the hope that this would improve stock-keeping, but most had failed.[104] The drought of 1978–9 instigated another series of integrated development products in Machakos, Kitui, Baringo and Turkana.[105] The Kenya government and donors also introduced a special arid and semi-arid lands programme in 1979. Some projects began to support pastoral lifestyles by restocking rather than encouraging sedentarisation, irrigation or the breakup of common grazing.[106] In Maasailand, however, population pressures, economic changes and political pressure were driving the demarcation and subdivision of the Kajiado group ranches, creating individual ranches that were barely economic and further speeding change in Maasai society.[107]

The Somali of the North-East, still mainly nomadic, remained a thorn in the side of the security forces. Although the *shifta* war was long over, banditry continued. The province still hosted significant military forces to deter Somali attack, including a new airbase, a GSU battalion and a tank squadron, and was closed to most outsiders. Kenyan Somali were still required to carry a special identity card to prove they were citizens, and were viewed with suspicion elsewhere. The local provincial administration, magistrates and police were almost all from other Kenyan communities, and behaved much like an occupying military power; Kenyatta for example had never visited the province as president. There were mass killings by security forces in November 1980 in Garissa after some upcountry officials were murdered. PC Benson Kaaria chillingly warned, 'a thousand Somalis will die' for every civil servant killed.[108]

Corruption and Prebendalism

In the early 1980s, the evidence grew that the Kenyan state was neither a powerless tool of foreign multinationals nor the puppet of domestic capitalists, but in part an independent actor. Its control over a large and valuable set of assets left them vulnerable to exploitation by those holding the levers of political power. Access to the resources that the state commanded and the ability to direct them for personal gain and political purposes was in fact a fundamental driver for competitive politics. The emergence of a predatory and prebendal state in the dying days of the Kenyatta regime and its enthusiastic exploitation by the Moi elite was to prove one of the main drivers of Kenya's economic and social malaise.[109]

State resources were increasingly diverted into the parasitic sector, the off-book sector of the economy in which insiders extracted resources from the state for private benefit via bribery, abuses of procurement and perks of office. Despite Njonjo's promise in 1978 to 'clean Kenya of corruption', it was worsened by Moi's takeover, since a shakier president needed to buy support more overtly.[110] There were some initial efforts at cleaning up corruption during 1978–82, including pressure to reverse the Ndegwa Report and end civil servants' involvement in private business. During a debate in 1981, it emerged that civil servants, who had been required to declare their interests in 1973 by the Ndegwa Report, had refused to do so unless politicians were required to do the same. Shikuku quoted from a Sessional Paper on how far the situation had already declined:

> ... some public servants utilise Government facilities in order to benefit themselves. Some are said to tender for Government supplies and to see to it that their tenders are always successful. Others are said to be in the habit of accepting rewards for work they are paid to do by the Government.[111]

In September 1982, the government again demanded civil servants declare their interests.[112] Again, it was ignored. A year later, the government commissioned a National Code of Conduct, which yet again recommended a register of interests, the abolition of civil servants' right to engage in private business, the appointment of an ombudsman and the sacking of officials under investigation for misdeeds. As usual, though, nothing was done. Talk was easy, but real action was to take another 20 years.

There was also evidence that the *harambee* movement was becoming an informal taxation system: chiefs were extorting money for unspecified projects, while *harambee* committees embezzled funds. Although *harambee* was a devolved local development scheme, from which the poor benefited in general more than the rich, there was as much politics as ever and less voluntarism.[113]

The cooperative movement also experienced problems, including widespread allegations of malpractice and misuse of funds. Like most other aspects of society, cooperative unions were best developed in Central Province, which contained about one-third of rural cooperative members. Now, however, reports emerged of the embezzlement of millions of shillings during the 1970s, mostly in (not coincidentally) Central Province and Meru, and several cooperative unions collapsed as a result. There were growing delays in the payments to farmers, reflecting profitability and liquidity problems within the marketing chain. To reduce the politicisation of the cooperative movement, Moi demanded in late 1981 that all politicians resign from posts with the unions, but this did not prevent them competing by proxy. During 1982, there was a campaign against corruption in the movement and many cooperatives were liquidated.

Despite Kenya's difficulties, the best connected prospered. Minister Oloitipitip, for example, boasted in 1982 that he could spend Ksh150 million (US$12 million) on his son's wedding, and in a conflation of material and affective assets, claimed in 1981 that independence had been so good for him that he had 'six cars, two big houses, 12 wives and 67 children'.[114] Most ministers, unlike backbenchers, soon became wealthy. Senior politicians and civil servants took advantage of their positions to acquire land, take loans without any intent to pay, and receive payments in return for political protection. The Bank of Baroda case was a high-profile example. When the staff of this bank discovered that it had engaged in illegal currency transactions, they published documents showing this and went on strike in protest. Rather than investigating, the Labour Ministry declared the strike illegal. Soon afterwards, it was alleged that Attorney-General Kamere, Minister for Labour Titus Mbathi and the deputy public prosecutor (all allies of Njonjo) had recently received substantial unsecured loans from the same bank, in which they did not hold accounts. The magazine *Africa Now* claimed that officials received US$1 million in bribes to hush up the bank's misbehaviour.[115]

There was a wide variety in attitudes to enrichment opportunities. Some leaders seized them with open arms; others avoided any indication of personal gain. In general, civil servants were more careful than politicians, but all were exposed to temptation and the expectation of enrichment, even where it had not occurred. Poor bureaucratic hygiene allowed a weakening of controls even where it did not result in losses.[116] Donor projects were a particularly fertile source of resources, with far more interest in obtaining the funds than in spending them wisely.[117]

It was widely believed, though unprovable, that by 1982 the nexus of accumulation was shifting from the Kikuyu to the Kalenjin. Moi himself was rapidly acquiring assets, generally in other names. As well as his investments via ALCS, his Baringo ally Henry Cheboiwo bought a controlling interest in a transport company in 1981. Asian executive Naushad Merali and his company Sameer Investments, formed in 1983, almost immediately acquired 51 per cent of the US Firestone Company in curious circumstances. Local tyre dealers were refused foreign exchange to prevent a counter-bid. Sameer's other directors were Kanyotu and a law firm that often acted as Moi's nominee.[118]

Regional and International Relations

While Moi was experiencing troubles at home, Kenya was playing a more assertive role internationally. Moi's foreign policy differed little from Kenyatta's but, unlike Kenyatta, Moi could travel, and he did so frequently. Moi paid his first state visit to the UK and the Netherlands in June 1979, where he met the British royal family and Prime Minister Margaret Thatcher. The British queen visited Kenya in 1983, to a rapturous response, her first state visit since independence.

Moi cultivated the US even more assiduously. Following a state visit in February 1980, he was back in September 1981, during which he met its new president, Ronald Reagan. Kenya's tilt to the US became more noticeable. During the early 1980s, US private business made several new investments in Kenya, including the arrival of IBM, and by 1980, the US was Kenya's third-largest bilateral aid donor after the UK and West Germany.

Relations between Kenya and China also improved after Moi's accession, with ambassadorial level representation restored. Moi visited Beijing in 1980 and Zhao Ziyang, premier of the State Council, repaid the compliment in 1983. Seeing Kenya as a market and potential ally, China began to cultivate the country more diligently. It donated education and technical assistance under a 1980 cultural cooperation treaty, and helped build a sports centre in Nairobi (the Moi International Sports Complex). Trade remained minimal, though.

Inside Africa, Moi served as OAU chairman from 1981 until 1983. He was extremely active in trying to resolve African issues, and hosted several events in Nairobi. South Africa remained a particular challenge. Like his predecessors,

Foreign Minister Robert Ouko was publicly critical of apartheid and South Africa. Kenya still required that South Africans be security-vetted before receiving visas, and discouraged such visits. Njonjo, however, ensured that contacts continued and campaigned in the government against its South African policy. It later emerged that Njonjo and Gethi had links with the South African mercenaries who tried to overthrow the government of Albert René of the Seychelles in 1981.[119] Almost as controversially, Njonjo also maintained links with Israel. Biwott, too, had strong links with Israel, originating from his business ventures and marriage to an Israeli wife. The Israelis continued to maintain security links with Kenya (they supplied surface-to-air missiles for Kenya's patrol boats, for example). Although diplomatic relations were not restored, El Al resumed flights to Nairobi in 1983.

Inside East Africa, Kenya's position remained difficult. Trade levels were low and tensions high. As Moi was assuming the presidency, in October 1978 Uganda had invaded northern Tanzania and claimed part of the common border. Tanzania responded in kind and its troops entered Uganda. Gradually, in chaos and fear, the Amin regime collapsed. Amin fled, and in April 1979, Tanzania installed a puppet regime. Kenya watched without intervening, but closed its Ugandan border in 1978 and 1979. The Tanzanians remained in Uganda for three years. In 1980, their preferred candidate, Milton Obote, was elected as president. Nonetheless, civil strife continued, and several guerrilla movements emerged. The Kenyan elite continued to harbour deep suspicions of Uganda, particularly as the Luo had cultural and economic links with their cross-border cousins. This was one of the reasons used to justify discrimination against the Luo in the military.

Relations with Tanzania improved slightly after Moi's accession. He had cordial meetings with Nyerere in 1979, and all three East African presidents met for the first time in a decade in January 1980. However, there was no true thaw until Njonjo's departure. November 1983 saw a final agreement on the division of the assets of the EAC: Kenya and Tanzania agreed to compensate Uganda for the assets seized in 1976–7, and the Kenya–Tanzania border reopened. Tanzania meanwhile had also come close to collapse, bankrupted by its policies, the oil shock, bad weather and the Uganda war.

In the north-west, relations with Somalia remained difficult, and Kenya reaffirmed its anti-Somali military cooperation agreement with Ethiopia's Marxist government in 1979.

The Crisis Begins, February–July 1982

In February 1982, Kenya entered a period of crisis that began with a Cabinet reshuffle and ended with an attempted coup. As the year advanced, relations deteriorated in the inner circle, while radical politicians sought to break KANU's monopoly of power.

On 25 February 1982, Moi reshuffled the Cabinet for a second time in 18 months. In a dramatic announcement that caught ministers unaware, he declared, 'nobody should consider himself indispensable.'[120] Moi was finally stepping out from the shadow of his handlers. He downgraded both Kikuyu combatants: Kibaki moved from Finance to Home Affairs, but kept the vice-presidency; Njonjo lost Home Affairs and the CID to the OP, leaving him with only Immigration and Elections, a clear demotion. As a consolation, Moi appointed Magugu, Njonjo's ally, as minister of finance. Moi also moved elsewhere both his ministers of state in the OP, G. G. Kariuki and Biwott, who had clashed several times. He was signalling the end of the era of shared rule.

Just as Kenyatta had done, Moi was developing an inner circle or kitchen cabinet of loyalists alongside his official advisers in the Cabinet and the civil service. Amongst these Kalenjin insiders were Biwott (from Elgeyo-Marakwet), Isaac Salat (from Kipsigis), Assistant Minister Stanley Metto (from Nandi, a family friend) and Cheboiwo (Moi's business partner and Tugen neighbour). Other senior Kalenjin inside the state apparatus now included permanent secretaries Joseph arap Leting and Aaron Kandie, Comptroller of State House Andrew arap Limo and the managing director of KPTC, arap Ng'eny. Unlike the non-Kalenjin, these men owed their loyalties directly to Moi (although some were business partners or allies of Njonjo as well). Politically, KADU-era Moi supporters such as Matano and Tipis were also moving up the 'greasy pole', the latter being elevated to minister of state in the OP in June 1982. It was already clear that Moi rewarded loyalty above all else. Those who prospered were those who had backed him when times were hard. Njonjo had been most loyal of all, the man who had handed him the presidency, and for a decade it had seemed that Njonjo could do no wrong. Now, however, the situation was changing.

In parallel, by early 1982, Odinga and his allies had decided that enough was enough. As late as January, Odinga had still been trying to play a role in KANU – of which he was nominally a member – announcing that he would contest the planned KANU polls. However, he had also been preparing since 1981 to take KANU and the single-party state on directly. His allies in this high-risk venture included his son Raila, MP George Anyona, long-time ally Oyangi Mbaja, lawyer Oki Ombaka and lecturers Anyang' Nyong'o and Mukaru Ng'ang'a. In February 1982, Odinga began an assault that was to last for the next decade, and eventually to end in triumph. It began with a public statement criticising foreign and domestic exploitation, corruption and the way in which the IFIs were dictating Kenya's policies.[121] Odinga also denounced Kenya's poor relations with its neighbours and the deteriorating economic position. He informed Nyerere and others that he intended to found a new political party. Moi in return castigated Odinga (without naming him explicitly), accusing him indirectly of subversion and attacking the 'cheap slogans and the outworn dialectic' of his socialism, the continuation of a debate between the two that went back to 1965.[122] In March, Odinga tried to set up a NGO, which the government refused to register, and in May, he attacked the US military deal. At the same time, anti-government leaflets began to appear on the streets, and rumours spread that the radicals were about to launch a new political party.

In April 1982, Moi warned that he had not abolished detention without trial and ordered MPs to stop criticising corruption in Parliament. In one of the off-the-cuff utterances that revealed his sometimes-simplistic thinking, he asked: 'How can those who are unable to look after their beards be expected to look after the interests of other people?'[123] The socialist and Marxist challenge to KANU was now open, as represented in *(In)Dependent Kenya*, a book-length critique of Kenya's post-independence politics and economics published in 1982. It described the imperial presidency as 'nascent fascism', castigated Moi's rule as one of 'divine right' and 'a new chapter in the history of incompetent leadership', and called for acts of mass defiance against the regime.[124] The stage was set for a confrontation. Western governments, still tightly linked to Kenya's establishment and wary of Odinga, appeared to give little or no support to the dissenters.

In May 1982, it became clear that Odinga was indeed about to launch a new party, to be known as the Kenya African Socialist Alliance (KASA). He made a speech in London to British Labour MPs, arguing that there was 'A ruling class that has arisen out of massive corruption and misuse of power' and called for a mass party of peasants, workers and proletariat.[125] Anyona was even more open, saying, 'through the formation of another political party, the people of Kenya will decide, by free and democratic elections, who their leaders shall be . . .'[126] Most of the political class were aligned with the establishment, but a significant minority (including 20 or so MPs) were willing to challenge the system. Although most Kenyans remained locally focussed and unmoved by such calls, providing tacit support to the one-party system, many students, academics and Luo supported Odinga. The popularity of Odinga's views in other communities remains unknown, but would probably have been significant if voters had been permitted a free choice.

On 27 May 1982, the crisis broke and detention without trial was back. The first detainee was not a radical, though, but a Kikuyu insider, the long-serving deputy director of intelligence (the operational head of Special Branch), Stephen Muriithi.[127] In 1981, Muriithi had been transferred to head the Uplands Bacon Factory, a punishment posting. It was variously suggested that Muriithi had fallen out with Njonjo, Kanyotu or Moi. Muriithi had led the Special Branch investigation that had prepared the ground for the Muthemba trial.[128] In an unprecedented move, however, Muriithi refused to accept his appointment and went to court, arguing that the president did not have the authority to fire him from the police; only the Public Service Commission could do so. He lost, as the courts decided that the president could retire any civil servant he chose; Muriithi had planned to appeal, but was detained.[129] The most likely reason for his imprisonment was that Moi and his advisers could not accept that anyone had the right to challenge their authority.

Meanwhile, KASA's formation had forced the regime to legalise its monopoly of power. Although its registration could have been rejected administratively, the involvement of senior politicians forced the leadership to declare its hand. Within days of their plans becoming public, Odinga and Anyona were expelled from KANU and the party's Governing Council resolved to convert Kenya from a de facto to a *de jure* one-party state. To prevent public demonstrations against the change, several activists were detained without trial.[130] Anyona was detained on 31 May, and was followed by his lawyer John Khaminwa and by four university lecturers during June–July, including Alamin Mazrui and Ng'ang'a.[131] Others were arrested and charged with sedition. In a chilling warning to students, Moi commented that tough action was needed at the university to root out dissent: 'If you spare the rod, you will spoil the child.'[132] He warned of a plot by lecturers to arm students and cause chaos.[133] Seeing what was coming, several lecturers resigned their posts.

On 9 June 1982, the nineteenth constitutional amendment converted Kenya into a *de jure* one-party state. It added the later-infamous Section 2A to the Constitution: 'There shall be in Kenya only one political party, the Kenya African National Union.'[134] In Parliament, Njonjo led the campaign for its passage, claiming that it purely regularised an existing fact, that Kenya could not afford the luxury of another party and that 'more than 99 per cent of the population want and support this one party system.'[135] Kibaki seconded the motion, claiming that unity had led the country towards development and avoided chaos, and blamed Marxism and foreign ideologies for creating the pressure for a second party: 'If somebody questions the legitimacy of this Government, how in all serioussness can he expect sympathy or even the freedom to go on questioning the legitimacy of the Government?'[136] The Constitution was also amended to require that MPs would lose their seats if they ceased to be members of KANU. Similar amendments were made to the electoral law, removing references to preliminary elections and converting them to general elections. The same amendment recreated the powerful colonial post of chief secretary, head of the civil service, with powers independent of those delegated by the president. The amendment was unopposed on both second and third readings. Those voting for the move included many who denounced it later, including Abuya, Orengo, wa Mwachofi, Mwithaga, Wamwere, Shikuku, Rubia, Karume, Keen, Michael Wamalwa and Oloo-Aringo. Wamwere suggested that MPs were threatened with detention if they did not back the proposal.[137] This sudden closedown was a precipitating factor for the coup.

With the reintroduction of detention and the declaration of the one-party state, students and exiles in London protested publicly, playing upon the government's ever-present concern about British opinions of Kenya.[138] *Standard* editor Githii also criticised the reintroduction of detention (as he had in 1966) and was immediately sacked as a result.[139]

As July 1982 advanced, there was growing tension in Parliament and the country. The socialist opposition had been driven underground, but the ruling elite was deeply divided. Njonjo still had the support of around a third of the parliamentary party and the Cabinet, but he appeared to be losing ground in the struggle to wrest the vice-presidency from Kibaki, and to have lost Moi's unequivocal support. His allies controlled many of the key offices of state and much of the government, including the post of chief secretary, which had been occupied by Kiereini, but his enemies were equally numerous and vociferous. In Parliament on 29 July 1982, there was a bitter exchange, during which Oloo-Aringo attacked those who were threatening that some politicians were 'finished', and suggested that MPs should never become 'spokesmen of other Hon. Members of Parliament because our loyalty is first and foremost to the President . . .'[140] In this tense mood, Parliament adjourned and MPs dispersed to their constituencies, bars and businesses.

The August 1982 Coup

On Sunday 1 August 1982, Kenya experienced its first true coup attempt. At around 2 a.m., non-commissioned officers, mainly Luo, from the air force rebelled. They took over Embakasi, Eastleigh and Nanyuki airbases, then seized Jomo Kenyatta International Airport, the post office and the Voice of Kenya. KAF troops moved through Nairobi, firing, inciting civilians to revolt and waving clenched fists with the slogan '*Pambana*' (power). Most of the army was in the north on exercises. The rebels' first nationwide radio broadcast at 6.30 a.m. declared, 'Rampant corruption, tribalism, nepotism have made life almost intolerable in our society. The economy of this country is in a shambles due to corruption and mismanagement.'[141] They announced the establishment of a People's Redemption Council and the release of all detainees. Most Kenyans hesitated in fear for the rest of that morning. In contrast, many University of Nairobi students openly supported the coup. Some had been deeply involved in its organisation.

Moi was up-country at his farm in Kabarak in northern Nakuru, protected by the Presidential Escort Unit. Coup plotters would normally have attempted to capture or kill the president, but on this occasion appear to have made little effort to do so. Moi was evacuated from his home into a maize plantation when the news broke. A trustworthy police officer was dispatched to the Lanet barracks to find out whether the army units there, headed by Brigadier John Musomba, were involved.[142] They were not. Moi was safe.

The coup failed. Neither the army nor the GSU rebelled in sympathy, despite KAF expectations of support. The coup was poorly organised, with many rebels drunk and looting rather than preparing for a counterattack. They failed to capture or kill any of the political leaders they had targeted and did not seize army headquarters. Without army support, the rebels had only surprise, their limited numbers and their aircraft as weapons. Two F5 fighters were loaded with bombs to attack the army and GSU headquarters, but the bomb loaders and pilots did not support the coup. They deliberately sabotaged the bombs and the pilots dropped them over forests rather than over the proposed targets.

For the rest of that day, there was fierce fighting in Nairobi between the KAF, with their student supporters, and troops loyal to the regime (see Figure 7.12). The government's immediate counterattack was led by the four remaining senior officers still in Nairobi, including Deputy Army Commander Mahamoud Mohammed and Sawe. The recapture of the Voice of Kenya radio station at about 9.30 a.m. and a subsequent broadcast that the rebels had been defeated contributed to the collapse of the coup as the 'bandwagon effect' ended. Eastleigh base, the nerve centre of the revolt, was the last major installation to fall, hit by missiles from an army helicopter. Seeing their plans disintegrating, two coup leaders, Hezekiah Ochuka and Pancras Okumu Oteyo (both Luo), hijacked a cargo plane and flew into Tanzania, seeking political asylum.

There was mass looting in the city by soldiers and then by civilians, taking advantage of the chaos. Dozens of women were raped, cars stolen and shops emptied. Asians were the particular victims of both KAF robberies and generalised looting

7.12: The army on the streets, 1 August 1982

Courtesy: Nation Group Newspapers

and violence. A deeply shocked Moi returned to Nairobi the same evening, escorted by an army platoon. The official death toll was 159, but unofficial estimates ranged from 600 to 1,800. The country was effectively under military rule for weeks. The airport remained closed for several days while the army conducted house-to-house searches for looted goods and escaped rebels.

Raila Odinga, deputy director of the Kenya Bureau of Standards, was amongst those arrested, following testimony from interrogated rebels that he and his father were involved in the coup.[143] He, a Luo journalist and a Luo professor were all charged with treason, a capital offence. Charges were eventually dropped, however, after advice that a conviction would be difficult and would further fuel international criticism following allegations that rebels and students were being tortured.[144] Instead, after weeks of interrogation, all three were detained in March 1983. Raila spent the next five years in jail.[145] His father Oginga Odinga was placed under house arrest and his ministerial ally Oloo-Aringo was sacked. Clearly, Moi believed the Odinga family and their allies were implicated.

There is little doubt that the Odinga family did have links with the plotters. Years later, the *Standard* published testimony from Ochuka and others that Raila and Jaramogi's ally Oyangi Mbaja had acted as the linkmen between Oginga Odinga and the plotters, helping to organise and providing funds for the coup. Raila's biography offered further confirmation from former rebels that he helped organise, fund and execute the plot.[146] The key actors were almost all Luo, and Ochuka was said to have used a car owned by Raila on the day of the coup. Morton's biography of Moi quotes ex-minister Omamo as saying, 'Before the coup a number of Odinga youth wingers left Luoland for Nairobi and said that they would return with the national flag.'[147] Raila admitted participating in secret anti-government activities, including the production of *Pambana* magazine, but denied direct involvement in the coup.

The origins of the coup were various. There were internal issues such as pay, the declining quality of services, and growing corruption in military procurement. Kikuyu dominance in the KAF leadership rankled with junior officers. Some linked the attempt to anger at Kenya's US military links.[148] There was also a link to the events of 1965–9. The political ideals that Odinga represented – socialist, anti-Western and redistributionist – had remained strong throughout the 1970s. Now, with the *de jure* one-party state, only military opposition remained. The KAF rebels cited corruption, repression and disenfranchisement of the masses, particularly of the Luo, as the drivers behind their actions. Ringleader James Diang'a in his memoir described how the deliberate blocking of promotion for Luo officers and concerns about the country's political direction had contributed to the coup attempt. He described it as the culmination of preparations that stretched back to February 1980, with the primary aim of preventing Njonjo seizing power.[149] The leaders of several countries, including Uganda, Tanzania and Zimbabwe, were alleged to have been aware of the plot, though there was no evidence they were actively involved.[150]

The biggest question however, is: were there two or even three coups planned for the same period? Much of the testimony that might have clarified this was heard *in camera*, or its truthfulness is uncertain, but what did emerge indicates plans for a second coup. *Africa Now* reported that there were two other ministerial coups in preparation.[151] Raila Odinga's arrest statement stated that Njonjo had been planning a coup for 5 August 1982, led by the GSU, and that GSU officials had told him that when the 'Luo coup' began, they did not know on which side to fight. Oteyo too claimed there was a 'conservative' coup planned by Kikuyu officers for 3 or 6 August. Others suggested it was planned to take place when Moi was attending the OAU in Libya on 6 or 8 August.[152]

Moi's response indicates that he doubted the loyalty of senior Kikuyu officials. It emerged later that Special Branch and military intelligence had been aware of the KAF plot for weeks, yet allowed it to proceed. The Air Force Commander Major-General Peter Kariuki (a Kikuyu) was jailed for four years for failing to prevent a mutiny (see Figure 7.13). He had been told a coup was imminent, but had replied that he already knew about it, and had gone to his farm for the weekend. Chief of Staff General Mulinge also admitted that he had known of the plans. He later told the *Nation*: 'Prior to August 1, we had received classified information that some junior ranks were planning a mutiny. Not only was I informed about the plan but I was also provided with names of the masterminds behind the planned coup . . .'[153] Mulinge claimed that he had ordered their arrest, but his orders were disobeyed, and that it had been obvious that the KAF were on the verge of revolt. Yet, Mulinge too 'went away for the weekend'. Kariuki claimed that he had told Mulinge of the plot, but that Mulinge was ordered not to testify in his defence.[154] The British security services had also been aware of coup plans via Kenyan officers training in the UK and had alerted the Kenyan military in June, but no action had been taken.[155]

Whether Njonjo was a beneficiary of these plans may never be known. The KAF rebels certainly believed they were striking before a pro-Njonjo coup. British insiders such as Colin Legum suggested that much of the government had known of the

7.13: Chief of Staff Mulinge and Major-General Peter Kariuki

Courtesy: Nation Group Newspapers

planned Njonjo coup, but had been taken by surprise by the Luo pre-emptive strike.[156] Raila Odinga reported that Police Chief Ben Gethi and GSU Commandant Mbuthia (both Kikuyu) had twice torn up his statement in which he claimed there was going to be a pro-Njonjo coup.[157] The managing director for Securicor Kenya suggested that Gethi had pulled all the police off the streets at midnight that night.[158] Gethi confirmed that he had been in communication with Njonjo at 4 a.m. on first news of the disturbances in Eastleigh, before speaking to Moi. The rebels hinted that they had been in communication with GSU headquarters on the morning of the attack and had been promised support. There were reports that early that morning some army units had been working with the KAF, but had then switched sides and opened fire on them.[159] Njonjo always denied any involvement in a coup plot, commenting years later, 'had I planned one, I would have succeeded'.[160]

Reconstruction and Response

Over the next few weeks, there were fervent demonstrations across the country, as politicians sought to demonstrate their continued loyalty (see Figure 7.14). It was a period of recrimination and doubt. Nairobi was under night curfew until September. The KAF was disbanded, almost all 2,000 airmen detained, and 900 were court-martialled. There were reports that confessions were extracted under torture. Ten airmen, mainly Luo, including Ochuka and Oteyo (who were eventually returned by Tanzania), were convicted of plotting the coup and executed in 1985. Nairobi University and Kenyatta College were closed for a year and dozens of students were jailed. The coup reinforced Moi's anti-intellectualism and his fear of both Marxists and Western-educated Kenyans, concerns that were to inspire the populist but oppressive actions of the second half of the decade.

The state seized the passports of many radical politicians, including those of Oginga Odinga, Mwachofi, Abuya, Orengo and Achieng-Oneko, and that of Githii. Odinga remained under house arrest for a year. Other anti-government individuals continued to be imprisoned. In August 1982, Wamwere and Nairobi law lecturer (later chief justice) Willy Mutunga became the eighth and ninth persons to be detained. Lecturer Maina wa Kinyatti was jailed for six years for possessing anti-government pamphlets. Journalists were also arrested and jailed. In November 1982, Orengo, on trial for forgery and theft, skipped bail and fled the country. Fellow Luo MP Onyango Midika was jailed for theft. The evidence introduced at the start of the trial that he had celebrated the coup may have assisted in his conviction.

The coup attempt was also the trigger for changes in the police and army, as Moi tried to ensure the security system would be loyal only to him. It had been a final warning that he had to change his style to survive. In the words of the *Standard*, the coup 'changed him from an easy-going, confident president, to a control-freak who wanted a direct handle on every important lever of State'.[161] It was clear that the political elite and the security forces were riddled with dissent. Moi had long been fearful of a Kikuyu coup and this botched attempt, which appears to have 'smoked out' many in the security forces whose loyalty was doubtful, left him more beholden to the army, but also secured him against an immediate rebellion. From now on, the authoritarian and paranoid aspects of the president's personality became dominant and his distrust of the Kikuyu sharpened. He had to create distance from his old allies and to rely only on those he knew he could trust, whatever their qualifications.

Both Gethi and Mbuthia were sacked and jailed within days, along with several mid-ranking Kikuyu officers. Kalenjin, pastoralist and northern officers began to be actively promoted. Perhaps surprisingly, given the role of the Luo community in the coup, Moi relied increasingly on Luo Rift Valley PC, Hezekiah Oyugi, who had been in Nakuru in August 1982 and had pledged his loyalty when many thought Nairobi was lost. Moi did not evict the Gema elites immediately from the security forces, however. In the police, Bernard Njiinu, Kenyatta's old Presidential

7.14: Loyalty demonstrations, August 1982

Courtesy: Nation Group Newspapers

Escort commander, became police commissioner on 21 August 1982, in a bizarre ceremony during which Moi and Kiereini jailed his predecessor.[162] A Meru, Erastus M'Mbijjiwe, who had been Rift Valley Provincial Police officer during the coup and had come to Moi's aid, took over the GSU (see Table 7.2). However, by 1984 three of the eight provincial heads of Special Branch, the new head of CID Noah arap Too and the deputy commissioner of the GSU were Kalenjin.[163]

The effects of the coup reverberated for years. It destroyed any plans Njonjo had to seize power and forced Moi to 'deconstruct' the Kenyatta state in order to survive.[164] In a curious way, therefore, Moi owed his survival to the radical Luo, whose intervention changed the course of Kenya's history. If they had not acted when they did, Kenya would probably have seen a pro-Kikuyu coup and a conservative, bureaucratic-elitist, Kikuyu-led government. It did not, though, signal the beginning of a series of coups and a descent into military rule, as in so many other African nations. It remains Kenya's only real coup attempt.

Although the appearance of normal life continued, there was paralysis at the top. The Njonjo faction was under deep suspicion. From the day of the coup, the collegiate presidency was gone. Moi withdrew into near-isolation; Morton says, 'Njonjo, Kariuki and other confidantes could no longer wander into State House and see the President when the mood took them.'[165] Neither Njonjo nor Kariuki could now join Moi in the presidential limousine. All ministers required clearance before entering State House, and Njonjo and G. G. Kariuki's security detail was withdrawn, a sign of severe displeasure.[166] Nyachae now controlled the OP and access to Moi, and he ensured that a distance was built between Moi and the Kikuyu triumvirate of Njonjo, Kariuki and Kiereini. There were indications that Moi loyalists were seeking evidence that Kikuyu leaders had been involved in the plot, but were unable to find proof. On several occasions, Moi warned that he no longer trusted those close to him, and that changes were in the offing. The *Weekly Review* summarised the crisis:

Table 7.2: Police and internal security heads in the early Moi years

Position	Name	Dates	Ethnicity
Police commissioner	Ben Gethi	1978–82 (sacked)	Kikuyu
	Bernard Njiinu	1982–8	Kikuyu
CID director	Ignatius Nderi	1973–84	Kikuyu
	Noah arap Too	1984–99	Kalenjin – Kipsigis
Head of Special Branch	James Kanyotu	1965–91	Kikuyu
GSU commandant	Peter Mbuthia	1978–82 (sacked)	Kikuyu
	Erastus M'Mbijjiwe	1982–7	Meru
Presidential Escort commander	Elijah Sumbeiywo	n/a	Kalenjin – Keiyo

Source: Various

. . . an air of uncertainty hangs over the political system. A sense of mistrust has been thrust into relations between politicians over the issue. No one knows who is and who is not implicated in the August 1 coup attempt, and until they know, politicians will continue to operate with the kind of tentativeness which now characterises most of their activities . . . the government machinery appears to be immobilised, with few top people doing anything really. All of them appear to be waiting. Waiting for the shake-up which they so dread.[167]

In the next few months, several provincial commissioners, permanent secretaries and the Central Bank Governor Duncan Ndegwa retired. Attorney-General Kamere, Njonjo's ally, was also forcibly retired.[168] Moi did not have the right to sack Kamere, as the Constitution stated that the attorney-general 'may be removed from office only for inability to exercise the functions of his office'. Moi did so nonetheless. Eyebrows were raised, but there was no lawsuit (since the last person to challenge an action by Moi in court had been detained). As in the security forces, there was no simplistic, wholesale ethnic purge. Moi was careful to 'boil the frog' of Kikuyu rule gently, allowing natural attrition to remove those not directly loyal to him. In 1983, most senior businessmen were still European or Kikuyu, and the majority of parastatal heads were still Kikuyu (including the heads of KPLC, the KCB, AFC, DFCK and KTDA), although there was a leavening of Kalenjin and others.

In the military, Moi relied increasingly upon Chief of Staff Mulinge. For nearly a year, he and other senior officers played a higher public role. The retirement age for senior officers was raised from 55 to 65, to allow Mulinge to stay on. The KAF was rebuilt and renamed the '82 Air Force, under the command of Mohammed, promoted to major-general. Eastleigh was renamed Moi Airbase, one of many institutions to be re-branded with the Moi prefix from this time on. It was not until 1 June 1983 that Moi released more than 8,000 jailed students and KAF members. Poor pay and living conditions had contributed to the coup. Now, new barracks were constructed and soldiers' pay increased.

In late 1982, Moi announced that a party revitalisation would soon begin, and that party elections, required every two years but not held since 1978, would take place in 1983. Although Moi's displeasure with his allies was apparent, the skirmishing between Kibaki and Njonjo continued. It was clear that Kibaki was going to face opposition for the vice-presidency of KANU if elections were held. By April 1983, just before the crisis broke and party elections were suspended, KANU had registered 1.7 million members, still a small proportion of the population, but showing for the first time a determination to create a mass party. Moi now placed more stress on KANU as an organ of legitimacy. He emphasised that KANU was a democratic party and that during KANU elections, 'democratic principles must be upheld in a manner which everyone can witness.'[169] However, theory and fact were different beasts. Lawyers were increasingly disturbed by the implications of KANU's ability to expel anyone from the party, denying them participation in politics without recourse to legal appeal and without any disciplinary procedures even being laid down.

Economic Reform and Recovery, 1982–3

As well as its security and political implications, the coup had serious economic effects. More than US$100 million of goods and equipment were damaged or looted, and the knock-on effects in jobs and private sector investment lost as a result of lost confidence were immense. Prices rose, creating an inflationary spike that left 1982 as the year of highest inflation since 1975. In the aftermath of the coup attempt, Moi introduced measures designed to assist economic recovery and help exports. However, rather than inflating the economy to satisfy political exigencies, as might be expected, he steered a different course. The government began to pay lip service, at least, to liberalisation and privatisation.

A Policy of Privatisation, 1982

In January 1982, still concerned about rising government spending, Moi had appointed a second working party, again led by Philip Ndegwa. Its brief was to get government spending within its income, rebalance the public and private sectors and improve the management of state spending. It reported just before the coup. It again demanded better spending controls, budgeting and planning. It also identified a 'fundamental structural problem' in the economy and the national accounts. Spending exceeded income and debt was rising, creating a spiral of rising interest payments. The team rejected a deficit-based inflationary solution, or 'printing money'. Instead, it adopted the emerging Western orthodoxy that only a reduction in the role of the public sector could solve Kenya's problems. As had been mooted in the 1979 Ndegwa Report and the Waruhiu Review, the state should cut its staff and focus on its core business.

The 1982 Working Party was even stronger in demanding an end to state investment in commercial activities. Government ownership of productive activities had helped decolonise the economy and promote development. It had probably been the only realistic option in the 1960s and early 1970s, when there was virtually no African private capital in the country. However, it had become an end in itself. There were now 147 statutory boards, plus 47 wholly owned companies, 36 where the government had a controlling interest and 93 where it had a minority holding.[170] This placed a vast burden on government, both financially and managerially. Most parastatals were drains on the Treasury, either directly or indirectly (most paid no taxes on their profits). The K£900 million invested in them so far was yielding less than 0.25 per cent in return. Resources were draining into poorly performing, over-staffed and politicised parastatals and boards that satisfied neither national interests nor consumer preferences.[171] The ICDC, for example (described as a 'miracle' in the 1978 *Weekly Review*), was now characterised as a financial 'black hole', which between 1964 and 1977 had paid almost nothing to the government. For the first time, the 1982 report suggested that the government introduce cost sharing for social services and develop a programme of divestiture to Kenyan investors.[172] These views were extremely controversial at the time. Twenty-five years later, they remain the core orthodoxy of privatisation and economic liberalisation. Implementing them in Kenya, however, was to prove a huge challenge.

In September 1982, the IMF visited Kenya to discuss further assistance. It made it clear that its support would have conditionalities, including spending cuts, import tariff cuts, higher interest rates and another devaluation of the shilling. In the unsettled conditions, initially no minister would even meet with them.[173] Only the economic policy-making triumvirate of Nyachae, new Central Bank Governor Philip Ndegwa and Treasury Permanent Secretary Harris Mule persuaded Moi to accept the package, though negotiations lasted into 1983. There was little public consultation on the issue, as the government itself was divided over such policies. Initially, the technocratic-rational view prevailed over the patrimonial. Moi adopted these views as government policy in his Kenyatta Day speech in October 1982. While state control had been essential for Africanisation and national identity, he noted, the state's role in allegedly free-market Kenya was more intrusive than in many socialist countries. Moi committed the government to borrowing and spending less, reducing subsidies to parastatals and ceasing to make major commercial investments itself.

It was a difficult decision, but the policy was to prove a qualified success. The result was a brief period of austerity. Although civil service numbers continued to grow, in dollar terms – including the effect of the devaluation – government spending fell by 30 per cent from 1980–1 to 1983–4 (see Figure 7.15). Real wages fell sharply in both the public and private sectors. As part of an effort to redistribute national resources and reduce poverty, Moi also announced a new decentralisation policy in September 1982, known as the District Focus for Rural Development. This aimed to shift more decision-making on rural spending from the ministries into the districts. In

7.15: Government spending, 1964–84 (in US$)

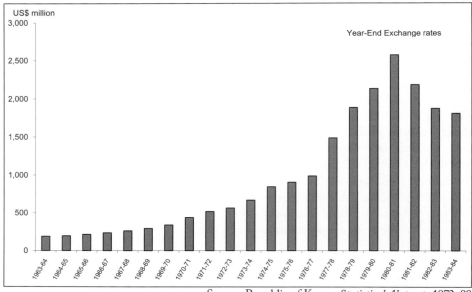

Source: Republic of Kenya, *Statistical Abstracts*, 1972–88

7.16: Imports and exports, 1969–89 (in US$)

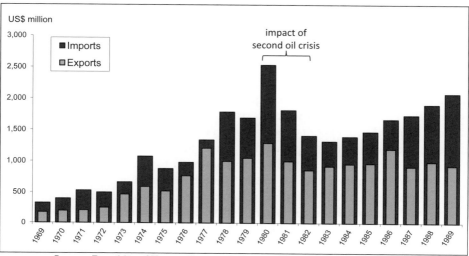

Source: Republic of Kenya, *Statistical Abstracts*, Various. Year-end exchange rate figures

December 1982, export compensation was reintroduced to encourage manufacturers to export, and cuts in tariffs began. A new US$150 million IMF deficit-financing deal followed in 1983 (though half was earmarked to repay previous IMF loans). The US chipped in balance of payments support and other loans, and the UK cancelled its remaining bilateral debts, moving to entirely grant-based aid. The World Bank, however, continued to refuse to release the rest of its structural adjustment loans approved in July 1982, relenting only in 1984.

By late 1983, the immediate crisis was over. A drop in oil prices to under US$30 per barrel, falling world interest rates and its recovery from recession stimulated the economy. The rains were good and the harvests healthy. Supported by another 15 per cent devaluation in 1983, the import–export balance came close to parity in 1983–4 after the unsustainable peak of 1978–81 (see Figure 7.16). The economy recovered, supported by donor aid, cuts in public spending and rising tea and coffee prices. The deficit as a percentage of GDP (after investments and loans to parastatals) fell back to 4 per cent.[174] But the long-term challenge of restructuring Kenya's economy remained.

A Changing Kenya

Kenya was gradually becoming a different country, more densely populated, more urban, better educated, less 'tribal' in the sense of distinct cultural traditions, but equally if not more driven by the perception – inspired in many cases by the reality – that decisions on resource allocation and appointments were made on the basis of ethnicity.

Health and Population

Kenya conducted its second national census since independence on 24–5 August 1979. The results showed that the country's population had risen to 15 million, an increase of 41 per cent in a decade and a 3.4 per cent compound growth rate, one of the highest in the world. The average number of children born per woman had also risen, from 7.6 in 1969 to 7.9 in 1979. The government was increasingly concerned about the implications: if population growth did not scale back, there was no way out of the economic crisis to come unless they could find some hitherto undiscovered source of growth. In 1982, it established a National Council for Population and Development, and a major population conference was held in 1984. However, 'pronatalist' religious and cultural factors continued to encourage high birth rates even as child mortality fell. The Catholic Church remained opposed to all forms of birth control, and the CPK opposed voluntary sterilisation as 'anti-African'.

Kenya's health statistics compared well with those elsewhere in sub-Saharan Africa. Life expectancy had continued to rise, from 49 in 1969 to 53 in 1979. Greater access to medical services and increasing prosperity had cut mortality rates from 2 per cent of the population per year in 1962 to 1.4 per cent in 1979. However, the state was having trouble in sustaining its levels of social provision. Hospital beds and cots per 100,000 people had doubled between 1973 and 1980, but started to fall from 1980, as funds could not keep pace with demand. Nairobi still topped the hospital statistics, followed by Central Province and the Coast (mainly Mombasa). Although state medical services had expanded, their quality remained poor. Kenyatta National Hospital was already notorious for drug shortages because

7.17: Population by ethnic group, 1969 and 1979

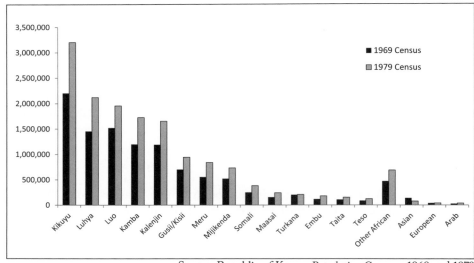

Source: Republic of Kenya, *Population Censuses*, 1969 and 1979

of funds being diverted or contracts issued for sub-standard or non-existent medicines. As a cheaper way to improve health, the government began a shift towards preventive rather than curative policies in the early 1980s, alongside more cost sharing (user charges for services).

The 1979 census also provided information on the sizes of ethnic groups, an issue of great importance to Kenyans (see Figure 7.17). The Kikuyu, Luhya and Kamba communities had all grown by nearly 45 per cent in 10 years. In contrast, the Luo and Gusii had grown by only 35 per cent. The Luhya were now the second-largest community in Kenya. Moi's Kalenjin were for the first time represented as an ethnic group with their own code, rather than as a collection of separate sub-tribes. This buttressed Moi's claims to represent a major community rather than just the tiny Tugen. Other ethnicities that the centralising and assimilationist Kenyatta government had not accepted as discrete identities were recognised for the first time, so it was possible to register now as Basuba (rather than Luo) or El Molo.

Urbanisation and Security

Many more Kenyans – 14.6 per cent of the population or 2.2 million people – were now living in urban areas. Nairobi's population had risen to 830,000 and Mombasa's to 340,000. Formal sector employment exacerbated the growing rural–urban divide. By 1984, nearly 60 per cent of all formal sector jobs were in Nairobi.[175] Far more men than women continued to migrate, leaving women as the heads of most rural households. With little agricultural development in their home areas, there was mass Luo emigration from rural Nyanza to Kisumu, Nairobi and Mombasa, and to the Kericho tea plantations. Nairobi was now only one-third Kikuyu, and one-third Luo and Luhya, up from a quarter in 1969.

Family and neighbourhood obligations remained the core of social relations, and family members often ended up in dependent relations with their more prosperous kin, but the circle who could be called upon for help gradually narrowed as social obligations in other contexts (work, urban life) and the pressures to succeed grew.

Crime was rising, particularly in urban areas, where older values and sanctions often failed to function. Kenya's 'get rich quick' ethos was placing an increased value on material goods and diminishing concern for how they were acquired. The arrival of thousands of penniless Ugandans fleeing repression and war also contributed to an upsurge in crime, which doubled between 1969 and 1982. Combined with unemployment, large differences in wealth, and a declining capacity to prevent and detect crime, the result was a gradual but inexorable breakdown in law and order. The police could do little. Prisons were increasingly overcrowded (the prison population more than doubled between 1963 and 1984) and conditions were appalling.

By the early 1980s, Kenya had become a major producer of another commodity with security implications – cannabis or marijuana. Seizures of cannabis destined for the European market were now substantial. Commissioner of Police Njiinu admitted that an average of 4 tonnes of Kenyan marijuana a year had been intercepted at

Heathrow Airport alone between 1982 and 1984.[176] Large commercial producers operated in the Mount Kenya region, alongside mafia-style import–export businesses based on the Coast. Marijuana was a common drug for the poor and wealthy alike, universally available and cheap. Kenya was also becoming a transit point for heroin from South-West Asia into West Africa, Europe and the US. The challenge that drug growth, use and export represented to the justice system was to become more severe over the next decade. Although it has been little explored due to its sensitivity, drug money became a growing influence on Kenya's politics.

Expanded Education

Moi's background as a teacher gave him a genuine concern for educational issues, and in these early years, he made education a cornerstone of his government. With his announcement of free primary education for Standards V and VI, primary enrolments jumped in 1979 from 3 million to nearly 4 million students. The numbers continued to rise thereafter, reflecting both high birth rates and Moi's announcement on 1 January 1980 that Standard VII primary pupils would also be exempted from fees. In 1980, the government declared that it had achieved its goal of free universal primary education: 92 per cent of primary school age children were now in school.[177] While nominally free though, schools still imposed fees for uniforms, equipment and to build classrooms. After 1983, parents had to buy their children's books, and by 1984, the government was contributing virtually nothing to schools apart from teachers' salaries.[178] Already reliant on *harambee* and private schools, education was one of the first services to see shift towards user charges.

The number of students in secondary education also continued to grow, though a secondary pass could no longer guarantee a job. Unaided schools now provided three-quarters of secondary places. Although the government recognised that there was little purpose in educating so many Kenyans to secondary level, local communities disagreed.

The End of Africanisation

The Moi government saw the effective end of Kenyanisation and of Africanisation. The civil service had been almost entirely Africanised, and non-citizens held only 1.3 per cent of formal sector jobs in 1982. However, Asian businesses remained in control of much of the manufacturing and trade sectors. As most Asians had now taken up Kenyan citizenship, the fiction that the issue was about citizenship rather than race no longer held water. There was pressure from hardline Africanisers such as Shikuku, but Moi, Njonjo and their allies had interests other than driving out the remaining Asians. Despite Moi's occasional references to the rights of 'indigenous Kenyans', discrimination on grounds of race was illegal.

Expatriate Europeans continued to hold roughly 10,000 senior positions in private businesses, jobs that some nationalists believed should be held by Kenyans. There were also foreigners in a few key positions in the KCB and NBK and in the judiciary, where high technical or professional qualifications were required and a lack of connection with the local population was seen as an advantage. Of 30 High Court judges in 1983–4, for example, only 10 were Kenyan Africans, the rest being British, Asian Kenyans or non-Kenyan Africans.[179]

A Traitor in our Midst, April–June 1983

Almost as soon as the 1982 coup was defeated, Moi had begun to isolate Njonjo and his allies. Whether Njonjo was really after Moi's job or Moi had had enough of being a mouthpiece for others may never be known. There were even rumours that there had been a secret deal that Njonjo would replace Moi after five years as Kenya's president, but that Moi now had no intention of relinquishing power.[180] For whatever reason, Njonjo had to go.

In April 1983, Moi's moves against Njonjo became public. A series of government members – Shikuku, Tipis, Elijah Mwangale and Keen, none of them Kikuyu or a friend of Njonjo – held public meetings at which they denounced MPs and ministers who were said to be dissatisfied with Moi's leadership and plotting subversion. Next, Shikuku claimed there was a plot to bring down the government through economic sabotage.[181] Moi remained silent, however, and the divisions within his government became open as Kikuyu leaders – including Kamotho and G. G. Kariuki – attacked those making the accusations. It appeared that Moi was 'flying a kite' preparatory to a Cabinet reshuffle, which he appeared to land on 1 May when he ordered ministers to stop washing their dirty linen in public.[182]

A week later, at a rally in Kisii on 8 May 1983, Moi himself claimed that foreign powers were grooming an unnamed person to take over the government, and he made it clear that Kibaki was not the traitor.[183] Rumours suggest that his intervention had been planned by a group including Oyugi, Biwott and Nyachae, and that their assault followed a warning to Moi by Kalenjin insiders including Barngetuny, Salat, his brother-in-law Eric Bomett and Philemon Chelegat that he must 'get rid of these people otherwise they will oust you'.[184] The British High Commission issued a statement denying that the UK was grooming anyone to take over the country, but suspicion grew that the president's ire was directed at Njonjo (who was conveniently in London). Most ministers refused to comment, unsure of what was happening. Soon, however, a witch-hunt began. Keen, Nassir, Tipis and others demanded the unmasking of the culprit, forcing other politicians to swear loyalty to the president. As more descriptions of the 'traitor' emerged, all eyes turned to Njonjo. Several ministers who had originally remained silent were forced to declare for Moi, although no one would publicly name the traitor.

On 15 May, Njonjo returned to Kenya at last. He denied he was the traitor, who was now described as a 'former Attorney-General', but admitted, 'it is in a situation like this that one knows who his friends and enemies are.'[185] It is reported that Njonjo was picked up by the security forces on his arrival home.[186] He tried to see Moi but was turned away. Moi still held back from naming Njonjo, and at a KANU Governing Council meeting in May 1983, he instead called a general election for

September, one year early, 'in order to clean the system'. Moi castigated the loyalty of some ministers, noting that,

> . . . I have been concerned and very disappointed with the performance of some people who I have appointed to senior positions as Ministers and in the civil service . . . At times, such people have conducted themselves in a manner which leads me to question their loyalty to me as the head of state, the government and this country.[187]

The pressure mounted on known supporters of Njonjo, as opponents sought to take advantage of the crisis. By this time, it was clear that Njonjo was losing the confrontation. His power had rested on his personal abilities, his alliance with Moi and his control of the government and legal machinery. He had had many allies but few friends, and his political constituency had always been weak. Many other allegations now emerged against him, including that he had been involved in the Seychelles coup of 1981, the 1982 coup attempt, the Muthemba case and in a plan to buy MPs to vote Moi out of office. Njonjo remained a minister, but Moi showed his distrust by transferring the office of supervisor of elections out of his care.

By early June, Njonjo was preparing a counterattack, with the message that he was the last defender of Kikuyu interests in the Cabinet. More and more Kikuyu parastatal executives and civil servants (probably Njonjo men) were 'being retired' as 1983 advanced. Kibaki in contrast appeared unable – like Moi before him – to defend his own people, hobbled by his closeness to the president and his duty to focus on national interests. However, one of Njonjo's first public moves in his re-election campaign misfired. On 12 June 1983, he attended a PCEA service in his constituency, where the preacher's sermon had been agreed with him in advance.[188] This sermon, in Gikuyu, referred to Daniel being thrown into the lions' den, but surviving by faith; it also referred to a 'limping sheep' that cannot lead the flock, and the need to find a new leader. The *Nation* headlined with the sermon, and the result was a torrent of abuse in the National Assembly. The association between the limping sheep and Moi was denounced, and finally, Mwangale named Njonjo in Parliament as the traitor.[189]

Njonjo's remaining allies ran for cover. Deputy Speaker Moses arap Keino was forced to resign after he refused permission to debate the issue in Parliament as a matter of national importance. Many MPs called for Njonjo's resignation and expulsion. Only a few, including Matano and G. G. Kariuki, were willing to stand by their colleague, who continued to defend himself. On 29 June, Shikuku tabled papers in Parliament showing large foreign payments to Njonjo's bank accounts. Allegations were made that he had businesses in South Africa, had smuggled arms into the country, and had bribed MPs to support him.[190] On the same day, Moi suspended Njonjo from the Cabinet and appointed a judicial commission of inquiry to investigate the allegations against him. Njonjo remained a free man, but was publicly humiliated. On 30 June, he resigned as an MP and was suspended from KANU soon after. The five ministers Shikuku had named as Njonjo's closest allies – G. G. Kariuki, Matano, Oloitipitip, Rubia and Kamotho – kept their jobs, but their authority was destroyed.

September 1983: The Snap Election

On 22 July, Moi dissolved Parliament in preparation for the election, to be held on 26 September 1983. The election was intended to purge the system of Njonjo supporters and to promote a new leadership which would owe its loyalty directly to Moi, rather than to intermediaries. It was the next step in the transition in policies and personnel that had begun with Moi's accession and accelerated after the coup attempt.

Voter registration had taken place in May–June 1983, adding 1.5 million names to the 1979 register (as there was no time for a full re-registration) and giving Kenya 7.2 million registered voters. The electoral processes were the same as in 1979, except that there was no longer any need to maintain the fiction that the elections were nominally party primaries.

Presidential and Parliamentary Nominations

As usual, civil servants had to resign their seats if they wanted to stand for election. Fewer decided to take the risk at short notice, but 20 parastatal heads – mostly defeated candidates appointed to sinecures in 1979 – contested. Candidates were now required by presidential diktat to have repaid all debts to the government.[191] Several of Moi's other announcements, such as his 1982 concession that life membership was no longer required to contest posts, were ignored. The KANU NEC, Governing Council and National Delegates' Conference met in August and reviewed 995 potential candidates. Only four were barred, the lowest number of any of the single-party elections. For the first time, all the ex-KPU leaders were free to stand (apart from Odinga, who had been expelled from KANU). Moi was unopposed as KANU's presidential candidate. To quash speculation, he announced that he would keep Kibaki on as vice-president after the election.

On 29 August, the parliamentary nominations took place. 730 candidates were nominated, roughly the same as in 1974 and 1979, an average of 4.6 candidates per seat. However, at least 22 were turned away because of 'problems' with their papers.[192] Ntimama, for example, trying once more to stand against Tipis (now minister of state for internal security) in Narok North, was forced to stand down under police pressure.[193] Moi was unopposed, as were Kibaki, Tipis, and two other incumbents. Candidates represented the usual range of occupations and responsibilities, most being businessmen, teachers or ex-civil servants. Only nine candidates (1 per cent) were women, the lowest proportion in any post-independence election. There were also fewer newcomers to parliamentary politics than in previous polls, indicating that the political elite was becoming more tightly defined and the barriers to entry rising.[194]

The Campaign

With open politicking near impossible (officials barred explicit mention of the traitor issue), candidates as usual stressed their development record and closeness to authority. Few could risk expressing anti-government sentiments of even the mildest kind. Candidates instead promised they would obtain roads, banks, schools and water facilities for the area if elected. They promised the subdivision of farms, title deeds for smallholders, and campaigned on the jobs and resources they had brought to the constituency. A few seats saw campaigns against the wealthy (such as that of Shikuku in Butere), but they were rare. The Ksh40,000 spending limit was ignored. Although many candidates condemned tribalism, clan and locational issues drove campaigning and voter preferences and the ethnicity of candidates was a key issue in the cities, multi-ethnic seats and the settlement zones. There was some anti-Asian and anti-white sentiment in Nairobi, where minority candidates were standing.

Factional contests for control of most districts continued, often entwining local and national alliances. With Kamotho crippled by his relationship with Njonjo, for example, Matiba used the traitor affair to consolidate his dominance of Murang'a. Nakuru demonstrated the growing influence of KANU Chairman Kariuki Chotara, a confidant of Moi.

There were indications of increasing ethnic tension in Nakuru North, where a candidate was cautioned for inflammatory statements about the Kikuyu having been 'sold to the Kalenjin' and jailed after the election, and another Kikuyu candidate was charged with fraud during the campaign. Nakuru North included Moi's Kabarak home, and was (controversially) won by the sole Kalenjin candidate. There was violence in Nyeri, where at least two died. There was also the usual bribery, importation of voters, campaigning by civil servants, destruction of voters' cards and corruption. There was more oathing of voters and use of witchcraft on the Coast to compel voters to back specific candidates.

This time, Moi did not actively involve himself in the campaign, preferring to maintain a more paternal stance. Indeed, candidates were ordered not to mention the president's name during their campaigns. Nonetheless, ministers and those close to Moi campaigned on their proximity to power and likelihood of appointment to an influential post. Although Njonjo's allies were the primary target of the poll, it appears that Kibaki's were a second. He ran a slate of allies in Nyeri, including Wamae and ex-PC Isaiah Mathenge. However, according to David Musila, the Central Province PC at the time, 'The Government did not want any leaders who were aligned to the Vice President to be elected. I received instructions to that effect.'[195] Moi's attention was already focusing on his next Kikuyu adversary.

The Results

Polling day (26 September) went smoothly. As before, the counts took place at the 41 district headquarters. There were many allegations of administrative bias, double voting, ballot box tampering and seals broken. Although administrative problems can easily be interpreted as rigging, it is likely that the level of electoral abuses was higher than in 1979.

Partly because of the short election timetable, 61 per cent of incumbent MPs were re-elected, the highest re-election rate of all elections. In spite of this, only half of Central Province MPs were re-elected, while the more loyal Coast, Western and Rift Valley MPs fared much better. Matiba was the sole survivor in Murang'a. Pork-barrel politicians were significantly more successful than in 1979. The new Assembly was the oldest yet, with an average age of 46, a decade older than the 1963 cohort. Only one woman, Asiyo, was elected. Many MPs won by very narrow margins, raising concerns that the political system was returning individuals with focused minority support and leading Moi to talk of introducing a primary or runoff system, to ensure victors had a broad-based mandate.

The 1983 contest decimated Njonjo's allies.[196] G. G. Kariuki was rigged out of his Laikipia West seat in favour of a local farmer whose vote rose from 22 per cent in 1979 to 62 per cent. Local officials campaigned against Kariuki, claiming, 'there is a need to uproot the tree in its totality.'[197] His agents were barred from polling stations. Njonjo ally and KANU Chief Whip Said Hemed lost narrowly in Mombasa, with two boxes apparently uncounted. In Murang'a, Kamotho lost to Michuki. Other prominent Kikuyu losers included ex-civil service head Kariithi, Josephat Karanja and Mungai's brother, Ng'ethe Njoroge. This again demonstrated that wealth and national status did not always translate into local support, especially when the political complexion had changed at the top. There were five ministerial losers. As well as Kamotho and Kariuki, Waiyaki lost in Mathare, Mbathi lost in Kitui and Luo John Okwanyo was questionably defeated in South Nyanza.[198]

However, the election did not achieve all that Moi desired. Several of Njonjo's allies were re-elected, including Oloitipitip in Kajiado, Rubia in Nairobi and Magugu in Kiambu. Njonjo's proxy, Peter Kinyanjui, also won in Kikuyu. Central Province returned a wealthy and outspoken group of Kenyatta-era technocrats, many close to Kibaki. In Murang'a, these included Matiba's allies Michuki and stockbroker Francis Thuo (ex-chairman of the Nairobi Stock Exchange). John Matere Keriri (the former managing director of the DFCK) won in Kirinyaga, Wamae in Nyeri and George Muhoho, Kenyatta's brother-in-law, in Kiambu. It appears that Moi henceforth lost confidence in his ability to dominate electoral politics without rigging.

In Nyanza, the Odinga factor was muted in the aftermath of the coup. Most ex-KPU leaders performed miserably, and Omamo was probably rigged back to stop a pro-Odinga candidate in Bondo.[199] In Western Province, ministers Mudavadi and Mwangale were comfortably re-elected as bosses of Kakamega and Bungoma districts, while Shikuku won a decisive victory in Butere. In the Rift Valley, there were several landslide victories and questionable results. In Baringo North, Cheboiwo was re-elected on an 83 per cent turnout, 30 per cent higher than in neighbouring seats. In Nandi, the GSU was deployed to ensure the re-election of Moi's allies, including Metto in Mosop.[200] Muliro, once Moi's equal in KADU, was again rigged out in Kitale East. The administration banned him from holding any rallies, and officials stuffed the ballot boxes with 14,000 pre-marked ballots.[201] Gumo's re-election was later annulled.

The overall turnout was low, at only 3.4 million, 46 per cent of registered voters, a substantial fall from 1979. Only 40 per cent or less of adults had voted, an unmistakable reflection of their disenchantment with the country's direction.

There were only 17 petitions against the 1983 elections, half those lodged after 1979, a reflection of the high costs and poor results achieved in previous court battles. For the first time, with Njonjo gone, African judges were allocated to hear petition cases. Four were successful, but several more were lost on technicalities.

The New Government

The new government of 1 October 1983 was slimmed down to only 22 ministers, plus Moi and the attorney-general. Kibaki remained vice-president. Several ministries were re-combined and the Constitutional Affairs Ministry abolished. The appointments were made over the radio, with most of those selected unaware until that moment of their preferment.[202]

There were five new entrants to the Cabinet. The able and opinionated Matiba became minister for culture and social services, reluctantly offering him the ministerial office he deserved, but parking him in a weak ministry that would limit his inevitable impact. A surprising choice as minister for finance and planning was nominated MP and KCB Chairman Professor George Saitoti (Figure 7.18). A political novice and ex-mathematics professor from Kajiado of ambivalent ethnic background, Saitoti was plucked from near-obscurity to play the 'technocrat' role, to bring greater professionalism to the Finance Ministry. He was soon to become part of the political establishment and to achieve even higher office. For the first time, the Somali (and the Muslim community) received a Cabinet post – Maalim Mohammed, younger brother of the air force commander.

Moi dropped two of Njonjo's re-elected allies, Oloitipitip and Rubia. Kisii MP and minister since 1969 Zachary Onyonka also lost his post, as he was in jail after a shooting incident during the campaign (some eyes turned to Nyachae as having instigated this). Luhya influence in the Cabinet increased, with Mudavadi at Local Government and Mwangale at Foreign Affairs. Biwott moved to the Ministry for Energy, where he stayed for the next decade.

7.18: George Saitoti

Courtesy: Nation Group Newspapers

7.19: Paul Muite and Charles Njonjo, 1984

Courtesy: Nation Group Newspapers

The Njonjo Inquiry and its Consequences

The commission of inquiry that Moi had appointed into the conduct of Charles Njonjo marked the end of the era of instability, and the confirmation of a new direction for Kenya. The protracted commission created sympathy for Njonjo amongst the Kikuyu, but also sealed the fate of the last man whose authority rivalled that of Moi.

The commission was composed of three Court of Appeal judges, chaired by Guyanese Cecil Miller, soon to become chief justice. Its brief was to investigate the many allegations made against Njonjo. It heard evidence for nearly a year from October 1983. Lee Muthoga, a Nyeri lawyer and long-time Njonjo enemy, led the prosecution. White Kenyan William Deverell and Paul Muite, Njonjo's protégé, led the defence (Figure 7.19).

The commission investigated in public every aspect of Njonjo's life and deeds that could conceivably be subversive, treasonable or anti-government. Dozens of witnesses testified, and indicted each other and Njonjo indiscriminately. Although the nature of life for the elite was exposed in fascinating detail, little could be pinned on Njonjo that was indisputably illegal. He was implicated in the misuse of funds from his charitable activities and the 1981 attempt to overthrow the government of the Seychelles. He had played fast and loose with the judicial system and had engaged in illegal currency dealings, but attempts to tie Njonjo to the 1982 coup failed. He had helped foreign friends import guns and military equipment in 1980–1, but those were probably for illegal hunting. The closest the investigation came to a 'smoking gun' was the evidence that the 1981 Muthemba coup preparations might well have been genuine. The commission was clearly under huge pressure to tar Njonjo with something, and the report contained odd rhetorical flourishes such as, 'To be evil is an art in itself.'[203] However, in the end, it was inconclusive. Miller presented his report to Moi in November, but it was not published.

For years, Njonjo had been the protector of the Asian community in Kenya and the beneficiary of its financial support. Now, some senior Asians, whose influence and vulnerability had been highlighted by the 1982 coup, felt exposed. Some of Njonjo's allies such as P. K. Jani quietly left the country for a while, but Moi soon assumed some of Njonjo's duties as 'protector'. In August 1983, the Asian community sent a large delegation to Moi to pledge loyalty. A similar effect was seen amongst multinationals that had cultivated Njonjo. Within a month of Moi's assault on Njonjo, for example, Lonrho boss Tiny Rowland flew to Kenya to meet Moi, and donated the title deeds for 3,000 acres (1,200 hectares) of land near Eldoret, to serve as the site for a proposed new university.[204]

In parallel with the inquiry, the purge of Njonjo supporters continued. Many of his associates lost their jobs, as did others who could be tarred with the same brush by their enemies. For example, G. G. Kariuki found his land-buying companies closed down, his *harambee* collections retrospectively audited and his family and allies under legal threat. In September 1984, Kamotho, G. G. Kariuki, Oloitipitip, arap Keino, Clement Lubembe, Jackson Kalweo from Meru and Hemed were all expelled from KANU.[205] All lost the right to participate in politics and Oloitipitip lost his parliamentary seat. In 1992, they were to return as some of Moi's strongest defenders, but for now they were national hate figures. Other Kalenjin and Coast politicians who had been linked with Njonjo – including Ng'eno, Kosgey and Nassir – were cleared. Everywhere, there were purges and tribunals to investigate disloyal tendencies.[206] The legal system continued to be used to pressurise uncooperative politicians, now focusing on MPs suspected of closeness to Njonjo. Oloitipitip had his loans called in by financial institutions in June 1984. Arrested for unpaid taxes, he paid in full but was jailed nonetheless. He died in January 1985, a broken man. Not a single MP dared attend his funeral, which was interrupted when his house caught fire in an arson attack. He had risen through intrigue and had fallen by the same means.

In the civil service, the exits were more honourable. Kiereini retired as chief secretary in July 1984, one of the last Kikuyu Kenyatta-era insiders to leave the inner circle. Nyachae took over the civil service, which he ran with a firm hand for the next three years. Kiereini was followed soon after by CID Director Nderi. Asian Deputy Public Prosecutor Sharad Rao had already gone, as had senior Asian police officers such as Sokhi Singh.

Njonjo had never been popular. The events of 1983–4, however, convinced many that anti-Kikuyu interests were using him as a scapegoat. Moi needed to avoid a backlash; while the inquiry had been inconclusive, Njonjo had unlimited ammunition about Moi's business and political life that would have damaged the president severely had it been made public. On 12 December 1984, therefore, Moi announced a full pardon for Njonjo, who thanked him in a muted manner. This almost certainly reflected a deal under which Njonjo would say nothing in return for his freedom. Moi announced that, although Njonjo had committed crimes, he took into account Njonjo's long service to the nation before he had begun entertaining 'misguided political ambitions' in 1980. Miller's report was published at the same time. Njonjo retired from active politics; his network of allies and supporters was eliminated, and Kenya entered a new era. The puppet had cut his strings, and Moi was alone at the top.

Conclusions

The instability of the presidential transition was over, and Moi was firmly ensconced as president. Njonjo's fall symbolised a second diminution of Kikuyu influence (the first, of 1978–81, he himself had orchestrated). The Kikuyu elite, for so long the dominant power in the state, had been divided and weakened as a political force. Moi had initially appeared a caretaker, but by dividing his opponents he had gradually brought his own loyalists into positions of power. Structural adjustment had come to Kenya, and the grand dance with Western powers had begun, which would dominate politics for decades. The beginnings were also emerging of a Kalenjin–Luhya–pastoralist alliance, replacing Kenyatta's Kikuyu–Kalenjin–Kamba coalition.

However, Moi's rule remained fragile and the economic situation dangerous, leading the state down a path of increasing authoritarianism. The 1982 coup had shocked the nation and changed its future. It also saved Moi from a pro-Kikuyu coup that would have taken Kenya along an equally authoritarian, less populist course. Knowing that it enjoyed limited support, the government was increasingly repressive. Although it remained in control, the combination of Moi's paranoia and the influence of a cabal of hard-line advisers would set Kenya on a course that was to damage the country's identity, economy, political stability and faith in government.

Chapter 8

Heavy Footsteps, 1984–1989

Brittle State

The late 1980s saw the maturing of the changes of 1979–83. Daniel arap Moi had already replaced most Kenyatta-era officials and introduced structural adjustment and the District Focus for Rural Development. He had restored the imperial presidency, neutralised Charles Njonjo and ended the era of Kikuyu supremacy. Now, he deepened his ethnically redistributive, populist but authoritarian rule. In parallel, there was a seizure of the state by Kalenjin elites, often in alliance with Kenyan Asians. This bought Moi short-term support, but at the price of sustained damage to the economy and the corrosion of state legitimacy.

Seeking legitimacy in new sources, KANU now asserted its primacy over all other institutions. Kenya briefly became a 'party-state'.[1] Mwai Kibaki clung to the vice-presidency until 1988, but was viewed with growing suspicion. No politician (especially Kikuyu) could follow an independent line or build a national-level coalition. Opposition to the government was treated as subversion, and the sole criterion for political success became loyalty to the president. The freedom of the press was constrained and intellectuals harassed and jailed.

Kenya showed signs of becoming a near-feudal society. The monarch (the president) ruled an apathetic population through force, with the support of military, church and political figures. Local barons (provincial and district commissioners, key ministers and favoured KANU chairmen) ruled their fiefdoms, maintaining private military forces (*askaris* or youth wingers) and extracting tribute from the populace. Surrounded by courtiers, the president maintained a personal fortune, often indistinguishable from the Treasury, which he dispensed to buy loyalty. The authority of an individual derived as much from his person as from his office.

These years also revealed a growing incapacity in the state. Many of the policy innovations of the era failed: some because they were misconceived; others because a civil service that was underpaid, overstaffed, politicised and tribalised was incapable of implementing them effectively and without rent-seeking. Moi himself was part of the problem, as his tolerance for corruption and tribalism became apparent, while his concern for the *wananchi* led to ad hoc interventions, which the command-and-control culture elevated into policy. There was an increasing centralisation in the Office of the President, which paralysed other departments and left their actions dependent on ratification from OP.

The state was also unable to implement policies – particularly unpopular ones such as civil service staff cuts – because of its own fragility. Moi was not particularly popular outside the Kalenjin, and his survival rested on a carefully constructed alliance between the Kalenjin, previously marginalised groups such as pastoralists and Muslims, sections of the Luo, Luhya, Kamba and Gusii, and individual Gema businessmen and politicians. Despite the apparent absolutism of the Moi state, its fragility meant that popular dissent would often initiate a change of direction, even as the perpetrators were punished. Although there was the appearance of stability, it was superficial and brittle, concealing deep dissatisfaction.

Meanwhile, Kenya faced hostile neighbours on all sides and an increasingly troubled relationship with the West. Western governments and the international finance institutions were irritated by Kenya's reluctant and partial response to their prescriptions of fiscal and economic reform, and under domestic pressure to act on allegations of human rights violations, yet this did not stop the flow of aid or the growth of Western tourism.

KANU Rules the Nation

With the Njonjo inquiry over, Moi and his allies sought new ways to assert their legitimacy and tighten their control. Kikuyu still dominated the civil service and business, and many were unhappy with their lower status in the hierarchy of distribution. Moi now began to use KANU as an alternate instrument of rule. For the first time in Kenya's history, during 1984–9 the party became a true focus of authority, relegating Members of Parliament and even the provincial administration to a subordinate position. Long the enemy of socialism, Moi briefly reinvigorated KANU to create a mass movement on East European lines.

This new stress on the party had little ideological content, however, apart from obedience to the president. This was encapsulated in Moi's *Nyayo* philosophy, which had gradually changed meaning from Moi's following in Jomo Kenyatta's footsteps, to that of everyone else following in Moi's. KANU was supreme, but this was because the president wanted it that way. Although Kenya took on the appearance of a party-state, time would show that it was an alternative expression of personal and elite rule. As US Ambassador Smith Hempstone later noted, Kenya was not a one-party state: it was a 'one-man state'.[2] While Kenyans pragmatically bowed their heads to this new order, when the opportunity for change came, they were happy to abandon the manufactured ideology of *Nyayoism*.[3]

The Rise of the Party-State, 1985–7

Late 1984 and early 1985 saw a major KANU recruitment drive, driven by the provincial administration, with the blurring of party and state near complete. Party membership jumped as a membership card became essential for jobs and access to local services. By mid-1985, 4.8 million members had paid their annual dues.

In June–July 1985, KANU finally held national elections, the first since 1978. Local polls elected delegates, who then chose their district team, which joined other Governing Council delegates to elect national officials. This year, the elections were conducted by queue voting (*mlolongo*). Voters lined up in public behind their candidate or his agent, at a time decided by the provincial administration, and were counted on the spot. Open to abuse without any permanent record of the result, the outcome was massive electoral fraud. Dissatisfaction was open, with even the pro-government *Weekly Review* suggesting:

> The party can hardly expect the rest of the country and its institutions to have respect for the constitution when the party itself does not adhere to its own constitution, and democracy is hardly likely to prevail when constitutions are treated with contempt.[4]

Loyalists and hardliners dominated the polls. In Kirinyaga and Nandi, there were protests over secret polling stations and falsified count records. District commissioners were actively involved in ensuring certain candidates won.

At the national level, party posts were allocated again according to an ethno-regional formula. This year, Moi's fixer Nicholas Biwott led the lobbying, as G. G. Kariuki had done in 1978. Moi was unopposed as KANU's president.[5] Kibaki was eventually unopposed as vice-president and Tipis remained treasurer, but the other five posts all changed hands, strengthening the hard-line wing of the party. Robert Matano was defeated after 16 years as secretary-general by Burudi Nabwera (now an ally of Moses Mudavadi). All the remaining seats were unopposed, as the other 30 candidates not on the state slate suddenly decided to stand down. Katana Ngala from the Mijikenda Coast became assistant treasurer, David Okiki Amayo (Luo) became chairman, while the Somali were represented by Maalim Mohammed.[6]

The party's assertiveness was also on the rise. Following the Njonjo expulsions of 1984, more and more party branches recommended the suspension or expulsion of politicians over factional disputes. After the 1985 elections, KANU established a National Disciplinary Committee (NDC) to adjudicate disputes and discipline those who brought the party into disrepute. Chaired by Amayo, its members included hardliners Shariff Nassir, Nabwera and Biwott. Within a few months, the NDC became a key organ of central control. It summoned and humiliated MPs and assistant ministers, inventing offences such as 'causing divisions amongst the people'. Several MPs were suspended from the party and lost their posts. By 1986, the mantra of KANU's supremacy was becoming a reality. Moi was now claiming that, 'Kanu was more powerful than any other institution in the country.'[7] In November 1986, he declared that the party had supremacy not only over Parliament, but also over the judiciary.[8] Civil servants were told that they must have party membership cards to keep their jobs. In some districts, non-members were barred from bars and markets or were required to join in order to obtain liquor licences or land allocations.[9]

However, dissatisfaction grew with the authoritarian and petty conduct of the NDC. In August 1986, Kibaki attacked the committee in Parliament, calling it a tool for intimidation by 'people who have no strength of their own'. In September 1987, concerned that the NDC was bringing the party into disrepute, in a characteristic volte-face, Moi abolished it entirely.[10] As he was to show again in 1990 and 1991,

Moi remained able to recognise when he had made a mistake, and was willing to change course, as long as it did not appear that he had been forced to do so.

For a brief period, the provincial administration moved into the background; its PCs speaking less often in public and rotating faster between posts. While Eastern Province had had two PCs between 1965 and 1978, for example (Eliud Mahihu and Charles Koinange), between 1980 and 1990 it had at least six, some of whose appointments were retrospective or overlapped. Its ethnic composition was also changing. Whereas half of all PCs had been Kikuyu between 1967 and 1979, there was only one Kikuyu PC between 1984 and 1989.

The Philosophy of Nyayo

Moi's political philosophy was centred in his own beliefs – in the importance of personal trust, ethnicity, the power of the common man, and of money. It was also based on patriarchal, even biblical concepts of discipline and obedience. He demanded others obey him, just as he had obeyed Kenyatta. In 1984, in a famous phrase, he spelled this out:

> I call on all ministers, assistant ministers and every other person to sing like parrots. During Mzee Kenyatta's period I persistently sang the Kenyatta tune . . . If I had sung another song, do you think Kenyatta would have left me alone? Therefore you ought to sing the song I sing. If I put a full stop, you should also put a full stop.[11]

A gradual reinterpretation of the Kenyatta presidency began, which glossed over Moi's KADU roots, and challenged the ethnic parochialism of the Kikuyu. All currency notes with Kenyatta's face on them were removed from circulation in 1985.

Seeking legitimacy in ideology, KANU also elevated Moi's *Nyayo* aphorisms into a political philosophy. His 1986 book, *Kenya African Nationalism*, wrapped the Christian theme of 'love, peace and unity' around Moi's speeches in an attempt to suggest an intellectual foundation to the regime.[12] By 1989, primary schools were teaching *Nyayo* philosophy.[13] The apparatus of the state was mobilised to reinforce the message of obedience. Parastatals, county councils and well-connected businesses such as Mugoya Construction and Lima Limited published eulogies to the dear leader on national anniversaries. In October 1988, for example, the Kenya Commercial Bank assured Moi of their 'total commitment to the *Nyayo* philosophy of Love, Peace and Unity . . .' while the Prudential Building Society hoped that God's blessings would 'shower in abundance upon our beloved President so that he may continue to lead us in peace to even greater heights in development'.[14] An Eastern European communist would have felt at home.

Moi's Loyalties and the Rise of the Populist Authoritarians

Although Moi was still following in Kenyatta's footsteps, in some aspects his approach had to differ from that of his predecessor. Kenyatta had never been challenged for the presidency after 1966. Safe in office, his criteria for selecting allies and agents had been loyalty and ethnicity, but also administrative efficiency. With a weaker popular base and surrounded by real and imagined enemies, competence was no longer the key criterion for success; it was loyalty. Loyalty could be demonstrated by blood: as Kenyatta had done, Moi surrounded himself with people from his own ethnic sub-group in key positions. In his Baringo Central constituency, Hosea Kiplagat – also chairman of the Cooperative Bank of Kenya – nurtured the constituency for its absentee MP. Other Tugen close to Moi included his cousin, Gideon Toroitich, managing director of the AFC for two decades. It could also be demonstrated by action. Moi was extremely loyal to those who had backed him during his rise to power and who helped him in moments of crisis, whatever their faults. Some of Moi's closest confidants in the 1990s, such as Joshua Kulei (already his personal assistant), Hosea Kiplagat and State House Comptroller Abraham Kiptanui, all Kalenjin, began as prison officers when Moi was home affairs minister (in charge of prisons), and rose alongside their mentor. Others such as PC Hezekiah Oyugi and police officer Philip Kilonzo had remained loyal during the 1982 coup attempt. Those who kept their distance and their options open (such as Kibaki) were treated with suspicion.

Moi was also a populist. Although he accepted the need for the apparatus of governance, his heart was elsewhere. He was more comfortable talking with security guards than with academics. He honestly felt the privations of the ordinary person, and believed that he could personally make a difference. He was spontaneous and generous. Without a powerful bureaucrat such as Njonjo or Nyachae at his side, he was inclined to snap responses to problems, which meant that a number of off-the-cuff speeches became government policy overnight. The plethora of *Nyayo* businesses which resulted (Nyayo buses, Nyayo hospital wards, Nyayo tea zones, Nyayo cars) – most of them services that the state should already have been providing, or commercial enterprises that the government had already committed itself to avoiding – caused despair to planners.

Moi also distrusted the Kikuyu-dominated administrative machinery he had inherited and expanded his personal network into most of Kenya's ethnic communities, ruling in parallel with the official organs of state. These were populist networks, linking him to grassroots operators – often of limited education and with a distaste for procedures or legality – whom he could trust to support him unquestioningly. The most obvious of Moi's hard-line allies was Biwott, minister, boss of Elgeyo-Marakwet District and Moi's right-hand man. Of near-equal importance was Mudavadi, minister and boss of Kakamega District. The illiterate Mulu Mutisya dominated Ukambani. In Nakuru, Kariuki Chotara was another classic Moi hardliner, an uneducated ex-Mau Mau detainee. He was the man who attacked Kenyatta in prison, and had been condemned to obscurity until Moi's accession. He then rose quickly to become KANU Nakuru District chairman and a nominated MP, and ruled Nakuru with an iron fist. Nandi was run by the primary-educated ex-soldier Ezekiel Barngetuny, while Kericho was under primary-educated Isaac Salat, who had been Moi's personal secretary until 1974. After 1986, William ole Ntimama (like Moi, once a primary school teacher) was the boss of Narok, brandishing the twin sigils of power: visits to State House and a seat alongside Moi in church. Mombasa was run by Nassir, the KANU chairman, who had been one Moi's strongest backers during the Change the Constitution movement. Oyugi, though a civil servant, was Moi's overseer in the Rift Valley. In contrast, Moi was also fascinated by academics and intellectuals, and promoted several to senior positions over the years, including Josephat Karanja, George Saitoti, Philip Mbithi, Samson Ongeri and Jonathan Ng'eno. Yet, while he used them as advisers, Moi never trusted them.

Somehow, throughout his time in power, Moi managed to maintain some distance from the worst excesses of his agents. He used and discarded advisers easily, and retained a measure of doubt as to whether he himself had sanctioned the violence, corruption and sycophancy that surrounded him. This was useful both at home and abroad, where foreign diplomats for years believed that Moi was simply badly advised.

Divide and Rule Amongst the Kikuyu

Having humbled Njonjo, Moi shifted his alliances amongst the Kikuyu for a second time. Now seeking to limit the influence of Kibaki and his allies, Moi briefly co-opted two groups for whom he had had little time in the past: the Kenyatta-era Kiambu elite and the ex-Mau Mau veterans of Nakuru and Nyeri. Again, he exploited divisions within the Kikuyu community, using individuals' willingness to work for the presidency in return for wealth and influence. In the Kiambu Kenyatta 'family', Moi focused on Ngengi Muigai (Kenyatta's nephew) and Njenga Karume, both assistant ministers. The Kenyatta family was still influential in Kiambu and their links with Moi remained close, particularly through Mama Ngina Kenyatta. Some Kikuyu believed that the first family sacrificed the interests of the broader Kikuyu community at this time in order to protect their own business interests.

Moi also tried to use Kikuyu ex-Mau Mau to win the support of poorer Kikuyu. During 1983–6, he brought into the fold several prominent ex-Mau Mau and used them to weaken the influence of Kibaki and the Kenyatta-era elites. In Nakuru, his point men were Chotara and ex-detainee Fred Kubai. In Nyeri, it was Waruru Kanja, like Chotara condemned to death but reprieved by the British, who re-emerged from political purgatory to help take on Kibaki.

Kibaki was now the most senior Kikuyu politician, and much of the political activity of 1984–8 was devoted to limiting his influence, as he was undermined by Moi or those around him. By the 1985 KANU elections, the attacks had become open. Foreign Minister Elijah Mwangale was particularly vocal, visiting Nyeri with gifts and funds, and campaigning to replace him as vice-president. Kibaki's response was a denunciation of what he called 'political tourists', but the pressure continued.[15] Luhya MPs denounced Kibaki in Parliament in April 1986 and it briefly appeared that Mwangale might be in line for the vice-presidency.

Inside Nyeri District, Kanja led the attack. In 1986, he organised the first convention of ex-Mau Mau fighters since 1964, targeting Isaiah Mathenge, the KANU Nyeri branch chairman, an ex-Home Guard and ally of Kibaki. Kanja's activities were well funded, and the state's preference for Kibaki's opponents was open.[16] However, Moi's use of Kikuyu ex-Mau Mau was short-lived. The legacy of the war no longer dominated Central Province. The more Moi made use of Chotara and Kanja, the more discredited they became, as it became clear that they could deliver little to their community and were in fact acting as agents for the dismantling of Kikuyu privilege.

By early 1988, it was clear that Moi was going to drop Kibaki as vice-president. The 'hawks' saw Kibaki as too soft and lukewarm in support of the president, and the time was right to dismantle another piece of the edifice of Kikuyu rule. Although Kibaki never experienced the vilification and humiliation faced by Njonjo and later Karanja, he was gradually stripped of authority, and restricted in his activity to his home district. Politicians close to him were harassed. In January 1988, for example, Moi sacked Taita minister Eliud Mwamunga from the Cabinet following a row over the whereabouts of Ksh1 million of *harambee* money. He was – not coincidentally – an ally of Kibaki and represented Kikuyu business interests in the district. A few days later, Philip Ndegwa resigned as governor of the CBK. The CBK had recently been criticised for pro-Kikuyu hiring policies and foreign exchange abuses; Ndegwa's departure removed another of Kibaki's allies from power.

The ethnic composition at the top continued to evolve, reducing the influence of the Kikuyu and increasing the number of Kalenjin. However, Moi did not automatically appoint Kalenjin to every post, but retained representation from all the main communities at every level. It was a dynamic balancing act, rewarding the loyal, punishing dissent, and seeking opportunities to incorporate all communities into his coalition. New Kikuyu appointments, for example, included Samuel Gichuru, who became managing director of KPLC in 1984 and Wilson Gacanja, appointed commissioner of lands in 1989. Whatever their ethnicity, though, Moi selected elites for preferment based on their willingness to meet his agenda, rather than their popularity or legitimacy in their community. True power lay elsewhere, in informal networks and – unlike the Kenyatta era – these conflicted with rather than aligned with existing power relations. The result was a gradual estrangement between the Kikuyu and the country's political leadership. The resulting impediments placed upon Kikuyu capital almost certainly weakened Kenya's economic performance during the 1980s.

Tightening His Grip

The inner circle found opposition increasingly intolerable. They appeared to be building a governance model in which – even more explicitly than in Kenyatta's day – all authority derived from a single figure, unfettered by law or custom; an absolutist monarchy.

Heavier Sticks

Election rigging became more common. KANU headquarters denied clearance to candidates unpopular with the regime, and the state sought to bankrupt others by calling in loans. 'Anti-establishment' candidates who did manage to contest elections found it difficult to hold meetings and faced well-funded opponents. When this was not enough, ballot boxes were stuffed. In April 1986, for example, Chotara and the Nakuru DC ensured that Eric Bomett, Moi's Tugen brother-in-law, won the Kikuyu-dominated Nakuru North by-election against the recently released Koigi wa Wamwere. Bomett had little support, but triumphed nonetheless. Chotara announced at a rally on 8 June, *'Ulituambia tumurigi Koigi tuchague Bomet. Koigi tumemurigi'* (You told us to rig out Koigi and elect Bomet. We have rigged him out).[17] Koigi soon fled overseas. In November 1986, a new MP was selected for Mathare in Nairobi, Dr Josephat Karanja. Former vice-chancellor of the University of Nairobi and unsuccessful Kiambu politician, his star was rising once more. The by-election was a farce, with only 9 per cent of those registered bothering to vote, and boxes of ballot papers neatly stacked up for Karanja. Karanja was already being groomed for office.

Public dissent was undermined by a combination of violence and patronage. Influential ex-ministers Charles Rubia and Masinde Muliro were continually in trouble, while Moi sacked Martin Shikuku as an assistant minister in 1985, and he was recommended for expulsion from KANU. All were soon to become leaders of the multi-party democracy movement. Sometimes the choices facing dissenters were quite overt. Muliro's protégé and Bukusu MP Michael 'Kijana' Wamalwa, for example, had his family farm invaded by squatters in 1989. He was summoned to see Moi, who told Wamalwa he had promised voters that Wamalwa's opponent would win the upcoming by-election. Wamalwa was offered a choice between losing his farm and being declared bankrupt, or having the squatters removed, receiving a car, school fees for his family and a parastatal post in return for not contesting the election. He decided not to stand.[18]

Internal opposition to the government was cowed, but did not vanish, and continued to be nurtured from outside. Concerned Western liberals supported Kenya's intellectuals in their struggles to maintain autonomy from the state, while the socialist-populist tradition remained strong in Kenya and outside. Both philosophies agreed that the presidency was too powerful, but disagreed whether its replacement should be pro-Western, capitalist, private sector-dominated, or a 'people's democracy': more socialist, less liberal and more in tune with the idealised self-reliant and egalitarian models of older African societies.[19]

There were few politicians left with both the credibility and the courage to speak out. The most prominent was Oginga Odinga. After four years of near-silence, on 1 July 1987, he returned to the public platform, calling for the reintroduction of multi-party democracy, saying, 'Public debate on national issues and policies have been stifled, and genuine constructive criticism of government and party policies is treated as sedition or treasonable offence.'[20] In August 1987, *Beyond* (the magazine of the Protestant NCCK) reproduced his letter to Moi, in which he declared Kenya's situation to be a 'tragedy', and called the claim that the ruling party was supreme 'a fallacy and an abrogation of the constitution'.[21] Soon after, Odinga said he would found a new party if the government would allow it:

> I firmly believe and trust that you will be able to reconsider, together with the party, the decision to expel me and others from the party . . . However, if that

is absolutely impossible, we demand that room be created for the formation of other political parties.[22]

There was no response.

Advisers and Rivals

Increasingly, Moi ruled like a combination of an American president and a mafia boss, with a set of advisers and fixers alongside the Cabinet and civil service. The Tugen and other favoured Kalenjin, many of them Keiyo, were his 'low' political advisers. At the national level, policy and practice were the subject of a tug of war between three powerful individuals, Nyachae, Biwott and Oyugi. Simeon Nyachae from Kisii, head of the civil service, was by far the most influential technocrat. Wealthy, able and arrogant, he had been an administrator (and therefore a politician) since independence and had showed his deep loyalty to Kenyatta and then to Moi many times. He was involved in several joint business investments with Moi.

Biwott was the most senior Kalenjin minister, with unlimited access to the president and his complete trust. Like Koinange a decade earlier, he was a back-room operator, who had few formal posts but attended every meeting and ran much of the government. His acumen was widely respected, and he was believed to handle most of Moi's investments. By the late 1980s, he was rumoured to be one of the richest men in Kenya. He part-owned two oil companies – Kobil (established when Mobil sold out to local investors in 1985) and Kenol (the Kenya National Oil Company) – some said with Moi as sleeping partner. He also part-owned the HZ and LZ group, the Lima agricultural machinery group and Air Kenya Aviation, along with cigarette production, farms, real estate and other businesses.[23]

The third rival for Moi's ear was Oyugi, a Luo from South Nyanza (Figure 8.1). In 1986, Moi elevated him from Rift Valley PC to the key post of permanent secretary for provincial administration and internal security. For the first time since 1965, the Luo had a representative in Kenya's highest councils, and Luo influence at the top

8.1: Hezekiah Oyugi

Courtesy: Nation Group Newspapers

grew. For five years, Oyugi ruled Nyanza, making the careers of Luo politicians such as John Okwanyo, Dalmas Otieno and Job Omino, and his home area of Rongo boomed into a modern town. Oyugi, known as 'the Governor', had Moi's complete confidence on security issues. Not only did he build a network of loyal officials and politicians, but he also established a security network that reported directly to him, bypassing long-serving intelligence head James Kanyotu.

Law, Justice and Detention without Trial, 1984–7

Although Western observers had not challenged the declaration of the one-party state, there was growing disquiet at Kenya's use of detention without trial. By November 1983, for example, Amnesty International had adopted George Anyona as a prisoner of conscience. Domestic pressure on Western governments to limit their support for Kenya was growing, despite the Kenya government's claim that the West was applying double standards and that in other countries people 'disappeared' entirely without Western protest.

At the same time as Njonjo's pardon in December 1984, Moi released four of the seven remaining detainees – Wamwere, Anyona and two of the university lecturers who had helped plan the Kenya African Socialist Alliance. In 1985 and 1986, he released two more, but Raila Odinga remained in solitary confinement, without a bed and with little medical attention or family contact. Rather than breaking his spirit, jail appeared to make Odinga stronger. His lawyers Gibson Kamau Kuria and Kiraitu Murungi were amongst the few willing to challenge (always unsuccessfully) the government's right to detain political prisoners without giving grounds for their detention.[24]

The law had always been a tool of the executive in Kenya, but the judiciary experienced a further decline in competence, probity and independence in the late 1980s. It was alleged that some judges 'bent over backwards to accommodate the wishes of the executive for financial and political rewards'.[25] At the top, politics played a key role in appointments, and partly as a result, Kenya went through four chief justices in five years. The first, the Njonjo-era Justice Alfred Simpson, retired in October 1985, to be replaced by the elderly and respected Asian judge Chunilal Madan. After only a year in office, in 1986, Madan, too, retired. He was replaced as Kenya's second African chief justice by Cecil Miller, a popular but controversial Guyanan and a friend of the president's who had presided over the Njonjo inquiry. A believer in Africanisation, Miller increased the independence of the judiciary from the attorney-general's office, but also gained a reputation as a *Nyayo* follower, willing to make contradictory or political decisions if the president desired them. In 1989, when Miller died, long-serving European judge Alan Hancox replaced him, ensuring this most sensitive of posts still remained outside the hands of a Kenyan African. There were other problems. Madan revealed that he had found the judiciary in an 'unbelievable' condition when he took over. Lawyers were insisting that certain judges heard cases to ensure inducements reached the right people, and there was a vast backlog.[26]

Judges were also finding it difficult to challenge the security apparatus. In August 1987, for example, Justice Derek Schofield resigned from the bench. He was a British judge working under the Overseas Development Administration scheme (which provided Kenya with Commonwealth judges and helped pay their salaries). He had been hearing a *habeas corpus* case for the release of a Kiambu farmer. Only after the order was obtained did the farmer's family discover he was dead. Schofield ordered the exhumation of the body, but police were unable to find it, despite opening 24 graves. Years later, it was revealed that the police had murdered the farmer and burnt his body near Nairobi. The press reported that reservist Patrick Shaw and a chief inspector of police were amongst the officers involved.[27] It appears that a 'Star Chamber' (death squad) process was operating inside the police, whereby suspected criminals who had escaped justice were hunted down. In frustration, Schofield threatened to have CID Director Noah arap Too jailed for contempt of court. However, rather than backing Schofield, Chief Justice Miller reassigned him to another case, at which Schofield immediately resigned.

Queues and Crosses, 1986

In April 1986, KANU decided to extend queue voting to the parliamentary polls. New regulations required KANU members to queue publicly behind their candidate or his nominee in a primary election before the main poll. Only those candidates achieving over 30 per cent of the vote would go forward to a secret ballot of all voters. Those who were supported by more than 75 per cent of those queuing would be declared the sole KANU candidate, and there would be no secret ballot. The party approved the changes in August 1986. The 75 per cent limit was reduced to 70 per cent in the process, heightening opportunities for abuse. Those who controlled the count could now rig the polls with greater ease, and KANU members, not the public, would have the first – and possibly final – say on who their MPs would be. Moi strongly supported the scheme because of the large number of minority victories in 1983 and its low cost to operate. Plans to take the changes to Parliament for approval were abandoned once the leadership realised they could implement the change without modifying the Constitution. The rules were first used in the 1988 general election.

The political elites did little to defend their electoral legacy. Although many were lukewarm about the proposals, Kibaki, Kenneth Matiba, Robert Ouko and other ministers backed them in public. Only a few brave or foolhardy MPs, including Muliro (Luhya), Abuya Abuya (Gusii), Rubia (Kikuyu) and Assistant Minister Kimani wa Nyoike (Kikuyu) dared defend the secret ballot publicly. Branded a dissident, wa Nyoike was sacked in 1987, suspended from KANU, then jailed in 1988. Abuya and Rubia were picked up by police and questioned. Muliro continued to protest through 1987, backed occasionally by other MPs who had fallen out of favour. But the state remained uncompromising.

The introduction of queue voting caused a schism between Church and state, and proved the foundation of civil society's engagement in active politics. The

NCCK and the Catholic Church both strongly opposed the change as divisive and undemocratic. Since the 1982 coup, the churches had become more open in their criticism of detention without trial, presidentialism, human rights abuses and inequality. A strengthening sense of social justice drove a more interventionist approach to domestic politics. Anglican CPK bishops were particularly critical, motivated by their sense of Christian duty but also reflecting the feelings of their parishioners, many of whom came from central Kenya.

The more interventionist mood inside the churches had strengthened in 1985, with the appointment of Methodist Samuel Kobia (from Meru) as the NCCK general secretary. The NCCK's national conference in August 1986 was the turning point, when church leaders spoke out in defence of the secret ballot. The leaders of this protest included Anglican Bishops David Gitari (Kikuyu), Henry Okullu (Luo) and Alexander Muge (Kalenjin), and the Rev. Timothy Njoya (Kikuyu) of the PCEA. Anglican Archbishop Manasses Kuria (Kikuyu) called the change 'un-Christian, undemocratic and embarrassing'.[28] *Beyond* magazine argued that Christians would find it difficult to vote publicly and suggested the system would prove a logistical nightmare. The Law Society of Kenya was equally hostile, claiming the proposals infringed voters' rights. Nonetheless, KANU refused to back down and instead condemned defenders of the secret ballot as tribalists and subversives in the pay of foreign governments. Unable to strike at the churches directly because of his long-standing public espousal of Christianity, Moi argued that churchmen should keep out of politics.

The result was a split within the churches. The mainstream churches and their mainly Kikuyu, Embu, Meru and Luo leadership were forced into confrontation with the government, while pro-government churches led by the AIC – of which Moi was a member – dissociated themselves and withdrew from the NCCK in November 1986. Although Moi announced exemptions from queuing for civil servants, religious leaders and soldiers, these were never implemented. The NCCK and Catholics continued to protest at the state's denial of democratic rights to its citizens, eliciting scathing attacks from politicians in response and forcing a disengagement of the churches from an explicitly Christian regime.

Another Amendment and the Departure of Nyachae, November 1986

In November 1986, the National Assembly passed the twenty-second constitutional amendment since independence. This had three objectives. First, the attorney-general and the controller and auditor-general (who monitored and audited the government's use of public funds) lost their security of tenure, making them subject to presidential pleasure (a clear message). Second, the amendment increased the number of constituencies from 158 to 188, ready for the upcoming constituency boundary review. Most significantly, the amendment abolished Nyachae's position of chief secretary. The situation reverted to be much the same as it had before 1982, with the permanent secretary at the OP first amongst equals rather than the final arbiter of civil service decisions. While Moi suggested that the post of chief secretary had delayed decision-making, in reality, the incumbent had fallen from grace, the first of several fallouts between Moi and his one-time ally. On 10 December 1986, the day after Moi gave final assent to the amendment, Nyachae was sent on compulsory leave and retired from the civil service, to take effect in 1987 when he actually reached the retirement age of 55.[29] Once again, the Constitution had been changed to resolve personal issues between individuals. The consequences went beyond this though: finance permanent secretary Harris Mule and others accompanied Nyachae into exile, the balance between technocrats and patrons in economic policy was disrupted and the decline of the bureaucracy accelerated.

The amendment was opposed by the LSK and the churches as further centralising power in the presidency, which in turn generated heated responses. Only two MPs – Rubia and Jonathan Njenga – had the courage to oppose the bill on its second reading in Parliament. Seconded and supported by Kibaki, the amendment was passed 130:2, and by 131:0 on the third reading, as by then Rubia had been ordered out of the house and Njenga had fallen silent.[30] Afterwards, the police held Rubia for five days without charge.

Security and the State

Moi and the Military

Despite the authoritarianism of the period, the Kenyan military remained calm and apparently loyal. It was defending a different elite, but remained faithful to presidential authority, its leadership tied to the regime by loyalty to the nation and its constitution, but also by patronage, with farms and parastatal positions available on retirement and sometimes before.

In 1985, Moi was warned that the growing proportion of Kalenjin amongst senior officers was creating discontent. In May, it was rumoured that 30 soldiers led by a Kikuyu major were jailed after secreting a cache of arms and ammunition for a coup attempt. In 1986, when General Mulinge finally retired, rather than making Kalenjin protégé John Sawe Chief of Defence Staff, Moi decided to retire him and instead promoted officers from other pastoralist groups. Mulinge was replaced by coup hero Mahamoud Mohamed (Somali), who remained Chief of General Staff for a decade, while Major-General James Lengees (Samburu), took over the army (see Table 8.1). Despite this, one-third of lieutenant-colonels and colonels were still Kikuyu, and the Kamba component was even larger. Kalenjin held only one-fifth of senior posts, though they included the rapidly rising and Sandhurst-trained Tugen Daudi Tonje.[31]

Military relations between the US and Kenya remained close, and the two countries engaged in joint manoeuvres in 1984.[32] Although the USA now provided most military equipment, Kenya was not tied to buy American. In 1989, for example, the government decided to buy another new generation of jet fighters. Biwott tried to make a deal with a British defence firm, but this was unsuccessful, and instead he entered into negotiations with a French firm. The French deal was eventually

Table 8.1: Military heads, mid- to late 1980s

Position	Name	Dates	Ethnicity
Chief of General Staff	Gen. Jackson Mulinge	1978–86 (retired)	Kamba
	Gen. Mahamoud Mohamed	1986–96	Somali
Army Commander and Deputy Chief of General Staff	Lt.-Gen. John Sawe	1981–6 (retired)	Kalenjin – Keiyo
	Lt.-Gen. James Lengees	1986–93	Samburu
Deputy Army Commander	Major-Gen. James Lengees	1983–6 (promoted)	Samburu
	Major-Gen. Daudi Tonje	1986–92	Kalenjin – Tugen
'82 Air Force Head	Lt.-Gen. Mahamoud Mohamed	1982–6 (promoted)	Somali
	Major-Gen. Dedan Gichuru	1986–9	Kikuyu
Navy Commander	Major-Gen. Simon Mbilu	1978–88	Kamba
	Major-Gen. Joseph Kibwana	1988–98	Mijikenda

Source: Various

completed, and Kenya bought 12 Mirage fighters and 60 automatic guns.[33] Security contracts were both expensive and not subject to parliamentary oversight, and therefore could be valuable sources of income for the inner circles via commissions and kickbacks.

Crime, the Police and Internal Security

Inside Kenya, the provincial administration remained the centre of rural authority, with PCs and DCs running tender boards, land boards and security and development committees. As in the Kenyatta era, they could act with full presidential authority and without the formality of law when circumstances required. After 1986, they answered to the permanent secretary for internal security, Oyugi.

The domestic security apparatus remained multi-ethnic, but loyalty was now the primary criterion for appointments and Kalenjin influence was growing. The first Kalenjin to take a top leadership position had been 38-year-old Noah arap Too at the CID in 1984. In 1986, Lazarus Sumbeiywo (later a well-respected envoy) was appointed director of military intelligence, straddling the military and civilian security services, and he was replaced in 1988 by another Keiyo, Wilson Boinett, who had been Moi's aide-de-camp until 1985. In 1987, the GSU also came under Kalenjin leadership; the particularly sensitive Presidential Escort had long been Kalenjin-led. At the top of the police force, Bernard Njiinu remained chief of police until his retirement in 1988, when he was replaced by Kilonzo. Kilonzo was an ally of Moi-insider Mutisya; he had zealously repressed Mwakenya (see below) as Nairobi assistant commissioner of police, and had stood by Moi during the 1982 coup. He was not an inspired choice, however. According to Njiinu, 'I knew Kilonzo well . . . and would have been the last person to recommend him as my replacement.'[34] Kilonzo remained police chief through the unsolved murder of a British tourist in the Maasai Mara in 1988 and the murder of Robert Ouko. Kanyotu was now the only Kikuyu, Embu or Meru security head (see Table 8.2).

Meanwhile, Kenya was becoming a dangerous place. Violent robberies were common and the wealthy began to leave central Nairobi for the northern and western suburbs. With the legal system in crisis, crime rates rising and oversight non-existent, prisons were increasingly overcrowded and unsafe. The police were notorious for beating and torturing suspects to obtain confessions, and for holding them for well over the legal limit of 24 hours. It was the embarrassment of the discovery of illegal detention by the police (when a Nakuru man died after being held for 24 days) that led to the 1988 change to the law to legalise up to two weeks of detention (which was sufficient to persuade most people to confess). Suspects routinely died in custody, bearing marks of torture, but the courts refused to find anyone responsible or to enforce the Constitution's guarantees of human rights.[35] Moi himself did denounce police violence on occasion, but little changed in practice.

Table 8.2: Police and internal security heads, mid- to late 1980s

Position	Name	Dates	Ethnicity
Permanent secretary for internal security	James Mathenge	1983–6	Kikuyu
	Hezekiah Oyugi	1986–91	Luo
Police commissioner	Bernard Njiinu	1982–8	Kikuyu
	Philip Kilonzo	1988–93	Kamba
CID director	Noah arap Too	1984–99	Kalenjin – Kipsigis
Head of Special Branch/ Directorate of Security Intelligence	James Kanyotu	1965–91	Kikuyu
GSU commandant	Erastus M'Mbijjiwe	1982–7	Meru
	Jackson arap Kosgei	1987–93	Kalenjin – Nandi
Head of Military Intelligence	Lazarus Sumbeiywo	1986–8	Kalenjin – Keiyo
	Wilson Boinett	1988–90	Kalenjin – Keiyo
Head of Presidential Escort Unit	Elijah Sumbeiywo	n/a	Kalenjin – Keiyo
	Stanley Manyinya	n/a	Kalenjin – Nandi
	Charles Kimurgor	to 1993	Kalenjin – n/a

Source: Various

In 1989, Chief Hancox reaffirmed Justice Norbury Dugdale's declaration that the bill of rights in the Constitution was 'unenforceable'.[36]

The state continued to detain its opponents without trial when it could not uncover or manufacture a criminal case. Those incarcerated included a journalist who had been investigating cases of prisoners shot dead in police custody. In January 1988, an American judge and doctor were deported after they attended the inquest into the death of another suspect who appeared to have died from torture after 22 days in police custody. For the first time, Kenyans lived in real fear of the security forces. Afraid of informers, few would say Moi's name out loud in public.

Violence in North-Eastern, 1983–9

North-Eastern Province remained isolated from the rest of Kenya. The area had effectively been under military rule since independence, as the emergency regulations remained in force, allowing arbitrary arrest and detention. Although the Somali community now had a minister for the first time, and a few civil service jobs in Nairobi followed, there was still virtually no economic development within the province. Apart from the civil service, most people were nomads; cattle herding and trading were the primary economic activities, and the province did not have a single tarmac road.

In 1983–4, the cattle raiding that characterised the region escalated into a full-scale war between the Degodia and Ajuran clans in Wajir District. In response, senior government officials authorised an operation later known as the 'Wagalla massacre'. On 10 February 1984, military based in Wajir rounded up 5,000 Degodia men and proceeded to shoot, beat and torture them for several days on the Wajir airstrip, in punishment for anti-government activities and insecurity in the area. Meanwhile, other troops raped women and robbed properties. Up to 2,000 people died in the massacre. It took years for the truth to emerge about these events, probably the worst single abuse of Kenya's citizens in its post-independence history. No one was indicted, nor has there been an official inquiry (though the North-Eastern PC Benson Kaaria was transferred soon after). The responsible minister, Justus ole Tipis, was unapologetic, and claimed in Parliament that only 57 people died. To hide the truth, the state banned relief agencies from the area and aid workers were deported. The mass graves remain to this day.[37]

During the 1980s, many Kenyan Somali were driven south and west by drought and the growing violence in Somalia into the grazing lands of the Borana, Samburu and Orma in Marsabit, Isiolo and Tana River Districts.[38] The result was an escalation of tension and fighting between pastoralists (over water) and between pastoralists and sedentary communities (mostly over grazing rights) as the ripple effects of their move buffeted northern agricultural settlements in Laikipia and Isiolo.

Although most ethnic Somali Kenyans had been required since the 1970s to undergo a screening procedure before obtaining a national identity card, in August 1989 the government introduced a re-screening procedure for all ethnic Somali. This process, which tested each Somali-speaker's background and ability to speak Swahili before granting them a special additional identity card, led to the deportation to Somalia of thousands of probably Kenyan ethnic Somali.[39] There were protests from foreign diplomats, the LSK and religious leaders. The bitterness against the government in the region deepened.

The Problem of Pokot

West Pokot District also posed special security problems. A remote pastoral area like North-Eastern, it was a thorn in the side of the government, yet as Moi's government aged, the Pokot were to provide some of its strongest defenders. A fierce and little-educated people, part of the Kalenjin family, the Pokot engaged in near-continuous cattle raids on their neighbours. Originally from Trans-Nzoia, and evicted by the British during the alienation of the white highlands, the Pokot had been severely affected by the collapse of Uganda and many had acquired automatic weapons. Half of the district had been administered by Uganda for 40 years – 'Kara-Pokot' was only returned to Kenya in 1970. The government responded by arming a Home Guard self-defence force, but the Home Guards themselves engaged in cattle rustling and banditry. The district also faced problems of land and ethnicity. There had been increasing immigration to Pokot during the 1970s, lured by low population densities and idle land, and by 1979 more than 10 per cent of the district was non-Pokot. The result was a wave of violence in 1982–3 aimed at removing outsiders.

In 1984, the government carried out a major security operation in the area using the GSU and helicopters to track down cattle raiders. Undeterred, banditry in Pokot and neighbouring Trans-Nzoia and Elgeyo-Marakwet continued, and there were indications that the Pokot political leadership was involved in these activities. The most prominent Pokot politician, Francis Lotodo, a little-educated nationalist, was sacked as an assistant minister in 1984 and expelled from KANU and Parliament for 'warlike activities'.[40]

Mwakenya

As open political opposition became impossible, protest went underground. A Marxist organisation called Mwakenya had been formed in 1983 as an offshoot of the shadowy December 12th Movement. It did not emerge into the limelight until March 1986, when the Kenya police made their first arrests, and followed these up with a campaign of repression against student, dissidents, academics and socialists.

The very existence of Mwakenya has been disputed. It was claimed to stand for Muungano wa Wazalendo wa Kukomboa Kenya (Union of Patriots for the Liberation of Kenya), but many suspected that it was a creation of the security forces to justify their violent repression. However, it appears from recent testimonies that some such organisation did exist, bringing together dissident intellectuals, workers and farmers in Nakuru and Nyeri, long centres of Kikuyu anti-government protest. Members admitted later to the distribution of the anti-government magazine *Pambana*, oathing and the sabotage of railway and telephone lines, though most denied the use of arms.[41] Mwakenya produced a manifesto known as the *Mwakenya Minimum Draft Programme* in 1987, though few actually saw it. It reflected the same anti-capitalist, anti-foreign, egalitarian, socialist, pro-Mau Mau strand of thought that can be traced from Bildad Kaggia through J. M. Kariuki to Ngugi wa Thiong'o. There were reports of oathing amongst the Kikuyu of Nakuru in 1986, and the district politics of the time were unprecedented in their ferocity, leaving most local Kikuyu activists in prison. It appears Oginga Odinga also had loose links with Mwakenya (through his ally Oyangi Mbaja), which in turn received covert assistance from Uganda, happy to discomfit Moi.[42]

Between March 1986 and March 1987, at least 75 journalists, academics, students and peasants were jailed for crimes such as the possession of seditious literature. Most were Luo or Kikuyu. Many were held illegally for weeks or even months and tortured by Special Branch. Some died in custody. The torture chambers of Nyayo House in Nairobi created a scar across the Kenyan psyche that has not yet healed. While normal business was conducted on other floors, the basement contained hidden flooded cells where captives were stripped, beaten, and held naked without food or water (Figure 8.2). The twenty-fourth floor hosted formal interrogations during which captives were beaten, burnt and assaulted.[43] The interrogations were led by a Kikuyu known as Machiri and by Superintendent James Opiyo, a Luo associate of Oyugi.

The survivors were brought to court suddenly, often at night, in front of an amenable judge and a courtroom of Special Branch, so that no press or defence counsel would be present. The chief prosecutor for almost all the criminal cases was again Luo, Deputy Public Prosecutor Bernard Chunga, reinforcing the impression

8.2: Nyayo House

Courtesy: Charles Hornsby

of an Oyugi connection. Most prisoners pleaded guilty to avoid further torture and were jailed for up to 15 years. In the words of Rumba Kinuthia, a non-conformist Kikuyu lawyer, 'The judiciary was so compromised that not a single person charged with Mwakenya was released.'[44] Lawyers were unwilling to represent the prisoners, because to do so was to risk the same fate, as happened to Kinuthia in 1990, when he was tortured and jailed for treason. The repression continued through 1988, gradually abating during 1989–90.

While most of those arrested were jailed, at least 10 academics and lawyers were detained without trial after interrogation failed to expose any crimes. These included three university lecturers, beginning with the (Kikuyu) ex-Dean of the Faculty of Commerce Isaac Ngotho Kariuki. Others included Odinga's allies Mbaja and Israel Agina, both managers at the Odinga family's East African Spectre LPG plant, and (Kikuyu) lawyers Mirugi Kariuki and Gibson Kamau Kuria. Kuria was openly told that he was detained in 1987 because he had acted for people the government considered a threat, having filed a lawsuit against the government alleging torture. His law partner Murungi continued operating but 'knew very well in what kind of situation he was operating, which amounted to an undeclared state of emergency'.[45] Many detainees remained in jail for years. The three who managed to file legal cases against their detention were held longest of all; Raila Odinga was only freed in February 1988, after nearly six years.[46]

Amongst those who told harrowing tales of their imprisonment and torture was Wanyiri Kihoro, a critic of the government since student days, later to become a Democratic Party MP. The tenor of the interrogations indicates that the police believed they were facing hardcore Mau Mau-style oathing. The interrogators' hatred of intellectuals and suspicion of atheism and communism were also clear. Many of those tortured and detained were permanently radicalised by the experience, and several opposition MPs and two presidential candidates in the 1990s had passed through the hands of the police in this period.[47]

How much of a threat Mwakenya was remains uncertain. Most evidence suggests that it was never a challenge to the state, but that the government used it as an excuse to crack down on opponents. However, the movement did have some support amongst radical Kikuyu and Luo. Who was responsible for the crackdown is also unclear. Most eyes have turned to Oyugi: distrusting Kanyotu, whom he believed was too close to Biwott, he had created a network of special district officers, intelligence police who answered directly to him. Final responsibility would normally lie with the Security Committee, the top government committee on security matters, which was chaired by Vice-President Kibaki, and consisted of Minister of State for Internal Security Tipis, Oyugi, Police Chief Njiinu, Chief of General Staff Mohamed, Kanyotu and CID Director arap Too. However, Njiinu suggested that Oyugi kept the committee in the dark about Mwakenya.[48] He also admitted that he was not in effective control of the police by this time. Real power lay elsewhere.

Two more revolutionary movements came to public attention in 1987–8: the Kenya Patriotic Front (KPF) which Koigi wa Wamwere claimed to have founded and the Kenya Revolutionary Movement. The KPF was based in Uganda, where the Museveni regime was far from friendly towards Moi's government. Neither movement caused much disruption and fizzled out by the end of the decade under heavy repression. Several more politicians were jailed for sedition or possession of prohibited materials. Raila Odinga, Agina and two more Luo were detained again in September 1988 (in Odinga's case after only seven months of freedom). Those under surveillance who could flee, did so.[49] The government had demonstrated its commitment to maintain control, but much else had been sacrificed.

External Relations

By 1986–7, Kenya's position as Africa's 'darling of the West' was under threat. Western governments were being pressured to cut aid and to protest to the Kenyan government about its actions. Amnesty International was amongst several human rights organisations that publicised the state's abuses and campaigned for an end to Western support. In 1985–6, Amnesty adopted more Kenyan detainees as possible prisoners of conscience. By 1986, concerned comment was surfacing in the European press. Amnesty coordinated a letter-writing campaign to Moi and Kenya's high commissioner to Britain, Sally Kosgei. Moi, always sensitive on issues of sovereignty, was infuriated by the idea that foreign NGOs could challenge his actions, and on Jamhuri Day, 12 December 1987, he declared, 'The so-called Amnesty International can go to hell,' though he released more detainees at the same time.[50] Independently, the humanitarian crisis in Ethiopia and the Live Aid response in 1985 began a process of politicisation of aid to African states, driving a permanent increase in engagement amongst Western audiences. Nonetheless, the West continued to offer economic and security aid to Kenya. The 1986 queue-voting controversy, Mwakenya and the 1988 elections did not provoke a crisis, and it was only in 1991 that foreign aid began to fall.

Kenya's relations with the US became more complex. The Reagan administration of 1980–8 saw Kenya as a bulwark against communism and the US continued to offer military assistance (US$16 million in 1989) and development, fiscal support and food aid (over US$60 million). However, the Americans also protested about human rights abuses in 1986, and at a March 1987 meeting between Ronald Reagan and Moi, the US asked the Kenyan government to investigate Kuria's allegations of torture of Mwakenya suspects. The US Congress was increasingly restive, briefly refusing to support further aid because of Kenya's poor human rights record in 1989, but the hawks that dominated American foreign policy remained well linked with Kenya's conservative security establishment.[51] By 1990, Kenya was the largest recipient of US aid in sub-Saharan Africa.

Relations with the UK remained warm, and the British continued to keep any criticism private. Moi visited the UK and met Margaret Thatcher in 1987, and Thatcher visited Kenya in turn in 1988, during which she expressed full support for Moi's 'wise' government, and questioned stories of human rights abuses. Britain continued to give large sums to Kenya (the second largest recipient of British aid) – GB£54 million in 1989 alone – and the UK remained one of Kenya's largest trading partners. Amnesty International's campaign received support from some British MPs, but at the government-to-government level, the UK saw Kenya as a friend and intelligence ally. In contrast, relations deteriorated sharply with Scandinavian donors, who were extremely concerned about human rights. By 1987, Kenya was in open conflict with Norway and Sweden, which worsened when the countries offered political asylum to Kenyan refugees.

An intriguing development was the growing relationship between Kenya and the East. During 1986–7, the Kenyan government visited and hosted delegations from both communist China and the Soviet Union. Moi visited China for a second time in October 1988. As well as strengthening economic links, it appeared that Moi was learning political tactics from the Chinese, something inconceivable under Kenyatta.

In the immediate post-Njonjo period, relations with Kenya's ex-EAC neighbours had improved, but this did not last. Tanzania was looking south for its economic links, and relations remained distant. The situation in Uganda had worsened sharply, with hundreds of thousands murdered during a brutal civil war, and relations with Kenya were very poor. Kenya provided sanctuary to Milton Obote when he was ousted for a second time by the military in July 1985. Moi also hosted peace talks in 1985 between the National Resistance Movement of Yoweri Museveni and the Military Council. Museveni reneged on the Nairobi Accords, however, and relations between the governments were frosty after he seized power in Uganda in 1986. A border clash in December 1987 led to deaths on both sides, there were more incidents in 1988, and Uganda continued to provide a haven for Kenyan dissidents. The Kenyans were also fearful of Uganda's relations with Libya and Cuba, and this was a feature of several Mwakenya cases. Chunga claimed that both Raila Odinga and Wamwere were recruiting Kenyans for guerrilla warfare training in Libya. Kenya expelled several Libyan diplomats in 1987 for spying, and in December 1987, closed their embassy entirely.

In the north, relations with Somalia improved, despite the chaos and influx of refugees, while dealings with Ethiopia were minimal. With Sudan, feelings were now hostile: the discovery of oil, Sudan's Islamic revolution of 1983 and the fall of the Numeiri regime in 1985 initiated a period of instability and growing north–south tension. In turn, Kenya provided support to Colonel John Garang's Sudan People's Liberation Army (SPLA). Garang lived in Kenya at the government's expense, from where he led his campaign for secularism and southern Sudanese autonomy, and he was well connected with the Kenyan elite. As conditions worsened, 250,000 southern Sudanese died from hunger and disease in 1988. In response, foreign aid agencies established a major relief operation in Lokichoggio in Turkana. In 1989, after a pro-northern and Islamic coup in Sudan, Moi tried to mediate a north–south peace deal, a task that would take 15 years to complete.

In 1988, Kenya controversially annexed the disputed Ilemi triangle north of Turkana, which it had administered since 1924. Following raiding from this near-lawless area, maps of the country (showing the original border with Sudan) were withdrawn and new maps issued showing Kenya owning all this land (see Figure 8.3).[52]

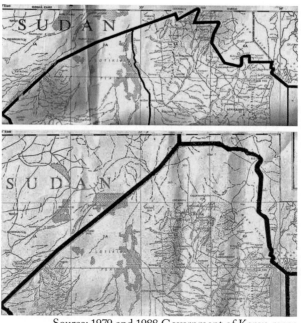

8.3: The annexation of the Ilemi triangle

Source: 1979 and 1988 Government of Kenya maps

A Failed Economic Transition

The state's insecurity and intolerance was in part a reaction to economic pressure. Although the economy was growing, it could not provide jobs for most of the 300,000 new entrants to the workforce every year. By 1989, 59 per cent of Kenyans were under 20, slightly fewer than in 1979, indicating that family planning and resource constraints were beginning to cut fertility, but far too slowly to help in the absence of explosive economic growth.

The *Development Plan, 1984–8* had been published in 1983. Like previous plans, it made implausible assumptions of rapid growth, but even its optimistic estimates implied little real per capita growth. The plan recognised that employment was growing far too slowly to create non-agricultural jobs for most people, and the larger workforce was not resulting in greater resource efficiency either. Foreign debt was an increasing burden and the plan argued that further development must be internally funded. Since there was now little opportunity to stimulate growth through state investment, the only way out of the crisis was to free up the domestic private sector and reduce state spending.

Since 1980, the government had been committed on paper to reducing the footprint of the state, liberalise trade and cut the deficit, but had struggled to deliver on its promises. While there was some fiscal liberalisation, in other sectors change was slow and inconsistent. Rather than cutting spending, the state actually expanded the civil service, established new parastatals and introduced expensive reforms such as the

8–4–4 education system (see below) and the expansion of the universities. The number of teachers doubled between 1981 and 1991. Financial controls weakened as ministries overspent their budgets without sanction. There remained a deep tension between the demands of bureaucratic efficiency and the patrimonial and prebendal interests of the elites. In the absence of strong popular support, Moi relied on buying the short-term support of key interest groups. But in Kenya these were not classical 'interest groups' such as urban workers or private business associations, but informal ethno-regional coalitions centred on individuals, including politicians, civil servants and others in cascading personalised hierarchies of distribution of both public and private goods. Cuts in state spending would dissolve the glue that held his fragile network together.

The Overall Economic Position

Kenya had been in deep trouble in 1983–4, mainly due to the drought. Exports and incomes had fallen, and the country needed US$200 million of maize imports and more oil to compensate for lower hydroelectric power. In contrast, during 1985–90 (the most repressive period in Kenya's history), GDP growth averaged over 4 per cent. Good rains, rising tourism, cheap oil and high prices for tea and coffee reduced the deficit and drove strong growth (see Figure 8.4), although official statistics were always questionable, as population estimates differed wildly and a high proportion of economic activity was 'off book'.

Foreign exchange reserves remained healthy, as Kenya now managed its exchange rate in line with IMF prescriptions. This had many benefits, but the shilling's resulting fall reflected Kenya's declining competitiveness and its inability to balance imports and exports. At 24 to the dollar in 1990, the shilling was worth less than a third of its value when Moi took office.[53]

The government deficit was now around 5 per cent of GDP, higher than its target but only half the level of 1978–83. However, Kenya was now a capital exporter, as debt repayment and interest exceeded inflows, a situation worsened by the declining exchange rate. Although the US, West Germany, Scandinavia, Great Britain and the

8.4: Real GDP growth, 1979–90

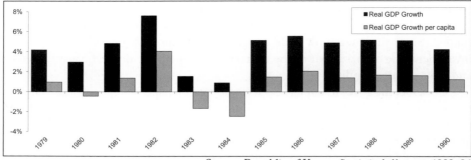

Source: Republic of Kenya, *Statistical Abstracts*, 1988–96

Netherlands wrote off US$700 million in debts between 1986 and 1992, the government owed six times as much in shilling terms in 1990 as it had in 1980 (see Figure 8.5). With between US$5.7 and $7.1 billion of external debt in 1990 (estimates were unreliable), Kenya's problem was modest by world standards, but debt servicing as a percentage of exports was around 33 per cent. Kenya continued to borrow more and more.

With domestic credit limited due to short-term government borrowing and foreign loans more risky, there was a decline in domestic private investment.[54] This was matched by reduced foreign investment, affected by price controls that restricted profitability, changes in world trade, politicised and arbitrary decision-making and the lack of a regional market. Although Kenya performed better than many other African countries in the 1980s, the whole continent was left behind.

Inflation was cut to 10 per cent in 1984–7 by better fiscal management, lower oil prices and falling worldwide inflation, but rose once more to 15–20 per cent in 1988–91. This was caused in part by price deregulation and the coffee boom of 1986, and in part by the rising deficit.

The IFIs and Structural Adjustment

Kenya's dependence on financial support from Western governments and the IMF and World Bank grew, as did their corresponding influence on economic policy. In 1984, with their previous aid package exhausted, Kenya once more promised macro-

8.5: Government debt, 1980–90

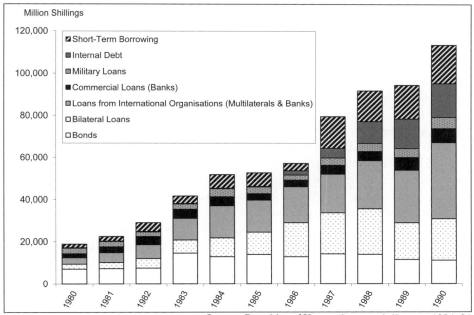

Source: Republic of Kenya, *Statistical Abstracts*, 1984–94

economic reform as a condition for IMF support: that it would cut government spending, reduce borrowing and inflation, promote exports, liberalise the economy and raise food prices. The response was another US$85 million stand-by loan in 1985. The IFIs still believed Kenya had some of the best economic policies in sub-Saharan Africa and was successfully adjusting, particularly fiscally (interest rates were positive for the first time in years). They placed their trust in 'technocrats' such as Nyachae, Mule and CBK Governor Ndegwa.[55] In 1985–6, however, with economic conditions improving, Kenya's dependence on IMF finance and interest in structural reform consequently waned. This time, unlike in 1977, the government took a high percentage of the profits from the coffee boom and there was a sharp rise in its spending. Within a year, the economic position had deteriorated once more.

After 1985, the IFIs focused on structural reforms that would promote growth, believing this would address the problems that developing countries were experiencing more effectively than fiscal reform alone. In 1986, the IMF introduced its structural adjustment facility, which became the enhanced structural adjustment facility (ESAF) in 1987. The ESAF programme offered concessional loans in return for policy changes. A neo-classical trend was sweeping the world, driving deregulation, free trade, competitive pricing and market liberalisation. Donor aid conditionalities tightened in response to this and to criticism of the effectiveness of Western aid when the policy environment was not conducive to growth.

In Kenya, these policies divided both state and society and faced resistance at every level. Senior economists (and some politicians) accepted the necessity of change and of opening up Kenya's economy, but they were a minority. Many politicians, administrators and opinion formers, in contrast, favoured a more self-reliant approach, were instinctively critical of Western prescriptions, or still looked to the Soviet model for inspiration. More cynically, some insiders feared that change would destroy the government by undermining the patronage system on which it rested, or would simply harm their personal interests. Structural adjustment was never popular amongst the *wananchi* either, who had been educated for decades in the virtues of self-reliance, Africanisation and a managed economy. The IFI-led liberalisation of import licensing regimes during 1984–5, for example, hurt some domestic producers and led to accusations that the state was deliberately 'crippling' indigenous production.[56] At times, the Kikuyu business establishment seemed more protectionist than the state itself. The result was a complex mosaic of reform and resistance that resulted in significant change in some sectors and stasis in others. This does not mean there was no reform in Kenya in the 1980s. Indeed, the level of fiscal reform is often underestimated because of the lack of progress on privatisation and the continued dominance of the state over resource allocation.

In 1986, the government issued *Sessional Paper No. 1* on 'Economic Management for Renewed Growth', a strategic review of the economy. This radical paper attempted to refocus Kenya for the challenges to come, before the pressure of population growth overwhelmed the economy's capacity to deliver.[57] For the first time, it suggested that the government would restructure or privatise some state corporations. Private enterprise was enshrined as the main engine of growth, though there were no specific commitments to privatise state assets. It reasserted Kenya's commitment to structural adjustment and acknowledged that the civil service could not expand indefinitely. It was now accepted that Kenya's import substitution industries were inefficient, high-cost producers, and that market incentives had to reward private investment better. The government also committed itself – reluctantly – to refocus expenditure away from health, education and basic needs, towards more immediately productive economic activities. Although criticism was already mounting of the side-effects of structural adjustment, policy-makers including Nyachae and Finance Minister George Saitoti argued that there was no other realistic option. Structural adjustment promised little in populist, nationalist or patronage terms, but a continuation of central planning and autarkist policies offered little hope. As in other developing countries, 'the shift toward privatization and liberalization that began in the late 1980s was less a natural response to shifting economic philosophy than a forced response to desperate economic circumstances.'[58]

Although the government made these commitments on paper, it struggled to execute them. To do so would require them to cut the civil service, improve parastatal productivity, sell state assets, charge for services that had previously been free, recover old debts and reduce corruption. None of this was easy or popular. In practice, state spending increased both in dollar terms and as a percentage of GDP, with recurrent expenditure on education and heath consuming an increasing proportion of funds. Budget deficits jumped again in 1986–7 and in 1989–91.[59] The *Development Plan, 1984–8* targeted a third of state expenditure to be committed to development, but in reality it did not rise above 23 per cent, because the state proved incapable of controlling its operating costs. The government's precarious base and the patrimonial political system left ministers unable to tackle overstaffing, waste or corruption. Indeed, the government itself was enlarged in 1986 and again 1987, increasing the size of the Cabinet to 29 members.

The closedown or privatisation of unprofitable state-owned enterprises proceeded grindingly slowly. A task force on divestiture sat from 1983 to 1986, but it had little effect. Some action was taken regarding the smallest and most unprofitable firms. Kenatco had been put into receivership in 1983. The National Construction Corporation and the Uplands Bacon Factory were wound up by 1988, and the Kenya Meat Commission was restructured in 1989 (but collapsed again in 1992). A small amount of equity in the KCB was sold on the Nairobi Stock Exchange (NSE) in 1988, Kenya's first sale of a state asset, but there were no true privatisations. The state's self-interest was at the core of this resistance, but there were other more palatable reasons. It was not clear, for example, whether there was sufficient private capital in the economy to support an indigenous privatisation programme. The NSE's capitalisation remained tiny compared to the size of the economy.

Instead, ad hoc efforts continued to improve the performance of parastatals without fundamental reform. These included the appointment of an auditor of state corporations in 1985 and the passing of the 1986 State Corporations Act, which imposed tighter controls on parastatal spending. These reforms cut the level of overall state subsidy to state-owned enterprises from 4.5 per cent of government spending in

1984–5 to 1 per cent in 1988–9.[60] However, they left the structure of state regulation intact. By the early 1990s, the state still owned or held an interest in 342 boards and commercial enterprises.[61] Productivity declined rather than increased and the entire parastatal sector contributed nothing to economic growth. The government had 'virtually lost control of expenditures made by these public bodies'.[62]

Nonetheless, the IFIs and donors continued to provide support. The pressure to increase aid to Africa was strong, both to overcome the continued slow-motion crisis and to help repay old debts. Budget shortfalls were met by larger loans from the Paris Club of bilateral and multilateral donors, still satisfied with Kenya's growth and macro-economic management. The IMF approved another arrangement for Kenya in 1987–8, and this was followed by a three-year ESAF loan in 1989, alongside large industrial, agricultural and financial sector reform loans from the World Bank. Despite the parallel political clampdown, Kenya was the fourth largest net aid recipient in the region during 1984–90 and aid (including loans, grants and write-offs of old loans) grew to US$1.1 billion in 1989. Although the economic situation improved, partly because of these capital infusions, compliance was poor. Each shortfall was met by requests for more loans based on proposals for change, which were either not fully implemented or did not solve the underlying problem.[63]

Equity Over Growth and the District Focus

Equitable development was another theme of the *Development Plan, 1984–8*: that development and services had to be more fairly distributed across the nation. Urban and rural surveys conducted in 1986 and 1988 showed that the top 10 per cent of households received 61 per cent of national income. Kenya was now one of the most unequal societies on earth.[64]

The government's policies were now openly redistributive, trying to provide equality of opportunity for the smaller ethnic groups, semi-arid areas and the pastoralists. State recruitment patterns shifted away from the Mount Kenya region and people. In the mid- to late 1980s, 'In the police, the armed forces, the universities, the civil service and the parastatals, social and tribal arithmetic was as much a factor in recruitment as proficiency.'[65] The urban areas and Central Province faced rapid declines in relative (and sometimes absolute) investment as the focus of activity moved into the Rift Valley. There was a renewed emphasis on smallholder production, driven by a combination of populism and the belief that land redistribution would increase productivity. The 1970s arguments for greater equality now appeared to have been adopted – 15 years later – by the state, keen to redirect resources away from central Kenya. As a side-effect, however, infrastructure investment declined in the most productive cash-crop areas, with knock-on implications for growth.

A key component of this strategy was the District Focus for Rural Development (DFRD), which was implemented during 1985–7.[66] The scheme was the brainchild of Nyachae and Mule, and had been considered (and rejected) in the Kenyatta era. It was a radical exercise in resource re-targeting, based on the principle of deconcentration of administrative power, rather than the devolution of political power. For the first time, an effort was made to ensure that every part of Kenya, even the most barren, received some form of development. Some officials were relocated into the districts and some decisions on rural development spending were decentralised to district development committees. Budgets would be disaggregated by district and an increasing proportion of spending would be committed locally and coordinated with other investments.

The rationale for the DFRD was both economic and political. Its primary goal was to refocus development at a lower level, with (it was hoped) better or more popular decisions. It also provided a means to refocus resources away from wealthier areas towards the less-developed pastoral areas that provided the bulk of Moi's support. The success of the plan is questionable. It transferred some staff and funds into semi-arid and less-developed areas, and resulted in a significant step forward for some communities for the first time.[67] It did nothing, however, for local government, which continued to limp on, financially unviable and deeply corrupt. There is some evidence that the rural project success rates increased, but the percentage of the budget at district discretion remained small.[68] Some suggested it actually channelled more development activity through the provincial administration, and thereby linked local development even more tightly to networks between local elites and the executive presidency.[69] The amount of government spending allocated under the DFRD was small and, in practice, planning processes gradually reverted to their old model.

What Moi did not do is almost as important as what he did. As one of KADU's leaders and architects of the *majimbo* constitution, just as he did not attempt to reopen the 'willing buyer, willing seller' land policy, Moi also made no overt effort during the 1980s to reactivate the federalism debate. Now he was leading the unitary state, he saw no need for devolution and there was little support for such ideas elsewhere. It was only after the reintroduction of multi-party democracy and the reassertion of ethnicity as the key line of political cleavage that *majimbo* returned to the political agenda.

Industry, Trade and its Liberalisation

Where Kenya did see real reform was in price and trade liberalisation. As the IFIs recommended, in 1987 tariffs were simplified or cut and help for exporters was improved.[70] The state gradually decontrolled domestic prices, reducing the number of commodities where it set prices by three-quarters between 1983 and 1991. In 1990, export processing zones (EPZs) were legalised, alongside facilities to recover duty and VAT on imports used as components for manufactured exports. There was already an export compensation scheme in place (though it soon fell victim to abuse). Regionally, the EAC's collapse had seriously damaged trade, but Kenya diversified its exports into the PTA region. Africa took between 21 and 29 per cent of Kenya's exports between 1978 and 1992, with Kenya running a strong surplus with its neighbours.

It was too little, too late, however. Despite 20 years of industrial development, Kenya still exported few manufactures outside Africa, and tea and coffee contributed half of its exports. Apart from the second coffee boom of 1986, the gap between imports and exports grew further. Export volumes increased, but the growth was more in primary products (mainly horticulture) than in manufactures. Despite the government's good intentions, Kenya was unable to kick-start an export-oriented manufacturing sector to replace the protected market of the 1960s and 1970s. Well-intentioned efforts to encourage manufacturing exports failed because Kenyan goods were often of poor quality or uncompetitive commercially, hampered by restrictions on intermediate imports, under-investment, inefficiencies protected by local monopolies, overmanning and corruption. Kenya was losing world market share. In a decade in which the GDP and share of world trade of the countries of the Pacific Rim grew rapidly, Kenya remained (like the rest of Africa) in a trough of slow growth and high debt.

Although there were capacity upgrades and capital injections, there were few new foreign investments during the 1980s. Some large companies (including US companies Bristol-Myers, Pepsi-Cola, Ford, John Deere and Caterpillar) shifted their African headquarters elsewhere, and despite amendments to the Foreign Investment Protection Act to improve the investment climate, a pattern of disinvestment began. Cadbury-Schweppes sold off its operations and exited in 1983–4; Firestone sold a chunk of its investments and Mobil left the market entirely. The delays in dividend remittance of the early 1980s eased, but foreign-owned business remained sceptical. Local industry continued to develop, and some sectors such as textiles saw a mini-boom, but there were too many companies chasing too small a domestic market and for most, export-oriented production remained a mirage. State regulation was unreliable and price control for political reasons hurt profitability in key products, while production costs were high and technical innovation levels low.[71]

There remained deep disagreement amongst Kenyans and academics alike about the merits of an open economy and liberal policies towards multinationals. Many still criticised the tendency of multinationals to make profits and export them, make decisions based on commercial rather than national interests and invest in capital-intensive rather than labour-intensive production.[72] The government was ambivalent, calling for more foreign investment and reaffirming its belief in free enterprise, yet simultaneously encouraging domestic ownership, making non-economic pricing and investment decisions, challenging foreign profit repatriation and bemoaning the effect of liberalisation on domestic production.

Every critique of multinational investment was challenged by the fact that these products succeeded in the Kenyan market because they were better quality or cheaper than the products they replaced. Transfer pricing to avoid taxes only made sense because taxation was higher in Kenya than elsewhere or because companies wished to export capital to use elsewhere and to bypass restrictions on doing so. There was no doubt that multinationals acted in their own interests, though they seldom saw the Kenyan market as a particularly desirable one. There were exceptions, but most multinationals would have preferred to source more locally if it was cheaper and more reliable to do so, but the economies of scale were difficult and the investment climate uncertain. The risk was not that they would produce goods locally that competed with indigenous manufactures, but that they would decline to do so, leaving Kenyans to import or make do with *jua kali* manufactures (see below). The independence of the nation-state was under threat globally, but while Kenyans might resent the shift of power away from governments and towards businesses, they could not legislate it away.

Infrastructure Parastatals in Trouble

Some infrastructure parastatals were now in serious trouble. While the Ports Authority and the Pipeline Company still performed well, and KPLC and KPTC were growing, the parastatals operating in deregulated sectors were struggling to survive. Kenya Railways was in a particularly serious state. Overstaffed and undercapitalised, costs remained too high and maintenance poor, resulting in a wholesale shift from rail to bus transport for passengers. Kenya Airways was also performing disastrously, operating old, inefficient aircraft, making huge losses, overstaffed and poorly managed. A restructuring and retrenchment programme began, routes were closed and fare deals done with other airlines, and in 1986 Kenya Airways took out large loans to acquire new planes. However, its performance remained appalling. At its low point in 1989, it had 4,000 employees for only 11 planes.[73] It had not filed annual returns since 1984.

A new transport parastatal joined the sector in 1986: the Nyayo Bus Service Corporation. This was one of Moi's ad hoc responses, this time to the endless queues of Nairobi commuters and schoolchildren. By 1988, there were 250 state-owned Nyayo buses, part-funded by overseas aid, competing with *matatus* and Kenya Bus Services. However, the Nyayo Bus Service proved commercially unsustainable, 'foundered on the rocks of nepotism, vandalism, corruption and inefficiency', and was liquidated in the 1990s.[74] In practice, the transport sector was dominated by *matatus*, the informal transport system, linked to Kenya's political, security and criminal classes, and able to defeat every effort to impose order. In 1984, the government passed a new law requiring annual inspections, limiting passenger numbers and setting minimum standards for drivers, but enforcement was difficult. A series of mass *matatu* strikes during 1986–8 against the rules resulted in massive disruption, and despite arrests and angry words, in practice the government abandoned all these controls.[75] These were not the actions of an all-powerful state, but of one that struggled to deal with organised popular resistance.

The Nyayo car project was another failed state intervention and a demonstration of the difficulties of self-reliance. The intention was to build a Kenyan car industry from nothing, using only technology available to Kenya and without the help of any large car manufacturer. Responding to the creation in 1985 of the Proton in Malaysia, in 1986 the University of Nairobi designed a low-cost car, which in theory could have been made locally. The government decided that since the best manufacturing facilities in Kenya were in Kenya Railways, that would be where they would be built. Efforts were made to obtain information about car manufacturing from foreign companies and 'the Project Team . . . were placed in very sensitive and strategic places

8.6: Moi demonstrates the Nyayo car, 1990

Courtesy: Nation Group Newspapers

all over the world, where the technology and information could be learned.'[76] Several prototype Nyayo pickups and a Nyayo car were produced, which Moi launched in February 1990 (see Figure 8.6). In 1990, the government formed the Nyayo Motor Corporation to oversee vehicle production, but no foreign investors would touch the project and there were no domestic funds available. Worse, the railways could not manufacture components sufficiently accurately to build a car. The government drip-fed funds to the project through the 1990s, but by 2001 it had collapsed.

New Banks and New Problems, 1982–6

In the financial sector, the 1980s saw private banks move ahead of their state competitors. In part, this was because redistributive pressures were directing parastatal finance away from urban areas and Central Province. Investments in less-developed areas assisted the disadvantaged, but did not achieve the same rates of return. An example of this was seen in the KCB, which was asked to broaden access to banking services by opening rural branches where other banks would not, and issuing large volumes of rural credit, increasing its costs without commercial return. In the words of the *Weekly Review*, 'KCB has been in constant consultation with the office of the president when making feasibility studies in order to determine in which rural township the next KCB branch or sub-branch should be opened.'[77] One estimate suggested that the KCB had forgone half its potential profits in the 1980s as a result.[78] There were other problems in the state sector. The NBK recorded losses in 1979 and 1984, and poor accounting concealed even worse performance. It wrote off huge bad debts every year, generating rumours that it was deliberately loaning money to the well connected, knowing it would never be repaid.

In 1984–6, Kenya suffered several bank failures, the first of a cycle of collapses. At this time, the CBK had few regulatory powers and the rules regarding capital adequacy were lax. This had allowed the foundation of several poorly managed and undercapitalised finance institutions. By 1986, there were 30 commercial banks and 50 building societies and non-banking finance institutions in the country, far more than could be viable in the long term. Most of the smaller institutions were Asian- or Kikuyu-led and owned, and predominantly served these communities. Most eventually collapsed, transferring large sums into the pockets of those who had borrowed from or otherwise exploited them.

In 1984, the CBK put the Rural–Urban Credit Finance Company chaired by Kikuyu MP Andrew Ngumba into receivership, the first Kenyan finance institution to go under. The cause was unsecured loans, many linked with Ngumba's election victory in 1983 in Mathare. The company had been founded only in 1982 and its main purpose appeared to have been to provide loans to Ngumba's constituents. In July 1986, Continental Bank and Continental Credit Finance (mainly Kikuyu-owned and managed, and with loans to senior Kikuyu including Kibaki and Matu Wamae's companies) also admitted liquidity problems. The Treasury and CBK revealed that the directors and shareholders had lent themselves over Ksh300 million (US$19 million). In 1986, Ngumba was accused of similar abuses and fled into exile. The CBK then put Union Bank, another Kikuyu-led bank, into receivership. There were knock-on effects as confidence weakened. The business model for many of these banks appeared unsound, with too little capital and high levels of risk. The cause of the crash was not solely the intrinsic weakness of these institutions, however. It was widely believed that Kikuyu-owned banks saw an outflow of government and parastatal funds, causing a cash crisis and the collapse of the weaker institutions. An angry Rubia alleged in October 1986 that the government was deliberately bringing Kikuyu-owned banks down. Moi in contrast claimed that he had been betrayed by some of those he had placed in positions of trust.

Alongside the 'Kikuyu' banks, the early 1980s had seen the formation of several Asian-managed banks with Kalenjin elite backers, which soon became known as the 'political banks'. In 1982, Mohammed Aslam, an Asian from Pakistan, founded Pan-African Bank. Its shareholders were reputed to include Moi himself, through Abraham Kiptanui and the company HEDAM (believed to stand for His Excellency Daniel Arap Moi).[79] Another new entrant was Trade Bank, led by Asian Alnoor Kassam, but 75 per cent owned by Gad Zeevi and Biwott. Other banks established in this period that soon became notorious included Trans-National Bank, founded in 1985 and associated with Moi and Nyachae, and Trust Bank, set up in 1988 by Ketan Somaia, Ajay Shah, Moi's son Gideon and others. Parastatals such as the NSSF, KNTC and the NHIF were pressured to deposit large sums with these political banks. These in turn issued large, often unsecured loans to senior politicians including Biwott, Hosea Kiplagat, Kiptanui, Kipng'eno arap Ng'eny and Mwangale and their companies. Trade Bank and Pan-African Bank were soon owed large sums by Biwott's companies, including Kobil and HZ Engineering, which was building Yaya Centre, an exclusive shopping mall. Trade Bank also loaned money to Kibaki's

Nyeri allies Wamae and Munene Kairu. By 1993, it had also loaned more than US$100 million to other companies owned by Kassam himself.

The government appeared to be trying to avoid further crises. In 1985, the CBK established a receiver for banks – the Deposit Protection Fund (DPF) – funded by contributions from institutions that accepted deposits, which guaranteed some returns for small depositors in a collapse, and could take over a failing bank. Financial reform was an IFI priority, fearing that the sector's weakness was distorting access to credit and foreign currency and interest rates. In response, the government launched a financial sector adjustment programme. The 1989 Banking Act increased capital requirements for banks and empowered the CBK to intervene in cases of illiquidity. The CBK then forced a merger of nine under-capitalised institutions, creating the state-owned Consolidated Bank of Kenya (funded by yet another World Bank loan). As 1991–3 was to show, though, process was no substitute for political will.

State Employment Peaks

The state remained the main employer for educated Kenyans, and in 1989 public sector employment hit 50 per cent of the formal sector workforce (see Figure 8.7). Whatever restructuring targets were established and instructions issued, each department, parastatal and council continued to hire staff, providing often-pointless jobs to their clients and thereby securing their personal position and collectively buying off discontent. The logic of neo-patrimonialism required the continued flow of state jobs and contracts to clients at every level and the explicit intervention of ethnicity into allocations of jobs, resources and even foreign aid projects. In the words of a foreign official who worked in Kenya's bureaucracy, 'Government-financed projects were proliferating with little or no regard to their potential contribution to economic and social development . . . because ethnic godfathers close to the center of power were pushing for projects in their home areas.'[80] Efforts to improve data collection and reporting, which would have exposed waste and partiality, were abandoned or hampered. A 1984 head count of civil servants revealed that salaries were being paid to 85,397 people who did not appear to exist.[81] The state's bureaucratic processes were also beginning to creak, as low wages, poor training and corruption undermined bureaucratic efficiency. As Robert Chambers wrote in the 1970s, a comment that now applied well to Kenya:

> As a government persistently tries to do too much and proliferates its organizations, whether departments or parastatals, the over-burdened, under-staffed and under-supervised machine becomes dysfunctional, demonstrating a spastic condition in which orders from the centre produce if anything unpredictable and often contrary twitchings in the extremities of the limbs. At the same time, the government bureaucracy continues to expand and lies as a deadening weight on the economy and the taxpayer.[82]

The conflict between the slow corrosion of patron–client patrimonialism and the public goods of bureaucratic efficiency and economic growth was increasingly clear.

8.7: Public and private sector employment, 1961–2007

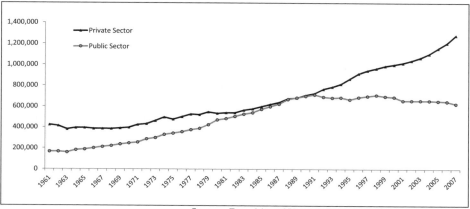

Source: Republic of Kenya, *Statistical Abstracts*, 1972–2009

Real wages continued to fall, driven by mass unemployment. Between 1979 and 1987, they fell by 5.9 per cent per annum in the private sector and 0.4 per cent in the public sector. At the same time, cost sharing for state services was beginning, and population pressure made access to basic services such as sanitation and water harder to deliver.[83] Life for most formal sector workers was far more difficult than for their parents.

Partly as a result, trade union membership grew. By 1985, 36 per cent of workers were union members, up from 29 per cent at independence. However, the unions could do little to defend their members' jobs or salaries. Kenya's largest employer, the state, had a strong interest in controlling wages. COTU remained the national trade union body, but it was effectively neutered. Open espousal of workers' interests remained unwise, and union officials represented their own interests as much as those of their members.

The NSSF remained the provident scheme for most workers. Nearly 2 million people were registered by 1989, up from 1.4 million in 1984. In 1987, the NSSF was converted from a government department into a state corporation, with a board representing the government, the Federation of Kenya Employers and COTU. This followed criticism that the NSSF was failing to look after its contributors' funds properly. In practice, however, the NSSF was soon involved in even more controversial investments.

Jua Kali

The *jua kali* (under the hot sun) informal sector continued to grow, as formal sector conditions grew more difficult. Unregistered and paying no taxes, *jua kali* manufacturing businesses produced hand-made items for consumers, using only basic equipment. Most were located in temporary structures on vacant government land. Characterised as small to medium enterprises, in the 1960s these textiles, woodworking and metalworking businesses had been seen as a transitional phenomenon, but had become an enduring provider of jobs, incomes and low-cost services in urban areas. In the 1980s, policy-makers identified what was now known as the informal sector as a key engine of growth – and a fundamental component of the economy – in their search for a way out of Kenya's problems. Foreign finance routed through NGOs such as Oxfam and the NCCK contributed significantly to the renewed attention on the sector. Statistics showed huge jumps in the number of informal sector workers (9 per cent per annum between 1980 and 1987), though this represented new methods of estimation and a search for hope as well as genuine growth.[84]

Moi himself initiated a notable piece of service provision in November 1985, when he visited informal sector workers at Kamukunji in Nairobi; seeing the difficult conditions in which they toiled under the sun, he promised them sheds. He returned four more times in 1985–6 to ensure that the sheds, water, electricity and even title deeds for the land were arranged. The *jua kali* sector was then highlighted in the 1986 Sessional Paper, which called for a direct stimulus to the informal sector for the first time.[85] By 1989, *jua kali* (now including all forms of private small-scale unlicensed enterprise) was part of the government's development planning, with its own Technical Training and Applied Technology Ministry.

It was now believed that Kenya had a 'missing middle' sector, a gap between large-scale manufacturing (with its origins in the European and Asian communities) and the micro-industries of the *jua kali* manufacturers. Government policy and regulatory systems with their Europeans origins and high standards had accidentally stifled this, and policies were now adapted to help *jua kali* enterprises grow. In practice, however, state support proved ineffectual and the sector grew more from Kenya's enforced liberalisation than from deliberate government action.[86] As Gavin Kitching described it, 'the "informal sector" is a place where people go whose only options are even worse . . .'[87]

Agriculture in the 1980s: A Mixed Performance

During the 1980s, agriculture, forestry and fishing generated roughly a third of Kenya's GDP, continuing its slow decline from 40 per cent at independence. Exports, though, continued to be primarily agricultural and (if agricultural transport, processing and trading were included) more than half the country's GDP was based on the sector, and three out of every four Kenyans depended on agriculture for their livelihoods. The performance of Kenya's economy in the 1980s, therefore, was linked to its inconsistent agricultural performance. This in turn was blamed on a combination of lack of investment, inflexible marketing systems, producer insensitivity to price changes, the weakness of the land market and lack of land title, and uneconomic pricing. Although there were successes in the export sector, especially compared to neighbours such as Tanzania, politicians promoted agricultural policies that would help them politically or personally, even at the expense of overall production. Kenyans also found themselves in a counter-cyclic system, with low production often accompanied by high prices, suggesting that agricultural production was not responsive to short-term price changes, especially in the slow-to-mature export crops.

The spilt in agricultural systems that had characterised pre-independence Kenya was now institutionalised in the African community. Most farms were small, family-owned subsistence or mixed farms, with a few thousand large commercial farms, mostly in the ex-white highlands, now almost entirely in African hands. The percentage of marketed produce (tea, coffee, sisal, sugar, wheat and maize) produced by large farms actually rose from 46 per cent in 1981 to 55 per cent in 1985.[88]

Increasingly, Central Province's development under Kenyatta was recognised as exceptional rather than the norm, driven by the combination of high-value cash-crop opportunities not available elsewhere and access to formal sector jobs in Nairobi. In other regions, mass labour migration, few cash-crop opportunities and lack of investment were leading towards mass pauperisation, but in a complex and inconsistent way, defying simple analysis.[89] However, land purchases and sales remained relatively uncommon, limited by the popular view of land as a sovereign asset in trust for future generations. Rural underemployment was widespread, reflecting structural inefficiencies in the rural labour market and further driving urbanisation. Urban remittances had fallen sharply since the mid-1970s, reducing the positive impact of employment on agricultural improvement. Inside Central Province, population growth and land shortage, the allocation of state resources elsewhere and setbacks in some of their key crops were changing the region's economic base.

Grain Politics

Maize remained Kenya's staple crop, produced by both small farmers and large commercial producers in the former white highlands. Wheat was increasingly popular and was grown mainly in the Rift Valley. The government, through the NCPB, controlled the pricing, movement and sale of both crops, although in practice large volumes of maize were still consumed or traded privately.

The year 1983–4 saw the worst drought and one of the worst agricultural performances in Kenya's history. With a very poor maize harvest (only 1.5 million tonnes), there was a real risk of famine, and coffee and tea production fell sharply at the same time. In marginal lands, food was unavailable even to those with money. However, few starved, as the government arranged large imports of American maize, and again the state took over maize transport and storage. DCs distributed free food in the worst-affected areas. Production then recovered and stabilised at around 2.5 million tonnes a year during 1985–92, reflecting good rains and relatively high producer prices. But Kenya's per capita food production continued to decline, by more than 2 per cent a year between 1980 and 1987, increasing the country's need to import food and becoming a serious concern to policy-makers.

In the second half of the 1980s, partly in response to the 1984 famine, rather than liberalising, Kenya tightened controls. Proposals to give maize millers the freedom 'to purchase their requirements direct from farmers without going through the

Maize and Produce Boards' had been planned since 1970, but never implemented.[90] The government promised the IFIs at least four times between 1982 and 1988 that it would liberalise maize marketing and agricultural finance and inputs, but on every occasion, it reneged on the agreement. As Peter Gibbon commented, 'A pattern emerged whereby Kenya would agree to conditionalities, bank the resulting flows of programme aid and then find reasons for non-compliance.'[91] The key issue facing the government was how to produce enough domestic maize to avoid shortages, and keep prices low for urban consumers without liberalising imports, which would hurt the grain barons of the Rift.

In June 1984, the government established a new cooperative, known as the Kenya Grain Growers Cooperative Union (KGGCU), as a competitor to the KFA. The KFA was a long-established cooperative with 10,000 members, with interests in farmers' inputs, machinery and fuels, which also acted as the government's agent in the purchase, storage and distribution of wheat, the purchase and distribution of fertilisers and the import of pedigree cattle. However, it was dominated by Kenyatta-era elites who owed little to Moi. The new KGGCU was established to compete with the KFA, offering lower prices for inputs, and Moi enrolled as KGGCU member no.1. In December 1984, the government ordered the KFA to hand over its operations to the new union. This made no commercial sense. The KGGCU had a capital base of only Ksh6 million, but was taking over the KFA's assets worth Ksh600 million.[92] As a side-effect, the control of key farming assets moved under state control, led by interim chairman Alfred Birgen (Kalenjin) and vice-chairman Nabwera (Luhya). Soon after, the KGGCU began to press to become the sole buyer of maize for the NCPB. It also extended services into Kalenjin lands, in contrast to the KFA's focus on the ex-white highlands, opening offices in Baringo and West Pokot within months.

In 1985, rather than liberalise prices and cut the NCPB out of grain marketing (as the IFIs required), the government did the opposite. The National Cereals and Produce Board Act formalised NCPB and KGGCU control of all aspects of the wheat and maize business, barring cultivation. It became a criminal offence to sell to anyone except the state. The NCPB remained both inefficient and corrupt, and in some areas the proportion of maize sold through the NCPB actually declined.

Coffee's Unstable Path

The 1980s also saw instability in the coffee industry, although it remained the country's largest foreign exchange earner until 1989 and its most profitable crop (see Figure 8.8). Two-thirds of Kenya's coffee now came from its 300,000 smallholders. Productivity per hectare was amongst the highest in the world. The KPCU (collectively owned by the farmers) was still the sole processor and main miller and the Coffee Board the sole marketer and regulator.

The country's overproduction was rewarded during 1984–6 by a second spike in world coffee prices, in which prices exceeded even the 1976–7 boom (see Figure 8.9). However, 1986 was the last year of real coffee profitability. World prices fell and farmers became increasingly dissatisfied as payments were 'eaten' by the chain of

8.8: Coffee and tea production, 1969–89

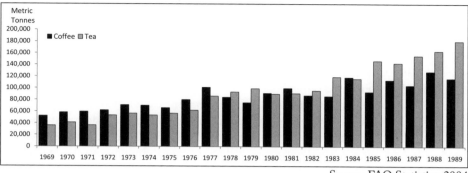

Source: FAO Statistics, 2004

8.9: Coffee and tea exports, 1963–93 (by value in US$)

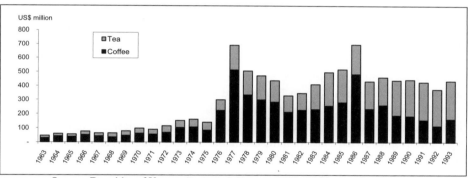

Source: Republic of Kenya, *Statistical Abstracts*, 1972–95. Year-end exchange rate figures

coffee organisations, including county councils, local cooperatives, the KPCU and the Coffee Board. The 3 per cent coffee cess (commodity tax) growers paid to the county council for local roads became a 6 per cent tax, of which 5 per cent went to the central government. The perception grew – though the evidence was mixed – that the government was taxing Kikuyu coffee (an area of competitive advantage) to fund investments elsewhere, especially Rift Valley grain growing.[93] There were disputes over the management of the KPCU, as farmers tried to retain control against state efforts to turn the cooperative into a parastatal. The Kenya Coffee Growers Association, a producers' union formed in 1981, was banned in 1989, in response to its growing militancy. The real problems, though, were yet to come.

Success Stories: Tea and Flowers

In contrast, the government's interest in expanding tea production was evident, and the industry prospered. Production doubled between 1980 and 1989 (see Figure 8.8), to the point where Kenya produced more than 10 per cent of world exports.

Smallholder production had increased, mainly around Mount Kenya, with the development of local factories and planting programmes supported by foreign donors. By 1985, smallholders contributed 43 per cent of all marketed tea, with most of the remainder coming from big plantations in Kericho District. The KTDA remained the regulatory and producing body, one of the most successful agricultural parastatals since the 1960s in delivering services and containing costs. It was no coincidence that it had few politicians on its board.

In 1986, in a change of direction, the government established a new parastatal, the Nyayo Tea Zone Corporation, to produce tea from farms inside forest reserves. The goal of the tea zones was to create a natural ecological barrier between peasant producers and forests, producing tea, reducing encroachment on the remaining forests, and providing jobs. The KTDA was not consulted regarding the decision. The new parastatal developed 17 boundary tea estates throughout the highlands over the next few years, from Mount Kenya to the Ugandan border. Tea production rose, but there were protests that the zones were undermining prices and that there were too few KTDA factories to process the new tea. The tea zones project was heavily politicised, managed directly by the OP and its head was Kalenjin ex-PC and Moi loyalist Isaiah Cheluget. Anti-government activists claimed that its covert aims included weakening control of the tea industry by (mainly Kikuyu) smallholders. The tea zones' mixed mandate of agricultural production and ecological protection proved difficult to maintain, but it remained self-financing.

Both smallholders and large farms contributed to Kenya's other success story: horticulture. By 1984, horticultural products – mostly flowers, but also green vegetables, pineapples, mangos and avocados – were already Kenya's third largest agricultural export earner and during 1984–8, the value of horticultural exports grew by a further 75 per cent. This mainly unregulated business was well suited to Kenya's high-potential land, and became a model of how to achieve export success without a controlling state marketing corporation.

Sugar Peaks

Kenya's sugar cane production was also growing, and peaked in 1989. Mumias Sugar, once considered marginal, had proved a success, now producing nearly half of Kenya's sugar. The sector faced many difficulties though. In 1988, the Ramisi factory in Kwale collapsed, as did Miwani in Kisumu. Nzoia Sugar embarked on a series of expensive expansions, which left it saddled with large loans and under-utilised equipment. Kenya's production was inefficient and returns to farmers were low, despite the fact that retail prices remained well above world market prices. This was in part because EEC quotas and the American preferential trade system depressed world prices and some producers exported surplus sugar at below cost. Kenya's demand now exceeded supply and from 1985 onwards, despite two decades of investment, Kenya became a sugar importer once more.

With the wide gap between local and import prices, domestic shortages, and a corrupt administrative environment, the consequence was sugar imports organised by insiders. In 1986, Muliro publicised a scandal whereby companies associated with civil servants and ministers had been licensed to import 26,000 tonnes of sugar during shortages.[94] By 1987, such imports were of increasing concern to Western donors. There were allegations that Moi and Abraham Kiptanui imported so much sugar during 1987 that the KNTC, the sole distributor, could not buy it all, and was unable to pay the factories for their deliveries for months.[95] It was also alleged that shortages were being artificially created, to allow pre-planned imports. In one case in 1990, critics alleged, 75,000 tonnes of sugar was imported and sold at prices more than double the state-controlled price. To ensure this happened, Ksh3 million were allegedly placed in a minister's account, Ksh500,000 into an official's, and Ksh1 million delivered to the OP.[96] There was a growing tension between policy and elite interests, which appeared ready to risk the survival of the industry for personal gain. Over the next three years, cane production fell, from its 1989 peak of 5 million tonnes to 4 million in 1992, leading to more imports. The worst problems with the mills appeared at the periods that sugar imports were landing at the docks. In 1992, bizarrely, Kenya was simultaneously exporting and importing large quantities of sugar.

Livestock Products

Although exports were modest, milk and meat remained key components of Kenya's agricultural sector. Roughly half of Kenya's cows were kept by pastoralists; the other half by commercial farmers and smallholders. Privatisation came early to meat processing, as the Uplands Bacon Factory and the Kenya Meat Commission, the state-owned processers, both collapsed in 1985. Both had suffered from private sector competition: they had no monopoly on processing, but could not vary their prices or offtake on commercial grounds.[97] Both had been in financial problems since 1976–7, which became self-reinforcing once farmers realised they could not trust them to pay on time.

The 1960s and 1970s had seen little growth in milk production. In contrast, 1985–9 saw a boom, with huge increases recorded year on year. Production marketed through the KCC's 11 factories doubled between 1982 and 1989 (see Figure 8.10), a result of greater production and the replacement of home consumption and local sales with cash sales. Much of this growth was in Kalenjin areas of the Rift Valley. In June 1989, the incumbent Kikuyu–Kalenjin leadership of the KCC was ousted by State House fiat, and a Luhya–Kalenjin dominated team took over.[98] From this time on, the organisation's leadership became more Kalenjin-dominated, and in parallel plunged into the red, losing money year on year.

The Performance of Kenya's Agricultural Parastatals

For decades, state regulation of agriculture had limited waste and maintained quality standards. However, many marketing boards were inefficient and some were being used as tools for a redistributive social policy. Liquidity was becoming a chronic problem, with knock-on effects in late payments to farmers. Between 1979 and 1981,

8.10: Milk production, 1963–93

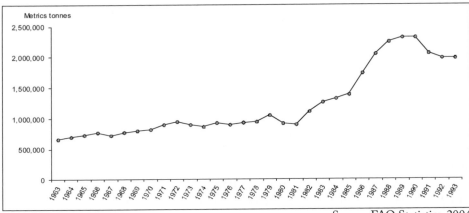

Source: FAO Statistics, 2004

most agricultural parastatals had begun to lose money; some never fully recovered. Like the government itself, they financed their losses by borrowing, but interest payments became an increasing component of their costs. The major factors affecting their performance were inflexible pricing, under-capitalisation (especially for the sugar factories), high levels of borrowing, and poor operational management – itself a product of politicisation, corruption and inefficiency. Although state regulation itself was not the cause of their decline, the inability to adapt prices to cycles in demand left them at risk, while the use of parastatals as tools of social policy caused a significant financial burden, and all were affected by predation.

The NCPB was probably the worst performer, its losses exacerbated by its obligation to provide numerous buying centres and to take all farmers' produce, irrespective of economics. It was widely believed that the NCPB and KGGCU favoured large growers in the Rift Valley, and that Kalenjin dominated their management.[99] The NCPB became a vehicle for quiet resource redistribution. By 1988, the board had accumulated Ksh10 billion (US$500 million) of debts, which the government duly wrote off.[100]

The AFC was also facing liquidity problems because of unpaid debts. It was financed by the Treasury and by cheap foreign loans to offer seasonal finance to farmers. Although terms were generous, many loans were never repaid.[101] By 1988, loan defaults were estimated at Ksh2.3 billion (US$125 million) out of a loan portfolio of Ksh3.6 billion. Most of the AFC's loans by value went to larger farmers, and it too was suspected of exhibiting both political and ethnic biases. Officials came under pressure from above and below to write off loans, ignore defaults or charge interest rates below commercial terms, another example of how administrative practices could be used (or suspected to be used) to subsidise certain communities and become a source of ethno-regional tension.

The Politics of Pastoralism

Pastoralism went through a resurgence of interest in the late 1980s and 1990s, reflecting a long-term shift in academic attention, but also one with political implications inside Kenya. From the mid-1980s, politicians from pastoral communities played an increasing role in Kenya's government, and social and political attention increasingly shifted towards them.

Since independence, the pastoralists of southern Kenya had been pushed back to marginal lands. The Maasai were the most affected by land sales, settlement, tourism and farming because of their proximity to Nairobi. This gradually made unavailable most dry-season water sources. The same process took place more slowly amongst the Orma of Tana River and the Kuria of South Nyanza. The situation was different for the northern pastoralists, where all land remained communal and almost everyone lived a nomadic lifestyle. Here, however, stock raiding was endemic and desertification and troubles in neighbouring countries were serious challenges.[102] The 1984 drought was a critical event. Many stock died, forcing northern herders to settle around urban settlements in search of food, creating a step-change in sedentarisation and dependency.

In the 1980s, development and the money economy reached previously neglected areas for the first time. This had many benefits, including education, reduced transaction costs for business and more profitable trade. There were side-effects though, with clan relationships and collective social obligations weakened. As had happened decades earlier amongst the Kikuyu, the moral economy that sustained rich and poor alike in bad times declined, and the rule of elders weakened.[103] Absolute inequality grew, sedentarisation increased, and most households diversified into non-cattle-related income sources. Studies suggested that pastoral communities were responding differently to the combination of drought, development and the market. Amongst the Orma and Kuria, for example, the net effect of the market economy remained positive, even for the poorest. In other communities, such as the northern Oromo, stock loss and sedentarisation were worsening absolute poverty.

Donor and state attitudes were changing and pastoralists were no longer seen as attached to an unsustainable lifestyle. It was realised that pastoralism might be the only sustainable use of arid and semi-arid lands.[104] The period 1989–92 saw the brief existence of a special Ministry for Reclamation and Development of Arid and Semi-Arid Lands, coordinating programmes across 14 districts, funded by eight different donors.

Changing perceptions amongst donors were associated with changes in Kenya's political landscape. There was a gradual shift in the 'balance of protection' from the agricultural communities to the pastoralists, as Moi's government sought to protect itself and to reassert idealised pre-colonial communal land rights in the Rift. Gradually, herders began to encroach onto small farms on the borders. There was an increasing feeling amongst long-disadvantaged pastoral communities and the Kalenjin (both farmers and herders) that they should fight to reclaim their land from rich 'foreign' settlers. Although no attempt was made to revoke the land settlements of the Kenyatta era, it became harder for 'non-indigenous' people to buy land north of Nakuru. Non-Kalenjin who had bought farms in Kalenjin-dominated areas found it increasingly difficult to get them demarcated or to obtain title deeds. Ethnicity played a growing role on the ground in the ex-white highlands; two-thirds of security officials and chiefs in Trans-Nzoia, for example, were now Kalenjin, although Kalenjin constituted only 21 per cent of the district's population.[105] By the late 1980s, despite policy being unchanged, in practice the 'willing buyer, willing seller' land model was dying.

Corruption, Tribalism and Resource Misallocation

Corruption Becomes Self-Sustaining

Corruption was now having an impact on international relations as well as on domestic economic efficiency, as donors recognised that their aid was being misspent or misappropriated and that many large contracts were being massively overpriced (to allow the payment of bribes to those approving them), causing lasting damage to and distorting the economy. Kenyan attitudes towards corruption remained inconsistent. Every person with a relative in a senior position would expect preferment as a result; yet everyone would criticise 'tribalism'. Everyone would expect a person in authority to make use of the office to enrich themselves; but at the same time, grand corruption was despised when practised by others. Generation to generation, a deliberate ambivalence built up around this sensitive matter, especially when dealing with foreigners. The 'economy of affection' – the personal, ethnic, religious and social relations between individuals – legitimised corruption to the benefit of one's own, but one denigrated the same actions by others.[106]

Corruption allegations are rarely proven, especially in Africa. However, it is widely accepted that by the late 1980s conflicts of interest were open at every level of government. Politicians and civil servants were players in the game they were refereeing, without effective scrutiny. Senior figures would own or be sleeping partners in businesses they were regulating and ensure they received contracts, licences, credit and information. There were no declarations of interests and little prospect of prosecution. The well connected continued to acquire government, council and private land with impunity. Although the European land frontier was closed, ADC-owned farms in the old white highlands were still being subdivided and sold (in principle) to the landless.[107] In practice, officials ensured that they, their families or proxies were allocated land at the same time.[108] The OP instructed plot allocation committees to allocate land cheaply to specific individuals.[109] Some allocations read like a roll call of the Kalenjin elite.[110]

Many allegations were later made that Moi and his family had stolen billions of shillings and salted them away abroad. There is little doubt that he and his allies received tens if not hundreds of millions of dollars in inducements, gifts and commissions, though exactly who received these funds is impossible to prove. A rare public example of the way business was done was given by the (Asian) manager of a Dubai business, who claimed that in 1989 he gave US$2 million in 'personal donations' for transmission to Moi, in return for the contract for the duty free business at Kenya's international airports.[111] Yet Moi remained an austere man personally. He was not particularly astute financially and was probably exploited by his various business managers. His real estate and business empire was worth tens of millions of dollars, but most of his assets were in Kenya, unlike some of his family and allies. Also, unlike his allies, he showed no sign of wanting to retire abroad. He probably spent most of the money his machinery brought in.

It could be argued that the corruption of the late 1980s was little worse than in the 1970s. The elephant herds, for example, were decimated under Kenyatta, not Moi. The perception of increased corruption could simply be a product of better international communications and growing foreign focus. The economy was no longer growing so fast, reducing the margins available. The argument that there was a genuine qualitative change in the 1980s is more convincing, however. It seems that the 10 per cent kickbacks of the Kenyatta era became 25–50 per cent, sinking some projects, while others appeared constructed primarily for the rent-seeking opportunities they gave. Moi's elites needed to extract more, more rapidly, because of their fragile political and economic position. They did not have the economic base that the Kikuyu had created (with government support). As the nation's resignation to corruption grew, so did corruption itself. Most internal restraints that limited abuses had now collapsed. Contracts were not given to the best vendors (which had never been the case), nor even to qualified vendors who had paid the necessary commissions. Now, they were given to vendors whose profits were so affected by the size of the commissions paid that they were incapable of doing a satisfactory job even if that had been their intent. The 'briefcase business' with no employees or products, whose sole objective was to fleece the state, was a feature of the 1980s and 1990s, not of the 1970s. The principle of elite corruption had been established under Kenyatta, but Moi practised it on a grander scale, and could not have stopped it even if he tried. His survival rested on fragile corruption-based elite alliances, and to have broken these would probably have destroyed his government within months.

One effect of rising corruption and declining capability in government was a rise in transaction costs for business and a reluctance to invest. The lack of foreign private investment in Kenya in the 1980s reflected the high level of bribes demanded as protection money as well as the economic environment. Some openly sought political protection as part of their business strategy. This was particularly clear in Lonrho's choice of senior African management. In the 1970s, 'family' member Udi Gecaga had been Lonrho's deputy chairman. In the Moi era, this would no longer do, and by 1984, Kalenjin Mark arap Too, a wheeler-dealer and Moi confidant, alleged by many to be his illegitimate son, was a director of Lonrho East Africa. By 1988, he was deputy chairman. When he fell from favour in 1991, Lonrho replaced him, but reappointed him in 1992 once he was back in Moi's good books.

Turkwell Gorge

In 1986, the government initiated the Turkwell Gorge hydroelectric plant, the most controversial development project in Kenya's history. Sited on the border between West Pokot and Turkana, this dam was a huge investment, intended to generate 100–150 megawatts of power and to provide irrigation and income-generating opportunities for local communities. After several feasibility studies, a French consortium backed by the French government funded the project, with Spie Batignolles the main contractor, a process that did not go to competitive tender.[112] The interest rates on the loans were higher than could have been obtained from other sources. The project cost was impossible to determine as it quickly became politicised, but there were rumours that the US$148 million budgeted cost eventually became between US$450 and $800 million. Turkwell was completed in 1991, but was not opened until 1993, when the dam was still less than a quarter full. The irrigation project was never implemented.

The Kerio Valley Development Authority (KVDA) was responsible for the project, and it fell under the responsibility of Minister for Energy and Regional Development Biwott. The project and the tendering process remain controversial, as allegations have been made that senior politicians received large kickbacks (US$25–30 million) on the contract, which were laundered through a local bank.[113] In March 1986, an angry memorandum written by the European Commission delegate to Kenya was leaked to the *Financial Times*. This stated that the contract price was more than double the amount Kenya would have had to pay for the project based on a competitive tender and that: 'The Kenyan government officials who are involved in the project are fully aware of the disadvantages of the French deal . . . but they nevertheless accepted it because of high personal advantages.'[114]

The project led to the cancellation of support for the Kenyan energy sector by foreign donors, as the evidence mounted that it was economically questionable and that the contract's value had been inflated. Spie Batignolles was named in other cases of bribery in connection with African dam projects.[115]

The Changing Shape of Tribalism

The late 1980s saw the maturing of the transition from Kikuyu to Kalenjin dominance. The overall ethnic arithmetic of state and parastatal appointments remained reasonably balanced. With Oyugi in a key role, the Luo – particularly from South Nyanza – were at their most influential since 1965. However, many Kikuyu believed that Kalenjin were taking a disproportionate share of government jobs and being promoted faster. The bitterness with which some viewed this was shown by an editorial in *Society* in 1992. In openly racist terms, it castigated, 'The massive invasion by poorly prepared, sparsely trained and highly inexperienced, awkward, haggard and sloppy looking humanity into responsible and senior positions . . .'[116]

The limited evidence available suggests that a change in hiring practice truly did occur, particularly towards the end of the decade, and it was particularly obvious at the top. As well as their key roles in the security system, for example, the head of the Public Service Commission, since 1980, Paul Boit, was from Nandi, the head of the civil service from 1986, Joseph arap Leting, was also Nandi and Eric Kotut (Tugen), became governor of the Central Bank in 1988. Chairmanships or chief executive roles in the ADC, AFC, KCB, KCC, HFCK, KNAC, ICDC, KPTC, sugar companies, NCPB and other agricultural boards were all held by Kalenjin, a pattern disproportionate to the size of the talent pool from that community.[117] It seems Moi and his allies were relying on ethnicity above ability, and trying to kick-start the development of a Kalenjin state elite.

There is some evidence that the same pattern existed in state resource allocation. Average earnings rose faster in Kalenjin (and Luhya) districts and, from a low base, Kalenjin districts saw some of the fastest improvement in educational levels and the most rapid rise in road mileage in the 1980s. But unlike the preferential treatment of Kikuyu under Kenyatta, Moi's refocusing of preference towards the periphery and the Kalenjin – more remote and more rural – generated less of a surplus. Not only did Moi have to take away before he could give, but what he gave generated less wealth, thereby damaging the economy and weakening popular consent elsewhere.

Kenyan Asians and the State

For years, Kenyan Asian-owned businesses had been a target for extortion by politicians. Formally driven out of most jobs and of trade (though in practice many had returned), those families who had remained in Kenya continued to dominate domestic manufacturing and some had built large capital bases. Now, the elite needed them in a different capacity. With the need amongst the Kalenjin elite to extract state resources and to challenge the commercial dominance of the Kikuyu, Moi and his allies turned to the Asians as the other source of indigenous private capital. While Kikuyu had acted as frontmen for Asians in the 1960s and 1970s, now Asians acted as frontmen for Kalenjin. Throughout the Moi era, senior politicians were engaged in a complex web of business relations with a network of Asian executives. Asian-African patron–client teams would compete on some deals and cooperate on others. Their primary target was government and parastatal contracts. Little has been written outside the popular press about the rise and fall of the flamboyant frontmen of Asian capital, in part due to the lack of reliable information and the risk of libel. However, the 'rags to riches' stories of some prominent Asian executives of the 1980s and 1990s are at the heart of Kenya's problems.

Ketan Somaia is the most public example. Somaia was a 26-year-old shop-owner in Kisumu when he began to be promoted by his political 'godfather' Hezekiah Oyugi, whose father had been a houseboy for the Somaia family. During Oyugi's period at the apex of power in 1985–91, Somaia's Dolphin Group grew to national prominence, with contracts to supply military equipment, computers and other goods. British tycoon Tiny Rowland was so incensed by Somaia's business practices that he wrote to Moi claiming that Somaia had shown him procurement forms from the OP with the spaces for prices left blank, to be filled in as he wished.[118] In 1988, Somaia bought the

Marshall's East Africa car dealership (another foreign divestment). He co-founded Trust Bank and in 1989 he acquired the Madhupaper International paper business from Kikuyu tycoon Samuel Macharia for only a third of the firm's book value. In 1990, he bought Miwani Sugar Mills and in 1991 took over the collapsed Bank of Credit and Commerce International in Kenya, renamed Delphis Bank. He also acquired the Nairobi International Casino. He appeared to have unlimited resources, was extraordinarily well connected and apparently untouchable.[119]

Another well-connected Asian entrepreneur, Naushad Merali, was also rising to prominence. He bought Firestone East Africa and Union Carbide, then the Commercial Bank of Africa and First American Bank. All were bought without public tender, based on discretionary access to hard currency to pay foreign investors. Merali also established the first private export processing zone as Sameer Investments in 1991. Many believe that he was fronting for Moi, Biwott or the Kenyatta family. Other Asian entrepreneurs such as Alnoor Kassam and Mohammed Aslam went into banking, backed by Moi or Biwott or both. They were supported by Asian businesses who wished to have 'trustworthy' figures handling their money, and to deposit cash obtained off book to avoid paying tax.[120]

There was also concern in public circles over Asian capital flight. Asian business-men were notorious for working with CBK officials to access hard currency to move overseas through over-invoicing and fake shipments. The government cracked down on these activities in 1987, arresting at least 20 businessmen and officials in Asian-owned banks for illegal currency transactions. Even for these small fry, the sums involved were huge, involving the failure to remit to the Treasury hundreds of mil-lions of shillings in foreign currency from coffee sales.[121] This is not to suggest, of course, that all Asian businessmen were enmeshed in corruption. Most Asian-owned groups avoided public scandals, though they still had to give *harambee* donations in return for protection.

The Decline of Local Government

Nairobi continued to mushroom, and the city council presided over a gradual decline in standards. Urban planning was never a priority after independence, and the plans that survived were poorly implemented. Ubiquitous municipal corrup-tion, involving embezzlement, extortion, land re-zoning and illegal allocations made the situation worse.

In 1983, Local Government Minister Mudavadi had suspended and then dissolved Nairobi City Council, and a probe revealed widespread malpractice, tribalism and corruption. An appointed City Commission ran the city for the next nine years. Initially, there was a crackdown on illegal plot allocations and attempts to cut over-manning, but the rot was already too deep. Although the council was corrupt and incompetent, these attributes were even more striking in the unanswerable, politically appointed commission. Investments in the city plummeted. The city's capital expenditure per capita for water and sewerage fell from US$28 in 1981 to $2 in 1987, and per capita maintenance expenditures fell from US$7 to $2 over the same period.[122] The fact that Fred Gumo, who had helped Moi remove Muliro from Parliament, was the chair of the Commission in 1989–92 indicates that Moi's priorities were not always impartial and efficient administration. A particularly rapid decline in services – the end of garbage collection, road craters and broken pipes and sewers – marked his watch. Gumo and the other commissioners rewarded themselves handsomely. For example, Gumo later admitted he had sold a plot to the CBK for Ksh300 million (US$800,000), on land that the Commission had sold to him while he was its chairman for Ksh11 million.[123] In most countries, this would have been a criminal offence.

Everywhere, local authorities remained ineffectual, politicised and corrupt. The rapid subdivision of councils of the early Moi era had made them even more financially unviable. They did not raise enough money to support the services they were supposed to provide, and were universally viewed as opportunities for private accumulation. Education and ability levels amongst councillors were low, the minister's nominations could be used to destroy what little representativeness they had, the choice of mayors was dominated by open treating and relations between councillors and council officers were poor. As local government minister from 1982–9, Mudavadi ruled local councils with an iron hand. In 1988, Parliament was even forced to pass legislation to legitimise his nomination of too many councillors to 22 councils, designed to ensure that 'his' mayors were elected.

Education, Health and Social Change

Declining Health Services and the Emergence of AIDS

The 1980s saw a gradual worsening of conditions in the health sector, a combination of bureaucratic indifference, politicisation, corruption and a shortage of funds. Some expectant mothers were forced to share beds, operating theatres had broken windows, and there was no water in some hospitals. The funds available for health services were increasingly stretched. Spending per capita was falling and performance indicators such as numbers of hospital beds per capita declined. Managers also seemed to lack the will to use the limited funds available to good effect. While donors subsidised or provided drugs to local dispensaries, the main hospitals had few; corruption in the central medical stores led to the theft of funds or the purchase of useless or out-of-date medicines.

AIDS (Acquired Immune Deficiency Syndrome) was recognised as a public health issue in 1981. It soon became clear that there was a locus of infection in East and Central Africa. The transmission method was mainly unprotected heterosexual contact. Kenya, like other African countries, initially refused to accept the existence of AIDS. Sensitivities were high: when doctors diagnosed the first case in Kenya in 1984, they were arrested for 'undermining tourism'. In 1985, reflecting the growing numbers of sick people and the worldwide focus on the disease, Kenya established a National AIDS Committee. There was no screening of blood for transfusions for several more years, however. In 1986, there were 80 confirmed cases, and in

1987, an AIDS control programme was introduced. A decade later, the disease had become a national disaster and it was still NGOs rather than the government who were leading the fight. For years, government personnel were hostile to AIDS prevention, viewing the illness as 'un-African', while the churches also found it difficult to respond apart from urging abstinence. This 'head in the sand' attitude cost Kenya many lives.

8–4–4: A New Education System

In many ways, the mid-1980s represented the peak of educational achievement in Kenya. In 1986, the state claimed that virtually every child received some primary schooling (see Figure 8.11).[124] By 1989, adult literacy had risen from 20 per cent at independence to 64 per cent, a major achievement.[125] The degree of capture could be shown by the rough parity at last between male and female primary students. Despite this, nearly half were failing to complete the primary course, and dissatisfaction at an old and sometimes inappropriate curriculum was widespread.

In 1984–5, for the first time since the 1960s, the government introduced a new education system, known as '8–4–4'. Based on the American model, it extended the length of primary education from seven to eight years, abolished the 'A' level and replaced it with the Kenya Certificate of Secondary Education as the end of four years of secondary education. This was followed by four years (replacing three) at university. The Certificate of Primary Education was abolished and replaced by a harder Kenya Certificate of Primary Education (KCPE). The new system also placed more emphasis on vocational education, reflecting a decade in which few secondary graduates could find a white-collar job.

The new system, designed and led by Education Minister Jonathan Ng'eno, required the recruitment of new teachers and the construction of classrooms in

8.11: Primary and secondary school enrolments, 1978–93

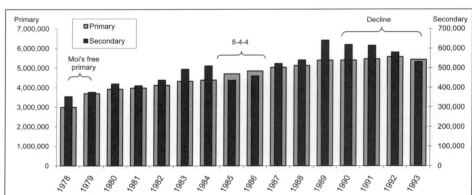

Source: Republic of Kenya, *Statistical Abstracts*, 1982–2003

almost every primary school to add another year of attendance. Moi took a personal interest in the change, organising academics to write textbooks and conducting *harambees* for classrooms. The World Bank helped fund the 8–4–4 system's development, but its implementation in January 1985 still caught teachers, parents and publishers by surprise and left schools in chaos. Although well intended, it was tendentious from the first, with too broad a curriculum, and it continued to be a source of dissatisfaction for decades.

At the same time, the government introduced an equally controversial change. Rather than secondary students being admitted to any state school (for which they could qualify scholastically and afford the fees), 85 per cent of students would now have to come from the province in which the school was situated. This quota system was controversial because it limited most of the intake to the local area, varied pass marks by region and meant many students would only meet those from other communities at university. The rationale was that it would allow students from underprivileged marginal areas access to equal education opportunities. It also gave parents a stronger interest in contributing to school *harambees* because their community would use the facilities they were supporting. It would also reduce the competitive advantage of the Kikuyu. This matched other changes in investment. Excluding Nairobi, Central Province had contained 27 per cent of Kenya's secondary places in 1981, but had steadily declined since then. The previously under-served Rift Valley was the main beneficiary (see Figure 8.12).

As well as being controversial, Kenya's education system was expensive: by 1989, the country was trying to educate more than 12 million people under 20 – the same number as the UK – with less than half the working-age population and a fraction of the income to finance it. In 1988, encouraged by the World Bank, the

8.12: Secondary school places in Central and Rift Valley Provinces, 1974–91

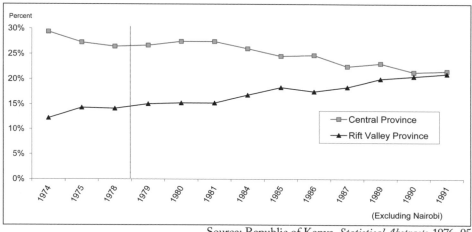

Source: Republic of Kenya, *Statistical Abstracts*, 1976–95

government committed itself to cost sharing for education, limiting its contribution to teachers' salaries only, and requiring that parents pay for buildings and all other costs in state schools. Levies and charges rose and enrolments dropped amongst poorer families.[126] From 1989 on, secondary enrolments began to fall, from 650,000 to 550,000 in 1993.

The Expansion of the Universities

Just as there was pressure on the lower levels of the education system, Kenya was also short of university places, as a degree was now essential for a professional job. The University of Nairobi could absorb only half of those who qualified for admission, and standards were falling. Many wealthy Kenyans sent their children abroad, but the government was unhappy with this, both because of the cost and because they believed a foreign education was irrelevant to the needs of the country.

Instead, the government expanded the university system, despite protests that Kenya did not need more universities, since it could not offer jobs even to its existing graduates. A 1981 report had recommended the creation of a second university, and Moi University near Eldoret opened in 1984. In 1985, Kenyatta College became Kenyatta University. Egerton University followed in 1986–7. The fifth, Jomo Kenyatta University College of Agriculture and Technology, was established in 1988–9 and became a university in 1994. Much of this expansion was funded by the UK, Japan and the US. From 1984, the university programme occupied between half and three-quarters of the capital budget for education. As a result, the number of state undergraduates in Kenya more than doubled, from 15,000 in 1987–8 to 36,000 in 1993–4. Students still received government loans for living costs, but in 1989 tuition fees were introduced as part of cost sharing.

Despite this, the system remained in crisis. The coup attempt had led to the university's closure for 13 months and forced deferred admissions, which had knock-on effects for several years. There was overcrowding and declining discipline. The atmosphere was repressive and lecturers feared to speak their minds; salaries were capped at levels that encouraged the best to leave. After two years of calm, there were student riots and a boycott in 1985 and the university was closed for several months. In 1987, there was more fighting between students and GSU, and more than 10,000 were expelled. The university was closed again in 1989, after students rioted over poor facilities and the banning of their union. This followed the double intake year of 1987–8 when the university took two years' worth of students to try to break the backlog. There was a second double-intake year in 1990–1, the effect of the 8–4–4 system, which left two years ready for university at the same time. There was severe overcrowding and stress on teaching staff.

Ethnicity also played a role inside the university. Although details remain sketchy, the government may have weighted university entrance requirements to give preference to those from poorer regions, and ordered the universities to follow an affirmative action policy to favour 'marginalised' (i.e. pastoralist and Kalenjin) areas in faculties such as law.

The Role of Women in the 1980s

There had been some change since the 1970s in attitudes towards women. The slow expansion in educational opportunities for women had begun to trickle through into their consideration for senior posts, though the top ranks of the business and political world remained closed. In 1982, for example, Moi appointed Kenya's first female judge. In the rural areas, however, the woman's lot as provider of subsistence agriculture and domestic work remained little changed. Most formal sector roles continued to be occupied by men, with women concentrated in nursing and teaching. Educational backgrounds, women's child-rearing responsibilities, employers' attitudes and self-selection by women all contributed to this. Although primary education was no longer gender-biased, secondary education remained 60 per cent male, and university education more than 70 per cent male.

The UN Decade for Women ended in 1985 with an international conference held in Nairobi. Still, little changed in Kenya. John Keen spoke for many African men, for example, when he declared that 'women getting to the height of political power is unacceptable . . . it is inconsistent with African culture.'[127] Moi too expressed similar views, commenting in 1984 that 'for women to be equal to men was to imply that God had erred when he made man the head of the family.'[128] Wife beating remained common, although increasingly frowned upon. Wife inheritance continued amongst some communities if a husband died, though by the late 1980s cases were occurring of women who refused to be 'inherited'.

The Rise of the NGO

While the state's dominance was unchallenged in Kenya's political sphere, international NGOs were increasingly important across Africa, beginning to become political actors in their own right, and spinning off local NGOs with a mix of developmental and political goals.[129] The number of NGOs in Kenya mushroomed from 125 in 1974 to over 400 in 1987.[130] This reflected the difficulties of seeking change through formal politics, and the resulting diversion of political energies into NGOs, churches and professional associations. It also reflected a Western consensus that Africa needed a better balance between the state and what was becoming known as 'civil society': NGOs seeking to execute collective political or economic activities outside the state, including charities, self-help groups, professional associations and churches. They captured a modest but growing proportion of overseas development aid and delivered a significant proportion of services such as health care. In Kenya, the government, concerned by the growing influence and independence of NGOs, began to talk of registration and monitoring.

Tourism and Ivory

Between 1972 and 1982, roughly 350,000 tourists a year, mainly British and West German, had visited Kenya. There was a downturn during 1981–3, the result of the coup attempt and foreign exchange shortages, then visitor numbers and game-park visits both rose during the late 1980s, a second boom for Kenya (see Figure 8.13).

8.13: International arrivals and visits to national parks, 1979–91

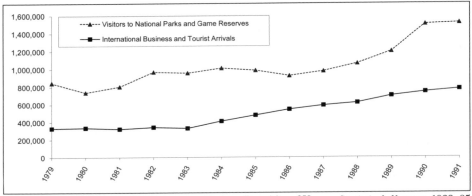

Source: Republic of Kenya, *Statistical Abstracts*, 1988–95

The government's pro-Western orientation, the availability of consumer goods, a realistic exchange rate and competitive pricing all helped the growth of mass tourism. Revenues rose to the point that earnings surpassed those from tea and coffee. Tourism now provided over 120,000 jobs and 12 per cent of the country's GDP. However, the picture was not entirely rosy; foreign impressions were hurt in 1988–9 by the depredations of poachers, the widely publicised murder of British tourist Julie Ward and the shooting of other foreigners. For Kenya itself, the industry remained a mixed blessing. Much of the income from tourism left the country again, to the airlines, tour operators and importers. Mass tourism was also causing growing environmental problems in the parks and on the coast.

Many tourists still came to Kenya for animal safaris, but the industry's existence was threatened by poaching, particularly of elephants.[131] High ivory prices, the availability of sophisticated weapons and the collapse of Somalia all contributed to the carnage, as many of the gangs were Somali *shifta*. In response, Moi issued shoot-on-sight orders in September 1988, but this achieved little. Poachers killed many game wardens in the poorly led and under-equipped anti-poaching units, and corruption remained endemic in the Ministry of Tourism and Wildlife. Lions, leopards, elephant and rhino had almost vanished outside the parks. Between 1973 and 1988, the number of elephants in Kenya was believed to have fallen from 167,000 to only 16,000, though statistics were uncertain, for obvious reasons. From 20,000 rhino in 1970, there were now only 350–400 left.[132]

Facing the near-extinction of the elephant and rhino, and under intense international pressure, in 1987 the government finally began to make real changes. In that year, Moi hired a new head of the Wildlife Department, conservationist Perez Olindo, who replaced park officials and reviewed lodge construction projects. In 1988–9, conservation responsibilities were transferred from ministerial control to a new parastatal, the Kenya Wildlife Service (KWS), less answerable to political pressure and with its own ranger force. The KWS was initially led by Olindo, but he was ousted after trying to take over the Maasai Mara game reserve from Narok County Council, and the killing of the last five white (square-lipped) rhino in 1988.[133] In April 1989, Olindo was replaced by the able but acerbic white Kenyan Richard Leakey, palaeontologist and long-time National Museums chairman. Leakey was outspoken and controversial, but Moi gave Leakey access to the presidential hotline and his complete support to take drastic action. This appointment started a chain of events and a love–hate association between Leakey and Moi that was to last for a decade.

Leakey immediately implemented Moi's 'shoot to kill' order, using former game wardens and hunters to create poacher-hunting gangs that killed more than 100 poachers in 1989. In July 1989, Leakey arranged for Moi to burn US$3 million worth of ivory, skins and tusks taken from poachers, to draw international attention to the crisis (see Figure 8.14). As a publicity event, it was extremely successful, and cemented the relationship between Moi and Leakey. Only a month later, the EEC banned ivory imports and the market for ivory collapsed. In October 1989, Kenya successfully supported placing the elephant on the Convention on International Trade in Endangered Species (CITES) Appendix 1 list of severely endangered animals, trade in the products of which was completely banned. The decline in animal numbers was halted.

8.14: Moi burning ivory, 1989

Courtesy: Nation Group Newspapers

Meanwhile, population growth continued to eat away at Kenya's forests, despite Moi's ad hoc efforts, such as his 1981 Permanent Presidential Commission on Soil Conservation. Although the state managed virtually all Kenya's forests, it seemed powerless to stop incursions. Gazetted forests were still burnt for charcoal and the land cultivated, sawmills exploited concessions without regulation, and primary forest was cleared for plantations. Water catchment areas were damaged and rainfall patterns changed. In 1984, there was a public outcry about deforestation around Mount Kenya, which led to a presidential ban on cutting of indigenous trees, but there is little evidence that this was effective. In 1988, Moi banned all forest timber cutting, but his order was again mostly ignored.

A Troubled Census

The 1989 census was the most controversial in Kenya's history. It was conducted in August 1989, but the results were not published until 1994. Doubts were raised about data quality, and the *post hoc* adjustment of numbers for political reasons. The population had grown by over 40 per cent since 1979, and now stood at 21.4 million, with a growth rate still at 3.4 per cent. Over half of all Kenyans were under 18. Decades of family planning had had little impact, and efforts to cut fertility were still hampered by conservative social views and religious opposition to contraception.

The key political issue lay in the ethnic totals, which showed that the Kalenjin had overtaken the Kamba to become the fourth largest community by only 10,000 people (see Figure 8.15). The highest growth rates were in communities seen as aligned to the government, membership of which might confer some advantages – the Kalenjin (49 per cent), Maasai (56 per cent) and Luhya (45 per cent). The Kikuyu, Embu and Meru grew more slowly, while the Luo remained the slowest growing of all major

8.15: Changes in population by ethnic group, 1969–89

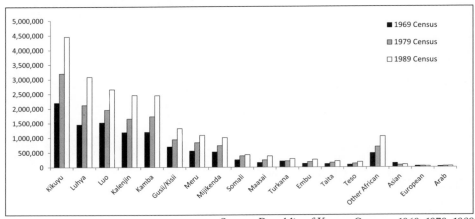

Source: Republic of Kenya, *Censuses, 1969, 1979, 1989*

8.16: Ethnic diffusion, 1969–89

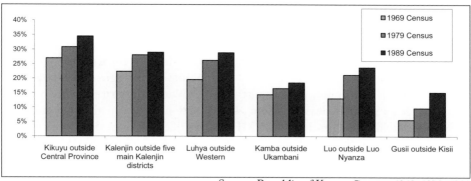

Source: Republic of Kenya, *Censuses 1969, 1979, 1989*

communities. There was concern that the state had manipulated the figures to ensure the Kalenjin came fourth, and thereby justified resource distributions in their favour, a statistical sleight of hand used in Nigeria in the past.

The census also revealed that migration and urbanisation were breaking down the historical relationship between ethnicity and geography. Whereas 27 per cent of Kikuyu had lived outside Central Province in 1969, now 34 per cent did so. The change was even more dramatic amongst the Luo, only 13 per cent of whom had lived outside Siaya, Kisumu and South Nyanza in 1969. Nearly a quarter did so now (see Figure 8.16).

Despite the introduction of a rural–urban balance strategy designed to reverse the flood of people to the cities, Kenya had one of the highest urbanisation rates in East Africa. Nairobi's population in 1989 was 1.3 million – a five-fold increase since independence. This was a growing threat to political stability, with failing services, slums, growing crime and deep poverty for the jobless. Whatever their ethnicity, the urban poor were the most disadvantaged sector of Kenyan society.

The 1988 General Elections

The February–March 1988 general elections saw the effective end to representative democracy in Kenya. The introduction of queue voting destroyed the National Assembly as a tool for political legitimacy. Henceforth, most MPs were tools of the centre, not local representatives, because their success was due in part or in whole to the state's rigging of elections.[134] The legitimacy of formal politics vanished, and only illegal protest was possible. The elections also unseated many popular Kikuyu, Luhya and Luo politicians. Many opposition leaders in the 1990s were KANU leaders who had been rigged out in 1988, who now recognised that only through confrontation could the 'system' be defeated.

Constituency Boundaries and Registration

The electoral process began with the establishment of new constituency boundaries. The first boundary review since 1966 was finally implemented during 1986–7 by the Electoral Boundaries Review Commission, increasing the number of seats from 158 to 188. However, the determinants of which new seats were created appeared more political than demographic. The changes did not abolish a single under-populated seat, and established no new urban constituencies. North-Eastern Province received two extra seats when it deserved none. If population had been the sole criterion, Nairobi would have been entitled to 16 MPs instead of eight. These decisions reflected a desire to maintain the over-representation of the semi-arid regions, to ensure that Parliament provided a counterweight to the economic power of the capital and of the agricultural communities.

The districts to benefit most were those where Moi's allies could dictate the recommendations.[135] There was also ethnic gerrymandering in some seats. Part of Lamu East was shifted to Lamu West, for example, to ensure that the Kikuyu in the settlement scheme did not take control of the seat. There were also alterations to district boundaries. Kerio South, Biwott's seat, grew dramatically, incorporating part of Uasin Gishu, and Moi's Baringo Central absorbed part of Laikipia. In the south, Baringo and Kericho both alienated a fragment of the ex-white highlands from Kikuyu-dominated Nakuru and broke the division between eastern and western Kalenjin homelands by creating a narrow corridor that cut off Uasin Gishu from Nakuru.[136] The review also reinforced the importance of ethnicity as a criterion for constituency design. The Commission split several seats populated by more than one ethnic group to create more ethnically pure constituencies. Nakuru North, for example, was partitioned to create one predominantly Kikuyu and one Kalenjin seat. Uasin Gishu was repartitioned to create a predominantly Keiyo seat in Eldoret East, and Trans-Nzoia was re-divided to create Cherangani constituency, covering the Kalenjin east of the district.

Voter registration took place from June to September 1987. The deadline was extended twice because of poor voter response. Despite this, only 6.1 million voters registered, 1.2 million fewer than in 1983, reflecting a growing disenchantment with the political system.[137] For the primary elections, only KANU members could vote; KANU claimed it had 4.3 million members, though in reality it was far fewer.[138]

The Blocking of Nyachae

One person conspicuous by his absence from the election was Simeon Nyachae. Forcibly retired in 1987, he had intended to enter Parliament as member for Nyaribari Chache, his home constituency in Kisii District. Like many other senior civil servants, he had long been active in district politics. He had donated generously to *harambees* and was well respected in the Gusii community. He had powerful opponents, however, including local minister Zachary Onyonka. Almost as soon as he retired, Nyachae faced a series of denunciations, and it appeared that Nairobi insiders were organising his humiliation. At the same time, Nyachae's business interests suffered, and government permits became difficult to obtain.[139]

When the 1988 elections were called, KANU barred Nyachae and all his Kisii allies (including Kenyatta-era ex-minister James Nyamweya) from contesting the election.[140] The reasons remain unknown. Some suggested a business deal with Moi had gone sour, while Morton pointed the finger of blame at Oyugi and Biwott.[141] Nyachae may simply have been too ambitious and Moi may have pre-emptively struck against a potential rival, as he was soon to do with Matiba.

Party and Parliamentary Nominations

As proposed in 1986, the 1988 primaries were fought under the queue voting system, in which KANU members lined up behind a candidate's representative in public. This was followed by a secret ballot run-off between the top two or three candidates if no candidate won 70 per cent of the vote in the primary. The changes to electoral processes were implemented administratively, treating the queue voting as 'primary' elections, private to KANU itself. Nonetheless, they were executed by the provincial administration, as if they were 'preliminary' elections as held in 1969–79, reflecting the ambiguity and probable unconstitutionality of the process.

Although Nyachae's team was barred, KANU cleared to stand several former Njonjo supporters and others suspended by the National Disciplinary Committee. Amongst those unable to contest, as they had been expelled from KANU, were George Anyona, Odinga, Jackson Kalweo and G. G. Kariuki. There were far fewer parliamentary candidates than in previous elections – only 668 contested the primaries. Fourteen candidates were unopposed, including Moi, Biwott, Mudavadi and Finance Minister Saitoti in Kajiado North, who had made the jump from technocrat to politician within five years.[142]

Moi was again unopposed as KANU's presidential candidate. Parliamentary nomination day was 29 February, with the three-week campaign ending with polling on 21 March. As usual, KANU released an election manifesto, but it contained little that was new, apart from an increased emphasis on family planning and the development of marginal lands for food production.

The Parliamentary Campaign

As with previous elections, local development, oratorical ability and experience were factors, as were the wealth and connections of the candidates. Candidates campaigned on their ability to resolve issues of particular concern to their community – sugar in Nyanza and Western, milk and tea in the central Rift Valley, coffee in Central, land adjudication on the Coast. Misuse of funds collected in *harambees* and by cooperatives was a common allegation. Religion played a role in Mombasa and Lamu, where Islamic fundamentalism was becoming stronger. Money was still critical for success, although in principle there was still a Ksh40,000 spending limit.

Clanism and locational voting were common in the ex-reserves, while ethnic voting was ferocious in the urban areas and the settlement zones in the Rift. In Narok North, home of many Kikuyu immigrants, the battle between Tipis and Ntimama was renewed, with Tipis representing the settlers as well as his own clan against Ntimama, a Maasai chauvinist who campaigned on an anti-Kikuyu ticket.[143] On the Coast, immigrant communities put up candidates in Lamu, Kwale and Taita-Taveta. In contrast, districts such as West Pokot and Tana River saw clan elders still deciding who their ethnic community would support. Moi did not campaign for a slate of candidates, but did indicate his preferences. In Mombasa, for example, he suggested in September 1987 that anyone planning to oppose Shariff Nassir was wasting his time.

Tensions were high in Central Province, where Matiba, Kibaki, Karume and others were under sustained state pressure. The churches continued to support a more open electoral process, and the Catholic Church published an eve-of-poll pastoral letter attacking bribery and rigging by 'prominent people'.[144] Nonetheless, the remaining liberals, allies of Kibaki, independently wealthy or influential MPs and those deemed 'anti-government' had great difficulties in campaigning.

The Results

The fears of the churches and others were well founded. The queue voting system greatly eased intimidation and malpractice, and the KANU primaries of 22 February 1988 saw blatant rigging. With a secret ballot unnecessary if 70 per cent of those queuing voted for the winner, it was easy for partisan officials to announce a fabricated result, as no recount was possible after the queues had dispersed. As even Moi acknowledged, 'the implementation of the queuing system of voting left a lot to be desired.'[145] At least one-third of the electoral contests (over 60 seats) were blatantly rigged.[146] The number of candidates scoring 70 per cent or more of the vote rocketed from 12 in 1983 to 47 in the 1988 primaries.[147]

Some of the most dubious results were those where candidates scored just above the 70 per cent hurdle. In Nairobi, for example, Rubia was rigged out in Starehe, where his opponent was declared elected with 70.5 per cent of the vote. When Rubia pointed out that the officials had miscalculated and his opponent's vote was only 63 per cent, the Nairobi PC simply added 1,500 votes to his total.[148] As a consequence, the official results did not even add up. Most Central Province primaries were also rigged. Of the 31 Kikuyu-dominated seats outside Nairobi, only 13 saw secret ballot elections at all. In Kinangop in Nyandarua, for example, wa Nyoike's opponent was announced to have won 72.9 per cent of the vote. Officials told his supporters that they would lose their businesses if they supported him, and his supporters were driven away from polling stations and his queue photos destroyed.[149] There were similar abuses in Kirinyaga, where hardliner James Njiru and ex-civil service head Geoffrey Kariithi were elected 'unopposed'. In Gatundu, Ngengi Muigai's opponent took 70.5 per cent, having lost to him 2:1 in 1983.

In the Rift, there was a similar change of guard. In Tinderet in Nandi, Henry Kosgey, who had been 'rigged in' in 1979, was now 'rigged out' by the KANU branch.

The minister's opponent, lawyer Kimaiyo arap Sego, secured 70.2 per cent of the queue vote (compared to the 5 per cent he had polled in 1983); CPK observers reported that Kosgey had actually won the queue voting poll 3:1.[150] Four out of five Nakuru seats were won at the primaries by allies of Chotara.[151] On the Coast, rigged primaries were used to remove ex-minister Mwamunga and independent wa Mwachofi alike. In Western Province, KANU Secretary-General Nabwera moved from 20 per cent of the vote in 1983 to 90 per cent, ready to become a minister alongside his patron Mudavadi. In South Nyanza, Hezekiah Oyugi's cousin Dalmas Otieno became Rongo MP with 78 per cent of the primary vote, despite never addressing a campaign rally.

The sole primary to have its result overturned was Kangundo in Machakos, where Paul Ngei lost to General Jackson Mulinge, who had entered politics after his retirement. Although Mulinge was Moi's proxy to remove the long-serving Ngei, it is rumoured that the evening after his victory, Mulinge was boasting that he would be appointed vice-president. To punish his impertinence, Moi ordered the polls rerun.[152] The rerun was inconclusive and Ngei won on the secret ballot.

Three more MPs ended up unopposed because their opponents stood down or were disqualified. As a result, on 21 March secret ballot elections only took place in 123 seats. Even in the allegedly secret ballot, there were blatant abuses: there were reports of presiding officers taking ballot boxes to hotel rooms in order to stuff them before returning them to the count; new boxes appeared filled with pre-marked ballots; others were lost, and obligatory recounts refused. Chiefs campaigned for candidates, voters were transported from elsewhere, and bribery was rife.[153]

Turnouts were no longer possible to determine, but were extremely low in the KANU primaries. Many MPs who won a 70 per cent victory were elected by fewer than 10 per cent of registered voters. On paper, 2.1 million voters turned out on the first ballot and 2.3 million on the second. No more than 37 per cent of the registered voters – and in reality probably less than 30 per cent – actually voted. Few educated Kenyans were willing to queue in public.

Only three ministers were defeated: Tipis, Kosgey and Ng'eno, all Moi loyalists now out of favour and another recycling of the inner circles. In Kisumu, Minister Robert Ouko only survived against opponent Job Omino (backed by Oyugi) because Moi had promised Ouko the Foreign Ministry and campaigned for him.[154] Most dissenters left the house, including Shikuku, who narrowly lost Butere after winning the primary 3:1.[155] In Central Province, Kibaki, Matiba and Karume won, but other Kikuyu heavyweights including Isaiah Mathenge, Wamae, Keriri and John Michuki were all defeated.

The verdict remains open on who the organisers of the 1988 rigging were. It was clearly directed from the top, as the intelligence services had instructed all PCs, DCs and chiefs on who they wished to win the polls. The evidence suggests a regional carve-up. Several foreign diplomats and journalists observed the polls. The *Weekly Review* reported that a British and an Ethiopian diplomat were satisfied at the evidence of 'practical democracy and political maturity'.[156] However, the Western press was critical, and there were attacks on the rigging in the US *Washington Post* and the British *Telegraph* and *Guardian*.[157] The mainstream Kenyan press, in contrast, fearful and abused, accepted the new order without public demur.

There were 25 petitions against the results of the 1988 elections. What was most notable was what was absent – any petitions against the primary polls. Several losers petitioned the High Court for redress, but the court decided it had no jurisdiction over KANU nominations, as KANU was a private society and the only right of appeal in KANU's rules was to its president.[158]

The New Government, March 1988

The new government appointed on 24 March 1988 saw the demotion of Vice-President Kibaki to the junior Ministry of Health. Although he and his allies discussed whether to refuse their posts, in the end Kibaki neither resigned nor protested publicly. Elite politics was now a dangerous game, and such an action could have had serious consequences. The new vice-president (and minister for home affairs) was Josephat Karanja. Karanja, another Kikuyu, was able, ambitious, and without a political constituency. Like Njonjo, the ex-high commissioner and vice-chancellor had the expensive tastes of the elite (and the close British connection that often went with this). His unpopularity was the key to his appointment.

Moi dropped three re-elected ministers, but the Cabinet grew to 34 members, its largest yet. Half of parliament was now subject to ministerial discipline. Following the East European model, Moi created a new Ministry of National Guidance and Political Affairs (responsible for promulgating *Nyayo* philosophy, and such reassuring functions as censorship). Two of the three newcomers who had beaten ministers in the elections were elevated to ministerial posts themselves – Sego and Ntimama. Waruru Kanja was appointed alongside Kibaki as a second 'minister for Nyeri', a deliberate recipe for confrontation. The Cabinet was now composed mostly of Moi-era loyalists. Only seven of the 34 members had been ministers under Kenyatta. Contrary to simplistic tribalist expectations there were twice as many Kikuyu (eight) as Kalenjin ministers (four).

Problems and Portents, 1988–9

Growing Pressure

During 1988–9, the state's efforts to control independent political thought reached a peak. It was the apogee of 'a culture of governance that rewards sycophancy, loyalty, and subservices and punishes innovation, merit, and critical analysis' that had its roots in the colonial era, but had been refined by both Kenyatta and Moi.[159] With queue voting deemed a success, in April 1988 KANU hawks, including Nassir, called for the complete abolition of the secret ballot. The arguments made for queuing included that it was 'authentically African', as opposed to the secret ballot, which was a colonial legacy. Defenders of the secret ballot, as in 1986, included Muliro and the churches. Anglican Bishops Alexander Muge and Henry Okullu, Catholic Bishop Ndingi Mwana a'Nzeki and others called for a referendum on the issue. Okullu alleged that 1988's queue voting 'produced some of the most blatant and cruel vote-rigging and cheating that has ever been practised in Kenya'.[160] In response, Church leaders were again criticised for involving themselves in politics and for having become tools of 'foreign masters' (the 'nationalist card'). However, in the end, the government backed down, fearful of its consequences.

Amongst the clerics, Nandi Bishop Muge of the CPK was a particularly sharp thorn in the government's side. In June 1988, Muge warned of famine in West Pokot, part of his diocese, which the government denied. Francis Lotodo and another Pokot MP supported Muge's claim. To oppose the government was to invite only one response, and the MPs were stripped of their party positions and therefore their parliamentary seats. Police were deployed to prevent worshippers attending Muge's sermons.[161] He was threatened with detention and MPs appealed to the CPK to defrock him.

In October 1988, Shikuku had another chance to return to Parliament, after the man rigged in to replace him died. The inevitable happened and the queue voting numbers were adjusted to ensure Shikuku lost again. The winner's official tally rose from 968 votes in February's election to 24,246, possibly the largest rise in popular vote ever seen.[162]

The main dailies, the *Nation* and the *Standard*, were under continual direct and indirect pressure and practised extensive self-censorship. In June 1989, Parliament even banned the *Nation* from covering its proceedings for three months, accusing it of bias and tribalism (many of the paper's staff were Kikuyu) following its veiled criticisms of corruption and the declining independence of Parliament. Hilary Ng'weno's *Weekly Review* was now a regime mouthpiece, a shift forced upon the owner by his financial problems. Ng'weno had also established the *Nairobi Times*, which – re-branded as the *Kenya Times* – was bought by KANU in 1983. In 1988, the newspaper was relaunched and its ownership transferred to a new body, the Kenya Times Media Trust. Controversial British businessman Robert Maxwell acquired 45 per cent shares in the trust, with a organisation called Kanu Investments Ltd owning 55 per cent. KANU therefore controlled the *Kenya Times*, and it propagated KANU's views. Journals that did not conform to government instructions were banned.[163] The government proscribed *Beyond* in March 1988, after their election special, 'Queue-Voting: Who Really Won'. Its editor, Bedan Mbugua, was jailed (for failing to submit annual sales returns). The broadcast media were even more firmly controlled: all local radio broadcasting remained state owned, as did KBC television, which was dominated by reports of Moi's activities from the Presidential Press Unit.

A controversial symbol of the government's approach was the construction of the Nyayo monument in Uhuru Park in Nairobi in 1988. This marble monument celebrated Moi's 10 years in power and showed his clenched fist, *rungu* (a traditional club) in hand, emerging out of Mount Kenya, the centre of traditional worship and cultural identity for the Kikuyu. Civil servants had their pay compulsorily docked to pay for the statue's construction. In the same year, 'Moi day' (the date of his accession as president) became a national holiday.

More Constitutional Changes

In August 1988, Parliament passed another constitutional amendment. This abolished the security of tenure of judges and members of the Public Service Commission. It also increased the period for which the police could hold suspects of capital crimes (deemed to include treason and therefore sedition, and therefore statements critical of the government) from 24 hours to 14 days (see above). Again, dissenting voices came only from the clergy and lawyers. A young Baptist priest, Mutava Musyimi, later to become a leader of the anti-government clergy, was the first to raise the alarm. Lawyers, including Murungi, Muite, Kuria and John Khaminwa also opposed the bill. However, fearful politicians backed the bill en masse and the Assembly passed the amendment 168 to 0.

The reason behind the abolition of the security of tenure of judges was not Moi's desire for unlimited power, but a personal dispute between Chief Justice Miller and a European judge. Miller had transferred the judge out of Nairobi, but he had refused to go, since it was formally the Judicial Service Commission who decided transfers. Unable to sack him, as judges had security of tenure, Miller sought the power to do so from Moi. As soon as the amendment was passed, the judge was fired.[164]

The Party Elections of September 1988

With the authoritarian state at its zenith, KANU held local and national elections again in September 1988. With Karanja now national vice-president, Kibaki also had to be replaced as KANU vice-president. The grassroots polls again used queue voting, which inspired more rigging, particularly in Central Province. Kibaki did not defend his vice-presidential seat, but there were still attempts to substitute delegates and modify results to prevent him becoming Nyeri branch chairman. Kibaki's response was devastating: 'Rigging has some intelligence. This scheme is by people who have no sense of intelligence. It is not rigging but direct robbery.'[165]

Similar rigging took place in Matiba's Kiharu and Shikuku's Butere, where delegate substitution and fraud resulted in the exclusion of both leaders.[166] In Kiambaa, the candidate who 'beat' Karume himself denied he had won the polls, but Karume's name was still missing from the list of winners. The polls were rerun, but the individuals affected were unable to participate in the rest of the elections.

The national polls that followed were orchestrated and every candidate was elected unopposed. Moi remained KANU president and Karanja replaced Kibaki. The other seats were again allocated on an ethno-regional basis, with (Luo) Minister Oloo-Aringo replacing Omolo-Okero as chairman and (Luhya) Mudavadi replacing Nabwera as secretary-general. Similarly, (Maasai) Ntimama replaced Tipis as treasurer; one Kamba (Kalonzo Musyoka, a 35-year old lawyer and Mutisya ally) replaced another; and the elderly Nyeri Kikuyu Davidson Kuguru replaced Kibaki.[167]

Omens and Portents

While KANU tightened its grip, the party was changing. Between 1987 and 1989, several of the hardliners who had helped build Moi's presidency died. In 1987, Kericho KANU Chairman Isaac Salat died, and in January 1988, Chotara too passed away (the residents of Nakuru celebrated with an impromptu party). They were followed in February 1989 by an even closer Moi ally, Mudavadi. Moi had used Mudavadi to control western Kenya, and he had been the only politician apart from Moi permitted to receive goodwill delegations. He dominated both politics and the administration, with the local DC and PC visiting his home to receive instructions.[168] After Mudavadi's death, Moi appointed to a ministerial post his son and successor as MP, Wycliffe Musalia Mudavadi, although he was only 29 and had no experience. Musalia was a childhood friend of Moi's own children. Mudavadi's appointment was one of five cases of 'political inheritance' between 1988 and 1990, where sons or brothers inherited seats on the death of an MP, the beginning of a dynastic model of political inheritance within political families.

A critical event in Kenya's history occurred in December 1988 when Kenneth Matiba, rigged out of the KANU chairmanship in Murang'a in September in favour of Kamotho, decided that he had had enough. He had forced a rerun of the elections in December, only for the same thing to happen again. On 9 December, Matiba resigned from the Cabinet.[169] For the first time since 1966, a minister had resigned rather than waited to be sacked. In fury, KANU stripped Matiba of his membership and he lost his parliamentary seat.

The Kiharu by-election to replace Matiba in February 1989 came to epitomise the regime's contempt for democracy. His old adversary Julius Kiano received over 90 per cent of the queue vote, only to be declared the loser. The provincial administration and Kamotho had decided that they would prefer a more pliable MP. To do so, they simply modified the results of the KANU primary, although the results had been photographed before they were changed.[170] Even the winner later admitted that he lost: 'I had no supporters. Kiano had about 9,000 genuine votes while I could not muster even 1,000. We took Matiba's previous figure of 24,000 and added it to mine . . .'[171]

Moi was running short of Kikuyu, Embu and Meru allies, and was forced into another recycling. Two of the Njonjo expellees – G. G. Kariuki and Jackson Kalweo – were readmitted to KANU, and Kamotho even replaced Matiba in the Cabinet.[172]

The Fall of a Second Vice-President

Political affairs became increasingly fevered, as the government was consumed in internecine fighting and clashed with donors, churches, lawyers and anyone who dared challenge its right to rule. In the most significant spasm, the new Vice-President Karanja was driven out of office after only a year.

The campaign against Karanja was launched in February 1989 from his native Kiambu District, by Minister Arthur Magugu and the little-known Director of Motor Vehicle Inspections Kuria Kanyingi. The little-educated (and otherwise unknown) Kanyingi's rise to prominence was apparently due to his once having, as a mechanic, repaired Moi's car when it broke down. Moi or his allies now gave Kanyingi immense sums of money to undermine Karanja. In the words of the *Nation*, 'Mr Moi, like a god, had created a political monster out of the dust whose raison d'être was to haunt and hound Dr Karanja out of office.'[173] Minor Kikuyu politicians attacked Karanja for claiming that the Kikuyu were being 'finished'. Moi, on returning from an overseas trip in March, commented that he had never appointed an acting president, implying that Karanja had tried to arrogate such powers to himself.[174] The anti-Karanja bandwagon grew in strength, and in April 1989 Karanja was named in the Assembly as the politician 'fomenting disunity'. On 27 April, the Assembly passed a unanimous vote of no confidence in him.[175] Karanja was not permitted to speak in his own defence; KANU branches throughout the country were ordered to condemn him. Like Njonjo six years before, Karanja resigned from the national and party vice-presidency and from Parliament on 1 May 1989.[176] Yet another senior Kikuyu had been used and discarded.

The reasons for Karanja's rapid downfall are unclear. While many saw Karanja as abrasive, his main failings seem to have been a greater than expected independence and a tendency to tread on the toes of the real power brokers. He was also becoming a rallying point amongst the Kikuyu, a concern to Moi's inner circle, for whom control of Kikuyu political activity remained a primary goal.

Moi now turned to his second choice. On the same day that Karanja resigned, Moi appointed Kajiado North MP Saitoti as vice-president. Officially, Saitoti was the first non-Kikuyu to hold the post under Moi, and was described as of 'Kikuyu-Maasai parentage', a suitably ambiguous description of his inconvenient background. His parents were actually Kikuyu from Limuru who had emigrated to Maasailand in the 1930s. He was born George Kinuthia Muthengi Kiarie, but had taken on a Maasai name and identity, a fact that was kept as quiet as possible, given that Saitoti did not even speak Maa.[177] This was well known amongst insiders, but was deliberately obscured by the press for nearly a decade.

The fallout from Karanja's demise continued for some months. Karanja and another MP were expelled from KANU, and two more MPs were suspended after Moi commented, 'The jigger [burrowing flea] has been removed but many little eggs remain in the wound and they must be killed.'[178] On 16 June 1989, the KANU National Delegates' Conference rubber-stamped another set of changes in party leadership in nine minutes. Saitoti replaced Karanja as KANU vice-president, Kamotho replaced the late Mudavadi and Ntimama stood down to avoid the Maasai districts holding two top posts.

Petitions, Rigging and Expulsions, 1989

Matiba, Karanja and their allies were only the most prominent among a flood of party expulsions and government sackings. There were 11 parliamentary by-elections in 1989, the largest number since the Little General Election of 1966. No one, not even a minister, was safe from the purges sweeping the party.

Just as Moi had shifted power into the party and away from Parliament, so in the 1980s power shifted away from his ministers. Kenyatta had encouraged a 'bottom-up' style of political activity, in which leaders had to demonstrate local popularity to win a place at the national table.[179] Moi favoured the reverse approach, in which ministers were representatives of the centre. When leaders developed their own popular support and patronage networks, it reduced their influence with him rather than enhanced it. Moi promoted, then demoted and disgraced his ministers with increasing frequency. Between 1988 and 1990, 12 ministers died, were sacked, resigned or lost their posts. Even hardline Kikuyu James Njiru was accused of trying to take over the government and his National Guidance Ministry abolished. Between January and May 1989, Moi sacked three more ministers as well as Karanja, and they and several other MPs were expelled from KANU. In November, Kibaki won a decisive victory when Kanja was suspended from KANU, abandoned by his patrons.[180] This divide and rule policy narrowed the regime's base of support, especially amongst the Kikuyu, alienating group after group without securing the stable support of their replacements.

Meanwhile, the few independent MPs who had survived the 1988 polls were cleared out. In July 1989, Muliro, whose election had been nullified by a petition, was rigged out of his seat for the second time.[181] One the same day, Joshua Angatia was also rigged out, also following a questionable petition judgement. Muliro's ally Wamalwa followed soon after.

Growing Opposition and Western Doubts

As the political system became more fevered and more paranoid, dissent sought alternative channels, as the popular and elite sense of injustice grew. Relations between Church and State remained hostile. The NCCK's opposition to queue voting aroused fury amongst MPs unable to accept the legitimacy of any challenge to the state-party's decision. Archbishop Gitari was abused and his home attacked after he preached sermons critical of the government and of KANU. Following the NCCK's Limuru conference in December 1989 – which called again for changes to queuing – the KANU Kirinyaga branch called for the deregistration of the NCCK.[182] Musyoka said queue voting was 'not negotiable'.

The legal profession was the second centre of challenge. Urban middle-class advocates such as Muite, Kuria, Khaminwa and Murungi (all Kikuyu or Meru) had been forced into confrontation with the government. Supported by Meru ex-lawyer Gitobu Imanyara's magazine *Nairobi Law Monthly*, they were increasingly critical of Kenya's poor human rights record and led several of Kenya's emerging human rights NGOs. By 1989, influenced by the changes taking place in Eastern Europe, some lawyers began to call for the restoration of multi-party politics, despite the risk to themselves. The government tried to silence the LSK through legal cases against Muite and other leaders and ensured the flow of legal work diminished.[183] However, they were watched over by their connections overseas, part of an emerging transnational human rights network that helped publicise their stance and protect them somewhat from the state's wrath, which was constrained by its public espousal of the rule of law. In 1988, the American Bar Association honoured Kuria, but he was unable to attend, as the state had seized his passport. In 1989, the Robert F. Kennedy Human Rights Foundation also gave Kuria an award. When the government again refused to allow Kuria to collect it, Muite spoke on his behalf, after which his passport was also withdrawn. When Moi mentioned the issue of multi-party democracy at all, it was to dismiss the idea entirely as tribalist or a foreign concept. Nonetheless, a culture of resistance was building that would soon blossom.[184]

One unexpected move came on 1 June 1989, when Moi freed the last seven political detainees, including Raila Odinga, Ng'ang'a, Mirugi Kariuki, Kihoro and Agina. Kenya was without official detainees for the first time since 1982 (although more than 40 Mwakenya convicts continued to serve out their sentences). Moi seemed newly tolerant, and at the same time issued an amnesty to exiles abroad. There were rumours that the release was intended to placate the Americans.[185]

Another example of the growing commonality of interest between domestic critics and foreign donors came with the KANU Towers project of 1989. This was a prestige project, a 60-storey skyscraper that would be the highest in Africa. It was to be built in Uhuru Park by the Kenya Times Media Trust. In front of it would be a bronze statue of Moi. It was to be funded by US$200 million in government-guaranteed loans.

Opposition to the project from the political classes was non-existent. However, for the first time, an environmentalist, Wangari Maathai of the Green Belt Movement, openly took on the government. Maathai, a US-educated ex-university lecturer from Nyeri, had founded the NGO in 1977, with the goal of planting trees to help reverse Kenya's deforestation. Following a letter-writing campaign to donors in November–December 1989, the internationally known Maathai sought an injunction to stop construction of the complex, as illegal and likely to cause environmental degradation. Her lawsuit was dismissed for lack of *locus standii* by Justice Dugdale, soon to become an irritant to multi-party democracy advocates. Maathai came under severe attack, with MPs including Keen attacking her as a woman and, worse still, a divorcee.[186] Moi demanded she obey like everyone else, suggesting that his critics had 'insects in their heads'.[187] Groundbreaking began on the project in November 1989, but Maathai's campaign had struck a chord with foreign diplomats, dismayed at Kenya's simultaneous begging-bowl strategy to donors and investment in prestige projects with no development return. Under donor pressure, the project was mothballed in 1990.

Conclusions

The mid- to late 1980s had seen the entrenchment of an increasingly corrupt, para-noid and autocratic government. The regime now relied on apathy and fear, with the active support only of Kalenjin and Abaluhya regions, pastoralists and Muslims, and a few military and political leaders, many of them unpopular at home. The dominance of Moi and KANU was unchallenged, but there was growing resistance – inside both the elite and the *wananchi* – to a repressive and ethnically partial administration that had squandered its legitimacy. Anger at the destruction of Kenya's participatory heritage – their right to vote and to choose their MPs, if not what they did once in office – was an important driver for the protests of 1990–1.

For the inner circle, both the risks and the rewards of power increased as corruption at the top grew more open. At the same time, the reconstruction of Kenya's economy at the expense of the Kikuyu deepened. This gradual transformation of the government from a 'Kikuyu first' to a 'Kalenjin first' model was an entirely contingent change, which only happened because Moi had come to power. It did not dislodge the Gema elites from their economic pre-eminence; rather, it overlaid their broad pyramid of influence with a thinner veneer of Kalenjin and Asian leaders, becoming wealthy through their state connections. The result was a deep-seated and widespread dissatisfaction amongst Kenya's largest and wealthiest community.

The economic picture was also looking ominous. The economy had been performing well recently, with good rains, good coffee prices and a stable economy. However, it was a short-term 'blip'. Kenya's debt was unsustainable, its balance of payments poor and inflation rising. It had failed to seize the opportunity to become a 'newly industrialising country'. Under international pressure, Moi, Nyachae and their colleagues had begun to liberalise and privatise, but had failed. Whatever the cries from technocrats about the need for reform, the state could not make tough decisions and stick to them. Individual elite interests conflicted with this goal, while at the same time Moi and his allies appeared to be using state resources to nurture a new Rift Valley commercial structure to compete with the Kikuyu. The West continued to bankroll Kenya, but its support could no longer be taken for granted. When the external environment changed, the government was unable to prevent an alliance between internal and external forces that was to end three decades of single-party rule.

Chapter 9

A Second Liberation? 1990–1992

Introduction

During 1990–2, the one-party state's edifice of central control cracked apart, and the rules of the game of Kenya's politics since 1969 were transformed by a resurgence of open political conflict. Deeper tensions were exposed, based on ethnic interests but catalysed around individuals, which had simmered for decades, held in check by the power of the single-party state. Kenya's democratisation was sudden and relatively peaceful: the product of a confluence of forces. External political changes included the end of the Cold War and a new assertiveness in the West in its dealings with African allies. At the same time, the tension between open and closed economic models of the 1980s came to a head. Had Kenya's economy been booming, Western donors might have been placated, but their patience was exhausted with the government's delays to economic liberalisation. Internally, the regime faced deep dissatisfaction amongst the political elite, the professional classes and much of the general population. The result was a twin crisis in November 1991 that forced President Daniel arap Moi to permit competitive multi-party politics once more.[1]

The reintroduction of democracy was the most dramatic change in the country's politics since 1969. By December 1991, Kenya was a multi-party state with a popular opposition that appeared ready to seize power. Nonetheless, after a year of political ferment, KANU and Moi triumphed in the 1992 general election. The opposition fragmented and foreign observers were unable to prevent substantial electoral malpractice, which ensured the outright victory of the governing party. Meanwhile, a process of forced and poorly planned economic liberalisation had begun, during which the state had been robbed to pay for KANU's victory, causing structural damage to the economy. In the same period, the conflation of politics and ethnicity and the exploitation of land-related tensions by those in power had led to widespread violence and severely damaged both the 'willing buyer, willing seller' land model and relationships between members of ethnic groups.

A Changing World

The period 1989–90 saw the most radical changes in world politics for 40 years, with the collapse of the Soviet empire in Eastern Europe and the fall of the Berlin Wall in 1989. In 1990, the Soviet Union disintegrated, ending the Cold War. The impact was swift and global. Not only had Africa's people been shown that authoritarian states could implode when faced with popular resistance, but Western powers could now remain neutral in struggles between incumbent regimes and their opponents without the risk of losing clients. A bandwagon effect of protest, reform and subsequent multi-party elections rippled through Africa. Military regimes fell in Mali and Niger, while one-party states in Ghana, Côte d'Ivoire, Benin, Zambia, Rwanda, Ethiopia and Angola were all forced to introduce multi-party politics between 1989 and 1992. Many old guard political leaders, successors of the founding fathers of independence, were ousted. These changes were 'the most far-reaching shifts in African political life since the time of political independence'.[2]

At the same time, Western views of Africa's misfortunes, which had long seen the continent's problems as primarily economic, were being displaced by perceptions that the problem might in fact be political. Not only did Africa require market economics, as the international financial institutions (IFIs) had been trying to persuade Kenya for years; it required democratic politics as well. The patrimonial, authoritarian state would stifle economic liberalisation, so only competitive politics and the diminution of that state could free Africa. The state also made bad decisions because it was not accountable to anyone for them. By 1989, the World Bank was arguing: 'political legitimacy and consensus are a precondition for sustainable development.'[3] Democratisation and liberalisation were mutually reinforcing, because private sector growth in turn created financial independence from the state.

As a result, Kenya was exposed to a second wind of change. For decades, the key US concerns in Africa had been communism and apartheid. With both now gone, the US acted as if its 'victory over communism' had confirmed its moral as well as military and economic ascendancy, and this powered a shift towards adherence to 'American values' as a criterion for assistance.[4] The US still saw most of Africa as of marginal interest. Without special assets to warrant special treatment, East Africa was fully exposed to America's new policy, by which it would promote peaceful change, pluralism and economic development, whether incumbent governments wanted it or not. Economically, the Americans also had little to lose. In 1992, there was only US$88 million of US private investment in Kenya.[5] The US was thus able to demand economic and political liberalisation at the same time, with little risk to its national interests.

In November 1989, with the victory of George Bush in the presidential elections, Kenya received a new US ambassador. Smith Hempstone, a journalist and old Kenya hand from the 1960s, was to play a key role in the changes to come. He soon proved a strong critic of Kenya's corruption and single-party rule, willing to speak out where a career ambassador would have been more cautious. On 3 May 1990, he publicly announced to Kenyans for the first time that in future, US aid would only go to nations that 'nourish democratic institutions, defend human rights, and practice multi-party politics'.[6] KANU leaders were apoplectic.

Hempstone initially appeared to be a loose cannon, but it soon became clear that many US congressmen shared his views. US loans and grants to Kenya dropped in 1990, as aid increasingly became subject to political conditionalities (see Figure 9.1) and US views in the IFIs shifted. Although the Bush administration had not ordered him to intervene, it would not repudiate Hempstone and he now provided

9.1: US grants and loans to Kenya, 1984–92

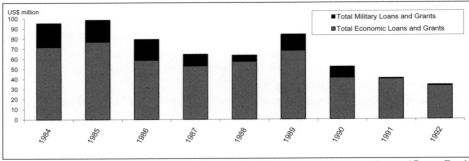

Source: *US Overseas Loans and Grants*, 'Green Book'

a lifeline to the repressed movement for change in Kenya. The stage was set for a confrontation between nations as well as within Kenya.

The Americans were not alone. Relations between Kenya and Scandinavia were already poor, and in October 1990 Kenya broke off diplomatic relations with Norway after it offered legal assistance for Koigi wa Wamwere (a Norwegian resident) and sent observers to his treason trial. Norway ended aid to Kenya in response. Initially, the attitude of the British was one of 'business as usual', defending Kenya in public and working behind closed doors to encourage reform. However, after Margaret Thatcher's fall in November 1990, their attitude, too, began to change.

The Kenyan government was unprepared for the resulting crisis. It had developed a sense of entitlement to aid over the decades because of its capitalist and pro-Western credentials, which made it disregard the warning signs. Moi was uneasy with the Western press, and reluctant to acknowledge its importance to Kenya (because of the country's dependence both on aid and tourism). He was also infuriated by what he saw as the West's hypocrisy in its criticism of Kenya in comparison to other African countries, and its assumption that those campaigning for change were doing so for altruistic motives. He felt that 'Western diplomats, journalists and aid workers unwittingly supported and complemented this false thesis of good versus evil, democracy versus authoritarianism, and corruption versus duty.'[7] However, KANU was unable to craft a non-confrontational response.

The Economic Challenge

Economic concerns lay behind both domestic protest and Western challenge. The Kenyan state was now seen as economically incompetent, as a result of its tolerance for corruption and its reluctance to privatise and liberalise. The 'Washington consensus' in favour of stabilisation, liberalisation and privatisation was now dominant amongst policy-makers. The free flow of capital, goods, technology and people between countries was the driver of world growth. Most experts agreed that institutional change was required: a remaking of the African state according to a Western model of private enterprise in which it would be a referee, not a player. Only by removing resources from the public domain and limiting the state could both growth and freedom be restored. Although many Africans blamed structural adjustment for the continent's difficulties in the 1980s, most economists blamed Africa's poor performance on its failure to adapt sufficiently quickly, though they often underestimated the difficulty of reforming state and society simultaneously.

The degree to which the popular protest of 1990–1 was created by Kenya's failure to liberalise economically, by the IFI-inspired structural adjustment policies it did implement, or by external and political factors alone remains controversial. By most economic measures, there was nothing unique about the economic conditions of 1989–91. Although Kenya's economy was in trouble, it had experienced a mini-boom in 1985–7 and the real economic crisis only occurred *after* democratisation. Foreign direct investment reached its highest for a decade in 1989, and Kenya reached its highest shilling GDP per capita in 1989–91 (see Figure 9.2). In 1990, the economy achieved a respectable 4.2 per cent GDP growth, but this fell to 2.2 per cent in 1991, with agricultural GDP falling for the first time since 1984.

The sell-off by multinationals continued. ICI sold Magadi Soda in 1991 to local investors, and Sadolin Paints was sold to an Asian group in the same year. Declining public infrastructure discouraged investment, while structural adjustment was changing the economics of domestic production versus global-scale production and imports. Some investors with connections in government, often Asian, were still happy to invest, but others took their money and ran, with capital flight in 1991 estimated at US$2.5 billion.[8]

9.2: GDP per capita, 1981–2002 (Ksh, 1982 constant prices, rebaselined)

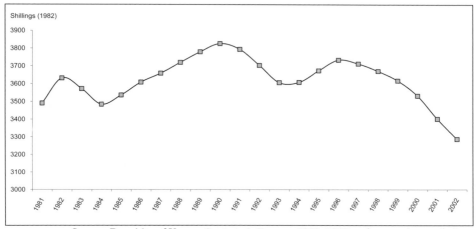

Source: Republic of Kenya, *Statistical Abstracts*, 1988–2003 and census interpolations

Genuine Fiscal Reforms, 1990–1

For a decade, analysts had argued for the liberalisation of Kenya's fiscal policies and a free-floating exchange rate, to allow the economy to adapt to changing world conditions. In 1990–1, in response, the government substantially liberalised Kenya's financial system.

Until 1990, the shilling had remained pegged to the SDR, a 'crawling' peg, in order to minimise speculation and short-term uncertainty. However, in 1990–1, the CBK abolished foreign exchange declarations, opening up the import and export of foreign exchange to those who could acquire it. In October 1991, the CBK also introduced a parallel currency system known as the foreign exchange bearer certificate (Forex-C). This was an open market tool to manage exchange rates and currency demand. Forex-C certificates were denominated in US dollars and were redeemable for dollars on demand. Alongside the official exchange rate, they offered a parallel open market rate for conversion of shillings into foreign exchange, and provided a buffer between the demand for foreign exchange and the state's actual supplies of it (which were limited).

In November 1990, the Treasury bills market was also liberalised, with rates determined by auction, and the government fully relinquished control of interest rates in 1991. Initially, things worked smoothly, as buyers and sellers for the first time negotiated over rates and spreads. However, inflation began to rise, driven by deregulation, expansion in the money supply and the effects of the Goldenberg scandal (see below). Base rates increased from 19 per cent in late 1991 to 29 per cent in March 1992, and worse was to come. Kenya also replaced its sales tax with value added tax (VAT) in January 1990, to broaden its tax base.

A Reluctant Reformer

Despite these reforms, international patience was exhausted at the Kenyan government's strategy of promising radical change but delivering only partial reform. Throughout the 1980s, the government had tried to satisfy Western donors, while protecting its own interests and leaving intact its patronage network. The process of privatisation had been particularly slow. In 1987, the government had sold 20 per cent of the KCB, and in 1990 it sold another 10 per cent. In late 1991, under intense Western pressure, it finally identified 139 parastatals as candidates for privatisation, but actual privatisations were meagre. Wholesale reform of the state sector would have disrupted Moi's fragile coalition and was deeply unpopular amongst the hundreds of thousands who depended on it for their livelihood, while some parastatals operated reasonably efficiently.[9]

As the donors demanded, the government had also begun to introduce cost sharing for social services, but this too was unpopular and both the implementation and the results were unsatisfactory. In 1989, for example, outpatient charges were imposed for medical services at most hospitals, with exemptions for the chronically sick and contagious illnesses. The process was poorly financed, managed and implemented, however, and was suspended in 1990, only to be then reintroduced in 1992. In 1991–2, the government also stopped paying full tuition fees for university students.

Aid Dependency

The real problem was that Kenya was responding too slowly to the changing world, and was structurally dependent on foreign aid. At its peak between 1989 and 1991, total aid inflows to Kenya exceeded US$1 billion a year, and direct government aid constituted 15 per cent of the budget and three-quarters of the development budget.[10] Foreign aid was funding more than 2,000 projects in 1991–2, while the government was committed to more than 150 foreign-funded structural reform programmes.[11] Although Kenya's aid (at 11–12 per cent of GDP) remained modest by the standards of the most indebted nations, it still left the government dependent on Western support. This income, similar to the unearned income from a sudden natural resource price increase, was not a function of productivity or internal economic efficiencies, but the opposite – a flow of resources that rewarded inefficiencies.

Laying the Foundations for Internal Challenge

While external pressure and events were the most important factors driving the changes of 1990–1, they would have had little effect without the courage and determination of Kenya's internal opposition. Despite sustained state pressure, elements in the churches, the legal profession, some NGOs and a few politicians had continued to contest the state's monopoly of power, intermittently supported by Western governments and activists. Observers have characterised this as 'a brief but effective cross-national alliance between politically active members of the professional middle classes and an international cartel of donors, journalists and human rights organisations'.[12] In reality, this alliance could only survive because of the deep discontent within Kenya, and it was sustained by political forces able to harness this dissent. Single-party rule was brought down by a four-way alliance – between politicians and their constituents, the churches, the urban professional classes and the West.

Since 1986, Church and State had been in confrontation. The churchmen who had led the 1986 protests remained in office and Moi's attempts to suppress their criticism had politicised a generation of clergy. The first open challenge to the government's authority therefore came from the churches. On 1 January 1990, PCEA Rev. Timothy Njoya delivered a sermon in which he asked how long it would be before the changes that had occurred in Eastern Europe would be seen in Kenya. He suggested that one-party states were undemocratic and isolated from popular opinion, which could only be expressed with the registration of new parties.[13] Debate grew on the merits of the single-party system and the need for change, though few politicians would support Njoya publicly. In April, emboldened by the recent release of Nelson Mandela and the legalisation of the African National Congress in South Africa, Bishop Henry Okullu restated Njoya's challenge, arguing that only multi-party politics would guarantee accountability and transparency.[14] Oginga Odinga too supported such calls.

Moi, opening the March 1990 parliamentary session, was firm:

> Kenyans are not opposed to the multi-party system because of ideological reasons or designs by those in leadership to impose their will on the people. What we have said is that until our society has become cohesive enough so that tribalism is of no significance in the economic and political activities of the nation, the strategy of a mass based democratic and accountable one-party system is best.[15]

The legal profession, too, was willing to take on the government. At its head was Paul Muite, who had become the link between the lawyers, the clergy and the politicians. As Kenneth Matiba's lawyer, he and Matiba met Okullu secretly several times during 1989–90 to plan a combined political, religious and legal challenge to the regime. In 1990, the radicals proposed him for the chairmanship of the LSK. When Muite lost in March, his backers sought to demonstrate that the results had been rigged.[16] Although they lost their lawsuit, the evidence of state-sponsored abuses inside their own professional body led many who had so far remained outside the political fray to declare themselves for the cause of change. Lawyers were to play key roles in the reintroduction of multi-party democracy.

Another source of succour for those willing to challenge KANU lay in the local media. There was little debate in the mainstream press or the broadcast media, but a few brave souls were now publishing dissenting views. The *Nairobi Law Monthly*, for example, called for debate on the possibility of multi-party politics and criticised attempts to subvert the constitution. In response, it came under heavy pressure. Between 1987 and 1991, its defiant editor Gitobu Imanyara was charged with printing a seditious publication, contempt of court and numerous criminal charges and was eventually jailed for theft. Njehu Gatabaki's *Finance* began political reporting in 1988 and Pius Nyamora's even more controversial *Society* began printing in 1988. Even at the height of its power, the state's control of political discourse was beginning to break down.

The Murder of Robert Ouko, 1990

Another driver for change had its origins purely inside Kenya. Early on the morning of 13 February 1990, Foreign Minister Robert Ouko was murdered and his body left near his farm in Nyanza. To this day, his murderers have not been found. The murder had many similarities with the murder of J. M. Kariuki 15 years before – again, the body showed signs of beatings, with a broken ankle, a bullet through the head as a *coup de grace*, and attempts to disguise the corpse's identity through burning.[17] Again, villagers found the body sooner than planned, and there were discrepancies in the reports of when it was found and by whom.[18] As with Kariuki, the government first suggested that Ouko had vanished. On 16 February, however, his body was found. As news of the murder spread, Kenyans moved from acquiescence into anger. Students rioted and Luo farmers broke into open revolt.

Ouko's murder was a rallying point for critics of the government and a catalyst for change. His murder and the revelations of the subsequent inquiries helped fuel the

9.3: Robert Ouko

Courtesy: Nation
Group Newspapers

campaign for multi-party democracy, crystallising concerns about corruption and the power of those close to the president, and further estranging the West from the government. Although he was not particularly popular, Ouko was one of the government's more capable administrators (Figure 9.3). He had acquiesced in the excesses of the 1980s, but had not benefited particularly obviously from them. His death was clearly not the work of anti-government forces. The question was, why was he killed and by whom?

For weeks, Kisumu was a scene of violence. There was trouble during a requiem mass and the burial, at which Moi spoke. More rioting followed in Kisumu and Mombasa, and in Nairobi the GSU fought protesters who tried to destroy the Nyayo monument. People were beaten, raped and killed.[19] Stories of government complicity were rife. In response, the state clamped down on potential dissent in Central Province as well. Many prominent Kikuyu – including Matiba, Josephat Karanja, Ben Gethi, Wangari Maathai and Gibson Kamau Kuria – were picked up by police for 'questioning'.[20] Tensions were building to breaking point.

Trying to quash rumours of the involvement of government figures in Ouko's death, Moi invited the UK's Scotland Yard to send experts to investigate the murder on 19 February. Their nominee, Chief Inspector John Troon, arrived soon after. However, he encountered hostility and interference from the authorities, particularly Permanent Secretary for Internal Security Hezekiah Oyugi. Oyugi insisted that Ouko had committed suicide. Police Chief Philip Kilonzo and Chief Pathologist Jason Kaviti claimed the same: Ouko had broken his own ankle, undressed, set himself on fire and then shot himself through the head. Troon and his forensic team, however, soon demonstrated that Ouko had been murdered.[21]

Discovering who had murdered Ouko and why proved more difficult. Throughout his investigations, the witnesses Troon was interviewing were threatened and beaten by Kenyan police before or after his sessions. Ouko's brother, for example, was taken away during a session with Troon to 'investigate relevant correspondence'. He was returned hours later having been beaten with rubber truncheons by police officers, trying to discover what he had told Troon. Ouko's sister was also 'visibly distressed' about speaking to Troon, and was ordered to tell Troon that Ouko had committed suicide. Police erased records of the phone calls made from Ouko's house on that night and Special Branch removed other records from the house before the discovery of his body.[22] None of the items found was dusted for fingerprints, and the murder weapon was only found some time later. Years afterwards, Troon reaffirmed that the authorities had 'used corrupt and incompetent law enforcement officers to promulgate a campaign of frustration and interference with investigations'.[23]

Troon himself was threatened and left Kenya before his investigations were complete. He handed his interim report to Attorney-General Mathew Muli in September 1990. It asserted that Ouko was murdered and proposed that Moi's closest ally Nicholas Biwott and Oyugi be investigated as the 'principal suspects', along with the Nyanza PC Julius Kobia and the Nakuru DC Jonah Anguka (a Luo ally of Oyugi's). This time-bomb would tick for a year before it became public. Rather than arresting the suspects or publishing Troon's report, in October 1990 Moi instead set up a second investigation – a judicial inquiry. For a year, Justices Evan Gicheru, Richard Kwach and Akilano Akiwumi heard evidence in public, and the testimony dominated the press during 1991. The inquiry pieced together a fuller picture of the dead man's last hours. Although no one would admit to seeing what had happened, Ouko appeared to have entered a white car late at night, probably meeting people he knew, to be murdered elsewhere and his body dumped and set up to simulate suicide. Some reports suggested that, in another echo of the Kariuki affair, his death at the hands of a senior minister had been unplanned.[24]

Three theories have been advanced as to who murdered Ouko and why. The first is that District Commissioner Anguka was the killer. Anguka was charged with the crime in 1991 but was acquitted after two trials. The motive was that Ouko was said to be over-friendly with Anguka's wife, Ouko's personal assistant. It is very unlikely that Anguka committed the murder though; not only was he acquitted, but the chance that a DC, acting alone, would murder the foreign minister and persuade the government to cover it up are minuscule.

The second theory was that Ouko was murdered by associates of Biwott, though such allegations have been the subject of several libel suits and we can do no more here than present some widely discussed possibilities. One motive that Troon investigated was that Ouko was working on a dossier on corruption in the rehabilitation of the Kisumu molasses plant.[25] It appeared that Ouko and Biwott had recently clashed over demands to BAK, an Italian–Swiss consulting firm, for large commissions during discussions over reviving the factory.[26] BAK had been cut out of the deal, and there were suggestions that other Italian business interests lay behind its sidelining.[27] There had been reports of angry exchanges between Ouko and Biwott and of threats made.[28] Troon observed: 'The BAK allegations of corruption and the dispute with Nicholas Biwott are key ...'[29]

The third explanation was that Ouko died because he had become a threat to Moi. He, Moi and others had recently returned on 4 February 1990 from a trip to the US, known as the 'Prayer Breakfast' visit. It was formally a private trip, whose purpose was to lobby against the threatened suspension of US military assistance to Kenya. Moi had no meeting planned with Bush, as the US was increasingly unhappy with

Kenya and had asked Moi not to come, though Bush did join the prayer breakfast with Moi. Relations soured between Moi and Ouko during the trip. It has been speculated that the US government showed itself too friendly to Ouko or indicated that it considered him suitable presidential material. Ouko's sister testified that during the visit, Biwott had started referring to Ouko as 'Mr President'.[30] The US government denied that Ouko was favoured, or that he had attended 'secret meetings' with Bush (although Ouko did meet Secretary of State James Baker).[31] However, Hempstone's report in *Rogue Ambassador* that he had received State Department photographs of Ouko and Bush shaking hands on the White House lawn, Moi nowhere to be seen, indicated his own views on the subject.[32] Ouko's sister noted that Ouko had been very distressed on his return from the US, commenting that 'the corruption allegations and the US press interviews would kill him.'[33] Moi was reported to be furious at the outcome of the trip and to have refused to allow Ouko to join his return flight. Ouko briefly saw Moi on 5 February, but the angry president ordered him to wait in Kisumu, where he was left with no passport or security. He had probably been sacked. His phone was tapped and he was involved in a suspicious road accident on 9 February, which he feared was a murder attempt.

Within two years of Ouko's death, more than a dozen witnesses or accessories were also dead. They included an employee of Ouko's on the farm on the night of the murder; one of the first people to see the body; a Special Branch officer and friend of Ouko; Anguka's bodyguard; Ouko's driver; the superintendent of police who participated in the investigation; the assistant commissioner who interrogated Biwott; one of Ouko's relatives to whom he spoke on the night of his disappearance; businessman Mohammed Aslam, who was named in connection with the corruption allegations; the first judge who tried Anguka; the senior commissioner of police who led the investigation; and Oyugi himself.[34] The herdsboy who found Ouko's remains vanished and neither he nor his body were seen again. A decade later, few were willing to speak about the events of that time.

Ouko's death was an unplanned catalyst for change. Whatever the truth about Moi, Biwott and Oyugi's involvement, it was clear that (at the very least) Moi had covered up the truth about the murder. The repercussions grew during 1990–1, and peaked at the exact moment that Western powers decided to end aid to Kenya.

The Kikuyu Uprising, May–July 1990

Matiba and Rubia's Challenge

On 3 May 1990, simultaneously with Hempstone's speech, a second front emerged in the movement for change. At a press conference, influential Kikuyu ex-ministers Matiba and Charles Rubia denounced corruption and blamed the government for the declining economy and the climate of oppression (Figure 9.4). The following week, they launched a campaign for the restoration of multi-party democracy. Only this, they argued, would ensure openness and accountability, while single-party rule had resulted in tribalism, mismanagement and embezzlement.[35] Since 1988, both

9.4: Matiba and Rubia's press conference, 3 May 1990

Courtesy: Nation Group Newspapers

had been driven from Parliament and their businesses had suffered. Now, they chose to fight back. For some time, Matiba had been working with a small circle of (mostly Kikuyu) allies including Muite, Kuria and Philip Gachoka (his business partner) to find others willing to make a stand in public. Rubia was willing to do so, though Mwai Kibaki, some say, was not. Other allies included out-of-favour Luhya ex-MPs Masinde Muliro and Martin Shikuku.[36]

During May–June 1990, Matiba and Rubia catalysed the long-repressed demand for multi-party democracy into a mass movement that for the first time threatened the elite's control. Their wealth, influence and ability to articulate the grievances of both the urban poor and the Kikuyu elite made them a far greater force than the long-repressed socialists. They also had the backing of many lawyers and churchmen.[37] To test the state's resolve, Matiba and Rubia announced that they would hold a mass rally at Nairobi's symbolic Kamukunji stadium on Saba Saba (7 July, or the seventh day of the seventh month). They were refused permission, but their supporters remained determined to make a stand. Kikuyu *matatus* played anti-government songs and the 'V' gesture for multiple parties (in contrast to KANU's single finger for one party) became a common gesture of defiance.

KANU's response was typically heavy-handed. Besides denouncing the ex-ministers for destabilising the country, and calling them 'puppets of foreign masters', the president informed a rally that Matiba and Rubia were plotting his assassination.[38] They were trailed and harassed by police. Matiba's house was attacked and his wife injured. Reinforcing the ethnic dimensions of the conflict, KANU MPs claimed that their campaign was simply an attempt to re-establish Kikuyu hegemony.

Another escalation in the crisis occurred on 25–6 May 1990, when the Nairobi City Commission demolished the Muoroto slums next to the main bus station. Facing growing urban protest, the Commission under Fred Gumo cleared slums with hitherto-unknown vigour during 1990. The objective of these clearances – as well as driving out the poor from Nairobi – was political. Most of Muoroto's inhabitants (like Matiba and Rubia) were originally from Murang'a, and had proved increasingly hostile to the government. In Muoroto, at least seven people were killed and 30,000 displaced during the clearances, and the fighting spread to other slums. The clearances inspired criticism in the press and led to the sacking of Minister Maina Wanjigi, in whose seat the slums were, after his outraged protests at Gumo's actions. Senior Anglicans including Archbishop Manasses Kuria were also inspired to protest. The urban poor had been reminded how little they owed the government.

Saba Saba, 7 July 1990

Three days before the Kamukunji meeting, the government called Matiba and Rubia's bluff. On 4 July 1990, both were arrested and detained, accused of being members of Mwakenya, subversion, organising an illegal meeting, and associating with 'foreign elements'. Rubia was arrested as he left the US 4 July celebrations at Hempstone's residence.[39] Although the state was unhappy about the prospect of the Kamukunji rally, Moi's inner circle was even more alarmed by a secret meeting that was said to have taken place between Matiba, Rubia, and Raila and Oginga Odinga, and the possible Luo–Kikuyu alliance it represented. Reports of this meeting suggest that when a reluctant Odinga complained that 'first marriage' between Kikuyu and Luo had brought few rewards for the Luo, Matiba and Rubia agreed that he should be the opposition's presidential candidate.[40] They also discussed the establishment of the post of prime minister, who would control government business, leaving the president as a symbol of national unity. Such a deal posed an imminent threat and, to head it off, the government detained Matiba and Rubia, along with Raila Odinga, Imanyara and two pro-opposition lawyers.

The result was an open confrontation. Thousands of supporters tried to gather at Kamukunji on 7 July, demanding Matiba and Rubia's release. Police dispersed them, igniting mass rioting in the slums of Nairobi, Kiambu, Nakuru, Thika and Nyeri, leaving between 30 and 100 dead. Protesters stoned and burnt vehicles, fought the police and tried to burn KANU offices. Despite Moi's personal order to local newsrooms, the press covered events fully. However, it was mainly a Kikuyu affair – Nyanza was tense but there was little fighting – and, after three days, the situation quietened. The state's response was fierce. Over the next few days, most opposition leaders were arrested and detained or went into hiding. More than 1,000 were jailed.

The detentions and Saba Saba riots were a critical moment in the fight for multi-party democracy. They revealed the degree of popular anger at KANU, created new symbols of resistance, and reinforced the growing Western consensus that change must come. In contrast to the Kisumu incident of 1969 (see Chapter 4), the result was not acquiescence but continued protest. It was no longer possible for the state to shoot rioters, detain critics and declare that the problem had been solved. The churches were increasingly united in calls for change and rejection of police brutality. Bishop Okullu and Rev. Njoya openly called in July for a new constituent assembly, free elections and the resignation of the government. Resistance tapes flourished in the underground Nairobi music scene – recordings of songs with political lyrics about the detainees, Saba Saba and the Muoroto clearances, and even Kenyatta's speeches and old Mau Mau songs.[41] But many in the political class remained loyal. Kibaki, for example, announced that '99.999' per cent of Kikuyu were behind the government.[42]

The USA, the Scandinavians and even Great Britain protested about the violence and detentions. The Americans were now openly committed to political change, and American legislators called for a freeze on aid to Kenya. Hempstone continued to develop his connections with opposition forces, granting political asylum in the US Embassy to Kamau Kuria and even meeting Oginga Odinga in August 1990. Relations between the two governments deteriorated as KANU took reprisals upon anyone foolish enough to associate with Hempstone and agitated for his recall.[43] Under congressional pressure, the US cut its military assistance in November 1990.

The IFIs, meanwhile, were pressing the government to reduce corruption, liberalise the economy and cut the civil service. Foreign donors were still unwilling to make a break, however. US military assistance was restored as a quid pro quo for Kenya's support in the Gulf War. In November 1990, Kenya's Paris Club of bilateral and multilateral donors met again. They considered cutting aid because of human rights concerns, but despite Saba Saba and the detentions, they concluded Kenya's economic performance was still satisfactory and again pledged over US$1 billion for 1991. In hindsight, this was probably a lost opportunity.

KANU Compromises, June–December 1990

The pressure on the government was growing from all sides. The Ouko murder remained a thorn in their side, the Kikuyu were in revolt, the professions and the churches remained hostile and questions were being asked in the West. As *Africa Confidential* predicted, it was time to compromise.[44] In June 1990, Moi had appointed a commission, chaired by Vice-President George Saitoti, to reform KANU's electoral and disciplinary procedures.[45] From July until October 1990, the committee provided a forum for indictments of the regime and calls for reform as it toured the country. Speakers complained about corruption, land theft, the autocratic behaviour of KANU officials and questioned the continuation of one-party rule. The resulting report recommended many changes, but did not recommend restoring multi-party democracy.[46] Peter Oloo-Aringo later claimed: 'The President was given a briefing that made him believe Kenyans were totally against multi-partyism.'[47]

Nonetheless, reform had begun, and it had its own momentum. In November 1990, a constitutional amendment restored the security of tenure of judges, the attorney-general, the controller and auditor-general, and the Public Service Commission. The same attorney-general prepared and the same Parliament passed legislation that reversed their amendments of two years before, without demur. Parliament was now truly a rubber stamp.

KANU's position was further weakened in August 1990 when CPK bishop and government critic Alexander Muge died in a car crash. Muge had recently appeared before the Saitoti Committee to demand an end to land grabbing, the restoration of pluralism and a two-term limit for the presidency. Suspicion focused on the government, which was made inevitable by minister Peter Okondo's public warning only days before that Muge should not visit Busia or he would not return alive. Muge had challenged Okondo to carry out his threat, leading a church delegation to the district. On his return journey, a truck hit Muge's car, killing him instantly. Popular anger erupted and Okondo was forced to resign from the Cabinet. Church leaders denounced the regime for being 'in league with the devil' and rumours circulated that the police had orchestrated the crash.[48] More than a decade later, there were still suggestions of police radios found at the scene and of bullet-wounds in Muge's body.[49] Some CPK leaders believed that Biwott had ordered Muge's death.[50]

When the KANU National Delegates' Conference assembled in December 1990 to discuss the Saitoti Committee's proposals, the mood was hostile. Nonetheless, Moi demanded that the conference accept the report *in toto*.[51] The most important concession was the abandonment of queue voting and the 70 per cent primary rule in parliamentary elections, to be replaced by secret ballot primaries. Moi and KANU Secretary-General Joseph Kamotho promised further reforms, and committed themselves to a programme of 'managed change'.[52] Moi appeared to be treading a narrow line, caught between his own hardliners and the manifest need to change tack.

Although the state's control was beginning to weaken, the leadership still made use of the law and the security forces to repress their critics. The police infiltrated and monitored student bodies, NGOs and other potential sources of disaffection. In July 1990, police arrested four opposition figures including ex-MP George Anyona and charged them with possession of seditious materials, including a press cutting from *Africa Confidential* describing the dominance of Kalenjin in the security forces. They were tortured, then jailed for seven years in 1991. In October 1990, Wamwere and three others were charged with treason, having been reportedly arrested in Nairobi, where he was accused of travelling with a cache of arms.[53] Wamwere maintained that Kenyan security agents kidnapped him in Uganda, and that the charges were fabrications. Their trial limped on until after the 1992 elections, at which point charges were dropped. In November 1990, Amnesty International again made allegations of abuses against Kenyan prisoners. Beatings, rapes and other abuses to force confessions remained commonplace, and the use of water torture in Nyayo House continued into 1990.[54]

Retreat and Resistance, November 1990–June 1991

Although his son was still in detention, Oginga Odinga was not cowed. In November 1990, he announced he intended to form a new political party and in a New Year's press release, he declared: '1991 is the year for political pluralism.'[55] In January 1991, Muliro and Shikuku also called for the repeal of Section 2A of the Constitution and the release of the detainees.

On 13 February 1991, Odinga announced that, for the third time in his life, he was forming a party to oppose KANU, to be known as the National Democratic Party (NDP).[56] Odinga's criticisms of the government echoed those of previous decades:

A master–servant relationship has emerged between the government as the master and the people as the supplicant servants. As the master harasses its servants, even courts of justice have been unable to come to the defence of the humble and meek.[57]

The government at first suppressed all news of the party, and when commentaries appeared in *Finance, Nairobi Law Monthly* and *Society* the magazines were confiscated by police. The registration of the NDP was, of course, refused. Odinga had been unable to attract many well-known politicians to his cause. However, he did have support from a group of young professionals, including Muite and ex-lecturer Peter Anyang' Nyong'o.[58] Over the next few weeks, Odinga continued to make statements in favour of multi-party politics and (embarrassingly for KANU) kept the NDP in the news by appealing the registrar's decision.

The legal community was another bastion of opposition. Finally elected as chairman of the LSK in March 1991, Muite took a confrontational stance, urging the government to register the NDP and challenging the competence of Chief Justice Alan Hancox and Justice Norbury Dugdale.[59] May 1991 saw another crack in the state carapace, when Moi replaced trouble-prone Attorney-General Muli with a more liberal, non-confrontational figure, who was to outlast all his predecessors in the post: Luhya lawyer Amos Wako. Inside the churches, too, anger was growing. Sermons from CPK leaders, particularly Gitari, edged closer to a call for open resistance to the state. By mid-1991, the mainstream churches were 'withdrawing the stamp of legitimacy that the Church had until then given to all of Kenya's governments'.[60]

Government policy zigzagged erratically, as reformers and hardliners struggled for Moi's ear. In April 1991, Rubia was freed from detention, in a serious condition (the detainees were kept in solitary confinement, with little medical attention). He spent the next two months receiving treatment in the UK. Soon after, Matiba suffered a stroke. Warned that Matiba was close to death and anxious to avoid so public a martyr, Moi released him, too, on 9 June 1991.[61] Matiba was immediately evacuated to the UK, where he remained for the next year, receiving treatment for what was found to have been two major strokes. Raila Odinga was released two weeks later, and he too went into exile. In June 1991, KANU abandoned primary elections entirely, returning the country to the pre-1988 situation. Candidates for office still had to be KANU life members, however, and receive party clearance.[62] These reforms alternated with more repressive actions. Imanyara was charged with sedition in March 1991, for example, after the *Nairobi Law Monthly* publicised the number of parastatals led by Kalenjin. Muite and other anti-government figures were followed by Special Branch, questioned and physically attacked by hired thugs. Editions of the radical press were regularly confiscated and vendors threatened not to sell them.

With the fracture between the Kikuyu community and the government growing more overt, the long-simmering issue of land in the Rift Valley was becoming a tinderbox. Political alignments, ethnicity and land rights were aligning into a 'them and us' confrontation in the former white highlands and in Narok and Kajiado (where Maasai elites maintained a fragile dominance, although a majority of the district was now non-Maasai). In February 1991, in a phrase that came to epitomise his violent, charged ethno-nationalism, Maasai minister and Narok 'big man' William ole Ntimama demanded that Kikuyu residents of Maasailand 'lie low like an envelope' or they would suffer the consequences.[63]

FORD and *Majimbo,* May–November 1991

The Formation of FORD

In May 1991, the informal alliance of Muite, ex-MP James Orengo, Anyang' Nyong'o and others persuaded Odinga to abandon his attempts to register the NDP. Instead, they decided to launch a new non-party organisation to emulate the Civic Forum movements in Czechoslovakia and East Germany. Since it would not technically be a political party, it did not have to be registered. Orengo coined the name 'FORD' – the Forum for the Restoration of Democracy – a name designed to echo the Civic Forum and draw American attention. There are hints that the US Embassy may have provided covert support for this plan.[64]

FORD's architects followed the example set by Matiba and Rubia the year before. They decided to provoke a crisis by calling a mass meeting to demand political change, which would demonstrate the government's waning legitimacy. Initially, this loose federation of lawyers, academics and politicians, now collectively known in the press as the 'Young Turks', planned a joint rally with Bishop Okullu and Archbishop Kuria, the NCCK and the LSK under the guise of a prayer meeting. However, the meeting collapsed after police threats, and subsequent efforts to unite the clergy and politicians also proved unsuccessful. Instead the group decided to recruit eight political elders – one from each province – to serve as frontmen for the movement. Odinga (from Nyanza) was already committed. The Central Province representative could only be Matiba, but he was ill and overseas, so the otherwise little known Gachoka became his representative. For Nairobi, both Munyua Waiyaki and Rubia were approached but declined.[65] However, Muliro from the Rift Valley and Shikuku from Western Province were happy to take a stand. Shikuku brought with him two lesser-known figures: Ahmed Bamahriz, an Arab councillor from Mombasa (Coast), and Kamba former MP George Nthenge (Eastern). The group now had representatives from all the provinces except Nairobi and North-Eastern. The decision to use these six brave but disparate individuals as FORD's frontmen had consequences that lasted for decades.

On 4 July 1991, Odinga announced the formation of FORD, though it was barely reported in the press. A month later, on 2 August 1991, the six frontmen – Odinga, Shikuku, Muliro, Nthenge, Bamahriz and Gachoka – tried again, calling a press conference at Chester House (the foreign press centre) and publicly announced FORD's foundation as a lobby group, not a political party. With only six members, the group was also small enough to avoid falling foul of the Societies Act. Although KANU attacked them, the government could do little legally. Despite a press blackout, the anti-government magazines reported the launch, and the public response was strongly positive.

Many Western diplomats supported their campaign, happy to assist those being harassed for demanding basic freedoms, and the tightening links between the opposition and foreign diplomats undermined the government's credibility both overseas and at home. The personal dislike between Hempstone and Moi, whom Hempstone accused of running the country like a 'personal fiefdom', was public knowledge. Hempstone was viciously critical of Moi, Biwott – 'a short pudgy, rather crude man with the predatory eyes of a ferret' – and Elijah Mwangale, whom he called 'a certified card carrying lickspittle'.[66] Moi in turn was furious at Hempstone for speaking in public about 'what should only have been discussed in private'.[67] KANU MPs denounced Hempstone for intervening in Kenya's domestic affairs, and called for his deportation. The American Embassy became a refuge for dissidents and, KANU believed, a source of covert funding for the opposition. The Americans were not alone; human rights organisations also kept up the pressure.[68] In August 1991, a reunited Germany appointed a new ambassador to Kenya, Bernd Mutzelberg, who soon joined Hempstone as a defender of the nascent opposition. The British, too, began to question their stance. Several times during 1991, British Prime Minister John Major and Foreign Secretary Douglas Hurd pressed Moi and his ministers to take action on corruption and to seek a compromise with the opposition, or risk isolation and the cessation of aid.[69]

Moi, however, was obdurate, claiming that the introduction of multi-partyism would be 'tantamount to suicide' for Kenya.[70] As tension mounted in August, he declared FORD an illegal organisation and ordered the arrest of its members.[71] In September, he called for FORD's supporters to be 'crushed like rats'.[72]

The Resurrection of Majimbo

From Kalenjin insiders came a stronger response, beginning with a speech by (Keiyo) Uasin Gishu MP Joseph Misoi on 15 August. Facing open dissent amongst Kikuyu, Luo and many Luhya, Kalenjin politicians sought to reactivate the concept of regional autonomy abandoned in 1964 – *majimbo* – in which foreign affairs and defence would be the responsibility of the central government, but the provinces would control most other affairs.

During September 1991, a series of mass rallies in Nandi and Kericho demanded the reintroduction of a federal political system. Most Kalenjin ministers and MPs participated (though Moi's own Tugen played only a minor role and Moi remained aloof). In subsequent rallies and press debates, non-Kalenjin supporters of *majimbo* included Saitoti and Ntimama for the Maasai, and Shariff Nassir for the Coast. Advocates of *majimbo* also incited pastoralist fears about their future without Moi as president. Rallies encouraged the Kalenjin to 'crush' FORD supporters and to expel those who had bought land within the Rift. Opposition leaders entering 'their' land were threatened with death. The notion of the Rift Valley as the sole entitlement of the Kalenjin, Maasai, Turkana and Samburu ethnic groups was affirmed publicly. The tension (latent since the 1960s) between liberal, individualist notions of property rights and communal and collective interests was now open.[73] It was a decisive shift of the terms of debate, with explicitly political origins, and its consequences were to continue to skew Kenyan politics for the next two decades.

KANU moderates such as Kibaki and Assistant Minister John Keen were horrified by such threats of partition and violence. However, the hardliners were in the ascendant, and in October 1991 Keen was sacked from the government.[74] Moi himself appeared unhappy with the *majimbo* campaign, trying to take a more moderate line during September and October, but he remained unwilling to meet his opponents, announcing in October 1991, 'We must plan our future on our own, and implement the necessary changes in a manner that does not disrupt the tempo and direction of our national development ...'[75] Change would only come through confrontation.

Confrontation at Kamukunji

In October 1991, FORD's leaders duly initiated the confrontation, calling another rally to promote change at Kamukunji stadium. When the Nairobi PC refused them a licence, they declared they would proceed whether the government licensed it or not. Their challenge aroused huge enthusiasm amongst the poor in Nairobi and Kikuyu areas, but the government was incensed. On the day of the rally, 16 November 1991, police barred people from making their way to Kamukunji and arrested Muite, Odinga, Imanyara and others before the rally even started. Muliro, Shikuku, Orengo and Gachoka, however, managed to lead a procession through the city before their arrest (see Figure 9.5), trailed by foreign diplomats.

Although the rally failed, FORD had won a valuable propaganda victory. They had demonstrated both their determination and their Western support. In protest at the arrests, the Germans briefly recalled Mutzelberg.[76] The US was incandescent and the British too expressed concern. In turn Kamotho demanded Hempstone's expulsion for what he alleged was open assistance to the opposition.[77] On 18 November, Kenya expelled 10 diplomats, including several Americans. With the next Paris Club meeting of donors due in days, this was a public relations disaster. The government

9.5: Shikuku, Muliro and Orengo, 16 November 1991

Courtesy: Nation Group Newspapers

attempted to defuse trouble by charging the arrested FORD leaders individually in their home districts rather than in volatile Nairobi. To its horror, however, it found dissent to be just as wide and vocal in the rural areas. Each trial turned into a focus for mass demonstrations; the government was losing control.

With the hardliners on the defensive, several influential politicians who had been driven out of Parliament but had not previously been public supporters of FORD now began to declare their colours. During November, Simeon Nyachae, ex-ministers G. G. Kariuki, Munyua Waiyaki and Wanjigi, and former Vice-President Josephat Karanja all called for compromise or the restoration of multi-party democracy.

The Crisis Breaks, November–December 1991

By November 1991, the regime was under intense pressure to liberalise both politically and economically. There was deep dissatisfaction in Nyanza, Central Province and elsewhere, and widespread (underground) support for FORD, while Western governments were openly hostile. Anger over the Ouko murder, repression and election rigging simmered. The party-state elite's bubble of invincibility and infallibility had been burst, as much by the Saitoti Commission as by the Saba Saba riots. The pressure was building to breaking-point.

Ouko and Troon

The Ouko judicial inquiry was one of their most public problems, with ramifications both domestically and internationally. At first, the inquiry had made little progress. It only sprang to life in August 1991, when Ouko's sister testified to Ouko's fears of Biwott and his concerns regarding the molasses plant. With British warnings still fresh, Moi decided to distance himself from his allies. On 27 October 1991, he retired Oyugi as permanent secretary and demoted Biwott to the Ministry of Industry.[78]

In November 1991, Troon returned to Kenya to read his report to the inquiry, and his testimony implicated Biwott, Oyugi, Kobia, Anguka and others.[79] Troon's evidence – serialised in the press – included allegations that huge kickbacks had been demanded in connection with the rehabilitation of the molasses plan and the construction of a cement factory (15 per cent for Biwott, of which some was for Moi, 10 per cent for Saitoti, 10 per cent for Mwangale, 10 per cent for Abraham Kiptanui and 5–10 per cent for Moi's banker Aslam, the head of Pan-African Bank).[80] Troon also suggested that Oyugi had been involved in Ouko's murder. He had concealed information, intimidated witnesses and might have been present that night at the farmhouse. Troon finished reading his report on 18 November, with the summary: 'By virtue of the motives I have outlined, I suspect that Mr Oyugi and Mr Biwott have some knowledge or involvement in the death of Dr Ouko . . . These two gentlemen are my principal suspects.'[81]

Under pressure both internally and from the West, Moi decided that he must sacrifice his closest ally to survive. Biwott was conveniently overseas, and (as he had done with Njonjo in 1983) Moi took the opportunity to strike. On 19 November, he sacked Biwott, possibly the most difficult and dangerous sacking of his presidency.[82]

Meanwhile, the Ouko inquiry continued. However, on the morning of 26 November 1991, Moi dissolved the Commission and asked the police to take over the investigation. At the same moment, the Commission had suspended itself, in protest at harassment by Special Branch, who had been discovered to be bugging the hotel rooms and phones of the judges and threatening them.[83] The reason for the shutdown probably related to the man who was due to testify that day – Hezekiah Oyugi. Fearing that Oyugi would 'name names' that afternoon, 26 November, police arrested both Biwott and Oyugi. Oyugi's house was searched and the testimony he had drafted to the Commission was seized.[84] Anguka and Kobia were sacked, and Anguka and others who had been implicated or who had testified to the inquiry were arrested.

The Paris Club Meeting, November 1991

By this time, most Western donors had decided that decisive action was required, as the pressure mounted on them to use their aid levers to drive political reform. In October 1991, Denmark had frozen new aid to Kenya, after an audit reported that Ksh1 billion had been spent on development projects that had produced virtually nothing over 17 years.[85] In November, in Britain's House of Commons, Minister

Lynda Chalker explicitly linked aid to Kenya to progress towards democracy.[86] In parallel, an international press campaign attacked corruption and Kenyans' holdings overseas, which the IMF estimated at US$2.6 billion. The government faced particular hostility from Lonrho and its boss Tiny Rowland, who had scores to settle inside Kenya. Using his British newspaper, the *Observer*, Rowland published a series of stories in late 1991 extremely critical of the Kenyan government, accusing Biwott of involvement in corruption and Ouko's death.[87] Meanwhile, Biwott had overreached himself financially, and his debts were mounting, risking the collapse of Trade Bank and Pan-African Bank. The *New York Times* reported that he had also borrowed Ksh320 million (US$11 million) from Citibank, but had blocked attempts to secure repayment.[88]

Over 25–6 November 1991, Kenya's aid partners met again in Paris.[89] To the government's surprise, the patience of most donors was exhausted. Influenced by the slow pace of reform and the worsening deficit, but equally by the furore surrounding Ouko, corruption and the political crisis, the donors suspended balance of payments and rapid disbursement aid. Further support, to be considered in six months' time, would be conditional upon decisive action. Kenya must redress macro-economic imbalances, improve the performance of parastatals and speed their divestment, cut the civil service and 'provide an environment that is consistently supportive of private investment and initiative'.[90] Political conditionalities, including pluralism, respect for human rights, freedom of assembly and action on corruption were also required. *The Times* spelt out the choice before the regime. 'Good government', an editorial observed, 'is now recognised as vital if aid is to be effective. President Moi continues to provide very bad government. Until he reforms, there should be no question of resuming foreign aid.'[91] Although in theory IFI assistance to governments was dependent only on economic criteria, in practice the two issues were now intertwined. It was one of the first (near-) united uses of aid to drive political reform in Africa.

The suspension of balance of payments support created a fiscal crisis. The Ministry of Finance reported that the government would need another Ksh12.2 billion (US$435 million) during 1991–2.[92] The decision deeply shocked the leadership, although its psychological effect was probably greater than its immediate economic impact, as donors continued to finance their existing project commitments and humanitarian assistance was unaffected.

The Restoration of Multi-Party Democracy

The decision to suspend aid, made on the same day that Biwott and Oyugi were arrested, broke the regime's resolve, and Moi was forced to make a snap decision. Moderate counsels persuaded him that the resumption of aid was conditional on political reform, and that KANU could still win a competitive election. Over the next few days, with Biwott and Oyugi still in jail, he prepared the ground for a shocking change in strategy.

Between 28 and 30 November, the state dropped all charges against the FORD leaders. On 2 December, Moi chaired a KANU Governing Council meeting, which

Kenya's top military officers also attended. There were rumours that the council had supported the reintroduction of multi-party democracy, though Moi himself had not spoken.[93] The next day, 3 December, the National Delegates' Conference met at Kasarani. It was only after two hours that National Organising Secretary Kalonzo Musyoka announced that delegates had been summoned to decide if opposition parties should be permitted. Either KANU leaders had only decided at the last minute that they would go through with the decision, or Moi was presenting hardliners with a *fait accompli*. The majority of speakers, including Musyoka, opposed the idea, arguing that Kenya would be torn apart by ethnic rivalries. But when Moi finally spoke, he announced that he indeed intended to repeal Section 2A of the Constitution and legalise political opposition. As in 1990, a stunned conference unanimously concurred.[94] On 5 December, nine days after the cessation of aid, Wako introduced a constitutional amendment formalising this change, which came into effect on 10 December 1991.[95] Foreign embassies applauded the decision. On 6 December, Smith Hempstone was photographed making the FORD 'V' sign in salute to demonstrators.

Moi's decision appears to have been forced on him, even though he had been on the path of reform since 1990. He was under particularly intense pressure between 25 November and 3 December, as he lost his closest allies, and found the West united against him. He denounced his own decision a few days later.[96] In a rare BBC interview in January 1992, he denied that he had changed his mind about the benefits of multi-party democracy,

> It is because of the Western media set against us, because of the economic setting today. The trend of the world economies are being controlled by developed countries, and I didn't want my people to be hammered and bothered for a long time . . . Don't you ever believe that in Africa with multi-partyism will produce stability in Africa. It will never.[97]

By acceding to the pressure for pluralism before it was inevitable, Moi seized the agenda and ensured that there was no mass breakdown of order. However, it did not mean that this would be a fair fight: the state apparatus remained partisan and hostile to the freedom of assembly, a free press and other norms of political liberalism. Moi and KANU would fight hard to win the forthcoming election, and their methods would be very questionable indeed.

Meanwhile, Biwott and Oyugi were still in GSU headquarters. Although reports of what happened there are of dubious veracity, it appears that while Biwott was treated well, Oyugi, who had intended to break the *omerta*, suffered more severely. On 10 December, having reached the legal 14-day limit, the police released both without charge. Biwott gradually rebuilt his power base, but Oyugi did not. Family sources suggested that, after his release, he never spoke coherently again. He only reappeared in the public eye when he travelled overseas for medical treatment. He died nine months later of motor neurone disease, which some claimed the security forces had induced through an injection.[98]

The New Opposition, December 1991–January 1992

Within three weeks, the reintroduction of multi-party democracy had resulted in the registration of two new mass political parties. FORD was registered formally on 31 December 1991 and hundreds of thousands of voters defected to the movement, along with Kikuyu elites such as Karanja, Wanjigi and former civil service head Geoffrey Kariithi. In Nyanza, although most Oyugi-era MPs remained in KANU, virtually every other Luo joined FORD, led by long-time Odinga supporters such as Orengo, Ramogi Achieng-Oneko, Denis Akumu and the recently sacked ex-minister Oloo-Aringo.

But it was Kibaki who registered the first new party. KANU moderates had initially seen the fall of Biwott and Oyugi and the reintroduction of multi-party democracy as an opportunity to reform KANU from within. However, something went seriously wrong with Kibaki's plans. On Christmas Day 1991, told by allies that the president was about to dismiss him, Kibaki persuaded Kenya Television Network (KTN) to interrupt its programmes to announce that he had resigned from the government, blaming his decision on the rigging of the 1988 elections and the dissolution of the inquiry into Ouko's death.[99] Two days later, Kibaki announced the launch of the Democratic Party of Kenya (DP) and declared his candidacy for the presidency. Many Kikuyu from Nyeri, Kiambu and Kirinyaga followed him, including the Kenyatta family, Njenga Karume and the entire political establishment in Nyeri.[100] Kibaki was also joined by senior non-Kikuyu allies including Eliud Mwamunga, Kyale Mwendwa and Keen.

The formation of the DP inspired angry responses from FORD leaders, who castigated Kibaki for only abandoning KANU after FORD had been victorious. Some even suggested that the DP was a KANU plot to divide the Kikuyu vote. In reality, Kibaki and the DP leadership appear to have been motivated by several factors when they decided to create a 'third force'. The DP represented the interests of the Kikuyu bourgeoisie, who were unwilling to let power slip out of Kalenjin hands only to be captured by Odinga and the Luo. They also represented a restoration of Kenyatta's conservative, Western-oriented, growth-focused, technocratic model of government, and were sceptical both of FORD's radicalism and its organisational chaos. The DP was the party of business, favouring liberalisation and the privatisation of parastatals, from which its core constituency around Mount Kenya was most likely to benefit. However, the DP did not initially receive much support outside Central Province, Embu, Meru and the Kikuyu diaspora. Even in Central Province, it was stronger in Kiambu and Nyeri than in Murang'a, where the support for FORD and Matiba was overwhelming. The party had no more than 20 safe parliamentary seats.

While the DP was a relatively unitary force, FORD's acephalous nature, populist origins and broader support left it subject to stronger pressures, which presaged its eventual destruction. There were soon divisions inside the party between the old guard politicians and the Young Turks; between socialists and liberals; between those who had suffered for decades to bring freedom and those who had only declared war after the battle was over; and between competing ethno-regional and personal interests. The tension between some of FORD's six frontmen and the Young Turks was soon obvious. Shikuku was particularly challenging, arguing that the lawyers and intellectuals should step aside and leave politics to the professionals, and that many of the Kikuyu elites now joining the party should be refused entry, because of their questionable history.

The party's launch on 5 December 1991 had already caused a crisis. Shikuku and his allies Nthenge and Bamahriz anticipated the launch by FORD's interim steering committee, and held a press conference a few hours earlier, at which they announced that Shikuku would be the party's chairman, and the six 'political' heads would hold all the leadership positions. A few hours later, the other 20 committee members called a second conference and denounced Shikuku (see Figure 9.6). Eventually, the split was papered over, but Shikuku's action ensured that the six founding fathers took all the leadership posts. Odinga became chairman, Muliro vice-chairman, Shikuku secretary-general, Nthenge treasurer, Gachoka organising secretary and Bamahriz assistant secretary.[101] It was an inauspicious start.

Several other politicians established their own smaller parties, including ex-minister Johnstone Makau, who established the Social Democratic Party (SDP) and the recently released Anyona, who refused to join FORD and established the Kenya Social Congress (KSC) instead. Political parties still had to be registered by the registrar of societies, and six were refused, most notably the fundamentalist Islamic Party of Kenya (IPK).

The Rift Valley 'Ethnic Clashes', 1991–2

The year 1991–2 saw some of the worst ethnic and political violence in Kenya's history, as Kalenjin 'warriors', instigated by KANU politicians and assisted by the state, wreaked havoc in virtually every district – bar Moi's Baringo – where Kalenjin

9.6: FORD's second press conference, 5 December 1991

Courtesy: Nation Group Newspapers

bordered with Kikuyu, Luo, Gusii and Luhya. This was not fighting over cattle or grazing, but a new phenomenon. Its causes were political and were inspired by the pressure for the restoration of multi-party democracy, but its roots reflected the 30-year struggle for the former white highlands between the Kalenjin and those from other communities who had bought land there.

The Clashes of 1991–2

Trouble began on 29 October 1991 in Nandi District, a few weeks after the *majimbo* rallies and before Moi's decision to reintroduce multi-party democracy. A long-running dispute over shares in a farm escalated into violence, pitting local Nandi against a mixed group of other communities, the original purchasers of the farm in the 1970s. Unlike 1984, when there had been similar clashes, the fighting spread rapidly to other farms in the area and to nearby Kisumu District. Organised groups of Kalenjin warriors armed with bows and arrows and machetes attacked Luo residents in Nandi and Kericho, looting and burning homes. Leaflets signed by 'Nandi Warriors' called on non-Kalenjin to leave the area.

In November, the trouble spread to Trans-Nzoia, with attacks on Luhya, and continued in Kericho, as Kalenjin burnt farms and drove out Luo and others from settlement-era farms. In December, the clashes spread to Mount Elgon in Bungoma District. This area was inhabited by pro-KANU Sabaot and Teso, and by pro-FORD Bukusu, who had bought land in previously Sabaot areas on the mountain. Sabaot politicians called on the community to drive out others and on 24 December the Sabaot began to burn the houses of non-Sabaot. Over the first few months of 1992, the clashes in Bungoma and Trans-Nzoia worsened, and some of the highest death-tolls occurred in this small region (Figure 9.7). The Sabaot were the aggressors, armed with bows and arrows and occasionally guns. The area had also seen Sabaot violence against Bukusu immigrants in 1963 and 1968. The underlying origins were the same. The Sabaot and Pokot, deported from Trans-Nzoia in the first years of colonial rule, remained determined to recover their 'stolen lands'.

With fighting continuing in Kericho, Nandi, Trans-Nzoia and Bungoma, in March–April 1992, it spread to a natural flashpoint: Molo and Olenguruone in Nakuru District. These areas were multi-ethnic as a result of decades of land buying, with Kikuyu in the majority, but many Kalenjin, Gusii, Luo and Luhya. Again, there were leaflets demanding that non-Kalenjin (*madoa doa*, or 'spots', in Kalenjin) leave the area, followed by arson and murder. Most weapons used were traditional, with the Kalenjin using bows and spears, and Kikuyu militia equipped with *pangas* and *rungus*. However, some Kalenjin appeared to have received military training, and there were reports of helicopters supporting the raiders and dropping arrows.[102] After rallies in February 1992 by Ntimama and Kipsigis hardliner Kipkalya arap Kones, the clashes spread to the Narok–Kipsigis–Kisii border. Here, the Gusii were the main victims, having bought land in Narok and Bomet Districts since independence.

The government response was extraordinary. Rather than repressing the violence, it appeared to do nothing. In February–March 1992, Kenya appeared on the brink of

9.7: Clash
victim, 1992

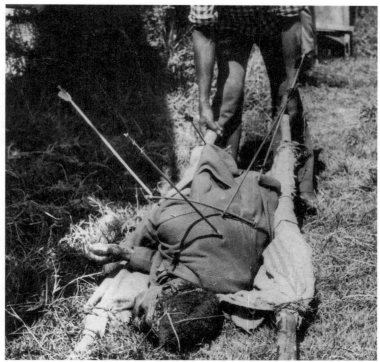

Courtesy: Nation Group Newspapers

civil war, as Kalenjin hardliners including Kones declared Kalenjin districts 'KANU
zones', banned FORD and DP members from entering the area and stated that
the Kalenjin had 'declared war' on the Luo. Kericho, Uasin Gishu, Trans-Nzoia,
Bungoma, Nakuru, Narok and Kisii were all ablaze. The opposition blamed KANU
for instigating the violence and there were retaliatory attacks against Kalenjin.[103]
Claims that Biwott had a tribal army hidden in the Maasai Mara contributed to
an atmosphere of confrontation and fear. KANU and the new civil service head
Philip Mbithi in turn blamed the clashes on Libyan-trained FORD supporters and
the American CIA and tried to ban newspapers from reporting the crisis, accusing
them of 'spreading lies'.[104] The churches prayed for peace, but in April also called
on Moi and the government to resign.[105] There was chaos in the Assembly as non-
Kalenjin KANU MPs openly called their Kalenjin colleagues 'murderers'. However,
the (Kalenjin) speaker, Jonathan Ng'eno, blocked all attempts to debate the clashes
until late April.[106]

   In May, MPs finally managed to appoint a Select Committee, led by Mombasa
MP Kennedy Kiliku, to investigate the clashes. At the same time, there seemed
to be signs of change in the government's attitude. The fighting abated and by
the end of July the government had the situation mostly under control. Trouble
continued though in Uasin Gishu, Mount Elgon and Trans-Nzoia. In the Burnt

Forest area of Eldoret South, the fighting and house burning did not begin until December 1992. Only three weeks before the general election, armed Kalenjin drove out 15,000 Kikuyu and Luhya. Meanwhile, the Select Committee visited clash sites and used material from an earlier report on the violence from the NCCK.[107] Its report blamed the violence on the return to multi-party democracy and the ethnic tensions that it had created.[108] It demanded the investigation of the politicians who had led the calls for *majimbo* and suggested they had financed and organised the killings.[109] Western countries were appalled, and saw parallels with events in former Yugoslavia. The phrase 'ethnic cleansing' was widely used, and the government's credibility was further shredded.

The Causes of the 'Clashes'

The causes of the clashes remained officially unknown, but the pattern of events suggested complicity at the centre. Long-repressed Kalenjin desires for a greater share of the former white highlands were legitimised by the exposure of Kenya's ethnic fault lines and supported by elements in the government who decided to seize the opportunity to drive out opposition supporters and create a pastoralist-dominated Rift Valley. Senior Kalenjin had incited ethnic hatred for months. Although the fighting took on its own momentum as other communities defended themselves, there were well-attested occasions where the trouble was initiated by armed men imported from elsewhere. There were reports that warriors were paid for each person killed and each house burnt.[110] The security forces were negligent or complicit: houses were burnt by Kalenjin while police officers watched, under 'orders from above' not to intervene.[111] When warriors were arrested, the police appeared unable to prosecute them. The government later reported that 1,324 people were prosecuted in connection with the 1991–2 clashes, of which 625 were Kalenjin and 430 Kikuyu.[112] No conviction numbers were reported, and it was believed that most Kalenjin were released without charge.

There was a widespread fear amongst the 'KANU tribes' in the Rift Valley that they would lose the upcoming election, and that their land rights would be lost, or that this was a last opportunity to reassert such rights. This was exploited by Kalenjin and Maasai leaders in order to create ethnically pure enclaves within which their land rights and KANU's victory would be secure. Local chiefs and security officials – the majority of them Kalenjin because of the government's partisan policies – supported the violence, believing that multi-party democracy was a ruse by the Kikuyu and Luo to retake power. As the Select Committee concluded, the clashes were 'politically motivated and fuelled by some officers in the Provincial Administration'.[113] In 1998, another inquiry was appointed to investigate the clashes, a judicial commission chaired by Justice Akiwumi.[114] Its report further stressed the political nature of the fighting and named politicians, administrators, army officers, policemen, chiefs and local councillors as financing, organising or abetting the violence. Investigations implicated Kalenjin politicians Wilson Leitich, Ezekiel Barngetuny, Biwott and Reuben Chesire, and Kalenjin

DCs Timothy Sirma (Kericho), William Chang'ole (Bungoma), Ishmael Chelang'a (Nakuru), Paul Lagat (Uasin Gishu) and Nicholas Mberia (Trans-Nzoia). Again, no action was taken.

The Victims and the Response

No one knows how many died, were displaced or lost property. The Select Committee report gave a total of 779 dead and 654 injured at that time.[115] At least 250,000 Kenyans fled their homes temporarily, and tens of thousands were left permanently homeless and landless. Thousands of displaced persons trekked to temporary camps at churches and other relief centres. Food prices rocketed and food production fell as farmers were unable to cultivate their crops and cattle were killed. Poor rains and the clashes combined to cut Kenya's wheat production from 195,000 tonnes in 1991 to 125,000 tonnes in 1992, and maize production fell to its lowest level since 1984. Education was disrupted as schools were closed or ethnically cleansed. Mixed communities were divided, and political cleavages – already polarised – were further aligned on an ethnic basis: supporting the opposition as a Kalenjin, or KANU as a Kikuyu or Luo became extremely dangerous.

The response of the government was callous even by Kenyan standards. Knowing that large camps of displaced persons would attract international attention, the regime made no attempt to feed or house most of the displaced. Instead, it actively harassed them during 1993–4, hoping that they would somehow disappear into the rural areas, far from the eyes of prying journalists. Several who returned to the most troubled areas were killed. Many Kikuyu ended up returning to Central Province, leading to a growing bitterness there, just as the return of squatters from the highlands had done in the late 1940s. While in some districts the displaced eventually returned, in other areas, land ownership patterns were permanently altered and tens of thousands were thrown into abject poverty. Many of those who lost their land were never resettled or compensated. Some had lost their title deeds when their houses were burnt by their neighbours, were joint owners of farms with block title deeds that had not yet been subdivided, or had bought land that had not yet been registered. Other refugees sold their land or swapped it for plots on the other side of the invisible ethnic border.[116] A decade later, thousands were still living in squatter camps.

Cracks in the Opposition, January–April 1992

With the reintroduction of multi-party democracy, FORD was transformed into a government in waiting with massive popular support, seemingly certain of victory at the next elections. However, its position was far from secure: it was less well established than KANU in most of the country, it faced active harassment from the provincial administration and it had not yet chosen a presidential candidate – the most hazardous process of all.

Popular but Disunited

In January 1992, the state authorised FORD to hold a series of rallies. Its first in Nairobi attracted a huge crowd of several hundred thousand. Odinga led the rally and introduced the themes that would become the cornerstones of the opposition's campaign. He promised that a FORD government would protect freedom of assembly and the right of Kenyans to live anywhere in the country, and would restore constitutional controls over executive action. He denounced the regime for killing, detaining or exiling its critics, and for its failure to stop the clashes. In contrast to his position in the past, he promised that FORD would support economic liberalisation and reduce state intervention in the economy.[117] All FORD's meetings nationwide attracted large crowds.

Nonetheless, FORD faced serious internal challenges. Odinga was old and frail, as much a figurehead as a leader in his own right. Speeches by Shikuku and Bamahriz raised concern that they were anti-Asian and anti-European. The lure of power also brought to the surface personal rivalries and generational conflicts. There were also signs of ethnic caucuses emerging inside the party, with Kikuyu, Luhya and Luo leaders all holding informal meetings in the cause of ethnic unity. The party also faced the daunting challenge of converting a protest movement into a political party with a coherent ideology, organisation and leadership. The precise powers of FORD's six founding fathers were unclear and FORD's formal structure inchoate.[118] The vagueness of the party's institutions, organisation and aims led to a tug of war, as politicians fought to direct the movement.

The Struggle for the Presidency

The presidency was the main point of tension. On 22 January 1992, the 80-year-old Odinga announced his candidacy for FORD's presidential nomination. Although many had hoped he would leave the post to Matiba, or allow Matiba to become an executive prime minister, Odinga remained determined to lead Kenya. However, while FORD had broad popular support, none of its leaders commanded a nationwide following alone. Thus the Luo rallied behind Odinga, the Luhya were split between Muliro and Shikuku, while most Kikuyu FORD supporters backed Matiba. Most FORD supporters owed allegiance simultaneously to a set of political ideals and to the collective self-interest of their ethnic community.

FORD's hastily written constitution stipulated that the party's presidential candidate would be chosen by a secret ballot of all members. However, Muite soon suggested that FORD might have to leave the nomination to the Annual Delegates' Conference, because direct party elections would be costly and hard to organise. Others, including Shikuku, Nthenge and Luhya human rights lawyer Japheth Shamalla, disagreed.[119] They also argued that only the Annual Delegates' Conference, and not the interim committee, could amend the party's constitution. This issue was more than procedural, as they feared Muite's proposal was an attempt to promote Kikuyu influence; these divisions deepened during March and

April 1992, although Muite won the support of Odinga and most Young Turks for his changes.

Matiba, meanwhile, was still in London, struggling to regain his health. Although it was kept secret, Matiba could neither read nor write since his stroke and his temper had become explosive. In spite of this, he maintained a high public profile, issuing statements calling for the appointment of an independent electoral commission, the release of political prisoners and the suspension of aid. He also welcomed the constitutional amendment bill (see below) that introduced the post of prime minister, arousing speculation that he might be interested in the post. However, Matiba too had his eyes set on the presidency. He was not only extremely wealthy, but also extremely popular, especially amongst poorer Kikuyu. His 1990 challenge had cemented his reputation as someone willing to take on Moi head to head, a 'man on horseback' who could lead the country to prosperity. He believed that his leadership of the 1990 movement and his sufferings in detention entitled him to seek the presidency. On 4 February 1992, Matiba announced that he would challenge Odinga. Efforts by Muite in April to persuade him to avoid a showdown and accept the vice-presidency under Odinga were unsuccessful.[120] The opposition would have at least three serious presidential candidates.

Skirmishes and Preparations

Tensions remained high, as the government and opposition parties skirmished. In April 1992, FORD led a nationwide general strike. Its original aim was to press the government to release all detainees and political prisoners, but the strike soon became a trial of strength, as opposition leaders added new demands, including the appointment of an independent electoral commission. In turn, the government threatened to sack striking civil servants and to prosecute strike organisers.[121] Although FORD called for trade unionists to back the strike, most remained loyal to KANU. FORD's call also divided the opposition, as both the DP and the churches were sceptical. The result was a draw. The strike succeeded in Nairobi and Kisumu, but over most of the country business continued as usual.[122]

Meanwhile, the opposition's campaign continued, never knowing when Moi might call a snap poll. In April 1992, FORD published its election manifesto, the *Charter for the Second Liberation*. FORD accepted that restructuring would be painful, but committed itself to cuts in the civil service, exchange rate liberalisation and to the privatisation or restructuring of parastatals. More controversially, FORD proposed to abolish the provincial administration and to devolve power to elected district councils. FORD also called for a limit to presidential powers, the establishment of a prime minister and the drawing-up of a new constitution for Kenya. FORD believed the 8–4–4 education system had been a disaster, and the universities had expanded too fast; Kenya needed workers with appropriate skills rather than more unemployable graduates.[123] FORD was equally critical of Kenya's health services, but, once again, it advocated a version of the government's policies, accepting the principle of cost sharing.

The opposition leaders had few policy differences. All agreed that corruption was bad, detention without trial and restrictions on freedom of speech and assembly must end, state intervention in the economy had gone too far, cash-crop producers needed more incentives, education and health care needed improving and political stability was needed to attract investment and tourism. They were united in their dislike of KANU and of Moi, conflating their removal with democratisation and social change. Their differences arose over the degree to which they would actually implement such radical – and divisive – reforms, and the personal, ethnic and regional interests that would be the main beneficiaries.

KANU's Response

The period from December 1991 to February 1992 was KANU's lowest ebb. Even then, all was not lost: Moi retained some personal respect, the government controlled the provincial administration and the security forces, and retained the support of most of the political establishment outside Central Province and Luo Nyanza. Defections never threatened KANU's control over the Rift Valley (outside Trans-Nzoia, Nakuru and Laikipia), the rural Coast or North-Eastern, while its opponents' penetration of Western, Eastern and Kisii was patchy. Moi could decide the date of the next election, and he chose to delay as long as possible, allowing his team time to recover and his opponents to fragment. Despite Moi's promises of free and fair elections, KANU did not intend to lose the polls. The tactics they used were a replay of those that had been so successful in 1966–9. The registrar of societies, the police and the civil service restricted the opposition's freedom to organise; youth wingers harassed them; they were accused of being tribalists and tools of foreign powers (the Americans this time, not the Chinese) and of subversion. Only detention was no longer an option.

Rebuilding Support

Inside Parliament, KANU quickly reasserted control. The 10 MPs (including Kibaki) who had defected to the opposition were relieved of their seats in Parliament under the 1966 KPU legislation. However, the speaker failed to declare their seats vacant until Parliament reassembled in March, and then Chesoni in turn refused to call the required by-elections. This (probably illegal) action left all 10 out of Parliament and their constituencies unrepresented for the entire year. The flow of MPs to the opposition halted.

During the first half of 1992, KANU used the time the opposition wasted in internal fighting to rebuild, and to reincorporate key actors from marginal communities. Party polls were held to replace defectors and remove the most compromised hardliners. KANU also sought out politicians who had been exiled in the 1980s, who might be persuaded to return to the fold. They succeeded in bringing many back on board, including William Omamo, rehabilitated to take on Odinga in Bondo, Henry Kosgey in Nandi, Njonjo's old ally G. G. Kariuki in Laikipia, Joshua Angatia in Kakamega, Pokot nationalist Francis Lotodo, Meru Jackson Kalweo and even

Simeon Nyachae. The wealthy Nyachae was the most significant catch – a surprising outcome after the events of 1986–8. His defection would have turned the Gusii entirely against KANU. However, a deal was done, in which Nyachae returned to the fold in return for a senior ministerial post, a free hand against his opponents in Kisii and the release of Anyona.[124] There were rumours that he, Musyoka and Mwangale had all been promised the vice-presidency if KANU won.

Moi also sought religious support, trying to counter the criticism of the mainstream churches by appealing to the smaller, African and evangelical churches and to biblical concepts of obedience to authority.[125]

The Power of the Presidency

Kenya had entered a dangerous period in which the political system had changed on paper, but these changes had not filtered down into supporting legislation or to the local level. The civil service and the security forces were still obedient to the president. The police remained intolerant and aggressive and loyalists still held key posts. The independence of the judiciary too was questionable. Many judges were closely linked financially or personally to the Moi elite, and it was widely believed that they continued to obey the government's instructions. The broadcast media too was mostly under state control.

FORD's first rallies had passed smoothly, but, as the year advanced, the disruption of opposition meetings became more common. The provincial administration and the police prevented FORD from establishing local offices and refused to license their meetings. Civil servants were told to support the government or face dismissal. Moi ordered that 'civil servants should not have divided loyalty or assume a neutral stand in the era of multi-party politics.'[126] The authorities also ignored attacks on opposition activists by KANU supporters. Meanwhile, Kalenjin 'warriors' and KANU supporters were driving out opposition-supporting communities from 'KANU zones' – areas declared the exclusive property of the ruling party. On 20 March, ostensibly to control the clashes, Moi banned all political rallies, provoking furious protests from the opposition.[127]

Divide and Rule

While Kenyatta and then Moi had tried to unite the nation under their rule, Moi was now forced to divide it, in order to retain power. Throughout 1992, the government and its mouthpiece the *Kenya Times* tried to divide the opposition, by whipping up ethnic tension between Kikuyu and Luo, and raising fears of a Kikuyu victory amongst other communities.

There were also suspicions that KANU was helping some opposition leaders in order to split the opposition vote. In early 1992, the focus was on Kibaki and the DP. By the end of the year, attention had shifted to Matiba and Shikuku. It is possible that the government assisted Matiba's presidential campaign in order to split both FORD and the Kikuyu vote. Insiders suggested that the state machinery had been used to boost the crowds that welcomed Matiba back to Kenya in May (see below) and his campaign was less harassed than the other opposition leaders. KANU tended to avoid direct criticism of him. Kamotho, for example, welcomed Matiba's declaration that he would vie for the presidency and the *Kenya Times* described Matiba as a 'capable administrator' and 'successful and very wealthy businessman' who was likely to fare better than Kibaki.[128] Shikuku fell under particular suspicion after he and Shamalla met Moi for a late-night private dinner ('midnight *ugali*', as it became known) at State House on 20 May. The result was a crescendo of personal attacks by other FORD leaders and rumours that Shikuku had received Ksh30 million (US$600,000) from Moi to finance his bid for FORD's presidential nomination, ensuring that the opposition would be further divided.[129] However, although there is circumstantial evidence that some FORD leaders were compromised, the truculent hatred Matiba later showed for Moi makes nonsense of any suggestion that the competition was stage-managed. If KANU did covertly support his FORD faction to fragment the opposition, it almost backfired, as by the end of the campaign Matiba was in danger of outpolling Moi and forcing a run-off.

The Fight for FORD, May–October 1992

During the summer of 1992, a series of miscalculations, leadership conflicts and deeper policy disputes forced FORD's fractious coalition into open warfare. The initial euphoria waned as the realities of organisation and the difficulties of bringing together a disparate coalition of individuals, united by nothing (not even their dislike of KANU, since many were opportunists), dragged down the leadership. The alliance FORD represented between Kikuyu, Luo and Luhya and between radicals and conservatives, was always going to face stresses. It was not inevitable that it would collapse – as NARC demonstrated in 2002, it was possible to sustain a trans-ethnic opposition alliance for a short period – but in 1992, time, a 'winner takes all' mentality, over-confidence and state manipulation ensured that the fledgling alliance shattered.

The Matiba–Odinga Split

The next step in FORD's disintegration came in May 1992, when Matiba returned to Kenya. Although still ill, he had to return if he was to seek the presidency. On 2 May, Matiba landed at Nairobi airport, to be welcomed by hundreds of thousands of supporters. However, it was mostly Kikuyu, Embu and Meru FORD leaders who were there to welcome him. Odinga was in Western Province, where he reaffirmed his intention to seek the party's presidential nomination and questioned Matiba's health.[130] Prominent non-Kikuyu claimed that the welcoming committee had snubbed them. Matiba's power base was among FORD's Kikuyu activists, and his association with senior Kikuyu such as Rubia, Karanja and Wanjigi aroused suspicion rather than confidence elsewhere.

Unwilling to back Odinga, Matiba now plunged FORD into a battle for control that shattered the party, split the Kikuyu vote and ensured Moi's re-election. FORD was gifted and cursed with two individuals who both felt they had a right to State House, and the hierarchical structure of political authority and the underlying 'winner takes all' model made it impossible for their supporters to control them in the collective interest.

In FORD, Matiba soon aligned himself with Shikuku, Nthenge and Bamahriz against Odinga and the Young Turks (while Muliro tried to remain outside the fray). All were suspicious of Muite, doubted Odinga's ability to lead and favoured the direct election of the party's presidential candidate. Shikuku further complicated the contest in May when he announced that he too was a candidate for FORD's presidential nomination. He had little chance of success, though, since he had no money, little elite support and was far from universally popular even amongst the Luhya. Despite their apparent rivalry, Shikuku and Matiba found themselves drawn together. Both were populists whose hopes of power depended on appealing to party members in a direct vote rather than relying on the support of intellectuals or the political elite.

The DP Strengthens

Although FORD was in the headlines, the more elitist, more conservative DP was playing a longer game. Until May 1992, the party had limited appeal outside Central and Eastern provinces. Kibaki and the DP had disassociated themselves from FORD's general strike and also refused to support a hunger strike by mothers of those imprisoned. As FORD's problems deepened, so the DP's fortunes improved. In May–June 1992, the party attracted several defectors, including senior Kalenjin, bolstering its claim to be a national force.[131]

KANU and the KBC now portrayed the DP in a more hostile light, as elitist and Gema-dominated, and trying to turn the clock back to the Kenyatta era. In May 1992, Moi even announced that the opposition parties were training armies to overthrow the government and that Keen (his assistant minister a few months before) was in charge of the DP's assassination squad.[132] As the DP made inroads into Kalenjin and Gusii areas, KANU responded with beatings and arrests of its supporters. As Kibaki toured the country during August and September, he encountered mounting harassment. Many of his rallies were cancelled, and his convoy was attacked several times by armed KANU youth. The *Kenya Times* even asserted that the DP had hired gunmen to assassinate Moi.[133]

FORD's Divisions Intensify, July–August 1992

In July 1992, Matiba went on the offensive, announcing that he would try to oust Odinga as chairman when FORD held national elections. Matiba also proposed that FORD's headquarters move from Agip House (the headquarters of Odinga's East African Spectre), to Muthithi House in Westlands, which had been loaned to Matiba for the party's use. Secretary-General Shikuku and some of the secretariat moved into Muthithi House, while Odinga's supporters stayed put. It was the first step towards a formal split.

Battle was now joined in earnest, with the fight against KANU almost a sideshow. Matiba began touring the country, funding a network of supporters nationwide. Unable to get his hands on FORD membership cards from the pro-Odinga secretariat, Matiba issued his own. Both factions focused on urban and densely populated districts, paying little attention to the pro-KANU Rift Valley or pastoral areas. The government did its best to keep Matiba within the Kikuyu districts, allowing his 'meet the people' tour inside Central and Laikipia, but imposing police roadblocks when he tried to enter Eastern Province in July.[134] In KANU's plan, Matiba's job was to split the Kikuyu, not take the Embu or Meru vote.

Perhaps oddly in retrospect, Matiba's assault was firmly supported by four of the original six FORD founders: by Shikuku, Bamahriz and Nthenge as well as Gachoka. On 27 July, the five announced that they had decided to call off FORD's upcoming elections and accused Odinga of plans to rig the polls.[135] Odinga, the Young Turks and the Agip House group, supported by a party apparatus that was increasingly dominated by Luo and the Odinga family, responded that Matiba and the 'gang of four' had no authority to override the decision of the party's national steering committee, its supreme governing body. The resulting propaganda war between the factions in the press further disillusioned supporters.

The Agip House FORD elections finally began on 1 August. With a boycott by pro-Matiba supporters and with few inroads into KANU zones, they demonstrated the patchy nature of Odinga's nationwide support, but they also showed that he controlled the majority of the party.[136] With the branch polls completed, the Agip House faction called a delegates' conference for the end of August to elect new officials and change the party constitution. Matiba and Shikuku had little choice but to split the party, and announced that they would hold their own elections.

As the rift widened, Masinde Muliro began to see himself as a compromise candidate. He announced his bid for FORD's presidential nomination – the fourth declaration – in July. However, none of the warring parties was willing to concede to him any more than to their opponents. Muliro was old, frail, lacked the hardcore support of either Odinga or Matiba and was on the verge of bankruptcy. Realising that his bid would fail, by August Muliro had decided to participate in the Agip House polls and back Odinga.[137] On 14 August 1992, however, Muliro suffered a heart attack and died at the airport after a flight from London. His death removed the last chance of reconciliation in FORD.

By August 1992, the split was irreconcilable. FORD's troubles stemmed above all from the ambitions of its two leaders, but their rivalry reflected deeper forces. Both factions were coalitions designed to seize power, consisting of a loose grouping of senior leaders with regional support, but centred on a single leader with a rock-solid ethnic base. Despite their common hostility to Moi's KANU, the antipathy between Kikuyu and Luo remained almost as strong. Many Luo considered that Nyanza had fared better under Moi than Kenyatta and some privately suggested that it was better to be dominated by the Kalenjin than by the Kikuyu. The Kikuyu–Luo tension within FORD became increasingly evident during August and September 1992. Kiambu FORD leaders were particularly outspoken, asserting that the Kikuyu would never tolerate Luo leadership. From the other side, the increasingly influential Raila Odinga declared: 'the country is not ready for another Kikuyu president . . .'[138]

In the same period, both the DP and FORD were weakened by a series of defections, particularly in Coast, Western and Eastern provinces. In part, this stemmed from the growing split in FORD, but it also reflected a cold-hearted calculation of the likely winner in these areas amongst aspiring MPs. There was a little-noted sub-text to KANU's frequent calls for opposition politicians to return home: appeals to Odinga to join KANU. Kalenjin MP Ezekiel Barngetuny, for example, appealed to the Luo in November to rejoin KANU and create 'one family from the west of the Rift Valley'.[139] Such a 'Nilotic alliance' was soon part of KANU's long-term survival strategy.

Congresses and Splits, September–October 1992

On 3–4 September, FORD (Agip House) held its national conference, which duly approved the changes to FORD's constitution and elected Odinga unopposed as chairman and therefore its presidential candidate. Agip House leaders tried to stage-manage the congress with an ethnically balanced leadership, to avoid claims that they were Luo dominated, but failed.[140] The plan was to ensure that a Luhya would be chosen as first vice-chairman, while a Kikuyu would become second vice-chairman. However, with Muliro dead, the Luhya vote was split, and delegates unexpectedly elected Muite as first vice-chairman. Wamalwa secured the second post, but it was too late. Agip House would have to fight the election without a vice-presidential candidate, since it could not put up a Kikuyu – especially the controversial Muite – for this post. This helped Matiba win more of the Luhya vote.

The success of the Agip House elections seemed to end Matiba's hopes, but the law took a different view. In September the registrar announced that he could not register Odinga's new officials.[141] No registered society could amend its constitution without minutes of a meeting approving the changes, signed by at least three officers of the society. After Muliro's death, however, Odinga was the only registered FORD official in the Agip House group. Thus, the congress could not amend FORD's constitution or elect officers. Although it ran contrary to public perception, Matiba had a strong case.

The Muthithi House team therefore continued the struggle and they in turn called locational and national FORD elections. However, many of Matiba's allies were unhappy, more interested in securing their parliamentary seats than in continuing the battle with Agip House. There was also growing dissatisfaction with Matiba's autocratic style. Although he held no office in FORD, he behaved as if Muthithi House was his personal fiefdom and was unwilling to listen to his colleagues. As a result, Rubia and others began to make contingency plans to form another party if Matiba's 'winner takes all' strategy failed.[142] Early in September 1992, this division became public, leaving FORD's most experienced leaders, including Rubia, Wanjigi, Kamba ex-minister Titus Mbathi and Kariithi arrayed against Matiba.[143] Far from compromising, though, Matiba pushed ahead, believing that he was so popular that he could capture power alone, and willing to risk his own fortune to prove it.[144]

FORD (Muthithi House) held constituency-level polls during September, but they were no better organised than those of Agip House, and no elections took place in Odinga's strongholds. Then, just before their National Delegates' Congress convened, Rubia and most of Matiba's allies abandoned him. The polls had shown that Matiba and Shikuku commanded a majority of delegates, so the fight to be recognised as the 'real' FORD would continue. Instead of trying to register another party, Rubia, Mbathi and the dissidents took over the moribund Kenya National Congress (KNC). This seemed the end of Matiba's hopes: abandoned by everyone except Shikuku, Nthenge, Bamahriz, Gachoka and Karanja. But Matiba was still unfazed. On 3 October, the FORD (Muthithi) congress duly elected him as its chairman and Shikuku as secretary-general. In fact, it appeared that Matiba's confidence might have genuine roots. More than 4,800 delegates from 45 districts attended the congress, which also confirmed Odinga's suspension and endorsed FORD's original constitution.[145]

Now that both factions had held elections, the registrar faced two rival slates of officials, and tensions mounted, because he was unable to register either without demonstrations or lawsuits. The government knew it had little to gain from an election if FORD could not effectively participate, as this would not restore aid or provide the government with international legitimacy. Attorney-General Wako therefore offered a solution, suggesting that both factions preserve the name 'FORD', with unique additional elements, following which he would register both parties.[146] With the election imminent, both sides agreed and during October 1992, two parties were formally registered. The Agip House faction became FORD-Kenya, while Muthithi House took the title FORD-Asili ('the original FORD'). FORD-Kenya secured FORD's lion symbol, although both parties used the party's colours and 'V' salute. It was a messy and bitter divorce, of which KANU was the main beneficiary.

All efforts to create electoral alliances or reunite the opposition parties failed. The most likely alliance was between the DP and FORD (Agip House). During August, the parties discussed a deal to fight the election with agreed prime ministerial, presidential and parliamentary candidates. The chaos in FORD, however, put Kibaki off.[147] In September 1992, a 'Middle Ground Group' was formed by FORD supporter Wangari Maathai, who was influential with Western donors, but this too failed to deliver a deal. Ambassadors Hempstone and Mutzelberg, exposing their partiality, also tried unsuccessfully to create a united anti-KANU front.[148] Nonetheless, last-minute efforts continued. In October, Mbathi and Rubia made a deal with the DP on a common slate and the KNC agreed to support Kibaki for president. Secret meetings also continued in parallel between the DP and FORD-Kenya, which outlined an agreement whereby Odinga would become their joint presidential candidate, but the deal was exposed too early, and fell through.[149] The opposition's last chance of unity before the polls was lost.

The Regional Basis of Electoral Politics

Alongside and beneath the high politics of Nairobi was a pattern of regional conflicts that became increasingly distinct as the year advanced. The ethnic sensitivities that had underlain politics in the single-party era became overt and self-reinforcing, a situation further inflamed by the state through its ethnic rhetoric and tolerance for ethnic violence, and by opposition leaders, who sought power through ethnic unity and were almost as concerned about the victory of their allies as they were about their enemies. Ethnicity proved the most effective mobilising factor for Kenya's politicians, triumphing over cleavages based on age, gender, wealth, religion, economic policy or attitudes to the state. The reasons for this remain controversial, but included the focus on individual leaders as patrons, Kenya's fractured ethnic history under colonial rule, new and weak parties, the short time between the reintroduction of multi-party democracy and the elections, the low level of political awareness amongst many Kenyans and the importance of ethnicity as a genuine social force.

Although it appeared that Kenya's parties were competing at a national level, in reality they were not. The election campaign was fought on different issues and between different parties in different regions of the country. By mid-1992, the country could be described as falling into 20 distinct regions. KANU controlled roughly one-third, as did the opposition, while the remaining seven were the key battlegrounds. The shape of this division reflected a complex combination of population geography, Kenya's history, the power of the state to reward its allies and the impact of individual leaders.

The Kikuyu of Central Province and the diaspora (21 per cent of the population) had virtually all joined the opposition. They were divided between the DP (stronger in Nyeri and northern Kikuyu areas) and Matiba's FORD (stronger in Murang'a and the south). Nairobi was also pro-opposition, but its melange of peoples ensured that no constituency was safe. In Eastern Province, the DP was strong amongst the Embu and Meru, but KANU remained a contender and FORD had a presence in a few seats. There was a house-to-house battle in Ukambani between KANU and the DP. In arid Isiolo, Marsabit and North-Eastern Province, KANU was dominant. Most of the rural, Christian Coast also appeared loyal, but KANU was likely to lose Mombasa and other seats dominated by Muslim or upcountry voters.

The Rift Valley was KANU's home, but also contained Kikuyu-dominated Nakuru and Laikipia and Luhya-dominated Trans-Nzoia, plus large minorities elsewhere. There were, therefore, five different sub-elections in the province. In the 'Kalenjin homelands' of Baringo, Nandi, Elgeyo-Marakwet, Kericho and the recently created Bomet District, KANU was overwhelmingly dominant. The second contest was in the 'pastoralist periphery' – the seats of Turkana, Samburu and West Pokot, plus southern Kajiado and Narok. Here KANU started ahead, but without the same monolithic ethnic identification with Moi. The third zone was a regional conflict between KANU and FORD for Uasin Gishu and Trans-Nzoia, the 'western borderlands' of the ex-white highlands. Laikipia voted with Nyeri. The last region covered the troubled borderlands between Kikuyu and Kalenjin in Nakuru, and between Kikuyu and Maasai in Narok North and Kajiado North.

The situation in Western Province was the most confused of all, and no one could be sure of the outcome. Most Luhya were FORD supporters, their commitment strengthened by the clashes. However, as the divisions in the party grew, Muliro's followers mainly backed Odinga, while Shikuku's backed Matiba. Support for KANU, by contrast, held up well in Mudavadi's Vihiga and in Busia. Nyanza Province divided into two zones. The Luo were committed to Odinga's FORD, while Kisii and Nyamira was a four-way marginal area, in which KANU, FORD and the DP had support, as did Anyona's KSC.

This ethnically dominated pattern was neither imposed nor absolute, but emerged from recent history, individual commitment and perceptions of community risk and opportunity. Such 'ethnic voting' was also a self-fulfilling prophecy: the more politicians couched their appeals in terms of ethnicity, the more voters perceived the political horserace as an ethnically driven zero-sum game, in which case the easiest way for politicians to win was to play the same game.

Economic Crisis and Response, 1992–3

External Demands for Reform

In November 1991, donors had withheld US$350 million of loans, to push Kenya into political and economic reform. As a condition for the restoration of aid, they demanded a detailed programme of reforms, including liberalisation of the marketing of most agricultural products, budget cuts, civil service reform, limits to the number of teachers, immediate and extensive privatisation and replacement of political managers. It was a recipe for a complete restructuring of Kenya's economy in a few months.

Desperate for money, the government did its best to meet their demands. In early 1992, it promised the privatisation of 130 state-owned industries. In July 1992, it published a paper committing itself to privatisation and set up a parastatal reform committee, led by Saitoti.[150] However, of the 240 enterprises with a part-public shareholding and commercial functions listed, 33 key parastatals, including the KPLC and KPTC were identified as 'strategic' and therefore slated for restructuring rather than privatisation. Actual privatisations remained meagre.[151]

More progress was achieved in agricultural liberalisation. In May 1992, the government liberalised milk imports, processing and marketing. In June, it introduced a variable tariff regime for food imports, including wheat, rice, milk, maize and sugar, to raise import prices to a set floor when the world price was lower than the domestic price. In the run-up to the election, some food prices were decontrolled and some duty-free import exemptions removed. In October 1992, the government also announced changes in the coffee industry, weakening the Coffee Board's monopoly on marketing and the KPCU's monopoly on processing.[152] They also announced a retention scheme to allow coffee and tea exporters to keep part of their proceeds in hard currency.

Throughout 1992, the government, led by Finance Minister Saitoti, tried to persuade Western governments that Kenya had liberalised and deserved to be rewarded. There was no response. Two IMF reviews were inconclusive, given the lack of progress on privatisation, continued abuses of sugar imports, corruption and the controversy over the fairness of the election. Saitoti came back empty-handed from every visit to solicit funds, with more and more emphasis placed by donors on political conditions. Only France restored direct bilateral aid in September. Even the World Bank's agricultural credit programme was scrapped in December after the government reintroduced grain movement controls.

The Economic Crisis

During 1992–3, Kenya's economy suffered severe and long-lasting damage. In part, this was a consequence of the suspension of donor support, but it was mostly the result of the tensions and uncertainties created by liberalisation and the election, the clashes and the state's actions to secure KANU's victory. Concerned by the risk of instability, businesses scaled down investment. Tourism, Kenya's largest foreign exchange earner, weakened as talk of 'tribal warfare' frightened visitors away. At the same time, the Goldenberg scandal (see below) bled the Central Bank dry of foreign exchange. Growth fell to near-zero in 1992 and 1993. At the same time, inflation was rising rapidly: to 20 per cent in 1991 and 27 per cent in 1992.[153]

In 1992, Kenya for the first time defaulted on its foreign debt, a response to the loss of assistance but also to Goldenberg, price and exchange rate liberalisation and rising state spending. The Central Bank devalued the shilling, but there was a growing

9.8: Dollar exchange rates and currency in circulation, 1978–98

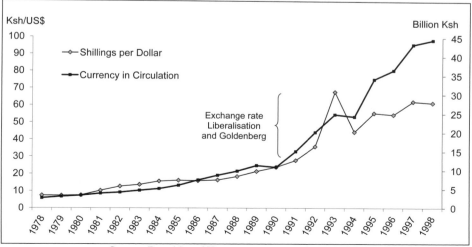

Source: Republic of Kenya, *Statistical Abstracts*, 1982–2003, year-end figures

discrepancy between regulated and deregulated rates.[154] Foreign exchange reserves fell to critical levels, with even international airlines refused foreign exchange.[155] The crisis can be seen in the exchange rate 'spike' of 1992–3, which reflected not only the effect of liberalisation but also the impact of gross market abuses (see Figure 9.8).

Some of the problems Kenya faced were genuinely external. The year 1992 saw the worst drought since 1983–4, which (combined with the clashes) led to a 4.5 per cent drop in agricultural output, which fell again in 1993. Kenya had to import large quantities of food. Despite their political differences with Kenya, famine relief came in bulk during 1992 and 1993 from the US and the EU. The states north of Kenya were also disintegrating. With the decline and fall of Somalia's government in 1990–2, more than 400,000 Somali took refuge in Kenya, creating a humanitarian crisis. There was a massive international relief effort in Garissa, led by the Red Cross and the United Nations High Commissioner for Refugees (UNHCR), financed by the Americans, to provide food, water and medicine for this exodus. The US also committed itself to a controversial military intervention in December 1992 to secure food supplies and restore order in Somalia. More than 100,000 Ethiopians too sought asylum in Kenya after the fall of the Mengistu regime during 1991–2. The situation worsened further in mid-1992, with a third influx of refugees from southern Sudan into Turkana.[156] Kenya could do little but appeal for help.

KANU's Cash Call and the Goldenberg Scandal, 1990–2

In the late 1980s, there had been a growing volume of gold and precious jewels passing through Nairobi's black market, one of the closest and most accommodating markets for goods smuggled out of Angola, Sudan, Rwanda and the Congo. This trade had come to the notice of the Central Bank and several businessmen and politicians, looking for some way to benefit. These included the Pattni family of Asian jewellers, who were acting as middlemen in buying and on-selling to other businesses, who would then (presumably illegally) export the goods to Europe for foreign exchange. To several groups, the same opportunity presented itself: could they not export the gold legally, earning foreign exchange for Kenya and a margin for themselves? The difference between the black market rate and the official rate for the shilling was a major obstacle though – illegal dollars from gold sold abroad could buy more shillings than legal ones. Extra compensation was needed to make it worth conducting the business legitimately.

According to 25-year-old Kamlesh Pattni, in 1990 he made contact with someone who might help at the highest level: Special Branch head James Kanyotu. Pattni claimed the volume of gold that could pass though Kenya was far higher than previous estimates. Kanyotu in turn saw an opportunity. If, as Pattni claimed, up to US$100 million worth could be exported through Kenya annually, this would provide a much-needed source of legal foreign exchange.[157] With the promise of such large sums, Kanyotu arranged for Pattni to meet Moi, who agreed to increase the level of export compensation on these items from 20 per cent to 35 per cent, to cover the exchange rate 'loss'. Moi also agreed to give the new venture, to be known as Goldenberg International Limited, a monopoly on exports of gold and diamonds. Pattni alleged that Moi asked to become a partner in the venture, to share the proceeds '50:50', with Kanyotu as his proxy. Pattni also claimed that he was asked to deliver a briefcase of Ksh5 million (US$200,000) in cash to Moi as a gift. In July 1990, Goldenberg was incorporated, with Pattni and Kanyotu (described as a 'farmer') as the sole shareholders. Moi flatly denied ever having been a partner in the business. However, relations were certainly close: Pattni had a presidential hotline phone installed in 1992 and the GSU guarded his house. There were also curious links between Biwott and Goldenberg. Pattni's driver, for example, became a director of Biwott's HZ International.[158]

In November 1990, Goldenberg's monopoly was formalised, on condition that the business would 'execute an agreement with Central Bank of Kenya, guaranteeing a minimum annual earnings of…US $50 million …'[159] The government also authorised the secret increase in export compensation, despite the opposition of Treasury officials and advisers. The Export Compensation Act, which set the compensation for non-traditional exports at 20 per cent, was not amended, leaving the payments illegal. Instead, a variance order was signed by Saitoti, paying another 15 per cent *ex gratia*. He also authorised compensation on diamonds, which were not eligible for such payments as no diamonds were mined in Kenya. Pattni alleged that he gave Saitoti a Ksh1 million *harambee* donation to smooth this process.[160]

Goldenberg began operating in December 1990 and quickly grew. A web of relationships developed that included Treasury officials, the Central Bank, the commissioner of customs and excise and the director of mines in order to declare, approve and execute the exports. At some point, someone became greedy. By June 1991, Goldenberg was falsifying invoices, massively overvaluing the gold being exported (to Switzerland and Dubai) in order to gain extra export compensation. By October 1991 Goldenberg was itself illegally importing gold in order to re-export it. This became known after an incident when customs officers seized 30 kilograms of gold dust from the Congo, and were pressured by the commissioner of customs, the commissioner of mines, Kanyotu and CID Director Noah arap Too to release it to Pattni.[161] At some point, someone realised there was no need to export gold at all in order to claim the export compensation. No customs duties were paid at the receiving countries, no documentation was supplied to prove the value of the items, many of the buying companies did not exist and no export documentation was supplied since the objects were all carried out 'by hand'. Where gold was actually exported, it was grossly overvalued. It had become a scheme to print money, and the result was 'exports' of gold worth (on paper) Ksh13 billion (US$400 million).[162] In return, Goldenberg received at least Ksh1.43 billion (US$45 million) (and probably more) in export compensation.[163] Goldenberg was also licensed in April 1991 to become a foreign currency dealer, making it easier to move foreign currency around in order to account for its alleged sales.[164] It was a carefully executed campaign at the highest levels to fleece the state, predating political liberalisation by a year.

Goldenberg and companies associated with Trade Bank, state-owned Post Bank Credit, Biwott and Moi's son Philip also benefited from a new pre-export finance scheme, introduced in December 1990, whereby the government made payments in advance of the actual export, to be repaid once the items had been shipped. Pattni reported that Goldenberg received Ksh8.9 billion (US$170 million) from the Treasury in pre-export finance. As the company had no intention of repaying it, it did not even distinguish the advances from income.[165]

A third front in the scandal opened when Pattni and Kanyotu were licensed to run their own bank, Exchange Bank. By June 1992, Exchange Bank was operating, but avoided actually having any customers. It appears that the bank's main purpose was to hide who was actually receiving the Goldenberg money, as its main commercial activity appeared to be to cash large sums from Goldenberg accounts to representatives of Post Bank Credit, Goldenberg and Youth for KANU '92 (YK'92), a KANU pressure group that played a major role in the 1992 election. Many of the names on the bank accounts to which funds were credited and from which cash was taken were later found to be fictitious.[166] Exchange Bank also handled requests for pre-shipment finance without the required documentation. The Central Bank failed to inspect or control the bank, though officials were suspicious. Meanwhile fraud was piling upon fraud. Fake dollars and stolen travellers' cheques were remitted to London banks, having been recycled through Exchange Bank, in order to demonstrate foreign currency receipts to support Goldenberg's claims for compensation.

KANU's War Chest

KANU knew it would need huge sums of money to fight the election, and by June 1992 it was seeking funds overseas. This included a fundraising appeal in the Middle East by Joshua Kulei and Pattni, but the trip was a disappointment.[167] After this, KANU decided that Goldenberg must finance the party's re-election. Over the next few months, Pattni claimed, Goldenberg, Exchange Bank and Post Bank Credit provided Ksh4.8 billion (US$90 million) in cash, cars and material to the KANU campaign. According to Pattni's records (which were disputed), his cash also found its way to PCs and DCs, lawyers, judges and even the Electoral Commission of Kenya (ECK) chairman. Pattni's money also funded the purchase of maize and rice from the NCPB stores by KANU candidates and DCs which was handed out as famine relief from KANU.[168] Pattni claimed that all this was a loan, to be repaid after the elections. The loans were indeed repaid in 1993, by taking funds from the Central Bank (i.e. taxpayers), a manoeuvre that was probably planned from the start.

While Goldenberg provided most of KANU's election funds, assistance came from many other sources. Indirect contributions were received from almost every parastatal, often by buying land from well-connected individuals. The NSSF was a key source of funds. Funds were believed to have moved from the NSSF to KANU via Mugoya Construction, for example, which was building its pricy Nairobi headquarters.[169] The NSSF also bought properties owned by KANU politicians and their retainers directly. The *Nation* broke one such scandal in November, when it documented how the NSSF had purchased two properties belonging to Sololo Outlets, a company part-owned by YK'92 leader Cyrus Jirongo, for Ksh1.2 billion, vastly more than their estimated value. In August 1992, an account was opened in Post Bank Credit in order to transfer NSSF funds to Sololo, although Post Bank was already insolvent and only surviving on cheque kiting (credit obtained in return for un-banked cheques), fake pre-shipment documents and funds from Goldenberg. In total, Ksh2.5 billion was transferred to Sololo, of which only Ksh900 million came from the NSSF. The rest came from Post Bank Credit itself, without any security, which led to the bank's collapse.[170]

This transaction was not unique. The NSSF made low-interest deposits in other troubled finance institutions, including the National Bank of Kenya, Exchange Bank, Trust Bank, Pan-African Bank, the Commercial Bank of Africa, Consolidated Bank of Kenya, Trans-National Bank and Trade Bank, which then on-lent funds to KANU. There were similar odd transactions in other parastatals. KPTC, under Kalenjin MD Kipng'eno arap Ng'eny, purchased plots of land at inflated prices in October 1992, at the height of the campaign, supplying funds that were believed to have been ended up with KANU. The Kenya Pipeline Company did the same. Mark arap Too was later sued concerning the whereabouts of a US$1 million donation from Rowland to the University of Nairobi, which went to Too in October 1992, but the university had not received.[171]

To get this money into the economy in a form it could use, the government bought bank notes. The currency in circulation more than doubled from Ksh11 billion to Ksh25 billion between 1990 and 1993 (see Figure 9.8).

New Electoral Processes

Although the government had committed itself to a multi-party election, the procedures governing the polls were still unclear. Their definition and fairness consequently became a point of contention between the government, the ECK, the opposition and Western diplomats. Because KANU had staked its survival on a constitutional victory, it had to maintain the image of a free and fair election, and through Parliament it could set the procedures as it wished. Its decisions could be challenged through the courts though, and here the opposition was stronger. Lawyers had led the multi-party movement, and in 1992 they sustained it through a succession of lawsuits contesting every aspect of the election. Western donors too scrutinised each plan for opportunities for rigging and forced the government into a series of concessions that made the process more evenly balanced, but which could still not guarantee the freedom of the polls.

A New Electoral Commission

One of the most controversial issues was the composition and conduct of the ECK, which was responsible for supervising the elections. Forced to take the process away from the provincial administration, in March 1992 legislation abolished the position of supervisor of elections and reinvested all powers in the moribund commission (which Moi still appointed). The 1992 election was therefore the first to be run by the

ECK. Its responsibilities and powers were disputed: the ECK argued for example that it had no authority for voter education, to ensure that the media were impartial or to issue permits for election rallies.[172]

The failure to replace the ECK with a neutral body was a key complaint for the opposition, and its behaviour was the focus of many protests. The ECK initially appeared unwilling to cooperate with or even meet the opposition. Its chairman was Zachaeus Chesoni, a Luhya lawyer whom Moi had appointed in September 1991. Accused by the opposition of incompetence, malevolence and dictatorial behaviour, he was a controversial figure. As the *Monthly News* in August 1992 revealed, Chesoni, once a High Court judge, had been declared bankrupt in 1990 and removed from the bench.[173] Moi had paid off his debts. The Commonwealth suggested (after the election was over) that his appointment was an 'unmistakable signal that the Government would use its powers to secure an advantage for the ruling party'.[174]

There were also disagreements within the ECK, and in November two (Kikuyu) commissioners publicly accused the ECK of 'leadership completely lacking in the basic rudiments of management and administration. It has been the kind of leadership that can only be described as doctored to suit somebody's "special" mission.'[175] In the face of the uproar over the election date and a warning from the Commonwealth, the ECK was forced to adopt a more open attitude (see below), and the situation improved thereafter.

Western Governments and the Election

Western governments and NGOs played a key role throughout 1992 in pressuring Chesoni and the government to hold a fair election. There were numerous visits by law and elections teams working on behalf of donors to force a fairer election. USAID and the International Foundation for Electoral Systems (IFES), for example, ensured that larger ballot boxes were introduced with better seals, and that ballot papers were printed outside the country. They also countered proposals to count presidential ballots for the whole country in one place. Much of the election was also paid for by the West, to ensure that it was conducted properly. The British provided Kenya with ballot boxes and training, for example, while the Americans provided the indelible ink and funded internal monitoring groups.

The Americans were the most vocal. Hempstone regularly pressed Moi to replace Chesoni and to level the playing field, and urged the ECK to meet the opposition. The US struggled to decide which party to prefer, but looked increasingly to the Young Turks, although the US remained doubtful of Odinga himself. KANU in turn distrusted the US and claimed that the CIA funded the opposition. Foreign foundations interested in promoting democracy certainly provided funds to opposition parties.[176] The Americans and Germans also supplied advice and supplies, if not actual cash.

British policy was to support a managed transition to democracy, without any presumption about who should be in power. The gradualist approach of the High Commission towards KANU faced growing criticism during 1992, and resulted in a mid-year change of guard, after which new officials established stronger relations with the opposition. Despite this, FORD remained fearful of covert British support for Moi. There was concern about the British Conservative Party's links with KANU, including their common use of the advertising company Saatchi and Saatchi for their election campaigns.

The Presidential Election Process and the '25 Per Cent Rule'

Victory in the presidential election was the main prize, but the procedures under which it was to be held were unclear, since Kenyans had never voted for a president before. There was a real fear in KANU in early 1992 that they could lose both presidency and Parliament. As a result, under Western pressure to reform the executive presidency, they decided to change the rules to increase Moi's chances of victory and to reduce the cost of possible defeat, while they still had control of the process.

On 3 March 1992, the *Kenya Gazette* published a Constitution of Kenya (Amendment) Bill. This proposed direct presidential elections, the abolition of the vice-presidency and the creation of a prime minister, chosen by the president, who would run the government. Future presidents would be limited to two five-year terms, and checks and balances on presidential powers would be introduced, including impeachment procedures, an end to the 'presidential veto' and provisions for referenda.[177] These proposals were extremely radical, and presaged those of the Constitution of Kenya Review Commission a decade later. Once they were published, however, criticism mounted on all sides. Only a week after it had been approved in Cabinet, the KANU Parliamentary Group rejected the bill and it was withdrawn.[178]

The proposed changes were reformulated over the summer and resubmitted as a new constitutional amendment, passed by the KANU-only Assembly in August 1992. This was far more conservative, making only three changes to the existing provisions. First, it restricted the president to two terms. Second, it prohibited the formation of coalition governments, reflecting KANU's concern that the opposition might win the presidency, but would not win Parliament because of the skewed constituency distribution. This made it far more difficult to create an opposition coalition since a victorious president could no longer share out ministerial rewards. Finally, the Act required that the winning presidential candidate must secure 25 per cent of the vote in at least five of Kenya's eight provinces (the '25 per cent rule'). If the leading candidate failed to achieve 25 per cent in five provinces, there would be a run-off between the two most popular candidates. This clause clearly favoured Moi. He was safe in the Rift Valley, North-Eastern and the Coast, and was likely to reach the 25 per cent mark in Western and Eastern, though he had little chance in Central and Nyanza. None of the opposition leaders had Moi's national coverage. The 25 per cent rule also made North-Eastern Province's 100,000 votes of near-equal importance to Central Province or Nyanza's 1 million. Both the West and the opposition criticised the rule, arguing that provinces were administrative structures and not entities requiring representation, but to little effect.

Voter Registration, June–July 1992

Voter registration lasted for six weeks during June and July 1992. Registration rates were low for the first month because FORD, the DP and church leaders boycotted the exercise. This was part of their campaign to replace the ECK with an impartial body and to force concessions on the issue of identity cards, which had not been distributed to many young Kenyans, most of whom were believed to favour the opposition. It was a failure, however; the government called their bluff, Western donors were sceptical of a boycott of the first multi-party polls since independence, and it was hard to persuade most politicians to abide by the policy either. Just before the closure date, the opposition conceded, and called for their supporters to register. Faced with thousands thronging the registration centres, the government granted two brief extensions, but registration closed with many still queuing.

The registration process saw widespread abuses. In many 'KANU zones', residence requirements were not checked and under-age voters were registered; pro-KANU Rift Valley seats showed extremely high registration rates. There were also claims that some officials made it difficult for people from opposition-supporting communities to register. As Hempstone acerbically noted, 'the same wonderful people (the provincial commissioners, district commissioners and KANU mayors) who gave Kenya the blatantly rigged election of 1988 are conducting the registration of voters today.'[179] The register was not computerised, so cross-checking for double-registration was not possible, and there was organised transport of voters from safe seats into marginal and urban areas, mostly by KANU. There were also changes in registration figures after the close of the exercise. There appears to have been a systematic process of registration continuing in secret in over 50 seats across the nation.[180] Overall, about 100,000 voters 'appeared' after the close of formal registration. The main beneficiaries were KANU and to a lesser extent FORD-Asili.

In the end, 7.9 million adults registered to vote, only a few more than in the last free elections in 1983. The Luo districts were particularly under-registered, reflecting the effect of FORD's boycott. The ECK insisted that only 9.6 million individuals were eligible, but others suggested that Kenya's adult population was much larger. The Commonwealth, for example, believed that the ECK had underestimated the number unregistered by 1 million.[181]

Election Mechanics

The constituency boundaries used for the 1992 election were unchanged. Although the Constitution had been amended in 1991 to expand the number of seats to 210, the ECK abandoned its review mid-way through. As a result, the predominance of the rural population over the urban and of the pastoral voters over more agricultural communities remained, favouring KANU. Although it did not affect the presidential election, the discrepancy in constituency size made it hard for a Kikuyu and Luo-centred opposition to win a parliamentary majority. The average safe KANU constituency had only 28,000 voters, while seats in pro-opposition areas averaged 52,000 voters.[182]

Parliament decided during the summer that voting would take place in the local government, parliamentary and presidential elections at the same time, and that, for the first time, votes would be counted in each constituency, rather than brought to district headquarters. This reduced opportunities for tampering with ballot boxes. For the first time since independence, the government also conceded that the returning and presiding officers not be officers of the provincial administration, because of concerns over malpractice. However, many of the chosen officials were retired members of the administration, soldiers or lower-rank officials. While most officials acted with probity, staff sympathetic to KANU took up positions in areas that the government saw as vital to its victory. Several presiding officers and deputies were later caught campaigning, mainly for KANU. There were also concerns about the clerks who would mark the registers, issue ballot papers and count votes. In targeted seats, their preferences for KANU were widely known.[183]

The ballot papers followed the British model, with the name of the candidate and his party, and a space for a cross to be inserted. The printing of the papers also became a point of contention, as the opposition feared the government would print extra ballots, to facilitate rigging. It was eventually agreed that they would be printed abroad. The 35,000 ballot boxes were also imported from Britain.

Setting the Date

The 1992 election followed the same pattern as previous contests, with one unique twist. The first stage was the dissolution of Parliament on 21 October; government employees then had to resign their positions, and the election date was announced. During this process, the government tried to catch the opposition unprepared by a blatantly illegal action that confirmed doubts about the independence and autonomy of Wako and Chesoni. In a legal notice on 23 October 1992, the attorney-general's office secretly 'corrected' the regulations governing the number of days between the party primaries and the nominations from 'not less' to 'not more' than 21 days, using his power to rectify a 'clerical or printing error' to a law. Clearly in collusion, on 3 November, Chesoni announced the election date as 7 December. Nomination day was set for 13 November, giving the opposition only 10 days to select their candidates. The government hoped to catch the opposition unprepared and to minimise defections from KANU.

The plan failed. The opposition immediately took the ECK to court and Justice Thomas Mbaluto bravely ruled on 12 November that no errors had been adduced in the law, so no correction was required, and that the attorney-general's action was illegal. On 16 November, therefore, Chesoni announced that the new nomination and polling days would be 9 and 29 December 1992.[184]

Observing the Elections

Back in April, Moi had invited the Commonwealth and other democracy watchdogs to observe the elections, in order to secure international recognition for his victory. As a result, unlike previous Kenyan elections, the 1992 polls were well monitored by foreign observers, though much of the monitoring was organised very late, and plans were handicapped by the change of election date, as many delegates were unwilling to miss Christmas at home. The main observer groups came from the International Republican Institute (IRI) and the Commonwealth, which both dispatched advance teams of Africanists and supplemented them by a larger number of delegates in the run-up to the polls. These teams helped raise awareness internationally and pressured the government to keep the electoral process fair. There were also 60 individual diplomats and observers from various countries and bodies.

Three observer teams were denied entry or withdrew before the election. The National Democratic Institute sent a delegation to Kenya in February 1992, but partly as a result of its critical report, the Kenyan government refused it permission to monitor the elections. The US Carter Center was also denied accreditation, and Germany withdrew its team since they believed the process was fatally flawed.

Although the international monitors received most attention, a domestic effort would have to provide the bulk of supervision on the ground. Western governments and foundations therefore funded and organised an internal monitoring process. Many religious and secular groups made funding requests to establish such bodies. Most were fused together into one alliance just before the elections, known as the National Election Monitoring Unit (NEMU). NEMU coordinated the recruitment and training of 5,000 observers. It focussed most of its attention on KANU, anticipating rigging and was often seen as pro-opposition – partly because it was operationally led by (Kikuyu) lawyer Grace Githu, chaired by the NCCK's Samuel Kobia (Meru) and including in its council of elders ex-CBK head Duncan Ndegwa (Kikuyu).[185]

The Election Campaign

With FORD's split, the election was under way. On 28 October, Moi dissolved Parliament, and over the next three weeks mass defections revealed how weak KANU's control had been, even of the 'class of 88'. Rather than sinking or swimming with their master, 10 per cent of KANU's MPs defected to the opposition, including another minister (Luo Onyango Midika), seven assistant ministers and the chief whip. Some had long been agents of the opposition in Parliament; others defected for personal advantage. The exodus was near-complete amongst Kikuyu MPs. If ethnicity had in part been the *means* of expression of conflict, it had by now broken free of its creators, and became the *essence* of competition in Central Province, the Kalenjin Rift and Luo Nyanza. Outside Kikuyu areas, the drift to the opposition was weaker, but they picked up important catches in Ukambani, Western, the Coast and North-Eastern. KANU's purse strings ensured that the exodus was limited, however.

The election campaign was fought at three different levels. Local government candidates fought as individuals, allied to parties, to parliamentary candidates and to their party's presidential nominee. Parliamentary candidates did the same, although they stressed national issues more strongly, while presidential candidates competed nationally through speeches, rallies and the media. Voters' preferences appeared to be driven primarily by whether they were for the government or for change, a choice driven by their community's perceived collective ethnic, regional, economic and patronage alignment as much as by individual self-interest. Voters who had decided to vote against KANU then tended to favour the strongest opposition party in the area, though the relationship between parties and wealthy and influential candidates was complex and bi-directional.

Although the result of the election had already been influenced by the registration of voters and by the ethnic cleansing of non-Kalenjin from the Rift Valley, KANU still faced a major challenge. More than 60 seats in Nairobi, Central Province, Nakuru, Laikipia, and Luo Nyanza were effectively lost to the opposition. Only wholesale rigging could have secured a KANU victory here, and such brazen manipulation could not be concealed. Roughly 60 seats were safe pro-government areas, so the real campaign was in the remaining 70 seats in the settlement zones and marginal communities. KANU and the government, almost indistinguishable in practice, walked a tightrope throughout. They had to hold an election that they could not blatantly rig, but could not afford to lose.

The Selection of Presidential Candidates

The first step for the parties was to select the presidential candidates who would represent their parties. There had never been a contested presidential primary in Kenya, and this changed little in 1992 – a reflection of the dominance of individuals in the political system. Moi was nominated unopposed for KANU, Kibaki was unopposed for the DP, while Odinga was selected automatically as he was FORD-Kenya's chairman.

The sole primary election took place inside FORD-Asili. Since the presidential nomination process had been one of the core points of disagreement between FORD factions, it was essential that Asili hold an open primary. Matiba and Shikuku were the main candidates, and the election was held by a secret ballot of all party members, carried out at the same time as the local government and parliamentary primaries on 10–12 November 1992. The result was a convincing win for Matiba by 850,000 votes to Shikuku's 440,000. The voting was ethnically polarised, with Matiba sweeping Kikuyu and Embu areas, while Shikuku won 96 per cent of the votes in Western. To the surprise of many who had predicted his defection to KANU, Shikuku accepted defeat and continued to work with Matiba. It is near-certain, however, that these figures were falsified to help FORD-Asili survive. The huge turnout in Western Province was imaginary, as was demonstrated when FORD-Asili polled less than half this number of votes in the general election proper. It did not reinforce impressions of the probity of FORD-Asili, but, aided by positive press coverage, the primary results helped it survive these crucial weeks.

The Parliamentary Primaries, November 1992

The second stage was to select each party's candidate for the 188 parliamentary constituencies and numerous civic seats. All candidates still had to be nominated by a political party, but with 10 parties now registered, most politicians were able to find a home. No formal procedure had existed for party nominations since 1982, as legislation only required that candidates be nominated in accordance with the rules of their party. Partly as a result, all the primaries were badly organised and subject to massive fraud. Rigging was particularly severe in KANU, but every party was willing to cheat, annul results and ignore its own procedures in order to ensure that particular candidates won or lost.[186] The sordid nature of the process was revealed as much in the reaction of the losers as the technicalities of the process. It was rare for losers in marginal seats to remain with their party. The press was full of defections and some candidates moved through three parties in three weeks.

In over half the constituencies, the primary would decide who would become the MP, as one party was clearly dominant. In many ways, therefore, these primaries resembled Kenya's previous general elections. This competition focused on personal and factional issues, many of them the same cleavages that had been articulated during the single-party era. A by-product was a dramatic opening of political space quite separate from (though driven by) the multi-party elections to follow. Parties could no longer impose unpopular candidates through rigged elections without risking mass defections. Each party therefore used the primaries to find the best candidate, sometimes even poaching candidates from other parties, against the wishes of local officials.

KANU's primaries were the best organised and the most abused. Whether conducted by queue voting or secret ballot, the result was chaos. KANU had no up-to-date registers of members and partisanship ran high. There were allegations of rigging in two-thirds of constituencies, ranging from violence to gross electoral fraud. The use of cash payments to queuing voters provided an easy means of fixing the result. PCs and DCs campaigned for particular KANU candidates or participated in electoral abuses in more than a dozen districts. Once the first cycle was completed, the battle started to reverse those results that did not satisfy the dominant local faction, or that had chosen candidates whom the central party thought too unpopular to win the seat. More than 100 protests were heard by an appeals tribunal, and over 30 primaries were eventually rerun, but little changed as a result. Many losers defected to the opposition, determined to return to Parliament on any party that would have them. At least six of FORD-Asili's and six of the DP's candidates were KANU primary losers, and the more desperate FORD-Kenya took 10. KANU also lured defectors from the opposition. At least seven of KANU's parliamentary candidates had been DP and FORD leaders a few weeks before, and KANU won two or three seats as a result. In the end, nearly half of KANU's 155 incumbents were defeated, including three out-of-favour ministers, while the 72-year-old Jeremiah Nyagah decided to retire, passing the political baton to his sons, two of whom were politically active.

Most of the other parties followed processes similar to KANU's, with greater efforts to ensure transparency, but faced similar difficulties where they were likely to win the election. Most FORD-Kenya nominations were held using an electoral college method, whereby local officials and delegates voted for the candidate in a secret ballot. As nomination day loomed, however, FORD-Kenya still had no candidates in many seats, and took defectors from other parties, regardless of the official processes. Just before the election, the unregistered IPK and FORD-Kenya formed a marriage of convenience, whereby IPK members received FORD-Kenya's nominations in Mombasa and Malindi in return for Muslim support for the party.

The DP held its primaries mainly by secret ballots of party members. In the Coast, the north-east, Western Province and Nyanza, they were poorly attended. In contrast, in Central and Eastern Provinces, Laikipia and Nakuru, turnouts were high and protests numerous. In the central Rift, candidates were selected rather than elected, since it was too dangerous to hold an open contest, but the DP now became KANU's main opponent, as several KANU losers, including Moi's old business partner Henry Cheboiwo, defected to the DP.

FORD-Asili's nominations were held by secret ballot at the same time as its presidential polls. Most of its candidates were unopposed outside Central and Western Provinces and Nakuru, reflecting its underdog status. The *Weekly Review* played up its nominations, reflecting KANU's desire to ensure that the factions remained balanced.

Parliamentary and Presidential Nominations

Parliamentary nomination day was 9 December. Over most of the country, candidates submitted their papers without hindrance. However, in the Rift Valley and neighbouring areas, at least 54 opposition candidates were refused nomination or were physically attacked in order to prevent them submitting their papers within the five-hour time window. These abuses affected 37 constituencies, mainly in Baringo, Elgeyo-Marakwet, Nandi, Kericho and Bomet, in Wajir in North-Eastern Province and in Kilifi and Busia.[187] There was open collusion between KANU, police and district officials. In Baringo and Elgeyo-Marakwet, 15 of the 16 opposition candidates were kidnapped by mobs, beaten or prevented from presenting their papers. In Turkana South, a policeman snatched the DP candidate's nomination papers at gunpoint. He was later promoted.[188] As NEMU noted, 'No-one was reported arrested or charged before a court of law for this perpetration of violence.'[189]

As a result, KANU was unopposed in 18 parliamentary seats, in only three or four of which was there genuinely no opposition. KANU would have won these seats in a fair fight, but it was a matter of pride that the party should demonstrate overwhelming popularity in its homelands. Party strategists wanted to save resources to use elsewhere, and to transport voters to marginal seats. In addition, by ensuring there would be no parliamentary elections in the Kalenjin areas, KANU ensured a far lower vote for the opposition presidential candidates.

The opposition parties were furious, and threatened to boycott the election if the ECK did not nullify the central Rift nominations. The British, Americans and the Commonwealth all protested. On 13 December, the Commonwealth advance team warned that the election would be '. . . severely compromised if the end result was that a substantial number of prospective candidates would be unable to contest the elections'.[190] In the end, opposition leaders decided that it was better to fight the election and win some seats than boycott and receive nothing. They had invested too much money and effort to withdraw without return, and central party control was too weak to prevent some candidates standing in any case. The ECK refused to help those who had been abducted, on the basis that electoral malpractice could only be remedied by a petition.[191]

Meanwhile, the opposition sought injunctions against elections taking place where their candidates had been barred. This briefly created a problem for KANU, since these seats were vital to its parliamentary majority. Victory in the courts was, therefore, essential. The first suit was that of the DP's Cheboiwo in Baringo North. The judge accepted Cheboiwo's argument and issued an injunction restraining the ECK from declaring his opponent as the MP.[192] KANU appealed, but the Appeal Court upheld the injunction. FORD-Asili had requested an identical injunction against Moi's unopposed election as MP for Baringo Central. This was a crucial case, since Moi would be ineligible for the presidency if he were not elected as an MP. The Baringo Central case, however, was heard separately from the others by the controversial British Judge Dugdale, who dismissed it on the grounds that it was 'wrongfully brought to court, was misconceived and premature'.[193] Dugdale refused to accept the Appeal Court's Cheboiwo ruling, which he was bound by law to follow.[194] The High Court eventually issued four more injunctions on behalf of FORD-Asili and DP candidates. How these cases differed from Moi's was not clear.

The result of the parties' existing regional focus and the abuses of nomination day was that while KANU had candidates in all 188 parliamentary seats, the other parties were far weaker. The DP was now KANU's strongest opponent, with 153 candidates.[195] Overall, 716 parliamentary candidates were nominated from nine parties. Many were new to the parliamentary process, as multi-party politics brought a new swathe of aspirants into the field. Still, it was no simplistic situation of compromised old KANU leaders versus innocent young opposition professionals. More than a third of the opposition's candidates had stood for Parliament under KANU's colours in 1983 or 1988. Permanent secretaries, ministers and senior figures from earlier governments loomed large in the ranks of the DP. Lawyers played a strong role in FORD-Kenya, while FORD-Asili was the party of the self-made men: small businessmen, many of them little-known. Multi-party elections did not change the need for candidates to have a birthplace or ethnic origin in the constituency. Outside the urban areas and the settlement zones, candidates directly reflected the ethnicity of their constituents.[196]

Unlike the parliamentary nominations, presidential nomination day on 14 December passed peacefully. There were eight nominated candidates: those of the four main parties, plus Chibule wa Tsuma for the KNC, Anyona for the KSC, David Mukaru Ng'ang'a for the Kenya National Democratic Alliance (KENDA) and John Harun Mwau, the enigmatic 'boss' of the Party of Independent Candidates of Kenya (PICK).

KANU's Campaign Strategy

KANU's campaign strategy was a conservative one, stressing that it was the party of 'Stability and Progress'. Its manifesto stressed the party's achievements since 1963 and its nationwide support. Under pressure from the opposition and the West, KANU promised 'accountability and transparency in the management of public affairs', the privatisation of all non-strategic parastatals and the complete removal of exchange controls.[197]

As incumbent governments often do, KANU targeted groups of voters with policy changes and benefits designed to ensure their support. During 1992, it created four new districts, bringing administration closer to the people and offering a patronage opportunity to local leaders. In May, Moi raised wages and announced the resumption of city commuter trains.[198] In July, the government revised the 8–4–4 education system, and raised salaries for teachers and civil servants.[199] In Nyanza and Western provinces, Moi ordered that farmers be paid for their sugar deliveries, that roads be resurfaced and factories rehabilitated. On 12 December, Moi raised the minimum wage, announced new benefits for women civil servants, directed that Muslims be allowed time off work on Fridays to pray and raised the amount of foreign currency they could take on the Haj.[200]

KANU's campaign in the field was somewhat different, and was based on the tactics of 'bribe and tribe'. In the Kalenjin homeland, KANU stressed that the presidency would be taken away unless the people voted for Moi. In the northern and southern periphery of the Rift Valley, North-Eastern, Isiolo and Marsabit, KANU used heavy administrative pressure to minimise the impact of defectors, and to ensure that the non-'indigenous' residents either did not vote or voted for KANU. The ruling party abandoned Central Province and Luo Nyanza (bar a few ministerial seats) and poured resources into Kisii and Coast, Eastern and Western.

KANU also relied heavily on negative campaigning. Its leaders condemned the opposition as tribalists. They accused the DP of being GEMA in disguise, suggesting that Karume was the real DP leader, and whipped up fears among pastoralists that a Kikuyu victory would mean that their land would be taken for Kikuyu settlement. It also worked to exacerbate Kikuyu–Luo rivalries, to ensure that the opposition did not negotiate an electoral pact. The *Kenya Times* and its unashamedly partisan 'KANU' Briefs' (written by journalists and academics for hire), for example, highlighted previous conflicts between the Kikuyu and Luo.[201] The opposition leaders were also targets for personal attack. Odinga was criticised as old, infirm, an atheist and having done nothing to develop Luoland. Kibaki was a 'fence sitter' and an alcoholic, who had mismanaged the economy as finance minister. Matiba was crippled and mad, and had resigned only when his own position was threatened. KANU also attacked Kibaki and Matiba for grabbing land and ethnic bias in their appointments when in power. In contrast, Moi was marketed as a Christian, in good physical and mental health.

KANU knew it was vulnerable on the issue of the ethnic clashes. Its response was classically authoritarian: to blame the opposition for the violence. Muite's comments that a rigged victory for Moi would lead inexorably to violent conflict were frequently repeated under the headline 'Muite Calls for Civil War'.[202] Throughout 1992, Moi attempted to deflect blame for the clashes through allegations of military preparations by the opposition and accusations that FORD had incited the clashes.[203] KANU even tried to blame them on the CIA.[204] On

20 November, Moi declared that 150 opposition-trained guerrillas had entered Kenya from Uganda and were poised to create chaos.[205] No one appears to have been charged concerning any of these incidents, and it is doubtful whether the claims had any basis in fact.

One of the most extraordinary aspects of the 1992 election was the role played by pressure groups for KANU in candidate selection, campaign organisation and the distribution of funds. The strongest of these organisations, Youth for KANU '92 (YK'92), was launched in March 1992 as a campaign organisation of young professionals. Its chairman, Cyrus Jirongo, a 31-year-old Luhya estate agent, was little-known prior to his emergence.[206] YK'92 soon set up campaign groups in most districts, and more than 30 smaller organisations were established to campaign for KANU, and to share in the vast sums that were made available to them.

These organisations had several aims. Most important, they were a means to transfer money into the political arena, bypassing the scrutiny that KANU itself faced. Second, YK'92 provided a means by which a few insiders could influence events in constituencies where they distrusted the local party machine. YK'92 served as the president's hit team during the primaries, and helped to remove ineffective or compromised incumbents in order to maximise Moi's vote. Its campaign was personalised around Moi, and many district KANU bosses distrusted it. Third, YK'92 was a public relations exercise. Media coverage focused on these young KANU leaders, more articulate and credible than the old hardliners.

The Cash Dispensers

In practice, KANU's strategy depended less upon policy than upon material considerations. The party spent extraordinary sums of money on its campaign, much of which came from Goldenberg. KANU candidates received large sums from the centre, and spared no expense in voter transport and rallies. KANU purchased hundreds of press advertisements and produced sophisticated television broadcasts, as well as financing posters, T-shirts and other gifts. Many candidates drove new Pajeros (courtesy of Pattni), while Moi and Saitoti used helicopters to move from rally to rally. Those attending its meetings were often paid in cash or kind. Moi made large personal donations to projects in Western Province in October and November. Parastatal loans were also used for political purposes. The *Nairobi Weekly Observer* alleged that the government's rural enterprise programme offered loans to voters on condition that they voted for KANU, and that the AFC had created the expectation amongst some of those receiving loans in the build-up to the election that they would soon be written off.[207]

The most successful tactic was the direct distribution of food and cash to voters. A 1992 amendment had removed the Ksh40,000 limit on election spending and as a result, KANU ran a campaign in which money was near-unlimited (though bribery was still technically illegal). KANU candidates bought votes house-to-house, paying cash for promises of support.[208] KANU was not the only party to hand out money: Matiba gave large sums for beer and treats for the voters and DP and FORD-Asili candidates also handed out money on polling day, but KANU's spending was on a different scale.

KANU also distributed famine relief at party meetings. In June 1992, the state had relaxed restrictions on the movement of maize. On 30 October, however, President Moi again banned maize movements, to suspicion that the ban was designed to increase the dependence of famine-hit areas on state largesse.[209] The World Bank cancelled its agricultural sector reform programme and loans as a result. In Ukambani, Embu, Meru, Tharaka-Nithi, Isiolo, Samburu, Turkana and North-Eastern Province KANU officials and chiefs are known to have distributed Goldenberg's food at KANU rallies or to KANU members only.[210]

KANU also used its financial power and administrative strength to target opposition parliamentary candidates. Between nomination day and polling day, more than 50 (10 per cent of their total) rejoined the ruling party. Such defections brought more than publicity; once nominated, a candidate could not be replaced on the ballot, but would garner little support. As a result, by 29 December KANU was unopposed in nine more seats. Nearly half of North-Eastern and the Rift Valley was theirs without a contest. In these areas, the state was powerful, the opposition candidates were poor and their chances of victory uncertain, leaving them vulnerable to intimidation and bribery. In the opposition heartlands, however, few defected. No matter how much the government offered, the risks associated with defection to KANU remained greater.

The Opposition Campaign

The opposition's campaigns addressed many of the same issues as KANU's and with some of the same tactics. Policy was not at the forefront of the debate and most voters were unaware of the parties' manifesto promises, which were targeted as much at Western donors as at Kenyans. Like KANU, the opposition targeted specific regions and mixed discussion of national issues with local promises and ethnic appeals. FORD-Kenya was the most policy-oriented of the parties, but suffered as a result, fighting a Western-style media campaign where on-the-ground organisation remained the key to success.

The presidential candidates criss-crossed the country with their entourages. Moi, Kibaki and Odinga all focused on marginal Western and Eastern provinces, the Coast and Nakuru. They also occasionally ventured into their rivals' strongholds in order to show that they had a national following. Matiba's campaign was different, leaving Western to Shikuku and focusing on Kikuyu areas, with his populist slogan 'Let the People Decide' and a simple message of unconditional trust and radical change. He articulated the grievances of the Kikuyu masses and drew support from the poorest in society.

Some unity of purpose remained amongst the non-FORD-Asili opposition, and they produced a joint (donor-funded) manifesto, the *Post Election Action Programme*, in November. FORD had already produced the *Charter for the Second Liberation*, and FORD-Kenya took this over with few changes. With most of the intellectuals backing Odinga, FORD-Asili wrote no manifesto, relying instead on eulogies of Matiba. The DP's manifesto outlined liberal economic policies similar to those of the others, but with more emphasis on the economy and private enterprise.[211]

All the opposition parties blamed KANU for the problems in Kenya's economy. The DP in particular received support from the business community, but there was no direct linkage between the parties and particular class or agricultural interests. Although KANU better represented pastoral and land-rich interests and those of large grain growers, all four big parties represented the full range of economic interests. As Steve Orvis noted, for example, coffee, tea and dairy farmers alike voted for KANU, the DP or FORD-Asili, their choice depending primarily on their ethnicity.[212] While all the parties promised to improve services and to address poverty, the populist FORD-Asili stressed action on unemployment more than liberalisation. Because Moi generally took a nationalist line, demanding indigenous solutions to Africa's problems, and the opposition saw Western governments as their lifeline of support, there was support for both economic and political liberalisation in the opposition parties. This was to prove only a temporary alliance.

Corruption had been one of the driving forces behind the move to multi-partyism, and FORD-Kenya took the lead in a series of press statements, letters to embassies, and advertisements publicising crimes in KPLC, the Kenya Meat Commission, the sugar industry and the Turkwell Gorge project.[213] Another theme was the state's use of violence against its opponents and its inability to maintain order. The ethnic clashes and the deaths of Ouko and Muge fuelled deep opposition anger. The DP press campaign highlighted photographs of a murdered clash victim, reminding voters of KANU's responsibility for the violence.

The opposition parties most clearly differentiated themselves from KANU by their emphasis on the need to improve human rights. They promised to end detention without trial, abolish the Public Order Act and the Chiefs Act, end the special identity card requirements for Somali Kenyans and restore the independence of the judiciary. While most politicians demanded a fair fight under the existing rules, some NGO leaders went further, calling for a constitutional convention to write a new constitution and for the formation of a government of national unity, similar to that of 1962. They lacked the capacity to bring this about, however, since KANU had no intention of complying.

The opposition parties also used their presidential candidates' achievements in their campaigns. Odinga's supporters stressed Jaramogi's history of dissent, his sacrifices and his ability to work with a team. Kibaki's supporters stressed his experience as a minister and his ability to create growth. FORD-Asili stressed Matiba's commercial acumen, his role in the campaign for multi-party politics and his willingness to stand up to Moi. There was little love between Matiba and the other opposition leaders: FORD-Kenya blamed Matiba for breaking up the party, while the DP saw him as standing in the way of Kikuyu unity. Both believed that he was too much of a megalomaniac to hold power. His opponents made less of Matiba's illness than one might expect, since the severity of his problem was only recognised after the election. FORD-Asili in turn castigated Odinga as senile and Kibaki as having already ruined the economy once. Matiba and his candidates also accused Kibaki of cowardice and betrayal, having failed to stand up for Kikuyu interests when he was vice-president or to speak out when Matiba was detained. The battle became increasingly fraught as Kikuyu voters moved towards FORD-Asili. In response, the DP promoted the idea that Matiba was a stooge of the ruling party and was receiving money from KANU.

Like KANU, the opposition parties also appealed to ethnic solidarity, particularly amongst the Kikuyu, Luo and Bukusu. Such tactics could only be employed in small-scale meetings, as all the parties needed to present themselves as nationwide organisations. Nonetheless, the economic importance of victory to the local ethnic community was quietly stressed. Sub-group and clan rivalries, while no longer dominant, still played a role, and districts such as Kisii saw clear alignments between clans and parties. Finally, opposition candidates campaigned on local issues. All parliamentary candidates stressed what they would do for the area in the traditional pork barrel style, demonstrating their political virility by their contributions to the constituency, in what was increasingly becoming an election tax.

None of the opposition parties could match KANU's financial resources. The DP was KANU's wealthiest competitor, funded by businessmen. FORD-Asili was founded on Matiba's personal fortune, though it too received contributions from the business community. FORD-Kenya was the poorest of the main parties. It could afford little advertising, and was appealing for funds up to polling day.

Church and State

The support of the mainstream churches was critical throughout 1992 in sustaining the opposition. While they did not actively campaign for particular parties, they supported the appointment of an impartial electoral commission and reforms in voter registration. They were most deeply angered, however, by the ethnic clashes, and openly intervened in the political system to demand action. In April 1992, a delegation of Catholic and NCCK bishops accused Moi of complicity in the clashes, saying: 'the people have lost confidence in you.'[214] Following demands from the Catholics and the NCCK in May that he should resign, Moi even threatened the NCCK with de-registration.[215]

Although the churches helped nurture the opposition and observe the election, they were far from united. The major denominations tacitly supported the opposition, while some independent churches and Moi's African Inland Church backed KANU. Different religious groups canvassed for different candidates, generally on an ethnic basis (in the CPK, for example, Kikuyu Archbishop Kuria backed FORD-Asili while Luo Bishop Okullu backed FORD-Kenya) and in some constituencies religious affiliation was an indicator of voter preference. More than a dozen parliamentary candidates were clergymen or prominent church members.

If the Christian churches were generally aligned with the opposition, Kenya's Muslims (5 to 8 per cent of Kenya's population) were hardly united behind the state either. Islam has played a growing role in Kenya's politics since the 1980s, and in 1990–2 many Arab, Swahili and Mijikenda Muslims turned against KANU. The

IPK did not vanish after it was refused registration, but continued to organise. Radical preachers, particularly 'Sheikh' Balala in Mombasa, used the mosques to criticise KANU and call for change. Balala built a coalition between Mombasa's Arab elite and the African faithful, drawing on their rejection of Western values and resentment at local economic difficulties. In response, KANU organised a Digo youth militia to fight the IPK and to intimidate upcountry voters.[216] The result was a violent conflict in Mombasa and Lamu, which led to street fighting and arrests in 1992–3 and proved to be the foundation for the more serious violence of 1997.

The Role of the Media

The period since 1990 had seen a flowering of independent weekly magazines, as *Society*, *Finance*, the *Nairobi Law Monthly* and later the *Nairobi Weekly Observer* and the *Economic Review* tapped into the market for anti-government material. They were popular amongst the educated elite, although they had little circulation outside the city. During 1992, these publications pushed the state's tolerance to the limit. The government, unused to criticism, responded aggressively, and all these journals experienced harassment, with thousands of copies of *Finance* and *Society* seized by police. Editors were arrested and faced libel and sedition charges, leading to more Western protests.[217] The OP also directed that no public institutions should advertise in any of these magazines.[218] Despite this, most were still publishing by polling day, and their invective against KANU ('Filth and Scum' was a characteristic headline in *Finance*) became even more bitter.

The most important medium for communicating issues and events remained the daily newspapers, though they practised self-censorship on the most sensitive stories; warnings from ministers or State House were frequent and journalists were questioned by police or attacked when they strayed where they were not wanted.[219] Nonetheless, during 1992, the Nation Group became the informal voice of the opposition. Attacked by the government for being Kikuyu-dominated, the *Nation* focused on scandals involving KANU and relations became extremely strained. The *Standard* in contrast generally favoured KANU, but coverage fluctuated as journalists, editors and proprietor Rowland contested the newspaper's line. The *Kenya Times* was unashamedly partisan and blacked out the opposition entirely, except to emphasise the ethnic rivalries in FORD and to blame multi-party democracy for the clashes. The print media also sensationalised the election, stressing conflict rather than policy. The foreign media reported frequently on the polls; most Western papers stressed recent tensions, fears of electoral abuses and 'tribal' divisions and were generally favourable to the opposition.

KANU retained stronger control on the broadcast media. Although in 1989 the Voice of Kenya had become the Kenya Broadcasting Corporation (KBC), making it 'semi-autonomous', it remained under government editorial control, with ex-minister Julius Kiano as its chairman. More variety emerged for Nairobi residents with the licensing of a competing broadcaster, the Kenya Television Network in 1990. KTN did try to chart an independent course, but it still suffered from editorial interference.[220] Despite more than 20 applications between 1985 and 1995, the state refused all investors' requests to set up truly independent commercial broadcasting.

As a result, throughout 1992 the opposition was prevented from advertising on radio or television, and its activities were ignored or denigrated. The KBC openly campaigned for KANU, devoting little time to the opposition parties. It reported only defections to, not from, KANU, and gave great prominence to YK'92. KTN gave more coverage to the opposition, but was only available in Nairobi. Control of radio broadcasting was even stricter.[221] KBC radio, broadcasting in English, Swahili and vernacular languages, was more influential and even more biased. Rural voters were less well informed, and KANU's victory depended upon control of the less-developed districts. It was only during the campaign proper that an effort was made to redress the balance. After a lawsuit from FORD-Kenya and pressure from the Commonwealth, the government announced in November that equal coverage would be given on both radio and television. Nevertheless, little changed. In November and December, KANU was the focus of half of KBC's television news time, while the opposition parties got less than 5 per cent each. On the radio, KANU received six times the airtime of the other parties combined. Moi was portrayed as a great leader and KANU as the party of national unity, while opposition leaders were tribal and trivial.[222]

News reports were not the only way for a party to communicate its message. For the first time, political parties advertised extensively in the press and on television, although KBC turned down all FORD-Asili and DP radio advertisements.[223] Kenya did not offer free airtime or state funding for parties; money thus played a key role and KANU again made full use of its advantage, festooning the papers, the radio and television with advertisements.

There were virtually no media-funded opinion polls, but NEMU published two polls that predicted the results reasonably accurately, showing a narrow lead for Moi, with Kibaki second, Matiba third and Odinga last.[224] Other KANU-funded polls were published with deliberate distortions, inflating Moi's results and reducing Kibaki's, to create a bandwagon effect in KANU's favour.

Violence, Intimidation and Administrative Bias in the Campaign

The provincial administration had always been an arm of the government. Now, DCs and PCs campaigned for KANU and harassed its opponents across at least half the country. They played a greater role in KANU's campaign than either YK'92 or the formal party apparatus. Even opposition presidential candidates were assaulted, threatened and refused permission to campaign in areas that KANU felt it should win. Opposition leaders were denied access to the Kalenjin 'KANU zones', and entry to North-Eastern Province, Tana River, Marsabit and Isiolo also proved very difficult, leaving their candidates isolated and vulnerable. Opposition presidential cavalcades were routinely stopped and searched. Although the 14 days' notice rule was waived, meetings still had to be licensed, and permits were frequently withdrawn at the last minute. FORD-Kenya ventured furthest into KANU territory, and consequently experienced the greatest intimidation. During November, Odinga's entourage was stoned, riot police dispersed his rallies, and many of his meetings were banned. When Kibaki toured Western Province and the western Rift in December, he too was harassed by the administration and his meetings were broken up by riot police or attacked by KANU youth.

KANU supporters, the provincial administration and the police ran a low-level campaign of violence and discrimination against opposition candidates throughout the country. Police trailed them and recorded whom they met. DCs cancelled opposition meetings at the last moment or restricted the number they could hold.[225] Opposition activists and candidates were attacked, arrested and had their loans called in. Opposition offices were frequent targets, particularly in marginal Western Province, Kisii and Trans-Nzoia, where the DP and FORD had several offices burnt down or looted. By contrast, the administration and the police assisted KANU candidates, and KANU youth wingers had effective immunity from prosecution. Throughout the country, state vehicles were used to campaign for KANU.

Electorally, civil servants were a key constituency, and came under heavy pressure to support KANU. Moi warned on 5 October that civil servants who sided with the opposition would be dismissed.[226] Most PCs and DCs demanded that their officials back KANU; they campaigned openly for KANU whenever foreign observers were not present, threatened to sack anyone who supported the opposition and made direct cash payment to KANU supporters.[227] Many officials had run the rigged elections of 1988. There was also a bias in the ethnic apportionment of these positions.[228] During the crucial pre-election period, 11 DCs were Kalenjin (25 per cent of the DCs but only 11 per cent of the population), while only nine were Kikuyu, Luo or Embu (for 40 per cent of the population).

The Kalenjin KANU heartlands of Nandi, Elgeyo-Marakwet, Baringo, Kericho and Bomet were entirely closed to the opposition. There were few reports of violence or intimidation because it was so pervasive that it was unwise even to enquire into what was happening. Much of the harassment of non-Kalenjin here was organised centrally, a continuation of the threats made during the *majimbo* rallies. Opposition in Moi's Baringo, for example, was not permitted. After ex-Moi confidant Cheboiwo defected to the DP in Baringo North his house was burnt down and his cattle killed. In Nandi, DP candidate Samuel arap Ng'eny, the former speaker of the National Assembly, received death threats and fled abroad. Even church leaders in Nandi ordered non-Kalenjin to vote for Moi or leave.[229] Kericho DC Sirma openly demanded that voters 'sing the song of Jogoo' or leave the area.[230]

The situation was similar in the Rift periphery. In Turkana, KANU candidates threatened non-Turkana in the area that if they failed to support KANU, 'we shall snatch from you all these businesses and you will have nobody but yourselves to blame.'[231] On 24 November, the West Pokot DC warned that bar owners who allowed their premises to be used by opposition parties would lose their licences.[232] The DP candidate fled after a rally attended by the DC resolved that everybody in West Pokot must support the party or leave the district.[233] In Uasin Gishu, KANU demanded: 'non-indigenous residents . . . should leave politics to the indigenous people.'[234] In Narok, the flashpoint was Ntimama's seat of Narok North, where several opposition supporters were killed, while Ntimama warned local Maasai that the Kikuyu would grab their land if they came to power. On 28 December, vehicles with loudspeakers moved around Kikuyu areas, warning them they would be evicted if they did not vote for KANU.[235]

In Central Province, in contrast, it was KANU's supporters who experienced intimidation. KANU also had severe difficulty in campaigning in Luo Nyanza, where many of their rallies were attacked by mobs. Here, state pressure could achieve little. Instead, communities were threatened with exclusion if they persisted in voting for the opposition. In Central Province, for example, DCs and ministers warned voters that they would lose jobs and development if they failed to vote for KANU, as it would form the next government anyway.[236]

Polling Day and the Count

Polling day, 29 December, was a national holiday. Over most of the country, the poll was calm, but heavy rainfall delayed the distribution of materials in the north and east. There were also errors in the ballot papers: in several seats, candidates' names and symbols had been mixed up or omitted and some papers were sent to the wrong district entirely. Polling was also delayed by the fact that Kenyans had never voted three times at once before, and the queues lasted long into the night. There were also problems with the secrecy of the ballot, due to the large number of illiterate voters. The presiding officer had to mark the paper for these voters, witnessed by the candidates' agents. Announcing the voter's preference in this way created a public rather than private vote, and in some districts this process was abused. The illiteracy rate became implausibly high, as KANU demanded in advance that all voters declare themselves illiterate, so that their agents could confirm they had voted Jogoo.[237]

Many marginal constituencies saw bribery and campaigning near polling stations. Reports revealed a massive distribution of cash by KANU to voters, particularly in Eastern and Western provinces, with prices ranging from Ksh10 to Ksh100 per vote. There was smaller-scale bribery by the opposition as well. It was possible for voters to take the cash but vote for others, but many voters felt an obligation to deliver when being watched by agents.

Once polling was over, the counterfoils were checked and the boxes sealed and transported to the 188 counting halls. Popular vigilance prevented much stuffing at this stage, but boxes did turn up unaccompanied in some key seats.

There were far more complaints about the count than the voting. Many officials failed to follow the letter of the law: agents' seals, for example, were often cut open without checking whether they were the originals. Counting also proceeded agonisingly slowly. Many halls were chaotic, with tired crowds held back by exhausted security personnel. By the end of the second day, there was growing concern that some counts were being delayed to facilitate rigging. After some preliminary counts indicated KANU might lose, new boxes arrived that altered the result. The last count ended on 4 January 1993, six days after the election.

The domestic observers had few problems in monitoring and covered three-quarters of the polling stations on polling day. However, all the observer groups were under-resourced for the counts, where the worst problems emerged. There was hostility towards observers in the Rift Valley and key marginals. NEMU and the NCWK reported that their people had experienced harassment in 22 seats, and this proved a good indicator of malpractice. The 160 foreign observers toured as many polling stations as they could, but there were no foreign observers at half the counts.

The Results

The results were a disaster for the divided opposition. KANU won the presidential and parliamentary elections, as well as the majority of civic contests. Moi took 37 per cent of the vote to Matiba's 26 per cent, Kibaki's 19 per cent and Odinga's 17 per cent, and KANU won an overall majority of 100 parliamentary seats to the combined opposition's 88. This result was predictable, given the divisions in the opposition, ethnic arithmetic, the authority of government and the tilted playing field. It was assisted, nonetheless, by electoral malpractice.

In the presidential poll, Moi won a minority victory, with nearly 2 million votes, half a million more than his nearest rival Matiba, who secured 1.4 million. Moi received 25 per cent of the vote in five (and only five) provinces, winning North-Eastern, the Rift Valley, the Coast and Western Province, and passing the 25 per cent barrier in Eastern. No opponent crossed the 25 per cent hurdle in more than three provinces. Matiba came closest, winning Central and Nairobi, and exceeding 25 per cent in Western. Kibaki won Eastern and secured 35 per cent in Central. Odinga won 76 per cent of the vote in Nyanza, but crossed the 25 per cent hurdle nowhere else. Each challenger had a regional centre of strength, but was weak elsewhere. Nonetheless, nearly two-thirds of the voters had voted against Moi.

Presidential voting proved predominantly regional and ethnic. Moi had the best-distributed vote, and outside Luo Nyanza and Central Province he polled strongly (see Figure 9.9). Matiba achieved spectacular results in Kiambu, Murang'a, Nairobi, Nyandarua, Nakuru and Shikuku's Kakamega, but elsewhere he polled only 10 per cent of the vote. Kibaki won Nyeri, Kirinyaga, Laikipia, and most of Meru and Embu, but nowhere else. His vote in Ukambani and Kisii was strong but variable, partly as a consequence of rigging. His support in his home bastion was so weakened by Matiba that he ended up stronger in Eastern than in Nairobi or Central. Odinga's fourth place reflected both state pressure and some aversion to a Luo president and to an aged leader with a radical past. He won Luo Nyanza, Mombasa (helped by the alliance with the IPK), Bungoma and Trans-Nzoia, and performed well in Nairobi. Elsewhere, he polled only 4 per cent of the vote. The other four candidates performed even more miserably.

The elections showed how polarised three of the five largest ethnic groups had become. The Kikuyu-dominated seats of Central Province, Laikipia and southern

9.9: Moi's percentage of the presidential vote, 1992

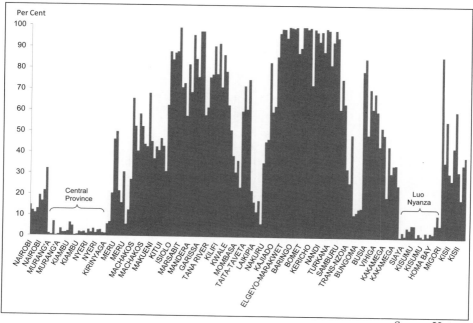

Source: Various

Nakuru cast 93 per cent of their votes for Kibaki and Matiba, 5 per cent for Moi and 2 per cent for Odinga. Luo Nyanza cast 95 per cent of its votes for Odinga, 4 per cent for Moi and 1 per cent for Kibaki and Matiba combined. The Kalenjin home districts plus two other Kalenjin-dominated seats voted 93 per cent for Moi (see Figure 9.10).

The parliamentary results followed a similar pattern. KANU won most of the Coast, Rift Valley and North-Eastern provinces, shared the honours in Eastern and Western, but did appallingly in Central Province, Nairobi and Nyanza. FORD-Asili and FORD-Kenya shared second place, with 31 MPs each, and the DP came fourth with 23. Numerous KANU ministers were defeated, including every Kikuyu and Luo. KANU won 53 per cent of the parliamentary seats with only 30 per cent of the parliamentary vote, due to the effect of the 'first past the post' system and the skewed distribution of constituencies. The DP was the main loser, winning 22 per cent of the vote but only 12 per cent of the Assembly, reflecting its more evenly spread support. Local issues and strong individuals were submerged by a pattern of ethno-regional voting, with a close relationship between a party's presidential, parliamentary and civic votes in most seats. Only 15 per cent of seats were truly marginal.

The turnout was 69 per cent, much the same as in 1979. While in Central Province, the Kalenjin Rift and Luo Nyanza voting was virtually compulsory, and some turnouts exceeded 90 per cent, elsewhere it averaged only 61 per cent. This was

9.10: Voting preferences of the largest communities in the presidential election, 1992

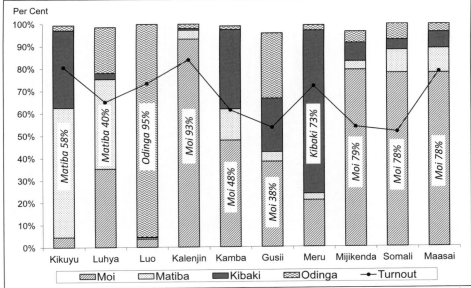

Source: Unpublished analysis of 1992 results.

Definitions: 'Kikuyu' vote: all Central Province, Laikipia and three Nakuru seats; 'Luo' vote: all Nyanza except Kuria, Kisii and Nyamira; 'Luhya': all Western Province except Amagoro and Mt Elgon; 'Kalenjin': all Baringo, Elgeyo-Marakwet, Kericho, Bomet, Nandi and Pokot plus Eldoret East and Mt Elgon; 'Kamba': Kitui, Machakos and Makueni; 'Gusii': Kisii and Nyamira; Mijikenda: all Kwale and Kilifi districts; 'Meru': Meru and Tharaka-Nithi; 'Somali': North-Eastern Province; 'Maasai': all Narok and Kajiado except Kajiado North. Multi-ethnic constituencies are not used in the analysis for simplicity and clarity.

strangely low for the first multi-party general election since independence. Ethnic groups without presidential candidates did not vote in the numbers expected.

Within an hour of Chesoni's declaring Moi the victor, on the morning of 4 January 1993 Daniel arap Moi was sworn in as Kenya's first elected multi-party president in front of a small crowd of diplomats and politicians.

How KANU won

KANU's victory was a product of three factors: first, the opposition failed to present a united front; second, the election was fought regionally, and in enough regions KANU had the edge; and third, state bias and electoral malpractice tipped the scales in crucial seats. Moi almost certainly won the presidency legitimately, in that he polled a larger number of genuine votes than any other candidate. In Parliament, however, KANU won no more that 80–5 seats fairly, and the result should have been a minority government.

A Divided Opposition

The explanation most frequently offered for the opposition's defeat was that it was divided.[238] The splits between the DP and FORD, then within FORD and finally within FORD-Asili allowed KANU to win on a minority vote. Arithmetic suggests that an electoral pact between any two of the three main opposition parties would have won both an overall majority and 25 per cent in five provinces in the presidency. In the parliamentary polls, if the opposition had fielded one candidate per seat against KANU (even assuming that 25 per cent of the supporters of the party running third would return to KANU), the government would have won only 87 seats, the opposition 101.

The reality is less clear. If Odinga had been the candidate of a united FORD, most Kikuyu would have voted for Kibaki. Equally, if Matiba had been FORD's candidate, many Luo would probably have opted for the 'devil they knew' – Moi. A FORD-Kenya/DP alliance was the most plausible combination, but Odinga would still have had difficulty delivering Luo votes to Kibaki, while Kibaki would have been incapable of delivering Kikuyu votes to Odinga with Matiba standing. As long as Matiba was in the race, KANU's chances were good.

Regional Strengths and Weaknesses

The second reason why KANU won was that it genuinely had broad support in the Kalenjin and in lightly populated, semi-arid and less-developed areas. Many pastoralists, rural coast voters and one-time supporters of KADU saw (and were encouraged to see) FORD and the DP as the vehicles of the 'majority tribes'. The contest accentuated the division between the land-rich pastoralists and those with a distinct culture they wished to preserve, and the wealthier, land-hungry, more numerous agricultural groups.

The 1992 election was not a nationwide contest between the same parties but a mosaic of smaller conflicts. There were five types of poll. The 'ethnic homelands' of the four main candidates in the Kalenjin homelands, Nyeri, Murang'a and Luo Nyanza respectively, one quarter of the seats, were one-party zones. Here, the presidential vote for the local man was overwhelming and the same party won every parliamentary seat by huge majorities. In these areas, it is unlikely that other parties had a fair chance to express their views. Turnouts were also extremely high as the main goal was to maximise the presidential vote.

In the 'allied territories', covering 35 per cent of the seats, powerful local leaders led one party to victory, but turnouts were lower and majorities smaller and there were occasional upsets. Thus, FORD-Kenya took Bukusu Bungoma, Shikuku delivered most of Kakamega for FORD-Asili and the DP won most of Embu and Meru. In the state-dominated North-East, Isiolo and Marsabit, Moi won the presidential poll everywhere, but KANU lost two parliamentary seats due to clan factors. The Coast also backed KANU outside Mombasa.

Ten per cent of seats were contested primarily between opposition parties, with KANU third or fourth. In Nairobi, KANU won only Westlands in the parliamentary

9.11: Presidential results by constituency winner, 1992

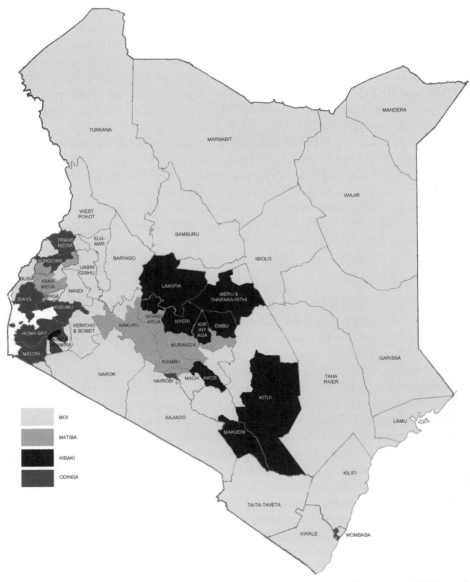

Source: 1992 ECK results

election and FORD-Asili took the presidential poll and the majority of seats. In Starehe, Rubia (KNC) went down to defeat, but Raila Odinga won Langata for FORD-Kenya. In Central Province, the contest was between the two Kikuyu heavyweights. Nyeri, Kirinyaga and Laikipia went to the DP, while Matiba won Murang'a and Kiambu, and Nyandarua split between the two parties. The great surprise was Matiba's victory in Kiambu, where defeated candidates included DP leaders Ngengi Muigai and Karume. The DP lost in part because it was seen as conservative and elitist, but its defeat was also a product of the radicalising effects of landlessness and peri-urbanisation. The sole exception to the FORD-Asili bandwagon here was Muite's victory in Kikuyu.

The 'ethnic borderlands' between Kalenjin or Maasai and pro-opposition communities formed the fourth group, covering 8–10 per cent of the country. These seats saw serious violence. In Uasin Gishu and Trans-Nzoia, FORD-Kenya took the Luhya-dominated west and KANU the south and east. In Nakuru FORD-Asili won four of the five seats, with the Kikuyu voting FORD-Asili or DP, and the Kalenjin supporting KANU. However, the results were rigged by both FORD-Asili and KANU, especially in Molo, where 10,000 Kalenjin voters were imported en masse to try to swing the seat to KANU.

Finally, 42 seats (22 per cent of the total) lay in the marginal communities: the Gusii, Kamba, Bajuni, Orma, Pokomo and the Luhya of Vihiga and Busia, where even by polling day it was not clear which party was going to win. Here, clan, personality and local factors dominated. There was still party voting, but communities voted for different parties from constituency to constituency, and votes went different ways in the parliamentary and presidential elections. It was here and in the ethnic borderlands that the election was won. Ukambani, for example, was closely contested between KANU and the DP. KANU won 12 of the 15 parliamentary seats, but only 10 in the presidential elections. There were electoral abuses in at least 10 seats. In the Gusii districts, honours were shared between KANU, FORD-Kenya, the DP and Anyona's KSC. Nyachae won easily, as did most of his allies, but again, the vote and count were rigged in KANU's favour in several seats.

The parallels between the 1963 and 1992 elections were striking. Comparing KANU's performance with that of KADU in 1963 (and the combined opposition's with that of KANU in 1963), in two-thirds of the districts, 1992 produced the same result to that seen three decades before. In 1963, KANU had won Nairobi and all the Kikuyu and Luo-dominated seats, just as the opposition did now. KADU had won the Coast (minus the Taita), the Kalenjin, Maasai and Samburu, as KANU did in 1992. In both elections, the Luhya split three ways. In 1963, the Kamba were divided between KANU and the African People's Party, in 1992 they were split between the DP and KANU. The Embu and Meru voted in both elections with the Kikuyu. The differences are also illustrative. Although Moi's coalition of 1992 was weaker in Bungoma and Mombasa, with the power of incumbency it proved stronger amongst the Gusii, Kamba, Meru, Taita, Turkana, Teso and Kuria.

Electoral Abuses

The third reason for KANU's victory was that it cheated. Just as it had used control of the state and state funds to tilt the campaign, so a partisan state manipulated the polls and rigged enough counts to ensure that KANU won both the presidency and Parliament. There is evidence of widespread falsification of the results, affecting at least 50 seats. In the contest for the presidency, the government piled up as many votes as possible in its strongholds. Over 30 per cent of Moi's vote came from the seats in the Rift Valley where opposition candidates had been excluded. In Parliament, KANU won a dozen marginal seats that they would otherwise have lost, through ballot-box stuffing and counting malpractices.[239]

In over 45 constituencies, the number of presidential and parliamentary ballots failed to match by more than 800 papers, a signal of stuffing or serious administrative issues. Twenty seats were won by a different party in the two elections; some of these victories were narrow, and were associated with imbalances in the number of votes cast. Turnouts exceeded 100 per cent in some polling stations. Such statistical anomalies can be cross-referenced with reports from observers, the press and participants to suggest what happened.

Credence cannot be given to all complaints, since Kenyan politicians cry foul at the slightest provocation. Nonetheless, there is little doubt that KANU did not win an overall majority in the parliamentary election. In marginal seats across the country, there was evidence of the introduction of ballot boxes full of stuffed papers, bribery of voters and of votes being counted against the wrong parties by partial clerks. In many pastoral areas, all voters were ordered to declare themselves illiterate and KANU agents noted down the names of those who refused to do so. A few polling stations were taken over by KANU and all voters forced to vote for it. In Samburu, Machakos, Garissa and Kisii, returning officers refused to allow observers into the count or threw them out mid-way through. In Saitoti's Kajiado North, someone may have ordered more ballot boxes than actually needed, and then reintroduced the (now-stuffed) spare boxes later, leaving the correct number at the end. In Tana River, where there had been gross stuffing, all the ballots were deliberately mixed up before the count began, preventing the detection of abuses.

Most of these malpractices benefited KANU, but in Nairobi, Murang'a and Nakuru there was also evidence of stuffing or forced voting in favour of FORD-Asili. In 1993, Oginga Odinga claimed that Matiba had printed 3 million ballot papers himself in order to rig the elections.[240] In a couple of seats, wealthy DP notables rigged the election in their own favour.

Overall, Moi's presidential tally was inflated by between 100,000 and 150,000 votes in 10 semi-arid or Kalenjin-dominated districts. Perhaps 250,000 of his 1.9 million votes were fabricated, while some opposition votes were probably destroyed to ensure that no opponent achieved 25 per cent in the Rift Valley and North-Eastern Province. Matiba's 1.4 million votes is probably a reasonable estimate of his vote, as FORD-Asili was the beneficiary of some malpractices and was not a contender in the North-East, central Rift Valley or Coast Province, where vote destruction is most likely. The vote for Odinga appears a slight underestimate. Kibaki's figure is also too low by 50,000–100,000 votes, particularly in the central Rift, Kisii and Eastern Province. Nonetheless, given the size of Moi's victory, rigging at this level did not change the result. Moi still appears to be 250,000 votes clear of his nearest rival. Whether Moi received 25 per cent of the vote in five provinces is less clear, but the evidence suggests that he did. He certainly polled 25 per cent in the Rift Valley, North-East, Coast and Western provinces, and he probably passed the 25 per cent hurdle in Eastern.

In the parliamentary elections, however, KANU should have won only 85–90 of its 100 parliamentary seats. In Eastern Province, KANU should have lost Kitui West, Mutito and Mutomo, and possibly three more. On the Coast, KANU should have lost Garsen, Galole, Lamu West and Msambweni; in Western Province, Emuhaya (and possibly two others); and in Nyanza, Kitutu Chache, North Mugirango, Nyaribari Masaba and Bobasi. The government arranged that the presidential results were counted first, and these results gave them enough information to work out which parliamentary seats they needed to rig to ensure a majority. The DP suffered most from the rigging.

The way this was done varied. In some cases, it relied on stuffing of boxes and the destruction or concealment of opposition ballots by clerks. There was also evidence of the insertion of properly marked ballot boxes full of stamped papers into the counting halls. Although theoretically impossible, there was evidence from more than a dozen seats that it had occurred. A clue as to how this might have been done was provided in 1993, when dissident Electoral Commissioner Habel Nyamu commented, 'to date, nobody in the world is prepared to tell the Commission [Kenya's] the whereabouts of 150 ballot boxes which were not received at the airport by the Commission's security force from the police.'[241]

Even accepting the huge difficulties of managing electoral processes in developing countries, there were at least six criteria on which the 1992 election failed the 'free and fair' test. First, the government abused the registration process, under-registering opposition supporters and over-registering KANU supporters. Second, the regime failed to sever the connection between party and state, using the provincial administration to campaign for KANU and frustrate the opposition. The climate of authoritarianism and fear that this created, intensified by the ethnic clashes, reduced opposition support in marginal areas and prevented the opposition functioning at all in KANU's heartlands. Third, KANU stole state funds to bribe voters and opponents. Fourth, government control of the media distorted coverage in favour of KANU. Fifth, pro-KANU thugs intimidated the opposition and prevented a tenth of their candidates even presenting their nomination papers. Finally, when all this was insufficient, KANU stuffed ballot boxes and rigged enough counts to ensure parliamentary victory.

It seems clear now that KANU had no intention of relinquishing power. As long as it thought it could win, it was willing to walk the tightrope of an election. If it had thought that it would lose, the election would have been disrupted. If Moi had not decisively won the presidential election, there would have been no second round –

no funds were allocated and no organisation had been made for a run-off between the two top candidates. The state did not intend to permit the opposition to unite behind a single candidate.

Observer, Donor and Popular Responses

The reaction of the election observers, both internal and external, was crucial. In each case, the audience for their reports was international more than domestic. Both the Commonwealth and the IRI were ambivalent and reluctantly gave the government the benefit of the doubt. The IRI initially failed to express a view, concluding: 'the people of Kenya will be the final arbiters of whether this process has produced a free and fair result.'[242] Its final report was harsher, but it still did not declare the result invalid. The Commonwealth observers were even more ambivalent. Their 1 January statement concluded:

> the evolution of the process to polling day and the subsequent count was increasingly positive to a degree that we believe that the results in many instances directly reflect, however imperfectly, the expression of the will of the people. It constitutes a giant step on the road to multi-party democracy.[243]

Their report stated that they 'neither saw nor heard of substantiated evidence' of stuffing.[244] On this basis, the Kenyan government was deemed by Western powers to have – narrowly – passed the test of electoral legitimacy. The internal monitors were more critical. NEMU concluded, 'the December 1992 elections were not free and fair.'[245] Western governments paid little attention to this; foreign diplomats reluctantly advised that the opposition should take up their seats and take on the government in the courts instead.[246] With time, the elections were recognised as flawed, but it was too late.[247]

The foreign observers failed to cry foul for five reasons. The first was practical: no group had the knowledge, support or staff to carry out a shadow count, and they were forced to rely on impressionistic evidence. They arrived late and unprepared to monitor well-organised manipulation. Second, their experiences were wildly different; some witnessing rigging, others not. They did not visit some of the areas where the problems were most acute, and most did not sit through the count, where many of the problems emerged. Third, the observers failed to cooperate; the production of numerous different reports weakened the impact of each. Fourth, they had no objective yardstick against which to measure the election. Even if all the information had been available, it is hard to see the observers producing unambiguous conclusions, since they had set themselves ambiguous questions. Finally, there may have been a predisposition towards the incumbent in a state of uncertainty. The Western press heavily criticised the foreign observers' reports, and there was debate as to whether the West had abandoned its commitment to democracy by legitimising the election.[248] The British *Independent* suggested that Western governments had thought that the presence of eminent persons would deter KANU from rigging, but had had their bluff called.[249]

The opposition believed it had been robbed. On 1 January 1993, Matiba, Kibaki and Odinga called a press conference to reject the results. However, the response from their supporters, the US government and the churches was hostile, with their defeat seen as punishment for their failure to unite. The losers could not agree on a common response and soon consented to take up their parliamentary seats and to pursue cases of rigging though the petition courts. Predictions of violent protest by the Kikuyu did not materialise: a combination of their regional successes, exhaustion, and a satisfaction that so many KANU stalwarts had been defeated.

Conclusions

Multi-party democracy had returned to Kenya as a result of a confluence of factors. Some fuses were slow-burning and systemic: corruption, ethnicisation and abuse of state power, dependence on Western aid and the alienation of the Kikuyu from the Moi state. Others, such as the fall of communism, the Ouko murder, Matiba and Rubia's 1990 rebellion, Odinga's protests and the cancellation of Western fiscal support, were actions or events that could easily have taken a different form. Although the outside world had changed, there was no inevitability about the ending of single-party rule in 1991. As the events of Saba Saba showed, the regime could still physically silence its critics. Moi's personal choices, first to resist and then embrace reform, were critically important. If in December 1991 Moi had called a general election that all Kenyans could contest, under the KANU banner but without any vetting or primaries, it is possible that the West would have accepted this as a step towards democratisation. Kenya would have moved towards a Ugandan model. Similarly, there was little evidence – apart from its dependence on foreign aid – that political change was a direct product of domestic economic crisis. Political change and economic change proved symbiotic and mutually reinforcing, without a simple linear cause and effect.

During 1992, a trans-ethnic movement for national renewal, human rights and economic liberalisation had rapidly disintegrated into hostile, ethnically focused teams, incapable of compromise in their quest to seize the state. As in the 1960s, the competition for power had been reduced to a contest between ethnic coalitions built around powerful individuals. For the majority of Kenyans, particularly those from ethnic groups with powerful, popular and wealthy presidential candidates, ethnicity proved the single most effective predictor of political preference. Of all the potential lines of cleavage, it was the three-way division between Kikuyu, Luo and Kalenjin/pastoralists that eclipsed all others. Deep tensions remained between the pastoral peoples of the arid and less-developed regions and the more numerous, land-hungry peoples of the centre. It was the struggle for land – particularly in the Rift – and its diversion into political channels that provided the dynamic for many events of the period.

KANU's victory was likely as soon as Kibaki, Odinga and Matiba all declared their candidacies. If Matiba had accepted the vice-presidency alongside Odinga, the opposition would have stood a good chance of victory, but Kibaki would then have taken more of the Kikuyu vote. Even a united FORD, therefore, might not have won. The opposition was never a single political movement, but a coalition of disparate social, ethnic and political forces, united only in their opposition to KANU.

The events of 1992 had also shown that elections alone were not enough to guarantee a successful democratic transition. The government had allowed a multi-party contest, but without reforming the country's political institutions or the state bureaucracy, and the incumbents retained powerful weapons of control, limited in their use more by fear of Western protest than by internal checks and balances. The inner circle's actions to secure their survival had intensified ethnic divisions and damaged the economy and the clashes had nearly driven Kenya into civil collapse. It was near-inevitable that multi-party elections would increase ethnic tensions in Kenya, as Moi had predicted. A political system based on locally elected community representatives competing for favours from and control of a centralised presidential power structure – combined with a history of ethnicised and personalised conflict – drove political parties to take on an ethnic flavour. The behaviour of both government and opposition leaders accentuated this trend.

The period showed the huge influence that Western donors exerted through their control of the country's purse-strings and their public opprobrium, but also their inability to control the changes they had instigated. They could not compel Kenya to make instant economic reforms, nor could they force a free election. Despite the rigging, Western governments continued to recognise and soon financially support Moi's government, a very different response to that seen when Kibaki faced similar allegations in 2007. By their actions and inaction, the donors and the IFIs were political actors on the domestic stage, whether they wished to be or not.

In this short period, Kenya had seen massive social and economic change. The country had begun an almost irreversible shift from an elite-led autocracy towards a form of pluralism. Despite the state's efforts, for the first time since independence some voters had been given the chance to choose their leadership and political path. The press had blossomed into a free – though partisan and venal – agent of information. Centres of independent political power began to roll back the state, at the same time as external pressure was forcing the state to divest itself of some instruments of economic control. However, true multi-party democracy, in which all voters could choose their government in an atmosphere of open competition, was not yet a reality. The economic problems facing Kenya had worsened. The looting of the economy took years to redress, economic liberalisation was slow and partial, and the loss of Western aid was only the first of many aid suspensions to come. Bribery and corruption were legitimised, while the clashes and the alignment of ethnicity and political preference ensured that the intertwined issues of ethnicity and land became once again the most serious political problem the country faced.

Chapter 10

Conflict and Change, 1993–1997

Introduction

Having won the elections, KANU strengthened its grip during 1993–6, while the opposition fragmented. The themes that had dominated 1990–2 – dependence on foreign aid, presidential authoritarianism, the corruption of politics, ethnically divisive policies and communal ethnic solidarity – continued to shape political discourse. Despite scrutiny from the opposition, the West and the independent media, officials and politicians continued to rob the state with impunity. The security situation deteriorated and violence continued in the Rift Valley on the borderlands between Kikuyu and 'indigenous' pastoralist groups, and broke out on the coast. At the same time, Kenya's economy liberalised and the democratic space expanded as the state's footprint contracted. Both changes were driven primarily by foreign pressure, and the relationship between donors and Kenya's political system deepened as Western countries tried to drive reforms and empower civil society. In the West, however, cynicism grew about the sustainability of the democratic changes they had nurtured since 1990 in Africa.

The government rewarded those regions and ethnic groups that had remained loyal, but its relationship with the Kikuyu community remained a point of deep division. President Daniel arap Moi and key allies wished to draw key Kikuyu leaders back into KANU on KANU's terms, but elsewhere his fragile claim to legitimacy lay in the Kikuyu's exclusion. The opposition parties weakened, divided and disillusioned. New parties emerged in the run-up to the 1997 election, but could offer no long-term challenge to KANU. The result in 1997 was an easier presidential victory for Moi, on a fairer basis, but built on the same divisions between his opponents and the same contest with the Kikuyu and Luo.

In the meantime, the debate over Kenya's Constitution had become the dominant political issue in the country. With the opposition parties in crisis, civil society, religious leaders and individual politicians made common cause in a crusade to reform or replace the Constitution. When combined with renewed Western economic and political pressure, this forced Moi into a significant change of direction in 1997. The state's decision to accede to mass civil disobedience and to compromise with moderate opposition leaders averted another crisis.

The New Government

Moi announced his new government on 13 January 1993. It reflected the need both to woo the donors and to assert KANU's authority. The number of ministries shrank from 32 to 23. Despite his promises to others, Moi reappointed George

Saitoti as vice-president, ensuring that someone without a strong ethnic base held the role.[1] Ministerial posts were given to those individuals and communities who had remained loyal in difficult times, including Joshua Angatia, Jackson Mulinge, Francis Lotodo and Simeon Nyachae. Moi also placed young professionals into key posts dealing with the West. The 32-year-old Musalia Mudavadi became minister of finance and 39-year old Kalonzo Musyoka foreign minister. Nicholas Biwott remained on the backbenches, but of the five Kalenjin home districts, only his Elgeyo-Marakwet received no Cabinet post, showing Moi's continued support for Biwott, as it meant that he faced no rival on his home turf. International reaction was generally negative.

As KANU now had no elected Luo or Kikuyu MPs, the ethnic composition of the Cabinet was the most imbalanced in Kenya's history (see Figure 10.1). To redress this at least partially, Moi nominated six defeated KANU candidates into Parliament and brought three into the Cabinet, including Dalmas Otieno and KANU Secretary-General Joseph Kamotho. Kenya now had a Kalenjin–Kamba–Luhya government (with Kalenjin holding Home Affairs and the OP as well as the presidency); the imbalance grew even further in 1998.

All attempts to remove Moi through electoral petitions failed. Although six presidential petitions were filed, each was dispensed with on procedural grounds. Matiba raised the most serious challenge, claiming massive vote rigging. In response, KANU challenged his petition's validity before the substantive hearing, arguing that Matiba's attorney, his wife, could not sign his petition papers (he still could not read or write). In July 1993, the petition court rejected KANU's case, since she had signed his parliamentary and presidential nomination papers, but no one had objected then.[2] However, the Appeal Court reversed the judgment in February 1994, ensuring

10.1: Ethnicity of Cabinet appointments, 1963–98

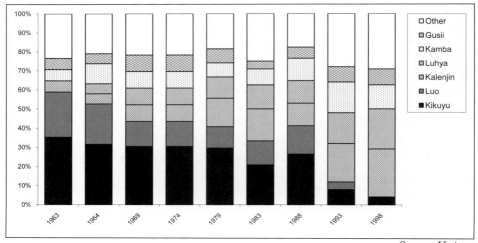

Source: Various

Matiba's evidence was never heard.[3] Within a year, two of the three inconvenient petition court judges were gone, their contracts not renewed.

Losers also launched petitions against the victors in 84 parliamentary constituencies, nearly half the country's seats. Only half of these were against KANU, since KANU petitioned opposition victors in some areas, and the two FORD parties also petitioned against each other. The result was a slow and expensive series of hearings that identified many malpractices, but were more adept at nullifying opposition victories than government ones. In total, of 44 parliamentary petitions against KANU, none was successful. Of 40 petitions against opposition winners, five were successful. These figures reflect a consistent – though unprovable – pattern of judicial interference and inconsistent application of the law.

Post-Election Politics, 1993–5

The first theme of 1993–5 was the government's attempts to restore control of the political agenda. It disorganised and repressed the opposition while rewarding its supporters, to demonstrate the effect that failure to be reincorporated would have on the economic health of opposition communities and the personal security of their leaders. But this strategy, so successful in the 1960s, did not eliminate the opposition entirely, which was now better protected by the space created by economic and political liberalisation and by Western attention.

Carrots and Sticks

The Parliament that assembled in January 1993 was very different from its predecessors. Gone were the 'class of '88', replaced by assertive opposition MPs and some equally confrontational KANU politicians. The opposing sides of the House once more took on their original meaning, as opposition MPs sat to the left of the speaker, KANU MP Francis ole Kaparo, while KANU MPs took the seats to the right. KANU MPs had to run a gauntlet of opposition demonstrators as they arrived. The Assembly was then prorogued until March. When it reopened, KANU took revenge. Armed *moran* bussed in from Maasailand assaulted opposition demonstrators in front of watching police.[4] It was an early example of the use of private security forces to repress the opposition, a 'privatisation' of political violence that came to characterise Kenya in the 1990s.

Attacks on the press and restrictions on the media continued. In 1993–4, more editions of *Finance*, *Society* and other journals were impounded, their editors arrested, copies destroyed by police, the printers charged and their presses dismantled.[5] There were protests from Western governments and a motion of condemnation in the British House of Commons. Some magazines truly pushed the limits. For example, *The Watchman* in January 1993 headlined with 'Moi – Rejected by God' and continued, 'his mission has been and still is the programmed murder of the non-Kalenjins, the church is his camouflage.'[6] This was fighting talk. The situation was little better in the television world. KBC continued to toe the government line, while KTN's independence was far from assured. In March 1993, KTN stopped covering local news for several months, under intense pressure over their coverage of opposition politicians.[7] Kenneth Matiba, meanwhile, had written a book, *Kenya: Return to Reason*, which detailed the corruption and abuses of the government. In January 1994, police seized all 15,000 copies from the printers and the book was banned.[8]

KANU spent most of 1993–4 rebuilding itself, finding more popular leaders to take up positions in opposition areas after the chaos of 1992. There was a clean-out of old guard KANU chairmen, including Burudi Nabwera, Elijah Mwangale, Jackson Angaine, Mulu Mutisya and Julius Kiano. Moi and his ministers also nominated several defeated KANU candidates to head parastatals, offering them a consolation prize, a platform for 1997 and future patronage opportunities for KANU.

KANU also executed a sustained campaign to undermine the opposition. Moi openly admitted that he did not intend to allow free and fair political competition. In 1996, he asserted, 'Politics in Africa is not like football, deserving a level playing ground. Here, you try that and you will be roasted.'[9] As the colonial government and Kenyatta had done, the government did everything it could to deny legitimacy to its opponents, refusing to respond to their complaints and taking legal, administrative and coercive reprisals against them and their families. Meanwhile, KANU continued to blame political violence in Kenya on the opposition and 'the evils of multipartyism'.[10] Although they never descended to the level of mass detentions or mass murder, the security forces and administration severely harassed opposition MPs. More than 20 were arrested and charged during 1993, mainly with crimes such as addressing their constituents without permission or publishing alarming statements. They were harassed when moving around their constituencies, and permits for rallies were denied or cancelled at the last minute. There were no such restrictions on KANU politicians. As William ole Ntimama admitted in 1997,

> . . . for the last nine years I have been a minister in the government, I have never been required to have a license either for a public or a private function. I do not know of any cabinet minister who is asked for licences.[11]

On several occasions, KANU threatened that areas that had voted for the opposition would receive no development aid.

Meanwhile, opposition MPs found that the politics of development required deep pockets. Although their constituents had voted against KANU, they still expected handouts from their MPs. Without the spoils of office, the pressure to defect to KANU grew. Opposition MPs were offered large inducements, and by October 1994, 10 (12 per cent of the total) had done so: one from the DP, seven from FORD-Asili and two from FORD-Kenya. Several other MPs claimed they had been offered between Ksh5 million and Ksh20 million to defect.[12] The actual defectors, of course, admitted nothing.

Although KANU had won the elections, it had lost control of many local authorities, but it had ways to limit the opposition's impact. First, council officials were answerable to the ministry, not the council; Local Government Minister Ntimama used this power to undermine local authority decisions. He even declared town and county council clerks the spokesmen of the councils rather than the elected mayors and chairmen.[13] Second, he could withhold their funds, as almost all councils were dependent on central grants for their survival. Finally, the Constitution permitted the nomination of up to one-third of councillors. It had not been modified to require that nominations be proportional to political parties. Ntimama, therefore, nominated pro-KANU councillors up to – and in some cases beyond – the limit of the law.[14]

The Fall of YK'92

KANU experienced internal stresses during the first years of multi-partyism – the result of unfulfilled promises, jockeying for power and the emboldening of regional political bosses who now had real leverage. The party's greatest fear was the defection of major representatives from swing communities, who for the first time since 1966 could hold the government to ransom. KANU experienced problems in maintaining the loyalty of the Somali, who were suffering from famine and banditry. There were also signs of schisms within the Kalenjin, with dissension amongst the Kipsigis and Nandi. In practice, however, the combination of threats and rewards, plus the lack of a plausible alternative, kept KANU united to an extent the opposition could not emulate.

KANU's leadership also had to deal with some unfinished business from their electoral victory. Some were increasingly unhappy about the 'Frankenstein's monster' they had created in YK'92. Within days of the election, its Chairman Cyrus Jirongo was under attack, while in turn YK'92 openly challenged the Kamotho–Biwott–Saitoti team inside KANU. Secretary-General Kamotho called for YK'92 to be disbanded in February, but Moi initially defended the organisation.[15] After a direct attack by Jirongo on Saitoti in April, however, Moi suspended its operations entirely.[16]

Vengeance was swift. Within a few months lawsuits abounded, Jirongo's companies were put into receivership, the NSSF's housing project was re-awarded to Mugoya Construction, and Jirongo received a Ksh272 million income tax bill with only days to pay. Jirongo pleaded publicly for forgiveness. The conduit of state funds to Jirongo was blocked by the removal of the managing trustee and finance manager of the NSSF and the head of Post Bank Credit (like Jirongo, all Luhya), though none was charged in court. The Luhya community – seeing some of its most prominent individuals ousted – was restive.

The New Parliament

Kenya's first multi-party Parliament since 1969 proved a disappointment. Predictions that the opposition would out-debate and occasionally out-vote the government proved wildly optimistic. Despite verbal victories, the opposition was unable to convert Parliament into a significant legislative organ or a true watchdog on the executive. MPs were inexperienced in the niceties of multi-party competition, requiring the regular intervention of the speaker. The Assembly also had little institutional support. The president controlled its timetable and its administrative resources were under executive direction. MPs had no proper offices or research services; there were few effective parliamentary committees and the state refused to accept Parliament's right even to be informed on security issues.

KANU had a clear majority and votes were heavily 'whipped', so the opposition rarely defeated the state on matters of importance. It was so divided internally that its effective strength was no more than 70, and several opposition MPs soon proved to be closet KANU supporters. Most efforts to bring the government to account (for example a motion by FORD-Kenya MP James Orengo to establish a Parliamentary Select Committee to reinvestigate the Ouko murder in 1995) were unsuccessful, defeated on a party vote. Another problem was Matiba's policy of extra-parliamentary action, which made him more dangerous to KANU, but weakened FORD-Asili's parliamentary effectiveness. From June 1993, he boycotted Parliament as 'a waste of time'.[17]

There were 30 by-elections between 1993 and 1997, 13 due to opposition defections, 10 called because of the death of MPs, five as a consequence of petitions, and two following resignations. In every single poll, KANU sustained or improved its share of the vote, and the opposition fell back. Several elections saw allegations of violence and fraud. In each poll, KANU sent high-level delegations, promising government jobs and services if KANU was victorious. After the Lugari by-election in 1994, FORD-Kenya even accused Moi of bribing voters on polling day in the company of ECK Chairman Zachaeus Chesoni's wife.[18] KANU gained 10 more seats as a result, taking it from 100 elected MPs to 110 (plus 12 nominees) and reducing the opposition from 88 to 78. This left them just short of two-thirds of the House. KANU easily lost all seven by-elections in Nyanza and Central provinces, however, discouraging potential defectors from the opposition heartlands. Thus, while KANU's victories increased the pressure on waverers in the marginals and virtually obliterated FORD-Asili in Western Province, the by-elections actually reinforced Luo and Kikuyu solidarity.

The Opposition Weakens

As elsewhere in Africa, Kenya's opposition parties struggled to compete with a government that was renewed and refreshed by its multi-party election victory. Like all Kenyan parties since the 1950s, they were elite-led, ethnically focused patronage parties, despite their rhetoric of mass appeal. They were designed to obtain power, with scant policy foundation, and therefore had little to hold them together when there were no direct material benefits. Their financial positions were shaky and they survived on donations from wealthy individuals and voluntary labour. Opposition leaders also faced the 'prisoner's dilemma', whereby the best course for them individually was to defect as soon as possible, even though they might all have gained if all had held out together. The majority held firm, but politicians in pro-government and marginal communities returned to KANU one by one. Opposition remained most determined in the communities that were most embittered (where ethnic solidarity was more powerful than state pressure) and best able to withstand the lack of state support. Only the Kikuyu, and to a lesser extent the Embu and Meru, had a self-sustaining economic base generating a sufficient surplus to finance an opposition party.

The pressure of defeat, personal self-interest, state harassment and divisions on crucial policy questions led to a period of reconstruction. As a result, all three main opposition parties experienced tensions between younger, more confrontational elites and the old guard. In the aftermath of defeat, the informal alliance between DP and FORD-Kenya expanded. However, FORD-Asili, the official opposition in the House, remained aloof, and the bitterness between Oginga Odinga and Matiba undermined all attempts at unity.

FORD-Kenya in Turn Splits

Inside FORD-Kenya, tensions were caused by the dominance of the Luo and the elderly Odinga. Conflicts also swirled around First Vice-Chairman Paul Muite, a Kikuyu in a party with no Kikuyu support, who was on paper in line to inherit the chairmanship when Odinga departed. However, the Kikuyu, Embu and Meru Young Turks in FORD-Kenya were increasingly sidelined for having failed to 'deliver' in 1992.[19]

The greatest problem was Odinga's blossoming relationship with KANU. In May 1993, he introduced a policy of cooperation with the enemy, to aid the development of Nyanza. Although committed to KANU's defeat, Odinga believed from bitter experience that in a multi-party state the only way to ensure that the Luo community obtained access to state resources was to cooperate with the government. FORD-Kenya was the poorest of the main parties. More fundamentally, the Luo had spent 25 years on the periphery and had no deep-rooted economic base, and were vulnerable to the lure of a 'Nilotic alliance' with KANU. Most Luo MPs, who saw the Kikuyu as the real long-term threat, supported Odinga's tactics. Odinga tried to retain some independence, criticising Moi as often as applauding him, but the strain soon began to show.

Odinga's behaviour was controversial for other reasons. In July 1993, he admitted that he had received a gift of Ksh2 million (US$55,000) to fight some upcoming by-elections, in cash, in a shoebox, from the chairman of Goldenberg and Exchange Bank, Kamlesh Pattni.[20] Although Odinga claimed that he did not know who this 'patriotic Kenyan' was, it was widely believed that he had been quite aware of his visitor's identity.[21] FORD-Kenya was in the middle of a campaign to bring down Pattni and Saitoti over the Goldenberg scandal, and few could believe it was not a bribe. Secretary-General Gitobu Imanyara openly alleged that Pattni's gift was intended to 'shut Odinga up' over Goldenberg.

The result was another split. Many Luo MPs (including Orengo, Peter Anyang' Nyong'o and Jaramogi's son Raila) were deeply unhappy with Odinga's tactics, but they could do little because of his vice-like hold on the Luo vote. His control over the non-Luo was weaker, but this group was divided over the succession. Second Vice-Chairman Michael 'Kijana' Wamalwa and his Luhya colleagues suffered excruciating contortions in order to justify Odinga's policy, as they knew that if Muite,

Imanyara and Kiraitu Murungi left the party, they would inherit the chairmanship. In September 1993, led by Raila Odinga and Wamalwa, FORD-Kenya's National Executive Committee duly sacked Imanyara and he resigned from the party. He was followed by Muite, Murungi and another MP, who resigned their posts but did not leave the party (as this would have forced a by-election).[22] Most other party members remained loyal, forced into acquiescence by the practicalities of politics and their hostility to what some saw as Muite's pro-Kikuyu agenda. This left Wamalwa as Odinga's sole heir.

With many of the Young Turks gone, Odinga moved closer still to KANU. In October–November 1993, he presided with Moi over the opening of the Turkwell Gorge hydroelectric scheme and held talks with the British about a coalition with KANU. Kalenjin Minister Jonathan Ng'eno even suggested that Odinga might be Moi's successor as president.[23]

FORD-Asili and the DP

While FORD-Kenya split, FORD-Asili imploded: the result of its focus on the seriously ill Matiba. Although the party recaptured Charles Rubia and the KNC defectors in 1994, Matiba remained authoritarian and unwell, refusing to hold party elections and treating the party as his personal property. The result was a leadership vacuum, which led other FORD-Asili leaders to call for his retirement. Martin Shikuku's Luhya allies defected to KANU en masse, leaving the party by late 1994 with only two MPs in Western Province (from seven two years before). By 1995, the party barely existed outside Murang'a, Kiambu, Nairobi and Nakuru, though Matiba retained an outlaw constituency amongst poor Kikuyu.

The DP survived, retaining northern Kikuyu and Meru support and that of the Kikuyu commercial elite and picking up some Matiba supporters, but it too was weakened. The party was less Kikuyu-dominated than FORD-Asili, with only half its MPs from Central Province and the Kikuyu diaspora. However, this left it more vulnerable to state pressure, and many of its non-Kikuyu leaders defected to KANU, including Secretary-General John Keen, Vice-Chair Agnes Ndetei and ex-ministers Eliud Mwamunga and Kyale Mwendwa. By the time of its 1996 National Delegates' Convention, the DP had lost 11 national officials. The party's finances deteriorated, with creditors besieging headquarters for payment. Kibaki did little to stem the losses. He remained reclusive, with the image of a beer-drinking golfer more comfortable with his Kenyatta-era friends than with the harsh realities of contemporary life. Instead, younger DP members made common cause with a cross-party 'ginger group' that became the main opposition grouping in the House.

By 1996, divisions, disillusionment and the exercise of state power had systematically weakened the opposition. They could not even put up candidates in by-elections in Turkana and Elgeyo-Marakwet in 1996, leaving KANU's candidates unopposed. Politically, 1996 was the high point for KANU in the multi-party era, with divided and ineffective opponents, good relations with the West and an economic mini-boom.

The Death of Odinga and the End of Cooperation

On 20 January 1994, the 82-year-old Oginga Odinga died of a heart attack. He had influenced Kenya's political life for 40 years, and had often taken a courageous – though sometimes foolhardy – stance in conflict with authority. He was a traditionalist and a Luo to the core; his socialism was more strongly linked to his belief in equity than to any political theory.

Odinga's death sparked a national outpouring of grief. His recent cooperation with KANU was downplayed, and he became once more a symbol of opposition resistance. The funeral cortege's progression through western Kenya was reminiscent of that for Mboya. His funeral in Bondo was an extraordinary event that brought the DP and FORD-Kenya closer, with Kibaki speaking emotionally and calling for unity.[24] Moi's courageous decision to attend the funeral almost led to a repetition of the Kisumu incident, with the danger that the 300,000-strong crowd would try to storm the Presidential Escort. In the event, Moi spoke with discretion, and he and his ministers escaped unscathed. However, he was infuriated by the personal attacks on him during the funeral.[25] With the only man who could hold FORD-Kenya in alliance with KANU gone, Moi saw little chance of continuing their accommodation. Using the funeral as an excuse, he announced, 'I will not accept to be abused, and, therefore, I will not cooperate with them . . .' and called on neighbouring districts to ostracise the Luo.[26] FORD-Kenya and KANU were again at loggerheads.

As the sole remaining member of the triumvirate elected in 1992, Wamalwa became the first Luhya to head a major political party when he was elected (unopposed) as FORD-Kenya chairman in March 1994. His new first vice-chairman was not Raila Odinga, surprisingly, but Orengo, who, with Wamalwa's support, narrowly beat Odinga to the post.[27] Neither Wamalwa nor Orengo were populist, charismatic or machine politicians, but both were excellent speakers, clever and committed to change. Initially, the Luo appeared to accept Wamalwa's inheritance, and the party made some inroads into Western Province. Over the next three years, however, Wamalwa achieved little more. Although his hold on the Bukusu vote remained firm, he failed to seize the advantage amongst the broader Luhya, while his support in Nyanza faded as Raila, increasingly alienated, built a political machine that was loyal primarily to him. FORD-Kenya split in two.

Security and Ethnicity

Although Kenya's borders remained mostly secure, the government struggled to maintain law, order or personal security for the majority of Kenyans, with serious long-term implications for its legitimacy and for the economy.

The Clashes Continue, 1993–5

Violence between Kalenjin, Maasai and Samburu and the Kikuyu continued in the Rift Valley throughout 1993 and 1994. KANU had threatened during the campaign that those who did not vote for Moi would suffer: as a poll monitor in Nakuru had observed, 'there is a plan to remove non-Kalenjins who are residing in Rift Valley Province for failing to vote for KANU Govt.'[28] Fighting restarted in Uasin Gishu and Trans-Nzoia in January–March 1993. To divert attention, Moi accused NGO leader Wangari Maathai and the churches of inciting the clashes.[29] In August 1993, Kalenjin warriors again attacked Molo and Burnt Forest, killing and burning Kikuyu-owned houses.[30] Opposition MPs called for UN intervention. In September 1993, with the situation deteriorating, the government again declared Molo, Burnt Forest and part of Kericho security zones and continued to exercise emergency powers until 1995, restricting the entry of journalists and observers. There were more attacks on Kikuyu squatters and refugees in Narok, Kericho, Laikipia and Uasin Gishu in early 1995, when at least 30 lives were lost. Although the situation gradually stabilised, 25,000–30,000 more people were driven from their homes.

International observers, diplomats, human rights monitors and journalists all blamed the government for the clashes. Each time, there were rumours that government vehicles had transported attackers and that police were under orders not to intervene. The judiciary appeared unable to convict arrested Kalenjin, but non-Kalenjin were prosecuted with vigour.[31] It was widely believed that elements in the predominantly Kalenjin Rift Valley administration and political class were organising the attacks. Some KANU officials in the Rift Valley and Coast still talked of *majimbo*, making clear that their goal was regional ethnic purity. It appeared that the events of 1990–2 and the alignment of politics and ethnicity had damaged the evolution of Kenya's national identity, particularly amongst the Kikuyu and Kalenjin. Under threat, individuals' affinities shifted downwards, reinforcing the focus of their citizenship on their ethnic rather than their national identity, and associating ethnic identity and political preference in a way not seen since the 1960s.[32]

While the violence in the former white highlands was a continuation of the previous year's events, a new front opened up in 1993 in Narok. Since 1988, relations between the Kikuyu and Maasai had been fragile, and there had been killings and intimidation of non-Maasai during 1991–2. In 1993, however, Ntimama took more substantive action, driving out many of the 30,000 Kikuyu who had settled in the forested north of his constituency, often without land title. First, the immigrants were ordered to leave by the administration, and the area was declared a water catchment zone. Then, during September and October 1993, Ntimama visited the region and ordered all Kikuyu to go. On 15 October 1993, an unofficial Maasai militia of hundreds of *moran*, game wardens and administration police conducted a coordinated night assault on Kikuyu homes in the Enoosupukia area, burning houses and driving out settlers.[33] More than 20 were killed. The police did nothing. The Akiwumi Report was explicit: 'The clashes in William ole Ntimama's Narok North constituency did not just happen. They were planned and executed for a political motive.'[34] Ntimama was unrepentant, suggesting that the Maasai were 'provoked' and fighting for their rights.[35] There were angry opposition protests in Parliament, but all efforts to force Ntimama to resign failed, with some FORD-Kenya MPs cynically voting with KANU to protect him.[36] Moi refused to sack him and Attorney-General Amos Wako declined to prosecute him either.

The Maasai leadership, meanwhile, made it clear that none of those displaced from Enoosupukia would be allowed back into Narok. Moi ordered their resettlement, but the administration was unable or unwilling to comply and most stayed in a makeshift camp in Nakuru. On 23 December 1994, police forcibly rounded up 2,000 Kikuyu from the camp and dumped them at what the government said was their 'ancestral' homes in Central Province. The camp was destroyed.[37] The message was clear: leave the Rift Valley.

Messages of ethnic hatred and political inflexibility continued during 1993. The implication was always the same: the Rift Valley was for the Kalenjin and pastoralists; the Kikuyu and other opposition-supporting communities must leave, fall silent or support KANU to avoid death or eviction. In October 1993, for example, minister Francis Lotodo demanded that all Kikuyu leave West Pokot within 48 hours or they would be dealt with 'mercilessly'.[38] There were similar anti-Kikuyu threats in Turkana. In March 1994, minister Kipkalya arap Kones threatened to lynch or expel all Luo in Kericho and Bomet if they continued to support FORD-Kenya.[39] Repeatedly, Kikuyu were warned that they must toe the line in Maasailand or they would be punished.[40] No minister was even reprimanded for such incitement to violence. The 'willing buyer, willing seller' model was dying, and Kenya appeared to be heading towards a Balkan model of ethnic fragmentation and the institutionalisation of ethnic discrimination.

Meanwhile, aid agencies were trying to support the 300,000 left homeless and destitute by the clashes. The largest group were Kikuyu in Uasin Gishu and Nakuru, but thousands of Luo, Luhya, Gusii and Teso were also affected.[41] The United Nations Development Programme (UNDP) was the primary vehicle for this assistance, trying to provide rehabilitation back to the land or productive occupations for the internally displaced. Their programme proved unsuccessful, since it focused on the mechanics of integration without recognising the lack of political will. The environment for the returnees was not yet secure, new clashes were taking place and many had lost their land for good. Although tens of thousands did return, and some communities did reintegrate, the UNDP programme ended in 1995, with at least 150,000 still homeless. Other agencies castigated it for having 'ignored the political, human rights, and development dimensions of the displacement'.[42]

Few of those dispossessed made use of the law to obtain justice, fearful of the police and the near-impossibility of negotiating Kenya's legal minefield without money. After the Kituo Cha Sheria (Legal Advice Centre) NGO helped some clash victims in litigation, its offices were firebombed in 1995. Others who tried to help the victims were harassed and some journalists attempting to find out what was happening were beaten or arrested and charged with subversion or incitement.

Despite harsh words, there was no serious consideration given to mediation by Western governments, and foreign aid was not made conditional on the restoration of peace in the Rift.[43] Concerned about Kenya's stability and balancing economic, political and security issues, this turning of a blind eye implicitly condoned the use of violence to achieve political ends. From March 1995, however – for reasons which have never been explained (perhaps they had achieved their goal; perhaps the lessons of Rwanda were heeded; perhaps new alliances were in the offing) – the violence abated.

Less serious ethnic and political confrontations also occurred elsewhere. On the Coast, supporters of the IPK continued their fight with pro-KANU militia for control of the Muslim vote. In September 1993 ethnically based fighting took place in Kwale, and residents presciently accused the government of 'planning to start tribal clashes between the local Digos and people from upcountry'.[44] In Mombasa, three died in clashes between Luo and coastal people in December 1993. There was also an attack on Luo residents in Kilifi in May 1994 that drove away 2,000 upcountry people. All this presaged the trouble to come in Likoni in 1997. There was also violence in Laikipia, following incursions by pastoralists from Baringo and Samburu. Forced out of their home areas by lack of water (in part the result of forest excisions and logging), they invaded predominantly Kikuyu farms. The government's reluctance to evict them led to tension here also.

FERA, 1994–5

In contrast, the government cracked down hard on an illegal anti-government organisation operating in Western Kenya known as FERA – the February 18th Revolutionary Army.[45] FERA probably did exist (though some suspect, like Mwakenya, that it was a creation of the security forces) but had no coherent ideology or objectives, being driven rather by the reverberations of the ethnic killings in 1992 in Bungoma, which had radicalised some Luhya into believing that state-sponsored violence could only be met by violence in response. FERA was based in camps in Uganda and had its headquarters in Kampala. It had small arms, grenades, and some trained military personnel, and received some support from the Ugandan military (and money from Libya) but did not pose any real threat to the state.[46] FERA had connections with Uganda intelligence, and possibly with President Yoweri Museveni himself. Its military leader, John Odongo, a Luo from Siaya, had fought with Museveni in the National Resistance Army.[47]

This group was the rationale for another bout of repression by the security forces and the death or imprisonment of 300 Bukusu (and a few Luo) in Bungoma and Trans-Nzoia in 1994–5. As ever, there are no proper records of those killed by the state. The crackdown focused on opposition sympathisers and those who had fought against the Sabaot in 1992 or had criticised the government's handling of the clashes. More than 20 were killed and buried in prison.[48] Assassination squads killed others inside Uganda. Many were tortured, despite a multi-party system and active human rights organisations, unable to prevent what was occurring. The torture teams still included James Opiyo, who had tortured Mwakenya suspects in 1985–6.[49] Bukusu political leaders raised the matter in Parliament, but could do little in the face of state claims that the movement was real. The Western Province legal fraternity did little to defend the accused.

Crime

The 1990s saw a deepening security crisis. Statistics suggest a step-change increase in crime after 1992, reflecting the difficult economic situation, the legitimisation of political violence, the atomisation of urbanisation and the alienation of Kenyan youth (see Figure 10.2). Murder and rape were now daily events, and robbery and assault barely worth reporting. The security situation even affected senior politicians.[50] Nairobi was now one of the most dangerous cities in the world. Tourists began to seek safer places, and much of the city became a 'no go area'. There were growing numbers of street children, reflecting the impact of AIDS, poverty and the effects of the clashes. Bank robberies and carjackings became more frequent. Many businesses relocated to the safer western and northern suburbs.

Northern Kenya too was an increasingly dangerous place. The knock-on effects of the clashes, easy access to weapons, the creation of vigilante self-defence forces, the decline of police efficiency and the growing use of armed conflict as a political tool were seen everywhere. Fighting between the Pokot, Samburu and Turkana intensified, and more than 50 died in a pitched battle in December 1996 and another 40 in September 1997. There were frequent incursions by Pokot raiders into Turkana, Trans-Nzoia and Marakwet, which the police appeared unable to counteract. More than 1,000 Ethiopian cattle raiders crossed into Kenya in April 1997, killing more than 80 people, including 17 police. In another incident, the DC for Samburu District died when raiders shot down his helicopter.

The Police

The reintroduction of multi-party democracy resulted in no improvement in the conduct or accountability of the police force, which remained (as in most of Africa) incompetent, violent and corrupt. It was widely believed to commit many crimes

10.2: Murder figures and population aged over 15, 1962–2000

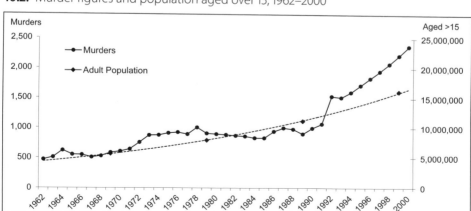

Source: Republic of Kenya, *Statistical Abstracts*, 1972–2001

itself. Poorly paid and trained, the force was low on morale and facilities and unable to conceive of any response to crime that did not involve reciprocal violence. The police were outgunned and at grave risk when dealing with serious crime. As a result, they appeared to be following an undeclared shoot to kill policy, and extra-judicial executions became more common. The traffic police, extracting bribes from *matatus* and drivers, appeared the most efficient part of the force. The first Kenya Urban Bribery Index, collated in 2001 by Transparency International, suggested the police were the most corrupt institution in the country, and that 'only one out of 10 people who regularly deal with the organization obtains satisfactory service without paying a bribe.'[51] Reform efforts were undermined by the knowledge at the top that change would undermine a key weapon in their armoury of political control.

The public face of Kenyan justice was now a facade, covering a far more corrupt, abusive and violent legal and penal system than most would admit.[52] The police and even chiefs could arrest, rob, beat, torture, jail and occasionally even murder Kenyans with effective impunity. All but the wealthiest and best-connected lived in fear of the police and the prisons – instruments of a chaotic, informal 'secret state' that served KANU's purposes but was only loosely under its control. There was a vast gulf between the 'paper' law and the 'real' law: of power, connections and money. The picture was not entirely one of decline, however. One positive step came with the reconstruction of Special Branch. Its head from 1995, Wilson Boinett, led the transformation of Special Branch into the National Security Intelligence Service (NSIS), changing its direction from the suppression of dissent towards intelligence-gathering on terrorism, organised crime and drugs.

In the late 1990s, Kenya's role in the worldwide drugs business became more prominent. This created both new commercial opportunities and new threats to the state, as drug growers and traffickers could entrench themselves, buying police protection and political power. In 1998–9, following protests by Kibaki and Archbishop Gitari, the police found and destroyed some cannabis plantations, but the efforts soon petered out. There were several high-profile seizures of drug cargoes in the mid- to late 1990s, but the traffickers and their goods vanished long before they reached the courts, having bought off the police. Kenya also became a transhipment point for hard drugs entering the country through its long and porous coastline.

The Legal and Penal System

The legal system meanwhile neared collapse. Between 1994 and 1997, Kenya's chief justice was Abdul Majid Cockar, the country's ninth and the first indigenous Kenyan since 1971 (and of Asian origin). Although personally a spartan man, he was unable to reverse the decline in standards, and faced growing clamour for the appointment of an African chief justice. Attorney-General Wako continued to take over and terminate private lawsuits against KANU leaders. The judiciary continued to respond informally to Moi's directives, such as his 1996 order that the courts not intervene in party disputes. Tension grew over the apparent partisanship of senior judges.[53]

Relations between (often pro-opposition) lawyers and (often pro-government) judges and magistrates reached a new low.

High-profile political cases were heard more fairly – because of media and foreign interest – than routine cases. With few lawyers outside the major urban areas and little legal aid, most of those arrested were unrepresented in court. Some magistrates and judges were for sale whether the case was small or large, and discriminated against those who obtained legal representation. Lawyers charged high fees and some stole compensation meant for their clients. Officials lost files or managed cases to ensure that pre-paid judges heard them. Judgments were no longer reported, making it impossible to use case law. Badly written law left entire sections of the legislative system in limbo.[54] These failures underpinned the survival of the government, since it could not have continued to rule if an impartial judiciary had held it to account. Meanwhile the number of open cases grew inexorably, some lasting 20 years.

Like those of many other African states, Kenya's prisons remained filthy, over-crowded, violent, corrupt and secretive. There was a steep rise in prisoners, with 75 per cent more inmates in 2002 than in 1995.[55] Only four new prisons had been built since independence, leaving the service catering for three times the population with virtually the same facilities. The government admitted to 1,800 deaths in prison in 1994 alone.[56] In September 2000, in a notorious incident, warders beat to death six inmates at a prison in Nyeri. Their bodies were thrown over the prison walls to make it appear they had died while escaping. When this was discovered, however, the resulting furore did bring about greater openness.

Kenya retained a mandatory death sentence for treason, murder and robbery with violence, but no executions were carried out after 1988.[57] Although the country had signed up to the UN Convention against Torture and Other Cruel, Inhuman or Degrading Treatment or Punishment in 1997, torture remained routine, as confessions made solely to police remained admissible.[58] In 1999, DP MP Norman Nyagah claimed that more than 1,700 people had died from police torture.[59] Despite reports by Amnesty International, UNESCO, foreign governments and even a new standing committee on human rights, little changed. It was increasingly unclear whether the police were there to protect the politicians, or the politicians were there to protect the police. Human rights activists increasingly targeted the police force as in need of fundamental reform.

As the police and courts' efficiency declined, local communities took the law into their own hands. There was growing use of informal elders' courts, as people could not afford the fees and bribes needed for a legal case and even if police did arrest criminals, they could be back on the streets within weeks if they could pay the right people. The lynching of suspected thieves became more frequent, with 500 lynchings in 1993 alone. Kenyans' strong belief in the immaterial combined with the decline in the rule of law to result in literal witch-hunts within 30 minutes' drive of Nairobi.[60] Seeking for explanations in an increasingly complex and arbitrary world, witchcraft and Satanism became daily fare in the national press.

The Military

The Kenyan military remained a relatively professional force. There was now little likelihood of external invasion and instead the army turned to UN peacekeeping, which offered both experience and a source of income for the army and its soldiers. Although other agreements had lapsed, the British continued to train annually in Kenya, with 4,000 troops on exercises in 1997. The American military influence, which had been cut back in 1990–1, was gradually restored. The US continued to train Kenyan officers and joint exercises recommenced in 1996, although direct military assistance did not resume until 2002.

Though the military remained outside active politics, senior appointments were viewed by the public with an ethnic lens. The top leadership demonstrated how much had changed since Kenyatta's day (see Table 10.1). By 1994, ex-KADU communities dominated the military, and there were no Kikuyu in top posts at all. Although the Kalenjin influence was not overwhelming, positions at the next level, including logistics, intelligence and barracks command, were more Kalenjin-dominated.[61] In 1996, on General Mahamoud Mohamed's retirement, a Kalenjin took command of the military for the first time. Tugen Daudi Tonje's rise, like Sawe's before him, had been rapid, with four promotions from head of the Defence College to Chief of General Staff in three years.

The government's financial problems affected the army as well. Spending fell to its lowest ever in dollar terms in 1994, leaving the military unable to maintain adequate training or replace ageing equipment. There was unrest in 1995, with NCOs complaining

Table 10.1: Military heads, 1990–9

Post	Name	Dates	Ethnicity
Chief of General Staff	Lt.-Gen. then General Mahamoud Mohamed	1986–96	Somali
	General Daudi Tonje	1996–2000	Kalenjin – Tugen
Deputy Chief of General Staff	Lt.-Gen. Daudi Tonje	1994–6	Kalenjin – Tugen
Army Commander	Lt.-Gen. James Lengees	1986–93	Samburu
	Lt.-Gen. Daudi Tonje	1993–4	Kalenjin – Tugen
	Lt.-Gen. Augustine arap Cheruiyot	1994–8	Kalenjin – Nandi
'82 Air Force/ KAF Commander	Major-Gen. Dedan Gichuru	1986–9	Kikuyu
	Major-Gen. D. K. Wachira	1989–94	Kikuyu
	Major-Gen. Nick Leshan	1994–2000	Maasai
Navy Commander	Major-Gen. Joseph Kibwana	1988–98	Mijikenda

Source: Various

over low pay and lack of facilities. In November of that year, soldiers heckled and walked out on General Mohamed.[62] A review of conditions soon followed.

The New Tribalism of 1990s Kenya

Driven by the alignment of political party and ethnicity, the multi-party Moi state shifted from an informal quota model for senior roles to one which was clearly biased towards 'insider' communities.

The Kalenjin Veneer

Given the paucity of educated, experienced (and obedient) Kalenjin, to possess such qualities was an immediate avenue for preferment. Kalenjin were parachuted at every level into parastatals, universities and the civil service, and held many of the top jobs in the police, the provisional administration, finance, telecommunications and agricultural parastatals. Even private businesses saw it was in their interest to ensure that the president's community were represented in their management team.

Senior police posts were particularly Kalenjin dominated, as they had been Kikuyu dominated in the 1970s. The country went through four police commissioners during the decade, none of whom was Kalenjin. However, the police commissioner was in many ways a figurehead; the real decisions were made by his operational assistants and by the heads of the CID, Special Branch and GSU. On sensitive matters they reported directly to State House, where a Kalenjin line ran direct from Moi and the permanent secretary for internal security into all the security services (See Table 10.2). This was so obvious it was almost unremarked.

Increasingly, ethnic groups saw positions held by their kin as 'their property', and treated the sackings of any leaders from their communities as ethnically motivated attempts to 'finish' their community at the national level. A popular expectation of an ethnic entitlement system was maturing in the administration, as in politics. There were choruses of disapproval from the Luhya, for example, when Jirongo and his allies were evicted in 1993–4; from the Mijikenda when the Kenya Ports Authority was purged in 1996; and from Kamba politicians when policemen William Kivuvani and Philip Kilonzo retired.

Ethnic Identities

During the 1990s, recognising the importance of numbers and of unity in the struggle for the state, Kalenjin leaders reinforced the community's common identity and interests and tried to downplay the cultural differences and sometimes conflicting interests of the Tugen, Keiyo, Nandi, Kipsigis, Pokot, Marakwet and Sabaot. They also began to manufacture a new supra-ethnic identity. Increasingly, KANU referred during 1993–4 to the common interests of the 'Kamatusa' communities (*Ka*lenjin, *Maa*sai, *Tu*rkana and *Sa*mburu), shaping a new identity amongst Nilotic pastoralists with few roots in history, languages or culture, but centred on their

Table 10.2: Police and internal security heads, 1991–2002

Post	Name	Dates	Ethnicity
Permanent Secretary for Provincial Administration and Internal Security	Wilfred Kimalat	1991–8	Kalenjin
	Zakayo Cheruiyot	1998–2003	Kalenjin
Police Commissioner	Philip Kilonzo	1988–93	Kamba
	Shadrack Kiruki	1993–6	Meru
	Duncan Wachira	1996–9	Kikuyu
	Philemon Abong'o	1999–2003	Luo
GSU Head	Jackson arap Kosgei	1987–93	Kalenjin
	Charles Kimurgor	1993–9	Kalenjin
	Samson Cheramboss	1999–2002	Kalenjin
	David Kimaiyo	2002–3	Kalenjin
CID Head	Noah arap Too	1984–99	Kalenjin
	Francis arap Sang	1999–2003	Kalenjin
Special Branch/ NSIS Head	William Kivuvani	1991–5	Kamba
	Wilson Boinett	1995–2006	Kalenjin
Presidential Escort Unit Head	Charles Kimurgor	n/a–1993	Kalenjin
	Samson Cheramboss	n/a –1999	Kalenjin
	David Kimaiyo	1999–n/a	Kalenjin
	Nixon Boit	n/a–2003	Kalenjin

Source: Various.

Data on presidential escort heads are difficult to acquire.

common economic position, lifestyle and influence on the government. Although there were countervailing tendencies, multi-party competition was driving the aggregation of ethnic identities to higher levels, just as in the 1950s and 1960s. Again, the goal was to create something akin to a 'minimum winning coalition': an identity big enough to secure both political power and control of land, particularly in the Rift Valley.[63]

As the same time, Kikuyu, Embu and Meru politicians were trying to rebuild an older, cross-party and cross-ethnic identity – that of the Kikuyu, Embu and Meru (Gema) or 'Mount Kenya' peoples. Calls for the reactivation of the GEMA organisation, a proxy institution to defend the collective interests of these communities, began in August 1993.[64] Muite, Imanyara and other Young Turks participated, as did DP leaders Njenga Karume and Ngengi Muigai and Mama Ngina Kenyatta. However, such approaches were easily portrayed as part of the tribalist agenda of Kikuyu hegemony, and all attempts to create such formal institutions foundered.

The Politics of Discrimination

Most Kikuyu believed they were being systematically weakened by government policies, undermined by the chaotic and corrupt administration of their cash-crops, physically driven out of the Rift and discriminated out of their jobs. As Kikuyu politician Rumba Kinuthia said in 1993, 'For many years during the Nyayo era, Kikuyu and other Gema communities have been openly discriminated against and their leaders systematically persecuted through detention, imprisonment, torture and personal economic annihilation.'[65]

There is some evidence that there was indeed a campaign at this time to drive senior Kikuyu and Luo out of the civil service, on the grounds that they were politically suspect.[66] Whatever the truth, there was no doubt that the Kikuyu *believed* that the government undermined their infrastructure, sacked their tribesmen and stole their profits. Many felt that Moi had 'a strong, deep-rooted hatred for the Kikuyu',[67] though this theory was to be challenged in 2002. In response, the Gema communities revealed their own chauvinistic elitism. Kikuyu criticism of Moi focused on how more backward ethnic groups had destroyed the country, whereas Kenya had prospered under their rule. Such messages were also a way for politicians to secure their ethnic constituency: communicating a message of discrimination by a partisan government reinforced (especially for Kikuyu and Luo) the need for unity in order to deliver the numbers needed to seize the state.

Although both elites and masses protested vocally, most did little but complain. Many of the same triggers existed for mass violence as in the late 1940s – landlessness, impoverishment, discrimination and forcible removal from land in the Rift – but there was no second Mau Mau. Most Kikuyu opposition leaders had too much to lose to support open conflict: some were still in business with their KANU opponents; others did not wish to risk what they had acquired by supporting violent protest. Moi also rewarded those who were loyal to him from any community. There were many Kikuyu such as Kamotho, Philip Ndegwa (Kenya Airways), Erastus Mureithi (Cooperative Bank) and Samuel Gichuru (KPLC) happy to work for the government. The greatest danger for reciprocal violence lay in the urban youth and the dispossessed peasants of the Rift. During 1993–5, there were attacks on police stations to steal weapons, and dozens of Kikuyu were convicted of oathing to defend their land. The clashes and disenfranchisement of the Kikuyu in this period helped spawn the Mungiki movement (see Chapter 11).[68]

Ethnic Parleys

Although Moi believed that he was the 'father of the nation', he also played the role of a Kalenjin chief. To address the clashes, for example, in May 1993 he took the extraordinary step of organising a tribal council. Twenty conservative elders from the Gema communities (including Karume, Isaiah Mathenge, Muigai and Geoffrey Kariithi) met 60 Kalenjin and Maasai to discuss how to end the violence in the Rift.[69] During 1995, more parleys took place between Kikuyu and Kalenjin, culminating in a 52-MP session in Molo, where a peace accord was reached.

However, talks ended in September 1995 when KANU lost the Kipipiri by-election, despite a campaign during which Moi visited the seat five times. KANU expected to win, but the DP won a decisive victory with 80 per cent of the vote. The opponents of a strategy of wooing the Kikuyu – Nyachae, Ntimama and Kones – once more denounced the Kikuyu community as isolationist and irreconcilably hostile to KANU. The electricity poles that KPLC had brought, to show how power would come to the seat if KANU was elected, were removed a week later. The deal with the Kikuyu would have to wait.

Aid, the West and the Economy

The year 1993 was one of pain and retrenchment. Agricultural production was low, affected by poor weather and the clashes. Inflation was out of control and the foreign currency crisis worsened, exacerbated by capital flight and the Goldenberg scandal. GDP growth for 1992–3 was only 0.4 per cent, the lowest since independence, and the country defaulted on its foreign debt repayments in 1994.

Liberalisation and De-Liberalisation, January–April 1993

In January 1993, the election over, Kenya's donors met to discuss the resumption of budgetary support and non-project aid, but concluded that Kenya's economic record, governance and levels of corruption were so poor that no new aid was justified for at least six more months.[70] The government's main hopes lay with the IMF and the World Bank, whose enthusiasm for political conditionality had always been weaker. Just before the IMF's next visit, on 19 February 1993, the government fully floated the exchange rate and abolished Forex-Cs. It also relaxed price controls on fuel, wheat, maize and sugar, liberalised wheat marketing and allowed tourist businesses to keep half their foreign exchange earnings. This was forced policy-making, driven by the need to do a deal with their financiers. The government hoped that the IMF would report positively and aid would resume, propping up the shilling.

However, the IFIs remained unconvinced. Negotiations broke down as Kenya refused to accept IMF demands for 45 per cent interest rates and leadership changes in key parastatals and the Central Bank. As a result, the economy entered a period of crisis as businesses panicked. The shilling fell from 36.5 to the dollar to 55 in a few days.[71] In the background, Goldenberg continued to drain funds from the economy. The Kenyan government was furious, accusing the West of 'shifting the goal posts every time we are about to score by coming up with new aid conditions . . .'[72] On 19 March 1993, Moi announced that the government was abandoning 'economically suicidal' structural adjustment policies. Believing that the country was on the verge of collapse and an explosion of discontent, Moi backed the hardliners against Saitoti, Mudavadi and the reformers. Three days later, Mudavadi reimposed controls on foreign exchange and prices.[73]

Within days though, the Kenyans were back-pedalling. The economy was seizing up, with oil companies unable to import and airlines unable to buy fuel. The government was forced to compromise with the IFIs, who feared in turn that they would be held responsible for Kenya's collapse. To meet the short-term liquidity crisis, the Treasury and CBK sold billions of shillings of Treasury bills. The government reaffirmed its commitment to privatisation and liberalisation. During April, Forex-Cs were reintroduced and interest rates were raised to 45 per cent, as the IMF had demanded. In return, the World Bank released US$85 million of aid. In parallel, the CBK began to clean up the political banks. In March, it had already abolished the pre-shipment finance scheme, in the face of overwhelming evidence of its abuse.[74] Soon after, it abolished import licences and reintroduced foreign exchange retention accounts. The crisis was over.

Crisis in the CBK, January–July 1993

In early 1993, the true extent of the Goldenberg scandal became public. Following reports from the auditor-general, FORD-Kenya and the *Nation* newspaper, Kenyans gradually learnt of the degree to which their banking system had been hijacked for private gain. In return for monopoly access and preferential compensation, Goldenberg and its backers had smuggled in gold, exported phantom products, bribed officials, extracted billions for themselves and funded KANU's re-election campaign. Between 1991 and May 1993, it seems that Pattni effectively ran the CBK. In 1993, facing a black hole in its accounts caused by theft and hubris, Goldenberg and its satellite companies kited cheques and conducted bank frauds that took the economy close to collapse and ratcheted inflation to 60 per cent.[75] The discovery of what was going on inspired huge Western concern and delayed the resumption of financial support.[76] The donors demanded changes at the top, particularly in the CBK.[77]

With the closing down of the gold export scam after its exposure in early 1993, the action shifted elsewhere, as Pattni and his backers sought every loophole to keep their operations running. First, Goldenberg (and other insider companies) bought as many Forex-Cs as they could, with the exposure rising to Ksh3.6 billion (US$70 million). The CBK was short of foreign exchange and had issued more certificates than it could redeem. Pattni alleged that he had an agreement with CBK Governor Eric Kotut that Goldenberg would purchase the certificates (with shillings from the original scam), but not redeem them for dollars. In return, the CBK would buy the certificates from Goldenberg at a shilling premium, thereby removing Forex-Cs from the market (and rewarding Goldenberg for doing precisely nothing). The CBK also bought foreign exchange at market rates and then sold it to Goldenberg at the official rate – foreign exchange that eventually ended up in the US to be declared as the proceeds of the imaginary exports. At least five banks also engaged in cheque kiting against the Central Bank, to the tune of Ksh10 billion or more in April 1993. In parallel, Central Bank officials secretly reissued millions of dollars' worth of already-redeemed Forex-C certificates.

The CBK may even have resorted to loans from Goldenberg, to fake foreign currency reserves that the country did not possess. Pattni claimed in 2004:

> On one such occasion around May 1993, I was requested by the governor through Deputy Governor Eliphaz Riungu to assist them in achieving certain monetary targets set for them by the IMF/World Bank by arranging a back to back deposit of $210 million of foreign exchange receipts and the sale of Treasury Bills amounting to Sh25 billion . . . The purpose of this was a book entry to boost the foreign exchange reserves of the country for a temporary period coinciding with the inspection/study of the finances of the country and the Central Bank by the IMF/World Bank.[78]

The state later charged Pattni with the theft of Ksh13.5 billion in this way, since he had allegedly taken the shillings, but bribed officials to fake the dollar deposits. It was an extraordinary story of greed, intrigue and incompetence.

With the election won, though, Pattni was a liability. Allegedly under instruction from Moi (a claim that was never proven) Treasury Permanent Secretary Wilfred Koinange ordered the repayment of Pattni's 'loans' to KANU by transferring another Ksh5.8 billion (US$85 million) of export compensation in three secret transactions from the Consolidated Fund to Goldenberg accounts between April and July.[79] Pattni's position became increasingly precarious as donor pressure increased. His hotline was disconnected in May 1993. As the extent of the scandal emerged, the prosecutions began; Pattni was first arrested in 1994 and was in court for most of the next 15 years, although he remained extremely wealthy.

As Goldenberg unravelled, at least 15 finance institutions collapsed in 1993 due to insider lending, under-capitalisation and bad debt. The most prominent was Trade Bank, which fell in April 1993 as owner Alnoor Kassam fled the country.[80] In April, the Deposit Protection Fund took over 11 more smaller financial institutions. In May–June 1993, Post Bank Credit went under, crippled by its unsecured loans to Sololo, and in July Exchange Bank and Pan-African Bank followed.[81] In every case, huge sums were lost by depositors and by the state. Trans-National Bank was the sole political bank to continue to receive parastatal deposits and unsecured credit from the CBK. It too had a Ksh500 million hole in its accounts, but Moi organised a loan from coastal tycoons to keep it afloat.[82]

The clean-up was now well under way. On 23 July 1993, Kotut finally resigned as CBK governor. His replacement, Micah Cheserem, was also a Kalenjin (and Moi's personal assistant Joshua Kulei's brother-in-law), but his reputation and that of the government now rested on cleaning up Goldenberg (while avoiding indicting the true beneficiaries).

A Deal is Done, November 1993

Between May and October 1993, negotiations continued between the IFIs and the government. In September, before the next IMF meeting, Kenya once more abolished exchange controls, floating the shilling in a more structured fashion. The government relaxed maize movements again and allowed private maize imports.

In November 1993, two years after the freeze, the Paris Club finally agreed a new package for Kenya. There would be US$850 million of aid, including $170 million in balance of payments support.[83] In return, Kenya promised to reduce corruption, mop up the excess money in circulation, demonstrate strict administration of the CBK, cut the civil service, end the clashes, liberalise the maize industry and enhance press freedom. The meeting also agreed a seven-year period during which Kenya would repay its US$715 million of debt arrears. However, it was only two months before Mudavadi was back in Paris, where Kenya was granted a full rescheduling of US$540 million of its overdue debt for the first time.[84] Requests for rescheduling to the London Club of commercial creditors followed. Estimates of Kenya's overseas liabilities varied from US$5.6 billion to $6.4 billion: either way, Kenya could not pay.

Macro-Economic Recovery, 1994–6

The restoration of aid, the end of foreign exchange controls, trade liberalisation, the one-off benefits of privatisation and the ending of the Goldenberg frauds saw the economy bounce back during 1994–6 (see Figure 10.3). There were particular successes in the services sector (in tourism, transport and financial services), which grew to more than 50 per cent of GDP. The Nairobi Stock Exchange boomed, doubling in 1993 and again in 1994. The shilling experienced a similar recovery. It had plunged from Ksh28 to the dollar in 1991 to 68 in 1993, when dollar reserves were almost exhausted. The year 1994 saw an appreciating currency, reaching Ksh44 to the dollar

10.3: GDP growth, 1990–8

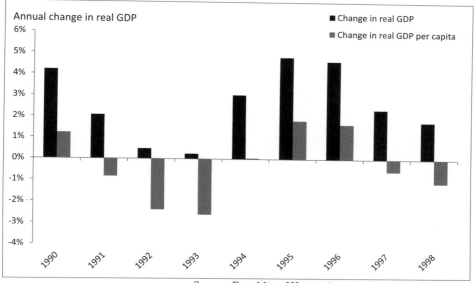

Source: Republic of Kenya, *Statistical Abstracts*, 1995–2001

as the Goldenberg scams unwound and the economy rebounded.[85] Dollar reserves improved with large foreign inflows and strong exports.

This was not the result of foreign private investment, which was virtually zero in 1992–4 and rose to only US$40 million a year in 1997, a fraction of the investments in Uganda and Tanzania. Although Kenya was more 'business friendly' than in the 1980s, the state's venality and incapacity remained a challenge and the investors were no longer multinationals but private businessmen, some of questionable reputation.

Inflation, which had peaked in 1993 at 46 per cent, fell back to 29 per cent in 1994 and to 1.6 per cent in 1995. Tight monetary policies kept inflation low for the rest of the Moi era (see Figure 10.4). Interest rates followed a similar pattern, but remained far higher. A side-effect of the government's efforts to control inflation and support the shilling by sales of Treasury bills at high interest rates was to make domestic borrowing extremely expensive, while encouraging speculative capital inflows.[86]

Exports boomed in 1993–6, benefiting from liberalisation, high coffee and tea prices, good horticultural production and falling real wages.[87] The export processing zone legislation began to be used, with the first zone set up in 1993, offering duty exemptions, tax holidays and a strike ban. In 1993, Kenya signed up to the Common Market for East and Central Africa (COMESA), the successor to the PTA, which soon became a key market for Kenyan manufactures. Import tariffs were simplified and absolute levels cut. In 1995, Kenya also joined the World Trade Organization (WTO).

However, Kenya's industrial productivity remained low, and the country struggled to adopt new technologies or to exploit its relatively low labour costs. The decline of the roads, railways and power sectors due to under-investment, corruption and an unreliable legal framework were often cited as reasons why growth was not faster. Kenya's manufacturing sector was also troubled by legitimate and black market

10.4: Inflation rates, 1978–2007

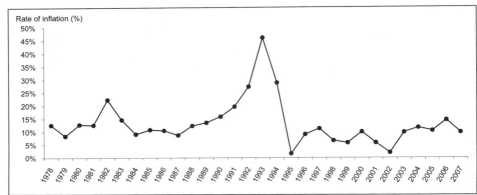

Source: CBS website, www.cbs.go.ke, 2010

imports and the diversion of goods for export back into the economy, at huge cost to the Treasury.

Key functions in the government were becoming more independent from direct political control. In 1995, the Kenya Revenue Authority (KRA) was established to create an integrated, semi-independent and professional tax collection body. This was encouraged by Western donors in order to make tax collection more efficient and, by raising more money, restore some of the diminished capacity of the state.[88] Estimates suggested that half of the revenue due to the government was not collected, as a result of low compliance, poor administration and corruption.[89] In 1996, following the trend in other countries, the Central Bank of Kenya Act gave the CBK autonomy to set monetary policy independently of the state. Its objectives were to limit inflation, maintain the value of the shilling and preserve the stability of the banking system. The Act also limited the government's overdraft to a ceiling of 5 per cent of state revenue and gave the CBK governor security of tenure.[90]

Debt servicing exceeded 35 per cent of exports, moving Kenya into the category of 'highly indebted nations'. With the successes of the mid-1990s, Kenya's debt fell in dollar terms between 1994 and 1997 (see Figure 10.5), but the state of Kenya's debt register was so poor that few placed trust in its figures. Even the government later described the register as 'incomplete and unreliable'.[91]

10.5: Internal and external debt, 1982–2002

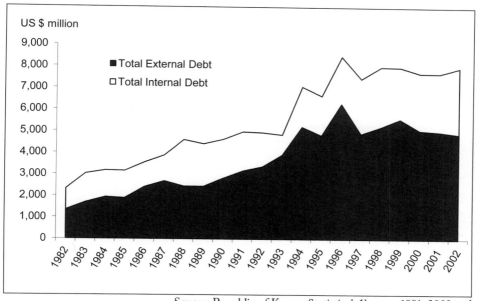

Source: Republic of Kenya, *Statistical Abstracts*, 1991–2003 and
Public Debt Management Report, 2005–6, year-end dollar rates and debt.
The domestic numbers for 1995 are an interpolation as originals were felt to be unreliable.

Tourism and Wildlife

In the tourism sector, the decline of 1991–2 was reversed and the mid-1990s saw a brief recovery. The 1996 peak of 924,000 visitors should have represented a boom era, but the industry was not entirely healthy. The world market was changing and total receipts from tourism fell from 1994. Causes included the decline in security, environmental degradation and the poor state of the roads. Better global communications propagated reports of ethnic violence and political instability to a fearful Western public, as the sharp falls in visitor numbers in 1992–3 and 1997–8 indicate (see Figure 10.6).

Kenya's tourism still depended on its wildlife. During 1990–3, Richard Leakey's reforms in the KWS achieved spectacular successes in cutting poaching. Combining commitment, efficiency, a thick skin towards politicians and strong donor support, Leakey turned around what had become a catastrophe: over four years, he raised more than US$100 million towards wildlife conservation; he retired 2,300 rangers – nearly half the force – recruited militarily trained professionals to replace them, armed them with semi-automatic weapons and new vehicles and put into practice Moi's controversial shoot to kill policy in the parks. Poaching was nearly eradicated in four years. Between 1991 and 2001, not a single rhino was poached in Kenya. From an all-time low of fewer than 20,000 elephants in 1989, by the mid-1990s, their number had risen to 25,000 and was growing by 1,000 a year.[92] In one of its few consistent policy positions, the government opposed any relaxation of the international ban on ivory sales and refused all foreign inducements to soften its position.

In 1994, tensions grew between Leakey and Moi. Although Leakey had done what Moi had wanted, he was too independent, and Moi felt uneasy about the uncritical (and sometimes racist) support he received from overseas. Like Perez Olindo before

10.6: International arrivals and visits to national parks, 1964–2002

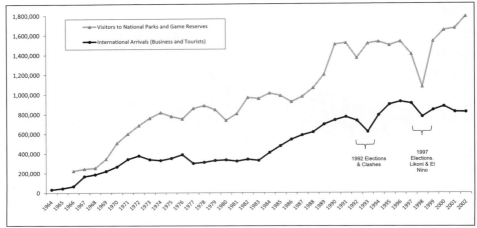

Source: Republic of Kenya, *Statistical Abstracts*, 1972–2003

him, Leakey also failed to persuade Moi to convert the Maasai Mara into a national park administered by the KWS, which would have removed a key patronage resource from the Maasai leadership of Narok. Leakey was driven out of his role in March 1994, partly because of his reluctance to implement new policies requiring that much of the KWS's funds be spent outside the national parks and that its revenues be shared with neighbouring communities.[93]

Aid, Donor Relations and Reform, 1994–7

Although the machine continued to turn, overall overseas aid was significantly lower than in 1989–91 (see Figure 10.7) and in real terms was below the level of 1980. Its origins had also changed. World Bank loans were less important, with bilateral (mostly grant) aid now 75 per cent of the total. Kenya continued to receive aid from dozens of nations, but Japan and Germany (not the US or UK) were Kenya's largest donors.[94]

The Aid Cycle

Having entered the political fray in Kenya in 1990–1, the West was unable to disengage. The political and economic conditionalities it had established for the disbursement of aid left it enmeshed in Kenya's internal affairs, granting or withholding aid, choosing projects and auditing outcomes, and driving policy via lobbying, aid conditionalities and NGOs alike. Western governments focused their public rhetoric on governance, privatisation and democratisation, but remained deeply concerned about security and stability as well, issues which sometimes pulled them in different directions.[95]

Both bilateral donors and the IFIs used money as a carrot and its suspension as a stick with which to beat the government to implement reforms it would otherwise

10.7: Overseas development aid, 1978–96

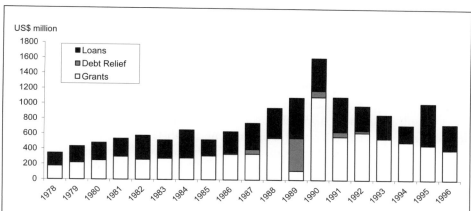

Source: O'Brien and Ryan: *Kenya*, pp. 471, 520–1

have delayed or abandoned. However, donors were unable to translate this power into direct control of government policy. They often overestimated the state's capacity and underestimated the difficulty of structural reform in a situation of low civil service competence and institutional corruption. There was a huge dependence on a few highly visible individuals. The government fought certain reforms, popular opinion opposed others, and the donors themselves were far from united. While the government and the IFIs battled, NGOs and opposition politicians sometimes exploited naive diplomats and agencies, covertly campaigning for regime change through their influence on donors.

The relationship with the donors waxed and waned on an annual cycle, which seemed only loosely related to actual policy changes. In November–December 1994, the Paris Club pledged another US$800 million of aid, including US$200 million in balance of payments support, at the same time as human rights agencies and the US Congress were damning the government for the clashes and its harassment of the opposition. Despite this, the Kenyans persuaded the IFIs that the economy had turned the corner.[96]

Still, donors kept the pressure on the government both for privatisation and for action on corruption, increasingly using the language of 'good governance', a surrogate for political openness since the IFIs were barred from interfering in the domestic politics of member states.[97] During 1995, relations worsened. Although Kenya's ESAF loans were extended, there were crisis meetings over delays in the privatisation and reform programme and protests that donors were trying to destabilise the government. In September, the IMF suspended the next $90 million ESAF payment.

By March–April 1996, relations had improved again. With privatisations flowing, better fiscal management and less opposition harassment, the Paris Club pledged new aid, and the IMF offered a new three-year loan programme worth US$220 million, of which US$36 million was disbursed. In June, the World Bank loaned $127 million for public sector and civil service reform. In return, the government promised autonomy for the Central Bank, faster civil service retrenchment, an end to the NSSF's monopoly, the restructuring of the insolvent KNAC, commercialisation of the NCPB, part-privatisation of KPTC and the restructuring of the KPA. In protest at their apparent endorsement of KANU, the opposition accused the IFIs of betrayal.

But the stop–start game continued, with knock-on economic effects. The second ESAF tranche in October 1996 was again withheld due to the slow pace of parastatal reform, poor monetary discipline and foot-dragging over corruption. Yet an IMF/World Bank Mission in April 1997 recommended the release of funds once more, describing the government's reform programme as 'satisfactory'.[98] This followed last-minute reforms – including privatisations, liberalisation of the energy sector, the restructuring of the NSSF and the break-up of KPTC – which looked to have been done entirely in order to get the money. It was a messy, inconsistent, destabilising and entirely political process.

International Relations

After the restoration of financial support in 1993, foreign governments took a lower profile in Kenyan affairs. The Clinton presidency of 1992–2000 reflected its lessened interest in Africa by replacing Smith Hempstone with a less senior diplomat in 1993. She was in turn replaced by the more assertive Prudence Bushnell in 1996. Although the US continued to defend the legitimacy of Kenya's opposition and criticise the government, it was far less vocal – a reaction to Hempstone's intemperance – and the US relied significantly on Kenya as a security partner during the crises in Rwanda and Somalia. There was growing US scepticism about the value to either party of foreign aid, and US aid to sub-Saharan Africa halved from US$1.2 billion in 1985 to $600 million in 1996.[99] After 1993, US aid to Kenya was well below the levels of the 1980s and military assistance virtually zero.[100] Relations between the UK and Kenya remained cautious, and dominated by aid.

In 1996, Kenya was elected to the UN Security Council for the second time since independence; again, this was seen as an endorsement of the government's position. In the same year, Kenya hosted a visit by Chinese premier Jiang Zemin, which ended with an agreement on Ksh1.2 billion of Chinese loans and grants. Trade increased substantially from 1994 on, mainly imports of Chinese manufactured goods.

Inside Africa, Moi remained active in conflict resolution, including efforts to save the life of Nigerian activist Ken Saro-Wiwa in 1995. Locally, linkages improved with Tanzania and Uganda, though progress was slow. However, all else was overshadowed by the events in Rwanda. In 1994, following the killing of the Rwandan and Burundian presidents, Rwandan Hutus murdered more than a million of their fellow-citizens in a genocidal orgy of violence. Although they had no shared border, the horrors in Rwanda affected Kenya. Not only did it show the risks involved in the violent ethnic politics being pursued in the Rift Valley, the war also came to Kenyan soil: over the next few years, several senior Hutu exiles were murdered in Kenya by agents of the new Rwandan Patriotic Front government.

Privatisation and Liberalisation in the 1990s

Although it had defended its capitalist credentials for 20 years, and private enterprise was deep-rooted by African standards, it had taken place in a state-defined framework, dominated by state corporations and joint ventures in which political and administrative insiders dominated. During 1991–4, however, Kenya began a reluctant transition into a genuine capitalist open market economy, eventually becoming one of the most liberalised in Africa. This change agenda was driven by an unstable alliance between the IFIs, a small group of technocrats, the private sector and elements in both the government and the opposition.

Still divided over the merits and costs of change, the state liberalised, relaxing fiscal controls, exchange control and tariffs before it privatised, creating a situation where some state industries, insufficiently restructured, faced the winds of external competition and suffered. All remaining price controls were removed by 1994.

Domestic import substitution businesses such as beer and cigarettes, previously de facto monopolies, began to face imports from abroad. From 1994 on, the privatisation process in turn moved into top gear. The process was slow, contested and incomplete, and it caused the failure of a number of industries, but it also contributed to a brief period of relative prosperity.

The Privatisation Programme, 1994–7

The government had committed itself to privatisation in 1986 and again in 1991, reflecting the belief amongst foreign advisers and local technocrats that it would bring greater efficiency and better financial performance.[101] The government had established a privatisation unit, and identified 240 state bodies as having commercial functions that rendered them candidates for sale. Yet it had privatised almost nothing. There were good reasons for this. Some of the enterprises were unprofitable and therefore hard to sell. The government remained committed to greater local ownership of the economy and feared that alliances of Kenyan and foreign capital would acquire state assets too cheaply. Equally important, the parastatals were avenues for nepotism, patrimonial appointments and corruption, all of which would diminish with privatisation. The inevitable restructuring would result in job losses, which would hurt the popularity of the government and of the patrons who had created these jobs. There were also concerns that the misappropriations and poor investments of the past would be exposed, revealing the degree to which some parastatals had already been run into the ground.

Despite the state's caution, it managed a series of quick wins during 1994–6, driven, financed and micro-managed by the World Bank. The revenues went into supporting the deficit. By the end of 1996, 141 of the 207 parastatals identified for privatisation had been sold. These included the KTDC, KNAC, the Industrial Development Bank and the Cotton Lint and Seed Marketing Board as well as many fully commercial investments. From this process, the government realised between Ksh9.6 billion and Ksh10.4 billion (US$200 million), a modest figure in comparison to total government revenue.[102] Many realised less than their accumulated debts. The Nyayo Bus Corporation, for example, attracted no buyers and was liquidated in 1997. African Tours and Hotels, once the centrepiece of the government's ownership of the tourism industry, was put up for privatisation in 1997 and found to have been insolvent for years.

Four methods of privatisation were used. The first was open competitive bidding. By December 1996, the state had sold 14 companies this way, mostly hotels or cotton mills.[103] In the same period, shares in 36 enterprises had been sold to their employees or existing shareholders who had pre-emptive rights to offer for them. These included well-known businesses of the 1960s and 1970s such as the Pan-Afric Hotel, Firestone, Kenya Cashewnuts, Associated Vehicle Assemblers and Kenya Vehicle Manufacturers.[104]

The most popular European mode of privatisation – the sale of shares to the public – was only used if a business was a large, going concern. Only five companies were partially or fully floated on the Nairobi Stock Exchange between 1992 and 1996: Kenya Airways, the NBK, Uchumi Supermarkets, the HFCK and the Kenya National Capital Corporation.[105] Such privatisations were extremely popular amongst investors, though, showing the depth of indigenous private capital, in stark contrast to the 1960s. Kenya Airways was a particular success story. Restructured for privatisation, the company became profitable for the first time in 1993–4. In 1995, it began a partnership with KLM, and the government took over its Ksh4.6 billion external debt. In 1996, the company was privatised: KLM bought 26 per cent for US$137 million, the government kept 26 per cent and 48 per cent was sold to local and international investors. The company soon proved one of the strongest and most profitable carriers in Africa.

The final category of privatisations covered a dozen smaller businesses (including Kenatco and several textile mills) that were in receivership, and were sold off to anyone willing to take them. In an intensively political exercise, in 1996 Raila Odinga's Spectre International won an auction for the derelict Kisumu molasses plant, on the promise of reviving it.[106]

Although it was modest in scale, corruption and nepotism played a role here as well. IMF and World Bank officials, who were funding the programme, were increasingly concerned that some parastatals were being sold off too cheaply to politically connected companies. In the case of Kenya Fluorspar, for example, it was alleged that the sale price was below the market value, and claims that the buyers included local MP Biwott.[107] The Milling Corporation, which operated flour mills nationally, was sold in 1994, but there was a near-revolt in Parliament after claims that it was valued at Ksh550 million and sold for 150 million. A year after the sale, most of the money had still not been received; the owners were rumoured to include Moi, Biwott and Kulei.[108] The privatisation unit, led by (Tugen) Lawi Kiplagat, refused to explain the tendering process. The auditor-general asked for the sale to be cancelled.[109]

Most of the 33 state assets the government had deemed strategic remained in state hands, including the KPTC, KPLC, KPA and Kenya Railways. Despite their generally poor performance and strong donor pressure, there was little national support for privatisation of such core services. In these sectors, the state's strategy was to create more professional management structures, increase user charges to cover costs, remove government guarantees for loans, segregate regulatory and commercial functions, allow greater competition and only then to look for private equity.

Restructuring the Energy Sector, 1994–7

In October 1994, the government deregulated the petroleum industry. Oil companies could now set their own prices and import from wherever they wished. The result was a flood of small entrants into the retail market, and a price war that drove margins down and undermined the established players. Although Kenyans benefited from lower fuel costs, there was a rapid fall in safety standards. This coincided with mass dumping of kerosene into diesel and abuses of the (duty-free) export system to Uganda to divert product back into western Kenyan petrol stations. In parallel, the extension of the Kenya Pipeline Company network to Kisumu and Eldoret in the early 1990s was a long-term boost to the economy, reducing costs and taking most tankers off Kenya's roads.

In 1996, under donor pressure, restructuring of the state-owned electricity sector began, separating responsibilities for production, distribution and sale from regulation, permitting competing entrants, and raising user charges to commercial levels. In 1997, the Kenya Power Company (later renamed KenGen) took over responsibility for all power generation, leaving KPLC responsible only for transmission and distribution. This split was designed to allow competition with independent power producers (IPPs). Drought and a decade of under-investment had left Kenya with a systemic power deficit, and liberalisation saw the licensing of two foreign IPPs to supplement KenGen. Both contracts later proved controversial, as tariffs were high, tendering processes were odd and there were allegations that ministers, a permanent secretary, Moi insiders and KPLC officials had received bribes from or had interests in both companies.[110] Western donors were extremely unhappy with the IPP contracts; stronger supervision of the sector became one of their key demands.

Privatisation and Restructuring in the Finance Sector

The crises of 1993 did not end the financial sector's growth or the controversy over its practices. Banking was now dominated by the big four – the KCB, Barclays, Standard Chartered and the NBK – but there were many smaller operations, including 53 commercial banks, 16 non-bank financial institutions and four building societies. Interest rates remained high, reflecting a credit shortage, low repayment rates and cartel-like practices by the banks. Bad debt – much of it politically connected – remained the heart of the problem.

While the largest private banks, Barclays and Standard Chartered, continued to make healthy profits, the main state-owned financial institutions were part-privatised during 1996–8, and in both cases the result was the exposure of a structural problem. The KCB had been the first state-owned bank to raise funds on the market. Between 1996 and 1998, the state divested a further 35 per cent. However, the company's loan portfolio was terrifying, with Ksh3.3 billion loaned to Mugoya Construction, its largest debtor, and dozens of non-performing loans to companies associated with politicians, policemen, civil servants and bank officials.[111] By 1999, the bank was in serious trouble. Non-performing loans rose to Ksh18.8 billion, and the bank posted a Ksh2.2 billion loss. It continued to lose money in 2000, dividends fell to zero, and the bank started shutting branches to cut costs.

The same occurred with the NBK. In 1994 and 1996, the government sold chunks of the NBK on the stock exchange, reducing the state's holding to 70 per cent. But investors had been 'sold a pup': while the bank had been profitable in 1997, it lost Ksh2.6 billion in 1998, Ksh3.5 billion in 1999 and Ksh1.6 billion in 2000.[112] Restructuring under new management followed, but it remained close to insolvency, with 30 per cent of its loans non-performing, valued at over Ksh7.5 billion (US$100 million). It was only sustained by government support.[113] Again, poor credit practices and a disregard for profitability had brought a state-owned enterprise near to collapse.

The Civil Service Stops Growing

The civil service remained one of Kenya's most intractable challenges: underpaid, underemployed, and riddled with corruption and nepotism. From a workforce of 60,300 at independence, central government numbers had risen to a peak of more than 275,000 in 1989.[114] Only in 1992 had the government taken reform seriously. For the first time in 30 years, the public sector workforce shrank in 1992 and it remained almost flat for a decade (see Figure 10.8).

Under the IFI-inspired retrenchment programme, 48,000 central government employees were retired during 1993–6, taking numbers back to the level of 1983. Parastatals, including Kenya Railways, Kenya Airways and KPTC also cut staff. Nonetheless, growing teacher numbers and expansion in other parastatals meant that total public sector numbers barely changed. Less effort, meanwhile, was put into increasing the skills, remuneration, accountability, ethics or motivation of the civil service – an issue of increasing concern to the IFIs.[115]

Agricultural Liberalisation under KANU

Tea, coffee, sugar, horticultural products, maize and livestock remained the core of Kenya's agricultural production, and agriculture the core of the economy, employing three-quarters of the labour force and accounting – including trading, transportation and processing – for half of Kenya's GDP. Agriculture was now far more intensive than in the 1960s, with greater use of tractors and fertilisers. However, agriculture's performance was poorer than for the economy as a whole, with sharp drops in

10.8: Public sector wage employment, 1963–2002

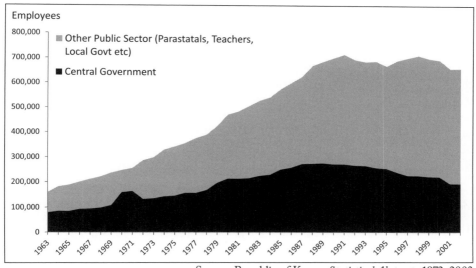

Source: Republic of Kenya, *Statistical Abstracts*, 1972–2003

agricultural GDP in 1991–3 and 2000. Kenya's vulnerability was shown both by repeated drought and unpredictable changes in the prices of its main exports.

The liberalisation of crop marketing had been a fundamental goal of reformers since the early 1980s. Despite many promises, change had been slow and the benefits limited. During the 1990s, helped (or driven) by the World Bank and other donors, structural adjustment changed the playing field in most commodities, but the consequences were often negative in the short term. Coffee, milk, maize, sugar, cotton and cashewnuts all experienced problems, and Kenya saw successes only in tea and horticulture. It is sometimes hard to understand the reasons for the timing of liberalisation and privatisation decisions, or the manner of their freeing. Several were hasty or poorly coordinated, damaging the industries they were supposed to liberate.

The government withdrew from services to the sector as well as removing controls on it. State spending on agricultural development fell from 10 to 4 per cent of GDP between the 1980s and the late 1990s. Access to credit also declined, as the key lenders to the sector (the AFC and the cooperatives) collapsed under the weight of non-performing debt. The pricing, production and distribution of seeds, pesticides and fertilisers was liberalised during 1990–6, and the government cut back on agricultural extension support. However, the free market did not always adapt to fill gaps in state provision. The resulting price rises for inputs, when combined with Kenya's high inflation, were politically difficult. Many farmers cut their inputs and productivity followed suit.

Small farms now contributed 70–80 per cent of agricultural GDP, but many farmers could no longer – with land subdivision and the decline of cash-cropping – produce enough to live sustainably.[116] The majority relied on off-farm incomes. The collapse during the 1990s of many agricultural cooperatives (due to embezzlement and mismanagement) put further pressure on the sector. There was growing doubt whether Kenyan peasants could respond rapidly enough to free market forces, because of their lack of access to capital or seasonal labour, the long growth cycle of their crops and the inefficiency of the micro-farm model.[117]

The relatively low productivity of peasant agriculture also reflected the desire to spread risk, growing food as well as cash-crops and seeking off-farm income rather than relying on an increasingly untrustworthy and unstable set of marketing boards and world prices. There was continued tension amongst both policy-makers and farmers between the need to grow profitable crops for export at the expense of domestic food production and the need for local food self-sufficiency, mirroring the broader divide between the closed and open economic models. The government affected to favour the open model, but, like the opposition, its heart was never fully in it.

Maize and Food Crops

The cereals sector was one of the slowest to liberalise, because of concerns about the ability of a free market to respond to shortages, the risk of destroying Kenya's food sufficiency through imports and, in part, the influence of large farmers and ethno-regional patronage. The NCPB had been a financial disaster for years, with a cumulative operating loss of Ksh3.85 billion between 1988 and 1992, yet it was still unable to maintain a strategic food reserve. The KGGCU (renamed the KFA in 1996) was also near-bankrupt.

Kenyan maize farmers remained relatively inefficient, many of their farms now too small for viability (average farm sizes fell below 1.6 hectares in 1992), although political considerations and cultural factors still discouraged large-scale land consolidation. Drought, poor seed quality and lack of inputs meant both maize and wheat production stagnated and higher and higher imports were needed to meet demand. Per capita maize production fell to half its 1976–7 peak (see Figure 10.9). There was no more land to cultivate safely; population pressure had forced the subdivision of many smallholdings; urbanisation and cash-cropping removed land from food crops, and access to credit and to fertilisers had fallen.

Maize transport was deregulated again in 1993, but the state still used the NCPB to prop up farm prices, while keeping retail prices low. In 1995, the government announced that the NCPB would act on a fully commercial basis, but it continued to intervene in the market. It was not until 1996–7 (and another World Bank project) that the private sector fully took over the grain trade and nationwide maize movement was freed. Although imports were deregulated, they were still tariffed, keeping local prices above world market prices and protecting domestic producers at the cost of consumers.[118] Wheat production remained concentrated amongst a few large producers in Narok, Nakuru and Uasin Gishu. Local production could now meet only 40 per cent of Kenya's demand, but import tariffs remained in effect, protecting these producers.

Rice production was also liberalised in the early 1990s, but the result was disastrous. In 1997, the government even reimposed import controls and duties to protect domestic producers. Nonetheless, all the rice-growing schemes created in the 1950s and 1960s eventually collapsed amid disputes with the NIB. The Ahero scheme and the Kano plains project failed in 1998, and in 1999 rice farmers violently drove out NIB officials from the huge Mwea scheme.

10.9: Per capita maize production, 1963–2007

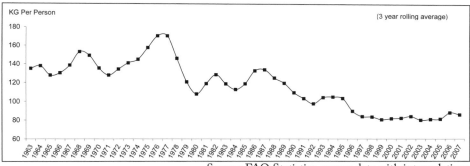

Source: FAO Statistics, census data with interpolations

Global climate change was a growing concern; when coupled with population growth and environmental degradation, the consequence was food shortages and even famine. There were shortages in 1993–4, after poor rains and the loss of crops caused by the clashes. Four million people were at risk of starvation, a situation worsened by the presence of 400,000 refugees from Somalia, Ethiopia and Sudan.[119] The ban on maize import was relaxed and the US donated large quantities.[120] After two years of good harvests, there was drought in 1996–7 in northern and eastern Kenya, a second one in 1998 and a third even more severe drought in 1999–2000. Hundreds died, but mass starvation was averted by a coordinated public and private campaign. By 2000, 4 million Kenyans were dependent on famine relief (mostly US imports routed through the World Food Programme), with each cycle of neglect, drought and emergency aid worsening the situation for the long term.

Coffee and Tea

Although coffee had experienced problems during the 1980s, the real crisis began with the collapse in 1989 of the International Coffee Agreement. From 1990 on, prices were determined on the futures markets. Increased supply combined with global market dominance by four large marketing and roasting companies to cut producer prices. An Oxfam report in 2002 accused the companies of the deliberate exploitation of farmers.[121] Alongside drought, under-investment and misappropriation in the Coffee Board and the cooperatives, world prices halved between 1999 and 2002. In 2001, coffee prices were at their lowest since independence. Farmers were paid less than they spent raising the crop.

Kenya's production had peaked in 1988 at 128,000 million tonnes, but then declined for five consecutive years. A recovery began in 1994, and production peaked once more in 1995–7, when prices reached their highest since 1977, but it collapsed again in 1997–8. Kenya remained a relatively high-cost producer. The country's market share had also fallen for other reasons: better technology allowed easier switching of coffees; there was a worldwide trend towards less acidic coffees; and Kenya's inability to produce consistent products or volumes had turned buyers elsewhere.

In the same period, the industry was incompletely and incompetently liberalised. Until 1992, the Gema-dominated KPCU had been the sole miller. Now, the Coffee Board, as part of its liberalisation plan, licensed three more millers. The transition to a deregulated market did not go well, however, as the board and KPCU resisted change, while fighting amongst themselves. In 1997, the government again announced – as Moi had five years before – an end to the board's marketing monopoly. But disputes again followed over how liberalisation should proceed and how funds should be remitted to the various parties. With a new assertiveness buttressed by their alignment with the opposition, there was growing popular resistance to regulatory initiatives amongst coffee farmers.

Drought and lack of credit accentuated the collapse. Farmers owed billions to EU and World Bank financing schemes designed to stabilise export earnings. Most loans were channelled through the Cooperative Bank, which lent to farmers

10.10: Coffee and Tea production, 1989–2007

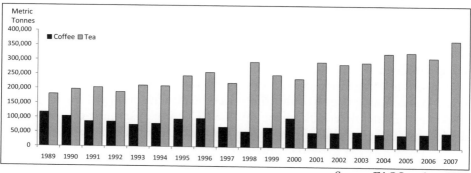

Source: FAOStat data, 2010

to buy inputs and finance crop picking; by 2002, coffee farmers owed the bank Ksh6 billion (US$80 million). However, after the split of the giant societies, some of the new units bypassed the Cooperative Bank and borrowed elsewhere at higher rates to avoid having to repay old loans. The costs of the coffee factories increased rapidly after liberalisation, and there were allegations that some cooperatives, under less supervision, were being run for the personal enrichment of directors.

The result was the pauperisation of smaller coffee farmers, facing ruin from spiralling debt and declining returns. Factories and growers declared independence from the cooperatives or tried to break them up. Nyeri, Kenya's coffee capital, was the worst affected district. There were pitched battles in 1999–2001 as farmers fought for the control of cooperative society assets. These 'coffee wars' were encouraged by the new millers, competing for the limited coffee available. The effect on Central Province was severe, with poverty, crime and social problems increasing. Thousands of smallholders in Central Province and Kisii uprooted their coffee trees and planted food instead. Coffee smuggling into Uganda became common – a reversal of the movements of the 1970s – to avoid payment delays (by 2001, some farmers had still not been paid in full for 1998–9) and to avoid repaying old debts. Production in 2001–2 was less than it had been 30 years before.

Tea, in contrast, was still performing well; it was now Kenya's most important cash-crop and export earner. Both volumes and prices rose during the 1990s, and production nearly reached 300,000 tonnes in 1998, 16 times 1963's level (see Figure 10.10). Kenya now produced 8 per cent of the world's tea. The industry was also changing: the *Nyayo* tea zones were in decline, while the KTDA's monopoly over smallholder planting, fertilisers, quality control, processing and marketing was under growing pressure. In 1999–2000, the state liberalised the industry, and smallholders took over the KTDA and its 45 small tea factories, converting it into a private company.

Milk and Meat

Like coffee, the milk industry was also in trouble. Rapid liberalisation, combined with internal predation, led directly to the collapse of the KCC. A national institution since 1925, with 11 factories and a near-monopoly on the purchase, distribution, storage and sale of milk, the KCC had been losing money even before the industry was opened to competition in 1992. Prices were then decontrolled, the Kenya Dairy Board licensed more than 40 competitors over the next five years and an unregulated market in unpasteurised milk sprang up. The KCC faced particular competition in the lucrative urban markets from players such as Limuru Dairies and Brookside Dairies (owned by the Kenyatta family).

In 1995, the government placed the KCC under a task force after a nationwide outcry over catastrophic losses in 1994. An audit revealed serious mismanagement – operating costs exceeded revenue and liabilities exceeded assets. Price competition, imports, poor marketing, looting by officials and uneconomic decision-making lost the KCC another Ksh1.8 billion in 1995 and Ksh1.7 billion in 1996. The government chipped in Ksh800 million to keep it afloat, despite donor protests. Farmers evicted the chairman and directors in 1996, but resisted pressure to break the organisation up.

However, the KCC still behaved like a parastatal, overmanned and taking surplus milk during glut periods but incapable of competing during shortages. Staff cuts came too late. In 1999, it was put into receivership, unable to pay more than Ksh500 million (US$7 million) it owed to farmers, Ksh1 billion to the KCB and more than 1 billion to others. Its failure, alongside the coffee crisis, further hurt the smallholders who had been the foundation of Kenya's growth. Farmers saw millions of litres of milk go to waste as the factories shut or cut their inputs. While private producers and traders flourished, the collapse satisfied neither political nor economic rationality, as the Rift highlands and the Kalenjin districts were some of the largest producers. The government was appalled by the effects of its own liberalisation policies, but its response was typically ad hoc and self interested – to set up a private company, KCC 2000, which bought the KCC's assets cheaply and without tender.

The situation was also deteriorating for meat producers. Cattle remained the main commercial product from the semi-arid lands, for slaughter to feed urban consumers. Here too, the government progressively withdrew from the sector, cutting support for artificial insemination and ceasing to enforce disease control laws, resulting in outbreaks of trypanosomiasis and rinderpest. The private sector struggled to fill the gap, and the result was a drop in production. The breakdown of security in the north also made commercial livestock production more risky.

The Near-Collapse of the Sugar Industry

Kenya's state-owned sugar industry also remained in difficulties, the result of poor and politicised management, excessive processing costs, under-investment, misappropriation and international price competition.[122] As the industry was both politically sensitive and close to failure, liberalisation was risky and long resisted. Retail prices were freed in 1994, but wholesale prices remained controlled and the KNTC continued to control marketing and distribution. Duties remained high, keeping prices up to three times higher than world prices, which fell sharply after 1997. Demand consistently outstripped supply, but stocks of unsold sugar built up in the factories and cane rotted or dried in the fields while imports continued. Shortages were used to justify import quotas for favoured firms, which were then sold on the open market. Dutiable refined sugar was misdeclared as low-duty 'industrial sugar', while duty-free sugar en route elsewhere was diverted into the domestic market.

Under COMESA rules, the country was supposed to permit unlimited imports of sugar at a 35 per cent tariff. However, Kenya was forced to use an emergency anti-dumping clause to protect its industry, through a quota and a 120 per cent tariff. The tension was now overt between the needs of sugar farmers and the factories (high prices and import protection), those of consumers and economic liberals (low prices and free imports) and those of cartels of sugar importers (high prices and restricted imports). The cartels had strong allies. Sugar imports were believed to have financed KANU in every multi-party general election. The problem continued throughout the decade; every attempt to cut imports (such as that made by Nyachae in 1996) was reversed by Moi, under pressure from importers and liberals alike, arguing that a ban was contrary to Kenya's liberalisation programme and restricted free trade.[123] Efforts by Mudavadi and the KRA to cut the diversion of duty-free sugar into the domestic market by companies associated with KANU tycoons in 1997 were also resisted by the OP.[124] A whistle-blower suggested that more than Ksh700 million (US$11 million) had been evaded on sugar imports during 1997.[125] Partly as a result, Kenya continued – according to FAO figures (see Figure 10.11) – to import and export sugar at the same time.

Production flattened off at between 4.5 and 5 million tonnes of cane, and fell in 2001–2 to less than 4 million tonnes. By 1999, Kenya's white sugar demand was 600,000 tonnes, with production only 400,000 tonnes (780,000 tonnes could have been produced had the industry been operating at full capacity). Poor husbandry, under-investment and the appalling financial position of the factories were all contributors. Costs were high and financial management poor within the mills, which were treated as cash-cows by politically appointed managers. Most of the factories were insolvent, with net liabilities of Ksh20 billion (US$260 million).[126]

In 2001, Parliament passed a Sugar Act to help farmers, but it achieved little. There seemed no way out of the impasse as long as world prices remained low and Kenyan prices high. Debt relief for the millers, lower taxation, more protection from COMESA or investment in better milling technology were all expensive or ran contrary to the wisdom that in the long term you could not fight the market. Privatisation of the industry had been on the agenda since 1998, but only Mumias was profitable (it was part-privatised in 2001). In the end, the state was forced to put the Miwani and Muhoroni factories into receivership.

10.11: Imports and exports of raw equivalent sugar, 1963–2002

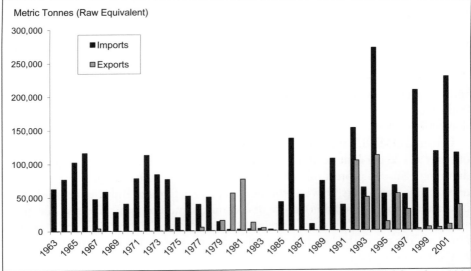

Source: FAOStat data, 2004

Cotton

The cotton industry was also hastily liberalised in 1991–3, with farmers free to sell to anyone they wished. As the state withdrew from the sector, the cooperatives and cotton ginneries lost their access to credit and to certified seeds, and several collapsed. The situation was worsened by textile import restrictions imposed by the US in 1994, liberalised imports of refined cotton and second-hand clothes, and world price instability. As with rice, most of the cotton-growing irrigation projects established in the 1970s failed and farmers reverted to food crops. The Cotton Lint and Seed Marketing Board collapsed in 1996, leaving many farmers unpaid. By 2004, Kenya was importing most of its clothing and only 8 of the 54 mills operating in 1983 remained.[127]

Horticulture and Other Cash Crops

While most other crops suffered, the high-input, high-output flower sector remained the fastest-growing part of the economy, increasing by 10 per cent a year. By 2003, horticulture (mostly flowers and vegetables) was second only to tea in foreign exchange earnings, at 22 per cent of Kenya's exports.[128] The flower market was now worth US$100 million a year and Kenya was the leading supplier of flowers to Western Europe. Growth was private-sector driven, an example of investment by private capital in irrigation, production and storage. Almost all production came from large commercial farms.

Pyrethrum remained a small but profitable crop and a significant foreign exchange earner, since Kenya produced 60–80 per cent of the world's traded product. However, the story of coffee was repeated here on a smaller scale. The growth of the 1980s was followed by production crashes that left output in 2000 the same as it had been at independence, and the Pyrethrum Board bankrupt.

Cashewnut production was also in crisis. The crop had once covered 30 per cent of arable land in Coast Province. In the early 1990s, the recently privatised Kilifi Cashewnuts factory (the only one in East or Central Africa) collapsed with huge debts, and shut its doors in 1998.[129] The failure was a product both of mismanagement and of liberalisation: farmers had bypassed the factory to sell raw nuts to intermediaries in India willing to pay higher prices, but with the factory closed, cashew prices then collapsed. Although production for raw export continued, 3,000 workers were left unemployed.

Kenya was also a major grower of the quasi-legal *miraa* or *khat*, a mild chewing narcotic used mostly by ethnic Somali. The business brought US$250–300 million a year into Meru, where most of the crop was grown, replacing coffee as the dominant crop in the region.[130]

Health and Social Services

Kenya's straitened financial position and the government's focus on macro-economic and fiscal rectitude resulted in lower relative spending on social services. Expenditure on pensions, health care and social benefits fell from 2.6 per cent of GDP in 1990 to 2 per cent in 1996.[131] The minimal safety net against poverty, ignorance and disease promised in the 1960s had long ago frayed away.

Kenya's life expectancy had risen to nearly 60, one of the highest in Africa. However, the combination of AIDS, population growth, economic stagnation and structural adjustment meant that from the mid-1980s the government struggled to sustain medical services. Its real per capita health spending hit an all-time low in 1993. AIDS was spreading rapidly, and by 1996, 7.5–8 per cent of Kenyan adults were believed to be HIV-positive. Death rates climbed, with the Coast and Nyanza worst affected. After a decade, sexual behaviours were changing, but it appeared too little, too late. Malaria, under control in the 1950s and 1960s, also became more common, the result of a decline in prevention activities and growing drug resistance. Donor assistance helped to stem a major outbreak in 1994–5, but the El Niño rains of 1997–8 initiated a second epidemic, killing more than 1,000, again only halted by foreign intervention.[132] By the late 1990s, malaria caused 20–30 per cent of hospital admissions.

By 2000, life expectancies had fallen to 52. In the rural areas, more than half of all households still had no access to safe water, over a third of children were stunted and a quarter were not fully immunised. Medical services remained thinly spread, government dispensaries often had no drugs or expired materials, and cartels built up between public and private providers, which forced even the poor to use private services. Preventive care services such as immunisation were now among the worst in Africa. There was a doctors' strike over low pay in 1994, during which a three-month walkout by most of the 1,200 state doctors led to the deaths of many poor people who were unable to afford private treatment. Facing an uncompromising employer, hundreds of state doctors resigned and sought jobs overseas or in private practice, leaving only 600 in the country. Although the number of people per hospital bed remained roughly constant, the Ministry of Health now provided only half of Kenya's medical services. The private sector, church hospitals and local councils provided the rest.

A new policy framework was inaugurated in 1994, after which health spending increased, but it was not the government's money. From this point, the government effectively admitted that it was unable to fund any new health care services. The money would have to come from donors, social insurance, patient charges or *harambee* activities. Between 1992 and 1996, donors provided 80 per cent of the Ministry of Health's budget for new services. Donors – particularly the WHO, the German GTZ, USAID and the Danish International Development Agency (DANIDA) – also supported the recurrent budget, funding drugs, immunisation, AIDS control and family planning.

Structural Adjustment: A Profit and Loss

Opinion remains divided on whether the reform and liberalisation process that had begun in 1980 but had taken nearly two decades to implement had been of genuine benefit to Kenya (or to the rest of Africa). Many local experts and politicians damned the process unreservedly, looking back to the golden years of Kenyatta and associating the decline of the 1980s and 1990s with structural adjustment. Although the economy had benefited in some areas, other sectors had completely collapsed. By 2004, 20 years of adjustment had had no positive effect on Kenya's overall balance of physical imports to exports (see Figure 10.12).

Some argued that only a much larger infusion of aid could change Africa's future. Others focused on the social costs of structural adjustment and argued that reform could only have negative implications without parallel reforms in land use, state services to the poorest, trade policy and access to regional markets.[133] There was little doubt that user charges and resource transfers away from social services had hurt Kenya's educational provision and health services, and that the urban poor had suffered the most. Despite both development aid and budgetary support, numbers in poverty continued to rise. On paper, 7.5 million Kenyans (28 per cent of the population) could not feed themselves adequately, even if they spent all their income on food.[134] As far as could be estimated, income inequalities were also growing.

Few disagreed that the state sector had become a dead weight, however. Its inefficiency became evident when the government tried to sell it. Indeed, one of the main benefits from privatisation was the end of subsidies, and the consequent improvement in the deficit in 1995–2001.[135] Responding to the challenge, the IFIs agreed that the results had been disappointing in Kenya and elsewhere (and they had adjusted their policies accordingly), but still believed that no other course had been

10.12: Ratio of imports to exports, 1964–2004

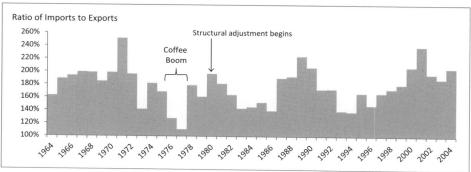

Source: Republic of Kenya, *Statistical Abstracts*, 1972–2005

feasible, and instead criticised the slow, poorly managed, corrupt and inconsistent implementation of structural adjustment. As Nicholas van de Walle suggested, 'political institutions hold the explanatory key to the African crisis and there will not be successful economic reform without a prior reform of the region's politics.'[136] From this perspective the problem was not *what* the politicians were doing but *how* they were doing it: slowly and with their own interests paramount.

Another focus of attention in the 1990s was whether Kenya's institutional framework (including its legal system, physical security, land law, capital market and banking system, government regulatory capability and infrastructure quality) was mature enough to generate growth in a liberalised market or to handle the rapid transfer of businesses from the state sector.[137] It was now recognised that the African state's capacity to implement and sustain change, both technically and politically, had been overestimated. Much of the donors' agenda in the late 1990s was therefore driven by the desire to stabilise and improve institutional frameworks (alongside the ever-present need for fiscal rectitude and the sale of the remaining state corporations).

The Moi State

Moi's Personal Style

President Moi remained a curious mix of opposites. As vice-president he had been formal, but also a populist. He had opposed the corrupt Kiambu elites, but as president he had cultivated a level of corruption amongst his allies that exceeded that of his mentor. He survived through a combination of paranoia, excellent political antennae and a clear understanding of two negative aspects of Kenyan society, which he used and accentuated: tribalism and a willingness to be bought. Moi used ethnicity to divide and rule, and money to buy loyalty. Rather than bringing gifts, most delegations to the president took them away. As a result, he had an insatiable need for cash, less for personal gain than to buy support.

Moi remained an interventionist, impatient and keen for action, though internal and external constraints now limited his ad hoc policy formation. He still had little respect for chains of command and often worked through direct and personal relations in order to get things done. Although he was tribalist and authoritarian, aspects of his personality still appealed to Kenyans: the patriarch, the populist, the man of action. He was deeply religious and a good friend to those he trusted. As head of state, however, he was dependent on others and his policies oscillated as his trust in advisers waxed and waned. His violent furies at bad news reinforced a culture of sycophancy. But Moi was mellowing as the years passed, taking his first overseas holiday for years and even meeting opposition leaders privately on occasion.

As he aged, Moi relied (as Kenyatta had done) on his kitchen cabinet of trusted advisers. The Tugen 'mafia' remained at the centre of events (and became extremely wealthy as a result), including Hosea Kiplagat (Moi's nephew and Cooperative Bank chairman), Philemon Chelegat (mayor of Kabarnet and his Baringo political manager), nephew Gideon Toroitich (managing director of the AFC), General Tonje (who was married to Moi's sister) and Kulei (Chelegat's nephew). Kulei was particularly influential; another ex-prison officer while Moi was vice-president, he had become Moi's personal assistant and managed most of his investments, taking over after Biwott's fall from grace. By 1997, Kulei was a director of dozens of companies, including CMC Holdings, Bamburi Cement, CFC Bank, NAS Airport Services, Heritage AII Insurance, the American Life Insurance Company and Mitchell Cotts.[138] He owned farms, flower exporters and dairies, both directly and on behalf of Moi, and many suspected him (like Biwott) of salting away millions overseas. In the wider Kalenjin community, as well as Biwott, key figures included successive State House Comptrollers Abraham Kiptanui and Franklin Bett. Another influential figure was youthful wheeler-dealer Mark arap Too.

The Succession Question

As the 1990s advanced, the issue of the succession grew in significance. As in the 1970s, the result was a conflict within KANU between supporters of two rival presidential tickets. The KANU A faction was led by Nyachae (its most likely presidential candidate), Kones and Ntimama, with Mudavadi and Musyoka loosely aligned and with ambitions of their own. It represented a more economically reformist but sometimes anti-Kikuyu perspective and sought to ally Moi's Kalenjin-pastoralist heartland of support not with the centre (the Mount Kenya communities) but with the west: the Gusii, Luo and Luhya. It contained some of the most aggressive supporters of *majimbo*. KANU B, in contrast, was a more Nairobi-focused team, led by Biwott, Saitoti (its most likely presidential candidate) and Kamotho, with control over the KANU central party and the support of Kalenjin kitchen cabinet members. It represented a more Central Province-focused team, aiming to bring the Kikuyu back into the fold, but more associated with elite corruption and divided over economic liberalisation.[139] There were no simplistic 'good guys' or 'bad guys' in this conflict.

The growing tension led to demands to hold KANU national elections (last held in 1988), which were resisted by the KANU B incumbents. Factionalism increased, as KANU B tried to oust its opponents. Nyachae came under attack at home and in Maasailand, Ntimama and Keen made common cause on an anti-immigrant ticket, while Saitoti openly admitted his Kikuyu origins.[140] Moi equivocated between the two factions.

During 1996–7, Moi and KANU B again tried to build bridges with the Kikuyu community, using a new tactic, the Central Province Development Support Group. This was a group of Kikuyu civil servants (including four permanent secretaries and the Nyanza PC), wealthy executives and parastatal heads (including Gichuru of the KPLC). These men were willing to risk their money and personal safety to campaign for KANU in the next election (loyalty had its rewards, of course). They led a focused effort to win over Kikuyu voters, with hints of a second Kalenjin–Kikuyu alliance. There was talk of a Kikuyu successor to Moi, though most eyes were on Saitoti. In the prescient words of the *Economic Review*,

> Moi . . . firmly believes that the Kikuyu . . . are a forgiving people who would not seek vengeance. He also believes that the community values stability, development and the pursuit of wealth, more than it does perpetual agitation, unlike the Luo, who he believes are incorrigible opportunists who engage in political confrontation at the expense of everything else.[141]

This strategy was criticised by western KANU A leaders as a wasted effort.[142]

Corruption in the Multi-Party State

One of the drivers behind Western demands for multi-party democracy had been the belief that a competitive political system would reduce corruption and increase transparency. In practice, however, some of the worst corruption scandals in Kenya's history occurred in the multi-party era. The governing elite had an insatiable demand for funds, in part because of the fragility of their coalition, which required continual injections of resources to sustain, and in part because many were in politics for the money, not the other way round. Although opposition politicians and civil society frequently exposed corrupt behaviour, this did not translate into practical restrictions on elite actions.

Politicians and officials continued to be accused of corrupt practices by auditors, the opposition and donors alike. Parastatals continued to bank with extraordinary incompetence, with the NSSF, NOCK, NHC, KPTC and KTDC losing hundreds of millions in the political banks. Contracts were issued without proper processes, import duties evaded, privatisations botched and officials refused to cooperate in investigations without sanction. In every aspect of the state's operations where money flowed in or out, doubts existed as to the probity or transparency of transactions.[143] Even import duties on goods passing through Jomo Kenyatta International Airport went missing for a while, and VAT exemptions were issued irregularly.[144] The controller and auditor-general's annual reports were filled with examples of waste, incompetence and disregard for procedures. In 2001 the Public Accounts Committee estimated that between 1991 and 1997 the government had lost Ksh475 billion (US$9 billion) in fraud, theft and illegal spending.[145]

There was now intense cynicism about the government's commitment to fight corruption, given the absence of action in even the most flagrant cases, and it was universally believed that it began at the top. Until the 'dream team' era, only once was a senior Kalenjin jailed for corruption.[146] Moi and his colleagues shrugged off criticism, protected by a subservient judiciary, a culture of state omnipotence and KANU's political skills and resources.

Two projects were particularly notorious in this period. In 1995, construction started on Kenya's third international airport at Eldoret. This project was controversial for two reasons. First, its Ksh2.7 billion (US$50 million) cost was spent without authorisation from Parliament and was therefore illegal. It was charged directly to the Consolidated Fund, despite the constitutional clause that specified that,

> . . . all revenues or other moneys raised or received for the purposes of the Government of Kenya shall be paid into and from a Consolidated Fund from which no moneys shall be withdrawn except as may be authorized by this Constitution or by an Act of Parliament . . . or by a vote on account passed by the National Assembly.[147]

Second, there were doubts about the airport's viability, given its location far to the north and on a high plateau. Many believed it was built specifically to benefit the Kalenjin community. Western donors refused to finance it.[148] Similarly questionable was the construction of the US$80 million Eldoret bullet factory, paid for in the same way.[149]

Another well-publicised incident concerned the contract for the supply of police vehicles, which was allocated without competitive tender to the Kamsons group in 1994. The Kamani family's company supplied hundreds of Mahindra jeeps from India, but they proved unsuitable for use in Kenya and were alleged to have been purchased at double the real cost.[150] The same company was involved in supplying unserviceable boilers to the prison department and in secret national security contracts.[151] The Kamani family were to become even better known in the Kibaki era. Another target for concern was any contract associated with Ketan Somaia, who was forced to flee overseas in 1995. After Moi's retirement, Somaia's companies collapsed and he briefly ended up in prison.

Many Kenyans, although verbally scathing, were in practice resigned to corruption as the sole reliable means of transacting government business, part of a culture of reciprocal favours and prebendal authority. Corruption was now routine throughout the polity. Most people had to give or receive bribes simply in order to live in Kenya.[152] In 1996, a donor-funded NGO study reported: 'corruption has eaten into the very fabric of Kenyan society, right from the top political levels to the family unit.'[153] It remained a negative-sum game, reducing the country's worth by the misallocation of resources from productive efforts and from the poor to those with rent-seeking opportunities. However, in a situation where the corruption of others was a given, it was rational to participate oneself. Whenever someone alleged corruption, there was a standard arsenal of responses: allegations were ignored, then defended as the result of misunderstandings or weak accounting practices; then, in the last resort, blamed on an ethnic witch-hunt. Clients universally defended their patrons, reflecting the greater moral weight put on rewarding the community than on the means by which these rewards were obtained. The moralities of the ethnic community appeared to have been shredded and reconstituted in a very different form.

Sales of Government Land

With privatisation eliminating some avenues of rent-seeking, the KANU barons' attention during the 1990s focused on state-owned land. The Ministry of Lands and Settlement was a treasure trove of opportunities, with the well-connected acquiring government land in disregard of both formalities and the presence of existing occupants.[154] In one small but well-documented example, the allocation register for Kitale Prison's land included PCs and DCs, army officers, judges and parastatal heads, many of them Kalenjin.[155] Nairobi City Council too had been notorious for land grabbing for decades, and virtually every open space or public institution, including parks, bus stations, mortuaries and road reserves, was now 'privatised', often without payment of any sort. Moi regularly issued directives that public land be repossessed, but the government did nothing. City council houses were sold off irregularly, payments forgotten, debts written off and title deeds irregularly issued.[156]

Forest excisions increased after the reintroduction of multi-party democracy, both legally and illegally, though international concern was also growing. Estimates suggested that 3 per cent of Kenya's forests were lost every year.[157] During the 1990s, the state degazetted and sold at least 60,000 hectares of forest reserve, much of which was used for private small-scale settlements (in return for political support). In 1995–6, the key gatekeeper, the commissioner of lands, sold part of Nairobi's northern Karura forest to developers, despite the fact that it had never been degazetted.[158] Parastatals were forced to buy the land from middlemen and thus fund the elite's coffers. Inevitably, the files for the buyers were 'missing from Companies House'. Even when not excised, forests were valuable assets, as illegal logging was rampant, supervised by corrupt forestry officers.

The NSSF was pushed close to collapse by a series of land purchases from politically connected vendors. The NSSF spent Ksh32 billion (more than US$700 million) between 1990 and 1995 on plots throughout the country, many of which were grossly overpriced.[159] This included the purchase of plots in Karura forest from companies associated with KANU.[160] A decade later, some plots were valued at only 10 per cent of what was paid.[161] In another example, Mugoya Construction sold to the NSSF land that was designated as a road reserve. Mugoya was also commissioned to build a huge housing estate and paid Ksh12.4 billion (US$220 million) for a project originally priced at Ksh2.5 billion, even though the estate was less than half-complete 10 years later.[162]

The 'KANU Districts'

During the 1990s, the government adopted a policy of bringing administration closer to the people through the subdivision of districts. Between 1988 and 1992, six new districts had been established; during 1993–2002, the government created at least 26 more. Some subdivisions made sense, but some new districts such as Kuria, Mount Elgon, Mwingi, Trans-Mara and Teso seemed designed primarily for political reasons and to be implementing a quiet policy of ethnic segregation, separating pro-government and pro-opposition communities into different administrative areas.

These new boundaries had implications for ethnic identity and land ownership (whatever the law said). The excision of pro-KANU Mount Elgon from Bungoma District, for example, institutionalised the ethnic cleansing of 1991–2. At the inauguration of the district, Sabaot leaders declared they would not allow any non-Sabaot to buy land in the area.[163] Pro-KANU Teso District's creation was followed by attempts to annexe other historically Iteso areas into the district, equating administrative boundaries with ethnic identity. When pro-KANU Kuria was hived off from pro-opposition (Luo) Migori, the result was clashes in 1996–7 as communities forced those from the 'wrong' ethnic group across the border. In 2000, there was fighting between Pokomo and Somali over the boundaries of the new Ijara District, and between Tharaka, Igembe and Tigania Meru sub-groups over the boundaries of their new districts. Such trouble demonstrated the risks of devolution of power to the district level.

By 2002, Kenya had at least 72 districts, though few knew which they were and most new districts had virtually no facilities. Although they did bring administration closer to the people, they were an additional cost to the local community, who were asked to pay for the buildings required to house the new officials through *harambees*. The legality of most of these districts was questionable, as their boundaries had not been officially demarcated, nor had they been approved by Parliament.

Blurring Boundaries: Politics and Civil Society

Kenya did not see a refocusing of political activism through formal political parties after 1992, but a continuation of the prominent role that civil society organisations – NGOs, churches and professional associations – had played in the reintroduction of multi-party politics. While Kenya's parties struggled, civil society's challenge to the state intensified.

The Era of the NGO

The number of NGOs rose rapidly during the 1990s, a response both to the shrinking state and to the growing resources available from the West.[164] While donors were prohibited from funding opposition parties directly, there were no such restrictions on support for governance-focused civil society organisations, and USAID and other bilateral donors funded dozens of NGOs whose main purpose was to encourage democracy. Foundations such as the German Friedrich Ebert Stiftung and Friedrich Naumann Stiftung funded projects on education, health, land and conflict resolution, but also financed efforts to create a united opposition and to reform the Constitution. Believing that civil society was more democratic than the state, foreign agencies actively bypassed the state in resource distribution.[165] By 1996–7, USAID routed 85 per cent and Britain 40 per cent of its aid through non-government channels.[166]

The result was a plethora of NGOs to exploit this seam of funds, and to fight KANU by other means. Between 1991 and 1995, groups working on election monitoring, human rights, civil education and gender empowerment expanded into a network of more than 100 organisations, often with overlapping memberships. In 1993, NEMU metamorphosed into the Institute for Education in Democracy (IED), with a remit to promote democracy and political education. It continued to monitor by-elections and generally cause trouble.[167] The Kenyan Human Rights Commission (KHRC), founded in 1991–2 by exiles in the US and the Release Political Prisoners group played an important part in publicising state abuses. Other NGOs focused on civil education, capacity building in political parties or conflict resolution. NGOs concentrating on economic policy included the influential Institute for Economic Affairs. By the late 1990s, Kenya had the highest concentration of NGOs in sub-Saharan Africa. The Kenyan state, pilloried, chronically short of funds and appallingly mismanaged, was the ugly sister at the ball.

As far as can be determined, every political NGO was entirely funded by Western donors and through the NGOs they influenced state policy and nurtured opposition to KANU.[168] Whether or not the goal was explicit, this flow of funds helped sustain opposition politics. NGO activists were usually politically active, almost entirely within the opposition.[169] NGO activism in Kenya was not an alternative to politics, but politics by other means, an alternative route into the political class, and NGO and civil society figures featured heavily in political debate.[170] In turn, the state became suspicious of NGOs, seeing them as fronts for their opponents, especially as many were Kikuyu- or Luo-led.[171]

The Churches

The churches remained critical to Kenya's political evolution. Religious beliefs ran deep and many Kenyans believed that the decline of social mores and the corruption of the state had spiritual as much as material origins. The mainstream churches had been disappointed by KANU's victory, and as in the political sphere, defeat turned attention inward. By 1995, however, churchmen were becoming more politically active once again. Although they retained diverse followings and social and religious objectives, church leaders tended to represent the interests of their constituents and their own experiences, drawn from specific ethnic and social strata. The newer churches and those centred in less-developed areas (such as the AIC) tended to take a more evangelical, less political orientation, while the older churches tended to be more confrontational and socially active.[172] The Catholics, Presbyterians and Anglicans continued to represent the interests of the 'settled tribes', particularly the Kikuyu and Luo, sometimes quite overtly.

In parallel, the 'religious sector' was changing. The number of churches were mushrooming, many promising salvation or personal wealth through God, a response to the lack of hope in many Kenyans (and offering money and influence to the successful pastor).

The independence-era religious leadership had lasted longer than its political counterparts, but its time was drawing to a close. Its successors were more politically active. In 1997, after 24 years in office, Catholic Cardinal Maurice Otunga retired, and the pope appointed Archbishop Ndingi Mwana a'Nzeki his successor as archbishop of Nairobi. Influential dissenter David Gitari replaced Manasses Kuria as CPK archbishop in 1997.[173] Anti-establishment cleric Mutava Musyimi became the NCCK's general secretary in 1993, while the elderly head of the PCEA also retired. The overall effect was a hardening of their attitude towards the incumbent government. Gitari's inaugural speech was a fervent call for constitutional reform.[174] Churchmen often joined NGO leaders to mobilise opposition to corruption, human rights abuses and authoritarian government and the divide between religious and political spheres was increasingly blurred (although the churches generally avoided backing specific opposition parties).[175] In the post-Odinga vacuum, CPK Bishop Henry Okullu, who retired in 1994, seriously considered standing as an opposition presidential candidate, while Musyimi was in a similar position in 2002 and actually became an elected MP in 2007.

Safina

The formation of Safina further blurred the boundary between politics and civil society activism and drew the West further into Kenya's domestic politics. In 1995, Muite and other FORD-Kenya exiles made common cause with an unlikely ally, Leakey. The ex-Kenya Wildlife Service head was increasingly concerned about the country's future. He had lost both his legs in 1993 in a plane crash, but remained determined to play a role. Andrew Morton reports that Leakey met Moi in April 1995 and warned him that he was considering forming a new political party, and suggested instead that Moi appoint him head of the civil service. Moi refused.[176]

A few weeks later, Muite and Leakey established a new party, Safina ('the ark' in Swahili), with Leakey as its secretary-general. Its core base was not ethnic but amongst civil society and the ex-Young Turks and it aroused great foreign media interest. Leakey was important not only because of his abilities and government connections, but because his high profile in environmental matters and his British heritage gave him a strong influence with donors. He and Safina received positive press from the West, which ignored Moi's previous support for Leakey and instead applauded the image of an underdog European taking on the might of the African presidency. This infuriated Moi as showing the 'ill-disguised racism and colonial arrogance of the international media'.[177]

Leakey's influence also caused problems for the new party. Moi went on the offensive against Leakey, denouncing him as a foreigner, a traitor, a Ku Klux Klan member and an atheist. He vowed that a white man would never again rule Kenya. In August 1995, Leakey and other Safina activists visiting the trial of Koigi wa Wamwere were whipped by thugs in front of the press. Kenya and Moi's reputations were further damaged.[178] Safina was not registered, on the grounds that its religious symbolism was not appropriate to a political party. In spite of this the party continued to operate. Although it never achieved mass popularity, it sustained the opposition agenda during its lowest ebb in 1995–6.

Cultural and Social Issues

Cultural Changes

With greater political freedom, trade liberalisation and the creation of global communication networks, Kenya was more exposed to Western influences. Foreign television and consumer products, magazines, advertising and ideas were changing Kenyan society, reducing its cultural distinctiveness while broadening choice for the wealthier. This change reflected and reinforced a deeper loss of national pride. Until the 1980s, many Kenyans had believed that they could find their own way to prosperity and development. The events of the late 1980s, the 1990–2 crisis and Moi's flawed triumph saw many younger elites turn to the West as a guide, no longer trusting any vision of the future sold to them by their own leaders. Many African Christian leaders, in contrast, blamed the West for Africa's condition and for the loss of its cultural and spiritual identity and sought to blame external actors (missionaries, donors, multinationals, even NGOs) for the crisis experienced by the Kenyan state and its people.[179] Whether victim or aspirant, few denied the pervasive impact of Western media.

Meanwhile, the children of the independence elite were reaching adulthood and taking up businesses and jobs, mostly in the private sector. Class formation – the reproduction of an elite with a distinct economic interest and a clear perception of its interest – was becoming a reality. At the same time, this elite was losing its rural links and becoming more urban in orientation and in language.

Gender

Gender issues became increasingly important, reflecting both the growing size of the female educated elite and the availability of international funding and support for gender equality. Many Kenyan NGOs were led by or focused on women and were increasingly vocal on gender issues.[180] Old barriers continued to fall. In 1995, Moi appointed Kenya's first female Cabinet minister, Winifred Nyiva Mwendwa.[181] In 1996, he appointed the first female DC and in 2000 the first female PC. The IPPG-inspired 1997 amendments made discrimination based on gender unconstitutional for the first time.

Despite this, most Kenyan men's attitudes to women remained traditional, with little support for female political leadership. The Beijing Conference on Women in 1995, a symbol of empowerment for professional women, was criticised by Moi as 'promoting lesbianism' and was a source of jibes by male Kenyans for a decade. Women still needed the approval of their fathers or husbands to apply for a passport or obtain a bank loan. The electoral system, with its reliance on money, tight linkages within an existing male elite and physical violence, combined with a reluctance to see women as leadership material, continued to discourage all but the most determined female politicians.

The Media

If the 1990s was a period of decline in many aspects of life, the media was one area where multi-party democracy and liberalisation had unequivocally changed things for the better. There were now far more opportunities for access to news and entertainment, both domestic and foreign.

This did not mean that the media avoided political bias; indeed, it remained institutionalised. The Moi family, though Mark arap Too, bought the *Standard* from Lonrho in 1995 and Too became its chairman. KTN's TV service was sold to them in 1997 (it had been part-owned by them for some time). Stellavision, the only other private TV broadcaster, was also suspected to be part-owned by Moi, his proxies or the Kenyatta family, though no one knew for sure. KBC improved its transmission periods and diversified its output, but continued to be pro-KANU with ex-minister Julius Kiano at the helm. Although the state reluctantly accepted that KBC would become only one amongst many TV and radio channels, they fought a rearguard action against suppliers who would not follow the government line. The politically suspect but commercially successful Nation Group was repeatedly denied a broadcasting licence, despite the unused TV transmitter on the roof of its new headquarters.

In the print media, the *Nation* remained the most popular newspaper and in general anti-KANU, while the *Standard* was broadly pro-government, though it sometimes took an independent stance. The sole radical newspaper was Matiba's 1993 creation, *The People*, which managed sales of up to 80,000 in its heyday. While several anti-government magazines closed down, crippled by legal cases and falling demand, a new arrival on the scene in 1992 was the *Economic Review*, which supplanted the *Weekly Review* as Kenya's definitive weekly magazine. Newspapers could now publish open criticism of the state, even cartoons lampooning the president – something unthinkable a few years earlier. State pressure on editors was more muted, but there were still occasional attacks on and arrests of overly inquisitive or hostile journalists.

In 1996, Wako tried to pass legislation requiring all journalists to be registered and licensed, but withdrew the proposals after a national and international outcry. However, the government succeeded in amending the law to increase the penalties for libel. After 1995–6, there was a steady increase in recourse to the libel laws against the press.

A Changing Contest

At the end of 1996, KANU appeared on course for an easier election victory, with the opposition weak and divided. During 1997, however, there were dramatic changes in the political landscape. With Western support, a loose alliance of opponents centred on political NGOs emerged outside formal party structures. When energised by populist politicians, they succeeded in driving real changes to the Constitution for the first time since the 1960s.

Constitutional Reform: The Prelude, 1993–6

The 'failure' of 1992 had led some in the opposition, the churches and civic society to re-evaluate their goals. While many politicians believed that change could best be achieved through opposition unity and the removal of the most misused provisions of the Constitution, others argued that no true change would be possible without radical constitutional change. This new tendency, which emerged from Kenya's NGOs, universities and lawyers, built a consensus around the need for a new constitution for Kenya for the first time since 1964.

Wako had promised a systematic review of Kenya's laws in 1993, and during 1993–4 the Catholics, the NCCK, the LSK and KHRC all called for a new constitution. KANU hardliners such as Biwott, Ntimama and Nassir also called for change, though their focus was on the restoration of *majimbo*. The KHRC went furthest, however, in actually drafting a new constitution, funded by American and German donors. In November 1994, they, the LSK and the International Commission of Jurists published the *Proposal for a Model Constitution*, which reduced the power of the presidency and abolished many 'colonial' laws.[182] In response, Moi promised a review of the Constitution, but quickly backtracked, suggesting only minor amendments were needed.[183] A few days later, a new NGO was formed to popularise the need for a new constitution, the Citizens Coalition for Constitutional Change (4Cs), whose leadership included ex-law lecturers and prison graduates Willy Mutunga, Gibson Kamau Kuria and Kivutha Kibwana. It soon became influential amongst donors, though it had little credibility with the government or opposition politicians.[184]

During 1995–6, the issue of constitutional reform simmered under the surface. The call for radical change was increasingly popular and a re-evaluation of Kenya's constitutional history began, which denigrated Kenyatta's 1960s centralisation. Most political NGOs and church leaders now agreed on the need to cut presidential powers, create a prime minister to serve as head of the government, entrench human rights and reconstruct the ECK. Abolition of the provincial administration and the removal of the 25 per cent rule in presidential elections remained more controversial, while few had time for *majimbo*.[185] The main opposition political parties supported a national constitutional convention in principle, but were unwilling to submit to extra-parliamentary leadership. As a result, in May 1996 they were excluded from a new committee of legal, political and church organisations (again foreign funded), to promote the idea of a National Convention to create a new constitution.[186] There has been a consensus that the mainstream opposition parties 'wanted to alter the regional patterns of distribution in favour of their regions, but not to change the overall parameters of distribution and leadership'. In contrast, NGOs were 'genuinely interested in wide-ranging democratic reforms'.[187] The reality was more complex, as the events of 2003–7 were to show.

Another key event came in late 1996, when the NCCK and the Catholic Church committed themselves to a set of minimal reforms before the elections, including an independent Electoral Commission, a repeal of many old laws, an end to detention, legalisation of independent candidates, the repeal of the 1992 bar on coalition governments, changes to the rules for the 12 nominated MPs, and the replacement of the presidential 25 per cent rule with a requirement to receive at least 50 per cent of the national vote.[188] These demands were to become the centrepiece of the reform movement. While KANU leaders acknowledged that the repeal of some legislation was unavoidable, both Moi and Wako refused to consider fundamental reform before the elections.

The Rise of Raila and the fall of FORD-Kenya, 1995–7

Meanwhile, Raila Odinga had emerged as his father's heir. During 1995–6, he rebuilt his father's political machine amongst both urban and rural Luo. Unwilling to play second fiddle in FORD-Kenya to Wamalwa, he began a long-running battle for the party's leadership. In 1995, allegations that Pattni had bribed Wamalwa as Public Accounts Committee chairman to exonerate the government over Goldenberg ended in a court case and an open split between Raila and Wamalwa factions (Figure 10.13). An attempted party coup by Odinga in November failed. This unedifying struggle culminated in party elections in April 1996, which collapsed in violence and disarray, with two competing slates elected.[189] It was a repeat of the events in FORD during 1992. The process ended in December 1996 with a formal split. Odinga walked out, and Wamalwa was re-elected unopposed as the much-diminished head of FORD-Kenya and its presidential candidate.

Now without a party, Raila bought and reactivated the moribund National Democratic Party (NDP), the party name that his father had used in 1991. In just a few months, he established it and its tractor symbol (*tinga*) as a new political force. He took most of the Luo political organisation with him, reflecting its enduring commitment to the Odinga dynasty. The FORD-Kenya establishment in several other districts also joined him, though most Luhya did not. Demonstrating his willingness to take risks, Raila voluntarily defected to his new political vehicle, the NDP, forcing a by-election in Langata. This he decisively won in March (both Kibaki and Matiba backed him, while Wamalwa actually backed KANU's candidate). The split was good news for KANU, as the Luo, Kikuyu and Luhya were now in competing parties, virtually guaranteeing Moi's presidential re-election. KANU barely campaigned for its own Langata candidate and the *Weekly Review* called it a 'blessing in disguise'.[190]

10.13: Raila Odinga (*left*) and Kijana Wamalwa (*right*)

Courtesy: Nation Group Newspapers

Opposition Alliances, 1995–7

While most opposition parties were fragmenting, efforts to build some form of cross-party unity continued in parallel. In November 1995, the DP joined FORD-Kenya, Safina and Shikuku's faction of FORD-Asili in Kenya's first opposition National Alliance. They initially hoped they could agree a single presidential candidate to face Moi, but made little progress. In February 1997, their alliance was further weakened after Wamalwa wrote letters as PAC chairman that appeared to exonerate Ketan Somaia from corruption charges. Both Orengo and Kibaki distanced themselves from him (something conveniently forgotten soon after).[191]

Matiba and Odinga opposed this alliance, ostensibly because it would involve imposing a leader without seeking a popular mandate to do so, but also because it might require them to stand down for someone else. In 1996, they established a competing Solidarity Alliance.[192] They were soon calling for an election boycott unless constitutional reforms were introduced (which Kibaki, Wamalwa and Shikuku all opposed). Odinga and Matiba had much in common: each commanded an ethnically exclusive, passionate and sometimes-violent mass movement, composed mainly of the poor from their respective communities. They were committed to radical change, but only if they were to lead it.

In the meantime Matiba had lost his own party. Although he was still popular amongst the Kikuyu masses, he proved unable to retain an effective organisation or work with others. In 1995, he had fallen out irrevocably with Secretary-General Shikuku in yet another factional split. Two years of infighting followed, but Matiba never managed to oust Shikuku or assert legal control over FORD-Asili. Eventually, in the run-up to the 1997 elections, Matiba walked away from the party, leaving his remaining MPs isolated and leaderless.

By January 1997, with all the opposition parties in trouble, some were looking for a compromise candidate such as a senior churchman to reunite their warring factions. However, no solution emerged, mainly because none of their leaders was willing to subsume his interests to that of the broader opposition. And time was in short supply.

Charity Ngilu Makes Waves, 1997

Instead, a fourth opposition presidential candidate emerged from a surprising quarter: an alliance between women's organisations, Kamba elites and radical intellectuals. DP MP Charity Ngilu had been vocal in the seventh parliament, but had not demonstrated any special qualities. She was not the first Kamba woman MP, had no real financial resources and only moderate organisational skills. Ngilu had been tested from the moment of her election, however, by a sustained campaign of pro-KANU harassment, which had hardened her resolve. She declared her candidacy in March 1997.

Initially, Ngilu tried to take on Kibaki inside the DP, but realising this was futile, in July she defected to the Social Democratic Party (SDP). This moribund party had recently been reactivated by two radical ex-academics, Peter Anyang' Nyong'o and Apollo Njonjo, who saw Ngilu as potential presidential material. Unlike most other Kenyan parties, the SDP was explicitly socialist. Ngilu's election campaign was hostile to structural adjustment, focusing on issues such as user access charges for health services. This was popular amongst urban voters, while rural women warmed to Ngilu as the vanguard of women's rights.[193] However, ethnicity was also a factor. Ngilu's base was in Kitui and it was amongst the Kamba that she elicited the most support. The DP organisation there defected to her en masse, and by September 1997 it was clear that Ngilu was going to win most votes in the region. The argument was that since every other major community had a candidate, the Akamba might as well back theirs. Despite her inexperience and the virtual non-existence elsewhere of her party, she had become 'the personification of Akamba ambitions to the presidency'.[194] Now, all five of Kenya's largest ethnic groups had their own candidate.

There was to be only one serious Kikuyu candidate, however. FORD-Asili supporters were stunned in June when Matiba announced that he had not registered as a voter and called on his supporters to burn their voters' cards if constitutional reform was not introduced.[195] It was a powerful message, but one that would have little effect if the other parties participated. For Kibaki, it was a godsend.

Growing Strains in KANU

With the election looming, strains within KANU over the distribution of the rewards of office became more open. Intra-Kalenjin tensions had been deepening since Moi came to power, just as the Kenyatta regime had seen divisions between the Kiambu and other Kikuyu. During 1997, for example, Marakwet and Pokot elites both demanded a greater share of the revenues from the Turkwell Gorge dam. Gradually, the Marakwet drifted away from KANU, forced into revolt by continued Pokot cattle raiding, which the government appeared unable to quell. Fighting between these Kalenjin groups continued into the election.[196]

There were also signs of weakening loyalty among the Nandi – the consequence in part of the KCC's problems and the East African Tannin Extract Company (EATEC) controversy. In 1979 and again in 1994, the government had bought EATEC farms from Lonrho and used them settle Kalenjin, but they had been mostly Keiyo and Tugen.[197] The proposed sale of the last 20,000 acres (8,000 hectares) of EATEC land in Eldoret South now became a major issue, as local Nandi were unable to afford to buy it and the state declined to assist them. Nandi anger at land sales on the Uasin Gishu plateau, which they claimed as their ancestral lands, remained deep (although the historical truth of these claims was questionable, given that the plateau had been grazed by Maasai until just before the arrival of the British). In the run-up to the polls, the Nandi KANU chairman for Uasin Gishu defected to FORD-Kenya, and Nandi maverick Kipruto arap Kirwa openly criticised Moi from within KANU.

Moi Changes his Mind, Twice, January–July 1997

On 15 January 1997, Moi signalled his commitment to KANU B over KANU A (Figure 10.14). After five years on the backbenches, a reshuffle brought Biwott back to the Cabinet as minister of state in the OP. He no longer controlled KANU as he once had, but remained a key figure in the state and the Kalenjin community, admired and hated in equal measure.[198] Opposition politicians termed it a disgrace, and the foreign media were universally hostile; indeed, it took only six months for the West to end aid to Kenya again. At the same time, Moi demoted KANU A leaders Ntimama and Nyachae and sacked Kones outright. Biwott's return suggested Saitoti's chances for the succession had improved. It also represented a reassertion of central authority against the regional bosses.[199]

Moi's rapprochement with KANU B proved short-lived however. His 'western strategy' of using Too to build bridges with the Luo and Luhya appeared to be bearing fruit, while Biwott's rapprochement with the Kikuyu was not, and there was some disquiet in the Tugen inner circle at Biwott's resurgence. The reshuffle caused discontent amongst the Kipsigis, Maasai, Kamba and Gusii. In June 1997,

10.14: KANU A: (*top, from left*) Nyachae, Ntimama, Kones and KANU B: (*bottom, from left*) Kamotho, Biwott and Saitoti

Courtesy: Nation Group Newspapers

therefore, with the international environment worsening, Moi put out feelers to Nyachae, Ntimama and Kones. Kones made a widely publicised 'plea for forgiveness' in July, which Moi accepted. Nyachae was rewarded with the removal of the pro-KANU B Nyanza PC in July. The struggle inside KANU continued, culminating in a tense Delegates' Conference in September, which decided to defer national elections yet again.

Preparations for Elections

As the 1997 election approached, pro-democracy and anti-government forces were pressing for legal and constitutional reforms, as were foreign donors.[200] However, KANU was obdurate that the polls would be fought on the same (unfair) basis as in 1992. In the run-up to the polls, Moi reappointed Chesoni as ECK head, while the broadcast media remained state dominated and the provincial administration partisan.

In 1996, in accordance with the law specifying that reviews should take place every 10 years, the ECK had reviewed constituency boundaries, increasing the number of seats from 188 to 210. The review used much the same criteria to define boundaries as before, targeting the same number of inhabitants as 'reasonably practical', but allowing for the need to represent sparsely populated areas, geographical features, communities of interest and administrative boundaries. Again, the ECK decided not to abolish any seats, only to add new ones. The Rift Valley received five new seats, Central, Western and Eastern four each, Nyanza three, the Coast and North-Eastern one each and Nairobi none (the excuse being that MPs could traverse a Nairobi seat easily). This maintained the over-representation of the semi-arid areas and under-representation of the urban areas that had existed since independence and which served to maintain KANU's dominance in Parliament.[201]

Some seats were distributed in a reasonable approximation to fairness, but there were many anomalies that appeared to benefit individuals, and half the new seats probably helped KANU's electoral prospects.[202] For example, Murang'a and Kiambu districts had recently been reorganised to recreate Thika District and Kangema in Murang'a was now split to help Kamotho's candidacy, while Gatundu was split in two, creating a more winnable seat for 35-year-old Uhuru Kenyatta (first-born son of Jomo by Mama Ngina). Ethnicity was again a driver for constituency redesign. Tense Molo in Nakuru was split along ethnic lines, creating a Kikuyu Molo and a Kipsigis Kuresoi, while Gwasi constituency in Suba District was formed to separate local Basuba from their Luo assimilators.

Voter registration took place during May and June 1997, again with two extensions to deal with the inevitable late rush. In the end, 9 million of the estimated 12.5 million adults had registered, roughly the same percentage as in 1992. The process was more effective and less biased than in 1992. For the first time, the ECK used an optical character recognition system to scan registration forms, with entries copied locally into a 'black book'. There were indications of registration continuing in the handwritten 'black books' after its formal closure, but there was nothing like the 1992 level of protest and 'no evidence of a deliberate and systematic process of manipulation'.[203] The new system helped identify and remove 20,000 double-registrations.[204] The issue of identity cards still remained controversial; it was frequently claimed that 2 million young Kenyans were unable to register as they did not have ID cards, and that restrictions on ID cards were targeting certain regions. The ECK accepted that it was a genuine issue, but believed the number to be fewer than 1 million.

Another 'Change the Constitution' Movement

During 1997, those committed to constitutional reform managed to stitch civil society activists, donors and opposition politicians together into a brief but effective alliance that, backed by Western protests and aid suspension, briefly threatened KANU's hold on power.

'No Reform, No Elections', April–June 1997

In April 1997, the 4Cs organised the first National Convention Assembly (NCA) of 600 activists and opposition politicians in Limuru, an attempt to create a national conference that would rewrite the constitution. The assembly agreed to press for constitutional reforms before the elections and to threaten a boycott if its demands were not met. What had been an academic debate about rights and norms was becoming a trial of strength. Attendees included Kibaki, Wamalwa, Shikuku and Ngilu. Neither Matiba nor Raila attended, but they sent messages of support. It was the beginning of a brief but powerful alliance between the mainstream parties and civil society. Some churches were already nervous of the project however; Timothy Njoya of the PCEA attended as did Methodist and Muslim leaders, but the Catholics did not and the NCCK only sent observers.[205] The conference was part-funded by the US Ford Foundation and several diplomats attended to show their support.

The NCA's goals were familiar – to curb the power of the presidency, repeal oppressive laws, resettle clash victims and change the electoral system – all of which would weaken KANU. Its long-term goal was a new constitution, but there could be no compromise on the need for minimal changes before the 1997 polls. The assembly elected a National Convention Executive Council (NCEC) of 25 members as its executive organ, led by non-party activists, including lawyers Kibwana, Mutunga and Davinder Lamba. The NCEC threatened an escalating campaign of civil disobedience if its demands were not met.

With political leaders and the anti-government intelligentsia aligned, buttressed by donor support, the result was a rapid deterioration in security. There was violence on 3 May 1997 during the first NCEC demonstration, which was designed to infringe the Public Order Act, although the police let politicians speak.[206] Kibaki, Wamalwa, Shikuku, Muite, Orengo and Ngilu all joined the NCEC in a rare show of unity, but the churches avoided breaking the law. Again, Odinga and Matiba were absent. Pro-KANU vigilantes, known as the Jeshi la Mzee (the Old Man's Army), responded, attacking anti-government activists in Nairobi.

By mid-May, fearful of a breakdown of order and its ripple effects on the region and angry at KANU's intransigence, 22 Western donors were pressuring Moi to introduce minimum reforms before the elections. The NCCK and the Catholics committed themselves to reforms to the Constitution, electoral law and the ECK, plus parliamentary confirmation of presidential appointments.[207] Moi was determined, however: there would be no dialogue with unelected activists and no reform before the elections. Again, change would only come through confrontation.

On 31 May 1997, riot police disrupted the second NCEC protest, setting off two days of unrest. As a palliative, on 1 June, Moi promised reform of the Public Order Act, but nothing else, as 'the atmosphere in the country is not conducive to holding serious and meaningful discussions on a subject of national importance such as the constitution.'[208] More clashes took place on 3 June. Unemployed, alienated and criminalised urban youth were the core of the protesters. On 19 June, placard-waving MPs drowned out Finance Minister Mudavadi during the budget speech, their protests broadcast on live TV. The same day, pro-reform lawyers submitted two model reform bills to address the most urgent constitutional issues.

Saba Saba and KANU's Response

The government banned the third NCEC protest, to be held on 7 July 1997 (Saba Saba), but thousands attended anyway. The resulting demonstrations degenerated into nationwide violence in which at least 14 people died. It was a replay of the events of 1990. MPs were beaten, and the GSU attacked pro-opposition clergy at prayer, leaving Reverend Njoya unconscious and bloodstained in front of journalists. The shilling fell 10 per cent against the dollar in a day, and donors were increasingly jittery. Foreign governments and newspapers criticised violence against peaceful protesters and urged another aid freeze. The agenda for the upcoming talks with Kenya's aid donors shifted dramatically from economic to political reform. There were daily confrontations between students and police.

Moi was already moving towards compromise and, as he was changing partners within KANU, he also changed approach on the Constitution. On 5 July, before Saba Saba, he had met church leaders and Wamalwa to discuss how to calm the situation. On 11 July, Moi publicly admitted that some form of reform was necessary. On 17 July, the KANU NEC supported proposals to create a constitutional reform commission and to introduce other reforms close to those proposed by the reform lobby. Western diplomats tried to facilitate meetings between Moi and his opponents, to synthesise a deal acceptable to both sides.

The gap now widened between the opposition doves – including the DP and FORD-Kenya – and the hawks, including the NCEC leaders, Kuria, Njoya, Odinga, Orengo, Matiba and Muite.[209] Seeing KANU's willingness to compromise, activists and harder-line politicians rejected piecemeal changes, continuing their demands for a boycott, and demanded that the NCEC be the only forum mandated to negotiate with KANU. On 26 July, opposition politicians and activists united at a rally in Mombasa, with the cry, 'no reforms, no elections'. The government, now keen to compromise, licensed the rally. Matiba called for a constitutional conference to take control of the country and Orengo and others began to talk of a revolution. Mutunga later described the situation as one in which 'a civilian coup against the Moi-KANU regime was imminent and possible.'[210] The mainstream opposition, in contrast, saw a real opportunity for consensual change, and increasingly questioned the right of the 'amorphous and unelected' NCEC to negotiate with the state. On 27 July, a cross-party meeting of 110 MPs, a majority of the Assembly, committed itself to minimum reforms before the elections.

Aid is Suspended Once More, July–August 1997

Frightened by the unrest, the West now returned to the field they had abandoned in 1993. Little had changed since 1996, save the fact that there was now the risk of mass unrest if no compromise was reached. Always risk averse, and with the echoes of Rwanda ringing in their ears, the US and other donors increased the pressure on the government to make a deal. On 31 July 1997 (after KANU had agreed to minimum reforms in principle), under strong US pressure, the IMF suspended its short-lived ESAF indefinitely, ostensibly in protest at the government's failure to tackle corruption and meet governance criteria. Diplomats warned Moi that he must address the concerns of demonstrators to avoid civil unrest. The donors appeared to be lining up with Kenya's political opposition.

Moi was defiant, calling the US$400 million of lost loans 'peanuts', but the result – in a market more open to capital movements – was panic selling of Treasury bills and the shilling. Talks with IMF representatives failed. Western officials were particularly angered by the misuse of sugar imports to fund KANU's election campaign.[211] In response, KANU hardliners called Mudavadi and Cheserem 'lackeys' of the IMF and claimed that donors were trying to bring down the government.[212] With the hardliners in the ascendant, several pro-reform officials were fired or transferred, and Mudavadi's promises of reforms in the energy sector were disowned. In frustration, the IFIs declared all agreements with the government void. A $125 million World Bank investment in the power sector was lost, alongside many other IFI and bilateral contributions. Mudavadi was forced into an emergency mini-budget, raising taxes and cutting spending. The shilling fell to 70 to the dollar and interest rates rose. The financial crisis coincided with the Likoni clashes and the resulting fall in tourism, and was soon followed by concessions to teachers, police and civil servants, worsening the problem.

The IPPG Seizes the Initiative, August–September 1997

The spectre of mass civil disorder and Western ostracism convinced KANU leaders that reforms to the laws around elections, meetings and movement were inevitable. In early August, Wako therefore published two reform bills, based on the NCEC's proposals. The first made several changes reducing centralised authority, including abolition of the Outlying Districts Act, and amendments to the Public Order Act and Societies Act. KANU also made proposals for a constitutional review commission to create a new draft constitution. However, the opposition response was negative, mostly due to the lack of prior dialogue.[213]

On 8 August, known as Nane Nane, the NCEC called a general strike, during which up to 40 people died in violent clashes. This time, the DP, NDP and Safina supported the strike, but FORD-Kenya and Matiba did not. Foreign donors (who were still funding the NCEC) again protested at the government's inflexibility and called for reforms, but were increasingly fearful of the situation they had helped create. The NCCK and Catholics too were nervous at the way in which the crisis was spiralling into violence. In the midst of this, passions were inflamed by the Likoni killings (see below). On 26–8 August, the National Convention Assembly met for the second time. Muite, Leakey, Orengo, Sheikh Balala, Odinga and Ngilu attended. The NCA rejected KANU's attempts to control the reform process and reaffirmed its 'no reforms, no elections' position. It made radical calls for action, including a proposal to transform itself into a constituent assembly. There were even calls for an 'armed struggle'.[214] The stakes were rising, leaving both the NCEC and the government on dangerous ground.

Simultaneously, moderates on both sides were crafting a compromise. A series of meetings between KANU MPs (led by Saitoti) and opposition MPs (led by Wamalwa) began on 26 August, and established a new body, known as the Inter-Parties Parliamentary Group (the IPPG), with the goal of negotiating a compromise.[215] The IPPG formed several committees to negotiate minimum changes, which turned out to surpass anything that KANU had been expected to concede. With growing support amongst politicians, churches and donors, by 9 September, a deal had been done, despite furious opposition from the NCEC, Matiba, the NDP, Safina and Orengo.[216] Most politicians were willing to break ranks with the NCEC, in part because it had become a competitor, but also because many believed they had a genuine opportunity for consensual change. When this package came to Parliament in October 1997, the pro-NCEC radicals were in a minority, with only 26 MPs voting against the final constitutional amendment, to 156 in favour. Moi gave his presidential assent on 8 November. Amid blood and recriminations, another crisis had been averted.

The resulting package contained three types of reform. The first category reduced state authority. The most widely heralded change was the end to preventative detention, with the abolition of the Preservation of Public Security Act. The Vagrancy Act, the Outlying Districts Act and the Special Districts Act were also repealed, and sedition laws were abolished. The Chief's Authority Act was amended to reduce the powers of chiefs. The Public Order Act was amended to remove the requirement for a licence before meetings, replacing it with a need to 'notify' the police three days beforehand. The Broadcasting Act was changed to provide free airtime for all political parties and to require the KBC to keep a fair balance of political viewpoints. The Societies Act was amended to require the registrar to respond 'reasonably' to all requests for registration within 120 days.

Second, there were changes to electoral regulations. The Election Offences Act was altered to make the falsification of voters' registers and the destruction, sale and purchase of voting cards offences.[217] A constitutional amendment gave new powers to the ECK for voter education and provided for the 12 nominated MPs to be chosen on a pro rata basis by the political parties. The requirement that the president appoint a Cabinet only from his own party was abolished, allowing coalition governments. The number of electoral commissioners was raised to 22, with 10 extra commissioners chosen by the opposition parties participating in the IPPG deal (although they were still formally appointed by the president). However, the NCEC's proposals for a '50 per cent rule' to replace the '25 per cent in five provinces' rule in presidential polls and to permit independent candidates were deferred.

Third, preparations were made for a fundamental review of the Constitution. The resulting 1997 Constitution of Kenya Review Commission Act provided for the president to appoint a commission to collect Kenyans' views on constitutional change after the elections. Here, KANU's approach dominated. The only limit imposed on Moi's freedom was that he had to appoint its members from amongst those nominated by the parties and civil society.

The IPPG deal remains a source of deep disagreement. NCEC supporters condemned it as a sell-out that had set back democratisation. Nevertheless, the IPPG did deliver substantive changes in an environment of confrontation. As to the 'what if': a failure to reach agreement would have left the Constitution unchanged, as there was little prospect of KANU conceding legitimacy to the NCEC. The election would have been boycotted by more parties (though not by all); the legitimacy of the government would have been weakened further and the country would have moved closer to being ungovernable. Though the reforms achieved in 1997 were imperfect, they permitted a significant opening of political space.

The Opposition Fragments

In the wake of a deal that satisfied many, the opposition split. The DP, SDP and FORD-Kenya backed the IPPG reforms, while the NCEC, NDP, Safina and Matiba continued their campaign. However, the government now had a freer hand to deal with radical elements. During October, police disrupted several NCEC rallies and beat pro-NCEC politicians in full view of the press. The NCA met once more, in October, but it was the end of their programme of mass action. The mood of the nation had moved against them, the rug pulled from under them by the IPPG changes, and their voices were drowned out by the election campaign; popular energies were now diverted to the electoral contest.

Of the pro-NCEC parties, Odinga's NDP, Safina and Orengo (still technically in FORD-Kenya) eventually contested the polls under protest. Matiba and his supporters were the sole group who boycotted them completely, losing their seats in Parliament as a result. Matiba formed a further FORD offshoot, known as Saba Saba Asili, which campaigned against the elections, talking implausibly of a Philippines-style revolution in which his supporters would storm State House, but he was unable to persuade even his own FORD-Asili MPs to boycott the polls. In October, the pro-participation FORD-Asili MPs formed yet another FORD spin-off, FORD-People, led by Kimani wa Nyoike, to allow them to stand.

In party terms, too, fragmentation was occurring. With the new rules on party registration, the registrar of societies now approved 16 more parties, most of them tiny. Safina was the last, registered on 26 November 1997, just a month before the elections. Conspiracy theorists noted that many of these parties were Kikuyu-led and might fragment the Kikuyu vote.

Lurching from Crisis to Crisis

Likoni

While the government was damping down dissent through political reform, it faced a series of security and economic crises, most of which were of its own making. In August 1997, the clashes started again, this time on the Coast. Over a period of several months, up to 1,000 Digo Mijikenda, including ex-servicemen, had been recruited into a paramilitary force and received rudimentary military training in Kwale District.[218] Some of the group's leaders were believed to be military or police figures from outside the area. The local (Digo) police were aware that trouble was coming, but did nothing.

Their first major attack, on Likoni police station in Mombasa, occurred on 13 August 1997. During the raid, more than 100 armed men killed six police and seven civilians, and robbed the station armoury of guns. An attack had been planned for some time, but there were indications that it was a rushed reaction to the recent arrest of an officer privy to their plans.[219] Either way, the militia was now empowered to act, and over the next few weeks, they roamed Likoni and the south coast of Kwale, killing and maiming between 70 and 100 upcountry people (mainly Luo and non-Muslims) and burning their houses. Initially, the local security forces appeared unwilling or incapable of responding. The army and navy were drafted into action and then recalled; the police investigation team was transferred to other duties; arrested raiders were mysteriously released. Many believed the same process had begun as in the Rift in 1991–2.

The origins of the Likoni violence lay in a deep-seated feeling amongst the Mijikenda that their land and jobs had been stolen, by both Arabs and upcountry people.[220] Economically, the Mijikenda were amongst the most disadvantaged of rural Kenyans, with little political influence and few cash-crops, and their major asset, the coast itself, had been long lost to the political elites. With many Muslims amongst their number, the growing assertiveness of Islam worldwide offered a call to action. Fed by a government for whom anti-upcountry feeling was useful, the formation of this tribal militia was probably part of a broader plan to reassert *mwambao* – coastal autonomy – as in the run-up to independence. It was a response to the NCEC's recent success, just as *majimbo* and the clashes of 1991–2 had been a response to the pressure for multi-party democracy. If upcountry voters could not be persuaded to vote KANU, perhaps they could be persuaded to leave entirely, and leave their land and jobs behind them too.

There was uproar in Parliament and the nation; tensions rose and tourist bookings slumped. Under pressure to act, and with the IPPG deal done, this time the government responded in kind. Once they began hunting the raiders in October, the GSU ruthlessly repressed the local community, robbing, beating and raping their way through Kwale.[221] Fighting continued through November and isolated killings continued into 1998, including a second attack on a police station in May, but the militia was crushed as a military force. Over 700 people were arrested and 200 raiders were jailed.

The leaders, however, escaped unscathed. Several KANU MPs and Mijikenda politicians including Emmanuel Karissa Maitha were implicated, as was KANU's coastal financier Rashid Sajaad, who was reported to have provided money that ended up with the raiders, and even to have visited them.[222] Maitha later claimed both Sajaad and Biwott were involved but that Moi was unaware of the plans.[223] None of the alleged leaders was convicted; several of the indicted chiefs were reinstated and local officials appeared to be concealing evidence. One investigating officer admitted he had been pressured to release suspects and to take care when investigating senior leaders: 'My Lords, in a political Government, we have got to be cautious. This is a political government.'[224] Most of those implicated were not even interviewed by the police, who were too frightened to do so.

The logic behind the Likoni events remains impenetrable at a national level, as the consequences included massive damage to the tourism infrastructure in which many KANU elites had investments. KANU benefited little, as there was a backlash amongst the Digo in Mombasa and Kwale that saw many desert the ruling party for a new federalist party, Shirikisho. It is likely that the events were instigated by local politicians to secure their own victory by driving away upcountry voters. However, it probably had the connivance of the Kalenjin security establishment, related to the fear of NCEC-led civil insurrection in July–August. Once the IPPG compromise had calmed tensions, the raiders were dispensed with.

Trouble in the South-West

In October and November, there was a second outbreak of ethnic violence, this time between Maasai and Gusii. Tensions had been building over the presence of thousands of Kuria, Kipsigis and Gusii in Maasai Trans-Mara District, where they had bought, leased or occupied land in the 1960s and 1970s. By now, the majority of voters in the seat were Gusii or Kipsigis, and the result was growing tension, accentuated by the differing political orientations of the communities and by the ongoing subdivision of group ranches. At least 25 people died in the resulting fighting. There was also fighting between Luo and Gusii and between Kuria and Luo that left 20 dead during October. In each case, local issues were inflamed by conflicting party sentiments. There was little logic behind the allegations that KANU organised this, because KANU undoubtedly lost more Gusii swing support as a result than it gained amongst the pastoralists.

A Perfect Storm

In parallel with these outbreaks of violence, the state also faced an economic challenge from public sector workers. Both teachers and nurses took advantage of the upcoming election to press their demands. After years of declining real incomes, on 1 October 1997 all Kenya's 287,000 teachers struck, demanding a 150–200 per cent wage increase, the recommendation of a recent salary review committee. It was the first full teachers' strike since 1969. The government was in agony: to grant such increases would leave their wages policies in tatters, and could even bankrupt the country, so large was the number of teachers; yet to refuse a deal would lose KANU the votes of teachers and their families and keep schools closed. After a two-week dispute, the government cracked. Bypassing the ministers of labour and education, Moi conceded to the KNUT's demands, but to be phased over five years. This was to have serious fiscal consequences, at a time when donors were demanding spending cuts. By November, with tourism in decline and foreign assistance cut, the state had trouble paying civil servants' salaries and was pressing against its 5 per cent borrowing limit.

On 29 November, state nurses also struck, demanding a 500 per cent salary increase; at least 60 people died because of lack of treatment as a result. This time, however, the government sacked all 30,000 nurses rather than negotiate.[225]

Finally, the weather too intervened to punish KANU. From October 1997 to February 1998, Kenya experienced the effects of the El Niño weather system (a periodic violent disruption in the ocean weather system in the Pacific). This caused mass flooding, especially in the Coast and North-Eastern Province. In November, Wajir received twice the amount of rainfall that had fallen in the whole of 1996. Everywhere, roads and bridges were washed away, animals drowned and crops flattened. Hundreds died and 300,000 lost their homes. Cholera was rife. Tourist bookings fell and roads, railways and airports were closed, causing knock-on damage to the economy and to government finances. For a while in January 1998, the Mombasa road itself – the lifeline for East Africa – was closed. Despite the aid stalemate, foreign donors and aid agencies again responded with millions of dollars in food and supplies for the disaster zones.

The 1997 Elections

Although some of the actors had changed, the 1997 election was in many ways a repeat of the 1992 polls.[226] Despite a majority of hostile voters, Moi and KANU again beat a divided opposition, although their parliamentary victory was narrow. In other ways, the 1997 election was a watershed. Multi-party democracy requires not just that many parties contest elections, but that the defeat of the incumbent be a realistic possibility. By this criterion, the 1997 elections were the first democratic elections in Kenya's history. By the end of 1997, the issue was no longer whether the opposition would survive, but how long the government could remain balanced on top of a society that consistently voted against it.

The Administration and Monitoring of the Polls

With the IPPG deal done, on 10 November Moi dissolved Parliament, and Chesoni announced that the elections would be held on 29 December 1997. This year, the government announced that (for reasons of national sovereignty) it would fund them itself. Despite much controversy, the ECK decided to use the same ballot boxes as in 1992.[227] However, the ballot papers were not printed by De La Rue as in 1992, but by a new vendor, Smith and Ouzman of the UK. The design and delivery of these papers was to become one of the most contentious issues of the election. Smith and Ouzman were not familiar with local conditions, while the ECK was struggling to cope with the rise in the number of parties, new civic wards, and the addition of the 10 new, inexperienced commissioners. The result was that the printers 'did not receive full, final and detailed information' in time.[228] Many amendments had to be made during printing, and packaging was done incorrectly. The last batch of papers did not arrive in Kenya until 26 December. The packages were not opened, but sent directly to the constituencies.

An extraordinary event occurred on 2 December, when, following the retirement of Chief Justice Majid Cockar, Moi appointed Chesoni as Kenya's new chief justice. He was only the second Kenyan African chief justice, but it was a deeply unpopular choice. The LSK called it a 'ridicule of the entire legal profession' (which ended its relationship with the new chief justice immediately).[229] Chesoni left the chairmanship of the ECK vacant only four weeks before the election. His vice-chairman since 1992, Samuel Kivuitu, a Kamba lawyer and ex-MP, took up the role with trepidation.

Amongst election monitoring groups, lessons had been learnt from 1992, and the election saw a better-organised international presence and better coordination between domestic and international observers. The donor organisations were similar: 22 national embassies, the EU and the UNDP, led by the Americans, the Scandinavians, the Netherlands and the British, working through a coordinating body, the Donors for Development and Democracy Group (DDDG). This year, they created a shared Election Observation Centre that tracked events and coordinated observers throughout November and December.[230] There were no large-scale observer missions, reflecting disillusionment with the election tourism of 1992. Instead, the donors relied on local diplomats and a small staff of Africanists.

Internally, the environment was also better monitored than in 1992. Many of the same organisations participated from the religious and secular arms of civil society, strengthened by five years of external financing and competence development. The IED, the Catholic Justice and Peace Commission (CJPC) and the NCCK all made monitoring proposals, but were brought together at Western request as a condition for funding.[231] The domestic observers monitored the campaign, including election violence and media coverage, as well as deploying 28,000 poll watchers and count certifiers, five times more than in 1992. Both domestic and international observers organised high-level vote tabulations and cross-checked observer reports with published results, shadowing the ECK. The donors also funded civic education programmes run by NGOs and the churches.

The Party Primaries, November–December 1997

As in 1992, all the party primaries were a shambles, marred by violence, malpractice and incompetence, but KANU's were again the most contested and the most abused. Every party saw the direct nomination of senior figures, the overturning of elections and substitution of candidates, lack of materials and poor coordination. Candidates picked parties and parties picked candidates based on their chances of victory. Where one party was clearly going to win, all candidates competed for this party's nominations. The losers then defected to the second most popular party and the process continued. Where there was no local consensus, the process reversed, and parties competed for the most powerful candidates. There were now 27 registered parties, so every candidate could find a home. Now headless, most FORD-Asili MPs fled elsewhere, to the DP, FORD-People, the SDP, and even the NDP and KANU. Most Luo MPs followed Raila into the NDP, while Muite stood on a Safina ticket and his Meru ally Murungi sought ethno-regional safety in the DP.

KANU's nominations were mostly conducted by queue voting, but this year the provincial administration was ordered not to run them and, partly as a result, they were even more confused and corrupt than in 1992. Some candidates apparently polled three times as many votes in the party primary as they did in the final poll, an indicator of open rigging. The deep divides within KANU were also revealed. State House backed candidates to take on Nyachae and Ntimama, now described as 'KANU rebels' in party briefings. Both ministers won, but their allies fared less well. Having lost several supporters during the primaries, Nyachae backed a slate of Gusii opposition candidates against his KANU opponents, with the result that during 1998–2002 he fronted a cross-party Gusii alliance, showing how light an overlay 'party' was on the real ethno-regional divisions. In Kwale, reflecting but also grounding the anger felt after Likoni, all three incumbent KANU MPs lost. Elsewhere, free primaries resulted in the election of several independent figures, ensuring KANU's victory but leaving rebels with the party ticket. More than 20 KANU candidates had been opposition candidates in 1992 and KANU won three or four seats as a result.[232] There were seven ministerial losers, and others survived only through interventions from party headquarters.

The DP used a secret ballot system, while the NDP used a combination of the delegate system, direct nomination and queue voting. Safina and the SDP adopted a 'first come first served' model. Outside the areas where they expected to win, the opposition's primaries were low key. Voters participated in several primaries if it was worth their while, demonstrating the importance of money in luring them to the ballot boxes.

The problem of defection was even worse than in 1992: more than a quarter of the final candidate list had been in a different party a few weeks before. The most extreme case was in Limuru in Kiambu. There, MP George Nyanja decamped from FORD-Asili to FORD-People (where he was refused entry), returned to FORD-Asili (where he had by now lost the party's nomination), then defected to the SDP and finally the NDP. His opponent Kuria Kanyingi defected from KANU to FORD-People, then back to KANU and finally to FORD-Asili.

The number of newcomers to parliamentary politics was the highest since 1969. KANU newcomers included ex-YK'92 leaders Jirongo in Western and 31-year-old Nandi William Ruto in Uasin Gishu, who used the experience and money they had gained in 1992 to springboard themselves into national politics.

Parliamentary and Presidential Nominations, 3–9 December

The presidential nominations of 3 and 4 December were calm and uncontested. An unprecedented 15 presidential candidates were nominated; as well as the big five, the parade of minnows included Koigi wa Wamwere (KENDA), Shikuku (FORD-Asili), Wangari Maathai (Liberal Party), Munyua Waiyaki (United People's Party), wa Nyoike (FORD-People) and Anyona (KSC). The Kikuyu particularly suffered from a surfeit of second-rank leaders who believed that in Matiba's absence they had a chance at power.

The new climate of cooperation and KANU's confidence of victory also led to less trouble at the parliamentary nominations. These were spread across two days, 8 and 9 December, which gave time to resolve paperwork issues. More candidates (884) were nominated than in 1992, mainly because of the proliferation of splinter parties. KANU again put up a candidate in every constituency (210), while the DP had 134, NDP 109, the SDP 105 and FORD-Kenya 103. The opposition parties did not try to create a national ticket and focused only on winnable seats, having learnt their lesson from 1992. There was no opposition alliance at the parliamentary level, but the DP did not put up a candidate against Ngilu or FORD-People's John Michuki. FORD-Kenya did not field candidates in most Central and Eastern seats, while the DP did the same in Western. They still competed, however, in Nairobi, the Coast and Kisii, where both believed they were strong.

Moi himself faced an opponent in Baringo Central, the first time a president had ever been opposed. Moi accepted this with good grace, publicly shaking his opponent's hand, but the candidate was unable to visit the constituency for the rest of the campaign after receiving death threats.[233] In 12 seats, 11 of which were in the

10.15: Women parliamentary candidates and elected MPs, 1963–2007

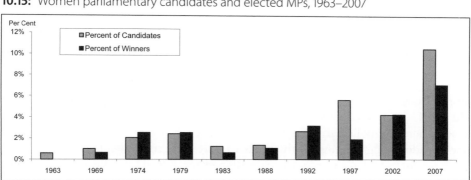

Source: Various

Rift Valley, KANU was unopposed, and the party won two more seats after all its opponents withdrew during the campaign.

There were 50 female candidates (6 per cent), the largest number yet. Ngilu's SDP fielded a particularly high proportion. However, partly as a result of the SDP's aspirational pro-female focus, female candidates performed extremely poorly (see Figure 10.15).

The Campaign

Unlike 1992, the 1997 campaign changed little. Opinion polls at the beginning predicted the results well. Kibaki was the main gainer, drawing in the undecided and ex-Matiba voters. This year, Moi faced four main opponents, each strong in one region and hoping to reach outside, but with little chance of victory nationwide. The SDP took on KANU in Ukambani, FORD-Kenya led the charge in Western, the NDP dominated Luo Nyanza and the DP Central Province, Embu and Meru. The key marginal communities were again the Gusii, Kamba and southern Luhya, plus the settlement areas, Nairobi and Mombasa.

In most seats, the election followed a similar pattern to 1992. Candidates competed within parties and then across them, promising local development as well as addressing national issues. Clanism dominated the poll in northern Kenya, Kisii, Kuria, parts of Meru and Embu, most of Western, Tana River and Maasailand. Ethnic politics dominated the settlement zones and the cities. Personal abilities and local sectionalism were critical in winning the favoured party's nomination. Money was extremely important, with wealthier candidates able to promise and deliver development to their areas. Insecurity played a greater role in the north, and the consequences of the Likoni clashes dominated the coastal strip. Problems with cash-crops and cooperatives characterised campaigns in Embu, Meru, Central and Kisii. Land allocation, squatters and delays or corruption in the issue of title deeds were issues everywhere.

Although Matiba did not stand or endorse another candidate, he continued to glower from the sidelines and launched another last-minute assault on Kibaki in December, part of an increasingly confused stream of pronouncements.[234] Homeless, many FORD-Asili voters backed wealthy populists on an 'anything but KANU' ticket. Kiambu and Thika were suffering from falling cash-crop incomes, land inequalities and growing poverty. An army of near-landless unemployed Kikuyu were now turning away from the stable, personalised politics of the past towards an unstable cocktail of ethnically exclusive, aggressive and populist policies.

The competition in 1997 was fairer than in 1992, though still unequal. The inclusion in the ECK of commissioners nominated by the opposition allayed concerns, while the IPPG laws eased candidates' abilities to campaign. There were still dozens of cases where the police arrested opposition MPs for crimes that no longer existed, such as addressing meetings without a licence. KANU continued to campaign using government vehicles and officials campaigned for KANU candidates in Turkana, Keiyo, Migori and elsewhere.[235] There was no attempt to declare exclusive KANU zones, but it was still extremely difficult for opposition supporters to campaign in Baringo, Nandi, Kericho, Bomet or Narok.

The election campaign was violent, with more than 12 killed, many in Nyanza. Open threats were again made against opposition supporters. In Samburu, Assistant Minister Peter Lengees threatened that 'Outsiders who are not ready to sing the Samburu song and are out to provoke them would be ejected from the district.'[236] The provincial commissioner warned non-Pokot not to participate in the West Pokot KANU nominations, and there were attacks on non-Pokot in December. Odinga was barred – as his father had been – from campaigning in North-Eastern Province by KANU supporters barricading the airstrip.[237]

All the parties made use of electoral bribery. There was buying of voters' cards, to destroy or use in multiple voting. More common were simple cash payments (from 20 shillings upwards) in return for promises of support. Food and drink were again distributed at party meetings. The patron–client politics of the past were evolving into more cash-based transactions, with fewer mutual long-term obligations.

KANU's dominance of the media changed little. The KBC was still partisan and unwilling to cover opposition activities unless it could place a negative slant on them.[238] Ngilu was blacked out almost entirely. This year, however, the IPPG agreement did allow a series of party political broadcasts on the KBC. In the print media, the *Kenya Times*, *Standard* and *Weekly Review* were pro-government, the *Nation* veered between neutrality and opposition, while *The People* and several new flimsy or 'grey' weeklies were anti-KANU. Whatever the medium, most reports on the election were personalised and sensationalised.

KANU's Campaign

KANU went into the campaign in the lead, and all the opinion polls predicted a victory for Moi. The party produced a glossy campaign manifesto, pledging good governance, employment, gender sensitivity and economic growth.[239] Despite their nationwide credentials and modern messages, however, their campaign was coordinated by a Kalenjin-dominated team, a glimpse into where real power still lay.[240]

KANU again had the largest campaign budget. The party raised Ksh100 million (US$1.6 million) in one American-style fundraising, attended by such magnates as Pattni and Chris Kirubi. Asian businesses were another target; Gideon Moi was reputed to have organised fundraisings amongst his Asian business partners.[241] Some claimed that sugar imports helped fund KANU's campaign and coastal tycoon Sajaad admitted to having spent Ksh17 million (US$270,000) on KANU's campaign.[242] Entreaties were again made to Middle Eastern governments for support. In contrast to the profligacy of 1992, however, there was no Goldenberg-style looting of state coffers, and no jump in inflation or fall in the shilling.

As this was probably Moi's last election, the competition for the succession was also heating up. Although most public attention concentrated on Saitoti, Mudavadi and Nyachae, insiders were already mulling over a shocking shift in strategy. There were hints that Moi was toying with the idea of nominating a non-Kalenjin – worse, a Kikuyu – as his successor. Moi already had his eye on Uhuru Kenyatta, elected in April as KANU chairman for Thika District, who was standing for the first time as a parliamentary candidate in his father's old seat.[243]

The Opposition Campaign

None of the four main opposition parties went into the election expecting outright victory. Without an electoral alliance, the best they could hope for was to deny Moi 25 per cent in five provinces, thereby forcing him into a second-round contest. But none stood down.

There were few major differences between the parties on policy issues. Kibaki and the DP campaigned on the platforms 'We Need Sanity Back in Kenya' and 'Unity and Justice', with an emphasis on better economic management and fighting corruption. Harking back to 1963, the DP manifesto referred to Moi's as a 'KADU-KANU' government.[244] The NDP stressed social programmes strongly, though Raila did not openly espouse the socialism or land redistribution of his father. All made promises on education, health and gender equality. Several parties called for further constitutional reform, with the NDP offering devolution and parliamentary approval of appointments.[245] All the opposition parties devoted most of their energy to a negative campaign, calling for an end to Moi's corruption and misrule. Odinga took a particularly strong line, suggesting: 'the only thing his government will be remembered for is corruption, land grabbing, instigation of ethnic clashes, and a ruined education system.'[246] This was to prove ironic given the aftermath. All the opposition parties reminded voters of the ethnic clashes and events in Likoni.

The enduring wealth of the Asian community remained a source of frustration for populists such as Matiba, Odinga and Shikuku, who all accused them of corruption during the campaign and of 'diabolical collusion' with KANU.[247] Matiba even threatened to expel all Asians should he take over the country.[248]

Ngilu's campaign initially made waves, delighting urbanites with its focus on basic needs and its criticism of structural adjustment and the 'vagaries of blind liberalisation'.[249] However, it faded in the last two weeks, as her meagre financial resources and lack of a wide network of local operators took their toll. The SDP's stress on youth and women's issues was a refreshing contrast to the machine politicians, but Ngilu struggled outside her core constituencies in Ukambani and amongst urban women.

Polling Day and the Count

Polling day (29 December) and the count saw less rigging than in 1992, but poor preparation and bad weather caused administrative nightmares for the ECK. Ballot papers, staff or vehicles to transport them were missing across much of the country. The ECK sent thousands of ballot papers to the wrong constituencies, affecting more than 10 per cent of seats. Other papers had incorrect candidate information.[250] Fewer than half the polling stations opened on time with enough materials. The lack of ballots particularly affected KANU zones of the Rift Valley, and Saitoti himself was unable to vote on 29 December. Meanwhile, bad weather delayed voting over much of the Coast and North-Eastern, also pro-KANU areas. Concerns over rigging became almost irrelevant in the face of the logistical chaos. While the ECK could do little about the weather, the distribution of ballot papers was evidence of incompetence or malice. The foreign observers later concluded, 'The distribution of ballot papers was flawed at three stages: first from the printers in Britain; secondly, from central stores of the Electoral Commission of Kenya, and finally by the Returning Officers in many constituencies.'[251]

KANU's reaction was extraordinary. It accused the Electoral Commission of rigging it out of office. On 30 December, the *Standard* headlined with a photo of a furious President Moi and a full-page quote, 'They're Rigging Me Out', after Moi accused the ECK of deliberately disrupting the polls in government areas.[252] The ECK eventually ordered polling to continue for a second day in 30 per cent of seats. Kivuitu also postponed the count in the rest of the country until the next morning, for reasons that were less clear.[253] The second day of voting proved almost as chaotic as the first. Officials were unsure which stations were supposed to reopen and which were not. The ballot boxes had had to be stored overnight using makeshift arrangements, open to abuse. By the end of the 30th, voting had still not begun in five seats, and in parts of Garissa it never took place at all. As in 1992, the count was agonisingly slow. The last few seats in Parliament were closely contested, and the late polling meant that the final results were long delayed.

The Results

As expected, Moi was re-elected as president. He won 2.5 million votes, and polled 25 per cent or more in the same five provinces as in 1992, with a higher percentage of the vote (up from 37 to 40 per cent). He easily won North-Eastern, the Rift Valley and Coast, matched Ngilu in Eastern and came second in Western to Wamalwa. He remained the sole candidate with a national constituency. Kibaki came second with 31 per cent of the vote, a dramatic improvement on his 1992 performance. With Matiba not a candidate, he won Central (89 per cent), Nairobi (43 per cent) and came third in Eastern. He received almost all the Kikuyu vote, and also polled well in Meru and Kisii (see Figure 10.16).

The other three candidates were regionally strong but had no national constituency. Odinga decimated FORD-Kenya in Luo areas, but elsewhere, he received less than 3 per cent of the vote. Wamalwa won Western Province, but had little success outside Luhya seats. Ngilu won two-thirds of the Kamba vote but she polled less than 4 per cent elsewhere (see Figure 10.16).

That the vote was not simply an 'ethnic vote' is shown by the fact that the other 10 presidential candidates received little support and only one (Anyona) even won his parliamentary seat. Voters voted for presidential candidates with resources, networks and some chance of winning, who would best represent their communal

10.16: Presidential voting preferences of the 10 largest communities, 1997

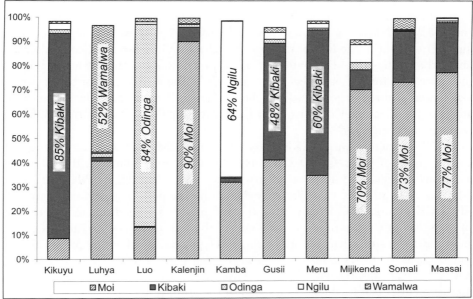

Source: Percentage of the vote in mostly mono-ethnic rural constituencies

and regional interests, rather than for their local candidate. Religion also played a role, with Muslim voters in North-Eastern and Coast provinces more pro-KANU.

In Parliament, the results followed a similar regional pattern. KANU took a narrow majority of 107 to the opposition's combined 103 seats (see Table 10.3). Kenya nearly ended with a hung Parliament and KANU needed some last-minute vote rigging to ensure a working majority. The DP became the official opposition with 39 elected MPs. KANU candidates received only 38 per cent of the parliamentary vote, but won 51 per cent of the seats, due to the uneven constituency sizes and the first past the post system. As elsewhere, the single-member model encouraged the emergence of a two-party system, but in Kenya, because of the ethno-regional and patron–client nature of party allegiance, the result was a series of semi-independent two-party systems. KANU (the party of government) ran first or second in 90 per cent of constituencies, competing against four regional parties.

The most obvious losers were FORD-Asili (none of their incumbents was re-elected under the party banner) and FORD-Kenya. However, the biggest loser was KANU, declining from 59 per cent to 51 per cent of the house. Its ability to focus money, development and intimidation on one small region had gained it 11 seats in by-elections since 1992, yet with the Assembly enlarged, its number of seats fell.

10.17: Presidential election results, 1997

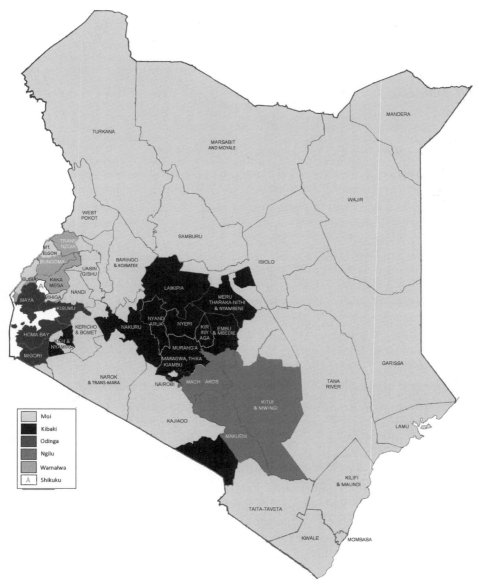

Source: ECK 1997 Results

Table 10.3: Elected MPs by party, 1992–7

Party	1992 Election	1997 Dissolution	1997 Election
KANU	100	110	107
DP	23	22	39
NDP	0	1	21
FORD-Kenya	31	31	17
SDP	0	0	15
Safina	0	0	5
FORD-People	0	0	3
FORD-Asili	31	23	1
KSC	1	1	1
Shirikisho	0	0	1
KNC	1	0	0
PICK	1	0	0
TOTAL	188	188	210

Source: Various

Note: Two seats were vacant in 1997 due to deaths – the incumbent party is recorded here.

Regional Results

The Nairobi results were a reversal of the DP's defeat of 1992. Without Matiba, Kibaki won most Nairobi votes and five of the eight seats ended up in the DP's hands, though Odinga triumphed in Langata. In Central Province, Kibaki won the presidential ballot in every constituency. Ex-FORD-Asili members who had joined FORD-People, the SDP or Safina won every parliamentary seat in south Central, apart from Njenga Karume (DP), who won Kiambaa, and Muite, re-elected in Kabete. Moi's Central Province Development Support Group was eliminated without a whimper and Kenyatta lost easily, evidence that patronage politics could not overcome the power of ethnicity when deployed behind a single leader. Roughly 150,000 southern Kikuyu voters boycotted the polls.

In Eastern Province, most Embu, Mbeere and Meru continued to vote DP, although KANU won two more seats. In Ukambani, Ngilu won the presidential poll in every seat bar one, but KANU won eight parliamentary seats, a reflection either of split ticket voting or malpractice.[254] Moi won all the semi-arid north and North-East again. KANU also continued to dominate the rural Coast. In Mombasa, Shirikisho won Likoni; the DP won one seat and KANU two. The DP picked up support in Taita-Taveta, and managed to win Voi, their first rural Coast victory.

In the Rift Valley, KANU and Moi continued to dominate all the Kalenjin constituencies. FORD-Kenya's challenge amongst the Nandi and Marakwet was brushed aside with ease. The ethnic borderlands followed a similar pattern to 1992. FORD-Kenya again won two seats to KANU's one in Trans-Nzoia and in Uasin-Gishu, KANU held every seat against a split opposition. The DP again dominated Laikipia. Without Matiba, the DP swept up most of the Nakuru Kikuyu vote. In Maasailand, the DP won both presidency and Parliament in Kajiado South, but KANU held the remaining five seats.

In Western Province, FORD-Kenya retained the Bukusu vote and did well in Kakamega. KANU again won Mount Elgon, Teso, Vihiga and Busia. Shikuku narrowly lost Butere. Luo Nyanza voted overwhelmingly for Odinga and the NDP. The party won all 21 Luo-dominated Nyanza seats in the presidency by massive margins and 19 of them in Parliament. Only Orengo in Ugenya and Joe Donde in Gem were re-elected for FORD-Kenya.[255] Other 'off-message' Luo MPs such as Anyang' Nyong'o (SDP) were decisively defeated. In Kisii, the picture was confused, dominated by the pro- and anti-Nyachae battle. Kibaki won five of the 10 presidential votes, without his candidates taking a single parliamentary seat. In Parliament, KANU won seven seats, the opposition three.

Despite the administrative problems and bad weather, turnout at 70 per cent was much the same as in 1992. Again, the Kikuyu and Kalenjin showed the highest turnouts, but the picture was healthier than in 1992, with turnouts falling in the most politicised regions in 1992 and rising elsewhere. The lowest turnouts were in Mombasa, where the clashes drove out many upcountry people, and many voters were out of town during the holiday.

How Fair Was Polling Day and the Count?

The 1997 election was far freer than in 1992. There was still state-sanctioned mal-practice, but it was more limited and focused on the Kalenjin homelands and marginals. Nonetheless, KANU still bribed, intimidated and finally rigged its way into an overall majority of the house. Concerns relate to relatively few seats, but with a governing majority of only four, malpractice in two seats determined whether the government would have a majority or not.

The administration was more neutral and security officials were rarely involved in abuses. However, campaigning in and around the polling stations was widespread. The practice of bribing or threatening voters to vote for a party, then ensuring they delivered by demanding that they declare themselves illiterate compromised fairness again in many areas.[256] Financial incentives again proved important in determining voting preferences. There were reports of bribery by KANU agents outside polling stations in more than 30 seats, with the going rate Ksh100 to Ksh200. In a few seats, there were similar allegations about the opposition. The IED/CJPC/NCCK report on the elections criticised an 'Unabashed greed and a corrosive beggar mentality . . .' that undermined the whole process.[257]

Ballot box stuffing and multiple voting on polling day was less common, though there were a few polling stations where the count revealed more votes than voters. Meru, Kisii and Nakuru all saw reports of ballot paper pre-marking and stuffing. In the rotten borough of Baringo North, presiding officers filled in all the missing votes for KANU after the polls closed, resulting in a splendid 96.4 per cent turnout.[258] Other presidential polls saw similar vote inflation, including Konoin in Kericho, where the 'total votes casted was subtracted from spoiled on[es] and remain was said for Jogoo [KANU]'.[259]

In 1992, many of the worst abuses had occurred during the count. Here too 1997 was better, though some abuses may have been concealed by the chaos associated with the second day of polling. Again, some seats saw counting clerks mix the votes for one candidate with votes for another, thereby over-counting one and under-counting the other. Unmarked ballots once more escaped from the ECK machinery and into the hands of individuals in up to 40 seats. People were found with multiple ballots; ballots were inserted folded in sequence; or boxes arrived with no seals on them or with broken or makeshift seals. These included eight seats in Eastern, 13 in the Rift Valley and six in Nyanza.[260] In several cases, this was associated with statistical anomalies in the results, with far more presidential than parliamentary voters or vice versa (though the nationwide totals matched to within 40,000 votes).

In most seats, the margin of victory was large enough that this malpractice did not change the result, but in five or six seats it probably changed the parliamentary winner. Most notably, KANU's Fred Gumo won Westlands in a violent election that was marred by rigging during the last moments of the count. After a visit from State House operatives, the returning officer announced a different result from that collated from the ballot boxes, refused the statutory recount and left the hall surrounded by security police. The last results were coming in, and KANU knew it was close to losing control of the House. Other results that were probably altered included Kitui West, Butere (where Shikuku appeared to have won the presidential vote but lost the parliamentary poll), Changamwe in Mombasa and Bomachoge in Kisii.

Observer and Donor Views

Both domestic and foreign observers viewed the 1997 elections as better organised and executed than in 1992. The IED/CJPC/NCCK interim statement castigated the ECK for incompetence, but confirmed that, 'The results do, on the whole, reflect the will of the Kenyan voters.'[261] The final report took the same view: the election had been administratively incompetent and unfair, but this had not changed the presidential winner. Voter education remained woeful and bribery and violence were growing concerns. However, the ECK itself had been cooperative.[262]

The foreign diplomats had visited 500 polling stations and attended 50 counts. Their interim report on 4 January accepted that Moi had won, but challenged several parliamentary results and alleged that KANU had not won a legitimate parliamentary majority due to 'serious irregularities' in some parliamentary polls. In the absence of conclusive evidence and given that an election petition was expected, the DDDG edited these conclusions into more diplomatic language. One unhappy embassy leaked these changes, which led to much protest later.[263] The international press was guardedly positive.

Moi was sworn in for his sixth and final term as Kenya's president on 5 January 1998. Unlike 1993, the event was a formal occasion at Uhuru Park, attended by presidents Museveni of Uganda and Benjamin Mkapa of Tanzania.

Conclusions

On the surface, 1997 ended in much the same vein as 1992, with KANU victorious, a split opposition and conflict with the West. Corruption appeared to be worsening, and although the economy had recovered during 1994–6, it was in trouble once more. Voters re-elected KANU despite its questionable record, reflecting the limited role played by the performance of the government in voting decisions. The arguments over constitutional change, land and presidential powers continued. The increasing use of violence for political ends appeared an unwelcome side-effect of democratic change. Even without state involvement, ethnicity continued to divide the opposition, and their protestations of unity proved superficial. Communal identities remained the primary determinant of electoral preference, reflecting long-term and self-reinforcing differences of interest between the KANU- and KADU-voting communities of the 1960s and between Kikuyu and Luo. Politics and economics blended into a three-way 'us and them' model between Kikuyu, Luo and the emerging 'Kamatusa complex', with the Kamba, Luhya and Gusii as swing communities. Ethnic identities were badges of political orientation as well as assertions of cultural and linguistic identity.

Behind the scenes, however, much was changing. Liberalisation and privatisation were well advanced, though there were still holdouts. The changes of the IPPG–NCEC period had enlarged political freedoms, and attention had shifted decisively to the Constitution and the need to rebalance the political landscape away from the executive presidency. These themes were to dominate the next decade. The run-up to the polls, dominated by political strife, the Likoni violence, economic crisis and the loss of Western support, had placed severe strains on the political system, but it had survived. The government's bad luck, poor management and poor relations with the West had reinvigorated the opposition, but it remained too divided to win. Kenya was now an example of what scholars called 'competitive authoritarianism', a regime that was far from democratic, but in which elections were real contests. Divided, the opposition and civil society organisations were no real threat, but the fragments had briefly aligned in 1997 with donor interests and forced the government to compromise, even though it had taken bloodshed to achieve change. Now, the final act of Moi's presidency was beginning, and economic decline, constitutional reform and the succession were to be the dominant themes.

Chapter 11
Unnatural Succession, 1998–2002

Decline and Fall

KANU had now won two multi-party general elections and appeared firmly in power. However, its success rested upon Daniel arap Moi himself. Although never popular after 1980, he had outlived or out-competed most opponents, and even those who denounced him accepted that he was a formidable opponent and the heart of KANU's coalition. The 1992 constitutional changes had allowed him only two more terms in office; he was now a lame duck president. For the next five years, politics was dominated by two intertwined debates: over the succession and over constitutional reform. Arguments over the choice between a presidential system and devolution or power sharing blurred with debates over the people who might occupy such posts. With no clear successor, a deeper embedding of democratic processes and the further liberalisation of the economy, the dominant one-party system of the 1990s evolved into a true multi-party system. At the same time, political parties themselves proved fragile or irrelevant, as every party fragmented and restructured around different and deeper relationships. When the time to choose a successor came, Moi kept his promise to retire, but passed over the obvious candidates in the party and selected a young Kikuyu as his replacement, a decision that split KANU and resulted in the victory of the opposition in the 2002 elections.

In parallel, Kenya's economic problems deepened, and relations with the country's donors were increasingly unstable. Internal struggles over corruption, privatisation and deregulation continued, while foreign governments further embedded themselves as actors in Kenya's political system and further eroded Kenya's policy autonomy. But neither democratic debate nor external oversight could limit the acquisitiveness of the ruling elite. With little popular goodwill, they bought power one day at a time.

The New Government

As in 1993, Moi appointed his government entirely from within KANU. This time, however, he was more limited in his choices, as he could choose only half the 12 nominated MPs (the IPPG agreement required them to be allocated proportionally amongst parliamentary parties).

The government Moi announced on 8 January contained some surprises. The biggest was that Moi dropped George Saitoti as vice-president. With KANU B now facing presidential displeasure, Moi left the position open, both to keep alive the hopes of Simeon Nyachae, Musalia Mudavadi and others, and as a lure for cooperation

11.1: The January 1998 Cabinet

Courtesy: Nation Group Newspapers

with the opposition to secure a working majority in Parliament. KANU A once more returned to prominence. Nyachae replaced Mudavadi at Finance, responsible for government spending and IMF relations, and Kipkalya arap Kones returned to the Cabinet. Nicholas Biwott was demoted to a new Ministry for East African and Regional Cooperation. Kalonzo Musyoka lost Foreign Affairs, to be replaced by Bonaya Godana (Kenya's first Boran, Rendille or Gabbra minister). There were nine newcomers to the Cabinet, including the former managing director of Kenya Airways, Joseph Nyagah (son of minister Jeremiah, another example of political inheritance from the independence generation), and ex-KPTC head Kipng'eno arap Ng'eny. Within a month, Moi had added four more ministers, including Joseph Kamotho, taking the Cabinet's size back up to 28 (see Figure 11.1). The government included no Luo, as KANU had no Luo MPs. Kamotho and Saitoti were the only Kikuyu. The number of Kalenjin (including Moi) rose from five to seven, with five Luhya and four Kamba. All were men.

In the civil service, Moi retained the low-key Pokomo Phares Kuindwa as head of the Public Service, but Kalenjin held key permanent secretaryships, including Internal Security and Provincial Administration, Finance, and Foreign Affairs.

Post-Election Problems

More Political Violence

As in 1993, the post-election period was characterised by violence. In January 1998, 60 people, most Kikuyu, died in fighting between Samburu and Pokot pastoralists and Kikuyu farmers in Laikipia.[1] A few days later, killings began again in Nakuru. Kalenjin with bows and spears fought Kikuyu armed with *pangas* and *rungus*. More than 120 died in January and February in these cycles of violence, seen by many as punishment for DP-supporting regions of the Rift Valley. Leader of the Opposition Mwai Kibaki and other opposition politicians argued that the Kikuyu community had a right to self-defence and should protect itself. Some Kikuyu talked of genocide against them. The DP and SDP disrupted the first sitting of Parliament in February 1998 in protest at the killings. Led by Kibaki, MPs waved placards and chanted 'Warlord!' at Kones and William ole Ntimama. The churches too castigated Moi for his failure to respond, but by April, with curfews and reinforcements, the state had brought the situation under control.

There were local issues behind the troubles, including competition for water, grazing and self-sustaining cycles of retaliation, but it was widely believed that local (Kalenjin) security officials had been complicit in the violence. It was a reminder of the continued tension between pastoralists and Kikuyu, and the close connection between political allegiances and land-related violence.[2] Despite Moi's messages of conciliation, the government no longer consistently had the will to stop such clashes, if it wanted to.[3] Every cycle of violence weakened national unity and reinforced sub-national ethnic identities.

In July 1998, Moi announced a judicial inquiry (chaired by Justice Akilano Akiwumi) into all the clashes since 1991. It completed its investigations in 1999, but the report was withheld until 2002 because of the sensitivity of its conclusions. The government disowned the final report in an unsigned statement, and the police and attorney-general prosecuted no one. The perpetrators again went unpunished.

Protests and Petitions

Following their defeat, opposition leaders again denounced the elections. This time, Kibaki and Raila Odinga were the most vociferous, issuing a joint statement on 2 January 1998 accusing KANU of rigging and demanding a new poll. The SDP, Safina and FORD-Kenya accepted the results as legitimate, though they objected to weaknesses in the process. The churches, keen to avoid civil disorder, pressed the opposition to compromise.

Odinga soon changed his mind, congratulating Moi on his victory on 6 January. Kibaki and the DP did not, and challenged Moi's election in the courts, despite Kalenjin threats that KANU would treat this as 'an incitement to violence'.[4] The DP's petition demanded a recount and alleged presidential vote rigging, particularly in Coast and North-Eastern provinces. They claimed that the government printed two sets of ballot papers with similar serial numbers in order to facilitate Moi's win.[5] However, the Appeal Court dismissed the case on the well-documented but bizarre precedent that no election petition was valid unless personally served on the respondent. Since there was no way in which anyone could serve a petition on the president, as his security detail prevented the servers getting near him, in practice no one could now challenge irregularities in a presidential election.

There were also 26 parliamentary petitions against the 1997 elections, less than half of them against KANU. As usual, most failed on procedural grounds. Several cases (including that against Saitoti) were withdrawn, with rumours that some petitioners had been bought off. Only one MP lost his seat, and it was, inevitably, a DP member. By the 2002 election, not a single KANU MP had lost his seat in the multi-party era due to an election petition.

Succession and Cooperation, 1998–9

President Moi and his inner circle now faced a decision that would change Kenya's future: to whom should they pass the baton of leadership? There seemed no plausible Kalenjin successor (as Biwott was unelectable), and the country would be unlikely to accept a dynastic model whereby Moi would pass on the presidency to one of his sons. A rotation of leadership between ethnic communities was hard-wired into popular perception. Whatever happened, the new president would need to bring in his own people, as Moi had done, and that would inevitably diminish the commercial and political influence of the Kalenjin elites. Worse still, if no plausible successor could be found, could the opposition actually win the next election? Although the West looked favourably upon Kibaki, the prospect of restored Kikuyu hegemony still frightened many non-Kikuyu. Moi had been so successful that few could imagine how the succession would work. As cartoonist Gado presciently observed in 1999, he might well be his own worst enemy (see Figure 11.2).

As the succession battle heated up, KANU was torn apart and reconstructed once more. Potential successors including Saitoti, Nyachae, Musyoka, Mudavadi and Katana Ngala manoeuvred and postured, trying to demonstrate their dominance of a large enough section of the ethnic body politic to warrant their elevation. If they could not be the president themselves, then they could at least sell their support to another for handsome rewards.

Meanwhile, Moi sought alliances outside KANU to sustain his narrow parliamentary majority. There were rumours that Moi had offered Kibaki the vice-presidency if he would bring the DP back into KANU, but he had refused. The opposition leaders from western Kenya – Kijana Wamalwa and Odinga – proved more flexible. As his father had done in 1993–4, Raila Odinga soon made a (cynical) deal with his greatest foe.[6] By February 1998, the 'cooperation' between NDP and KANU and between the Luo and Kalenjin was sealed. This alliance was to last for four years, during which the NDP supported KANU's thin majority in Parliament in return for Luo access to the 'fruits of Uhuru' (including investments in the cotton industry and the Kisumu molasses plant) and progress on constitutional reform. As a 'sweetener', Moi dangled a few parastatal posts before the Luo, and appointed Luo Philemon Abong'o as commissioner of police, and Sandhurst and US-educated Lieutenant General Daniel Opande as vice-chief of the General Staff. The NDP alliance was essential to secure KANU's control of Parliament and of the constitutional review process. In October 1998, for example, the NDP voted with the government to defeat a motion of no confidence from James Orengo.[7] Odinga was simultaneously positioning himself for a second shot at the presidency. By mid-1998, there was even talk of a coalition government.

For such a vocal critic of Moi, Odinga's deal was a huge gamble and was deeply unpopular amongst civil society, opposition politicians and even his own family. The protests within the NDP grew, resulting in the resignation of its deputy chairman, secretary-general and other officials. However, while most non-Luo abandoned the party, the vast majority of Luo politicians, elites and voters alike remained with Odinga, demonstrating an astonishing loyalty to a man who had never held political office and had spent nearly a decade in prison.

Secret talks also took place between Wamalwa and Moi. When Parliament reassembled in 1998, most FORD-Kenya MPs voted with KANU and the NDP against the DP and SDP in the election for speaker and deputy speaker. However, with Odinga in the bag, KANU had little need for Wamalwa, who was unable to persuade colleagues such as Mukhisa Kituyi and Orengo to back a deal. Although in June 1998, Moi and Wamalwa were still talking of cooperation, FORD-Kenya was back in the opposition.[8]

While the Luo were moving closer to KANU, the Gusii were moving away. On 18 February 1999, after only a year as finance minister, Nyachae resigned from the government. His relationship with Moi had become increasingly frosty. Nyachae had committed the government to a major austerity programme in 1998, to manage the

11.2: Moi's chess game, 1999

Courtesy: Nation Group Newspapers

effects of the 1997 crisis. He had admitted at a cross-party forum that the economy was in crisis because of 'mafia-like' looting and that the current level of public spending was unsustainable, a view shared by the IMF but not by Moi.[9] Nyachae had also published a list of debtors to the NBK, which included 'people who dine with' Moi.[10] In February 1999, Moi demoted Nyachae to the Ministry of Industry, but Nyachae instead walked out of the government in fury. His public rationale was Moi's tolerance for corruption and lack of support for his austerity programme, but his position in the succession struggle was also a motive for his departure.[11] In the next few months, the wealthy and confrontational Nyachae opened up a new front in Kenya's near-endless factional conflict. Although he remained technically within KANU, he and his supporters were now Moi's sworn enemies, and with much of the Gusii community already pro-opposition, Kisii was lost to KANU outright. In response, Nyachae's house was bugged and investigations begun into his tax affairs.[12]

In April 1999, Moi announced at a roadside stop that he would reappoint Saitoti as vice-president. Stories suggested that Saitoti's backers such as Biwott no longer supported his ambitions, but to subdue competition and avoid an upcoming legal challenge, someone had to occupy the seat. Moi dulled the blow to the aspirations of other hopefuls by making it clear that Saitoti was a stopgap.

Saitoti's reappointment was far from popular inside KANU, especially in the emerging 'western alliance' between Kalenjin, Luo and Luhya leaders. Efforts to remove Saitoti from inside the NDP and KANU itself culminated in a motion of no confidence against him in June 1999, proposed by an NDP MP. To win that motion, in yet another bizarre realignment, Saitoti was forced to meet the DP's Njenga Karume and to request 'Gema' (Kikuyu, Embu and Meru, i.e. DP) support. He received it, and won the motion.[13] But Saitoti struggled to achieve much legitimacy as vice-president, since no one believed he was Moi's preferred successor, a choice that remained shrouded in uncertainty. By 2000, the leading light inside KANU was probably Mudavadi, while Musyoka and Saitoti waited in the wings and Odinga staked his claim via the NDP.

The Shambles of Constitutional Reform: Part I, 1998–2000

A key theme of the next decade was the failure of all efforts to reform Kenya's ageing Constitution. An issue on which the nation was apparently united concealed huge differences over the nature of the reforms people actually wanted, and it took another 12 fractious years for an agreement to be reached. The 1997 IPPG changes had created a more level playing field, but had not met the aspirations of liberal anti-government elites, who continued to demand devolution and reduced presidential powers. Some believed that only a new constitution could change Kenya; others held that reform was the best tactic to weaken KANU. Meanwhile, KANU too wanted the Constitution changed, but its agenda included the return of *majimbo* and a change to the two-term limit to allow Moi to remain president. The result was chaos, revealing both the determination of those in power to retain the executive presidency and the entrenched ethnic interests in Kenya's politics.

Moi had defused the 1997 crisis with a promise to set up a Constitution of Kenya Review Commission (CKRC). The result was a series of meetings during 1998 known as the Bomas of Kenya and Safari Park talks, between the churches, NGOs, MPs and political parties on how to create a new constitution. The talks ended in deadlock over the objectives and membership of the CKRC, but did agree a three-tier structure for the review, consisting of district fora, the commission itself and a national consultative forum. The resulting legislative compromise in 1998 established a 25-person CKRC (13 nominated by political parties and 12 by civil society groups), plus a chairman and vice-chairman and was mandated to deliver a new constitution by mid-2001. However, it failed to unblock the process. The Act contained serious technical weaknesses, while the political parties could not agree how to allocate their seats. The deadlock continued throughout 1999. There were street demonstrations and accusations of bad faith.

The reform process eventually split in two. Frustrated by what they saw as KANU's delaying tactics and attempts to hijack the process, on 15 December 1999 the 'Ufungamano House' alliance of religious groups (the NCCK, Anglicans, PCEA, Methodists, the AIC, Muslim Consultative Council, the Supreme Council of Kenya Muslims (Supkem) and the Hindu Council) moved from facilitating to driving reform. Under their aegis, a group of civil society organisations and religious figures led by Mutava Musyimi established a 'stakeholder' or 'people-driven' reform process, chaired by ex-FORD-Kenya MP Oki Okoo-Ombaka.

KANU and the NDP opposed this, arguing that Parliament was the only constitutionally sanctioned place to discuss such issues. As Moi challenged, 'a mob beating up a thief in a city street is people-driven.'[14] Although opinion polls suggested that voters opposed a Parliament-only process, the government remained determined that the review would not fall into its opponents' hands and believed that the Assembly was less hostile than either civil society or the churches. On the same day, 15 December, the National Assembly created a Parliamentary Select Committee to manage the constitutional review, its membership dominated by KANU and the NDP. Odinga became its chairman. In solidarity with Ufungamano, most of the proposed opposition nominees refused to serve.

The result was a confrontation that lasted throughout 1999 and 2000. It spilled over into street violence, in which gangs of armed KANU and NDP youth joined forces to break up opposition demonstrations in Nairobi and beat politicians and churchmen, in front of the watching police, instructed not to intervene.[15] There were state-sponsored attacks on Ufungamano leaders and attempts to blackmail them using state security files.[16]

In April 2000, the Select Committee reported, proposing that MPs should choose a smaller 15-member CKRC, and KANU and the NDP pushed this change through Parliament in May.[17] The result was more legislation, deeper confusion, and a further entrenchment of positions. The day after the adoption of the committee's report, the Ufungamano group swore in their own commission. While the Ufungamano exercise was more popular, however, it had no money or means to implement its ideas. The reform process seemed close to collapse, since neither exercise had both popular and legal legitimacy.

KANU meanwhile went on a sales drive for federalism. Despite its association with the ethnic clashes, KANU hawks once more called for *majimbo*, seeking (as in 1962–3) to secure the interests of their core constituency through regional government. Although the Kikuyu and Luo were universally hostile, as were some civil society activists, fearful it would break up the country and lead to ethnic violence, foreign donors were ambivalent. Many supported decentralisation at home, while the US generally acted as a patron of federalism.

A Fragmented but Assertive Parliament

More Party Fragmentation

The election over, Kenya's newer political parties again fragmented and realigned. Rather than solidifying into cross-community national alliances, tiny splinter groups emerged, while the real fault lines no longer matched party allegiances at all. Having learnt their lesson, most MPs now remained in their old parties, refusing to resign in writing to avoid losing their seats, but acted as if they had changed alignments, creating a situation of extreme confusion.

Safina's fortunes declined rapidly after the election. Richard Leakey gave up his nominated parliamentary seat in 1998 to resume his duties at the KWS. Soon after, even cynical Kenyans were shocked to hear that Kamlesh Pattni had not only paid Oginga Odinga in 1993 but he had also given Ksh20 million (US$300,000) to Paul Muite. A Law Society investigation concluded that Pattni had indeed paid Muite the money, which he had used to clear his debts, but that Muite had not committed a crime by receiving it.[18] Muite's image was in tatters, however, and his political career severely damaged.

In 2001, a dispute between the intellectuals who had masterminded Charity Ngilu's 1997 bid for the presidency and Ngilu herself also destroyed the SDP. New proposals requiring presidential candidates to have a university degree were designed to exclude Ngilu from standing in 2002, leaving space for ex-lecturers Apollo Njonjo or Peter Anyang' Nyong'o to bid for the presidency themselves (however poorly they were likely to perform). After months of factional conflict, Ngilu abandoned the SDP and formed her own National Party of Kenya (NPK). The NPK inherited some of Ngilu's influence in Ukambani, but had little impact elsewhere, and KANU's position strengthened amongst the Kamba.[19]

At the same time, Orengo and some other pro-NCEC MPs had established yet another opposition force, known as Muungano wa Mageuzi (United Movement for Change), to campaign for radical constitutional reform. It too was short-lived. The movement was repressed by the police after Moi declared it 'revolutionary' and barred it from holding any meetings. In 2001, this group also split, between those who refused to accept the legitimacy of traditional politics, and others like Orengo who were seeking an alternative political home. In October 2001, Orengo struck a deal with the SDP rump. He and his allies joined the party, and he became the SDP's presidential candidate.[20] In response, in 2002 the SDP split for a second time, with Anyang' Nyong'o leading the other part. Another once-national party was in factional ruins.

All the opposition parties remained structurally weak: divided ethnically and by patron, with no proper secretariats and few funds. Even the DP struggled to raise enough money to operate.[21] Most of its funds came from contributions by businesses in exchange for future favours, just as with the government, though on a smaller scale because of its limited influence and lower expectation of victory. There was no requirement for a party to disclose where its money came from or how it spent it. Four times after 1992, Parliament passed motions calling for state funding for political parties, but they were ignored.

KANU too experienced internal stresses. As well as losing most of the Gusii, the long-simmering discontent in the Nandi finally emerged in the formation of the United Democratic Movement (UDM) in 1998, led by MPs Cyrus Jirongo (Luhya) and Kipruto arap Kirwa, John Sambu and William Ruto (like Jirongo, a wealthy YK'92 alumnus), all Nandi.[22] It was powered by Nandi anger over the sale of the EATEC farms and the crisis in the KCC, and by the personal interests of its leaders, trying to demonstrate their importance to KANU. The registrar of societies conveniently refused to register the UDM, but it continued to operate informally in alliance with the opposition, further destabilising the House. The DP and FORD-Kenya, in contrast, remained relatively united, their constituencies in the Kikuyu, Embu and Meru and Bukusu Luhya respectively still safe.

The Growing Power of Parliament

While the influence of president and of party declined, the power of Parliament grew. The eighth Parliament was probably the most assertive in Kenya's history, rivalling 1969–74 for the difficulties the state had in passing legislation. With a wafer-thin majority, the government – divided on constitutional reform, donor relations, economic liberalisation and the succession – struggled to take a coherent position on anything.[23] In theory, KANU lost its majority in 1999 when Nyachae and his supporters defected, but it retained control with the help of the NDP and rogue opposition members. While the government won 'no confidence' motions in 1998 and 1999, it lost several motions in the House.

With Moi a lame duck and greater political freedom, there was less fear of the presidency. By late 1998, backbenchers were openly defying Moi's wishes in KANU Parliamentary Group meetings.[24] The executive's once-formidable power over Parliament was being whittled away. In 1998, MPs were given their own offices and secretarial facilities and, in 1999, Parliament passed a constitutional amendment that transferred the power to appoint the clerk of the House from the president to Parliament. Soon after, another amendment established a Parliamentary Service Commission with its own budget, answerable to the house. In 2000 and 2002, Luo elder statesman Peter Oloo-Aringo even introduced bills (unsuccessfully) to permit the impeachment of a president and to allow Parliament to set its own timetable.

Although the West was seeking a deal with the government on the economy, it continued to finance efforts to reduce the powers of the presidency, build capacity in the opposition and Parliament and develop Kenya's civil society. The euphoria of the early 1990s over the democratic credentials and potential of civil society in Africa had begun to fade. Critics now saw some democracy NGOs as 'the fiefs of powerful and not particularly democratic individuals or small factions, a donor-induced façade over personal and ethnic identity and action'.[25] Bruce Berman suggested that in Africa the Western concept of civil society as independent institutions 'taming the state' did not exist, and that civil society was as factionalised, unequal and divided by ethnicity, class, and gender as any other part of Kenya's society.[26] However, the opposition's demands for reduced presidential powers still struck chords with the West, and donors provided better facilities for Kenyan MPs and advised them on how to manage relations with the executive.[27] NGO pressure also grew to revise constituency boundaries or consider introducing proportional representation, though there was no consensus in the House on such changes.

Polling the Polity

The period 1998–2002 saw a flowering of public opinion polling, both on the political horserace and on current issues. While there were still methodological problems, these polls were far more accurate than in the past. Foreign donors funded several polls on social questions, encouraging the state to pay more attention to issues such as poverty. In turn, this offered a propaganda opportunity for KANU. In the words of the *Kenya Times*:

> . . . a new wave of anti Moi, KANU campaign is currently being bankrolled by a number of foreign countries through the civil society programme . . . The campaign is to focus on a public discontent, popularise a public uprising and force the President out of office through street violence and alleged public opinion polls campaigns to depopularise the presidency and the Government.[28]

The Nation Group also sponsored several polls during 1998–2000. Most produced results highly critical of the government, which in turn condemned them as 'a product of sheer imagination' or 'cooked up'.[29] Amongst potential successors to Moi explored in such polls, Saitoti performed strongly within KANU; 47.5 per cent of those polled preferred him in 1999, 13 per cent supported Mudavadi, while 1.9 per cent of voters opted for the low-profile Uhuru Kenyatta.[30] The American IRI also funded a series of polls that showed KANU and the government to be deeply unpopular, with the economy, constitutional reform and corruption the key issues. Such polls also revealed that voters were deeply divided over both the creation of a post of prime minister and devolution.

A New Cadre Emerges, but the Problems Remain the Same

Meanwhile, civil society's movement into formal politics continued. By 2003, there were a dozen (mostly opposition) Members of Parliament who had built their political careers in this way. These included Kituyi (NORAD), Kivutha Kibwana (NCEC), Wangari Maathai (Green Belt Movement), Linah Kilimo (a campaigner against cattle rustling and female circumcision) and others with backgrounds in Oxfam, World Vision, Plan International, UNESCO and the World Food Programme. As civil servants had been the aspiring politicians of the 1970s, NGO activists were the aspiring politicians of the 1990s. Although these 'millennium politicians' differed in many ways from those of previous generations, they retained an insatiable need for money. Mass poverty and the dependency culture that independent Kenya had built meant that most constituents expected their politicians to be all-purpose providers, both individually – paying school fees and contributing to *harambees* – and using their proximity to power to encourage the government to tarmac roads, site government offices or build boreholes in their constituency. MPs had become a personal safety net for those constituents willing to pledge fealty.

The absence of government largesse was a particular problem for the opposition. The need to raise funds from 'well-wishers' put those MPs who were not already dollar millionaires under intense pressure, and forced many into uncomfortable compromises. One study suggested MPs were spending hundreds of thousands of shillings a month on local contributions.[31] Government ministers, in contrast, never appeared short of funds, often from unclear sources. During 2000–2, Moi was the largest donor to *harambees* nationwide, contributing at least Ksh75 million (US$1 million), followed by Kenyatta, Saitoti, Mudavadi and Kamotho.[32] Those MPs without independent means to sustain them could face disaster. One Kikuyu MP defeated in 1992, for example, ended up as a second-hand car salesman, while another ended up selling soup, goats' heads and intestines in Nairobi housing estates. In 2000–1, partly as a result, MPs approved a dramatic increase in their own remuneration. Not only did this make it possible for the first time since the 1960s to perform the role of an MP without independent means, it also inflated popular demands on the role.

Although the political playing field was less tilted in favour of the incumbent, the state could still be roused to anger. Opposition legislators still ended up in hospital or prison. The police refused to accept that the law on meetings had changed in 1997, and continued to act as if they had the power to ban meetings. Although such charges could not be upheld in the courts, the police regularly arrested opposition supporters and broke up demonstrations anyway. Luo leaders who refused to support Odinga were particular targets, and Orengo and Anyang' Nyong'o experienced sustained state harassment.

Both Kenyan elites and voters now viewed politics consistently in an ethnic light, not as an intrinsic tribal struggle, but as a zero-sum competition for preference in which victory lay in unity behind their gladiatorial champion, to deliver the numbers needed to win State House. Whatever the reality, the perception was that an ethnic preference in resource allocations was inevitable. This lesson, learnt since independence, made it harder for senior politicians to make a deal to support a leader from another community, for fear of risking a haemorrhage of support to a more intransigent colleague.[33] Ethnic politics had become self-reinforcing. The consequence was a political sphere consisting of two forces, neither of them actually political parties. On one side sat the 'in team' or 'government' – a cross-ethnic and cross-party alliance held together by state patronage and centred on the ethnic group of the incumbent president. On the other side sat the 'opposition' – a set of several ethnically focused parties, able to mobilise strong anti-government dissent but united only by their dislike of the 'in team', and unable to present a united front without the patronage that government offered.

Aid, Donor Relations and the 'Dream Team', 1999–2001

Kenya's relations with the IFIs remained strained through 1998, following the loss of the ESAF loans in 1997. Hopes of an African renaissance began to fade by the millennium, with wars, the rollback of democracy and fragile economic growth continent-wide. In Kenya, the donors were 'stuck' with the same politicised, unpopular and corrupt leadership they had negotiated with for the last two decades.

Western powers remained committed – albeit with doubts – to their strategy of economic development through liberalisation, democratic choice and peace and stability in the less-developed world. The de-patrimonialisation of the Kenyan economy therefore remained a key goal, believing that this would both improve economic performance and reduce state power. However, while multi-party politics might permit a change of government, there was some evidence in Kenya that it actually slowed reform. The models of 'new institutional economics' suggested that governments facing imminent threat were likely to be more short-term and to placate interest groups directly, and Kenya appeared typical of this. The opposition was more hostile to structural adjustment than the state and succeeded in defeating foreign-inspired economic liberalisation initiatives several times during 1999–2002. Indeed, for a decade the West had to use one of the least democratic parts of Kenya's polity – KANU – to impose economic liberalism.

A Loveless Marriage

Western circles saw KANU's 1997 election victory as a mandate for Kenya to continue its (reluctant) path of economic reform. Within a few weeks, the 'dance' between foreign institutions and the government had resumed. The conditions set by the World Bank and IMF for the restoration of aid remained structurally the same as in the early 1990s, though the specific actions they required had changed. The result was another five difficult years, during which the donors became overtly involved in Kenya's internal politics, unable to avoid appearing to side with either the opposition or the state. Nonetheless, the West could not force Kenya to pass laws its government (and often its people) did not support. The louder the donors protested about delays, the more KANU could play the self-reliance card and obtain legitimacy from their defence against foreign intervention.

In February 1998, the London Club of commercial creditors agreed (after a five-year gap) to reschedule Kenya's remaining US$70 million of overdue debt. With the formation of the Kenya Anti-Corruption Authority (KACA) and reasonable macro-economic stability, an IMF team recommended that Kenya had met most preconditions for the resumption of aid. Despite regular meetings, however, no IFI funds were forthcoming during 1998. The country's economic challenges, its failure to address the Goldenberg scandal, and tightening political conditions kept KANU under pressure. Most opposition parties called for the aid taps to be kept closed, though they in turn faced criticism for trying to keep Kenyans poor.

Moi remained unpopular in the US, his reputation worsened by the publication of Smith Hempstone's book, *Rogue Ambassador*, in 1997. American President Bill Clinton bypassed Kenya on his 1998 tour of Africa, but relations improved during 1998, as the US edged Moi towards support for constitutional reform. The donors also faced a worsening security environment, the consequence of the growing influence of Al Qaeda and the US Embassy bombing (see below), strengthening the need for global security cooperation. This pushed Western governments into closer links with Kenya's incumbent government than they might otherwise have desired.

The year 1999 saw the lowest level of foreign aid to Kenya for a decade, only a third of its 1989 peak. While the IFI taps remained dry, however, bilateral project aid continued to flow into the country. The British government estimated it had GB£164 million of ongoing commitments in Kenya in 2001, from goat restocking to AIDS prevention.[34] Oxfam and UN agencies continued their programmes, while US aid (mostly food) increased sharply once more in 1998 (see Figure 11.13). All US and British aid was now in grant form.

The West as a Competing Patron

Although the West's leverage was limited when fiscal aid had already been halted, donors had an alternative tool to influence domestic politics: NGOs. During the 1990s, the West increasingly directed its aid outside the government, routing it instead

11.3: US grants to Kenya, 1992–2002

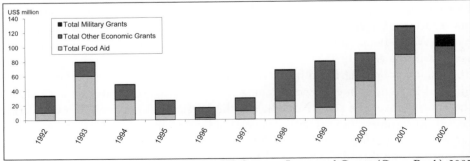

Source: US Overseas Loans and Grants (Green Book), 2005

to NGOs, Christian development organisations and charities and building up civil society as an alternative source of influence. Donors could drive policy more directly this way, because of NGOs' financial dependence and project-based approach. They in turn could lobby the government to follows external prescriptions.

Reflecting both the divide between popular opinion and state policy and the availability of foreign resources, political NGOs blossomed after 1990, with 13 major democracy, law and human rights organisations by the mid-1990s for whom foreign donors and diplomats were the core constituency.[35] Kenyans gave virtually no funds to any political NGO, whether for election monitoring or constitutional reform. A network developed of experienced actors, able to speak the international language of reform. Many were Luo or from the Gema communities and relations with the state were often tense. For some, NGOs were a business opportunity, while for others they were a political strategy to weaken KANU. Some aspiring politicians even created or used NGOs as stepping-stones into the parliamentary arena. In practice, most Kenyan NGOs were institutions of personal rule as much as was the state and Western donors accentuated this through their reliance on a few articulate, high-profile leaders.

Gradually, a competing patronage structure developed in which donors, through their developmental bureaucracies, selected and funded both short- and long-term projects and institutions, bypassing a distrusted state. The combined effect of the liberalisation and privatisation programme and this diversification of income sources was a dilution in state patronage. Districts such as Turkana benefited more from donor relief than any action by the government. NGOs now provided 30–40 per cent of all Kenyan development spending.[36] The result was a diversification of dependency: from one source, the all-powerful state, to a multitude of donors and their local gatekeepers, though they had little more accountability for their decisions than the state. KANU leaders saw the implications of this, but could do little to stop it. Morton expressed Moi's frustrations, in his comment that, 'The belief that there is a "shadow government" based in Paris, London or Washington which monitors the activities of the KANU administration inevitably unsettles the political process.'[37] Moi's opposition to the external orientation and dependence on Western funds of the younger elites was a common thread throughout his time in office. He consistently criticised Kikuyu such as Muite for looking to the West rather than creating African solutions to their problems. The contrast was clear between an externally oriented, foreign-educated, well-paid 'edge culture' of urban elites and Kenya's larger heartland of traditional values, domestically focused, locally educated and sceptical of both foreign capital and oversight, epitomised by Moi.[38]

There were other unfortunate side-effects to this diversification of dependency. Most obvious was the brain drain: able, educated individuals would not work for the state if they could avoid it, but would go into civil society (or private business). There was also a form of moral hazard. In many areas, the state now provided no services at all, able to divert its revenue elsewhere because of the well-meaning assistance of Western aid agencies and charities, offering a safety net for the state as well as for the less fortunate.

Leakey and the 'Dream Team', 1999–2001

Relations between the Kenyan government and the West improved dramatically between 1999 and 2001, during which the two entered into a form of coalition government. On 23 July 1999, in a stunning move, Moi appointed his opponent Richard Leakey as the head of the civil service and secretary to the Cabinet. Leakey had been enticed back to head the KWS in 1998, with a rehabilitated Charles Njonjo as his chairman. Nonetheless, his appointment was an astonishing gamble for both Leakey and Moi. It was forced by external pressure for radical change to restore donor confidence. Moi was reluctant to bring the abrasive Leakey into the centre of power, but was pressured by the international community, impressed by Leakey's role in negotiations with the donors in the past. Moi needed a salesman for Kenya with integrity and an international reputation. The deal was done directly between Moi and World Bank President James Wolfensohn, with Njonjo amongst others as advisers. Amid concern about the recent financial meltdown in the Far East, it was an unprecedented IFI intervention for Africa.

As part of the deal, Leakey brought with him a new team, including respected figures from the Kenyan private sector and the World Bank, on private sector salaries funded by the donors. The key aims of this 'Dream Team' (as it became universally known) were to combat inefficiency and corruption in the civil service, re-energise the privatisation programme and restore the government's finances. Moi promised Leakey his 'complete and undivided support'. The move was welcomed both nationally and internationally.

The opposition looked on in impotent fury, sidelined by a deal that vested power in a non-African, directed by foreigners, and implicitly endorsed the government. Their allies had again become their opponents, and this realignment was to create ripples for the next two years. At the same time as Leakey and the government were trying to restore foreign aid, many in the opposition were trying to stop the move, arguing that the West's conditions had not been met, and that aid would legitimise the regime and be misappropriated. They also pointed out that the funds were only needed because Kenya had received so many loans in the past, the repayment of which now consumed 25 per cent of the budget.

Once in office, Leakey focused on streamlining the chaos and corruption in the civil service. Almost immediately, he sacked several parastatal heads. Financial controls were tightened and the Dream Team reduced the number of 'pending bills', a Kenyan phrase for unpaid invoices to government. By 2000, nearly Ksh12 billion (US$150 million) of these off-book liabilities had piled up (as the government budgeted on a cash basis), of which the government disputed more than Ksh5.5 billion.[39] The Dream Team also brought extra-budgetary transactions (purchases made outside the budget) under control, the Office of the Controller and Auditor-General was strengthened and procurement processes improved.

As ever, however, politics limited what could be achieved. In September 1999, under pressure to cut costs, Moi executed a bizarre reshuffle. He reduced the number of ministries from 27 to 15, but left all his existing ministers in place, creating two ministers in most ministries. The number of assistant ministers even rose by two.[40] The reshuffle was widely criticised. Donors, promised cuts, were shocked, and even the NDP was lukewarm.

Despite this, negotiations continued between Leakey, Finance Minister Chrisantus Okemo and the IFIs, who were now stipulating that officials declare their wealth and demanding stronger action against corruption, more civil service retrenchments and Treasury reforms in return for their money. Leakey reported that at one point a Cabinet committee had to sit for more than 13 hours to debate over 100 IMF conditionalities before taking the document to the Cabinet for approval.[41] The IMF and World Bank both visited in early 2000, reporting positively, but there was still no money. In June 2000, Kenya stopped paying its commercial creditors, hoping for another debt rescheduling. They were soon lobbying the IMF, talking of litigation. Another London Club rescheduling followed in 2001.

The Kenya Anti-Corruption Authority and the Fight against Corruption, 1998–2001

Corruption remained a particularly painful issue for Western governments, infuriated by indications that their aid was being misappropriated, though there was seldom the unambiguous smoking gun they needed to be able to prove it. The record of the early months of Leakey's term in combating corruption was substantial. There was carnage amongst the agricultural parastatals. The heads of the coffee and tea boards were sacked, Coffee Board officials were suspended, while ex-KCC Chairman Stanley Metto was accused of theft.[42]

Nairobi's City Hall was still a hotbed of corruption, particularly in the allocation of urban land. All attempts to sort out the mess had failed in the face of the complexity of the problem, the incompetence, indifference and corruption of both councillors and officials, and the sheer cost of remedial action. In the Leakey era, it briefly appeared that political connections were no longer a guarantee of protection. The wife of a minister was charged with fraud against the council, as was the KANU Kisii branch chairman.[43] The road construction sector, too, had long suffered from severe predation. Leakey announced in December 1999 that Ksh11.2 billion (US$140 million) had been paid to contractors for road projects that had been abandoned or were behind schedule.[44] An ex-permanent secretary for public works was charged with abuse of office.[45]

Even senior Kalenjin appeared no longer immune. National Housing Corporation Managing Director Lawi Kiplagat was suspended in April 2000 for selling the corporation's houses at throwaway prices. In the same month, a (Kalenjin) permanent secretary and the (Kalenjin) commissioner for customs and excise were also sacked and charged.[46] In July 2000, KACA finally charged minister Kipng'eno arap Ng'eny in connection with a fraud worth Ksh186 million (US$2.4 million) against KPTC, conducted during the 1992 election campaign, when he had been its head. He was the first serving minister to be charged in court with corruption. Now fair game, Ng'eny was also sued for more than Ksh100 million of bank loans taken in 1994 and never repaid. However, Ng'eny refused to resign and Moi declined to sack him. The

KANU leadership played both sides: part of the government that was prosecuting him, but keen to exonerate him in practice.[47]

While the Dream Team had significant successes, the original tool created to control corruption, the special autonomous KACA proved a failure. Established in 1997, Moi's extraordinary choice for its first head was 1992 PICK presidential candidate and former police marksman John Harun Mwau. Mwau was not free from the taint of corruption himself. The origins of his very substantial wealth have never been clear and there have been frequent rumours of links with drugs and organised crime. He was also politically partisan, having defected to join KANU in 1997 and given it Ksh1 million at the time.[48] Once appointed as KACA director, Mwau did little to inspire confidence. After a conflict with Nyachae in 1998, when Mwau arrested several Treasury officials, Moi was forced to sack him and he was declared incompetent.

Mwau's successor was more reassuring: Solicitor-General Aaron Ringera, Kiraitu Murungi's old law partner from Meru. However, KACA was on shaky constitutional foundations, and it only became fully operational in October 1999. The donors saw KACA's effectiveness as a litmus test of Kenya's commitment to fight corruption, and the campaign against corruption (and the resource misallocation implicit in patronage politics) as key to economic renewal.[49] However, Moi and Leakey failed to get KACA operating effectively or to push the legislation the West was demanding through Parliament. Parliament was no more effective as a watchdog than KACA. In May 2000, for example, a select committee on corruption published a report naming many senior names (known as the 'list of shame'), but KANU MPs and their allies voted to have all the names expunged.

Aid is Restored, August 2000

In the middle of 2000, Moi and Leakey finally persuaded the donors to resume funding. In July 2000, the Kenyan government requested SDR150 million under the IMF's Poverty Reduction and Growth Facility (PRGF), agreeing to all its conditions.[50] The PRGF had replaced ESAF in 1999, when the IMF changed its approach, now focussing on poverty reduction in the context of a 'growth-oriented economic strategy'. The IMF required that poverty reduction plans be prepared with the participation of civil society and other development partners, though access to the money was also conditional on more traditional balance of payments reforms. In August 2000, the World Bank and IMF approved a three-year PRGF loan of US$190 million for Kenya, with US$50 million more in October. This was the second-largest PRGF loan in 2000. KANU was buoyed by the reintroduction of support, which was headlined as a triumph for Leakey and Okemo.

The government had promised the earth to achieve this. Fiscally, it had offered better budgetary management and reduced debt, restrictive monetary policies, tariff reform, reduced import exemptions, higher VAT, new banking legislation and a review of pending bills. Other promises including 30,000 more jobs cut from the civil service, more privatisation, the reform of tea and coffee marketing (see Chapter 10), a code of conduct for public officials including the declaration of assets, and the passage of an anti-corruption and economic crimes bill.

The government had also promised to check the expansion of poverty in the country, soon to become one of the Millennium Development Goals of the UN, although how they were going to do this was unclear, since poverty-reduction initiatives usually involved spending more, not less in the short term. The UN reported that Kenya's Human Development Index (a measurement of life expectancy, education and incomes) was lower in 2002 than in the 1980s.[51] Other studies concurred that a higher proportion of Kenyans were poor than at independence, a consequence of many factors including poor health, lack of land, insecurity, lack of capital and technology, macro-economic failures, the effects of structural adjustment and cultural and social factors.[52] The Luo appeared to be suffering particularly severely, with the nation's difficulties compounded by Nyanza's limited cash-crop opportunities, AIDS and the spread of the invasive water hyacinth, which was causing serious economic and ecological problems in Lake Nyanza.

Kenya agreed to the rescheduling of another US$288 million of its external debt with the Paris Club in 2000, reducing its servicing obligations further.[53] It did not qualify, however, for the Highly Indebted Poor Countries Initiative, launched in 1996 to reduce the debt of the world's most indebted countries, as Kenya was expected to achieve sustainability under traditional mechanisms. Again, Kenya fell between two stools: too rich for charity; too poor to pay.

Corruption Continues

Despite the efforts of the Dream Team, both grand and petty corruption remained endemic. The country still had a functioning bureaucracy on paper, but formal processes were of little relevance. In 1999, the anti-corruption NGO Transparency International (TI) rated Kenya as one of the most corrupt countries in public perceptions, at 90 out of 99, and it was ranked 96 out of 102 in 2002.[54] Degrees and bursaries were on sale in the Education Ministry, birth certificates in the Home Office, passports at the Immigration Department, and business licences at Trade and Industry. Foreign exchange bureaux were used to launder the proceeds of corruption into overseas accounts and evade import duties.

Although the true extent will never be known, it is widely believed that government coffers were systematically emptied in corrupt deals between vendors and politicians in the period. For example, later investigations indicted the Kenya Pipeline Company for procurement abuses, overemployment and poor investments, including the purchase of overpriced and illegally excised Ngong forest land.[55] NOCK was indicted for issuing unsecured credit, inflated contracts and fraud. The properties sold by Kenya Railways to improve its financial position were bought cheaply by influential individuals and then sold to the NSSF at massive profits. KPLC was accused of double payments, theft, procurement abuses, overpayment for land and undercharging for assets sold to employees. The KTDC was brought to the brink of collapse by incompetence and embezzlement. Even in the private sector, the ability of Kenyans to develop innovative scams was widely respected. While attention concentrated on public utilities, private firms also suffered from cartels that drained millions of dollars via product thefts, deliberately unsecured credit and sale of discounts. Expatriate managers at one large manufacturer discovered a third production run operating at night in their own factories, using company raw materials, entirely for private gain.

Meanwhile, the Goldenberg prosecutions struggled ineffectively through the courts, stymied by their complexity and sensitivity. Eleven criminal cases were initiated between 1994 and 1999 around the events of 1991–3, most of which ended inconclusively.[56] Kamlesh Pattni spent years in court or in jail, yet somehow remained both wealthy and influential. In 1999, for example, despite his appalling record, he acquired the World Duty Free complexes at Nairobi and Mombasa airports, which in turn resulted in an international lawsuit against the Kenyan government.

The government's anti-corruption institutions remained on shaky ground. In August 2000, the Anti-Corruption and Economic Crimes Bill demanded by the IMF was published. This improved the institutional foundations of KACA, broadened Kenya's definition of corruption and gave KACA powers to investigate those living beyond their means. However, it never reached Parliament. KACA itself was dissolved in December 2000, after the courts ruled that the organisation was unconstitutional, as only the attorney-general and the police had the right to initiate prosecutions. Its cases were handed over to the regular police force, to go no further. Some were happy to see it go.

Eventually, the government decided to pass a constitutional amendment to reintroduce KACA alongside an updated Anti-Corruption and Economic Crimes Bill. However, Parliament voted this down in August 2001, in a trial of strength that pitted the KANU–NDP alliance against the opposition. Despite President Moi himself appearing as an MP and voting for the bill (something he had never done before), it narrowly failed to achieve the two-thirds majority needed. Resistance to the re-establishment of KACA was not focused on the body itself, as stronger action on corruption was a key opposition demand. The true reasons for KACA's rejection were three-fold. The first lay in a clause in the bill pardoning all crimes committed before 1997, which many saw as a pardon for Goldenberg. Second, the government was testing whether it now commanded the two-thirds majority needed to change the Constitution; its defeat indicated that it did not. Finally, there was growing domestic resistance to donor-imposed conditionalities. The donors were again forced to line up behind the government and against the opposition.

The End of the Dream Team, 2000–1

The deal with the IMF and World Bank was far from universally popular inside Kenya, as it became clear that the government had ceded sovereignty in return for aid. Not only were the opposition unhappy, but many KANU leaders were uncomfortable with the implications of the deal for their personal positions, their party's survival and the country's autonomy. Recognised as one of the toughest sets of conditions ever imposed on an African country, the agreement specified that precise financial data be sent weekly. The conditionalities of the PRGF facility, with disbursements locked to the achievement of specific targets, were a shock to the government. In response, KANU's mouthpiece the *Kenya Times* played the anti-foreigner card, asking, 'Is the World Bank our New Colonial Master'?[57]

To the government's frustration, only US$43 million of the promised funds were disbursed, as Kenya failed to meet the IFIs' conditions. In December 2000, after only four months, the fund suspended further loans when the court declared KACA unconstitutional, and other donors followed suit. Regular IMF visits ended in no more money, with a lengthy list of unmet preconditions, including the re-establishment of KACA, the privatisation of Telkom Kenya and modifications to the Donde Bill (see below). It was clear that Leakey's claims that he could bring change into the government could no longer be sustained.

In March 2001, frustration and disillusionment on all sides led to Leakey's resignation, and most of his team followed. His dismissal was said to have the tacit approval of the World Bank, concerned about his inability to deliver, and allegations that his team was overpaid and ineffective. A month later, CBK Governor Micah Cheserem also departed, having angered hardliners by his willingness to follow donor conditionalities.[58] The Dream Team was a bold but unsuccessful experiment. It changed the political agenda for 18 months, punished dozens of cases of corruption, improved public finances and reduced waste. But it was unable to secure its own survival, as change was too slow and the IFI cash did not materialise. Appointed in Leakey's place – in the same month that Moi had announced in an off-the-cuff speech that women did not get the top jobs because they had 'little minds' – was Sally Kosgei, Kenya's first female civil service head.[59] A Nandi, Kosgei had served with distinction both as high commissioner to Britain and as finance permanent secretary and had built a close rapport with Moi. She, unlike Leakey, was an insider.

Despite Okemo's promises, the next IMF visit in 2001 ended with a clear statement that aid would not be forthcoming. Again, Kenya appeared close to financial collapse, facing a US$300 million hole in the budget.[60] Hardliners were incensed, and Okemo launched an angry broadside against the donors at a public meeting.[61] Whatever the reality, Kenya's perceived dependence on foreign aid was soon demonstrated, as within three weeks Okemo had been reshuffled out of the Treasury. His replacement, Chris Obure, funded the growing budget deficit through high interest rates and high domestic borrowing, leaving more problems for his successor. Despite the passage of anti-corruption legislation and macro-economic stability, there were no IMF funds in 2002 either. This time, the divorce between KANU and the IFIs had been final.

Macro-Economic Decline

The last years of the Moi regime were a period of economic decline. Despite the government's prudent macro-economic policies, the economy stuttered downwards from 2 to 1 per cent annual growth in GDP. Kenya's economy was the slowest growing in the region. The drought of 2000 led to the country's worst economic performance since independence (forcing it into the IMF deal), and 2001 and 2002 were not much better.

While the government had introduced many reforms during 1991–6, its programme faltered after 1997. The quick wins had already been taken, leaving only the hardest problems to solve. Because the government no longer had a clear mandate, it was also more beholden to populist interests, which were hostile to SAP. As in other African countries, 'broad support for Structural Adjustment programmes is generally lacking . . .'[62] Price increases and redundancies directly harmed interest groups, while general economic improvement was a more indirect benefit. Although cuts were made, they were slow and painful since a weak government could not afford to take the political hit.

In per capita terms, Kenyans were getting poorer (see Figure 11.4) as the population was still growing at nearly 3 per cent a year. Apart from the brief spurt of 1994–6, real GDP per person (in shillings, let alone in US dollars) fell year after year. However, since the *jua kali* economy was only roughly estimated and the 'parasitic economy' was entirely unrecorded, the accuracy of all these statistics is questionable. GDP per head estimates were further distorted by an inability to determine how many people lived in the country, statisticians' estimates proving more than a million out in 1989 and again in 1999.

The shilling devalued further in 1999–2000, from 62 to the dollar to nearly 80, reflecting the country's macro-economic woes. Exports also declined in 1997–2001, hurt by interest rates running at 20–30 per cent, in turn driven by government borrowing, high levels of bad debt and capital market liberalisation. However, exchange rates stabilised during 2001–2, foreign exchange reserves remained high and inflation stayed stable at around 2 per cent, evidence of conservative fiscal policies during the transition.

The literature on Kenya's economy grew during the 1990s, as the IFIs became more deeply involved in restructuring Africa's economies, and many explanations

11.4: Change in real and per capita GDP, 1991–2002 (1982 shillings)

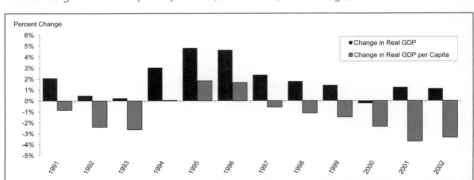

Source: Republic of Kenya, *Statistical Abstracts*, 1998–2007

were advanced for Kenya's declining performance after 1996. Despite its macro-economic reforms, Kenya, like other African countries, was not growing as fast as the IFIs had expected when they forced structural adjustment on a reluctant government. In practice, lower private sector investment seemed to coincide with lower state investment, in part a response to deteriorating public infrastructure. Other explanations included the effects of corruption, institutional weaknesses, high interest rates, the cost of debt servicing, poor terms of trade, political and policy instability, poor health and low education levels, and the changing global economy.[63] This lack of consensus on the real causes of Kenya's problems made them near intractable.

Most proposed solutions followed the orthodoxy that more liberalisation and privatisation would stimulate growth, since a development path based on state ownership and protectionism had failed. However, Kenya and other African states had been following a version of the prescribed macro-economic policies for years, while the IFIs themselves had a growing body of evidence that uncontrolled or too-rapid change might create instabilities and cause the collapse of national assets. The Goldenberg incident remained a salutary lesson that changes intended to bring positive outcomes could be misused. Attention began to shift from relying on liberalisation and structural adjustment per se towards political institutions, infrastructure, corruption and patron–client politics as reasons why structural adjustment was not delivering. There also remained many Kenyans, though they were usually kept away from the macro-economic levers, who were sceptical of the entire 'mission to market', believing that a more regulated and protected economy – in which price and market stability could be maintained, infant industries grown and jobs protected – might prove a better overall development route for less-developed countries.

Debt and Deficit

From 1994, the government's budget oscillated between surplus and deficit, reflecting a complex interaction of economic growth, investment and aid. The outlook was particularly gloomy in 1997–8, following the suspension of direct assistance and the El Niño rains. In his year at the Treasury, Nyachae produced an austerity budget that came closer to balancing, made possible by a 20 per cent cut in shilling spending and huge domestic borrowing. A small surplus in 1999–2000 was followed by another huge deficit in 2001–2, as government hopes of donor aid did not materialise and spending rose in an election year.

The budget was now dominated by recurrent expenditure, mostly salaries. New development investments hit an all-time low in 1997–9, when 90 per cent of state spending was on recurrent items, and virtually all of the rest was foreign funded (see Figure 11.5).

The country experienced a net outflow of foreign capital during 1998–2002, with foreign direct investment minimal apart from the mobile phone auction of 2000. Popular attitudes to foreign aid were complex, simultaneously desired yet disliked

11.5: Development as a proportion of government expenditure, 1964–2002

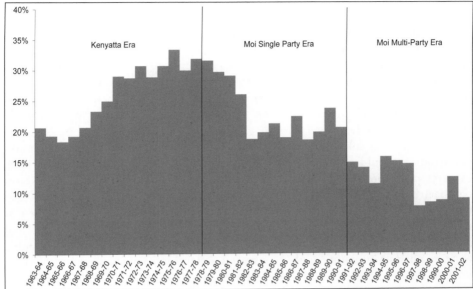

Source: Republic of Kenya, *Statistical Abstracts*, 1972–2005

as creating a culture of dependency. As Saitoti commented in 2002, a very different view from that of the 1960s, 'Foreign aid cannot result in sustained economic growth.'[64] Some observers blamed this on the self-serving nature of some aid. Others argued that aid shielded bad governments from the consequences of their policies, or that the unpredictability of foreign cash was intrinsically destabilising. All these arguments had some merit in the Kenyan case.

The debt burden continued to grow beyond the imagination of most Kenyans. Externally, Kenya was paying back more interest and principal than it was receiving in new aid.[65] From 1997 on, foreign aid in short supply, there was a steady rise in domestic debt, as short-term Treasury bills and (increasingly) longer-term bond sales were used instead to fund the deficit. By 1999, servicing the debt cost US$1.5 billion a year, or US$55 per person. By the end of 2002, the government owed at least US$8–9 billion, of which $5 billion were loans from multilateral agencies and foreign governments. Such vast debts – two-thirds to three-quarters of Kenya's GDP and between two and three times the budget for the year – were deemed sustainable by the IFIs, as foreign debt servicing took up only 25 per cent of foreign exchange earnings, but the situation was grimmer from the Kenyan perspective. Kenya had rarely run a surplus excluding aid, so the generation of sufficient surplus to repay the debts already incurred was implausible unless capital expenditure ceased entirely. If Kenya was a business, it had been making a net loss year on year, and borrowing heavily ostensibly to invest, but only to invest it poorly or spend it on operations. Although it continued to generate enough cash to service its loans, there was little prospect that it could clear its debts.

The Civil Service in Decline

Kenya's civil service remained a costly obstacle to reform. Its size (larger than Uganda and Tanzania's combined) had finally been capped. Central government numbers had been falling since the early 1990s, and from 1998 onwards, the numbers of teachers and parastatal employees began to follow suit (see Figure 11.6). Nonetheless, there were still too many ministries and parastatals performing overlapping functions. There were also too many staff, particularly at lower grades. Absenteeism was common, morale poor and pride in the job non-existent. There were growing tensions over civil service pay, with the desire to improve professionalism in conflict with pressure to cut costs. The salary bill jumped after awards to civil servants in 1994 and 1997 and after the 1997 increases for teachers.

Apart from the brief Leakey era, in which discretion was advisable, public officials continued to engage in pervasive corruption. The auditor-general issued report after report cataloguing waste, theft and illegal activities in the government. For some staff, rent and transport costs were more than their salary, leaving corruption as their only option. Unlike the European 'black economy' of cash transactions and unpaid taxes on business activities, this 'parasitic economy' produced nothing. It was a structure built alongside the government, extracting resources at every level, some for personal use, others for diversion to the private contractors that sustained and profited from it. Government contracts would involve kickbacks at every level or were issued to companies that civil servants owned. Junior officials were set private revenue targets by their line managers, part of a parallel network of resource extraction – none of which went through the books – which ran to the top in most departments. This trickle-up effect funded the opulent lives of the top elites.

11.6: Public sector employees by type, 1982–2007

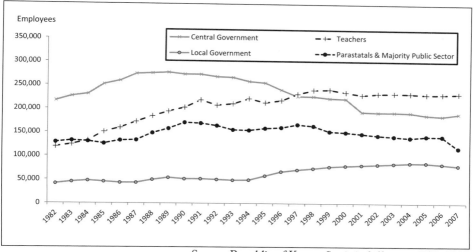

Source: Republic of Kenya, *Statistical Abstracts*, 1972–2009

Slowing Privatisation and the Telkom Debacle

The government had made good progress in privatising smaller state assets during the mid-1990s, but progress was now painfully slow. Of the 33 strategic enterprises and public utilities originally identified, two had been liquidated and six restructured, but none fully divested. Many remained drains on the Exchequer. Although the state re-committed itself to a stronger programme of privatisation in 2000–1, this posed economic and political dilemmas. The remaining institutions were large and complex, major employers and had been subject to severe predation. Privatisation also remained unpopular, reflecting decades in which Kenyans had been told they were building national assets for the future.

One of the most visible failures was in telecommunications, the monopoly of KPTC and the top target for the government and the donors. The inefficiencies of KPTC's network were legendary, with 120,000 people waiting for lines and corruption and mismanagement everywhere. By the late 1990s, the development of communications technology was exposing Kenya as a backwater, with one of the worst networks in the region. The pressure became intense both to liberalise (by introducing competition) and privatise (by selling off KPTC).

As in the electricity sector, the first step in 1999 was a split of functions. The Postal Corporation of Kenya took over mail services, Telkom Kenya operated voice and data communications, and a regulatory agency, the Communications Commission of Kenya (CCK) was established to regulate Telkom and future entrants into the market.[66] The state also signed up to the World Trade Organisation (WTO) General Agreement on Trade in Services for telecoms, to provide confidence that future foreign investors would be protected.[67] For now, though, Telkom would retain a five-year monopoly. Soon afterwards, the state wrote off US$262 million in taxes due from the parastatal, in recompense for it having subsidised services to unprofitable areas in the 1980s.[68] Reluctant to liberalise, the government initially tried to create competition inside Kenya by licensing regional service providers, while Telkom retained a monopoly on the international network and Nairobi. This failed, however, because the businesses were not viable concerns.

With Telkom segregated, but with over-manning endemic and little improvement in services, donor pressure mounted for full privatisation. However, the attempted sale of 49 per cent of the parastatal in 2000 led to a disastrous public tender that pitted six international telecoms companies, each with local allies, against each other.[69] The resulting dirty tricks and bribery allegations were a major scandal. The process led to a single preferred bidder, the Mount Kenya Consortium, a grouping of international telecoms businesses and local investors including wealthy Kikuyu insider Chris Kirubi. Their bid of US$305 million was far lower than the government wanted, however, and officials violated tender procedures and approached the second bidder to see if it would outbid them. After months of negotiations, in October 2001, the government used a due diligence investigation to discredit the consortium and the deal was off.[70] Kenya had failed another international test.

Drought and Power Problems, 1999–2000

Kenya's problems were worsened by poor rainfall in 1999–2000 (the aftermath of El Niño) and electricity rationing, exacerbated by a systemic failure to build capacity to meet growing demand. Agricultural GDP fell, the cities ran short of water and the hydroelectric dams, which contributed three-quarters of Kenya's power, were crippled. By June, residential power was cut from sunrise to sunset. The crisis depressed a weak economy further, leading to factory closures, job losses and crime. After the shutdown of the hydroelectric schemes, Kenya relied on the Kipevu diesel plant, Olkaria's geothermal supplies, power from Uganda and the oil-burning plants of the new IPPs. The IPPs were now crucial in keeping the lights on, but there was growing controversy over the way in which they had been awarded the licences, as the contract terms and costs became clear.

Foreign investment in the electricity industry had dried up since the Turkwell Gorge scandal, and World Bank loans to prepare for privatisation had been cancelled in 1997. Only when the crisis broke in 2000 did the state try to reactivate stalled projects. Rising world oil prices worsened the situation. The IPPs produced more than 10 per cent of Kenya's electricity in 2000, but at huge cost. Kenya had to seek an emergency US$72 million loan simply to buy fuel for the generators.[71] By 2002, as a result of the 2000 crisis and structural over-manning, KPLC and KenGen had both defaulted on their foreign loans and KPLC was insolvent, having lost Ksh14 billion in four years.

Trade and Industry

Kenya's exports were still bifurcated: agricultural products to Europe and low technology manufactures to Africa. The Lomé Convention had helped exports to Europe since 1975, but this expired in 2000. Its successor, the Cotonou Agreement, required the gradual reduction of preferential treatment between 2000 and 2007. It also made explicit reference to political conditionalities in its aid provisions.

In 2000, the US offered a new export opportunity for manufactured goods – the African Growth and Opportunity Act (AGOA). This cut US tariffs and quotas on imports from African countries, if African countries liberalised their trade relations. Once the US allowed Kenya to export clothing duty free for four years, foreign companies took advantage of this, creating 30,000 EPZ jobs as a result. Even so, it made little difference to the balance of trade between the two countries.[72]

World trade was growing fast, driven by the WTO and tariff reform, but Kenya's international competitiveness was not. Manufacturing's percentage of GDP remained stuck at 13 per cent. The apparently irreversible march of globalisation and global production networks appeared to be driving out inefficiencies in domestic production without the country developing areas of competitive advantage apart from cash-crops, since it lacked natural resources, political stability, a skilled workforce, good power, water, transport and communications infrastructure or a buoyant domestic economy. Instead, Kenya saw an influx of Asian-produced manufactures.

Foreign investment remained low and multinationals continued to close down smaller manufacturing centres. In the pharmaceutical industry, for example, both Johnson & Johnson and Pfizer partially sold up. The owners of Crown Berger paints sold out to a Rwandan consortium in 1999. Several potential foreign investments, including an Italian bid for KCC and the acquisition of Ken-Ren by a South African firm, collapsed before completion. The automotive industry too was in crisis. Lonrho Motors was put into receivership in 2000. The three surviving vehicle assembly plants (General Motors Kenya, Kenya Vehicle Manufacturers and Associated Vehicle Assemblers) saw their profitability decline, the result of poor economic conditions and liberalisation of import rules for second-hand cars. There were threats to withdraw from Kenya entirely unless the government increased protection for the industry, reflecting a classic tension between consumer benefit (cheap second-hand vehicles), local business interests (protection and profits), workers' interests (employment), donor pressure (free trade) and the national interest (a trade-off with no obvious winner). The Nairobi Stock Exchange declined for a decade after its peak of 1993–4 (see Figure 11.7).

One exception to the general stagnation was the drinks sector, which in 1997–8 saw an attack on Kenya Breweries Limited (KBL)'s monopoly by South African Breweries' subsidiary Castle, setting the two largest brewers in Africa head-to-head. The brewery that Castle built at Thika and its aggressive actions to compete with the Guinness-dominated KBL led to the 'beer wars' of 1997–2002. The industry went through massive changes, with new products, aggressive marketing and even violence. A key asset to Castle was its recruitment of members of the Kikuyu elite: its managing director was Joe Wanjui, while beer distributor and MP Njenga Karume was poached from KBL and owned one-third of the Thika plant. The investment generated tension between South Africa and Kenya, as many Kenyans viewed Castle

11.7: Nairobi Stock Exchange Index, 1964–2002

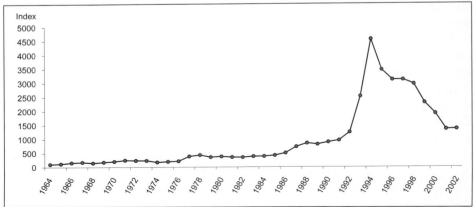

Source: Republic of Kenya, *Statistical Abstracts*, 1976-2003

as foreign. However, Castle was unable to achieve the profitability or scale it needed. It was hampered by KBL's tight links with political and business leaders and barley farmers.[73] There was also strong brand loyalty to Tusker and its sister brands as 'Kenyan'. In 2002, Castle conceded defeat, swapping the Thika brewery for one in Tanzania. KBL (once more renamed East African Breweries) closed the plant down, the end to one of the largest investments in Kenya for 15 years.

Transport Trouble

Kenya's railways were now in a disastrous state. In 2001, KR suspended passenger services to Kisumu, no longer able to operate a safe or economically viable service along the line created a century before. This left Nairobi–Mombasa as its only long-distance route. Despite asset sales, KR could not service its loans or offer a safe service, as was demonstrated by a series of horrific crashes in 1999 and 2000. Foreign pressure grew on the government to award a private sector concession to run the railways, leaving KR as the regulator. Although it had been restructured since 1999, Kenya Ports Authority too retained a reputation for high charges, inefficiency and corruption.

The situation on the roads was not much better. For decades, road contracts had been a favourite tool for predation, and the result was a deteriorating road stock. This fragile situation was tipped over the edge by the El Niño floods of 1997. The World Bank funded an El Niño rehabilitation programme in 1998, but the problem remained so bad that the Bank itself took over supervision of key road repair contracts. The results were little better: the programme was suspended in 2000 amid corruption allegations.[74]

The poor state of the roads was reflected in the accident statistics, which showed a doubling of deaths and serious injuries between 1985 and 2002. Kenya now had the highest rate of road accidents per vehicle in the world. Private bus companies, most owned by wealthy and well-connected individuals, were some of the worst killers. Poor roads and vehicle standards combined with institutionalised corruption, poverty and a lack of respect for the law to create a system in which dog eat dog was the only law. The *matatu* industry was also growing, with 4,000–6,000 minibuses plying the roads in a complex and little-regulated network of informal employment, collective self-help and criminal gangs. The success of the industry in the 1980s and 1990s, based on its adaptability and low costs, had created jobs for unskilled male youth. However, as most buses were overloaded, untaxed, dangerous and badly driven, *matatus* also relied on police corruption in order to operate. The large sums of money made by such quasi-legal networks increasingly represented a destabilising phenomenon.

The End of Urban Services

A continual concern to all city-dwellers was the collapse of public services. In Nairobi, tensions between the ministry and the opposition-controlled council further undermined failing water supplies, garbage collection and road maintenance.[75] The systematically looted Nairobi City Council was bankrupt by 1997, unable to pay its taxes or salaries. Most services became intermittent or ceased entirely.

The government, following Western and IFI advice, considered the privatisation of the most poorly performing utilities, including Nairobi's water supply. However, it was not an easy decision. The experience of water privatisation in Africa in the 1990s was positive compared with the appalling performance of state utilities, but still mixed.[76] Although studies were carried out (funded inevitably by donors) to look at privatisation or foreign management, the political cost of such a change was high. The admission of incompetence to run basic services without foreign help was a political minefield, while commercial firms would not touch such deals without cast-iron guarantees (such as the right to disconnect government offices for non-payment) and freedom to raise charges, which the state was unwilling to give. In 2002, the Water Act finally separated regulatory from service delivery functions, paving the way for private sector service delivery.

Employment, Labour and Trade Unionism

With cuts in civil service and parastatal staff, privatisation, a static industrial sector and the need to create more than 450,000 jobs a year, Kenya's employment crisis deepened. Between 1988 and 1998, public sector employment barely changed, and shrank sharply during 1998–2002. Privatisation, export-led growth and domestic recovery drove strong growth in the private sector in the 1990s, but this too slowed thereafter (see Figure 11.8).

11.8: Changes in formal sector employment, 1951–2007

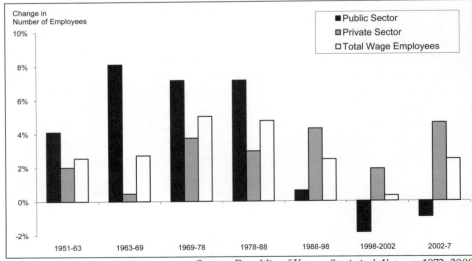

Source: Republic of Kenya, *Statistical Abstracts*, 1972–2009

The labour market too was liberalised in the mid-1990s, with easier hiring and firing rules, fewer wage guidelines and a reduced role for the Industrial Court. This was in part a reaction to growing competition from imports, which had led to the complete collapse of local textile and shoe production. It was a very different world from the one that workers had faced in 1963. School leavers at independence had been three times more likely to find a job and formal sector workers had been paid far more in real terms.[77] Despite a generation of education, gender inequalities in the labour market remained institutionalised, with far higher unemployment amongst women than men and salaries far lower.

COTU and the trade union movement continued to exist on paper, but had little relevance on the ground. Formally, Kenya had 37 unions with 400,000 members. However, they had been in decline for years. The days of tripartite deals were long gone, and strikes were rare in a situation of mass unemployment even amongst the educated. COTU's leaders seemed more concerned with national politics than workers' benefits. This did not prevent strikes, but tended to mean they were unofficial, and often resulted in mass dismissals.

The labour-intensive *jua kali* sector continued to grow, as far as surveys could estimate. Virtually every Kenyan now engaged in multiple occupations, whether as a civil servant with his own business, a factory worker doing evening work, or a farmer selling his labour. Hawkers and kiosks mushroomed as people sought ways to make a living. Policy-makers continued to stress the vibrancy of the informal sector, but for most it remained a last resort.

The NSSF in Crisis

The NSSF struggled to pay meaningful benefits to retiring workers. Workers' contributions had been fixed at Ksh80 a month in 1975, and were not increased until the end of the 1990s, so even if the funds had been well invested, the result after decades of inflation would have been a provident fund that could provide for virtually nothing. As it was, the NSSF's financial position was untenable given its excesses of the past. By 2000, the auditor-general of public corporations reported that the NSSF had accumulated losses of Ksh7.9 billion (US$100 million) because of 'imprudent past investment decisions'. Its records were so poor that Ksh7.3 billion were sitting in a suspense account, with no evidence of who had paid it in.[78]

Although the NSSF was no longer buying land, its management remained tightly linked to the political establishment and it was still used to prop up ailing political banks. This included Ksh256 million transferred to Euro Bank in 2002, which collapsed immediately thereafter.[79]

Banking Crises and the Donde Act

In 1998, 2000 and 2002, the country witnessed another series of banking collapses. Accused of making monopoly profits, yet holding massive non-performing debt portfolios (estimated at 40 per cent of all loans), the sector remained dangerously unstable. The main banks were now KCB, Barclays, Standard Chartered, the Cooperative Bank, Trust Bank and Citibank, but the country had 55 banks, far too many to be viable.

Cheserem, CBK governor until 2001, had stabilised the banking system after the chaos of 1992–3. There had been no inflationary spike in 1997–8, and the CBK gradually tightened the capital requirements for financial institutions, theoretically reducing the risk of collapse. However, the smaller banks were dangerously exposed, and there were six bank failures in 1998 due to lack of liquidity, fraud and insider loans. The largest was Trust Bank, Kenya's fifth largest bank. The bank, led by Asian Ajay Shah, was alleged to have operated an off-book banking system, with funds from the Asian community passing through a parallel *chopdi* system that was not recorded on the main bank computers (presumably to avoid paying tax). Relatives had extracted at least US$33 million in non-performing loans before its collapse, but depositors lost more than Ksh13 billion. Shah fled the country.

Reliance Bank followed it into liquidation in 2000. Again, the bank was Asian run and the managing director was accused of asset stripping. There was evidence once more of cheque kiting, money laundering and tax evasion. In the 2002 Euro Bank collapse, Ksh3 billion (US$40 million) was lost, including the NSSF's funds and deposits from Post Bank, Kenya Pipeline Company, the NHIF, Kenyatta National Hospital, the KTDC and the Pyrethrum Board.[80] As in other such cases, most of the parastatal heads who had made such poor investment decisions were Kalenjin or Luhya.

The part-privatised NBK, meanwhile, was still in crisis, with an unsustainable portfolio of bad debt and large loans to politicians such as Kones, Biwott and Ntimama, much of which had been invested in real estate. It could not even pay interest on its loans from the NSSF. Eventually, the state had to bail out the NBK, with a new management team imposed by the World Bank.

The worst problem for the banking industry, however, was the passage of the Central Bank of Kenya (Amendment) Act in 2000. This was a rare private member's bill, introduced by Luo FORD-Kenya MP Joe Donde. A popular and populist measure, it limited the maximum interest rates on loans to 4 per cent above the Treasury bill rate, provided that the interest on a debt could not exceed the principal, and set a minimum rate that banks must pay on deposits. It responded to the perception of the banks as exploiters, the high rates charged on personal loans, and the many cases of banks shaming prominent individuals for unpaid debts. MPs were fertile ground for this argument, as dozens were in court every year.[81]

The result was a contest between backbenchers and the public on one side and the government, the banks and the IMF on the other. The government's attempts to defeat the legislation failed and the Donde Bill was passed in December 2000. However, under pressure from donors appalled at this return to regulation, Moi refused to sign the Act, and returned it to the House in 2001. An amended version was reintroduced in 2002 and again passed by a cross-party consensus, despite opposition from the IFIs.[82] As with the defeat of KACA, the government suffered from its inability to control Parliament and the perception that it was kowtowing to

IFI demands. The result was confusion and a reduction in banks' willingness to lend to high-risk customers. The courts then threw the Act out as unconstitutional, but the Court of Appeal ruled it could be reinstated, with a new commencement date. In the end, the Act remained pending, in limbo.

Education and Health

Education

Since 1964, Kenya's education system had undergone at least 10 reviews. Nonetheless, it was still under-performing and many of the proposed remedies were controversial. The country's level of spending on education as a percentage of GDP was one of the highest in the world. Dissatisfaction with the 8–4–4 system was widespread, but criticism was often treated by KANU as politically motivated and designed to discredit it. Partly as a consequence, since 1988 the government had failed to implement any of its own policy papers. Nonetheless, KANU had promised a review of 8–4–4 in the 1997 election, and in 1998 Moi duly set up yet another commission of inquiry. The resulting report castigated the system for over-emphasis on examinations rather than skills acquisition, and recommended its abolition. It called on the state to offer 12 years of compulsory education (one year elementary, seven primary and four secondary).[83] It also argued for the abolition of the district quota system. However, Moi rejected the report as 'confusing and . . . likely to breed corruption since there would be no exams . . .'[84] He praised his 8–4–4 system once more, and another report vanished into the archives (though, characteristically, some of its recommendations were implemented once the political cost was containable).

Gross primary enrolments as a percentage of school-age children had fallen sharply during 1989–93, and continued to decline during the 1990s. Fewer than half those who started primary education now completed it. Of 1 million pupils who entered Standard I in 1994, for example, only 495,000 sat the KCPE exams in 2001. Estimates suggested that two-thirds of dropouts were due to charges and fees, including uniforms, sports equipment and building levies. In 2001, Moi abolished primary school fees yet again, without any plan for how they were to be funded instead. Things carried on much as before.

Public and private schools could now only provide secondary places for half of those who sat the KCPE. Enrolment rates had declined during the 1990s, and three-quarters of Kenya's children still received no secondary education. The competition for limited places remained intense and disparities in access to a quality education between rich and poor were huge. Both gender and ethno-regional inequalities also remained significant, with the arid and semi-arid lands consistently showing the lowest enrolment rates and Central Province the highest (though Moi's Baringo had the highest teacher–pupil ratio).[85]

The expansion of the universities slowed in the mid-1990s. Although tertiary education continued to absorb a large percentage of the education budget, rising fees cut enrolments by 15 per cent between 1995 and 1997. The introduction of the Higher Education Loans Board (HELB) in 1995 had begun the reorganisation of student funding, which by 1996 was suffering from a legacy of Ksh7 billion of unpaid student debts going back to 1974 (another example of the structural difficulties in debt management which had dogged Kenya since independence).[86] However, the HELB in turn proved politicised and incompetent. Despite promises to the World Bank to refocus resources away from the universities, from 2000 onwards student numbers rose once more, as Maseno University came on stream in 2001, and Kenyatta and Moi universities grew. By 2002, more than 40,000 students a year qualified for admission. Of these, 15,000 took places at the six public universities, and another 3,000 at six private universities (including Moi's own Kabarak University) that had been allowed to issue degrees since 1999. More than 10,000 students attended foreign universities. Local mid-level colleges and polytechnics took 5,000, leaving 10,000 a year to leave the education system.

The government still spent 15–20 per cent of its budget on education, much the same as in the 1970s and 1980s. However, more than 85 per cent of the ministry's budget was consumed by salaries, leaving little for maintenance or books. By 2001–2, the number of teachers had risen from 37,000 in 1967 to 233,000 and the Teachers Service Commission was the largest public sector employer in East and Central Africa. Having promised increases of 150–200 per cent over five years to the teachers during the 1997 election, the state now refused to pay them. Claiming that it simply did not have the money, the government had only paid the first increase in 1997. In October 1998, the argument escalated into a nationwide teachers' strike that paralysed learning and led to mass arrests. Another strike followed in 2002, just before the elections, when the state formally cancelled the deal it had made in 1997.[87] The government was in an impossible position, crippled by promises it had made for short-term gain, but without the funds to pay and under intense IFI pressure to cut costs.

Health and Population

HIV/AIDS was now Kenya's number one health issue. Infection numbers continued to grow, fuelled by poverty, limited access to condoms, and norms of social and sexual behaviour (including polygyny, wife inheritance and the widespread acceptance of commercial sex transactions). Recorded deaths from AIDS numbered 180,000 in 1999, dwarfing other causes of death. The result was a crash in life expectancy, from 61.9 in 1989 to 56.6 in 1999. The economic impact was huge. AIDS mainly killed adults between 20 and 40, and although the number of people per hospital bed had remained constant, AIDS patients now occupied most of these beds, taxing the medical system to the limit. Labour productivity declined and there were believed to be 300,000 AIDS orphans.[88]

The taboo surrounding AIDS had endured longer in Kenya than in most other countries, but was now broken, led mainly by NGOs. In 1997, the government published Sessional Paper No. 4, *Aids in Kenya and the National Strategic Plan*, and in 1999 it formed a National Aids Control Council and declared AIDS a national disaster. However, little changed in practice. In 2001, the council received US$50 million from the World Bank to fight AIDS, but virtually all of it was stolen or misused.[89] Religious organisations opposed to family planning also found themselves in a terrible dilemma; the Catholic Church, for example, continued to oppose the distribution of condoms and sex education in schools.

Actual infection numbers were disputed. There were complex issues surrounding the statistics, as higher rates encouraged more foreign aid. In 1999, estimates put the number of HIV-positive individuals between 1.5 and 1.9 million. In 2000, the minister for medical services announced that 1.5 million Kenyans had died of AIDS and that 2.2 million were HIV positive.[90] Kenya was reported to have one of the highest infection rates in the world, at 14 per cent of adults.[91] However, the 2003 Demographic and Health Survey suggested the adult infection rates were only half this, at around 7 per cent.[92]

Kenya's sixth census took place in August 1999. Kenya now had 28.7 million people, more than a million fewer than estimated, leaving it with the same population as Algeria but less than Tanzania. The census had good news in that the rate of population growth had slowed to 2.9 per cent per annum. 'Only' 44 per cent of the population was under 15, down from 49 per cent in 1989. This was a result of the wider use of contraception and better education for women, but also worsening economic and health circumstances. Western, Eastern and Nyanza's share of the population all declined due to out-migration and mortality.

Nonetheless, Kenya's population had nearly tripled since 1969, with the Rift Valley growing from 2 million to 7 million (see Figure 11.9). Thirty-five per cent

11.9: Census data by province, 1969 and 1999

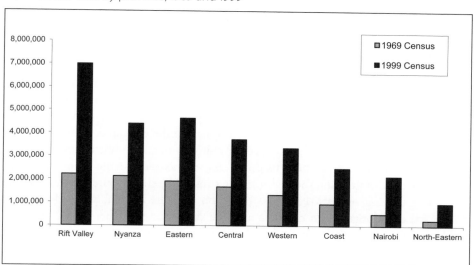

Source: Republic of Kenya, *1999 Population Census*, Vol. 1 and 1969 Census

of the population was now urban, with Nairobi's population exceeding 2.1 million. Many people lived in urban areas that had barely existed in the 1960s. The ex-settler and coastal cities had grown far more slowly than the African townships, so that Mumias in Western, for example, was larger than Nyeri.[93] Nairobi remained the main draw, however.

The government promised to publish the detailed results, including ethnic figures, in 2000.[94] They failed to do so, however, in part because of the politicised ethnic competition that had resulted each decade, in part to conceal unwelcome messages about the impact of the ethnic clashes. In 2000, the *Nation* published unauthorised results, disowned by the government, which showed the Kikuyu at 5.3 million (down to 18 per cent of the population), the Luhya up to 14 per cent and the Luo down to 11 per cent. It appeared there were now more Kalenjin than Luo.[95]

Cultural and Social Issues

Social Change, Gender and Traditional Values

Globalisation was increasingly affecting Kenyans, in their social relations as much as in their economy and politics. The increasingly rapid whirlwind of foreign images, ideas and peoples moving through the country, particularly the urban areas, was sweeping away many of the attributes of 'old Kenya', including some that Kenyans still saw as fundamental to their national or ethnic identity. The nature and characteristics of the 'tribe' to which virtually all Kenyans ascribed themselves had changed over the years. The long-awaited 'detribalisation' of urbanisation was well advanced, but the symbology and ascriptive elements of ethnic identities had endured even though many of their original characteristics had vanished. Many Nairobi residents in their twenties and thirties were born and educated there, and did not view the rural areas as home. Some wealthier children did not even speak their 'local language' – only English and Swahili. They still knew their 'tribe', however. The poor remained closer to their rural roots and their ethnicity as a point of identity and cleavage.

Forty years after independence, marriage practices were changing. Arranged marriages were now rare outside pastoral areas, and most Kenyans opted for Christian marriages.[96] There was a gradual conversion of the extended family to the nuclear family, though the Kenyan family still spent more time with its relatives than did its Western counterpart. Some men – rich and poor – still married multiple wives, though the practice was rare amongst the young and the educated. Even in nuclear families, polygyny continued in practice for many men, taking mistresses once their economic status permitted them to do so. As submissions to the Constitution of Kenya Review Commission showed, a strong rural lobby still favoured both polygyny and the outlawing of birth control.[97] Abortion remained illegal, as in the rest of East Africa. Amongst slum dwellers and the dispossessed, male–female relations had become transient and atomised, with many women without permanent partners. With unskilled labour now little valued, the payment of bridewealth amongst poorer communities declined.[98] Violence against women in all forms remained common.

Female 'circumcision', now described as female genital mutilation (FGM), remained widespread, although the pressure to stop it was growing. To put an end to the practice was a key target of women's groups, for which Western donors provided substantial funding. Although it had been 'banned' by presidential decree in 1982 and 1989 and by law in 2001, and government hospitals would not carry out the procedure, between 30 and 40 per cent of women in Kenya were still circumcised. Although uncommon amongst the better educated, the Luhya and Luo, FGM rates rose to 90 per cent or more amongst the Kisii, Maasai and Somali.[99] Those who defended Kenya's indigenous cultural traditions (and the politicians who hoped to benefit from their espousal) actively supported its continuance.

In northern Kenya, traditional Somali and Oromo values continued to dominate other forms of social organisation. Community leaders remained resolute that not only was Islam the foundation of their society, but that it denied the equality of men and women. Generation-set leadership models that had collapsed in the 1950s in the Kikuyu remained functional in communities such as the Gabbra in the 1990s. Violence was rife, with communities engaging in banditry, rape and murder, and occasional open warfare using automatic weapons. Families still paid blood money as compensation for murder. Development remained near non-existent, with most people nomadic and fewer than 10 per cent of children in school.

The 'Liberated' Media

From 1998, facing an international explosion in communications, the government abandoned most overt media controls. While the media were liberated from direct censorship, however, politicians now owned most media channels. In 1995–7, the Moi family and Kulei had bought the *Standard* and KTN, which gave them a strong influence over public opinion. KANU retained control over the *Kenya Times*, while Kenneth Matiba retained majority ownership and editorial control over the daily but diminished *People*. Moi's attempts to purchase an interest in the Nation Group were, however, unsuccessful.

The late 1990s also saw an explosion of numerous low content, high-shock-value weeklies such as *Kenya Confidential*. Some were owned or bankrolled by politicians and all emphasised partisan, sensational and often untrue stories. Some were used for extortion, threatening to reveal politicians' improprieties if not paid off. The glossy weeklies, in contrast, were failing. In 1998, the *Economic Review* got into financial trouble and closed down, and the *Weekly Review* shut its doors in 1999. All state attempts to regulate the press more tightly were rejected by an alliance of MPs, civil society, journalists and donors, but libel cases multiplied and the state still occasionally harassed journalists and editors.

In the broadcast media, KBC remained the government mouthpiece and continued to pander to the presidency. The Moi family owned KTN, while the Kenyatta family had an interest in Hilary Ng'weno's Stellavision. In 2001, Nation TV finally managed to start broadcasting. After years of failed applications, in 1998 the company had changed tack, buying up a shell company that did have a licence and frequency.

A furious government did everything it could to stop this, including sacking the sellers, withdrawing the licence and disputing the company's true ownership.[100] Eventually, however, the government realised it could not blackball the Nation Group indefinitely while licensing dozens of others, and by 1998 the group had reluctantly been granted a licence, which it then enthusiastically exploited.

In the radio sphere, it was not until 1996 that the government licensed the first private station. In 1997, two more were licensed, and after the formation of the Communications Commission in 1998, the number mushroomed. In 2000, the first private local-language station, Kameme FM, began broadcasting in Gikuyu and was followed by many more in other languages.[101] By 2001, Kenya had nine private TV broadcasters and 19 radio stations. It was an entirely different world from that of the 1980s.

Mobile Phones, Computers and the Internet

The broader availability in the late 1990s of personal computers, the Internet and mobile phones had dramatic effects inside Kenya. Moi was not alone in believing that 'the new information civilisation erodes the identity and functions of the nation-state . . .', because it allowed the rapid dissemination of Western culture.[102] With computers, for the first time it was possible for wealthy individuals to analyse government data and produce high-quality publications. The development of the Internet gave Kenyans independent access to world news and allowed them fast and cheap international communications. From one Internet service provider (ISP) in 1994, by 2002, there were 70 ISPs and 400,000 users. The *Nation's* local website received more than a million hits per day by 2002. However, the law still required all ISPs to use Telkom Kenya's 'backbone'. No private satellite dishes (which Telkom could not switch off and did not generate revenue), were licensed, in contrast to the approach elsewhere.

Mobile phones were even more significant as an economic and cultural phenomenon, allowing cheap communications even in rural areas and bringing the heartland of rural Kenya closer to the city. KPTC had initially retained a monopoly on mobile phone technology. It had set up the Safaricom service in 1997, but there were few subscribers and prices were high. This changed in 1999 and 2000. Safaricom was part privatised, with 40 per cent sold to Vodafone for US$30 million. The CCK also auctioned the licence for a second GSM operator, which was won by Kencell Communications (a partnership between Vivendi, a French communications and entertainment consortium, and the Kenyan Sameer Group). The investment in these two networks was the largest foreign investment in Kenya for years.

With money came both politics and corruption. There were rumours that Biwott and Gideon Moi had a commercial interest in Safaricom and that a 5 per cent stake in the company had moved offshore.[103] There were also indications of questionable practices around the Vivendi–Sameer win, with competitors who submitted higher bids disqualified in favour of Kencell's US$55 million. Each of the bidding consortia recruited senior politicians, there was intense intra-elite competition over who would win, and rumours that the NSIS had even tapped Trade Minister Biwott's telephone.[104]

The result of liberalisation was an explosion in mobile communications. Within two years, Kencell and Safaricom had equalled the 300,000 landlines installed by KPTC over 50 years. With a product that met local needs, driven by foreign expertise and honed by intense competition, by the end of 2002, there were more than one million subscribers. Despite its controversial origins, it was one of Kenya's most successful 'privatisations'.

Money and Power

Kenya was now an extremely stratified society, with a few thousand elite African, Asian and European families at the top, a significant (and often under-estimated) urban middle class, a small working class of urban and rural workers, a large, family-dominated agricultural sector and a growing underclass of *jua kali* workers, urban and rural unemployed and landless.

At the very top were a few dozen families. Almost all these super-rich Kenyans fell into one of three categories. In the first were the old money families of the 1960s and 1970s, mainly Kikuyu. They were exemplified by the Kenyatta family, the family of ex-CBK Governor Philip Ndegwa (owner of insurance companies and a large property portfolio), Duncan Ndegwa and his family, Unilever boss Joe Wanjui, John Michuki (owner of the Windsor Hotel and Golf Club) and the investment triumvirate of Njonjo, Jeremiah Kiereini and James Kanyotu. Nyachae and his Sansora food-processing companies were in this category, as would Matiba have been if he had not bled his businesses dry in 1992. There had been other insiders in the 1970s who had not survived the decades of Moi's rule.

In the second group were those Africans who had made their money in the 1980s and 1990s, mostly associated with Moi. These included the key Kalenjin elites – the Moi family, Biwott, Kulei, Hosea Kiplagat, ex-CBK Governor Kotut and others from the Tugen heartlands. They also included favoured sons from other communities, such as Saitoti, Kirubi and Samuel Gichuru amongst the Kikuyu. By 2002, Moi himself had seven private residences, as well as investments, businesses, buildings, farms and ranches. He always denied having foreign bank accounts, but there was little dispute than he, his family, his proxies and Biwott together owned the largest chunk of Kenya's economy in private African hands. Rather than working together, however, Kulei, Biwott, Gideon Moi, Franklin Bett, Kiplagat and others often competed over deals. All used Moi's name as the authority for their transactions.

In the third group was the Asian business community, which still owned most of the manufacturing industry in Kenya and much else, sparking periodic debate over the reason why this remained the case.[105] Several groups of families coexisted (independent of divisions based on origins and religion). First, there were the high-profile frontmen of the late 1980s and early 1990s such as Pattni, Somaia and the Shah banking families, *nouveaux riches* who had lost their lustre. Other Asian businesses had close links to ministers, and were extremely successful at winning government contracts, but were more careful. These included Mukesh

Gohil (who until 2002 was Gideon Moi's business colleague); Sunil Behal, owner of a road construction company (Saitoti's regular *harambee* donor); and the Kamani family (owners of the Kamsons Group), linked with Kulei. Harbinder Singh Sethi was close to Biwott and Gideon Moi, commodity dealer Harish Devani worked with Kiplagat and Gichuru and architect Harbans Singh was an ally of Saitoti.[106] A dozen more well-known Asian businessmen had close links to permanent secretaries, other ministers and military officers.

Other Nairobi Asian families were longer established and less dependent on state largesse, although many needed links with either the Moi or Kenyatta families. These included Naushad Merali (Sameer), the Comcraft Group, Moi and Njonjo's business partner P. K. Jani, the Popat family (holders of the Mitsubishi vehicle franchise and owners of Imperial Bank), Lalit Pandit (East African Building Society) and Manish Shah and family (owners of Kingsway Motors, Charterhouse Bank and the Village Market shopping complex).[107] A final group of Arab and Asian tycoons had made their money by commodity trading, transportation and import–export, most based in Mombasa. These included Rashid Sajaad, Twahir Said Sheikh, Mohamed Bawazir and Abdallah Zubedi, who helped fund KANU during the 1992 and 1997 general elections. Others included the Bayusuf group (transport) and the Akasha family (later accused of drug smuggling).

This picture reconfirms the close interrelationship of business and politics. Almost all the wealthiest families had close government links, good business acumen and a flexible attitude to the law. One was not sufficient without the others. There were wealthy and successful politicians such as Kibaki (who held shareholdings in many companies) who were not in the super-rich league because they lacked the 'killer instinct' or an appetite for gross corruption. Others – such as Paul Ngei – had had the contacts and the willingness to use the system, but not the business acumen. The wealthiest elites knew each other, schooled their children together and were in business together. Their struggles to consolidate resources into their mini-*chaebol* (family-controlled conglomerates) lay behind many of the country's political battles, and they funded both KANU and opposition leaders for their own reasons.

The European community, meanwhile, remained wealthy and influential, but in a more ephemeral form. Most resident Europeans were expatriates, diplomats or businesspeople, almost all living in Nairobi and often politically naive. A few white settlers remained, influential behind the scenes, but were rarely seen in the city.

Military and Security Issues

The gradual decline in security throughout Kenya became a major threat to both development and governance in the late 1990s. Neither the cities nor the pastoral north were now safe. While Kenya had avoided wars and coups, Moi had proved unable to maintain security within Kenya's own borders. This failure systematically weakened the state's legitimacy, but also helped secure KANU's survival in the short term.

Nairobi under Siege

Most of Nairobi now lived in violence and fear. While foreigners and the local elite inhabited secure compounds, much of the city was under the control of criminals and private militia. The decline in police capability, the politicisation of violence, poverty, joblessness, inequality and a lack of hope merged to create a culture of crime. Even the city centre was under attack, with daily bank robberies, carjackings and attacks on diplomats and tourists during 2000–1.[108] Without physical security, few foreigners were willing to invest. Local residents paid protection money to militia such as the Taliban, Kamjesh and Mungiki to help secure their estates, to which the police turned a blind eye. Many militias had an explicit ethnic orientation, and there were complex links between such organisations and Nairobi's confrontational politics.

War in the North

Much of the country north of Isiolo was now lost to the security forces, as drought-stricken pastoralists engaged in cattle rustling with automatic weapons, and bandits proliferated on the roads. Education, agriculture and tourism were disrupted or abandoned in Marakwet, Pokot, Turkana, Samburu and North-Eastern Province. In December 1999 and January 2000, one of the worst periods, there were more than 25 mass killings in Pokot, Marakwet, Turkana, Marsabit, Samburu, Isiolo, Tana River, Baringo and Garissa districts. Hundreds were killed in fighting over cattle, pasture and blood feuds, which the police and military appeared unable to counter. The northern border with Ethiopia and the Sudan had been a source of insecurity since the 1980s, exacerbated by the presence of the SPLA in southern Sudan. Although Kenya stayed out of the war, it supported the SPLA, and suffered from a continued influx of refugees and weapons. The situation was much the same in the north-east, worsened by competition for declining grazing. Garissa District saw conflicts between Ogaden Somali clans during 1999–2000 in which at least 70 died. In Wajir, clan fighting over land between Garre and Ajuran Somali, which had begun in 1993, reached a peak in 2000, despite government efforts to maintain peace.[109]

Isiolo, too, saw deteriorating security, associated with the southern movement of Somali away from drought and war. In 1991, 3,000 Degodia had crossed with their livestock into Isiolo. They, the Samburu and the Borana (the main occupants of the district), competed for pasture and water, a process exacerbated by the 1997 election, which channelled these tensions into party competition. In May 2000, 100 Borana and Somali died during clashes.[110] In Laikipia, there were killings by Samburu or Turkana raiders, with political overtones created by the alignment of KANU with the pastoralists and the Kikuyu with the DP. There were more allegations that plain-clothes GSU officers were involved.[111]

Amongst the Kalenjin, the Marakwet continued to suffer from Pokot cattle raiding. Hundreds died and thousands were made homeless. The Pokot terrorised their neighbours with apparent impunity, protected by minister Francis Lotodo and the Pokot's importance to KANU. Lotodo's influence was so broad that he could 'hire and fire' district commissioners at will. Even after his death in 2000, the Pokot near-insurrection continued. Their quest to drive out all foreigners from the district essentially complete, they increasingly turned their attention to Trans-Nzoia, much of which they claimed as their 'ancestral' land.

In the south, too, there were tensions inside pastoral areas and on the borders with settled communities, as drought, population pressure, poverty and politics combined. In 1999, several died in clashes between Kipsigis and Maasai.[112] There was also fighting between Maasai and Gusii. More than 100 were killed in 1999 and 2001 in the once-quiet Tana River, due to what the press called 'tribal warfare' between Orma and Somali clans, and then between the pastoral Orma and Wardei and Pokomo farmers.

Some claimed this apparently inexorable onset of ethnic violence was a side-effect of globalisation and the harm caused to the nation-state by structural adjustment. Others believed it was a deliberate strategy by the government to divide and repress its opponents. It also reflected an enduring tension between the individual freehold model of land ownership and communal ownership, and the risks to pastoralism of enclosure and demarcation.[113] Whatever the causes, endemic crime and out-of-control community violence were destroying the legitimacy of the state and its hopes for development.

The Military

The army's strength was now 18,000–20,000, six times its size at independence, with an air force of 3,000 and 5,000 GSU. However, Kenya's financial difficulties were also straining its military capability. In 1998–9, defence spending stood at less than 2 per cent of GDP and 4 per cent of the budget, too little to maintain training or replace ageing equipment.[114] As a result, when combined with the growing terrorist challenge, military spending rose once more during 2000–2. The army continued to be helped with training and equipment by the British, who in return still made use of the 1964 training arrangements, though the supply of arms to Kenya became increasingly sensitive after the Labour Party came to power in 1997, committed to an ethical foreign policy. UN duties remained a source of both experience and finance, and by 2000, Kenya had soldiers on peacekeeping activities in 12 countries.

Chief of General Staff Daudi Tonje embarked on a restructuring of the army in 1997. He created a new position of Vice-Chief of General Staff, to which all service commanders reported, and in 1998 the army shifted from a British to an American model of command. Army head Augustine Cheruiyot retired in 1998, but the Kalenjin and pastoralist influence remained strong (see Table 11.1). On Tonje's retirement, UK- and US-trained Joseph Kibwana replaced him, the first navy professional to head the military. Lieutenant-General Opande, the most senior Luo in the military, was sidelined to a UN role. There were no Kikuyu at the top.

Although Tonje was commended for increasing professionalism, corruption and tribalism were embedded in the army too, and political 'godfathers' had a strong influence on appointments.[115] The late 1990s saw several allegations of procurement

Table 11.1: Military heads, 1997–2003

Chief of General Staff	General Daudi Tonje	1996–2000	Kalenjin–Tugen
	General Joseph Kibwana	2000–5	Mijikenda
Vice-Chief of General Staff	Lt.-Gen. Jackson Munyao	1997–8	Kamba
	Lt.-Gen. Daniel Opande	1998–2000	Luo
	Lt.-Gen. John Koech	2000–3	Kalenjin–Kipsigis
Army Commander	Lt.-Gen. Augustine Cheruiyot	1994–8	Kalenjin–Nandi
	Lt.-Gen. Abdullahi Aden	1998–2000	Somali
	Lt.-Gen. Lazarus Sumbeiywo	2000–3	Kalenjin–Keiyo
Air Force Commander	Major-Gen. Nick Leshan	1994–2000	Maasai
	Major-Gen. Simon Mutai	2000–3	Kamba
Navy Commander	Major-Gen. Joseph Kibwana	1988–98	Mijikenda–Giriama
	Major-Gen. Aboud Rauf Raouf	1998–2001	Bajuni
	Major-Gen. Pasteur Awitta	2001–3	Luo

Source: Various

malpractices and the jailing and early retirement of senior officers.[116] There were even rumours in 1999 of a coup plot and six soldiers were jailed for planning a mutiny in 2000.[117]

Rediscovering the Law

Political and economic liberalisation had another concomitant: the reaffirmation of the law as a tool for arbitration and conflict resolution, more transparent than bribery or violence. However, attempts to restore a functioning legal system in Kenya faced a mire of bureaucracy, inefficiency and corruption. The tight links between judges, senior politicians and, in some cases, criminal syndicates reflected the 'for hire' status of many in the legal system. In 1998, for example, a report by Justice Richard Kwach damned the judicial system as inept, corrupt and partial. It was 'a mouse squeaking under the chair of the executive'.[118]

Kenya now had no detainees and few political prisoners, but the state still initiated punitive cases against the most recalcitrant student leaders, politicians and civil society activists. Attorney-General Amos Wako still took over and terminated private prosecutions, and courts often used technicalities to avoid ruling against the government. The real problem, however, was not political but economic: only the wealthy could afford lawyers. The police were uninterested in solving crimes unless paid to do so, and police beatings and torture to extract confessions remained common, part of a culture of violence that permeated society. The courts were chaotic and overloaded, and there were allegations of corruption against almost everyone. Where no money was involved, prosecutions could drag on for a decade. In 2004, in Meru alone, there were 26,000 pending legal cases and 32,000 in the North Rift.

In 1999, to great surprise, Moi appointed (Luo) Director of Public Prosecutions Bernard Chunga as chief justice, replacing Zachaeus Chesoni, who had died of a heart attack. There was widespread distaste at the promotion of the man who had led the Mwakenya trials to become the defender of judicial independence. Although his appointment was tarnished, Chunga did try to address some of the structural reasons behind the delays, with the establishment of special courts for specific subjects and efforts to better manage judges' workloads. In 2001, Chunga even published rules for applications to the High Court for the enforcement of fundamental rights, which had been lacking for the previous three decades. In 2002, written law reports recommended after a 19-year gap.

Nonetheless, the state of the judiciary remained a public scandal and a political football. In early 2002, with elections looming, lawyers, reformers and opposition politicians began a campaign for judicial reform. The CKRC invited five senior Commonwealth judges to review the state of administration of justice and advise how to bolster confidence in Kenya's legal institutions. The judges' report was deeply critical, expressing their alarm at the depths to which standards had fallen, and recommended both fundamental reform and 'a short sharp shock' to drive out endemic corruption.[119] Chunga and Moi rejected these conclusions outright, but the shock the judges prescribed was to come in 2003.

International Relations

The Nairobi Bomb Blast and US Relations

On 7 August 1998, Islamic terrorists allied to Osama bin Laden bombed the US Embassy in Nairobi. They killed 250 people and injured 5,600, including Kamotho and US Ambassador Prudence Bushnell. Nairobi was completely unprepared for the attack or the resulting carnage, and the bombing changed popular attitudes both to Islam and to the Americans. US President Clinton vowed to track down those responsible, and cooperation between the US and Kenyan security forces improved as they hunted together for the bombers. The US eventually paid US$40 million in compensation to Kenyans killed or injured in the blast.

Over the next few years, the US provided substantial anti-terrorist assistance to Kenya, still positioning itself as America and the West's strongest ally in the region (a role that it had jealously guarded since independence). Joint exercises with the US took place in 1999 and 2000, completing the transition from a UK-focused to a US-focused military that had been under way since 1976. In 2000, Kenya agreed to join the African Crisis Response Initiative, and formal US military assistance resumed in 2002, a decade after it had been suspended.

Relations with the US improved even further after the 11 September 2001 attacks on the World Trade Center and the Pentagon. Moi saw the events as an opportunity to improve relations and was among the first African leaders to sign up to the 'war on terror'. Kenya publicly backed the Americans and allowed Western countries to base warships in Mombasa to support the war in Afghanistan. The anti-Israeli Paradise Beach Hotel suicide bomb and the failed missile attack on an Israeli airliner in Kenya in November 2002 emphasised Kenya's need for a stronger anti-terrorist strategy, given the country's large Western interests, porous borders, poverty, growing Islamic fundamentalism on the coast and proximity to Somalia. Kenya provided intelligence to the US on Al Qaeda supporters on the Coast and in Somalia to help US Special Forces in their missions. There was growing concern amongst liberals that the US might subordinate democracy to security, particularly after George W. Bush became president in 2001.

The worldwide debate about the relationship of Islam and democracy had particular sensitivity in Kenya because of the Muslim communities of the Coast and North-Eastern's political alignment with KANU.[120] Muslim influence in the government had grown in the 1990s: six assistant ministers and two ministers were Muslims in 1998. However, Muslim interests were associated with the IPK and the opposition as well, and many Muslims still claimed to be disadvantaged.[121] The bombings and Kenya's participation in the 'war on terror' severely damaged Kenya's relations with its Arab and Muslim minorities, leading to protests, the de-registration of several Muslim NGOs and allegations of police torture during the hunt for terrorists. One Muslim MP called on the government to be neutral, since Osama bin Laden, like other terrorists before him (such as Jomo Kenyatta and Nelson Mandela) might end up as 'father of the nation'.[122]

Regional Integration and the New EAC

After more than two decades, in November 1999 Kenya, Uganda and Tanzania re-established the East African Community (EAC). The process had begun with a 1993 treaty to restore some common institutions. In 1996, with tensions reducing between Uganda and Kenya, efforts began to align fiscal policies, and a secretariat had been established. Now, the partners committed themselves to a customs union, a common market and (eventually) a monetary and political federation. This reflected the unwelcome reality that East Africa's economies remained individually too small to support competitive manufacturing industries in a 'world without borders'.[123] Nonetheless, the issue of trade between the three countries and Kenya's industrial dominance remained unresolved. Each country maintained its customs regimes and there were still tariffs on Tanzanian imports to Kenya and vice versa. In virtually no areas – customs, taxation, telecommunications, currencies, power, water, product standards, education or health – had common institutions or policies survived, leaving the region's economies less integrated that at any time since the colonial invasion. Despite the re-formation of the EAC, there was little evidence that Kenyans took federation seriously.

Kenya was also a member of another preferential trading area: COMESA. By 2000, the COMESA bloc of 20 countries was Kenya's biggest trading partner. Exports from Kenya grew from an average of US$170 million in 1990–2 to US$664 million in 1996–8.[124] However, COMESA's main goals remained unfulfilled: promises of a free trade zone were not met, countries continued to produce competing goods and compensation mechanisms to address imbalances in benefit did not exist. In any case, the opportunity to cut tariffs was not appreciated by most Kenyans, whose protectionist streak remained strong. There were demands to pull out from COMESA because of the tariffs forgone on imports (whatever the benefits to consumers) and the competition with domestic producers, particularly in sugar. The willingness to sacrifice jobs, factories or state revenue for collective benefit appeared minimal. Tensions also existed between the goal of regional integration – and a tariff preference for regional products – and global pressure to dismantle all trade barriers.

On Kenya's northern border, in contrast, relationships remained difficult. Ethiopian troops crossed the border several times into northern Kenya while fighting secessionists. Kenya assisted in a reconciliation of sorts between Uganda and Sudan in 1999, and Moi committed himself in 1997 to mediation in the Sudan, which finally bore fruit in 2004. However, insecurity on the border with Somalia remained acute. In 2001, Kenya was still hosting more than 135,000 Somali refugees. Moi remained active in his regional peacekeeping missions. He was reported to have chaired at least 12 peace initiatives on Somalia between 1991 and 2001, all of which had failed.

Elsewhere in Africa, in 1998 Kenya re-established diplomatic relations with Libya after a decade and became part of the African Union when it replaced the discredited OAU in 2002. South Africa became increasingly influential as an investor in Africa after the end of apartheid in 1994. By 2002, South Africa was Kenya's third largest source of private investment, and there were large imports of South African products into Kenya. However, South Africa's businesses struggled for popular acceptance, and Castle's failure was used an example of Kenya's hidden protectionism.[125]

Succession Politics, 2000–1

On the all-important matter of the succession, Moi still refused to make his intentions clear, assuring donors in 2001 that he was determined to stand down as constitutionally required, but unwilling to say so openly for fear of launching an immediate succession battle. With Nyachae out of favour, the main competitors were Mudavadi and Saitoti in KANU and Odinga in the NDP. Whoever was the victor, the government seemed likely to win the next election, under whatever system emerged from the constitutional review.[126]

The NDP–KANU Alliance

The alliance between the NDP and KANU deepened. A key indicator of Raila's progress into the heart of KANU was his role in the constitutional review process, where he was now Moi's most loyal ally. In June 2001, Odinga finally received a reward for his cooperation, when Moi formed Kenya's first coalition government since

1963. He appointed Raila as minister for energy, his colleague Adhu Awiti became planning minister and two more NDP MPs became assistant ministers.[127] Most NDP MPs crossed over to the government bench, and moves began to formalise their partnership into a merger. Raila looked to have done a deal that would leave him well placed to succeed Moi, and Nyanza celebrated in response. However, there was strong opposition inside KANU from the Kamotho–Saitoti axis, concerned about their future. They resisted Moi's 'western alliance' throughout 2001, arguing that KANU's constitution did not permit a merger, and had to be overridden by Moi. The parties eventually held a joint Delegates' Conference on 24 August 2001 at Kasarani Sports Stadium, an event that became known as 'Kasarani I' (see Figure 11.10).

The strengthening alliance had side-effects. In December 2001, Kisumu became Kenya's second city, overtaking Mombasa, which received its own promotion a few weeks later. In the same month, fighting broke out in the Kibera slums of Odinga's Langata constituency after Moi visited the area and ordered rents to be cut. The mainly Luo tenants initiated a rent boycott and the landlords (mainly Nubian and Kikuyu) fought back. For days, Kibera was a battlefield, with 12 killed and hundreds arrested. Meanwhile Raila's personal wealth was rumoured to be growing, based on oil import deals between firms he owned (while minister of energy) and Saudi Arabia and Libya. In 2001, Odinga's Spectre finally acquired both the Kisumu molasses plant and the land on which it sat, a transaction that the government had refused when Raila was in the opposition.

11.10: KANU–NDP alliance, 24 August 2001

Courtesy: Nation Group Newspapers

Nyachae Goes it Alone

In December 2000, the KANU National Governing Council suspended six rogue MPs from the party, including Nyachae, Kones, Kipruto arap Kirwa and Jirongo. The effect was to make KANU technically a minority government, though via their alliance with the NDP they still controlled the Assembly. In practice, party was increasingly irrelevant, as, by now, a dozen KANU MPs were effectively in the opposition, while most of the NDP and several DP MPs were with the government. Ethnic caucusing was the norm.

In January 2001, believing like Matiba that he had the ability, resources and support to go it alone, Nyachae decided that he would not join an existing opposition party, but build his own vehicle to win power. There are hints that the DP had refused Nyachae's condition for joining them: that he, not Kibaki, would be their presidential candidate.[128] Instead, Nyachae acquired the semi-moribund FORD-People and his supporters took over the party.[129] Most Gusii politicians and many of Kones's allies in Kericho followed them. Nandi rebels such as Kirwa also flirted with the party and it appeared FORD-People might become an alternative to KANU in KANU's home areas. Although centred in the Gusii and Kipsigis, the party also had some Kikuyu support, because of its Kikuyu roots. Nyachae was preparing a slate of candidates for Parliament and had a well-oiled and professional machinery for his inevitable presidential bid.

'Project Uhuru' and a New Generation, September–November 2001

At the same time as Moi was luring Raila into an alliance, he was also raising the profile of Jomo Kenyatta's son, Uhuru. Despite his protégé's defeat in 1997, Moi had appointed the 40-year-old as chairman of the Tourism Board and he was already Thika KANU chairman. By 1998, insiders including Kosgei and Kulei were quietly marketing Uhuru as a potential presidential candidate. In October 2001, Moi nominated Uhuru to Parliament, replacing the now-disgraced Mark arap Too.

At first, Kenyatta was seen as another ally for Mudavadi, Ruto, Odinga and Sunkuli, but as time passed, Moi's praise for Uhuru began to rouse expectations that he might be a candidate in his own right. In the same month, Moi publicly stated for the first time that he would hand over power to a younger leader.[130] This was the signal for an effusion of support for what became known as the 'dot.com' generation of young, media-friendly KANU politicians; the new 'KANU Young Turks'. The resulting media focus on Uhuru appeared to signal a convergence of interests between the youthful majority of the country and the Moi elite, who believed they had found an electable – and controllable – Kikuyu. In November 2001, Moi appointed Kenyatta (and a rehabilitated Jirongo) to the Cabinet, Kenyatta's first government post, only a year before the elections were due.[131]

Kenyatta had another asset apart from his youth, name and connections: his money. The Kenyattas were probably the wealthiest African family in Kenya. They owned the Heritage Hotels chain, the Hilton Hotel, and hotels in most of the main parks. The family owned Brookside Dairies, which had taken over much of the urban market for milk. They still had vast tracts of land in the Rift Valley, on the coast and along the Nairobi–Thika road.[132] They were rumoured to possess farms and businesses in Brazil, and to be worth more than Ksh20 billion (US$250 million). Moi had remained friendly with Mama Ngina, and the Moi and Kenyatta families were in business together. The Commercial Bank of Africa and Euro Bank were believed to be part-owned by the two families. They also had joint interests in transport, shipping, hotels, the media and land. These links gave Moi another reason to favour a Kenyatta as his replacement. Without clear institutional mechanisms or any precedent to protect him, Moi had reason to be fearful of his future under another president.

What Moi did not do was promote his own children as potential successors. He and his estranged wife Lena had eight children. They were now all adults, and increasingly active both politically and economically. However, Moi appeared dissatisfied with several of his sons. Raymond Moi was a quiet individual with a chequered business past, who had been vice-chairman of KCC before its collapse and a director of a failed bank. Philip Moi was alleged to have links with foreign criminals and to be associated with customs evasion at Mombasa port.[133] Jonathan Moi had stayed close to his mother after they split. The only Moi brought into the 'family business' was his youngest, Gideon. By the end of the decade, he was grooming Gideon to take over his Baringo Central seat when he retired.

Unresolved Land Problems

Land Theft and Land Rights

Land rights and land law remained one of Kenya's most intractable problems. In November 1999, Moi appointed a presidential commission of inquiry into land issues, headed by Njonjo. The commission toured the country, taking submissions on land policies, squatters, the clashes and theft and misappropriation cases. It reported in November 2002, just before the elections.[134] It did not rake over old misdeeds, but its recommendations included a complete overhaul of national land law, with more stress on agrarian reform alongside private land registration, and a new national land authority.

Nonetheless, state land continued to be stolen. Public toilets, playgrounds, parks, schools and medical centres were all alienated and sold. In 2000, it emerged that donors had refused to fund the revival of the Kenya Meat Commission after they discovered that Jackson Mulinge (ex-minister for lands) had acquired the site.[135] Even the KWS saw attempts to grab parts of national parks and to obtain mining concessions inside Tsavo.[136]

Disputes over settler immigration to the Rift Valley continued. Ntimama continued to espouse 'indigenous' land rights, and sought international support for his campaign to restore Kajiado and Narok to primordial ethnic purity or to receive compensation from the British or the Kenyan state for the Maasai dispossessions of the 1900s, reaffirming the significance of the communal model of historical land rights, at least in some communities.[137]

The future of Lonrho's EATEC farms continued to divide the Kalenjin and to challenge the 'willing buyer, willing seller' model in the Rift. By 1997, Lonrho wished to sell its remaining land in Eldoret South. Over the next three years, local Nandi tried to raise funds to buy the farms or to have the state buy them and allocate land for settlement schemes. They were, however, frustrated by the 'willing buyer, willing seller' model, which valued the land at prices higher than they could pay, and by backroom deals that saw chunks allocated to powerful individuals.[138] The same process took place and the same tensions developed elsewhere in Uasin Gishu when farms came up for sale. The popular perceptions that the 'land of your ancestors' was eternally yours (even if your family had never lived there) and that the poor had a right to land remained strong, 45 years after the creation of individual land title. Ethnic nationalism amongst the Nandi deepened, and MPs Kirwa, Sambu and William Ruto took advantage of this to cement their popular credentials.

Land Ownership and Registration

Over most of the country, formal and informal land subdivision continued, alongside a parallel consolidation into fewer, larger producers. In some areas, at least, the processes of differentiation begun during colonial rule appeared to be reaching the predicted outcome. A study of a Makueni village showed that in 1965 the richest 20 per cent of farmers owned 40 per cent of the land. By 1996, this had grown to 55 per cent, while the share of the poorest had dwindled from 8 to 3 per cent.[139] With virtually no empty land left, the poorest subsistence households now had to survive on their shrinking landholdings, work for larger farmers, or abandon agriculture to chance their fortunes in the urban areas. Off-farm incomes were now near essential to survival for small farmers. Farmers with access to salaried employment had better education, housing, food and savings, and could buy land and labour from others. With declining social mobility as formal employment opportunities shrank, families without such access suffered from Kenya's unstable producer prices and collections, a lack of cash and a spiral of declining investment and yields.

Consolidation into a few large farms was slowed, however, by population growth and by unusually strong cultural factors. The desire for land remained deep-rooted, even in those born and bred in the city. Even though many elites did not intend to cultivate their lands personally, the acquisition and exploitation of land (using the labour of others) remained a near-universal goal. The little available data suggested that commercial land sales inside the ex-reserves remained uncommon, in part because of informal discrimination that made it hard for people from other ethnic groups to buy land. Local land control boards usually insisted that sellers demonstrate that they had other land elsewhere before approving sales.[140]

The debate continued on the long-term merits of the 'privatisation' of communal land (individual land demarcation and registration). While individual land title might be economically advantageous in high-potential areas, most farmers did not use their title to obtain credit anyway. Attention now centred on the policy's broader social and political implications for land use, inequality and poverty. The process itself proceeded with incredible slowness, beset by multiple contested claims and an absence of alternative land for those eventually dispossessed. Most northern pastoralist regions were still Trust Lands, without individual land title, and even Meru was not fully demarcated. In western Kenya, although registration had been conducted in the 1970s, few residents had collected title deeds or regularised their inheritance or sale. Land registration processes appeared inconsistent, with some types of rights confirmed immediately, while others took decades to establish. KANU appeared to be using registration, like everything else, as a political tool, with surveyors deployed in constituencies where support for the party was stronger.[141]

The Politics of Forest Excisions

Most of Kenya's forest cover was now gone, legally or illegally excised for settlement or cut down for timber, often with the help of the foresters paid to protect it. Unconstrained logging in water catchment areas in Mount Kenya, Mau Narok and the Aberdares was drying up riverbeds and reducing water levels in dams. Most hardwood trees were gone, logged for handicrafts. Population growth drove further cultivation, and urban development consumed land, forcing agriculture outwards.

As a result, politicians regularly demanded that forests be degazetted for settlement or cultivation. Ministers duly degazetted large tracts in 1999 and 2001 (some of which had been cleared long ago), much of which ended up in the hands of senior individuals. The list of those allotted land in the Mau Narok, released a decade later, included the commissioner of lands himself, Moi's family and close allies. Given the value (both financially and politically) of state land, it was not coincidence that the chief conservator of forests and the commissioner of lands were both now from Moi's Baringo Central constituency.

In response, the 1990s saw a concerted effort by NGOs to resist the destruction of Kenya's remaining forests. The Green Belt Movement of Wangari Maathai was the most effective, creating huge publicity and claiming by 1999 to have planted more than 20 million trees.[142] In 1999, logging was banned in most forests, closing down much of the sawmill industry, but nonetheless it continued in secret.

Forest land was particularly valuable and therefore at risk in Nairobi. There were violent conflicts over the demarcation, sale and clearance of parts of Karura forest in north Nairobi in 1999. During 1995–7, the government had secretly excised then sold dozens of plots to well-connected individuals, who then sold them to parastatals and wealthy Asians. Most records showing to whom the land had been sold or given had vanished or the companies buying it appeared not to exist. The result was more violence, as activists, led by Maathai, tried to disrupt the land demarcation and plant seedlings. Police, GSU and security guards injured more than 30 people in January and February 1999, including opposition MPs. The conflict not only raised Maathai's international profile, but also raised the stakes around such corruptly acquired lands, indicating that it might not remain forever in the hands of those who had acquired it. However, it did not lead to trees being replanted.

The Challenge to Pastoralism

The challenge to pastoralism as a lifestyle and economic model continued. There was evidence of a structural pauperisation of northern pastoralists since the 1980s, with stock levels falling below sustainability, and more forced into urban areas by drought, insecurity, the availability of food aid and the commoditisation of the rangelands.[143] Government services in northern districts remained almost non-existent, with no bituminised roads, and few schools or medical facilities in the North-East, 40 years after independence. For the southern pastoralists, the picture was more mixed. Sedentarisation, land subdivision and straddling were widespread, and inequality was growing, but successful commercial meat production was raising household incomes and access to food.[144]

There was at the same time, a resurgence of academic interest in pastoralism.[145] This reflected both a new understanding of the sustainability of pastoral societies and a conscious effort by the Kenya government to promote pastoralist identities. Ntimama was a particularly assertive representative of Maasai identity and the pastoralist lifestyle at home and overseas. Ironically, however, a government that settled agriculturalists saw as grossly biased in favour of pastoralism was seen by academics as presiding over its decline. The growing commercialisation of livestock production (with massive increases in the number of cattle sold commercially during the 1990s) weakened networks of mutual assistance amongst pastoral communities, as had been seen amongst agriculturalists decades earlier.[146] There was growing evidence that those taking up sedentary occupations were more exposed to drought than those who remained herders.[147] Poverty alleviation programmes were now discouraged from forcing sedentarisation on pastoralists.

The threat to pastoralism was worsened by the security crisis and the expansion of cattle raiding, which now affected virtually every pastoral district. As a mobile asset, cattle had always been a target, but until the 1980s, most raiding was for personal wealth and status. From that time on, commercial stock theft became an increasing problem. In the words of Suzette Heald, 'Today raiding can be regarded as yet another branch of the informal economy with its widespread corruption.' With the inflow of guns from Somalia, Ethiopia, Sudan and Uganda and the complicity of government officials, stock keeping became increasingly dangerous. Heald noted here that, 'long term, this may sound the death knell not only of cattle rustling as an occupation but for the pastoral sector as a whole: agro-pastoralism will give way to agriculture.'[148]

The Shambles of Constitutional Reform: Part II, 2001–2

The Constitution of Kenya Review Commission

Out of the chaos of the constitutional reform initiative, a new hybrid CKRC emerged in January 2001, a last chance for consensual reform. In 2000, Odinga's Parliamentary Select Committee had appointed renowned Kenyan Asian constitutional lawyer

Yash Ghai to lead its review. However, Ghai recognised the impossibility of solving the problem without a dramatic change in attitude. The Ufungamano group, too, was ready to compromise, having been unable to sustain its momentum. In March 2001, despite concerns amongst hardliners in both KANU and the NCEC, Ghai persuaded the Ufungamano group to merge with the CKRC. The resulting constitutional amendment of May–June 2001 (a fourth layer of legislation) reconstituted the CKRC as a 27-person hybrid, combining both Select Committee and 10 Ufungamano commissioners, merging competing visions of the future. The opposition took up their Select Committee seats and the stage was set for a last chance.[149]

The goal was still a new constitution before the 2002 elections. The 2001 Act specified that the CKRC had until October 2002 to do its work. Once the new constitution was ready, it had to be submitted to a National Constitutional Conference and the resulting product would be put to Parliament, which could vote only to accept or reject the constitution *in toto*. If it was not adopted, a national referendum would be held. However, the Act was not entrenched in the Constitution, so Parliament could still vote to change this process if it saw fit.

Over the next year, the CKRC travelled and conducted civic education throughout Kenya and received 35,000 submissions from individuals, districts, NGOs and parties on how to reconstruct the political system. It soon acquired substantial legitimacy, which in turn led a nervous government to try to delay, weaken or undermine it.[150] Western governments were extremely supportive. The American government supported the CKRC both materially and technically and in parallel, donors gave Ksh2 billion to NGOs to conduct nationwide civic education, to enhance voters' understanding of their rights. However, by early 2002, the CKRC had not decided any substantive issue. The key choices it faced were whether to support *majimbo*, devolution or unitary government; the merger or replacement of the provincial administration with elected local government; and the choice of a prime minister or an executive president – much the same issues as had been debated in 1962–3. The battleground between competing visions for Kenya and competing power groups had shifted inside the CKRC. Many groups lobbied the commission, but there seemed no clear direction, and the timetable was impossibly tight.

The result was yet another crisis. With the 2002 elections approaching, no one knew whether they would be fought under the old system, a new constitution or a hybrid of some sort. Opinion polls confirmed that most Kenyans wanted the elections held on time, preferably under a new constitution, but, if not, then under the old. In June 2002, KANU members of the Parliamentary Select Committee, which continued to shadow the CKRC, proposed that Parliament be extended by four months (thereby also extending Moi's term) so that the CKRC could complete its work. This created an agonising conflict of interest between those favouring a new constitution, which would require Moi to stay on longer, and those favouring a quick opportunity to defeat KANU. Once the request became public, all 11 opposition members of the Select Committee resigned, opposing any delay to the polls. There was also opposition to an extension from civil society leaders, the British and Americans.[151] KANU issued the usual protests at interference in

Kenya's internal affairs, but in reality, Moi was ambivalent if not opposed to the extension. As it needed a two-thirds majority, which it was unlikely to obtain, the idea was shelved in July. In the end, the Assembly gave the CKRC an extension until January 2003.[152]

The Ghai Constitution

On 18 September 2002, at the last possible moment, the CKRC delivered a completely new constitution, informed by a strong decentralising and human rights spirit.[153] It had been written by Ghai himself and a few key aides. The constitution, which was widely published in the media, re-established a bicameral National Assembly, with a district- and province-based National Council sitting above the House, as the original Senate had done. A mixed-member proportional electoral system combining locally elected MPs and party lists would replace the first past the post scheme. The president would still be directly elected, but the 25 per cent rule was reduced to 20 per cent and the requirement added that he win an absolute majority of the vote. His powers were reduced, although he retained the power to declare war and a limited veto over legislation. The Assembly would have the right to approve presidential appointments. As expected, a prime minister would run the government (with two deputies), appointed by the president but chosen from amongst MPs and answerable to them. Devolution would return, with elected district and provincial councils (like the original *majimbo* regions) with the power to make law in restricted domains. The judiciary would be reformed, as would the police and the administration of public land. Constitutional amendments would require a 75 per cent majority of both houses, except for 'specially entrenched' provisions, which would also require a referendum. It was the most radical restructuring of Kenya's constitutional framework since independence, with many similarities to the original 1963 *majimbo* constitution, and it would have changed the nature of politics and the apparatus of government fundamentally.

On 17 October 2002, Select Committee chairman Odinga presented the bill for the new constitution to the National Assembly. The next stage was to convene the constitutional conference to ratify it. However, it was too late. Although Raila strongly supported the proposals, Moi and other KANU leaders denounced the work they had commissioned, calling the constitution a 'fantasy', 'alien', 'outrageous' and suitable for Europe, not Africa.[154] They were distressed by its sudden publication just as the succession was being settled and with the elections looming. The work required to implement the new constitution in time would have been immense and the impact uncertain. Although the CKRC argued that there was still time for it to be enacted, Moi feared that his plan for the succession was crumbling, and decided on a snap election to force the issue, while many of the opposition were also anxious for the 'final battle'. As a result, Moi dissolved Parliament on 25 October, eliminating a key component of the conference and ensuring there was no time to enact its proposals. Ghai could do nothing but postpone the conference. The reform process was frozen once more, to reawaken in 2003.

Succession Politics, January–June 2002

During the first half of 2002, the political tide flowed towards KANU in its quest for a third multi-party election victory. It seemed that the opposition was going to lose again, weaker than in 1997 and still leaderless. Moi's 'western' strategy, which appeared to position Odinga and Mudavadi as contenders for the top jobs, was paying dividends. Only the presidential succession stood in the way of victory.

The KANU–NDP Merger

On 18 March, the NDP and KANU formally merged in a conference at Kasarani stadium (known as 'Kasarani II'), where 6,000 delegates dissolved the NDP and elected a new KANU leadership. Odinga had worked tirelessly for this merger, although many of his allies feared they were embedded in a complex plot. Odinga believed that, with an opposition victory implausible, he would play a key role in the merged party, with a strong chance at the presidency. There were intense factional fights between the presidential contenders in the build-up to the merger, during which it became clear that the Rift Valley elite had abandoned Saitoti and Kamotho in favour of the new leadership of Kenyatta and Odinga. Moi was open that he wanted someone from this younger generation to succeed him.[155]

In a carefully choreographed election, Raila became secretary-general of the enlarged party, replacing Kamotho. The party kept the name KANU, but 'New KANU' briefly became its campaign slogan (along the lines of New Labour in the UK). Moi's position of party chairman was given additional powers, to ensure his continued influence after his presidency ended. At the same time, with echoes of the 1966 Limuru party conference, KANU's constitution was changed to keep its leadership options open, by creating four party vice-chairmen rather than one. As expected, Mudavadi took one post for Western, Ngala the second for the Coast and Musyoka the third for Eastern. There was one newcomer amongst the four: Kenyatta (Figure 11.11).[156] To his horror, Saitoti found that his name had been removed from the list of vice-chairmen he had seen the night before. Saitoti had been Moi's vice-president for as long as Moi had been Kenyatta's, but despite the recent undermining of his position by State House, Saitoti could not believe that he could be dumped so humiliatingly. He was wrong, and cameras captured the angry debate between Saitoti and Moi, during which Moi ordered him to *kimya* (shut up).[157] With voting by 'acclamation', Saitoti could do nothing. As a result, the vice-president lost his chance at the succession, turning him into a bitter enemy who would reward Moi's betrayal a few months later. The Kalenjin, meanwhile, were increasingly concerned about its future without Moi. Biwott was elected national organising secretary, but the community's loyalties were divided, with other lobbies backing Moi's son Gideon and Ruto (now director of elections) as future leaders.

Over the next few weeks, there were messy integration struggles in Nyanza reminiscent of the KANU–KADU merger of 1964–5. Oginga Odinga's old FORD headquarters in Kisumu was repainted in KANU colours. The unity was superficial,

11.11: Moi and the new KANU chairmen, March 2002

Courtesy: Nation Group Newspapers

though. Odinga tried to take control of KANU headquarters, but was frustrated at every turn by Moi loyalists. Although the Saitoti–Kamotho axis was out of contention, KANU still had at least five potential presidential candidates (Mudavadi, Musyoka, Ngala, Kenyatta and Odinga), four of whom were the sons of previous presidents, vice-presidents or ministers (see Figure 11.12). Like the general population, many KANU barons were uncertain about who would emerge as their candidate, and adopted a 'wait and see' attitude. Gradually, Raila and Kenyatta emerged as the frontrunners, with Mudavadi, Ngala and Musyoka pushed to the sidelines.

With KANU committed to a dot.com strategy, Moi was ebullient, confident that there was no doubt of victory. April–June 2002 was KANU's high-water mark. Everywhere, reports suggested that KANU was heading for a decisive victory. Key districts in Western and Coast provinces 'knew only KANU'.[158] Several opposition MPs defected to the ruling party during April, May and June.[159] The opposition's support appeared limited to the Kikuyu, Embu and Meru, the Bukusu and Kamba. In June 2002, the *Nation*'s view was that if he stood, 'Mr Kibaki will this time have to work even harder to retain his base as the leading Kikuyu candidate, let alone extending his appeal across ethnic boundaries.'[160] Despite Kenya's economic problems, insecurity and corruption, KANU appeared about to win a third victory.

Opposition Alliances

The opposition was also preparing for the elections. On 18 January 2002, the first step towards a change of government occurred when the three opposition leaders established another national alliance. Known as the National Alliance for Change

11.12: Political dynasties

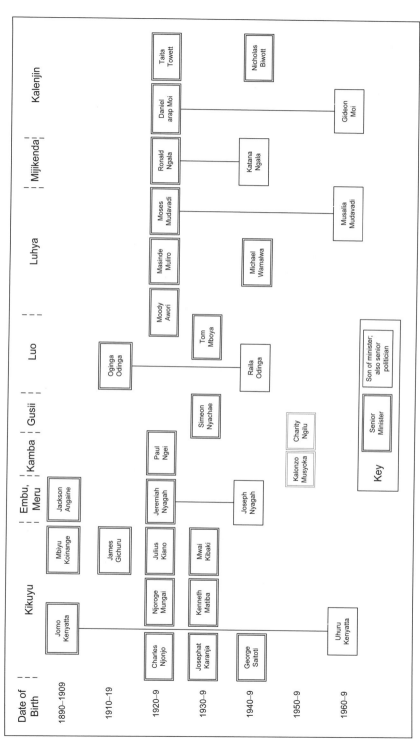

Source: Various

(NAC), it combined Kibaki's DP, Wamalwa's FORD-Kenya and Ngilu's NPK. Several other groups, including part of the SDP, Willy Mutunga for the KHRC and Kibwana from NCEC also signed the NAC 'memorandum of understanding' (MoU) in February. However, their unity was superficial: no presidential candidate had been agreed, while FORD-Kenya luminaries such as Kituyi were seeking an alliance with Nyachae instead.

Overshadowed by events in KANU, NAC struggled to make much impact. Efforts to find a neutral presidential candidate (an NGO or church leader such as Musyimi) failed. Not only would such a choice undermine the electoral machines of their leaders, but it was probably too late to build up a political unknown into a potential president. Instead, NAC seized on the CKRC's proposal to create the position of prime minister, as this would allow them more posts to share out. Talk began of a new party that all the NAC allies would join, matching the KANU–NDP alliance. In June 2002, Kirwa's UDM also joined the NAC alliance. There was still a fear amongst the other opposition parties of being swallowed up by the DP, leading to the idea of an 'alliance constitution' that could bind all parties together, but allow each to keep its distinct identity. By June, however, NAC still had no presidential candidate. Local factions jostled for advantage, as NAC had declared it would field only one candidate in each constituency.[161] Many parliamentary candidates campaigned without declaring which party they were for, uncertain of both the government and the opposition candidate, and so unable to tell which side to join.

Meanwhile, Nyachae, Kones and their allies were developing FORD-People as the base of a third national alliance, luring figures such as John Keen and Gitobu Imanyara into the party, and making overtures to other ex-KANU A leaders such as Ntimama. Nyachae's alliance was known as the Kenya People's Coalition (KPC), consisting of FORD-People, Safina, the Labour Party of Kenya, and individuals from the NCEC. Unlike NAC, however, everyone knew they were supporting Nyachae's candidacy. Seeing the crisis to come when KANU and NAC chose their candidates, Nyachae positioned the party to take on unhappy leaders from both alliances. He established links with disaffected KANU figures from the Coast and made inroads in the Rift and Central Province.

In July 2002, NAC and FORD-People held talks about a shared ticket or alliance. However, the deal fell through and, soon after, Ngilu's supporters registered a change of name for the National Party of Kenya to become the National Alliance (Party) of Kenya or NAK. NAK would be the host party for the alliance.[162] Wisely, NAK announced it would not nominate a presidential candidate until KANU announced its own.

Roles Reversed and a Fatal Mistake

Moi Passes the Baton, July 2002

By early 2002, President Moi was set on passing the baton. Although some suggested that he finesse the constitutional reform crisis into a sixth full term, he wanted to retire. In fact, he had already decided by 1998 to give the party's nomination to Kenyatta. He was influenced in this choice by younger politicians, particularly his son Gideon. Moi wished to pass on a united country to his successor, and believed that only a KANU Kikuyu president could achieve this. Although the fiction of a contest continued, it is likely that the seduction of Raila into KANU was a fraud from the start, and that Moi never intended to hand over the state to a man he had imprisoned for nine years. However, he delayed his announcement as long as possible, and instead used his younger allies, such as the recently rehabilitated Ruto (35) and Julius Sunkuli (41), to build up Uhuru ('Project Uhuru'). During the first half of 2002, these brash ministers bragged that they were Moi's successors, and endorsed Kenyatta as their candidate.[163] The bandwagon in favour of Uhuru gained speed, with the backing of most Rift Valley MPs (although Biwott remained sceptical).

On 29 June 2002, Moi confirmed that he would stand down and would soon name his successor. He still refused to anoint Kenyatta explicitly though: many in the party were hostile, believing the choice of a Kikuyu was a fatal mistake. Odinga was the centre of resistance. There were reports that Moi asked Musyoka, Ngala and Odinga to endorse Uhuru as his successor at State House on 5 July, but they refused to commit themselves. Instead, Raila took Moi on head to head, with a series of statements in which he set himself directly against Moi's wishes. Nonetheless, on 28 July 2002, Moi took the plunge and declared formally that Kenyatta would be his successor. The other contenders now appeared committed to back an amiable Kikuyu who had never been elected to anything, and whose main credentials for office were his family's name and wealth, and his inexperience.

The same day, 28 July, NAC launched the National Alliance (NAK) in Mombasa, with a logo of a flaming torch.[164] Political parties qualified for 'corporate membership' in the new body. Despite rumours of rifts over the choice of presidential candidate, NAK appeared to be preparing to fight as a bloc.

'Project Uhuru', Mungiki and the Kikuyu

At this point, there were stirrings of resentment, but KANU's grip remained strong. Politicians from all over the country declared themselves for Uhuru, despite the fact that many had not even met him until recently.[165] The *Standard* and *Kenya Times* supported Uhuru's candidacy, with some backing from the *Nation* as well. Television saw wall-to-wall coverage of him, replacing Moi as the lead in almost every KBC bulletin. An opinion poll in August now put Uhuru ahead of all the other candidates.[166]

As Uhuru toured Central Province and Nairobi in May–August 2002, he received a rapturous reception from ex-opposition supporters, now converted to support KANU by the lure of power for the Kikuyu. Without a clear opposition candidate, it appeared inevitable that KANU would win Central Province, and dozens of southern Kikuyu opposition leaders defected to KANU.[167] Particularly galling for Kibaki was the defection of his old ally Karume in August. One Safina MP was given a Cabinet post in return for his defection.

Meanwhile, Uhuru and KANU were preparing for the election. There were reports that Uhuru's campaign budget was Ksh15 billion (US$200 million), to be raised from foreign donations, allies and the Kenyatta family fortune.[168] The state machinery was reluctant, but there were signs that it was stirring into action in his support. Uhuru was receiving briefings from the intelligence services, while his security detail was seconded from the state. Behind the scenes, a team of Rift Valley leaders was coordinating his campaign, including Gideon Moi, Hosea Kiplagat, Ruto, Sunkuli, State House Comptroller John Lokorio and Biwott.

There was now another link between KANU and the Kikuyu: a Kikuyu religious sect, known as Mungiki ('the Multitude', 'the masses' or 'a united people'). Part traditionalist religion, part self-help group and part criminal mafia, it had emerged from the growing sense of alienation amongst poor Kikuyu. Mungiki espoused a return to animist religions and opposed women's liberation, Western influences and Christianity.[169] It also represented a revival of the Kikuyu ethnic nationalism that had underlain Mau Mau and which British victory and independence had delegitimised. During the 1990s, it had gained immense influence amongst poor young Kikuyu. The sect's origins were in Laikipia in the 1980s, and many early members had been radicalised during the 1992–3 ethnic clashes, evicted from their lands like the squatters of the 1940s. It also drew strength from the poverty that KANU's policies and structural adjustment seemed to have brought on the Kikuyu. Mungiki provided a social welfare organisation for the poorest of the poor, crusading against drunkenness, drug addiction and prostitution. It used oathing and religious techniques to build and retain loyalty.

As a violent, Kikuyu-focused movement appealing to the marginalised and talking of revolutionary change, Mungiki raised echoes of Mau Mau.[170] It was therefore a serious concern to the government, which outlawed the group in 2000, repressed its meetings and jailed its members. Despite this, the movement grew, centred in Kiambu, Nairobi, Laikipia and Nakuru, and was believed to have 2 million members by 2002.[171] It was well organised and financially secure. Acting as a criminal mafia, Mungiki took over *matatu* routes during 2000–1, and operated mob justice in Kikuyu-dominated shantytowns. There was evidence of the sect's involvement in drug dealing and murder. At some point, the movement also acquired wealthy Kikuyu allies, including incumbent MPs and even ministers. This reflected a common radical ethno-nationalism, but equally important was the desire of some politicians to use Mungiki to support their own agenda.

In the run-up to the elections, there was a bizarre change of stance by KANU. In late 2000, Moi had made a secret deal with Mungiki, fearful of the security implications of the group's alleged conversion to Islam, giving it more of a free hand.[172] In 2001, KANU entered into a brief alliance with the outlawed sect, seeking Kikuyu youth support for Uhuru. After Mungiki leaders declared their support for Uhuru in March 2002, police harassment abated, despite the group's killing of 23 people (most Luo) in a Nairobi slum in the same month. There was a remarkable rally on 21 August 2002 during which several thousand armed Mungiki members marched through Nairobi, under police protection, and the sect campaigned for Kenyatta in the 2002 elections.

Several Mungiki officials were nominated as KANU parliamentary candidates, and they were supplied with army Land Rovers to help them campaign for Uhuru.

It was not to last. The negative reactions to the association of the educated Uhuru with a Kikuyu-chauvinist mafia contributed to a sudden reversal of policy before the polls. Uhuru flatly disowned Mungiki on 6 October and its Chairman Maina Njenga, KANU's candidate for Laikipia West, had his nomination revoked.

The Rainbow Alliance, July–September 2002

During July and August, Moi's strategic mistake in forcing the nomination of Uhuru and sidelining his strongest supporters became apparent. Rather than obeying Moi as expected, there was a mass rebellion. Seven senior ministers – Vice-President Saitoti, Kamotho, Odinga, Musyoka, Ngala, Mudavadi and Ntimama – defied Moi's orders and made common cause in demanding a free election for KANU's presidential candidate. Mudavadi, Odinga, Ngala, Musyoka and Saitoti each declared their candidacies for the nomination between 27 July and 14 August and received support from many in their respective ethnic communities. Odinga and his supporters openly challenged Moi to a street brawl over the nominations. There was booing and heckling when Moi tried to endorse Uhuru in a visit to Kisumu.

In early August, the seven ministers began touring the country under a new banner, that of the 'Rainbow Alliance'. They were campaigning for a change of plan by Moi, and for a fair vote in the KANU presidential nominations. Still KANU secretary-general, Odinga was the most aggressive rebel, the originator and organiser of the Rainbow Alliance idea. Over the next few weeks, the rebels held rallies nationwide, while the pressure mounted on them either to obey Moi or to resign from KANU. Although leaders from various ethnic groups and factions continued to declare their support for Uhuru, it became clear that there was little enthusiasm for Moi's choice outside the southern Kikuyu.

Moi's response to this unexpected rebellion was measured. Rather than a mass sacking, he followed two strategies in parallel. First, he tried to persuade the rebels one by one to obey his wishes. On 7 August, he succeeded in 'turning' the long serving but politically unambitious Ngala, who withdrew from the race and announced his support for Uhuru.[173] Coast residents excoriated Ngala as cowardly, showing the degree to which central control was already slipping. Moi's second strategy was to threaten the real rebels by sacking their lieutenants. The first to fall were assistant ministers Fred Gumo and Kamotho, sacked as warnings respectively to Mudavadi and Saitoti. However, a meeting of KANU leaders on 14 August ended in chaos, as the dissidents still refused to submit to Moi's will, and the rebellion continued. Secretary-General Raila announced that there would be a secret ballot to choose KANU's presidential candidate, though few believed him. Attempts to summon an emergency Cabinet meeting were thwarted, as the dissidents refused to attend. On 30 August, Saitoti himself was sacked, only minutes before he resigned from the government.[174] The split in KANU was widening. By September 2002, most Central, Rift Valley and North-Eastern Province KANU leaders had declared for Uhuru;

Eastern and Coast were divided; while Nairobi, Western and Nyanza leaders were overwhelmingly against.

On 5 September, Mudavadi also blinked. Bowing to Moi's entreaties, he too abandoned his quest for the nomination and declared his support for Uhuru. His constituents, fired by the rebellion, were disgusted. In his place, the rebels persuaded the elderly Moody Awori to represent Luhya interests, and their campaign continued.

On 7 September, Moi launched Uhuru's campaign at a rally in Nakuru that was attended by 20 Cabinet ministers, 80 KANU and opposition MPs and six district commissioners.[175] Their Rainbow opponents held a parallel rally in Mombasa, still demanding a free ballot in the KANU polls. During September, Moi sacked three more pro-Rainbow assistant ministers, but rather than falling silent, each dissident reaffirmed his commitment to the rebellion, and their popularity in turn encouraged further defiance. As influential leaders in their own right, the Rainbow rebels' meetings attracted large crowds in traditional KANU strongholds (see Figure 11.13). Most were not harassed, there were no police assaults; rather it was several pro-Uhuru rallies that were disrupted. As the rebellion mounted, KANU candidates began to drift to safer parties, fearful that the electorate was about to revolt. Moi accused his ex-supporters of betrayal.

11.13: Rainbow rebels, 6 September 2002, *left to right:* Kamotho, Musyoka, Saitoti and Odinga

Courtesy: Nation Group Newspapers

NAK Chooses Kibaki

In September, the Rainbow Alliance began meetings with NAK to determine if there was common ground if they were forced out of KANU. The alliance, while it was a powerful force, knew it could not stand alone and by definition it had no leader. On 15 September, NAK, the KPC and the Rainbow Alliance held a joint public rally for the first time.

Before any deal was announced, however, on 18 September NAK unexpectedly declared that it had already selected Kibaki as its presidential candidate.[176] This was a pragmatic choice. With Uhuru as KANU's candidate, to nominate a non-Kikuyu would drop the entire Kikuyu vote into KANU's hands, while Kibaki was the most experienced politician with the broadest popular base. He also had the advantage, from the viewpoint of his allies, of being elderly, aged 71, and having apparently promised (without putting it in writing) to give up the post after one five-year term.[177] Wamalwa was announced as NAK's vice-president, and Ngilu as its future prime minister, in the expectation that such a role would be created with the implementation of the new constitution.

Work to build a three-way 'super alliance' continued, though it was dampened by Kibaki's selection. FORD-People began to back away from a deal, but Nyachae continued parallel talks with the Rainbow leaders.

Rainbow Defects, 13 October 2002

Raila and others continued to demand a fair vote at the KANU nominations, and Moi's last-minute efforts to bring them back on board failed. Finally, with the 'Kasarani III' Delegates' Conference a day away, on 13 October Odinga, Ntimama, Awiti and Awori all resigned from the government. Odinga declared: 'We have publicly disagreed with Moi over candidates. We have requested for a level playing ground. Our requests have fallen on deaf ears. There is no possibility of reconciliation . . .'[178] A still-hesitant Musyoka followed the day after. The break was now complete.

The Rainbow Alliance announced that it had taken over the moribund Liberal Democratic Party (LDP). Rainbow leaders appointed themselves as interim LDP officials, choosing Kamotho as secretary-general and Luo Job Omino as chairman. The defectors' decision not to join NAK or FORD-People but to create a third opposition structure was to resonate through 2003–10. Soon after, the LDP signed a second memorandum of understanding with FORD-People, committing them to fielding one presidential candidate.

The Rainbow revolt was elite led, with virtually no ideological content, but it condemned the regime to defeat. If the Rainbow team had not left, KANU would have surged to another victory, as NAK and FORD-People were far too weak to defeat it. If he had wanted a KANU victory, Moi had mishandled every stage of the revolt. He should not have offered the presidency to Kenyatta, whatever the wishes of the dot.com generation. If he had to do this, then he should have ensured that it appeared a fair and legitimate victory. He had also mishandled the Rainbow

Alliance. Not only did his divide and rule tactics fail, but his drip-fed sackings only emboldened them. Finally, after the Rainbow defection, facing a real prospect of opposition victory, he could have used state harassment to weaken the opposition and rig the ballot. He did none of these.

October 2002: The Die is Cast

KANU lost the election on 14 October 2002, though its death throes continued for two more months. On that day, the 4,500 KANU delegates elected Kenyatta (see Figure 11.14) unopposed as their presidential candidate. Accepting the nomination, he committed himself to constitutional reform and the fight against corruption.

On the same day, NAK, the LDP and the KPC announced their transformation into an umbrella party, to be known as NARC (an acronymic blend of National Alliance and Rainbow Coalition).[179] A rally in Nairobi attended by 100,000 people inaugurated the new 'super alliance', at which the coalition's leaders, including Kibaki, Saitoti, Nyachae, Odinga, Musyoka, Wamalwa, Ngilu, Awori and Orengo declared that they would choose a single presidential candidate to face Uhuru. To the surprise of many, and the anger of other contenders, Odinga unexpectedly offered Kibaki the job, with his rallying call '*Kibaki anatosha*' (Kibaki is enough).[180] It was a radical shift from his previous alliance with Nyachae, designed to ensure that the Kikuyu community remained with the opposition, and that the argument over the presidency did not split NARC as it had KANU and FORD.

Over the next few days, virtually the entire Luo community defected from KANU to the LDP, the third time Raila had led them through a shift of party. Many other KANU supporters followed suit. NARC announced it would field a single candidate for each parliamentary seat. Thirteen smaller parties also joined the coalition, including the Anyang' Nyong'o wing of the SDP, and NGOs such as the KHRC openly backed the anti-KANU ticket.

A week later, on 22 October, NARC formally endorsed Kibaki as its presidential candidate (Figure 11.14). In reality, there was little choice. Inside NAK, Wamalwa and Ngilu had already conceded. From the LDP, Saitoti lacked a mass following. The opposition needed a senior Kikuyu to avoid a rout in Central Province, and the choice of Odinga would have divided both the nation and alliance, since most Kikuyu would have joined an 'anyone but Raila' party at the drop of a hat. There was, of course, no open election as the rebels had demanded when in KANU. Although Kibaki was undisputed as their presidential candidate, there was little else that NAK, the Raila group and the other Rainbow dissidents had in common. It was an alliance of convenience. Their sole basis for unity was their opposition to Moi's choice of successor, and their belief that they had a real chance of victory. All else – policies, principles and memoranda – must be subordinated.

The sole exception was the KPC, which continued to insist on an election for the combined candidate, and on 20 October, Nyachae abandoned the alliance and declared he would go it alone.[181] There were rumours that KANU encouraged this, hoping to split the opposition as it had done in 1992 and 1997.

11.14: Mwai Kibaki (*left*) and
Uhuru Kenyatta (*right*), 2002

Courtesy: Nation Group Newspapers

To cement their partnership, NAK and the LDP agreed a third memorandum of understanding. In this, the parties agreed a power-sharing formula. In return for allowing Kibaki the presidency and Wamalwa the vice-presidency, Odinga would become prime minister, and a number of other senior appointments were agreed, to take effect once the constitution was reformed.[182] There were, however, two versions of the MoU agreed at different times: a private one with specific positions for specific individuals, and the other made public on 22 October, with a general commitment to a government of national unity and an 'equitable' distribution of seats. NARC also established an informal 'summit' of eight leaders to coordinate activities, chaired by elder statesman Awori. NARC chose as its symbol NAK's African torch, but also used the Rainbow symbol in its campaign.

The 2002 Elections

Election Mechanics and Monitoring

The long-awaited election campaign finally began when Moi dissolved Parliament on 25 October and the ECK announced that elections would be held on 27 December. The terms of office of Kivuitu and the 10 commissioners appointed in 1997 expired just before the polls, leading to concerns that Moi might drop Kivuitu and the election might be disrupted. However, he reappointed the independent lawyer.

For the first time for decades, non-election-related voter registration drives had been conducted in 2000 and 2001, the first step towards continuous registration, which was introduced in late 2002. A final opportunity was given to register in February 2002. In the end, there were 10.5 million registered voters, four times as many as in 1963. Far more men (5.6 million) than women (4.8 million) registered, reflecting enduring differences in political participation. Kenya's population had finally started to age, however: only a third were under 30.[183] The registration process proceeded well this time, but many people were still unable to obtain ID cards. Worse, many of those on the register had died, as there was no effective process to remove them.[184]

The anomalies created in 1962–3 continued to distort Parliament's representativeness. A vote in Ijara in North-Eastern Province, for example, was 10 times more powerful than a Nairobi vote. However, the boundary changes of 1996 had rebalanced the ethnic books a little. While the over-representation of pastoralists and the Kalenjin continued, outside the urban areas there was no obvious bias amongst other major groups (see Figure 11.15).

The election process was much the same as in 1997. The main difference was that this year, the ballots would be counted and announced at each of the 14,000 polling stations, reducing the risk of stuffing during the transfer to constituency headquarters. Voters could now also mark ballots with any symbol, rather than just an 'X', while illiterates could nominate a friend to help them. Presidential candidates now had to be supported by at least 100 voters from at least five provinces, and to pay a Ksh50,000 nomination fee, to deter spoiler candidates.

For the first time, the elections were computerised, with the ECK distributing details of candidates, registration statistics and polling stations electronically in advance. As a result, they deleted at least 133,000 double registrations.[185] Because of concerns about abuse, it was decided to rely only on the electronic registers, not the manual 'black books', to reduce concern over the addition of names between register publication and polling day. Learning the lesson from 1997, the ECK was also more careful in preparing the ballot papers, which it distributed to the districts well before polling.

Both local and foreign observers monitored the election once more, as usual funded by the donors. In contrast to 1997, the donors' response in 2002 was slow, and election tourism made a return to popularity. The EU provided the largest foreign team, with 22 long-term and 138 short-term observers. The US Carter Center, the African Union and the Commonwealth also sent smaller teams. There was no central observation centre. On the domestic side, the religious groups who had played a role in 1997 (the CJPC, Hindu Council, Supkem and NCCK) came together once more.

11.15: Registered voters per seat by ethnic group, 2002

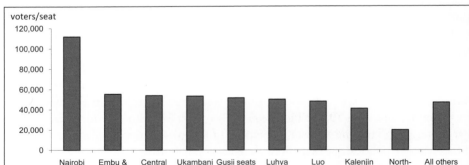

Source: Electoral Commission of Kenya, *Registered Voters per Constituency (Revised October 2002)* (13 November 2002)

This faiths-led initiative was expanded in June into a broader team, known as the Kenya Domestic Observation Programme (K-DOP), with the addition of the IED, Transparency International and the Media Institute. This 'forced marriage' was again driven by donor demands for unity (in return for money). Other donors funded the IED to put observers in each constituency and conduct a parallel count. This year, the domestic observers worked closely with the ECK in the run-up to the polls.

Civic education was a stronger feature of the run-up to the polls. The donors had funded a major civil education campaign in 2001–2.[186] The ECK and donors also supported NGO-led voter education campaigns and a monitoring programme for electoral violence.

KANU Crumbles

As November progressed, KANU's campaign was going nowhere. Moi had run out of room to manoeuvre. The economy was in crisis, the party split in two, the government near-leaderless as Moi prepared for retirement and the opportunities for electoral malpractice had been reduced by years of reforms. KANU faced a crisis like that of 1991–2, but this time, it could not wait a year for the opposition to split.

Seeing the growing wave of support for NARC, politicians deserted KANU en masse. Even before the party primaries, for example, Minister Joseph Nyagah and ex-insider Mark arap Too had joined NARC. The later they left it to defect, the fewer rewards would be available for them and their communities if NARC won. Ex-MP Jarso Falana eloquently expressed why he and the people of Marsabit had abandoned KANU: 'Kanu has run out of pasture and water and we now have to move to greener pastures.'[187]

On 4 November 2002, after the dissolution of Parliament, Moi appointed Kenya's eighth vice-president: Musalia Mudavadi, chosen to sustain KANU's waning support in Western Province.[188] It was a year too late. Mudavadi did his best, noting that he was the first Luhya vice-president, but his unpopularity even in his own constituency was obvious. With Awori's LDP and FORD-Kenya united, safe KANU seats in Western began to crumble.

The Party Primaries

The 2002 party primaries were even more chaotic and corrupt than previous polls. K-DOP called them 'the most shameful, dirtiest, and violent phase of the 2002 general elections'.[189] There were now 51 registered parties, but the vast majority were one-man shows or of only regional significance. Effectively, there were three competing national coalitions.

Most primaries were conducted between 20 and 24 November. Many KANU and NARC polls were abortive and there were increasingly frantic reruns as the nomination date approached, but this year, the award for most abused process shifted to NARC. Several people were killed, most in Luo Nyanza, where NARC's victory was certain. There was also extensive violence in Western, also now an opposition stronghold, very often between LDP (ex-KANU) and FORD-Kenya factions. Returning officers were bribed to change results, voters driven away, boxes stuffed and voters imported. Bribery was rife in both NARC and KANU primaries: in Nyanza, the *Daily Nation* noted that 'Cash handouts to woo voters in four Migori constituencies marked the home stretch to today's NARC nominations for civic and parliamentary seats. Candidates' campaign teams criss-crossed villages throughout the night dishing out money to voters.'[190] Virtually every constituency reported cash handouts to voters, with rates varying from 20–50 shillings per person in poorer areas to several hundred shillings in Central Province. Patronage politics had reached its logical conclusion.

NARC held its primaries by 'secret ballot', using buckets as ballot boxes. It was difficult to tell who was a NARC member, however, so anyone who wanted to vote could do so. Much unhappiness was caused by NARC's decision to exempt its senior leadership from the bother of primaries, freeing them for the national campaign. Kibaki, Odinga, Awori, Ngilu, Saitoti, Wamalwa, Musyoka, Ntimama, Kirwa, Murungi, Kamotho, David Mwiraria, Noah Wekesa, Najib Balala and Omino were all declared nominated unopposed, to the frustration of their opponents. There was in-fighting everywhere between NAK and LDP candidates, enemies until a few weeks ago. In the event, honours were shared, with some seats in Kikuyu areas going to LDP rather than DP candidates and a couple of Luo seats won by non-NDP leaders. Losers included Kibaki's oldest allies Matu Wamae and Matere Keriri, both of whom lost the NARC nominations to newcomers, but Kibaki did not intervene to save them.

As before, most of KANU's nominations were conducted by queue voting. Voters queued up to find that counts had already occurred, or milled around waiting, while agents bribed them to change queues. A disturbing fact for KANU was that more than 30 of their candidates were unopposed: it was no longer an asset to be associated with the party. The FORD-People nominations were generally quiet, with little interest outside Gusii areas, where they were oversubscribed, chaotic and rigged. Elsewhere, the party acquired many last-minute defectors from other parties.

The need for rules to avoid serial defections was again apparent. Of the 210 incumbents, fewer than half ended up as the candidate of the same party as the one they had represented at the dissolution (even assuming that DP, FORD-Kenya and NPK candidates for NARC were effectively in the same party). More than a third of candidates had changed party at least once between September and November.

Presidential and Parliamentary Nominations

The presidential nominations on 18 and 19 November went smoothly. The three main candidates presented their papers without incident. Orengo refused to stand down (as NARC would not give him their parliamentary nomination), and his rump SDP nominated him as its candidate. The only other candidate was David Waweru Ng'ethe of the tiny Chama Cha Umma party.

Parliamentary nominations were also conducted over two days, 25–6 November. To some surprise, the ECK permitted candidates from the various parties under the NARC umbrella to stand as 'NARC' candidates, rather than as candidates of their own party. This decision was a key contributor to their victory. Without it, the parties would have had to agree somehow which one was going to be the NARC candidate. The result would have been that other candidates would have reverted to and stood on their home parties, fragmenting the alliance vote – as was to happen in 2007. There was little violence and little evidence of state malpractice. KANU still had the most candidates – covering 209 of 210 seats, while NARC had 208. FORD-People was the only other party with a national coverage (185 seats), while the SDP had 96 and Safina 59. There were 1,035 candidates in total from 38 parties, the highest number yet: 60 per cent were newcomers to the ballot paper. Only 44 (4 per cent) were female.

For the first time, the ECK decided that, rather than accepting whoever was nominated on the day, it would take whoever the parties listed as their candidate, whether they had turned up to be nominated or not. As a result, there were angry protests when candidates found that their names had been removed from ECK records. In several seats, one party had nominated two candidates, because a candidate had forged his nomination papers or different factions in party headquarters had issued competing certificates, and now the party had to pick one. In a few seats, NARC abandoned its own nominees because of suspicions about their intentions, and in some Kalenjin seats it replaced its candidate with the loser in the KANU primary, deeming them to have a better chance. Nothing would stand in the way of victory.

NARC's fragile unity nearly collapsed in the last days of the primaries, when Wamalwa signed nomination papers for three unsuccessful Bukusu candidates to stand on a FORD-Kenya ticket against the official NARC nominee. Evidence of infighting amongst the FORD-Kenya leadership, Wamalwa's candidates were to compete against the most prominent Bukusu leaders apart from himself – Musikari Kombo, Kituyi and Wekesa. However, Wamalwa was forced to backtrack and his nominees were somehow removed from the ballot papers (even though they had been formally nominated in the meantime).

This year, no one was completely unopposed and few candidates were willing to concede defeat during the campaign either. The only unchallenged candidate was the wealthy and controversial 38-year-old Gideon Moi, who duly replaced his father as MP for Baringo Central after all his (already nominated) opponents conveniently decided to stand down.

The Campaign

For the first time, the opposition went into the election with a real expectation of victory. The state was mostly neutral and KANU was not flush with funds, as the Central Bank had countenanced no inflationary money printing. As a result, all three presidential candidates were working from a similar base: well funded and relying on modern communications techniques to sell their messages.

Much of the action in the early stages was based around individual civic and parliamentary candidates. Once the nominations were over and the candidates chosen, however, campaigning became more structured and made more use of national issues. Money was even more influential than in 1997. Poverty had now privatised the voting system, so that the majority of voters saw their vote as a commercial asset, and reports from all over the country suggested that voters were no longer willing to vote for free.[191] There was bribery with cash, clothes, *chang'aa, busaa,* bread and sodas. Although money alone could not win an election, it was essential to be able to compete. Candidates who rejected personal development responsibilities and argued that the government should provide such services from taxation were increasing rare and usually unpopular.

Regional agricultural issues dominated the debate: sugar in Western, coffee in Central and Kisii, milk in Central and the Rift. Insecurity was a serious concern, and a driver for anti-government feeling in more than a third of districts. Clanism and localism remained important in much of the country. In the north and North-East, clan elders still met before the nominations to decide which candidate to support.

The choice of two Kikuyu candidates de-ethnicised the national campaign, a notable change from previous polls.[192] Anxious to avoid a violent backlash, both Kibaki and Kenyatta promised no witch-hunt against Moi after the polls, effectively offering him amnesty for past misdeeds, although others were not so forgiving. There was little direct bias by the provincial administration. Few candidates were harassed or had their meetings banned. There was some violence, and two died in clashes between supporters. For the first time, the ECK fined some candidates for inciting violence. There was more trouble on the Gucha–Trans-Mara–Migori border between Maasai, Gusii and Luo, merging tensions over land and livestock with differing party allegiances, but the result appeared unaffected.

With the experience of two multi-party elections to call on and better survey methods, opinion polls became more accurate. All told a similar story. Kibaki would win with between 50 per cent and 68 per cent of the presidential poll to Uhuru's 28–40 per cent, with Nyachae at 6–15 per cent, though analysts predicted a far closer parliamentary poll, factoring in the skewed constituency distribution and KANU's expected dirty tricks.

NARC's Campaign and Campaign Promises

The NARC presidential campaign team criss-crossed the country, reaffirming their unity. Although it did not need any policies to win, NARC had clear views on the changes needed in Kenya and made extravagant promises that would come to haunt it in office. Education was a major campaign theme; an often-repeated promise was the introduction of free universal compulsory primary education. NARC also undertook to reform public universities, review the 8-4-4 system and to pay teachers the salary increments that KANU had said the country could not afford.[193] This gained it the support of teachers nationwide.

An end to corruption was another easy pledge to make. Kibaki promised 'zero tolerance for corruption' and a mandatory declaration of wealth for all officials and politicians.[194] The party promised root and branch reform of the civil service, the police and the judiciary. NARC also pledged to restart the constitutional review process and implement a new constitution within 100 days. This was the centrepiece of the deal between NAK and the LDP, which would create enough senior positions to share amongst its unwieldy leadership.

Other commitments included improved security, administration and tax collection, the reconstruction of infrastructure and rapid economic growth as a result. Little attention was paid to the economic effects of most of their promises, however, or to the likely reaction of foreign donors, who had already suggested financial support would not immediately be restored whoever won, and who were demanding continued commitment to the government's expenditure framework. There was a widespread and naive hope that simply stopping corruption would provide much of the needed money.

The real action, as ever, was in local organisation, financial inducement and negative campaigning against the corruption and incompetence of the government. In Western Province, Mudavadi was a particular target, with Musyoka travelling to rallies in Western in order to dismiss him: 'Mudavadi is a coward. We started the Rainbow Alliance with him, then he was frightened and he bolted out.'[195] Awori predicted that Mudavadi would be Kenya's only vice-president never to attend Parliament in that capacity.

Both NARC and KANU made extensive use of newspaper, radio and TV adverts and billboards (see for example Figure 11.16) and produced campaign manifestos, though few bothered to read them. It was rumoured that Saitoti funded NARC's advertising costs; other funds were raised from Kenyans abroad.[196] NARC's campaign was enlivened by the omnipresent song 'Who Can *Bwogo* [scare] Me?' which was bought and converted into a tribute to NARC and its Luo leadership during their campaign. As a result, KBC refused to air it by November.[197] NARC also made use of SMS (text messaging) for the first time to criticise KANU and sell itself outside formal media channels.

A key moment in the campaign came on 3 December, when Kibaki was involved in a near-fatal car crash. With a broken arm and ankle, he was sent for emergency treatment in London. Wamalwa too was ill and in London. NARC's campaign continued undaunted, however, with Raila taking up some of Kibaki's engagements and the team splitting into two or even three groups. Kibaki returned to Kenya on 14 December to a hero's welcome.

Uhuru and KANU's Campaign

In the hands of the Young Turks, and without some of the key 'machine' politicians who had moved to the LDP and FORD-People, KANU fought a very different campaign from that of 1997. For the first time, there was a real split between party and state. Rather than Moi, PCs and dignitaries assembled on the dais, a youthful

11.16: NARC billboard, Nairobi

Courtesy: Charles Hornsby

Kenyatta mingled with the people. He appeared at times to present himself as the underdog, eschewing (unless Moi was there) most of the apparatus of power. He ran his campaign with a team of public-relations specialists and journalists more suited to an American than a Kenyan election. Uhuru campaigned enthusiastically in the final stretch, visiting Central Province, Eastern, Kisii, Trans-Mara, North-Eastern, the Coast, Baringo and Nairobi between 16 December and the end of campaigning on 24 December. Even though he did everything that could be expected from a youthful, media-friendly politician, he struggled to deliver the vote on the ground without the cash and intimidation of the past.

In policy terms, KANU and Uhuru were far from explicit. They promised a new start, and contrasted their youth and vigour with the aged heavyweights of the opposition. Uhuru made a generalised commitment to change and to a new constitution, but his room for manoeuvre was limited. Photographs of President Moi dominated KANU's manifesto, and their campaign was overshadowed by the legacy of the patriarch and the issue of his future role.[198] When he did campaign, Moi backed Uhuru, defended KANU's record and criticised the LDP defectors as unprincipled 'tribal chiefs'.[199] However, Moi was clearly tiring and had little enthusiasm for the campaign. There was growing speculation that he had no fundamental objection to a Kibaki presidency, as long as some accommodation could be reached on his security and that of his family and business associates. His visit to Kibaki and Wamalwa in hospital in London on 7 December was – many believe – the point where he conceded defeat.

Uhuru's stronghold was his family's home turf in Kiambu and Thika districts. There, his candidates – many of them ex-opposition leaders who had joined him when his chances looked good – had the edge. In much of the Rift and the semi-arid areas, the KANU machine worked as before, albeit without the enthusiasm or money of the past. In the opposition strongholds, Kamba and Luhya areas, however, it disintegrated completely. The provincial administration began to distance itself and NARC leaders to behave like ministers in waiting.

There was some desultory use of state resources to campaign for Uhuru. Government vehicles were used to transport KANU supporters, and administrators campaigned for KANU in safe seats such as Baringo, North-Eastern, Lamu and Mount Elgon, but the mass abuses of the past were over. There were no ethnic clashes. The freedom to abuse state resources and divert funds had diminished as governance practices tightened and privatisation moved on. In a break from the past, the NSIS declined to provide political intelligence to KANU, leading to friction with State House.[200] Money was in shorter supply. Few campaign organisations like YK'92 emerged, and those that did collapsed once they realised that KANU leaders were unwilling to spend their own funds on Uhuru's campaign. Moi too was reported to be giving little to support Uhuru.[201] There were reports that insiders raised some funds through the hurried payment of questionable 'pending bills' to contractors, but it did not appear to be large enough to change the course of events.

The sole area where the presidential machine functioned as before was in the KBC, which gave TV airtime overwhelmingly to Uhuru's campaign. The IPPG legislation, which required public broadcasters to give coverage to all opinions, was ignored. In September 2002, KBC gave 92 per cent of its political airtime to Kenyatta or Moi, 7 per cent to Kibaki and virtually none to anyone else.[202] Even when the KBC covered opposition events, it frequently managed to lose the film or the soundtrack of their speeches. After Uhuru's presidential nomination was broadcast live, for example, KBC reported a 10-minute technical hitch that lasted exactly as long as Kibaki's nomination.

The difference now was that KBC was no longer the sole broadcaster. Although competing broadcasters were available only in urban areas, KTN and Nation TV took a different line, both giving a slight excess of coverage to NARC and Kibaki.[203] On the radio, the position was similar – Uhuru's campaign dominated KBC, with 76 per cent of the coverage. However, the six main private stations offered a more balanced picture in the areas they reached.[204] On the positive side, there were few direct KBC attacks on NARC, and KBC did accept opposition advertisements. The mainstream press was reasonably neutral in the campaign proper, with only the *Kenya Times* and *The People* openly biased.

Nyachae's Campaign

Despite an active and well-funded campaign, Simeon Nyachae saw his support dwindle. When KANU was strong and the opposition split, Nyachae had looked like a serious contender, and politicians flocked to him. Now that Kibaki had a united alliance behind him, it was clear that Nyachae would come third. As a result, despite his strong candidates and deep pockets, there was little he could do but watch his support shrivel outside the Gusii.

Where KANU and NARC's campaigns were a combined effort, with many leaders and interests represented, FORD-People's presidential campaign was a one-man show, based around Nyachae's financial muscle and experience (in his wife's words, a 'product not a project'). As with Matiba in 1992, he emphasised his experience, ability and business acumen as proof that he could pull Kenya out of the doldrums. Nyachae too made ambitious commitments, promising to reform the 8–4–4 system, create 1 million jobs in two years, increase incomes by 50 per cent, and introduce constitutional reform within 90 days.[205]

Polling Day and the Count

Polling day, 27 December, was wet. Voters were slower to assemble, having learnt from the past. There was little trouble and the process was smooth. However, there was some violence and bribery and campaigning near polling stations.[206]

This year, the count was conducted at each polling station, in front of observers and party agents. It still took a full two days and nights, as officials struggled to obtain the correct paperwork, and then to check, collate and report the results. Bad weather delayed polling and counting in some seats; in others, a paralysis appeared to set in as the result became clear. NARC's lead gradually grew, until by the morning of 29 December, observers reported that Kibaki's (uncertified) presidential margin was greater than that of the remaining seats to declare. With the winner clear, but without all seats declared, the ECK summoned a press conference on the afternoon of 29 December. Despite stating that the criteria for election had not been formally satisfied, as many presiding officers had failed to send in their tallies, Kivuitu bowed to massive pressure and declared Kibaki the winner, based on the provisional results. He announced:

> Hon. Kibaki had the majority votes having scored 25 per cent of the registered votes in seven out of the eight provinces in the country. He therefore provisionally satisfies the criteria upon which a presidential candidate must be declared. The ECK therefore declares Hon. Kibaki the President of Kenya.[207]

Official results were only announced on 3 January 2003, days after Kibaki's swearing-in. Luckily, they differed little from the provisional results. Kivuitu was not to have such freedom of manoeuvre five years later.

The Results

As predicted, Kibaki won an easy presidential victory. With 3.6 million votes, he took 61 per cent of the poll, double Kenyatta's 1.8 million, and won Nairobi, Central, Eastern, the Coast, Western and Nyanza. He also took 25 per cent or more of the vote in all eight provinces, the first time this had happened. He was far more popular than NARC's parliamentary candidates. Kenyatta won only the Rift Valley and North-Eastern. Nyachae polled virtually nothing outside the Gusii community, where he took the entire vote. For the first time, voting (outside the Luo and Gusii) was not obviously ethnic. The Kikuyu, Meru, Mijikenda, Somali and Maasai all split their votes. Amongst the largest ethnic groups, only the Kalenjin and Somali backed Uhuru en masse, and even then only by a 2:1 margin (see Figure 11.17).

In Parliament, NARC did just as well, winning 125 seats to KANU's 64, as the electoral system began to favour them as the largest party (see Table 11.2). KANU's parliamentary losers included 10 ministers, amongst them once-untouchable figures such as Sunkuli, Mudavadi and Shariff Nassir. Biwott was one of the returnees, however, as were other senior Kalenjin. New faces from KANU's side included insiders such as former CID Director Noah arap Too and ex-PC Yusuf Haji. Amongst NARC's winners were several radicals, including Maathai, Koigi wa Wamwere, Mirugi Kariuki and the former NCEC head Kivutha Kibwana. In FORD–People, while the Gusii candidates were all successful, Kones lost in Bomet. There was little comfort for the minor parties either. George Anyona was overwhelmed by the Nyachae wave, and all the SDP candidates, including Orengo, were defeated.

The new Assembly was the oldest yet, with an average age of 50. Although the LDP was extremely influential in NARC, the coalition's direct inheritance of personnel from KANU was modest.[208] Of the 1963 MPs, only two remained: Kibaki himself and G. G. Kariuki. Nine women were elected, the largest number yet.

11.17: Presidential voting preferences of the largest communities, 2002

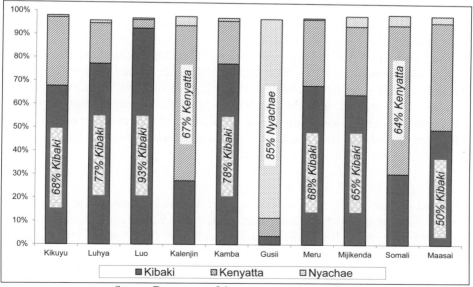

Source: Percentage of the vote in mostly mono-ethnic rural constituencies

Table 11.2: Parliamentary results by party, 2002

Party	Seats Won	% of Seats	% of Votes
NARC	125	59.5	50
KANU	64	30	28
FORD-People	14	7	8
Safina	2	1	4
Sisi kwa Sisi	2	1	1
FORD-Asili	2	1	1
Shirikisho	1	0.5	0
SDP	0	0	3
Others	0	0	4
Spoilt	0	0	1
TOTAL	210	100	100

Source: Various

KANU's stronghold in rural Coast Province delivered the biggest surprise of the election. KANU lost vote share in 20 of 21 seats, most dramatically in Giriama areas, reflecting disenchantment with Ngala's desertion of the Rainbow rebellion and years of neglect. KANU won only seven seats and even Ngala himself lost, defeated by an outsider who admitted he had never expected to win.[209] Western Province also voted overwhelmingly for NARC, and voters even evicted Mudavadi. The Kamba did the same. In Nyanza, NARC achieved a clean sweep of the Luo seats, and Raila delivered 93 per cent of the Luo vote to Kibaki, though the turnout was much lower than in 1997. In the Gusii districts, in contrast, Nyachae and FORD-People won all 10 seats and 85 per cent of the vote.

The collapse of KANU's Rift Valley vote was also dramatic, and had more impact than KANU's unpopularity in Western and Nyanza combined. Figure 11.18 shows the absolute vote received by KANU in the 1992, 1997 and 2002 presidential polls by province. The failure to mine the Rift Valley vote – due to reduced rigging and the loss of their patron – contributed as much to KANU's defeat as did its poor showing elsewhere. If every Luo had voted for Uhuru, Kibaki would still have won.

Turnout

One odd feature of what was otherwise a successful election was the low turnout. At 6 million of the 10.4 million voters, it was only 57 per cent, the lowest of all the multi-party polls. The highest turnouts were seen in Kibaki's Nyeri and Moi's Baringo, the lowest (again) in Mombasa and Nairobi. A contributory factor was the high number of dead voters on the register, since the registrations of deaths process in rural areas was ineffective; 7–10 per cent of the voters on the register had probably

11.18: KANU's presidential votes by province, 1992, 1997 and 2002

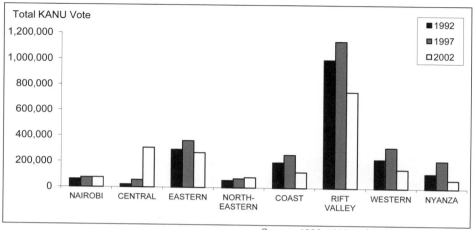

Source: 1992, 1997 and 2002 election results

11.19: Change in actual presidential vote, 1997–2002

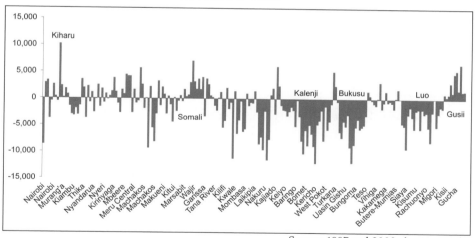

Source: 1997 and 2002 election results

died. Excluding the register-ageing effect by looking at the change in actual votes from 1997, turnouts fell most dramatically amongst Luo, Bukusu and Kalenjin, reflecting the absence of Odinga, Wamalwa and Moi from this presidential contest (see Figure 11.19). Another reason may have been a reduction in electoral abuses. In contrast, the vote rose amongst the Gusii and the Somali.

Why Did NARC win?

NARC's win was a victory for the same type of organisation and momentum previously created by KANU. The alliance was a national coalition, superficially united, and it benefited from a short-term bandwagon effect. With Moi out of contention, the 2002 election was always going to be difficult, but his choice of a Kikuyu as his successor broke his 'social contract' with his strongest supporters and infuriated key lieutenants, while the Kikuyu did not desert Kibaki for Kenyatta en masse.

Over a decade, KANU had frittered away its remaining legitimacy in violence, corruption and economic inefficiency. It could still buy individual elites, but there was little pleasure in supporting the ruling party, even in its strongholds. The formidable machine that Moi had built over three decades had seen him through in 1997, but Moi's heart never seemed to be in this election. The machinery of government splintered with so many members of the elite now in NARC. Kibaki, Musyoka, Saitoti, Kamotho, Ntimama and Awori gave the opposition the gravitas, experience and money that at times made KANU seem the opposition party. There was almost as much tradition and experience in NARC's parliamentary candidates as in KANU's.[210] Though KANU had more ministers and more years of ministerial office, it was unable to match the combination of Kibaki's gravitas and Odinga's energy.

The final reason for the size of NARC's victory was that, in the end, KANU faced a single opponent. Nyachae's campaign collapsed in the last three weeks. Although he had sustained the momentum up to the presidential nominations, the NARC wave was so overwhelming that his loss became predictable and therefore inevitable.

Was the Election Free and Fair?

The government also lost so decisively because it did not cheat. For the first time, the elections were basically free and fair. None of the parties had allowed a free choice of its presidential candidate, but the polls and counts went smoothly, the only ones since Kenya's re-democratisation so far to do so, and not coincidentally, the only ones in which ethnicity did not dominate. There was violence, bribery and government interference in the campaign, but it did not change the result. There were few cases of overt abuse during the vote or count, and those that did occur were small scale. There was still pressure to vote according to the preference of the majority in an area, and some voters were coerced to vote for candidates – mainly NARC – but the sustained abuses of the past were absent. KANU fought this election fairly, in part because it chose to, in part because cheating was more difficult. Not only were officials more experienced, rules tighter and communications better, but the size of the gap made it hard to persuade officials to cheat, since it was clear that Kibaki was going to win. Only in a close poll could rigging change a result.

There were some questionable results. In Nambale in Western, officials were caught bringing blank ballot papers, ink and seals into one count and there were reports of substituted polling station returns.[211] There were also concerns about the result in Kaiti in Ukambani and Tinderet in Nandi. There were 37 election petitions submitted after the polls. In these, more allegations emerged, such as the issuance of title deeds for land in Kiambaa before the election by Karume and Mama Ngina Kenyatta.[212] In Fafi in North-Eastern Province, the loser claimed that chiefs had threatened voters that their wells would be poisoned if NARC won.[213] There were many other allegations of irregularities, including the bribery of returning officers.[214] In fact, there was evidence of bribery by all parties in virtually every constituency. Transparency International cynically noted that the reason the 2002 election was considered free and fair was the outcome as much as the process, since bribery could well have influenced the result.[215]

There was talk that KANU leaders had considered a last-minute vote injection on 29 December as their defeat became clear, but no such event occurred. The parallel counts conducted by observers provided detailed results online, which were picked up by international news organisations, so the abuse would have had to be large scale and blatant. Finally, the margin was just too great. If the results had been close, the temptation to intervene might have been irresistible, but only the most grotesque abuse could reverse the NARC tide. There were reports that a meeting of government leaders on 29 December discussed the possibility of obtaining an injunction against Kibaki being declared president, due to 'serious irregularities', which would see Moi remain in power until new elections would be held. NSIS head Boinett's opposition to the idea, on the grounds it would cause chaos, helped them decide to accept the results.[216] Moi similarly dismissed suggestions by some military allies of a coup.[217] Kenyatta too made an explicit choice to avoid chaos and accept the results. Soon after Kivuitu announced Kibaki's victory, Uhuru issued a personal statement: 'I accept your choice, and, in particular, now concede that Mr Mwai Kibaki will be third President of the Republic of Kenya. Kanu and I will respect him and his position in accordance with the Constitution.'[218] Because of Moi and Uhuru's decisions, a potential disaster became a triumph of democracy.

Observer Responses

Both foreign and domestic observers were delighted with the elections. The Commonwealth observers called them the 'best the country has ever had'.[219] The EU and the Carter Center agreed. K-DOP described them as '. . . a big step forward for democracy in Kenya', though it decried the violence and bribery of the party nominations and the behaviour of the KBC.[220] K-DOP's 18,000 observers noted virtually no ballot box stuffing, vote theft, counting abuses or substitution of results, and independent counts confirmed both presidential and parliamentary results in almost every case. The IED noted, '. . . Kenya has come of age in the democratisation process; the political preferences of Kenyans and voters were generally respected.'[221] The ECK's performance was unanimously praised. Because of the results of the election, there was little real interest in the final reports of any of the observers. As far as most Kenyans and foreign governments were concerned, the elections were manifestly free and fair, because KANU had lost.

A New President

With KANU defeated, the state security apparatus began to break down. Without any rules for a presidential transition, on the night of 29 December, police abandoned State House, unsure of their loyalty to or role in a Kibaki administration. Nonetheless, within 24 hours, a bloodless transition was complete.

On 30 December 2002, Kibaki was inaugurated as Kenya's third president, in a chaotic all-day event in Uhuru Park that transfixed the nation. He was sworn in by Chief Justice Chunga while seated in a wheelchair, in front of 500,000 people and the presidents of Tanzania, Uganda and Zambia. It was the first presidential handover to take place through the ballot box in Kenya's history.

The handover saw Moi make a regretful but supportive speech of departure. However, he was humiliated by a booing and resentful crowd, and his former assistant pulled few punches about the task that he faced. Kibaki said he was taking over in a country 'ravaged by years of misrule and ineptitude'. He promised economic renewal, an end to corruption, cabinet government and functioning institutions and announced that: 'The era of road-side decisions and declarations is gone. My government will arrive at decisions through teamwork. We will restore the authority of Parliament and the independence of the judiciary.'[222] A shocked Moi left the inauguration ceremony that afternoon, said farewell to his weeping staff in State House and departed by helicopter for Kabarak. His 47 years in Parliament were over. NARC's problems were just beginning.

Conclusions

KANU did not lose the 2002 elections because of economic decline, insecurity, corruption or administrative incompetence. It lost because its coalition was torn apart by a factional and personal dispute over the presidency. Change would have come in the end. Liberalisation had challenged the control of the state, eliminating entire areas of patronage. The playing field had been levelled, driven by the combination of popular protest and Western patronage. However, KANU's defeat in 2002 was the result of the decisions and passions of a few powerful political grandees in an environment that had become more conductive to change. Out of defeat, KANU had also achieved something no one expected: it had conceded gracefully and handed over power to a cross-party coalition with widespread support and a mandate for structural reform. Kenya was now a true democracy, it appeared. There was a powerful outpouring of emotional support for Kenya's ability to change its course.

Change was needed in most areas of state policy and practice. Corruption, economic decline, collapsing services, the police, the legal system, land policy, the education sector: each was a vast problem with no easy solution. The years since 1990 had shown how intertwined politics and economics were in Kenya. The fledgling NARC coalition's economic achievements were soon to be overshadowed by their political side-effects.

Chapter 12

Back to the Future, 2003–2008

A New Era

The year 2003 awoke more hope in Kenyans than any since 1963. Forty years after independence, expectations were high and the NARC government had huge goodwill, both domestically and internationally. However, President Mwai Kibaki's administration was unable to shake off its legacy as an ad hoc merger of combatants. The brief honeymoon period soon ended and deeper pressures drove the allies apart. Just as in 1963–5, there were intrigues within the ruling alliance, and again it seemed the goal was to keep an Odinga out of power. A resurgence of ethnic and leadership disputes, combined with the unremitting debate over constitutional reform, left the government fighting too many battles. The new inner circle increasingly behaved as its predecessor had done: corrupt, intolerant and ethnically chauvinist. Dissatisfaction with the entire political system grew amongst many intellectuals, the underclass and the Luo and Kalenjin communities. As Stephen Ndegwa had predicted in 2003, the reform agenda stalled, NARC split along ethnic lines, economic recovery was not accompanied by structural transformation of state or society, and the 'disparate and ideologically unfocused' coalition fractured.[1]

NARC's priorities lay in the restoration of the public goods of the Kenyatta era: economic renewal, an end to ethnic violence and a campaign against corruption. After a slow start in 2003–4, the economy coughed into life, with improved resource efficiency and better performance in most sectors. Foreign aid resumed and the economy recovered, refreshed by greater economic rationality and less overt rent seeking in state decision-making. NARC's policies were little different to KANU's, but were implemented with greater enthusiasm and legitimacy. By 2006, Kenya was in a mini-boom. Security also improved, though here success proved harder to sustain. Initially, the anti-corruption crusade was simple and vote-winning, since so many KANU leaders were so corrupt and unpopular that it had little political cost. As well as cleansing the judiciary and evicting many parastatal executives, the government restarted the Goldenberg investigations and new revelations emerged. However, the lure of office and the insatiable demand for money to feed the political machine soon undermined these achievements. By 2005, the inability of the government to address corruption was apparent.

In parallel, resource allocation disputes, the implications of policies for different communities and the struggle to reform the constitution tore the coalition apart. Every decision was coloured by a resurgence of the same themes of cleavage that had dogged Kenya since the early 1960s. The ethnicisation of politics and zero-sum attitude to resource allocation decisions that had emerged with the executive presidency and been strengthened by its abuse left every decision and its ethnic and patronage implications contested. A series of constitutional conferences saw increasingly tense disputes over two issues: whether Kenya should introduce devolution and whether it should have an executive president or a division of powers between president and prime minister. Initial differences gradually turned into all-out war, destroying NARC from within.

By 2006, Kenya's political map had been redrawn into a new two-party model, in which ethnicity once more played a key role. Kenya went into the 2007 election in an atmosphere of increasing tension, in which the opposition appeared set for victory.

The New Government

Kibaki announced his government on 3 January 2003. His new team represented both wings of the NARC alliance, but created enduring problems. The Cabinet was slightly slimmed down, consisting of Kibaki, 24 ministers and long-serving Attorney-General Amos Wako, who had security of tenure. Only five (Kibaki, Raila Odinga, Kalonzo Musyoka, George Saitoti and Wako) had ever held ministerial office. Michael Wamalwa, like Oginga Odinga in 1964, was given the sinecure of vice-president without portfolio, responsible for 'national reconstruction'. Odinga received only a ministry, but a powerful one – Roads, Works and Housing, responsible for the rebuilding of the country's infrastructure. Ministerial dockets were restructured (Home Affairs recovered the police, for example) and the number of assistant ministers was cut back sharply, from 39 to 23, as a sign of the state's commitment to prudence. The government formed the smallest percentage of the House since independence (22 per cent).

The Cabinet was far better balanced ethnically and regionally than Moi's last two governments, with all eight provinces represented and only the Gusii amongst the major communities excluded, as NARC had no Gusii MPs (see Figure 12.1). Kikuyu representation was roughly the same as under Moi in the single-party era. Nonetheless, the Kikuyu and Meru influence in the Cabinet and amongst senior officials was considerable. David Mwiraria was a key appointment as finance minister. Shadow finance minister for many years, he was a close ally of Kibaki's, having been permanent secretary in Kibaki's Home Affairs Ministry in the 1980s. His Imenti neighbour Kiraitu Murungi became minister of justice and constitutional affairs (the same ministry Charles Njonjo had held in 1980–3). Nyeri MP Chris Murungaru became minister of state in the OP, responsible for internal security, taking on Nicholas Biwott's role as the president's 'fixer'.

NAK leaders dominated the Cabinet, taking nearly twice as many seats as the LDP. Kibaki bypassed most LDP ex-KANU ministers, including Joseph Kamotho, William ole Ntimama and Joseph Nyagah. The distribution of seats amongst the coalition partners was supposed to be based on the MoU of October 2002, which had agreed a distribution between NAK (13 seats) and Rainbow (9). However, NAK did better than agreed, with 14 ministers to the LDP's six to eight.[2] Two ministers came from neither party: Peter Anyang' Nyong'o (SDP) and Kipruto arap Kirwa

(UDM). The LDP's list of ministerial nominees was ignored. The LDP was furious and Kamotho and Ntimama led 26 MPs in a public protest, though Odinga remained quiet, recognising the public mood favoured consensus over confrontation.

The new administration contained five different interests. First, there were the old guard Gema technocrats of the 1970s, typified by Kibaki, Mwiraria, John Michuki, Matere Keriri and Kibaki's kitchen cabinet of Kikuyu allies such as Joe Wanjui and George Muhoho.[3] Second, there were the Young Turks of the 1990s who had entered politics as lawyers, academics and activists, typified by Murungi, Anyang' Nyong'o, Charity Ngilu and Musikari Kombo, though all were now part of the political establishment. Third, there were the newcomers, many of them businessmen with loose political allegiances, such as Amos Kimunya and Raphael Tuju (a Luo MP but with little loyalty to Raila). Fourth, there were the other Luo MPs, united in support of Odinga, who was also backed by several non-Luo who owed their loyalty primarily to him. Finally, there were the other ex-KANU Rainbow ministers and their allies, including Saitoti, Musyoka and Moody Awori.

The parties also chose their 12 nominated MPs. This year, with gender balance a major issue, most were women. Women also did well in the government; for the first time, three (Ngilu, Martha Karua and Linah Kilimo) were appointed to Cabinet posts.

At the top of the civil service there were also changes. Sally Kosgei lasted only four weeks as civil service head before she was forcibly retired. Zakayo Cheruiyot, Moi's permanent secretary for internal security, was sacked and questioned by police, and several other permanent secretaries were replaced, as was the commissioner for lands. Kibaki's old friend Keriri became State House controller, a key gatekeeper appointment. The LDP was also unhappy about the lack of consultation in the appointment of permanent secretaries. A surprising but popular appointment was

12.1: Ethnic composition of the Cabinet, 1963–2008

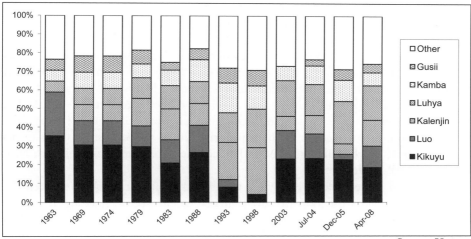

Source: Various

that of the director of Transparency International John Githongo, a Kikuyu journalist and anti-corruption consultant, as permanent secretary in the OP, responsible for leading the government's fight against corruption.[4] Working directly for Kibaki from inside State House, Githongo was to prove extremely effective, indeed too effective for the system to countenance.

Tragedy struck the new government within days. On 24 January 2003, a plane crash killed Labour Minister Ahmed Khalif and injured several others.[5] This was the first of eight deaths amongst NARC MPs in their first two years in office, in which four ministers (Khalif, Geoffrey Parpai, Wamalwa and Karissa Maitha) died, an extraordinary run of bad luck.

Flaws in the Government

Kibaki's government contained two crucial flaws from the moment of its formation: the divide between the LDP and NAK, and the health of its leader.

NARC was always an opportunistic alliance, with no ideology except KANU's defeat. Its leaders had been frank during the campaign that the goal of their alliance was power. Perhaps unluckily, its new parliamentary party was evenly split: 50 NARC MPs were LDP members and around 60 were in the NAK camp. The remaining 15 or so, most from the Coast and Rift Valley and with little loyalty to anything except NARC, held the balance of power. Kibaki understood the need to balance the factions in the party, both within NAK (between the DP, NPK and FORD-Kenya) and within NARC. However, he did not feel bound to ethnic or party parity, or to offer all elements equal weight in his counsels. Kibaki was a centrist, a believer in economic rationality and the best interests of all Kenya. He paid less attention – initially – to the need to balance regional and ethnic interests. As he had announced, his appointments would be made on merit, but his failure to give all parties equal weight in the Cabinet and as his advisers eventually undermined his other achievements.

The government's second key flaw was the health of the president. Kibaki's first days in office were marred by his car injuries. Then, in late January he suffered a stroke, which left him incapacitated for most of 2003. Although it was concealed as much as possible, he was visibly unwell in his few public appearances. As late as October 2003, during his visit to Washington, a Kenyan diplomat confided that he had introduced all his ministers in turn as 'Finance Minister Mwiraria'. By the end of 2003, Kibaki's health had improved – he had been forced to give up alcohol completely – but he never recovered the focus or eloquence of his earlier years. The effect was to create a vacuum at the top during 2003, and ministers and officials close to him (mostly Kikuyu or Meru) filled the gap. Confusion reigned, with ministers settling old scores.

Kibaki had never been renowned as a workaholic or decision-maker. As president, his hands-off 'non-executive' management style, choosing the right team and leaving them to get on with the job, was a novelty when compared to Moi's interventionism, but it faced serious challenges when the team captain

12.2: Gado cartoon on Kibaki's 'style'

Courtesy: Nation Group Newspapers

was ill, and the team contained historic enemies and conflicts of interest, as the Gado cartoon in Figure 12.2 suggests. Despite good intentions and a message of trust, accountability and transparency, in practice ministers set policy with little coordination or commitment to collective responsibility. Many Kenyans interpreted his style as weakness. In the words of the *Standard* in 2004: 'It beggars belief that a man boasting the vast political experience and glowing academic credentials Kibaki possesses would wilfully preside over the stunning mess that the coalition he heads has turned out to be.'[6]

By 2005 the analogy was more between Kibaki and another aged president: Jomo Kenyatta. Even after he recovered, Kibaki remained reclusive. The infighting between ministers continued, while Kibaki's personal authority was weakened by a series of embarrassing incidents in 2003–5 involving his wife Lucy, during which the existence became public of a second customary wife, Mary Wambui. There was growing evidence of behind-the-scenes Gema elite cartels – linking relatives and friends of the president with ministers, civil servants and security officials – similar to those around Kenyatta.

Many believed that Kibaki's accident and its effect on his health were the cause of the vacuum at the top, and that this led to the assumption of power by his Kikuyu and Meru allies, the continuation of corruption, and the splintering of the coalition. However, the truth is probably different. The conflict of interest in NARC was deep and the coalition fragile from the moment of its foundation. An active and assertive president could have controlled it, but nothing could disguise the deep-rooted differences between the ex-KANU and Odinga-dominated LDP and Kibaki's DP. Less than a month after the government had taken office, senior ministers were already predicting it would collapse.[7]

Reform and Restitution, 2003–5

The new government immediately embarked on changes in personnel, policy and style. In comparison with the last days of Moi, its achievements were substantial, but they could never satisfy the expectations they had aroused during the campaign. Inevitably, they blamed their predecessors for their problems, with Raila explaining 'We took over the government only to find empty coffers.'[8] Nonetheless, 2003–4 saw notable successes in education, the civil service, anti-corruption, the judiciary, parastatal reform, transport and land.

Educational Successes

One of NARC's greatest achievements was to deliver on its promise to bring the 3 million missing primary-age children into school. On taking office, ex-university lecturers Saitoti (education minister) and Kilemi Mwiria (assistant minister) faced the task of implementing the end to all primary school fees announced by Kibaki at his inauguration. Although enormously popular, the side-effects included a rush to the better schools, overcrowded classrooms, teacher shortages, and a Ksh5 billion hole in the government's accounts. Foreign donors helped where they could. The World Bank, which had pushed cost-sharing under Moi, backed Kibaki's populist commitment.

Despite a chaotic start, it was a success. By 2004 there were 1.3 million more children enrolled than in 2002 (see Figure 12.3). Gross enrolment rates jumped to over 100 per cent of eligible children. This achievement was trumpeted by luminaries such as Bill Clinton as one the greatest turnarounds in state provision for years in Africa. Others were more cynical. KNUT and some NGOs claimed that large class sizes and overstretched facilities had caused a decline in teaching standards, since teacher numbers remained frozen. It also further advantaged private schools, which already filled a disproportionate number of secondary places. The government also stressed that not only was education free, it was compulsory. In 2003, they rounded up more than 1,000 street-children in Nairobi and sent them to school.

Secondary student numbers also rose rapidly. In 2006, for the first time, more than 1 million children were in secondary school (though half still left school with only primary education).[9] Although the state provided most teachers, secondary fees for tuition, buildings, utilities and facilities remained high. By 2006, consideration was

12.3: Primary and secondary school enrolments, 1993–2008

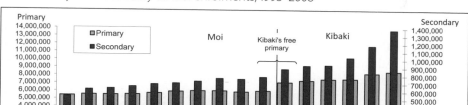

Source: Republic of Kenya, *Statistical Abstracts*, 2005, 2007, 2009

being given to abolishing secondary fees as well, and in mid-2007, during the election campaign, Kibaki committed himself to their progressive end. The government also quietly cut the 1985 quota system (by which 85 per cent of students in provincial and district schools had to come from the area) to 60 per cent, lessening the positive discrimination that the Moi government had preferred. Promises to abolish the 8–4–4 system, however, were dropped.

At the university level, numbers continued to grow, with nearly 80,000 under-graduates in six public universities by 2006 and 20,000 more in 11 private universities.[10] In 2007, Masinde Muliro University was established, finally giving Western Province its own university.

The second major challenge the government faced in the education sector was the payment of the 1997 salary award to teachers, which KANU had partially abrogated, but NARC had promised to honour during the campaign. However, the IFIs proved no more willing to countenance additional public expenditure under NARC than under KANU. Initially, therefore, NARC too refused to pay the 1997 award, citing 'resource constraints', but slipped the rises gradually through, culminating in the election year of 2007, when the government made the final Ksh9.8 billion of payments. In 2006–7, 21 per cent of the budget was devoted to education, a huge burden on the workforce.

A New Team, but the Same System

The new leadership soon cleared out Moi's nominees from most parastatals as well as the top of the civil service. During 2003–4, almost every Kalenjin parastatal executive was sacked, many tainted with grand corruption. Those evicted included the Kalenjin chairmen of the Communications Commission of Kenya, Kenya Airports Authority, KTDC, Nyayo Tea Zones, Kenya Revenue Authority and Telkom Kenya; the chairman and the chief executive of the Consolidated Bank of Kenya; and the managing directors of the ADC, Chemelil Sugar Company, East African Portland Cement, Kenya Seed Company and the Kenya Pipeline Company.

Some were questioned by police and a few charged with abuse of office. Two decades of Kalenjinisation were swept away in a year, and other Moi allies were also evicted, including Samuel Gichuru, fired as managing director of KPLC, and Uhuru Kenyatta's brother, sacked as chairman of the Kenya Reinsurance Company. Although a few senior Kalenjin did survive (and there were some new Kalenjin appointments), there were furious allegations of a witch-hunt.[11] Facing state displeasure for the first time since 1978, the Kalenjin community retreated into itself, seeking unity in adversity. The government's approach may have been rational, but it was certainly not politically sensitive.

Respected professionals replaced many KANU notables, but the clear-out also saw NARC loyalists take plum positions. A dozen defeated NARC parliamentary candidates (including Kalenjin Reuben Chesire, Tabitha Seii, Andrew Kiptoon and Francis Mutwol) were given diplomatic or parastatal posts, ex-KAF Commander Peter Kariuki and George Muhoho, Kibaki's campaign manager in 1997, also received parastatal jobs, as did NARC's director of elections and the DP's deputy secretary-general, while Wanjui became chancellor of Nairobi University. The government had shown that it shared its predecessor's view that parastatals were political sinecures and sources of patronage.

Reforming the Civil Service

One of the most urgent structural improvements NARC made in its first year was the clean-up of the OP, which had been a controlling hand on all ministries and had run many of the most lucrative portfolios directly, including the KWS, famine relief and AIDS control. There were also changes in the provincial administration. NARC's leaders swiftly removed the officials who had most obstructed them in the KANU era. Within a month of taking office, six of Moi's PCs had been removed (leaving only the one Luo and one Kikuyu PC), and by 2006 all eight had gone, just as Moi had done in 1979–82.

The new government was committed to cleaning up the civil service, cutting staff numbers but improving pay and conditions for those who remained. Salaries jumped for civil servants in 2004, to improve professionalism and reduce the incentive for corruption. It also permitted the restoration of the Kenya Civil Servants Union, banned by Moi. However, the tension remained acute between the finance ministry and the donors, looking for a lean civil service and lower spending, and the spending ministries, looking to improve conditions and services. Politically difficult retrenchment plans for another 21,000 staff remained on hold until 2004, but then began to take effect. A civil service strike in protest in 2005 was defeated. Performance contracts were introduced for parastatal heads and permanent secretaries. The government also introduced computerisation and electronic document management for key registries, including the Register of Companies, to improve services and reduce corruption. Another major change came in 2006, when Kibaki ordered that 30 per cent of all civil service recruitment be reserved for women, reflecting a growing nationwide focus on gender issues.

Cleaning up the Judiciary, 2003–4

While the civil service and parastatal system was cleansed, it remained intact. The judiciary, on the other hand, underwent root and branch reform. Within weeks of Kibaki's accession, Chief Justice Bernard Chunga resigned, rather than face a tribunal accusing him of partisanship and misconduct. He was replaced by court of appeal judge Evan Gicheru (a respected judge since 1988, and a Kikuyu). It was the first step in a programme of radical surgery. In October 2003, the state suspended from office 23 judges and 82 magistrates, nearly half the judiciary, following an investigation by (Meru) ex-KACA head Aaron Ringera that made shocking allegations of illegal and unethical behaviour.[12] Judges had routinely been bribed to give favourable judgements and had consorted and done business with criminals. Under intense donor pressure, Chief Justice Gichuru demanded those named by Ringera either retire or face investigative tribunals. Most chose to go quietly, though a few cleared their names.

The reform of the judiciary was one of the most radical changes of NARC's first year. Even so, it could not eliminate the vast backlog of cases, eradicate corruption in the courts or improve facilities; indeed, the lack of judges further delayed many legal cases. Also, where some lost, others gained, which in turn created new jealousies and fears. Some KANU-era lawyers were now frozen out of work, to be replaced by high-profile ex-opposition (Kikuyu) activists such as Kamau Kuria and John Khaminwa, who finally profited from their years of suffering. Further radical reforms of the judiciary were in the pipeline in 2005, but faded away as the country's political problems grew. By 2007, there were allegations of politicisation and tribalism in the appointment of NARC-era judges as well.

Fighting Corruption and Impunity

NARC's first 18 months were a period of great openness and the government's anti-corruption programme was ambitious, beginning with Githongo's appointment as Kibaki's anti-corruption adviser. Immediately after they came to power, the government seized back Kenyatta International Conference Centre from KANU. It had been built with government funds, but had become KANU property in the single-party era. By April 2003, Parliament had passed the two key laws donors were demanding: the Anti-Corruption and Economic Crimes Act and the Public Officer Ethics Act. All civil servants were given 90 days to declare their sources of income and assets (although the declarations remained secret). By 2004, KACA, now known as the Kenya Anti-Corruption Commission (KACC), had been restored and a permanent Kenya National Human Rights Commission established, alongside a special Cabinet committee on corruption and a commission on the irregular allocation of public land.[13] Western donors enthusiastically supported this and funded much of it directly. There was a mood of renewal and optimism.

For Moi insiders, 2003–4 was a period of great difficulty.[14] Their businesses faltered, relations deteriorated and corruption charges seemed imminent. Story after story emerged of blatant theft, and many of Moi's allies found themselves facing court proceedings, including Gichuru, investigated over US$2 million paid by IPP Westmont Power into the offshore bank accounts of a company he owned.[15] Hosea Kiplagat was forced to give up his chairmanship of the Cooperative Bank, and came under investigation for suspect property transactions. In 2004, ex-minister William Ruto and Commissioner of Lands Sammy Mwaita were charged with fraud and Gideon Moi, Joshua Kulei and ex-Commissioner Wilson Gachanja were questioned over the sale of government land.[16] The eponymous head of Mugoya Construction saw his once-untouchable company collapse and ended up a wanted man.[17] Nicholas Biwott was barred from entering the US under new legislation that allowed the US government to ban those suspected of benefiting from corruption. Many of the scandals mentioned in previous chapters became public at this time. The declaration of wealth process led to investigations into public officers who declared disproportionate assets, while several thousand were sacked for refusing to declare their assets at all. Thousands of forestry officers and procurement officers were suspended and vetted before being allowed to return to office. The police force too, found themselves the subject of reform efforts, facing exposures of malpractice at every level.[18]

Long-time insiders such as Kulei and Kiplagat tried to blend into the background, relinquishing their seats on many company boards and struggling to avoid indictment. Some, including Kulei, managed to obtain residency abroad, in case the situation worsened. In November 2003, Kulei gave up his nominee roles in most companies, and Moi's children took over their father's interests directly.[19] In 2003, the government hired Kroll Associates to investigate offshore assets held by Moi-era leaders, particularly Kulei, Gideon Moi and Biwott. Their April 2004 report traced at least Ksh78 billion (US$1 billion) in assets overseas, including cash in banks, real estate and hotel investments.[20] In March 2005, the UK *Observer* revealed more details of Kroll's investigation, suggesting that Ksh73 billion transferred overseas by 'influential officials' was in London.[21] Although accounts were frozen in the UK, little if any was actually recovered. Worse, the revelations harmed efforts to obtain more Western aid, as the evidence of its misappropriation in the past mounted.[22]

Amongst all this, former President Moi remained untouched. Throughout the Kroll investigations, Moi denied he had a single cent abroad. Despite the eviction of his allies, he was never charged with any crime. He appeared protected from retribution by an unwritten deal with Kibaki and the NARC leadership that offered him immunity from prosecution in return for his silence and tacit support for his successor, however difficult this must have been for both parties.[23] His backing for a peaceful transition in 2002 contributed to this grudging consensus at the top, as did the potential for violence if they did indict him. Western diplomats appear generally to have taken a similar view, that – much as in 1963 – peace and stability trumped righting old wrongs.

There were also revelations from another Goldenberg Commission of Inquiry, appointed in 2003 to find out what had really happened a decade before. The judicial inquiry, chaired by Judge Samuel Bosire, dominated the news for months, as testimony from Kamlesh Pattni and Central Bank officials exposed the scale and complexity of the thefts that had occurred. The report, presented to Kibaki in February 2006, concluded that Ksh27 billion (US$600 million) had been lost or stolen under the export compensation scheme, pre-shipment finance, foreign exchange abuses, unsecured loans and cheque kiting.[24] It indicted Pattni, Saitoti, James Kanyotu, Erik Kotut, Eliphaz Riungu, three permanent secretaries and other officials in illegal acts, and recommended them for investigation and possible prosecution. As a result, Saitoti resigned from the Cabinet.[25] Pattni, Kanyotu, Kotut, Riungu and Permanent Secretary Wilfred Koinange were eventually charged in court, but Saitoti managed to have the findings against him quashed. However, the inquiry concluded that while Moi must have been aware of what was going on, there was no proof that he had authorised his officials' actions. Pattni's statement that Moi had been a 50–50 partner in Goldenberg and had been paid his share in cash was disregarded as untruthful.[26] Moi was not forced to testify.

In 2004, another investigation began into Robert Ouko's death 14 years before. New testimony to a Parliamentary Select Committee reinforced suspicions that Special Branch or the GSU had murdered Ouko, and again implicated Biwott, Jonah Anguka, Hezekiah Oyugi and others.[27] It confirmed that witnesses had been bribed and threatened in order to give false testimony to previous inquiries. It seemed that President Bush had indeed met Ouko and jocularly suggested he might be a suitable successor to Moi. Inspector Troon testified in London that Moi had personally provided him with information, but had prevented him interviewing Biwott.[28] Evidence emerged that a key witness, the BAK Group representative, had been Moi's lover since 1980 and that Moi himself might have part-owned BAK, adding further confusion to an already murky picture.[29] This inquiry too fizzled out in 2005. Its report was drafted but not submitted until five years later, when it was unexpectedly tabled (and rejected) in Parliament. It alleged (subject to parliamentary privilege) that Ouko had been murdered in State House, Nakuru, in the presence of a minister, fearful that Ouko was seeking foreign support for an attempt at the presidency.[30]

There was now open discussion of the torture chambers of Nyayo House, to be turned into a national monument to remind Kenyans of their past.[31] The government also commissioned a report (funded by American donors) that recommended the establishment of a South African-style Truth and Reconciliation Commission, to review injustices since independence, but little came of the review.[32]

Land

The changes in the controls around government land were immediate. Lands Minister Kimunya revoked all the land transactions and forest excisions of the past four years, while Local Government Minister Maitha revoked recent local government allocations. The pressure grew on beneficiaries to return illegally allocated land before it was seized by force.

In June 2003, Kibaki appointed another commission to investigate the land abuses of the past. The Ndung'u Commission's report, presented to Kibaki in July and reluctantly published in December 2004, was political dynamite.[33] It indicted virtually every senior KANU leader, including Moi himself, his family, politicians, civil serv-ants and military officers for profiting from illegal government land transactions, housing allocations and forest excisions, and demanded that most of these awards be revoked. It suggested that 200,000 fake or illegal title deeds had been registered over the last 10–15 years, in many cases as a result of the actions of the president, the commissioner for lands and his deputies. The 'grabbed' land was mainly state or Trust land, including offices, military establishments, road reserves, public parks, bus parks, forests and cemeteries.[34] Much had then been on-sold to parastatals for vast profits, creating overnight millionaires who would then gratefully donate much of their gains to the politicians who had facilitated the transaction. To pre-empt further criticism, Moi himself offered a full audit of all his land acquisitions, and agreed to return anything that had been irregularly acquired.[35] The report also tarred some close to Kibaki, including Karume and Mama Ngina Kenyatta.[36] The system-atic nature of the abuses was further evidence – if any were needed – of the complete moral bankruptcy of the KANU administration and of the significance of land both as a patronage resource and as a source of easy money.

In the meantime, the damage done to the NSSF by a decade of resource extraction had become clear, and auditors reported that it had net liabilities close to Ksh14 billion. The NSSF committed itself to cut its land portfolio, but it was too late. Efforts to plug the gap by selling assets were ineffectual, as many of its plots were near-worthless because of their over-valuation, questionable legal status or occupation by squatters. Its administrative expenses were consuming the contributions of all workers to the scheme (Ksh1.9 billion a year).[37] The net effect was that most formal sector workers' pensions had been lost or stolen. In November 2004, Kibaki ordered the NSSF to initiate prosecutions against dozens of companies and individuals who had fleeced the organisation of Ksh15 billion over the years.

NARC had come to power committed to ending the destruction of Kenya's forests, and its MPs included environmentalist Wangari Maathai, awarded the Nobel Peace Prize in 2004. A Forests Act was eventually passed in 2005, to help secure Kenya's remaining forests and encourage commercial forestry. Illegal logging was reduced and some parts of Karura and Ngong forests repossessed, although the administration proved more reluctant to act when politicians and senior officials had been allocated the land.

Roads, Public Works and Urban Services

NARC came to power committed to improving services. Odinga, with one of the most high-profile ministries, faced a particularly daunting task. He quickly began closing down suspect payments to road contractors that had left the Treasury nearly empty before the election. During 2003, he also bulldozed without compensation houses built on land allocated for road reserves and for a Nairobi bypass, which had been illegally excised and sold, a brave and tricky action. Meanwhile, he tried to tackle the ubiquitous corruption in his ministry, which saw engineers and surveyors awarding contracts to companies that they themselves owned. A special investigation (funded by the UK) under ex-minister Andrew Kiptoon examined road construction bills and recommended the blacklisting of virtually every contractor.[38] The government began to prepare designs for a new road network for Nairobi, to ease the city's congestion. However, progress was painfully slow; internal politics also seemed to be involved. There were claims, for example, that the Treasury repeatedly delayed Odinga's plans to build 150,000 new houses, to avoid his obtaining the political credit.

The privatisation of failed public services continued, albeit slowly. The 2002 Water Act had allowed the part-privatisation of water services, moving control from the ministry and local government to regional boards. Services in Nairobi were then outsourced to a commercial subsidiary of the council in 2003, despite fears for the impact on the poor.[39] The World Bank provided a Ksh3.4 billion grant to help reconstruct the country's water infrastructure. Garbage privatisation also began. Despite an arson attack on City Hall in 2004, the council's performance and transparency improved, revenue collection rose and real efforts were made to restore services. Other councils also cut corruption, shed staff and restarted services. In a major decentralisation innovation, 2 and then 5 per cent of income tax revenue was allocated to the Local Authorities Transfer Fund to get councils back on their feet.

Transport and Security

Another major achievement was the introduction of order into the *matatu* industry, which had long been plagued by violence and controlled by criminal cartels linked with Mungiki or police officers. In 2003, Michuki took on the industry and won. Leveraging their political legitimacy, the NARC government first attacked the touts and cartels controlling routes. It then forced drivers to wear uniforms and demanded that they hold valid driving licences and have no criminal records. It faced down a strike by 25,000 *matatus* in November 2003 against plans to limit the number of seats in vehicles and to make seatbelts and speed governors mandatory. In February 2004, when the new rules came into force, police arrested hundreds and impounded both *matatus* and buses.[40] Although inconvenient, this was the type of robust action that voters expected. The number of deaths and serious injuries on the roads fell by a third in 2004 (but then resumed their steady rise, as the predictable slide back into disorder began). Financially damaged, Mungiki and other groups reorganised and the violence continued, but their power was weakened.[41] When he moved from Transport to Internal Security in 2005, Michuki vowed to wipe Mungiki out entirely.

In the aviation sector, Eldoret airport was closed for a year after reports that it was being used as a conduit for guns and drugs and to bypass customs duties. It reopened in 2004, with most officials replaced. The rebuilding of Jomo Kenyatta International Airport, which had been unaltered since Kenyatta's day, began in 2006, to relieve congestion, improve services and eventually allow direct flights from the US once more.

In another symbolic but important step, Christmas 2003 saw the restoration of passenger rail services from Nairobi to Kisumu, suspended in 1997. The insolvent Kenya Railways was finally broken up, much as electricity and posts and telecommunications had been. In 2005, the safety and regulatory aspects of the corporation were split off from the transport business, to allow the actual business of transportation to be delivered by private companies.

Health

The NARC era also saw improvements in drug availability and health provision, with facilities, medical personnel and immunisation levels all rising faster than population growth. Infant mortality rates fell, deaths from malaria halved due to the distribution of treated mosquito nets, and after 20 years of decline, life expectancies began to rise once more.[42] As in other areas, the improvement owed less to radical new policies than to a greater stress on efficiency, reduced resource extraction and more consistent implementation. Health Minister Ngilu's one great policy innovation, a new compulsory nationwide state-run health insurance scheme, although popular, faced huge cost obstacles (it was estimated it would cost Ksh40 billion) and was eventually killed off by Kibaki.

A surprise announcement in 2004 was a fall in the estimated number of Kenyans with HIV. The new figures put the national prevalence in 2003 at 6.7 per cent, in contrast to the National Aids Control Council's 9 per cent, which had reduced its estimate from 14 per cent three years earlier as a result of better information, better access to low-cost retroviral drugs and better lifestyle choices.[43] One million Kenyans fewer were estimated to be HIV-positive, though, as the *Nation* commented, 'What this basically adds up to is that nobody really knows the exact number of people in Kenya, or any other country, infected by HIV.'[44] Estimates of prevalence were down to 4.6 per cent by 2007.[45]

Kenya's Problems Continue

Despite the government's many achievements, all was not rosy. The new leadership soon adopted the practices of its predecessors, and while the economy improved, they were unable to deliver sustained improvements in security or an environment free from corruption.

Although it was understood that many of NARC's campaign promises, such as that of 500,000 jobs, could not be fulfilled in the timescales promised, the speed and ease with which they were abandoned was still impressive. Some of the blame could be placed on the institutional incapacity that had built up in the administration and on NARC's inheritance of personnel from KANU. Others pointed to the control exerted over government policy by Western donors and their reluctance to support any reform that did not result in reduced spending or privatisation. However, it mainly reflected the corrosive effect of the NAK–LDP divide, which converted every decision into a political football, and every reform into a conflict in which the winners and losers were more important than the game being played.

12.4: The 'Meru mafia': Murungi, Mwiraria, Muthaura and Ringera

Courtesy: Nation Group Newspapers

The 'Mount Kenya Mafia'

Perhaps the most obvious warning sign was that, as Kalenjin executives and Moi's business partners were evicted, a high proportion were replaced by people from the Gema communities, more often described now as the 'Mount Kenya' people. Particular venom was reserved amongst KANU, LDP and FORD-People alike for the preponderance of Meru in key roles. In part, this reflected Kibaki's promise to appoint only the most qualified people. The Meru had many educated, able administrators. They had tended to play a background role to the Kikuyu in the 1960s, 1970s and early 1980s, and their main channels of influence had been in public service rather than business. It was also a consequence of the support the Meru had given to the DP since 1992. Now, Kenya not only had justice and finance ministers from Meru, but the new head of the civil service, Francis Muthaura, and Ringera, head of the anti-corruption authority after its re-establishment, were also Meru (Figure 12.4). So too were several permanent secretaries and the heads of parastatals including the Nyayo Tea Zones, the Pyrethrum Board, the AFC and the Industrial Development Bank.

Other Mount Kenya insiders whose influence over Kibaki in 2003–4 gave cause for concern included State House Comptroller Keriri from Kirinyaga and Security Minister Murungaru from Nyeri. The perception became widespread (and contained some truth) that tribalism had intensified as ministers – given greater autonomy from the presidency – built their own structures of patronage.[46]

As with both previous presidents, a kitchen cabinet (this time, elderly and Kikuyu) began to prosper. The TransCentury business group, owned by some of Kibaki's Kikuyu allies, began to acquire large shareholdings in other companies, including Rift Valley Railways, KPLC, Equity Bank and East African Cables. Freed of Moi-era restrictions, Kikuyu businessmen once more became the dominant economic power in the land, with their control of large corporations, banking and finance near-complete. Both the community's natural talents and its perception of entitlement and superiority were again let loose.

A Purge of the Security Services

The security services suffered the inevitable purge. Immediately after Kibaki's inauguration, the (Kalenjin) head of the Presidential Escort was replaced. In February 2003, Kibaki dropped Philemon Abong'o as commissioner of police and the (Kalenjin) CID and GSU heads were removed. Although Kibaki retained Moi's personal bodyguard for a year, in January 2004 the whole Presidential Escort was replaced (see Table 12.1).

NARC's first team did not last long; although it demonstrated greater transparency, there was no dramatic fall in crime. The leadership also fell victim to NARC's internal problems. Some appeared to believe that their preferment owed as much to Odinga as to Kibaki. After only a year, Luo police chief Edwin Nyaseda was sacked after he provided state security for Odinga during a mixed official and political visit to the Coast.[47] As a result, a second team arrived on the scene in 2004, led by Kenya's first soldier (and first Muslim) to become police commissioner, Brigadier Mohammed Hussein Ali. Ali was given a freer hand than previous police heads to strike at the roots of crime and to use a more 'military' approach (more draconian, but expected to

Table 12.1: Police and internal security heads, 2003–8

Role	Name	Dates	Ethnicity
Permanent Secretary for Provincial Administration and Internal Security	Zakayo Cheruiyot	1998–2003	Kalenjin
	Dave Mwangi	2003–6	Kikuyu
	Cyrus Gituai	2006–8	Embu
Commissioner of Police	Philemon Abong'o	1999–2003	Luo
	Edwin Nyaseda	2003–4	Luo
	Mohammed Hussein Ali	2004–9	Somali
GSU Head	David Kimaiyo	2002–3	Kalenjin
	Lawrence Mwadime	2003–5	Taita
	Mathew Iteere	2005–9	Meru
CID Head	Francis arap Sang	1999–2003	Kalenjin
	Daniel Ndung'u	2003–4	Kikuyu
	Joseph Kamau	2004–6	Kikuyu
	Simon Karanja Gatiba	2006–10	Kikuyu
NSIS Head	Wilson Boinett	1999–2006	Kalenjin
	Michael Gichangi	2006 on	Kikuyu
Presidential Escort Unit	Nixon Boit	to 2003	Kalenjin
	Mathew Iteere	2003–5	Meru
	Benson Githinji	2005–10	Kikuyu

Source: Various

be less corrupt). He proceeded with vigour to purge the police force. In 2006, Wilson Boinett's retirement also posed a risk, given the sensitivity of his post. He was replaced, unsurprisingly, by a Kikuyu. As a result, by 2006, the permanent secretary for internal security, and the CID, GSU, Presidential Escort and NSIS heads – all Kalenjin in 2002 – were all Kikuyu, Embu or Meru. It may have been rational, but it was clearly influenced by trust, and trust by ethnicity.

Kibaki also reshuffled the military three times in as many years. The overall effect was again to retire or sideline the most senior Kalenjin and Luo and increase Kikuyu (and Kamba) representation (see Table 12.2). Retiring military heads often went into politics (as John Koech did) or were appointed as parastatal heads (Joseph Kibwana, for example, moved to head the Ports Authority and his successor Jeremiah Kianga retired to run the railways).

Security Problems Continue

While the security position in rural areas improved, trouble continued on the Ethiopian and Somali borders. Fighting over pasture and water between Somali clans remained common. Violence between the Garre and Murille in 2004–5 claimed at least 50 lives, which was addressed not through arrests but by the customary payment of 'blood money' for each death.[48] Although the tensions between the Marakwet

Table 12.2: Military heads, 2003–8

Chief of General Staff	Major-Gen. Joseph Kibwana	2000–5	Mijikenda
	General Jeremiah Kianga	2005–11	Kamba
Vice-Chief of General Staff	Lt.-Gen. John Koech	2000–3	Kalenjin – Kipsigis
	Major-Gen. Nick Leshan	2003–5	Maasai
	Lt.-Gen. Julius Karangi	2005 on	Kikuyu
Army Commander	Lt.-Gen. Lazarus Sumbeiywo	2000–3	Kalenjin – Keiyo
	Lt.-Gen. Jeremiah Kianga	2003–5	Kamba
	Lt.-Gen. Augustino Njoroge	2005 on	Kikuyu
Deputy Army Commander	Major-Gen. Jeremiah Kianga	2000–3	Kamba
	Major-Gen. Augustino Njoroge	2003–5	Kikuyu
	Major-Gen. Jones Mutwii	2005–8	Kamba
Air Force Commander	Major-Gen. Simon Mutai	2000–3	Kamba
	Major-Gen. Julius Karangi	2003–5	Kikuyu
	Major-Gen. Harold Tangai	2005 on	Taita
Navy Commander	Major-Gen. Pasteur Awitta	2001–4	Luo
	Major-Gen. Samson Mwathethe	2004–11	Mijikenda

Source: Various

and Pokot reduced, and thousands of guns were handed in during amnesties, cattle raiding continued in most northern pastoralist communities, part of a cycle of retribution that appeared impossible to break.

In the Rift, land tensions that had simmered in the 1990s again broke out into violence. The marginalised Ogiek took up arms in protest in Mount Elgon in 2004, the legacy of a decade of disputes over land allocated to them as squatters. There was also fighting between Maasai and Kipsigis in Trans-Mara in 2004. Water and land rights were the cause of an outbreak of fighting in January 2005 in Naivasha between Maasai and Kikuyu, with 15 people killed and houses burnt. Local villagers were reinforced by Maasai *moran* from Narok and Kikuyu from Nairobi, ready to fight, a warning that the risk of violence over land rights remained ever-present. Increasingly, the old opposition's claims that the government was the cause of Kenya's insecurity appeared hollow. Worse was to come in 2007, when the Sabaot Land Defence Force wreaked havoc in Mount Elgon, killing hundreds in a dispute over grabbed land and settlement rights.

There were some improvements in the behaviour of Kenya's police. A taskforce on police reform was set up in 2004, and Parliament changed the law so that only confessions made in court were admissible, to reduce the use of torture to extract confessions. However, this made it more difficult to convict the guilty as well, and this policy was soon under review. In 2004, the police received their first pay rises for 15 years.

However, there was no step-change fall in crime, long blamed on the Moi government's disdain for human rights and alienation of the masses. The poor state of security continued to be a thorn in the side of both foreign investment and popular support. According to a NGO report, at the turn of the millennium Kenya was one of the 10 most unequal societies on earth, with more than half the population living in absolute poverty and huge variations in access to health services, water and education.[49] One consequence was that crime could not be controlled either. Police numbers remained low as a percentage of Kenya's population, pay and conditions poor, training weak and trust in their competence and probity non-existent.

Mungiki's activities in Nairobi, Central Province, Nakuru and Laikipia were repressed, but the organisation survived as a mafia-like secret state, with its own tax collectors, land allocation processes, courts, money, armouries and protectors in the political system, including MPs and even ministers. Parts of Nairobi remained no-go areas. In 2005, Internal Security Minister Michuki ordered a shoot to kill policy for those found carrying weapons.[50] There was open warfare between Mungiki and the police. In their quest for order, elements in the police carried out hundreds of extra-judicial executions of 'known criminals' every year, many of them Mungiki supporters.[51]

Justice and Independence

As the risks of pursuing the corrupt declined, so the pressure on those who had profited multiplied. The problem for NARC was to obtain justice without seeming to be conducting a witch-hunt against their predecessors, which would set a precedent when NARC itself departed and inspire protest from those under threat.

Some NARC leaders had been KANU insiders a few months earlier, and there were few with completely clean hands. Partly as a result, Kibaki and others promised on various occasions to let 'bygones be bygones'. While many parastatal heads and civil servants were evicted, virtually no one ended up in jail. The KANU top leadership remained immune from prosecution, defended by good lawyers, deep pockets and their continued influence, which strengthened after 2005 when Moi and Biwott were backing Kibaki rather than opposing him.

The government's attitude to the law also proved almost as flexible as that of its predecessor. Again and again, ministers were slapped with injunctions barring them from taking decisions, but took them anyway.[52] The attorney-general declined to cite them as in contempt of court. The state also appeared to be targeting those who were opposing them on the issue of constitutional change (see below). Anti-corruption and malpractice investigations seemed to focus on supporters of Odinga: Kisumu City Council (Odinga's home) was targeted for reform in 2005, and Spectre's acquisition of the Kisumu molasses plant came under scrutiny in 2004–6 as pro-government figures searched for evidence of malpractice. Such accusations of selective justice blurred the boundaries between right and wrong. Although 65 MPs who refused to declare their assets were scheduled for prosecution in 2005, this went nowhere, and other prosecutions of MPs for expenses fraud were delayed until after the 2007 elections.[53] A proposed freedom of information bill never made it onto the statute books.

The NGOs and civic society organisations that had proved so adept at taking on KANU struggled to adapt to a situation in which their allies and their own leaders were now at the centre of government. The 'movement' gradually bifurcated between those who believed that NARC represented the best available option for Kenya, and those who held to the same precepts of challenge that had motivated their opposition to KANU. The Nation Media Group, long an independent voice, also found itself dangerously close to the government. The Moi family-owned *Standard*, in contrast, soon became a supporter of the opposition.

The Intractable Problem of Land

Although NARC's reforms helped expose the sins of the past, greater transparency did not result in greater equity. Indeed, the problem worsened as more and more cases of grabbed land came to light, bringing the entire structure of individual land rights built since 1954 into question. The Ndung'u Commission's report provided ammunition for those who argued for a fundamental review of land rights, recommending the establishment of a land title tribunal to investigate every dispute (a near-impossible task). In practice, few of the report's recommendations were implemented. Chaos in land markets and the finance sector had ensued as soon as the government had threatened to repossess fake or illegal title deeds, since many had been resold or were security for bank loans.[54]

The coexistence of two competing systems of land rights – one based on clan and inheritance, the other on registration and purchase – sat at the heart of Kenya's troubles. Increasingly, politicians from the Luo and ex-KADU communities stressed the importance of collective or 'people's' rights, as contrasted with the liberal view of rights as residing in individuals (which all governments in Kenya since independence had formally supported). Ntimama continued to demand the restoration of much of the Rift Valley to the Maasai, based on their pre-colonial occupation and the expiry of the century-old 1904 agreement.[55] In 2006, the government's eviction of Samburu herders from Kikuyu-owned farms in Laikipia led to demonstrations from those who claimed access based on 'ancestral rights'. There was a growing body of opinion that Kenya needed a fundamental review of its land policy, to pay greater attention to indigenous, communal land rights and to challenge the inviolability of individual title. A draft national land policy to this effect was drawn up by NGOs and submitted to the Cabinet in 2007. While this was a vote-winner in many quarters, it risked reopening every major problem in Kenya's history, from the British conquest through the settlement schemes of the 1960s to the ethnic clashes.

Another problem was that the land demarcation and registration process begun in the 1950s was still incomplete. Although NARC had promised title deeds for all, progress remained slow: some residents in parts of Central Province still had no deeds in 2007. Land continued to be both a popular desire and a source of divisions. During the election campaign, Kibaki travelled the country, issuing title deeds to farmers and winning friends and enemies in equal measure. By 2007, distrust in presidential favour was so intense that the draft National Land Law removed the power to allocate state land from him entirely.

The Lure of Power

While NARC's victory replaced many of the players, it did not change the game, and whatever its initial convictions, the new leadership tended to play the game in the same way as its predecessors. During by-elections, NARC used police and government vehicles to campaign (though it disingenuously claimed that they had paid for them).[56] It was caught pressuring the press not to print stories regarding corruption and misbehaviour by NARC MPs and it banned rallies by both KANU and the LDP.

As well as enjoying their new power, some NARC politicians also found office rewarding. Government officials spent Ksh878 million (US$12 million) on luxury cars in their first 20 months in office.[57] There was also a rapid swelling in their bank balances and lifestyles, which could only in part be accounted for by their higher salaries. As the press suggested,

> Those who, just a year ago, were living in some low-class hotels in Nairobi are now the proud owners of homes in plush residential estates . . . a year of Narc in power has changed the lifestyles of some Cabinet ministers beyond their wildest dreams.[58]

Stories circulated of ministers who had acquired large houses and full wallets within months of taking office. Local Government Minister Maitha followed in an older tradition in marrying a fourth wife after he achieved office and acquiring a substantial new rural home. He was linked to several corruption allegations and procurement anomalies, and admitted 'finding' Ksh5 million left in a suitcase outside his office by a developer. Ministers Murungaru, Kirwa, Peter Ndwiga, Chirau Mwakwere, Michuki and Mukhisa Kituyi too faced allegations of corruption or partiality. Transparency International alleged in March 2005 that one minister had deposited Ksh750 million in domestic and foreign bank accounts during 2004.[59]

While the state had made good progress in its anti-corruption drive in 2003, by late 2004 its campaign was fading.[60] Old networks of exploitation were resurfacing, reinforced by the LDP–NAK divide. Kenya's political system still ran on money, and, unable to win fairly, ex-DP insiders were gathering funds to use against their opponents by the same methods as under Moi (see below). Although the police were prosecuting more of those accused of corruption, and fewer criminals were buying their way out of jail, the trouble at the top was corrosive of public perceptions. By 2006, Transparency International's bribery survey suggested Kenya was almost as corrupt as it had been under Moi.

The Decline of the Opposition, 2003–4

Without Moi, without political power and without a clear leader, the party that had governed Kenya for 40 years withered within a year into a pastoralist alliance, a small rump around Uhuru Kenyatta and an embittered Kalenjin, infuriated at their eviction from the state apparatus. In the seven by-elections in 2003–4, KANU was unable to recover any ground. Kenyatta, their presidential candidate but not party leader, was isolated. Not only had most of Central Province voted NARC, by October 2003 most of his Kikuyu KANU MPs had deserted him for an ethnically motivated cohabitation deal with Kibaki, abandoning Uhuru for the same reason they had joined him. Several Luhya and Kamba KANU leaders also defected to the LDP, FORD-Kenya or NARC itself, including Musalia Mudavadi and Cyrus Jirongo. When Moi retired as KANU chairman in September 2003, there were expectations that a new leadership would emerge, but it was not to be. Racked by infighting between potential leaders Kenyatta, Biwott, Ruto and Chris Okemo, the party repeatedly postponed elections and the struggle continued for three more years.

The core of KANU, meanwhile, remained the Kalenjin. They spent 2003–4 in shock, as their leaders were evicted from post after post, resources no longer came their way and they felt bereft of influence. Angry at both Kenyatta and Kibaki, they pursued an ethnically separatist agenda, with Kalenjin KANU MPs warning of violence if Moi was disrespected, threatening secession and talking of an ethnically Kalenjin party.[61] Moi in contrast spent more than a year in retirement, rarely making public pronouncements. Despite the harsh words said about him and his allies, Moi defended Kibaki's government on several occasions. It was not until the referendum crisis of 2005 that he tried to reclaim the leadership of the Kalenjin.

In December 2003, recognising they were both too weak to survive alone, Kenyatta and the other 2002 loser, Simeon Nyachae, made common cause. KANU and

FORD-People announced a Coalition of National Unity (CNU), of which Nyachae was the chairman and Uhuru the deputy. However, the CNU was far from popular in either party. Theoretically able to muster 80 votes, in practice it had neither the numbers nor the will to challenge the government. KANU hardliners rejected the alliance because Nyachae was the leader, while KANU was the larger party, while Gusii KANU leaders who had fought Nyachae for years felt betrayed. In practice, the coalition proved short-lived. It agreed on little, and in July 2004, with Nyachae's appointment to the Cabinet, it collapsed completely.

In the interim, some KANU MPs were also entering into a working arrangement with disenchanted LDP leaders, to counter what they saw as the Gema inner nexus of power. During August 2003, a series of joint rallies between Kalenjin MPs led by youthful Secretary-General Ruto and Odinga's Luo supporters established an alliance that would blossom into a common front and a new political party in 2005–6.[62]

The Shattering of NARC

No sooner had NARC been victorious at the ballot box than the debate over who and what the party truly was began. With KANU imploding, it was clear there was going to be little opposition from outside the coalition. As in 1963–5, the real fault lines lay within. Although the policy differences were more blurred and more nuanced than in the 1960s, the same centralism versus devolution and liberal versus protectionist debates continued, both genuine issues and veneers for the ethnic battle for resources. Most of the tensions centred on Raila Odinga. Still commanding fanatical support in his Luo community, he also had a network of allies and associates in the LDP who saw him as a bulwark against the return of Kikuyu domination. In turn, the 'Gema elite' seemed unable to resist the lure of striking against him. The result was three years of conflict that eventually reconstructed Kenya's political parties on entirely different lines. By the end of 2003, with the constitutional reform debate out of control and the economy still sluggish, tempers were rising and NAK MPs were demanding that the LDP fully participate in NARC and cease to act as a 'party within the party' or pull out completely.[63] The struggle not only tore NARC in two along the lines of the original LDP–NAK split, but also split KANU and FORD-People as the government sought allies here also. A series of arguments over constitutional reform, the distribution of jobs and resources, party structures, economic policies and corruption forced the uncommitted to choose a side. By 2005, the party existed only in name.

The Memorandum of Understanding, the NARC Summit and the Party

The first disputes were over procedural issues, proxies for the perceived marginalisation of the LDP by those around Kibaki. It was a strange series of debates, in which Kibaki rarely participated directly, leaving the work to be done by Murungi, Murungaru and others, and Odinga too avoided expressing his personal opinion, though everyone knew where he stood.

The first of these issues was the 2002 MoU, which LDP supporters believed Kibaki had reneged on. It now emerged there were at least two different agreements. The protagonists had signed an early, non-specific MoU privately, while there was a more detailed, public, but unsigned version. The LDP's copy stated there would 50–50 power sharing; the copy on the NAK website said only that jobs would be shared out 'equitably'.[64] In August 2003, the LDP also demanded that the MoU be honoured by Odinga's appointment as prime minister even before the constitutional review had been completed, but Kibaki declared this impossible.[65]

NAK and LDP members were also divided on the role of the NARC Summit, created in October 2002 as the governing body of the coalition. The LDP was represented by Chairman Awori, Saitoti, Odinga and Musyoka, while NAK's team consisted of Kibaki, Wamalwa, Ngilu and Kirwa. Within a few weeks of the 'betrayal' of the Cabinet appointments, the LDP realised that the Summit might be a way to control NAK. Calls for it to meet made it clear that the aim was to keep Kibaki out of the clutches of his GEMA advisers: 'The Summit has to be retained as an advisory council to the President. That is the only way we will take care of the Mount Kenya group forming a wall around him.'[66]

NAK, by contrast, was clear that the president governed the country, and would not answer to an unelected advisory body. As a result, although the Summit was on paper NARC's supreme organ, it did not meet for nine months, despite both pleadings and threats by LDP members. Eventually, in December 2003, NAK allowed the summit's reconstitution but simultaneously undermined it, packing its membership with pro-NAK leaders while Kibaki himself withdrew, leaving it unable to mandate him via its decisions

A debate over whether NARC was a political party or an umbrella of individual parties further deepened the divide. Although elected under the NARC banner, the 15 parties in the coalition had retained their independent existence. NARC's constitution stated that it was a coalition of parties, and that only parties, not individuals, could be members. The ambiguity that had been used to advantage in 2002 became a serious problem. The same teams again took opposite sides. Most ex-NAK members (particularly those from the DP) supported dissolution of all constituent parties on the grounds that voters had voted for NARC, and NARC was the sole body with a mandate. However, fearing that absorption into 'NARC' meant subordination to Gema interests, the LDP and FORD-Kenya both refused to play ball. Even when Kibaki joined the debate in December 2003, proposing that all the sub-parties in NARC be dissolved as 'obsolete', the response was dismissive.[67] Although some LDP ministers backed Kibaki, most flatly rejected plans for a NARC membership drive.

In early 2004, NARC began to establish its own identity and membership register and to prepare for grassroots elections, but both FORD-Kenya and the LDP refused to participate and the attempt was abandoned in April. This left the inner core of the government, which needed to lose the old 'DP' label, without a party of its own. Some tried to reactivate the moribund DP, while others focused on trying to re-energise NARC. However, they faced another obstacle. The NPK, which had become NAK and then NARC, was still controlled by Ngilu, and although generally favouring

Kibaki more than the LDP, she proved unwilling to hand over operational control of the party.[68] After she manoeuvred her way to retaining the chair of NARC in early 2005, which automatically made her the party's presidential candidate, NARC itself became useless to Kibaki as a re-election vehicle. The result was conflict, lawsuits, abortive 'NARC' elections and continued instability throughout 2005.

A New Vice-President

Wamalwa had been unwell for years, and his condition deteriorated during 2003. He was transferred to hospital in London suffering from pancreatitis, but his condition worsened and he died on 23 August 2003.

With the most powerful post held by a Luhya now up for grabs, Kibaki needed a replacement, but there was no obvious choice. After a month of uncertainty, in September 2003, he appointed Moody Awori as Kenya's eighth vice-president. The oldest MP in the house at 76, he was also Luhya, but Samia, not Bukusu. He was already chair of the NARC Summit and had played a key role in bringing the Luhya to NARC in the dying days of the Moi regime. Hopes were dashed that Kibaki might appoint Raila, thereby ending the furore over the non-existent position of prime minister, and the ambitious Musyoka was also deeply disappointed, but the LDP was at least satisfied that one of its own had been chosen. Awori proved a conciliatory figure, but soon showed himself to be closer to Kibaki than to Odinga. FORD-Kenya meanwhile chose Kombo, like Wamalwa a Bukusu, as their party chairman, and Kombo duly joined the Cabinet soon after.

The LDP Changes Sides

As the tension in NARC grew, the LDP's influence in Cabinet weakened. The party was divided internally between pro-Odinga and pro-Musyoka wings, manoeuvring for the succession. Meanwhile, several nominally LDP ministers appeared to be backing the NAK/DP faction, including Tuju, Saitoti, Awori and coastal appointees Mwakwere in 2003 and Morris Dzoro in 2005. Despite efforts by both wings to maintain a veneer of unity, including parliamentary group meetings, retreats and appeals, nothing seemed to allay the fears of the LDP or NAK's determination to dominate the coalition. Kikuyu MPs openly targeted Odinga as the 'enemy within' and demanded his sacking. Raila repeatedly declared his loyalty to Kibaki, but he too was preparing for battle. Amid calls for elections and resignations, both sides sought allies elsewhere. NAK had already brought on-side all the Kikuyu MPs except Kenyatta. In return, Kalenjin MPs sided with their old LDP colleagues, infuriated by the events at Bomas (see below) the return of Gema dominance and the witch-hunt against them.[69] Although the biggest fault lines were around constitutional reform, political power and ethno-regional preference, some of the bitterness between NARC factions had its origins in the KANU years, when NAK's Ngilu and KANU's Musyoka had been at loggerheads in Ukambani, as had FORD-Kenya and Mudavadi and Awori's KANU in Western.

By the end of 2003, both Odinga and Musyoka from the LDP were already talking of pulling out of NARC and standing for the presidency in 2007. They were not the only candidates. Although it had been widely understood in 2002 that the 71-year-old Kibaki would not seek a second term, the rules changed once he was on the presidential dais. As cynics predicted, by the end of 2003 it was clear that Kibaki would stand again, though it was no longer clear for which party he would stand.

In August 2004, the government's problems were worsened by the death of Karissa Maitha, NAK's most outspoken leader on the Coast. The Kisauni by-election in December 2004 precipitated an open split. The LDP managed to get its candidate nominated in the NARC primaries, after which NAK's MPs successfully backed a defector to a minor party against the official NARC candidate.[70] From now on, in different disguises, every by-election would be contested between the erstwhile allies.

The Media and Perceptions of the Government

The love affair between NARC and the media was brief. Press freedom, which the opposition had used to good effect during their time in the wilderness, was now extremely inconvenient. During 2004 the government cracked down on the gutter press, while also keeping the lid on true but unwelcome stories. By 2005, the Moi-owned *Standard*, which had remained close to Kenyatta, was unrelenting in its criticism.

Like KANU since 1997, NARC faced a bracing climate of scrutiny, with many opinion polls critical of its approach and delivery. Catholic and Protestant churchmen also pronounced on contemporary issues, almost always critically. The optimism of 2003 was gone, and between 2004 and mid-2005, satisfaction with the government fell from 50 to 40 per cent. By 2005, while education and public transport were seen as their main achievements, dissatisfaction at the state of the economy, housing, land reform, constitutional reform and unemployment were widespread, with two-thirds of those polled unhappy with Kibaki's achievements.[71] Disappointment with NARC did not, however, translate into support for other parties. Only one-third to one-quarter of those sampled preferred Kibaki as president, but Odinga was a non-starter, with only 3–6 per cent believing he had the experience and gravitas for the presidency. Musyoka was the most popular candidate, with 20 and 35 per cent of the vote in three polls during late 2005, while KANU supporters backed Kenyatta.[72]

A series of Afrobarometer polls onwards also explored Kenyans' views on social, political and economic issues, and compared them with those elsewhere in Africa. These showed initial euphoria with NARC and a similar disenchantment by 2005, although views on Kibaki's performance varied sharply with the respondents' ethnicity. There was a clear preference for greater state regulation in agriculture, regulated, tariffed trade and a low-wage, high-employment economy.[73] There remained a deep vein of egalitarianism, with some of the continent's strongest opposition to wide gaps between rich and poor.

A New Constitution: Part III, 2003–4

NARC had promised a new constitution within 100 days of taking office. However, it was unable to deliver on this pledge, because of the divisive issues that underlay it. The NAK wing soon backtracked from its previous support for dramatic reform, in part since it would now be the loser. Divisions were particularly apparent over the role of prime minister. The deal that Raila would become Kenya's prime minister had been made before NARC's victory. Now, ex-NAK leaders denied that it had ever been on offer. Gradually, the argument over centralised executive power, which combined disputes over the role of the presidency, a struggle for regional control of land and an ethnicised attempt to control a resurgent Kikuyu elite, forced everyone to take sides, just as had happened in 1963–5.

Bomas I and II, 2003

On 28 April 2003, the 629-member National Constitutional Conference assembled at the Bomas Cultural Centre (as planned in 2002), to review the draft constitution prepared by the CKRC. Its members consisted of all 222 MPs, representatives from parties, civil society and religious groups and 210 district delegates (three per district, enshrining the district as a unit of representation, whatever its size), chaired by Yash Ghai (Figure 12.5). The conference sat until late September, but proved an acrimonious affair, reviewing the new constitution line by line, but struggling to reach consensus.

Despite pressure from NAK leaders, the delegates continued to back a devolved constitution with an executive prime minister and a ceremonial president. Their model might well have been the regional constitution of 1963, with its governor-general, prime minister, regional government and bicameral assembly. Most Kenyans also supported the Bomas process and constitution, believing that only by radical change to the legal framework governing the country's politics could it truly be reformed (what the 2008 post-election review commission later castigated as 'societal change by means of statutory amendment').[74]

In the view of many around Kibaki, however, this was a disaster. The history of federal constitutions in Africa (in Sudan, Ethiopia, Nigeria and Senegal-Gambia) was poor, and many believed federalism would fail in Kenya. Opponents argued that devolved government would be too expensive and complex, the same accusations made against regionalism 40 years before. Nyachae agreed. 'As a former Finance minister,' he said in November 2003, 'I foresee serious financial implications arising from implementation of a new constitution.'[75] It was also claimed that federalism would weaken national identity and lead to ethnic Bantustans in which the rights of 'indigenous' people would be paramount over those from elsewhere in Kenya. Less charitably, after 20 years in opposition, some were hungry for wealth and power, and Bomas seemed to be taking their trough away before they could taste the food. Some admitted that they had only supported an executive prime minister as long as Moi was in power. Now, with their man in the driving seat, the idea had outlived its usefulness. The key fault line, though, was Odinga and the role of executive prime

12.5: The Bomas Talks

Courtesy: Nation Group Newspapers

minister. As an LDP MP put it in July, 'That the country should have a prime minister is not for debate, and the fact that the office-bearer will be Mr Raila Odinga is not negotiable . . .'[76] Gradually, most NAK leaders turned against Bomas, though Kibaki himself said little.

While a majority of NARC were uncomfortable with the draft constitution, led by Justice and Constitutional Affairs Minister Murungi, KANU and the LDP retained a working majority amongst delegates, in alliance with the original drafters of the constitution. The Cabinet was officially united around proposals for a constitution that included a relatively weak prime minister, but in reality their differences were already irreconcilable by mid-2003. Demands from ex-DP ministers that the constitution be put to a referendum (rather than passed or rejected *in toto* by Parliament) surfaced in August–September 2003, once it was clear that the constitution would survive Bomas II intact.[77] Odinga and others opposed this as changing the rules after losing the debate. Acrimony grew when the (Luo) chairman of the Bomas Devolution Committee was murdered in September.[78]

In December 2003 and January 2004, with the split widening, NAK insiders Murungaru, Murungi and Assistant Minister Kivutha Kibwana called for the scrapping of the Bomas conference entirely. They claimed that the majority of delegates were 'KANU moles' and that they were introducing constitutional changes to advance the position of specific individuals (meaning Odinga).[79]

Bomas III, January–March 2004

The final part of the Bomas process began in January 2004. A last review of the draft left the basics unaltered. Kenya would have a complex system of devolution, with four levels of government: national, regional, district and locational. There would be an end to the provincial administration; limits to land ownership; a two-chamber house with women making up at least one-third of members; and a division of executive powers, with a president and a strong prime minister who chose the Cabinet. Working together, the LDP, KANU and civil society representatives retained a majority in Bomas. All efforts by supporters of a centralised administration to modify the draft or introduce new drafts failed. However, the picture was different in Parliament, where 150 of the 222 MPs backed the government's view that the House (not Bomas) should have the final decision.[80] Many NAK MPs boycotted Bomas entirely. The process ended in March 2004 with a constitution (the 'Zero Draft') ready to be presented to Parliament, but an open split between those supporting a centralised state and those supporting a division of powers. Most other issues faded into the background (apart from whether to retain Islamic (Kadhi's) courts in the constitution). The LSK and the churches too were divided. Most Western diplomats, in contrast, supported the review.

With tensions rising, a last-minute effort by DP, FORD-Kenya and NPK ministers to restore a strong presidency was rejected by the conference. Despite frenzied state lobbying, delegates refused to be cowed. In response, Awori led a walk-out by NAK ministers and their allies, but Raila and the LDP stayed on. A furious Murungi publicly accused Odinga of being a traitor. On 15 March 2004, the remaining delegates passed the constitution unchanged and a confrontation seemed imminent.[81]

Within days, though, the situation had changed. Ruling on a lawsuit by Bishop Timothy Njoya and other Bomas delegates, the High Court led by Ringera declared unconstitutional (by a majority verdict) the legislation under which the whole review process had been conducted. It rejected the idea that Parliament or the National Constitutional Conference were empowered to enact a new constitution, and required that any new constitution be approved by a constituent assembly or referendum.[82] Another opportunity had been created for compromise, or to undermine the popular will. Ghai called the ruling 'weakly reasoned, misapplied and a tragedy'.[83]

The Government of National Unity, 2004

On 30 June 2004, Kibaki executed his first major government reshuffle. With a divided Cabinet and party, constitutional reform stalled and evidence emerging of state corruption, many had expected dramatic action. In the event, he fired none of the LDP ministers (who had declared they would stand or fall together), but instead added 18 newcomers to his government, including MPs from FORD-People and KANU. The effect of this 'Government of National Unity' or GNU was to split the opposition parties and the Kalenjin and Gusii along the same lines that NARC itself was split. It brought in those opposed to the Bomas constitution and left out those supporting it. It strengthened Kibaki's uncertain parliamentary majority, but left the position of the LDP within NARC fatally unclear. It had echoes of Jomo Kenyatta's incorporation of KADU in 1964, with much the same result.

In the reshuffle, Nyachae became minister for energy, accompanied by two FORD-People assistant ministers, though some of the party's MPs refused to follow their leader. KANU too was peeled apart. Against the wishes of Kenyatta, three KANU MPs (including Karume) were appointed as ministers, and four assistant ministers (including Kipkalya arap Kones) also took the DP shilling. LDP member Ntimama rejoined the Cabinet, reuniting the KANU A team (Nyachae, Ntimama and Kones) that had been so vocally anti-Kikuyu in a Kikuyu-led government. There were reports that some of those enticed into government were paid.[84] The second major change was the demotion of LDP ministers. Musyoka was moved from Foreign Affairs to Environment, while Odinga had Housing clipped from his ministry. Although the LDP ministers took their posts and remained tight-lipped, their anger was obvious.

The government's enlargement to 71 members, one-third of the Assembly, was criticised by NGOs and donors alike as wasteful, diverting attention from constitutional reform, and designed to force the LDP to resign. Both sides were clear what had happened. In the words of a pro-NAK assistant minister:

> Shut up or lose your job, is the message Kibaki has sent to these rebels . . . The coalition, if you ask me, is as dead as a dodo and what NAK should do now is look for other partners in Parliament.[85]

LDP supporters were equally open that it symbolised the end of NARC. Some were critical of Kibaki, something they had previously tried to avoid.[86] Dissatisfaction was worsened by the transfer (and immediate reversal) of Githongo from the OP to report instead to Murungi's Justice and Constitutional Affairs Ministry, in the middle of extremely sensitive anti-corruption investigations (see below). Githongo's direct line to the presidency was seen as a key indicator of the government's determination to fight corruption. The reshuffle also reaffirmed the continued power of the last few members of the independence generation, with the ageing Kibaki, Awori, Karume, Michuki, Nyachae and Ntimama still holding key offices.

Throughout 2005, tensions in the government grew, as the LDP leadership was sidelined. Just as in 1964–5, internal divisions poisoned relationships and undermined the government's genuine achievements. This time, however, the LDP was stronger than Oginga Odinga's group had been in the 1960s: they had allies elsewhere, and the global and national political environment had changed. There would be no easy win for Kibaki in this battle.

The Anglo-Leasing Scandal

During 2004–5, evidence grew that, despite its rhetoric, Kibaki's government had adopted the same kleptocratic attitude to state funds as its predecessors. The resulting scandal nearly brought it down and permanently tarnished its reputation.

There was widespread public shock and anger in May and June 2004 when KANU MP Maoka Maore exposed the first fraud. This contract, a Ksh3.4 billion passport deal between Awori's Home Affairs Ministry and a British lease finance company Anglo-Leasing, had been signed in 2003. The deal was found to involve the violation of procurement processes, tripled prices and the legal non-existence of the supplying company itself. It was followed by the discovery of another Ksh4 billion contract with Anglo-Leasing to build a forensic laboratory for the CID. This decision had been taken by KANU in 2001, but NARC ministers had continued to make payments on the contracts when they took office. Investigations revealed a web of fake companies that appeared to link back to the Kamani family, owners of Kamsons, who had been the winners of many government contracts under KANU, and less directly to the son of an ex-minister, and thence to ministers and officials.[87] Amid frantic denials, investigations by Githongo, the Public Accounts Committee and KACC gradually exposed the full extent of the scandal.

Githongo had been investigating the Anglo-Leasing contracts even before they were made public. With the issue now in the spotlight, the people behind Anglo 'anonymously' wired back nearly Ksh1 billion that the government had already paid, in an unsuccessful attempt to persuade Githongo and the KACC to go easy on the investigation.[88] Others took this as an admission of guilt. When Murungi called Anglo-Leasing 'the scandal that never was', few were convinced.[89]

More and more questionable contracts emerged. It was discovered that a Ksh4 billion ship being built in Spain for the Kenyan navy had been the subject of curious arrangements and inflated costs. It also involved a well-known arms dealer who had been involved in military procurement under Moi and was now a supporter of Kibaki.[90] This was followed by the revelation of other suspicious security contracts (not subject to normal tendering processes or parliamentary scrutiny). A communications network for the administration police worth Ksh4.4 billion had been commissioned from another company associated with the Kamani family; this company also appeared not to exist. There were projects to provide computer and video equipment for the police (Ksh4.5 billion), security vehicles for the police (Ksh6.75 billion), and equipment for the intelligence services (Ksh3 billion). Each had been issued by Murungaru's security department in the OP during 2003 and 2004 and signed off by Mwiraria's Treasury. All were based on the principle of debt financing, which had the effect of disconnecting the debt payments (from the Consolidated Fund) from the actual services and did not need parliamentary approval. Most appeared overpriced or showed evidence of corrupt practices. Hundreds of millions of dollars were being stolen.

During 2004, although in theory an insider (a Kikuyu from a family who had long supported Kenyatta and later Kibaki), Githongo came under increasing pressure from Murungi and Murungaru.[91] It gradually became apparent that the contracts had been designed to steal taxpayers' money to fund the government's re-election (or 'resource mobilisation' as Murungi was alleged to have described it).[92] It seemed the Kikuyu–Meru core of the government (including Muthaura, Murungi and Murungaru) were well aware of what had happened, and were more concerned about keeping Githongo quiet than about taking action. Alienated and realising the need for irrefutable evidence, Githongo began secretly to tape record his conversations. In February 2005, having finished his investigations and passed a file to KACC, but distrusted by his government colleagues, Githongo was warned that he was about to be fired, and that his life might be in danger. While overseas, he resigned and went into exile.

Donors were infuriated by the discovery that while the Kenyan government was begging for aid, it appeared to be stealing sums of a similar size to the entire aid budget. During July–October 2004, virtually every foreign embassy criticised the government openly. By this time, half the Cabinet had been named in corruption allegations, each becoming public footballs that further damaged confidence. In 2005, with Githongo's departure, the US and Germany suspended support for the anti-bribery campaign and threatened to cut off aid entirely. Murungaru became one of the first ministers to be refused a visitor's visa by both Britain and the US because of information linking him to corruption.[93] Transparency International's 2005 Corruption Perception Index placed Kenya at an all-time low of 144 out of 148 countries.

To dampen down protest, in February 2005 Kibaki swapped Murungaru for Michuki in the OP and sacked three permanent secretaries over the Anglo-Leasing scams. Both they and ex-Permanent Secretary Cheruiyot were later charged in court. However, the changes were universally seen as cosmetic, as Kibaki had not fired any ministers, and protests continued. LDP, FORD-Kenya and NPK ministers all used these events as further evidence of the inner (Gema) government's corruption. The LSK privately prosecuted Awori, Wako and Mwiraria over the passports and forensic lab deals, but Wako took over the case and terminated it (just as he had done under Moi).

In May 2007, Kimunya summarised the government's position on the Anglo-Leasing frauds. There had been 18 suspect contracts with a value of Ksh54 billion (US$700 million) issued between 1997 and 2004, of which half by value were KANU's and half NARC's. The promissory notes on six contracts worth Ksh25.1 billion had been cancelled and no payments made since 2005.[94] Of the remainder, three had been completed and paid for. The rest were stalled because the state had suspended payment. The money lost or stolen was undisclosed. Some argued that the government's liabilities were higher than estimated because the commitments had been irrevocable promissory notes, which could not be cancelled.[95]

International and Donor Relations

The government's first year in power was a honeymoon period with the donors, to whom many of its members had been close for a decade. Committed to compliance with international prescriptions, many expected that the aid taps would be rapidly turned on, and that Kenya would experience an economic boom as a result of Western investment, proper financial management and an end to corruption. Things did not work out that way. NARC found that the IFIs continued to apply the same requirements to them as to KANU. While greater trust in the government's probity and capacity inspired stronger support for state-led development (rather than via NGOs), the government's internal divisions and inability to address corruption soon frustrated the donors. While Kibaki wanted to take a more independent line towards the West than Moi had done, he could not insulate Kenya from aid-related disputes, while differing goals between Western governments, populations and aid bureaucracies produced contradictory and inconsistent outcomes.

Aid is Restored, but Donors are Wary

In November 2003, the IMF finally approved a new three-year PRGF loan to Kenya for US$253 million, satisfied with Kenya's combination of anti-corruption zeal and fiscal probity. However, only the first of the three PRGF tranches had been received by July 2004. The rest was again on hold, as under KANU, awaiting faster privatisation for Telkom Kenya, KPLC and the remainder of the KCB. Donors were also worried by the evidence they were uncovering of corruption. The EU suspended aid in July 2004 in protest at the handling of Anglo-Leasing. Although the anti-corruption legislation the donors demanded had been passed, they remained doubtful about Kenya's privatisation speed and expansionary spending plans. There was disappointment at the delay to constitutional reform and the divisions between the LDP and NAK. Meanwhile, it was KANU that was arguing that the government was reforming too little, too late, and that aid should not be disbursed.

Eventually, the IMF released the next tranche in September 2004 to fill the growing budget deficit, which had been exacerbated by rising oil prices, and even raised Kenya's loan entitlement to US$326 million in December. Most other donors followed suit. The April 2005 consultative group meeting, which was expected to punish the government, proved abortive. Further disbursements planned for late 2005 were delayed by the sacking of the Cabinet, but IMF reviews were still positive. Total aid disbursements actually rose from US$454 million in 2002 to US$677 million in 2005.

World Bank and British aid continued into 2006. However, a partial break came in 2006. With the international climate changing, the *Standard* raid and the Armenian saga (see below) cost the country dear, and the PGRF was suspended again in March 2006. As under KANU, however, politics and economics often conflicted, and PGRF support was restarted in March 2007, just before the elections.

International Relations

Relations with the US remained complex, driven by contradictory security, political and economic criteria. The US still viewed Kenya as an anchor state in East Africa, the centre of its regional security initiatives and the site of its largest African embassy. Kibaki's conservative and growth-focused politics went down well in the Bush administration of 2001–8, particularly in contrast to Odinga's socialist rhetoric. However, concerns over state corruption often conflicted with this close security engagement.

Kenya under Kibaki continued to be a fairly reliable ally in the 'war on terror', allowing the FBI to search for Al Qaeda suspects on the Coast and taking advantage of free American training for its security forces (though Kenya declined to join the US invasion of Iraq). Kenya allowed the Americans to set up a small US military base in Lamu to support operations. In return, the US provided significant security assistance to Kenya. Kenyan, American and British security forces worked together secretly to detain and extradite for 'rendition' elsewhere more than 100 Kenyans, Somali and others fleeing Somalia in 2007.[96] However, there was a price to pay at home. Heavy-handed searches and interrogations by Kenyan and US intelligence services worsened relations with coastal Muslims, and anti-American sentiment grew. The government's failed 2003 Suppression of Terrorism Bill roused passions because of the perception that it targeted Muslims, violated constitutional freedoms and had been dictated by the US.

A rare exception to this pattern was the surge of popular interest in US Senator Barack Obama, whose father was a Luo from Alego. His ascent of the US political tree from 2004 became a symbol (particularly for Luo) of the difference between the 'meritocracy' of the US and the 'big man' tribalism of Kenya. It also reaffirmed local perceptions of patronage and obligation, in which the Luo (including Odinga) tried to 'capture' Obama for themselves and create an obligation for him and the US to develop their region and ethnic community.[97]

Relations with the UK worsened under NARC, as the government found the British 'special relationship' an uncomfortable legacy. British High Commissioner Edward Clay, a political officer in Kenya in the early 1970s, emerged as a strong critic of the new government, with a series of critiques of state corruption that raised his profile as high as that of former US Ambassador Smith Hempstone in the 1990s. As with Hempstone, the British government, while far from happy, could not condemn him directly, since British policy was publicly hostile to international corruption. Popular pressure in the West and the desire in Tony Blair's government to increase aid to Africa jarred with the reality that much of that aid was being misused. Clay's protests culminated in a notorious speech in July 2004, as the Anglo-Leasing scandal became public, in which he accused the government of 'vomiting' over the shoes of donors and Kenyans in their gluttony. This aroused commendation and condemnation in equal measure.[98] Clay was back in the news in February 2005 with more pungent criticism of the Anglo-Leasing contracts, when he announced that he had handed over information to Kibaki regarding 20 cases of grand corruption, half related to internal security, worth over Ksh40 billion (US$525 million).[99] Pro-Kibaki ministers responded robustly, suggesting that British interests had been 'well represented in the Kenyatta and Moi governments' and that they were targeting NARC because NARC refused to do their bidding.[100] Foreign Minister Mwakwere called Clay a 'congenital liar'. Kimunya threatened to have Clay arrested, and to charge with treason civil servants who had leaked information to him.[101]

The relationship was further affected by the 2003 travel advisory warning and a series of legal cases alleging rape by British soldiers training in Kenya and injuries caused by unexploded munitions left over from decades of exercises in Samburu and

Laikipia. After Murungaru was barred from the UK, the Kenyans prevented British troops training for the first time since 1964.[102] Further damage was done by a furore over two books criticising the colonial power for its actions during Mau Mau.[103] Lawyers representing Mau Mau veterans also filed lawsuits against the British government alleging torture. Eventually, defence minister Karume and the British did a deal and training recommenced in 2006, but relations remained strained.

Kenya, like other African countries, was now looking wider afield for economic assistance, since both the US and the UK had proved unreliable patrons. From the east, Japan had long been a major donor, particularly in education and energy. China was another significant ally, as the new giant sought resources and entered into agreements with fewer strings attached than the more squeamish West. Kibaki visited China in 2005, seeking investment and trade, and the Chinese premier signed an oil exploration deal when he visited Kenya in 2006. Chinese companies tripled their exports to Kenya between 2001 and 2005.[104] Their road-building businesses prospered, Chinese tourism increased and in 2007 the Chinese even offered military assistance to Kenya. Western donors feared both the loss of their 'soft power' in Africa and a hardening of state resolve against their aid conditionalities.

Regional Changes and East African Federation

Regionally, Kibaki continued the activist policies of his predecessor and only gradually replaced KANU's diplomats and envoys. Eventually, Kenya managed to broker peace deals in both Somalia and the Sudan under his watch, initiatives that Moi had long championed.

There were also successes within the East African region, again building on a decade of work by the Moi government. In March 2004, the leaders of the EAC agreed a full customs union with a common external tariff. Kenya allowed the other two countries to export manufactured products to it duty free, while Uganda and Tanzania retained small tariffs on Kenyan products, which were gradually to be phased out. In previous decades, it would have been a major step, but the impact when it came into effect on 1 January 2005 was modest.

In November 2004, the three states also committed themselves to full federation in 2010, with a federal parliament and government, the same goal they had sought in 1963.[105] They agreed a six-year timetable for regional integration, including a new federal constitution by 2007. However, this fast-track plan proved over-ambitious, as there was still fear of domination by Kenya, the economic giant of the region. In 2007, history was made when Rwanda and Burundi joined the EAC, its first expansion, creating a regional market of over 100 million people. Planning continued, but even a revised 2013 target for political federation and a common market and monetary union (modelled on the EU) was wildly optimistic. There was huge goodwill for the community, but the politics and economics alike remained unclear and the prospects for common currencies, parliaments and governments very uncertain.

The Effect on the Economy

Growth and Macro-Economic Performance

Economic growth, absent in the last days of KANU, reignited. A disappointing 2.9 per cent growth in GDP in 2003 became 5.1 per cent in 2004, 5.8 per cent in 2005, 6.1 per cent in 2006 and 7.1 per cent in 2007, the highest for 20 years (though this was also a side-effect of a new system of national accounts). It was the strongest period of sustained growth for decades, and reflected improvements in virtually every sector of the economy. GDP per capita also turned upwards in 2004 for the first time since 1996 (see Figure 12.6). Although there was frustration about the slow pace of change in 2003 and 2004, which contributed to the general feeling of disappointment, most Kenyans agreed that the government had delivered on its economic promises. But it did this through better administration rather than structural reforms, and through higher public spending. Its policies were little different to KANU's: the difference was in their execution and the external response. Most of the growth was driven by domestic investment, rather than aid or foreign private sector inflows.

The Nairobi Stock Exchange saw spectacular growth to a new high in 2006–7, with the index quadrupling from its 2001–2 low point. Foreign investors drove much of this growth (although rules requiring 25 per cent local ownership remained).

The recovery took place despite the rapid rise in world oil prices during 2003–6, which worsened Kenya's terms of trade, cut growth and fuelled inflation. However, Kenya's liberalised economy was more robust than in the 1970s and 1980s. Inflation rose above 10 per cent a year, but then slackened, actively managed by the Treasury and Central Bank. The shilling appreciated against the dollar, rising from its low of nearly 80 in 2001 to 62 in December 2007. Kenya's liberalised economy became more open and its balance of payments improved, with rising exports and higher foreign reserves.

The manufacturing sector grew steadily but unspectacularly. COMESA continued to offer a vibrant market for Kenyan manufactures, but the percentage of GDP generated by manufacturing remained at around 10 per cent (revised down from 13

12.6: Changes in GDP and GDP per capita, 1997–2007 (constant prices)

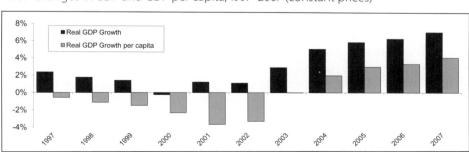

Source: Republic of Kenya, *Statistical Abstracts*, 2001–9

per cent according to new estimation methods). Unit labour costs remained relatively high and infrastructure poor, particularly in the power and transport sectors, import procedures were still lengthy and weaknesses in the legal system remained hurdles to overcome.[106] New jobs remained rare. Public sector jobs continued to shrink, while formal private sector jobs grew at 4 per cent a year in 2002–6, a performance little different from that of 1988–98. As before, most new arrivals in the labour market were deemed to have joined the informal sector.

Incomes grew in the private sector and amongst the wealthier, but the government's strategy was slow to deliver for the poorest. The UN's human development and security indicators for Kenya improved fractionally after 2005, but the percentage of people living in poverty was estimated to have increased from 45 per cent in 1992 to 56 per cent in 2005, while the wealthiest 10 per cent of Kenyans received 42 per cent of the country's income.[107] Nyanza, the rural Coast and North-Eastern Province had the highest poverty levels in the country; Central Province and Nairobi the lowest. By most indices (life expectancy, poverty, child mortality, malaria, AIDS/ HIV), Nyanza performed particularly badly, providing real ammunition for the Luo community's perception of marginalisation.

Taxation and Debt

Tax receipts increased substantially with less corruption and more efficiency in tax collection, exceeding projections by nearly Ksh30 billion a year, a valuable safety net that helped to finance higher government spending. While domestic borrowing continued to grow, the government's overseas borrowings dropped from 35 to less than 25 per cent of GDP between 2002 and 2007.[108] The duty and tariff reforms of the last decade continued to deliver gains, and the position was helped by the stronger enforcement of import tariffs and anti-dumping measures. Kibaki also established a special committee in 2005 to review the government's 'pending bills', which totalled Ksh100 billion (US$1.5 billion) by 2007.[109] Most were found to be invalid.

External debt servicing was now modest in comparison with the 1980s as a percentage of GDP. The Paris Club rescheduled another Ksh27 billion (US$350 million) in debts in January 2004 to allow the government to invest more in poverty reduction. However, with public spending regularly exceeding budgets, difficulties in meeting donor aid conditions and large spending programmes, the government had to borrow on the domestic market, to the point that in 2007 domestic debt exceeded foreign debt, again threatening to crowd out private sector investment. Key parastatals including Telkom, KBC, KenGen, Kenya Railways and Nzoia Sugar remained unable to service their debts to the government or pay their taxes. Total debt continued to rise, exceeding US$10 billion in 2006.[110]

In an unprecedented gesture, in 2007, Kenya opened its foreign debt register as of 2002 to the public, revealing more than US$5 billion in liabilities for education, agriculture, roads, water, housing, health, energy, security and Paris Club loans going back decades.[111] This was part of a campaign to encourage foreign governments to cancel old debts. It showed many loans for controversial, overpriced projects or for projects that simply never took place. From 2004 on, the government ceased to budget for IFI aid (except for committed funding), to avoid the damaging fiscal effects if it was delayed or denied.

Privatisation

NARC was committed to the privatisation of Kenya's remaining parastatals. In practice, however, it could move little faster than its predecessor, and its successes were built on the foundations laid in the Moi era. The government eventually unwound some of the worst problems, but the process proceeded slowly, vexed by legal and political disputes. The key problem NARC faced – like KANU before it – was that external pressure to privatise and cut the civil service would improve economic efficiency, but result in mass unemployment without a flexible and rapidly expanding private sector. KenGen (the hydroelectric power generator) was part-privatised on the stock exchange in 2005–6, as was another chunk of Mumias Sugar. The KNTC, founded in 1965, was wound up in 2006, and 40 per cent of Kenya Reinsurance was sold in 2007, but other planned privatisations failed. After years of planning, Kenya Railways was franchised out in 2006 under a 25-year concession to a South African and Kenyan consortium, and began shedding staff, but it struggled financially because of the appalling state of the track and wagons it had inherited. The Kenya Ports Authority was restructured, and its performance improved.

The government faced pressure, as its predecessor had done, to sell assets only to locals and to avoid privatisations that advantaged foreigners. A donor-inspired Privatisation Act was rejected by Parliament in 2004, then passed in 2005, but never put into effect. Critics said it was likely to 'become a vehicle for corrupt practices, covert sale of public assets and unnecessary "foreignisation" of our economy'.[112] The belief that the IFIs were working at the behest of international capital and against Kenyan interests remained widespread.[113]

The Quagmire of Telecommunications

The most significant remaining candidate for restructuring and sale was Telkom Kenya. After a decade of equivocation, the state operator was losing more than US$25 million a year, services were poor and costs high. Privatisation and the end of its monopoly had been planned for 2003–4, but did not actually take place until 2007. Telkom was in chaos, and the risk of complete collapse and its political consequences forced NARC into delay after delay. Privatisation plans were hampered by three drawbacks: many of the company's assets had already been 'sold' and the proceeds embezzled; the workforce was grossly overmanned; and Telkom was financially near collapse. The pressure on Kenya mounted as donors demanded action as a condition for World Bank loans, but the political cost was too high. Although subsidies were cut, plans to license a second national operator in 2004 fell apart.[114] In 2006 and 2007, staff numbers were cut and the government announced that a strategic investor would be brought in and a third of the company sold on the stock exchange. However, allegations of dirty tricks in the bidding and protests at the sale of strategic assets to foreigners proved political footballs between the government and the new opposition. Eventually, in 2007, just before the elections, the state tendered 51 per cent of Telkom. To do so, it had to write off Ksh64 billion of debt (US$900 million) owed to pensioners, staff and shareholders to give the company a clean balance sheet. The scale of the mismanagement was stunning. A France Telecom-led consortium bought it for US$390 million.[115]

In parallel, in 2006, the CCK licensed a (foreign) second operator to compete against Telkom in fixed and mobile voice, Internet and international communications. It had also franchised a third mobile operator in 2003, but this resulted in lawsuits when the state tried to cancel the licence (since the mandatory Kenyan partner could not pay its share of the licence fees). Instead, to raise money, the state sold another 25 per cent of Safaricom in 2007–8. At Ksh200 billion, it was the largest privatisation in Kenya's history. Odinga tried to stop the sale, claiming that Kenyans were being fleeced by the government in alliance with foreign capital.[116] Nonetheless, the offering proved extremely successful, demonstrating both the depth of local capital and the value mobile phones offered to countries such as Kenya.

Energy

The energy sector saw a new focus on rural electrification, which increased access from 5 to 10 per cent of the population between 2003 and 2007. Donor support to the sector resumed with changes at the top of KPLC. A new Energy Act was passed in 2006 and under World Bank pressure, the management of KPLC was finally franchised in 2007 to a Canadian firm (though it inspired protests at 'whites' running national institutions and being paid more than locals).[117] Prices were still subsidised to support consumers. Installed capacity grew with the coming on stream of a new geothermal plant in 2004 and the long-delayed Japanese-funded hydroelectric scheme at Sondu-Miiru was commissioned in 2008.

The Mombasa oil refinery – the only one left in East and Central Africa – posed more of a problem, as its operations were increasingly uneconomic. The multinationals eventually sold their half to an Indian corporation in 2008–9. In the oil marketing business, ExxonMobil divested in 2007 and BP pulled out of Africa entirely, while the other majors continued to struggle against competition from low-cost independents. Shell divested in 2011. Kenya's 40-year search for oil continued, but nothing had yet been found.

More Problems in Banking

The banking sector continued to suffer from predation and the after-effects of previous misbehaviour. Although Barclays posted healthy profits, more than half of Kenya's 50 banks would have been insolvent if non-performing loans were written off.[118] Bank failures continued. In 2003, Euro Bank collapsed, costing parastatals millions and CBK Governor Nahashon Nyagah his job, and it was followed by the collapse of Daima Bank. Allegations of drug-money laundering and tax evasion inspired a state takeover of Charterhouse Bank in 2006 (though the beneficiaries were not disclosed).[119] A cut-down version of the Donde Act finally became law in 2007, limiting the total interest on any debt to double the principal.

Agricultural Recovery

Kenya's agricultural performance improved under NARC, though the government's main contribution to this was the write-off of old debts and the reactivation of collapsed state-owned enterprises (which KANU had resisted under IFI pressure). Tea, horticulture, sugar and livestock all performed well. Kenya remained the world's largest tea exporter, and the crop continued to produce a quarter of the country's export earnings. The growth of horticulture continued, to the point where Kenya overtook Israel as a flower exporter and horticultural exports exceeded those of tea.

Coffee production in contrast struggled, down to only 4 per cent of Kenya's exports. Its institutions had virtually collapsed and many growers had abandoned the crop. To restore the industry, once the basis of Central Province's profitability, was a priority for NARC. The 2001 Coffee Act had begun truly liberalising the sector, freeing marketing from the Coffee Board. In 2004, the government promised to write off Ksh5.8 billion of old debts to the Cooperative Bank, despite the cost to the Exchequer and the political implications of benefiting particular individuals and communities.[120] It also forced a re-merger of small cooperatives to improve efficiency, and licensed dozens of new marketing agents. Prices rose, but the industry still suffered from over-regulation and over-capacity. Production remained around 50,000 tonnes a year and Kenya's market share continued to decline.

Sugar production rose, but this sector too remained troubled. In 2004, the industry entered another crisis, caused again by COMESA imports during a period when the main plants were closed for maintenance. There were more allegations of price fixing and of cartels buying up sugar to inflate prices. There was conflict between the Sugar Board and the Kenya Revenue Authority, which the board accused of corruptly authorising duty-free imports. Agriculture Minister Kirwa walked a tightrope between economic liberals and coastal sugar tycoons (who supported more imports) and protectionists and those in Nyanza and Western Province whose livelihoods depended on the industry (who supported protection). Eventually, a new COMESA quota was agreed, but the disputes continued. The underlying issue remained the high local price of sugar and the inability of Kenyan producers to compete internationally. Efforts to restore Muhoroni and Miwani (still in receivership) continued, but privatisation of the factories (apart from Mumias) remained impractical, even though the state wrote off Ksh4.8 billion of debts.

Although maize production hit an all-time peak in 2006, Kenya remained in a structural food deficit, requiring regular maize imports. This was worsened by exports of maize stocks by the state-owned NCPB, raising money to clear its debts to farmers. Drought followed by floods led to food shortages in 2004 and again in 2005–6 in northern Kenya, part of what appeared an endemic cycle of suffering. Donors and the government spent at least US$230 million on food aid. Despite state commitments to the full commercialisation of the NCPB, it continued to intervene in the market and provide subsidised products to farmers.

The state also intervened in other sectors, recapitalising struggling institutions such as the AFC and writing off old debts. It bought back and reactivated the KCC, reconstituted as the 'New KCC' and by 2005, chaired by Kibaki's old ally Matu Wamae, it was growing rapidly, sustained by government loans, and milk production was back to the level it had reached before the KCC's collapse. The state also managed to revive the Bunyala and Ahero irrigation schemes. Not all was rosy, however. While payments to farmers from some marketing boards improved, others remained three to six years behind in their accounts. In the pyrethrum sector, farmers were only paid in 2007 for their 2003 crop.

Tourism, Wildlife and the Environment

With the furore over Al Qaeda, the Mombasa attacks in 2002 and British and American travel alerts, tourism flattened out in 2003. The country's image improved in 2004; visitor numbers and receipts grew, and there was substantial investment in the marketing of tourism. Earnings grew rapidly, to the point where tourism became the country's largest foreign exchange earner, and visitor numbers reached all-time highs (see Figure 12.7).

For Kenya's wildlife, however, the period was mixed. The tension continued between those who believed the interests of animals were paramount and those

12.7: International tourist and business arrivals, 1963–2009

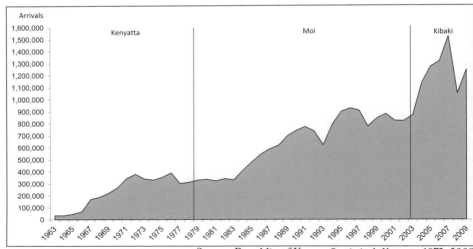

Source: Republic of Kenya, *Statistical Abstracts*, 1972–2009

who believed that human needs should dominate. Amboseli National Park was controversially degazetted in 2005, relaxing controls on land use and moving control to the Ol Kejuado Council. There were even proposals, eventually abandoned, to franchise all the national parks to a private company.

Parliament and Opposition

The Performance of Parliament

Many expected an explosion of energy in the National Assembly, driven by a well-educated, cosmopolitan, second generation of Young Turks. However, in practice Parliament became less rather than more effective, and lost rather than gained credibility. Popular perceptions of MPs' performance were hostile, influenced by the tripling of salaries and allowances that they awarded themselves in 2003 (MPs still set their own salaries).[121] MPs were now very well paid, with an untaxed income of US$150,000 a year plus benefits. Some appeared indifferent to the public or even the local good, and simply in it for the money. Some were obviously for sale, taking cash for asking questions and casting their votes.[122]

Although on paper the government had a massive majority, it was so divided that its true parliamentary strength was uncertain, and it came under sustained attack from the LDP, but also from FORD-Kenya and NPK MPs, determined to assert their independence from the *kiama* (council) around Kibaki. More and more time was lost in inconclusive debates on constitutional reform and partisan sniping. By 2004, LDP backbenchers were effectively free to vote against the government when they wished, and the state lost several motions and bills. Parliament's failure to hold the government to account on Anglo-Leasing cost it dearly, as did the confusion over which parties MPs were in, which became systemic in 2006–7.

Parliament was also less vigorous in asserting its independence from the executive. The parliamentary committee structure continued to strengthen, but the most significant reform, the reintroduction in 2004 by KANU MP Charles Keter of the bill to allow Parliament to set its own timetable, became mired in the same disputes over the power of the presidency seen in Bomas (because it ended the link between presidential and parliamentary tenure), and was never passed. The Public Accounts Committee fell further and further behind, not debating its 1999/2000 report until 2007. Several bills were passed by Parliament but were refused presidential assent by Kibaki, including Ngilu's health insurance scheme, which an alliance of social reformers, populists and critics had forced on a reluctant government. Kibaki's veto was supported by Western pressure to control state spending and limit Kenya's tax burden. Kibaki also rejected a bill that would have allowed hunting to resume in Kenya's national parks. Several private members' bills, however, did become law.

Probably the biggest change in the role of the MP came with the Constituency Development Fund (CDF), a legislative initiative passed in 2003. This guaranteed that 2.5 per cent of all government development funds would be set aside, to be spent on projects within each constituency, managed by the local MP and his nominees;

75 per cent of the grant was a fixed amount, with 25 per cent set according to local poverty levels. It was designed to give local communities the power to choose the projects of most benefit to them, like the District Focus for Rural Development of the 1980s. It was intended not only to address disparities in regional development, but also to reduce the pressure on the politician as provider. It proved simultaneously an example of decentralised decision-making and a patronage opportunity for the incumbents, whose powers to distribute the funds were almost unchecked.

The result was an explosion of road repairs, classroom building, water projects, health centres and police posts, for some areas the first visible state-funded projects for decades. However, there were not always funds or staff to maintain these investments, and the CDF committees experienced widespread politicisation, theft and abuse. Despite this, the CDF budget was increased to Ksh10 billion (US$145 million) in 2006. By the 2007 elections, it had become a liability to most incumbents, since they could no longer blame central government or claim lack of resources for projects, and because of the widespread belief that they had abused the system for their own benefit.

Election Petitions

Although the 2002 elections had been the freest and fairest yet, there was the usual crop of parliamentary petitions: 27 were filed, the same number as in 1997. In contrast to previous elections, the winning party faced only eight challenges, while NARC and its allies challenged 17 of KANU's seats. Most were again thrown out on technicalities, despite the courts now permitting petitions to be served through radio or TV advertisements, rather than in person in exceptional circumstances. In the end, only one MP lost his seat as a result. However, the shortage of judges led to the situation that by the 2007 general election eight of the petitions against the 2002 election had not been heard. This was a systematic failure of controls over electoral malpractice.

Transitions

The period saw a stream of deaths amongst Kenyatta and Moi-era political heavy-weights. Those who passed away in 2003 included George Anyona, Wamalwa and Julius Kiano. In 2004, Elijah Mwangale, Matthew Muli, Mulu Mutisya, Paul Ngei, Joshua Angatia, Andrew Omanga, Maitha and Kihika Kimani followed them. Shariff Nassir and Bildad Kaggia died in 2005, Isaiah Mathenge, Kamwithi Munyi and Bonaya Godana in 2006, and Ramogi Achieng-Oneko, Darius Mbela and Taita Towett in 2007. The old era was finally passing.

The Lost Constitution, March 2004–November 2005

For 18 months after the crisis of March 2004, the government equivocated, divided and with many searching for a way to modify the Bomas 'Zero Draft' of the constitution. They eventually succeeded in using Parliament to modify the Bomas proposals, creating a new draft known as the 'Wako Constitution'. The result was a catastrophe.

A Year of Stalemate, 2004–5

According to the law, Attorney-General Wako was supposed to receive the new constitution from Bomas, then publish a bill within 14 days to introduce it, but a series of lawsuits had derailed the process. Despite Kibaki's reassurances that his government would follow a consensus approach, there was no consensus to follow. Many in the government were determined not to implement the Zero Draft, and they had the legal demand for a referendum in their pocket. Their opponents were more numerous, angry and committed to a structural change in the relationship between citizen and state. It was stalemate. The CKRC adjourned and Ghai resigned in frustration. MPs caucused and argued as their self-imposed 30 June 2004 deadline passed. There were violent protests at the delay.[123] The government banned these demonstrations, as KANU had done, breaking up protesters with water cannon, leading to expressions of concern by the Americans and messages of support for the new constitution from Western donors. The calls grew to sack Raila and the other LDP ministers, though they still avoided a direct confrontation.[124]

The Cabinet (including the LDP leaders, whose position was becoming extremely difficult) eventually instructed Wako to introduce legislation to allow Parliament to amend the Bomas Draft. In August 2004, Parliament duly passed yet another Constitution of Kenya (Review) Act, giving it control of the process. However, it included an amendment from the new Parliamentary Select Committee (PSC) Chairman Ruto that required a 65 per cent majority to make any changes. Kibaki therefore refused to sign the bill into law, it was returned for amendment, and Parliament – with the GNU now holding a working majority – modified this to a simple majority. Kibaki finally assented to the bill in January 2005, giving him control over the Constitution once more.[125] Meanwhile, in November 2004 the PSC had agreed a compromise: there would be two levels of government only (national and county), and an ambiguous power sharing between president and prime minister.

The process dragged on into 2005, searching for an agreement that could then be put to a referendum. Relations with Bomas supporters deteriorated, since the PSC was now dominated by pro-government figures and chaired by Nyachae. At a conference in Kilifi, the PSC agreed yet another set of amendments. Devolution would be to the district level, there would be only one house in the Assembly, and the prime minister would be a presidential nominee accountable to the president and with limited powers: an 'errand boy', in Odinga's trenchant language.[126] The subsequent report was acrimoniously approved by Parliament on 21 July by 102 votes to 61, amidst street demonstrations.[127] The government split in two. While most ministers were in favour, Odinga, Anyang' Nyong'o, Balala and George Ayacko voted against, as did KANU's Kenyatta, Moi and Ruto.[128] The LDP was now effectively in the opposition.

The Referendum Debacle, November 2005

The resulting constitution, known as the 'Wako Draft', published in August, had to be put to a referendum, Kenya's first. However, the country was deeply divided both on the merits of the new constitution and the process by which it had been cobbled together. The result was a final split in NARC, and the ignominious rejection of the proposals.

The campaign began in August, and in October ministers were 'given time off' to campaign, as the split in the Cabinet was irrevocable.[129] The LDP and seven ministers drove the 'No' campaign, led by Odinga and Musyoka and by former civic society figures Anyang' Nyong'o and Kilimo, whose position was based more on their support for Bomas than hostility to the government per se. Most KANU leaders, including Kenyatta, Ruto, Moi and even the elderly Charles Njonjo, joined them, as did influential organisations such as the KNUT and many churches. The rest of the 30-member Cabinet and most of NAK campaigned in favour, including Ngilu, Kombo, Awori and Saitoti, some KANU MPs, FORD-People and some church leaders. Kibaki himself was initially equivocal, asking voters to decide for themselves, but buying support through new projects, salary rises for councillors, new districts and allotment letters for squatters, and criticising the 'No' lobby as lying to Kenyans and seeking power by the back door.[130] In an eve of poll television address, he asked Kenyans to vote 'Yes'.

The ECK supervised the referendum, and allocated the supposedly content-free symbols of a banana (pro-new constitution) and an orange (against) to the two factions. From the start, however, the Orange team had the better organisation, branding and popular reception, drawing parallels with the recent Orange revolution in the Ukraine. Its leaders built an increasingly confident machine that reduced NAK's frontmen Murungi and Nyachae to impotence. Although the 'Yes' campaign still had a narrow majority of MPs behind it (118 to 90, with 14 declining to take a position) the country's mood was hostile.[131] From what was initially predicted to be a reasonably easy win, the contest moved against the Wako Draft. Much of the hostility was based on the process by which the draft had been created, rather than its content. The issues at stake included not only the constitution itself, but also land (as there were fears that the constitution's centralised land provisions might once more support a Kikuyu 'return to the rift'), the role of the Kadhi's courts, and the performance of the government since 2002. The campaign was violent, with eight or nine killed in fighting and hundreds injured.[132] There was widespread campaigning by civil servants and misuse of government resources by the Banana side. Observers noted that 'Tribal sentiments, hate speech ethnic hatred tribal polarisation and emotions were whipped up' by both sides, a sign of trouble to come.[133]

On 21 November 2005, the nation voted, with only one ballot paper and two options: 'Are you for' (Banana) and 'Are you against' (Orange). The Banana team was decisively defeated, by 3.6 million votes (58 per cent) to 2.6 million (41 per cent). Nyanza, the Coast, the Rift Valley, North-Eastern and Western (the KANU and LDP heartlands) all voted Orange; Eastern and Nairobi split down the middle; only Central Province voted overwhelmingly in favour.[134] Although there was widespread intimidation and bribery, 5,000 (donor-funded) domestic monitors reported that the referendum was well-conducted, voting was generally free and fair, and an exit poll produced similar results.[135] Turnout was low, at 54 per cent.

The reasons for the government's defeat were simple. First, the draft constitution appeared to fly in the face of the CKRC and Bomas's achievements over many years. Second, Kibaki's allies and enemies both turned it into a referendum on the government's performance, and the government was unpopular outside the Mount Kenya region. Third, the Orange camp had Odinga – whose energy and organisational ability was unparalleled – plus other influential ethno-regional leaders, particularly Musyoka in Ukambani. Fourth, devolution was genuinely popular, particularly in the ex-KADU Rift and the Coast, while the Luo were determined to see their champion as Kenya's second prime minister. Finally, the 'Yes' team ran a poor campaign. They appeared to be expecting a win until the last minute.[136]

The numbers were damning. Since 2002, Kibaki had lost the Luo, the Kamba, the non-Bukusu Luhya and the Mijikenda, and only picked up support amongst the Kikuyu, Embu and Meru and Gusii (see Figure 12.8). His efforts to woo KANU supporters in Kalenjin and pastoral areas had resulted in defeat there also.

With the Wako Draft rejected, Kenya retained the 1964/1969 republican Constitution. The Orange Democratic Movement (ODM), as the 'No' group dubbed itself, called for the reactivation of the constitutional review process. However, the CKRC soon shut down, having spent Ksh4 billion (US$50 million) over five years for nothing. The ODM also called the result a referendum on the government's performance, and demanded either a snap election or Kibaki's resignation. The government of course rejected such calls. Kibaki himself accepted the result stoically. As he said, 'The people have made a choice and, as I have always said, my Government would respect the choice of the people.'[137] It was the signal, however, for the long-awaited restructuring of Kenya's political system.

12.8: Difference between Kibaki's 2002 presidential vote and 2005 referendum yes vote

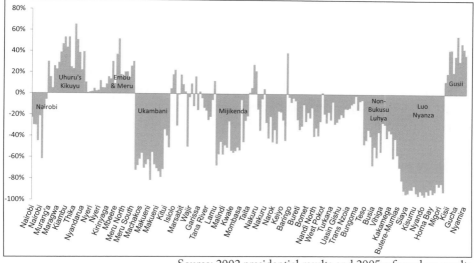

Source: 2002 presidential results and 2005 referendum results

Dissolution and Reconstruction, November–December 2005

Once the constitution's defeat became public, on 23 November 2005, Kibaki dissolved the entire government mid-term, for the first time in Kenya's history. Rather than calling elections, which he knew the NAK wing would lose, he restructured the government in an unprecedented manoeuvre that left the county leaderless (apart from himself, the vice-president and attorney-general) for two weeks. During this period, he cloistered himself with a small team of advisers, and reached out to some of those who had opposed him in the past, including ex-president Moi. In the meantime, fearful of some form of non-violent revolution following the model of events in the Ukraine, the government banned all Orange rallies as a 'threat to national security'.[138]

After a period of desperate negotiations, Kibaki announced his new administration on 7 December.[139] He finally dropped all the Orange leaders, including Odinga, Musyoka, Balala, Ntimama, Ayacko, Anyang' Nyong'o and Kilimo, who had again maintained a united front, demanding that they all be reappointed or fired together. Kibaki chose to sack them. He moved Murungi out of Justice and Constitutional Affairs (replacing him with Kikuyu lawyer Martha Karua), and dropped Murungaru entirely (though he remained influential behind the scenes). Instead, he promoted several NAK assistant ministers and tried to persuade individual LDP and KANU MPs to join him. Negotiations continued until the last minute, but failed. The result was a disaster. Three ministers and 15 KANU, FORD-Kenya, LDP and NPK assistant ministers rejected their appointments, unwilling to abandon the ODM or holding out for more. There was a week-long stand-off, during which Ngilu and Kombo refused to accept their posts until their parties were given more jobs, holding the government to ransom. Worse, FORD-Kenya demanded that it (and the Luhya community) receive a percentage allocation of ambassadors, permanent secretaries and parastatal posts, a public admission that ethnicity and party played a role in the selection of senior civil servants.[140]

Eyeball to eyeball, Kibaki blinked. On 13 December 2005, FORD-Kenya and the NPK negotiated themselves an extra four Cabinet posts and five assistant ministerial roles, in what was now explicitly a coalition government. Half the Cabinet was Kikuyu or Luhya. Tuju was the only Luo willing to risk Raila's wrath (he would pay the price in 2007). The government's size rose to 85, with 35 ministers, its largest number yet. Kibaki was buying support anywhere he could find it, and the price had to be paid in salaries and expenses. The donors were disappointed and said so publicly.[141]

Embattled and Isolated

Unpopular, enmeshed in corruption allegations, haemorrhaging ministers and without even a political party on which to base itself, the first three months of 2006 were Kibaki's low point.

To address the deep national frustration, Kibaki pledged a fresh start on constitutional reform in January 2006, and set up another Committee of Eminent

Persons to investigate what should be done. However, the nation was tired of this frustrating and unproductive process. There was little interest amongst either the government or the opposition in a compromise. The beleaguered government viewed the ODM as irreconcilably hostile, and since it preferred the current constitution to any devolved power system or power sharing, there seemed little incentive to reach out. Although Kibaki promised a bill to revive the constitutional review process, even a set of minimum reforms agreed by all parties faded away in the run-up to the polls. The battle would be fought on the same terms as in 2002.

Kibaki also turned to his old nemesis, Daniel arap Moi. In a series of private meetings between November 2005 and February 2006, Moi committed himself to backing Kibaki. There was talk of the restoration of the Kikuyu–Kalenjin alliance that had sustained the country in the late 1960s. Odinga alleged that Kibaki agreed to go slow on the Kroll corruption investigation in return for Moi's support.[142] Many believed that Moi had made a deal to protect himself at the expense of his community, and he found it unexpectedly difficult to bring his old KANU supporters to Kibaki's side.[143]

Resignations and Dismissals, 2006

The government also proved unable to quiet the Anglo-Leasing furore, fuelled by popular and international anger. Parliamentary questions and foreign protests buttressed the investigations of the KACC and the Public Accounts Committee (chaired by opposition leader Kenyatta). Despite Kibaki's requests that Kenyans not 'waste our energies on unproductive politics', many refused to obey his wishes.[144]

After a year of preparation, in January 2006, Githongo finally went public from London with his corruption allegations in the *Nation*. His evidence suggested that Awori, Murungaru, Muthaura, Murungi and Mwiraria had all tried to stop investigations into the Ksh50 billion Anglo-Leasing contracts because of the involvement of Kibaki insiders in the deals. The suspicion grew that Kibaki had been aware of what his closest allies were doing, but had maintained deniability.[145] The LDP and the emerging ODM alliance called for the government to resign or establish a commission of inquiry, and FORD-Kenya and the NPK also demanded action. Under intense foreign and domestic pressure, Kibaki reaffirmed his commitment to root out corruption. He introduced a new ministerial code of conduct, banning ministers from doing business with the departments they headed.[146] The government also suspended payments on the 18 security contracts until the issue was resolved.

With his credibility at an all-time low, Kibaki was forced to ditch his own closest allies in order to survive. During February 2006, Mwiraria, Saitoti and Murungi all 'resigned', because of evidence associating them with corruption. In Saitoti's case, his resignation followed the publication of the Goldenberg Inquiry's report, which recommended his prosecution for the illegal payment of extra export compensation. Mwiraria and Murungi stood down after the publication of evidence (including tape recordings made by Githongo and broadcast by the BBC) that suggested that they had indeed used the Anglo-Leasing deals to raise money for the inner circle's re-election, and that Murungi had tried to blackmail Githongo to 'go slow' on his investigations. Awori, Wako and Muthaura also came under pressure to resign.

Although Kibaki had shown that he could act against those closest to him, his fragile alliance was further weakened. Although his national popularity improved, the Meru community rallied round their hard-pressed leaders, claiming (just as KANU had done) an ethnic conspiracy against them. The accusations became wilder. Murungaru alleged the entire Anglo-Leasing scandal was a conspiracy hatched by NARC's opponents. Awori claimed the anti-corruption investigations were an attempt by foreign countries to bring down a successful African nation.[147]

The Armenians and the Press

On the night of 1–2 March 2006, the government's remaining credibility was lost when 80 armed, masked police burst into the offices of the *Standard* and KTN, took the TV station off the air, burnt the presses and dismantled equipment, in an intimidatory raid unlike anything seen since 1993. There were suggestions that the raid was connected with the *Standard*'s plans to publish links between relatives of the president and drug smugglers. The government was hopelessly divided, with Police Commissioner Ali denying knowledge of the raids, while the CID director and Security Minister Michuki (both Kikuyu) appeared to admit responsibility.[148] The press was incensed and unbowed: proof it was truly 'free' and no longer subject to the whim of the state, and Western diplomats were openly disgusted at the reversion to the practices of the KANU era. Kibaki was almost certainly unaware in advance of what had occurred. Senator Obama, in Kenya at the time, was amongst those who were publicly critical of the government.

The next few months were dominated by the bizarre events surrounding two well-connected, well-muscled, gold-draped Armenian businessmen, the Artur 'brothers' (as they were known, though they were not in fact Armenian and not related), who had been photographed leading the *Standard* raid. This culminated in an unprecedented drama at Jomo Kenyatta International Airport when officials insisted on inspecting goods they were importing, after which the brothers broke out of the airport at gunpoint. Their house, when raided by reluctant police, uncovered police and Presidential Escort weapons and materials, and evidence that one of them had been appointed as deputy police commissioner with unrestricted access to sensitive installations.[149] They were hurriedly deported.[150] It was discovered that the Arturs had visited State House in February and were linked to Kibaki's daughter by his (alleged) customary wife Mary Wambui. The belief that the inner circle had called on foreign mercenaries and drug dealers to help repress its opponents was universal. Parliament was furious and set up another inquiry, which damned the state's behaviour in its 2007 report. The government suspended CID chief Joseph Kamau but did everything it could to stop further investigations and refused to release the report of its own inquiry for reasons of 'national security'. The Gema inner circle was reaching a point of desperation.

The International Response

In early 2006, several donors suspended aid to Kenya, frustrated by the Anglo-Leasing saga, the attacks on press freedom, the collapse of constitutional reform and delayed privatisation. This did not affect their project commitments in areas such as free primary education and health, however. For the remainder of the NARC-era, the UK and most other Western countries were hostile, damning Kenya's corruption and also accusing it of being 'wide open' to drug cartels and terrorists.[151] However, the World Bank continued funding as did most donors in the project space. US aid (mostly food aid and anti-AIDS campaigns) was back up to US$500 million in 2007. It was a confused message from donors.

Phoney War: The Orange Democratic Movement and NARC-Kenya

During 2006 and early 2007, the consequences of the 2005 referendum played themselves out. Kenyan politics had been restructured and the compromises and ambiguities of 2003–5 resolved. Odinga and the Luo community had moved decisively into opposition to a Gema-led government, as had most Kamba, some Luhya and Kalenjin and the pastoral and coastal ex-KANU regions of the country, supporters of a more decentralised, communal model of political authority. The world had changed over four decades, but at times it seemed the protagonists were playing the same three-way game that their fathers had played in 1960–6.

Political instability increased as party labels became less relevant. KANU was split into several factions; the LDP was mostly in ODM; the government did not really have a party at all; while FORD-Kenya and the NPK moved in and out of NARC as they pleased. Sub-regional and ethnic caucusing became open. With no clear national slates, politicians consolidated their home support. Voters were increasingly confused and focused their support further on their own ethnic community and its patrons.

KANU Fractures

KANU national elections were finally held in January 2005, the first since 1988 and the first without state support. The main contenders for the post of chairman were Kenyatta and Biwott. The polls ended with a chaotic conference at which Uhuru's faction (backed by Ruto, Julius Sunkuli and Gideon Moi) outnumbered the Biwott team. Sensing defeat, Biwott's team walked out and Kenyatta was overwhelmingly elected. Moi, showing his disappointment at the state to which his party was reduced, stayed away.

Just before the polls, pro-Biwott officials registered another splinter party, echoing the splits that had engulfed the opposition after their 1992 defeat.[152] From this time on, a four-way split in KANU deepened, between Uhuru's faction, Biwott's faction, the KANU MPs who had joined the government, and most Kalenjin MPs, who saw their future as lying with Odinga and the LDP. This last group found a champion in the influential William Ruto, who seized the opportunity Moi's departure created and in 2005–6 declared his candidacy for the presidency under both KANU and the ODM banner, the first Kalenjin to challenge Moi's pre-eminence directly.[153] As a political party, KANU had almost ceased to exist.

The LDP, KANU and the ODM

The LDP was now the core of Kenya's opposition. Odinga declared himself a candidate for the LDP's presidential nomination in January 2006, as did Musyoka and Mudavadi. In May, the LDP held its first grassroots polls, but they exposed the deep divisions in the party, and plans for national elections were deferred.

The LDP was also part of the broader Orange movement. Invigorated by their victory, the LDP, KANU and the civil society alliance gradually morphed into a political party, the Orange Democratic Movement. Its six most senior leaders (the LDP's Odinga, Musyoka, Mudavadi and Balala, and KANU's Kenyatta and Ruto) announced in early 2006 that the movement would turn their alliance into a national party and field one candidate against Kibaki in the 2007 elections.[154] The six candidates campaigned together nationwide against the government during 2006, under the slogan 'The Future is Orange'. In September 2006, ODM-Kenya was registered as a political party, with a constituent membership of individual parties, much like NARC's (the name 'ODM' was already taken). However, many in KANU remained reluctant to subsume their party into ODM-Kenya, while Ruto and several others wanted exactly that.

It was also unclear how the ODM-Kenya presidential candidate would be chosen. It was originally planned that the winners from independent KANU and LDP primaries would face each other in a run-off. However, by early 2006, a dispute was building between those who favoured a delegates system (including Odinga), those who favoured a national ballot of party members (which Musyoka wanted) and those who preferred a 'smoke-filled room' deal and a compromise candidate such as Mudavadi. It was the same issue that had split FORD in 1992.

With Ruto backing ODM-Kenya, the Kalenjin community was split, as Moi and Biwott were now supporting the government and opposing any deal with the LDP. Extraordinarily, it seems Kibaki came close to appointing Biwott to his Cabinet in May 2005.[155] Moi campaigned nationwide against Odinga and Ruto during 2006, accusing the ODM of 'Balkanising' Kenya into ethnic blocs. Although Kenyatta had backed a no vote in the 2005 referendum, he was far from comfortable with an Odinga presidency. His support in Central Province would be severely tested and his commitment to devolution was uncertain. Kenyatta and most registered KANU officials moved steadily closer to Kibaki, while Ruto, Nandi ex-minister Henry Kosgey and others insisted that KANU remained part of ODM. Under pressure from inside his community, in June 2007 Uhuru finally declared that (his faction of) KANU would abandon the ODM and go it alone in the elections.

From NARC to NARC-Kenya

Unable to control NARC because of the unreliability of Ngilu, the government also created a new party. NARC-Kenya was registered in early 2006 as a new home for the pro-Kibaki parts of NARC, and soon won the support of most ex-DP, FORD-People and KANU MPs who were supporting the government. The aim was to create a new umbrella party broad enough to capture and retain the support not only of the Kikuyu, Embu and Meru, but also of other individuals and communities who were backing Kibaki. Finally, it seemed the government had a viable party, though MPs could not defect to it without losing their seats. In July 2006, after five MPs died in a plane crash, the resulting by-elections pitted NARC-Kenya against KANU and the LDP (who entered into an electoral pact). NARC-Kenya won three, a good result, though its performance was assisted by the use of state resources in the campaign.

However, the perception soon became widespread that NARC-Kenya was the DP in disguise. NARC-Kenya ended up competing with rather than absorbing FORD-Kenya and the NPK. Nervous and uncertain, Kombo and Ngilu both refused any merger. Indeed, both also held talks with the ODM, contemplating a mass defection, but eventually decided to stay in and support the government, if not its party.[156] When NARC-Kenya tried to hold national elections in early 2007, they too proved acrimonious and badly organised. Kibaki, while appearing to back NARC-Kenya as late as June 2007, never explicitly declared his membership or support for it either.

Crude Conflicts, 2006–7

With two competing super-alliances, all else was subordinated to victory. Plans for further policy reforms, which required unity and a strong mandate, were abandoned. Instead, with the elections due in 2007, the government tried to buy support, much as KANU had done, announcing 38 new districts (taking the total to 108), raising civil service salaries, issuing title deeds to squatters, promising roads and factories, paying farmers' arrears, creating a Ksh1 billion Youth Development kitty, and committing itself to expansionary spending plans. In 2007, the government even unveiled a monument to Dedan Kimathi in Nairobi, 50 years after the Mau Mau leader had been hanged, reminding Kenyans of their debt to the Kikuyu community. Campaigning in the Rift Valley, Kibaki effusively praised former President Moi. The civil service was mobilised to support the government (at least in part), with Internal Security Minister Michuki asking civil servants to campaign for it in February, saying: 'We expect you to reciprocate the good salaries that you have been given by ensuring that citizens are happy with this government.'[157] There were also allegations of a discretionary allocation of funds to pro-government districts and neglect of pro-opposition seats.

The KACC's Anglo-Leasing investigations became bogged down as the increasingly strident government blamed ODM leaders for the contracts issued in the

KANU era. The Public Accounts Committee had recommended Awori, Murungi, Murungaru and Mwiraria for police investigation in 2006, and also proposed that security contracts be subject to parliamentary scrutiny.[158] When KACC proposed in October 2006 that ministers and others be prosecuted, however, Wako refused. Despite the publication of Githongo's tapes, the attorney-general discredited the evidence and returned the cases for further investigation. Ringera's KACC continued to investigate thousands of corruption allegations and to pursue the recovery of assets, including cases against Mudavadi, Noah arap Too and Biwott's companies, but it failed to make headway against state insiders, despite Western exhortations. The KACC and Ringera's credibility were severely affected.[159]

The political seesaw teetered between the two coalitions during 2006–7, with no one sure who would be the candidates or for which parties they would stand. In early 2006, polls placed Musyoka first in a nationwide presidential contest, with Kibaki second, Kenyatta third, Odinga fourth (with around 11 per cent) and Ruto fifth.[160] Federalism remained the main policy divide, but the voting patterns were as much ethnic and personal. By the end of 2006, Kibaki was back on top (with between 42 and 43 per cent) and Musyoka and Raila roughly equal with between 13 and 20 per cent.[161] In June 2007, with election fever now rampant, Kibaki was still the favourite with 45 per cent of the vote, but Odinga's popularity was up to 25 per cent and Musyoka's down to 11, with all the other candidates irrelevant.[162] But ODM-Kenya was consistently the most popular party. Attitudes to the presidency remained divided and variable. Although there was strong support for reduced presidential powers, especially amongst the Kalenjin, Luo and Kamba, there was stronger support for the presidency as an institution than for most other aspects of the political system.[163]

ODM-Kenya conducted an ethnically charged campaign, publicising instances of Kikuyu dominance and inciting protests at Gema tribalism. Odinga called for a Malaysian-style system of ethnic quotas in state appointments.[164] In early 2007, a list of senior appointments circulated on the Internet, alleging that Kikuyu held a disproportionate number of state posts, particularly in the Treasury, the Kenya Revenue Authority, the Central Bank and the finance sector. Opposition MPs took up the call, simultaneously implying both tribalism and a Kikuyu love of money.[165] In response, in April 2007 the government published the entire list of public service and parastatal heads, trying to dispel the 'myth of Kikuyu bias', though it thereby also pandered to the growing conception of ethnic quotas. Ethnic pressures were building in the rural areas too. Well before the polls, ex-KANU ODM leaders were warning non-Kalenjin in the Rift, as they had in 1991–2, to toe the line or face the consequences.[166]

The government sought support wherever it could find it, while some of its original NAK allies were falling away. During 2006–7, Kombo's FORD-Kenya split in two, and Ngilu's NPK/NARC too was severely diminished, each hurt by their ambiguous position half-way between Kibaki and Odinga. Instead, the government appealed to its core Mount Kenya supporters. In November 2006, Kibaki reappointed both Saitoti and Murungi to the Cabinet, their names 'cleared' by their period of purdah, although the Western press was hostile.[167] Mwiraria also returned to the Cabinet in July 2007, and Kibaki appointed yet more KANU MPs. By the end of 2007, less than half of the administration had been in office in January 2003 and one-quarter were from KANU or FORD-People. The political system was in such chaos that the Speaker of Parliament refused to recognise either the GNU or the ODM as legitimate political parties. The political system had gone 'off book'.

Two Oranges and Two Flames

With a year-end election in mind, the coalitions skirmished and prepared. The result was further restructuring and the creation of two new national political parties during 2007.

ODM-Kenya Splits

Like so many of its predecessors, ODM-Kenya split in mid-2007, once more over the issue of who would be its presidential candidate. Odinga was the organisational and popular powerhouse, but some believed he was too controversial and too closely associated with the Luo community's interests to garner nationwide support. Musyoka, long positioning himself for the succession, was still popular in opinion polls but slipping back, with Mudavadi running third. Unable to agree on either a presidential nomination method or on the registered officials of the party (the same issues that had broken FORD in 1992), ODM-Kenya duly fractured in July–August. The registrar threatened to deregister the party if the dispute was not resolved swiftly. In the end, Odinga and his supporters took over a similarly named party (ODM) and its orange symbol. Musyoka defected to the small Labour Party of Kenya, but remained in control of the ODM-Kenya 'party of parties' and brand, with fanatical support in Ukambani, ex-LDP and KANU allies nationwide, a symbol of two oranges and a hatred of Odinga. Only a few months before the general election, it appeared a golden opportunity for Kibaki to secure victory, as Moi had done in 1992, through the division of his opponents.

However, the split was uneven. Demonstrating his growing stature and ability to build a cross-ethnic coalition, Odinga managed to maintain the loyalty of most Orange leaders, including Mudavadi and Ruto, even after he beat them in the election to become ODM's presidential nominee. Many Kalenjin saw Odinga as their best chance for revenge against the Kibaki government. Most Kipsigis and Nandi rejected Moi's entreaties and backed Ruto, Raila and the ODM, while the Keiyo, Tugen and Pokot communities were divided. The ODM established a 'Pentagon' (like 'FORD', an appropriation of an American word of power), of five leaders, to gather the support behind them of their respective communities. Its members were Odinga (Luo), Mudavadi (Luhya), Ruto (Kalenjin), Balala (Arab from the Coast) and Joseph Nyagah (Mbeere). Ngilu also joined the Pentagon in October when she finally walked out of an administration in which she had long ago lost confidence. It was a powerful coalition of ethno-regional leaders, with alliances at every level.

KANU Backs Kibaki, 2007

In response, the Biwott and Uhuru factions of KANU drew closer together and to Kibaki. In August, Moi declared that he would back Kibaki's presidential bid. In September 2007, Uhuru Kenyatta, officially the leader of the opposition, announced that he would not even stand and instead committed himself to Kibaki's re-election.[168] Many saw this decision through an ethnic lens – a reassertion of Kikuyu unity – though it was also a pragmatic choice, as Uhuru faced inevitable defeat in a four-horse race. In return, Uhuru obtained the pro-Kibaki parliamentary nomination for himself and many KANU leaders, a seat in the next government, and a shot at the presidency in 2012. The three non-ODM factions of KANU were now on the same side, and the party reunited to face the polls.

The Party of National Unity

While finally committing himself publicly to a second term in January 2007, Kibaki still did not have a party on which to contest. With NARC under Ngilu's control and NARC-Kenya hard to sell outside the Kikuyu, Embu and Meru, in August 2007 the government invented yet another umbrella alliance: the Party of National Unity (PNU). On 16 September, only three months before the polls, Kibaki announced he would stand on a PNU ticket.[169]

This manufactured party, created specifically to support his re-election, was both a party and a coalition of a dozen independent Kibaki-friendly parties. It absorbed most of the DP, on which its leadership was centred, but was designed as an umbrella movement for a set of regionally strong parties, all of whom supported Kibaki for the presidency. It was a naked political process that pandered to precisely the fissiparous pressures of ethnicity that Kibaki had previously sought to deny. The PNU itself dominated Central Province and had some support elsewhere; KANU was the government's vehicle in the Rift Valley, pastoral areas and North-Eastern; both FORD-Kenya and its factional enemy New FORD-Kenya in Western; Nyachae's FORD-People in Gusii areas; and Shirikisho on the coast. NARC-Kenya, a few weeks ago the party of choice, was allowed to wither, as was the DP. Safina, Mazingira and 18 other micro-parties joined the coalition, but paid little attention to its rules. Although the PNU established the apparatus of a single electoral entity, its creators failed to establish the procedures needed to agree a single candidate in each seat, which had been an essential part of NARC's 2002 success. Instead, they agreed that their constituent parties (including the PNU itself) would put up candidates under their own names. Although this was designed to harness the ethno-regional forces of established parties behind Kibaki, the time to organise was too short and controls proved ineffective. It was a major mistake.

The three national alliances squared up for a bruising campaign that appeared to repeat the ethnic, personal and factional battles of decades before. The Luo were unanimously in the ODM, as were the western Kalenjin and (non-Bukusu) Luhya. The Mount Kenya peoples were with Kibaki, wherever he was, and the Kamba were with Musyoka. The Gusii, the Coast, the pastoralists and smaller groups were split. Odinga had the momentum and was more popular than Kibaki, but no one was confident of the final result.

The 2007 Elections

The 2007 elections were the most closely contested, controversial and violent in Kenya's history, and ran contrary to the trajectory of the last three multi-party polls, which had shown a deeper embedding of electoral democracy and acceptance of the rules of the game. The formal contest began when Kibaki dissolved Parliament on 22 October 2007, and the ECK announced that polling day would again be 27 December.

Boundaries, Mechanics and Monitoring

The ECK's regular constituency boundary review took place in 2006–7 and recommended the creation of 42 new seats. In August 2007, the government had duly proposed to amend the Constitution to create 40 more constituencies and to add 50 special seats for women. However, Parliament, unhappy with the addition of the special seats, failed to pass the amendment by the two-thirds majority required. This left the ECK only able to tinker with boundaries, and left the anomalies in constituency size (which a court had declared unconstitutional in 2002) unchanged. Kenya had the most uneven set of constituencies in the world, with a 19:1 variation between the largest and smallest seat.[170]

Voter registration was now continuous, but most voters only registered during the ECK's periodic drives, the last of which took place in June–July 2007. Proposals from the ECK to build a common database for elections and ID cards were not taken forward. There were the usual concerns about voter card buying and reports of unusual registration behaviour. As many as 420,000 multiple registrations were detected (most were due to people moving between polling stations – more than 1.5 million people had done so by mid-2006, a surprisingly high number).[171] There were suggestions that some ODM strongholds were suffering more from registration anomalies than usual. Some districts, including Uasin Gishu and Kajiado, showed more than 100 per cent registration and others much lower percentages, suggesting mass voter importation to marginal seats.[172] In the end, 14.3 million voters registered, a 71 per cent registration rate. The number of dead voters on the register had grown even larger because of the lack of a reliable process for the registration of deaths.[173]

This year, with more polling stations, the polls were due to close an hour earlier, at 5 p.m., to minimise the need to vote and count at night. Again, votes were counted at the polling station. Tallying was then done at the constituency level, this time using new laptops. Donor support via IFES had made significant improvements to the technology available to the ECK. However, limited training in the use of these IT systems was given and the final communication of the result was still manual.

The ECK went through several personnel changes during 2007, as the tenure of 15 of its 22 commissioners and the chairman expired. Rather than taking nominations from other parties as agreed in the IPPG reforms in 1997, Kibaki unilaterally nominated the commissioners' replacements, to great disquiet. There were prescient warnings that many of Africa's coups and rebellions had followed disputed elections, and that popular rejection of the results often stemmed from the perception of bias more than from rigging per se. As a consequence, only five of the ECK's members had actually overseen an election before, and some of the newcomers may have been pro-government. Reports that he was to drop the respected and independent Chairman Samuel Kivuitu proved false, however, and Kibaki reappointed him in November, a decision that all parties (and donors) welcomed at the time.[174]

With the election heating up, every administrative problem led to accusations that the ECK was partial, and every decision – even the choice of polling date – inspired ODM allegations of rigging.[175] Although Kenyans and diplomats alike had built some confidence in local electoral processes after the 2002 and 2005 results, it was clear by 2006 that this might unravel and that a 'closely fought election is likely to be violent'.[176] Once reappointed, Kivuitu was accused of being a government stooge. Although the ECK chairman went confidently into the election, the opposition's campaign had built a groundwork of concern over potential rigging.

As in previous elections, NGOs and churches banded together to create a domestic monitoring body, known as KEDOF (the Kenya Elections Domestic Observation Forum). Funded by UNEP, it trained poll watchers for 17,000 of the 27,000 polling stations. The National Democratic Institute (NDI) also funded training for party agents and the ECK conducted a (government- and Western-funded) civic education campaign. The largest international observer groups came from the EU, the IRI and the Commonwealth, with smaller teams from the EAC and COMESA. The foreign observers were on the ground throughout the campaign.

Party Primaries

As usual, the party nominations were violent, corrupt and incompetently run. This year, the ECK tried to manage them more strictly than before. In August, it demanded that parties follow their constitution in their primaries and threatened to disqualify candidates who were not nominated in accordance with their party's rules.[177] The ECK also demanded that parties declare their candidates at least five days before nomination day, limiting the time available for losers to find another party. In practice, this proved impossible, as even the largest parties struggled to deliver an approved set of primary winners in time. The rule was abandoned, and the primaries lasted up until nomination day. The ODM directly nominated 50 of its most senior candidates and the PNU at least 40. Bribery was near-universal, with one study suggesting Ksh1 billion had been handed out to influence the results.[178]

In September 2007, Parliament had finally passed a Political Parties Act to provide state funding for parties, which also contained requirements for gender balance and national representation in party officials and restricted the ability of candidates to switch parties. However, this legislation, potentially disruptive to virtually every political interest, had not come into effect by the time of the dissolution.

A warning sign for the government was that across most of western Kenya, there was little interest in the PNU ticket: the ODM nomination was what everyone wanted. Many NAK MPs defected to ODM, seeing the writing on the wall. On the government side, many senior Kikuyu, Embu and Meru were amongst the PNU primary losers, including Murungaru, Kamotho, Norman Nyagah and Keriri. Fewer MPs were felled in the primaries than normal and (as in 2002) almost all of the losers defected elsewhere.[179] Reflecting the chaotic personalisation of party politics in Kenya, only 40 of the 210 elected MPs stood on the same party as had claimed their allegiance at the dissolution.

Presidential and Parliamentary Nominations

The presidential nominations took place on 15–16 November 2007. As well as Odinga, Kibaki and Musyoka, Kenneth Matiba put his name forward again, though few were aware of his intentions beforehand and his candidacy was regarded with sadness rather than excitement. There were five other minor candidates, with no prospect of success.

With MPs' salaries far higher, interest in parliamentary seats was correspondingly stronger. When this was combined with the absence of a clear national winner, the consequence was an explosion in the number of candidates. In the parliamentary nominations on 23–4 November, 2,547 candidates were nominated, more than twice as many as in 2002. This caused great difficulties for both the ECK and for voters.[180] There were now over 300 registered parties, of which 117 fielded candidates, which left everyone able to find some party on which to stand, no matter how hopeless the quest. Even Goldenberg architect Kamlesh Pattni emerged as the head of a party, KENDA, which fielded 170 candidates for the elections. Ten per cent of candidates were women, the highest proportion yet.

The ODM had candidates in 190 of 210 seats (it abandoned Central Province without a contest). They were a mixed bunch: Moi-era insiders in Kalenjin areas, a few incumbent MPs, grassroots political operators and many newcomers to parliamentary politics. They included several evangelical Pentecostal ministers, reflecting ODM's appeal to the poor and to those who believed that success came through God's gift.[181] In contrast, the government's coalition proved a failure. The PNU itself was the largest component, but the other parties had been allowed to put up candidates in some seats, because the PNU was not truly a party, and tensions within the coalition were high. The result was chaos. At least 26 parties claimed to be pro-PNU. The loosely affiliated Shirikisho, Safina, NARC-Kenya, KANU and even the DP refused to bow to the result of the PNU primaries in various seats, or did not even participate, and nominated their candidates to compete against the 'PNU' candidate. PNU factions overrode deals and nominated competing candidates. In dozens of seats, several serious pro-government candidates competed. Although Kibaki and his allies tried to indicate their preferred candidate, it had little effect.

Kivuitu blocked attempts by the PNU to prevent affiliated parties putting up their own candidates and ran a 'first come, first served' model.[182] Eventually the PNU put up 135 candidates, KANU 91, Safina 88, the DP 86, NARC-Kenya 59, Mazingira 50, FORD-People and FORD-Kenya each 43 and Shirikisho 17. ODM-Kenya, the third force, covered 133 seats.

The Campaign

The campaign proved open and closely fought, with all candidates able to travel and speak freely. The running was made by the three main presidential contenders. All had been campaigning since 2006, so there were few surprises, but there was concern about the growing ethnic polarisation amongst the Kikuyu and Luo, and Kibaki and Odinga mostly avoided each other's strongholds. In October, opinion polls gave Odinga a clear lead. He was dominant everywhere except Eastern, Central and Nairobi.[183] Most gave him 50 per cent of the vote to Kibaki's 35 per cent and Musyoka's 15 per cent. In response, the PNU called these results 'fabrications', accusing the media of favouring the opposition. As KANU had done a decade before, Kibaki's supporters alleged an American plot to undermine their leader.[184]

The official campaign began on 3 December. Nationwide, three quite different elections were fought. In Kikuyu and Luo areas, it was a 'census vote', with the aim of turning out as many voters as possible and ethnicity the sole criterion for presidential preference, irrespective of religion, occupation or socio-economic status. In the ex-KADU regions (the Kalenjin, Luhya and Coast), there was a strong pro-ODM wave, which was partly counterbalanced by the PNU's sub-regional alliances amongst the Giriama and Bukusu and with individual ministers. In the rest of the country, it was a neck-and-neck contest in which every issue mattered.

At the constituency level, the election was fought on much the same issues as before, on individual achievements and capability to bring jobs and development. Broader issues included poverty, infrastructure, landlessness and insecurity. In Nairobi, ethnicity played a role, with the PNU putting up mostly Kikuyu candidates and the ODM mostly Luo and Luhya. Sugar politics dominated much of Western and Nyanza provinces; in Kericho it was tea and around Mount Kenya, coffee. Lack of tarred roads, water projects, delayed revival of agricultural processing centres, land adjudication, electrification and lack of title deeds were common campaign issues. Increasingly, candidates campaigned not on the government resources they had brought to the constituency, but on the private sector and NGO resources they could command or influence.[185] The CDF was an issue in almost every constituency, with incumbents under pressure to demonstrate it had not been misused. Despite the efforts of KANU and PNU ministers in Kalenjin and coastal areas, the desire for change was palpable. There was a growing sense of popular anger.

Mudavadi was chosen as Odinga's running mate and led the attack in Western. In contrast, Awori remained vice-president, but was not anointed as Kibaki's running mate. Aged 80, he lacked the energy for the fight and was in trouble at home, facing both the ODM and Musyoka's running mate Julia Ojiambo. Both

Lucy Kibaki and Ida Odinga campaigned for their respective partners, for the first time in Kenyan history.

Kibaki campaigned mostly on his government's economic record, on a platform of security and stability, and opposition to devolution and the risk of what the PNU called the 'Balkanisation' of Kenya. The PNU's slogan was '*Kazi iendelee*' ('Let the work continue'). He promised an end to corruption, free secondary education, gender balance, investments in infrastructure and a doubling of Kenya's growth rate to 10 per cent a year.[186] His 'pork barrel' promises on the campaign trail included the creation of yet more districts (149 by 2008), roads, land grants and the construction of new facilities. In the traditional fashion, civil servants were given pay increases in November 2007. Kenya's teachers also received their final payment on the 1997 deal and were promised more rises and promotions, in return for which their unions promised to back him.[187] Kibaki's allies also engaged in negative campaigning, questioning Odinga's fitness to rule, and accusing him of planning to create a socialist state and to ban people from owning land outside their 'district of origin'.[188] Finance Minister Kimunya alleged that the donors might suspend aid to Kenya if Odinga won and pro-government businessmen castigated him as a communist. In contrast, Musyoka was treated with care. Both the ODM and PNU thought his withdrawal would help their opponent.

Odinga dominated the agenda and was the most widely travelled candidate.[189] He was well funded, with many contributions from the 1.8 million strong Kenyan diaspora abroad, and rumours that he had backers amongst influential politicians and even heads of state in Libya, Nigeria, South Africa, the Congo and the US.[190] His campaign focused on the issues of constitutional reform, federalism, corruption, security, unemployment and poverty, but in parallel also worked the seam of concern amongst other communities over Kikuyu rule. It combined a spectrum of appeals: to Luo identity, to those disappointed at the performance of the government, to pastoralists and supporters of *majimbo* and to the (non-Kikuyu) young and dispossessed in Nairobi and Mombasa. He personified a popular movement for radical change, while Kibaki was positioned as leader of a reactionary, tribalist, old guard that had mismanaged Kenya in the past. Economic policy was also an issue. As well as opposing recent privatisations, ODM leaders took an egalitarian and anti-structural adjustment position, with their ex-academic Secretary-General Anyang' Nyong'o, for example, declaring that structural adjustment was 'imposed on us to perpetuate structural inequality in the global economy in the interest of imperialism'.[191]

Odinga too made many promises, including the reconstruction of infrastructure, reduced waste and corruption, and increasing annual GDP growth to 14 per cent a year.[192] Top of his agenda, however was devolution and constitutional reform. He promised what Kibaki had failed to deliver in 2002: a new constitution in six months. The ODM campaigned on a platform of *majimbo* and implementation of the Bomas Draft, arguing that Kenya's centralised constitution was one of the main reasons why poverty and inequality were so widespread, and that only its proposals to redistribute 60 per cent of state funds to the regions would ensure equity. It even created regional manifestos. This struck chords in historically marginalised areas, but not around Mount Kenya, where *majimbo* was seen as code for the expulsion of the Kikuyu, Embu and Meru. The debate over devolution, *majimbo* and federalism, though blurred, was the most significant policy issue of the campaign. Musyoka and ODM-Kenya advocated a less radical programme of federalism, and also promised transparency and economic regeneration, though with few details. In an unusually visible example (for Kenya) of social pressure driving policy, all three candidates for the first time promised free secondary education by 2010, despite the Ksh20 billion a year price tag.

Religion played a more public role than in previous polls. Most senior politicians used religious functions to campaign, sometimes overtly. One Nairobi evangelical pastor stood for president on a minor party ticket and some churchmen declared themselves for the Catholic Kibaki. The new (Kikuyu) Catholic Archbishop John Njue, for example, openly opposed federalism as 'disastrous', as did some PCEA, Methodist and Anglican clergy. In contrast, Luo clergy from the same denominations backed *majimbo*.[193] There were accusations that Odinga was not even a Christian, designed to raise doubts about his fitness for office.[194] There were also attempts to smear Odinga over a memorandum of understanding he had signed with Muslim leaders, in which they promised to support him in return for the redress of discrimination against the community.[195] Most coastal Muslims indeed backed Odinga.

There was some use of government vehicles and resources to campaign for the PNU, though probably not enough to change the result. As under Moi, some DCs campaigned for the incumbent. The state-owned media again proved partial to the president, and 76 per cent of KBC's radio coverage went to the PNU. Now, however, there were so many news outlets (more than 50 radio and TV broadcasters) that the effect of the KBC's bias was muted and commercial broadcasters took a variety of lines.[196] The PNU received half the press coverage across the main media, with the rest split between ODM and ODM-Kenya.[197] In the press, there was a slight preference to Kibaki in the *Nation* and for Odinga in the *Standard*, but commercial considerations inhibited an overt declaration. Ethnicity was an ever-present issue, though media houses and speakers used roundabout means by which to express it. Both main candidates made use of Western campaign strategists and media consultants. All the parties advertised heavily in the media and on billboards, often attacking each other. The PNU, with the largest war chest, outspent the ODM by 4:1, its two flaming torches and blue colour scheme raising echoes of the British Conservative Party.[198] Kibaki's re-election campaign reached out to many of the same donors who had backed KANU – coastal business tycoons, construction companies, local businessmen (now Kikuyu rather than Kalenjin) and Asian entrepreneurs. All the main parties used mass text messaging to woo voters and insult their opponents, and there was some use of the Internet as a campaigning medium amongst elites. There was again widespread bribery, now considered normal.

The level of violence was higher than in 2002 and up to 40 people died.[199] In the Kalenjin Rift, there were threats against local Kikuyu, and leaflets once more circulated warning that outsiders would be evicted if the ODM won. In Mount Elgon (where several hundred had died since 2006), the fighting worsened. An ethnic militia known as the Sabaot Land Defence Force (SLDF) made the district near-ungovernable and killings spread into Trans-Nzoia, as Sabaot groups fought each other and the Ogiek/Ndorobo over Kenyatta- and Moi-era land settlements. Trouble also worsened in Kalenjin-dominated Kuresoi in Nakuru (involving Kalenjin, Kikuyu and Ogiek), resulting in dozens of deaths. Leaflets had circulated since 2006 warning the Kikuyu to leave or die. Thousands were displaced from their homes. There was the growing expectation in pro-ODM areas in the Rift Valley, incited by politicians, that after their victory, the introduction of *majimbo* would result in the permanent dispossession of Kikuyu and Gusii who had bought land in 'their' districts. On the Coast, there were similar pro-*majimbo* expectations around Mombasa, with both land and jobs at stake, and leaflets calling on the Kikuyu to leave. In contrast, some Nairobi landlords evicted Luo tenants after reports that Odinga had promised to 'regulate' (reduce) rents if he won.

Moi continued to campaign passionately against Odinga in Kalenjin areas. Rumours suggested that he believed Odinga to be too dangerous to hold power and blamed him both for the 1982 coup and the 'betrayal' of 2002. However, his efforts and those of Biwott and KANU's Kalenjin ministers were unable to reverse Odinga's momentum, particularly amongst the Kipsigis and Nandi, where the ODM's Ruto, ex-civil service head Kosgei and Kosgey dominated the agenda. Western Province, too, appeared lost and the Coast was teetering. In Luo Nyanza, Odinga was unchallenged, while in Kisii, the 75-year-old Nyachae (ready to retire) was unable to convince the community to stand behind Kibaki.

The contest narrowed to a two-horse race, with the poorly financed Musyoka shunted to the sidelines with 10 per cent of the vote, just as Nyachae had been in 2002. The PNU's conservative campaign, stressing Kibaki as a safe pair of hands, appeared to strike some chords with the undecided in the last weeks of the campaign. The PNU clawed back some of the ODM's lead, and the last opinion polls before Christmas put the presidency as 'too close to call', with Steadman showing Raila ahead by 45 to 43 per cent, and Gallup putting Kibaki ahead by 44 per cent to 43 per cent.[200] Fearing he would be outmatched, or would concede too much to Odinga, Kibaki refused to debate with him in public.

Polling Day and the Count

Polling day, 27 December, went well. As it was the fourth election under the same system, there were few administrative problems. There was a high turnout and voting was mostly peaceful. However, at least four died on polling day. The government's deployment of several thousand off-duty administration police to Luo Nyanza to ensure the polling went fairly, or to rig the elections to the PNU's advantage (depending on the interpretation), was abandoned after several were killed by enraged locals.[201]

However, the presidential count proved a disaster. Although the polling station counts were mostly uncontroversial, the process of tallying and reporting the results back and collating them centrally turned into a nightmare for the ECK and the country. In several seats, the returning officer refused to provide observers with the station-by-station results, a worrying sign.[202] The first results suggested a decisive victory for Odinga, but the results from Kikuyu, Embu and Meru areas were heavily delayed, and rumours abounded of modified or unverified results being communicated to the ECK that favoured the PNU. Photocopies were delivered instead of originals and documents had been clumsily altered. Observers agreed that some of the results in the ECK did not accord with those announced locally. It emerged that there were no regulations for how central tallying should be done, nor how it could be verified.

The Parliamentary Results

The parliamentary results saw a victory for the ODM throughout the non-Kikuyu Rift Valley, the Coast, Western and Luo Nyanza. In Gusii areas, Nairobi and North-Eastern, honours were shared. The PNU was forced back to its home amongst the Kikuyu, Embu and Meru and the Bukusu, though they won seats in every province. Twenty-two ministers lost their seats – including the old guard of Awori, Mwiraria, Joseph Munyao, Karume and Nyachae, but also Kirwa, Kombo and Kituyi – and only 11 survived. Outside the Mount Kenya region, even strong candidates who had not joined the ODM did very poorly. Their KANU ally was decimated in Kalenjin areas, and losers included Biwott, Gideon Moi, his brothers Raymond and Jonathan and ex-State House Comptroller John Lokorio, all overwhelmed by the ODM wave. Moi's patronage appeared to be a liability rather than an asset, and the ODM won 26 of the 30 Kalenjin-dominated seats in the Rift. Musyoka's ODM-Kenya swept Ukambani, but performed poorly elsewhere. Ngilu was a rare survivor there on a pro-Odinga NARC ticket. Around Mount Kenya, in contrast, the PNU did well, and even ODM Pentagon member Joseph Nyagah performed appallingly (his vote fell from 11,000 in 2002 to 2,000 in 2007).

While the headline numbers suggested a massive win for ODM, by 99 to 43, the real picture was more complex. The Kibaki-friendly parties under the PNU umbrella won 78 seats, while ODM and its affiliates (NARC and the UDM) polled 103 (see Table 12.3). For the first time, the ECK annulled one result and delayed another before the MP had even been declared, because rigging had been detected. One seat was declared a tie.

More non-mainstream party MPs were elected than ever before, and voters split their tickets across many candidates, reflecting weaker ticket voting than in any previous poll. Less than half the winners were elected with a plurality of the vote. The influence of Islam grew further, with several Muslim MPs elected outside the coast and north-east. Fifteen MPs were women (7 per cent of the House), the largest proportion yet. Only 71 of 210 incumbents were re-elected. In general, it was a rejection of the old generation and an appeal for change. This did not mean the ODM's MPs were all new to power, however. Kalenjin newcomers included Moi's Internal Security Permanent Secretary Cheruiyot, his civil service head Kosgei, ex-State House Comptroller Franklin Bett and ex-Commissioner for Lands Mwaita, while ODM-Kenya's MPs included ex-PC Peter Kiilu and Moi's lawyer Mutula Kilonzo.

Table 12.3: Parliamentary election results, 2007

Party	Seats	%
ODM	99	48
PNU	43	20
ODM-Kenya	16	8
KANU	14	7
Safina	5	2
NARC-Kenya	4	2
NARC	3	1
FORD-People	3	1
New FORD-Kenya	2	1
DP	2	1
PICK	2	1
Sisi Kwa Sisi	2	1
Others	12	6
Delayed/annulled	3	1
TOTAL	210	100

Coalition	Seats	%
ODM + allies	103	49
PNU + allies	78	37
ODM-Kenya	16	8
Others	10	5
Delayed/annulled	3	1
TOTAL	210	100

Source: Various

The Presidential Results

In the presidency, the result was the most extraordinary in the country's history. On Friday 28 December, Odinga was leading by nearly 900,000 votes, with half the ballots counted. With parliamentary results suggesting he had swept the country, victory seemed assured.[203] However, during Saturday, Kibaki clawed back his position. At midday, ECK reports suggested Odinga was 300,000 votes ahead of Kibaki. By 2 p.m., the gap was down to only 100,000 votes. By mid-afternoon, the PNU was claiming victory.

The result was uproar. Reports that ECK officials were doctoring results to inflate Kibaki's total rapidly gained credence. There was evidence of basic arithmetical errors and extraordinary incompetence amongst officials. Some returning officers were unavailable (although they had mobile phones), and the results for pro-Kibaki seats such as Molo and Nithi were hotly disputed at ECK headquarters. As Odinga's lead slipped away, ODM leaders claimed rigging, and tension grew as they demanded the results be reassessed and the announcement delayed. The ECK appeared paralysed, with some officials disowning their own results. Kivuitu began to express doubts about his own organisation. Press announcements and tabulations of the presidential results ceased, as did updates to the ECK website. No one else seemed to be running a presidential vote tabulation or to be willing to publish it. Observers and NGOs were aghast.[204] Around 4 p.m. on 29 December, officials attempted to announce the results but ODM protests disrupted their reading.

All Saturday night and Sunday morning, tired and tense officials, agents and observers tried to validate the results, as tension escalated, but 47 results remained disputed. On Sunday 30 December, under huge pressure to announce a winner, the ECK battened down the hatches and excluded observers as it prepared for the crisis to come. In parallel, ODM leaders went public in a press conference with allegations of rigging in 48 constituencies, claiming that results were still being modified in ECK headquarters.[205]

At 4.30 p.m. on Sunday 30 December, Kivuitu declared that Kibaki had won the presidential election, by 4.6 million votes to 4.4 million for Odinga and 0.9 million for Musyoka (see Table 12.4), although he had not received a certified set of original forms from at least 40 constituencies. Kivuitu was permitted legally to do this, as he had in 2002, but only if the uncertified results could not change the final total, which in this case was far from clear. Unable to announce the results in public because of ODM and observer protests, Kivuitu retreated upstairs, and the announcement was made under GSU guard, reinforcing suspicions.

An hour later, Kibaki was sworn in at State House in a hurried ceremony, but Kenya was already falling apart. While central Kenya celebrated, the ODM declared Odinga the real winner. At a press conference in which dissenting ECK officials confirmed rigging, the ODM rejected an election petition, since Kibaki 'controlled' the courts, and announced the formation of a parallel government. As the pressure rose on Kivuitu, on the evening of 1 January 2008 he admitted that he was no longer sure who had won.[206]

The official ECK results, published on its website between 8 and 11 January, reconfirmed Kibaki's victory by only 200,000 votes (see Table 12.4 and Figure 12.9). He had also passed the 25 per cent hurdle in seven of eight provinces (excluding

Table 12.4: Presidential election results, 2007

Province	Kibaki PNU	Odinga ODM	Musyoka ODM-K	Others	Rejected	Total
Nairobi	**313,448**	288,922	52,974	1,845	4,819	662,008
Central	**1,741,086**	34,046	11,702	7,199	9,099	1,803,132
Eastern	**835,481**	90,955	719,402	13,229	18,670	1,677,737
North-Eastern	**97,263**	91,440	4,498	333	614	194,148
Coast	197,354	**353,776**	38,881	5,937	5,462	601,410
Rift Valley	818,445	**1,580,880**	33,843	12,300	21,752	2,467,220
Western	312,300	**639,246**	6,729	11,417	18,309	988,001
Nyanza	262,627	**1,280,978**	4,488	7,160	11,243	1,566,496
Total	4,578,004	4,360,243	872,517	59,420	89,968	9,960,152
%	46.0	43.8	8.8	0.6	0.9	100

Source: ECK final results from ECK website, with typographic errors corrected.
Bold indicates the winning party

12.9: ECK presidential election results, 2007

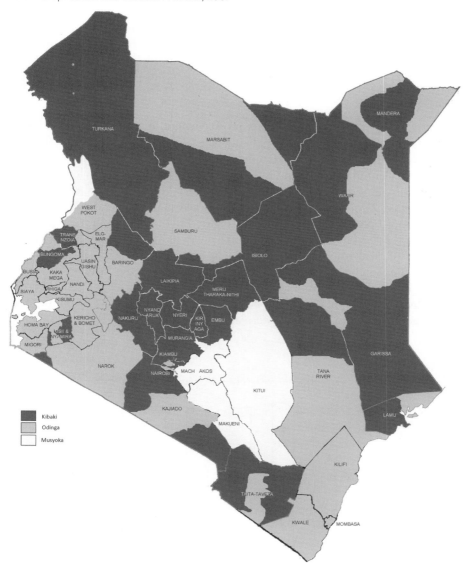

Source: ECK final results, from ECK website, with typographic errors corrected

Nyanza). Odinga had won 4.4 million votes and 25 per cent in six provinces, while Musyoka's 9 per cent of the vote came entirely from Ukambani (elsewhere, he polled virtually nothing). The other candidates were irrelevant. There were differences between the original results and the final totals, but no huge discrepancies.

According to the ECK's results, 80 per cent of which were undisputed, Kibaki had won at least 95 per cent of the rural Kikuyu, Embu and Meru vote (of every age or gender), while Odinga had taken 99 per cent of the Luo and at least 85 per cent of the Kalenjin vote (see Figure 12.10). The Luhya, Mijikenda and Maasai voted two-thirds for Odinga, while the Gusii and Somali split down the middle. Urban adults voted according to a similar pattern, with Nairobi split in half, Nakuru and Thika backing Kibaki, and Mombasa, Kisumu and Eldoret backing Odinga.

Turnout

Turnout was higher than in 2002, at around 70 per cent, and was implausibly high in some seats: 10 million people had apparently voted, 4 million more than in 2002 (and a million more than in the 2010 referendum to come). The highest turnouts were in Luo Nyanza, Central Province and Kalenjin districts. Turnouts were close to 100 per cent in some polling stations in Kibaki's Othaya and Moi's Baringo Central.

The number of votes cast rose by 66 per cent across the board and 75 per cent or more in Nairobi, Nyanza and Central (see Figure 12.11). Even given the huge media attention and polarisation of this election, this was an extraordinary increase, given the number of dead voters on the register. The signs of stuffing and the breakdown of controls in the parties' homelands were clear. However, the increase in votes in Kikuyu-, Embu- and Meru-dominated districts was only slightly higher than average. In contrast, turnouts in Luo Nyanza jumped dramatically. Turnout actually fell in Western Province, North-Eastern and Kisii.

12.10: Ethnic voting patterns, 2007

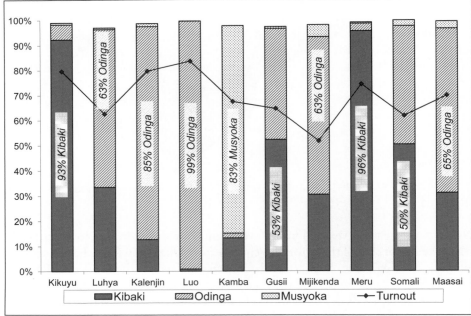

Source: Calculated from results in mostly mono-ethnic constituencies

12.11: Presidential votes cast by province, 1992–2010

Source: ECK final results, typographic errors corrected and other election and referendum results

Observer Opinions

All observers took seriously the ODM's claim that at least 300,000 votes had been crudely added to Kibaki's total to give him victory. The EU Observer Mission expressed concern about the accuracy of the presidential results in its preliminary statement of 1 January 2008, and reported pro-Kibaki doctoring of results in constituencies in Central Province and Meru, though it was more comfortable with the parliamentary polls.[207] Its final report asserted: 'The 2007 General Elections in Kenya fell short of key international and regional standards for democratic elections.'[208] The IRI believed that 'electoral fraud took place and condemns that fraud'.[209] The Commonwealth similarly suggested that things had gone well until the count, but the process thereafter 'fell short of acceptable international standards'.[210]

KEDOF's preliminary statement on 31 December also commended the voting and expressed serious concerns about the tallying.[211] It noted delays in the transmission of results and a refusal to let its observers sign forms in many places. They too reported discrepancies between the ECK results and those announced by returning officers, the overstatement of results in some seats, and their reduction or suppression in others. In some seats, the number of presidential votes was far higher than the parliamentary tally, suggesting stuffing or vote inflation. Although they did not directly accuse the government of rigging, most civil society organisations were convinced that it had happened.[212] The Kenyan media equivocated, fearful of stoking the violence. The Western media took a stronger line, with headlines such as 'Twilight Robbery, Daylight Murder' in *The Economist* and a suggestion to suspend Kenya from the Commonwealth in *The Times*.[213] The credibility of Kibaki's victory and of the ECK were irrecoverably damaged.

Unhappy and confused, many African and Western governments refused to congratulate Kibaki on his victory and limited contacts with the government. The US government initially declared the election free and fair, then reversed its position. The British declined to recognise Kibaki's government and the British foreign secretary stated: 'we do not recognise the current Kenyan government as representing the democratic will of the Kenyan people.'[214] Few came to the defence of a government that was now equated with that of Zimbabwe.

Kenya Burns

With the announcement of the PNU's victory and the widespread belief that they had rigged the result, violence erupted across the country. ODM supporters rioted, demonstrated and exacted revenge on the Kikuyu in the Rift Valley, Nyanza and the slums of Nairobi. What began on 31 December as a non-violent protest, in which Odinga called for a million-man march against State House's 'civilian coup', descended into mass slaughter.

Over the New Year, Kenya cracked apart in the worst outbreak of ethnic violence in the country's history. By 1 January, protests at the elections had become pogroms against pro-government ethnic groups. Text messages ('41 on 1') circulated, inciting other communities to rise up against Kikuyu election rigging. Over the next week, the Luo, Kalenjin, Mijikenda and Maasai took up arms against pro-PNU communities in their midst. The government appeared in shock, unprepared for the scale of the violence. On 30 December, to limit the tit-for-tat spread of the chaos, the government (illegally) banned all live broadcasts, to further international disquiet. However, the blackout had little effect. In Uasin Gishu, northern Nakuru and Trans-Nzoia, hundreds were murdered as gangs of Kalenjin armed with crude weapons took revenge on local Kikuyu and Gusii, raping and murdering strangers and neighbours alike. Some attackers were organised and transported in chartered lorries. In the most shocking incident, 28 Kikuyu women and children were burnt alive on 1 January 2008, when the church to which they had fled for safety was set on fire.[215] Throughout Kalenjin and Luo areas, other communities fled, as their houses burnt. Local security forces were overwhelmed, afraid and in some cases divided, with some Kalenjin chiefs and police joining the attacks and some Kikuyu police forcibly disarming their Kalenjin colleagues.[216] The centre of Kisumu was gutted as protesters destroyed shops and houses belonging to pro-government communities and looted what remained, shouting 'No Raila, no peace'. There were also days of rioting in Western Province, though most of the killing and burning was in the Rift Valley. In the shanties of Nairobi, gangs of armed ODM and PNU youth (essentially Luo and Kikuyu) fought pitched battles in which dozens were killed, a few miles from where their more fortunate cousins had just celebrated the conversion of the Nairobi Stock Exchange to fully electronic trading. Railway lines were torn up in Kibera and transport across western Kenya became nearly impossible.[217]

As the days passed, the balance of terror shifted. With tens of thousands of displaced Kikuyu seeking refuge, in late January the Kikuyu responded. Kikuyu militia including Mungiki began to kill and drive Luo and Kalenjin out of Central Province and south-eastern Nakuru.[218] On 26 January alone, 48 people died in Nakuru housing estates; the day after Kikuyu crowds murdered another 40 (mostly Luo) in Naivasha. There were indications that some Kikuyu politicians financed and supported their actions.[219] The army was briefly called out. Everywhere, invisible boundaries were drawn between ethnic groups; to cross risked death, as militia dragged from their vehicles and murdered those unable to speak the right language. Convoys trucked east and west to places of ethnic safety, bringing with them tales of murder and destruction. Everywhere, workers outside their home districts took sanctuary in offices, churches and camps for the displaced. Ethnic 'self-defence' units in the worst trouble spots became more organised and were supported by local politicians. With echoes of the Rwandan genocide, local-language radio stations contributed to the climate of hate and fear. Demonstrations, barricades and looting continued across Nyanza and the Rift Valley. Food shortages worsened. Factories ground to a halt as their workers fled and supply lines were cut. Billions of shillings of property were burnt. Kisumu was gutted and many Asian and Kikuyu businessmen fled, never to return. The shilling collapsed; foreign tourism virtually ceased, horticultural exports declined, the stock exchange dropped 25 per cent and the economy went into free fall.

Although no state of emergency was declared and the army was little used, the police were merciless in restoring order. Facing looting and violence, the GSU and police indiscriminately shot demonstrators in Kisumu in front of international camera crews, to more international consternation. Odinga in turn accused the government of the mass murder of Luo: in Nyanza and Western, two-thirds of the dead had been shot by police.[220]

Kibaki meanwhile refused to resign and Odinga refused to accept his victory. Both sides initially seemed willing to hold a recount or another election, but both options were practically impossible. A recount would be pointless if rigging had genuinely occurred, because papers might have been further tampered with in the meantime. A new election was financially impossible for both parties; in any case it would have produced quite a different result in areas where voters had been killed or driven away and might have inflamed the violence further. Initial efforts at foreign mediation achieved nothing and a series of 'mass action' demonstrations by ODM in mid-January ended in more violence. The killing continued into February in Uasin Gishu, Kericho, Nakuru, Nairobi and Mombasa. Gradually order was restored, as the consequences of what had happened became apparent. Just as the situation had begun to quieten, however, two ODM MPs were murdered in late January: one by gangsters in his Nairobi home, the other shot dead in what was probably a marital dispute.[221] However, in the tense atmosphere of the time, the ODM claimed an assassination programme designed to eliminate its narrow parliamentary majority and there were more spasms of violence. In the end, over 1,100 people had been killed (more than 400 shot dead by police), and 3,500 injured. More than 350,000 had been displaced from their homes. The world's reporters were simultaneously horrified and fascinated by this sudden descent into anarchy of a country they had become used to treating as stable.

To some extent, this eruption was a predictable response to the growing divide in the nation since 2005 and to Kibaki's narrow victory. It had been clear long before the results were announced that the ODM was unlikely to accept defeat with equanimity, and a close result was an invitation to mass protest. The fact that the elections had – at least in part – genuinely been rigged added fuel to the flames. There were deeper causes, however. As Susanne Mueller notes, Kenya had seen the increasing use of violence as a political tool and the emergence of mono-ethnic youth militia. Chaos empowered the young, the violent and the zealous and became self-sustaining. Many politicians and voters appeared to share a 'winner takes all' model of political power and a general acceptance of violence as an inevitable, and to an extent legitimate, response to state machinations.[222] Popular confidence in the impartiality of state institutions had been undermined by decades of abuses and the universal perception that the hidden hand of the presidency could corrupt every institution.

What was not sufficiently appreciated at first was that the origins of the violence were very different. For the urban Luo, it was an expression of anguish, mostly by unemployed youth in Nairobi and Kisumu and was probably encouraged (at least initially) by the ODM leadership to pressure Kibaki and the PNU to reconsider. In the former white highlands, where the death toll was higher, the violence also reflected anger at Kikuyu 'rigging', but it was fuelled by the long-running resentment over land and a well-established antipathy to the Kikuyu that politicians used for their own ends, uniting their people in a pogrom against a minority in their midst. A seam of popular hatred was exposed here which deeply shocked the nation. The same areas of the Rift Valley – Uasin Gishu, north and western Nakuru – had seen much of the violence in 1991–2. The perception of Kalenjin marginalisation since 2003 had deepened antagonism to the Kikuyu, even though Moi and other Kalenjin leaders had backed Kibaki. For two years, ODM leaders had been urging Kalenjin unity against Kikuyu dominance.[223] There were credible reports that senior Kalenjin politicians had organised some of the violence, either to press the government to change course, or to take revenge for old wrongs.[224] The post-election investigative commission's report described, for example, a Nandi oathing ceremony in August 2007 that committed local youth to evict foreigners from the north Rift, while other witnesses reported that preparations for mass violence had begun by 28 December and named Kalenjin politicians as inciting, organising and financing the attacks in order to drive the Kikuyu out of the Rift Valley and acquire their land, as many had feared would be the outcome of the *majimbo* constitution.[225]

Were the 2007 Elections Rigged?

We will never know who truly won the elections. It is clear that something went seriously wrong in the ECK. There were problems with the results that would bring them into question in any country. However, intense analysis of the seat-by-seat results and other supporting evidence was unable to demonstrate whether the problems were the result of systematic rigging by pro-PNU officials or 'simply' administrative errors and partially counteracting local rigging and bias. The 2008 Independent Review Commission (IREC) investigation similarly concluded: 'The conduct of the 2007 elections was so materially defective that it is impossible – for

IREC or anyone else – to establish true or reliable results for the presidential and parliamentary elections.'[226]

From observers' reports of polling day, no major concerns arose, except the prevalence of census voting in the candidates' homelands and the high level of illiteracy declarations, which were bought, as before. There was intimidation and violence in urban areas and ODM and PNU strongholds, and several suspicious ballot boxes were seized and burnt by angry crowds during the count, even before the results became clear. There were accusations of rogue ballot boxes or tallies being introduced in at least six counts, including marginal Nairobi and Kajiado North.[227] There were numerous reports of agents being evicted from polling stations or the count.

Turning to the count and the tallying, a strong case can be made that Odinga was rigged out of the presidency. More than half of Kibaki's votes (2.8 of 4.6 million votes) came from just 20 per cent of the country's seats. Odinga was clearly far more popular nationwide, while Kibaki dominated only in Central Province, Embu, Meru, Nakuru and Laikipia, and polled well amongst the Bukusu and Gusii. The IRI's unpublished exit poll gave a clear win to Odinga.[228]

There was evidence of sloppy or abusive procedures during the collation and reporting of the results in 30–40 constituencies. There were well-documented reports of results being 'corrected' after the event to make them more plausible. In numerous seats, mostly in Central Province, observers reported that the results for Kibaki recorded in ECK headquarters were thousands of votes larger than those recorded locally.[229] The paperwork was a mess, and numerous forms were missing, incomplete or altered.[230] In Maragwa in Central Province, the official forms showed a turnout of 115 per cent, but the returning officer was allowed to correct it to a more 'reasonable' 85 per cent.[231] In other PNU wins, including Turkana North and Dagoretti, the official results were so implausible that they could not be true. More than 40 of the published presidential tallies on the ECK website did not even add up arithmetically.[232] The US later refused visas for three ECK Commissioners, on suspicion of accepting bribes to fix the result.[233]

Even in the final validated results, there were 185,000 more presidential than parliamentary ballots, a total similar in size to Kibaki's majority (it is rare in reality for a voter to vote in only one of the three simultaneous elections). Considering both excesses and shortfalls in a constituency as potentially suspicious, there were 450,000 mismatched ballots. In comparison, in 2002, there had been only 190,000. In 22 seats, the turnout for the presidential poll was more than 5 per cent larger than that for parliament, including pro-Kibaki seats such as Mathioya, Limuru, Igembe and Kajiado North.[234] There were probably pro-Kibaki phantom voters in North-Eastern Province, where the number of registered voters had nearly doubled in 10 years and had risen by 20 per cent since January 2007.[235]

All this is not enough, however, to be sure the wrong candidate was declared president. Although some actions are inexplicable without malicious intent, the majority of the final tallies are consistent with the provisional results, the presidential and parliamentary results match reasonably well, and turnout is consistent with the result of previous elections. The post-election inquiry took a similar view, concluding that the evidence of rigging was 'unconvincing'.[236] In the confusion and tension, with the result so close, mistakes took on sinister intent. Turnouts were no higher in pro-government than in opposition areas. Some of the results questioned by observers (such as Molo and Kieni) proved accurate when the final results were examined. While the ECK's first results suggested there were 350,000 more presidential than parliamentary ballots, by the time the final results were published this had halved and seats with too many presidential ballots included eight seats in Luo Nyanza, where all the votes went to Odinga. There was no automatic connection between presidential–parliamentary discrepancies and pro-Kibaki abuses.

The situation where ODM won parliament and Kibaki the presidency, though counter-intuitive, was quite plausible. First, the Kibaki alliance was a coalition of parties, and the coalition lost to ODM by 103:78 in Parliament, a defeat but not a rout. Second, Kibaki's allies split their parliamentary votes, with competing candidates losing a dozen seats to ODM as a result (including Embakasi, Makadara, Cherangani, Rongai and South Mugirango). If they had put up a single pro-Kibaki candidate, the parliamentary result would have been neck and neck. Kibaki-friendly parties polled 4.3 million parliamentary votes, far more than the Odinga-friendly parties (3.6 million), though as 1.4 million votes went to parties not obviously aligned to any of the three candidates, this is not conclusive. Third, pro-government constituencies had 24 per cent more registered voters on average than those in the rest of the country, a legacy of high registration rates and Moi's pastoralist gerrymandering. Finally, some of the problems that observers noted were the results of tiredness, administrative incompetence or frustration rather than malice. They probably occurred in 2002 as well, but were not objected to then. With hindsight, Kivuitu robustly defended the ECK's performance, suggesting that he was being subjected to a witch-hunt and that the results were not invalidated by a 'small tallying error' in the presidential poll.[237]

The true result will never be known. Although some of the evidence of malpractice faded with better data, the suspicion remains that Kibaki's votes were inflated in his strongholds and that some government ministers were rigged into Parliament. With the result so close, whichever candidate had won, the other would have claimed rigging and would have had grounds for this claim. As the IREC report noted, this was exactly what the people of Kenya deserved, since while they were supporters of democracy in principle, they had tolerated or endorsed bribery, violence and ethnic hate speech, the misuse of public resources and a culture of impunity for the 'big men' of every party.[238]

The Grand Alliance

The elections and the violence were a severe shock to Kenya's psyche and to the country's international standing. Everyone demanded a political solution, but it took nearly three months to be crafted, in the face of the gulf between the parties. Both sides appeared convinced they had won and were unwilling to concede. During January and early February, international mediation by UN Secretary-General Kofi Annan and a succession of African leaders brought the combatants closer together, but weeks passed with no deal. Kibaki and his supporters – who appeared to take a harder line as the killing continued – refused to concede any form of power sharing. Raila in turn demanded Kibaki's resignation and a transitional government, while ruling out any deal whereby he would become prime minister to Kibaki's president.[239] ODM leaders came under pressure from below (including explicit threats of violence) that they must return from negotiations having won the presidency.

On 8 January, at the peak of the violence, Kibaki appointed a new Cabinet. His shock choice as Kenya's tenth vice-president was his ODM-Kenya opponent Musyoka, who had secretly made a deal during the campaign to join an alliance with Kibaki if he won, in return for the vice-presidency.[240] This gave the government 94 seats in parliament, but also reaffirmed the national centre–periphery divide. However, Kibaki only filled 17 Cabinet posts and appointed no assistant ministers, which left open the prospect of the ODM joining the government as a junior partner.[241] The ODM would have none of it. When Parliament reassembled in mid-January, the ODM demonstrated it could control Parliament, winning the vote to choose the speaker by 105:101.[242]

The US and the UK placed intense pressure on both sides to make a deal, including a ban on visits by Kikuyu and Kalenjin politicians and businessmen they believed had been involved in the violence. There were even suggestions that the Americans might try to impose a solution directly.[243] Bilateral donors and the World Bank warned they might end aid permanently if a settlement was not reached.[244] The fear of more mass killings was everywhere. Eventually, with tempers (nationally and internationally) fraying to breaking point, and backed by high-level US diplomatic intervention, Annan and a panel of eminent African persons managed to broker a settlement on the only plausible basis: to create a coalition government. On 28 February 2008, despite protests from within both their parties, Kibaki and Odinga signed a power-sharing National Accord by which Odinga would take up the prime minister's post for which he had long been earmarked, able to 'co-ordinate and supervise the execution of the functions and affairs of the Government', while Kibaki remained president.[245] A constitutional amendment and a National Accord and Reconciliation Act were rushed through Parliament in March, establishing new posts of prime minister and two deputy prime ministers, and providing for a Grand Coalition between the parties based on their strength in parliament. After 44 years, Kenya once more had a prime minister and its first power-sharing arrangement since Jomo Kenyatta had shared power with Malcolm MacDonald. However, the powers of the prime minister were left loosely defined, the same issue that had bedevilled Bomas in 2003–4.

Odinga duly took up his post, and after six weeks of horse-trading about every detail, on 13 April 2008 Kibaki announced a new 42-minister coalition government. This matched pro-Kibaki and pro-Odinga members one to one, with Musyoka vice-president, Odinga prime minister and Mudavadi from the ODM and Kenyatta from

12.12: Size of Cabinets, 1963–2008

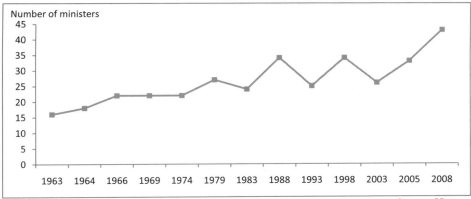

Source: Various

the PNU as deputy prime ministers. New ministries had to be created to represent every interest and ethnic group, resulting in the largest Cabinet since independence (see Figure 12.12). With 94 MPs in the government, there was virtually no one to occupy the role of official opposition. On paper, Kenya had almost become a one-party state. All the ODM Pentagon leaders received spending ministries, while the PNU retained Internal Security, Defence, Justice and Finance.[246] Incorporation triumphed over justice as well as efficiency, with some describing the new government, caustically, as a coalition of Goldenberg and Anglo-Leasing.

Conclusions

Kenya was now in uncharted waters, with a true division of central authority for the first time, a recent history of political and ethnic violence and an angry, empowered and divided society. Having failed to agree on constitutional reform for a decade, it had been forced on the country after a period in which its darker side had become visible and the 'hatred of the other' implied in the competitive model of ethnicity, driven by real and perceived marginalisation, had been allowed full rein. With the country unable to craft a deal internally, foreign governments had used their moral and financial leverage to force a solution. A groundbreaking coalition had been built to paper over deep divides, but it faced greater suspicion and deeper fissures than any previous government. It was a bandage, designed to allow the wound to heal. Everyone knew that battle would be joined again and that, unless a miracle happened, the same ethno-regional divisions would come into play.

Chapter 13

Cold War and Compromise, 2008–2011

Muddling Through

Although on paper the PNU and ODM were united in the Grand Coalition, their divisions were as large as ever, and the conflict moved inside the government. It was an ugly, messy process, but the only possible solution. Many of the issues the country faced were intractable and a managed delay in which 'politics' and 'development' would coexist was the only option. Despite challenges from hardliners on both sides, the coalition endured and Kenya gradually recovered, its leaders knowing they had no alternative. The fragile power-sharing mechanism created in 2008 survived, though the role of Prime Minister Raila Odinga and his influence over the government remained a point of continued contention. Gradually, the country recovered its confidence and credibility and began to invest once more.

While the divisive legacy of the 2007 elections and the violence dominated much of the political agenda, there was one unexpected achievement. In 2010, out of a decade of chaos, a new draft constitution emerged, with both mass and elite support across the political spectrum. Almost miraculously, it was enacted following a second referendum. 2011 began on a note of optimism, although few could predict what was to come as the new constitution came into effect.

A Shaky Coalition

There was a desperate desire on all sides to avoid another outbreak of violence, but the friction between ODM and PNU was continuous and the 'ceasefire' always under threat. The role and responsibilities of the prime minister were poorly defined, and he contradicted President Mwai Kibaki, Vice-President Kalonzo Musyoka and Civil Service Head Francis Muthaura repeatedly, as the principals tried to agree a pecking order in the absence of legislative guidance.

Although the government remained legally balanced between the coalition partners, the close relationship between ethnicity and party converted every public sector appointment into a quota debate and institutionalised an ethnic power-sharing model. Although each party strived for regional balance, the underlying relationship was obvious (see Figure 13.1). The same pattern was seen elsewhere – every civil service and parastatal appointment for a Kikuyu was seen as the PNU's; every Luo as ODM's. Both coalition partners packed bodies under their control with ethnic allies and even family members.[1] Positions were allocated depending on which side's 'turn' it was, not always with regard for merit. The National Cohesion and Integration Act's requirement that no state department be staffed more than 30 per cent by one ethnic group was generally ignored.

13.1: April 2008 coalition government, by party and ethnic origin

Source: Various

Many in the ODM felt they had conceded too much and that the PNU did not treat the ODM as an equal partner. Kibaki made key appointments without consulting ODM ministers, and ODM leaders openly criticised their PNU colleagues. Throughout 2008 and 2009, collective responsibility was a myth as ministers battled each other in public. Only fear of the consequences of failure and loss of the rewards of office kept them together. The elderly Kibaki tried to keep the fragile coalition together, but the sniping and intrigue was continuous, and decision-making difficult when agreement was required by two opposed ethno-regional coalitions. Odinga frequently had to swallow his pride and accept Kibaki's choices.

Popular perceptions were soon hostile, with opinion polls showing that most voters felt the coalition – often seen in zero-sum terms – was failing to deliver. While Kibaki and Odinga seemed committed, extremists blossomed on both side, arguing that the compromises were too many and that unwieldy coalition prevented real decision-making. Few seemed to be gaining much credibility from the arrangement, though few could think of a safe alternative.

Peeking Inside Pandora's Boxes

The parties had agreed as part of the African Union mediation in February 2008 to an independent public inquiry into the election and the ECK's performance, led by eminent persons from overseas. This risked fuelling the flames of violence once more, so the inquiry declared at the outset that it had no intention of determining who had actually won the poll.[2] The investigation's report (the IREC or Kriegler Report) concluded that virtually all the results announced were arithmetically incorrect, the register was defective, voting was not free and fair in many PNU and ODM strongholds, and that it was impossible to determine the real winners.[3] However, it also noted that when revalidated, the results of 19 disputed constituencies contained a 'litany of errors' but no systemic bias, and accused the ECK of incompetence rather than malice. Nonetheless, Samuel Kivuitu and his ECK departed in disgrace in December 2008, to be replaced by an Interim Independent Electoral Commission (IIEC).

The Post-Election Violence Investigation and the ICC

Another even more controversial inquiry (the Committee to Investigate Post-Election Violence), chaired by Justice Philip Waki, investigated the violence of 2007–8. Its recommendations in October 2008 included the establishment of a special tribunal to hear cases against those accused of serious crimes, with the threat of recourse to the International Criminal Court (ICC) in The Hague if action was not taken. A sealed list of 20 offenders was handed to Kibaki and Kofi Annan, which included ministers, MPs and officials (alleged to be mostly Kalenjin or Kikuyu).[4] However, in February 2009, MPs refused to support the constitutional amendment to establish a special tribunal; some in order to protect the guilty, others to ensure that the guilty would be tried in The Hague rather than Kenya. The ODM split, as Odinga supported plans for the tribunal, while many Kalenjin MPs, fearing their community's leaders were the main suspects, objected. Another year was lost in failed attempts to reach consensus, while the ICC decided that, in the absence of Kenyan action, its investigation must begin.

Inside Kenya, virtually no investigations of who had committed the murders of 2007/8 took place. The nation was divided over whether there should be an amnesty (favoured by the ODM) or whether the state should prosecute all those involved. The security forces were fearful or unwilling to reopen the wounds, and those affected too afraid to testify in court. A special witness programme was put in place in 2009 to protect those willing to testify to the ICC, their lives increasingly in danger.

On 15 December 2010, having spent months collecting evidence and with Kenya having failed to establish a local tribunal, the ICC Prosecutor Luis Moreno-Ocampo called the politicians' bluff, and issued public pre-trial notices for crimes against humanity against six Kenyans. Summoned to The Hague were ODM presidential aspirant William Ruto, ODM Chairman and minister Henry Kosgey, Kalenjin radio station head Joshua arap Sang (for the Kalenjin-on-Kikuyu violence in the Rift), PNU Deputy Prime Minister Uhuru Kenyatta (accused of organising and financing Mungiki revenge attacks), Police Chief Hussein Ali (for shoot to kill orders against demonstrators) and the influential civil service head and national security committee chairman Francis Muthaura (also accused of organising revenge attacks after the first anti-Kikuyu violence).[5] Kenya was again in dangerous waters, although no one knew if the charges would stick.

Rather than throwing their tainted leaders to the wolves, the Kikuyu and Kalenjin political classes played the ethnic and nationalist card. MPs caucused and postured to protect their presidential contenders, Kenyatta and Ruto, alleging a hidden foreign agenda to support Odinga. Within weeks, Parliament had passed a motion to withdraw from the ICC, and Kibaki and Musyoka led an unsuccessful effort at the African Union and UN to delay the investigation long enough to reinstate a (more malleable) local tribunal. Western countries were unsympathetic, as were

NGOs and Odinga (his supporters unaffected by the cases). As pre-trial hearings began, a 'pariahs' alliance' against Odinga was cobbled together between Kenyatta and Ruto (both accused of crimes against each others' communities), though it would inevitably collapse once no longer needed.

The Security Quagmire

While there was no new outbreak of mass ethnic and political violence, security remained a ever-present challenge. Both state and private violence continued, reflecting a culture of impunity, chaos at the top, the legitimisation of violence as a political tool and the intractability of reducing crime in a situation of poverty, inequality and disrespect for law.

Mungiki killings continued, as did lynch law killings and extrajudicial executions by police. Hundreds of Mungiki members were murdered by police death squads, part of a systemic effort to bypass the judicial process and prosecute an undeclared civil war against the Kikuyu-dominated movement, a conflict with increasing parallels to the repression of Mau Mau. A UN special observer confirmed serious allegations against the security forces in 2009.[6] The police seemed have formed covert alliances with some vigilante groups to defeat others, a further slide into lawlessness. There were no convictions for extrajudicial executions (even when photographed by passers' by), suggesting that protection came from the top.[7]

Table 13.1: Key military positions, 2008–11

Chief of General Staff	General Jeremiah Kianga	2005–11	Kamba
	General Julius Karangi	2011 on	Kikuyu
Vice-Chief of General Staff/ Defence Forces	Lt.-Gen. Julius Karangi	2005–11	Kikuyu
	Lt.-Gen. Samson Mwathethe	2011 on	Mijikenda
Army Commander	Lt.-Gen. Augustino Njoroge	2005–8	Kikuyu
	Lt.-Gen. Jack Tuwei	2008–10	Kalenjin
	Lt.-Gen. Njuki Mwaniki	2010–11	Kikuyu
	Lt.-Gen. John Kasaon	2011 on	Kalenjin
Deputy Army Commander	Major-Gen. Jones Mutwii	2005–8	Kamba
	Major-Gen. Njuki Mwaniki	2008-10	Kikuyu
	Major-Gen. Maurice Oyugi	2010 on	Luo
Air Force Commander	Major-Gen. Harold Tangai	2005–11	Taita
	Major-Gen. Joff Otieno	2011	Luo
Navy Commander	Major-Gen. Samson Mwathethe	2004–11	Mijikenda
	Major-Gen. Ngewa Mukala	2011 on	Luhya

Source: Various

The army was unleashed in 2008 in Mount Elgon to crush the SLDF militia, though this was achieved only with heavy fighting, allegations of torture and several hundred killed. Kenya also faced embarrassing though trivial incursions from Ugandan troops on an island in Lake Victoria and in West Pokot in 2009. Violence continued in the north-east and on the Ethiopian border.

Kibaki and Odinga's security appointments showed how the coalition was working in practice. Kikuyu and Meru continued to dominate domestic security, heading the security ministry (via George Saitoti), the police force, NSIS and CID. Fearful of the risks of change, Kibaki and the defence council kept several senior soldiers on past their normal retirement ages. When change finally came in 2011, it was obvious, with Kenya's first Kikuyu COGS, but every other position held by non-Gema (and non-Kamba leaders), including two Luo and one Luhya for the first time (see Table 13.1).

Land and Ethnicity

The tension over land rights continued. Although the government set up a special resettlement programme to help more than 350,000 displaced people return home and paid Ksh10,000 to every returnee, tens of thousands were still living in makeshift camps a year later. Some who returned were driven away once more by their neighbours. The government resorted to setting up new police posts (allegedly manned by Kikuyu officers) in some of the most difficult areas.

The Mau Forest

Odinga faced a particularly difficult land-related issue in 2009 – a dispute over the Mau forest in north Narok. Blaming Kenya's declining rainfall partly on the destruction of the forest water catchment, the government tried to end forest destruction and recover forest land illegally allocated to 20,000 Kalenjin and Ogiek families (and to Moi-era insiders) in the 1990s. Divisions between the Kalenjin and non-Kalenjin inside the ODM grew, as Odinga courageously joined PNU (and some other ODM) leaders in favouring the forest's recovery and replanting, while Ruto and most Kalenjin opposed any evictions or demanded full compensation.[8] Furious at the resulting evictions, most Kalenjin elites abandoned Odinga and once again began to chart a separate political course. Ruto declared his intention to contest the presidency in 2012 – this time for real.

The 2009 Census

In August 2009, Kenya conducted its fifth decennial census. Donors questioned the merit of asking Kenyans their ethnicity (given its sensitivity and that the results of the 1999 census in this regard remained secret), but the decision was taken to continue. When the results were published in August 2010, they showed Kenya's population had reached 38.6 million, of which more than a quarter lived in the Rift Valley. One-third of Kenyans were now urban, with 3.1 million people living in Nairobi alone.[9]

The Kikuyu remained the largest community, with the Luhya and Kalenjin second and third and the Luo now only fourth, their growth suppressed by AIDS and high infant mortality.

For the first time, the government disowned some results of a census – those for North-Eastern Province and Turkana (the Somali population had apparently increased by 850 per cent since 1989), and a repeat exercise was planned. Including the questionable northern results, Kenya's population growth rate had risen to 3 per cent once more.

Competitive Corruption

Power sharing appeared not to have reduced corruption, but it certainly became more visible, particularly after the Wikileaks releases of confidential US documents describing in detail the embassy's suspicious of corruption against ministers and officials. The new government was – in the now-public opinion of US ambassador Michael Rannenberger – a 'rogues' gallery' in which many were tainted with grand corruption.[10] A series of scandals in 2008 and 2009 tarnished ODM and PNU ministers alike and weakened the government's credibility, as the coalition partners indicted each other for alleged misdeeds. Finance Minister Amos Kimunya was forced to resign in July 2008 over the controversial sale of the Grand Regency Hotel. A series of scandals rocked the Kenya Pipeline Company. Undutied sugar imports continued, protected by senior police officers. Subsidised maize imports, introduced in May 2008 to stabilise prices after the post-election violence, were exploited to skim off large sums. All these received widespread negative publicity, suggesting that tolerance for such behaviour might finally be beginning to fade.[11]

However, decisive action against corruption was almost impossible for three years. There was near-chaos when Raila announced in February 2010 the sacking of Minister for Agriculture Ruto (after an audit named him in connection with the skimming of maize subsidies) and of Education Minister Samson Ongeri, only to have Kibaki veto his sackings. Ongeri's troubles came after the discovery by the British government that Ksh4.2 billion ($48 million) of British and American aid for the free primary education programme had been misappropriated between 2005 and 2009, by the simple but effective process of inventing imaginary schools.

On 20 October 2010, Ruto was finally suspended from office, after the High Court ruled he must stand trial in connection with $1.2 million of payments arising from land deals involving Kenya Pipeline Company in 2001.[12] The new constitution (see below) required all public officers facing criminal charges to stand down. The same clauses claimed other scalps, including PNU Foreign Minister Moses Wetang'ula, who stepped aside in October 2010 after the misuse of ministry funds, and Industrialisation Minister Kosgey, who stood down in January 2011 over corruption charges (after being named as one of the organisers of the post-election violence).[13] The KACC, meanwhile, led by P. L. O. Lumumba after Aaron Ringera resigned, was investigating three more ministers (including Charity Ngilu) and conducting 'lifestyle audits' of 45 parastatal heads. Ongeri was close to dismissal, while the British suspended further aid and pursued the Kenyans, demanding their money back. Kenya had never seen such carnage at the top over corruption, and more heads were expected to roll.[14] In May 2011, in an extraordinary sequence of events, Samuel Gichuru, long-time KPLC boss, was charged by the British courts in Jersey with bribery and money laundering committed during the Moi era, and ex-Finance Minister Chris Okemo was also indicted as having been paid off. More than a billion shillings in payments were involved. Transparency International continued to name the police as the most corrupt institution in the country, but broadened its focus to also look at aid organisations, recognising that their wealth made them an increasing target for predation.

More than a dozen officials and ministers, including Attorney General Amos Wako, had meanwhile been banned from the UK or US because of concerns over corruption or their role in protecting it. Bans were also requested on Kosgey and Ringera.[15] The US banned four Kenyan officials and businessmen due to links with drug trafficking in 2010. In December 2010 it publicly named MP John Harun Mwau as an international drug smuggler and in 2011 froze all his US assets.[16] Three other surprisingly wealthy MPs were named by Saitoti in Parliament as being drug lords or crime bosses, according to the Americans.[17]

After the one-off ivory sale approved by CITES, poaching worsened sharply, with 271 elephants killed by poachers in 2009 and numerous seizures of ivory bound for the Far East and Nigeria. In 2011, as a publicity exercise, Kibaki emulated Moi two decades before and burnt a huge pile of ivory, seized from smugglers.

A Miracle: A New Constitution at Last

Yet Another Draft Constitution

The constitutional reform process restarted, with yet another Constitution of Kenya Review Act in 2008. This established another Committee of Experts, mandated to produce a new constitution, while taking into account all previous drafts and issues. They published their 'harmonised draft' in November 2009. This generally pro-Orange draft retained both a devolved system of government and embedded the role of the prime minister as head of government.[18] The Parliamentary Select Committee then restructured it, under the leadership of a neutral MP, managing to reach a new and delicate political consensus, despite protests from civic society. The Committee of Experts incorporated this feedback and produced a refined draft in February 2010.[19]

In this draft, the Senate was restored, with membership combining elected district (now renamed county) representatives, plus special seats for women, young people and disabled people. The lower house was based on a combination of 290 parliamentary constituencies, plus 47 special seats for women elected by the counties (and 12 nominees). As in 1962, the Senate had veto rights but limited powers over money bills. The voting system would remain first past the post, but constituency boundaries would be redrawn to make consistencies more equal. Politicians faced potential recall, a process likely to generate significant tension.

The three-layer system of devolution initially proposed by the experts was simplified by the Committee to a two-tier system, with powers split between 47 county governments (almost identical to the districts of 1991–2), each with a governor and county assembly, and the national government. The provincial administration would (eventually) be merged into the devolved governments. Government land would be allocated between central and county governments, with an independent National Land Commission to administer it. Community land (including Trust land and group lands) would be managed at county level. Parliament was mandated to fix the maximum acreage of land which could be owned by an individual (and foreigners could no longer own, only lease, land). The administration police and regular police would be merged and an independent police oversight commission created.

The president remained head of state, directly elected in a national election. The two-term limit was retained, as was the runoff system, but an impeachment process was introduced for the first time.[20] However, in the PSC's deliberations in late January, an unexpected shift occurred, as the prime minister's role – previously considered so fundamental and so contentious – was abolished, apparently with Raila's support.[21] The lesson from two years of power sharing was that it just did not work. Although Odinga would remain in office until 2012, the prime minister vanished from the constitution. The president would appoint a deputy president, (effectively the vice-president), and ministers (renamed Cabinet secretaries, and prohibited from being MPs, a surprising outcome that would inevitably drive a more technocratic approach to policy). Presidential appointments would require parliamentary approval. Essential to obtaining the support of the incumbent elites, all incumbent officials and politicians would retain their seats for a while after the constitution's enactment.

The final draft went to the National Assembly in March 2010, with politicians still divided over its merits, despite several retreats and caucuses. Although more than 100 amendments were proposed, all failed to achieve the required quorum, as no group held the two-thirds majority required. As a consequence, the draft was approved without amendment on 1 April 2010, with both Kibaki and Odinga supporting the deal and with support from many foreign governments and eminent persons.[22] The new 179-page constitution was published by perennial survivor Wako on 6 May 2010.

Kenya's Second Referendum, August 2010

The IIEC prepared with trepidation for Kenya's second referendum, which was held on 4 August 2010. The respective camps were allocated the campaign colours of green for 'Yes' and red for 'No'. The IIEC also conducted a full re-registration with new voters' cards during March–May. This registered only 12.6 million of the estimated 18 million eligible voters, 89 per cent of those registered in 2007. This confirmed suspicions that there were more than 2 million dead or invented voters on the 2007 register, more than a million of which had apparently voted (See Figure 13.2).

13.2 Registered voters and actual votes, 1963–2010

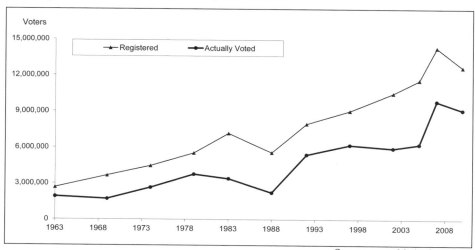

Source: unpublished analysis

Most politicians were in favour, as were most civil society groups and trade unions. Odinga was its strongest supporter, and Kibaki also actively campaigned for a yes vote, seeing it as his legacy and the best chance Kenya had to overcome the divisions of the past. However, most churches opposed the draft, objecting to the clauses permitting abortion (though it was only when the mother's life was in danger) and embedding the Kadhi's courts in the constitution. Ex-president Moi also campaigned for a 'no', as did supporters of the presidential aspirations of the increasingly alienated Ruto (including most Kalenjin MPs), fearful of the land-related clauses in the draft and of the implications of victory for the upcoming presidential contest. Polls during May indicated that 57–65 per cent would vote yes and 20–25 per cent no, but a number of voters remained undecided.[23] There were some 'watermelon' yes supporters (green on the outside, red on the inside), including allies of the church-backed Vice-President Musyoka in Eastern, also fearful of the boost a yes vote would give Raila's chances for the succession.

The results were, as expected, a decisive victory for the yes team, by 67 per cent to 31 per cent, with 9 million votes cast. Turnout was 72 per cent.[24] Most observers were satisfied, and foreign governments welcomed the verdict. There was little or no violence, despite fears of another outbreak in the Rift. The only warning signs were a decisive 88 per cent no vote in Kalenjin districts (every single Kalenjin-dominated constituency voted no, on very high turnouts, showing the strength of the pro-Ruto vote), a 50–50 result in Ukambani and a high number of spoilt votes (2.4 per cent) overall. Again, the Luo community proved the most monolithic, voting 99 per cent for Odinga's latest project (see Figure 13.3). Western governments and media endorsed the result, although the press decried the 'tribal loyalty' of Kenya's voting.[25]

13.3: Referendum results by ethnic group, 2010

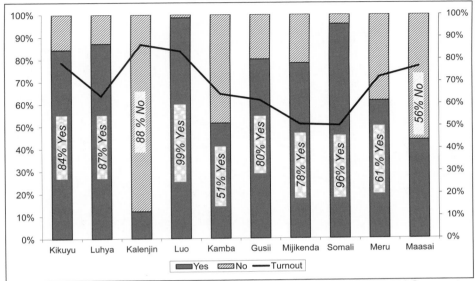

Source: Interim Independent Electoral Commission,
'Comprehensive Final 2010 Referendum Results', 10 August 2010, www.nation.co.ke

The Second Republic

The new Constitution was promulgated by Kibaki on 27 August 2010, in a mass ceremony in Nairobi's Uhuru Park, in front of 10 heads of state (see Figure 13.4). It was hailed with hyperbole as the start of Kenya's 'Second Republic' and a new era of freedom and opportunity.

Led by ODM-Kenya's Minister for Justice and Constitutional Affairs Mutula Kilonzo, Kenya's legislators and a (theoretically non-political) Constitutional Implementation Commission now faced the daunting task of crafting 49 pieces of complex legislation which would implement the new Constitution within one to five years, while preparing for a very different electoral contest in 2012–13. The competition for the posts of senator and governor in each county began immediately, though the future role of the provincial administration (undefined in the Constitution) remained unclear. Without the possibility of ministerial office or the reality of patronage, the MP's role suddenly looked less attractive. Devolution seemed to promise real power to county governors (the name redolent of colonial rule) and tension between them and central government was almost inevitable.

Most observers agreed that the new Constitution was a reasonable compromise and better than the existing structure. But there were concerns. The Constitution had embedded the use of ethnic quotas in state jobs, including army recruitment. By creating a technocratic Cabinet of non-politicians, the Constitution had

13.4: Kibaki and the new Constitution, August 2010

Source: Nation Group Newspapers

removed a key tool (patronage) for crafting unity between competing political factions. Most significantly, devolution remained unproven. There were concerns that the county governments might face some of the problems of Nigerian states, with a devolution of corruption, a 'winner takes all' competition within ethnically divided districts such as Uasin Gishu and Nakuru, and the deliberate discrimination against minority groups. Despite recent state investment, many of Kenya's local authorities (the closest equivalent to future country governments) remained poorly run and heavily indebted.

Some did not live to see this day. Although Moi and Njonjo soldiered on, apparently impregnable, few of the independence generation remained. Jeremiah Nyagah (who had retired from politics in 1992) passed away in 2008, as did Robert Matano, Eliud Mahihu and Kipkalya arap Kones.

Crafting the Future

During 2011, the attorney-general's office, politicians, the presidency and NGOs worked together to engineer the legislative structures which would govern Kenya for the future, in a combined mood of optimism and concern (that old structures of exploitation would re-emerge in a new guise). Parliament passed laws establishing a new Supreme Court and rules for vetting judges as well as the new Independent Electoral and Boundaries Commission, though no one was yet clear how these new institutions would work. The Constitutional Implementation Commission, chaired by Charles Nyachae (lawyer, compromise candidate and son of Simeon), struggled to prepare and obtain MPs' endorsement for the raft of legislation required on the original timetable. While the debates were superficially about constitutional matters, the various political interests competed behind the scenes as every law was drafted and commission reported, always seeking or fearing advantage.[26]

As planned in the new Constitution, Chief Justice Evan Gichuru retired, and – in an appointment shocking to many 'family values' Christians – Odinga and Kibaki jointly agreed to appoint liberal activist Willy Mutunga (ex-detainee and founder of the Kenyan Human Rights Commission) as chief justice in May 2011. It was the most radical judicial appointment made for decades.[27] It was also the first time the House had formally vetted and approved presidential nominations, further evidence of the true separation of powers in the new Constitution, though the probity, competence and independence of Parliament all remained long-term risks to this balance .[28] Mutunga had his work cut out. The legal system was almost as inefficient and corrupt as it had been under Moi. Estimates now suggested there were 1 million pending legal cases.[29]

African and Western governments and their media houses were generally pleased with Kenya's progress, though they demanded even faster action (if roles were reversed, one would doubt progress would have been as rapid). But there remained a fear that the new constitutional structure was too devolved to allow clear decision-making and that corruption, tribalism and incompetence in some county governments would require intervention from the centre. Some gave the Constitution less than five years before a unitary system was reimposed.

Economic Performance

Economic growth, the talisman of Kibaki's first presidency, was shaky in 2008, with GDP growth cut to 1.7 per cent by the violence. Agricultural production and tourism were worst affected (international arrivals fell by 31 per cent in 2008, its biggest fall ever). The shilling declined against the dollar for the first time since 2000, and inflation exceeded 26 per cent, its worst since 1991–3.[30] The economy was further stressed in 2009 by the world credit crunch and falls in overseas demand and investment. There were maize and power shortages in 2008 and 2009 following poor rainfall. In 2010, Parliament even passed a bill to reintroduce price controls on essential commodities, abolished for a decade.[31]

However, Kenya weathered the worst of the recession, with GDP growing at 2.9 per cent in 2009 and 5.6 per cent in 2010, though growth in 2011 was expected to be lower because of the drought. IMF loans continued, with a $200 million exogenous shocks loan and a US$350 million SDR allotment in 2009. Treading carefully since the 2007–8 violence, donor talk of conditionalities was perfunctory. Tourism reached a new all-time high. Government revenues again exceeded targets, but the deficit (excluding grants) as a percentage of GDP grew steadily, to 8.4 per cent in 2010–11. Kenya's public debt continued to grow, financing an investment programme in roads, railways and electricity of huge long-term potential value but some medium-term risk. With rising inflation – reaching 13 per cent in mid-2011 – the shilling fell to an all-time low. In December 2008 the government announced plans to privatise another tranche of state assets, including the NBK, KenGen, the Kenya Pipeline Company and the Kenya Ports Authority, although progress thereafter was typically slow.

As long as its politics remained peaceful, Kenya remained the region's powerhouse, with strong tourism, good growth expectations and a vibrant private sector. With submarine fibre-optic networks finally reaching Kenya, the opportunity existed to enter the IT and business process outsourcing markets, mobile phone networks having demonstrated the innovative and technically savvy nature of the Kenyan market. Growth was constrained mainly by a reluctance to invest: a product of corruption, insecurity, non-tariff barriers and fears for the country's political future. Multinationals continued to struggle and more divestments took place, with Chevron and Shell exiting the oil industry. However, the Kenyan diaspora continued to pour billions back into the country, particularly after the new Constitution permitted dual citizenship.[32] With the positive referendum result and unity of most of the political and business classes, the brakes on investment and growth appeared – superficially – to have been removed. The hope, enunciated in 2008's Vision 2030 strategy, remained that Kenya would become a middle-income economy by 2030.

Trade, Aid and International Relations

Western donors continued to offer project assistance, with US aid rising to $900 million by 2009.[33] They also continued to involve themselves in Kenya's domestic affairs: a product of their continued financial support for the government and their key role in the 2008 crisis. The Americans worked hard behind the scenes to sustain the coalition and praised its achievements publicly, despite their scepticism over elite corruption, a view which became embarrassingly public in 2010 and 2011 when Wikileaks acquired and published internal US government communications in which both their high-level access and contempt for the corrupt practices of the Kenyan government were equally clear.[34] Relations with the UK were likely to be strained by the continued progress of the lawsuit alleging torture during Mau Mau.

Kenya continued to diversify its trade and aid partners away from the West, with stronger engagements with Brazil and Far Eastern countries. Closer to home, on 1 July 2010, the five-country EAC implemented its common market protocol, the next step towards the free movement of goods, people and services in a market of 120 million people, with federation still the end goal. Trade increased (Kenya had a billion dollar surplus with the EAC in 2010–11), but the country continued to rely on tariff walls in maize, wheat and particularly sugar, where the survival and privatisation of the five remaining state-owned mills still depended on exemptions from COMESA's free trade rules.

Independence in Southern Sudan, finally achieved on 1 July 2011, caused an influx of money to its southern neighbour as well.[35] China, Kenya's new preferred aid and trade partner, began to invest significantly in Kenya's infrastructure, willing to make big investments for long-term returns. These included a new port in Lamu (first mooted in the 1970s) and a new railway line to Ethiopia and Sudan to export Sudanese oil and import commodities. In mid-2011, China was estimated to be investing in projects worth Ksh57 billion in Kenya, including a new Nairobi–Thika super-highway and a new teaching hospital (although much of this money was in loans, storing up more trouble for the future, and there were rumours of large backhanders for contracts).[36] China was now the third largest exporter to Kenya after the UAE and India and even began building cars in Thika, fast becoming part of an extended Nairobi conurbation.

Food and Famine

Food pricing once more became a political issue, as world food prices rose steadily after 2004. The increase was driven by growing demand and by structural changes such as the increasing use of farmland for biofuels, and by 2011 prices had doubled in seven years.[37]

In 2010–11, the spectre of famine once more faced the Horn of Africa and northern Kenya. The drought, following heavy El Niño rains in 2009–10, was feared to be the worst for 60 years, with 10 million people affected. Kenya estimated it would grow no more than 60 per cent of the maize it needed. Hundreds of thousands of starving Somali fled into Kenya, hoping for help. Western aid agencies appealed for help as the Dadaab refugee camp, the biggest in the world, exceeded 380,000 people by July 2011, while the Kenyans wrestled with the security implications of another influx of impoverished Somali, some supporters of militant Islamic groups. Donors and IFIs gave generously once more.

The Succession Puzzle

No Party, No Leader

While the rival teams prepared for the next electoral battle in 2012 or early 2013, it was not yet clear who was the PNU's candidate, with Kibaki ineligible for a third term. Finance Minister and Deputy Prime Minister Kenyatta was the leading contender from the Kikuyu, with George Saitoti, rebel Martha Karua from NARC-Kenya and low-key Murang'a minister Peter Kenneth an outside chance (though Uhuru's political survival rested on the outcome of the ICC prosecutions). But Kibaki declined to make Moi's mistake and anoint a successor.

Some PNU insiders recognised that they should not put up a Kikuyu candidate once again: not only would a third Kikuyu president reinforce the belief in the unwillingness of the Gema elites to allow others to rule, it would inevitably result in a second ethnic head-to-head with Odinga. Vice-President Musyoka from ODM-Kenya was the most obvious non-Kikuyu aspirant but, to many, he lacked backbone and leadership qualities. They seemed to have little choice but to pick

Uhuru and repeat the 1960s with a Kenyatta-versus-Odinga competition: one which Odinga (the better tactician, organiser and with an unquenchable desire for office) might well win.

The PNU itself, created as a vehicle for the 2007 elections, remained a party more on paper than in practice. Its non-Gema constituent parties began to prepare to go it alone. As in 2006, the political forces centred on Kibaki and the Mount Kenya peoples appeared in deep trouble. But as 2006–7 had shown, a year was a long time.

A Trial Separation

Odinga, meanwhile, remained the ODM's sole presidential candidate, his credibility boosted by a series of difficult decisions taken as prime minister and by his referendum success. A September 2010 opinion poll gave him 47 per cent of the vote, head and shoulders above his competitors, with Kenyatta at 10 per cent and Musyoka 8 per cent.[38] However, his 2005–7 alliance had fractured, as Kalenjin and Luo leaders drifted apart in a series of disputes over land rights, corruption and the treatment of post-election violence suspects. Raila in turn tried to broaden his appeal, making inroads into Kamba districts (with Ngilu) and even Meru areas during 2011. A joint Odinga–Mudavadi ticket was the most popular and most likely winning ticket in mid-2011, with a Kenyatta–Musyoka ticket a distant second. The issue of the running mate had become more significant as the Constitution required a US-style formally nominated joint ticket and the deputy president would take over from his boss in the event of his death.

Ruto, eventually sacked from the Cabinet, became Kenya's third force and Odinga's leading critic. He had channelled religious and land-focused concerns about the Constitution into a Kalenjin 'no' vote in the referendum, positioning himself for the 2012 contest on his old UDM party ticket (if he had not been jailed for corruption or crimes against humanity in the interim). Other Kalenjin ministers reluctantly followed his lead. While Nyanza and Western Province remained solid behind Odinga, it was no longer clear how monolithic his support was elsewhere. Kenyatta, Ruto and Musyoka's bizarre Kikuyu-Kalenjin-Kamba (i.e. anti-Raila) alliance appeared to be holding.

Gambler's Luck

Much depended on whether the ICC would convict Ruto, Kenyatta or both. The court's action had the potential to shock the system severely. If both Kenyatta and Ruto were convicted, Odinga would romp home. If Kenyatta went down and Ruto did not, again Odinga would probably win, whoever the PNU–ODM-Kenya alliance put forward. If both were acquitted, a Kenyatta–Ruto alliance would match Odinga head to head. If Ruto went down and Kenyatta did not, there would be trouble. The Kalenjin would be alienated; it would still a very close race, and there might well be trouble in Kikuyu–Kalenjin boundary areas. By most assessments, a runoff was the most likely option, no candidate having won 50 per cent of the vote nationwide and 25 per cent in at least half the counties (as the new Constitution required). In such a troubled environment, all bets would be off and security would be an ever-present concern for Odinga.

A New Generation?

The urban middle class, which had expanded significantly since the mid-1980s, continued to offer some hope for the future. Less tribal and less embedded in the politics of the past, some believed Kenya's next generation of city-dwellers would drive both economic revival and a true renewal of the political elite in 2012–13, disenchanted with the corruption, partisanship and machine politics of both parties. But it remained likely that the main parties would find some way to harness this dissent – as they had in 1992 and 2002 – behind existing structures, rather than allowing the creation of a new third force. And while the destitute, disempowered, undereducated urban underclass was currently quiet, no one was sure it would stay that way.

Conclusions

The year 2011 showed signs that Kenya was – despite the heavy legacy of the past – moving towards a new deal, with a new Constitution, less encumbered by institutional failures, and its economy growing in a way which seemed more robust than in the stop–start days of Moi. The reality, though, was more sobering. A new Constitution changed the rules of the game, but the players remained the same, and they still appeared to be playing to win. No one could confidently make any forecasts; much depended on the PNU's strategy and whether it could, somehow, accept that an Odinga victory might in the long run be better for Kenya, even at some economic and personal cost. But the lesson of history was that no one was president of Kenya for only five years. In any case, few Gema leaders could stomach the idea of Odinga as president, even with reduced powers, even for a day. Whatever the outcome, the 2012–13 elections were going to be confused, corrupt and unpredictable until the event itself, and the risk of trouble remained high. As this book goes to press, everything is still to play for.

Chapter 14

Conclusions

Kenya in 2011

In the 48 years since independence, Kenya's population has increased nearly fivefold, urbanisation has been rapid and chaotic, global technology, communications and marketing waves have swept across the nation and the spread of agriculture and settlement has consumed most of its forests and wildlife. Politically, some of the issues of the early 1960s have become history. The white settlers are a distant mirage, a tourist trap. Single-party rule has come and gone. Kenya is a more open, more liberal society than at any time in its history. However, other lines of division have endured. Kenya remains closely linked to its colonial history and dominated by the events of its independence. Lines of conflicts that had been contingent, near-accidents in the 1960s have become institutionalised and continue to play out across a different set of actors in a changed world.

The economy remains structured along colonial lines, with a relatively large manufacturing sector serving regional markets and strong cash-crop agricultural exports, though the economic stranglehold of the state has loosened. External financial support and its implications for internal politics remains as important as in 1963, though the donors involved and their conditions for support have changed. 'Tribalism', the propensity of those with authority to distribute resources on an ethno-regional basis and of individuals to behave differently towards their 'own' and those from 'other' ethnic communities, remains widespread. At the national level, the contest for political power is as structured and dominated by ethnicity – particularly amongst the Kikuyu, Kalenjin and Luo – as it was in 1963. Although the constitutional convention of the monarchical presidency had been unchallenged for two decades, the reintroduction of multi-party democracy and the realignment of politics on an ethnic basis in 1991–2 reawoke the debate over federalism, and it blazed with as much fervour in 2002–7 as it had in 1962–4. Land remains a key fault line, contested between rich and poor and between ethnic communities alike. The Kenya of 2011 is an extremely unequal society. The colour of the ruling elites has changed, but the struggle for resources and the tension between redistributive and growth-oriented policies was as apparent between Raila Odinga and Mwai Kibaki in 2007 as between Tom Mboya and Oginga Odinga in 1963.

The role of Kenya's history in driving its political culture remains strong and yet, to a degree, manufactured. Kenya's history is poorly understood by most Kenyans, and is often simplified into linear narratives of development, corruption or repression. Accepted wisdom and reality often differ. Yet Kenyans have been determined to replay the divisions of the past, and real and imagined injustices have merged to create conflicts and entitlements that in turn drive contemporary politics. The exploitative money-grabbing Kikuyu, the corrupt incompetence of the Kalenjin and the anti-government socialism of the Luo are stereotypes, all with some historical root, but all contemporary political messages for political effect. Few remember Kenya's 'real' history and the origins of contemporary divisions. Less than 3 per cent of Kenyans now remember colonial Kenya as an adult.

This concluding chapter explores a number of threads, drawing some general conclusions about post-colonial Kenya's evolution but casting doubt on others. It cannot be a summary of a nation's history, which is multi-layered and multi-directional. In fact, Kenya's history suggests that there are no easy generalisations about the intertwined challenges of politics, development, security and national identity. Accident and design intermingle; political necessity and economic rationality often conflict; and even the most basic assertions about successes and failures are contested.

In aggregate, looking at events since 1963, one is left with the feeling of stoic endurance, but also of promises unfulfilled and opportunities missed. Unlike many other African countries, Kenya has survived nearly five decades as a functioning nation-state with its borders intact, without fighting a single war and without a complete breakdown of law and order or the imposition of military rule. Its institutions endured and economic growth (intermittently) continued. However, although Kenya has become a nation-state, it has never achieved its longed-for autonomy from foreign aid, and has abandoned attempts to maintain a distinct cultural identity. It has failed to deliver adequate material living conditions for most of its people; and its politics have failed to transcend its history. In 2005–11, Kenyans were fighting over many of the same issues that had divided them five decades before: over land, ethnicity and power. Their leaders, some coming from political families that had become dynasties in just two generations, were fighting old wars with new troops.

Continuity and Change

Like all states, Kenya's history has been strongly influenced by world-scale events (such as oil crises and the end of the Cold War) and by social, economic and technological change, though uniquely mediated by the circumstances it faced at independence and the acts and omissions of its people since. Alongside the slower currents – of population growth and urbanisation; rising inequality; mass education; the spread of agriculture and of land registration; the gradual breakdown of gender barriers – the country has seen four episodes of political and then economic change, separated by longer periods of semi-stasis. Each involved a gradual build-up of tension, an overt discontinuity, and then a period of consequential change in both policy and practice. None was inevitable. Of these, the first was the most important, setting the direction for the next five decades.

The Independence Settlement, 1962–5

The first years of independence saw a continuation of the pre-independence conflict over the direction of the state, which became a battle to control the levers of power. The Cold War of the period was won by the forces of 'stability and progress', to which the British handed over power. The capture of the state by Jomo Kenyatta and his allies in 1962–5 remains the single most important factor in understanding Kenya's subsequent trajectory. Right or wrong, Kenyans (or more accurately Kenyan elites) chose a more conservative, inegalitarian, pro-Western and authoritarian path, for reasons that were ideological, personal, ethnic and pragmatic in equal measure. Although radical changes were taking place in society, the country's political institutions soon reverted towards those of colonial rule and away from the instruments designed in 1962 for a democratic state. Even before independence, the federal model had been mortally wounded and a centralised constitution soon replaced it. Political parties withered away or became a fig leaf on executive power and the presidency was elevated to a height analogous to that recently commanded by the colonial governor, able to rule by decree and periodically seeking endorsement from a near-advisory Parliament.

Two different conflicts were under way at the same time. The first was the contest between region and centre, and the tension that underlay this between models of citizenship that focused on the individual (a model which the Kikuyu community came to epitomise) and those that concentrated on the rights of groups, generally ethnic groups, and particularly rights to land (which Kalenjin, coastal and Maasai leaders championed). Central authority triumphed, and the consequence was both the evolution of the monarchical presidency and the continuation of the 'willing buyer, willing seller' model of individual land rights. The second conflict was between east and west, capitalism and socialism, and increasingly, between Kikuyu and Luo. A conservative Kikuyu-dominated elite defeated the more populist, communal and socialist elements in KANU and society. Their representatives were driven into the political wilderness, where they were to remain for decades, creating a model of alienation and disempowerment for the Luo that continues to drive behaviour today.

The institutions, policies and personnel that gained ascendancy in this period survived almost unaltered until Kenyatta's death. For 15 years, a conservative Kikuyu-centric regime entrenched itself, and co-opted, excluded or in a few cases murdered its competitors. Kenyatta had no intention of submitting to, let alone losing, a competitive election – no one ever directly voted for him after his release from prison. His Kenya was ruled by a capable, assertive and accumulative elite that offered an implicit 'social contract' of Western backing, development and security in return for obedience. The strongest threat to this contract was from Kenya's left, a blend of principled dissent, socialism and anti-foreigner and anti-immigrant populism, associated with the Luo, intellectuals and landless Kikuyu squatters.

Many in this conservative elite genuinely believed they were acting in the public good, and they were supported for more than 20 years by Western governments, unwilling to challenge the politics or economics of one of their few strong allies in the region. A centralised, rational-bureaucratic model of the nation-state was presented to its people and its foreign patrons, but it was one in which some regions (Nairobi, Central Province and the Kikuyu diaspora) benefited more than others. Political competition was inhibited or diverted into controlled channels. This served both to sustain national identity (as the multi-party era showed, fears about the impact of competitive politics on Kenya's national identity, stability and growth were far from idle) and to protect the elite's control of the bureaucracy and the informal systems that operated beneath it.

The Moi Presidency, 1980–3

Kenyatta's death and the succession of Daniel arap Moi in 1978 'unfroze the mould' and forced a restructuring of the political system. Although there was no electoral process accompanying his elevation, it was a regime transition as profound as if it had been executed through the ballot box. Moi's accession was followed by a period of growing tension that culminated in the economic crisis of 1981–2, the 1982 declaration of the one-party state, the coup attempt and Njonjo's fall in 1983.

The result of the discontinuity of 1982–3 then rippled out in changes to policy and the gradual emergence of a second political and economic elite. By 1984, Moi was beginning to restructure Kenya's politics and economics, introducing redistributive policies that benefited new groups and less-developed regions. Unlike Kenyatta, however, he needed to take away before he could give.[1] This hurt the existing Kikuyu-dominated commercial class and slowed Kenya's growth. For a decade, Kenya would chart a praetorian course, populist without being socialist, and would fail to grasp the challenge of structural adjustment. The Kikuyu and the urban poor were disadvantaged and disenfranchised, and economic rationality as a criterion in decision-making was often abandoned in the interests of regime survival.

Although Moi introduced new policies during 1984–7, it was in the 'shadow state' of practice rather than policy – of land grants, appointments, contracts, police actions, political violence and ethnic arithmetic – that the biggest changes occurred. With the dismantling of Kikuyu privilege, growing corruption, economic difficulties, the decline of the (previously stable) patron–client system and the consolidation of a new Kalenjin elite, grasping and contemptuous of democracy, the state became increasingly authoritarian in order to control dissent. In parallel, the economy was stuttering and increasingly dependent on aid. Although some in Kenya's small cadre of technocrats saw the need for structural reform, the shadow state, the parasitic class of 'briefcase businessmen', and the survival interests of neo-patrimonialism delayed or diverted many of the changes the West demanded. Moi's failure to satisfy either domestic or foreign interests led to crisis when the world shifted around it. His model of governance was little different from that of Kenyatta: he had learnt carefully at the feet of his predecessor. But the model was struggling both politically and economically and the external environment had changed, less tolerant of corruption, authoritarianism and state capitalism, even when it delivered stability.

The Incomplete Transition of 1991–3

The third major period of change was the result of limitations built into Kenya's economic strategy, Western pressure, unique events such as the murder of Robert Ouko, and frustration at the corrupt, undemocratic and divisive policies of the government. These tensions became apparent in 1990, and grew until a third discontinuity occurred in 1991–3.

The reintroduction of multi-party democracy in 1991 and the reforms that followed were the most dramatic changes in the country's path since 1965. Kenya's politics and economics were both restructured into a more liberal, competitive model, and as a side-effect the importance of ethnicity and of external influences on the country's path were reasserted. From that time on, the state was in retreat in every sphere. This change would have been impossible without sustained pressure from Western donors, flexing their financial, diplomatic and even moral authority. However, the donors could not force regime change itself, and KANU survived, winning the 1992 elections by a combination of guile, electoral abuse, divisions in the opposition and genuine concern over a return to rule by the 'majority tribes'. Moi and his allies reinvented themselves to win the polls, creating a new anti-Kikuyu coalition that survived for another decade. It was more flexible than Moi's previous structure of support, but built around the same bastions of state abuses, money and ethnicity. Kenya reformed, but it was a hard-fought and incomplete process. Seeking its own survival above all else, the government zigzagged between conflict and cooperation throughout the next decade.

Moi represented a 'third way' in Kenyan politics. He was not pro-capitalist or pro-socialist. Indeed, he appeared to see this as less of an issue than whether Kenya was free to take its own economic and political decisions. Although personally austere, his regime survived through corruption. He was, above all, a Kalenjin of the old school, whose moral values had been built in a different time. It was Moi, however, who broke KANU's monopoly of power. His choice of Uhuru Kenyatta to lead the party into the 2002 election and his refusal to permit a free contest for the succession infuriated key allies and fragmented his coalition. KANU's resulting defeat ended a 20-year diversion of history.

The Twin Discontinuity of 2003–5 and 2007–8

The period 2003–5 saw a second chance for renewal, and the nation witnessed rapid changes in both policy and practice. However, the momentum for change soon dissipated: a consequence of bad luck, the scale of the problems NARC had inherited from KANU and the tension between ethno-regional interests in the disparate coalition. The rot of politicisation, corruption and tribalism was too deep to be cleared out by a fractious coalition led by an ageing Kikuyu, his every decision viewed through a zero-sum ethnic lens.

Gradually, political conflict hardened around the same three-way stereotypical division as in 1963: between the (conservative, centralising, individualist, expanding, growth- and wealth-focused) Kikuyu, the (more socialist, egalitarian, protectionist and instinctively anti-government) Luo and the (pro-devolution, communal, self-reliant, anti-Kikuyu) Kalenjin, usually supported by other ex-KADU pastoralist, Luhya and coastal communities. The economic realities had changed, but the same battles continued. Tension built until the first discontinuity – the referendum crisis of 2005 – which drove apart Kikuyu and Luo, forced many liberals and intellectuals to declare their hand against the government and divided supporters of regionalism from those believing in a strong central executive. Unlike 1965, however, this time the decentralisers and the critics of Kikuyu dominance united, and the state froze. The government was unable to defeat its opponents, but unwilling to concede to them either.

After two years of phoney war, battle was joined in the 2007 elections between two manufactured alliances that represented different futures for Kenya. While Kibaki and the PNU were the 'party of government', representing security, efficiency, stability, growth, inequality and Kikuyu, Embu and Meru interests, Odinga and the ODM represented an alliance of the disenfranchised, pro-devolution, anti-Kikuyu, communal and redistributive elements of Kenya's society. Kibaki's disputed victory and its brutal fallout shocked the world and forced all parties into an uneasy power-sharing deal, but there was no clear winner and the internal struggle continued within the administration.

The next three years of the Grand Coalition and power sharing showed that little has changed. Corruption remained rampant, ethnicity has been institutionalised in the administration and security remained elusive.

One More Chance, 2010–11

The only bright spot as this story closed was the enactment of the new Constitution. Its implementation, in parallel with the events at the ICC, had the potential to catalyse a change more fundamental than anything since 1965. It could allow Kenya to break free of the past, but could also reinforce ethnic segregation, devolve corruption and create administrative chaos. Only time will tell.

Bureaucracy, Corruption and the Strength of Institutions

The strong, centralised and undemocratic political institutions that Kenya had operated until independence and restored in 1964–5 have weakened over the decades. The 'public good' of a politically neutral, depersonalised bureaucracy, an ideal inherited from the British, was soon corrupted (if it ever truly existed), and the state was near privatised in the 1990s, its capacity weakened in myriad ways. Whatever the formal process, by the 1970s there was already a second state of clientelism, corruption and connections, fuelled by poverty and politics, entwined with and running beneath the formal processes of government. But in Kenya – unlike some African societies, where formal process all but collapsed – the two operated in parallel. Kenya is not a Congo or a Nigeria, in which office is purely prebendal, a licence to accumulate. The formal system was sustained in part by foreign pressure, investment and expertise, in part by the individual efforts of administrators and politicians, and in part by the wealth and relative sophistication of the country's economy, able to afford an educated elite and more vulnerable to the distorting effects of clientelism and predation. You can steal, but you must work as well, and you must steal cleverly to avoid detection. Kenya is complex because there are always layered processes: formal and informal and seldom one answer for why decisions are made or who gains.

There are three related – though distinct – ways in which Kenya failed to achieve the bureaucratic ideal: the dominance of *patron–clientelism* and the personalisation (and ethnicisation) of decision-making; *corruption* and the commercialisation of the state; and the *limited capacity* of the bureaucracy to execute policy.

Kenya's history is largely a history of *patron–client politics*. Everyone knows that 'who gets what' is crucially important, and that despite the efforts of technocrats and advisers, policy is set or applied in order to favour particular groups. There is also a disconnect between policy and practice. Ever since independence, Kenya's leadership has hidden behind (theoretically neutral) bureaucratic processes, but tilted them in such a way as to ensure particular groups gained (for example through access to state loans, land, jobs and development resources). Deliberately opaque processes concealed partial and self-interested decision-making. Change is promised and begins with each round of new leadership, but falters after roughly three years. Every president has then taken a route forced upon him by the practicalities of survival: of a return to the bastions of loyalty through a shared ethnic identity, resource extraction and authoritarianism.

Bruce Berman suggests that African politics is – in line with Bayart – 'personal, materialistic and opportunistic', and that ideology, principle and policy have been relatively unimportant.[2] This is true to a great degree, but there are exceptions in Kenya: particularly the struggle over economic policy, where principle eventually overcame patronage politics, the result of economic necessity and external pressure. Similarly, while opportunism has dominated the behaviour of many political actors, it is not the sole driver of choice. December 1991 would not have seen the restoration of multi-party democracy if there had not been a sustained campaign by pro-pluralist elites during the 1980s, at great personal cost. Similarly, while the Rainbow Alliance's defection in 2002 met all of Berman's criteria, NARC itself would never have existed if Kibaki and his allies had not held firm for a decade.

In Kenya, there is little doubt that patron–client politics and patronage are the bedrock of political perception and very often of political reality. Such networks of hierarchical personal relationships (often with an ethnic dimension) cover the private sector, the churches, civil society and the professions as well as the state itself. Such relationships are not static, however, but have evolved as the years passed. Politicians' relationships with state decision-makers are now being eclipsed by equally valuable relationships with NGOs, private businesses and donors. In the political sphere, what were once semi-stable and personalised clientelist relationships have become more transient and cynical: driven by money, less trust based and more ethnicised. Many Kenyans no longer vote for free, while the moral obligations of the rich towards the poor have weakened as the number of the poor has grown and the links that connected urbanites to rural life have weakened. The 'man-eat-man' life of Nairobi has always been a pressure cooker in which obligations were gained and lost faster than in rural Kenya. Urbanisation has created huge, poverty-stricken, violent, lawless and disenfranchised communities which require urgent attention from the state in order to avoid complete social collapse and which are now a destabilising political force.

At the level of national politics, voting patterns have also become more ethnicised and less personal. Kikuyu men and women did not vote for Kibaki, Luo for Odinga or Kamba for Kalonzo Musyoka in 2007 because they were good men, because they espoused specific policies, as part of a deep network of reciprocal obligations, or because they thought they would do something directly beneficial for them. They voted for them because voters understood politics as an ethnic duel of champions, a gladiatorial contest in which winning the game was more important than what you actually did once you had won.

Corruption lies at the heart of the Kenyan political system. For many in the early years of independence, the wealth of the state was an occult wealth. It was 'free money', there to be seized by those able to do so.[3] It seems that the larger the unit within which funds were raised, the weaker the moral obligations to guard it. Although it only became an international issue in the 1980s, the challenge of corruption was already visible by the 1960s, and during the 1970s the elites abused their access to land, state coffers and resources to make money, some of which they recycled as handouts to their constituents. Glorified as *harambee*, it became part of a parallel economic cycle, matching the 'tax and spend' model of government. During the 1980s, the situation worsened. At the top, the Moi elite's financial needs were greater than those of the Kenyatta 'family'. Because of the fragility of their coalition, the lack of a deep economic base in most Kalenjin districts, the community's minor role in Nairobi (where the real money was made), and the visceral hostility of the Gema peoples, they relied on money to buy support. Some of the grand corruption of the late 1980s and early 1990s can be laid at this door.

It is far from clear that representative democracy has reduced corruption; indeed, democracy without civil liberties may in the short term have increased it. After the discontinuity of 1991–3, the elite's need for funds was greater, its time in office uncertain, the constraints imposed by representative democracy inadequate, and administrative oversight ineffective (since the state itself remained partial). In practice, Western governments were the only constituency of which the state had to be careful. Until the police and judiciary are genuinely independent, the fear of foreign discovery is far more significant than the reaction of domestic voters, lured by the sirens of 'bribe and tribe'.

The years of independence have seen an evolution of rent-seeking opportunities. In the 1960s, there were government contracts to be won, but the biggest benefits lay in Africanisation of the civil service, of Asian businesses and of European-owned land. In the 1970s, as the land frontier closed, poaching, natural resource extraction and the abuse of licences became the key opportunities. In the 1980s, the centre of exploitation shifted to the parastatals. Their new bosses, weakly ensconced, resorted to over-rapid rent extractions, which – combined with genuine economic difficulties – drove several close to bankruptcy. Throughout, state-owned banks were a fertile source of loans, never to be repaid. With the need to finance the election of 1991–2, there was frantic resource extraction from the Treasury and the banking system. In the 1990s, the theft of government land in the cities and forests became rampant, as privatisation and liberalisation reduced opportunities elsewhere. Privatisation also gave opportunities to a few wealthy insiders. In the 2000s, with a new government, new commitments to transparency and stronger institutional constraints, petty corruption declined, but the Anglo-Leasing scandal proved that grand corruption was still flowing beneath the surface, and the inability of its anti-corruption organisations to convict any senior person of anything reinforced Kenya's culture of impunity. The subsequent scandals of the Grand Coalition suggest little had changed in elite behaviour, but the tolerance for such practices is changing globally. The new Constitution imposes new constraints and controls which are making headlines, but it is uncertain whether they will truly change behaviour. In the 50 years since Ronald Ngala first became leader of government business, no incumbent or ex-minister has been convicted of any economic crime.

For at least four decades, corruption has been structural to Kenya's politics, economics and society. There are many reasons for this. These include widespread poverty; a systematic and deliberate destruction of controls and sanctions; a societal lack of respect for law; the need for money to finance the political process; the ethnicised pork barrel electoral system; and the self-reinforcing nature of such activity. In addition, to a degree, corruption works. Many Kenyans find the payment of commissions for services to be a reasonably reliable way to transact business, and accept it as inevitable. For junior civil servants, the system is redistributive, because funds flow from the wealthy to the poor, but the aggregate effect is the opposite, because of the larger gains made by the briber than by the bribee and the 'trickle-up' system that takes a cut from the receiver and gives it to their boss in order to keep their job.

Kenya's history also shows that politics and economics are intertwined, with access to money, both at the nation-state and the individual level, the hidden hand behind much behaviour. For decades, access to state resources has been key to the accumulation of wealth and to political success. This linkage is now weakening, but the result is a 'privatisation of politics' that will be more unstable and dominated instead by private sector and overseas money. As the Orange referendum victory and the ODM wave of 2007 showed, for a short time, even non-Kikuyu elites can now finance a national coalition, able to compete directly with the state's largesse.

Ironically, the single-member 'first past the post' electoral system that has tied the elites to their rural roots, ensured policies were not fundamentally damaging to rural interests, and maintained some regional balance in Parliament and the government is partly to blame. The system's costs may have outweighed its benefits. It has created a resource competition (an election tax) that forces politicians into abusive behaviour as the price for survival, and which converts the competition for limited resources into a local, regional and ethnic struggle. It consumes huge sums, creates 'winner takes all' models wherever ethnic or clan differences exist and reinforces corruption, because small electorates can genuinely be bought. In a multi-party system, it may also result in the complete un-representation of particular ethnic groups locally (as in all three Uasin Gishu constituencies in the period since 1992, for example) and nationally (for example the absence of Kikuyu and Luo in the 1992 and 1997 governments and of Gusii in 2002). A multi-member system based around Kenya's districts (now counties) might better serve the nation. The new Constitution's rule that ministers cannot be politicians is another 'game changer' of unknown impact. It should encourage a stronger technocracy, but such a divorcing of executive authority from popular control will be disruptive to Kenya's clientilist coalitions. I suspect it will not survive.

The state's third challenge was in its *capacity to implement change*. There have been few well-planned and well-executed policy changes in Kenya since the 1960s (if then). From the Nyayo buses, the DFRD and the 8–4–4 education system to cost sharing, financial liberalisation and agricultural privatisation, policies have been poorly designed or poorly implemented. Despite a capable cadre of senior civil servants and long-term donor support for the operation of the bureaucracy (including experts, policies and information systems), change has proved difficult. This is partly because the civil service cannot implement it, partly because interest group resistance is instinctive (and losers always couch their protests in ethnic terms), predation is easier in periods of transition, and partly because the complexity of contemporary society means change is genuinely harder. It is still far from clear that Kenya's leaders have the administrative capabilities and political toughness simultaneously to strengthen Parliament, create the Senate, abolish the provincial administration and devolve money and power to the counties. Something will go seriously wrong.

Some have argued that the Kenyan state had been weakened by two decades of liberalism, the sale of state assets and the flow of foreign resources through non-state channels. There is some truth in this. However, the decline of the state cannot be blamed on this alone. Capacity issues were apparent long before liberalisation. In principle, indeed, the opposite should have happened. The reduction in the state's burden (fewer businesses to run and fewer, better-paid civil servants) should have enhanced its scope of control. There is nothing intrinsic to privatisation that weakens a state, if it retains the ability to create and enforce policy. Kenya's problem was that the state was already rotten, and poor and partial parastatal management was replaced by poor policy and partial supervision. Professionalism improved under Kibaki, but there remains a long way to go.

However, Kenya is not a country in which the state has collapsed. Although this book offers a catalogue of weaknesses and tragedies, it does so against a backdrop of 'business as usual'. Corrupt, incompetent and partial, the state still works; soldiers and rebels do not roam the streets; businesses still make money; tourists visit: achievements that were deeply appreciated by the first post-independence generation. Kenya is a true neo-patrimonial state – not one in which the state is a veneer, a fig leaf, but one in which bureaucratic process and norms compete with and coexist with personal authority and prebendalism.

As the decades passed, the popular assumption of state impartiality has been lost, and with it a key component of its legitimacy. Today, Kenya faces a systemic lack of trust in the efficiency and neutrality of its administrative processes, unless there is a private patron–client relationship to secure that trust. The state is not seen as impersonal, but a coiled mass of interests, harnessed by a partial bureaucracy towards the wishes of the dominant political thread, but always pulling in multiple directions. The partisan hatred with which every action of every government has been greeted in the multi-party era is in many ways as dangerous as its actual decisions, since it has created a perception of pervasive, malicious incompetence and undermined the legitimacy of many legitimate decisions. The state no longer has a presumption of innocence but of guilt. This reflects both a genuine decline in its capability and impartiality and a 'conspiracy theory' model of political events in which every accident has a secret purpose, and every decision is made for ethnic or personal benefit.

State and Security

The second 'public good' identified in the introduction as key to understanding Kenya's history is security, an area often underemphasised in works of political economy but which is fundamental to the existence of the nation-state and remains one of the most controversial areas of state policy and practice in every society. Under this broad umbrella lie three linked issues: the ability of the government to maintain national boundaries, public order and a monopoly of force; its ability to rely upon its security forces without fear of a coup or revolt; and people's ability to live their lives without fear of state or private violence or crime.

The application of force was fundamental to the creation and sustenance of the colonial state and to its successor. The military has rarely been deployed on active service inside Kenya, has never seized power and has generally declined to become involved in political engagements either in support or in opposition to the government. Kenyatta, Moi and Kibaki all succeeded in keeping the army in its barracks where others failed: in part because of British and American military support and training; in part because of active management to ensure the military retained common interests with its politicians; in part because success was self-reinforcing in the same way as failure. Kenya also avoided military intervention in other countries or open war, its boundaries were (mostly) secure and since 1967, it has never faced a real prospect of secession. In part, this reflects the more distributed, agricultural basis of Kenya's wealth: there are no diamonds or oil revenues to fight over, which would continue to hold their value in war. In contrast, Kenya's tourism, cash-crop exports and strong industrial sector would become near worthless in such a conflict. Kenyans have never brought their country to the depths to which so many African states have fallen: the civil wars and mass murder of Uganda, Rwanda, Burundi, Congo, Angola, Mozambique, Sudan, Ethiopia, Somalia, Liberia, Sierra Leone, now even Côte d'Ivoire. Neither Kibaki nor Odinga were the architects of the 2007 violence, though they helped create the conditions in which it bred, and they have worked at some personal risk to reduce the chance that Kenya will follow this well-travelled descent into horror.

For the first three decades of its life, the state retained a monopoly on the means of coercion, and was willing to exercise it. Kenyatta relied on and believed in the importance of security, not only for personal protection, but also for the nation's development. However, the security forces' remit has been challenged since the genie of ethnic violence was unleashed in 1991, and its limited capacity to maintain this monopoly has become apparent. While groups have seldom taken up arms in a formal sense against the government, low-level non-state violence remains common, particularly in the northern half of the country, which has never been fully assimilated into the modern state. Although the majority of coercive force lay with the police, GSU and army, violence between supporters of opposing factions as a political tool has been an ever-present challenge throughout the nation-state's existence. The regular resurgence of political violence against immigrants and strangers and the inability of the state to prevent or punish this since 1991 have had a corrosive effect on popular expectations. Although Kibaki's government performed better than Moi's until 2007, the belief in violence as a legitimate response to state machinations remains.

Regarding its ability to offer security against both crime and abuses by the security forces, the state's failures have been apparent since the 1980s, and worsened during the 1990s. The Kenyatta and then Moi governments steadily lost control of crime, to the point where many communities abandoned all hope of protection from the police, courts and prisons, and took the law into their own hands. The Kibaki government's reform of the judicial system and improvement to the police force have not solved the problem. Repeatedly, the state has been unwilling or unable to enforce the existing laws of the country. The leadership was partial, the police violent, incompetent and corrupt, the judiciary pliable, and the population appeared to view the law as an instrument of repression, to be flouted whenever it was safe to do so. One of the ironies of the lengthy argument over constitutional reform is that obedience to and enforcement of their existing Constitution is often beyond the Kenya state or its people.

Indeed, the state has long been part of the problem as much as the solution, as the statistics on police torture and extra-judicial executions show. Kenyatta consistently used the language of violence during his time in power, and while Moi was gentler in words, in deeds he behaved in much the same way. Political killings, the Mwakenya repression, the abuses of pro-pluralist elites, the clashes and the war on Mungiki all point to a blurring of the lines between state and private violence and a willingness to use force to destroy as well as maintain public order.

An Aborted Take-Off?

The third 'goal of government' that threads through Kenya's history has been its search for economic growth and development. Headline growth and per capita GDP have been the driving forces behind many policies, from Mboya's open arms to foreign investment in the 1960s to tariff reform in the 1980s and privatisation in the 1990s. The fight against poverty, ignorance and disease was also one of the most public commitments of the early years of independence. In practice, this too depended on the country's ability to generate wealth (though also on its ability to share such wealth).

In the 1960s and early 1970s, Kenyatta's government delivered rapid growth, but it was founded on the one-off springboard of smallholder cash-crop expansion into under-developed lands and on Western loans and investment. By 1973, the combination of the first oil crisis, changing terms of trade and the heavy hand of state and crony capitalism were slowing this growth. Since that time, it has spectacularly failed to convert its advantages into sustained take-off. Between 1990 and 2003, Kenyans became poorer year after year, whether measured by GDP per capita or income poverty, food security or life expectancy. Real per capita GDP was lower when Moi retired than when he took office 22 years earlier. Kenya's GDP per head had fallen by 2002 to place it 201 out of 231 countries, to levels officially below those of Togo and Rwanda (though significant parts of Kenya's economy were in truth invisible). Moi's redistributive policies damaged some competitive sectors (particularly the coffee industry), while the florid corruption of an isolated elite, when combined with poor infrastructure, political instability, crime and violence undermined its industrial achievements. All this could have been tolerable in a world of rapid growth, but the environment was far more difficult for less-developed countries without oil after 1980. Not only was there too little to go around, but what the economy did produce was extremely unequally distributed, a legacy of early colonial investment patterns, the dominance of Nairobi, the country's growth-oriented policies and elite-centred practices.

Kenya achieved a higher degree of import substitution with local manufacturing than many other African states, but this could not shield it forever from world markets. This import substitution model has been dismantled since the early 1990s under Western pressure, and most of the industries created in the independence years have since been privatised or have collapsed. Its agricultural sector has performed erratically, with some successes alongside great failures. Productivity per acre was seldom high or unit costs low. Food security remained a concern in 2011 just as in 1963. There were nearly five times as many people to feed from the same land, and drought, climate change, deforestation, urbanisation, export-oriented specialisation, world price rises and protective tariff walls meant many Kenyans were still hungry.

Kenya's high-input, high-output economy, its dependence on tourism and imported oil and its lack of major natural resources (apart from agriculture and tourism) left it subject to both positive and negative price shocks (1973, 1977, 1979) and social shocks (1991–3, 1997 and 2007–8). The government has always found predicting and planning difficult, taking into account such shocks, alongside the distortions of budgeted but delayed aid. Kenya has also been subject to the amplification effects of foreign journalism, reinforcing positive and later negative perceptions of the country, thereby affecting both aid and tourism.

As expected, Kibaki made economic recovery a priority, and delivered a period of strong growth and improving services as the brakes of self-serving and non-economic decision-making were removed. It is becoming clear that liberalisation has delivered some long-term benefits to Kenya, but the change has been painful and the country has not yet reached a point of stability in the new world order. Kenya retains the capability and the will to become a regional industrial powerhouse, with one of the largest, most influential and assertive middle classes on the continent, but it still struggles to compete outside Africa (where it is strong in both manufacturing and services) and its cash-crop and tourist heartland.

The Intractable Problem of Land

One thing that has not changed is Kenya's dependence on smallholder agriculture. Although urbanisation has been rapid and land subdivision and socio-economic differentiation has grown, smallholder agriculture has remained a political and economic constant.

The land problems of Kenya's independence were both symbolic and central to the issues the country has faced since. At independence, there was already land-hunger amongst peasants and huge inequalities in land ownership (between whites and blacks). Forty-eight years later, both poverty and land inequality have increased. Although there was a limited acceptance that the emergence of a landed and landless group was inevitable, the manner in which this took place has been a source of confusion and popular anger. All attempts to limit the size of individual land holdings failed, resisted by liberals concerned to nurture a capitalist, production-oriented, commercial farming model (and their own substantial share in that). But Kenya has not switched to a large farm model either. In practice, cultural factors proved stronger, and the 'right' of people to live on and cultivate a plot of land remains strong in the popular mind, long after the economic basis for doing so has passed. This desire for land has also been overlaid, conflated with and redirected into a second competition, over who (which ethnic group, specifically) owns the land, works in the nearby towns and exercises political influence. The evidence suggests that after a period of state-sponsored loosening in the 1960s and 1970s, in which densely populated communities migrated into land-rich areas, the ethnic noose has been tightening, and outside the cities, it is becoming hard to own land if you are not from the majority community in that area.

Kenya's land policy has failed. This failure takes at least four forms. The foremost is the failure to convince Kenyans that there is no inalienable link between specific areas of land and the ethnic communities who had inhabited that land at the time of the colonial incursion. John Harbeson's introduction to his 1973 book suggested that one of the Kenyatta government's key goals had been 'to make land a symbol of national unity for all the people of Kenya instead of a symbol of unity for divergent African communities'.[4] It has failed. Despite 50 years of 'willing buyer, willing seller' policies, the idea of land as the specific entitlement of one ethnic community remains strong. Communal land rights remain a potent myth: a politicised strategy by the economically disenfranchised (and their leaders) to protect their access to land. They are a myth because few if any of the ethnic groups 'frozen' in place in the 1900s had been grazing or cultivating their land for more than a few generations, and most occupancy rights were based on exactly the same principles of conquest, purchase or labour investment as those of subsequent generations of occupants.

The Kenyatta regime downplayed this connection, reflecting a combination of national and Kikuyu interests, but the Kalenjin era shifted this focus. In fact, Moi (perhaps surprisingly) never changed state policy. It was practice – as in the racial segregation of colonial Kenya – that changed. But his rule inevitably reopened questions some would have preferred lie quiet, and the ethnic clashes, the *majimbo* debates, the Balkanisation of the Rift Valley and the carnage in Uasin Gishu and Trans-Nzoia of 2007–8 were the direct consequence of this failure. The 1955 Royal Commission's goal of the free movement of land, labour and capital across the country remained contested at every level. Nairobi remains a 'free for all', but outside the city boundaries, land is still for many a communal right, labour is accepted on sufferance and while capital can move freely, it cannot always be applied to the best effect.

Secondly, although the 'willing buyer, willing seller' model has endured and land inequalities have grown (as planned), their legitimacy has never been fully accepted. Wealth and land remain directly associated in the popular mind, and two generations after independence, the desire for land remains strong. Land redistribution and land ceilings have occasionally come to the front of the agenda, but they run counter to Kenya's liberalisation policy, which aims to allow market forces to reign. For the high-production agricultural specialisation model to take root fully, Kenya needs to complete the transition to a non-farm society, where there is no expectation of land for most and where further subdivision of smallholdings is reversed. The reduced stress on land ownership amongst contemporary urban youth suggests this is possible, but it will be another generation before such a change matures.

The third failure is of land registration. Fifty years later, the process of land adjudication, registration and creation of inalienable individual title is still incomplete. Where formal title does exist, sales and purchases are often unregistered and boundaries and ownership in dispute. In part, this was because the process was intrinsically difficult (particularly in the pastoral lands and on the coast); in part because of institutional failures in the machinery of government; in part the tendency of peasants to avoid the state because of costs and bureaucracy they did not understand; and in part because of endemic corruption.

Finally, the elite has corruptly stolen vast quantities of state land and given or sold it to themselves and their allies. The wealthy took advantage of their connections at independence and after to acquire large tracts of European-owned land cheaply. Then, government land was alienated to private use – often for nothing – leaving cities and towns without schools, mortuaries, road reserves, hospitals, bus parks and toilets. With 200,000 land titles fraudulent or disputed in 2005, Kenya was sitting on a time bomb. A new land policy must be delivered, but the process of rectification will be lengthy, contested, politicised and will again bring to the forefront lines of ethnic cleavage that the country is trying to paper over.

The Enduring Power of Ethnicity

Despite a gradual blurring of real differences (as people migrated, communications improved and cultural differences attenuated) and state-led attempts at nation building, tribalism and ethnicity remain potent political issues. Between 1969 and 1991, information was controlled and ethnically partial activitism repressed, to ensure that the state's own tribalist policies were unchallenged, but also to avoid inflaming sentiment. Since that time, the alignment of politics and ethnicity has reinforced divisions and strengthened a desire for government by quota, independent of ability.

Tribalism is certainly not an intrinsic phenomenon, or something unique to Kenya or Africa: it is primarily a form of competition between individuals and groups for wealth, power and status. But it is not arbitrary: the processes of definition, tightening and aggregation always reflects common socio-economic interests, culture or language. What is called tribalism inside national borders becomes 'defending national interests' in supra-national bodies, and clanism or sectionalism inside a particular ethnic community. In the European Union, a supra-national body with some of the same faults and strengths of post-independence African states, ethnicity remains a dominant feature of political debate. The ethnicity of every official is discussed openly, political parties are ethno-regional and every decision is conceptualised by the popular press in terms of which ethnic groups (the French, the Germans, the British) gains or loses. Ethnicity is also simply a natural point on which to compete. Since politics is intrinsically a contest for resources, it is a reasonable expectation that this would become a cleavage point in Africa, as in any other place where a larger structure was laid over distinct communities of language, culture and economic interests.

Outside the cities and the settler farms, Kenyan ethnicity was regional in 1963, and this remains broadly true today. The areas of social integration have broadened as a result of urbanisation, migration and land settlement on the coast and former white highlands, but the result of high population densities, informal restrictions and historical linkages is that most of the old 'reserves' (especially those of the Luo and Kikuyu) remain mono-ethnic to an extraordinary degree. Where other communities live within their boundaries, they are few in number, and do not seek or receive representation outside the urban areas. In the Rift Valley, the most cosmopolitan of Kenya's rural provinces because of the settler farms, these tensions were the primary source of political violence in the 1990s.

As to why ethnicity has proved so potent a rallying cry in Kenya, there are both necessary and contingent elements. The complex ethnic distribution in the country, with more than 40 ethnic communities, a few larger ones but no single dominant group, favoured a system in which coalitions of communities were required in order to seek and maintain power. The history of Kenya's stunted democracy before 1963 and the Mau Mau war discouraged the emergence of class-based or national parties. Kenya's first parties – KANU, KADU, the APP, the BPU and NPUA – were all regional.

The politicisation of ethnicity was in part a creation of the British: within the ethnic reserves and provincial administration, then through district parties and the *majimbo* Constitution, but it is an evolution to which Africans have consented, through the behaviour they have rewarded. It has changed its nature, however. What were to some extent accidents – such as the positioning of the Luhya community in KADU rather than KANU, in part because of the antipathy between Masinde Muliro and Mboya – were institutionalised and became accepted wisdom.

Part of the power of ethnicity can also be traced to the political institutions Kenya inherited at independence. The single-member 'first past the post' system nurtures a political system based on concentrated local support. Voters back politicians whom they believe will represent their interests, and the person seen as most likely to do this has almost always been someone from the same ethnic community as themselves. Since 1963, it has proved virtually impossible for anyone from outside a rural community to represent it at the parliamentary level. Kenya's Parliament was poorly designed to 'ground' ethnicity or geographically focused cleavages, especially in a multi-party state.

Successive governments also operated a political system that exalted ethnicity. From the establishment of constituency boundaries through the allocation of Cabinet posts to the employment practices of parastatals, ethnicity has permeated the Kenyan state. This was a deliberate policy, in part in order to ensure that political competition was based on a 'safer' ethnic basis instead of a disruptive class basis. The elites had a common interest in ensuring that outsiders did not throw them down from their new castles, and the older generation of politicians genuinely viewed political events through an ethnic lens. Although the early politicians spoke and worked for national integration, their actions often indicated a far more direct view of political ethnicity. Kenya's ruling classes have used ethnicity for their own purposes, but it is not only an act of deliberate deception, but one they are forced to follow, and which in part they believe.

There were and remain major differences between ethnic communities in the degree to which they have been incorporated into, profited from and differentiated as a result of the nation-state economy. The geographical and therefore ethnic basis of wealth remains clear. Forty years after a Kiambu Kikuyu became president and despite 20 years of Moi's redistributive policies, the 11 richest constituencies in Kenya in 2004 were all in Central Province, the top four of which were in Kiambu District.[5] Ethnicity and regional preference is not solely an 'imagined' frame of reference, but a real one.

The single-party state repressed most public expressions of such attitudes, but politics continued to be structured on an ethno-regional basis even within the one-party state. Kenyatta and then Moi built and managed the polity through balancing ethnicity and regions, incorporating and exiling influential individuals in order to retain control of a fissiparous nation. They managed the ever-present danger of ethnic cleavage by forcing tensions underground or routing them through institutions they could manage, in part because this was to their advantage, in part because it genuinely helped to build a national identity. Although the 'lever' for change in 1991 was American pressure and the withholding of Western aid, the pressure from within was ethnic as much as economic.

Ethnicity as an overt frame of political reference was reinforced by the reintroduction of multi-party democracy. Such cleavages were inflamed by the state-sanctioned clashes of 1991–2 and the 'Kamatusa first' (Kalenjin, Maasai, Turkana, Samburu) politics of the state in the 1990s. The clashes created an enduring wound in Kenya's social fabric that has never healed. Despite its other benefits, there is little doubt that multi-party democracy drove the alignment of political position and ethnicity. Although the government exacerbated it, it was working a genuine seam of difference, and pro-opposition politicians worked the same seam from the other side, seeking unity against their opponents. To be a Luo was to support an Odinga; to be a Kikuyu was to support a Kikuyu leader (Kibaki, Matiba or a Kenyatta); to be a Kalenjin was to support Moi. But to be clear, Kenyans vote ethnically, but ethnicity is not sufficient to gain their vote. In every election, there were other individuals from the same background, with closer links to particular communities, who were ignored in the grand battle for the presidency. The electorate voted for symbols: Odinga, Kibaki, Matiba, Moi, Charity Ngilu, Kenyatta, Simeon Nyachae or Musyoka, and the confluence of interests and policies that they represented.

Once cleavages are established, they tend to become self-sustaining. The 'Kikuyu–Luo' conflict, which did not exist before 1961, was a political struggle that lasted only five years, but has dominated events and attitudes since. As Bratton and van de Walle noted, 'Political behaviour is not just the consequence of structural precedent but also an independent social force and analytical factor in its own right.'[6] Western attitudes to ethnicity as a point of cleavage and as a unifying symbol for communities have generally been hostile, and tribalism has been blamed for many of the troubles still facing Africa. Both liberals and Marxists have seen ethnicity as a distracting irrelevance from the real issues of production, exchange and accumulation. The evidence from Kenya, however, is that ethnicity is a real and enduring political phenomenon that single-party rule papered over but never eliminated. The concept of 'negative ethnicity' has become widely understood amongst both Kenya's elites and observers, but has itself become a political tool, used to criticise the established order wherever its ethno-regional roots might lie. Challenges to the tribalism of others are sometimes a cover for a form of envy at the achievements of others and a desire to level down rather than up, something seen particularly clearly in 2006–7.

Another lesson from Kenya is that ethnicity can become the end of political competition rather than its means. The ethnicity of the 2000s is not an old phenomenon, a cultural ghost refusing to die, but something new, masquerading under the same name. It is sharpened, politicised, shorn of much of its history or cultural basis, and defined by conflict and difference as much as by commonality; more situational or 'functional' than in the past. In Daniel Posner's analogy of a card game, of 'repertoires of identity' and incentives to play the cards that you have been given, the cards themselves have changed.[7] The perception is also unstable and self-reinforcing. Allegations of ethnic favouritism are mirrored into exclusive or sectional campaigns by politicians, which in turn reinforce such situational ethnicity. 'Negative' ethnicity (the desire to get your share or take the share of others simply because they are other) has limited what is possible for governments to achieve, creating a 'tribal veto' on policies and recasting every economic decision in an ethnic lens.

Like class, religion represents a potential counter-cut to ethnicity in Kenya. Kenya has seen relatively little political competition based on religion: some tensions on the coast between Christians and Muslims; some support for anti-government parties amongst the main Christian denominations in the 1990s; some influence from religious communities in electing particular parliamentary candidates. However, its influence is growing. For Muslims, the position of Islam was always a political issue, but because Islam was institutionally disadvantaged and centred in a few communities (Somali, coastal Digo, Swahili, Arabs and Asians) it never became a national issue. Today, Islam is playing a stronger role, and the number of Muslim politicians is rising, at the same time that religion appears to be more divisive politically than ever before. It may become one of Kenya's new challenges.

Majimbo, Power Sharing and the Imperial Presidency

The thread of conflict between centralisation and decentralisation has run through-out Kenya's history, though centralisation dominated between 1965 and 1984. Once the regional constitution was dismantled, the arena of conflict shifted to the deeper question of access to land and resources: mediated and allocated through a powerful central bureaucracy. Regionalism has rarely been a point of true political principle, but rather a struggle for autonomy from the *par excellence* centralisers, the Kikuyu, and a demand for a more even share of national resources. It has also been a desire to secure land. There remains an enduring cleavage between those communities 'with land' and those 'without', built around competing conceptions of the validity of the 'willing buyer, willing seller' policy. This underlay the arguments over Kikuyu rights within Maasailand in the 1950s and over the EATEC land in the 1990s. It under-pinned the Nandi Hills declaration in 1969 and the ethnic clashes of 1991–4. It was the power behind the first *majimbo* movement and the second. The association of ethnicity and geography also means that decentralisation becomes a euphemism for preference for locals over in-migrants. Although there are many arguments for power sharing and a reduced role for the presidency, they are rarely viewed on their merits, but for what they will bring to individuals and communities.

The fight for constitutional reform and the reining-in of the imperial presidency has become enmeshed in the debate over decentralisation. Where in the past Nairobi would dictate and enforce through the provincial administration, in the new Constitution 47 elected county governments will decide. With the 2003 Constituency Development Fund, local politicians can already decide on investment priorities, the exact opposite of a technocracy. The corruption and incompetence of local government has been even worse than that of central government, which does not bode well for the future.

One less-recognised strength that emerges from the sound and fury of domestic politics is the ability and willingness of key elites to compromise, even when it is against their ethno-regional interests. Kenya's stability has been reinforced by a willingness to step back from the edge when politics had pushed the country into genuine crisis. Kenyatta did this in 1969, Moi in 1991 and in 1997, and Kibaki and Odinga demonstrated the same capacity in 2008. Despite hard-line pressure to fight to the finish, the men at the top saw that the national interest required that a deal must be done (though this was driven by foreign desire to mediate a compromise more than internal forces).

Capitalism, Socialism and Non-Alignment

The foreign and economic policy of Kenya has remained capitalist and Western oriented for five decades. It was founded in the crucible of independence, and by 1965 the central question of Kenya's political direction was settled. However, the popular legitimacy of this was always in doubt. Although they were never permitted to express an opinion, Kenyans would probably have preferred a more socialist, egalitarian, pan-African and non-aligned domestic and foreign policy. As a result, the state enmeshed itself in a multi-layered fiction. It portrayed itself as the non-aligned successor of the struggle for independence, implementing 'African socialism', while following policies that were the exact opposite. The government parlayed its moderate stand in international affairs for preferential treatment from Western states. It did little apart from posture on African or UN issues, since its basis for rule rested on its capitalist–socialist hybrid, and that in turn rested on Western financial, military and political support.

Under pressure from the 'radicals', Mboya, Kenyatta and the 'moderates' portrayed what was essentially a deal to maintain a capitalist economic model and foreign investment rights as 'socialism'. However, to broadcast their socialist credentials too aggressively might kill the goose that laid the golden egg of international confidence. What they created (or maintained, as it was based on the colonial model) was a state-capitalist system in which free enterprise operated under the protection and constraints of boards and tariffs, and the government part-owned and actively participated in most aspects of the economy.

The authoritarianism of Kenya's first generation of post-independence leaders was sustained by the consent of Western governments. The support for pro-capitalist strongmen against their more socialist opponents worldwide, led by the US but supported by the UK and other countries, is well known. In addition, the 1960s and 1970s saw a liberal timidity or relativism that suggested that democracy might be right for the West but it was not suited to Africa, where the challenges of development and nation-building came first and individual choice was seen as of little consequence, either politically or economically.

In fact, the struggle against socialism was a key theme of the whole period from the early 1960s until the collapse of the Soviet Union and of communism as an alternative model. There is now little challenge to capitalism per se, but the debate still rages over the degree to which capitalism should be regulated to benefit locals over foreigners, small over large investors and to protect the nation against the vagaries of price and production in world markets. Raila Odinga, educated in East Germany, academic Peter Anyang' Nyong'o and others in the ODM still represent a stream of thought more hostile to unfettered capitalism than either Moi or Kibaki's governments have proved.

State Capitalism and Structural Adjustment

Kenya has passed through at least five phases in its economic history since 1963: the public–private expansion of the 1960s, the state capitalism of the 1970s, the fiscal liberalisation and neo-patrimonialism of the 1980s, the contested privatisation of the 1990s and the mini-boom of the mid-2000s. For the last 25 years, however, the liberal orthodoxy has dominated, and while the details have changed, the basic principles of fiscal rectitude, an external orientation and free markets continue to be enshrined, though hedged about with conditions built from bitter experience.

Economically, the state was less liberal or pro-free enterprise in the 1960s and 1970s than was perceived at the time. Although international capital was extremely influential, it worked within a framework that limited foreign influences and built domestic capital. The state controlled the vast majority of investments, taking ownership or equity in most industrial projects. Corruption did not appear to interfere with the execution of the board or company's functions, but state bureaucracy, fixed pricing, non-economic decision-making and undercapitalisation all did damage. Although this 'public–private partnership' model has been criticised from all sides, it is difficult to see what alternative could have been followed in the absence of domestic private capital and the political conditions of the time.

The challenge for the Moi government in the 1980s was to reverse this model without political support or much to offer in compensation apart from foreign aid. It was only in the mid-1990s, under intense Western pressure and globalisation, that privatisation began and the state began to be rolled back. But the state fought this, trench by trench, and though it did not really have an alternative policy, it managed to delay change. This may have allowed some state-owned businesses to flourish post-privatisation, but many others, such as Telkom and the railways, were doomed by the same process.

Although most of its goals were eventually achieved, the overall record of structural adjustment in Kenya is unsatisfactory. The changes proposed in the early 1980s took 20 to 30 years to deliver. The process was slow, incomplete, poorly planned and contested by both the government and the population. Kenya was not forced into reform entirely against its will. Just as in the political sphere, foreign interests allied themselves with domestic actors in challenging the status quo. In the economic sector, however, the reformers were few in number and mostly inside the administration. Since 1979, Kenya has always had a core of able technocrats who have favoured liberalisation policies, their confidence reinforced by regular injections of technical specialists from Western countries.[8] But though senior technocrats knew what was required, they were never fully divorced from domestic political pressures (Nyachae and Saitoti, for example, were technocrats but also local and national politicians). Implementation was dependent on elite support as much as the availability of foreign funds. Nonetheless, it did occur. Kenya has completely changed its economic structure over 25 years. It has a vibrant and liberal middle class. It has privatised most state industries and liberalised exchange rates, interest rates, prices, exports and imports. It is well integrated into the global economy. Although there are still a few areas of the state yet to fall – such as the sugar factories – privatisation and liberalisation have proceeded further than in many other African (and Asian) economies.[9] Indeed, the fashion has started to move in the other direction with the world credit crisis and recession, as belief in the value of state ownership and government-based stabilisation grows once more.

The 'rollback of the state' since the 1980s has probably reached a natural end, or such an end is close. The capacity of the state to implement its policies must strengthen if it is to perform even the most basic functions. Devolution risks further diminution. Privatisation also contains a fundamental flaw in a corrupt political and administrative environment. It relies on a small, able, rational, disinterested elite to manage contracts and to control private competition and its potential conflict with public goods. There is little evidence, however, that, when tendering large contracts and overseeing the performance of private utilities, Africa's leaders are any less corrupt than when owning and operating them.

It is far from true that international capitalism has taken over the country as a result of a decline of the state. Indeed, international capital works at a disadvantage in an environment when the state has rotted, because it generally lacks the 'shadow state' personal and financial linkages that indigenous capital can build and sustain. It is riskier for multinationals to bribe, because the cost of exposure is far higher. An environment of state weakness in fact rewards indigenous wealth. Multinational capital would prefer an environment where the rule of law applied and the civil service worked reliably.

Despite Western efforts, there remains deep cynicism amongst Kenyans (as elsewhere in Africa) at the efforts of the IMF and World Bank to force structural reform on Kenya. In the words of ex-minister Kirugi M'Mukindia in Parliament in 2006, for example, 'For the last 20 years, this country has been moved from one prescription to another by the IMF and the World Bank, and none of these has worked. Kenyans have become poorer and poorer by the day.'[10] Some still look to a more closed development model, seeing the achievements of China, South Korea, India and Taiwan. Many African intellectuals argue that structural adjustment and neo-liberalism have – as well as freeing politics and the media – returned countries such as Kenya to a state of dependency and marginalisation, as powerless clients of the West and their multinationals, though they do not have a clear alternative solution.[11]

In reality, the country never ceased to be dependent on or marginal to the world economy. It was Kenya's failure to achieve self-sustaining growth in the 1970s and 1980s that left it reliant on Western aid, and therefore on Western economic and political prescriptions. Change was probably unavoidable, and its impact probably more positive than most other available options, but it is true that the effect has not been what the IMF expected. What appeared simple and obvious in the late 1980s proved the exact opposite, as a decade of experience showed how fragile and complex economic change could be. Kenya – like much of Africa – struggled to compete in the absence of a consistent policy, political stability, good infrastructure, the unquestioned rule of law and a strong bureaucracy. It started off the blocks too slowly in the early 1980s, and has struggled to catch up since.

Why Africa has failed to incubate newly industrialising countries and to achieve growth without aid is one of the biggest unanswered questions about the continent. Kenya can contribute some lessons, but no overall answer. The colonial export-orientation was long blamed for Kenya's externalisation and dependency, but this external alignment is now a competitive advantage in a globalised economy. Kenya's education system was and is relatively good, its cost competitiveness variable but never poor. It is clear, however, that in Kenya politics has undermined development. The ethnic and personal competition for assets became more important than the creation of such assets. Corruption and self-interested policy-making shackled Kenya's economy for decades, directly through non-economic decision-making and rent-seeking, but also through the revelation of such behaviour, which has turned Western eyes away from the continent. Kenya has exploited some areas of comparative advantage – coffee (for a while), tea, horticulture, tourism and regional manufactures – but has wasted others. it has also seen a continued tension between popular, 'Kenya first' policies – such as protecting local industries and factories through tariffs, throwing out highly paid expatriates, and relaxing quality standards – and growth-maximisation strategies, which would often suggest the opposite course, allowing some sectors to collapse and ploughing the resources instead into Kenya's areas of greatest comparative advantage. In principle, Kenya remains today one of the best chances in Africa to escape the aid and dependency trap and to establish itself (without oil, but far stronger as a result of liberalisation) as a regional powerhouse. Whether it will do so depends on its internal politics, security and, of course, events in the rest of the world.

Debt and Dependency

Kenya has always been in a dependent relationship with Western governments and international institutions: militarily, financially, economically, technologically and culturally. The country has been a supplicant for its entire lifetime, borrowing for development, security or simply fiscal convenience. Its lenders have used this leverage to require specific policies of the country, from the land settlement schemes of the 1960s to the privatisations of the 1990s and anti-corruption initiatives of the 2000s, either because they believed them right or (in a few cases) for more selfish reasons.

Partly as a result, the hand of Western powers, donors and NGOs can be seen in every aspect of Kenya's politics, economics and society, encouraging some types of change and discouraging others. One of the reasons Kenya endured without disruptive violent change or state failure was the steady stream of financial support to the state and later to NGOs and the continued presence of expatriate advisers and professionals in key areas such as the military and the Treasury and Planning Ministry. There was continuous gentle (and sometimes harsh) pressure for compromise, moderation and 'deals' that would avoid violent and unpredictable change (as was seen most obviously in 1997 and 2008). Although the foreign actors were seldom united, and policy itself see-sawed due to external factors, there is no doubt that their chequebooks stabilised the regime in the first three decades, then destabilised it in the 1990s.

The management of private and public loans and consequent debt has been at the heart of the Kenya state and many of its problems. The nation, like many of its people, was for many years comfortable to borrow today to repay tomorrow, but struggled to deliver the principal back, let alone the interest, having failed to invest the loans productively. In every sector, credit was misused and debts unpaid, and as a result funds for more sustainable investments were diverted, institutions collapsed and interest rates remained high, crippling domestic investment. Although the achievements of the Kibaki era were notable in contrast to the declining days of Moi, the write-off of farmers' and cooperatives' old debts once more demonstrated that – in the end – the state would act as the guarantor of last resort.

The Kibaki government demonstrated a new will to reduce Kenya's dependency on Western aid, no longer factoring it into the budget and increasing the proportion of the national debt that was funded domestically. This reflected a disenchantment with the pervasive influence of Western governments, finance institutions and NGOs. A pro-capitalist Kikuyu-led government proved more hostile to foreign funds and interventions and more willing to challenge the unfettered market than the sceptical Moi. We shall see how easy China finds it to get its loans repaid in the decades to come.

In Kenya, political legitimacy has come from and been sustained externally as much as internally. Both Kenyatta and Moi understood the patron–client model and played much the same game with foreign donors as they played at home. The British, interested to protect their investments, to ensure that white farmers and Asians were not evicted, and to retain international allies, propped up the regime throughout the 1960s and early 1970s. By the late 1970s, however, Britain's influence was declining and its own economic weakness prevented it giving preferential treatment to the Kenyans. The 1980s were the American era and Moi led this alignment, giving loyalty in return for financial support throughout the decade. However, in 1990–1, his patron abandoned him. From the late 1980s on, the IFIs and structural adjustment took over, and the next two decades were dominated by an endless debate. There was no one patron, with the IMF the closest equivalent. Under Kibaki, since 2006, Kenya has no obvious patron at all, but China is stepping into the breach with alacrity.

Virtually every policy initiative and investment in Kenya's history since 1963 has been either inspired by or financed by foreign donors. They have supported everything from the 8–4–4 education reforms to the Truth and Reconciliation Commission; from land settlement to the Bomas constitution; from pastoral restocking to road building; from fiscal probity to opinion polling, election monitoring and parliamentary capacity building. Although most interventions were beneficial individually, the result has been a drain on the state's competences and its accountability for tax and spend decisions. Western states were there to protect Kenyans from their mistakes, and Kenyans did not need to decide for themselves between competing priorities. The country became addicted to aid. But while the West could finance, even force, particular policies, it could not dictate their timing or the outcome.

More People, Changing Cultures

Many of Kenya's problems can be attributed to its rapid population growth before and in the first two decades after independence. In a perfect world, the economy could have sustained such a rise indefinitely, but Kenya was never in this position. Experts knew that one of the highest population growth rates in the world was unlikely to be matched with the fastest economic growth in the world. Kenya had an almost uniquely rapid demographic transition, which in only five decades has nearly quintupled the population. Some of today's poverty, youth alienation, loss of identity and politicised ethnicity can be blamed on the cultural attenuation of such rapid growth in a period of unparalleled complexity and foreign influence.

By the late 1980s, economic factors, better access to contraception and the AIDS pandemic began to reduce fertility and increase mortality. Nonetheless, even in 2010, abortion remained illegal and religious restrictions and cultural preferences result in high birth rates. Kenya's population could reach 50 million by 2025. Land shortages, forest destruction, desertification and environmental degradation have been the consequence, and the environmental situation continues to worsen, exacerbated by rising temperatures and increasing climate instability.

As well as being more numerous, the people of Kenya are far more educated, cosmopolitan and sophisticated than those of 1963. Their beliefs and behaviours have become more 'Western', as with most other societies in the world. Parts of Nairobi could be any capital city. Efforts by Kenyatta, Moi and others to protect Kenya's traditions and cultures were unsuccessful. Although Kenya is more Westernised than many other African countries, however, Kenyans are not 'black Europeans'. International norms of behaviours are laid over deeper roots that in some areas diverge sharply from Western practices. The Mungiki, cattle rustling and blood money, tribalism, patron–client obligations, bridewealth, female circumcision, the widespread belief in witchcraft, strong religious convictions, a deep resistance to gender equality and the low value placed on human life all clash with contemporary European morality.

Kenya's women remain a subservient majority. They have gradually achieved rights that Western women had expected for decades, such as the right to a passport, to loans or to inherit property, yet many Kenyan men (as elsewhere in Africa) still see them as second-class citizens and as unsuitable for leadership. The reintroduction of multi-party democracy did little to change this. While women have stormed many bastions once reserved for men, and have even stood for the presidency, popular views lag decades behind.

The urban poor have been the most disadvantaged and disenfranchised group in Kenya (save perhaps for the Somali). Their land rights have been lost, government services are virtually non-existent and their political impact has been minimised by their massive under-representation in Parliament. Increasing numbers of Somali refugees from the north are stressing the urban environment even further. As a dangerous, 'lumpen' community – for many of whom formal sector work is an impossible dream and whose poverty and alienation often lead to criminal activity – they have proved one the most powerful weapons for political change and one of the greatest threats to political stability in Kenya. Properly enfranchising and assisting them is one of the greatest opportunities and risks for Kenya's government today.

Kenya remains uneasily on the cusp between two models of the world and of social behaviour, a tension and bifurcation that replays across many aspects of society. Although the 'world of the formal' had spread massively since 1963, bringing many people fully into the world of government, salaries, computers, records and accountants, the 'world of the informal' still sits alongside it, adapting and shaping formal processes in unpredictable ways. The conversion from collective to individual land ownership has failed; patron–client relationships still motivate much bureaucratic endeavour, as do the invisible mathematics of ethnicity; spiritual and immaterial beliefs still drive behaviour; and networks of crime and corruption grow alongside and within the formal architecture of bureaucracy and government.

Dilemmas of Democracy

The relationship between Kenya's rulers and its people has always been ambivalent. Although Kenyatta's autocracy appeared to have popular support, and the institutions of democracy apparently flowered after 1991, in each case the reality was somewhat different. Kenya's economic and social policies have been driven by competing interests, of which the popular will is only one. Kenyan governments have seldom done what voters wanted. They have always held the view that voters required education and that the government represented their best interests, even when the voters did not see it that way. Neither Kenyatta nor Moi came to power democratically. They rose to pre-eminence through political tactics and elite bargaining. Neither was willing to submit voluntarily to electoral competition (though Moi was forced to do so in 1991). Kibaki, a decade younger than Moi, in this respect is slightly different, apparently more sanguine about losing power, though the Anglo-Leasing scandal and the 2007 rigging suggest a harder core. Kenya's next president will have no choice but to submit (and sometimes pander) to the popular will.

There are many examples in Kenya's recent history of policies that were popular but disadvantageous, or unpopular but necessary. These include the rapid departure of foreigners from senior positions in the 1960s; the state socialism of the mid-1970s; the civil service retrenchments, privatisation and cost sharing of the early 1990s; tariff reduction and interest rate liberalisation; greater cash-crop production at the expense of food self-sufficiency; and the control and decontrol of prices and interest rates. The state could argue that authoritarian polices were in the national interest and that Kenya's democracy must remain 'guided'. The resulting lack of democratic accountability and of policy debate meant that public opinion was rarely a factor for Kenya's presidents when reaching a decision. Accountability was lost and oversight came from outside as much as from within.

In the 1960s, efforts by more socialist members of the new elite to redirect Kenya's path made appeals to democratic accountability, but were undermined by more conservative, Kikuyu-centric interests, who feared democracy would benefit neither themselves nor the country. Others, such as Martin Shikuku and J. M. Kariuki, also called for more popular democracy, sometimes on its own merits, but often as a means to deliver redistributive, socialist or personally beneficial changes. The Moi era of 1984–90 represented a new variant of this debate, as Moi attempted to create a new form of populist authoritarianism. His reach often exceeded his grasp, however, and by 1991 the debate had returned to familiar ground. The changes of 1992 opened up Kenya to more democracy than it had ever seen before, though it took several years for the change to be institutionalised. One result has been a more explicit articulation of public opinion into policy. In the early 1990s, both Kenneth Matiba and Moi were populists with little commitment to democratic accountability, but they spoke the language of mass appeal and promised benefits to the poor and downtrodden (even though the constituencies to which they appealed were different). Raila Odinga often sounds much the same. As the NARC era and then the Grand Coalition showed, however, the easy rhetoric of democracy in opposition becomes much harder when leaders face choices with real impact, in which some must lose, and they see how fickle, ethnicised and malleable popular choice can be.

Electoral democracy in Kenya is now deep rooted. Since 1963, suffrage has been universal (save for the 1988 primaries and the distortions implied by constituency boundary design and the presidential 25 per cent rule). Repeated execution of the process of electoral competition has embedded it in the public psyche as a public good. However, it is far from an unambiguous good, and since 1992 competitive elections have not helped the development of a national identity, while democracy is not the only concept that has been embedded by repetition. Elections have been institutionalised as 'winner takes all' trials of strength between elites, affirmations of communal identity and opportunities to 'eat' the ill-gotten gains of putative parliamentarians. Although public protestations exalt electoral democracy, in practice neither voters not politicians behave as if this were true. The tension between politicians and administrators has been high, and will become only stronger if the 2010 Constitution truly divorces ministerial office from political representation.

While political competition has always been elite led, multi-party politics is having strange results in a situation of mass impoverishment. There is a gradual move towards populist imperatives and away from technocrat elitism, associated with the perception that pro-Western technocratic elites have failed Kenya, without there being a clear alternative. Inevitably, the leadership of the ODM – a populist mass movement as well as an ethno-regional coalition – has adapted to the realities of office, but the popular sense of injustice and alienation remains: the belief that there are solutions to Kenya's problems that the elites do not take because of their own self-interest. There is also a deeply engrained mental model of competition for central resources that is focused on the presidency as the 'spider at the centre of a web'. Kenya's history constrains its actors inside a model of behaviour that no longer meets the interests of the country. The new Constitution appears to offer an alternative, devolved model, but there is a strong risk that the 'great spider' will become 47 spiders, smaller, but just as authoritarian and venal.

One thing multi-party democracy did achieve was a far greater openness in speech and writing. The reports of presidential goings-on, of scandals, government abuses and political alliances and enmities, premiered by magazines such as *Society* and *Finance*, have permeated down into the mainstream media. The openness created by the Internet was also a significant contributor after 1997, as international media became instantly available to Kenyans with money. This was a complete break from the previous 30 years, in which only 'positive' stories were permitted, investigative journalism was non-existent, and regime changes could only be discerned by a variety of Kremlinology as to who was 'in' and 'out'. Today, everything is public, though telling truth from fiction becomes harder by the day.

The relationship between economic development, industrialisation and urbanisation and political liberalisation and democracy has been debated for decades. It was argued by donors in the 1980s and 1990s that political liberalisation was essential for economic growth and democracy for development. The evidence for both theses remains ambivalent in Kenya. Political liberalisation underpinned and sustained economic change, but economic change was forced more by Western donors and their control of the purse strings than by internal pressures. The converse theory, that development encourages democracy, and more specifically that economic liberalisation finances and fuels democracy, finds more support. Kenya's history suggests that differentiation and growth – when combined with greater awareness of examples in the outside world – encourages a form of political competition that is more overt, conflict driven and less easily controlled than the politics of agrarian societies. Electoral competition is more open (for example, more candidates stand for election) in wealthier and more differentiated districts of the country. But this does not mean they are more democratic, only more competitive. Kenya's history since independence suggests that sustainable multi-party democracy relies on the existence of a differentiated society, but as much on the existence of a wealthy baronial elite, capable of balancing the state, as on a middle class or an urban working class. The absence of an influential middle class underpinned the single-party state. Every other community apart from Kenya's wealthiest made an accommodation with KANU during 1992–2002. The shrivelling of the state and the maturing of the urban middle class in the late 1990s is changing this pattern, though the final form is not yet clear. This analysis is made more complex by the fact that Kenyans are not actually becoming wealthier, only more differentiated, by the continued existence of the smallholding agricultural and pastoral sectors, and by the size of the informal sector in urban areas.

Parties and Politics

The 50 years since the British permitted national party politics suggest that there has been no such thing as an enduring political party in Kenya. The party as a shared ideology and organisation with aims, objectives and structures that transcend specific communities and the abilities and interests of its leadership, does not exist. Parties represent individuals and communities first and any other interests, including political philosophy or policy, second. All significant Kenyan parties have either been 'state-parties' (arms of government), ethnic parties or short-term alliances.

The single-party era was not one in which one party was in government; it was one in which the government was in one party. In reality, Kenya was a no-party state, in which KANU was a fig leaf on the state bureaucracy. The same phenomenon was seen in the late Kibaki era, when the government manufactured a party on which to fight the elections, based on a commonality of interest in retaining power, with a single ethno-regional core, but leveraging state resources to build a cross-ethnic coalition. All other national parties have been fragile alliances of convenience built up from sub-parties with distinct ethnic roots (such as KADU, FORD, NARC, the LDP and ODM) or, when forced back to their ethnic bailiwick, rooted in one specific ethnic sub-nationalism (such as the NDP, FORD-Kenya after 1994, the SDP/NPK, and FORD-People after 2002). Only the state has had the organisational and financial strength to sustain a nationwide political party for much longer than a year. The sole exception to this rule, the DP, survived in opposition intact for a decade for two reasons: first, the ethnic sub-nationalism it represented was Kenya's largest and most alienated; second, it was its wealthiest, which allowed the party to survive despite the lure of the state.

Raila Odinga represents an extreme example of this phenomenon. The focusing of Luo identity around him is unique in Kenya, driven by the community's perceived and real economic, social and political exclusion. His rise to prominence followed a tempestuous apprenticeship with his father, which included three periods of detention, involvement in the 1982 coup, Mwakenya, the struggle for multi-party democracy and the establishment of FORD and FORD-Kenya. After his father's death, he took his place as the informal *ker* (spiritual leader of the Luo community), and led the Luo out of FORD-Kenya into the NDP, then into alliance with KANU. In 2002, his ambitions thwarted, he was the prime mover behind the Rainbow Alliance's defection and NARC's victory. Then, in 2004–6, he led the LDP and the Luo into the Orange Democratic Movement (ODM-Kenya). Finally, he left ODM-Kenya acrimoniously and shifted to the closely related ODM. He had been through seven parties in 15 years, and his community had near-unanimously followed him every time, even delivering the holy grail of a Luo vote for a Kikuyu in 2002, which many had believed impossible.

Class in Kenya

As well as taking an ethnic and patrimonial form, Kenya's history supports a form of class-based analysis, without any normative assumptions about one particular group's success being desirable. Kenya's elites certainty see themselves as a 'class', with a distinct identity and socio-economic interest, albeit one that is also fractured on ethnic and racial lines. The urban poor increasingly see themselves as collectively disadvantaged, and competitive politics has given them greater influence through mass protest and the electoral power of sheer numbers. Workers are generally a privileged minority, and their political representation has been erratic. The interests of the business community have always been well represented, though more as members of other elite organisations than as a collective bargaining force. The unemployed and informal workers have felt increasingly frustrated at the absence of effective representation of their problems, which was some of the pressure behind the Matiba wave in 1992, and the subsequent fragmentation of Nairobi and Central Province politics.

Kenya has been ruled for five decades by an emerging political aristocracy, the first generation of which arrogated to itself the powers and privileges of the Europeans at independence. While some of those who prospered and dominated the independent state were old colonial families – the children of the senior chiefs of the 1940s and 1950s – the vast majority of those who made their names and fortunes were children of ordinary peasants, teachers and clerks. A generation of young, lucky, educated, able politicians and administrators, in their 20s and early 30s as independence approached, were given a one-off boost that propelled them into an enduring dominance of Kenyan society. Today, this elite is far more closed, unless political connections grant special access. For a Kenyan today to reach the rank of permanent secretary or PC would take at least 20 years of service, whereas for men such as Matiba it took five.

Not only did the 'independence elite' effectively run the country for the next 40 years, but as they aged, their relatives took over. Many noted the extraordinary spectre of the son of Jomo Kenyatta opposing the son of Oginga Odinga for the KANU nomination in 2002, while the children of Daniel arap Moi, Ronald Ngala and Moses Mudavadi played supporting roles. Kibaki's family were also influential behind the scenes once he took the presidency, though they remained outside competitive politics. Although it can be over-stressed, since most of the early political heavyweights did not establish dynasties, politics is becoming an inherited vocation, played out between wealthy families and supported by a culture that increasingly sees representative power as inherited. By the 2000s, most of the independence elite had retired or died, but the social and political structures that they built had replicated themselves into both 'political families' and huge inequalities in wealth and influence.[12] As in other developing nations, these families have become enduring 'brands', short-cuts evoking strong positive (and negative) feelings.

As in so many other countries, money is power and power is money. The atomisation of patron–client relations and the abuse of state resources for political and private gain have created a self-fulfilling expectation that high politics can only be sustained by vast financial resources, and that the route to power and wealth is through connections and the ruthless exploitation of opportunities. Kenya has become a society that worships wealth, although many know its questionable provenance. History truly shows that here, 'behind every great fortune is a great crime.' The second generation, the children of the airlifts, and the third, the Moi elites, have had less than 20 years to build their structures for survival. The accumulation of the Kalenjin elites and their politically safe Asian partners produced a serious competitor for the Kikuyu at the top ranks of business and government, but they were unable to replicate this in state or society. Not only were the Kalenjin numerically fewer, especially in Nairobi, but their slower economic development left their elites precariously balanced on a narrow socio-economic pyramid. A Luo presidency would almost inevitably have the same outcome.

The Future

Kenya is arguably no longer 'post colonial' but entering a third era, mid-way between the centralised authoritarianism and development focus of the independence era and something else, though few agree on what the future will or should hold.[13] It will probably be a state with stronger private (though not always multinational) business, possibly more externally engaged and entrepreneurial than in its past. It may be more democratic and devolved, but not necessarily so, and not much less corrupt. It may still descend into mass ethnic violence, if the political bargain that has sustained it since 2008 collapses acrimoniously in 2012. It is unlikely to match idealised expectations of a liberal, democratic, bureaucratic, capitalist, developmental society. Despite the risks, Kenya today needs a stronger (though less authoritarian) state and bureaucracy. After nearly 30 years in which the state was damned as evil, corrupt and incompetent, Kenyans need once more to invest in their state.

Whether there will be a second chance for popular national renewal remains unknown, as would be the nature of the policies a new leadership might implement. At the time of writing, this opportunity still exists. The Grand Coalition stumbles forward, like a runner in a three-legged race: slow, bruised, but with popular goodwill. The country faces a fortuitous combination of the new Constitution, the retirement of the two-term presidential incumbent and the disruption to ethnic politics threatened by the ICC prosecutions. But it is not clear from where the leader of such a 'third liberation' could come. The 1992 crop of Young Turks such as Odinga, Kiraitu Murungi, Anyang' Nyong'o, James Orengo, Paul Muite and Ngilu are now elderly, fully socialised Kenyan politicians. Their experience of 15 years of ethnic tension, violence and money politics has not left them idealised democrats. The prospect that an Odinga presidency could create a radical renewal is unlikely. In part, this is because he brings with him a weighty historical baggage of divisiveness. It is also because of the cynical populism he has sometimes shown and (not always of his own making) because of the response that his accession would bring amongst the Luo, anxious for their turn in the sun, and the Kikuyu, who would withdraw their consent to be governed in a thousand ways. But the game may change a dozen times between now and the final poll, and each change could shift the result. Behind the Young Turks loom a fourth generation of political elites who are entering the arena in their 30s and early 40s, more numerous, wealthier, better educated, more international than any previous generation, but who grew up under Moi and Kibaki.

Can they truly break the mould? Will the increasingly influential diaspora drive politics towards a more Western model?

Although the country has become far more ethnically blurred and more mixed in reality, Kenyans continue to deploy ethnicity in multiple arenas. The younger foreign-educated elites do not view the state or their community in the same way as the older generations. They mix freely socially and intermarry more easily, but they still understand that power in Kenyan politics is about creating and exploiting division, and that the easiest division to exploit remains ethnicity, even if these communities are more imagined than real. For many, the aggregated, imagined, situational tribalism of Nairobi is as real as the 'real' ethnic groups of their grandparents, and ethnic strife remains likely.

Meanwhile, the landless, urbanised, impoverished youth remain politically powerless, ruled by the older and the wealthy. Mungiki was in part a reaction to this powerlessness, and more successors to Mungiki are likely in a dog-eat-dog society in which young men have little to offer except violence and little to lose from it. An overcrowded, poor, badly-educated, violent, alienated majority who have experienced more than 20 years during which coercion dominated over any other form of state service has little attachment to any government.

The bargain hammered together to end the violence has lasted, but it will face a severe test in 2012 or 2013. Although the most likely outcome remains one of managed change, the divisions in society remain strong and the sense amongst the poor that violence remains a legitimate response to exploitation and that somehow, something important has been taken from them is palpable. The legacy of history weighs far more heavily in contemporary politics than in many other countries. There is a bitterness at the outcome of independence which demands expression. Federalism may deliver this opportunity, but it is far from guaranteed. If the elites cannot find a means to rule without appearing to view all issues through the lenses of corruption, ethnicity and self-interest, the danger remains that this logjam will break, and that future is clouded. To avoid this, to show their ability to seek the common good, and to accept short-term individual and community disadvantage in the interest of all, is the challenge that Kenyans now face.

Notes

Chapter 1: Introduction

1 For an account of structural and contingent explanations of democratisation, see Bratton, Michael and van de Walle, Nicholas, *Democratic Experiments in Africa: Regime Transitions in Comparative Perspective* (Cambridge, 1997), pp. 20–7.

2 Berman, Bruce, 'Up from Structuralism' in Berman, Bruce and Lonsdale, John, *Unhappy Valley, Book One: State and Class* (London, 1992), p. 199.

3 Allen, Chris, 'Understanding African Politics', *Review of African Political Economy*, No. 65 (1995), p. 316.

4 See for example Leonard, David K., *African Successes: Four Public Managers of Kenyan Rural Development* (Berkeley, 1991), pp. 284–5.

5 World Bank, '2007 World Development Indicators Online' (Washington, DC: The World Bank, 2007), http://earthtrends.wri.org/text/economics-business/variable-638.html

6 Lonsdale, John, 'African Pasts in Africa's Future', in Berman and Lonsdale: *Unhappy Valley, Book One*, p. 205.

Chapter 2: Independence!

1 See Ominde, S. H. (ed.), *Population and Development in Kenya* (Nairobi, 1984), Chapter 1.

2 See Thompson, Vincent B., 'The Phenomenon of Shifting Frontiers: The Kenya–Somalia Case in the Horn of Africa, 1880s–1970s', *Journal of Asian and African Studies*, Vol. 30, No. 1–2, (1995).

3 The phrase 'ethnic group' is used here to describe Kenya's various communities of shared origin, language, culture, traditions or interests – even though Kenyans and the Kenyan government mostly use the word 'tribe' – because of the latter word's connotations with primitiveness and primordial origin. It is critical to Kenya's politics that all such terms reflect both a relational and an absolute construct. They are relational in that ethnic groups define themselves and are defined by others situationally; for specific purposes, and in the context of the actions of others. They are also absolute in that there is rarely (if ever) an absence of common characteristics (language, appearance, kin-relations, common food and social practices, myths of origin) from which to build such an identity. There is no assumption of genetic homogeneity or common socio-economic interest implied in the use of the term. Generally, African scholars have tended to see ethnicity as reflecting a more absolute model, while Western scholars have tended to see ethnicities as relational constructs.

4 For histories of Kenya's ethnic groups, see Ochieng, William R., *A History of Kenya* (London, 1985), pp. 1–35 and Spear, Thomas T., *Kenya's Past: An Introduction to Historical Method in Africa* (London, 1981).

5 See Muriuki, Godfrey, *A History of the Kikuyu, 1500–1900* (Nairobi, 1974) and Kershaw, Greet, *Mau Mau from Below* (Oxford, 1997), pp. 13–37.

6 See Ogot, Bethwell, *History of the Southern Luo* (Nairobi, 1967) and Ochieng, William R., *An Outline History of Nyanza up to 1914* (Nairobi, 1974).

7 The Tachoni were of Kalenjin origin, for example, while the Bukusu were recent arrivals from Uganda. For a history of the Abaluhya, see Were, Gideon S., *A History of the Abaluyia of Western Kenya, c.1500–1930* (Nairobi, 1967).

8 Whether due to recent migration, urbanisation or other phenomena, Kamba generally did not consider clans and lineages as significant culturally or politically as did other Bantu communities such as the Gusii.

9 See for example Mwanzi, Henry A., *A History of the Kipsigis* (Nairobi, 1977).

10 According to Kipkorir, the Marakwet people were not a single people but five related communities (the Almo, Cherang'any, Endo, Markweta and Kiptanai) who were formed by the British into 'Marakwet' division. Kipkorir, Ben E. with Welbourn F. B., *The Marakwet of Kenya* (Nairobi, 1973), pp. 4–5.

11 For a collection of studies of the Maasai, see Spear, Thomas and Waller, Richard (eds), *Being Maasai: Ethnicity and Identity in East Africa* (London, 1993).

12 Ominde: *Population and Development*, p. 36. I refer to the mostly white settlers as 'Europeans' for simplicity in most contexts, although some were South African.

13 Himbara, David, *Kenyan Capitalists, the State and Development* (Boulder, 1993), pp. 37–40.

14 After the independence of India and Pakistan, it became common in East Africa to refer to the peoples whose origins lay in the Indian sub-continent as 'Asians'.

15 Kipkorir: *The Marakwet*, p. 1.

16 Lonsdale, John, 'The Conquest State', in Berman, Bruce and Lonsdale, John, *Unhappy Valley, Book One: State and Class* (London, 1992), p. 38.

17 See Ayot, Henry Okello, *A History of the Luo-Abasuba of Western Kenya from A.D. 1760–1940* (Nairobi, 1979).

18 Lonsdale, John, 'Soil, Work, Civilisation and Citizenship in Kenya', *Journal of Eastern African Studies*, Vol. 2, No. 2 (2008), p. 306.

19 See for example Carey-Jones N. S., *The Anatomy of Uhuru* (New York, 1966), pp. 61–9. On the early years of European settlement, see also Sorrenson, M. P. K., *Origins of European Settlement in Kenya* (Nairobi, 1968).

20 See Matson, A. T., *Nandi Resistance to British Rule, 1890–1906* (Nairobi, 1972) and Maxon, Robert M., *Conflict and Accommodation in Western Kenya: The Gusii and the British, 1907–1963* (Cranbury, 1989), pp. 36–45.

21 Clayton, Anthony and Savage, Donald, *Government and Labour in Kenya 1895–1963* (London, 1974), pp. 1–6.

22 Before the British arrival, there was no formal trans-community land title system, with clearance, inheritance and violence combining to secure use. Most farmland was held in common by a clan or lineage.

23 Maloba, Wunyabari O., *Mau Mau and Kenya: An Analysis of a Peasant Revolt* (London, 1993), p. 27; Tiffen, Mary, Mortimore, Michael and Gichuki, Francis, *More People, Less Erosion: Environmental Recovery in Kenya* (Chichester, 1994), p. 48.

24 Lonsdale: 'Conquest State'.

25 See for example, *Daily Nation*, 26 August 2004, when Sabaot leaders showed a document said to be a copy of the 99-year lease to the press, and laid claim to most of the western Rift Valley.

26 Sorrenson: *Origins*, pp. 190–209.

27 Lonsdale: 'Conquest State', p. 21; Kipkorir, Ben E., 'The Alliance High School and the Origins of the Kenya African Elite, 1926–1962', D.Phil. dissertation, St John's College Cambridge, 1969, pp. 11–20.

28 See Maxon: *Conflict and Accommodation*, pp. 35–6 on the choice of Gusii chiefs.

29 Berman, Bruce, *Control and Crisis in Colonial Kenya: The Dialectic of Domination* (London, 1990), pp. 73–127. In this book, the word 'state' generally relates to the entire apparatus of administration and rule, both political and bureaucratic, while 'government' refers to political structures.

30 Berman, Bruce, 'The Concept of Articulation and the Political Economy of Colonialism', in Berman and Lonsdale: *Unhappy Valley, Book One*, p. 137.

31 Sorrenson: *Origins*, p. 146.

32 See for example Maxon: *Conflict and Accommodation*, p. 78.

33 Ogutu, G. E. M., 'History of Religion', in Ochieng, William R. (ed), *Themes in Kenyan History* (Nairobi, 1990), p. 86.

34 Governor Sir Philip Mitchell, in Maloba: *Mau Mau*, p. 33.

35 Protestant missionary, quoted in Sorrenson: *Origins*, p. 268.

36 Rosberg, Carl G. and Nottingham, John, *The Myth of Mau Mau* (London, 1966), pp. 36–55; Singh, Makhan, 'The East African Association 1921–25', in Ogot, Bethwell (ed.), *Hadith 3* (Nairobi, 1971).

37 See Atieno Odhiambo, E. S., *Siasa: Politics and Nationalism in East Africa, 1905–1939* (Nairobi, 1981) and Bennett, George, *Kenya: A Political History* (London, 1963), pp. 1–52 on tensions between Indian and white settlers in the early years.

38 Clayton and Savage: *Government and Labour*, pp. 33–38; Frost, Richard, *Race against Time: Human Relations and Politics in Kenya before Independence* (London, 1978), pp. 103–29.

39 Clayton and Savage: *Government and Labour*, pp. 28–30; Berman, Bruce and Lonsdale, John, 'Crises of Accumulation, Coercion and the Colonial State', in Berman and Lonsdale: *Unhappy Valley, Book One*.

40 Berman and Lonsdale: 'Crises of Accumulation', pp. 101–20.

41 See for example Kanogo, Tabitha, *Squatters and the Roots of Mau Mau, 1905–63* (London, 1987).

42 These included the Young Kavirondo Association (1921), Kavirondo Taxpayers Welfare Association (1923), North Kavirondo Central Association (1932), Ukamba Members Associations (1938) and Taita Hills Association (1939).

43 Mueller, Susanne D., 'Political Parties in Kenya: Patterns of Opposition and Dissent, 1919–1969', Ph.D. dissertation, Princeton, Princeton University, 1972, pp. 9–18; Berman, Bruce, 'Bureaucracy and Incumbent Violence', in Berman, Bruce and Lonsdale, John, *Unhappy Valley, Book Two: Violence and Ethnicity* (London, 1992), pp. 239–42.

44 Murray-Brown, Jeremy, *Kenyatta* (London, 1972), pp. 40–75.

45 See for example, Kershaw: *Mau Mau*, pp. 189–93; Lonsdale, John, 'The Moral Economy of Mau Mau', in Berman and Lonsdale, *Unhappy Valley, Book Two*, pp. 386–97.

46 Kipkorir: 'The Alliance High School', p. 147a. Although its dominance faded as educational access grew, Alliance continued to produce future leaders into the 1960s.

47 For studies of the state as a political and economic actor in colonial Kenya, see Berman: *Control and Crisis* and Berman and Lonsdale, *Unhappy Valley, Book Two*.

48 Kitching, Gavin, *Class and Economic Change in Kenya: The Making of an African Petite Bourgeoisie 1905–1970* (London, 1980), pp. 62–73.

49 Maxon: *Conflict and Accommodation*, pp. 101–4.

50 Berman: 'Bureaucracy', pp. 245–6.

51 Kitching: *Class and Economic Change*, pp. 280–97; Sorrenson, M. P. K., *Land Reform in the Kikuyu Country* (Nairobi, 1967), p. 40.

52 See for example Anderson, David, *Eroding the Commons: Politics of Ecology in Baringo, Kenya, 1895–1963* (Oxford, 2002), pp. 157–89; Rosberg and Nottingham: *Myth*, pp. 164–74.

53 Kenyatta, Jomo, *Facing Mount Kenya: The Tribal Life of the Gikuyu* (London, 1938). The book was accused in later years of mythologising Kikuyu life, and many saw it as a work of politics as much of anthropology. See for example Arnold, Guy, *Kenyatta and the Politics of Kenya* (London, 1974), pp. 68–82.

54 Murray-Brown: *Kenyatta*, pp. 163–71.

55 Arnold: *Kenyatta*, p. 32; Andrew, Christopher, *The Defence of the Realm: The Authorised History of MI5* (London, 2010), p. 455.

56 Berman: 'Bureaucracy', p. 242.

57 Throup, David W., *Economic and Social Origins of Mau Mau, 1945–53* (Oxford, 1987), pp. 21–5; Maloba: *Mau Mau*, p. 56.

58 See for example the views of British-born permanent secretary for agriculture until 1964 in Carey-Jones: *Anatomy*, pp. 35–41.

59 Leys, Colin, *Underdevelopment in Kenya: The Political Economy of Neo-Colonialism 1964–71* (London, 1975), pp. 33–6.

60 Berman, Bruce, 'Structure and Process in the Bureaucratic States of Colonial Africa', in Berman and Lonsdale, *Unhappy Valley, Book One*, pp. 162–3.

61 There was empty Crown land (land designated waste or unoccupied and therefore state-owned), but most of it was dry or infested by tsetse fly.

62 For example Kaggia, Bildad, *Roots of Freedom, 1921–63* (Nairobi, 1975), pp. 16–20, 26–8.

63 Anderson: *Eroding the Commons*, pp. 216–17.

64 Sorrenson: *Land Reform*, pp. 54–71.

65 Barnett, Donald L. and Njama, Karari, *Mau Mau from Within* (London, 1966), p. 34; Kanogo, however, suggests there were only 125,000 'registered' Kikuyu squatters in 1945. Kanogo: *Squatters*, p. 126.

66 See Throup: *Origins of Mau Mau*, pp. 91–119; Furedi, Frank, *The Mau Mau War in Perspective* (London, 1989), pp. 32–7.

67 Throup: *Origins of Mau Mau*, pp. 120–38.

68 Youé, Christopher, 'Settler Capital and the Assault on the Squatter Peasantry in Kenya's Uasin Gishu District, 1942–63', *African Affairs*, Vol. 87, No. 348 (1988).

69 See Spencer, John, *KAU: The Kenya African Union* (London, 1985), pp. 128–73. Teachers were a particularly influential group at this time because of the relatively high educational standards required to be able to teach and their key gatekeeper role, given the excess of demand over supply for education.

70 Mueller: 'Political Parties', p. 22.

71 It has been disputed whether the oathing movement had its origins in the reserves or the highlands. See Furedi: *The Mau Mau War*, p. 84, and Kanogo: *Squatters*, pp. 116–17.

72 Mbiyu Koinange was the first Kikuyu to receive a bachelor's degree, and the first Kenyan African to be awarded a master's.

73 Arnold: *Kenyatta*, pp. 99–100.

74 Kershaw: *Mau Mau*, pp. 200–1, 211.

75 Mueller: 'Political Parties', pp. 29–33; Spencer: *KAU*, pp. 156–84; Maloba: *Mau Mau*, pp. 52–3.

76 Berman: 'Bureaucracy', p. 249.

77 Throup: *Origins of Mau Mau*, pp. 171–202; Maloba: *Mau Mau*, pp. 40–4.

78 Furedi: *The Mau Mau War*, p. 5.

79 Clayton and Savage: *Government and Labour*, pp. 265–89, 328–33.

80 See Kaggia: *Roots*, pp. 25–59; Itote, Waruhiu, *Mau Mau General* (Nairobi, 1967), pp. 23–9.

81 Spencer: *KAU*, pp. 221–8.

82 Kaggia: *Roots*, pp. 96–8, 107–15.

83 Percox, David A., *Britain, Kenya and the Cold War* (London, 2004), pp. 29–30.

84 Furedi: *The Mau Mau War*, pp. 115–18; Branch, Daniel, *Defeating Mau Mau, Creating Kenya: Counterinsurgency, Civil War and Decolonization* (New York, 2009), pp. 25–6.

85 Itote: *Mau Mau General*, pp. 44–69.

86 Kershaw: *Mau Mau*, p. 240; Maloba: *Mau Mau*, p. 70; Murray-Brown: *Kenyatta*, pp. 245–6.

87 Rosberg and Nottingham: *Myth*, p. 275; Kaggia: *Roots*, p. 114; Anderson, David, *Histories of the Hanged: The Dirty War in Kenya and the End of Empire* (New York, 2005), p. 41.

88 Corfield F. D., *The Origins and Growth of Mau Mau*, Sessional Paper No. 5 of 1959/60 (Nairobi, 1960), pp. 159–62; Percox: *Britain, Kenya*, pp. 48–51.

89 Odinga, Oginga, *Not Yet Uhuru* (Nairobi, 1967), p. 115.

90 Anderson: *Histories*, pp. 230–88.

91 Maloba: *Mau Mau*, pp. 16–17.

92 Edgerton, Robert B., *Mau Mau: An African Crucible* (London, 1990), pp. 104–5.

93 Branch: *Defeating Mau Mau* explains how the loyalist vs Mau Mau division was as much a product of the violence as a precursor to it, and how many straddled that boundary, unless forced by personal circumstance to take a side. The term 'loyalist' is used here in the same sense as in Branch – as a Kikuyu opponent of the Mau Mau, for whatever reason.

94 Maloba: *Mau Mau*, pp. 82–97.

95 Cleary, A. S, 'The Myth of Mau Mau in its International Context', *African Affairs*, Vol. 89, No. 355 (1990), p. 240; also see Leakey, Louis S. B., *Defeating Mau Mau* (London, 1954).

96 Barnett and Njama: *Mau Mau from Within*, pp. 125–6 describes how oaths had antecedents in Kikuyu cultural practices; See also Maloba: *Mau Mau*, pp. 104–9.

97 See Lonsdale, John, 'Introduction', in Kershaw: *Mau Mau*, pp. xxii–xxvii, Maloba: *Mau Mau*, p. 13.

98 Anderson: *Histories*, pp. 200–20.

99 Kimathi was executed in prison on 18 February 1957 and buried secretly, creating a martyr for later generations.

100 Corfield: *Origins and Growth of Mau Mau*, p. 316; Anderson: *Histories*, p. 4; Elkins, Caroline,

Britain's Gulag: The Brutal End of Empire in Kenya (London, 2005) quotes Fitz de Souza as suggesting that more than 100,000 died, p. 89.

101 Chege, Michael, 'Mau Mau Rebellion Fifty Years on', *African Affairs*, Vol. 103, No. 410 (2004); Anderson: *Histories*, pp. 258–61, 291–3.

102 Anderson: *Histories*, pp. 297–327; Edgerton: *Mau Mau*, pp. 142–72.

103 Branch: *Defeating Mau Mau*, pp. 66–88.

104 Anderson: *Histories*, p. 5; Elkins: *Britain's Gulag*, pp. 91–232.

105 Anderson: *Histories*, pp. 313–14.

106 Elkins: *Britain's Gulag*, pp. 314–40.

107 Maloba: *Mau Mau*, pp. 137–46; Edgerton: *Mau Mau*, pp. 173–201.

108 Corfield: *Origins and Growth of Mau Mau*, p. 316; Odinga: *Not Yet Uhuru*, p. 172.

109 *Guardian*, 1 July 1985; Macharia, Rawson, *The Truth about the Trial of Jomo Kenyatta* (Nairobi, 1991).

110 Arnold: *Kenyatta*, pp. 133–48.

111 Sorrenson: *Land Reform*, pp. 110–12; Elkins: *Britain's Gulag*, pp. 235–50.

112 Sorrenson, *Land Reform*, pp. 104–8.

113 Sorrenson: *Land Reform*, pp. 113–34.

114 Berman: *Control and Crisis*, pp. 379–84.

115 Swainson, Nicola, *The Development of Corporate Capitalism in Kenya, 1918–1977* (Berkeley, 1980), pp. 99–169.

116 Swainson: *Corporate Capitalism*, p. 181.

117 See Ogonda, R. T, 'Colonial Industrial Policies', in Ochieng, William R. and Maxon Robert M. (eds), *An Economic History of Kenya* (Nairobi, 1992), p. 168.

118 One of the best known was the Chandaria family (the Comcraft group), which invested in aluminium and steel milling and small goods manufacturing. Other businesses included the Manji family's trading and food products businesses, the Patel family's glass factories and the Madhvani agro-industrial group, based in Uganda, which dominated sugar, edible oils, textile and soap production and moved into Kenya in the 1960s. See Himbara: *Kenyan Capitalists*, pp. 51–9; Swainson: *Corporate Capitalism*, pp. 126–30.

119 Elkins: *Britain's Gulag*, pp. 171–5.

120 Throup, David, 'Render unto Caesar', in Hansen, Holger Bernt and Twaddle, Michael (eds), *Religion and Politics in East Africa* (London, 1995), p. 144.

121 Maurice Otunga was the first Kenyan African to become a full bishop in 1960. He rose to head the Catholic Church. The first bishops of the ACK appointed in 1955, Obadiah Kariuki and Festo Olang', rose to head the ACK.

122 Kipkorir: 'The Alliance High School', p. 302.

123 Republic of Kenya, *Ministry of Education Triennial Survey 1961–63* (Nairobi, 1964).

124 Van Zwanenberg R. M. A. with King, Anne, *An Economic History of Kenya and Uganda, 1800–1970* (London, 1975), pp. 12–22. For the history of the East African medical profession to independence, see Iliffe, John, *East African Doctors: A History of the Modern Profession* (Kampala, 1998), pp. 7–135.

125 For the life of Tom Mboya, see Goldsworthy, David, *Tom Mboya: The Man Kenya Wanted to Forget* (London, 1982).

126 Goldsworthy: *Mboya*, pp. 18–20.

127 Mboya's trans-ethnic base can be ascribed to his upbringing on the sisal estate and the ambiguous position of the Abasuba within Luo culture, as well as to his own labour movement career. Goldsworthy: *Mboya*, p. 4.

128 Stichter, Sharon, *Migrant Labour in Kenya: Capitalism and African Response, 1895–1975* (Harlow, 1982), p. 142.

129 Goldsworthy: *Mboya*, pp. 50–64.

130 Goldsworthy: *Mboya*, pp. 156–60.

131 See Bogonko, Sorobea N., *Kenya 1945–1963: A Study in African National Movements* (Nairobi, 1980), pp. 98–115.

132 There are accounts of the 1957 election in Engholm, G. F., 'African Elections in Kenya, March 1957', in Mackenzie, W. J. M. and Robinson, Kenneth (eds), *Five Elections in Africa* (Oxford,

1960); Goldsworthy: *Mboya*, pp. 67–72; Roelker, Jack R., *Mathu of Kenya: A Political Study* (Stanford, 1976), pp. 125–6.

133 Branch, Daniel, 'Loyalists, Mau Mau and Elections in Kenya: The First Triumph of the System, 1957–1958', *Africa Today*, Vol. 53, No. 2 (2006), pp. 29–37.

134 Atieno Odhiambo, E. S., "Seek Ye First the Economic Kingdom': A History of the Luo Thrift and Trading Corporation (LUTATCO) 1945–56', in Ogot, Bethwell (ed.), *Hadith 5: Economic and Social History of East Africa* (Nairobi, 1976). Also, Odinga: *Not Yet Uhuru*, pp. 76–94.

135 Roelker: *Mathu*, pp. 134–42; Goldsworthy: *Mboya*, pp. 69–72.

136 Roelker: *Mathu*, pp. 137–9.

137 On this period, see Odinga: *Not Yet Uhuru*, pp. 142–55, and Mboya, Tom, *Freedom and After* (London, 1963), pp. 119–26.

138 Goldsworthy: *Mboya*, pp. 76–80.

139 Anderson: *Histories*, pp. 83–4.

140 Percox: *Britain, Kenya*, p. 187.

141 Gertzel, Cherry, *The Politics of Independent Kenya, 1963–8* (Nairobi, 1970), pp. 13–15; Odinga: *Not Yet Uhuru*, pp. 167–8.

142 Odinga: *Not Yet Uhuru*, pp. 156–61.

143 Mboya's indecision in 1958 on the Kenyatta question is described in Goldsworthy: *Mboya*, pp. 102–4.

144 Oruka, H. Odera, *Oginga Odinga: His Philosophy and Beliefs* (Nairobi, 1992), pp. 58–60.

145 See Kipkorir, Ben E., 'The Inheritors and Successors: The Traditional Background to the Modern Kenya African Elite; Kenya c.1890–1930', *Kenya Historical Review*, Vol. 2, No. 2 (1974).

146 Rothchild, Donald, *Racial Bargaining in Kenya: A Study of Minorities and Decolonisation* (London, 1973), p. 208.

147 See for example on Nyachae, Leonard, David K., *African Successes: Four Public Managers of Kenyan Rural Development* (Berkeley, 1991), pp. 50–4.

148 Goldsworthy: *Mboya*, pp. 116–19.

149 As this 'second generation' elite moved into leadership roles, so attitudes to the US warmed.

150 Odinga: *Not Yet Uhuru*, pp. 187–8.

151 After the political crisis that followed, few of the students trained in the East achieved national prominence, and their degrees were considered second-class qualifications after independence.

152 Anderson: *Histories*, p. 332.

153 Ng'ang'a, David Mukaru, 'Mau Mau, Loyalists and Politics in Murang'a 1952–1970', *Kenya Historical Review*, Vol. 5, No. 2 (1977).

154 Zeleza, Tiyambe, 'The Colonial Labour System in Kenya', in Ochieng and Maxon, *An Economic History of Kenya* (Nairobi, 1992), p. 179.

155 Kanogo: *Squatters*, pp. 150–2.

156 Leys: *Underdevelopment*, pp. 56–7.

157 Kyle, Keith, *The Politics of the Independence of Kenya* (Basingstoke, 1999), pp. 99–102.

158 The first Lancaster House Conference is described in Odinga: *Not Yet Uhuru*, pp. 178–82, and Kyle: *Politics*, pp. 102–8.

159 Goldsworthy: *Mboya*, pp. 137–8.

160 Wasserman, Gary, *Politics of Decolonization: Kenya Europeans and the Land Issue, 1960–65* (Cambridge, 1976), pp. 41–2, 67–8.

161 Salim A. I., 'The Movement for 'Mwambao' or Coast Autonomy in Kenya, 1956–63', in Ogot, Bethwell (ed.), *Hadith 2* (Nairobi, 1970).

162 Renison, quoted in Murray-Brown: *Kenyatta*, p. 301.

163 Kaggia: *Roots*, pp. 145–9.

164 Murray-Brown: *Kenyatta*, pp. 294–5.

165 Rothchild: *Racial Bargaining*, p. 373.

166 Large-scale disinvestment was possible because the shilling was locked to and convertible with sterling.

167 International Bank for Reconstruction and Development (IBRD), *The Economic Development of Kenya* (Baltimore, 1963), pp. 38–9.
168 Wasserman: *Decolonization*, pp. 59–61.
169 Wasserman: *Decolonization*, pp. 158–9. The CDC was originally known as the Colonial Development Corporation.
170 Leo, Christopher, *Land and Class in Kenya* (Toronto, 1984), pp. 73–86.
171 The best source on the 1961 election is Bennett, George and Rosberg, Carl, *The Kenyatta Election: Kenya 1960–61* (London, 1961). The registration of voters for the elections took place from August to October 1960. Since no census had been taken since 1948, no one knew how many eligible voters there were, and registration was made even more complex by the various 'fancy franchises'. However, difficulties in applying these rules led them to break down in several areas, creating a near-universal franchise. A British-style secret ballot was used for voting.
172 This is the only case in Kenya's history to date of multi-member constituencies in which the two most popular candidates were elected.
173 Bennett and Rosberg: *The Kenyatta Election*, p. 133; Odinga: *Not Yet Uhuru*, pp. 201–2; Goldsworthy: *Mboya*, p. 177.
174 Kyle: *Politics*, pp. 130–1; Karume, Njenga, *Beyond Expectations* (Nairobi, 2009), p. 312.
175 Odinga: *Not Yet Uhuru*, pp. 213–14.
176 Wasserman: *Decolonization*, pp. 89–90.
177 'Conclusions of a Meeting of the Cabinet', 27 July 1961, in CAB 128/35, pp. 5–6.
178 Murray-Brown: *Kenyatta*, p. 304.
179 Some believe that Odinga and Mboya '. . . had little doubt that they would be able to control Kenyatta, whom they believed to be elderly, alcoholic, feeble and out of touch . . .' (Edgerton: *Mau Mau*, p. 209).
180 Macmillan, quoted in Kyle: *Politics*, p. 142.
181 Maudling, Reginald, 'Conclusions of a Meeting of the Cabinet', 9 November 1961, in CAB 128/35, p. 6.
182 The son of a Murang'a colonial chief resigned his seat to allow him to contest.
183 Wassermann: *Decolonization*, pp. 98–100; Kyle: *Politics*, pp. 137–8; Sanger, Clyde and Nottingham, John, 'The Kenya General Election of 1963', *Journal of Modern African Studies*, Vol. 2, No. 1 (1964), pp. 9–13.
184 Anderson, David M., '"Yours in Struggle for Majimbo": Nationalism and the Party Politics of Decolonization in Kenya, 1955–64', *Journal of Contemporary History*, Vol. 40, No. 3 (2005), pp. 553–6.
185 Harbeson, John, *Nation-Building in Kenya: The Role of Land Reform* (Evanston, 1973), p. 115.
186 Furedi: *The Mau Mau War*, pp. 175–9.
187 Harbeson: *Nation-Building*, p. 122.
188 Kenyatta, Jomo, *Suffering Without Bitterness: The Founding of the Kenya Nation* (Nairobi, 1968), pp. 163–4.
189 Kenyatta, in Arnold: *Kenyatta*, p. 156.
190 Maudling, in Proctor, J. H., 'The Role of the Senate in the Kenya Political System', *Parliamentary Affairs*, Vol. XVIII, No. 4 (1965), p. 391.
191 Ghai, Yash and McAuslan, J. P. W., *Public Law and Political Change in Kenya* (Nairobi, 1970) were caustic about its coherence, see pp. 196–201.
192 Wasserman: *Politics of Decolonization*, p. 120.
193 *Report of the Kenya Constitutional Conference* (London, 1962), Annex C pp. 29–30; Hughes, Lotte, 'Malice in Maasailand: The Historical Roots of Current Political Struggles', *African Affairs*, Vol. 104, No. 415 (2005), pp. 209–11.
194 Leo: *Land and Class*, pp. 91–4.
195 Maudling, Reginald, 'Memorandum by the Secretary of State for the Colonies', C (62) 22, 6 February 1962, p. 2, in CAB 129/108.
196 Kyle: *Politics*, p. 151; Odinga: *Not Yet Uhuru*, pp. 230–1.
197 Odinga: *Not Yet Uhuru*, pp. 189–92, 200–1.
198 Oruka: *Oginga Odinga*, p. 49.
199 Oruka: *Oginga Odinga*, p. 75.

200 Anderson: 'Yours in Struggle for Majimbo', pp. 557–60.
201 Kenya Regional Boundaries Commission, *Report of the Regional Boundaries Commission* (London, 1962).
202 Carey-Jones: *Anatomy*, p. 157.
203 Leo: *Land and Class*, p. 111.
204 Wasserman: *Decolonization*, pp. 147–50.
205 Wasserman: *Decolonization*, pp. 171–5.
206 On 12 August 1963, Kenyatta met a delegation of 300 white settlers and, in a famous speech, won their support to stay and farm in an independent Kenya.
207 Leo: *Land and Class*, p. 132.
208 *Daily Nation*, 13 June 2004, online edition.
209 Goldsworthy: *Mboya*, pp. 199–203.
210 Kenya Northern Frontier District Commission, *Report of the Northern Frontier District Commission*, CMD 1900 (London, 1962); Ghai and McAuslan: *Public Law*, pp. 184–6.
211 *The Times*, 19 March 1963.
212 Goldsworthy: *Mboya*, pp. 208–210.
213 Ngei speaking at an election meeting, reported in *East African Standard*, 3 May 1963.
214 Colonial Office, *Kenya Report of the Constituencies Delimitation Commission* (London, 1963).
215 Kenya African Democratic Union, *KADU Election Policy 1963: Uhuru na Majimbo sasa!* (Nairobi, 1963).
216 Ngala, quoted in *The Times*, 16 May 1963.
217 Lamb, Geoff, *Peasant Politics: Conflict and Development in Murang'a* (Lewes, 1974), pp. 28–30.
218 'The Kenya General Elections, KANU paper for Discussion', N.D., in Murumbi Archives MAC/KEN/38/1 Kenya Political Organisations. Kenya African National Union (KANU) – General and Local Government Elections 1963–69.
219 Njoroge Mungai, in *Daily Nation*, 6 May 1963, p. 2.
220 *Daily Nation*, 19 June 2000, p. 9.
221 *The Times*, 25 May 1963.
222 Sammy Omari, quoted in *Daily Nation*, 6 May 1963.
223 Letter from George Githii to Murumbi, part of series 17 March 1964–5 February 1965, in Murumbi Archives MAC/KEN/38/1 Kenya Political Organisations. Kenya African National Union (KANU) – General and Local Government Elections 1963–69.
224 Sanger and Nottingham: 'The Kenya General Election', pp. 1–40.
225 *Kenya Gazette*, 11 June 1963, GN. 2465.
226 Kipkorir, 'The Alliance High School', p. 2.
227 Odinga: *Not Yet Uhuru*, pp. 242–5.
228 Odinga: *Not Yet Uhuru*, p. 247.
229 In return, Ngei became chairman of the Maize Marketing Board, one of the first examples of the leadership appointing politicians to head parastatals as a reward for loyalty.
230 There were quotas for each major ethnic group, with the Kamba allocated 34%, the Kalenjin 39%, the northern pastoralists 12.5% and the Samburu 7.5% in 1959. See Parsons, Timothy, *The 1964 Army Mutinies and the Making of Modern East Africa* (Westport, 2003), p. 38.
231 Parsons: *Army Mutinies*, p. 46.
232 Parsons: *Army Mutinies*, pp. 82–3.
233 Parsons: *Army Mutinies*, pp. 61–8, 74.
234 Parsons: *Army Mutinies*, p. 89.
235 Parsons: *Army Mutinies*, p. 81.
236 Mboya: *Freedom and After*, p. 237.
237 For example, the KAR had no artillery or engineers, and shared signals units with the British army.
238 Letter from R. S. Havell, head of S6 to the Air Ministry, 'Formation of a Kenyan Air Force', 9 January 1963, p. 1, in CO 968/874 Proposed Formation of a Kenyan Air Force, 1963–4.
239 Ugandan and Tanganyikan politicians had done the same before independence.
240 *Standard*, 23 August 2004, online edition, based on letters to and from Kenyatta from 1962–64; Itote: *Mau Mau General*, pp. 236–48.

241 Itote: *Mau Mau General*, pp. 261–6. See also Arnold: *Kenyatta*, pp. 153–4.

242 Odinga: *Not Yet Uhuru*, pp. 277–8.

243 *Standard*, 8 February 2004, quoting a letter to Kenyatta dated 5 November 1963.

244 'Conclusions of a Meeting of the Cabinet', 21 November 1963, in CAB 128/38, p. 5.

245 Okoth, P. Godfrey, *United States of America's Foreign Policy toward Kenya, 1952–1969* (Nairobi, 1992), pp. 38–59.

246 *The Times*, 6 June 1963.

247 Sandys, in the House of Commons, in *The Times*, 28 June 1963.

248 Seroney, in *Daily Nation*, 6 March 2004, online edition.

249 Kyle: *Politics*, pp. 190–2.

250 *Daily Nation*, 6 March 2004, online edition, quoting private papers of Robinson Mwangi.

251 Note to Sir Burke Trend, 'Kenya', 11 October 1963, in CAB 21/5284 Kenya.

252 'Amendments and Additions to be made to the Constitution', *Kenya Independence Conference 1963*, Cmnd 2156 (London, 1963), pp. 12–22

253 Ngala, in *The Times*, 22 October 1963.

254 Letter from Kenyatta, *Kenya Independence Conference 1963*, Cmnd. 2156 (London 1963), Annexe C.

255 Kenyatta, Jomo, *Harambee!* (Nairobi, 1964), p. 14.

Chapter 3: Struggle for the State, 1964–1965

1 For convenience, I use Gertzel's distinction between 'radicals' and 'conservatives' (or 'moderates'), as – although the division was complex in origins, reflecting policy, individual and communal interests – it took on a more ideological component as time passed. Gertzel, Cherry, *The Politics of Independent Kenya, 1963–8* (Nairobi, 1970), pp. 44–58.

2 Bienen, Henry, *Armies and Parties in Africa* (New York, 1978), p. 73.

3 Goldsworthy, David, *Tom Mboya: The Man Kenya Wanted to Forget* (London, 1982), pp. 223–4.

4 Proctor, J. H., 'The Role of the Senate in the Kenya Political System', *Parliamentary Affairs*, Vol. XVIII, No. 4 (1965), pp. 409–10.

5 Mueller, Susanne D., 'Political Parties in Kenya: Patterns of Opposition and Dissent, 1919–1969', Ph.D. dissertation, Princeton, Princeton University, 1972, pp. 74–81.

6 Kenyatta, 2 July 1963, quoted in Kenyatta, Jomo, *Harambee!* (Nairobi, 1964), p. 12.

7 Kenyatta, paper on one-party systems in Africa, *Daily Nation*, 14 August 1964, reprinted in Gertzel, Cherry, Goldsmidt, Maure and Rothchild, Donald (eds), *Government and Politics in Kenya* (Nairobi, 1969), pp. 111–13.

8 See for example Coleman, James S., 'The Concept of Political Penetration', in Cliffe, L., Coleman J. S., and Doornbos, M. R. (eds), *Government and Rural Development in East Africa* (The Hague, 1977).

9 Mboya, quoted in *East African Standard*, 18 June 1964. Also see Mueller: 'Political Parties', pp. 79–81.

10 Only one man refused to join KANU: maverick Butere MP Shikuku, who sat as an independent until 1969.

11 *Sunday Nation*, 17 February 2002, online edition.

12 *The Times*, 20 November 1963, p. 9.

13 *The Times*, 27 December 1963, p. 6.

14 *Sunday Standard*, 18 January 2004, online edition.

15 Schlee, Gunther, *Identities on the Move: Clanship and Pastoralism in Northern Kenya* (Nairobi, 1994), p. 19.

16 Republic of Kenya, *1962 Census Advance Report of Vols 1 & 2* (Nairobi, 1964), and Republic of Kenya, *Kenya Population Census 1969, Vol. 1* (Nairobi, 1969).

17 Parsons, Timothy, *The 1964 Army Mutinies and the Making of Modern East Africa* (Westport, 2003), pp. 108–17.

18 Parsons: *Army Mutinies*, pp. 118–30.

19 Arnold, Guy, *Kenyatta and the Politics of Kenya* (London, 1974), p. 163; Odinga, Oginga, *Not Yet Uhuru* (Nairobi, 1967), p. 281; Parsons: *Army Mutinies*, pp. 135–6.

20 Parsons: *Army Mutinies*, pp. 140–1.

21 *Daily Nation*, 6 May 1964, n.p.

22 Parsons: *Army Mutinies*, p. 6.

23 'The Entire Memo of Intention and Understanding Regarding Certain Financial and Defence Matters of Mutual Interest to the British and Kenya Government (as Approved by British Minister)', signed by Kenyatta and Geoffrey de Freitas, 3 June 1964, p. 2, in FCO 31/375 Kenya Defence: Consolidation: Claims; Counter Claims: 'Memorandum of Intention and Understanding'.

24 *Pathé News*, 1753_24 Defence Talks (1964).

25 Note from R. G. Tallboys to E. G. Le Toq (EAD), 'Kenya Memorandum of Intention and Understand [sic] Regarding Certain Financial and Defence Matters of Mutual Interest to the British and Kenya Governments', 15 January 1969, in FCO 31/375 Kenya Defence: Consolidation: Claims; Counter Claims: 'Memorandum of Intention and Understanding'.

26 Note from P. H. Lawrence, 'Use of British troops in the North-Eastern Region of Kenya', 3 April 1964, FO 371/ 178532 British Military Support to Kenya, 1964. Also Defence and Overseas Policy Committee, 'Item 3: British Troops for Kenya', 8 April 1964, FO 371/ 178532 British Military Support to Kenya, 1964.

27 Note from R. S. Scrivener, 'Military Assistance to Kenya', 22 May 1964, FO 371/178534 British Military Aid to Kenya: Shifta Raids from Somalia, 1964.

28 'Letter to Secretary of State from L. B. Walsh Atkins, Commonwealth Relations Office, Downing Street, Kenya: Military Aid', 21 May 1964, in FO 371/178534 British Military aid to Kenya: Shifta Raids from Somalia. 1964. Also, Letter from Foreign Office to J. E. Killick Washington, 9 June 1964, in FO 371/ 178532 British Military Support to Kenya, 1964.

29 Throup, David, 'Crime, Politics and the Police in Colonial Kenya, 1939–63', in Anderson, David and Killingray, David (eds), *Policing and Decolonisation: Nationalism, Politics and the Police, 1917–65* (Manchester, 1992).

30 Odinga: *Not Yet Uhuru*, p. 277.

31 *Daily Nation*, 1 May 1967, p. 1.

32 *The Times*, 14 December 1963.

33 Parsons: *Army Mutinies*, p. 107.

34 Arnold: *Kenyatta*, pp. 174–5.

35 Van Zwanenberg R. M. A. with King, Anne, *An Economic History of Kenya and Uganda, 1800–1970* (London, 1975), p. 249.

36 Murray-Brown, Jeremy, *Kenyatta* (London, 1972), p. 320.

37 MacDonald, in Kenyatta: *Harambee!*, p. ix.

38 There is an issue regarding Moi's relations with the British that remains unexplained: why, in the British National Archives, are there a dozen references to him where sections have been redacted and the original retained for longer than the 30-years rule? From the context, Moi may have been providing information on occasion to the British.

39 Kenyatta: *Harambee!*, p. 47.

40 Hilton, Michael, 'Malcolm Macdonald, Jomo Kenyatta and the Preservation of British Interests in Commonwealth Africa, 1964–68', M. Phil thesis, Trinity College Cambridge, 2009, pp. 55–79.

41 Winkgates, James, 'US Policy Towards East Africa: Crisis Response amid Limited Interests', in Magyar, Karl (ed.), *United States Interests and Policies in Africa: Transition to a New Era* (Basingstoke, 2000), p. 107.

42 Attwood, William, *The Reds and the Blacks: A Personal Adventure* (New York, 1967), pp. 191–217.

43 Kenyatta, Jomo, *Suffering Without Bitterness: The Founding of the Kenya Nation* (Nairobi, 1968), pp. vi–viii.

44 *Daily Nation*, 18 May 1964, p. 2, reporting a joint Kenyan–Soviet communiqué.

45 Various in DO 213/214, Ministerial Delegation from Kenya Visiting China via Soviet Union, 1964.

46 *Sunday Nation*, 20 June 2000, p. 8.
47 Oruka, H. Odera, *Oginga Odinga: His Philosophy and Beliefs* (Nairobi, 1992), p. 82.
48 See for example Murray-Brown: *Kenyatta*, and Arnold: *Kenyatta*.
49 Murray-Brown: *Kenyatta*, pp. 118–19, 132, 182–3.
50 *Standard*, 22 August 2004, quoting Kenyatta family correspondence.
51 The Ndung'u report of 2004 on the illegal allocation of public land described some of Kenyatta's activities. See for example *Daily Nation*, 17 December 2004, online edition.
52 Gertzel: *Politics*, pp. 34–8 and Gertzel, Cherry, 'The Provincial Administration in Kenya', *Journal of Commonwealth Political Studies*, Vol. IV, No. 3 (1966), pp. 201–15.
53 Mueller: 'Political Parties', pp. 67–73.
54 Masinde Muliro, in Republic of Kenya, *House of Representatives Official Report* (*HoROR*), 1 February 1966, col. 336.
55 See for example Matiba, Kenneth, *Aiming High* (Nairobi, 2000), p. 75.
56 Good, Kenneth, 'Kenyatta and the Organization of KANU', *Canadian Journal of African Studies*, Vol. 2, No. 2 (1968).
57 Goldsworthy: *Mboya*, pp. 238–9.
58 'Neo-patrimonial' is a widely used term to describe states such as Kenya, where despite the formal structures of modern bureaucracies, the state operates on patrimonial principles, with personalised political authority, weak checks on private appropriation of public resources and pervasive clientelism.
59 Mueller: 'Political Parties', pp. 91–9.
60 Lamb describes the differing factional interests in Murang'a politics in the mid-1960s and similar stories could be told about other districts. Lamb, Geoff, *Peasant Politics: Conflict and Development in Murang'a* (Lewes, 1974), pp. 39–51.
61 Okoth-Ogendo, H. W. O., 'The Politics of Constitutional Change in Kenya since Independence, 1963–69', *African Affairs*, Vol. 71, No. 282 (1972), p. 21.
62 *Daily Nation*, 28 April 1965, p. 1.
63 Charles Njonjo, in Republic of Kenya, *The Senate Official Report* (*SAOR*) *(Vol. IV)*, (Nairobi) 5 May 1965, col. 972.
64 See Werlin, Herbert H., *Governing an African City; A Study of Nairobi* (London, 1974), pp. 180–200.
65 Personal communication, 2004.
66 Achieng-Oneko, in *The Times*, 16 July 1963.
67 *The Times*, 28 November 1963, np.
68 Branch, Daniel, *Defeating Mau Mau, Creating Kenya: Counterinsurgency, Civil War and Decolonization* (New York, 2009), p. 180.
69 *The Times*, 19 December 1963, np.
70 *The Times*, 9 January 1964, np.
71 See Buijtenhuis, Robert, *Mau Mau Twenty Years After* (Leiden, 1973), pp. 49–72.
72 Atieno Odhiambo E. S. and Lonsdale, John, 'Introduction', in Atieno Odhiambo, E. S. and Lonsdale, John (eds), *Mau Mau and Nationhood* (Oxford, 2003), p. 4.
73 Kenyatta: *Suffering*, p. 189.
74 Odinga: *Not Yet Uhuru*, p. xii.
75 See for example Ogot, Bethwell, 'Mau Mau and Nationhood: The Untold Story', in Atieno Odhiambo and Lonsdale: *Mau Mau and Nationhood*, and Lonsdale, John, 'The Moral Economy of Mau Mau', in Berman, Bruce and Lonsdale, John, *Unhappy Valley, Book Two: Violence and Ethnicity* (London, 1992).
76 Harbeson, John, *Nation-Building in Kenya: The Role of Land Reform* (Evanston, 1973), pp. 266–7 has one of the best scheme summaries.
77 Leo, Christopher, *Land and Class in Kenya* (Toronto, 1984), pp. 119–24.
78 Business Daily Supplement, *Daily Nation*, 9 November 2009, summarised government archives on this subject.
79 Wasserman, Gary, *Politics of Decolonization: Kenya Europeans and the Land Issue, 1960–65* (Cambridge, 1976), p. 155.

80 Letter from B. Greatbatch to W. G. Lamarque, Ministry of Overseas Development, 'Kenya Land Settlement Account: CAG Refused to Certify Accounts, 1964–65', 3 February 1965, p. 2, in DO 156-15, Kenya land Settlement Account, 1964–5.

81 Wasserman: *Politics*, pp. 155–6.

82 Wasserman: *Politics*, pp. 151–3.

83 Lamb: *Peasant Politics*, pp. 12–14.

84 Sorrenson, M. P. K., *Land Reform in the Kikuyu Country* (Nairobi, 1967), p. 212.

85 Lamb: *Peasant Politics*, pp. 15, 133–4.

86 Republic of Kenya, *Report on the Mission of Land Consolidation and Registration in Kenya, 1965–1966* (Nairobi, 1966), pp. 33, 49.

87 Kenyatta, 20 September 1963 and June 1964 in Narok, in Kenyatta: *Harambee!*, pp. 111–12.

88 Sorrenson: *Land Reform*, pp. 215–18.

89 Kenyatta: *Harambee!*, p. 3.

90 Rothchild provides statistical evidence of African attitudes to non-Africans and vice versa in 1966. See Rothchild, Donald, *Racial Bargaining in Independent Kenya: A Study of Minorities and Decolonisation* (London, 1973), pp. 159–82.

91 Ghai, Yash and McAuslan, J. P. W., *Public Law and Political Change in Kenya* (Nairobi, 1970), pp. 192–6.

92 Carey-Jones N. S., *The Anatomy of Uhuru* (New York, 1966), p. 110.

93 Bharati, Agehananda, *The Asians in East Africa: Jayhind and Uhuru* (Chicago, 1972), pp. 23–94; Rothchild: *Racial Bargaining*, pp. 36–51.

94 See Bharati: *The Asians*, pp. 83–8 and Oded, Arye, *Islam and Politics in Kenya* (Boulder, 2000), pp. 12–18.

95 International Bank for Reconstruction and Development (IBRD), *The Economic Development of Kenya* (Baltimore, 1963), p. 212.

96 Republic of Kenya, *African Socialism and its Application to Planning in Kenya, Sessional Paper No. 10* (Nairobi, 1965), p. 21.

97 Koinange, Mbiyu, in Republic of Kenya, *National Assembly Official Report* (Nairobi), 22 March 1967, col. 1423.

98 See for example on the Kenya Meat Commission, Dresang, Denis L. and Sharkanksky, Ira, 'Sequences of Change and the Political Economy of Public Corporations: Kenya', *Journal of Politics*, Vol. 37, No. 1 (1975).

99 Kenyatta, in Rothchild, Donald, 'Kenya's Africanization Program: Priorities of Development and Equity', *American Political Science Review*, Vol. 64, No. 3 (1970), p. 741.

100 Kenya: *African Socialism*, p. 21.

101 Rothchild: 'Kenya's Africanization Program', p. 738, 745.

102 Rothchild: *Racial Bargaining*, pp. 244–8.

103 Swainson, Nicola, *The Development of Corporate Capitalism in Kenya, 1918–1977* (Berkeley, 1980), p. 195.

104 Ghai and McAuslan: *Public Law*, pp. 367–78.

105 Ghai and McAuslan: *Public Law*, p. 402.

106 Ghai and McAuslan: *Public Law*, pp. 385–6, 403–6; Mwangi, Paul, *The Black Bar* (Nairobi, 2001), pp. 23–7.

107 Goldsworthy: *Mboya*, pp. 203–4.

108 IBRD: *Economic Development*, pp. 153–4.

109 Kenya: *African Socialism*, p. 29.

110 Wolf, Jan J. de, *Differentiation and Integration in Western Kenya: A Study of Religious Innovation and Social Change among the Bukusu* (The Hague, 1977), p. 103.

111 Kitching, Gavin, *Class and Economic Change in Kenya: The Making of an African Petite Bourgeoisie 1905–1970* (London, 1980), pp. 325–30.

112 Lamb: *Peasant Politics*, pp. 83–109.

113 Leonard, David K., *African Successes: Four Public Managers of Kenyan Rural Development* (Berkeley, 1991), pp. 125–9.

114 Republic of Kenya, *Statistical Abstract*, 1972, Table 60 c.

115 EAD, 'Brief for the Parliamentary Secretary's Meeting with Mr Bruce McKenzie, Kenya

Minister for Agriculture and Hugh Fraser MP, on 17th August (1966)', in DO 214/86 Sugar Industry in Kenya, 1964–66.

116 Hyden, Goran, 'Government and Cooperatives', in Hyden, Goran, Jackson, Robert H. and Okumu, John J. (eds), *Development Administration: The Kenyan Experience* (Nairobi, 1970).

117 See Kanogo, Tabitha, 'Cooperatives', in Ochieng, William R. (ed.), *Themes in Kenyan History* (Nairobi, 1990), pp. 178–9

118 Lamb: *Peasant Politics*, pp. 110–31.

119 Mboya, Tom, *The Challenge of Nationhood* (Nairobi, 1970), p. 14.

120 Sandbrook, Richard, *Proletarians and African Capitalism: The Kenyan Case, 1960–1972* Cambridge, 1975), p. 87.

121 Sandbrook: *Proletarians*, pp. 100–11.

122 Sandbrook: *Proletarians*, p. 134.

123 Sandbrook suggests that Kenyatta provided funds (some via Pinto) to use against Mboya until January 1965. See Sandbrook, Richard, 'Patrons, Client and Unions: the Labour Movement and Political Conflict in Kenya', *Journal of Commonwealth Political Studies*, Vol. 10, No. 1 (1972).

124 Amsden, Alice, *International Firms and Labour in Kenya, 1945–70* (London, 1971), pp. 122–8.

125 Kenya: *African Socialism*, p. 30.

126 Kenya: *African Socialism*, p. 30.

127 Holmquist, Frank, 'Class Structure, Peasant Participation and Rural Self-Help', in Barkan, Joel D. (ed.), *Politics and Public Policy in Kenya and Tanzania*, second edition (New York, 1984), pp. 174–9.

128 Private European and Asian schools retained high fees, religious practices and informal discrimination that skewed access towards their original constituency.

129 Rothchild, Donald, 'Ethnic Inequalities in Kenya', *Journal of Modern African Studies*, Vol. 7, No. 3 (1969).

130 Bogonko, Sorobea N., *A History of Modern Education in Kenya (1895–1991)* (Nairobi, 1992), pp. 124–5.

131 Bienen, Henry, *Kenya: The Politics of Participation and Control* (Princeton, 1974), pp. 49–57.

132 Bogonko: *Modern Education*, p. 127.

133 Bogonko: *Modern Education*, pp. 14–15.

134 In Itote, Waruhiu, *Mau Mau General* (Nairobi, 1967) and Itote, Waruhiu, *Mau Mau in Action* (Nairobi, 1979), for example, several senior Mau Mau survivors are pictured in NYS uniforms.

135 *The Reds and the Blacks* was the title of the revealing book by the ex-US ambassador to Kenya on his tour of duty in Africa and role in fighting communism. Attwood: *The Reds and the Blacks*.

136 Oruka: *Oginga Odinga*, p. 63.

137 Odinga: *Not Yet Uhuru*, p. 266.

138 *East African Standard*, 25 March 1966, np.

139 Interview with John Keen, 19 July 2004.

140 Odinga: *Not Yet Uhuru*, p. 116.

141 Goldsworthy: *Mboya*, p. 246.

142 *Daily Nation*, 28 April 1964, editorial p. 6.

143 'Replies to 'Soapy's' Depcirtel on 'New Policy for Africa'' Memorandum from Ulric Haynes to Robert W. Komer of the National Security Council (Washington, May 18, 1965)', Johnson Library, National Security File, Haynes Files, CHRONO (Haynes), 3/1/65-6/15/66. *Foreign Relations of the United States, 1964–1968*, Volume 24, Africa (Washington, US Department of State), www.state.gov/www/about_state/history/frusonline.html.

144 Attwood: *The Reds and the Blacks*, pp. 160–2.

145 Attwood: *The Reds and the Blacks*, pp. 186–7.

146 Attwood: *The Reds and the Blacks*, p. 180.

147 Oduya, quoted in Goldsworthy: *Mboya*, p. 237.

148 Goldsworthy: *Mboya*, p. 235.

149 Goldsworthy: *Mboya*, p. 238.

150 Thomas, Gordon, *Gideon's Spies: The Secret History of the Mossad* (London, 1999), p. 259.

151 Goldsworthy: *Mboya*, pp. 234–5.
152 *Sunday Standard*, 11 July 2004, online edition.
153 Intelligence summaries 12 October 1964 and 30 October 1964, in DO 213/159, HQ BLFK Weekly Intelligence Summaries.
154 Odinga: *Not Yet Uhuru*, p. 278.
155 Intelligence summary 21 December 1964, in DO 213/159, HQ BLFK Weekly Intelligence Summaries.
156 Goldsworthy: *Mboya*, pp. 234–5.
157 Kenya: *African Socialism*, p. ii.
158 *Daily Nation*, 20 June 2000, pp. 8–9 and 24 June 2000, pp. 8–9.
159 *Daily Nation*, 28 June 2000, pp. 1–2, 4.
160 Attributed to Pinto, *Daily Nation*, 13 April 1965, p. 1.
161 *Daily Nation*, 19 June 2000, pp. 8–9.
162 *Daily Nation*, 21 June 2000, pp. 8–9.
163 *Daily Nation*, 3 April 1965, p. 16.
164 *Daily Nation*, 2 April 1965, p. 1.
165 *Daily Nation*, 9 April 1965, p. 20.
166 Kenyatta, *Daily Nation*, 12 April 1965, p. 9.
167 Kenyatta on 11 April 1965 quoted in Thiong'o, Ngugi wa, *Detained: A Writer's Prison Diary* (London, 1981), p. 89.
168 Kaggia, *Daily Nation*, 22 April 1965, p. 8.
169 Cipher from Mr MacDonald Nairobi to Commonwealth Relations Office (CRO), Telegram No. 630, 9 April 1965, p. 1 in PREM 13/2743 1965–1969 Kenya.
170 Adams, C. C. W., 'Brief for Commonwealth Secretary for the Cabinet Defence and Overseas Policy Committee Meeting', 12 April 1965, in CAB 21/5284 Kenya, 1963–65.
171 Cipher No. 931 from CRO to Nairobi, 14 April 1965, p.1 in PREM 13/2743 1965–1969 Kenya.
172 Cipher No. 931, from CRO to Nairobi, 14 April 1965 and Cipher No. 651 from Mr MacDonald, 14 April 1965 in PREM 13/2743 1965–1969 Kenya.
173 *Daily Nation*, 23 and 29 April 1965, reporting on House and Senate debates; *SAOR*, 28 April 1965, cols 828–35.
174 Mungai, quoted in *Daily Nation*, 15 April 1965, p. 1.
175 Cipher No. 651, from Mr MacDonald, 14 April 1965, pp. 2–3 in PREM 13 /2743 1965–1969 Kenya.
176 Secret Intelligence cipher, date unclear, April 1965 in DO 213/159 HQ BLFK Weekly Intelligence Summaries
177 Attwood: *The Reds and the Blacks*, p. 246.
178 *Daily Nation*, 17 April 1965, p. 5.
179 Attwood: *The Reds and the Blacks*, p. 246.
180 James Nyamweya, *Daily Nation*, 24 April 1965, p. 4.
181 *Daily Nation*, 26 April 1965, p. 1.
182 *Daily Nation*, 28 April 1965, p. 20.
183 Cipher No. 640, from Nairobi to CRO, 29 April 1965, in PREM 13/1588, 1964–67 Kenya.
184 Cipher No. 746, from McDonald to CRO, 29 April 1965, in PREM 13/1588, 1964–67 Kenya.
185 *Time Magazine*, 7 May 1965, online edition.
186 Military intelligence summary, 17 May 1965, in DO 213/159 HQ BLFK Weekly intelligence Summaries.
187 Parsons: *Army Mutinies*, p. 187.
188 Kenya: *African Socialism*, p. 12.
189 Kenya: *African Socialism*, p. 39.
190 Kenya: *African Socialism*, p. 38.
191 Attwood, *The Reds and the Blacks*, p. 249.
192 Goldsworthy: *Mboya*, pp. 234–47; Gertzel, *Politics*, pp. 57–72; Mueller: 'Political Parties', pp. 100–2; Odinga: *Not Yet Uhuru*, pp. 297–300.

193 Wanguhu Ng'ang'a, *Daily Nation*, 31 July 2003, Kenya @40 special, online edition.
194 Mueller: 'Political Parties', p. 184.
195 Kenyatta: *Suffering*, p. 276.
196 Republic of Kenya, *Kenya Gazette* (Nairobi), January–December 1965.
197 Gertzel: *Politics*, pp. 69–70.
198 *East African Standard*, 29 July 1965, p. 1; Hakes, Jay, 'The Parliamentary Party of the Kenya African National Union', Ph.D. dissertation, Duke University, 1970, chapter 4.
199 Henry Wariithi, in *HoROR*, 26 January 1966, cols 147–56.

Chapter 4: Multi-Party, but not Democracy, 1966–1969

1 Mueller, Susanne D., 'Political Parties in Kenya: Patterns of Opposition and Dissent, 1919–1969', Ph.D. dissertation, Princeton University, 1972 provides the most detailed account available of the KPU.
2 Letter reporting results of secret defence review, 5 May 1966, in DO 213/128 External Threat to Kenya, 1965–1966.
3 Republic of Kenya, *House of Representatives Official Report* (*HoROR*), 15 February 1966, cols 899–905.
4 Tom Mboya, in *HoROR*, 15 February 1966, cols 915–16.
5 Bruce McKenzie, in *HoROR*, 26 January 1966, cols 94–105.
6 *Weekly Review*, 24 November 1975, p. 10.
7 See Gertzel, Cherry, *The Politics of Independent Kenya, 1963–8* (Nairobi, 1970), pp. 71–2, and Mueller: 'Political Parties', pp. 210–14.
8 Mueller suggest there were 49, not 51, see Mueller: 'Political Parties', p. 213.
9 Lamb, Geoff, *Peasant Politics: Conflict and Development in Murang'a* (Lewes, 1974), p. 22; Mueller, Mueller: 'Political Parties', p. 216.
10 Attwood, William, *The Reds and the Blacks: A Personal Adventure* (New York, 1967), p. 266.
11 Letter from Peck (British High Commission) to Bolland (Far East Department, Foreign Office), 26 July 1966, p. 1, in FO 371/187002 Political Relations Kenya.
12 Mueller: 'Political Parties', p. 218.
13 Odinga, Oginga, *Not Yet Uhuru* (Nairobi, 1967), p. 299.
14 Bennett, George, 'Kenya's 'Little General Election'', *The World Today* (August 1966), p. 340.
15 Odinga, *East African Standard*, 15 April 1966.
16 Goldsworthy, David, *Tom Mboya: The Man Kenya Wanted to Forget* (London, 1982), pp. 241–6.
17 Gertzel: *Politics of Independent Kenya*, p. 75; Koff, David, 'Kenya's Little General Election', *Africa Report*, Vol. 11, No. 7 (October 1966).
18 Interview with Tom Okelo-Odongo, 25 November 1984.
19 Kenyatta, Jomo, *Suffering Without Bitterness: The Founding of the Kenya Nation* (Nairobi, 1968), pp. 301–7.
20 Moi, 24 April, in *The Times*, 25 April 1966.
21 Mueller: 'Political Parties', pp. 395–7.
22 Kenyatta, in Kyle, Keith, *The Politics of the Independence of Kenya* (Basingstoke, 1999), p. 200.
23 *East African Standard*, 21 April 1966, p. 1.
24 KPU-supporting MPs from Baringo, *East African Standard*, 30 April 1966, p. 3.
25 *HoROR*, 28 April 1966, cols 2018–122.
26 These including Anyiene, who had been elected as an independent in 1963, but that inconvenient fact was simply ignored and the error legalised later.
27 Interview with Sheila Murumbi, 1 September 2000.
28 *KPU Manifesto*, 1966, reprinted in Gertzel, Cherry, Goldschmidt, Maure and Rothchild, Donald (eds), *Government and Politics in Kenya* (Nairobi, 1969), p. 150.
29 On the campaign, see Harbeson, John W., 'The Kenya Little General Election: A Study in Problems of Urban Political Integration', *IDS Discussion Paper No. 52* (Nairobi, June 1967) and Gertzel: *Politics of Independent Kenya*, pp. 73–94.
30 Mueller: 'Political Parties', pp. 295–6.
31 Lamb: *Peasant Politics*, p. 44.

32 Mueller: 'Political Parties', pp. 243–4. See also Gertzel: *Politics of Independent Kenya*, p. 91.
33 Gertzel: *Politics of Independent Kenya*, pp. 95–112.
34 Mueller: 'Political Parties', pp. 240–2.
35 Throup reports that a senior police officer told Kaggia later, 'he and his colleagues had 'manufactured' the result, writing thousands of false ballots and burning votes for Kaggia.' Throup, David W., 'The Construction of the arap Moi State and Elections in Kenya', unpublished article, pp. 1–2; See also Mueller: 'Political Parties', p. 244; Lamb: *Peasant Politics*, pp. 44–5.
36 Mueller: 'Political Parties', pp. 244–8.
37 Murray-Brown, Jeremy, *Kenyatta* (London, 1972), pp. 323–5.
38 Kenyatta in Mombasa, in *Daily Nation*, 29 August 1966.
39 *Daily Nation*, 6 January 1967, p. 1.
40 Morton, Andrew, *Moi: The Making of an African Statesman* (London, 1998), p. 91.
41 Anyang' Nyong'o, Peter, 'State and Society in Kenya: The Disintegration of the Nationalist Coalitions and the Rise of Presidential Authoritarianism, 1963–78', *African Affairs*, Vol. 88, No. 351 (April 1989), p. 230.
42 Gertzel: *Politics of Independent Kenya*, pp. 167–9.
43 Bienen, Henry, *Kenya: The Politics of Participation and Control* (Princeton, 1974), p. 60.
44 On the role of the National Assembly, see Hornsby, Charles, 'The Member of Parliament in Kenya, 1969–1983', D.Phil. dissertation, St Antony's College Oxford, 1985, pp. 22–35.
45 Ghai, Yash and McAuslan, J. P. W., *Public Law and Political Change in Kenya* (Nairobi, 1970), pp. 334–57.
46 M. J. Seroney, in *HoROR*, 2 March 1966, col. 1647.
47 Mohammed Jahazi, in *HoROR*, 24 February 1966, col. 1396.
48 See Hakes, Jay, 'The Parliamentary Party of the Kenya African National Union', Ph.D. dissertation, Duke University, 1970.
49 Sandbrook, Richard, *Proletarians and African Capitalism: the Kenyan Case, 1960–1972* (Cambridge, 1975), p. 20.
50 Ghai and McAuslan: *Public Law*, pp. 214–15.
51 Mueller: 'Political Parties', pp. 331–4.
52 This was to become a subject of controversy when a similar extension was proposed in 2002.
53 See for example Stren, Richard, 'Factional Politics and Central Control in Mombasa 1960–1969', *Canadian Journal of African Studies*, Vol. 4, No. 1 (Winter 1970).
54 Loughran, Gerald, *Birth of a Nation* (London, 2010), p. 90.
55 Most detainees were held for no more than a year. The reasons for their release appear to relate to their willingness to denounce the KPU to their jailers and beg for release, plus the declining ability of the KPU to pose a credible threat.
56 Mueller: 'Political Parties', pp. 264–81.
57 *Kenya Gazette*, Supplement, 16 February 1968, reprinted in Gertzel, Goldschmidt and Rothchild: *Government and Politics*, pp. 167–74.
58 Mueller: 'Political Parties', pp. 285–6.
59 Gertzel: *Politics of Independent Kenya*, p. 147.
60 Mueller: 'Political Parties', pp. 276–8.
61 See *Daily Nation*, 3 July 1968, pp. 1, 16, and 4 July 1968, pp. 1, 5.
62 Mueller: 'Political Parties', pp. 375–6.
63 Mueller, Susanne D, 'Government and Opposition in Kenya, 1966–1969', *Journal of Modern African Studies*, Vol. 22, No. 3 (1984), pp. 419–20.
64 Mueller: 'Government and Opposition', pp. 413–15.
65 Mueller: 'Political Parties', pp. 379–85.
66 Osogo, in *Sunday Nation*, 29 May 1966, reprinted in Gertzel, Goldschmidt and Rothchild: *Government and Politics*, p. 497.
67 The carrot and stick metaphor has been commonly used, but was probably first applied to Kenya in depth by Mueller.
68 Mueller: 'Political Parties', pp. 337–8.

69 *East African Standard*, 8 August 1968, p. 3.

70 Note for File from R. G. Tallboys (EAD), 7 August 1968, p. 1, in FCO 31/206 Political Affairs (Internal). Political Parties: Kenya African National Union, 1967– 68.

71 See for example Wolf, Jan J. de, *Differentiation and Integration in Western Kenya: A Study of Religious Innovation and Social Change among the Bukusu* (The Hague, 1977), p. 177, 180; Frost, Richard, *Race against Time: Human Relations and Politics in Kenya before Independence* (London, 1978), pp. 39–40.

72 Anderson, David, *Histories of the Hanged: The Dirty War in Kenya and the End of Empire* (New York, 2005), pp. 227–8.

73 See for example Diang'a, James Waore, *Kenya, 1982: The Attempted Coup-the consequence of a one-party dictatorship* (London, 2002), pp. 100–1.

74 Wolf: *Differentiation and Integration*, p. 110.

75 Njonjo, in *HoROR*, 17 February 1966, col. 1116.

76 Discussion with ex-civil servant, May 2004.

77 By the late 1960s, Kenyatta had abandoned the leopard-skin attire of a tribal chief, now appearing in public in a conservative pinstriped suit.

78 *Sunday Nation*, 20 January 1968, reprinted in Gertzel, Goldschmidt and Rothchild: *Government and Politics*, p. 92.

79 Shikuku, Martin, *HoROR:* 14 October 1966, reprinted in Gertzel, Goldschmidt and Rothchild:, *Government and Politics*, p. 46.

80 Leonard, David K., *African Successes: Four Public Managers of Kenyan Rural Development* (Berkeley, 1991), pp. 86–8 and Appendix A; Nellis, John, *The Ethnic Composition of Leading Kenyan Government Positions*. Research Report No. 24 (Uppsala, 1974).

81 Rothchild, Donald, 'Ethnic Inequalities in Kenya', *Journal of Modern African Studies*, Vol. 7, No. 3 (1969), pp. 704–5.

82 Military document 'Integer Ditons' reference RTP (West) No.10 and CICC (West) 110/68, probably 1968, in CAB 164/630 Kenya: Position of UK Nationals 1968–1970.

83 Letter from R. J. S. Edis to Mr Steele, Mr Mountain, H of C, 'Report of Meeting with Achieng-Oneko', 22 August 1969, in FCO 31/352: Kenya Political and Administrative Affairs (Internal) Political Parties: Kenya People's Union (KPU) 1968–69.

84 Letter from E. G. le Toq (EAD) to Goodall (Nairobi), 6 October 1969, p. 1, in FCO 31/352: Kenya Political and Administrative Affairs (Internal) Political Parties: Kenya People's Union (KPU) 1968–69.

85 'Record of a Meeting between Bruce McKenzie and Mr George Thomas, Minister of State for Commonwealth Affairs, 3 April 1967', p. 1, in DEFE 13/581, Kenya.

86 Hazelwood, Arthur, 'The End of the East African Community: What Are the Lessons for Regional Integration Schemes?', *Journal of Common Market Studies*, Vol. 18 No. 1 (September 1979), p. 42.

87 Maxon. Robert, *East Africa: An Introductory History* (Nairobi, 1986), p. 246.

88 Such as a 1968 railway line in Tanzania, which Kenya backed down from supporting after Power and Communications Minister Nyamweya had already signed the agreement.

89 Njoroge Mungai, as foreign minister, in Republic of Kenya, *National Assembly Official Report* (*NAOR*), 28 March 1972, col. 165.

90 *HoROR*, 16 December 1966, cols 2897–917.

91 'Note for Record' of meeting between McKenzie and Defence Secretary E. G. Norris, 13 April 1967, in DEFE 13/581, Kenya.

92 A. D. Blighty, 'Record of a Private Conversation between the Secretary of State and Mr. Bruce McKenzie, Kenya Minister of Agriculture', 30 August 1968 p. 2, in PREM 13/2743 1965–1969 Kenya; Andrew, Christopher, *The Defence of the Realm: The Authorised History of MI5* (London, 2010), p. 473.

93 Letter from Goodall to Tallboys (EAD), 'Tribalism in the Kenya Army', 4 July 1969 and letter from Edis to P. Seymour (EAD), 12 November 1969 'Tribal Breakdown of the Kenya Armed Forces', in FCO 31/384 – Tribalism. 1969.

94 Parsons, Timothy, *The 1964 Army Mutinies and the Making of Modern East Africa* (Westport, 2003), p. 175.

95 Letter from Edis to Tallboys, 'Tribal Breakdown of Senior Army Posts', 20 June 1969, in FCO 31/384 – Tribalism. 1969.

96 'Bamburi Agreement Message from the Prime Minister to Kenyatta', delivered 25 January 1967, in FCO 31/375 Kenya Defence: Consolidation: Claims; Counter Claims: 'Memorandum of Intention and Understanding'.

97 'British Military Assistance to Kenya in the Event of Somali Aggression', COS 17/68, 16 February 1968, in DEFE 13/581, Kenya.

98 Nellis, John, *Who Pays Tax in Kenya?* Research Report No. 11 (Uppsala, 1972).

99 *East African Standard*, 4 February 1964, n.p.

100 US Embassy spokesman, quoted in National Christian Council of Kenya (NCCK), *Who Controls Industry in Kenya?* (Nairobi, 1968), p. 199.

101 Lacey, Robert, 'Foreign Resources and Development', in Hyden, Goran, Jackson, Robert H. and Okumu, John J. (eds), *Development Administration: The Kenyan Experience* (Nairobi, 1970), p. 65.

102 Republic of Kenya, *Statistical Abstract 1972*, Table 49.

103 See Mboya, Tom, 'A Development Strategy for Africa: Problems and Proposals', reprinted in Mboya, Tom, *The Challenge of Nationhood* (Nairobi, 1970).

104 Swainson, Nicola, *The Development of Corporate Capitalism in Kenya, 1918–1977* (Berkeley, 1980), p. 165.

105 Swainson: *Corporate Capitalism*, pp. 276–8.

106 Leys, Colin, *Underdevelopment in Kenya: The Political Economy of Neo-Colonialism 1964–71* (London, 1975), pp. 119–22.

107 NCCK: *Who Controls Industry*, pp. 167–70.

108 Leys: *Underdevelopment*, p. 136.

109 Herman, Barry, 'A Case of Multinational Oligopoly in Poor Countries: Oil Refinery Investment in East Africa', in Kaplinsky, Raphael (ed.), *Readings on the Multinational Corporation in Kenya* (Nairobi, 1978).

110 NCCK: *Who Controls Industry*, p. 89.

111 Ogonda, R. T., 'Post-Independence Trends in Development of Transport and Communications', in Ochieng, William R. and Maxon Robert M. (eds), *An Economic History of Kenya* (Nairobi, 1992), p. 314.

112 Marris, Peter and Somerset, Anthony, *African Businessmen: A Study of Entrepreneurship and Development in Kenya* (Nairobi, 1971), pp. 69–72.

113 Marris and Somerset: *African Businessmen*, pp. 55–76.

114 These included Magadi Soda, East African Portland Cement, the Inchcape Group, Mitchell Cotts, Shell/BP, BAT, Metal Box, Gailey and Roberts, East African Industries, East African Breweries, Consolidated Holdings, East African Oxygen and Marshalls East Africa.

115 NCCK: *Who Controls Industry*, pp. 144–6.

116 See Hyden, Goran, 'Basic Civil Service Characteristics', in Hyden, Goran, Jackson, Robert H. and Okumu, John J. (eds), *Development Administration: The Kenyan Experience* (Nairobi, 1970).

117 NCCK: *Who Controls Industry*, p. 134.

118 Collier, Paul and Lal, Deepak, *Labour and Poverty in Kenya, 1900–1980* (Oxford, 1986), p. 66; Kitching, Gavin, *Class and Economic Change in Kenya: The Making of an African Petite Bourgeoisie 1905–1970* (London, 1980), pp. 388–97.

119 Republic of Kenya, *Ministry of Labour Annual Report* (Nairobi, 1969).

120 Amsden, Alice, *International Firms and Labour in Kenya, 1945–70* (London, 1971), pp. 113–18; Sandbrook: *Proletarians*, p. 136.

121 Sandbrook: *Proletarians*, p. 52, notes that strong men ran their unions 'regardless of the niceties of these constitutions'.

122 *East African Standard*, 7 October 1969, p. 1.

123 The colonial government had banned the killing of large animals by Africans except for reasons of self-defence, and this policy continued, despite the frequent deaths and damage to crops caused by animals in nearby communities. The tension between protecting wildlife (generally supported by central government and foreign donors) and helping local development (the goal of local politicians even at the expense of wildlife) was to continue for decades.

124 See for example Heyer, Judith, 'Agricultural Development Policy in Kenya', and Cowen, Michael, 'Commodity Production in Kenya's Central Province', in Heyer, Judith, Roberts, Pepe and Williams, Gavin, *Rural Development in Tropical Africa* (Basingstoke, 1981).

125 Republic of Kenya, *Development Plan, 1970–74* (Nairobi, 1969), p. 24.

126 Maxon, Robert, 'Small-Scale and Large-Scale Agriculture since Independence', in Ochieng and Maxon: *An Economic History of Kenya*, p. 276.

127 Kenya Human Rights Commission, *Ours By Right, Theirs by Might: A Study on Land Clashes* (Nairobi, 1996), p. 19.

128 Wasserman, Gary, *Politics of Decolonization: Kenya Europeans and the Land Issue, 1960–65* (Cambridge, 1976), p. 173.

129 Widner, Jennifer A., *The Rise of a Party-State in Kenya: From Harambee! to Nyayo!* (Berkeley, 1992), p. 81, quoting the unpublished thesis of Apollo Njonjo.

130 Republic of Kenya, *1962 Census Advance Report of Vols 1 & 2* (Nairobi, 1964) and Republic of Kenya, *Kenya Population Census 1979, Volume 1* (Nairobi, 1981).

131 Collier and Lal: *Labour and Poverty*, p. 75.

132 Clayton, Eric S., 'A Comparative Study of Settlement Schemes in Kenya', *Cooperative Paper No. 3* (Agrarian Development Unit, December 1978).

133 Kitching: *Class and Economic Change*, pp. 364–72.

134 Kenya: *Statistical Abstract 1972*, Table 92; *Statistical Abstract 1976*, Table 93.

135 See Campbell, David J., 'Land as Ours, Land as Mine', in Spear, Thomas and Waller, Richard (eds), *Being Maasai: Ethnicity and Identity in East Africa* (London, 1993), pp. 258–72.

136 Rothchild, Donald, *Racial Bargaining in Independent Kenya: A Study of Minorities and Decolonisation* (London, 1973), pp. 192–203.

137 'Kenya@40', *Daily Nation*, 1 May 2004, online edition.

138 Rothchild: *Racial Bargaining*, p. 362.

139 Leys: *Underdevelopment*, pp. 152–6.

140 Rothchild: *Racial Bargaining*, p. 50.

141 JIC (A) (70) 17 (Final) copy No. 4 , 'The Outlook for British Interests in Kenya up to 1975', 27th May 1970, p. 1, Joint Intelligence Committee (A), Edward Peck, Chairman, JIC, in PREM 15/509: 1971 Kenya.

142 Ominde S. H. (ed.), *Population and Development in Kenya* (Nairobi, 1984), pp. 41–53.

143 Ominde: *Population*, pp. 71–3.

144 Obudho R. A. and Obudho, Rose A., 'The Post-Colonial Urbanisation Process' in Ochieng and Maxon: *An Economic History of Kenya*, p. 429.

145 Leys, Colin, 'Politics in Kenya: The Development of Peasant Society', *British Journal of Political Science*, Vol. 1, No. 3 (1971), p. 315.

146 Dutto, Carl A., *Nyeri Townsmen* (Nairobi, 1975), pp. 176–83.

147 Kenya: *Statistical Abstract 1972*, Table 188.

148 Sindiga, Isaac, 'Health and Disease' in Ochieng, William R. (Ed), *Themes in Kenyan History* (Nairobi, 1990), pp. 140–1.

149 Kenya: *Statistical Abstract 1972*, Table 225.

150 By 1971, 42% of primary and 30% of secondary school pupils were girls. Kenya: *Statistical Abstract 1972*, Tables 177 and 178.

151 Wipper, Audrey, 'Equal Rights for Women in Kenya?', *Journal of Modern African Studies*, Vol. 9, No. 3 (1971).

152 Mwendwa, in *HoROR*, 9 March 1966, col. 1886.

153 Dutto: *Nyeri Townsmen*, pp. 115–25.

154 Thus, those from Nyeri were often Catholic, many Kiambu Kikuyu were Anglican members of the Church of the Province of Kenya (CPK), and the Bukusu were mostly Quakers.

155 Sabar, Galia, *Church, State and Society in Kenya: From Mediation to Opposition, 1963–1993* (London, 2002), pp. 70–4.

156 Oded, Arye, *Islam and Politics in Kenya* (Boulder, 2000), Chapter 1.

157 Before independence, there were limits on the number of Muslims permitted to go to Makerere, development in the nominally autonomous strip was limited and there were legal and cultural restrictions on Muslims. Educationally, they fell far behind the Christian communities.

158 JIC (A) (70) 17 (Final) copy No. 4, 'The Outlook for British Interests in Kenya up to 1975', 27 May 1970, p. 15, Joint Intelligence Committee (A), Edward Peck, Chairman, JIC, in PREM 15/509: 1971 Kenya.

159 *Daily Nation*, 14 August 2003, online edition.

160 See Gertzel: *Politics of Independent Kenya*, pp. 154–5; Ghai and McAuslan: *Public Law*, pp. 221–7.

161 Murray, J., 'Succession Prospects in Kenya', *Africa Report*, Vol. 13, No. 8 (November 1968).

162 Ghai and McAuslan: *Public Law*, p. 230; Gertzel: *Politics of Independent Kenya*, pp. 160–1.

163 Miller, Norman, 'Assassination and Political Unity: Kenya –Implications of the Assassination of Tom Mboya', *East Africa Series*, Vol. VIII, No. 5 (Kenya) (September 1969), p. 6.

164 'Kenya: First Impressions' from Norris to Rt Hon. Michael Stewart Sec of State for Foreign and Commonwealth Affairs, 2 May 1969, p. 3, in FCO 3/350 Kenya: Political and Administrative Affairs: (Internal Political Situation), 1968–69.

165 *Africa Confidential*, No. 4 (1968).

166 *The Times*, special report, 12 December 1969, p. 1.

167 Letter from Norris to E. G. le Toq, 'Kenya: Talks with the Americans', 3 February 1969, p. 2, in FCO 31/350 Kenya: Political and Administrative Affairs (Internal Political Situation), 1968–69.

168 Letter from Edis to Tallboys, 'Kenya Internal Politics', 6 November 1968, p. 2, in FCO 31/350 Kenya: Political and Administrative Affairs (Internal Political Situation), 1968–69.

169 A. D. Blighty, 'Record of a private conversation between the secretary of state and Mr. Bruce McKenzie, Kenya Minister of Agriculture', 30 August 1968, p. 2, in PREM 13 /2743 1965–1969 Kenya.

170 Letter from Edis to Tallboys, 25 November 1968, p. 2 in FCO 31/350 Kenya: Political and Administrative Affairs (Internal Political Situation), 1968–69.

171 Letter from Goodall to Tallboys, 'Kenya Internal Politics', 16 December 1968 p. 1, in FCO 31/350 Kenya: Political and Administrative Affairs (Internal Political Situation) 1968–69.

172 McKenzie, quoted in letter from Goodall to le Toq, 24 March 1969, in FCO 31/350 Kenya: Political and Administrative Affairs (Internal Political Situation) 1968–69.

173 Siaya and Kisumu districts had been carved out of the old Central Nyanza in 1968, one of only two changes in district boundaries until the 1990s.

174 See Okumu, John J., 'The By-Election in Gem: An Assessment', *East African Journal*, Vol. VI, No. 6 (June 1969).

175 Miller: 'Assassination', p. 1; Ogot, Bethwell, *My Footprints on the Sands of Time: An Autobiography* (Kisumu, 2003), pp. 228–32.

176 Letter from Norris (BHC) to St John Johnston (FCO), 16 July 1969, p. 2, in FCO 31/356 Kenya: Political and Administrative Affairs (Internal) Mr Tom Mboya 1968–69.

177 Cipher from Norris to FCO, 'Mboya's Death', 12 July 1969, in FCO 31/356 Kenya: Political and Administrative Affairs (Internal) Mr Tom Mboya 1968–69.

178 *Daily Nation*, 23 June 2000, p. 9.

179 *East African Standard*, 13 August 1969, n.p.

180 Telex from Norris to FCO, 19 November 1969, in FCO 31/356 Kenya: Political and Administrative Affairs (Internal) Mr Tom Mboya 1968–69.

181 Letter from R. M. Purcell to Goodall, 'Mboya Case', 5 September 1969, in FCO 31/356 Kenya: Political and Administrative Affairs (Internal) Mr Tom Mboya 1968–69.

182 Mboya, in Goldsworthy: *Tom Mboya*, p. 275.

183 Letter from Norris to St John Johnston (FCO), 16 July 1969, in FCO 31/356 Kenya: Political and Administrative Affairs (Internal) Mr Tom Mboya 1968–69.

184 Letter from Goodall to Purcell, 'Mboya Assassination', 27 August 1969, in FCO 31/356 Kenya: Political and Administrative Affairs (Internal) Mr Tom Mboya 1968–69.

185 Cipher No. 367 from Sir T. Bromley to FCO, 21 July 1969 and letter from Norris to St John Johnston, FCO, 16 July 1969, in FCO 31/ 356 Kenya: Political and Administrative Affairs (Internal) Mr Tom Mboya 1968–69.

186 *The People*, 5 July 1999, p. 14.

187 Telex from Norris to FCO, 19 November 1969, pp. 1–2, in FCO 31/356 Kenya: Political and Administrative Affairs (Internal) Mr Tom Mboya 1968–69.

188 Goldsworthy: *Tom Mboya*, pp. ix–xii.

189 Letter from Edis to Mr Steele, Mr Mountain, House of Commons, 'Report of Meeting with Achieng-Oneko', 22 August 1969, p. 2, in FCO 31/352 Kenya Political and Administrative Affairs (Internal) Political Parties: Kenya People's Union (KPU) 1968–69.

190 Kershaw, Greet, *Mau Mau from Below* (Oxford, 1997), pp. 223–36.

191 Murray-Brown: *Kenyatta*, pp. 317–19.

192 Njenga Karume describes the oathing in detail in Karume, Njenga, *Beyond Expectations* (Nairobi, 2009), pp. 205–7.

193 Taita Towett, *Kenya Weekly News*, 15 August 1969, p. 15.

194 Okelo-Odongo, *East African Standard*, 12 August 1969, p. 1.

195 *Daily Nation*, 22 September 1969, p. 20.

196 Letter from T. J. Bellers to Purcell, 29 September 1970, p. 1, in FCO 31/597 Political Developments in Kenya 1970 Part 'B'.

197 *Daily Nation*, 20 September 1969, p. 1.

198 *Daily Nation*, 29 September 1969, p. 24; Nyamora, Pius, 'The Role of Alternative Press in Mobilization for Political Change in Kenya 1982–1992: Society Magazine as a Case Study', M.A. thesis, University of Florida, 2007, pp. 68–9.

199 Kiano, in *Daily Nation*, 29 September 1969, p. 24.

200 Oruka, H. Odera, *Oginga Odinga: His Philosophy and Beliefs* (Nairobi, 1992), p. 60.

201 Hornsby: 'The Member of Parliament', p. 82.

202 Letter from J. S. Arthur to EAD, 2 December 1968 and letter from Arthur to EAD, 3 February 1969, in FCO 31/348 Political Parties: Kenya African National Union 1968–69. Also, letter from F. W. Hall to Tallboys, 3 April 1969, in FCO 31/350 Kenya: Political and Administrative Affairs: Internal Political Situation 1968–69.

203 *Africa and the World*, November 1969, p. 7.

204 *Daily Nation*, 24 June 2000, p. 9. Also, see Tetley, Brian, *Mo: The Story of Mohammad Amin* (London, 1988), pp. 102–4.

205 Reports of the number killed differ. Luo talked of up to 100 killed. Tetley reports 15. Tetley: *Mo*, p. 104.

206 Njiinu, in *Sunday Nation*, 2 March 2003.

207 Transcript of VOK, evening of 27 October, reported in *East African Standard*, 28 October 1969.

208 Moi in the National Assembly, *East African Standard*, 29 October 1969, p. 1.

209 *East African Standard*, 31 October 1969, p. 1.

210 Copy of a call for a protest march for Sunday 2 November 1969, Hyde Park Corner, in FCO 31/352 Kenya Political and Administrative Affairs (Internal) Political Parties: Kenya People's Union (KPU) 1968–69.

211 *Africa and the World*, November 1969, p. 7.

212 The best study of the 1969 election is Hyden, Goran and Leys, Colin, 'Elections and Politics in Single Party Systems: the Case of Kenya and Tanzania', *British Journal of Political Science*, Vol. 2, No. 4 (1972).

213 Save for retiring civil servants and a few ex-KPU members specifically exempted by Kenyatta.

214 The ECK had been established in 1963, and consisted of 10 commissioners, now appointed by the president. However, its only function by this time was to revise electoral boundaries.

215 For example, Peter Kinyanjui resigned as KNTC chairman to stand in Starehe, and was appointed chairman of the East African Harbours Corporation after he lost.

216 Some of the principles behind this were described in Barkan, Joel D. and Okumu, John J., 'Semi-Competitive Elections, Clientelism and Politics Recruitment in a No-Party State: The Kenyan Experience', in Hermet, Guy, Rose, Richard and Rouquié (eds), *Elections without Choice* (London, 1978).

217 Hyden and Leys: 'Elections and Politics', p. 401.

218 M. J. Seroney, in *NAOR*, 2 April 1974, cols 562 and 564.

219 J. M. Kariuki, in *NAOR*, 2 April 1974, col. 578.
220 Letter from Edis to BHC Nairobi, 10 December 1969, p. 1, in FCO 31/355 Political (Internal) Kenya General Elections December 1969.

Chapter 5: 'Golden Years', 1970–1974

1 Note from Purcell (EAD), 'The Elections and the New Administration', 3 February 1970, p. 1, in FCO 31/595 Elections and New Administration in Kenya, 1970.
2 Kariuki, in *Daily Nation*, 11 December 1969, p. 1.
3 See for example Barkan, Joel D. and Okumu, John J., 'Semi-Competitive Elections, Clientelism and Politics Recruitment in a No-Party State: The Kenyan Experience', in Hermet, Guy, Rose, Richard and Rouquié (eds), *Elections without Choice* (London, 1978).
4 Despite the assertiveness of the Assembly there was often no parliamentary quorum, as most MPs felt that (unless a major event was expected), time in the House was time wasted that could be spent making money or building popular support.
5 Martin Shikuku, in Republic of Kenya, *National Assembly Official Report* (*NAOR*), 4 March 1971, col. 387.
6 *Standard*, 22 January 2005, online edition.
7 *Daily Nation*, 25 September 1972, quoted in Widner, Jennifer A., *The Rise of a Party-State in Kenya* (Berkeley, 1992) p.90.
8 For a list of investments see the *East African Standard*, 11 April 2004, online edition, and FCO 31/1192 Reports on Leading Personalities in Kenya, 1972.
9 Letter from Edis to Steele, Betters and Arthur, 'J. M. Kariuki', 15 September 1970, in FCO 31/597 Political Developments in Kenya Part 'B', 1970.
10 Kariuki, in *East African Standard*, 26 October 1970, p. 5.
11 Letter from Edis to Purcell, 'Kenya Internal: Kenya Parliamentary Group', 3 November 1970, p. 2 in FCO 31/597 Political developments in Kenya Part 'B', 1970.
12 Kariuki, quoted in letter from Edward Clay to A. Joy (EAD), 'National Assembly', 13 October 1971 in FCO 31/853 Affairs of the National Assembly in Kenya, 1971. Also see letter from Edis to Steele, Betters and Arthur, 'J. M. Kariuki', 15 September 1970, in FCO 31/597 Political developments in Kenya Part 'B, 1970.
13 *NAOR*, 17 April 1973, col. 619; 7 December 1973, col. 1015.
14 *Daily Nation*, 30 March 2000, p. 10.
15 This was extensively documented in the March–April 2000 *Nation* series on McKenzie, 'The Spy in Kenyatta's Cabinet'.
16 *Daily Express*, 26 May 1978.
17 *Sunday Nation*, 7 May 2000, p. 14. Even before the hijack, there was active security cooperation between Kenya and Israel.
18 *Guardian*, 3 April 1970.
19 *East African Standard*, 4 April 1970, p. 1.
20 Letter from P. B. Hall to S. Darling (EAD), 'Luo MPs', 11 January 1974 in FCO 31/1707, Political situation in Kenya, 1974.
21 Kamau Ngotho, *Daily Nation*, 3 April 2000, online edition.
22 British High Commission (BHC), 'An Army Coup in Kenya', March 1971, p. 1 in FCO 31/850, Succession to the Presidency in Kenya, 1971.
23 BHC: 'An Army Coup', p. 2.
24 BHC: 'An Army Coup', pp. 8–9.
25 *Sunday Standard*, 26 March 2000, p. 11. Given that Muga and co were asking for money and military equipment on 6 April, a coup date of 8 April is impossible, which raises questions about the veracity of all the claims made.
26 *Sunday Standard*, 26 March 2000, p. 12.
27 Telex from Norris to FCO, No. 923, 'Political Detainees', 26 March 1971 in FCO 31/856 Political Detentions in Kenya, 1971.
28 Diang'a, James Waore, *Kenya, 1982: The Attempted Coup – The Consequence of a One-Party Dictatorship* (London, 2002), p. 111.

29 *East African Standard*, 24 June 1971.

30 Mutiso, quoted in *Sunday Nation*, 2 April 2000, online edition.

31 Letter from Clay to Joy, 'Sedition Trial', 9 June 1971, in FCO 31/856, Political Detentions in Kenya, 1971.

32 *Sunday Nation*, 26 March 2002, p. 2, and *Sunday Standard*, 26 March 2002, p. 12.

33 MOD, 'Country Assessment Sheet Kenya', January 1974, in DEFE 24/582, Kenya General, 1973–74.

34 'Brief for SoS for Defence BAC167 Strikemaster Aircraft for Kenya. Visit of Dr. Mungai - Kenyan Minister of Defence and Mr. McKenzie – Kenyan Minister of Agriculture', July 1969, in DEFE 13/581, Kenya.

35 'Letter from J. Thomas (Defence Dept) to Mr Duggan', 1 September 1971, in FCO 31/850 Succession to the Presidency in Kenya, 1971.

36 See for example the letter from Harold Wilson to Kenyatta, 5 September 1974, in FCO 31/1725, Bamburi Understanding between Kenya and UK, 1967.

37 In 1971, Kenya bought armoured cars from France and trucks from West Germany, despite Kenyatta's doubts and British complaints.

38 British High Commissioner Norris to the Secretary of State for Foreign and Commonwealth Affairs, 'British Defence Interest in Kenya', 3 January 1969, p. 2, in FCO 31/375 Kenya Defence: Consolidation: Claims; Counter Claims: 'Memorandum of Intention and Understanding'.

39 Senior figures at the next level down (majors or lieutenant-colonels) included two future military commanders: Daudi Tonje, a Tugen who was married to Moi's sister, and Mahamoud Mohamed, the most senior Somali in the military.

40 Colonel R. M. Bebbie (Defence Adviser, Nairobi), 'Annual Report on Kenya', 22 April 1974, in DEFE 11/652, Kenya, 1974.

41 BHC: 'An Army Coup'.

42 Letter from Edis to Purcell, 'The President's Escort and Personal Bodyguard', 17 November 1970, in FCO 31/597, Political Developments in Kenya Part 'B', 1970.

43 *Daily Nation*, 14 August 1968, quoting the Africanisation report of 1968.

44 See for example, Okullu, Henry, *Church and Politics in East Africa* (Nairobi, 1974), p. 35.

45 Swainson, Nicola, *The Development of Corporate Capitalism in Kenya, 1918–1977* (Berkeley, 1980), pp. 192–3; Himbara, David, *Kenyan Capitalists, the State and Development* (Boulder, 1993), pp. 61–4.

46 Mwai Kibaki, quoted in *Daily Express*, 16 April 1970.

47 See for example, letter from Rose to Sir S. Crawford, 'Military Assistance', 2 January 1973, in FCO 46/955, New Money Projects to Provide Military Assistance to Kenya, Thailand and Oman, 1973, and 'Conclusions of a Meeting of the British Cabinet on Thursday 15 March 1973', CM (73) 16th, in CAB 128/51/17.

48 He was later found to have been murdered by one of Amin's senior officers over money.

49 'Report on a Visit to Kenya by Mr D. M. Biggin of IRD (Information Research Department, FO/CO)', 4–11 October 1971, in FCO 31/850 Succession to the Presidency in Kenya, 1971.

50 Letter from High Commissioner Norris to Le Toq, 'Report of Meeting with Vice-President Moi', 25 August 1970, in FCO 31/596, Political Developments in Kenya Part 'A', 1970.

51 Note from G. A. Duggan (EAD) to Counsell and Le Toq, 'Kenya's Comments on Rhodesia', 12 November 1971, p. 1, in FCO 31/857, Foreign Policy of Kenya, 1971.

52 Telex Nairobi to FCO, 'Mungai's Statement Today on Rhodesia', 26 November 1971, in FCO 31/857, Foreign Policy of Kenya, 1971.

53 Winkgates, James, 'US Policy towards East Africa: Crisis Response amid Limited Interests', in Magyar, Karl (ed.), *United States Interests and Policies in Africa: Transition to a New Era* (Basingstoke, 2000), p. 107.

54 Republic of Kenya, *Development Plan, 1970–74* (Nairobi, 1969), p. iii.

55 Githinji, Mwangi wa, *Ten Millionaires and Ten Million Beggars: A Study of Income Distribution and Development in Kenya* (Aldershot, 2000), pp. 16–20.

56 Killick, Tony, 'Kenya 1975–71', in Killick, Tony (ed.), *The IMF and Stabilisation: Developing Country Experiences* (London, 1984), p. 169.

57 Grosh, Barbara, *Public Enterprise in Kenya: What Works, What Doesn't, and Why* (Boulder, 1991), p. 58.
58 Kitching, Gavin, *Class and Economic Change in Kenya: The Making of an African Petite Bourgeoisie 1905–1970* (London, 1980), pp. 416.
59 Republic of Kenya, *Statistical Abstract 1976* (Nairobi), Table 210.
60 Mutiso, Gideon Cyrus, *Kenya: Politics, Policy and Society* (Nairobi, 1975), pp. 132–61.
61 See for example Mutiso: *Kenya*, pp. 113–14.
62 Swainson: *Corporate Capitalism*, p. 190.
63 Langdon, Steven, *Multinational Corporations in the Political Economy of Kenya* (London, 1981), p. 31.
64 Republic of Kenya, *Statistical Abstract 1972*, Table 66 (a); *1976*, Table 59(a); Hazelwood, Arthur, *The Economy of Kenya: The Kenyatta Era* (Oxford, 1979), p. 75.
65 *Daily Nation*, 21 June 1974, p. 15.
66 See Eglin, Richard, 'The Oligopolistic Structure and Competitive Characteristics of Direct Foreign Investment in Kenya's Manufacturing Sector', in Kaplinsky, Raphael (ed.), *Readings on the Multinational Corporation in Kenya* (Nairobi, 1978).
67 Wagacha, Mbui, 'Analysis of Liberalisation of the Trade and Exchange Regimes in Kenya since 1980', in Kimenyi, Mwangi S., Mbaku, Mukum John and Mwaniki, Ngure (eds), *Restarting and Sustaining Economic Growth and Development in Africa: The Case of Kenya* (Aldershot, 2003), pp. 160–1.
68 See Langdon: *Multinational Corporations*, pp. 127–39.
69 Langdon, Stephen, 'Multinational Corporations in the Political Economy of Kenya' in Kaplinksy: *Readings*, pp. 192–4.
70 *NAOR*, 28 March 1972, cols 177–180.
71 Hazelwood: *Economy of Kenya*, pp. 98–9.
72 Collier, Paul and Lal, Deepak, *Labour and Poverty in Kenya, 1900–1980* (Oxford, 1986), p. 94.
73 *East African Standard*, 9 September 1970, p. 1.
74 International Labour Office, *Employment, Incomes and Equality: A Strategy for Increasing Productive Employment in Kenya* (Geneva, 1972).
75 Leys, Colin, *Underdevelopment in Kenya: The Political Economy of Neo-Colonialism 1964–71* (London, 1975), pp. 260–5.
76 Collier and Lal: *Labour and Poverty*, p. 74.
77 *Daily Nation*, 17 August 1974, p. 1.
78 Leys, Colin, 'Politics in Kenya: The Development of Peasant Society', *British Journal of Political Science*, Vol. 1, No. 3 (1971).
79 Leys: *Underdevelopment*, pp. 106–10.
80 While commercial production was based on imported cattle and crossbreeds, most smallholders relied on hardy, disease-resistant, but lower-yielding zebu.
81 See for example Ensminger, Jean, *Making a Market: The Institutional transformation of an African Society* (Cambridge, 1992), pp. 81–8.
82 Moses arap Keino, in *NAOR*, 24 October 1973, col. 1422.
83 Maxon, Robert, 'Small-Scale and Large Scale Agriculture since Independence', in Ochieng, William R. and Maxon, Robert M. (eds), *An Economic History of Kenya* (Nairobi, 1992), p. 282.
84 See Leys: *Underdevelopment*, pp. 93–102.
85 Okullu: *Church and Politics*, p. 28.
86 Collier and Lal: *Labour and Poverty*, pp. 263, 269.
87 Maxon: 'Agriculture', p. 277; Leys: *Underdevelopment*, pp. 79–82.
88 Leo, Christopher, *Land and Class in Kenya* (Toronto, 1984), pp. 182–5.
89 The number of Maasai, Turkana and Samburu pastoralists also grew dramatically, which was less noted.
90 Mutiso: *Kenya*, pp. 113–14.
91 *East African Standard*, 3 October 1970, p. 7.
92 Osman Araru, in *NAOR*, 23 November 1973, col. 535.
93 Moses arap Keino, quoted in *East African Standard*, 26 April 1974, p. 1.

94 See for example letter from T. J. Bellers to Counsell, 'Kenya Internal', 28 April 1971, in FCO 31/854 Political Developments in Kenya, 1971.

95 Letter from Clay to Joy, 'National Assembly', 13 October 1971, in FCO 31/853 Affairs of the National Assembly in Kenya, 1971.

96 During the colonial period, many Kikuyu had settled in Maasai lands, farming or working for Maasai. Thousands were expelled from Ngong and Loitokitok during the emergency back to Central Province.

97 Jackson Angaine, in *NAOR*, 15 September 1971, col. 98.

98 *Daily Nation*, 2 January 1976, p. 1.

99 Maxon, Robert M., *Conflict and Accommodation in Western Kenya: The Gusii and the British, 1907–1963* (Cranbury, 1989), p. 20.

100 *Daily Nation*, Business Daily, 12 and 13 November 2009, online edition.

101 Leonard, David, 'Class Formation and Agricultural Development', in Barkan, Joel D. (ed.), *Politics and Public Policy in Kenya and Tanzania*, second edition (New York, 1984), pp. 145–51.

102 Leonard: 'Class Formation', p. 165.

103 Eliud Mahihu, quoted in *Sunday Nation*, 10 May 1998, online edition.

104 Influential non-Kikuyu permanent secretaries included Titus Mbathi and John Kyalo (Kamba) and Geoffrey Boit and John Koitie (Kalenjin).

105 Nellis, John, *The Ethnic Composition of Leading Kenyan Government Positions*, Research Report No. 24 (Uppsala, 1974), Table III reinterpreted.

106 Legum, Colin, *Africa Contemporary Record 1973–74* (New York, 1974), B. 172.

107 Karungaru, B. M., in the Assembly, reported in *East African Standard*, 30 May 1970, p. 3.

108 KANU Briefs, *Kenya Times*, 23 December 1992, p. 16.

109 Atieno Odhiambo, E. S., 'Ethnicity and Democracy in Kenya', lecture, University of Nebraska-Lincoln (Lincoln, Arts & Sciences Publications Department, 25 September 1998), pp. 15–21.

110 Ogot, Bethwell, 'Mau Mau and Nationhood', in Atieno Odhiambo, E. S. and Lonsdale, John (eds), *Mau Mau and Nationhood* (Oxford, 2003), p. 11.

111 *Daily Nation*, 5 July 1974, p. 1.

112 Letter from Clay to Joy (EAD), 'The President's Style of Government', 28 July 1971, in FCO 31/854 Political Developments in Kenya, 1971.

113 *Daily Nation*, 10 July 1974, p. 1.

114 After Kenyatta's death, MPs were allowed to debate in both English and Swahili. Virtually all chose to speak English.

115 Morton, Andrew, *Moi: The Making of an African Statesman* (London, 1998), p. 9.

116 See Bienen, Henry, *Kenya: The Politics of Participation and Control* (Princeton, 1974), pp. 98–119.

117 Bienen: *Politics*, pp. 8–24; Berg-Schlosser, D., 'Modes and Meanings of Political Participation in Kenya', *Comparative Politics*, Vol. 14, No. 4 (July 1982).

118 See for example Bienen: *Politics*, pp. 121–9.

119 The patron–client system was well embedded in pre-colonial African societies. Cattle herders assisted cattle owners, younger family assisted their elders and familial relationships were characterised by the exchange of labour for social and economic goods. A critical element in relations was the creation of a structure of common interest around the achievement of the patron's goals.

120 See recently, Hyden, Goran, *African Politics in Comparative Perspective* (New York, 2006), pp. 72–93.

121 See for example Barkan and Okumu: 'Semi-Competitive Elections'.

122 Barkan, Joel, 'Legislators, Elections and Political Linkage' in Barkan: *Politics and Public Policy*; Hornsby, Charles and Throup, David, 'Elections and Political Change in Kenya', *Journal of Commonwealth and Comparative Politics*, Vol. 30, No. 2 (1992), p. 187.

123 Such as Kariuki Njiiri, the man who resigned for Kenyatta in 1961.

124 See Hornsby, Charles, 'The Member of Parliament in Kenya, 1969–1983', D.Phil. dissertation, St Antony's College Oxford, 1985, pp. 284–8.

125 See for example the D. T. Dobie Mercedes story, reported after Ngei's death in *Daily Nation*, 18 August 2004, online edition.

126 In October 1974, the Housing Finance Company of Kenya (HFCK) won an order to repossess Ngei's land and buildings. In 1975, bailiffs seized his motorboat.

127 Letter from P. H. G. Molloy to Miss Leonore Storar (FCO), 16 October 1974, in FCO 31/1707, Political Situation in Kenya, 1974.

128 Letter from Purcell to Counsell, 'Kenya', 29 May 1970, in FCO 31/596 Political Developments in Kenya Part 'A', 1970.

129 Letter from P. R. A. Mansfield to M. K. Ewans (EAD), 'Corruption', 7 May 1974, in FCO 31/1707 Political Situation in Kenya, 1974.

130 Conversation with ex-Cabinet minister, 11 December 1992.

131 *Daily Nation*, 18 October 1972, p. 40.

132 Legum, Colin, *Africa Contemporary Record 1974–75* (New York, 1975), B. 203.

133 Correspondence with Tom Wolf, 2004.

134 Republic of Kenya, *Report of the Commission of Inquiry (Public Service Structure and Remuneration Commission) 1970–71 (The Ndegwa Report)* (Nairobi, 1971).

135 *Daily Nation*, 5 June 1974, p. 4.

136 Nabwera in the Assembly, *Daily Nation*, 5 June 1974.

137 *Daily Nation*, 6 June 1974, p. 4.

138 Legum, Colin, *Africa Contemporary Record 1972–73* (New York, 1973), p. B152.

139 After his release, he was elected as an MP, corruption being no disqualification for office in the eyes of his constituents.

140 Letter from Bellers to Joy, 'National Assembly', 24 November 1971, in FCO 31/853 Affairs of the National Assembly in Kenya, 1971.

141 Sabar, Galia, *Church, State and Society in Kenya: From Mediation to Opposition, 1963–1993* (London, 2002), pp. 156–9.

142 *Daily Nation*, 23 September 2002, p. 11.

143 Kenyatta, quoted in Legum: *Africa Contemporary Record 1972–73*, B. 146.

144 'Kenya @40: 1972', *Daily Nation*, 28 August 2003, p. 3.

145 Hazelwood: *Economy of Kenya*, pp. 140–1. This did not take into account the resources invested into *harambee* schools.

146 Republic of Kenya, *Economic Survey, 1969*, Table 10. 3. Numbers exceeded 100% due to in-migration of students to study.

147 North-Eastern's primary numbers quadrupled between 1970 and 1980 and the Rift Valley's tripled.

148 Republic of Kenya, *Statistical Abstract, 1982* (Nairobi), Table 192(b).

149 By 1980, more than 90 per cent of Kiambu teachers had formal training, but this was true of only half of Kisii and Kakamega teachers. Martin Shikuku, in *NAOR*, 11 June 1980, col. 1783.

150 Letter from Ministry of Education, *Weekly Review*, 6 March 1978.

151 *NAOR*, 7 December 1973, col. 994.

152 *NAOR*, 7 October 1980, col.1340.

153 On the Harambee Institutes of Technology, see Abreu, Elsa, *The Role of Self-Help in the Development of Education in Kenya, 1900–1973* (Nairobi, 1982), pp. 230–45, and Mbithi, Philip M. and Rasmusson, Rasmus, *Self-Reliance in Kenya: The Case of Harambee* (Uppsala, 1977), pp. 90–6.

154 Ogot, Bethwell, *My Footprints on the Sands of Time: An Autobiography* (Kisumu, 2003), pp. 245–56.

155 *NAOR*, 16 November 1973, col. 187.

156 Bogonko, Sorobea N., *A History of Modern Education in Kenya (1895–1991)* (Nairobi, 1992), pp. 202–3.

157 Their leaders included Luo law student James Orengo, who later became a nationally known figure.

158 Letter from Edis to Purcell, 'One Party System in Kenya', 29 June 1970, in FCO 31/596 Political Developments in Kenya 1970 Part 'A'.

159 On the formation and leadership of GEMA, See Karume, Njenga, *Beyond Expectations* (Nairobi, 2009), pp. 156–81.

160 Elijah Mwangale, in *NAOR*, 7 December 1973, cols 1027–8.
161 Len Allison (BHC), 'Minute for File', 9 August 1972, in FCO 31-1193, Political Parties in Kenya 1972.
162 Note from Purcell, 'Kenya the Internal Political Situation', 4 August 1970, p. 2 in FCO 31/597 Political Developments in Kenya Part 'B', 1970.
163 Osman Araru, quoted in a letter from Bellers to Mr Steele House of Commons, 12 February 1971, p. 1, in FCO 31/854 Political Developments in Kenya, 1971.
164 Fairhall, John, in *Guardian*, 13 February 1971.
165 *East African Standard*, 1 March 1973, p. 1.
166 See for example Robert Matano, in *Weekly Review*, 30 March 1984, p. 11.
167 Hornsby: 'The Member of Parliament', pp. 80–1.
168 *East African Standard*, 16 May 1973, p. 1.
169 Kenyatta, quoted in *Daily Nation*, 1 April 1974, p. 1.
170 Kenyatta, quoted in *Daily Nation*, 1 April 1974, p. 1.
171 Kenyatta, in *Daily Nation*, 3 June 1974, p. 3.
172 Kenyatta in Nakuru, *Daily Nation*, 15 June 1974, p. 1.
173 See *Daily Nation*, 3 April 1974, p. 4 and editorial p. 6, and 4 April 1974, p. 4.
174 Government statement, *Daily Nation*, 15 May 1974, p. 1.
175 J. M. Kariuki, *Daily Nation*, 16 May 1974, p. 3.
176 *Daily Nation*, 22 and 23 August 1974.
177 *Daily Nation*, 29 June 1974, p. 5.
178 *Daily Nation*, 1 October 1974, p. 24.
179 *Daily Nation*, 16 September 1974, p. 1.
180 Eliud Mahihu, in *Daily Nation*, 4 September 1974, p. 1.
181 *East African Standard*, 26 September 1974, p. 1.
182 See for example *Daily Nation*, 4 September 1974. Also, see Loughran, *Birth of a Nation*, p. 114.
183 *Daily Nation*, 6 September 1974, p. 1, and Njoroge Mungai, in *Daily Nation*, 7 September 1974, p. 9.
184 Amongst the Bukusu, for example, Masinde Muliro campaigned jointly with Bungoma leaders Mwangale and Nathan Munoko and his Trans-Nzoia running mate Wafula Wabuge, all Bukusu.
185 Odinga's son Raila was amongst those who campaigned against incumbent Nyanza MPs for having 'sold out' to Kenyatta.
186 *Daily Nation*, 11 October 1974.
187 Hornsby and Throup: 'Elections and Political Change', pp. 178, 185–8.
188 Barkan Joel D., 'Bringing Home the Pork: Legislator Behavior, Rural Development, and Political Change in East Africa', in Smith, Joel and Musolf, Lloyd (eds), *Legislatures in Development* (Durham, 1978); Barkan and Okumu: 'Semi-Competitive Elections'; Barkan: 'Legislators, Elections'.
189 *The Times*, 24 October 1974, p. 18.

Chapter 6: Rigor Mortis, 1975–1978

1 See his autobiography, Karume, Njenga, *Beyond Expectations* (Nairobi, 2009).
2 Oruka, H. Odera, *Oginga Odinga: His Philosophy and Beliefs* (Nairobi, 1992), p. 63.
3 *Sunday Nation*, 27 March 1975, p. 3.
4 J. M. Kariuki, in *Weekly Review*, 3 March 1975, p. 8.
5 Kenyatta, *Daily Nation*, 8 March 1975, p. 1 and 10 March 1975, p. 1.
6 *The Mirror*, 15 December 2001, pp. 1–3.
7 *Daily Nation*, 13 March 1975, p. 1.
8 Moi in the National Assembly, *Daily Nation*, 14 March 1975, p. 1.
9 Geoffrey Kareithi, *Daily Nation*, 12 March 2000, p. 22.
10 *East African Standard*, 8 April 1975, p. 1.
11 Information from a European diplomat who was close to opposition leaders in this period, 1993.

12 _Echo_, September 1991, p. 32.
13 Nathan Munoko, like Muliro a Bukusu, took Kenyatta's shilling and replaced him in the Cabinet.
14 _Daily Nation_, 7 March 2000, p. 2 and 11 February 2002, online edition.
15 _Daily Nation_, 7 March 2000, p. 2. More details were given in the _Nation_ of 11 and 12 February 2002.
16 _Daily Nation_, 5 March 1975, p. 6.
17 _Daily Nation_, 11 February 2002, online edition.
18 _Daily Nation_, 11 March 1975, p. 1 and p. 20.
19 _Daily Nation_, 12 February 2002, online edition.
20 _Sunday Nation_, 23 March 1975, special edition, p. 1.
21 Mbiyu Koinange, in _Weekly Review_, 12 May 1975, p. 15.
22 Kenyatta, in _Africa Confidential_, Vol. 16, No. 12 (20 June 1975), p. 8.
23 Kenyatta, in _East African Standard_, 23 May 1975, p. 1.
24 _East African Standard_, 13 May 1975, p. 1.
25 Ngei, in _Weekly Review_, 24 November 1975, p. 5.
26 _Weekly Review_, 24 November 1975, p. 4.
27 Moi, in the Assembly, _Weekly Review_, 22 December 1975, p. 6.
28 _Weekly Review_, quoting Shikuku and Seroney, 20 October 1975, p. 4.
29 To reduce the inevitable impact, Achieng-Oneko and two other detainees were released at the same time.
30 _Sunday Times_, 19 October 1975.
31 Wamwere, Koigi wa, _Conscience on Trial_ (Trenton, 1988), pp. 1–10; pp. 87–8.
32 See _Africa Confidential_, Vol. 16, No. 21 (24 October 1975), and _Guardian_, 17 October 1975.
33 _East African Standard_, 7 October 1976, p. 1.
34 Ngotho, Kamau and Odindo, Joseph, 'A Spy in the Cabinet', _Echo_, June 1992; _Weekly Review_, 16 May 1977, pp. 3–6.
35 Kariithi, in _Sunday Nation_, 12 March 2000, p. 22.
36 Although it was a constitutional requirement that the Electoral Commission review constituency boundaries every decade, there was no review in 1976. There was no way such a hot potato could be managed without unity at the centre.
37 Killick, Tony, 'Kenya, 1975–81', in Killick, Tony (ed.), _The IMF and Stabilisation: Developing Country Experiences_ (London, 1984), pp. 185–9; Ikiara, G. K. and Killick, T., 'The Performance of the Economy Since Independence', in Killick, Tony (ed.), _Papers on the Kenyan Economy: Performance, Problems and Policies_ (Nairobi, 1981), p. 8.
38 Killick, Tony and Mwega, F. M., 'Monetary Policy in Kenya 1967–88', _ODI Working Paper 39_ (July 1990), p. 48; Bevan, David, Collier, Paul, Gunning, Jan Willem with Bigsten, Arne and Horsnell, Paul, _Controlled Open Economies: A Neoclassical Approach to Structuralism_ (Oxford, 1990), pp. 143–4.
39 Killick: 'Kenya', pp. 173–5.
40 Republic of Kenya, _Statistical Abstract 1972_, Table 195 and _1982_ Table 212(a).
41 Hazelwood, Arthur, _The Economy of Kenya: The Kenyatta Era_ (Oxford, 1979), pp. 17–19.
42 Killick: 'Kenya', p. 177.
43 Killick: 'Kenya', pp. 196–202.
44 O'Brien, F. S. and Ryan, T. C. I., 'Kenya', in Devarajan, S., Dollar, D. and Torgny Holmgren (eds), _Aid and Reform in Africa_ (Washington, 2001), pp. 520–1.
45 Anonymous, _(In)Dependent Kenya_ (London, 1982), p. 81.
46 Harden, Blaine, _Africa: Dispatches from a Fragile Continent_ (London, 1991), pp. 177–82.
47 A key institutional investor was the National Social Security Fund (NSSF), set up in 1965 as a state-run provident fund for formal sector workers.
48 Young, Crawford, 'The End of the Post-Colonial State in Africa? Reflections on Changing African Political Dynamics', _African Affairs_, Vol. 103, No. 410 (2004), p. 33.
49 Grosh, Barbara, _Public Enterprise in Kenya: What Works, What Doesn't, and Why_ (Boulder, 1991), pp. 96–100.
50 Anyang' Nyong'o, Peter, 'The Possibilities and Historical Limitations of Import-Substitution

Industrialization in Kenya', in Coughlin, Peter and Ikiara, Gerrishon K. (eds), *Industrialisation in Kenya: In Search of a Strategy* (Nairobi, 1988), p. 43.

51 Grosh: *Public Enterprise*, pp. 105–17.

52 Republic of Kenya, *Review of Statutory Boards (the Ndegwa Report)* (Nairobi, 1979), p. 3.

53 Anonymous: *(In)Dependent Kenya*, pp. 101–2.

54 Gachuki, David and Coughlin, Peter, 'Structure and Safeguards for Negotiations with Foreign Investors', in Coughlin, Peter and Ikiara, Gerrishon K. (eds), *Industrialisation in Kenya: In Search of a Strategy* (Nairobi, 1988), pp. 95–103; Anonymous: (*In*) *Dependent Kenya*, pp. 104–6.

55 Langdon, Steven, *Multinational Corporations in the Political Economy of Kenya* (London, 1981), pp. 9–10.

56 See Langdon: *Multinational Corporations*, pp. 186–93.

57 Eliud Mwamunga, quoted in Langdon: *Multinational Corporations*, p. 199.

58 Letter from C. M. leQuesne to S. Y. Dawbarn, 'LonRho', 5 December 1972, in FCO 31-1201 Political Relations Between United Kingdom, and Kenya, 1972.

59 Grosh: *Public Enterprise*, p. 67.

60 Leys, Colin, *Underdevelopment in Kenya: The Political Economy of Neo-Colonialism 1964–71* (London, 1975), pp. 16–25.

61 Leys: *Underdevelopment*. For critiques, see Berman, Bruce, 'Up from Structuralism' in Berman, Bruce and Lonsdale, John, *Unhappy Valley, Book One: State and Class* (London, 1992); Leo, Christopher, *Land and Class in Kenya* (Toronto, 1984), pp. 12–23. See also Hazelwood: *Economy of Kenya*, pp. 81–5.

62 Himbara, David, *Kenyan Capitalists, the State and Development* (Boulder, 1993), pp. 18–19.

63 Swainson, Nicola, *The Development of Corporate Capitalism in Kenya, 1918–1977* (Berkeley, 1980), p. 216.

64 Swainson: *Corporate Capitalism*, p. 189.

65 Swainson: *Corporate Capitalism*, pp. 209–11.

66 See Leonard, David K., *African Successes: Four Public Managers of Kenyan Rural Development* (Berkeley, 1991), pp. 137–42.

67 Swainson: *Corporate Capitalism*, p. 283.

68 See Matiba, Kenneth, *Aiming High* (Nairobi, 2000), Chapter 8.

69 See for example Bates, Robert H., *Markets and States in Tropical Africa 2005 Edition* (London, 2005).

70 Leonard: *African Successes*, pp. 210–12.

71 Bates: *Markets and States*, pp. 26–8.

72 Bates, Robert H., *Beyond the Miracle of the Market: The Political Economy of Agrarian Development in Kenya* (Cambridge, 1989), pp. 106–9.

73 Charles Njonjo, in *Daily Nation*, 26 May 1979, p. 1.

74 See for example Mulaa, John, 'The Politics of a Changing Society: Mumias', *Review of African Political Economy*, Vol. 20 (January–April 1981).

75 *Africa Confidential*, Vol. 19, No. 4 (17 February 1978), p. 2.

76 Members of land-buying companies usually came from a single ethnic group.

77 House of Commons, *Hansard*, Vol. 960, 15 January 1979, col. 575.

78 Department of Settlement records, quoted in Oucho, John O., *Undercurrents of Ethnic Conflict in Kenya* (Leiden, 2002), pp. 155–6.

79 Maxon, Robert, 'Small-Scale and Large Scale Agriculture since Independence', in Ochieng, William R. and Maxon, Robert M. (eds), *An Economic History of Kenya* (Nairobi, 1992), p. 279.

80 Republic of Kenya, *Statistical Abstract, 1972*, Table 92; *1982*, Table 82.

81 Republic of Kenya, *Statistical Abstract, 1976*, Table 5.

82 Haugerud, Angelique, *The Culture of Politics in Modern Kenya* (Cambridge, 1995), pp. 173–6.

83 Haugerud: *Culture of Politics*, p. 188.

84 Grosh: *Public Enterprise*, pp. 82–3.

85 Grosh: *Public Enterprise*, p. 88.

86 Grosh: *Public Enterprise*, p. 100.

87 Hazelwood: *Economy of Kenya*, p. 157.
88 Chege, Michael, 'The Political Economy of Agrarian Change in Central Kenya' in Schatzberg, Michael G. (ed.), *The Political Economy of Kenya* (New York, 1987), pp. 106–9.
89 Hazelwood: *Economy of Kenya*, p. 39.
90 Cowen, Michael, 'Commodity Production in Kenya's Central Province' in Heyer, Judith, Roberts, Pepe and Williams, Gavin (eds), *Rural Development in Tropical Africa* (Basingstoke, 1981).
91 Maxon: 'Agriculture', p. 291.
92 Kitching, Gavin, *Class and Economic Change in Kenya: The Making of an African Petite Bourgeoisie 1905–1970* (London, 1980), pp. 420–30.
93 Carlsen, John, *Economic and Social Transformation in Rural Kenya* (Uppsala, 1980), pp. 76–90, 220–5.
94 Cowen, Michael and MacWilliam, Scott, *Indigenous Capital in Kenya: The 'Indian' Dimension of Debate* (Helsinki, 1996), pp. 160–1.
95 On poverty in 1970s Kenya, see Killick: *Papers on the Kenyan Economy*.
96 Carlsen: *Transformation*, pp. 52–60.
97 Martin Shikuku, in Republic of Kenya, *National Assembly Official Report* (*NAOR*), 11 October 1973, col. 1016.
98 Ogingo Migure, in *NAOR*, 3 May 1973, col. 1039.
99 Wafula Wabuge, in 'Kenya@40: 1979', *Daily Nation*, 18 September 2003, p. 9.
100 Okullu, Henry, *Church and Politics in East Africa* (Nairobi, 1974), p. 13.
101 Okullu: *Church and Politics*, p. 9.
102 Sabar, Galia, *Church, State and Society in Kenya: From Mediation to Opposition, 1963–1993* (London, 2002), pp. 165–6.
103 *Weekly Review*, 18 July 1977, p. 3.
104 O'Brien, Donal B. Cruise, 'Coping with the Christians: The Muslim Predicament in Kenya', in Hansen, Holger Bernt and Twaddle, Michael (eds), *Religion and Politics in East Africa* (London, 1995), p. 201.
105 Oded, Arye, *Islam and Politics in Kenya* (Boulder, 2000), p. 23.
106 *Guardian*, 29 October 1977.
107 *Africa Confidential*, Vol. 16, No. 13 (1975), pp. 6–7 See also Ochieng', Philip, *I Accuse The Press* (Nairobi, 1992).
108 Loughran, Gerald, *Portrait of a Nation* (London, 2010), pp. 1–11.
109 Oucho, John O., *Urban Migrants and Rural Development in Kenya* (Nairobi, 1996), pp. 126–40.
110 Moi in the National Assembly, *Weekly Review*, 16 May 1977, p. 7.
111 See for example the surveys in Berg-Schlosser, Dirk, 'Ethnicity, Social Classes and Political Process in Kenya', in Oyugi, Walter O. (ed.), *Politics and Administration in East Africa* (Nairobi, 1994), pp. 251–4.
112 For a recent study of Luo perceptions of alienation and disadvantage, see Morrison, Lesa, 'The Nature of Decline: Distinguishing Myth from Reality in the Case of the Luo of Kenya', *Journal of Modern African Studies*, Vol. 45, No. 1 (2007).
113 *Sunday Times*, 24 August 1975.
114 Mounter, Julian, 'The Biggest Game in Kenya', *The Listener*, 9 June 1977.
115 Jones, Brenda, in *Guardian*, 11 October 1976, p. 4.
116 *Sunday Times*, 24 August 1975.
117 Marnham, Patrick, 'Repression in Kenya', *Spectator*, 21 January 1978.
118 Njehu Gatabaki, in *Weekly Review*, 14 April 1975, p. 9.
119 In 1975, for example, the East African Legislative Assembly discovered Ksh140 million in a secret account in the East African Harbours Corporation.
120 *Sunday Times*, 10 August 1975, p. 12.
121 *Weekly Review*, 8 March 1985, pp. 9–15.
122 All from the *Sunday Times*, 17 August 1975, pp. 5–6.
123 *East African Standard*, 3 May–25 June 1975.
124 *Weekly Review*, 26 April 1976, p. 6.

125 Kenya had a pink-coated hunt in Limuru until 1977.
126 See *Standard*, 8 January 2005, online edition.
127 Staudt describes this situation amongst the Idakho Luhya of Western Province in Staudt, Kathleen A., 'Sex, Ethnic and Class Consciousness in Western Kenya', *Comparative Politics*, Vol. 14, No. 2 (January 1982).
128 *Weekly Review*, 30 January 1978.
129 *Weekly Review*, 11 and 18 August 1978.
130 Thomas, Gordon, *Gideon's Spies: The Secret History of the Mossad* (London, 1999), pp. 149–51.
131 Pincher, Chapman, *Inside Story* (London, 1978), pp. 354–6.
132 *Sunday Nation*, 7 May 2000, p. 14.
133 Telegram 166469, Department of State to the Embassy in Kenya, 4 July 1976, 0034Z, and Telegram 173878, Department of State to the Embassy in Kenya, 14 July 14 1976, 0105Z, in *Foreign Relations of the United States, 1969–1976*, Vol. E-6, Documents on Africa, 1973–1976 (Washington, U.S. Department of State, 2006).
134 Pincher: *Inside Story*, pp. 355–6.
135 *Weekly Review*, 3 August 1984, pp. 5–6.
136 *The Times*, 5 June 1978.
137 Hazelwood, Arthur, 'The End of the East African Community: What Are the lessons for Regional Integration Schemes?', *Journal of Common Market Studies*, Vol. 18, No. 1 (September 1979), p. 40.
138 Hazelwood: 'End of the East African Community', p. 49.
139 Hazelwood: 'End of the East African Community', p. 54.
140 *Daily Nation*, 1 April 2000, p. 8.
141 Republic of Kenya, *Statistical Abstract, 1982*, Table 53 (year-end exchange rates used).
142 *Daily Nation*, 1 April 2000, p. 8.
143 Interview with Abdullahi Yusuf, *Daily Nation*, 30 July 2003, online edition.
144 Bienen, Henry, *Armies and Parties in Africa* (New York, 1978), pp. 12–13.
145 Major-Gen. Mans and Air Commodore Howlett, 'Draft Report on the Kenyan Armed Forces', DMAO/89/3, in DEFE 11/652, Kenya, 1974.
146 Karimi, Joseph and Ochieng, Philip, *The Kenyatta Succession* (Nairobi, 1980), pp. 127–61.
147 See for example Martin, Paul, 'Kenya's Uncertain Future', *Spectator*, 18 March 1978.
148 Odinga too suggested Kenyatta 'did not take him seriously', Oruka: *Odinga*, p. 124.
149 *Echo*, September 1991, pp. 27–33.
150 Kareithi, *Echo*, September 1991, p. 29.
151 Karimi and Ochieng: *The Kenyatta Succession*, pp. 147–8.
152 *Africa Confidential*, Vol. 16, No. 21 (24 October 1975).
153 On the Change the Constitution movement, see Karimi and Ochieng: *The Kenyatta Succession*, pp. 20–38.
154 Widner reports several meetings between Odinga and family members in the period, in Widner, Jennifer A., *The Rise of a Party-State in Kenya: From Harambee! to Nyayo!* (Berkeley, 1992), p. 114.
155 Ngei, *Weekly Review*, 4 October 1976, p. 3.
156 *Daily Nation*, 12 October 2002, online edition.
157 Njonjo, *Daily Nation*, 7 October 1976, p. 1.
158 *East African Standard*, 9 October 1976, p. 1; *Daily Nation*, editorial 7 October 1976, p. 6.
159 *East African Standard* and *Daily Nation*, 9 October 1976, both p. 1.
160 *East African Standard*, 9 October 1976, p. 1.
161 *Daily Nation*, 11 October 1976, p. 1, 16.
162 Karimi and Ochieng: *The Kenyatta Succession*, pp. 27–35.
163 Karimi and Ochieng: *The Kenyatta Succession*, pp. 22–4.
164 See *Weekly Review*, 11 April 1977, pp. 4–8 and *Africa Confidential*, Vol. 19, No. 4 (17 February 1978).
165 *Sunday Nation*, 12 March 2000, p. 23.
166 Eliud Mahihu, in 'Kenya @ 40: 1978', *Daily Nation*, 18 September 2003, p. 5.
167 Karimi and Ochieng: *The Kenyatta Succession*, p. 170; *Standard*, 27 October 1978, p. 1.

168 *Daily Nation*, 16 August 2004, online edition.
169 Republic of Kenya, *Constitution of Kenya, Revised Edition (1992)* (Nairobi, 1992), 6 (3).
170 *Africa Confidential*, Vol. 21 (20 October 1978), pp. 6–7; Karimi and Ochieng: *The Kenyatta Succession*, p. 5.
171 *Echo*, September 1991, p. 33.
172 *Daily Nation*, 30 April 2000, online edition; Mwangi, Paul, *The Black Bar* (Nairobi, 2001), p. 71.

Chapter 7: Too Many Cooks, 1978–1983

1 *Weekly Review*, 15 September 1978, pp. 2–6; 6 October 1978, pp. 9–13; and 13 October 1978, pp. 10–17.
2 Kariuki, Godfrey Gitahi, *The Illusion of Power* (Nairobi, 2001), pp. 74–5.
3 Robert Matano, in *Standard*, 23 October 1978, p. 1.
4 *Weekly Review*, 29 December 1978, p. 8.
5 *Weekly Review*, 15 December 1978, pp. 3–4.
6 *Weekly Review*, 10 November 1978, pp. 6–7. Republic of Kenya, *National Assembly Official Report (NAOR)*, 1 July 1993 col. 1331.
7 Karimi, Joseph and Ochieng, Philip, *The Kenyatta Succession* (Nairobi, 1980).
8 *Sunday Nation*, 18 November 1979, p. 4.
9 *Daily Nation*, 19 July 2001, online edition.
10 Keegan, John, *World Armies*, second edition (London, 1983), pp. 336–7.
11 Prinslow, Karl E., 'Building Military Relations in Africa', *Military Review*, Foreign Military Studies Office (May–June 1997).
12 *Weekly Review*, 1 December 1978, p. 8.
13 *Daily Nation*, 'Kenya's Rich List', 24 November 2003, online edition.
14 *Weekly Review*, 27 January 1984 p. 9; *Daily Nation*, 24 November 2003, online edition.
15 There were rumours that a new left-wing opposition party might be formed, but they came to nothing. See Kiereini, Jeremiah in *Sunday Nation*, 18 November 1979, p. 1.
16 Cross S., 'L'Etat C'est Moi: Political Transition and the Kenya General Elections of 1979', *University of East Anglia Discussion Paper No. 66* (Norwich, n.d).
17 Njonjo in the National Assembly, *Daily Nation*, 10 May 1979, p. 1, 4.
18 Moi, in *Weekly Review*, 17 August 1979, p. 15.
19 Studies of contests in the 1979 election include Mulaa, John, 'The Politics of a Changing Society: Mumias', *Review of African Political Economy*, Vol. 20 (January–April 1981); Wanjohi, Nick Gatheru, 'The Politics of Ideology and Personality Rivalry in Murang'a District, Kenya: A Study of Electoral Competition', *Working Paper No. 411* (Nairobi, September 1984); Chege, Michael, 'A Tale of Two Slums: Electoral Politics in Mathare and Dagoretti', *Review of African Political Economy*, Vol. 20 (January–April 1981); Alila, Patrick O., 'Luo Ethnic Factor in the 1979 and 1983 Elections in Bondo and Gem', *Working Paper No. 408* (Nairobi, June 1985) and Kareithi, Peter, *Weekly Review Guide to Politics in Kiambu* (Nairobi, 1979).
20 *Daily Nation*, 1 November 1979, p. 4.
21 Ochieng', Philip, *I Accuse the Press* (Nairobi, 1992), p. 168. Polls made it harder to manipulate the results.
22 Hornsby, Charles, 'The Member of Parliament in Kenya, 1969–1983', D.Phil. dissertation, St Antony's College, Oxford, 1985, pp. 190–2.
23 Interview with Koigi wa Wamwere, 1985. See also *Standard*, 8 November 1979, p. 1.
24 George Mwicigi, in *Daily Nation*, 6 August 2000, online edition.
25 The account's purpose was confirmed in Morton, Andrew, *Moi: The Making of an African Statesman* (London, 1998), p. 142.
26 His closest friend dead and his power base lost, Koinange retired from politics and died two years later.
27 Wandibba, Simiyu, *Masinde Muliro: A Biography* (Nairobi, 1996), pp. 30–1.
28 See Wandibba: *Muliro*, pp. 29–31; *Sunday Nation*, 11 November 1979, p. 30; *Daily Nation*, 12 November 1979, p. 5 and 13 November 1979, p. 1. Supervisor of Elections Montgomery resigned in 1980.

29 Weekly Review, *1979 Election Handbook* (Nairobi, 1979), p. 45; Seroney, in *Daily Nation*, 17 November 1979, p. 4.
30 See Barkan, Joel D., 'Bringing Home the Pork: Legislator Behavior, Rural Development, and Political Change in East Africa', in Smith, Joel and Musolf, Lloyd (eds), *Legislatures in Development* (Durham, 1978), pp. 265–88; Hornsby: 'The Member of Parliament', pp. 165–211.
31 Hornsby: 'The Member of Parliament', pp. 173–4.
32 See Hornsby: 'The Member of Parliament', pp. 94–131, for irregularities in the 1969–83 polls.
33 *Standard*, 28 November 1979, p. 1.
34 Bates, Robert H., *Beyond the Miracle of the Market: The Political Economy of Agrarian Development in Kenya* (Cambridge, 1989), pp. 109–11.
35 Bates, Robert, 'The Politics of Food Crises', in Schatzberg, Michael G. (ed.), *The Political Economy of Kenya* (New York, 1987), pp. 86–9.
36 *Daily Nation*, 19 July 2001, online edition.
37 Kibaki, in Parliament, *Weekly Review*, 24 October 1980, p. 9.
38 Sabar, Galia, *Church, State and Society in Kenya: From Mediation to Opposition, 1963–1993* (London, 2002), pp. 178–88.
39 *Daily Nation*, 3 November 2002, online edition.
40 Ogot, Bethwell A., 'The Construction of a National Culture', in Ogot, Bethwell and Ochieng, William (eds), *Decolonisation and Independence in Kenya, 1940–93* (Nairobi, 1995), p. 220.
41 Ogot: 'Construction of a National Culture', p. 230.
42 Matiba, Kenneth, *Aiming High* (Nairobi, 2000), p. 194.
43 Samuel arap Ng'eny, in *NAOR*, 23 June 1982, col. 395.
44 Hornsby: 'The Member of Parliament', p. 247.
45 *Weekly Review*, 17 August 1979, p. 9. See also Hornsby: 'The Member of Parliament', pp. 175–9.
46 See Hornsby: 'The Member of Parliament', pp. 288–290.
47 *Weekly Review*, 25 September 1981, p. 7.
48 Kibaki, at Special Delegates' Conference, *Standard*, 27 March 1980, p. 1.
49 *Echo*, September 1991, p. 30.
50 *Africa Confidential*, No. 12 (4 June 1980); *Weekly Review*, 11 July 1980 pp. 7–9 and 24 October 1980, pp. 7–9.
51 Moi, in *Weekly Review*, 25 July 1980, n.p.
52 *Weekly Review*, 14 November 1980, p. 9.
53 Fred Omido, in the National Assembly, *Daily Nation*, 11 July 1990, p. 4.
54 See for example *Standard*, 10 October 2004, online edition.
55 *Daily Nation*, 26 September 2002, online edition.
56 *Weekly Review*, 3 October 1980, pp. 3–11.
57 Interview with David Anderson, 6 November 1985; *Daily Nation*, 19 July 2001, online edition..
58 See *Weekly Review*, 27 March – 27 May 1981.
59 *Weekly Review*, 20 July 1984, pp. 4–9.
60 *Weekly Review*, 24 April 1981, p. 7.
61 *Africa Now*, June 1982, p. 21; Loughran, *Birth of a Nation* (London, 2010), pp. 152-3.
62 Diang'a, James Waore, *Kenya, 1982: The Attempted Coup – The Consequence of a One-Party Dictatorship* (London, 2002), pp. 148–85.
63 Although radicals campaigned for an alternative candidate, the seat was won by a pro-government figure, with several ballot boxes found with their seals broken.
64 Morton: *Moi*, p. 141.
65 *Africa Now*, June 1982, p. 21.
66 Ochieng: *I Accuse*, pp. 63–9.
67 *Sunday Nation*, 1 November 1981, p. 10.
68 *Daily Nation*, 2 November 1981, p. 4.
69 Moi, in *Daily Nation*, 31 October 1981, p. 1.

70 Moi, in *Standard*, 19 February 1982, p. 1 and 27 February 1982, p. 1.
71 Republic of Kenya, *Statistical Abstract 1972 (Nairobi)*, Tables 48(a) 193(b); *Statistical Abstract 1982*, Table 38(a); *Statistical Abstract 1984*, Table 190 (b).
72 Bevan, David, Collier, Paul, Gunning, Jan Willem with Bigsten, Arne and Horsnell, Paul, *Controlled Open Economies: A Neoclassical Approach to Structuralism* (Oxford, 1990), pp. 143–257, discusses the implications of the coffee boom for Kenya.
73 Republic of Kenya, *Report of the Civil Service Review Committee, 1979–80 (The Waruhiu Report)* (Nairobi, 1980), pp. 36, 39, 105.
74 *East African Standard*, 3 September 2002, online edition.
75 Philip Ndegwa came from Kirinyaga, and was unrelated to Duncan Ndegwa.
76 Republic of Kenya, *Review of Statutory Boards (Ndegwa Report)* (Nairobi, May 1979), May 1979.
77 Kenya: *Review of Statutory Boards*, p. 18.
78 Republic of Kenya, *Statistical Abstract 1979*, Table 222; *Statistical Abstract 1982*, Tables 38(a) and 208; *Statistical Abstract 1988*, Table 38(a).
79 Killick, Tony, 'Kenya, 1975–81', in Killick, Tony (ed.), *The IMF and Stabilisation: Developing Country Experiences* (London, 1984), pp. 202–5.
80 Boughton, James M., *Silent Revolution, the International Monetary Fund, 1979–1989* (Washington, 2001), p. 595.
81 On Kenya's first experience with structural adjustment in 1980–2, see Hecox, Walter, 'Structural Adjustment, Donor Conditionality and Industrialization in Kenya', in Coughlin, Peter and Ikiara, Gerrishon K. (eds), *Industrialisation in Kenya: In Search of a Strategy* (Nairobi, 1988), pp. 200–11.
82 Killick: 'Kenya', pp. 206–10.
83 Republic of Kenya, *Development Plan, 1984–88* (Nairobi, 1984), p. 107.
84 Grosh, Barbara, *Public Enterprise in Kenya: What Works, What Doesn't, and Why* (Boulder, 1991), pp. 146–8.
85 Grosh: *Public Enterprise*, pp. 134–40.
86 Kenya Power and Lighting Company, *Annual Report* (Nairobi, 1983).
87 Ikiara, Gerrishon, 'Government Institutions and Kenya's Industrialisation', in Coughlin and Ikiara: *Industrialisation in Kenya*, pp. 229–30.
88 *Daily Nation*, 20 August 2004, online edition; Juma, Calestous, 'Investment Strategy and Technology Policy', in Coughlin, Peter and Ikiara, Gerrishon K. (eds), *Kenya's Industrialization Dilemma* (Nairobi, 1991), pp. 26–56.
89 Ikiara, Gerishon and Killick, Tony, 'The Performance of the Economy since Independence', in Killick, Tony (Ed) *Papers on the Kenyan Economy: Performance, Problems and Policies* (Nairobi, 1981), pp. 13–15.
90 Maxon, Robert and Ndege, Peter, 'The Economics of Structural Adjustment', in Ogot and Ochieng: *Decolonisation and Independence in Kenya*, p. 159.
91 Bates: *Beyond the Miracle*, pp. 85–9.
92 Ikiara, Gerrishon, Jama Mohamud and Amadi, Justus O., 'The Cereals Chain in Kenya: Actors, Reforms and Politics', in Gibbon, Peter (ed.), *Markets, Civil Society and Democracy in Kenya* (Uppsala, 1995), p. 32.
93 Food and Agriculture Organisation, *FAOSTAT Production Data* (2004); Faostat.fao.org.
94 Maxon, Robert, 'Small-Scale and Large Scale Agriculture since Independence', in Ochieng, William R. and Maxon, Robert M. (eds), *An Economic History of Kenya* (Nairobi, 1992), pp. 289–90.
95 *NAOR*, 25 September 1980, col. 1113. A sixth factory, the private West Kenya Sugar Company in Kakamega, was established in 1981.
96 Kenya: *Statistical Abstract 1988*, Table 80.
97 *Standard*, 26 February 2006, online edition.
98 See for example on settlement schemes in Kilifi during 1979–84, Kanyinga, Karuti, *Re-Distribution from Above: The Politics of Land Rights and Squatting in Coastal Kenya*, Research Report No.115 (Uppsala, 2000), pp. 72–9.
99 *Daily Nation*, 24 December 1981, n.p.

100 Homewood, Katherine, Coast, Ernestina and Thompson, Michael, 'In-Migrants and Exclusion in East African Rangelands: Access, Tenure and Conflict', *Africa*, Vol. 74, No. 4 (2004), p. 596.

101 Haugerud, Angelique, *The Culture of Politics in Modern Kenya* (Cambridge, 1995), pp. 151–4, Orvis, Stephen Walter, *The Agrarian Question in Kenya* (Gainesville, 1993), pp. 94–101.

102 Collier, Paul and Lal, Deepak, *Labour and Poverty in Kenya, 1900–1980* (Oxford, 1986), p. 124

103 Collier and Lal: *Labour and Poverty*, pp. 129–37.

104 Harden, Blaine, *Africa: Dispatches from a Fragile Continent* (London, 1991), pp. 198–203.

105 Ndege G. O., 'History of Pastoralism', in Ochieng and Maxon: *An Economic History of Kenya*, p. 107.

106 Hogg, Richard, 'Re-Stocking Pastoralists in Kenya: A Strategy for Relief and Rehabilitation', *Overseas Development Institute Paper 19c* (February 1985).

107 Campbell, David J., 'Land as Ours, Land as Mine', in Spear, Thomas and Waller, Richard (eds), *Being Maasai: Ethnicity and Identity in East Africa* (London, 1993), pp. 266–9.

108 Africa Watch, *Kenya: Taking Liberties* (New York, 1991), pp. 272–3.

109 Prebendalism is the state in which the revenues of an office are appropriated or exploited by its officeholder (and this is seen by some as legitimate or at least unavoidable and accepted). Its use in explaining African politics is usually credited to Richard Joseph on the basis of his work on Nigeria.

110 Njonjo, speaking to the BBC, *Weekly Review*, 22 December 1978, p. 9.

111 Para 268, report of Civil Service Review Committee No. 10, quoted by Shikuku, in *NAOR*, 8 April 1981, col. 923.

112 *Weekly Review*, 29 October 1982, p. 18.

113 Barkan Joel D. and Holmquist, Frank, 'Peasant–State Relations and the Social Base of Self-Help in Kenya', *World Politics*, Vol. 41, No. 3 (April 1989).

114 *Weekly Review*, 30 March 1984, p. 6.

115 *Africa Now*, April 1982, p. 289.

116 Leonard, David K., *African Successes: Four Public Managers of Kenyan Rural Development* (Berkeley, 1991), pp. 250–1.

117 See for example on Turkana, Harden: *Africa: Dispatches*, pp. 197–8.

118 *Standard*, 8 January 2005, online edition.

119 See Rene's accusations in *Weekly Review*, 19 March 1982, pp. 4–6.

120 Moi, in *Standard*, 26 February 1982, p. 2.

121 *Standard*, 10 February 1982, p. 1.

122 Moi, in *NAOR*, 9 March 1982, col. 4.

123 Moi, in *Weekly Review*, 23 April 1982, p. 8.

124 Anonymous, *(In)Dependent Kenya* (London, 1982), pp. 14, 30, 34.

125 Odinga, in *Africa Now*, June 1982, p. 18.

126 Anyona, in *Weekly Review*, 21 May 1982, p. 6.

127 *Weekly Review*, 4 June 1982, pp. 5–6.

128 *Weekly Review*, 20 May 1983, p. 7. Wanyiri Kihoro suggested that it might have been connected with private property deals between Moi and Muriithi that went wrong. Kihoro, Wanyiri, *Never Say Die: The Chronicle of a Political Prisoner* (Nairobi, 1998), p. 93.

129 *Nairobi Law Monthly*, No. 18 (September/October 1989).

130 Badejo, Babafemi A., *Raila Odinga: An Enigma in Kenyan Politics* (Lagos, 2006), pp. 89–91.

131 A small law firm agreed to help several detainees challenge their detention. All of its members – Kiraitu Murungi, Gibson Kamau Kuria and Aaron Ringera – were to rise to prominence.

132 Moi, in *Weekly Review*, 4 June 1982, p. 6.

133 Ogot, B. A., 'The Politics of Populism', in Ogot and Ochieng: *Decolonisation and Independence in Kenya*, p. 199.

134 *Weekly Review*, 22 June 1982, pp. 4–6.

135 Njonjo, in *NAOR*, 9 June 1982, col. 77.

136 Kibaki, in *NAOR*, 9 June 1982, cols 81–2.

137 Widner, Jennifer A., *The Rise of a Party-State in Kenya: From Harambee! to Nyayo!* (Berkeley, 1992), p. 145.
138 Ex-student radical Wanyiri Kihoro was a leading figure in the Committee for the Release of Political Prisoners, formed in July 1982, which campaigned against Moi and Njonjo and for the release of the detainees.
139 Kibaki led the attack. See *NAOR*, 21 July 1982, col. 1325 and Ochieng: *I Accuse*, pp. 57–8.
140 Oloo-Aringo, in *NAOR*, 29 July 1982, cols 1721–2.
141 PRC Broadcast, quoted in Anyang' Nyong'o, Peter, 'Struggles for Political Power and Class Contradictions in Kenya', *Contemporary Marxism*, No. 7 (1983).
142 *East African Standard*, 23 March 2004, online edition.
143 *Weekly Review*, 1 October 1982, pp. 3–4; *Sunday Standard*, 14 March 2004, online edition.
144 *Sunday Standard*, 14 March 2004, online edition.
145 Amnesty International took up their cases as possible prisoners of conscience.
146 *Sunday Standard*, 14 March 2004 and *East African Standard*, 15, 17, 19 and 20 March 2004, online editions; Badejo: *Raila Odinga*, pp. 95–9, 106–8.
147 William Omamo, in Morton: *Moi*, p. 137.
148 See Anonymous, 'Kenya: The Politics of Repression', *Race and Class*, Vol. XXIV (Winter 1983), pp. 237–8; Thiong'o, Ngugi wa, *Barrel of a Pen: Resistance to Repression in Neo-Colonial Kenya* (London, 1983), p. ix.
149 Diang'a: *Kenya, 1982*.
150 *East African Standard*, 17 March 2004, online edition.
151 *Africa Now*, September 1982, p. 14.
152 See for example *East African Standard*, 16 March 2004, online edition.
153 Mulinge, in *Daily Nation*, 1 August 2002, p. 25.
154 Mwangi, Paul, *The Black Bar* (Nairobi, 2001), pp. 137–8.
155 *East African Standard*, 20 March 2004, online edition.
156 Interview with Colin Legum, 3 May 1985.
157 Gethi denied everything. Republic of Kenya, *Report of Judicial Commission Appointed to Inquire into Allegations Involving Charles Mugane Njonjo* (Nairobi, 1984), pp. 28–31.
158 Informal interview with managing director of Securicor, 2004.
159 Anonymous: 'Kenya: The Politics of Repression', p. 236.
160 *Daily Nation*, 30 July 2006, online edition.
161 *Daily Nation*, 1 August 2002, online edition.
162 *Sunday Nation*, 2 March 2003, online edition.
163 *Africa Confidential*, Vol. 26, No. 1 (2 January 1985), p. 7.
164 Throup, David, 'The Construction and Deconstruction of the Kenyatta State', in Schatzberg, Michael G. (ed.), *The Political Economy of Kenya* (New York, 1987).
165 Morton: *Moi*, p. 138.
166 *Weekly Review*, 8 October 1982, p. 8.
167 *Weekly Review*, 20 December 1982, p. 22.
168 He was replaced in January 1983 by Matthew Muli, from an influential Machakos family.
169 Moi's Jamhuri Day speech, in *Weekly Review*, 17 December 1982, p. 7.
170 Republic of Kenya, *Report and Recommendations of the Working Party on Government Expenditures* (Nairobi, 1982), p. 40.
171 For a critique of Kenya's parastatal performance, see Aseto, Oyugi and Okelo, Jasper, *Privatisation in Kenya* (Nairobi, 1997), pp. 98–119.
172 Kenya: *Working Party*, p. 43.
173 Leonard: *African Successes*, pp. 215–16.
174 Kenya: *Statistical Abstract 1982*, Table 208; *Statistical Abstract 1988*, Table 191.
175 Zeleza, Tiyambe, 'The Labour System in Independent Kenya', in Ochieng and Maxon: *An Economic History of Kenya*, p. 349.
176 Njiinu, in *Weekly Review*, 3 May 1985, p. 12.
177 Kibaki would declare this to be the government's goal once again in 2003.
178 Bogonko, Sorobea N., *A History of Modern Education in Kenya (1895–1991)* (Nairobi, 1992), pp. 116–17, 196.

179 *Weekly Review*, 16 November 1984, pp. 11–12.
180 Karume, Njenga, *Beyond Expectations* (Nairobi, 2009), p. 246.
181 Shikuku, in *Weekly Review*, 22 April 1983, pp. 4–5.
182 *Weekly Review*, 6 May 1983, pp. 4–5.
183 *Standard*, 9 May 1983, pp. 1–2.
184 *Standard*, 20 June 2004, online edition.
185 Njonjo press statement, 16 May 1983, in *Weekly Review*, 20 May 1983, p. 6.
186 *Standard*, 20 June 2004, online edition.
187 Moi, in *Weekly Review*, 20 May 1983, p. 5.
188 Rev Timothy Njoya, in the *Sunday Standard*, 18 June 2000, pp. 12–13.
189 *Weekly Review*, 17 June 1983.
190 Transcripts of National Assembly debates, in *Weekly Review*, 8 July 1983, pp. 8–28.
191 *Weekly Review*, 17 June 1983, p. 21.
192 They included Tabitha Seii, trying to stand against Biwott, who had her language proficiency certificate declared invalid.
193 Hornsby: 'The Member of Parliament', p. 99.
194 See Hornsby: 'The Member of Parliament', p. 69 and subsequent calculations.
195 David Musila, in *Daily Nation*, 11 July 2003, pp. 31–2.
196 *Weekly Review*, 23 September 1983, pp. 3–9; 30 September 1983, pp. 3–9; 28 October 1983, pp. 3–6.
197 Kariuki: *Illusion of Freedom*, p. 97.
198 Okwanyo lost by 800 votes with an exceptionally high 1,430 spoilt votes (6.4 per cent of the total).
199 Alila, Patrick O., 'Kenya's Parliamentary Elections: Ethnic Politics in Two Rural Constituencies in Nyanza', *IDS Discussion Paper No. 282* (Nairobi, July 1986), p. 32.
200 Throup, David, 'Render unto Caesar', in Hansen, Holger Bernt and Twaddle, Michael (eds), *Religion and Politics in East Africa* (London, 1995), p. 149.
201 See Wandibba: *Muliro*, p. 33, and *Weekly Review*, 16 March 1984, p. 15.
202 Matiba: *Aiming High*, pp. 203–4.
203 Kenya: *Njonjo Commission*, p. 26.
204 *Africa Now*, September 1983, p. 55.
205 *Weekly Review*, 21 September 1984, pp. 3–9.
206 *Weekly Review*, 5–26 October 1984.

Chapter 8: Heavy Footsteps, 1984–1989

1 See Widner, Jennifer A., *The Rise of a Party-State in Kenya: From Harambee! to Nyayo!* (Berkeley, 1992).
2 Hempstone, Smith, *Rogue Ambassador: An African Memoir* (Sewanee, 1997), p. 39.
3 Throup, David W. and Hornsby, Charles, *Multi-Party Politics in Kenya* (Oxford, 1998), p. 38.
4 *Weekly Review*, 7 June 1985, p. 5.
5 Use of the term president for any role except that of Kenya's president had been long banned, but KANU ignored the law.
6 *Weekly Review*, 7 June–5 July 1985; Widner: *Party-State in Kenya*, pp. 150–97.
7 Moi, in *Daily Nation*, 2 December 1986, p. 1.
8 Moi in Kiambu, *Weekly Review*, 21 November 1986, p. 9.
9 *Weekly Review* 29 March 1985, p. 7.
10 *Weekly Review*, 18 September 1987, pp. 4–14.
11 Moi, 13 September 1984, in Africa Watch, *Kenya: Taking Liberties* (New York, 1991), pp. 26–7.
12 Moi, Daniel T. arap, *Kenya African Nationalism: Nyayo Philosophy and Principles* (London, 1986).
13 Mailu, David G., *The Principles of Nyayo Philosophy, Standard 7 and 8* (Nairobi, 1989).
14 *Weekly Review*, 9 October 1988, pp. 29, 51.
15 *Weekly Review*, 22 February–8 March 1985.

16 Widner: *Party-State in Kenya*, pp. 154–8.

17 'Uchaguzi Weekly Briefing', *East African Standard*, 24 November 2002, online edition.

18 *East African Standard*, 16 February 2003, online edition.

19 Kanyinga, Karuti, 'Contestation over Political Space. The State and Demobilisation of Party Politics in Kenya', *CDR Working Paper 98/12* (Copenhagen, November 1998), p. 3.

20 Odinga, in *Guardian*, 2 July 1987; *Beyond*, August 1987, p. 19.

21 Odinga, in *Beyond*, August 1987, p. 19.

22 Odinga, in *Weekly Review*, 14 August 1987, p. 5.

23 *Weekly Review*, 22 November 1991, pp. 7–8.

24 *Weekly Review*, 27 April 1984, p. 11.

25 Mutua, Makau, 'Justice under Siege: The Rule of law and Judicial Subservience in Kenya', *Human Rights Quarterly*, Vol. 23, No. 1 (2001), p. 113.

26 *Daily Nation*, 16 December 1986, p. 1.

27 *Daily Nation*, 1 May 2004, online edition.

28 Manasses Kuria, *Weekly Review*, 29 August 1986, p. 5.

29 *Daily Nation*, 11 December 1986.

30 *Weekly Review*, 5 December 1986, pp. 3–11.

31 Throup, David, 'The Construction and Destruction of the Kenyatta State', in Schatzberg, Michael G. (ed.), *The Political Economy of Kenya* (New York, 1987), pp. 65–7; Mohammed's brother was a minister from 1983 onwards. Lengees's brother was an MP.

32 *Africa Confidential*, Vol. 26, No. 1 (2 January 1985).

33 Some commentaries on this subject are rather more incendiary. See for example George Ayittey, 'The Looting of Africa 3 – Kenya', Jaluo.com, 4 December 2007, www.jaluo.com/wangwach/200704/George_Ayittey041107.html.

34 *Sunday Nation*, 2 March 2003, online edition.

35 See for example *Weekly Review*, 5 February 1988, p. 8, 1 July 1988, pp. 9–10; Africa Watch: *Kenya*, pp. 98–120.

36 Kibwana, Kivutha, *Fundamental Rights and Freedoms in Kenya* (Nairobi, 1990), pp. 84–5.

37 See for example *Daily Nation*, 17 February 2003, online edition.

38 Schlee, Gunther, *Identities on the Move: Clanship and Pastoralism in Northern Kenya* (Nairobi, 1994), p. 52.

39 Africa Watch: *Kenya*, pp. 298–322.

40 He was jailed for 18 months for parliamentary mileage fraud, but eight years later became a government minister.

41 Kang'ethe Mungai, *Sunday Nation*, 12 March 2000, p. 2.

42 Diang'a, James Waore, *Kenya, 1982: The Attempted Coup – The Consequence of a One-Party Dictatorship* (London, 2002), pp. 227–32.

43 See Kihoro, Wanyiri, *Never Say Die: The Chronicle of a Political Prisoner* (Nairobi, 1998), Chapters 3, 4 and 5; Citizens for Justice, *We Lived to Tell: The Nyayo House Story* (Nairobi, 2003).

44 Kinuthia, in *Sunday Nation*, 12 March 2000, p. 20.

45 Kihoro: *Never Say Die*, p. 205.

46 *Weekly Review*, 12 February 1988, pp. 29–30.

47 As well as Raila Odinga himself, these included David Murathe, Wanyiri Kihoro, Mghanga Mwandawiro, Adhu Awiti, Mirugi Kariuki, Mukaru Ng'ang'a and George Katama Mkangi.

48 *Sunday Nation*, 2 March 2003, online edition.

49 Wamwere sought political asylum in Norway, where he continued his campaign against the government. Awiti, director of the World Bank housing programme, was jailed and subsequently escaped into exile. Maina wa Kinyatti, sacked lecturer and Mwakenya activist, fled to Tanzania and then the US.

50 Moi, quoted in *Nairobi Law Monthly*, Nov/Dec 1987, p. 3.

51 Kenya also restored diplomatic relations with Israel in 1988, to muted protest from Kenyan Muslims.

52 Mburu, Nene, 'Delimitation of the Elastic Ilemi Triangle: Pastoral Conflicts and Official Indifference in the Horn of Africa', *African Studies Quarterly*, Vol. 6, No. 4 (2003), http://web.africa.ufl.edu/asq/v7/v7i1a2.htm.

53 Republic of Kenya, *Statistical Abstract 1982*, Table 144; *Statistical Abstract 1995*, Table 124.

54 Killick, Tony and Mwega, F. M., 'Monetary Policy in Kenya 1967–88', *ODI Working Paper 39* (July 1990), pp. 40–4

55 Murunga, Godwin R., 'The State, its Reform and the Question of Legitimacy in Kenya', *Identity, Culture and Politics*, Vol. 5, Nos 1–2 (2004), pp. 197–8.

56 *Weekly Review*, 17 May 1985, p. 27.

57 Republic of Kenya, *Economic Management for Renewed Growth, Sessional Paper No. 1 of 1986* (Nairobi, 1986), Preamble.

58 Boughton, James M., *Silent Revolution: The International Monetary Fund, 1979–1989* (Washington, 2001), p. 33.

59 Maxon, Robert and Ndege, Peter, 'The Economics of Structural Adjustment', in Ogot, Bethwell and Ochieng, William (eds), *Decolonisation and Independence in Kenya, 1940–93* (Nairobi, 1995), p. 179.

60 Adam, Christopher, 'Privatization and Structural Adjustment', in Geest, Willem van der (ed.), *Negotiating Structural Adjustment in Africa* (New York, 1994), pp. 143–6.

61 Aseto, Oyugi and Okelo, Jasper, *Privatisation in Kenya* (Nairobi, 1997), pp. 83–9.

62 Cohen John M. and Wheeler, John R., 'Improving Public Expenditure Planning: Introducing a Public Investment Program in Kenya', *Harvard Institute for International Development, Development Discussion Paper, No. 479* (Harvard, March 1994), p. 7.

63 Boughton: *Silent Revolution*, p. 595.

64 Githinji, Mwangi wa, *Ten Millionaires and Ten Million Beggars: A Study of Income Distribution and Development in Kenya* (Aldershot, 2000), pp. 26–43.

65 Morton, Andrew, *Moi: The Making of an African Statesman* (London, 1998), p. 149.

66 Republic of Kenya, *District Focus for Rural Development (Revised March 1987)* (Nairobi, 1987).

67 See for example Ensminger, Jean, *Making a Market: The Institutional transformation of an African Society* (Cambridge, 1992), pp. 159–61, on the effect of DFRD on the Orma of Tana River.

68 Leonard, David K., *African Successes: Four Public Managers of Kenyan Rural Development* (Berkeley, 1991), pp. 207–8.

69 Kanyinga, Karuti, 'The Changing Development Space', in Gibbon, Peter (ed.), *Markets, Civil Society and Democracy in Kenya* (Uppsala, 1995), pp. 107–9.

70 Wagacha, Mbui, 'Analysis of Liberalisation of the Trade and Exchange Regime in Kenya since 1980', in Kimenyi, Mwangi S., Mbaku, Mukum John and Mwaniki, Ngure (eds), *Restarting and Sustaining Economic Growth and Development in Africa: The Case of Kenya* (Aldershot, 2003), pp. 156–84.

71 Coughlin, Peter, 'Gradual Maturation of an Import Substitution Industry', in Coughlin, Peter and Ikiara, Gerrishon K. (eds), *Kenya's Industrialization Dilemma* (Nairobi, 1991), pp. 127–52.

72 See for example Nzomo, M., 'External Influence on the Political Economy of Kenya: The Case of MNCs', in Oyugi, Walter O. (ed.), *Politics and Administration in East Africa* (Nairobi, 1994).

73 *New African*, August 1989, p. 29.

74 Morton: *Moi*, p. 147.

75 Widner: *Party-State in Kenya*, p. 183.

76 *Daily Nation*, 18 May 2000, p. 23.

77 'Financial Review Supplement', *Weekly Review*, 15 March 1985, p. 6.

78 Grosh, Barbara, *Public Enterprise in Kenya: What Works, What Doesn't, and Why* (Boulder, 1991), p. 74.

79 *Society*, 9 March 1992, p. 48.

80 Cohen, John M., 'Ethnicity, Foreign Aid and Economic Growth in Sub-Saharan Africa: The Case of Kenya', *Harvard Institution for International Development, Paper No. 520* (1995), p. 27.

81 *Weekly Review*, 26 April 1985, p. 15.

82 Chambers, Robert H., 'Creating and Expanding Organizations for Rural Development', in Cliffe, L., Coleman J. S., and Doornbos, M.R. (eds), *Government and Rural Development in East Africa* (The Hague, 1977), pp. 135–6.

83 Zeleza, Tiyamba, 'The Labour System in Independent Kenya', in Ochieng, William R. and Maxon, Robert M. (eds), *An Economic History of Kenya* (Nairobi, 1992), p. 356.
84 Zeleza: 'The Labour System', pp. 354–6.
85 Republic of Kenya, *Economic Management for Renewed Growth, Sessional Paper No.1 of 1986* (Nairobi, 1986).
86 King, Kenneth, *Jua Kali in Kenya: Change and Development in an Informal Economy 1970–95* (London, 1996), pp. 14–18, 189.
87 Kitching, Gavin, *Class and Economic Change in Kenya: The Making of an African Petite Bourgeoisie 1905–1970* (London, 1980), p. 406.
88 Maxon, Robert, 'Small-Scale and Large Scale Agriculture since Independence', in Ochieng and Maxon: *An Economic History of Kenya*, p. 279.
89 See for example Githinji, Mwangi wa and Cullenberg, Stephen E., 'Deconstructing the Peasantry: Class and Development in Rural Kenya', *Critical Sociology*, Vol. 29, No. 67 (2003).
90 Republic of Kenya, *Development Plan, 1974–78* (Nairobi, 1974), p. 234.
91 Gibbon, Peter, 'Markets, Civil Society and Democracy in Kenya', in Gibbon: *Markets*, p. 13.
92 *Weekly Review*, 3 May 1985, p. 3.
93 Lofchie, Michael, 'The Politics of Agricultural Policy', in Barkan, Joel D. (ed.), *Beyond Capitalism vs. Socialism in Kenya and Tanzania* (Boulder, 1994), pp. 158–64.
94 *Weekly Review*, 1 August 1986, pp. 8–9.
95 *Weekly Review*, 4 September 1987, p. 21.
96 *Sunday Times*, 24 November 1991.
97 Grosh: *Public Enterprise*, pp. 49–50.
98 Republic of Kenya, *Kenya Gazette*, 9 June 1989, G.N.2806.
99 Ikiara, G., Jama, M. and Amadi, J. O., 'The Cereals Chain in Kenya', in Gibbon: *Markets, Civil Society and Democracy*, pp. 33, 63.
100 Himbara, David, *Kenyan Capitalists, the State and Development* (Boulder, 1993), p. xii.
101 In 1985, farmers had repaid only two-thirds of the credit granted to them between 1980 and 1984.
102 Broch-Due, Vigdis, 'Remembered Cattle, Forgotten People', in Anderson, David and Broch-Due, Vigdis (eds), *The Poor are Not Us: Poverty and Pastoralism in Eastern Africa* (Oxford, 1999), pp. 85–6.
103 See for example Ensminger: *Making a Market*, pp. 28, 78–108, 172–6.
104 Anderson, David, 'Rehabilitation, Resettlement and Restocking', in Anderson and Broch-Due: *The Poor are Not Us*.
105 Muliro, *Weekly Review*, 10 July 1987, p. 12.
106 See also Bayart, Jean-Francois, *The State in Africa: The Politics of the Belly* (London, 1993), p. 238.
107 In 1973, there were 24 ADC farms in Trans-Nzoia; by 1989, there were nine.
108 See for example *Weekly Review*, 24 May 1991, pp. 6–10.
109 See for example *Weekly Review*, 4 May 1984, pp. 11–13.
110 See *Society*, 11 May 1992, p. 34 for an example from 1990.
111 See for example *Daily Nation*, 9 February 2004, online edition.
112 A British firm was the design consultant, supported by the British Export Credits Guarantee Department.
113 Biwott successfully sued *The People* newspaper for libel in connection with such allegations in 2002.
114 Achim Kratz, in Ozanne, Julian, 'Mr Biwott the Businessman: A Look at the Former Kenyan Minister's Road to Riches', *Financial Times*, 27 November 1991.
115 See for example Pottinger, Lori, 'Major Dam Companies Caught in African Bribery Scandal', *World Rivers Review*, Vol. 14, No. 5 (Berkeley, International River Network, October 1999).
116 *Finance*, 31 July 1992, p. 11.
117 In November 1991, Kikuyu MP Njenga Mungai tried to table in Parliament a list of 220 parastatal positions held by 'one ethnic community' (i.e. the Kalenjin).
118 Rowland, *Weekly Review*, 15 November 1991, p. 28.

119 Somaia was also associated with the British Conservative Party and made large donations to them. He did business with Mark Thatcher, and British minister Cecil Parkinson became chairman of his Dolphin Group.

120 The apparent undercapitalisation of some Asian banks may be attributed to this off-book funding.

121 Mukonoweshuro, Eliphas, 'Authoritarian Reaction to Economic Crises in Kenya', *Race and Class*, Vol. 31, No. 4 (April–June 1990), pp. 53–4.

122 'Africa', Globenet Enda Preceup (Urban Popular Environment Economy Programme) website, September 1999, www.globenet.org/preceup/pages/fr/chapitre/etatlieu/approchr/d/a_e.htm.

123 *Daily Nation*, 23 April 2003, online edition.

124 KANU, *Kenya Pays Tribute to President Moi* (Nairobi, 1986), p. 31.

125 Republic of Kenya, *Kenya Population Census 1989, Volume I* (Nairobi, 1994), Table 5.

126 Bedi, Arjun S., Kimalu, Paul, Manda, Damiano and Nafula, Nancy, 'The Decline in Primary School Enrolment in Kenya', *KIPPRA Discussion Paper No. 14* (May 2002), pp. 7–9, 25–6.

127 Keen, in *Weekly Review*, 10 November 1989, p. 7.

128 Moi, in *Weekly Review*, 17 September 1984, p. 10.

129 See Ndegwa, Stephen N., 'Civil Society and Political Change in Africa: The Case of Non-Governmental Organizations in Kenya', *International Journal of Comparative Sociology*, Vol. 41, No. 4 (1994).

130 *Weekly Review*, 4 November 1988, p. 30.

131 For example, the *Independent*, 11 October 1988, p. 11.

132 World Wildlife Fund (WWF) website, www.panda.org.

133 *Daily Nation*, 1 November 1988, p. 1.

134 Hornsby, Charles and Throup, David, 'Elections and Political Change in Kenya', *Journal of Commonwealth and Comparative Politics*, Vol. 30, No. 2 (1992), pp. 195–6; and Throup, David, 'Elections and Political Legitimacy in Kenya', *Africa*, Vol. 63, No. 3 (1993), pp. 383–7.

135 In Kakamega, a new constituency was created for Bahati Semo, a long-term opponent of Moses Mudavadi. Machakos received three new seats while Kitui received none because of Mulu Mutiso's importance. Nyeri received two new constituencies in order to bolster the anti-Kibaki faction and divert attention from Kibaki's impending demotion.

136 Throup and Hornsby: *Multi-Party Politics*, pp. 250–3.

137 Estimates of 9 million eligible adults were cut to 7.3 million to make the registration percentages look better. However, the 1989 census showed there were indeed at least 9 million eligible adults.

138 *Weekly Review*, 12 February 1988, p. 18.

139 These including factories, flour mills, and joint businesses with the Kalenjin elite such as Kenindia Assurance and Trans-National Bank. See letter to *Society*, 14 December 1992, p. 6.

140 *Weekly Review*, 19 February 1988, pp. 10–11.

141 Morton: *Moi*, p. 156.

142 Moi personally persuaded Saitoti's opponent John Keen to stand down, to allow 'the professor' an elected post; in return for which he nominated Keen to Parliament. Interview with John Keen, 19 July 2004.

143 *Weekly Review*, 11 March 1988, p. 10.

144 In 1988, the Catholics established the Catholic Peace and Justice Commission, a more activist body, mandated to eradicate injustice, which played a major role in monitoring elections in the 1990s.

145 *Weekly Review*, 7 December 1990, p. 15.

146 Throup and Hornsby: *Multi-Party Politics*, pp. 42–5.

147 See Hornsby and Throup: 'Elections and Political Change', Table 7, p. 194.

148 *Beyond*, Election Special, March 1988, pp. 18–19.

149 *Beyond*, March 1988, pp. 16–17; *Weekly Review*, 26 February 1988, pp. 14.

150 Kariuki, Godfrey Gitahi, *The Illusion of Power* (Nairobi, 2001), pp. 116–17; *Beyond*, March 1988, pp. 9–10.

151 These elections were administered by DC Jonah Anguka, who was to appear soon in the Ouko case.
152 *Daily Nation*, 16 August 2004, online edition.
153 *Weekly Review*, 29 April 1988, pp. 17–39.
154 Morton: *Moi*, pp. 157–8.
155 Shikuku's agents were locked out of the polling stations and hundreds of his votes were found hidden after the count.
156 *Weekly Review*, 26 February 1988, p. 15.
157 See for example *Telegraph*, 23 March 1988; *Guardian*, 24 February 1988.
158 *Weekly Review*, 18 March 1988, pp. 16–17.
159 Mutua, Makau, *Kenya's Quest for Democracy: Taming Leviathan* (Boulder, 2008), p. 75.
160 Bishop Okullu, in *Weekly Review*, 29 April 1988, p. 13.
161 Throup, David, 'Render unto Caesar', in Hansen, Holger Bernt and Twaddle, Michael (eds), *Religion and Politics in East Africa* (London, 1995), p. 157.
162 Personal observation, Butere by-election, 31 October 1988.
163 The *Financial Review* was banned in April 1987 and its editor later detained. He and the editor of another publication, the *Nairobi Law Monthly*, were charged with failing to file financial returns.
164 *Nairobi Law Monthly*, No. 18, September/October 1989.
165 Kibaki, in *Weekly Review*, 23 September 1988, p. 4.
166 On Kiharu, see Matiba, Kenneth, *Aiming High* (Nairobi, 2000), pp. 240–1.
167 *Weekly Review*, 30 September 1988, pp. 4–17.
168 *Sunday Standard*, 5 May 2002, online edition.
169 Matiba: *Aiming High*, pp. 242–4.
170 Throup and Hornsby: *Multi-Party Politics*, p. 44.
171 Matiba: *Aiming High*, p. 319.
172 *Daily Nation*, 20 December 1985, p. 1.
173 *Sunday Nation*, 8 February 2004, online edition.
174 *Weekly Review*, 24 March 1989, p. 3.
175 Parliamentary procedure did not provide for a motion of no confidence in an individual minister.
176 *Weekly Review*, 28 April 1989, pp. 3–9; 5 May 1989, pp. 9–16.
177 *Weekly Review*, 5 May 1989, pp. 3–6; *Daily Nation*, 18 February 2002, online edition; *Finance*, 15 March 1992, p. 10.
178 Moi in *Weekly Review*, 12 May 1989, p. 6.
179 Hornsby and Throup: 'Elections and Political Change', pp. 189–90.
180 *Weekly Review*, 24 November 1989, pp. 5–7.
181 The victor was a young Nandi teacher called Kipruto arap Kirwa, who later rose to prominence.
182 See *Daily Nation*, 4–9 December 1989.
183 Press, Robert Maxwell, 'Establishing a Culture of Resistance: The Struggle for Human Rights and Democracy in Authoritarian Kenya 1987–2002', D.Phil. thesis, University of Florida, 2004, pp. 121–2
184 Press: 'Establishing a Culture of Resistance', pp. 130–1.
185 *New African*, August 1989, p. 18.
186 Maathai, Wangari, *Unbowed: One Woman's Story* (London, 2007), pp. 184–98.
187 *The Economist*, 13 January 1990, p. 69.

Chapter 9: A Second Liberation? 1990–1992

1 This chapter draws extensively on Throup, David W. and Hornsby, Charles, *Multi-Party Politics in Kenya* (Oxford, 1998).
2 Bratton, Michael and van de Walle, Nicholas, *Democratic Experiments in Africa: Regime Transitions in Comparative Perspective* (Cambridge, 1997), p. 3.
3 World Bank, *Sub-Saharan Africa: From Crisis to Sustainable Growth* (Washington, 1989), p. 60.

4   Hempstone, Smith, *Rogue Ambassador: An African Memoir* (Sewanee, 1997), pp. 88–91.
5   Committee on International Relations, *Kenya Economic Policy and Trade Practices, Country Report on Economic and Trade Practices, 1993* (Washington, 1994).
6   Hempstone: *Rogue Ambassador*, p. 91.
7   Morton, Andrew, *Moi: The Making of an African Statesman* (London, 1998), p. 166.
8   Saitoti, George, *The Challenges of Economic and Institutional Reforms in Africa* (Aldershot, 2002), p. 60.
9   Grosh, Barbara, *Public Enterprise in Kenya: What Works, What Doesn't, and Why* (Boulder, 1991), p. 154.
10 World Bank, *World Development Report: The Challenge of Development* (New York, 1991), Table 20, Official Development Assistance: Receipts, p. 242; Republic of Kenya, *Statistical Abstract 1995*, Table 118(b); O'Brien, F. S. and Ryan, T. C. I., 'Kenya', in Devarajan, S., Dollar, D. and Holmgren, Torgny (eds), *Aid and Reform in Africa* (Washington, 2001), p. 471.
11 Cohen, John M., 'Ethnicity, Foreign Aid and Economic Growth in Sub-Saharan Africa: The Case of Kenya', *Harvard Institution for International Development, Paper No. 520* (1995), p. 9.
12 African Rights, *Kenya Shadow Justice* (London, 1996), p. 125.
13 *Weekly Review*, 5 January 1990, pp. 5–6; 12 January 1990, pp. 3–9.
14 *Weekly Review*, 4 May 1990, pp. 6–9, 15–17.
15 Moi, quoted in Morton: *Moi*, p. 168.
16 Mwangi, Paul, *The Black Bar* (Nairobi, 2001), pp. 156–65.
17 *Weekly Review*, 23 February 1990, pp. 3–27; 2 March 1990, pp. 4–28; 9 March 1990, pp. 4–10; 16 March 1990, pp. 10–12; 23 March 1990, pp. 4–10.
18 *Weekly Review*, 30 November 1990, pp. 27–8; Cohen, David W. and Atieno Odhiambo, E. S., *The Risks of Knowledge: Investigations into the Death of the Hon Minister John Robert Ouko in Kenya, 1990* (Nairobi, 2004), pp. 120–31; Anguka, Jonah, *Absolute Power: The Ouko Murder Mystery (*London, 1998), pp. 126–31
19 *Weekly Review*, 2 March 1990, pp. 4–28.
20 *Weekly Review*, 9 March 1990, pp. 4–22.
21 Stern, Chester, *Iain West's Casebook* (London, 1997), pp. 97–104.
22 Anguka: *Absolute Power*, p. 48.
23 Troon, in *Sunday Nation*, 12 February 2000, p. 5.
24 *Sunday Times*, 26 April 1992, p. 15; *New African*, June 1992, p. 16.
25 See *Weekly Review*, 16 August 1991, pp. 8–12 and 23 August 1991, pp. 17–29; Anguka: *Absolute Power*, pp. 84–92.
26 *Weekly Review*, 8 November 1991, p. 6.
27 Cohen and Atieno Odhiambo: *The Risks of Knowledge*, pp. 200–2.
28 Barack Mbaja, Ouko's brother, in *Daily Nation*, 27 February 2004, online edition.
29 Troon, in *Weekly Review*, 29 November 1991, p. 7.
30 *Daily Nation*, 10 and 11 August 1991.
31 Cohen and Atieno Odhiambo: *The Risks of Knowledge*, p. 12.
32 Hempstone: *Rogue Ambassador*, p. 71.
33 *Sunday Standard*, 13 February 2002, p. 9.
34 *Sunday Standard*, 13 February 2002, p. 12; Anguka: *Absolute Power*, pp. 219–29.
35 Throup and Hornsby: *Multi-Party Politics*, pp. 60–1.
36 Interview with Paul Muite, Nairobi, November 1993.
37 Kenya's churchmen were far from united, with some calling only for greater democracy within the one-party state. See Sabar, Galia, *Church, State and Society in Kenya: From Mediation to Opposition, 1963–1993* (London, 2002), pp. 215–16.
38 *Daily Nation*, 5 May 1990, p. 1; *Weekly Review*, 6 July 1990, pp. 9–10, 12.
39 *Weekly Review*, 13 July 1990, pp. 16–19.
40 Muite, *Daily Nation*, 8 April 2002, online edition.
41 Haugerud, Angelique, *The Culture of Politics in Modern Kenya* (Cambridge, 1995), pp. 29–30.
42 Kibaki, in *Daily Nation*, 11 July 1990, p. 4.
43 Hempstone: *Rogue Ambassador*, pp. 126–8, 131–4.
44 *Africa Confidential*, Vol. 32, No. 11 (31 May 1991), p. 5.

45 *Weekly Review,* 27 July 1990, pp. 3–8.
46 The Saitoti report was reprinted in *Weekly Review,* 7 December 1990, pp. 37–59.
47 Interview with Oloo-Aringo, *Sunday Standard,* 9 September 2001, pp. 15–17.
48 *Weekly Review,* 17 August 1990, pp. 4–11; 24 August 1990, pp. 4–21.
49 *Daily Nation,* 2 August 2004, online edition. The truck driver was jailed, but murdered in prison before his release.
50 Throup, David, 'Render Unto Caesar', in Hansen, Holger Bernt and Twaddle, Michael (eds), *Religion and Politics in East Africa* (London, 1995), p. 171.
51 *Weekly Review,* 7 December 1990, pp. 4–21.
52 Kamotho, in *Weekly Review,* 1 February 1991, pp. 10–11.
53 *Weekly Review,* 12 October 1990, pp. 4–11
54 Africa Watch, *Kenya: Taking Liberties* (New York, 1991), p. 107.
55 *Daily Nation,* 2 January 1991, p. 36.
56 The NDP was the name chosen by Kaggia, Kubai, Ngei and Karumba during their colonial detention.
57 Odinga, 'NDP Launch', *Finance,* April 1991, p. 39.
58 Murungi, Kiraitu, *In the Mud of Politics* (Nairobi, 2000), p. xi.
59 *Daily Nation,* 10 March 1991, p. 1; *Weekly Review,* 17 May 1991, p. 15.
60 Sabar: *Church, State and Society,* p. 238.
61 *Daily Nation,* 10 June 1991, p. 1.
62 *Daily Nation,* 22 June 1991, p. 1; 23 June 1991, p. 1.
63 Ntimama, in *Daily Nation,* 20 February 1991. Ntimama said later he had been misquoted, and he had demanded they lie low like an 'antelope', but the misquotation stuck.
64 Interview with Paul Muite, Nairobi, November 1993; Badejo, Babafemi A., *Raila Odinga: An Enigma in Kenyan Politics* (Lagos, 2006), p. 158.
65 Interview with Paul Muite, Nairobi, November 1993; *Weekly Review,* 9 August 1991, pp. 20–2.
66 Hempstone: *Rogue Ambassador,* p. 53; p. 290.
67 Morton: *Moi,* p. 164.
68 In July 1991, Africa Watch issued a book-length report – *Kenya: Taking Liberties* – claiming that a systematic and state-sponsored destruction of the rule of law had taken place.
69 Throup and Hornsby: *Multi-Party Politics,* p. 74.
70 Moi in Kisii, *Daily Nation,* 12 August 1991, p. 28.
71 *Daily Nation,* 24 August 1991, p. 1.
72 *Weekly Review,* 30 August 1991, pp. 4–7; 4 October 1991, pp. 4–7.
73 Ndegwa, Stephen N., 'Citizenship and Ethnicity: an Examination of Two Transition Moments in Kenyan Politics', *American Political Science Review,* Vol. 91, No. 3 (September 1997).
74 *Weekly Review,* 4 October 1991, pp. 10–11; 18 October 1991, pp. 10–13.
75 Moi, in Morton: *Moi,* p. 173.
76 *Weekly Review,* 22 November 1991, pp. 13–15.
77 *Daily Nation,* 19 November 1991, p. 1.
78 In the same reshuffle, Kenya acquired a new civil service head, Philip Mbithi, a Kamba academic and ex-vice-chancellor of Nairobi University.
79 *Weekly Review,* 15 November 1991, pp. 4–10.
80 See for example *Daily Nation,* 14 November 1991, pp. 17–18.
81 Troon, in *Daily Nation,* 16 November 1991, p. 1; 19 November 1991, p. 1.
82 The day before, in a curious coincidence, Mohammed Aslam, who had recently been named by Troon, died in hospital. Rumours circulated that he had been murdered.
83 *Daily Nation,* 26 November 1991, pp. 1, 28; Anguka: *Absolute Power,* pp. 112–17.
84 *Daily Nation,* 27 November 1991, p. 2.
85 *Daily Nation,* 19 October 1991, p. 1.
86 *Daily Nation,* 22 November 1991, p. 32.
87 *Observer,* 27 October 1991, p. 23; Rowland, in *Weekly Review,* 15 November 1991, pp. 28–32.
88 *Weekly Review,* 25 October 1991, p. 10.

89 *Weekly Review*, 6 December 1991, pp. 25–6; Aseto, Oyugi and Okelo, Jasper, *Privatisation in Kenya* (Nairobi, 1997), pp. 44–7.
90 World Bank, 'Press Release: Meeting of the Consultative Group for Kenya' (Paris, 26 November 1991).
91 *The Times*, 27 November 1991.
92 *Weekly Review*, 29 November 1991, p. 28.
93 *Daily Nation*, 3 December 1991, p. 1.
94 *Weekly Review*, 6 December 1991, pp. 7–9.
95 At the same time, the Assembly repealed the North-Eastern Province and Contiguous District Regulations, which had restricted freedom of movement in these areas since 1966, although most other restrictions remained in force.
96 Moi, in *Daily Nation*, 7 December 1991, p. 1.
97 Moi, in BBC Interview, Kenya Television Network (KTN), 16 January, *Summary of World Broadcasts*, 18 January 1992.
98 See for example *Society*, 3 January 1993, p. 23.
99 Furious at being taken by surprise, Moi immediately fired Special Branch head James Kanyotu.
100 Their election symbol was the lantern, Njenga Karume's election symbol since 1979.
101 *Weekly Review*, 13 December 1991, pp. 3–8.
102 Republic of Kenya, *Report of the Parliamentary Select Committee to investigate Ethnic Clashes in Western and Other Parts of Kenya (Kiliku Report)* (Nairobi, 1992), pp. 14–15.
103 Human Rights Watch/Africa Watch, *Divide and Rule: State Sponsored Ethnic Violence in Kenya* (New York, 1993), pp. 23–5.
104 *Weekly Review*, 27 March 1992, p. 11.
105 *Society*, 18 May 1992, pp. 19–20.
106 *Society*, 11 May 1992, pp. 8–15.
107 National Christian Council of Kenya, *The Cursed Arrow: A Report on Organised Violence Against Democracy in Kenya, Volume 1: Contemporary Report on the Politicized Land Clashes in Rift Valley, Nyanza and Western Provinces* (Nairobi, 1992).
108 Kenya: *Kiliku Report*.
109 Kalenjin MPs rejected its conclusions as both based on hearsay and ethnically biased, and Parliament rejected the report in October. *Weekly Review*, 23 October 1992, p. 12.
110 See for example Kenya: *Kiliku Report*, pp. 49–51; Republic of Kenya, *Report of the Judicial Commission Appointed to Inquire into Tribal Clashes in Kenya (Akiwumi Report)* (Nairobi, 1999), p. 121.
111 Kenya: *Kiliku Report*, pp. 71–3.
112 Wako, in *East African Standard*, 19 October 2002, online edition.
113 Kenya: *Kiliku Report*, p. 82.
114 Kenya: *Akiwumi Report*.
115 Kenya: *Kiliku Report*, p.78.
116 Kenya Human Rights Commission, *Killing the Vote: State Sponsored Violence and Flawed Elections in Kenya* (Nairobi, 1998), pp. 29–30; Human Rights Watch/Africa Watch, *Failing the Internally Displaced: The UNDP Displaced Persons Programme in Kenya* (New York, 1997).
117 *Weekly Review*, 24 January 1992, p. 8.
118 By the end of January 1992, for example, Odinga had established a 108-member national steering committee, and a 14-member executive council, even though they were not mentioned in FORD's constitution. *Weekly Review*, 7 February 1992, pp. 5–7; 6 March 1992, pp. 11–12.
119 *Weekly Review*, 6 March 1992, pp. 11–12.
120 *Society*, 27 April 1992, pp.6–9; *Weekly Review*, 17 April 1992, pp. 3–6; *Finance*, 15 April 1992, pp. 18–23.
121 *Weekly Review*, 3 April 1992, p. 8.
122 *Weekly Review*, 10 April 1992, pp. 1, 4–10.
123 Forum for the Restoration of Democracy, *FORD Manifesto: Charter for the Second Liberation* (Nairobi, 1992), pp. 41–3.
124 Throup and Hornsby: *Multi-Party Politics*, pp. 204–7.

125 Gifford, Paul, *Christianity, Politics and Public Life in Kenya* (London, 2009), pp. 216–19.

126 Moi, 6 February 1992, in *Summary of World Broadcasts*, 8 February 1992.

127 *Weekly Review*, 3 April 1992, p. 9. Under pressure from the opposition, the NCCK and Western governments, Moi lifted the ban in May.

128 KANU Briefs, *Kenya Times*, 23 December 1992, pp. 14–15.

129 *Society*, 8 June 1992, pp. 8–14; *Weekly Review*, 29 May 1992, pp. 4–7.

130 *Weekly Review*, 8 May 1992, pp. 4–14.

131 These included Gusii former minister James Nyamweya and Keiyo Charles Murgor, a former provincial commissioner.

132 *Society*, 1 June 1992, pp. 8–13.

133 *Daily Nation*, 17 September 1992, pp. 1, 14.

134 *Weekly Review*, 24 July 1992, p. 6.

135 *Weekly Review*, 7 August 1992, pp. 4–6.

136 While four of the six founders supported Matiba, all the other 10 national executive members backed Odinga. Only six FORD branches backed Matiba's faction, 27 remained loyal to Odinga, while 13 were divided.

137 *Weekly Review*, 14 August 1992, pp. 10–11.

138 *Weekly Review*, 28 August 1992, pp. 18–19.

139 Ezekiel Barngetuny, in *Society*, 23 November 1992, p. 27.

140 Throup and Hornsby: *Multi-Party Politics*, pp. 142–5. To avoid accusations of nepotism, Raila Odinga took the minor position of deputy director of elections.

141 *Weekly Review*, 11 September 1992, p. 3; *Standard*, 10 September 1992, p. 1.

142 They also opened negotiations with Odinga, but their terms were too high, a lost opportunity for unity. *Weekly Review*, 18 September 1992, pp. 3–5; *Nairobi Law Monthly*, No. 45 (August–September 1992), pp. 16–18; *Daily Nation*, 17 September 1992, p. 3.

143 *Weekly Review*, 18 September 1992, pp. 3–5; 2 October 1992, pp. 9–10.

144 Matiba's proprietal attitude to Muthithi House stemmed from the fact that he was bankrolling the enterprise.

145 *Society*, 19 October 1992, pp. 21–2.

146 *Weekly Review*, 16 October 1992, pp. 5, 11.

147 *Society*, 14 September 1992, pp. 21–3.

148 Hempstone: *Rogue Ambassador*, p. 304.

149 *Daily Nation*, 2 November 1992, p. 2; 3 November 1992, p. 24.

150 Aseto and Okelo: *Privatisation*, pp. 129–32.

151 The sale of government shares in the HFCK and Uchumi Supermarkets in November–December 1992 were the first true Nairobi Stock Exchange privatisations.

152 *Weekly Review*, 20 November 1992, pp. 20–3. However, the changes were resisted by the board, the KPCU, major growers and the agriculture ministry alike, and were not implemented.

153 Details from Central Bureau of Statistics website (2006), www.cbs.go.ke.

154 By December 1992, Forex-C rates were Ksh21 per dollar over the official rate, reflecting the near-absence of foreign exchange.

155 *Weekly Review*, 27 November 1992, p. 20.

156 The town of Kakuma became another refugee camp, run by the UNHCR.

157 Kamlesh Pattni, Goldenberg Inquiry testimony, *Daily Nation,* 21 May 2004, online edition.

158 Goldenberg Commission testimony, *Standard* 7 May 2004, online edition.

159 Letter from Charles Mbindyo, permanent secretary for finance, to Goldenberg International, 1 November 1990, Ref. CONF 153/01, FORD-Kenya, The Goldenberg File (May 1993).

160 *Standard*, 21 May 2004, online edition.

161 *Daily Nation*, 13 June 2003, online edition.

162 Republic of Kenya, *Report of the Judicial Commission of Inquiry into the Goldenberg Affair. (Chair Justice Bosire) (Goldenberg Inquiry Report)* (Nairobi, 2005), p. 75.

163 Kibwana, Kivutha, Wanjala, Smokin and Okech-Owiti (eds), *The Anatomy of Corruption in Kenya* (Nairobi, 1996), p. 90; Kenya: *Goldenberg Inquiry Report*, p. 102.

164 *Kenya Gazette*, Supplement No. 3, 10 January 1992. Letters from the Kenya government Exports Division to the registrar of companies, Swiss Embassy and Office for Trade Promotion

in Switzerland. Internal government documents querying the payment of compensation in FORD-Kenya: Goldenberg File.

165 Pattni, Goldenberg Inquiry testimony, in *Daily Nation*, 2 July 2004, online edition.

166 Goldenberg Inquiry testimony, in *Daily Nation*, 18 and 19 June 2004, online edition.

167 Documents and testimony from Pattni, Goldenberg Inquiry, *Standard*, 2 July 2004, online edition.

168 Pattni, Goldenberg Inquiry testimony, *Daily Nation*, 2 July 2004, online edition.

169 *Economic Review,* 7 December 1992, pp. 4–8.

170 Goldenberg transcripts, *Daily Nation*, 4 May 2004, online edition.

171 *Daily Nation*, 27 January 1996.

172 *Economic Review*, 16 November 1992, p. 5.

173 Commonwealth Observer Group, *The Presidential, Parliamentary and Civic Elections in Kenya 29 December 1992* (London, 1993), p. 64.

174 Commonwealth Observer Group: *Report*, p. 10.

175 *Daily Nation*, 7 November 1992, p. 1.

176 The German Friedrich Ebert Stiftung, for example, financed both the printing of the *Charter for the Second Liberation* and inter-party unity conferences.

177 Republic of Kenya, *Constitution of Kenya (Amendment) Bill, 1992, Kenya Gazette Supplement No. 16* (3 March 1992).

178 *Weekly Review*, 13 March 1992, pp. 3–13.

179 Hempstone, in Hempstone: *Rogue Ambassador*, p. 266.

180 Throup and Hornsby: *Multi-Party Politics*, pp. 262–4; International Human Rights Law Group, *Facing the Pluralist Challenge: Human Rights and Democratization in Kenya's December 1992 Multi-Party Elections* (Washington, 1992), p. 7.

181 See Commonwealth Observer Group: *Report*, pp. 3, 11.

182 Throup and Hornsby: *Multi-Party Politics*, p. 255.

183 Throup and Hornsby: *Multi-Party Politics*, pp. 264–6.

184 Mbaluto was soon transferred from Nairobi, some believed as a punishment. Mutua, Makau, 'Justice Under Siege: The Rule of Law and Judicial Subservience in Kenya', *Human Rights Quarterly*, Vol. 23, No. 1 (2001), p. 111.

185 NEMU coordinated the work of the main churches, the International Federation of Women Lawyers, the International Commission of Jurists and the Professional Committee for Democratic Change. There were also three other smaller observer groups.

186 Throup and Hornsby: *Multi-Party Politics*, pp. 308–35.

187 Throup and Hornsby: *Multi-Party Politics*, pp. 389–96.

188 *Daily Nation*, 13 January 1993, p. 4.

189 National Election Monitoring Unit, *The Multi-Party General Elections in Kenya 29 December, 1992: The Report of the National Election Monitoring Unit* (Nairobi, 1993), p. 51.

190 Commonwealth Observer Group, 'Commonwealth Team Urges Action on Nominations', press statement (13 December 1992).

191 Chesoni, in *Kenya Times*, 14 December 1992, p. 3; letter to Raila Odinga, 15 December 1992. However, they did reinstate five candidates whose papers had been wrongly rejected by the returning officer, reducing the number of unopposed seats to 16.

192 *Kenya Times*, 17 December 1992, p. 2; 22 December 1992, p. 3.

193 *Kenya Times*, 25 December 1992, p. 2.

194 *Kenya Times*, 29 December 1992, p. 2.

195 FORD-Asili had 142 candidates, with big gaps in the Rift and Nyanza. FORD-Kenya had 139, with few candidates in the Rift Valley or Central Province.

196 Every Central Province candidate was Kikuyu; every candidate in Ukambani was Kamba; every one in Luo Nyanza was Luo or Basuba; in Kisii, Gusii.

197 KANU, *KANU Manifesto and Policy Document 1992* (Nairobi, 1992), p. 13.

198 *Society*, 18 May 1992, p. 32.

199 *Society*, 10 August 1992, p. 35.

200 *Weekly Review*, 18 December 1992, p. 15; *Kenya Times*, 13 December 1992, pp. 1–2.

201 See for example KANU Briefs, *Kenya Times*, 23 December 1992, p. 16.

202 *Standard*, 14 December 1992, p. 1.
203 *Economic Review*, 30 November 1992, p. 8.
204 Moi, in *Daily Nation*, 17 October 1992, p. 2.
205 Moi, at Kiganjo Police Training College, in *Daily Nation*, 21 November 1992, p. 1.
206 He was believed to be a frontman for Moi's sons Jonathan and Philip. *Weekly Express*, 23 December 1992, p. 2; *Nairobi Law Monthly*, October/November 1992, p. 26.
207 *Nairobi Weekly Observer*, 20 November 1992, p. 9.
208 See also for example testimony from Reuben Otutu, *East African Standard*, 13 October 2004, online edition.
209 Moi, *Daily Nation*, 31 October 1992, p. 1.
210 Throup and Hornsby: *Multi-Party Politics*, p. 359.
211 Democratic Party of Kenya, *Democratic Party of Kenya Manifesto 1992* (Nairobi, 1992).
212 Orvis, Stephen Walter, *The Agrarian Question in Kenya* (Gainesville, 1993), pp. 150–6.
213 See for example, FORD-Kenya advertisement in *Daily Nation*, 1 December 1992, p. 5; 2 December 1992, p. 11 and *Weekly Mail*, 7 January 1993, p. 23.
214 *Weekly Review*, 8 May 1992, p. 21.
215 *Society*, 8 June 1992, pp. 21–5; 6 July 1992, pp. 18–19; and 13 July 1992, pp. 35–9.
216 Kenya: *Akiwumi Report*, pp. 254–5; Oded, Arye, *Islam and Politics in Kenya* (Boulder, 2000), pp. 150–5. KANU activist Karissa Maitha later admitted that the DC, local police and CID supported and financed their activities.
217 Throup and Hornsby: *Multi-Party Politics*, pp. 364–5; Nyamora, Pius, 'The Role of Alternative Press in Mobilization for Political Change in Kenya 1982–1992: Society Magazine as a Case Study', M.A. thesis, University of Florida, 2007, pp. 89–99.
218 US foundations helped finance them instead.
219 Africa Watch: *Taking Liberties*, pp. 199–203; Throup and Hornsby: *Multi-Party Politics*, p. 363.
220 KTN's ownership was unclear; only later did it emerge that it was a joint venture between KANU and the British Maxwell Communications Corporation.
221 The government licensed no private radio stations until 1996.
222 NEMU: *Multi-Party General Elections*, pp. 57–60.
223 Throup and Hornsby: *Multi-Party Politics*, p. 366.
224 *Daily Nation*, 7 December 1992, p. 1.
225 Throup and Hornsby: *Multi-Party Politics*, pp. 377–8.
226 *Daily Nation*, 6 October 1992, p. 2.
227 Throup and Hornsby: *Multi-Party Politics*, pp. 372–7.
228 See *Kenya Times*, 24 December 1992, p. 14.
229 *Daily Nation*, 3 December 1992, p. 32.
230 Timothy Sirma, in *Daily Nation*, 21 October 1992, p. 3. *Jogoo* is Swahili for cockerel, the KANU symbol.
231 Francis Ewoton, *Daily Nation*, 8 December 1992, p. 4.
232 *Standard*, 25 November 1992, p. 4.
233 *Kenya Times*, 28 December 1992, p. 22.
234 Jackson Kibor, in *Daily Nation*, 26 November 1992, p. 5.
235 Throup and Hornsby: *Multi-Party Politics*, pp. 380–1.
236 See for example Onyonka, in *Daily Nation*, 19 October 1992, pp. 1–2.
237 NCWK, *Report of the Election Monitoring Exercise: A Project of the National Council of Women of Kenya* (Nairobi, 1993), p. 26.
238 See, for example, the views of foreign journalists and observers in the *Financial Times*, 31 December 1992; Andreassen, Bard-Anders, Geisler, Gisela and Tostensen, Arne, *A Hobbled Democracy: The Kenyan General Election, 1992* (Norway, 1993), p. 31.
239 Throup and Hornsby: *Multi-Party Politics*, pp. 453–518.
240 Oginga Odinga, in *Daily Nation*, 30 August 1993, p. 4.
241 Habel Nyamu, in *Daily Nation*, 5 June 1993, p. 16.
242 International Republican Institute, *Preliminary Statement of Findings, Kenyan General Elections, December 29, 1992* (Nairobi, 1 January 1993), p. 4.

243 Commonwealth Observer Group: *Report*, p. 40.
244 Commonwealth Observer Group: *Report*, p. 37.
245 NEMU: *Multi-Party General Elections*, p. 90.
246 Brown, Stephen, 'Authoritarian Leaders and Multiparty Elections in Africa: How Foreign Donors Help to Keep Kenya's Daniel arap Moi in Power', *Third World Quarterly*, Vol. 22, No. 5 (2001), pp. 731–2.
247 Bratton and van de Walle: *Democratic Experiments*, p. 120.
248 *Africa Confidential*, Vol. 34, No. 1 (8 January 1993).
249 *Independent*, 25 January 1993, p. 18.

Chapter 10: Conflict and Change, 1993–1997

1 *Standard*, 14 January 1993, p. 1.
2 *Weekly Review*, 9 July 1993, p. 14.
3 Matiba, Kenneth, *Aiming High* (Nairobi, 2000), p. 281; conversations with senior lawyer, 2004.
4 *Sunday Nation*, 28 March 1993, p. 1.
5 Throup, David W. and Hornsby, Charles, *Multi-Party Politics in Kenya* (Oxford, 1998), p. 544.
6 *The Watchman*, January 1993, p. 8.
7 *Daily Nation*, 2 March 1993, p. 1.
8 *Weekly Review*, 21 January 1993, p. 18.
9 *Daily Nation*, 25 July 1996, p. 2.
10 Moi blamed the carnage in Rwanda on this. *Weekly Review*, 15 April 1994, p. 7. Shariff Nassir even called for a return to single-party rule in 1994.
11 Ntimama, *Weekly Review*, 25 April 1997, p. 11.
12 *Weekly Review*, 12 March 1993, p. 4; 23 July 1993, p. 24; 20 August 1993, p. 18.
13 *Weekly Review*, 26 March 1993, p. 12.
14 Southall, Roger and Wood, Geoffrey, 'Local Government and the Return to Multi-Partyism in Kenya', *African Affairs*, Vol. 95, No. 381 (October 1996).
15 *Society*, 22 February 1993, p. 21.
16 *Weekly Review*, 30 April 1993, pp. 3–8.
17 Matiba, in *Daily Nation*, 12 June 1993, p. 1.
18 *Weekly Review*, 15 April 1994, pp. 11–12.
19 Badejo, Babafemi A., *Raila Odinga: An Enigma in Kenyan Politics* (Lagos, 2006), pp. 170–1.
20 *Weekly Review*, 30 July 1993, pp. 3–5. According to diplomats, Odinga may have received far more than he declared. *Africa Confidential*, Vol. 35, No. 3 (February 1994), p. 4.
21 There were indications that other FORD-Kenya MPs received donations from Pattni.
22 See *Weekly Review*, 24 September 1993, pp. 3–13.
23 *Daily Nation*, 1 November 1993, p. 1.
24 See *Weekly Review*, 11 February 1994. Matiba refused any reconciliation, saying he saw no reason to attend Odinga's funeral since there had been no love lost between them.
25 Particularly from James Orengo, who called Moi a hypocrite, one of those '. . . who tortured and detained this great man, and now come here in false praise of his greatness', Orengo, *Weekly Review*, 11 February 1994, p. 7.
26 Moi in Kericho, in *Weekly Review*, 18 February 1994, p. 3.
27 *Weekly Review*, 25 March 1994, pp. 4–11; Badejo: *Raila Odinga*, pp. 172–3.
28 NEMU Count Certifier Report, Nakuru Town, 1992.
29 *Weekly Review*, 5 March 1993, pp. 13–14.
30 *Weekly Review*, 3 September 1993, pp. 3–5.
31 Human Rights Watch/Africa Watch, *Divide and Rule: State-Sponsored Ethnic Violence in Kenya* (New York, 1993), pp. 49–52.
32 On citizenship and ethnic identities in the 1990s, see Ndegwa, Stephen, 'Citizenship and Ethnicity: An Examination of Two Transition Movements in Kenyan Politics', *American Political Science Review*, Vol. 91, No. 3 (September 1997).

33 Republic of Kenya, *Report of the Judicial Commission Appointed to Inquire into Tribal Clashes in Kenya (the Akiwumi Report)* (Nairobi, 1999), pp. 165–70; *Economic Review*, 25 October 1993, pp. 4–8.

34 Kenya: *Akiwumi Report*, p. 172.

35 *Weekly Review*, 29 October 1993, p. 12.

36 *Society*, 8 November 1993, pp. 22–24.

37 *Weekly Review*, 13 January 1995, pp. 4–9.

38 *Economic Review*, 1 November 1993, p. 8.

39 *Weekly Review*, 8 April 1994, p. 4.

40 *Sunday Nation*, 18 June 1995, p. 3.

41 Rogge, John, 'The Internally Displaced Population in Kenya, Western and Rift Valley Provinces: A Need Assessment and a Program Proposal for Rehabilitation' (Nairobi, 1993).

42 Human Rights Watch/Africa Watch, *Failing the Internally Displaced: The UNDP Displaced Persons Programme in Kenya* (New York, 1997).

43 See Brown, Stephen, 'Quiet Diplomacy and Recurring "Ethnic Clashes" in Kenya', in Sriram, Chandra Lekha and Wermester, Karin (eds), *From Promise to Practice: Strengthening UN Capacities for the Prevention of Violent Conflict* (Boulder, 2003).

44 *Standard on Sunday*, 5 September 1993, p. 2.

45 Named for the date the British hanged Dedan Kimathi.

46 *East African Standard*, 23 April 2004, online edition.

47 Odongo, like Diang'a in the 1980s, was motivated by anger at the government and its treatment of Odinga and later of Robert Ouko. He had been one of those Odinga had sent to be trained in Bulgaria in the 1960s.

48 See the *East African Standard*, 21, 22 and 23 April 2004 on FERA and the government crackdown.

49 Wekesa Barasa, *East African Standard*, 21 April 2004, online edition.

50 The KANU chief whip and his deputy were shot and left for dead in 2000.

51 Transparency International-Kenya, 'Corruption in Kenya: Findings of an Urban Bribery Survey' (2001).

52 See for example Rodley, Sir Nigel, 'Civil and Political Rights, Including Questions of Torture and Detention: Report of the Special Rapporteur: Addendum Visit of the Special Rapporteur to Kenya', United Nations Economic and Social Council Commission on Human Rights, E/CN.4/2000/9/Add.4 (9 March 2000).

53 Munene, Macharia, *The Politics of Transition in Kenya, 1995–98* (Nairobi, 2001), pp. 30–7.

54 These included the rights of women to inherit their husband's land, recognised on paper but rarely in practice.

55 Republic of Kenya, *Statistical Abstract 2001*, Table 212; *2003*, Table 216.

56 Republic of Kenya, *Statistical Abstract 1995*, Table 226.

57 Commissioner of Prisons, in *Sunday Nation*, 25 June 2000, p. 16.

58 African Rights, *Kenya Shadow Justice* (London, 1996), pp. 150–68.

59 *East African Standard*, 1 July 1999, p. 8.

60 See for example *Kenya Times*, 22 September 1995.

61 *Finance*, 28 February 1993, pp. 24–5.

62 *People*, 24–30 November 1995.

63 Posner, Daniel N., *Institutions and Ethnic Politics in Africa* (New York, 2005), pp. 4–7.

64 *Weekly Review*, 13 August 1993, pp. 3–11; 8 October 1993, pp. 3–12.

65 Rumba Kinuthia, *Society*, 8 November 1993, p. 15.

66 *Weekly Review*, 8 March 1996, p. 6.

67 Wangari Maathai, in *Society*, 8 November 1993, p. 18.

68 For oathing, see for example *Weekly Review*, 30 July 1993, p. 12.

69 *Weekly Review*, 28 May 1993, pp. 3–9.

70 Hempstone, Smith, *Rogue Ambassador: An African Memoir* (Sewanee, 1997), p. 313.

71 *Economic Review*, 8 March 1993, pp. 4–12.

72 Musyoka, during meeting with the British high commissioner, reported in *Society*, 22 February 1993, p. 5.

73 *Weekly Review*, 26 March 1993, pp. 14–20.
74 This left Goldenberg with Ksh8 billion of credit advanced through various banks. Republic of Kenya, *Report of the Judicial Commission of Inquiry into the Goldenberg Affair (Chair Justice Bosire)* (Nairobi, 2005), p. 119.
75 Economist Intelligence Unit, *Kenya, Country Report, 1st Quarter 1994* (London, 1994), p. 10.
76 See for example the *Independent*, 8 June 1993, p. 16. Robert Shaw of FORD-Kenya had an extensive dossier of Goldenberg materials that he took round Western capitals in 1993 (personal copy, 1993).
77 Edward Jaycox, *Weekly Review*, 23 July 1993, p. 30.
78 Pattni testimony to Goldenberg Inquiry, in *Daily Nation*, 27 February 2004, online edition.
79 *Economic Review*, 16 March 1998, online edition.
80 *Weekly Review*, 16 April 1993, p. 20; 16 April 1993, pp. 13–18.
81 *Weekly Review*, 23 July 1993, p. 27; 30 July 1993, p. 19.
82 *Economic Review*, 21 April 1997, pp. 4–7. KANU was amongst those with large loans from Trans-National; Joshua Kulei was a director and there were rumours that Moi, Biwott and Kulei actually owned the bank.
83 World Bank, 'Press Release: Meeting of the Consultative Group for Kenya' (Paris, 23 November 1993).
84 *African Business*, March 1994, p. 32.
85 The shilling then continued its steady decline.
86 Ndung'u, Njuguna S., 'Liberalization of the Foreign Exchange Market in Kenya and the Short-Term Capital Flows Problem', *AERC Research Paper 109* (Nairobi, 2001). O'Brien, F. S. and Ryan, T. C. I., 'Kenya', in Devarajan, S., Dollar, D. and Holmgren, Torgny (eds), *Aid and Reform in Africa* (Washington, 2001), p. 491.
87 Glenday, Graham and Ndii, David, 'Export Platforms in Kenya', in Kimenyi, Mwangi S., Mbaku, Mukum John and Mwaniki, Ngure (eds), *Restarting and Sustaining Economic Growth and Development in Africa: The Case of Kenya* (Aldershot, 2003), pp. 87–122.
88 On revenue authorities in Africa, see Fjeldstad, Odd-Helge and More, Mick, 'Revenue Authorities in Sub-Saharan Africa', *Journal of Modern African Studies*, Vol. 47, No. 1 (March 2009).
89 KRA Commissioner General, reported in *Economic Review*, 6 October 1997, p. 16.
90 Although it was a government bill, Moi refused to sign the Act into law until forced to do so by Western pressure. *Weekly Review*, 25 April 1997, pp. 18, 20.
91 Republic of Kenya, *Annual Public Debt Management Report, July 2005–June 2006* (Nairobi, 2007), p. v.
92 Kenya Wildlife Service, *Annual Report* (Nairobi, 1995), p. 16.
93 *Weekly Review*, 21 January 1994, pp. 16–17; 25 March 1994, pp. 17–18.
94 O'Brien and Ryan: 'Kenya', pp. 473, 524.
95 On the use of various levers to encourage democratisation in countries such as Kenya and the arguments for and against intervention, see Clinkenbeard, Stephen, 'Donors versus Dictators: The Impact of Multilateral Aid Conditionality on Democratization: Kenya and Malawi in Comparative Context, 1990–2004', BA dissertation, Brown University, 2004, pp. 26–51.
96 See for example, Versi, Anwer, 'Kenya: First of the African "Tigers"?', *African Business*, 1 January 1995.
97 Clinkenbeard: 'Donors vs Dictators', pp. 49–50.
98 *Weekly Review*, 25 April 1997, p. 20.
99 Winkgates, James, 'US Policy Towards East Africa: Crisis Response amid Limited Interests', in Magyar, Karl (ed.), *United States Interests and Policies in Africa: Transition to a New Era* (Basingstoke, 2000), p. 124.
100 *US Economic and Military Assistance (Loans and Grants), 'Green Book'* (1999).
101 See for example Aseto, Oyugi and Okelo, Jasper, *Privatisation in Kenya* (Nairobi, 1997), pp. 6–13; Saitoti, George, *The Challenges of Economic and Institutional Reforms in Africa* (Aldershot, 2002), pp. 181–202.
102 *Weekly Review*, 18 April 1997, pp. 21–2; Republic of Kenya, *Privatisation of State Corporations and Investments* (Nairobi, 2005), p. 10.

103 Aseto and Okelo: *Privatisation*, pp. 176–82.

104 Aseto and Okelo: *Privatisation*, pp. 183–5.

105 Aseto and Okelo: *Privatisation*, pp. 187–9; Kenya: *Privatisation of State Corporations*, Annexe 3.

106 Spectre successfully commissioned the plant in 2005.

107 *Economic Review*, 25 August 1997.

108 Kroll, 'Project KTM', 27 April 2004, p. 13, published on Wikileaks, 2004.

109 Aseto and Okelo, *Privatisation*, pp. 178–80. Kiplagat was moved out of the role in 1995.

110 See for example *Post on Sunday*, 21 December 1997, pp. 4–15.

111 *Daily Nation*, 7 May 2002, online edition.

112 All figures from the National Bank of Kenya, *Annual Reports and Accounts, 1996–2000*.

113 *The Analyst*, May 2000, p. 13.

114 Kenya, *Statistical Abstract*, 1995, Table 202.

115 See for example Olowu, Bamidele, 'Redesigning African Civil Service Reforms', *Journal of Modern African Studies*, Vol. 37, No. 1 (1999).

116 Institute for Economic Affairs/Society for International Development, *Kenya at the Crossroads: Scenarios for our Future* (Nairobi, 2001), pp. 30–1.

117 See for example Orvis, Stephen Walter, *The Agrarian Question in Kenya* (Gainesville, 1993).

118 Institute for Economic Affairs: *Kenya at the Crossroads*, pp. 39–40.

119 The number who died of hunger was unknown, however, as officials were instructed not to report deaths.

120 They insisted that the World Food Programme distribute it, as they no longer trusted the government.

121 *Daily Nation*, 24 September 2002, p. 8.

122 Wanyande, Peter, 'Management Politics in Kenya's Sugar Industry: Towards an Effective Framework', *African Journal of Political Science* Vol. 6, No. 1 (2001).

123 *Weekly Review*, 1 March 1996, pp. 14–15.

124 *Economic Review*, 30 June 1997, pp. 6–9.

125 *Economic Review*, 11 August 1997, p. 26.

126 Odek, Otieno, Kegode, Peter and Ochola, Shem, 'The Challenges and Way Forward for the Sugar Sub-Sector in Kenya' (Nairobi, 2003), p. 25.

127 World Bank, 'Kenya: Growth and Competitiveness', *Report No. 31387-KE* (27 January 2005), p. 67.

128 Kenya: *Statistical Abstract*, 2005, Table 41(c).

129 Waithaka, J. H. G., 'Kenya: Assessment of the Situation and Development Prospects for the Cashew Nut Sector' (UNCTAD/WTO, July 2002).

130 Labrousse, Alain and Laniel, Laurent, *The World Geopolitics of Drugs, 1998/1999* (Dordrecht, 2001), pp. 241–6.

131 This compared with a 1990 average for Africa of 4.3 per cent, 16.6 per cent in North America and 24.8 per cent in Europe. International Labour Organisation, *World Labour Report 2000* (Geneva, 2000).

132 Snow, R. W., Ikoku, A., Omumbo, J. and Ouma, J, 'The Epidemiology, Politics and Control of Malaria Epidemics in Kenya: 1900–1998', report prepared for Roll Back Malaria, Resource Network on Epidemics (World Health Organisation, July 1999).

133 See for example Geest, Willem van der, 'Introduction', in Geest, Willem van der (ed.), *Negotiating Structural Adjustment in Africa* (New York, 1994), p. 3.

134 *Economic Review*, 2 June 1997, p. 11.

135 Aseto and Okelo: *Privatisation*, p. 23.

136 Van de Walle, Nicholas, *African Economies and the Politics of Permanent Crises, 1979–1999* (Cambridge, 2001), p. 14.

137 Aseto and Okelo: *Privatisation*, pp. 137–41; Kimenyi, Mwangi and Mbaku, John Mukum, 'Institutions and Economic Growth', in Kimenyi, Mbaku and Mwaniki: *Restarting and Sustaining Economic Growth and Development*, pp. 13–34.

138 *Economic Review*, 7 July 1997, online edition.

139 See for example Cowen, Michael and Kanyinga, Karuti, 'Kenya: The 1997 Elections', in Cowen, Michael and Laakso, Liisa (eds), *Multi-Party Elections in Africa*. (Oxford, 2002), pp. 152–5.

140 Munene, Macharia, *The Politics of Transition in Kenya, 1995–98* (Nairobi, 2001), pp. 16–20.

141 *Economic Review*, 2–8 June 1997, p. 9.

142 *Economic Review*, 2–8 June 1997, pp. 6–9.

143 See for example the 1996/7 Public Investments Committee report in *Economic Review*, 6–12 October 1997, pp. 9–15 and the controller-general's report in *Economic Review*, 24 November 1997, online edition.

144 Kibwana, Kivutha, Wanjala, Smokin and Okech-Owiti (eds), *The Anatomy of Corruption in Kenya* (Nairobi, 1996), pp. 70–1.

145 *Daily Nation*, 19 April 2001, online edition.

146 Ex-Commissioner of Cooperatives Alfred Birgen was sentenced in 1996 for the theft of Ksh3.9 million.

147 Republic of Kenya, *Constitution of Kenya, Revised Edition (2001)* (Nairobi, 2001), Section 99.

148 Eldoret airport opened in 1998 and proved of limited benefit, with few airlines using it. Farmers continued to truck their goods to Nairobi.

149 Some also feared that the factory would also fuel insecurity in northern Kenya.

150 *Economic Review*, 10 November 1997, online edition.

151 *Daily Nation*, 26 January 2006, online edition.

152 For an analysis of corruption in Africa, see De Sardan, J. P. Olivier, 'A Moral Economy of Corruption', *Journal of Modern African Studies*, Vol. 37, No. 1 (March 1999).

153 Kibwana, Wanjala, Okech-Owiti: *The Anatomy of Corruption*, p. 3.

154 See for example Kanyinga, Karuti, *Re-Distribution from Above: The Politics of Land Rights and Squatting in Coastal Kenya*, Research Report No. 115 (Uppsala, 2000), pp. 87–94.

155 *East African Standard*, 5 October 2006, online edition.

156 See for example Klopp, Jacqueline, 'Can Moral Ethnicity Trump Political Tribalism? The Struggle for Land and Nation in Kenya', *African Studies*, Vol. 61, No. 2 (2002).

157 Institute for Economic Affairs/Society for International Development: *Scenarios*, p. 87.

158 See for example the NSSF's failed purchase of land in 1995, which resulted in a court case in 2004, reported in *Daily Nation*, 16 February 2004, online edition.

159 Ndung'u report, *Daily Nation*, 8 October 2004, online edition.

160 *Standard*, 17 April 2004, online edition.

161 *Daily Nation*, 15 August 2004, online edition; *Economic Review*, 11–17 March 1996, p. 8.

162 *Economic Review*, 27 May 1996, pp. 4–7.

163 Kenya: *Akiwumi Report*, p. 224.

164 Kanyinga, Karuti, 'The Changing Development Space', in Gibbon, Peter (ed.), *Markets, Civil Society and Democracy in Kenya* (Uppsala, 1995), pp. 100–1.

165 US Ambassador Bushnell, for example, in 1996 explicitly declared that the US would shift aid towards NGOs and private investors, because of US dissatisfaction with the government's performance.

166 Carol Peasley, USAID, in 'Kenya's Election Crisis', *Committee on International Relations, House of Representatives*, 30 July 1997, p. 18; House of Commons, *Hansard*, Written Answers for 18 November 1997 (pt 1) [12553].

167 The author worked with NEMU in 1992 and the IED in 1997 and 2002. Comments on the organisation may therefore lack independence.

168 See for example Orvis, Stephen Walter, 'Kenyan Civil Society: Bridging the Urban–Rural Divide?', *Journal of Modern African Studies*, Vol. 41, No. 2 (2003), p. 248.

169 Orvis: 'Kenyan Civil Society', p. 254.

170 Some NGO heads were open about their goals. Makau Mutua, for example, said in his book: 'As a lifelong reformer, and as chair of the Kenya Human Rights Commission (KHRC), the country's leading NGO, I put on my hard hat and went to work to oust KANU.' Mutua, Makau, *Kenya's Quest for Democracy: Taming Leviathan* (Boulder, 2008), p. vii.

171 Holmquist, Frank and Ford, Michael, 'Kenyan Politics: Towards a Second Transition', *Africa Today*, Vol. 45, No. 2 (April–June 1998), p. 240.

172 Ngunyi, Mutahi, 'Religious Institutions and Political Liberalisation in Kenya', in Gibbon: *Markets, Civil Society and Democracy*, pp. 145–76.

173 In 1998, the name of the church was changed from the Church of the Province of Kenya (CPK) to the Anglican Church of Kenya (ACK).

174 *Weekly Review*, 24 January 1997, pp. 12–14.

175 On the relationship between religious belief and politics in Africa in the 1990s, see Ellis, Stephen and Ter Haar, Gerrie, 'Religion and Politics in Sub-Saharan Africa', *Journal of Modern African Studies*, Vol. 36, No. 2 (1998).

176 Morton, Andrew, *Moi: The Making of an African Statesman* (London, 1998), p. 194.

177 Morton: *Moi*, p. 189.

178 See for example *Financial Times*, 11 August 1995, p. 5.

179 Gifford, Paul, *Christianity, Politics and Public Life in Kenya* (London, 2009), pp. 71–81.

180 These included the IED, the Coalition of Violence against Women, the National Commission on the Status of Women, the Education Centre for Women in Democracy, the Federation of Women Lawyers, the Green Belt Movement, and the League of Women Voters.

181 She was the wife of an ex-minister, rather than a completely independent political force.

182 Mutunga, Willy, *Constitution-Making from the Middle: Civil Society and Transition Politics in Kenya, 1992–1997* (Nairobi, 1999), pp. 48–73.

183 *Weekly Review*, 6 January 1995, pp. 4–9.

184 Peters, Ralph, 'Civil Society and the Election Year 1997 in Kenya', in Rutten, Marcel, Mazrui, Alamin M. and Grignon, François (eds), *Out for the Count: The 1997 General Elections and Prospects for Democracy in Kenya* (Kampala, 2001), pp. 32–8.

185 See for example, Okech-Owiti (ed.), *The Electoral Environment in Kenya: A Research Project Report* (Nairobi, 1997).

186 Mutunga: *Constitution Making*, pp. 111–25.

187 Peters: 'Civil Society', p. 37. See also Mutunga: *Constitution Making*.

188 *Weekly Review*, 16 August 1996, pp. 4–5.

189 See for example *Economic Review*, 22 April 1996, pp. 4–8.

190 *Weekly Review*, 14 March 1997, p. 3.

191 'The Democratic Party is committed to good governance, transparency, total accountability and integrity and cannot, therefore, continue associating itself in whichever way with a person like Wamalwa, whose character negates all these principles . . .' DP press release, in *Weekly Review*, 14 February 1997, p. 9.

192 *Weekly Review*, 15 March 1996, pp. 4–5.

193 There were rumours that the Americans saw Ngilu as a moderate non-Kikuyu candidate they could support.

194 *Weekly Review*, 31 October 1997, p. 5.

195 *Economic Review*, 7 July 1997, pp. 4–5.

196 Kagwanja, Peter, 'Politics of Marionettes: Extra Legal Violence and the 1997 Elections in Kenya', in Rutten, Mazrui, and Grignon: *Out for the Count*, pp. 81–4.

197 Klopp: 'Moral Ethnicity', pp. 277–8.

198 He received congratulations on his reappointment from 21 heads of state corporations, indicating how deep his influence remained. *Weekly Review*, 24 January 1997, p. 5.

199 KANU elections followed in Central Province, Kericho, Bomet, Trans-Nzoia and Uasin Gishu, reaffirming the resurgence of 'KANU B'.

200 For example, an IFES report in 1996 stressed the need to repeal several laws, reform the ECK, redistribute boundaries and end state bias. Klein, Keith, Scallan, Andrew, De Assuncao, Celio Santos and Dauphinais, Denise, 'Towards Credible and Legitimate Election in Kenya: Recommendation for Action', unpublished report (Washington, April 1996).

201 Embakasi in Nairobi had nearly as many registered voters (114,000) as all 11 constituencies in North-Eastern Province together (167,000). For more on the boundary redistribution, see Fox, Roddy, 'Bleak Future for Multi-Party Elections in Kenya', *Journal of Modern African Studies*, Vol. 34, No. 4 (1996).

202 See Aywa, Francis Ang'ila and Grignon, Francis, 'As Biased as Ever?', in Rutten, Mazrui and Grignon, *Out for the Count*, pp. 109–17; and Institute for Education in Democracy/Catholic

Justice and Peace Commission/National Council of Churches in Kenya (IED/CJPC/NCCK), *Report on the 1997 General Elections in Kenya 29–30 December 1997* (Nairobi, 1998), pp. 39–43.

203 IED/CJPC/NCCK: *Report on the 1997 General Elections*, p. 48.

204 Electoral Commission of Kenya, 'ECK Report on the 1997 General Elections (Final Draft)', typescript, 1999, p. 48.

205 Mutunga: *Constitution Making*, pp. 159–69.

206 Peters: 'Civil Society', p. 40.

207 *Weekly Review*, 30 May 1997, pp. 15–18.

208 Moi, *Weekly Review*, 6 June 1997, p. 16.

209 *Weekly Review*, 25 July 1997, pp. 4–10

210 Mutunga: *Constitution Making*, p. 9.

211 *Africa Confidential*, Vol. 38, No. 18 (September 1997).

212 *Weekly Review*, 22 August 1997, p. 22.

213 Both bills were shelved, though in practice they provided the basis for the final settlement.

214 *Economic Review*, 1 September 1997, online edition.

215 See *Weekly Review*, 12 September 1997, pp. 4–11.

216 *Economic Review*, 15 September 1997, pp. 6–12; Mutunga: *Constitution Making*, pp. 209–12.

217 A more controversial change was the repeal of its Section 15, which barred treating; this effectively legitimised electoral bribery.

218 Kenya: *Akiwumi Report*, pp. 33–5, 42–3; Kenya Human Rights Commission (KHRC), *Kayas of Deprivation, Kayas of Blood: Violence, Ethnicity and the State in Coastal Kenya* (Nairobi, 1997), pp. 21, 25.

219 Kenya: *Akiwumi Report*, pp. 241–51; KHRC: *Kayas of Deprivation*, p. 26; Kenya Human Rights Commission (KHRC), *Kayas Revisited: A Post-Election Balance Sheet* (Nairobi, 1998), p. 10.

220 The KHRC reported that in 1997, over 80% of businesses sampled in Kwale belonged to non-locals. KHRC: *Kayas of Deprivation*, p. 13.

221 KHRC: *Kayas of Deprivation*, pp. 43–8.

222 On Sajaad, see Kenya: *Akiwumi Report*, pp. 272–3 and KHRC: *Kayas of Deprivation*, p. 22.

223 KHRC: *Kayas Revisited*, p. 9.

224 Francis Gichuki, in Kenya: *Akiwumi Report*, p. 268.

225 They eventually reinstated the nurses and reviewed their terms and conditions nonetheless.

226 The literature on the 1997 election is extensive, including Rutten, Mazrui and Grignon: *Out for the Count*; IED/CJPC/NCCK: *Report on the 1997 General Elections*; Cowen and Kanyinga: 'The 1997 Elections in Kenya'; Southall, Roger, 'Moi's Flawed Mandate: The Crisis Continues in Kenya', *Review of African Political Economy*, Vol. 25, No. 75 (January 1998); and Steeves, Jeffrey S., 'The Political Evolution of Kenya: The 1997 Elections and Succession Politics in Kenya', *Journal of Commonwealth and Comparative Politics*, Vol. 37, No. 1 (March 1999).

227 ECK: Report on the 1997 General Elections, p. 59.

228 ECK: Report on the 1997 General Elections, p. 63.

229 *Weekly Review*, 5 December 1997, online edition.

230 On the foreign monitors, see Braakhuis, Norbert, 'International Election Observation during the 1997 General Election', in Rutten, Mazrui and Grignon: *Out for the Count*; and Rutten, Marcel, 'The Kenyan General Election of 1997: Implementing A New Model for International Election Observation in Africa' in Abbink, J. and Hesseling, G. (eds), *Election Observation and Democratization in Africa* (New York, 2000).

231 Akatsa-Bukachi, Marren, 'Domesticating Election Observation: Experience from the 1997 General Elections', in Rutten, Mazrui and Grignon: *Out for the Count*.

232 These included Chris Okemo, Jembe Mwakalu and Francis Nyenze. Most defected in the belief that their prospects would be better in KANU.

233 IED/CJPC/NCCK: *Report on the 1997 General Elections*, p. 64.

234 *Weekly Review*, 19 December 1997, pp. 4–6.

235 IED/CPJC/NCCK: *Report on the 1997 General Elections*, pp. 59–62.

236 *Daily Nation*, 29 December 1997, p. 4.

237 IED/CPJC/NCCK: *Report on the 1997 General Elections*, p. 62.
238 IED/CPJC/NCCK: *Report on the 1997 General Elections*, pp. 95–99.
239 KANU, *KANU Manifesto 1997: Our Vision into the Next Millennium* (Nairobi, 1997).
240 This included former Controller Abraham Kiptanui, Special Branch head Boinett, managing director of the NCPB Major William Koitaba, managing director of the Kenya Airports Authority Peter Lang'at, military intelligence head Lazarus Sumbeiywo, Permanent Secretary Sally Kosgei and Zipporah Kittony, chair of Maendeleo ya Wanawake. *Africa Confidential*, Vol. 38, No. 24 (May 1997).
241 *Kenya Confidential*, 19 December 1997, p. 7.
242 *Daily Nation*, 23 October 1998, n.p.
243 See for example Versi, Anwer, 'Kenya's Watershed Elections', *African Business*, December 1997.
244 Democratic Party of Kenya, *Election '97 Manifesto* (Nairobi, 1997), p. 9.
245 *Economic Review*, 17 November 1997, online edition.
246 Raila Odinga in Migori, in *Daily Nation* 18 December 1997, online edition.
247 *Economic Review*, 6 May 1996, p. 4; Raila Odinga, advertisement, *Daily Nation*, 31 July 1997.
248 See for example, *East African Standard*, 9 April 1997.
249 Ngilu, in Nairobi, *Daily Nation*, 18 December 1997, online edition.
250 IED/CPJC/NCCK: *Report on the 1997 General Elections*, pp. 67–79.
251 DDDG, 'Executive Summary Final Statement of 26 January 1998', submitted 2 February 1998 to ECK.
252 *East African Standard*, 31 December 1997, p. 1.
253 Hornsby, Charles, 'Election Day and the Results', in Rutten, Mazrui and Grignon: *Out for the Count*, pp. 136–7.
254 Hornsby: 'Election Day', pp. 180–3.
255 The scale of the rout was visible in the performance of Ramogi Achieng-Oneko, who received only 3 per cent of the vote for FORD-Kenya, compared to the 94 per cent he had received in 1992.
256 IED/CPJC/NCCK: *Report on the 1997 General Elections*, p. 76.
257 IED/CJPC/NCCK: *Report on the 1997 General Elections*, p. 31.
258 Hornsby: 'Election Day', p. 162.
259 IED/CJPC/NCCK, *Rapid Count Reports*, Konoin, 1997.
260 Hornsby: 'Election Day', pp. 163–9.
261 Mutava Musyimi, press conference, 31 December 1997.
262 IED/CPJC/NCCK: *Report on the 1997 General Elections*.
263 Munene: *The Politics of Transition*, p. 84; personal observation, EOC, 1997–8.

Chapter 11: Unnatural Succession, 1998–2002

1 Republic of Kenya, *Report of the Judicial Commission Appointed to Inquire into Tribal Clashes in Kenya (the Akiwumi Report)* (Nairobi, 1999), p. 142; Rutten, Marcel, '"Fresh Killings": The Njoro and Laikipia Violence in the 1997 Kenyan Election Aftermath', in Rutten, Marcel, Mazrui, Alamin M. and Grignon, François (eds), *Out for the Count: The 1997 General Elections and Prospects for Democracy in Kenya* (Kampala, 2001).
2 Kagwanja, Peter Mwangi, 'Facing Mount Kenya or Facing Mecca? The *Mungiki*, Ethnic Violence, and the Politics of the Moi Succession in Kenya, 1987–2002', *African Affairs*, Vol. 102, No. 406 (January 2003), p. 27.
3 Kenya Human Rights Commission, *Killing the Vote: State Sponsored Violence and Flawed Elections in Kenya* (Nairobi, 1998).
4 *Daily Nation*, 18 January 1998, online edition.
5 *Daily Nation*, 22 January 1998, online edition.
6 Badejo, Babafemi A., *Raila Odinga: An Enigma in Kenyan Politics* (Lagos, 2006), pp. 182–94.
7 *Sunday Nation*, 18 October 1998, online edition.
8 See for example *Weekly Review*, 12 June 1998, online edition.

9 Southall, Roger, 'Re-forming the State? Kleptocracy and the Political Transition in Kenya', *Review of African Political Economy*, Vol. 26, No. 79 (March 1999), pp. 96–7.

10 Nyachae, in *Sunday Nation*, 26 August 2001, p. 3.

11 *Sunday Nation*, 26 August 2001, pp. 1, 3.

12 *Kenya Confidential*, Vol. 3, No. 6, 4–10 March 1999, p. 3.

13 *East African Standard*, 1 July 2000, pp. 1–2.

14 Moi, 23 September 1999, quoted in *Daily Nation*, Kenya@40 1999.

15 The battle around Parliament of 10 June 1999, for example, during which Rev. Timothy Njoya was beaten, raised international indignation once more.

16 *East African Standard*, 27 April 2000, p. 3.

17 *East African Standard*, 27 April 2000, p. 8.

18 *Finance*, 29 July 1999, pp. 4–27.

19 In November 2001, for example, the NPK was humiliated with 10 per cent of the vote in a by-election in Machakos.

20 *Daily Nation*, 15 October 2001, online edition.

21 Following the 1997 elections, the DP was sued for non-payment of a Ksh1 million bill for the printing of membership cards and party registers. *Daily Nation*, 21 December 1999, p. 20.

22 *Weekly Review*, 8 January 1999, pp. 10–11.

23 Kibaki, in contrast, was unchallenged as leader of the opposition, and his 39 seats underestimated his strength, as Ngilu's supporters generally voted with the DP.

24 *Daily Nation*, 28 April 1998, online edition.

25 Orvis, Stephen Walter, 'Kenyan Civil Society: Bridging the Urban–Rural Divide?', *Journal of Modern African Studies*, Vol. 41, No. 2 (2003), p. 248.

26 Berman, Bruce J., 'Ethnicity, Patronage and the African State: The Politics of Uncivil Nationalism', *African Affairs*, Vol. 97, No. 388 (1998), p. 340.

27 For example, USAID funded the National Assembly to build its capacity and independence from the executive in 2001. USAID, *Kenya Activity Data Sheet No. 615-006* (2001).

28 *Kenya Times*, 15 June 1999, p. 1.

29 *Daily Nation*, 14–16 September 1999.

30 *Daily Nation*, 30 December 1999, pp. 1, 16–17.

31 See for example Transparency International-Kenya, 'Paying the Public or Caring for Constituents?' (Nairobi, November 2003).

32 Transparency International-Kenya, 'An Analysis of Reported Harambee activity, January 2000–September 2002' (n.d.).

33 Hulterström, Karolina, 'The Logic of Ethnic Politics: Elite Perceptions about the Role of Ethnicity in Kenyan and Zambian Party Politics', in Hulterström, Karolina, Kamete, Amin Y. and Melber, Henning, *Political Opposition in African Countries: The Cases of Kenya, Namibia, Zambia and Zimbabwe, Discussion Paper 37* (Uppsala, 2007).

34 House of Commons, *Hansard* (Various), Written Answers, 4 April 2001 col. 194W, online edition.

35 African Rights, *Kenya Shadow Justice* (London, 1996), pp. 199–218.

36 African Rights: *Shadow Justice*, p. 207.

37 Morton, Andrew, *Moi: The Making of an African Statesman* (London, 1998), p. 185.

38 Shell International, *2001 Global Scenarios: People and Connections* (London, 2001).

39 Okemo, Chrisantus and Cheserem, Micah, 'Memorandum of Economic and Financial Policies of the Government of Kenya, 2000–03', Letter to Horst Kohler, IMF (12 July 2000), at www.imf.org.

40 *Daily Nation*, 7 September 1999, online edition.

41 *East African Standard*, 12 April 2004, online edition.

42 *Daily Nation*, 1 December 1999, p. 1; *East African Standard*, 12 January 2000, p. 4; *Kenya Times*, 7 January 2000, p. 32.

43 *Daily Nation*, 12 May 2000, p. 1.

44 *Daily Nation*, 20 December 1999, p. 1.

45 *Kenya Times*, 8 December 1999, p. 1.

46 *East African*, 1 May 2000, online edition.

47 This case dragged on until 2002, when the High Court decided that the KPTC's directors had acted with KPTC authority all along in their actions. See *Daily Nation*, 20 April 2001 and 20 February 2002, online editions.

48 In 2011, the United States openly accused Mwau of drug trafficking and banned all contact with him.

49 See the argument that patron–clientelism and forms of corruption may, contrary to accepted wisdom, have assisted some less-developed countries to grow, in Yoo, Hyung-Gon Paul, 'Corruption, Rule of Law, and Civil Society: Why Patronage Politics is Good for Developing Markets and Democracies', *International Affairs Review*, Vol. XIV, No. 1 (Spring 2005).

50 Okemo and Cheserem: 'Letter'.

51 *East African Standard*, 25 July 2002, online edition.

52 Saitoti, George, *The Challenges of Economic and Institutional Reforms in Africa* (Aldershot, 2002), pp. 71–3.

53 *Daily Nation*, 18 December 2001, 'Business Week', p. 2.

54 Transparency International website (2008), www.transparency.org.

55 *Daily Nation*, 11 December 2003, online edition.

56 *Daily Nation*, 26 February 2003, online edition.

57 *Kenya Times*, 24 August 2000, p. 13.

58 *East African*, 9 April 2001.

59 Moi, in *Daily Nation*, 7 March 2001, online edition.

60 *African Business*, 1 October 2001.

61 *Daily Nation*, 30 October 2001, 'Business Week', p. 1.

62 Kjaer, Anne Mette, 'Old Brooms Can Sweep Too! An Overview of Rulers and Public Sector Reforms in East Africa', *Journal of Modern African Studies*, Vol. 42, No. 3 (2004), p. 392.

63 Ndungu, Njuguna, 'Kenya Macroeconomic Management', in Kimenyi, Mwangi S., Mbaku, Mukum John and Mwaniki, Ngure (eds), *Restarting and Sustaining Economic Growth and Development in Africa: The Case of Kenya* (Aldershot, 2003), pp. 55–69.

64 Saitoti: *Challenges*, p. 6.

65 In the same period that the PRGF payments were made, Kenya made 40 million SDRs of repayments to the IMF. International Monetary Fund, *Annual Report* (Washington DC, 2001), Appendix II, Table II.5 and II.8.

66 The political significance of the sector was shown by the fact that Moi appointed Kalenjin to head all three organisations.

67 Kerretts-Makau, Monica J. J., 'At a Crossroad: The GATS Telecom Framework and Neo-Patrimonial States: The Politics of Telecom Reform in Kenya', D.Phil. thesis, University of New South Wales, 2006, pp. 72–4, 123–4.

68 *East African*, 2 June 1999, online edition.

69 Rules required at least 30 per cent local ownership.

70 'Kenya Telkom Sale Stalls', *African Business*, 1 May 2002.

71 Oludhe, Christopher, 'An Assessment of the Potential Benefits of Seasonal Rainfall Prediction in Relation to Hydro-Electric Power Generation in Kenya: A Case Study of the Impacts of the 1999/2000 Drought and the Accompanied Power Rationing', University of Nairobi, n.d.

72 US figures on trade balance between Kenya and the US, 2003. African Growth and Opportunity Act, website (2005), www.agoa.info.

73 KBL had Jeremiah Kiereini as its chairman and other senior figures as shareholders.

74 Two Swedish businessmen were later jailed for bribing bank officials for contracts under the programme. *Daily Nation*, 6 February 2004, online edition.

75 The failure to maintain roads and infrastructure almost certainly slowed economic growth in the urban areas. World Bank, *Entering the 21st Century: World Development Report, 1999/2000* (New York, 2000), p. 126.

76 Bayliss, Kate, 'Water Privatisation in Africa', *Journal of Modern African Studies*, Vol. 41, No. 4 (2003).

77 The price of commodities such as flour had increased more than 80-fold, while average earnings had risen between 23 and 26 times, leaving the average Kenyan far poorer in purchasing power.

78 'Report of the Auditor General (Corporations) on the Accounts of National Social Security Fund for the Year Ended 30 June 2000' (14 March 2002). www.nssfkenya.com/docs/auditor_general.pdf.

79 *Daily Nation*, 17 September 2002, p. 1.

80 *Daily Nation*, 28 February 2003, online edition.

81 Wamalwa, Orengo, Muite and Kones, for example, were all in the bankruptcy courts between February and July 2002.

82 *Sunday Nation*, 28 April 2002, pp. 1–3.

83 Tuitoek, Kiboswony, 'Educational Commissions as an Inquiry of Education Policy in Kenya: A Case Study of the Koech Commission', D.Ed. thesis, University of Birmingham, 2005, pp. 45–63, 118–22.

84 Moi, quoted in *Sunday Nation*, 16 April 2000, p. 32.

85 Society for International Development, *Pulling Apart: Facts and Figures on Inequality in Kenya* (Nairobi, 2004), pp. 33–4

86 *Economic Review*, 20 May 1996, p. 10.

87 *Sunday Nation*, 29 September 2002, online edition.

88 Bollinger, Lori, Stover, John and Nalo, David, 'The Economic Impact of AIDS in Kenya', *The Policy Project Working Paper* (Futures Group International, September 1999).

89 *Standard*, 28 and 29 April 2005, online edition.

90 *Daily Nation*, 20 December 2000, online edition.

91 See for example Saitoti: *Challenges*, p. 159.

92 Republic of Kenya, *Kenya Demographic and Health Survey 2003: Preliminary Report* (Nairobi, 2003), p. 37.

93 Republic of Kenya, *The 1999 Population and Housing Census, Vol. 1* (Nairobi, 2001).

94 Ndambuki, in *Kenya Times*, 1 March 2000, p. 1.

95 *Daily Nation*, 1 March 2000, online edition.

96 Hetherington, Penelope, 'Generational Changes in Marriage Patterns in the Central Province of Kenya, 1930–1990', *Journal of Asian and African Studies*, Vol. 36, No. 2 (2001).

97 See for example Constitution of Kenya Review Commission, 'Ikolomani Constituency Committee Report' (2002), www.constitutionnet.org/files/IKOLOMANI%20CONSTIT UENCY%20%20COMPLETE1.pdf, p. 19.

98 Hetherington: 'Generational Changes'.

99 Kenya: *Kenya Demographic and Health Survey*, p. 30.

100 *Weekly Review*, 20 March 1998, online edition; *Economic Review*, 23 March 1998, online edition.

101 This took place despite fears that such stations could incite ethnic divisions. Tanzania in contrast banned all private local-language stations.

102 *Foreign Affairs Bulletin*, Vol. II, No. 7 (December 1999), p. 2.

103 Kroll UK, *Project KTM*, 27 April 2004, published on Wikileaks (2004), p. 14; *The Economist*, 7 June 2008.

104 *Africa Confidential*, Vol. 40, No. 25 (17 December 1999).

105 See for example Himbara, David, *Kenyan Capitalists, the State and Development* (Boulder, 1993).

106 See *Economic Review*, 12–18 February 1996; *Daily Nation*, 23 November 2003, 11 February 2004; *People*, 24–30 January 1997.

107 *Daily Nation*, 24 November 2003, online edition.

108 See Kaumutunga, Musambayi, 'A City Under Siege: Banditry and Modes of Accumulation in Nairobi, 1991–2004', *Review of African Political Economy*, No. 106 (2005).

109 Korre, Abdulwahab H., Hassan, D. A. and Omar, Isaac, *The Gharri Experience in Northern Kenya* (2001).

110 *Daily Nation*, 20 May 2000, p. 4.

111 *Daily Nation*, 20 January 2000, p. 4.

112 *East African Standard*, 24 December 1999, p. 5.

113 Kagwanja, Peter Mwangi, 'Globalising Ethnicity, Localising Citizenship: Globalisation, Identity Politics and Violence in Kenya's Tana River Region', *Africa Development*, Vol. 28, Nos 1 and 2 (2003).

114 Department of State, *Annual Report on Military Expenditures, 1998, Submitted to the Committee on Appropriations of the U.S. Senate and the Committee on Appropriations of the U.S. House of Representatives* (19 February 1999), www.fas.org/irp/world/98_amiex2.html, p. 3.

115 Waihenya, Waithaka, *The Negotiator* (Nairobi, 2006), pp. 42–4.

116 See for example *People*, 4–10 September 1998, *Daily Nation*, 9 December 1999, 3 July 2000.

117 *People*, 6 December 1999; *Daily Nation*, 8 December 1999, p. 1; *People*, 3 July 2000.

118 Kwach, Richard quoted in Schmidt, S. and Kibara, G., *Kenya: On the Path to Democracy? An Interim Evaluation* (Nairobi, 2002), p. 28.

119 Constitution of Kenya Review Commission, 'Report of the Advisory Panel Of Eminent Commonwealth Judicial Experts' (17 May 2000), www.commonlii.org/ke/other/KECKRC/2002/index.html , p. 35.

120 Bratton, Michael, 'Briefing: Islam, Democracy and Public Opinion in Africa', *African Affairs*, Vol. 102, No. 408 (2003).

121 Oded, Arye, *Islam and Politics in Kenya* (Boulder, 2000), pp. 140–6.

122 Fahim Twaha, in Parliament, in *Daily Nation*, 1 November 2001, p. 3.

123 Mitry, Percy, 'Africa's Record of Regional Cooperation and Integration', *African Affairs*, Vol. 99, No. 397 (2000).

124 Glenday, Graham and Ndii, David, 'Export Platforms in Kenya', in Kimenyi, Mbaku and Mwaniki: *Restarting and Sustaining Economic Growth*, pp. 115–19.

125 'South African Investors Cry Foul', *African Business*, September 2002.

126 Throup suggested for example that KANU was 'well placed to win the next election . . .' Throup, David W., 'Kenya: Revolution, Relapse or Reform?', *Africa Notes, No. 3* (Washington, November 2001), p. 1.

127 *Daily Nation*, 12 June 2001, online edition.

128 Throup: 'Kenya: Revolution', p. 6.

129 See *Daily Nation*, 13 June 2001, online edition.

130 *Sunday Nation*, 21 October 2001, online edition.

131 *East African Standard*, 22 November 2001, p. 1.

132 *Daily Nation*, 26 September 2002, online edition.

133 *Finance*, 30 March 2000, pp. 8–17.

134 Republic of Kenya, *Report of the Commission of Inquiry into the Land Law System of Kenya on Principles of a National land Policy Framework, Constitutional Position on Land and New Institutional Framework for Land Administration (Chairman Charles Njonjo)* (Nairobi, Government of Kenya, 2002).

135 *Daily Nation*, 2 November 2000, online edition.

136 *Weekly Review*, 29 May 1998, online edition.

137 See for example *East African Standard*, 18 May 2002, p. 8.

138 Klopp, Jacqueline, 'Can Moral Ethnicity Trump Political Tribalism? The struggle for land and nation in Kenya', *African Studies*, Vol. 61, No. 2 (2002), pp. 285–6.

139 Murton, John, 'Population Growth and Poverty in Machakos District, Kenya', *Geographical Journal*, Vol. 165 (March 1999).

140 Kanyinga, Karuti, *Re-Distribution from Above: The Politics of Land Rights and Squatting in Coastal Kenya*, Research Report No.115 (Uppsala, 2000), pp. 110–15.

141 *Daily Nation*, 16 February 2006, online edition.

142 Maathai, Wangari, *The Green Belt Movement: Sharing the Approach and the Experience* (New York, 2004), p. 64.

143 Anderson, David, 'Poverty and the Pastoralist', in Anderson, David and Broch-Due, Vigdis (eds), *The Poor Are Not Us: Poverty and Pastoralism in Eastern Africa* (Oxford, 1999), pp. 4–5; Nunow, Abdirazak Arale, 'Pastoralists and Markets: Livestock Commercialisation and Food Security in North-Eastern Kenya', *African Studies Centre Research Report*, (n.d. 2000?), pp. 47–60.

144 Zaal, Fred and Dietz, Ton, 'Of Markets, Meat, Maize and Milk: Pastoral Commoditization in Kenya', in Anderson and Broch-Due: *The Poor Are Not Us*.

145 Books on Kenyan pastoralism include Spear, Thomas and Waller, Richard (eds), *Being Maasai: Ethnicity and Identity in East Africa* (London, 1993); Anderson and Broch-Due: *The Poor Are*

Not Us; Anderson, David, *Eroding the Commons: Politics of Ecology in Baringo, Kenya, 1895–1963* (Oxford, 2002); Ensminger, Jean, *Making a Market: The Institutional transformation of an African Society* (Cambridge, 1992); Aguilar, Mario, *Being Oromo in Kenya* (Trenton, 1998); Fratkin, Elliot, *Aariel Pastoralists of Kenya: Surviving Drought & Development in Africa's Arid Lands* (Needham Heights, 1998); Schlee, Gunther, *Identities on the Move: Clanship and Pastoralism in Northern Kenya* (Nairobi, 1994).

146 Nunow: 'Pastoralists and Markets', pp. 8–9.

147 See for example Fratkin, Eliot, Nathan, Martha and Roth Eric, 'Health Consequences of Pastoral Sedentarisation amongst Rendille of Northern Kenya', in Anderson and Broch-Due: *The Poor Are Not Us.*

148 Heald, Suzette, 'Agricultural Intensification and the Decline of Pastoralism: A Case Study from Kenya', *Africa Magazine*, Vol. 69 (22 March 1999), p. 9.

149 This process is described in Mutua, Makau, *Kenya's Quest for Democracy: Taming Leviathan* (Boulder, 2008), pp. 119–27.

150 There was a staged public outcry over the commissioners' (substantial) allowances and expensive vehicles. In September 2001, Moi attacked Commissioner Ombaka, the blind ex-MP and human rights activist, claiming in one of his notorious off-the-cuff speeches, 'Certain people are blind and yet you insist they should lead the constitutional review process. What message are you sending God?' Moi speaking in Kiswahili, translated by *Daily Nation*, 29 September 2001, p. 3.

151 See for example the American ambassador, in *Election Africa News*, June–July 2002, online edition.

152 *Daily Nation*, 2 August 2002, p. 1.

153 Constitution of Kenya Review Commission, *Draft Bill: The Constitution of the Republic of Kenya*, 27 September 2002, CKRC website (2002).

154 *Daily Nation*, 20 September 2002, online edition; *East African Standard*, 28 October 2002, online edition.

155 *Daily Nation*, 9 March 2002, online edition.

156 The Kenyatta family apparently donated US$3.6 million to pay for the conference.

157 *Daily Nation*, 20 March 2002, online edition.

158 *Daily Nation*, 1 April 2002, online edition.

159 *East African Standard*, 7 May 2002, online edition; *Sunday Nation*, 26 May 2002, p. 5.

160 *Daily Nation*, 17 June 2002, online edition.

161 *East African Standard*, 23 May 2002, online edition.

162 Ngilu's supporters retained their formal leadership positions, which was to prove an issue later.

163 See for example *East African Standard*, 24 May 2002, online edition.

164 *East African Standard*, 29 July 2002, online edition.

165 See for example the commitment by all 11 North-Eastern MPs in *East African Standard*, 25 July 2002, online edition.

166 *East African Standard*, 12 August 2002, online edition.

167 See for example *Daily Nation*, 6 May 2002, p. 1.

168 *Expressions Today*, 26 June 2002.

169 For more on Mungiki, see Wamue, Grace Nyatugah, 'Revisiting our Indigenous Shrines through Mungiki', *African Affairs*, Vol. 100, No. 400 (2001); Anderson, David M., 'Vigilantes, Violence and the Politics of Public Order in Kenya', *African Affairs*, Vol. 101, No. 405 (October 2002); Kagwanja: 'Facing Mount Kenya'.

170 See for example Kagwanja, Peter Mwangi, 'Power to Uhuru: Youth Identity and Generational Politics in Kenya's 2002 Elections', *African Affairs*, Vol. 105, No. 418 (October 2005).

171 Kagwanja: 'Facing Mount Kenya', p. 34.

172 *Sunday Nation*, 24 June 2007, online edition.

173 *Daily Nation*, 8 August 2002, p. 1.

174 *East African Standard*, 31 August 2002, online edition.

175 *Sunday Standard*, 8 September 2002, online edition.

176 *Daily Nation*, 19 September 2002, online edition.

177 *Standard*, 28 January 2007, online edition.
178 Raila Odinga, in *East African Standard*, 14 October 2002, online edition.
179 What was little understood at the time was that NARC was not actually a new political party, but a renaming of Ngilu's NAK, and the NPK/NAK officials duly became NARC's officials.
180 Badejo: *Raila Odinga*, pp. 230–2.
181 In response, Safina switched support to Kibaki, though it contested the polls as an independent party.
182 *Daily Nation*, 22 and 23 October 2002, online edition.
183 Electoral Commission of Kenya, *Distribution of Voters by Age Nationally* (7 November 2002).
184 Institute for Education in Democracy, *Registration of Voters in 2002: An Audit* (Nairobi, 2002).
185 The reports were confusing. Three different figures were quoted in Institute for Education in Democracy (IED), *Enhancing the Electoral Process in Kenya: A Report on the Transition General Elections 2002* (Nairobi, 2003), pp. 31, 55, 91.
186 Kenya Domestic Observation Programme (K-DOP), *When Kenyans Spoke: 2002 General Election* (Nairobi, 2003), pp. 41–4.
187 *Daily Nation*, 16 November 2002, p. 3.
188 *East African Standard*, 5 November 2002, online edition.
189 K-DOP: *When Kenyans Spoke*, p. 65.
190 *Daily Nation*, 20 November 2002, p. 14.
191 Institute for Education in Democracy, *Constituency Observer Reports*, November and December 2002.
192 Asingo, Patrick O., 'The Political Economy of Transition in Kenya', in Oyugi, Walter O., Wanyande, Peter and Odhiambo-Mbai C. (eds), *The Politics of Transition in Kenya: From KANU to NARC* (Nairobi, 2003) p. 39.
193 Kibaki, Nyayo National Stadium, 18 November 2002, quoted in *Daily Nation*, 19 November 2002, p. 12.
194 *Standard*, 25 November 2002, online edition.
195 *Daily Nation*, 15 November 2002, online edition.
196 There were rumours that Odinga and Kibaki also sought financial support from foreign governments, including Libya.
197 See Nyairo, Joyce and Ogude, James, 'Popular Music, Popular Politics: Unbwogable and the Idioms of Freedom in Kenyan Popular Music', *African Affairs*, Vol. 104, No. 415 (April 2005).
198 KANU, *KANU Manifesto 2002, Laying a Solid Foundation for Kenya* (Nairobi, 2002).
199 Moi speaking in Mwingi, *Daily Nation*, 27 November 2002, online edition.
200 *Daily Nation*, 16 January 2004, online edition.
201 *Africa Confidential*, 6 December 2002, p. 1.
202 K-DOP: *When Kenyans Spoke*, p. 133.
203 European Union Election Observation Mission, *Kenya General Elections 27 December 2002 Final Report* (2003), pp. 28–31.
204 K-DOP: *When Kenyans Spoke*, pp. 132–42.
205 See for example Nyachae's presidential nomination rally speech, *Daily Nation*, 20 November 2002, online edition.
206 See IED: *Enhancing the Electoral Process*, pp. 89–93 and K-DOP: *When Kenyans Spoke*, pp. 109–11.
207 Kivuitu press statement, 29 December 2002, quoted in *Daily Nation*, 30 December 2002, p. 3.
208 Of the 125 NARC MPs, only 23 had been KANU MPs in September 2002, though another half-dozen had been KANU members at some point in the previous decade.
209 Joseph Kingi, in *Coast Express*, 3 January 2003, online edition.
210 Of the NARC parliamentary candidates, 39 had been in government at some point since independence, including two vice-presidents and 13 ministers.
211 IED: *Enhancing the Electoral Process*, p. 99; See also Throup, David W., 'The Kenya General Election: December 27, 2002', *Africa Notes No. 14* (Washington, January 2003), p. 5.

212 *Daily Nation*, 29 January 2003, p. 6.
213 *Daily Nation*, 17 January 2003, p. 5.
214 *Daily Nation*, 23 November 2004, online edition.
215 K-DOP: *When Kenyans Spoke*, pp. 152–8.
216 *Daily Nation*, 16 January 2004, online edition.
217 There were rumours of a US-brokered 'immunity' deal for Moi, perhaps the price for a peaceful transition.
218 Uhuru Kenyatta, quoted in *Daily Nation*, 30 December 2002, p. 32.
219 Commonwealth press statement, quoted in *Standard*, 3 January 2003, p. 5.
220 Kenya Domestic Observation Programme (K-DOP), *A Big Step Forward for Democracy in Kenya*, press release, 29 December 2002.
221 IED: *Enhancing the Electoral Process*, p. 124.
222 Kibaki, 30 December 2002, quoted in *Daily Nation*, 31 December 2002, p. 1.

Chapter 12: Back to the Future, 2003–2008

1 Ndegwa, Stephen N., 'Kenya: Third Time Lucky?', *Journal of Democracy*, Vol. 14, No. 3 (July 2003), p. 157.
2 Luo businessman Raphael Tuju was nominally in the LDP but owed little to Odinga, while Ahmed Khalif Mohammed died soon after taking office.
3 Barkan, Joel D., 'Kenya After Moi', *Foreign Affairs*, Vol. 83, No. 1 (January/February 2004), pp. 9–10.
4 Wrong, Michaela, *It's Our Turn to Eat: The Story of a Kenyan Whistleblower* (London, 2009), pp. 15–18. She describes how the appointment was arranged by some of Kibaki's closest allies, who had founded TI, including Muhoho, Wanjui and Harris Mule.
5 *Daily Nation*, 25 January 2003, p. 1.
6 *Sunday Standard*, 25 July 2004, p. 12.
7 *Daily Nation*, 3 February 2003, online edition.
8 Raila Odinga, *Daily Nation*, 3 February 2003, online edition.
9 Of the 588,000 who sat the Kenya Certificate of Primary Education in 2003, 317,000 (54 per cent) found no state place.
10 Republic of Kenya, *Statistical Abstract 2007*, Table 161(a).
11 See for example *Daily Nation*, 3 February 2003, online edition.
12 *East African*, 7 October 2003, online edition.
13 Lecture by John Githongo, 26 March 2006.
14 See the series of special reports in the *Daily* and *Sunday Nation* during February 2004.
15 *Daily Nation*, 1 December 2003, online edition.
16 See for example *Daily Nation*, 16 April 2004, online edition.
17 *Standard*, 9 January 2007, online edition; *Daily Nation*, 29 July 2007, online edition.
18 *Daily Nation*, 21 December 2005, online edition.
19 Kroll UK, *Project KTM*, 27 April 2004, published on Wikileaks (2004), p. 9.
20 *Daily Nation*, 29 April 2004, online edition; Kroll: *Project KTM*.
21 *Daily Nation*, 3 July 2005, online edition.
22 *Daily Nation*, 7 March 2005, online edition.
23 See Wolf, Thomas P., 'Immunity or Accountability? Daniel Toroitich arap Moi, Kenya's First Retired President', in Southall, Roger and Melber, Henning (eds), *Legacies of Power: Leadership Change and Former Presidents in African Politics* (Cape Town, 2006).
24 Republic of Kenya, *Report of the Judicial Commission of Inquiry into the Goldenberg Affair. (Chair Justice Bosire)* (Nairobi, 2005).
25 *Daily Nation*, 17, 18 and 22 February 2006, online edition.
26 *East African Standard*, 9 June 2004, online edition.
27 See for example *East African Standard*, 18 and 26 March 2004, online edition.
28 *Daily Nation*, 21 February 2005, online edition.
29 *East African Standard*, 21 November 2004, online edition.
30 *Saturday Nation*, 11 December 2010, online edition.

31 Citizens for Justice, *We Lived to Tell: The Nyayo House Story* (Nairobi, 2003).
32 Republic of Kenya, *Report of the Task Force on the Establishment of a Truth, Justice and Reconciliation Commission* (Nairobi, 2003).
33 *Daily Nation*, 11 December 2004, online edition.
34 *East African Standard*, 3 July 2004, online edition; Southall, Roger, 'The Ndung'u Report: Land and Graft in Kenya', *Review of African Political Economy*, Vol. 32, No. 103 (March 2005).
35 *East African Standard*, 22 April 2004, online edition.
36 See for example, *Daily Nation*, 17 December 2004, online edition.
37 KPMG audit of the NSSF, reported *Daily Nation*, 15 August 2004, online edition.
38 However, business continued in a similar way in some jurisdictions, just with more care than in the past. A Nairobi road resurfaced by the city council in 2003, for example, was already impassable two years later.
39 K'Akumu, O. A., 'Privatization of the Urban Water Supply in Kenya: Policy Options for the Poor', *Environment and Urbanization*, Vol. 16 (2004).
40 *Daily Nation*, 2 February 2004, online edition.
41 See for example Kagwanja, Peter Mwangi, 'Power to Uhuru: Youth Identity and Generational Politics in Kenya's 2002 Elections', *African Affairs*, Vol. 105, No. 418 (October 2005), pp. 65–73.
42 United Nations Development Programme (UNDP), *Kenya National Human Development Report* (Nairobi, 2006), pp. 39–45.
43 The preliminary report of the *Kenya Demographic and Health Survey*, reported in *Daily Nation*, 2 February 2004, online edition.
44 *Daily Nation*, 2 February 2004, online edition.
45 Republic of Kenya, *Statistical Abstract 2007*, Table 9(b).
46 See for example, *East African Standard*, 13 November 2004, online edition.
47 *East African Standard*, 11 April 2004, online edition.
48 *Daily Nation*, 26 March 2005, online edition.
49 Society for International Development, *Pulling Apart: Facts and Figures on Inequality in Kenya* (Nairobi, 2004).
50 *Daily Nation*, 27 March 2005, online edition.
51 *Daily Nation*, 6 November 2007, online edition.
52 See a summary of such cases in *Daily Nation*, 19 October 2005, online edition.
53 *Daily Nation*, 16 September 2005, online edition.
54 See for example, *East African*, 26 April 2004, online edition.
55 Interview with Ntimama, *Daily Nation*, 29 August 2004, online edition.
56 *Daily Nation*, 17 April 2003, online edition.
57 Wrong: *It's Our Turn*, p. 80.
58 *Sunday Nation*, 18 January 2004, online edition.
59 In the *Daily Nation*, 19 March 2005, online edition, Murungaru was asked if he was that man.
60 Lecture by and conversation with John Githongo, 26 March 2006, London.
61 See for example *Daily Nation*, 23 February 2003 and 18 January 2004, online editions.
62 *Sunday Nation*, 10 August 2003 online edition.
63 *Daily Nation*, 21 December 2003, online edition.
64 *Daily Nation*, 6 January 2003, online edition.
65 *Daily Nation*, 19 August 2003, online edition.
66 Joe Khamisi, in *Daily Nation*, 16 March 2003, online edition
67 *Daily Nation*, 30 December 2003, online edition.
68 *East African Standard*, 26 January 2005, online edition.
69 William Ruto, in *Daily Nation*, 10 August 2003, online edition.
70 See *Daily Nation*, 18 December 2004, online edition.
71 Steadman Group, 'Referendum Opinion Poll Results, Quarter 3 2005', unpublished PowerPoint, October 2005.
72 *Daily Nation*, Steadman survey results, 21 December 2005, online edition.

73 See for example, Afrobarometer Network, 'Afrobarometer Round 2: Compendium of Comparative Results from a 15-Country Survey', *Afrobarometer Working Paper No. 34* (March 2004); Wolf, Thomas P., Logan, Carolyn and Owiti, Jeremiah, 'A New Dawn? Popular Optimism in Kenya after the Transition', *Afrobarometer Working Paper No. 33* (2004); Branch, Daniel and Cheeseman, Nic, 'Briefing: Using Opinion Polls to Evaluate Kenyan Politics, March 2004–January 2005', *African Affairs*, Vol. 104, No. 415 (2005).

74 Republic of Kenya, *The 2007 Elections in Kenya: Independent Review Commission (IREC) Report* (pdf download, 19 September 2008), p. 22.

75 *Daily Nation*, 3 November 2003, online edition.

76 Wycliffe Oparanya, quoted in *Daily Nation*, 21 July 2003, online edition.

77 *Daily Nation*, 30 September 2003, online edition.

78 *East African Standard*, 11 May 2004, online edition.

79 Murungaru and Murungi, *Daily Nation*, 22 December 2003, online edition.

80 See for example *Daily Nation*, 5 February 2004, online edition.

81 *Daily Nation*, 16 March 2004, online edition.

82 *Daily Nation*, 26 March 2004, online edition; Muthoni, Anne and Wendoh, Peter (compilers) and Kichana, Philip (ed.), *Constitutional Law Case Digest Vol. II* (Nairobi, 2005), pp. 111–32.

83 Yash Ghai, in *East African Standard*, 14 April 2004, online edition.

84 *Sunday Nation*, 22 January 2006, online edition.

85 Peter Munya, in *East African Standard*, 3 July 2004, online edition.

86 See for example, Otieno Kajwang', in *East African Standard*, 3 July 2004, online edition.

87 *Daily Nation*, 26 January 2006, online edition; 31 March 2006, p. 12; Wrong: *It's Our Turn*, p. 84.

88 *Daily Nation*, 31 March 2006, pp. 13–14; Wrong: *It's Our Turn*, p. 173.

89 Murungi, *Daily Nation*, 12 January 2005, online edition.

90 *Africa Confidential*, Vol. 45, No. 11 (May 2004), p. 2; Wrong: *It's Our Turn*, p. 85.

91 See for example, Wrong: *It's Our Turn*, pp. 94–7, 126.

92 Githongo, in *Sunday Nation*, 22 January 2006, online edition; *Daily Nation*, 31 March 2006, p. 13.

93 See for example, *Daily Nation*, 31 August 2005, online edition.

94 Amos Kimunya, in Republic of Kenya, *National Assembly Official Report (NAOR)*, 2 May 2007, pp. 1068–9.

95 Mars (Media Analysis and Research) Group, 'Illegally Binding: The Missing Anglo Leasing Scandal Promissory Notes', GAP Report No. 2 (2007), www.marsgroupkenya.org.

96 See for example, Muslim Human Rights Forum, 'Horn of Terror: Report of US-Led Mass Extraordinary Renditions from Kenya to Somalia, Ethiopia and Guantanamo Bay January – June 2007, presented to the Kenya National Commission on Human Rights, 6 July 2007, pdf version (Wikileaks, 2009).

97 Carotenuto, Matthew and Luongo, Katherine, 'Dala or Diaspora: Obama and the Luo Community of Kenya', *African Affairs*, Vol. 108, No. 431 (April 2009).

98 See for example *Daily Nation*, 15 July 2004, p. 1; Wrong: *It's Our Turn*, pp. 201–4.

99 *Standard*, 16 February 2005, online edition.

100 Murungaru, *Daily Nation*, 15 February 2005, online edition.

101 *Daily Nation*, 26 February 2005, online edition.

102 *Daily Nation*, 18 September 2005, online edition.

103 Anderson, David, *Histories of the Hanged: The Dirty War in Kenya and the End of Empire* (New York, 2005); Elkins, Caroline, *Britain's Gulag: The Brutal End of Empire in Kenya* (London, 2005).

104 See Chege, Michael, 'Economic Relations between Kenya and China, 1963–2007', *Centre for Strategic and International Studies, Working Paper* (June 2008).

105 *Daily Nation*, 27 November 2004, online edition.

106 World Bank, 'Kenya: Growth and Competitiveness', *Report No. 31387-KE* (27 January 2005), pp. i–iii.

107 *Daily Nation*, 8 September 2005 and 23 May 2006, online editions; UNDP: *Human Development Report*, p. 58.

108 Organisation for Economic Cooperation and Development (OECD), *African Economic Outlook* (2007), p. 307.
109 Republic of Kenya, *Kenya Gazette*, 28 January 2005.
110 Republic of Kenya, *Statistical Abstracts*, 2001–7.
111 The Mars Group published on the Internet a pdf copy of Kenya's foreign debt register. Liabilities incurred since 2002 were rather more confidential.
112 Kihoro, Wanyiri, *Politics and Parliamentarians in Kenya 1944–2007* (Nairobi, 2007), p. 33.
113 See for example *East African Standard*, 29 April 2004, online edition.
114 Kerretts-Makau, Monica J. J., 'At a Crossroad: The GATS Telecom Framework and Neo-Patrimonial States: The Politics of Telecom Reform in Kenya', D. Phil thesis, University of New South Wales, 2006, pp. 184–99.
115 *Daily Nation*, 17 November 2007, online edition.
116 See for example Raila Odinga's campaign website, http://raila2007.wordpress.com./2007/11/15.
117 See for example, *NAOR*, 24 April 2007, Mars Group copies of Kenya Hansard.
118 More than half the KCB and NBK's loans were still non-performing in 2004.
119 Nyagah's successor was also replaced after he tried to investigate those behind Charterhouse Bank.
120 *Daily Nation*, 22 August 2004, online edition. It eventually wrote off Ksh3.2 billion.
121 See for example, Mars Group, 'The Case Against the Members of the Ninth Parliament', (2007), www.marsgroupkenya.org.
122 See for example Khamisi, Joe, *The Politics of Betrayal* (2011), pp. 245–7.
123 *East African Standard*, 4 July 2004, online edition.
124 See for example *Daily Nation*, 27 September 2004, online edition.
125 *Standard*, 25 January 2005, online edition.
126 Odinga, *Daily Nation*, 7 September 2005; Republic of Kenya, *The Proposed Constitution of Kenya*, Kenya Gazette Supplement, 22 August 2005.
127 *NAOR*, 21 July 2005, col. 2651.
128 See Badejo, Babafemi A., *Raila Odinga: An Enigma in Kenyan Politics* (Lagos, 2006), pp. 275–8.
129 *Daily Nation*, 17 October 2005, online edition.
130 *Daily Nation*, 7 September 2005; 11 September 2005; 18 October 2005, online editions; *Standard*, 17 November 2005, online edition; Kenya Civil Society Observation Programme (KCSOP), *Report on the Referendum on the Proposed New Constitution of Kenya, 21st November 2005* (Nairobi, 2006), p. 51.
131 *Daily Nation*, 12 September 2005, online edition.
132 *Daily Nation*, 24 November 2005, online edition.
133 KCSOP: *Report on the Referendum*, p. vi.
134 All results were published on the ECK website; Electoral Commission of Kenya, *Presidential and Parliamentary Election Results, 2007*, www.eck.or.ke.
135 KCSOP: *Report on the Referendum*, pp. 30, 34.
136 *Daily Nation*, 24 November 2005, online edition.
137 Kibaki, *Daily Nation*, 23 November 2005, online edition.
138 Awori, quoted in *Daily Nation*, 28 November 2005, online edition.
139 *Daily Nation*, 7 December 2005, online edition.
140 *Daily Nation*, 9–14 December 2005, online edition.
141 See for example the German ambassador, in *Daily Nation*, 12 December 2005, online edition.
142 Raila Odinga, in *Daily Nation*, 20 October 2007, online edition.
143 Lynch, Gabriella, 'Courting the Kalenjin: The Failure of Dynasticism and the Strength of the ODM Wave in Kenya's Rift Valley Province', *African Affairs*, Vol. 107, No. 429 (October 2008), pp. 549–50.
144 Kibaki, in *Daily Nation*, 13 December 2005, online edition.
145 *Daily Nation*, 23 January 2006, online edition; Wrong: *It's Our Turn*, p. 174.
146 *Daily Nation*, 20 January 2006, online edition.
147 Awori, *Daily Nation*, 6 April 2006, online edition.

148 *Daily Nation*, 7 March 2006, online edition.
149 *Daily Nation*, 11 June 2006, online edition.
150 *Daily Nation*, 10 June 2006, online edition.
151 UK junior minister, in *The Economist*, 18 November 2006, p. 54.
152 *Standard*, 29 January 2005, online edition.
153 Lynch: 'Courting the Kalenjin', p. 546.
154 *Daily Nation*, 10 March 2006, online edition.
155 *Standard*, 6 May 2005, online edition.
156 *Daily Nation*, 5 June 2006, online edition.
157 Michuki, in *Standard*, 14 February 2007, online edition.
158 *Daily Nation*, 19 April 2006, online edition.
159 Kenya Anti-Corruption Commission, *Annual Report, 2006–7* (Nairobi, October 2007). www.kacc.go.ke; Lawson, Letitia, 'The Politics of Anti-Corruption Reform', *Journal of Modern African Studies*, Vol. 47, No. 1 (2009).
160 Steadman opinion poll, in *Daily Nation*, 1 April 2006, online edition.
161 *Daily Nation*, 4 November 2006, online edition.
162 *Daily Nation*, 14 July 2007, online edition.
163 Steadman Group, 'Using Multi-Party Democracy in Kenya' (August 2006), pp. 39–41.
164 *Daily Nation*, 16 May 2007, online edition.
165 Ojode, Joshua, in *NAOR*, 22 March 2007, pp. 83–4.
166 See for example Linah Kilimo, in *Daily Nation*, 1 June 2007, online edition.
167 See for example, *Financial Times*, 16 November 2006, p. 5.
168 *Daily Nation*, 14 September 2007, online edition.
169 *Daily Nation*, 17 September 2007, online edition.
170 Embakasi was the largest with 250,000 voters, Lamu East the smallest with 13,000. Kenya: *IREC Report*, p. 76.
171 USAID, *Assessment of the Pre-Electoral Environment* (USAID, May 2006), p. 19.
172 ECK, *Daily Nation*, 5 July 2007, online edition.
173 The IREC report later estimated 1.2 million. Kenya: *IREC Report*, p. 8.
174 *Daily Nation*, 13 November 2007, online edition.
175 See for example, *Daily Nation*, 2 November; 15 December 2007, online editions.
176 USAID: *Pre-Electoral Environment*, p. 2.
177 *Daily Nation*, 24 August 2007, online edition.
178 Results of a voter bribery survey, *Daily Nation*, 29 November 2007, online edition.
179 Only 20 of 210 incumbents (less than 10%) did not stand or accepted their primary defeat, compared to 20% in 2002.
180 In one Gusii seat, voters were faced with 33 candidates from which to choose one MP.
181 Kavulla, Travis R., 'Our Enemies are God's Enemies: The Religion and Politics of Bishop Margaret Wanjiru, MP', *Journal of Eastern African Studies*, Vol. 2, No. 2 (July 2008); Gifford, Paul, *Christianity, Politics and Public Life in Kenya* (London, 2009), pp. 114–18.
182 *Daily Nation*, 23 November 2007, online edition.
183 *Daily Nation*, 14 and 21 October 2007, online edition.
184 Kibaki in Mombasa, in *Daily Nation*, 14 October 2007, online edition.
185 In 2008, all three of Turkana's elected MPs were ex-aid workers for Oxfam or the World Food Programme.
186 Party of National Unity, *Manifesto 2007* (Nairobi, 2007), pp. 2–3
187 *Daily Nation*, 12 May 2007; 27 June 2007; 5 December 2007, online editions.
188 Mwiraria and Murungi, in *Daily Nation*, 21 October 2007, online edition.
189 While the incumbents could 'readily use their occupancy of political office to draw on the material and coercive responses of the state, opposition movements often hold the ideological advantage . . .', Bratton, Michael and van de Walle, Nicholas, *Democratic Experiments in Africa: Regime Transitions in Comparative Perspective* (Cambridge, 1997), pp. 26–7.
190 WorldNet Daily, 'Obama Raised $1 Million for Foreign Thug's Election' (14 October 2008), www.wnd.com/?pageId=78035.
191 *Daily Nation*, 7 July 2007, online edition.

192 Odinga in Kericho, in *Daily Nation*, 7 December 2007, online edition.
193 Gifford: *Christianity*, pp. 59–60.
194 PNU leaders in Meru, in *Daily Nation*, 21 October 2007, online edition.
195 See *Daily Nation*, 20 November 2007, online edition.
196 See Rambaud, Brice, 'Caught Between Information and Condemnation: The Kenyan Media in the Election Campaigns of December 2007', in Lafargue, Jérôme (ed.), *The General Elections in Kenya, 2007*, Cahier No. 38 (Nairobi, 2008).
197 European Union Election Observation Mission (EUEOM), *Kenya Final Report, General Elections 27 December 2007* (2008), pp. 25–6.
198 Willis, Justin, 'What Has he Got up his Sleeve? Advertising the Kenyan Presidential Candidates in 2007', *Journal of Eastern African Studies*, Vol. 2, No. 2 (July 2008), pp. 266–7.
199 Kenya Human Rights Commission, *Violating the Vote: A Report on the 2007 General Elections* (Nairobi, 28 February 2008), pp. 17–22.
200 *Sunday Standard*, 23 December 2007, p. 10.
201 Republic of Kenya, *Commission of Inquiry into Post-Election Violence (CIPEV)* (Nairobi, 2008), pdf download, pp. 406, 412; *Standard*, 10 April 2010, online edition.
202 EUEOM: *Kenya Final Report*, pp. 32–3
203 *Daily Nation*, 29 December 2007, online edition.
204 Kenya: *IREC Report*, p. 2.
205 Throup, David, 'The Count', *Journal of Eastern African Studies*, Vol. 2, No. 2 (July 2008), p. 298.
206 *Standard*, 2 January 2008, online edition.
207 Recording of EU Mission press conference, 1 January 2008 (courtesy Sebastian Elischer).
208 EUEOM: *Kenya Final Report*, p. 1.
209 International Republican Institute, *Kenya Presidential, Parliamentary and Local Elections, December 2007: Election Observer Mission Final Report* (Washington, 2008), p. 4.
210 Commonwealth Observer Group, *Kenya General Election 27 December 2007* (London, 2008), p. 28.
211 KEDOF, 'Preliminary Press Statement and Verdict of 2007 Kenya's General Elections' (31 December 2007). It never published its final report.
212 See for example, Kenyans for Peace with Truth and Justice (KPTJ), 'Count Down to Deception: 30 Hours that Destroyed Kenya', final press release (18 January 2008); and Ndii, David, 'Preliminary Results from the 2007 Presidential Election Results Received by the Electoral Commission of Kenya' (January 2008).
213 *The Economist*, 3 January 2008. For Western press reactions see *Daily Nation*, 7 January 2008, online edition.
214 David Milliband, in *Daily Nation*, 14 February 2008, online edition.
215 Kenya: *CIPEV Report*, p. 46. Original reports had the death toll at 35. *Daily Nation*, 2 January 2008, online edition.
216 Kenya: *CIPEV Report*, p. 110.
217 Areas such as the Coast (despite their history of political and ethnic violence during 1992–7) remained mostly calm in comparison, with few spontaneous assaults and no sign of a coordinated pogrom. See Mghanga Mwandawiro, 'Usipoziba Ufa Utajenga Ukuta: Land, Elections, and Conflicts in Kenya's Coast Province' (Nairobi, 2011).
218 Kenya: *CIPEV Report*, pp. 102, 117, 214–15; *Standard*, 27 January 2008, online edition.
219 Kenya: *CIPEV Report*, pp. 104–6, 121–3.
220 Kenya: *CIPEV Report*, pp. 170, 343
221 *Daily Nation*, 1 February 2008, online edition.
222 Mueller, Susanne D., 'The Political Economy of Kenya's Crisis', *Journal of Eastern African Studies*, Vol. 2, No. 2 (2008).
223 Kenya: *CIPEV Report*, pp. 40–1.
224 See for example, Anonymous, 'The Truth About the Kenyan Genocide', 5 January 2008, http://kenyangenocide.blogspot.com/2008/01/truth-about-kenyan-genocide.html; and Kenya: *CIPEV Report*.
225 Kenya: *CIPEV Report*, pp. 69–70, 92.

226 Kenya: *IREC Report*, p. 9.

227 On Kajiado North, see *Daily Nation*, 29 December 2007, online edition.

228 Gibson, Clark and Long, James, 'The Presidential and Parliamentary Elections in Kenya December 2007: Evidence from an Exit Poll', *Electoral Studies*, Vol. 23, No 3 (2009); *New York Times*, 20 January 2009, online edition; Gibson, Clark and Long, James, 'What Explains the African Vote? Using Exit Poll Data from Kenya to Explore Ethnicity and Government Performance in Vote Choice', slide pack (San Diego, 5–6 December 2008), slide 50.

229 EUEOM: *Kenya Final Report*, p. 34.

230 Kenyans for Peace with Trust and Justice (KPTJ), 'Kenyan Election Observers Log December 29–30, 2007, unpublished (January 2008).

231 KPTJ: 'Observers Log'.

232 ECK: www.eck.or.ke.

233 Cable 08NAIROBI420, February 2008, from Rannenberger to US State Department, published by Wikileaks.

234 Other discrepancies vanished when the results were reviewed by the ECK and arithmetical errors corrected.

235 By the 2010 referendum, the number of registered voters had fallen again by 27%, suggesting at least 10% of the Somali votes were spurious.

236 Kenya: *IREC Report*, p. 124.

237 Kivuitu, in *Standard*, 16 March 2008, online edition.

238 Kenya: *IREC Report*, p. 23.

239 Raila Odinga, in *Daily Nation*, 25 January 2008, online edition.

240 *Daily Nation*, 3 March 2011, online edition, reporting US diplomatic cables from 2007 published by Wikileaks; also Khamisi, *Politics of Betrayal*, pp. 200–10; 216–20.

241 *Daily Nation*, 11 January 2008, online edition.

242 A narrow victory, since the government had acquired the support of most minor party MPs in the interim. *Daily Nation*, 16 January 2008, online edition.

243 *Daily Nation*, 31 January 2008, online edition.

244 *East African*, 28 January 2008, online edition.

245 Lindenmayer, Elisabeth and Kaye, Josie Lianna, 'A Choice for Peace? The Story of 31 Days of Mediation in Kenya', UN Studies Programme (n.d). http://kofiannanfoundation.org/sites/default/files/Microsoft%20Word%20-%20A%20Choice%20for%20Peace.pdf.

246 Republic of Kenya, 'Organization of the Government of the Republic Of Kenya', *Presidential Circular No.1/2008, Kenya Gazette* (May 2008).

Chapter 13: Cold War and Compromise, 2008–2011

1 *Nairobi Law Monthly*, January 2011, lists in painful detail the number of relatives of ministers in diplomatic and parastatal posts, including Odinga's wife, sister and nephew.

2 *Daily Nation*, 18 April 2008, online edition.

3 Republic of Kenya, *Report of the Independent Review Commission on the General Elections Held in Kenya on 27 December 2007* (Nairobi, pdf download, September 2008).

4 A list of offenders with their alleged crimes was published on a website within a week: www.mashada.com/blogs/You_Missed_This/2008/10/23/Alleged_Perpetrators_Of_Post_Election_Violence (23 October 2008).

5 *Daily Nation*, 15 December 2010, online edition. Redacted pre-trial notices and the accusations were immediately available on the Internet.

6 Alston, Philip, press statement (16–25 February 2009), www.eastandard.net/downloads/pressfinal.doc, pp. 2–3.

7 A police officer who had testified to his involvement in multiple murders was himself murdered.

8 *Daily Nation*, 15 November 2009, online edition. In the heat of the debate, ODM's William ole Ntimama was caught on camera claiming that his Maasai had killed 600 already while defending their land, and threatening war against the Kipsigis over the forest. Nation TV, 24 July 2008, www.youtube.com.

9 Kenya National Bureau of Standards, '2009 Population and Housing census highlights' (28 August 2010), www.knbs.or.ke/Census%20Results.

10 *Daily Nation*, 3 March 2011, online edition, reporting US cables from June 2008 released by Wikileaks

11 Kenya's politicians were under the spotlight continually, partly as a result of the work of the Mzalendo team and particularly of the Mars group, who had made a name for themselves by publishing much otherwise unavailable information on parliamentary performance and government scandals. See www.mzalendo.com and www.marsgroupkenya.org.

12 He was eventually acquitted due to lack of evidence.

13 Kosgey had also been named in Wikileaks documents as (in the view of the US) having been involved in massive corruption.

14 Some Moi-era figures were also in trouble, particularly ex-Commissioners for Lands Mwaita and Gacanja, who faced 300 legal cases against them filed by KACC for illegal land allocation. *Daily Nation* 27 March 2010, online edition.

15 *Nairobi Star*, 15 July 2011, online edition.

16 *Daily Nation*, 2 June 2011, online edition. They had been saying this in confidential cables since 2004, as the Wikileaks releases showed. Mwau resigned, but the Kenyan police said they had no evidence linking Mwau to drugs.

17 Saitoti, *National Assembly Official Report*, 22 December 2010 p. 25.

18 Committee of Experts on Constitutional Review, 'Harmonised Draft, Constitution of Kenya' (17 November 2009), www.nation.co.ke/blob/view/-/687282/data/113624/-/tvxtiqz/-/draft.pdf.

19 Committee of Experts on Constitutional Review, taking into account the consensus of the Parliamentary Select Committee, 'Proposed Constitution of Kenya' (23 February 2010), www.nation.co.ke.

20 The gradual demystification of the presidency was already well under way, with Kenyatta Day rebranded to Mashujaa (Heroes) Day and Moi Day no longer even a holiday.

21 *Daily Nation*, 28 January 2010, online edition.

22 *Daily Nation*, 1 April 2010, online edition.

23 Nation TV, 29 May and 4 June 2010, www.youtube.com; Capital FM, 24 July 2010, reporting results of Infotrak and Synovate polls.

24 Interim Independent Electoral Commission, 'Comprehensive Final 2010 Referendum Results' (10 August 2010), www.nation.co.ke.

25 See for example, *The Economist*, 12 August 2010, online edition.

26 There was huge trouble, for example, over the election boundaries review in 2010, headed by ex-MP Andrew Ligale, which was alleged to have been biased towards pro-ODM regions. Its proposals were not implemented and the problem passed to the Independent Electoral and Boundaries Commission in 2011. See for example *Daily Nation*, 20 November 2010, online edition.

27 Kibaki had tried unilaterally appointing his nominees but failed.

28 *Daily Nation*, 15 June 2011, online edition. Live transmission of parliamentary proceedings improved debating quality and encouraged attendance, but confidence in MPs was not enhanced when they voted themselves more large pay increases in 2010 and then refused in 2011 (despite the new constitution) to pay tax on them.

29 *Daily Nation*, 6 May 2011, online edition.

30 Federation of Kenya Employers, 'Highlights of the 2009 Economic Survey' (2010), http://fke-kenya.org/download/econsurvey2009.pdf.

31 Kibaki rejected it but it was re-passed and enacted in 2011.

32 *Daily Nation*, 6 May 1011, online edition.

33 *US Economic and Military Assistance (Loans and Grants), (Green Book)* (2009).

34 The Wikileaks diplomatic cables concerning Kenya were published in batches in November 2010 and March 2011. American embarrassment was huge. See for example *Nairobi Star*, 1 March 2011, *Daily Nation*, 3 March 2011, online editions.

35 Long a supporter of South Sudan, Kenya helped arm it against potential trouble in 2009, allowing it to tranship Russian tanks through the country.

36 KBC News, 17 June 2011, online edition.

37 Food and Agriculture Organisation, 'World Food Price Index, 2011', www.fao.org/worldfood situation/wfs-home/foodpricesindex/en.
38 Synovate Poll, in *Standard on Sunday*, 26 September 2010, online edition.

Chapter 14: Conclusions

1 Mueller, Susanne D., 'The Political Economy of Kenya's Crisis', *Journal of Eastern African Studies*, Vol. 2, No. 2 (July 2008), p. 188.
2 Berman, Bruce J., 'Ethnicity, Patronage and the African State: The Politics of Uncivil Nationalism', *African Affairs*, Vol. 97, No. 388 (1998), p. 338.
3 Lonsdale, John, 'Threads and Patches: Moral and Political Argument in Kenya', essay (24 April 2008), www.kenyaimagine.com.
4 Harbeson, John, *Nation-Building in Kenya: The Role of Land Reform* (Evanston, 1973), p. vxii.
5 See *East African Standard*, 26 June 2004, online edition.
6 Bratton, Michael and van de Walle, Nicholas, *Democratic Experiments in Africa: Regime Transitions in Comparative Perspective* (Cambridge, 1997), p. 42.
7 Posner, Daniel N., *Institutions and Ethnic Politics in Africa* (New York, 2005), pp. 3, 7.
8 O'Brien, F. S. and Ryan, T. C. I., 'Kenya' in Devarajan, S., Dollar, D. and Torgny Holmgren (eds), *Aid and Reform in Africa* (Washington, 2001), p. 506.
9 To cite a personal example, living in Malaysia, despite its many virtues, I live today in a country with preventive detention, bans on opposition rallies, state control of key prices such as fuel, large state industries and pervasive subsidies.
10 Kirugi M'Mukindia, in Republic of Kenya, *National Assembly Official Report* (Nairobi), 26 July 2006, col. 2403.
11 Van de Walle, Nicholas, *African Economies and the Politics of Permanent Crises, 1979–1999* (Cambridge, 2001), p. 149.
12 Kibaki is now the only MP who was in the House of Representatives in December 1963.
13 Young, Crawford, 'The End of the Post-Colonial State in Africa? Reflections on Changing African Political Dynamics', *African Affairs*, Vol. 103, No. 410 (2004).

Bibliography

Unpublished Primary Sources

British Government Archives (Public Records Office, London and Online)

Series CAB (Cabinet Records) 21, 128, 129 (Various).
Series CO (Colonial Office) 822, 968 (1960–4).
Series DEFE (Ministry of Defence) 11, 13, 24 (1967–74).
Series DO (Commonwealth Relations Office) 156, 213, 213, 214 (1964–6).
Series FCO (Foreign and Commonwealth Office) 31 (1967–74) and 46 (1973).
Series FO (Foreign Office) 371 (1964–6).
Series PREM (Prime Minister's Office) 11, 13, 15 (1963–73).

US Government Archives (Online)

Foreign Relations of the United States 1964–1968, Volume 24, Africa (Washington, US Department of State, 2006) www.state.gov/www/about_state/history/frusonline.html.
Foreign Relations of the United States, 1969–1976, Volume E-6, Documents on Africa, 1973–1976 (Washington, US Department of State, 2006). www.state.gov/r/pa/ho/frus/nixon/e6/c17634.htm.

Kenya National Archives (Murumbi Collection)

MAC/KEN/38/1 *Kenya Political Organisations. Kenya African National Union (KANU) – General and Local Government Elections 1963–69.*

Daily Nation Archives

Questionnaire and Candidate Declarations for Elections, 1979–2002.

Institute for Education in Democracy/NEMU Archives

Institute for Education in Democracy, *Constituency Observer Reports*, 2002.
National Election Monitoring Unit, *Count Certifier Reports*, 1992.
National Election Monitoring Unit, *District Liaison Officer Reports*, handwritten, 1992.
National Election Monitoring Unit, *Poll Monitors Reports, Various Polling Stations*, handwritten, 1992.
NCCK/IED/CJPC, *Observers/Poll Watchers Checklists, Various Constituencies*, handwritten, 1997.
NCCK/IED/CJPC, *Rapid Count Reports, Various Constituencies*, handwritten, 1997.

Interviews and Private Correspondence

Conversation with ex-Cabinet minister, 11 December 1992.
Conversations with senior lawyer, 2004.
Conversations and interviews with NEMU and IED teams, 1992, 1997, 2002.
Conversation with Njenga Mungai, November 1993.
Conversations with Robert Shaw, 1993, 1998.

Correspondence with Tom Wolf, 2004.
FORD-Kenya, *The Goldenberg File*, a collection of documents relating to the Goldenberg affair passed to the author, May 1993.
Interview with David Anderson, 6 November 1985.
Interview with Chris Hart, 1992–3.
Interview with IRI election observer, December 1992.
Interview with John Keen, 19 July 2004.
Interview with Gibson Kamau Kuria, Nairobi, December 1992.
Interview with Colin Legum, 3 May 1985.
Interview with Paul Muite, Nairobi, November 1993.
Interview with Sheila Murumbi, 1 September 2000.
Interview with Tom Okelo-Odongo, 25 November 1984.
Interview with former managing director of Securicor, 2004.
Interview with Koigi wa Wamwere, 1985.
Lecture by and conversation with John Githongo, 26 March 2006, London.
Personal communications with Susanne Mueller, various.
Personal communications with John Lonsdale, various.
Personal observation, Butere by-election, 31 October 1988.
Recording of EU Mission press conference, 1 January 2008.

Published Primary Sources

Kenyan and British Government Publications

Colonial Office, *Kenya Report of the Constituencies Delimitation Commission* (London, HMSO, 1963).
Committee on International Relations, *Kenya Economic Policy and Trade Practices, Country Report on Economic and Trade Practices, 1993* (Washington, US Department of State, 1994).
Corfield, F. D., *The Origins and Growth of Mau Mau, Sessional Paper No. 5 of 1959/60* (Nairobi, Government Printer, 1960).
House of Commons, *Hansard* (1988 on). www.parliament.uk/business/publications/hansard/.
Kenyan Hansard, 2006–7. Pdf copies available at Mars (Media Analysis and Research) Group, www.marsgroupkenya.org/pdfs/governance/Hansards/.
Kenya Independence Conference 1963, Cmnd 2156 (London, HMSO, 1963).
Kenya Northern Frontier District Commission, *Report of the Northern Frontier District Commission*, CMD 1900 (London, HMSO, 1962).
Kenya Regional Boundaries Commission, *Report of the Regional Boundaries Commission* (London, HMSO, 1962).
'Kenya's Election Crisis', Hearing before the Subcommittee for Africa of the Committee for International Relations, House of Representatives, 30 July 1997 (Washington, Government Printing Office, 1997).
Report of the Kenya Constitutional Conference (London, HSMO, 1962).
Republic of Kenya, *1962 Census Advance Report of Vols 1 & 2* (Nairobi, Economics and Statistics Division, Ministry of Economic Planning and Development, 1964).
Republic of Kenya, *The 1999 Population and Housing Census, Volume 1* (Nairobi, Government Printer, 2001).
Republic of Kenya, *The 2007 Elections in Kenya: Independent Review Commission (IREC) Report* (Nairobi, 19 September 2008), pdf download from http://www.communication.go.ke/media.asp?id=719.
Republic of Kenya, *African Socialism and its Application to Planning in Kenya*, Sessional Paper No. 10 (Nairobi, Government Printer, 1965).
Republic of Kenya, *Annual Public Debt Management Report, July 2005–June 2006* (Nairobi, Debt Management Department, 2007). PDF version available at www.treasury.go.ke.
Republic of Kenya, *Commission of Inquiry into Post-Election Violence (CIPEV)* (Nairobi, Government Printer, 2008), pdf download from http://www.communication.go.ke/media.asp?id=739.

Republic of Kenya, *Constitution of Kenya (Amendment) Bill, 1992, Kenya Gazette Supplement No. 16* (3 March 1992).

Republic of Kenya, *Constitution of Kenya, Revised Edition (1992)* (Nairobi, Government Printer, 1992).

Republic of Kenya, *Constitution of Kenya, Revised Edition (2001)* (Nairobi, Government Printer, 2001).

Republic of Kenya, *Development Plan, 1970–74* (Nairobi, Government Printer, 1969).

Republic of Kenya, *Development Plan, 1974–78* (Nairobi, Government Printer, 1974).

Republic of Kenya, *Development Plan, 1984–88* (Nairobi, Government Printer, 1984).

Republic of Kenya, *District Focus for Rural Development (Revised March 1987)* (Nairobi, Government Printer, 1987).

Republic of Kenya, *Economic Management for Renewed Growth*, Sessional Paper No. 1 of 1986 (Nairobi, Government Printer, 1986).

Republic of Kenya, *Economic Survey* (Nairobi, Central Bureau of Statistics, Various).

Republic of Kenya, *House of Representatives Official Report* (Nairobi, Government Printer, 1963–6).

Republic of Kenya, *Kenya Demographic and Health Survey 2003: Preliminary Report* (Nairobi, Central Bureau of Statistics, 2003).

Republic of Kenya, *Kenya Gazette* (Nairobi, Government Printer, various).

Republic of Kenya, *Kenya Population Census 1962* (Nairobi, Government Printer, 1966).

Republic of Kenya, *Kenya Population Census 1969* (Nairobi, Statistics Division, Ministry of Finance, Economic Planning and Development, 1969).

Republic of Kenya, *Kenya Population Census 1979, Volume 1* (Nairobi, Central Bureau of Statistics, Ministry of Economic Planning and Development, 1981).

Republic of Kenya, *Kenya Population Census 1989, Volume I* (Nairobi, Government Printer, 1994).

Republic of Kenya, *Ministry of Education Triennial Survey 1961–63* (Nairobi, Government Printer, 1964).

Republic of Kenya, *Ministry of Labour Annual Report* (Nairobi, Republic of Kenya, 1969).

Republic of Kenya, *National Assembly Official Report* (Nairobi, Government Printer, 1967 on).

Republic of Kenya, 'Organization of the Government of the Republic Of Kenya', *Presidential Circular No.1/2008, Kenya Gazette* (May 2008).

Republic of Kenya, *Privatisation of State Corporations and Investments*, Draft Sessional Paper (Nairobi, 2005).

Republic of Kenya, *The Proposed Constitution of Kenya*, Kenya Gazette Supplement, 22 August 2005.

Republic of Kenya, *Report and Recommendations of the Working Party on Government Expenditures* (Nairobi, Government Printer, 1982).

Republic of Kenya, *Report of Judicial Commission Appointed to Inquire into Allegations Involving Charles Mugane Njonjo* (Nairobi, Government Printer, 1984).

Republic of Kenya, *Report of the Civil Service Review Committee, 1979–80 (the Waruhiu Report)* (Nairobi, Government Printer, 1980).

Republic of Kenya, *Report of the Commission of Inquiry (Public Service Structure and Remuneration Commission) 1970–71 (the Ndegwa Report)* (Nairobi, Government Printer, 1971).

Republic of Kenya, *Report of the Commission of Inquiry into the Land Law System of Kenya on Principles of a National land Policy Framework, Constitutional Position on Land and New Institutional Framework for Land Administration. (Chairman Charles Njonjo)* (Nairobi, Government of Kenya, 2002).

Republic of Kenya, *Report of the Independent Review Commission on the General Elections Held in Kenya on 27 December 2007* (Nairobi, September 2008), pdf download at www.communication.go.ke/media.asp?id=719.

Republic of Kenya, *Report of the Judicial Commission Appointed to Inquire into Tribal Clashes in Kenya (the Akiwumi Report)* (Nairobi, Government Printer, 1999).

Republic of Kenya, *Report of the Judicial Commission of Inquiry into the Goldenberg Affair. (Chair Justice Bosire)* (Nairobi, Government Printer, 2005).

Republic of Kenya, *Report of the Parliamentary Select Committee to investigate Ethnic Clashes in Western and Other Parts of Kenya (the Kiliku Report)* (Nairobi, Government Printer, 1992).

Republic of Kenya, *Report of the Task Force on the Establishment of a Truth, Justice and Reconciliation Commission* (Nairobi, Government Printer, 2003).

Republic of Kenya, *Report on the Mission of Land Consolidation and Registration in Kenya, 1965–1966* (Nairobi, Government Printer, 1966).
Republic of Kenya, *Review of Statutory Boards (the Ndegwa Report)* (Nairobi, Government Printer, May 1979).
Republic of Kenya, *The Senate Official Report* (Nairobi, Government Printer, 1963–6).
Republic of Kenya, *Statistical Abstract* (Nairobi, Government Printer, 1972–2009).

Political Party Materials

Democratic Party of Kenya, *Democratic Party of Kenya Manifesto 1992* (Nairobi, DP, 1992).
Democratic Party of Kenya, *Election '97 Manifesto* (Nairobi, DP, 1997).
Forum for the Restoration of Democracy, *FORD Manifesto: Charter for the Second Liberation* (Nairobi, Agip House, 1992).
KANU, *KANU Manifesto 1997: Our Vision into the Next Millennium* (Nairobi, KANU, 1997).
KANU, *KANU Manifesto 2002: Laying a Solid Foundation for Kenya* (Nairobi, KANU, 2002).
KANU, *KANU Manifesto and Policy Document 1992* (Nairobi, KANU, 1992).
KANU, *Kenya Pays Tribute to President Moi* (Nairobi, KANU, 1986).
Kenya African Democratic Union, *KADU Election Policy 1963: Uhuru na Majimbo sasa!* (Nairobi, KADU, 1963).
Party of National Unity, *Manifesto:2007* (Nairobi, PNU, 2007).

Company and Parastatal Accounts

Kenya Power & Lighting Company, *Annual Report* (Nairobi, KPLC, 1983).
Kenya Wildlife Service, *Annual Report* (Nairobi, KWS, 1995).
National Bank of Kenya, *Annual Reports and Accounts* (Nairobi, NBK, 1996–2000).

Election Observer Reports

Andreassen, Bard-Anders, Geisler, Gisela and Tostensen, Arne, *A Hobbled Democracy: The Kenyan General Election, 1992* (Norway, Michelsen Institute, 1993).
Commonwealth Observer Group, *Kenya General Election 27 December 2002: The Report of the Commonwealth Observer Group* (London, Commonwealth Secretariat, 2006).
Commonwealth Observer Group, *Kenya General Election 27 December 2007* (London, Commonwealth Secretariat, 2008).
Commonwealth Observer Group, *The Presidential, Parliamentary and Civic Elections in Kenya 29 December 1992* (London, Commonwealth Secretariat, 1993).
European Union Election Observation Mission, *Kenya Final Report, General Elections 27 December 2007* (2008).
European Union Election Observation Mission, *Kenya General Elections 27 December 2002 Final Report* (2003).
Institute for Education in Democracy, *Enhancing the Electoral Process in Kenya: A Report on the Transition General Elections 2002* (Nairobi, IED 2003).
Institute for Education in Democracy, *Registration of Voters in 2002: An Audit* (Nairobi, IED, 2002).
Institute for Education in Democracy/Catholic Justice and Peace Commission/National Council of Churches in Kenya, *Report on the 1997 General Elections in Kenya 29–30 December 1997* (Nairobi, IED/CJPC/NCCK, 1998).
International Republican Institute, *Kenya Presidential, Parliamentary and Local Elections, December 2007: Election Observer Mission Final Report* (Washington, IRI, 2008).
International Republican Institute, *Kenya: The December 29, 1992 Elections* (New York, IRI, 1993).
Kenya Civil Society Observation Programme, *Report on the Referendum on the Proposed New Constitution of Kenya, 21st November 2005* (Nairobi, IED, 2006).

Kenya Domestic Observation Programme, *When Kenyans Spoke: 2002 General Election* (Nairobi, K-DOP, 2003).

National Council of Women of Kenya, *Report of the Election Monitoring Exercise: A Project of the National Council of Women of Kenya* (Nairobi, NCWK, 1993).

National Election Monitoring Unit, *The Multi-Party General Elections in Kenya 29 December, 1992: The Report of the National Election Monitoring Unit* (Nairobi, NEMU, 1993).

Electoral Commission of Kenya Materials

Electoral Commission of Kenya, 'Distribution of Voters By Age Nationally' (7 November 2002).

Electoral Commission of Kenya, 'ECK Report on the 1997 General Elections (Final Draft)', typescript (1999).

Electoral Commission of Kenya, 'Presidential and Parliamentary Election Results, 2007. www.eck.or.ke (2008).

Electoral Commission of Kenya, 'Registered Voters per Constituency (Revised October 2002)', 13 November 2002.

Electoral Commission of Kenya. *Presidential, Parliamentary and Civic Election Results Database, 1997, 2002* (2007). www.eck.or.ke/index.php/Election-Results-Database/.

Secondary Sources

Books

Abreu, Elsa, *The Role of Self-Help in the Development of Education in Kenya, 1900–1973* (Nairobi, Kenya Literature Bureau, 1982).

Africa Watch, *Kenya: Taking Liberties* (New York, Human Rights Watch, 1991).

African Rights, *Kenya Shadow Justice* (London, African Rights, 1996).

Aguilar, Mario, *Being Oromo in Kenya* (Trenton, Africa World Press, 1998).

Amin, Mohamed and Moll, Peter, *One Man, One Vote: A Photo-Record of Kenya's 1974 General Elections* (Nairobi, East African Publishing House, 1975).

Amsden, Alice, *International Firms and Labour in Kenya, 1945–70* (London, Frank Cass, 1971).

Anderson, David, *Eroding the Commons: Politics of Ecology in Baringo, Kenya, 1895–1963* (Oxford, James Currey, 2002).

—— *Histories of the Hanged: The Dirty War in Kenya and the End of Empire* (New York, W. M. Norton, 2005).

—— and Broch-Due, Vigdis (eds), *The Poor are Not Us: Poverty and Pastoralism in Eastern Africa* (Oxford, James Currey, 1999).

Andrew, Christopher, *The Defence of the Realm: The Authorised History of MI5* (London, Penguin, 2010).

Anguka, Jonah, *Absolute Power: The Ouko Murder Mystery* (London, Pen Press, 1998).

Anonymous, *(In)Dependent Kenya* (London, Zed Press, 1982).

Anonymous, 'Kenya: The Politics of Repression', *Race and Class*, Vol. XXIV (London, Institute of Race Relations, Winter 1983).

Arnold, Guy, *Kenyatta and the Politics of Kenya* (London, J. M. Dent & Sons, 1974).

Aseto, Oyugi and Okelo, Jasper, *Privatisation in Kenya* (Nairobi, Basic Books Kenya, 1997).

Atieno Odhiambo, E. S., *Siasa: Politics and Nationalism in East Africa, 1905–1939* (Nairobi, Kenya Literature Bureau, 1981).

—— and Lonsdale, John (eds), *Mau Mau and Nationhood* (Oxford, James Currey, 2003).

Attwood, William, *The Reds and the Blacks: A Personal Adventure* (New York, Harper & Row, 1967).

Ayot, Henry Okello, *A History of the Luo-Abasuba of Western Kenya from A.D. 1760–1940* (Nairobi, Kenya Literature Bureau, 1979).

Badejo, Babafemi A., *Raila Odinga: An Enigma in Kenyan Politics* (Lagos, Yintab Books, 2006).

Barkan, Joel D. (ed.), *Beyond Capitalism vs. Socialism in Kenya and Tanzania* (Boulder, Lynne Rienner, 1994).

Barkan, Joel D. (ed.), *Politics and Public Policy in Kenya and Tanzania*, second edition (New York, Praeger, 1984).

Barnett, Donald L. and Njama, Karari, *Mau Mau from Within* (London, McGibbon & Kee, 1966).

Bates, Robert H., *Beyond the Miracle of the Market: The Political Economy of Agrarian Development in Kenya* (Cambridge, Cambridge University Press, 1989).

—— *Markets and States in Tropical Africa 2005 Edition* (London, University of California Press, 2005).

Bayart, Jean-François, *The State in Africa: The Politics of the Belly* (London, Longman, 1993).

Bennett, George, *Kenya: A Political History* (London, Oxford University Press, 1963).

—— and Rosberg, Carl, *The Kenyatta Election: Kenya 1960–61* (London, Oxford University Press, 1961).

Berman, Bruce, *Control and Crisis in Colonial Kenya: The Dialectic of Domination* (London, James Currey, 1990).

—— and Lonsdale, John, *Unhappy Valley, Book One: State and Class* (London, James Currey, 1992).

—— and —— *Unhappy Valley, Book Two: Violence and Ethnicity* (London, James Currey, 1992).

Bevan, David, Collier, Paul and Gunning, Jan Willem with Bigsten, Arne and Horsnell, Paul, *Controlled Open Economies: A Neoclassical Approach to Structuralism* (Oxford, Clarendon Press, 1990).

Bharati, Agehananda, *The Asians in East Africa: Jayhind and Uhuru* (Chicago, Nelson-Hall, 1972).

Bienen, Henry, *Kenya: The Politics of Participation and Control* (Princeton, Princeton University Press, 1974).

—— *Armies and Parties in Africa* (New York, Africana Publishing Company, 1978).

Blundell, Michael, *So Rough a Wind* (London, Weidenfeld & Nicholson, 1964).

Bogonko, Sorobea N., *Kenya 1945–1963: A Study in African National Movements* (Nairobi, Kenya Literature Bureau, 1980).

—— *A History of Modern Education in Kenya (1895–1991)* (Nairobi, Evans Brothers Kenya, 1992).

Boughton, James M., *Silent Revolution: The International Monetary Fund, 1979–1989* (Washington, IMF, 2001).

Branch, Daniel, *Defeating Mau Mau, Creating Kenya: Counterinsurgency, Civil War and Decolonization* (New York, Cambridge University Press, 2009).

Bratton, Michael and van de Walle, Nicholas, *Democratic Experiments in Africa: Regime Transitions in Comparative Perspective* (Cambridge, Cambridge University Press, 1997).

Buijtenhuis, Robert, *Mau Mau Twenty Years After* (Leiden, Mouton & Co., 1973).

Carey-Jones N. S., *The Anatomy of Uhuru* (New York, Praeger, 1966).

Carlsen, John, *Economic and Social Transformation in Rural Kenya* (Uppsala, Scandinavian Institute of African Studies, 1980).

Citizens for Justice, *We Lived to Tell: The Nyayo House Story* (Nairobi, Friedrich Ebert Stiftung, 2003).

Clayton, Anthony and Savage, Donald, *Government and Labour in Kenya 1895–1963* (London, Frank Cass, 1974).

Cliffe, L., Coleman J. S., and Doornbos, M. R. (eds), *Government and Rural Development in East Africa* (The Hague, Martinus Nijhoff, 1977).

Cohen, David W. and Atieno Odhiambo, E. S., *The Risks of Knowledge: Investigations into the Death of the Hon Minister John Robert Ouko in Kenya, 1990* (Nairobi, EAEP, 2004).

Collier, Paul and Lal, Deepak, *Labour and Poverty in Kenya, 1900–1980* (Oxford, Clarendon Press, 1986).

Coughlin, Peter and Ikiara, Gerrishon K. (eds), *Industrialisation in Kenya: In Search of a Strategy* (Nairobi, Heinemann, 1988).

—— and —— (eds), *Kenya's Industrialization Dilemma* (Nairobi, Heinemann Kenya, 1991).

Cowen, Michael and Laakso, Liisa (eds), *Multi-Party Elections in Africa* (Oxford, James Currey, 2002).

—— and MacWilliam, Scott, *Indigenous Capital in Kenya: The 'Indian' Dimension of Debate* (Helsinki, InterKont, 1996).

Diang'a, James Waore, *Kenya, 1982: The Attempted Coup – The Consequence of a One-Party Dictatorship* (London, Pen Press, 2002).

Dutto, Carl A., *Nyeri Townsmen* (Nairobi, East African Literature Bureau, 1975).

Economist Intelligence Unit, *Kenya, Country Report, 1st Quarter 1994* (London, EIU, 1994).

Edgerton, Robert B., *Mau Mau: An African Crucible* (London, I.B.Tauris, 1990).

Elkins, Caroline, *Britain's Gulag: The Brutal End of Empire in Kenya* (London, Jonathan Cape, 2005).

Ensminger, Jean, *Making a Market: The Institutional Transformation of an African Society* (Cambridge, Cambridge University Press, 1992).

Fratkin, Elliot, *Aariel Pastoralists of Kenya: Surviving Drought and Development in Africa's Arid Lands* (Needham Heights, Allyn and Bacon, 1998).

Frost, Richard, *Race Against Time: Human Relations and Politics in Kenya Before Independence* (London, Rex Collings, 1978).

Furedi, Frank, *The Mau Mau War in Perspective* (London, James Currey, 1989).

Geest, Willem van der (ed.), *Negotiating Structural Adjustment in Africa* (New York, UNDP, 1994).

Gertzel, Cherry, *The Politics of Independent Kenya, 1963–8* (Nairobi, East African Publishing House, 1970).

—— Goldschmidt, Maure and Rothchild, Donald (eds), *Government and Politics in Kenya* (Nairobi, East African Publishing House, 1969).

Ghai, Yash and McAuslan, J. P. W., *Public Law and Political Change in Kenya* (Nairobi, Oxford University Press, 1970).

Gibbon, Peter (ed.), *Markets, Civil Society and Democracy in Kenya* (Uppsala, Nordiska Afrikainstitutet, 1995).

Gicheru, H. B. Ndoria, *Parliamentary Practice in Kenya* (Nairobi, Transafrica, 1976).

Gifford, Paul, *Christianity, Politics and Public Life in Kenya* (London, C. Hurst & Co., 2009).

Githinji, Mwangi wa, *Ten Millionaires and Ten Million Beggars: A Study of Income Distribution and Development in Kenya* (Aldershot, Ashgate, 2000).

Goldsworthy, David, *Tom Mboya: The Man Kenya Wanted to Forget* (London, Heinemann, 1982).

Grosh, Barbara, *Public Enterprise in Kenya: What Works, What Doesn't, and Why* (Boulder, Lynne Rienner, 1991).

Hansen, Holger Bernt and Twaddle, Michael (eds), *Religion and Politics in East Africa* (London, James Currey, 1995).

Harbeson, John, *Nation-Building in Kenya: The Role of Land Reform* (Evanston, North-Western University Press, 1973).

Harden, Blaine, *Africa: Dispatches from a Fragile Continent* (London, HarperCollins, 1991).

Haugerud, Angelique, *The Culture of Politics in Modern Kenya* (Cambridge, Cambridge University Press, 1995).

Hazelwood, Arthur, *The Economy of Kenya: The Kenyatta Era* (Oxford, Oxford University Press, 1979).

Hempstone, Smith, *Rogue Ambassador: An African Memoir* (Sewanee, University of the South Press, 1997).

Heyer, Judith, Roberts, Pepe and Williams, Gavin (eds), *Rural Development in Tropical Africa* (Basingstoke, Macmillan, 1981).

Himbara, David, *Kenyan Capitalists, the State and Development* (Boulder, Lynne Rienner, 1993).

Human Rights Watch/Africa Watch, *Divide and Rule: State Sponsored Ethnic Violence in Kenya* (New York, Human Rights Watch, 1993).

Human Rights Watch/Africa Watch, *Failing the Internally Displaced: The UNDP Displaced Persons Programme in Kenya* (New York, Human Rights Watch, 1997).

Hunt, Diana, *The Impending Crisis in Kenya: The Case for Land Reform* (Aldershot, Gower, 1984).

Hyden, Goran, *African Politics in Comparative Perspective* (New York, Cambridge University Press, 2006).

Hyden, Goran, Jackson, Robert H. and Okumu, John J. (eds), *Development Administration: The Kenyan Experience* (Nairobi, Oxford University Press, 1970).

Iliffe, John, *East African Doctors: A History of the Modern Profession* (Kampala, Fountain, 1998).

Institute for Economic Affairs/Society for International Development, *Kenya at the Crossroads: Scenarios for our Future* (Nairobi, Institute for Economic Affairs and Society for International Development, 2001).

International Bank for Reconstruction and Development (IBRD), *The Economic Development of Kenya* (Baltimore, Johns Hopkins, 1963).

International Human Rights Law Group, *Facing the Pluralist Challenge: Human Rights and Democratization in Kenya's December 1992 Multi-Party Elections* (Washington, International Human Rights Law Group, 1992).

International Labour Office, *Employment, Incomes and Equality: A Strategy for Increasing Productive Employment in Kenya*, (Geneva, ILO, 1972).

International Labour Organisation, *World Labour Report 2000* (Geneva, ILO, 2000).

International Monetary Fund, *Annual Report* (Washington, IMF, 2001).

Itote, Waruhiu, *Mau Mau General* (Nairobi, East Africa Publishing House, 1967).

—— *Mau Mau in Action* (Nairobi, Transafrica, 1979).

Kaggia, Bildad, *Roots of Freedom, 1921–63* (Nairobi, East Africa Publishing House, 1975).

Kanogo, Tabitha, *Squatters and the Roots of Mau Mau, 1905–63* (London, James Currey, 1987).

Kanyinga, Karuti, *Re-Distribution from Above: The Politics of Land Rights and Squatting in Coastal Kenya, Research Report No. 115* (Uppsala, Nordiska Afrikainstitutet, 2000).

Kaplan, Irving, Dobert, Margaret, Marvin, Barbara J., McLaughlin James L. and Whitaker, Donald P., *Area Handbook for Kenya*, second edition (Washington, United States Government, 1982).

Kaplinsky, Raphael (ed.), *Readings on the Multinational Corporation in Kenya* (Nairobi, Oxford University Press, 1978).

Kareithi, Peter, *Weekly Review Guide to Politics in Kiambu* (Nairobi, Stellascope, 1979).

Karimi, Joseph and Ochieng, Philip, *The Kenyatta Succession* (Nairobi, Transafrica, 1980).

Kariuki, Godfrey Gitahi, *The Illusion of Power* (Nairobi, Kenway Publications, 2001).

Kariuki, Josiah Mwangi, *Mau Mau Detainee: The Account of a Kenya African of his Experience in the Detention Camps 1953–1960* (London, Oxford University Press, 1963).

Karume, Njenga, *Beyond Expectations* (Nairobi, East African Educational Publishers, 2009).

Keegan, John, *World Armies*, second edition (London, Macmillan, 1983).

Kenya Human Rights Commission, *Kayas of Deprivation, Kayas of Blood: Violence, Ethnicity and the State in Coastal Kenya* (Nairobi, Kenya Human Rights Commission, 1997).

Kenya Human Rights Commission, *Kayas Revisited: A Post-Election Balance Sheet* (Nairobi, Kenya Human Rights Commission, 1998).

Kenya Human Rights Commission, *Killing the Vote: State Sponsored Violence and Flawed Elections in Kenya* (Nairobi, Kenya Human Rights Commission, 1998).

Kenya Human Rights Commission, *Ours by Right, Theirs by Might: A Study on Land Clashes* (Nairobi, Kenya Human Rights Commission, 1996).

Kenya Human Rights Commission, *Violating the Vote: A Report on the 2007 General Elections* (Nairobi, Kenya Human Rights Commission, 2008).

Kenyatta, Jomo, *Facing Mount Kenya: The Tribal Life of the Gikuyu* (London, Secker and Warburg, 1938).

—— *Harambee!* (Nairobi, Oxford University Press, 1964).

—— *Suffering Without Bitterness: The Founding of the Kenya Nation* (Nairobi, East African Publishing House, 1968).

Kershaw, Greet, *Mau Mau from Below* (Oxford, James Currey, 1997).

Khamisi, Joe, *The Politics of Betrayal* (Bloomington, Trafford, 2011).

Kibwana, Kivutha, *Fundamental Rights and Freedoms in Kenya* (Nairobi, Oxford University Press, 1990).

—— Wanjala, Smokin and Okech-Owiti (eds), *The Anatomy of Corruption in Kenya* (Nairobi, Claripress, 1996).

Kihoro, Wanyiri, *Never Say Die: The Chronicle of a Political Prisoner* (Nairobi, East African Educational Publishers, 1998).

Killick, Tony (ed.), *Papers on the Kenyan Economy: Performance, Problems and Policies* (Nairobi, Heinemann, 1981).

Killick, Tony (ed.), *The IMF and Stabilisation: Developing Country Experiences* (London, Heinemann Education, 1984).

Kimenyi, Mwangi S., Mbaku, Mukum John and Mwaniki, Ngure (eds), *Restarting and Sustaining Economic Growth and Development in Africa: The Case of Kenya* (Aldershot, Ashgate, 2003).

King, Kenneth, *Jua Kali in Kenya: Change and Development in an Informal Economy 1970–95* (London, James Currey, 1996).

Kipkorir, Ben E. with Welbourn F. B., *The Marakwet of Kenya* (Nairobi, East Africa Literature Bureau, 1973).

Kitching, Gavin, *Class and Economic Change in Kenya: The Making of an African Petite Bourgeoisie 1905–1970* (London, Yale University Press, 1980).

Kyle, Keith, *The Politics of the Independence of Kenya* (Basingstoke, Macmillan Press, 1999).

Labrousse, Alain and Laniel, Laurent, *The World Geopolitics of Drugs, 1998/1999* (Dordrecht, Kluwer, 2001).

Lafargue, Jérôme (ed.), *The General Elections in Kenya, 2007*, Cahier No. 38 (Nairobi, Institute Français de Récherche en Afrique, 2008).

Lamb, Geoff, *Peasant Politics: Conflict and Development in Murang'a* (Lewes, Julian Friedmann, 1974).

Langdon, Steven, *Multinational Corporations in the Political Economy of Kenya* (London, Macmillan, 1981).

Leakey, Louis S. B., *Defeating Mau Mau* (London, Methuen, 1954).

Legum, Colin, *Africa Contemporary Record* (New York, African Publishers, Various).

Leo, Christopher, *Land and Class in Kenya* (Toronto, University of Toronto Press, 1984).

Leonard, David K., *African Successes: Four Public Managers of Kenyan Rural Development* (Berkeley, University of California Press, 1991).

Leys, Colin, *Underdevelopment in Kenya: The Political Economy of Neo-Colonialism 1964–71* (London, Heinemann, 1975).

Lindberg, Staffan I., *Democracy and Elections in Africa* (Baltimore, Johns Hopkins University Press, 2006).

Loughran, Gerald, *Portrait of a Nation* (London, I.B.Tauris, 2010).

Maathai, Wangari, *The Green Belt Movement: Sharing the Approach and the Experience* (New York, Lantern Books, 2004 edition, 2004).

—— *Unbowed: One Woman's Story* (London, Heinemann, 2007).

Macharia, Rawson, *The Truth about the Trial of Jomo Kenyatta* (Nairobi, Longman Kenya, 1991).

Magyar, Karl (ed.), *United States Interests and Policies in Africa: Transition to a New Era* (Basingstoke, Macmillan, 2000).

Mailu, David G., *The Principles of Nyayo Philosophy, Standard 7 and 8* (Nairobi, Mailu Publishing House, 1989).

Maloba, Wunyabari O., *Mau Mau and Kenya: An Analysis of a Peasant Revolt* (London, James Currey, 1993).

Marris, Peter and Somerset, Anthony, *African Businessmen: A Study of Entrepreneurship and Development in Kenya* (Nairobi, East African Publishing House, 1971).

Matiba, Kenneth, *Aiming High* (Nairobi, People Ltd, 2000).

Matson, A. T., *Nandi Resistance to British Rule, 1890–1906* (Nairobi, East Africa Publishing House, 1972).

Maxon, Robert, *East Africa: An Introductory History* (Nairobi, Heinemann Kenya, 1986).

Maxon, Robert M., *Conflict and Accommodation in Western Kenya: The Gusii and the British, 1907–1963* (Cranbury, Associated University Presses, 1989).

Mbithi, Philip M. and Rasmusson, Rasmus, *Self-Reliance in Kenya: The Case of Harambee* (Uppsala, Scandinavian Institute of African Studies, 1977).

Mboya, Tom, *Freedom and After* (London, Andre Deutsch, 1963).

—— *The Challenge of Nationhood* (Nairobi, East African Educational Publishers, 1970).

Miller, Norman and Yeager, Rodger, *Kenya: The Quest for Prosperity*, second edition (Boulder, Westview, 1994).

Moi, Daniel T. arap, *Kenya African Nationalism: Nyayo Philosophy and Principles* (London, Macmillan, 1986).

Morton, Andrew, *Moi: The Making of an African Statesman* (London, Michael O'Mara Books, 1998).

Munene, Macharia, *The Politics of Transition in Kenya, 1995–98* (Nairobi, Quest & Insight, 2001).

Muriuki, Godfrey, *A History of the Kikuyu, 1500–1900* (Nairobi, Oxford University Press, 1974).

Murray-Brown, Jeremy, *Kenyatta* (London, George Allen & Unwin, 1972).

Murunga, Godwin R. and Nasong'o, Shadrack W., *Kenya: The Struggle for Democracy* (London, CODESRIA/Zed Books, 2007).

Murungi, Kiraitu, *In the Mud of Politics* (Nairobi, Acacia Stantex, 2000).

Mutiso, Gideon Cyrus, *Kenya: Politics, Policy and Society* (Nairobi, East Africa Literature Bureau, 1975).

Mutua, Makau, *Kenya's Quest for Democracy: Taming Leviathan* (Boulder, Lynne Rienner, 2008).

Mutunga, Willy, *Constitution-Making from the Middle: Civil Society and Transition Politics in Kenya, 1992–1997* (Nairobi, SAREAT, 1999).

Mwangi, Paul, *The Black Bar* (Nairobi, Privately Published, 2001).

Mwanzi, Henry A., *A History of the Kipsigis* (Nairobi, East African Literature Bureau, 1977).

National Christian Council of Kenya, *Who Controls Industry in Kenya?* (Nairobi, East African Publishing House, 1968).

National Christian Council of Kenya, *The Cursed Arrow: A Report on Organised Violence Against Democracy in Kenya, Volume 1: Contemporary Report on the Politicized Land Clashes in Rift Valley, Nyanza and Western Provinces* (Nairobi, NCCK, 1992).

Nellis, John, *Who Pays Tax in Kenya? Research Report No. 11* (Uppsala, Scandinavian Institute of African Studies, 1972).

—— *The Ethnic Composition of Leading Kenyan Government Positions, Research Report No. 24* (Uppsala, Scandinavian Institute of African Studies, 1974).

Nzioki, Mutuku and Dar, M. B., *Who is Who in Kenya 1982–1983* (Nairobi, Africa Book Services, 1982).

Ochieng', Philip, *I Accuse the Press* (Nairobi, Initiatives Publishers, 1992).

Ochieng, William R., *An Outline History of Nyanza up to 1914* (Nairobi, East African Literature Bureau, 1974).

—— *A History of Kenya* (London, Macmillan Press, 1985).

—— (ed.), *Themes in Kenyan History* (Nairobi, East African Educational Publishers, 1990).

—— and Maxon, Robert M. (eds), *An Economic History of Kenya* (Nairobi, East Africa Educational Publishers, 1992).

Oded, Arye, *Islam and Politics in Kenya* (Boulder, Lynne Rienner, 2000).

Odinga, Oginga, *Not Yet Uhuru* (Nairobi, Heinemann Educational Publishers, 1967).

Ogot, Bethwell, *History of the Southern Luo* (Nairobi, East African Publishing House, 1967).

—— (ed.), *Hadith 2* (Nairobi, East African Publishing House, 1970).

—— (ed.), *Hadith 3* (Nairobi, East African Publishing House, 1971).

—— (ed.), *Hadith 5: Economic and Social History of East Africa* (Nairobi, Kenya Literature Bureau, 1976).

—— *My Footprints on the Sands of Time: An Autobiography* (Kisumu, Anyange Press, 2003).

—— and Ochieng, William (eds), *Decolonisation and Independence in Kenya, 1940–93* (Nairobi, East Africa Educational Publishers, 1995).

Okech-Owiti (ed.), *The Electoral Environment in Kenya: A Research Project Report* (Nairobi, IED, 1997).

Okoth, P. Godfrey, *United States of America's Foreign Policy Toward Kenya, 1952–1969* (Nairobi, Gideon S. Were Press, 1992).

Okullu, Henry, *Church and Politics in East Africa* (Nairobi, Uzima Press, 1974).

Ominde S. H. (ed.), *Population and Development in Kenya* (Nairobi, Heinemann, 1984).

Oruka, H. Odera, *Oginga Odinga: His Philosophy and Beliefs* (Nairobi, Initiatives Publishers, 1992).

Orvis, Stephen Walter, *The Agrarian Question in Kenya* (Gainesville, University Press of Florida, 1993).

Osolo-Nasubo, Ng'weno. *A Socio-Economic Study of the Kenya Highlands from 1900–1970: A Case Study of Uhuru Government* (Washington, University Press of America, 1977).

Oucho, John O., *Urban Migrants and Rural Development in Kenya* (Nairobi, Nairobi University Press, 1996).

—— *Undercurrents of Ethnic Conflict in Kenya* (Leiden, Brill, 2002).

Oyugi, Walter O. (ed.), *Politics and Administration in East Africa* (Nairobi, English Press, 1994).

—— Wanyande, Peter and Odhiambo-Mbai, C. (eds), *The Politics of Transition in Kenya: From KANU to NARC* (Nairobi, Heinrich Böll Foundation, 2003).

Parsons, Timothy, *The 1964 Army Mutinies and the Making of Modern East Africa* (Westport, Praeger, 2003).

Percox, David A., *Britain, Kenya and the Cold War* (London, I.B.Tauris, 2004).

Pincher, Chapman, *Inside Story* (London, Book Club Associated, 1978).

Posner, Daniel N., *Institutions and Ethnic Politics in Africa* (New York, Cambridge University Press, 2005).

Roelker, Jack R., *Mathu of Kenya: A Political Study* (Stanford, Hoover Institution Press, 1976).

Rosberg, Carl G. and Nottingham, John, *The Myth of Mau Mau* (London, Pall Mall, 1966).

Rothchild, Donald, *Racial Bargaining in Independent Kenya: A Study of Minorities and Decolonisation* (London, Oxford University Press, 1973).

Rutten, Marcel, Mazrui, Alamin M. and Grignon, François (eds), *Out for the Count: The 1997 General Elections and Prospects for Democracy in Kenya* (Kampala, Fountain, 2001).

Sabar, Galia, *Church, State and Society in Kenya: From Mediation to Opposition, 1963–1993* (London, Frank Cass, 2002).

Saitoti, George, *The Challenges of Economic and Institutional Reforms in Africa* (Aldershot, Ashgate, 2002).

Sandbrook, Richard, *Proletarians and African Capitalism: The Kenyan Case, 1960–1972* (Cambridge, Cambridge University Press, 1975).

Schatzberg, Michael G. (ed.), *The Political Economy of Kenya* (New York, Praeger, 1987).

Schlee, Gunther, *Identities on the Move: Clanship and Pastoralism in Northern Kenya* (Nairobi, Gideon S. Were Press, 1994).

Schmidt, S. and Kibara, G., *Kenya: On the Path to Democracy? An Interim Evaluation* (Nairobi, Konrad Adenaur Foundation, 2002).

Shell International, *2001 Global Scenarios: People and Connections* (London, Shell International Limited, 2001).

Sorrenson, M. P. K., *Land Reform in the Kikuyu Country* (Nairobi, Oxford University Press, 1967).

—— *Origins of European Settlement in Kenya* (Nairobi, Oxford University Press, 1968).

Spear, Thomas T., *Kenya's Past: An Introduction to Historical Method in Africa* (London, Longman, 1981).

—— and Waller, Richard (eds), *Being Maasai: Ethnicity and Identity in East Africa* (London, James Currey, 1993).

Spencer, John, *KAU: The Kenya African Union* (London, Routledge and Kegan Paul, 1985).

Stern, Chester, *Iain West's Casebook* (London, Warner Books, 1997).

Stichter, Sharon, *Migrant Labour in Kenya: Capitalism and African Response, 1895–1975* (Harlow, Longman, 1982).

Swainson, Nicola, *The Development of Corporate Capitalism in Kenya, 1918–1977* (Berkeley, University of California Press, 1980).

Tetley, Brian, *Mo: The Story of Mohammad Amin* (London, Moonstone Books, 1988).

Thiong'o, Ngugi wa, *Detained: A Writer's Prison Diary* (London, Heinemann, 1981).

—— *Barrel of a Pen: Resistance to Repression in Neo-Colonial Kenya* (London, New Beacon Books, 1983).

Thomas, Gordon, *Gideon's Spies: The Secret History of the Mossad* (London, Pan Books, 1999).

Throup, David W., *Economic and Social Origins of Mau Mau, 1945–53* (Oxford, James Currey, 1987).

—— and Hornsby, Charles, *Multi-Party Politics in Kenya* (Oxford, James Currey, 1998).

Tiffen, Mary, Mortimore, Michael and Gichuki, Francis, *More People, Less Erosion: Environmental Recovery in Kenya* (Chichester, John Wiley, 1994).

United Nations Development Programme, *Kenya National Human Development Report* (Nairobi, UNDP, 2006).

Van de Walle, Nicholas, *African Economies and the Politics of Permanent Crises, 1979–1999* (Cambridge, Cambridge University Press, 2001).

Van Zwanenberg R. M. A. with King, Anne, *An Economic History of Kenya and Uganda, 1800–1970* (London, Macmillan, 1975).

Waihenya, Waithaka, *The Negotiator* (Nairobi, Kenway Publications, 2006).

Wamwere, Koigi wa, *Conscience on Trial* (Trenton, African World Press, 1988).

Wandibba, Simiyu, *Masinde Muliro: A Biography* (Nairobi, East Africa Educational Publishers, 1996).

Wasserman, Gary, *Politics of Decolonization: Kenya Europeans and the Land Issue, 1960–65* (Cambridge, Cambridge University Press, 1976).

Weekly Review, *1979 Election Handbook* (Nairobi, Stellascope, 1979).

Were, Gideon S., *A History of the Abaluyia of Western Kenya, c.1500–1930* (Nairobi, East African Publishing House, 1967).

Werlin, Herbert H., *Governing an African City: A Study of Nairobi* (London, Africana Publishing Company, 1974).

Widner, Jennifer A., *The Rise of a Party-State in Kenya: from Harambee! to Nyayo!* (Berkeley, University of California Press, 1992).

Wiseman, John A. (ed.), *Democracy and Political Change in Sub-Saharan Africa* (London, Routledge, 1995).

Wolf, Jan J. de, *Differentiation and Integration in Western Kenya: A Study of Religious Innovation and Social Change Among the Bukusu* (The Hague, Mouton, 1977).

World Bank, *Sub-Saharan Africa: From Crisis to Sustainable Growth* (Washington, World Bank, 1989).

World Bank. *World Development Report: The Challenge of Development* (New York, Oxford University Press, 1991).

World Bank, *Entering the 21st Century: World Development Report, 1999/2000* (New York, Oxford University Press, 2000).

Wrong, Michaela, *It's Our Turn to Eat: The Story of a Kenyan Whistleblower* (London, Fourth Estate, 2009).

Articles, Chapters and Discussion Papers

Adar, Korwa G., 'Assessing Democratization in Kenya: A Post-mortem of the Moi Regime', *Journal of Commonwealth and Comparative Politics*, Vol. 38, No. 3 (November 2000).

Allen, Chris, 'Understanding African Politics', *Review of African Political Economy*, No. 65 (1995).

Anderson, David M., 'Vigilantes, Violence and the Politics of Public Order in Kenya', *African Affairs*, Vol. 101, No. 405 (October 2002).

—— 'Kenya's Elections 2002: The Dawning of a New Era?', *African Affairs*, Vol. 102, No. 407 (April 2003).

—— '"Yours in Struggle for Majimbo": Nationalism and the Party Politics of Decolonization in Kenya, 1955–64', *Journal of Contemporary History*, Vol. 40, No. 3 (2005).

Anyang' Nyong'o, Peter, 'Struggles for Political Power and Class Contradictions in Kenya', *Contemporary Marxism*, No. 7 (1983).

—— 'State and Society in Kenya: The Disintegration of the Nationalist Coalitions and the Rise of Presidential Authoritarianism, 1963–78', *African Affairs*, Vol. 88, No. 351 (April 1989).

Barkan Joel D., 'Bringing Home the Pork: Legislator Behavior, Rural Development, and Political Change in East Africa', in Smith, Joel and Musolf, Lloyd (eds), *Legislatures in Development* (Durham, Duke University Press, 1978).

—— 'Kenya: Lessons from a Flawed Election', *Journal of Democracy*, Vol. 4, No. 3 (July 1993).

—— and Ng'ethe, Njuguna, 'Kenya Tries Again', *Journal of Democracy*, Vol. 9, No. 2 (April 1998).

—— 'Kenya After Moi', *Foreign Affairs*, Vol. 83, No. 1 (January/February 2004).

—— and Holmquist, Frank, 'Peasant–State Relations and the Social Base of Self-Help in Kenya', *World Politics*, Vol. 41, No. 3 (April 1989).

—— and Okumu, John J., 'Semi-Competitive Elections, Clientelism and Politics Recruitment in a No-Party State: The Kenyan Experience', in Hermet, Guy, Rose, Richard and Rouquié, Alain (eds), *Elections Without Choice* (London, Macmillan Press, 1978).

Bayliss, Kate, 'Water Privatisation in Africa', *Journal of Modern African Studies*, Vol. 41, No. 4 (2003).

Bennett, George, 'Kenya's "Little General Election"', *The World Today* (August 1966).

Berg-Schlosser, D., 'Modes and Meanings of Political Participation in Kenya', *Comparative Politics*, Vol. 14, No. 4 (July 1982).

Berman, Bruce J., 'Ethnicity, Patronage and the African State: The Politics of Uncivil Nationalism', *African Affairs*, Vol. 97, No. 388 (1998).

Branch, Daniel, 'Loyalists, Mau Mau and Elections in Kenya: The First Triumph of the System, 1957–1958', *Africa Today*, Vol. 53, No. 2 (2006).

—— and Cheeseman, Nic, 'Briefing: Using Opinion Polls to Evaluate Kenyan Politics, March 2004–January 2005', *African Affairs*, Vol. 104, No. 415 (2005).

—— and Cheeseman, Nic, 'The Politics of Control in Kenya: Understanding the Bureaucratic-Executive State, 1954–73', *Review of African Political Economy*, Vol. 33, No. 207 (2006).

—— and —— 'Democratization, Sequencing and State Failure in Africa: Lessons from Kenya', *African Affairs*, Vol. 108, No. 430 (2009).

Bratton, Michael, 'Briefing: Islam, Democracy and Public Opinion in Africa', *African Affairs*, Vol. 102, No. 408 (2003).

Brown, Stephen, 'Authoritarian Leaders and Multiparty Elections in Africa: How Foreign Donors Help to Keep Kenya's Daniel arap Moi in Power', *Third World Quarterly*, Vol. 22, No. 5 (2001).

—— 'Quiet Diplomacy and Recurring "Ethnic Clashes" in Kenya', in Sriram, Chandra Lekha and Wermester, Karin (eds), *From Promise to Practice: Strengthening UN Capacities for the Prevention of Violent Conflict* (Boulder, Lynne Rienner, 2003).

Carotenuto, Matthew and Luongo, Katherine, 'Dala or Diaspora: Obama and the Luo Community of Kenya', *African Affairs*, Vol. 108, No. 431 (April 2009).

Chege, Michael, 'A Tale of Two Slums: Electoral Politics in Mathare and Dagoretti', *Review of African Political Economy*, Vol. 20 (January–April 1981).

—— 'Mau Mau Rebellion Fifty Years on', *African Affairs*, Vol. 103, No. 410 (2004).

Cleary, A. S., 'The Myth of Mau Mau in its International Context', *African Affairs*, Vol. 89, No. 355 (1990).

Cohen, John M., 'Ethnicity, Foreign Aid and Economic Growth in Sub-Saharan Africa: The Case of Kenya', *Harvard Institution for International Development, Paper No. 520* (1995).

Committee for the Release of Political Prisoners in Kenya, *University Destroyed: Moi Crowns Ten Years of Government Terror in Kenya* (London, CRPP, 1983).

Currie, Kate and Ray, Larry, 'State and Class in Kenya: Notes on the Cohesion of the Ruling Class', *Journal of Modern African Studies*, Vol. 22, No. 4 (1984).

De Sardan, J. P. Olivier, 'A Moral Economy of Corruption', *Journal of Modern African Studies*, Vol. 37, No. 1 (March 1999).

Dove, Linda A., 'Teachers and Politics in Ex-Colonial Countries', *Journal of Commonwealth and Comparative Politics*, Vol. 17, No. 2 (1979).

Dresang, Denis L. and Sharkanksky, Ira, 'Sequences of Change and the Political Economy of Public Corporations: Kenya', *Journal of Politics*, Vol. 37, No. 1 (1975).

Ellis, Stephen and Ter Haar, Gerrie, 'Religion and Politics in Sub-Saharan Africa', *Journal of Modern African Studies*, Vol. 36, No. 2 (1998).

Engholm, G. F., 'African Elections in Kenya, March 1957', in Mackenzie, W. J. M. and Robinson, Kenneth (eds), *Five Elections in Africa* (Oxford, Oxford University Press, 1960).

Fjeldstad, Odd-Helge and More, Mick, 'Revenue Authorities in Sub-Saharan Africa', *Journal of Modern African Studies*, Vol. 47, No. 1 (March 2009).

Fox, Roddy, 'Bleak Future for Multi-Party Elections in Kenya', *Journal of Modern African Studies*, Vol. 34, No. 4 (1996).

Gertzel, Cherry, 'The Provincial Administration in Kenya', *Journal of Commonwealth Political Studies*, Vol. IV, No. 3 (1966).

Gibson, Clark and Long, James, 'The Presidential and Parliamentary Elections in Kenya December 2007: Evidence from an Exit Poll', *Electoral Studies*, Vol. 28, No. 3 (2009).

Githinji, Mwangi wa and Cullenberg, Stephen E., 'Deconstructing the Peasantry: Class and Development in Rural Kenya', *Critical Sociology*, Vol. 29, No. 67 (2003).

Good, Kenneth, 'Kenyatta and the Organization of KANU', *Canadian Journal of African Studies*, Vol. 2, No. 2, (1968).

Hazelwood, Arthur, 'The End of the East African Community: What Are the Lessons for Regional Integration Schemes?', *Journal of Common Market Studies*, Vol. 18, No. 1 (September 1979).

Heald, Suzette, 'Agricultural Intensification and the Decline of Pastoralism: A Case Study from Kenya', *Africa Magazine*, Vol. 69 (22 March 1999).

Hetherington, Penelope, 'Generational Changes in Marriage Patterns in the Central Province of Kenya, 1930–1990', *Journal of Asian and African Studies*, Vol. 36, No. 2 (2001).

Holmquist, Frank and Ford, Michael, 'Kenyan Politics: Towards a Second Transition', *Africa Today*, Vol. 45, No. 2 (April–June 1998).

—— and —— 'Kenya: Slouching Towards Democracy', *Africa Today*, Vol. 39, No. 3 (1992).

Homewood, Katherine, Coast, Ernestina and Thompson, Michael, 'In-Migrants and Exclusion in East African Rangelands: Access, Tenure and Conflict', *Africa*, Vol. 74, No. 4 (2004).

Hornsby, Charles, 'The Social Structure of the National Assembly, 1963–83', *Journal of Modern African Studies*, Vol. 27, No. 2 (1989).

—— and Throup, David, 'Elections and Political Change in Kenya', *Journal of Commonwealth and Comparative Politics*, Vol. 30, No. 2 (1992).

Hughes, Lotte, 'Malice in Maasailand: The Historical Roots of Current Political Struggles', *African Affairs*, Vol. 104, No. 415 (2005).

Hulterström, Karolina, 'The Logic of Ethnic Politics: Elite Perceptions About the Role of Ethnicity in Kenyan and Zambian Party Politics', in Hulterström, Karolina, Kamete, Amin Y. and Melber, Henning, *Political Opposition in African Countries: The Cases of Kenya, Namibia, Zambia and Zimbabwe, Discussion Paper 37* (Uppsala, Nordiska Afrikainstitutet, 2007).

Hyden, Goran and Leys, Colin, 'Elections and Politics in Single Party Systems: The Case of Kenya and Tanzania', *British Journal of Political Science*, Vol. 2, No. 4 (1972).

K'Akumu, O. A., 'Privatization of the Urban Water Supply in Kenya: Policy Options for the Poor', *Environment and Urbanization*, Vol. 16 (2004).

Kagwanja, Peter Mwangi, 'Facing Mount Kenya or Facing Mecca? The *Mungiki*, Ethnic Violence, and the Politics of the Moi Succession in Kenya, 1987–2002', *African Affairs*, Vol. 102, No. 406 (January 2003).

—— 'Globalising Ethnicity, Localising Citizenship: Globalisation, Identity Politics and Violence in Kenya's Tana River Region', *Africa Development*, Vol. 28, Nos 1–2 (2003).

—— 'Power to Uhuru: Youth Identity and Generational Politics in Kenya's 2002 Elections', *African Affairs*, Vol. 105, No. 418 (October 2005).

Kanyinga, Karuti, 'Struggles Over Access to Land: The "Squatter Question" in Coastal Kenya', *Copenhagen, CDR Working Paper 98.7* (June 1998).

—— 'Contestation Over Political Space. The State and Demobilisation of Party Politics in Kenya', *Centre for Development Research Working Paper 98/12* (Copenhagen, Centre for Development Research, November 1998).

Kaumutunga, Musambayi, 'A City Under Siege: Banditry and Modes of Accumulation in Nairobi, 1991–2004', *Review of African Political Economy*, No. 106 (2005).

Kavulla, Travis R., 'Our Enemies Are God's Enemies: The Religion and Politics of Bishop Margaret Wanjiru, MP', *Journal of Eastern African Studies*, Vol. 2, No. 2 (July 2008).

Khapoya, Vincent, 'Kenya Under Moi: Continuity or Change?' *Africa Today*, Vol. 27, No. 1 (1980).

Kipkorir, Ben E., 'The Inheritors and Successors: The Traditional Background to the Modern Kenya African Elite; Kenya c.1890–1930', *Kenya Historical Review*, Vol. 2, No. 2 (1974).

Kjaer, Anne Mette, 'Old Brooms Can Sweep Too! An Overview of Rulers and Public Sector Reforms in East Africa', *Journal of Modern African Studies*, Vol. 42, No. 3 (2004).

Klopp, Jacqueline, 'Pilfering the Public: The Problem of Land-Grabbing in Contemporary Kenya', *Africa Today*, Vol. 47, No. 1 (2000).

—— 'Can Moral Ethnicity Trump Political Tribalism? The Struggle for Land and Nation in Kenya', *African Studies*, Vol. 61, No. 2 (2002).

Koff, David, 'Kenya's Little General Election', *Africa Report*, Vol. 11, No. 7 (October 1966).

Lawson, Letitia, 'The Politics of Anti-Corruption Reform', *Journal of Modern African Studies*, Vol. 47, No. 1 (2009).

Leys, Colin, 'Politics in Kenya: The Development of Peasant Society', *British Journal of Political Science*, Vol. 1, No. 3 (1971).

Lonsdale, John, 'Soil, Work, Civilisation and Citizenship in Kenya', *Journal of Eastern African Studies*, Vol. 2, No. 2 (2008).

Lynch, Gabriella, 'Courting the Kalenjin: The Failure of Dynasticism and the Strength of the ODM Wave in Kenya's Rift Valley Province', *African Affairs*, Vol. 107, No. 429 (October 2008).

MacWilliam, Scott, 'Rights and the Politics of Legality in Kenya', *Manchester Papers on Development*, Vol. 1, No. 1 (1985).

Marnham, Patrick, 'Repression in Kenya', *Spectator*, 21 January 1978.

Martin, Paul, 'Kenya's Uncertain Future', *Spectator*, 18 March 1978.

Mburu, Nene, 'Delimitation of the Elastic Ilemi Triangle: Pastoral Conflicts and Official Indifference in the Horn of Africa', *African Studies Quarterly*, Vol. 6, No. 4 (2003), web.africa. ufl.edu/asq/v7/v7i1a2.htm.

Mghanga Mwandawiro, 'Usipoziba Ufa Utajenga Ukuta: Land, Elections, and Conflicts in Kenya's Coast Province' (Nairobi, Heinrich Boll Stiftung, 2011).

Miller, Norman, 'Assassination and Political Unity: Kenya: Implications of the Assassination of Tom Mboya', *East Africa Series*, Vol. VIII, No. 5 (Kenya) (September 1969).

Mitry, Percy, 'Africa's Record of Regional Cooperation and Integration', *African Affairs*, Vol. 99, No. 397 (2000).

Morrison, Lesa, 'The Nature of Decline: Distinguishing Myth from Reality in the Case of the Luo of Kenya', *Journal of Modern African Studies*, Vol. 45, No. 1 (2007).

Mounter, Julian, 'The Biggest Game in Kenya', *The Listener*, 9 June 1977.

Mueller, Susanne D., 'Government and Opposition in Kenya, 1966–1969', *Journal of Modern African Studies*, Vol. 22, No. 3 (1984).

—— 'The Political Economy of Kenya's Crisis', *Journal of Eastern African Studies*, Vol. 2, No. 2 (July 2008).

Muigai, Githu, 'Amendment Lessons from History', *The Advocate*, Vol. 2, No. 3 (February 1993).

Mukonoweshuro, Eliphas, 'Authoritarian Reaction to Economic Crises in Kenya', *Race and Class*, Vol. 31, No. 4 (April–June 1990).

Mulaa, John, 'The Politics of a Changing Society: Mumias', *Review of African Political Economy*, Vol. 20 (January–April 1981).

Murray, J., 'Succession Prospects in Kenya', *Africa Report*, Vol. 13, No. 8 (November 1968).

Murton, John, 'Population Growth and Poverty in Machakos District, Kenya', *Geographical Journal*, Vol. 165 (March 1999).

Murunga, Godwin R., 'The State, its Reform and the Question of Legitimacy in Kenya', *Identity, Culture and Politics*, Vol. 5, Nos 1–2 (2004).

Muthoni, Anne and Wendoh, Peter (compilers) and Kichana, Philip (ed.), *Constitutional Law Case Digest Vol. II* (Nairobi, International Commission of Jurists, 2005).

Mutua, Makau, 'Justice Under Siege: The Rule of law and Judicial Subservience in Kenya', *Human Rights Quarterly*, Vol. 23, No. 1 (2001).

Ndegwa, Stephen N., 'Civil Society and Political Change in Africa: The Case of Non-Governmental Organizations in Kenya', *International Journal of Comparative Sociology*, Vol. 41, No. 4 (1994).

—— 'Citizenship and Ethnicity: An Examination of Two Transition Moments in Kenyan Politics', *American Political Science Review*, Vol. 91, No. 3 (September 1997).

—— 'Kenya: Third Time Lucky?', *Journal of Democracy*, Vol. 14, No. 3 (July 2003).

Ng'ang'a, David Mukaru, 'Mau Mau, Loyalists and Politics in Murang'a 1952–1970', *Kenya Historical Review*, Vol. 5, No. 2 (1977).

Nyairo, Joyce and Ogude, James, 'Popular Music, Popular Politics: Unbwogable and the Idioms of Freedom in Kenyan Popular Music', *African Affairs*, Vol. 104, No. 415 (April 2005).

O'Brien, F. S. and Ryan, T. C. I., 'Kenya', in Devarajan, S., Dollar, D. and Holmgren, Torgny (eds), *Aid and Reform in Africa* (Washington, World Bank, 2001).

Okoth-Ogendo, H. W. O., 'The Politics of Constitutional Change in Kenya since Independence, 1963–69', *African Affairs*, Vol. 71, No. 282 (1972).

Okumu, John J., 'The By-Election in Gem: An Assessment', *East African Journal*, Vol. VI, No. 6 (June 1969).

Olowu, Bamidele, 'Redesigning African Civil Service Reforms', *Journal of Modern African Studies*, Vol. 37, No. 1 (1999).

Orvis, Stephen Walter, 'Kenyan Civil Society: Bridging the Urban-Rural Divide?', *Journal of Modern African Studies*, Vol. 41, No. 2 (2003).

Pottinger, Lori, 'Major Dam Companies Caught in African Bribery Scandal', *World Rivers Review*, Vol. 14, No. 5 (October 1999).

Prinslow, Karl E., 'Building Military Relations in Africa', *Military Review* (May–June 1997).

Proctor, J. H., 'The Role of the Senate in the Kenya Political System', *Parliamentary Affairs*, Vol. XVIII, No. 4 (1965).

Rothchild, Donald, 'Ethnic Inequalities in Kenya', *Journal of Modern African Studies*, Vol. 7, No. 3 (1969).

—— 'Kenya's Africanization Program: Priorities of Development and Equity', *American Political Science Review*, Vol. 64, No. 3 (1970).

Rutten, Marcel, 'The Kenyan General Election of 1997: Implementing a New Model for International Election Observation in Africa', in Abbink, J. and Hesseling, G. (eds), *Election Observation and Democratization in Africa* (New York, Macmillan, 2000)

Sandbrook, Richard, 'Patrons, Client and Unions: the Labour Movement and Political Conflict in Kenya', *Journal of Commonwealth Political Studies*, Vol. 10, No. 1 (1972).

Sanger, Clyde and Nottingham, John, 'The Kenya General Election of 1963', *Journal of Modern African Studies*, Vol. 2, No. 1 (1964).

Southall, Roger, 'Moi's Flawed Mandate: The Crisis Continues in Kenya', *Review of African Political Economy*, Vol. 25, No. 75 (January 1998).

—— 'Re-Forming the State? Kleptocracy and the Political Transition in Kenya', *Review of African Political Economy*, Vol. 26, No. 79 (March 1999).

—— 'The Ndung'u Report: Land and Graft in Kenya', *Review of African Political Economy*, Vo. 32, No. 103 (March 2005).

—— and Wood, Geoffrey, 'Local Government and the Return to Multi-Partyism in Kenya', *African Affairs*, Vol. 95, No. 381 (October 1996).

Staudt, Kathleen A., 'Sex, Ethnic and Class Consciousness in Western Kenya', *Comparative Politics*, Vol. 14, No. 2 (January 1982).

Steeves, Jeffrey S., 'The Political Evolution of Kenya: The 1997 Elections and Succession Politics in Kenya', *Journal of Commonwealth and Comparative Politics*, Vol. 37, No. 1 (March 1999).

—— 'Presidential Succession in Kenya: The Transition from Moi to Kibaki', *Journal of Commonwealth and Comparative Politics*, Vol. 44, No. 2 (July 2006).

Stren, Richard, 'Factional Politics and Central Control in Mombasa 1960–1969', *Canadian Journal of African Studies*, Vol. 4, No. 1 (Winter 1970).

Tamarkin, Mordechai, 'From Kenyatta to Moi: The Anatomy of a Peaceful Transition of Power', *Africa Today*, Vol. 26, No. 4 (1979).

Thompson, Vincent B., 'The Phenomenon of Shifting Frontiers: The Kenya–Somalia Case in the Horn of Africa, 1880s–1970s', *Journal of Asian and African Studies*, Vol. 30, Nos 1–2, (1995).

Throup, David, 'Crime, Politics and the Police in Colonial Kenya, 1939–63', in Anderson, David and Killingray, David (eds), *Policing and Decolonisation: Nationalism, Politics and the Police, 1917–65* (Manchester, Manchester University Press, 1992).

—— 'Elections and Political Legitimacy in Kenya', *Africa*, Vol. 63, No. 3 (1993).

—— 'The Count', *Journal of Eastern African Studies*, Vol. 2, No. 2 (July 2008).

Versi, Anwer, 'Kenya: First of the African "Tigers"?', *African Business*, (1 January 1995).

Versi, Anwer, 'Kenya's Watershed Elections', *African Business* (December 1997).

Wamue, Grace Nyatugah, 'Revisiting our Indigenous Shrines through Mungiki', *African Affairs*, Vol. 100, No. 400 (2001).

Wanyande, Peter, 'Management Politics in Kenya's Sugar Industry: Towards an Effective Framework', *African Journal of Political Science*, Vol. 6, No. 1 (2001).

Willis, Justin, 'What Has He Got up his Sleeve? Advertising the Kenyan Presidential Candidates in 2007', *Journal of Eastern African Studies*, Vol. 2, No. 2 (July 2008).

Wipper, Audrey, 'Equal Rights for Women in Kenya?', *Journal of Modern African Studies*, Vol. 9, No. 3 (1971).

Wolf, Thomas P., 'Immunity or Accountability? Daniel Toroitich arap Moi, Kenya's First Retired President', in Southall, Roger and Melber, Henning (eds), *Legacies of Power: Leadership Change and Former Presidents in African Politics* (Cape Town, HSRC Press, 2006).

Yoo, Hyung-Gon Paul, 'Corruption, Rule of Law, and Civil Society: Why Patronage Politics is Good for Developing Markets and Democracies', *International Affairs Review*, Vol. XIV, No. 1 (Spring 2005).

Youé, Christopher, 'Settler Capital and the Assault on the Squatter Peasantry in Kenya's Uasin Gishu District, 1942–63', *African Affairs*, Vol. 87, No. 348 (1988).

Young, Crawford, 'The End of the Post-Colonial State in Africa? Reflections on Changing African Political Dynamics', *African Affairs*, Vol. 103, No. 410 (2004).

Theses

Clinkenbeard, Stephen, 'Donors Versus Dictators: The Impact of Multilateral Aid Conditionality on Democratization: Kenya and Malawi in Comparative Context, 1990–2004', B.A. dissertation, Brown University, 2004.

Hakes, Jay, 'The Parliamentary Party of the Kenya African National Union', Ph.D. dissertation, Duke University, 1970.

Hilton, Michael, 'Malcolm Macdonald, Jomo Kenyatta and the Preservation of British Interests in Commonwealth Africa, 1964-68', M.Phil. thesis, Trinity College Cambridge, 2009.

Hornsby, Charles, 'The Member of Parliament in Kenya, 1969–1983', D.Phil. dissertation, St Antony's College Oxford, 1985.

Kerretts-Makau, Monica J. J., 'At a Crossroad: The GATS Telecom Framework and Neo-Patrimonial States: The Politics of Telecom Reform in Kenya', D.Phil. thesis, University of New South Wales, 2006.

Kipkorir, Ben E., 'The Alliance High School and the Origins of the Kenya African Elite, 1926–1962', D.Phil. dissertation, St John's College Cambridge, 1969.

Mueller, Susanne D., 'Political Parties in Kenya: Patterns of Opposition and Dissent, 1919–1969', Ph.D. dissertation, Princeton University, 1972.

Nyamora, Pius, 'The Role of Alternative Press in Mobilization for Political Change in Kenya 1982–1992: Society Magazine as a Case Study', M.A. thesis, University of Florida, 2007.

Press, Robert Maxwell, 'Establishing a Culture of Resistance: The Struggle for Human Rights and Democracy in Authoritarian Kenya 1987–2002', D.Phil. thesis, University of Florida, 2004.

Tuitoek, Kiboswony, 'Educational Commissions as an Inquiry of Education Policy in Kenya: A Case Study of the Koech Commission', D.Ed. thesis, University of Birmingham, 2005.

Online and Other Sources

African Growth and Opportunity Act (2005), www.agoa.info.

Afrobarometer Network, 'Afrobarometer Round 2: Compendium of Comparative Results From a 15-Country Survey', *Afrobarometer Working Paper No. 34* (March 2004).

Alila, Patrick O., 'Kenya's Parliamentary Elections: Ethnic Politics in Two Rural Constituencies in Nyanza', *Institute for Development Studies Discussion Paper No. 282* (University of Nairobi, July 1986).

Alila, Patrick O., 'Luo Ethnic Factor in the 1979 and 1983 Elections in Bondo and Gem', *Institute for Development Studies Working Paper No. 408* (University of Nairobi, June 1985).

Alston, Philip, press statement, 16–25 February 2009, www.eastandard.net/downloads/pressfinal. doc.

Anonymous, 'The Truth About Kenyan Genocide', 5 January 2008, http://kenyangenocide. blogspot.com/2008/01/truth-about-kenyan-genocide.html.

Armstrong, Gina and Edgeworth, Linda, 'Kenya: A Pre-Election Assessment and Budget Analysis. July 3–10, 1992' (Washington, International Foundation for Electoral Systems. 1992).

Atieno Odhiambo, E. S., 'Ethnicity and Democracy in Kenya', lecture, University of Nebraska-Lincoln, Lincoln, Arts and Sciences Publications Department, 25 September 1998.

Ayittey, George, 'The Looting of Africa 3: Kenya', April 2007, www.jaluo.com/wangwach/200704/George_Ayittey041107.html.

BBC East Africa Unit, 'Kenyan Elections 1997: A Reference Guide', photocopy, December 1997.

Bedi, Arjun S., Kimalu, Paul, Manda, Damiano and Nafula, Nancy, 'The Decline in Primary School Enrolment in Kenya', *KIPPRA Discussion Paper No. 14* (Social Sector Division, Kenya Institute for Public Policy Research and Analysis, May 2002).

Bollinger, Lori, Stover, John and Nalo, David, 'The Economic Impact of AIDS in Kenya', *The Policy Project Working Paper, Futures Group International* (September 1999).

Central Bureau of Statistics, www.cbs.go.ke.

Chege, Michael, 'Economic Relations between Kenya and China, 1963–2007', *Centre for Strategic and International Studies Working Paper* (June 2008).

Clayton, Eric S., 'A Comparative Study of Settlement Schemes in Kenya', *Agrarian Development Unit, Cooperative Paper No. 3* (December 1978).

Cohen, John M. and Wheeler, John R., 'Improving Public Expenditure Planning: Introducing a Public Investment Program in Kenya', *Harvard Institute for International Development, Discussion Paper No. 479* (March 1994).

Committee of Experts on Constitutional Review, 'Harmonised Draft, Constitution of Kenya', 17 November 2009, www.nation.co.ke/blob/view/-/687282/data/113624/-/tvxtiqz/-/draft.pdf.

Committee of Experts on Constitutional Review, Taking into Account the Consensus of the Parliamentary Select Committee, 'Proposed Constitution of Kenya', 23 February 2010, www.nation.co.ke.

Commonwealth Observer Group, 'Commonwealth Team Urges Action on Nominations', press statement, 13 December 1992.

Constitution of Kenya Review Commission, 'Report of the Advisory Panel Of Eminent Commonwealth Judicial Experts', 17 May 2000, www.commonlii.org/ke/other/KECKRC/2002/index.html.

Constitution of Kenya Review Commission, 'Ikolomani Constituency Committee report', 2002, www.constitutionnet.org/files/IKOLOMANI%20CONSTITUENCY%20%20COMPLETE1.pdf.

Constitution of Kenya Review Commission, 'Draft Bill: The Constitution of the Republic of Kenya', 27 September 2002, www.constitutionnet.org.

Cross S., 'L'Etat C'est Moi: Political Transition and the Kenya General Elections of 1979', *University of East Anglia Discussion Paper No. 66* (n.d.).

Department of State, 'Annual Report on Military Expenditures, 1998, Submitted to the Committee on Appropriations of the U.S. Senate and the Committee on Appropriations of the U.S. House of Representatives', 19 February 1999, www.fas.org/irp/world/98_amiex2.html.

Donors for Development and Democracy Group, 'Election Observation Centre. Report on the 29th December 1997 General Elections in Kenya', 4 January 1998.

Donors for Development and Democracy Group , 'Executive Summary Final Statement of 26 January 1998', submitted 2 February 1998 to ECK.

EH Net Economic History Series, USD–GBP exchange rates website, eh.net/databases/.

Federation of Kenya Employers, 'Highlights of the 2009 Economic Survey', 2010, www.fke-kenya.org/download/econsurvey2009.pdf.

Food and Agriculture Organisation, 'FAOSTAT Production Data', 2004, www.faostat.fao.org.

Food and Agriculture Organisation, World Food Price Index, 2011, www.fao.org/worldfoodsituation/wfs-home/foodpricesindex/en.

Free Africa Foundation, www.freeafrica.org.

Gibson, Clark and Long, James, 'What Explains the African Vote?: Using Exit Poll Data from Kenya to Explore Ethnicity and Government Performance in Vote Choice', slide pack, San Diego, 5–6 December 2008.

Globenet Enda Preceup (Urban Popular Environment Economy Programme), www.globenet.org/preceup/pages/fr/chapitre/etatlieu/approchr/d/a_e.htm.

Harbeson, John W., 'The Kenya Little General Election: A Study in Problems of Urban Political Integration', *Institute of Development Studies Discussion Paper No. 52* (University College Nairobi, June 1967).

Hogg, Richard, 'Re-Stocking Pastoralists in Kenya: A Strategy for Relief and Rehabilitation', *Overseas Development Institute Paper 19c* (February 1985).

Hornsby, Charles, 'The History and Impact of Opinion Polls in Kenya', unpublished paper presented at ICAD/IRI Seminar on opinion polling, Nairobi, June 2001.

International Crisis Group, 'Kenya in Crisis', *Africa Report No. 137* (21 February 2008).

International Monetary Fund, 'International Finance Statistics', 2005, www.imf.org.

International Republican Institute, 'Follow-Up Statement IRI Observer Mission Kenya General Election 29–12–1992', press statement, Nairobi 4 January 1993.

International Republican Institute, 'Preliminary Statement of Findings, Kenyan General Elections, December 29, 1992', press statement, Nairobi, 1 January 1993.

KEDOF, 'Preliminary Press Statement and Verdict of 2007 Kenya's General Elections', 31 December 2007.

Kenya Anti-Corruption Commission, 'Annual Report, 2006–7' (Nairobi, October 2007), www.kacc.go.ke.

Kenya Domestic Observation Programme (K-DOP), 'A Big Step Forward for Democracy in Kenya', press release, 29 December 2002.

Kenya National Bureau of Standards, '2009 Population and Housing Census Highlights', 28 August 2010, www.knbs.or.ke/Census%20Results.

Kenyans for Peace with Trust and Justice (KPTJ), 'Kenyan Election Observers Log December 29–30, 2007', unpublished, January 2008.

Kenyans for Peace with Truth and Justice (KPTJ), 'Count Down to Deception: 30 Hours that Destroyed Kenya', final press release, 18 January 2008.

Killick, Tony and Mwega, F. M., 'Monetary Policy in Kenya 1967–88', *ODI Working Paper No. 39* (July 1990).

Klein, Keith, Scallan, Andrew, De Assuncao, Celio Santos and Dauphinais, Denise, 'Towards Credible and Legitimate Election in Kenya: Recommendation for Action' , unpublished report (Washington, International Foundation for Election Systems, April 1996).

Korre, Abdulwahab H., Hassan, D. A., Omar, Isaac, *The Gharri Experience in Northern Kenya* (2001), http://www.africanewsonline.com/The%20Gharri%20Eperience%20In%20Kenya.htm.

Kroll UK, *Project KTM*, 27 April 2004, published on Wikileaks (2004), www.wikileaks.org.

Lindenmayer, Elisabeth and Kaye, Josie Lianna, 'A Choice for Peace? The Story of 31 Days of Mediation in Kenya', UN Studies Programme, n.d., kofiannanfoundation.org/sites/default/files/Microsoft%20Word%20-%20A%20Choice%20for%20Peace.pdf.

Lonsdale, John, 'Threads and Patches: Moral and Political Argument in Kenya', essay (24 April 2008), www.kenyaimagine.com.

Mars (Media Analysis and Research) Group, 'Illegally Binding: The Missing Anglo Leasing Scandal Promissory Notes', GAP report No. 2 (2007), www.marsgroupkenya.org.

Mars (Media Analysis and Research) Group, 'The Case Against the Members of the Ninth Parliament', (2007), www.marsgroupkenya.org.

Mashada website. www.mashada.com/blogs/ You_Missed_This/2008/10/23/Alleged_Perpetrators_ Of_Post_Election_Violence (2008)

Muslim Human Rights Forum, 'Horn of Terror: Report of US-Led Mass Extraordinary Renditions from Kenya to Somalia, Ethiopia and Guantanamo Bay January–June 2007', presented to the Kenya National Commission on Human Rights on 6 July 2007, pdf version published on Wikileaks, 2009.

Mzandeleo Group, Eye on Kenyan Parliament Website, www.mzalendo.com.

Nation TV, on www.youtube.com (2010–11).

Ndii, David, 'Preliminary Results from the 2007 Presidential Election Results Received by the Electoral Commission of Kenya' (January 2008).

Ndung'u, Njuguna S., 'Liberalization of the Foreign Exchange Market in Kenya and the Short-Term Capital Flows Problem', *African Economic Research Consortium Research Paper No. 109* (Nairobi, 2001).

Nunow, Abdirazak Arale, 'Pastoralists and Markets: Livestock Commercialisation and Food Security in North-Eastern Kenya', *African Studies Centre Research Report* (n.d., 2000?).

Odek, Otieno, Kegode, Peter and Ochola, Shem, 'The Challenges and Way Forward for the Sugar Sub-Sector in Kenya' (Nairobi, Friedrich Ebert Stiftung Foundation, 2003).

Okemo, Chrisantus and Cheserem, Micah, 'Memorandum of Economic and Financial Policies of the Government of Kenya, 2000–03', letter to Horst Kohler, IMF, 12 July 2000, on IMF website at http://www.imf.org/external/np/loi/2000/ken/01/.

Oludhe, Christopher, 'An Assessment of the Potential Benefits of Seasonal Rainfall Prediction in Relation to Hydro-Electric Power Generation in Kenya: A Case Study of the Impacts of the 1999/2000 drought and the accompanied Power Rationing', unpublished paper, Department of Meteorology, University of Nairobi, n.d.

Organisation for Economic Cooperation and Development (OECD), *African Economic Outlook* (2007): Kenya, http://www.oecd.org/dataoecd/26/34/38562812.pdf

Pathé News, Broadcast 1753–24, Defence Talks (1964).

Raila Odinga's campaign website, raila2007.wordpress.com/2007/11/15.

'Report of the Auditor General (Corporations) On the Accounts of National Social Security Fund For the year ended 30 June 2000', 14 March 2002, www.nssfkenya.com/docs/auditor_general. pdf

Rodley, Nigel, 'Civil and Political Rights, Including Questions of Torture and Detention: Report of the Special Rapporteur: Addendum Visit of the Special Rapporteur to Kenya', United Nations Economic and Social Council Commission on Human Rights, E/CN.4/2000/9/Add.4 (9 March 2000).

Rogge, John, 'The Internally Displaced Population in Kenya, Western and Rift Valley Provinces: A Need Assessment and a Program Proposal for Rehabilitation' (Nairobi, UNDP, October 1993).

Rutten, Marcel, 'Parks Beyond Parks: Genuine Community-Based Wildlife Eco-Tourism or Just Another Loss of Land for Maasai Pastoralists in Kenya?', *Issue Paper No. 111* (Leiden University, 2002).

Snow R. W., Ikoku A., Omumbo J. and Ouma, J., 'The Epidemiology, Politics and Control of Malaria Epidemics in Kenya: 1900–1998', report prepared for Roll Back Malaria, Resource Network on Epidemics (World Health Organisation, July 1999).

Society for International Development, 'Pulling Apart: Facts and Figures on Inequality in Kenya' (Nairobi, Society for International Development, 2004).

Steadman Group, 'Referendum Opinion Poll Results, Quarter 3 2005', unpublished PowerPoint presentation, October 2005.

Steadman Group, 'Using Multi-Party Democracy in Kenya', August 2006.

Strategic Public Relations and Research Limited, 'Nationwide Exit Poll on the 21st November Constitutional Referendum in Kenya: Narrative Report' (Nairobi, Strategic, 2005).

Throup, David W., 'Kenya: Revolution, Relapse or Reform?', Centre for Strategic and International Studies, *Africa Notes, No. 3* (Washington, CSIS, November 2001).

Throup, David W., 'The Kenya General Election: December 27, 2002', Centre for Strategic and International Studies, *Africa Notes, No. 14* (Washington, CSIS, January 2003).

Throup, David W., 'The Construction of the arap Moi State and Elections in Kenya', unpublished article.

Transparency International website, www.transparency.org.

Transparency International-Kenya website, www.tikenya.org.

Transparency International-Kenya, 'Corruption in Kenya: Findings of an Urban Bribery Survey' (2001), www.tikenya.org.

Transparency International-Kenya, 'An Analysis of Reported Harambee Activity, January 2000–September 2002', n.d.

Transparency International-Kenya, 'Paying the Public or Caring for Constituents?' (Nairobi, Freidrich Ebert Stiftung and Transparency International, November 2003).

United States Bureau of Democracy, Human Rights and Labor, 'Human Rights Report: Kenya' (1999–2009), www.state.gov/g/drl/rls/hrrpt/.

US Economic and Military Assistance (Loans and Grants), (Green book), 1999, 2005, 2009, online editions, qesdb.cdie.org/gbk/index.html.

USAID, *Kenya Activity Data Sheet No. 615-006* (2001).

USAID, *Assessment of the Pre-Electoral Environment* (Washington, USAID, May 2006).

Waithaka, J. H. G., 'Kenya: Assessment of the Situation and Development Prospects for the Cashew Nut Sector' (UNCTAD/WTO, July 2002).

Wanjohi, Nick Gatheru, 'The Politics of Ideology and Personality Rivalry in Murang'a District, Kenya: A Study of Electoral Competition', *Institute of Development Studies Working Paper No. 411* (University of Nairobi, Institute for Development Studies, September 1984).

Wolf, Thomas P., 'Multi-Party Politics in Taita, 1963 vs. 1982: From KANU to KADU (or) from Uhoro (Principle) to Utumbo (Pragmatism)', draft paper (University of Nairobi, 1993).

—— Logan, Carolyn and Owiti, Jeremiah, 'A New Dawn? Popular Optimism in Kenya after the Transition', *Afrobarometer Working Paper No. 33* (2004).

World Bank, '2007 World Development Indicators Online' (Washington, World Bank, 2007), earthtrends.wri.org/text/economics-business/variable-638.html.

World Bank, 'Kenya: Growth and Competitiveness', *Report No. 31387-KE* (27 January 2005).

World Bank, 'Press Release: Meeting of the Consultative Group for Kenya' (Paris, 26 November 1991).

World Bank, 'Press Release: Meeting of the Consultative Group for Kenya' (Paris, 23 November 1993).

WorldNet Daily, 'Obama Raised $1 Million for Foreign Thug's Election' (14 October 2008), www.wnd.com/?pageId=78035.

World Wildlife Fund (WWF) website , www.panda.org.

World Wildlife Fund, 'Pachyderm No. 19' (World Wildlife Fund, Nairobi, 1995), www.african-elephant.org/pachy/pdfs/pachy19.pdf.

Yahya, Saad S., 'Who Owns the Kenya Coast? The Climaxing of Land Conflicts on the Indian Ocean Seaboard', unpublished paper, March 1998.

Index